Mark Wallace (Ed.)

Principles and Practice of Constraint Programming – CP 2004

10th International Conference, CP 2004
Toronto, Canada, September 27 - October 1, 2004
Proceedings

 Springer

Volume Editor

Mark Wallace
Monash University, Faculty of Information Technology
Building 63, Clayton, Vic 3800, Australia
E-mail: Mark.Wallace@infotech.monash.edu.au

Library of Congress Control Number: 2004112519

CR Subject Classification (1998): D.1, D.3.2-3, I.2.3-4, F.3.2, I.2.8, F.4.1, J.1

ISSN 0302-9743
ISBN 3-540-23241-9 Springer Berlin Heidelberg New York

This work is subject to copyright. All rights are reserved, whether the whole or part of the material is concerned, specifically the rights of translation, reprinting, re-use of illustrations, recitation, broadcasting, reproduction on microfilms or in any other way, and storage in data banks. Duplication of this publication or parts thereof is permitted only under the provisions of the German Copyright Law of September 9, 1965, in its current version, and permission for use must always be obtained from Springer. Violations are liable to prosecution under the German Copyright Law.

Springer is a part of Springer Science+Business Media

springeronline.com

© Springer-Verlag Berlin Heidelberg 2004
Printed in Germany

Typesetting: Camera-ready by author, data conversion by Olgun Computergrafik
Printed on acid-free paper   SPIN: 11320180   06/3142   5 4 3 2 1 0

Lecture Notes in Computer Science   3258

Commenced Publication in 1973
Founding and Former Series Editors:
Gerhard Goos, Juris Hartmanis, and Jan van Leeuwen

Editorial Board

David Hutchison
   Lancaster University, UK
Takeo Kanade
   Carnegie Mellon University, Pittsburgh, PA, USA
Josef Kittler
   University of Surrey, Guildford, UK
Jon M. Kleinberg
   Cornell University, Ithaca, NY, USA
Friedemann Mattern
   ETH Zurich, Switzerland
John C. Mitchell
   Stanford University, CA, USA
Moni Naor
   Weizmann Institute of Science, Rehovot, Israel
Oscar Nierstrasz
   University of Bern, Switzerland
C. Pandu Rangan
   Indian Institute of Technology, Madras, India
Bernhard Steffen
   University of Dortmund, Germany
Madhu Sudan
   Massachusetts Institute of Technology, MA, USA
Demetri Terzopoulos
   New York University, NY, USA
Doug Tygar
   University of California, Berkeley, CA, USA
Moshe Y. Vardi
   Rice University, Houston, TX, USA
Gerhard Weikum
   Max-Planck Institute of Computer Science, Saarbruecken, Germany

Preface

The 10th International Conference on the Principles and Practice of Constraint Programming (CP 2003) was held in Toronto, Canada, during September 27 – October 1, 2004. Information about the conference can be found on the Web at http://ai.uwaterloo.ca/~cp2004/

Constraint programming (CP) is about problem modelling, problem solving, programming, optimization, software engineering, databases, visualization, user interfaces, and anything to do with satisfying complex constraints. It reaches into mathematics, operations research, artificial intelligence, algorithms, complexity, modelling and programming languages, and many aspects of computer science. Moreover, CP is never far from applications, and its successful use in industry and government goes hand in hand with the success of the CP research community.

Constraint programming continues to be an exciting, flourishing and growing research field, as the annual CP conference proceedings amply witness. This year, from 158 submissions, we chose 46 to be published in full in the proceedings. Instead of selecting one overall best paper, we picked out four "distinguished" papers – though we were tempted to select at least 12 such papers. In addition we included 16 short papers in the proceedings – these were presented as posters at CP 2004.

This volume includes summaries of the four invited talks of CP 2004. Two speakers from industry were invited. However these were no ordinary industrial representatives, but two of the leading researchers in the CP community: Helmut Simonis of Parc Technologies, until its recent takeover by Cisco Systems; and Jean François Puget, Director of Optimization Technology at ILOG. The other two invited speakers are also big movers and shakers in the research community. We were delighted to welcome Bart Selman, previously at AT&T and now at Cornell, and Andreas Podelski, previously at Microsoft Research and now at the University of the Saarland.

A doctoral program was again organized to expose students to CP 2004, and 22 doctoral presentations are summarized as 1-page papers in the proceedings. Michela Milano brought to the doctoral program all the energy, tact, and organization that the CP community has come to recognise in her.

Finally, nine applications of CP were demonstrated at CP 2004, and 1-page descriptions of these demos have been included here.

The day before CP 2004, nine workshops were held, each with their own proceedings. Four tutorials were presented during the conference: "Modelling Problems in Constraint Programming" by Jean-Charles Regin; "Online Stochastic Optimisation" by Pascal Van Hentenryck and Russell Bent; "Symmetry Breaking in Constraint Programming" by Ian Gent and Jean-François Puget; and "Distributed Constraints – Algorithms, Performance, Communication" by Amnon Meisels. Barry O'Sullivan brought this excellent program together with his unique combination of charm and competence.

For conference publicity I'm very grateful for the hard work of Gilles Pesant, who took it on at the same time as moving his family across to Europe. He managed both with consummate efficiency.

Many thanks to the program committee, who reviewed and discussed all the submissions, and got nothing for their efforts but a free lunch. Nevertheless PC members took an enormous amount of trouble and the PC meeting was intense but also a lot of fun.

In preparing the proceedings, I'm grateful to Neil Yorke-Smith for generously volunteering to manage all the copyright forms, and Sevim Zongur who aided me in time of need.

Peter Van Beek and Fahiem Bacchus were nothing short of marvellous. I dread to think how much time and trouble they spent on budgeting, planning, booking, covering up for me and making it all work.

Finally heartfelt thanks to the many sponsors who make it possible for the conference to invite speakers, fund students and continue successfully for year after year. We are very grateful to IISI, Cornell; AAAI; Parc Technologies; ILOG; SICS; CoLogNET; Microsoft Research; NICTA, Australia; 4C, Cork; Dash Optimization; and the CPOC.

September 2004   Mark Wallace

Executive Committee

Conference Chair   Peter Van Beek, University of Waterloo, Canada
                      Fahiem Bacchus, University of Toronto, Canada
Program Chair   Mark Wallace, Monash University, Australia
Workshop Chair   Barry O'Sullivan, University College Cork, Ireland
Publicity Chair   Gilles Pesant, University of Montreal, Canada
Doctoral Chair   Michela Milano, University of Bologna, Italy

Program Committee

Pedro Barahona, Universidade Nova de Lisboa, Portugal
Frédéric Benhamou, University of Nantes, France
Christian Bessière, LIRMM-CNRS, France
Pascal Brisset, ENAC, France
Dave Cohen, Royal Holloway College, UK
Yves Colombani, DASH, UK
Rina Dechter, UC Irvine, USA
Boi Faltings, EPFL, Switzerland
Ian Gent, St Andrews, UK
Carmen Gervet, IC-Parc, UK
Filippo Focacci, ILOG, France
Gene Freuder, 4C, Ireland
John Hooker, CMU, USA
Ulrich Junker, ILOG, France
Narendra Jussien, ÉMN, France
Henry Kautz, University of Washington, USA
François Laburthe, Bouygues, France
Jimmy Lee, CUHK, Hong Kong
Pedro Meseguer, IIIA-CSIC, Spain
Michael Maher, Loyola University Chicago, USA
Laurent Michel, University of Connecticut, USA
Michela Milano, University of Bologna, Italy
Alexander Nareyek, CMU, USA
Barry O'Sullivan, 4C, Ireland
Gilles Pesant, Polytechnique Montréal, Canada
Jean-François Puget, ILOG, France
Peter Revesz, University of Nebraska-Lincoln, USA
Thomas Schiex, INRA Toulouse, France
Helmut Simonis, Parc Technologies, UK
Peter Stuckey, University of Melbourne, Australia
Michael Trick, CMU, USA
Mark Wallace, Australia
Roland Yap, NUS, Singapore

Referees

Dimitris Achlioptas
Farid Ajili
Ionut Aron
James Bailey
Vincent Barichard
Nicolas Barnier
Chris Beck
Nicolas Beldiceanu
Hachemi Bennaceur
Thierry Benoist
Julien Bidot
Bozhena Bidyuk
Stefano Bistarelli
Lucas Bordeaux
James Bowen
Marc Brisson
Ismel Brito
Ken Brown
Andrei Bulatov
Martine Ceberio
Samarjit Chakraborty
Andrew Cheadle
Jeff Choi
Marc Christie
Remi Coletta
Martin Cooper
Jorge Cruz
Joe Culberson
Victor Dalmau
Philippe David
Simon de Givry
Romuald Debruyne
Carmel Domshlak
Greg Duck
Renaud Dumeur
Susan L. Epstein
Andrew Eremin
Francois Fages
Helene Fargier
Alaaeddine Fellah
Spencer Furg
Philippe Galinier
Etienne Gaudin
Marco Gavanelli

Cormac Gebruers
Bernard Gendron
Daniel Godard
Vibhav Gogate
Frederic Goualard
Laurent Granvilliers
Martin Green
Christophe Guettier
Susanne Heipcke
Martin Henz
Emmanuel Herbrard
Brahim Hnich
Tudor Hulubei
Peter Jeavons
Olli Kamarainen
Kalev Kask
Tom Kelsey
Zeynep Kiziltan
Arun Konagurthu
Philippe Laborie
Vitaly Lagoon
Javier Larossa
Yat-Chiu Law
Claude Le Pape
Michel Leconte
Christophe Lecoutre
Olivier Lhomme
Vassilis Liatsos
Samir Loudni
Santiago Macho
Arnold Maestre
Margarida Mamede
Felip Manya
Radu Marinescu
Joao Marques-Silva
Kim Marriott
Robert Mateescu
David Mitchell
Eric Monfroy
John Mullins
Peter Nightingale
Stefano Novello
Angelo Oddi
Laurent Perron

Adrian Petcu
Thierry Petit
Emmanuel Poder
Steve Prestwich
Patrick Prosser
Jean-Charles Regin
Georg Ringwelski
Thomas Riviere
Jerome Rogerie
Andrea Roli
Francesca Rossi
Louis-Martin Rousseau
Andrew Rowley
Mihaela Sabin
Andrew Sadler
Lakhdar Sais
Marti Sanchez
Frederic Saubion
Hermann Schichl
Joachim Schimpf
Christian Schulte
Josh Singer
Barbara Smith
Zoltan Somogyi
Kostas Stergiou
Vincent Tam
Peter van Beek
Marc R.C. van Dongen
Maarten van Emden
Pascal Van Hentenryck
Willem van Hoeve
Brent Venable
Gerard Verfaillie
Paolo Viappiani
Marie-Catherine Vilarem
Xuan-Ha Vu
Rick Wallace
Toby Walsh
Nic Wilson
Quanshi Xia
Makoto Yokoo
Neil Yorke-Smith
Guy Yosiphon
Zhang Yuanlin

Tallys Yunes
Yuanlin Zhang

CP Organizing Committee

Krzysztof Apt, National University of Singapore
Christian Bessière, LIRMM-CNRS, France
James Bowen, University College Cork, Ireland
Carla Gomes, Cornell University, USA
Jean-François Puget, ILOG, France
Francesca Rossi, University of Padova, Italy
Peter Stuckey, Melbourne University, Australia
Pascal Van Hentenryck, Brown University, USA
Mark Wallace, Monash University, Australia
Toby Walsh, NICTA, Australia

Workshops

Cooperative Solvers in Constraint Programming
Preferences and Soft Constraints
Modeling and Reformulating Constraint Satisfaction Problems
Constraint Solving Under Change and Uncertainty
Local Search Techniques in Constraint Satisfaction
Symmetry and Constraint Satisfaction Problems
Workshop on CSP Techniques with Immediate Application
Distributed Constraint Programming
Constraint Propagation and Implementation

Sponsoring Institutions

Intelligent Information Systems Institute, Cornell
American Association for Artificial Intelligence
Parc Technologies Ltd.
ILOG Inc.
Swedish Institute of Computer Science
CoLogNET
Microsoft Research
National ICT, Australia
Cork Constraint Computation Centre
Dash Optimization Ltd.
Constraint Programming Organizing Committee

Table of Contents

Invited Papers

Constraints in Program Analysis and Verification 1
 Andreas Podelski

Constraint Programming Next Challenge: Simplicity of Use 5
 Jean-Francois Puget

Algorithmic Adventures at the Interface of Computer Science,
Statistical Physics, and Combinatorics 9
 Bart Selman

Challenges for Constraint Programming in Networking................. 13
 Helmut Simonis

Distinguished Papers

Consistency and Random Constraint Satisfaction Models
with a High Constraint Tightness 17
 Yong Gao and Joseph Culberson

Statistical Regimes Across Constrainedness Regions 32
 *Carla P. Gomes, Cèsar Fernández, Bart Selman,
 and Christian Bessiere*

Constraint-Based Combinators for Local Search...................... 47
 Pascal Van Hentenryck, Laurent Michel, and Liyuan Liu

Unary Resource Constraint with Optional Activities................. 62
 Petr Vilím, Roman Barták, and Ondřej Čepek

Full Papers

Constraint Propagation as a Proof System 77
 Albert Atserias, Phokion G. Kolaitis, and Moshe Y. Vardi

Backtrack-Free Search for Real-Time Constraint Satisfaction 92
 *J. Christopher Beck, Tom Carchrae, Eugene C. Freuder,
 and Georg Ringwelski*

Deriving Filtering Algorithms from Constraint Checkers 107
 Nicolas Beldiceanu, Mats Carlsson, and Thierry Petit

Leveraging the Learning Power of Examples
in Automated Constraint Acquisition 123
  *Christian Bessiere, Remi Coletta, Eugene C. Freuder,
  and Barry O'Sullivan*

Disjoint, Partition and Intersection Constraints
for Set and Multiset Variables 138
  *Christian Bessiere, Emmanuel Hebrard, Brahim Hnich,
  and Toby Walsh*

Decomposition and Learning
for a Hard Real Time Task Allocation Problem 153
  *Hadrien Cambazard, Pierre-Emmanuel Hladik,
  Anne-Marie Déplanche, Narendra Jussien, and Yvon Trinquet*

Quantified Constraint Satisfaction and 2-Semilattice Polymorphisms 168
  Hubie Chen

(Smart) Look-Ahead Arc Consistency
and the Pursuit of CSP Tractability 182
  Hubie Chen and Víctor Dalmau

Heuristic Selection for Stochastic Search Optimization:
Modeling Solution Quality by Extreme Value Theory 197
  Vincent A. Cicirello and Stephen F. Smith

A Complete Characterization of Complexity
for Boolean Constraint Optimization Problems 212
  David Cohen, Martin Cooper, and Peter Jeavons

Financial Portfolio Optimisation 227
  Pierre Flener, Justin Pearson, and Luis G. Reyna

Bounding the Resource Availability of Partially Ordered Events
with Constant Resource Impact 242
  Jeremy Frank

Monotone Literals and Learning in QBF Reasoning 260
  Enrico Giunchiglia, Massimo Narizzano, and Armando Tacchella

Streamlined Constraint Reasoning 274
  Carla Gomes and Meinolf Sellmann

A Domain Consistency Algorithm for the Stretch Constraint 290
  Lars Hellsten, Gilles Pesant, and Peter van Beek

A Hybrid Method for Planning and Scheduling 305
  John N. Hooker

Counting-Based Look-Ahead Schemes for Constraint Satisfaction 317
    Kalev Kask, Rina Dechter, and Vibhav Gogate

Completable Partial Solutions
in Constraint Programming and Constraint-Based Scheduling 332
    András Kovács and József Váncza

Set Domain Propagation Using ROBDDs 347
    Vitaly Lagoon and Peter J. Stuckey

Global Constraints for Integer and Set Value Precedence 362
    Yat Chiu Law and Jimmy H.M. Lee

Quality of LP-Based Approximations
for Highly Combinatorial Problems................................... 377
    Lucian Leahu and Carla P. Gomes

Constraint Satisfaction in Semi-structured Data Graphs 393
    Nikos Mamoulis and Kostas Stergiou

Strategies for Global Optimization of Temporal Preferences 408
    *Paul Morris, Robert Morris, Lina Khatib, Sailesh Ramakrishnan,
    and Andrew Bachmann*

ID Walk: A Candidate List Strategy with a Simple Diversification Device.. 423
    Bertrand Neveu, Gilles Trombettoni, and Fred Glover

Understanding Random SAT: Beyond the Clauses-to-Variables Ratio 438
    *Eugene Nudelman, Kevin Leyton-Brown, Holger H. Hoos, Alex Devkar,
    and Yoav Shoham*

Symbolic Decision Procedures for QBF 453
    Guoqiang Pan and Moshe Y. Vardi

Propagation Guided Large Neighborhood Search 468
    Laurent Perron, Paul Shaw, and Vincent Furnon

A Regular Language Membership Constraint
for Finite Sequences of Variables 482
    Gilles Pesant

Generating Robust Partial Order Schedules 496
    Nicola Policella, Angelo Oddi, Stephen F. Smith, and Amedeo Cesta

Full Dynamic Substitutability by SAT Encoding 512
    Steven Prestwich

Improved Bound Computation in Presence of Several Clique Constraints .. 527
    Jean-Francois Puget

Improved Algorithms for the Global Cardinality Constraint 542
  *Claude-Guy Quimper, Alejandro López-Ortiz, Peter van Beek,
  and Alexander Golynski*

Impact-Based Search Strategies for Constraint Programming 557
  Philippe Refalo

The Cardinality Matrix Constraint 572
  Jean-Charles Régin and Carla Gomes

Controllability of Soft Temporal Constraint Problems.................. 588
  Francesca Rossi, Kristen Brent Venable, and Neil Yorke-Smith

Hybrid Set Domains to Strengthen Constraint Propagation
and Reduce Symmetries 604
  Andrew Sadler and Carmen Gervet

Speeding Up Constraint Propagation 619
  Christian Schulte and Peter J. Stuckey

Theoretical Foundations of CP-Based Lagrangian Relaxation 634
  Meinolf Sellmann

A Constraint for Bin Packing 648
  Paul Shaw

Solving Non-clausal Formulas with DPLL Search 663
  Christian Thiffault, Fahiem Bacchus, and Toby Walsh

A Hyper-arc Consistency Algorithm for the Soft Alldifferent Constraint ... 679
  Willem Jan van Hoeve

Efficient Strategies for (Weighted) Maximum Satisfiability............ 690
  Zhao Xing and Weixiong Zhang

Short Papers

Preprocessing Techniques for Distributed Constraint Optimization 706
  Syed Muhammad Ali, Sven Koenig, and Milind Tambe

Variable Ordering Heuristics Show Promise 711
  J. Christopher Beck, Patrick Prosser, and Richard J. Wallace

The Tractability of Global Constraints 716
  *Christian Bessiere, Emmanuel Hebrard, Brahim Hnich,
  and Toby Walsh*

Support Inference for Generic Filtering 721
  *Frederic Boussemart, Fred Hemery, Christophe Lecoutre,
  and Lakhdar Sais*

Strong Cost-Based Filtering for Lagrange Decomposition
Applied to Network Design 726
    Wilhelm Cronholm and Farid Ajili

The Impact of AND/OR Search Spaces
on Constraint Satisfaction and Counting 731
    Rina Dechter and Robert Mateescu

A General Extension of Constraint Propagation
for Constraint Optimization 737
    Xiaofei Huang

How Much Backtracking Does It Take to Color Random Graphs?
Rigorous Results on Heavy Tails 742
    Haixia Jia and Cristopher Moore

Solving the Crane Scheduling Problem Using Intelligent Search Schemes .. 747
    Andrew Lim, Brian Rodrigues, and Zhou Xu

Algorithms for Quantified Constraint Satisfaction Problems 752
    Nikos Mamoulis and Kostas Stergiou

Improving the Applicability of Adaptive Consistency:
Preliminary Results 757
    Martí Sánchez, Pedro Meseguer, and Javier Larrosa

On-Demand Bound Computation for Best-First Constraint Optimization.. 762
    Martin Sachenbacher and Brian C. Williams

A New Algorithm for Maintaining Arc Consistency
After Constraint Retraction 767
    Pavel Surynek and Roman Barták

Computing the Frequency of Partial Orders 772
    Marc R.C. van Dongen

On Tightness of Constraints 777
    Yuanlin Zhang

Concurrent Dynamic Backtracking for Distributed CSPs 782
    Roie Zivan and Amnon Meisels

Doctoral Papers

Set Variables and Local Search 788
    Magnus Ågren

N–Kings for Dynamic Systems 789
    Konstantin Artiouchine

Relation Variables in Qualitative Spatial Reasoning 790
　　Sebastian Brand

Synchronous, Asynchronous and Hybrid Algorithms for DisCSP 791
　　Ismel Brito

Long-Term Learning for Algorithm Control 792
　　Tom Carchrae

Solution Extraction with the "Critical Path"
in Graphplan-Based Optimal Temporal Planning...................... 793
　　Tien Ba Dinh

Machine Learning for Portfolio Selection
Using Structure at the Instance Level................................ 794
　　Cormac Gebruers and Alessio Guerri

Local Search with Maximal Independent Sets 795
　　Joel M. Gompert

A Dynamic Restart Strategy for Randomized BT Search 796
　　Venkata Praveen Guddeti

A BDD-Based Approach to Interactive Configuration 797
　　Tarik Hadzic

Extending Super-solutions 798
　　Emmanuel Hebrard

Choosing Efficient Representations of Abstract Variables 799
　　Christopher Jefferson

A Hypergraph Separator Based Variable Ordering Heuristic
for Solving Real World SAT 800
　　Wei Li

Exploiting Symmetries via Permutations for PC Board Manufacturing 801
　　Roland Martin

Iterative Forward Search Algorithm: Combining Local Search
with Maintaining Arc Consistency and a Conflict-Based Statistics 802
　　Tomáš Müller

Programming Robotic Devices
with a Timed Concurrent Constraint Language 803
　　María del Pilar Muñoz and Andrés René Hurtado

Heuristics for the Distributed Breakout Algorithm 804
　　Adrian Petcu

Explanations and Numeric CSPs..................................... 805
　　Guillaume Rochart

Softly Constrained CP Nets 806
    Kristen Brent Venable

Online Constraint Solving and Rectangle Packing 807
    Alfio Vidotto

Modelling Chemical Reactions
Using Constraint Programming and Molecular Graphs 808
    Christine Wei Wu

Constraining Special-Purpose Domain Types 809
    Peter Zoeteweij

Demonstrations

PLASMA: A Constraint Based Planning Architecture 810
    Andrew Bachmann, Tania Bedrax-Weiss, Jeremy Frank,
    Michael Iatauro, Conor McGann, and Will Taylor

Applying Constraint Satisfaction Techniques to 3D Camera Control 811
    Owen Bourne and Abdul Sattar

Adaptive Enterprise Optimization Framework:
AEO Server and AEO Studio 812
    Alexander Brodsky and X. Sean Wang

CRE2: A CP Application for Reconfiguring a Power Distribution Network
for Power Losses Reduction 813
    Juan Francisco Díaz, Gustavo Gutierrez, Carlos Alberto Olarte,
    and Camilo Rueda

A Constraint-Based Planner Applied to Data Processing Domains 815
    Keith Golden and Wanlin Pang

CLab: A C++ Library
for Fast Backtrack-Free Interactive Product Configuration 816
    Rune M. Jensen

A Constraint-Based System
for Hiring and Managing Graduate Teaching Assistants 817
    Ryan Lim, Venkata Praveen Guddeti, and Berthe Y. Choueiry

A Web-Based Meeting Scheduling Solver
With Privacy Guarantees, Without Trusted Servers 818
    Marius-Călin Silaghi, Vaibhav Rajeshirke, and Richard Wallace

A Constraint-Based Graphics Library for B-Prolog 819
    Neng-Fa Zhou

Author Index 821

Constraints in Program Analysis and Verification
(Abstract of Invited Talk)

Andreas Podelski

Max-Planck-Institut für Informatik
Saarbrücken, Germany

Program verification is a classical research topic in core computer science. Recent developments have lead to push-button software verification tools that are industrially used e.g. to check interface specifications of device drivers. These developments are based on program analysis, model checking and constraint solving.

This Talk. After a short introduction to classical program analysis, we will illustrate how constraint solving is used to overcome two problems in the use of abstraction for verifying properties of program executions. The first problem is *infinite precision*: how can we abstract away enough irrelevant details to be efficient, but keep enough details to preserve the property we want to prove? The second problem is *infinite error length*: how can one abstract a program so that it preserves *liveness* properties?

Program Analysis. The term 'program analysis' refers to any method for verifying execution properties ("dynamic properties") that is or can be used in a compiler ("statically"). The original motivation has been compiler optimization. An optimization relies on a redundancy, which is a property that is valid throughout runtime. A typical verification problem is the question: "is the value of variable x always constant?" or: "is the value of variable x always different from 0?" The question is motivated by improving the efficiency respectively by avoiding an execution error.

Program Analysis vs. Model Checking vs. Program Verification. To fix our terminology, we distinguish the three prominent approaches to verification by whether they are (1) automated and (2) whether they deal with general purpose and hence *infinite* programs (where infinite refers to the space of data values for program variables). Program analysis satisfies (1) and (2), model checking satisfies (1) but not (2), and program verification (by applying deductive proof rules and possibly checking proofs mechanically) satisfies (2) but not (1). Program analysis uses *abstraction* to circumvent the manual construction of a finite model resp. the manual construction of an auxiliary assertion (such as an induction hypothesis). In fact, the methodic speciality of program analysis is abstraction. But what exactly is abstraction?

Program Analysis in 2 Steps. To simplify, we divide program analysis into two steps: (1) the transformation of the program P into a finite *abstract* program $P^\sharp$, and (2) the model checking of the property for $P^\sharp$. The finiteness of $P^\sharp$ refers to the number of its 'abstract' states.

The example program P shown below on the left (an extract from a Windows NT device driver) is transformed into the program $P^\sharp$ shown below on the right. The states of P are partitioned according to the values of the expressions $(z = 0)$ and $(x = y)$, which is recorded by the Boolean variables $b1$ resp. $b2$ of $P^\sharp$. An abstract state is thus bitvector, which in fact stands for an equivalence class (consisting of all states that satisfy the predicates or their negation, according to the value of the bit for the predicate).

Step (1) transforms each update statement in P to one in $P^\sharp$. Step (2) follows all execution traces of $P^\sharp$ until its (finite) state space is exhaustively explored. Step (2) determines that Line 9 in $P^\sharp$ can not be reached. This proves that P satisfies the correctness property (Line 9 in P can not be reached), because $P^\sharp$ simulates every possible execution of P.

```
[1]   do {                         [1]   do
[2]     z = 0;                     [2]     b1 := 1;
[3]     x = y;                     [3]     b2 := 1;
[4]     if (w){                    [4]     if (*) then
[5]       x++;                     [5]       b2 :=if (b2) then 0 else *;
[6]       z = 1;                   [6]       b1 :=0;
      }                                  fi
[7]   } while(x!=y)                [7]   while( b2 )
[8]   if(z){                       [8]   if (!b1) then
[9]     assert(0); }               [9]     assert(0);
```

First Problem: Infinite Precision. The abstraction is specified manually. I.e., the choice of the expressions $(z = 0)$ and $(x = y)$ is based on judicious insights regarding the program and the property. That is, that choice must be done anew for each program and each property. Moreover, once the abstraction is fixed (by a choice of expressions), the abstract statement corresponding to each statement in P is specified manually (e.g. b2 := if (b2) then 0 else * for the concrete statement x++). This must be done anew for each abstraction.

We take a more simple example to explain how constraint solving may come in to avoid the manual specification of an abstract statement. Classically, the table for the abstract addition of the three abstract values plus, zero, minus is specified manually. This is not necessary if one uses constraint solving to infer that

$$x > 0, y > \text{ implies } x + y > 0$$

and so on for the other entries in the table for the abstract addition of plus, zero, minus.

In the talk, we will explain the constraint-based construction of an abstract statement corresponding to each concrete statement in full generality. We will also explain how that construction lends itself to *counterexample-guided abstraction refinement*, where expressions such as $(z = 0)$ and $(x = y)$ are thrown in incrementally in an iterative process (a process that is iterated until either a counterexample is found in the concrete program P or the property is proven correct). This solves the problem of infinite precision.

Second Problem: Infinite Error Length. Let us take an example of a concurrent program for which we want to establish a liveness property, here that every execution eventually reaches ℓ_4 (and thus terminates). To give a more interesting example of a liveness property, from an interface specification of a device driver: "each time a lock is acquired, it will be eventually returned". The violation of a liveness property can be exhibited only on an infinite execution trace (and that is exactly the formal criterion that distinguishes it from a safety property). For liveness properties, one adds *fairness* assumptions to model that enabled transitions will eventually be taken (here, the transition from m_0 to m_1).

$$P_1 :: \begin{bmatrix} \ell_0 : \textbf{while } x = 1 \textbf{ do} \\ \quad \ell_1 : y := y + 1 \\ \ell_2 : \textbf{while } y \geq 0 \textbf{ do} \\ \quad \ell_3 : y := y - 1 \\ \ell_4 : \end{bmatrix} \; \| \; P_2 :: \begin{bmatrix} m_0 : x := 0 \\ m_1 : \end{bmatrix}$$

Finite-State Abstraction Does Not Preserve Liveness Properties. We take the previous example program with two threads; the variable y is set to some arbitrarily large value n and is then continually decremented, $0 \rightsquigarrow n \rightsquigarrow n-1 \rightsquigarrow \ldots \rightsquigarrow 1 \rightsquigarrow 0$. No terminating finite-state system is an abstraction of this program. I.e., every sufficiently long computation of the concrete program (with length greater than the number of abstract states) will result in a computation of the abstract system that contains a loop.

We thus need to come up with an extension of the idea of abstract states and their representation by constraints: abstract transitions and their representation by transition constraints.

Transition Constraints. An update statement such as x:=x-1 corresponds to the transition constraint $x' = x - 1$. A state s leads to state s' under the execution of the update statement if and only if the pair of states defines a solution for the corresponding transition constraint (where s and s' define the values of the unprimed respectictively primed version of the program variables).

An if statement corresponds to a transition constraint that contains the if expression as a conjunct (a constraint, i.e. the special case of a transition constraint over unprimed variables). For example, if(x>0){x:=x-1} corresponds to $pc = L0 \land x > 0 \land x' = x - 1 \land pc' = L0$.

The program statement L0: while(x>0){x:=x-1} L1: (at program label L0, with L1 in the next line) corresponds to the set (disjunction) of two transition constraints c_1 and c_2 below.

$$c_1 \equiv pc = L0 \land x > 0 \land x' = x - 1 \land pc' = L0$$
$$c_2 \equiv pc = L0 \land x \leq 0 \land x' = x \land pc' = L1$$

That is, a program corresponds to a set of transition constraints. A program states the relation between pre and post states. Hoare-style reasoning for partial and total correctness, and deductive verification and model checking of safety and liveness properties of (sequential, recursive, concurrent, ...) programs can be transferred to reasoning over transition constraints.

The sequential composition of statements $S_1; S_2$ corresponds to the logical operation $\circ$ over the corresponding transition constraints c_{S_1} and c_{S_2}, an operation that implements the relational composition of the denoted binary relations over states. We illustrate the operation $\circ$ on the transition constraints c_1 and c_2 introduced above.

$$c_1 \circ c_1 \equiv pc = L0 \land x > 1 \land x' = x - 2 \land pc' = L0$$
$$c_1 \circ c_1 \circ c_2 \equiv pc = L0 \land x = 2 \land x' = x - 2 \land pc' = L1$$

Abstract Transitions. We used a fixed finite set of expressions over states (which are constraints in unprimed variables) to partition the state space into finitely many equivalence classes; those were treated as abstract states. We now use a fixed finite set of 'atomic' transition constraints (which are constraints in unprimed and primed variables) to partition the space of state pairs into finitely many equivalence classes; we treat those equivalence classes as abstract transitions $c^\#$. For example, taking the set $\{x > 0, x' \leq x - 1\}$, we can abstract the set of all pairs (s, s') such that s leads to s' in an arbitrarily long sequence of transitions by the two abstract transitions $c_1^\#$ and $c_2^\#$ below.

$$c_1^\# \equiv pc = L0 \land x > 0 \land x' \leq x - 1 \land pc' = L0$$
$$c_2^\# \equiv pc = L0 \land x \leq 0 \land x' \leq x - 1 \land pc' = L1$$

A *transition invariant* $\mathcal{T}$ is a set of transition constraints that contains the transitive closure of the binary transition relation of a program. Partial correctness can be proven via the restriction of $\mathcal{T}$ to the entry and exit points of a program. Termination can be shown via the well-foundedness of each single transition constraint in $\mathcal{T}$, which corresponds to the termination of a corresponding single-while loop program and can be tested very efficiently (e.g. by a reduction, based on Farkas' Lemma, to a constraint solving problem). General safety and livess properties can be handled in a similar manner.

The construction of a transition invariant starts with the transition constraints c_i that correspond to the single statements of the program; iteratively, it takes each (new) transition constraint T in , composes T with each of the c_i's, approximates the result $T \circ c_i$ by an abstract transition $c^\#$, and adds $c^\#$ to $\mathcal{T}$; it terminates when no new abstract transitions are added.

Infinite Dimensions in Program Analysis. Constraints and logical operations over constraints as effective means to represent and manipulate infinite sets and relations, have been used to overcome the problem of infinite precision and the problem of infinite error length. There is quite a number of infinite dimensions in program analysis (local variables, memory cells, objects, abstract data types, control points, threads, messages, communication channels, ...) that still need to be addressed. Probably that number itself is infinite.

References

http://www.mpi-sb.mpg.de/~podelski

Constraint Programming Next Challenge: Simplicity of Use

Jean-Francois Puget

ILOG, 9 avenue de Verdun, 94253 Gentilly, France
puget@ilog.fr

1 Introduction

Constraint Programming (CP) is a healthy research area in the academic community. The growing number of participants to the CP conference series, as well as the number of workshops around CP is a good evidence of it. Many major conferences have a CP track, both in artificial intelligence, and in operations research. The existence of several commercial companies that offer CP tools and services is a further evidence of the value of CP as an industrial technology. ILOG is one of such companies. One of our uniqueness, as far as CP is concerned, is that the research and development team that produces our CP products is also responsible for the development of our mathematical programming (MP) tool, namely ILOG CPLEX. This provides a unique opportunity to contrast the way these products are developed, marketed and used.

In this paper we argue that current CP technology is much too complex to use for the average engineer. Worse, we believe that much of the research occurring in the CP academic community makes this even worse every year. The rest of the paper provides evidence for this claim, and suggests ways to address the issue of simplicity of use by looking at how a similar issue has been addressed in the mathematical programming community.

2 A Comparison Between Math Programming and Constraint Programming

A technical comparison between mathematical programming and constraint programming shows many similarities [8]. If we look at it from the angle of an industry user, then the two approaches also look very similar. For instance, problems are modeled in a very similar way, using variables, constraints, and an objective function. There are differences though. For instance, the set of constraint types that can be used is usually restricted in math programming to linear or quadratic constraints. CP systems usually support a much richer set of constraint types. There are also differences in the algorithms used under the hood to solve a problem once it is modeled. However, our point is that a typical industry user is not interested in understanding the differences in the way solutions are computed with a CP system as opposed to the way they are computed with an MP system. What matters is to know if one technology is applicable to the problem at hand, and, subsequently, how to best apply it. In this respect MP seems quite appealing.

Indeed, the paradigm of mathematical programming tools can be concisely defined as: "model and run". This means that the main thing one has to worry about is how the problem is specified in terms of variables, constraints and objective functions. There is no need to deal with how the search for solution should proceed for instance.

Let us contrast this with a typical CP application development. First of all, modeling is still a key component here. The problem must be stated in terms of variables, constraints and objective function if any. But, the richer set of modeling constructs available in a CP system creates a much larger of alternative formulations for a given problem. The choice of the right model requires an understanding of how the underlying algorithms work. For instance, it is usually interesting to use global constraints. This can induce significant changes in the way a problem can be modeled in CP. The second very important ingredient in a CP solution is the search part. Should the traditional tree search be used, or should a local search, or even a hybrid approach be selected? In the case of a tree search, the ordering in which decisions are explored is extremely important. Designing an ordering that is both robust and efficient can be challenging. A third ingredient can be the design of ad hoc global constraints, which again requires some expertise. One can argue that the variety of options allowed by CP is an asset[12]. This is true, provided the user is a very experienced CP user that understands many of those options in great detail.

The perceived value is the exact opposite for users that have no background in CP. The time needed to get an experience of a significant fraction of the available CP tools and methods may just be too important given the time allocated for developing a software solution.

3 Mathematical Programming at Work

The "model and run" paradigm has far reaching consequences. One can focus on the modeling part, regardless of which particular software will be used to solve that model. There exists modeling tools such as AMPL[1], GAMS[5], or OPL Studio[6][11] that let users create a model of the problem they want to solve independently of the MP software that will be used to solve the model. The existence of these modeling tools is possible thanks to the existence of a standard file format for expressing mathematical problems: the MPS format. Standardization is in turn very interesting for business users, because they can develop models without being tied to a particular software vendor. On the contrary, models written with one particular CP tool cannot usually be solved with another tool unless some significant rewriting occurs.

The identification of modeling as the main activity of interest has spurred the publication of books that focus on modeling, see [13] for instance. There is no description of algorithms in such books. Rather; these books are cook books for problem solving. Let us contrast this with CP books such as [11][10][9][2][7][4][3].

These books either focus on the description algorithms used to solve CSPs, or on the design of CP languages, or both. Some of them may also contain sections devoted to the modeling activity, but this is never their core.

Another consequence of the "model and run" paradigm is that MP systems are designed to support it. This means that typical MP systems such as ILOG CPLEX can read a model from a file, and can compute solutions to it without requiring any additional input[1]. On the contrary, CP systems are developments toolkits[2] with which one has to build an algorithm that solves a given problem. One could say that CP systems are not ready to use, whereas MP systems look more like a turnkey application.

Yet another consequence of the "model and run" paradigm is that the language in which models are stated is fixed in time. This means that improvements in the way models can be solved do not require model transformations. On the contrary, the typical way a given CP system is enhanced is by adding features to it. Let us just give some examples here. One typically adds new global constraints in order to benefit from improved domain reduction algorithms. One usually introduces new search constructs in order to support new search paradigms, or new hybridizations. A more specific example is symmetry breaking, where symmetries need to be provided as input. In order to benefit from these enhancements, models must be rewritten or augmented. One has to introduce statements that add global constraints for instance. This way of augmenting CP in order to improve its problem solving capacity permeates the academic research as well. Improvements are very often described in term of new global constraints, new modeling constructs, or new primitive and operators to program search.

4 A "Model and Run" Paradigm for CP

One way of decreasing the complexity of current CP systems, tools and techniques, it is to mimic what has been done in the MP community over the years. We propose to the CP community the following challenge: try to develop a "model and run" paradigm for CP. This means that the following items should be developed:

- A standard file format for expressing CP models.
- A library of CP algorithms that can get models as input, and produces solutions as output, without requiring additional inputs.
- Books that focus on modeling.
- Software improvements that do not require model rewriting.

---

[1] Tuning and more advanced interaction with MP algorithms is also available, but these advanced features are usually used by experienced users and academics. They are not used by typical industry engineers.

[2] ILOG provides software libraries, hence the analogy with a toolkit. Other vendors provide CP programming languages, usually in the form of specialized versions of the PROLOG language. To a great extent the argument we make is valid for both the library and the languages approaches.

We believe that the above items generate interesting research problems beyond the current ones actively pursued by the academic community. We further believe it is the long term interest of the academic community to make sure that CP technology can be used in the industry at large.

References

1. http://www.ampl.com/
2. Krzysztof Apt *Principles of Constraint Programming*, Cambridge University Press, 2003.
3. Philippe Baptiste, Claude Le Pape, and Wim Nuijten *Constraint-Based Scheduling: Applying Constraint Programming to Scheduling Problems*, Kluwer, 2001.
4. Rina Dechter *Constraint Processing*, Morgan Kaufmann, 2003.
5. http://www.gams.com/
6. http://www.ilog.com/
7. Thom Fruehwirth and Slim Abdennadher *Essentials of Constraint Programming*, Springer Verlag, 2003.
8. Irvin Lustig, and Jean-Francois Puget. "Program Does Not Equal Program: Constraint Programming and its Relationship to Mathematical Programming," Interfaces 31(6), pp 29-53.
9. Kim Marriott and Peter J. Stuckey *Programming with Constraints: an Introduction*, MIT Press, 1998.
10. Edward Tsang. *Foundations of Constraint Satisfaction*, Academic Press, 1993.
11. Pascal Van Hentenryck, with contributions by Irvin Lustig, Laurent Michel, and Jean-François Puget *The OPL Optimization Programming Language*, MIT Press, 1999.
12. Mark Wallace: "Languages versus Packages for Constraint Problem Solving" *In proceedings of CP'03*, F. Rossi (Ed.), LNCS 2833, Springer, pp. 37-52, 2003.
13. H. P. Williams *Model Building in Mathematical Programming, 4th Edition* Wiley, 1999.

Algorithmic Adventures at the Interface of Computer Science, Statistical Physics, and Combinatorics*

(EXTENDED ABSTRACT)

Bart Selman

Department of Computer Science, Cornell University, Ithaca, NY 14853, USA
selman@cs.cornell.edu

The challenge to solve worst-case intractable computational problems lies at the core of much of the work in the constraint programming community. The traditional approach in computer science towards hard computational tasks is to identify subclasses of problems with interesting, tractable structure. Linear programming and network flow problems are notable examples of such well structured classes. Propositional Horn theories are also a good example from the domain of logical inference. However, it has become clear that many real-world problem domains cannot be modeled adequately in such well-defined tractable formalisms. Instead richer, worst-case intractable formalisms are required. For example, planning problems can be captured in general propositional theories and related constraint formalisms and many hardware and software verification problems can similarly be reduced to Boolean satisfiability problems. Despite the use of such inherently worst-case intractable representations, ever larger real-world problem instances are now being solved quite effectively. Recent state-of-the-art satisfiability (SAT) and constraint solvers can handle hand-crafted instances with hundreds of thousands of variables and constraints. This strongly suggests that worst-case complexity is only part of the story. I will discuss how notions of typical case and average case complexity can lead to more refined insights into the study and design of algorithms for handling real-world computationally hard problems. We will see that such insights result from a cross-fertilization of ideas from different communities, in particular, statistical physics, computer science, and combinatorics.

Typical Case Complexity and the Role of Tractable Problem Structure.

The key to handling intractability is our ability to capture and exploit problem structure, a way of taming computational complexity. In general, however, the notion of structure is very hard to define. Recently, researchers have made considerable strides in correlating structural features of problems with typical case complexity. In particular, the study of phase transition phenomena is an emerging area of research that is changing the way we characterize the computational

---

* Work supported in part by the Intelligent Information Systems Institute at Cornell University sponsored by AFOSR (F49620-01-1-0076) and an NSF ITR grant (IIS-0312910).

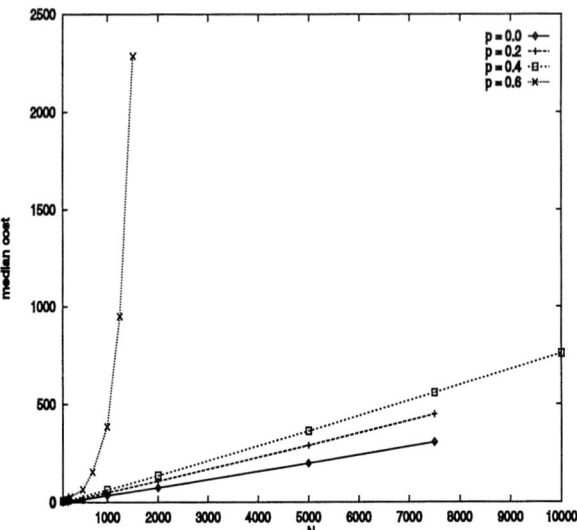

Fig. 1. Median cost of solving a 2+p-SAT problem for different values of p. We observe linear typical case scaling for a fraction of 3-SAT structure less than 0.4.

complexity of NP-Hard problems, beyond the worst-case complexity notion: Using tools from statistical physics we are now able to provide a finer characterization of the spectrum of computational complexity of instances of NP-Complete problems, identifying typical *easy-hard-easy* patterns as a function of the ratio of variables to constraints [1–3]. An interesting related structural concept involves the characterization of the complexity of a problem in the presence of tractable (sub)components. Monasson et al. [4, 5] introduced the 2+p-SAT problem to study the behavior of problems that are a mixture of 2-SAT and 3-SAT clauses. The fraction of 3-SAT clauses is defined by a parameter p ($0 \leq p \leq 1$). This hybrid problem is NP-complete for $p > 0$. However, somewhat surprisingly, Monasson et al. showed that the typical case complexity of the problem scales linearly as long as the fraction of 3-SAT clauses is below 0.4. See figure 1. This is a promising result, suggesting that real-world instances of NP-complete problems may behave in a tractable way as long as they contain a reasonable amount of tractable substructure. Finding ways to exploit tractable substructure is very much aligned with work in the constraint programming community where one relies on special structure captured by global tractable constraints, such as the alldiff constraint.

Characterization Hidden Problem Structure.

In recent work, we have pursued a more general characterization of tractable substructure to explain the wide range of solution times – from very short to extremely long runs – observed in backtrack search methods, often characterized by so-called heavy-tailed distributions [6]. We introduced the notion of a special subset of variables, called the *backdoor* variables [7]. A set of variables forms a

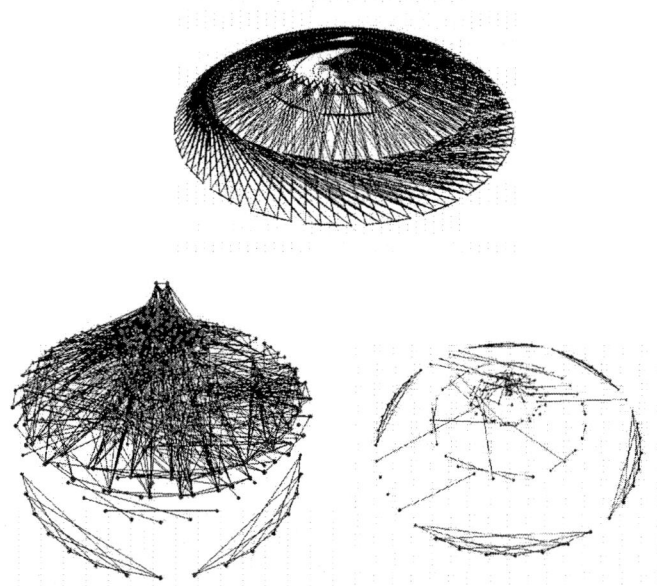

Fig. 2. A visualization of a SAT-encoded logistics planning instance (logistics.b.cnf, containing 843 vars and 7301 clauses). Each variable is represented as a node, and variables belonging to the same clause are connected by an edge. At the top: the original logistics formula. Bottom left: simplified instance after setting 5 backdoor variables. Bottom right: simplified instance after setting 12 backdoor variables. We observe that the formula is dramatically simplified after setting just a few backdoor variables. (Figure by Anand Kapur.)

backdoor for a problem instance if there is a value assignment to these variables such that the simplified instance can be solved in polynomial time by propagation and simplification mechanisms. Another way of stating this is to say that after setting the backdoor variables the simplified instance falls in a polynomially solvable class. Note however that we do not require for this class to have a clear syntactic characterization.

Structured problem instances can have surprisingly small sets of backdoor variables. When considering SAT encodings of logistics planning problems, we found that, for example, the logistics-b planning problem instance has a backdoor set of 15 variables, compared to a total of over 800 variables in the formula. Figure 2 provides a visualization of the logistics-b planning problem instance. We have found similarly small backdoors for other structured problems instances, such as those from bounded model-checking domains.

Of course, in practice, the small backdoor set (if it exists) still needs to be uncovered by the solver itself. In [7], we show that even when taking into account the cost of searching for backdoor variables, one can still obtain an overall computational advantage by focusing in on a backdoor set, provided the set is sufficiently small. Heuristics, incorporated in many current CSP/SAT solvers, also implicitly search for backdoor variables, by uncovering those variables that cause a large number of unit-propagation.

Survey Propagation and Random Walks

An exciting recent development is the discovery of a completely new class of satisfiability and constraint solving methods that effectively solve very large (satisfiable) instances near phase transition boundaries [8]. The approach is called survey propagation, and is based on advanced techniques from statistical physics used to study properties of disordered system. Survey propagation is an extended form of belief propagation. At an intuitive level, the method estimates the probability that a given variable has a certain truth value in the set of satisfying solutions. The method incrementally sets variables to their most likely values. After each variable setting, propagation is used to simplify the problem instance and new probability estimates are computed. The strategy is surprisingly effective – random 3-SAT instances with up to 10^7 variables very near the phase transition boundary can be solved. This is an improvement of almost two orders of magnitude over the previous best approach on hard random instances based on biased random walks (WalkSAT) [9]. However, WalkSAT and related methods are much more widely applicable and more robust on structured problems. The challenge is to adapt survey propagation methods for structured problems instances. One potential strategy is to use biased random walks to sample from near-solutions [10] as a complementary method for estimating probabilities for variable settings.

References

1. Hogg, T., Huberman, B., and Williams, C.: Phase Transitions and Search Problems. *Artificial Intelligence* Vol. 81 (1-2) (1996) 1–15.
2. Kirkpatrick, S. and Selman, B.: Statistical physics and computational complexity. In Ong, N.P., Bhatt, R.N., eds.: *More is different – fifty years of condensed matter physics*. Princeton University Press (2001).
3. Gomes, C. and Selman, B.: Satisfied with Physics. *Science*, Vol. 297 (2002) 784–785.
4. Monasson, R., Zecchina, R., Kirkpatrick, S., Selman, B., and Troyansky, L.: Determining Computational Complexity from Characteristic Phase Transitions. *Nature*, Vol. 400(8) (1999) 133–137.
5. Achlioptas, D., Kirousis, L., Kranakis, E., and Krizanc, D.: Rigorous results for (2+p)-sat. *Theo. Comp. Sci.* Vol. 265 (2001) 109–129.
6. Gomes, C.P., Selman, B., Crato, N., and Kautz, H.: Heavy-tailed phenomena in satisfiability and constraint satisfaction problems. *J. Autom. Reas.* Vol. 24 (2000).
7. Williams, R., Gomes, C., and Selman, B.: Backdoors to Typical Case Complexity. In: *Proc. IJCAI-03* (2003).
8. Mézard, M., Parisi, G., and Zecchina, R.: Analytic and algorithmic solutions to random satisfiability problems. *Science*, Vol. 297 (2002) 812–815.
9. Selman, B., Kautz, K., and Cohen, B. Local Search Strategies for Satisfiability Testing, *DIMACS Series in Discr. Math. and Theor. Comp. Sci.* Vol. 26 (1993).
10. Wei, W., Erenrich, J., and Selman, B.: Towards Efficient Sampling: Exploiting Random Walk Strategies. In: *Proc. AAAI-04.* (2004).

Challenges for Constraint Programming in Networking

Helmut Simonis*

IC-Parc
Imperial College London
Exhibition Road
London SW7 2AZ
`helmut.simonis@icparc.imperial.ac.uk`

Abstract. In this talk we present a number of problems for network design, planning and analysis and show how they can be addressed with different hybrid CP solutions. Clearly, this problem domain is of huge practical importance, but it also provides us with interesting, complex problem structures. CP directly competes with MILP and local search approaches to these problems, with best results often obtained by a combination of different solution techniques. Teams at Parc Technologies and IC-Parc have been working in this field over the last years, with a number of applications now embedded in commercial products.

1 Introduction

In recent years computer networks have become ubiquitous, they are now part of everyday life. This has caused a rapid growth in traffic volume, but has also increased our dependency on their undisturbed operation. The current move toward 'converged' networks, which combine both connection-less (Internet) and connection-based (voice, video) traffic in a single IP network environment, increases the demand for reliable but cost-effective network services. Constraint programming can help to provide software tools for various aspects of network design and operations. In this talk we show five areas where constraint techniques are already used, most often in the form of hybrid solvers, combining constraints with LP or local search methods.

2 Network Design

In its simplest form, network design consists in selecting a capacitated topology of nodes and links which can transport predicted demands between customers. Links typically can only be chosen between certain locations and from few, predefined capacity types. The objective is to minimize investment cost, while allowing enough spare capacity for robust operation. Different solution approaches were

---

* Part of this work was done while the author was working for Parc Technologies Ltd.

compared in [1], and a branch and price scheme was presented in [2]. But the design problem has many variations, for example allowing multi-cast traffic [3], while optical network design may use a very different model [4].

3 Traffic Engineering

Traditionally, IP networks relied on destination-based routing to forward packets using routing protocols like OSPF. In this approach the shortest path (wrt link weights) between source and destination is used to transport packets. This can lead to bottlenecks in the network when multiple shortest paths use the same link. Traffic engineering(TE) tries to overcome this problem by permitting explicit paths for each source and destination pair. Choosing these paths taking connectivity and capacity constraints into account allows to spread the traffic over the whole network, removing bottlenecks in utilization. There are three main models for expressing TE problems:

- *Link based models* use 0/1 integer variables to express whether a demand is routed over a link or not. The model grows cubically with the network size, which makes a direct MILP solution impractical for large networks.
- *Path based models* choose some of the possible paths for each demand and select a combination of the possible paths which satisfies the capacity constraints. This approach lends itself to a column generation method with a branch and price scheme to generate new paths on demand as used in [2].
- *Node based models* use a decision variable for each node and demand, which indicates the next-hop for the demand. This model can be expressed with traditional finite domain constraints [5].

In recent years, many different techniques have been proposed to solve these problems. Hybrid models using constraints include Lagrangian relaxation [6, 7], local probing [8, 9], probe backtracking [10] and local search hybrids [11]. A decomposition method was introduced by [12].

4 Deducing the Demand Matrix

The models for traffic engineering and network design all rely on an accurate *demand matrix*, which describes the traffic size between nodes in the network. This matrix is surprisingly difficult to obtain. In traditional, connection-based networks this data is readily available by design, but IP networks typically only collect aggregate link traffic counters. The task is complicated by the fact that counter collection may be incomplete and inconsistent. Deducing the traffic matrix from link counters is the problem of traffic estimation [13], which can be seen as a constraint problem with incomplete and incorrect data [14, 15].

5 Network Resilience

The failure of a single network element (link, router) should have minimal impact on the operation of the network. Depending on the network technology used, we can provide different solutions for improved network resilience:

- In destination-based routed networks, we can predict the utilization of the network under element failure based only on current link traffic counters. This is achieved by a combination of bounds reasoning with a linear traffic model [16].
- In MPLS networks, it is possible to automatically reroute important traffic around an element failure, a technique called *fast re-route*. Parc Technologies has provided a solution for Cisco's *TunnelBuilder Pro* to automatically find such detours. This problem is related to the traffic bypass problem described in [17].
- For traffic engineered networks, we can provide secondary paths, which are node or link disjoint from the primary paths chosen. We can use these secondaries if one of the elements on the primary path fails. Depending on the capacity constraints used, this can lead to very challenging models.

6 Bandwidth-on-Demand

Traffic engineering considers the impact of a set of demands on the current network, all demands are active at the same time. We can generalize this concept where demands have fixed start and end times, and compete for resources only if they overlap in time. This is the problem of *Bandwidth-on-Demand*, where customers can reserve network capacity for future time periods, for example a video conference between multiple sites with guaranteed throughput and quality of service. The model of [5] extends to this case, an alternative, repair-based model for this problem has been proposed in [18, 19] in the context of an ATM network.

Parc Technologies and IC-Parc have developed a Bandwidth-on-Demand (BoD) system for Schlumberger's *dexa.net*, a global MPLS network providing services in the oil-field sector. This network combines traffic engineering, multiple classes of service and rate limiting at the ingress points to guarantee delivery of BoD requests without disrupting existing traffic.

References

1. Le Pape, C., Perron, L., Regin, J., Shaw, P.: Robust and parallel solving of a network design problem. In Van Hentenryck, P., ed.: Principles and Practice of Constraint Programing - CP 2002, Cornell University, Ithaca, N.Y. (2002)
2. Chabrier, A.: Heuristic branch-and-price-and-cut to solve a network design problem. In: Integration of AI and OR Techniques in Constraint Programming for Combinatorial Optimization Problems CP-AI-OR 03, Montreal, Canada (2003)

3. Cronholm, W., Ajili, F.: Strong cost-based filtering for Lagrange decomposition applied to network design. In Wallace, M., ed.: Principles and Practice of Constraint Programming CP-2004, Toronto, Canada (2004)
4. Smith, B.: Search strategies for optimization: Modelling the SONET problem. In: 2nd International Workshop on Reformulating Constraint Satisfaction Problems, Kinsale, Ireland (2003)
5. Ros, L., Creemers, T., Tourouta, E., Riera, J.: A global constraint model for integrated routeing and scheduling on a transmission network. In: 7th International Conference on Information Networks, Systems and Technologies. (2001)
6. Ouaja, W.: Integrating Lagrangian Relaxation and Constraint Programming for Multicommodity Network Routing. PhD thesis, IC-Parc, Imperial College London, University of London (2004)
7. Ouaja, W., Richards, B.: A hybrid multicommodity routing algorithm for traffic engineering. Networks **43(3)** (2004) 125–140
8. Kamarainen, O., El Sakkout, H.: Local probing applied to network routing. In: Integration of AI and OR Techniques in Constraint Programming for Combinatorial Optimization Problems CP-AI-OR 04, Nice, France (2004)
9. Kamarainen, O.: Local Probing - A New Framework for Combining Local Search with Backtrack Search. PhD thesis, IC-Parc, Imperial College London, University of London (2003)
10. Liatsos, V., Novello, S., El Sakkout, H.: A probe backtrack search algorithm for network routing. In: Proceedings of the Third International Workshop on Cooperative Solvers in Constraint Programming, CoSolv'03, Kinsale, Ireland (2003)
11. Lever, J.: A local search/constraint propagation hybrid for a network routing problem. In: The 17th International FLAIRS Conference (FLAIRS-2004), Miami Beach, Florida (2004)
12. Frei, C., Faltings, B.: Resource allocation in networks using abstraction and constraint satisfaction techniques. In: Principles and Practice of Constraint Programming - CP 1999, Alexandria, Virginia (1999)
13. Medina, A., Taft, N., Salamatian, K., Bhattacharyya, S., Diot, C.: Traffic matrices estimation: Existing techniques and new directions. In: ACM SIGCOMM2002, Pittsburgh, PA (2002)
14. Yorke-Smith, N., Gervet, C.: On constraint problems with incomplete or erroneuos data. In Van Hentenryck, P., ed.: Principles and Practice of Constraint Programing - CP 2002, Cornell University, Ithaca, N.Y. (2002)
15. Yorke-Smith, N.: Reliable Constraint Reasoning with Uncertain Data. PhD thesis, IC-Parc, Imperial College London, University of London (2004)
16. Simonis, H.: Resilience analysis in MPLS networks. Technical report, Parc Technologies Ltd (2003) submitted for publication.
17. Xia, Q., Eremin, A., Wallace, M.: Problem decomposition for traffic diversions. In: Integration of AI and OR Techniques in Constraint Programming for Combinatorial Optimization Problems CP-AI-OR 2004, Nice, France (2004) 348–363
18. Lauvergne, M., David, P., Bauzimault, P.: Connections reservation with rerouting for ATM networks: A hybrid approach with constraints. In Van Hentenryck, P., ed.: Principles and Practice of Constraint Programing - CP 2002, Cornell University, Ithaca, N.Y. (2002)
19. Loudni, S., David, P., Boizumault, P.: On-line resource allocation for ATM networks with rerouting. In: Integration of AI and OR Techniques in Constraint Programming for Combinatorial Optimization Problems CP-AI-OR 03, Montreal, Canada (2003)

Consistency and Random Constraint Satisfaction Models with a High Constraint Tightness

Yong Gao and Joseph Culberson

Department of Computing Science, University of Alberta
Edmonton, Alberta, Canada, T6G 2E8
{ygao,joe}@cs.ualberta.ca

Abstract. Existing random models for the constraint satisfaction problem (CSP) all require an extremely low constraint tightness in order to have non-trivial threshold behaviors and guaranteed hard instances at the threshold. We study the possibility of designing random CSP models that have interesting threshold and typical-case complexity behaviors while at the same time, allow a much higher constraint tightness. We show that random CSP models that enforce the constraint consistency have guaranteed exponential resolution complexity without putting much restriction on the constraint tightness. A new random CSP model is proposed to generate random CSPs with a high tightness whose instances are always consistent. Initial experimental results are also reported to illustrate the sensitivity of instance hardness to the constraint tightness in classical CSP models and to evaluate the proposed new random CSP model.

1 Introduction

One of the most significant problems with the existing random CSP models is that as a model parameter, the constraint tightness has to be extremely low in order to have non-trivial threshold behaviors and guaranteed hard instances at phase transitions. In [1,2], it was shown that except for a small range of the constraint tightness, all of the four classical random CSP models are trivially unsatisfiable with high probability due to the existence of the flawed variables. For the case of binary CSPs, the constraint tightness has to be less than the domain size in order to avoid the flawed variables. Recent theoretical results in [3,4] further indicate that even for a moderate constraint tightness, it is still possible for these classical models to have an asymptotically polynomial complexity due to the appearance of embedded easy subproblems.

Several new models have been proposed to overcome the trivial unsatisfiability. In [2], Gent et al proposed a CSP model, called the flawless random binary CSP, that is based on the notion of a *flawless conflict matrix*. Instances of the flawless random CSP model are guaranteed to be arc-consistent, and thus do not suffer asymptotically from the problem of flawed variables. In [1], a nogoods-based CSP model was proposed and was shown to have non-trivial asymptotic behaviors. Random CSP models with a (slowly) increasing domain size have also been shown to be free from the problem of flawed variables and have interesting threshold behaviors [5, 6]. However, none of these models have addressed the fundamental requirement of an extremely low constraint tightness in order to have a guaranteed exponential complexity. The flawless random CSP does have a true solubility phase transition at a high constraint tightness, but as we will show later, it still suffers from the embedded easy unsatisfiable subproblems at a moderate constraint tightness. In CSP models with an increasing domain size, the (relative) constraint tightness should still remain low. In the nogood-based CSP model, it is impossible to have a high constraint tightness without making the constraint (hyper)graph very dense.

In this paper, we study the possibility of designing non-trivial random CSP models that allow a much higher constraint tightness. For this purpose, we show that consistency, a notion that has been developed to improve the efficiency of CSP algorithms, is in fact the key to the design of random CSP models that have guaranteed exponential resolution complexity without the requirement of an extremely low constraint tightness. We propose a scheme to generate consistent random instances of CSPs that can potentially have a high constraint tightness. Initial experiments show that the instances generated by our model are indeed much harder at the phase transition than those from the classical CSP models and the flawless CSP models.

2 Random Models for CSPs

Throughout this paper, we consider binary CSPs defined on a domain D with $|D| = d$. A binary CSP $\mathcal{C}$ consists of a set of variables $x = \{x_1, \cdots, x_n\}$ and a set of binary *constraints* $(C_1, \cdots, C_m)$. Each constraint C_i is specified by its *constraint scope*, a pair of the variables in x, and a *constraint relation* R_{C_i} that defines a set of incompatible value-tuples in $D \times D$ for the scope variables. An incompatible value tuple is also called a restriction. Associated with a binary CSP is a *constraint graph* whose vertices correspond to the set of variables and edges correspond to the set of constraint scopes. In the rest of the paper, we will be using the following notation:

1. n, the number of variables; m, the number of constraints;
2. d, the domain size; and t, the constraint tightness, i.e., the size of the restriction set.

Given two variables, their constraint relation can be specified by a 0-1 matrix, called the *conflict matrix*, where an entry 0 at (i, j) indicates that the tuple $(i, j) \in D \times D$ is incompatible. Another way to describe the constraint relation is to use the *compatible graph*, a bipartite graph with the domain of each variable as an independent partite, where an edge signifies the corresponding value-tuple is compatible.

An instance of a CSP is said to be *k-consistent* if and only if for any (k-1) variables, each consistent (k-1)-tuple assignment to the (k-1) variables can be extended to an assignment to any other kth variable such that the k-tuple is also consistent. A CSP instance is called *strongly k-consistent* if and only if it is j-consistent for each $j \leq k$. Of special interest are the strong k-consistency for $k = 1, 2, 3$, also known as node-consistency, arc-consistency, and path-consistency.

Definition 1 (Random Binary CSP $\mathcal{B}_{n,m}^{d,t}$). *Let $0 < t < d^2$ be an integer. $\mathcal{B}_{n,m}^{d,t}$ is a random CSP model such that*

1. *its constraint graph is the standard random graph $G(n,m)$ where m edges of the graph are selected uniformly from all the possible $\binom{n}{2}$ edges; and*
2. *for each of the edges of G, a constraint relation on the corresponding scope variables is specified by choosing t value-tuples from $D \times D$ uniformly as its restriction set.*

$\mathcal{B}_{n,m}^{d,t}$ is known in the literature as the Model B. It has been shown in [1, 2] that for $t \geq d$, $\mathcal{B}_{n,m}^{d,t}$ is asymptotically trivial and unsatisfiable, and has a phase transition in satisfiability probability for $t < d$. This motivates the introduction of the flawless conflict matrix to make sure that the random model is arc-consistent [2].

Definition 2. ($\mathcal{B}_{n,m}^{d,t}[1]$, Flawless Random Binary CSP). *In the flawless random binary CSP $\mathcal{B}_{n,m}^{d,t}[1]$, the constraint graph is defined in the same way as that in $\mathcal{B}_{n,m}^{d,t}$. For each constraint edge, the constraint relation is specified in two steps:*

1. *Choosing a random permutation π of $D = \{1, \cdots d\}$; and*
2. *Selecting a set of t value-tuples uniformly from $D \times D \setminus \{(i, \pi(i)), 1 \leq i \leq n)\}$ as the restriction set.*

The reason that we use a suffix "[1]" in the symbol $\mathcal{B}_{n,m}^{d,t}[1]$ will become clear after we introduce the generalized flawless random CSPs later in this paper. By specifying a set of tuples $\{(i, \pi(i)), 1 \leq i \leq n)\}$ that will not be considered when choosing incompatible value-tuples, the resulting model is guaranteed to be arc-consistent and consequently will not have flawed variables. However, even though the flawless random binary CSP $\mathcal{B}_{n,m}^{d,t}[1]$ does not suffer the problem of trivial unsatisfiability, it can be shown that $\mathcal{B}_{n,m}^{d,t}[1]$ asymptotically has embedded easy subproblems for $t \geq d-1$ in the same way as the random binary CSP model.

Theorem 1. *For $t \geq d-1$, there is a constant $c^* > 0$ such that for any $\frac{m}{n} > c^*$, with high probability $\mathcal{B}_{n,m}^{d,t}[1]$ is asymptotically unsatisfiable and can be solved in polynomial time.*

A detailed proof outline of Theorem 1 can be found in the Appendix, Section 6.1. The idea is to show that for $\frac{m}{n} > c^*$, the flawless random CSP $\mathcal{B}_{n,m}^{d,t}[1]$ will with high probability contain an unsatisfiable subproblem called an r-flower. The definition of an r-flower can be found in the Appendix. Furthermore, if a binary CSP instance contains an r-flower, then any path-consistency algorithm will produce a new CSP instance in which the center variable of the r-flower has an empty domain. It follows that we can prove that it is unsatisfiable polynomially.

It should be noted that $\mathcal{B}_{n,m}^{d,t}[1]$ does have a non-trivial phase transition since it is satisfiable with high probability if $\frac{m}{n} < \frac{1}{2}$. Theorem 1 does not exclude the possibility that $\mathcal{B}_{n,m}^{d,t}[1]$ will also be able to generate hard instances when $\frac{m}{n}$ is below the upper bound c^*, in particular in the case of a large domain size. Further investigation is required to fully understand the complexity of $\mathcal{B}_{n,m}^{d,t}[1]$ in this regard.

3 Consistency, Resolution Complexity, and Better Random CSP Models

Propositional resolution complexity deals with the minimum length of resolution proofs for an (unsatisfiable) CNF formula. As many backtracking-style complete algorithms can be simulated by a resolution proof, the resolution complexity provides an immediate lower bound on the running time of these algorithms. Since the work of Chvatal and Szemeredi [7], there have been many studies on the resolution complexity of randomly generated CNF formulas [8, 9].

Mitchell [10] developed a framework in which the notion of resolution complexity is generalized to CSPs and the resolution complexity of randomly generated CSPs can be studied. In this framework, the resolution complexity of a CSP instance is defined to be the resolution complexity of a natural CNF encoding which we give below. Given an instance of a CSP on a set of variables $\{x_1, \cdots, x_n\}$ with a domain $D = \{1, 2, \cdots, d\}$, its CNF encoding is constructed as follows: (1) For each variable x_i, there are d Boolean variables $x_i : 1$, $x_i : 2, \cdots$, and $x_i : d$, each of which indicates whether or not x_i takes on the corresponding domain value; and there is a clause $x_i : 1 \vee x_i : 2 \vee \cdots \vee x_i : d$ on these d Boolean variables making sure that x_i takes at least one of the domain values; (2) For each restriction $\delta_1, \cdots, \delta_k \in D^k$ of each constraint $C(x_{i_1}, \cdots, x_{i_k})$, there is a clause $\overline{x_{i_1} : \delta_1} \vee \cdots \vee \overline{x_{i_k} : \delta_k}$ to respect the restriction.

In [10, 4], upper bounds on the constraint tightness t were established for the random CSPs to have an exponential resolution complexity. For random binary CSP $\mathcal{B}_{n,m}^{d,t}$, the bound is (1) $t < d-1$; or (2) $t < d$ and $\frac{m}{n}$ is sufficiently small. For a moderate constraint tightness, recent theoretical results in [3, 4] indicate that it is still possible for these classical models to have an asymptotical polynomial complexity due to the existence of embedded easy subproblems. The primary reason for the existence of embedded easy subproblems is that for a moderate constraint tightness, constraints frequently imply forcers which force a pair of involved variables to take on a single value-tuple.

In the following, we will show that it is not necessary to put restrictions on the constraint tightness in order to have a guaranteed exponential resolution complexity. Based on quite similar arguments as those in [10, 4, 11], it can be shown that if in $\mathcal{B}_{n,m}^{d,t}$, the constraint relation of each constraint were chosen in such a way that the resulting instances are always strongly k-consistent ($k \geq 3$), then $\mathcal{B}_{n,m}^{d,t}$ has an exponential resolution complexity no matter how large the constraint tightness is.

Theorem 2. *Let $\mathcal{B}_{n,m}^{d,t}[SC]$ be a random CSP such that (1) its constraint graph is the standard random graph $G(n, m)$; and (2) for each edge, the constraint relation is such that any instances of $\mathcal{B}_{n,m}^{d,t}[SC]$ is strongly k-consistent. Then, the resolution complexity of $\mathcal{B}_{n,m}^{d,t}[SC]$ is almost surely exponential.*

Proof. See Appendix.

Using the tool developed in [4], the requirement of strong k-consistency for CSP instances to have an exponential resolution complexity can be further relaxed. We call a CSP instance *weakly path-consistent* if it is arc-consistent and satisfies the conditions of path-consistency for paths of length 3 or more.

Theorem 3. *Let $\mathcal{B}_{n,m}^{d,t}[WC]$ be a random CSP such that (1) its constraint graph is the random graph $G(n, m)$; and (2) for each edge, the constraint relation is such that any instances of $\mathcal{B}_{n,m}^{d,t}[WC]$ are weakly path-consistent. Then, the resolution complexity of $\mathcal{B}_{n,m}^{d,t}[WC]$ is almost surely exponential.*

Proof. See Appendix.

The question remaining to be answered is whether or not there are any natural random CSP models that are guaranteed to be strongly k-consistent or weakly path-consistent. In fact, the CSP-encoding of random graph k-coloring problem is strongly k-consistent. Another example is the flawless random binary CSP $\mathcal{B}_{n,m}^{d,t}[1]$ that is guaranteed to be arc-consistent, i.e., strongly 2-consistent. In the rest of this section, we discuss how to generate random CSPs with a high tightness that are strongly 3-consistent or weakly path-consistent.

Definition 3. ($\mathcal{B}_{n,m}^{d,t}[\mathcal{K}]$, **Generalized Flawless Random Binary CSP**). *In the generalized flawless random binary CSP $\mathcal{B}_{n,m}^{d,t}[\mathcal{K}]$, $\mathcal{K}$ is a random bipartite graph with each partite being the domain D of a variable. The constraint graph is defined in the same way as that in $\mathcal{B}_{n,m}^{d,t}$. For each constraint edge, the constraint relation is specified as follows:*

1. *Generate the bipartite graph $\mathcal{K}$ satisfying certain properties; and*
2. *Select a set of t value-tuples uniformly from $(D \times D) \setminus E(\mathcal{K})$ as the restriction set.*

The idea in the generalized flawless random binary CSP is that by enforcing a subset of value-tuples (specified by the edges of the bipartite graph $\mathcal{K}$) to be always compatible, it is possible that the generated CSP instance will always satisfy a certain level of consistency. If we define $\mathcal{K}$ to be a 1-regular bipartite graph, then $\mathcal{B}_{n,m}^{d,t}[\mathcal{K}]$ reduces to the flawless random binary CSP model $\mathcal{B}_{n,m}^{d,t}[1]$.

The following result shows that a connected and l-regular bipartite graph $\mathcal{K}$ with sufficiently large l can be used to generate strongly 3-consistent random CSPs or weakly path-consistent random CSPs.

Theorem 4. *Let $\mathcal{K}$ be an l-regular connected random bipartite graph. Then, $\mathcal{B}_{n,m}^{d,t}[\mathcal{K}]$ is always*

1. strongly 3-consistent if and only if $l > \frac{d}{2}$; and
2. weakly path-consistent if and only if $l > \frac{d-1}{2}$.

Proof. We only prove the case for weak path-consistency; the case for the strong 3-consistency is similar.

Consider a path $x_1 - x_2 - x_3 - x_4$ and any assignment $x_1 = i$ and $x_4 = j$. There are l values of x_2 that are compatible to $x_1 = i$ and there are l values of x_3 that are compatible to $x_4 = j$. Since the conflict graph is connected, there are at least $l+1$ values of x_3 that are compatible to $x_1 = i$. Therefore if $l > (d-1)/2$, there must be a value of x_3 that is compatible to both $x_1 = i$ and $x_4 = j$.

To see the "only if" part, we will show that there is a connected bipartite graph $K(V,U)$ on two sets of vertices $V = \{v_1, v_2, \cdots, v_d\}$ and $U = \{v_1, u_2, \cdots, u_d\}$ such that the neighbors of the first l vertices in V are the first $l+1$ vertices in V. First, we construct a complete bipartite graph on the vertex sets $\{v_1, v_2, \cdots, v_l\}$ and $\{u_1, u_2, \cdots, u_l\}$; Second, we construct an l-regular connected bipartite graph on the vertex sets $\{v_{l+1}, \cdots, v_d\}$ and $\{u_{l+1}, \cdots, u_d\}$ such that (v_{l+1}, u_{l+1}) is an edge. We then replace the two edges (v_l, u_l) and (v_{l+1}, u_{l+1}) with two new edges (v_l, u_{l+1}) and (v_{l+1}, u_l). This gives the bipartite graph $K(V,U)$. □

The generalized random CSP model $\mathcal{B}_{n,m}^{d,t}[\mathcal{K}]$ with a connected regular bipartite $\mathcal{K}$ allows a constraint tightness up to $\frac{(d+1)d}{2}$. The above theorem also indicates that this is the best possible constraint tightness when using an arbitrary connected bipartite graph $\mathcal{K}$. To achieve higher constraint tightness, we propose a recursive scheme to generate a bipartite graph $\mathcal{K}$ that is more efficient in its use of edges.

Definition 4 (Consistency Core). *Let $D_1 = D_2$ be the domains of two variables with $|D_1| = |D_2| = d$. The consistency core for the domains D_1 and D_2 is a bipartite graph $\mathcal{G}_{core}(D_1, D_2)$ on D_1 and D_2, and is defined recursively as follows.*

1. *Let $\{D_{ij}, 1 \leq j \leq s\}$ be a partition of D_i such that $|D_{ij}| \geq 3$.*
2. *If $s < 3$, $\mathcal{G}_{core}(D_1, D_2)$ is equal to an l_0-regular connected bipartite graph on $D_1(\pi_1) = \{\pi_1(1), \cdots, \pi_1(d)\}$ and $D_2(\pi_2) = \{\pi_2(1), \cdots, \pi_2(d)\}$ where π_1, π_2 are two permutations of $\{1, 2, \cdots, d\}$ and $l_0 > \frac{d}{2}$.*
3. *For $s \geq 3$, let π_1, π_2 be two permutations of $S = \{1, 2, \cdots, s\}$ and*

$$G(S(\pi_1), S(\pi_2), l)$$

be an l-regular connected bipartite graph on $S(\pi_1) = \{\pi_1(1), \cdots, \pi_1(s)\}$ and $S(\pi_2) = \{\pi_2(1), \cdots, \pi_2(s)\}$. The edge set of $\mathcal{G}_{core}(D_1, D_2)$ is defined to be the union of the edge sets of all consistency cores $\mathcal{G}_{core}(D_{1i}, D_{1j})$ where i and j are integers such that $(i, j) \in G(S(\pi_1), S(\pi_2), l)$.

Theorem 5. *If a consistency core is used for $\mathcal{K}$, then $\mathcal{B}_{n,m}^{d,t}[\mathcal{K}]$ is*

1. *strongly 3-consistent if and only if $l > \frac{s}{2}$; and*
2. *weakly path-consistent if and only if $l > \frac{s-1}{2}$.*

Proof. By induction on the domain size and using the previous theorem.

Using the consistency core, we can define random CSP models with constraint tightness well above $\frac{(d+1)d}{2}$. For example, if the domain size d is 12, the random generalized random CSP model $\mathcal{B}_{n,m}^{d,t}[\mathcal{K}]$ with a consistency core $\mathcal{K}$ allow a constraint tightness up to $144 - 6 * 8 = 96$.

Example 1. Consider the consistency core $\mathcal{K}$ where the domain size is $|D| = 9$ and assume that all the permutations used in Definition 4 are identity permutations and $l = s = 3$. Figure 1 shows the consistency core where the edges connected to two vertices in the lower partite are depicted. Using such a consistency core, a constraint on two variables x_i, x_j in $\mathcal{B}_{n,m}^{d,t}[\mathcal{K}]$ with $t = 45$, has a set of restrictions

$$\{(i,j);\ i = 3a_1 + a_2 \text{ and } j = 3b_1 + b_2 \text{ are integers such that}$$
$$a_1 \neq b_1 \text{ and } a_2 \neq b_2\}.$$

An instance of this CSP model can be viewed as a generalized 3-colorability problem.

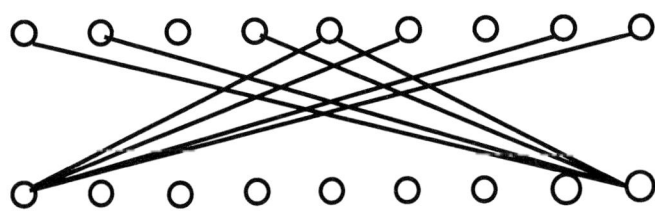

Fig. 1. A special type of consistency core with the domain size 9.

4 Experiments

In this section, we report results of two sets of preliminary experiments designed to (1) study the effect of an increase in the constraint tightness on the typical-case complexity; and (2) compare typical-case instance hardness between the classical random CSPs, flawless random CSPs, and the generalized flawless random CSPs.

4.1 Effect of an Increase in the Constraint Tightness

In [3, 4], upper bounds on the constraint tightness have been established for random CSPs to have an exponential resolution complexity for any constant constraint-to-variable ratio $\frac{m}{n}$. Molloy [4] further showed that for the constraint tightness above the upper bound, the existence of forcers can be compensated by sufficiently low constraint-to-variable ratio so that one can still have typical instances with exponential resolution complexity.

We have conducted the following experiments to gain further understanding on the effect of an increase in the constraint tightness (and hence an increase in the likelihood of the existence of a forcer in a constraint) on the typical-case hardness of random CSPs. The experiments also help understand the behavior of CSP models, such as the flawless CSP model, that only enforce arc-consistency (strong 2-consistency).

In the experiments, we start with a random 3-CNF formula whose clauses are treated as constraints. We then incrementally increase the tightness of each constraint by adding more clauses defined over the same set of variables. There are two reasons why we have based our experiments on random SAT models. First, the typical-case complexity of the random SAT model is well-understood and therefore, experiments based on the random SAT model will enable us to have an objective comparison on the impact of an increase in the constraint tightness. Secondly, the complexity of Boolean-valued random CSPs obtained by increasing the tightness of the random 3-CNF formula has been characterized in great detail. We have a clear picture regarding the appearance of embedded easy subproblems in these Boolean-valued random CSPs [3].

Let $\mathcal{F}(n, m)$ be a random 3-CNF formula with n variables and m clauses. We construct a new random 3-CNF formula $\mathcal{F}(n, m, a)$ as follows:

1. $\mathcal{F}(n, m, a)$ contains all the clauses in $\mathcal{F}(n, m)$;
2. For each clause C in $\mathcal{F}(n, m)$, we generate a random clause on the same set of variables of C, and add this new clause to $\mathcal{F}(n, m, a)$ with probability a.

In fact, $\mathcal{F}(n, m, a)$ is the random boolean CSP model with an average constraint tightness $1 + a$ and has been discussed in [3]. For $a > 0$, it is easy to see that $\mathcal{F}(n, m, a)$ is always strongly 2-consistent, but is not 3-consistent asymptotically with probability 1.

Figure 2 shows the median of the number of branches used by the SAT solver zChaff on 100 instances of $\mathcal{F}(n, m, a), a = 0.0, 0.1, 0.2$.

As expected, an increase in the tightness results in a shift of the location of the hardness peak toward smaller m/n. More significant is the magnitude of the decrease of the hardness as a result of a small increase of the constraint tightness.

From [3], the upper bounds on m/n for $\mathcal{F}(n, m, a)$ to have an exponential resolution complexity are 23.3 if $a = 0.1$ and 11.7 if $a = 0.2$. Since the constraint-to-variable rations m/n considered in the experiment are well below these bounds above which embedded 2SAT subproblems appear with high probability, it seems that the impact of forcers on the instance hardness goes beyond simply producing embedded easy subproblems. As forcers can appear at a relatively low constraint tightness even in CSP models such as the flawless model, approaches that are solely based on restricting constraint tightness to generate interesting and typically hard instances cannot be as effective as has been previously believed.

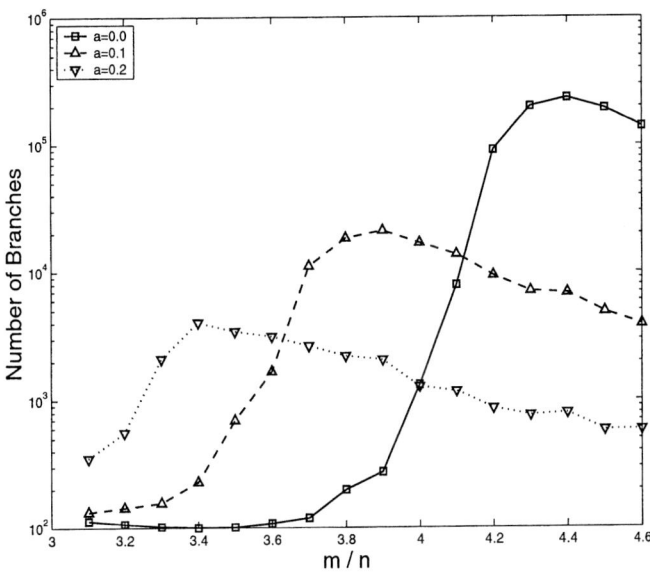

Fig. 2. Effects of an increase in the constraint tightness on the instance hardness for $\mathcal{F}(n, m, 0.0), \mathcal{F}(n, m, 0.1)$, and $\mathcal{F}(n, m, 0.2)$. $n = 250$.

4.2 Comparisons Between Three Random CSP Models

This set of experiments is designed to investigate the effectiveness of the generalized flawless random CSP model. We generate random instances of the classical random models $\mathcal{B}_{n,m}^{d,t}$, flawless random model $\mathcal{B}_{n,m}^{d,t}[1]$, and the generalized random model $\mathcal{B}_{n,m}^{d,t}[\mathcal{K}]$ with the domain size $d = 4$. For $\mathcal{B}_{n,m}^{d,t}[\mathcal{K}]$, we have used a 2-regular connected bipartite graph as $\mathcal{K}$. These instances are then encoded as CNF formulas and solved by the SAT solver zChaff [12]. It looks unnatural that we have tested random CSP instances by converting them to SAT instances and using a SAT solver. This is justified by the following considerations. First, all of the existing research on the resolution complexity of random CSPs have been carried out by studying the resolution complexity of a SAT encoding of CSPs as described in Section 3. We have used the same encoding in the experiments. Secondly, it has been shown that as far as the complexity of solving unsatisfiable CSP instances is concerned, many of the existing CSP algorithms can be efficiently simulated by the resolution system of the corresponding SAT encodings of the CSPs [13].

The experiments show that the threshold of the solution probability of the generalized random CSP model $\mathcal{B}_{n,m}^{d,t}[\mathcal{K}]$ is much sharper than those of $\mathcal{B}_{n,m}^{d,t}$ and $\mathcal{B}_{n,m}^{d,t}[1]$. More importantly, instances of $\mathcal{B}_{n,m}^{d,t}[\mathcal{K}]$ at the phase transition are much harder than those of $\mathcal{B}_{n,m}^{d,t}$ and $\mathcal{B}_{n,m}^{d,t}[1]$, as shown in Tables 1-3 where the median of the number of branches of zChaff for 100 instances of each of the three random CSP models is listed at different stages of the solubility phase

Table 1. Maximum Median Number of Branches of zChaff on random instances of three random CSP models, over all $\frac{m}{n}$. Domain size $d = 4$ and $\mathcal{K}$ is 2-regular.

	Number of Branches		
(n, t)	$\mathcal{B}_{n,m}^{d,t}$	$\mathcal{B}_{n,m}^{d,t}[1]$	$\mathcal{B}_{n,m}^{d,t}[\mathcal{K}]$
$(100, 6)$	230	224	399
$(300, 6)$	1830	1622	4768
$(500, 6)$	7152	6480	45315
$(300, 8)$	843	1010	2785

Table 2. Median Number of Branches of zChaff on random instances of three random CSP models at the smallest $\frac{m}{n}$ where the solution probability is less than 0.1. Domain size $d = 4$ and $\mathcal{K}$ is 2-regular.

	Number of Branches		
(n, t)	$\mathcal{B}_{n,m}^{d,t}$	$\mathcal{B}_{n,m}^{d,t}[1]$	$\mathcal{B}_{n,m}^{d,t}[\mathcal{K}]$
$(100, 6)$	116	154	241
$(300, 6)$	819	700	4768
$(500, 6)$	1398	1649	45315
$(300, 8)$	204	269	1118

Table 3. Median Number of Branches of zChaff on random instances of three random CSP models at the largest $\frac{m}{n}$ where the solution probability is greater than 0.9. Domain size $d = 4$ and $\mathcal{K}$ is 2-regular.

	Number of Branches		
(n, t)	$\mathcal{B}_{n,m}^{d,t}$	$\mathcal{B}_{n,m}^{d,t}[1]$	$\mathcal{B}_{n,m}^{d,t}[\mathcal{K}]$
$(100, 6)$	211	212	199
$(300, 6)$	1327	1595	2809
$(500, 6)$	7152	6450	8787
$(300, 8)$	843(0.67)	709	2785

transition: Table 1 is for the constraint density $\frac{m}{n}$ where the maximum median of the number of branches is observed; Table 2 is for the constraint density $\frac{m}{n}$ where the solubility probability is less than 0.1; and Table 3 is for the constraint density $\frac{m}{n}$ where the solubility probability is greater than 0.9.

It can be seen that while the classical random CSP model and flawless matrix CSP model have little difference, the proposed strong flawless random CSP model $\mathcal{B}_{n,m}^{d,t}[\mathcal{K}]$ with $\mathcal{K}$ being a connected 2-regular bipartite graph is significantly harder in all of the cases except row 1 in Table 3. It is also interesting to notice that the most significant difference in the hardness among the three models is at the phase where instances of the random CSP models are almost always unsatisfiable. A plausible explanation for this phenomenon is that consistency is a property that may also help improve the efficiency of search algorithms in solving satisfiable instances.

5 Conclusions

In this paper, we have shown that consistency, a notion that has been introduced in an effort to improve the efficiency of CSP algorithms, also plays an important role in the design of random CSP models that have interesting threshold behavior and guaranteed exponential complexity at phase transitions, while at the same time allow a much higher constraint tightness. We have also proposed a scheme to generate random consistent random CSPs by generalizing the idea of flawless random CSPs. Initial experiments show that the proposed model is indeed significantly harder than existing random CSP models.

References

1. Achlioptas, D., L.M.Kirousis, E.Kranakis, D.Krizanc, M.Molloy, Y.C.Stamation: Random constraint satisfaction: A more accurate picture. In: Proceedings of CP97, Springer (1997) 107–120
2. Gent, I., MacIntyre, E., Prosser, P., Smith, B., Walsh, T.: Random constraint satisfaction: Flaws and structure. Constraints **6** (2001) 345–372
3. Gao, Y., Culberson, J.: Resolution complexity of random constraint satisfaction problems: Another half of the story. In: LICS'03 Workshop on Typical Case Complexity and Phase Transitions. (2003)
4. Molloy, M., Salavatipour, M.: The resolution complexity of random constraint satisfaction problems. In: Proceedings of FOCS 2003. (2003)
5. Xu, K., Li, W.: Exact phase transitions in random constraint satisfaction problems. Journal of Artificial Intelligence Research **12** (2000) 93–103
6. Smith, B.M.: Constructing an asymptotic phase transition in random binary constraint satisfaction problems. Theoretical Computer Science **265** (2001) 265–283
7. Chvatal, V., Szemeredi, E.: Many hard examples for resolution. Journal of the Association for Computing Machinery **35** (1988) 759–768
8. Beame, P., Karp, R.M., Pitassi, T., Saks, M.E.: On the complexity of unsatisfiability proofs for random k -CNF formulas. In: ACM Symposium on Theory of Computing. (1998) 561–571
9. Achlioptas, D., Beame, P., Molloy, M.: A sharp threshold in proof complexity. In: ACM Symposium on Theory of Computing. (2001) 337–346
10. Mitchell, D.: Resolution complexity of random constraints. In: Proceedings Principles and Practices of Constraint Programming (CP-2002), Springer (2002) 295–309
11. Beame, P., Culberson, J., Mitchell, D., Moore, C.: The resolution complexity of random graph k-colorability. Electronic Colloquium on Computational Complexity, TR04-012 (2004)
12. Zhang, L., Madigan, C., Moskewicz, M., Malik, S.: Efficient conflict driven learning in a boolean satisfiability solver. In: Proceedings of International Conference on Computer Aided Design (ICCAD2001). (2001)
13. Mitchell, D.G.: The Resolution Complexity of Constraint Satisfaction. PhD thesis, Department of Computer Science, University of Toronto, Canada (2002)
14. Gao, Y., Culberson, J.: Consistency and random constraint satisfaction models. Technical Report TR04-13, Department of Computing Science, University of Alberta (2004)
15. Ben-Sasson, E., Wigderson, A.: Short proofs are narrow - resolution made simple. Journal of ACM **49** (2001)

A Appendix

In this section, we present more concepts related to the resolution complexity results stated in this paper and outline the proof of Theorems 1, 2, and 3. Detailed proofs can be found in [14].

A.1 Theorem 1

In this subsection, we outline the proof of Theorem 1. First let us formalize some definitions such as a forcer, a forbidding cycle, and an r-flower. Following [10], we call an expression of the form $x : \alpha$ a literal for a CSP. A literal $x : \alpha$ evaluates to TRUE at an assignment if the variable x is assigned the value α. A nogood for a CSP, denoted by $\eta(x_1 : \alpha_1, \cdots, x_l : \alpha_l)$, is a disjunction of the negations of the literals $x_i : \alpha_i, 1 \leq i \leq l$. A nogood is equivalent to a restriction $\{\alpha_1, \cdots, \alpha_l\}$ on the set of variables $\{x_1, \cdots, x_l\}$, and the restrictions of a constraint correspond to a set of nogoods defined over the same set of variables.

Definition 5 (Forcers [4]). *A constraint C_f with $\mathrm{var}(C_f) = \{x_1, x_2\}$ is called an (α, β)-forcer if its restriction set corresponds to the set of nogoods*

$$NG(C_f) = \{\eta(x_1 : \alpha, x_2 : \gamma); \gamma \neq \beta\}.$$

We say that a constraint C contains an (α, β)-forcer C_f defined on the same set of variables as C if $NG(C_f) \subseteq NG(C)$.

Definition 6 (Forbidding cycles and r-flowers [4]). *An α-forbidding cycle for a variable x_0 is a set of constraints $C_1(x_0, x_1), C_2(x_1, x_2), \cdots, C_{r-1}(x_{r-2}, x_{r-1})$, and $C_r(x_{r-1}, x_0)$ such that $C_1(x_0, x_1)$ is an (α, α_1)-forcer, $C_r(x_{r-1}, x_0)$ is an (α_{r-1}, α_r)-forcer $(\alpha_r \neq \alpha)$, and $C_i(x_{i-1}, x_i)$ is an (α_{i-1}, α_i)-forcer $(2 \leq i \leq r-1)$. We call x_0 the center variable of the cycle.*

An r-flower $R = \{C_1, \cdots, C_d\}$ consists of d (the domain size) forbidding cycles each of which has length r such that (1) $C_i, 1 \leq i \leq d$, have the same center variable x; (2) each C_i is an α_i-forbidding cycle of the common center variable x; and (3) these forbidding cycles do not share any other variables.

The following facts are straightforward to establish:

1. An r-flower consists of $s = d(r-1) + 1 = dr - d + 1$ variables and dr constraints;
2. The total number of r-flowers is $\binom{n}{s} s!(d-1)^d d^{d(r-1)}$.
3. A constraint in the flawless CSP model is an (α, β)-forcer only if the pair (α, β) is one of the pre-selected tuples in the flawless constraint matrix.

The probability for a constraint to contain a forcer and the probability for the flawless random CSP to contain an r-flower are given in the following lemma.

Lemma 1. *Consider the flawless random CSP $\mathcal{B}^{d,t}_{n,m}[1]$ and define $f_e = \dfrac{\binom{d^2-d-d+1}{t-d+1}}{\binom{d^2-d}{t}}$.*

1. The probability that a given constraint $C(x_1, x_2)$ contains an (α, β)-forcer is

$$\frac{1}{d} f_e. \tag{1}$$

2. Let R be an r-flower and let $c = m/n$,

$$P\{R \text{ appears in } \mathcal{B}^{d,t}_{n,m}[1]\} = O(1)(2cf_e)^{dr} \frac{1}{n^{dr}} \frac{1}{d^{dr}}. \tag{2}$$

Proof. Equation (1) follows from the following two observations: (A) $\frac{1}{d}$ is the probability for (α, β) to be one of the pre-selected tuples in the flawless conflict matrix; and (B) f_e is the probability for the rest of the tuples, $(\alpha, \gamma), \gamma \neq \beta$, to be in the set of t restrictions selected uniformly from $d^2 - d$ tuples.

To calculate the probability that a given r-flower R appears in $\mathcal{B}^{d,t}_{n,m}[1]$, notice that the probability of selecting all the constraint edges in R is

$$\frac{\binom{N-dr}{cn-dr}}{\binom{N}{cn}},$$

where $N = \binom{n}{2}$. And for each fixed choice of dr constraint edges in the r-flower, the probability for these constraints to contain the r-flower is $(\frac{1}{d}f_e)^{dr}$. □

The outline of the proof of Theorem 1 is given below.

Proof (**Proof of Theorem 1**). Let $c^* = \frac{d}{2f_e}$. We will show that if $c = \frac{m}{n} > c*$, then

$$\lim_n P\{\mathcal{B}^{d,t}_{n,m}[1] \text{ contains an r-flower}\} = 1. \tag{3}$$

Let I_R be the indicator function of the event that the r-flower R appears in $\mathcal{B}^{d,t}_{n,m}[1]$ and $X = \sum_R I_R$ where the sum is over all the possible r-flowers. Then, $\mathcal{B}^{d,t}_{n,m}[1]$ contains an r-flower if and only if $X > 0$.

By Lemma 1 and the fact that $s = dr - d + 1$, we have

$$E[X] = \sum_R E[I_R] = \Theta(1) n^{1-d} (2cf_e)^{dr}.$$

Therefore, if $c > c^*$ and $r = \lambda \log n$ with λ sufficiently large, $E[X] \to \infty$. An application of the second-moment method will prove the theorem. Details can be found in [14].

Remark 1. The relatively loose upper bound $c^* = \frac{d}{2f_e}$ in the above proof may be improved by a factor of d by further distinguishing among the r-flowers that share forcing values at a different number of shared variables.

A.2 Theorems 2 and 3

In this subsection, we give a brief introduction to the concepts and ideas required in the proof of Theorems 2 and 3.

Given a CNF formula $\mathcal{F}$, we use $\text{Res}(\mathcal{F})$ to denote the resolution complexity of $\mathcal{F}$, i.e., the length of the shortest resolution refutation of $\mathcal{F}$. The width of deriving a clause A from $\mathcal{F}$, denoted by $w(\mathcal{F} \vdash A)$, is defined to be the minimum over all the resolution refutations of the maximum clause size in a resolution refutation. Ben-Sasson and Wigderson [15] established a relationship between $\text{Res}(\mathcal{F})$ and $w(\mathcal{F} \vdash \emptyset)$:

$$\text{Res}(\mathcal{F}) = e^{\Omega(\frac{(w(\mathcal{F} \vdash \emptyset) - w(\mathcal{F}))^2}{n})}.$$

This relationship indicates that to give an exponential lower bound on the resolution complexity, it is sufficient to show that every resolution refutation of $\mathcal{F}$ contains a clause whose size is linear in n, the number of variables.

Let $\mathcal{T}$ be an instance of the CSP and $\text{CNF}(\mathcal{T})$ be the CNF encoding of $\mathcal{T}$. Mitchell [10] provided a framework within which one can investigate the resolution complexity of $\mathcal{T}$, i.e., the resolution complexity of the CNF formula $\text{CNF}(\mathcal{T})$ that encodes $\mathcal{T}$, by working directly on the structural properties of $\mathcal{T}$. A sub-instance $\mathcal{J}$ of $\mathcal{T}$ is a CSP instance such that $\text{var}(\mathcal{J}) \subset \text{var}(\mathcal{T})$ and $\mathcal{J}$ contains all the constraints of $\mathcal{T}$ whose scope variables are in $\text{var}(\mathcal{J})$. The following crucial concepts make it possible to work directly on the structural properties of the CSP instance when investigating the resolution complexity of the encoding CNF formula.

Definition 7 (Implies. Defined [10]). *For any assignment α to the variables in the CSP instance $\mathcal{T}$, we write $\hat{\alpha}$ for the truth assignment to the variables in $\text{CNF}(\mathcal{T})$ that assigns a variable $x : a$ the value TRUE if and only if $\alpha(x) = a$.*

Let C be a clause over the variables of $\text{CNF}(\mathcal{T})$. We say that a sub-instance $\mathcal{J}$ of $\mathcal{T}$ implies C, denoted as $\mathcal{J} \models C$, if and only if for each assignment α satisfying $\mathcal{J}$, $\hat{\alpha}$ satisfies C.

Definition 8 (Clause Complexity [10]). *Let $\mathcal{T}$ be a CSP instance. For each clause C defined over the Boolean variables in $\text{var}(\text{CNF}(\mathcal{T}))$, define*

$$\mu(C, \mathcal{T}) = \min\{|\text{var}(\mathcal{J})|; \mathcal{J} \text{ is a sub-instance and implies } C\}.$$

The following two concepts slightly generalize those used in [10, 4] and enable us to have a uniform treatment when establishing resolution complexity lower bounds.

Definition 9 (Boundary). *The boundary $\mathcal{B}(\mathcal{J})$ of a sub-instance $\mathcal{J}$ is the set of CSP variables such that for each $x \in \mathcal{B}(\mathcal{J})$, if $\mathcal{J}$ minimally implies a clause C defined on some Boolean variables in $\text{var}(\text{CNF}(\mathcal{J}))$, then C contains at least one of the Boolean variables, $x : a, a \in D$, that encode the CSP variable x.*

Definition 10 (Sub-critical Expansion [10]). *Let $\mathcal{T}$ be a CSP instance. The sub-critical expansion of $\mathcal{T}$ is defined as*

$$e(\mathcal{T}) = \max_{0 \leq s \leq \mu(\emptyset, \mathcal{T})} \min_{s/2 \leq |\text{var}(\mathcal{J})| \leq s} |\mathcal{B}(\mathcal{J})| \qquad (4)$$

where the minimum is taken over all the sub-instances of $\mathcal{T}$ such that $s/2 \leq |\text{var}(\mathcal{J})| \leq s$.

The following theorem relates the resolution complexity of the CNF encoding of a CSP instance to the sub-critical expansion of the CSP instance.

Theorem 6. *[10] For any CSP instance $\mathcal{T}$, we have*

$$w(\text{CNF}(\mathcal{T}) \vdash \emptyset) \geq e(\mathcal{T}) \tag{5}$$

To establish an asymptotically exponential lower bound on $\text{Res}(\mathcal{C})$ for a random CSP $\mathcal{C}$, it is enough to show that there is a constant $\beta^* > 0$ such that

$$\lim_n P\{e(\mathcal{C}) \geq \beta^* n\} = 1. \tag{6}$$

For any $\alpha > 0$, let $\mathcal{A}_m(\alpha)$ be the event $\{\mu(\emptyset, \mathcal{C}) > \alpha n\}$ and $\mathcal{A}_s(\alpha, \beta^*)$ be the event

$$\left\{ \min_{\frac{\alpha n}{2} \leq |\text{var}(\mathcal{J})| \leq \alpha n} \mathcal{B}(\mathcal{J}) \geq \beta^* n \right\}.$$

Notice that

$$P\{e(\mathcal{C}) \geq \beta^* n\} \geq P\{\mathcal{A}_m(\alpha) \cap \mathcal{A}_s(\alpha, \beta^*)\}$$
$$\geq 1 - P\{\overline{\mathcal{A}_m(\alpha)}\} - P\{\overline{\mathcal{A}_s(\alpha, \beta^*)}\}. \tag{7}$$

We only need to find appropriate α^* and β^* such that

$$\lim_n P\{\mathcal{A}_m(\alpha^*)\} = 1 \tag{8}$$

and

$$\lim_n P\{\mathcal{A}_s(\alpha^*, \beta^*)\} = 1. \tag{9}$$

Event $\mathcal{A}_m(\alpha^*)$ is about the size of minimally unsatisfiable sub-instances. For the event $\mathcal{A}_s(\alpha^*, \beta^*)$, a common practice is to identify a special subclass of boundaries and show that this subclass is large. For different random CSP models and under different assumptions on the model parameters, there are different ways to achieve this. Details about the proofs of Theorems 2 and 3 can be found in [14].

Statistical Regimes Across Constrainedness Regions*

Carla P. Gomes[1], Cèsar Fernández[2], Bart Selman[1], and Christian Bessiere[3]

[1] Dpt. of Computer Science, Cornell University, Ithaca, NY 14853, USA
{carla,selman}@cs.cornell.edu
[2] Dpt. d'Informàtica, Universitat de Lleida, Jaume II, 69, E-25001 Lleida, Spain
cesar@eup.udl.es
[3] LIRMM-CNRS, 161 rue Ada, 34392, Montpellier Cedex 5, France
bessiere@lirmm.fr

Abstract. Much progress has been made in terms of boosting the effectiveness of backtrack style search methods. In addition, during the last decade, a much better understanding of problem hardness, typical case complexity, and backtrack search behavior has been obtained. One example of a recent insight into backtrack search concerns so-called heavy-tailed behavior in randomized versions of backtrack search. Such heavy-tails explain the large variations in runtime often observed in practice. However, heavy-tailed behavior does certainly not occur on all instances. This has led to a need for a more precise characterization of when heavy-tailedness does and when it does not occur in backtrack search. In this paper, we provide such a characterization. We identify different statistical regimes of the tail of the runtime distributions of randomized backtrack search methods and show how they are correlated with the "sophistication" of the search procedure combined with the inherent hardness of the instances. We also show that the runtime distribution regime is highly correlated with the distribution of the depth of inconsistent subtrees discovered during the search. In particular, we show that an exponential distribution of the depth of inconsistent subtrees combined with a search space that grows exponentially with the depth of the inconsistent subtrees implies heavy-tailed behavior.

1 Introduction

Significant advances have been made in recent years in the design of search engines for constraint satisfaction problems (CSP), including Boolean satisfiability problems (SAT). For complete solvers, the basic underlying solution strategy is backtrack search enhanced by a series of increasingly sophisticated techniques, such as non-chronological backtracking, fast pruning and propagation methods, nogood (or clause) learning, and more recently randomization and restarts. For example, in areas such as planning and finite model-checking, we are now able to solve large CSP's with up to a million variables and several million constraints.

---
* This work was supported in part by the Intelligent Information Systems Institute, Cornell University (AFOSR grant F49620-01-1-0076).

The study of problem structure of combinatorial search problems has also provided tremendous insights in our understanding of the interplay between structure, search algorithms, and more generally, typical case complexity. For example, the work on phase transition phenomena in combinatorial search has led to a better characterization of search cost, beyond the worst-case notion of NP-completeness. While the notion of NP-completeness captures the computational cost of the very hardest possible instances of a given problem, in practice, one may not encounter many instances that are quite that hard. In general, CSP problems exhibit an "easy-hard-easy" pattern of search cost, depending on the constrainedness of the problem [1]. The computational hardest instances appear to lie at the phase transition region, the area in which instances change from being almost all solvable to being almost all unsolvable. The discover of "exceptionally hard instances" reveals an interesting phenomenon : such instances seem to defy the "easy-hard-easy" pattern, they occur in the under-constrained area, but they seem to be considerably harder than other similar instances and even harder than instances from the critically constrained area. This phenomenon was first identified by Hogg and Williams in graph coloring and by Gent and Walsh in satisfiability problems [2, 3]. However, it was shown later that such instances are not inherently difficult; for example, by renaming the variables such instances can often be easily solved [4, 5]. Therefore, the "hardness" of exceptionally hard instances does not reside purely in the instances, but rather in the combination of the instance with the details of the search method. Smith and Grant provide a detailed analysis of the occurrence of exceptionally hard instances for backtrack search, by considering a deterministic backtrack search procedure on ensembles of instances with the same parameter setting (see e.g., [6]).

Recently, researchers have noted that for a proper understanding of search behavior one has to study full runtime distributions [3, 7–10]. In our work we have focused on the study of randomized backtrack search algorithms [8]. By studying the runtime distribution produced by a randomized algorithm on a *single* instance, we can analyze the variance caused *solely* by the algorithm, and therefore separate the algorithmic variance from the variance between different instances drawn from an underlying distributions. We have shown previously that the runtime distributions of randomized backtrack search procedures can exhibit extremely large variance, even when solving *the same instance over and over again*. This work on the study of the runtime distributions of randomized backtrack search algorithms further clarified that the source of extreme variance observed in exceptional hard instances was not due to the inherent hardness of the instances: A randomized version of a search procedure on such instances in general solves the instance easily, even though it has a non-negligible probability of taking very long runs to solve the instance, considerably longer than all the other runs combined. Such extreme fluctuations in the runtime of backtrack search algorithms are nicely captured by so-called heavy-tailed distributions, distributions that are characterized by extremely long tails with some infinite moments [3, 8]. The decay of the tails of heavy-tailed distributions follows a power law – much slower than the decay of standard distributions, such as the normal or the exponential distribution, that have tails that decay exponentially. Further insights into the empirical evidence of heavy-tailed phenomena of randomized backtrack search methods were provided by abstract models of backtrack search that show that, under certain conditions, such procedures provably exhibit heavy-tailed behavior [11, 12].

Main Results. So far, evidence for heavy-tailed behavior of randomized backtrack search procedures on concrete instance models has been largely empirical. Moreover, it is clear that not all problem instances exhibit heavy-tailed behavior. The goal of this work is to provide a better characterization of *when* heavy-tailed behavior occurs, and *when it does not*, when using randomized backtrack search methods. We study the empirical runtime distributions of *randomized* backtrack search procedures across different constrainedness regions of random binary constraint satisfaction models[1]. In order to obtain the most accurate empirical runtime distributions, all our runs are performed without censorship (*i.e.*, we run our algorithms without a cutoff) over the largest possible size. Our study reveals dramatically different statistical regimes for randomized backtrack search algorithms across the different constrainedness regions of the CSP models. Figure 1 provides a preview of our results. The figure plots the runtime distributions (the survival function, *i.e.*, the probability of a run taking more than x backtracks) of a basic randomized backtrack search algorithm (no look-ahead and no look-back), using random variable and value selection, for different constrainedness regions of one of our CSP models (model E; instances with 17 variables and domain size 8). We observe two regions with dramatically different statistical regimes of the runtime distribution.

In the first regime (the bottom two curves in Fig. 1, $p \leq 0.07$), we see heavy-tailed behavior. This means that the runtime distributions decay slowly. In the log-log plot, we see linear behavior over several orders of magnitude. When we increase the constrainedness of our model (higher p), we encounter a different statistical regime in the runtime distributions, where the heavy-tails disappear. In this region, the instances become inherently hard for the backtrack search algorithm, all the runs become homogeneously long, and therefore the variance of the backtrack search algorithm decreases and the tails of its survival function decay rapidly (see top two curves in Fig. 1, with $p = 0.19$ and $p = 0.24$; tails decay exponentially).

A common intuitive understanding of the extreme variability of backtrack search is that on certain runs the search procedure may hit a very large inconsistent subtree that needs to be fully explored, causing "thrashing" behavior.

---

[1] Hogg and Willimans (94) provided the first report of heavy-tailed behavior in the context of backtrack search. They considered a *deterministic* backtrack search procedure on different instances drawn from a given distribution. Our work is of different nature as we study heavy-tailed behavior of the runtime distribution of a given *randomized* backtrack search method on a particular problem instance, thereby isolating the variance in runtime due to different runs of the algorithm.

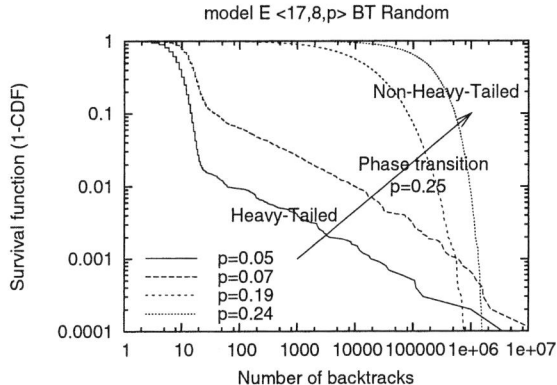

Fig. 1. Heavy-tailed (linear behavior) and non-heavy-tailed regime in the runtime of instances of model E $\langle 17, 8, p \rangle$. CDF stands for Cummulative Density Function.

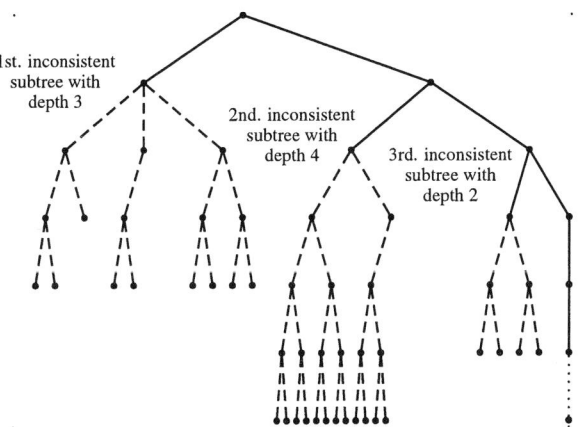

Fig. 2. Inconsistent subtrees in backtrack search.

To confirm this intuition and in order to get further insights into the statistical behavior of our backtrack search method, we study the inconsistent sub-trees discovered by the algorithm during the search (see Figure 2).

The distribution of the depth of inconsistent trees is quite revealing: when the distribution of the depth of the inconsistent trees decreases exponentially (see Figure 3, bottom panel, $p = 0.07$) the runtime distribution of the backtrack search method has a power law decay (see Figure 3, top panel, $p = 0.07$). In other words, when the backtrack search heuristic has a good probability of finding relatively shallow inconsistent subtrees, and this probability decreases exponentially as the depth of the inconsistent subtrees increases, heavy-tailed behavior occurs. Contrast this behavior with the case in which the survival function of the runtime distribution of the backtrack search method is not heavy-tailed (see Figure

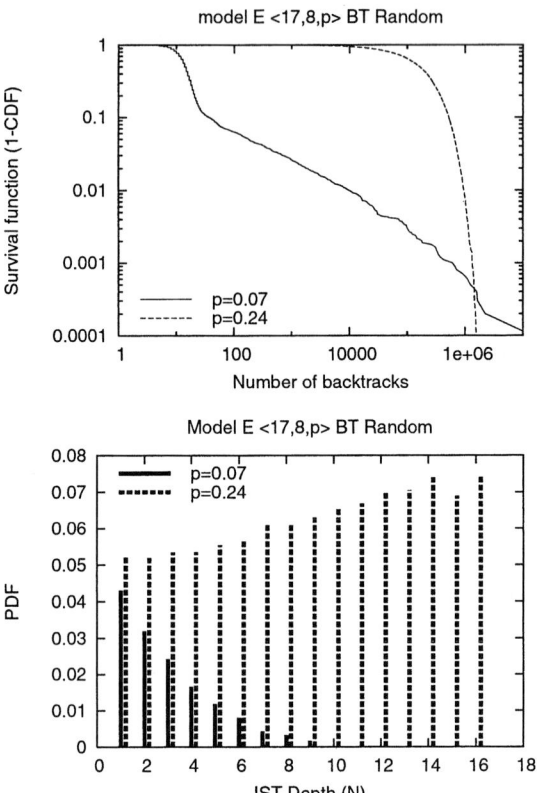

Fig. 3. Example of a heavy-tailed instance ($p = 0.07$) and a non-heavy-tailed instance ($p = 0.24$): (top) Survival function of runtime distribution, (bottom) probability density function of depth of inconsistent subtrees encountered during search. The subtree depth for $p = 0.07$ instance is exponentially distributed.

3, top panel, $p = 0.24$). In this case, the distribution of the depth of inconsistent trees no longer decreases exponentially (see Figure 3, bottom panel, $p = 0.24$).

In essence, these results show that the distribution of inconsistent subproblems encountered during backtrack search is highly correlated with the tail behavior of the runtime distribution. We provide a formal analysis that links the exponential search tree depth distribution with heavy-tailed runtime profiles. As we will see below, the predictions of our model closely match our empirical data.

2 Definitions, Problem Instances, and Search Methods

Constraint Networks. A finite binary *constraint network* $\mathcal{P} = (\mathcal{X}, \mathcal{D}, \mathcal{C})$ is defined as a set of n *variables* $\mathcal{X} = \{x_1, \ldots, x_n\}$, a set of *domains* $\mathcal{D} = \{D(x_1), \ldots, D(x_n)\}$, where $D(x_i)$ is the finite set of possible *values* for variable x_i, and a set $\mathcal{C}$ of binary *constraints* between pairs of variables. A constraint C_{ij} on the ordered set of variables (x_i, x_j) is a subset of the Cartesian product $D(x_i) \times D(x_j)$ that specifies the *allowed* combinations of values for the variables x_i and x_j. A *solution* of a constraint network is an instantiation of the variables such that all the constraints are satisfied. The constraint satisfaction problem (CSP) involves finding a solution for the constraint network or proving that none exists. We used a direct CSP encoding and also a Boolean satisfiability encoding (SAT) [13].

Random Problems. The CSP research community has always made a great use of randomly generated constraint satisfaction problems for comparing different search techniques and studying their behavior. Several models for generating these random problems have been proposed over the years. The oldest one, which was the most commonly used until the middle 90's, is *model A*. A network generated by this model is characterized by four parameters $\langle N, D, p1, p2 \rangle$, where N is the number of variables, D the size of the domains, p_1 the probability of having a constraint between two variables, and p_2, the probability that a pair of values is forbidden in a constraint. Notice that the variance in the type of problems generated with the same four parameters can be large, since the actual number of constraints for two problems with the same parameters can vary from one problem to another, and the actual number of forbidden tuples for two constraints inside the same problem can also be different. Model B does not have this variance. In *model B*, the four parameters are again $N, D, p1$, and $p2$, where N is the number of variables, and D the size of the domains. But now, p_1 is the proportion of binary constraints that are in the network (*i.e.*, there are exactly $c = \lfloor p_1 \cdot N \cdot (N-1)/2 \rfloor$ constraints), and p_2 is the proportion of forbidden tuples in a constraint (*i.e.*, there are exactly $t = \lfloor p_2 \cdot D^2 \rfloor$ forbidden tuples in each constraint). Problem classes in this model are denoted by $\langle N, D, c, t \rangle$. In [14] it was shown that model B (and model A as well) can be "flawed" when we increase N. Indeed, when N goes to infinity, we will almost surely have a *flawed* variable (that is, one variable which has all its values inconsistent with one of the constraints involving it). *Model E* was proposed to overcome this weakness. It is a three parameter model, $\langle N, D, p \rangle$, where N and D are the same as in the other models, and $\lfloor p \cdot D^2 \cdot N \cdot (N-1)/2 \rfloor$ forbidden pairs of values are selected with repetition out of the $D^2 \cdot N \cdot (N-1)/2$ possible pairs. There is a way of tackling the problem of flawed variables in model B. In [15] it is shown that by putting certain constraints on the relative values of N, D, p_1, and p_2, one can guarantee that model B is sound and scalable, for a range of values of the parameters. In our work, we only considered instances of model B that fall within such a range of values.

Search Trees. A *search tree* is composed of *nodes* and *arcs*. A node u represents an ordered partial instantiation $I(u) = (x_{i_1} = v_{i_1}, \ldots, x_{i_k} = v_{i_k})$. A search tree is rooted at the particular node u_0 with $I(u_0) = \emptyset$. There is an arc from a node u to a node u_c if $I(u_c) = (I(u), x = v)$, x and v being a variable and one of its values. The node u_c is called a child of u and u a parent of u_c. Every node u in a tree T defines a *subtree* T_u that consists of all the nodes and arcs below u in T. The *depth* of a subtree T_u is the length of the longest path from u to any other node in T_u. An inconsistent subtree (IST) is a maximal subtree that does not contain any node u such that $I(u)$ is a solution. (See Fig. 2.) The maximum depth of an inconsistent subtree is referred to the "inconsistent subtree depth" (ISTD). We denote by $T(A, P)$ the search tree of a backtrack search algorithm A solving a particular problem P, which contains a node for each instantiation visited by A until a solution is reached or inconsistency of P is proved. Once assigned a partial instantiation $I(u) = (x_{i_1} = v_{i_1}, \ldots, x_{i_k} = v_{i_k})$ for node u, the algorithm will search for a partial instantiation of some of its children. In the case that there exists no instantiation which does not violate the constraints, algorithm A will take another value for variable x_{i_k}, and start again checking the children of this new node. In this situation, it is said that a *backtrack* happens. We use the number of wrong decisions or backtracks to measure the *search cost* of a given algorithm [16][2].

Algorithms. In the following, we will use different search procedures, that differ in the amount of propagation they perform, and in the order in which they generate instantiations. We used three levels of propagation: no propagation (backtracking, BT), removal of values directly inconsistent with the last instantiation performed (forward-checking, FC), and arc consistency propagation (maintaining arc consistency, MAC). We used three different heuristics for ordering variables: random selection of the next variable to instantiate (random), variables preordered by decreasing degree in the constraint graph (deg), and selection of the variable with smallest domain first, ties broken by decreasing degree (dom+deg) and always random value selection. For the SAT encodings we used the Davis-Putnam-Logemann-Loveland procedure. More specifically we used a simplified version of Satz [17], without its standard heuristic, and with static variable ordering, injecting some randomness in the value selection heuristics.

Heavy-Tailed or Pareto-Like Distributions. As we discussed earlier, the runtime distributions of backtrack search methods are often characterized by very long tails or *heavy-tails* (HT). These are distributions that have so-called Pareto like decay of the tails. For a general Pareto distribution $F(x)$, the probability that a random variable is larger than a given value x, *i.e.*, its survival function, is:
$$1 - F(x) = P[X > x] \sim Cx^{-\alpha}, \ x > 0,$$
where $\alpha > 0$ and $C > 0$ are constants. I.e., we have power-law decay in the tail of the distribution. These distributions have infinite variance when $1 < \alpha < 2$ and

---

[2] In the rest of the paper sometimes we refer to the search cost as runtime. Even though there are some discrepancies between runtime and the search cost measured in number of wrong decisions or backtracks, such differences are not significant in terms of the tail regime of the distributions.

infinite mean and variance when $0 < \alpha \leq 1$. The log-log plot of the tail of the survival function $(1 - F(x))$ of a Pareto-like distribution shows linear behavior with slope determined by α.

3 Empirical Results

In the previous section, we defined our models and algorithms, as well as the concepts that are central in our study: the runtime distributions of our backtrack search methods and the associated distributions of the depth of the inconsistent subtrees found by the backtrack method. As we discussed in the introduction, our key findings are: (1) we observe different regimes in the behavior of these distributions as we move along different instance constrainedness regions; (2) when the depth of the inconsistent subtrees encountered during the search by the backtrack search method follows an exponential distribution, the corresponding backtrack search method search exhibits heavy-tailed behavior. In this section, we provide the empirical data upon which these findings are based.

We present results for the survival functions of the search cost (number of wrong decisions or number of backtracks) of our backtrack search algorithms. All the plots were computed with at least 10,000 independent executions of a randomized backtrack search procedure on a given (uniquely generated) problem satisfiable instance. For each parameter setting we considered over 20 instances. In order to obtain more accurate empirical runtime distributions, all our runs were performed without censorship, i.e., we run our algorithms without any cutoff[3]. We also instrumented the code to obtain the information for the corresponding inconsistency sub-tree depth (ISTD) distributions.

Figure 4 (top) provides a detailed view of the heavy-tailed and non-heavy-tailed regions, as well as the progression from one region to the other. The figure displays the survival function (log-log scale) for running (pure) backtrack search with random variable and value selection on instances of Model E with 17 variables and a domain size of 8 for values of p (the constrainedness of the instances) ranging from $0.05 \leq p \leq 0.24$. We clearly identify the heavy-tailed region in which the log-log plot of the survival functions exhibits linear behavior, while in the non-heavy-tailed region the drop of the survival function is much faster than linear. The transition between regimes occurs around a constrainedness level of $p = 0.09$.

Figure 4 (bottom) depicts the probability density function of the corresponding inconsistent sub-tree depth (ISTD) distributions. The figure shows that while the ISTD distributions that correspond to the heavy-tailed region have an exponential behavior (below we show a good regression fit to the exponential distribution in this region), the ISTD distributions that correspond to the non-heavy-tailed region are quite different from the exponential distribution.

---

[3] For our data analysis, we needed purely uncensored data. We could therefore only consider relatively small problem instances. The results appear to generalize to larger instances.

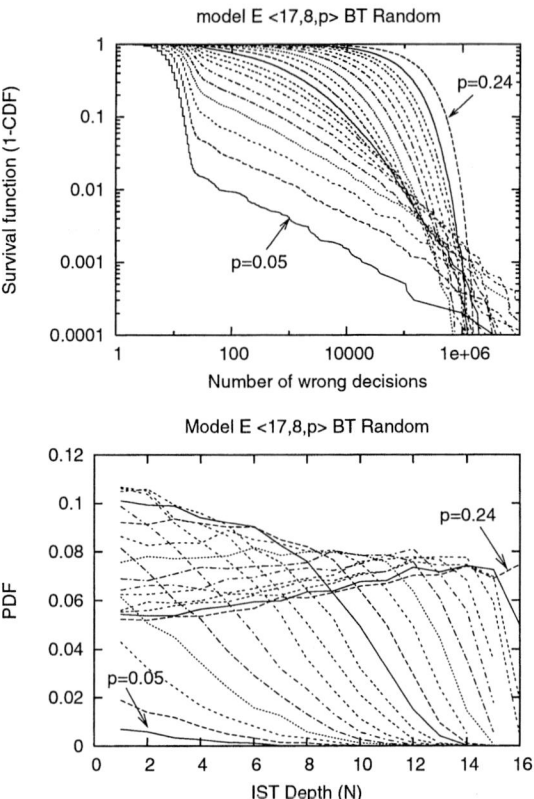

Fig. 4. The progression from heavy-tailed regime to non-heavy-tailed regime: (top) survival function of runtime distribution; (bottom) probability density function of the corresponding inconsistent sub-tree depth (ISTD) distribution.

For all the backtrack search variants that we considered on instances of model E, including the DPLL procedure, we observed a pattern similar to that of figure 4. (See bottom panel of figure 6 for DPLL data.)

We also observed a similar behavior – a transition from heavy-tailed region to non-heavy-tailed region with increased constrainedness – for instances of Model B, for different problem sizes and different search strategies. Figure 5 (top) shows the survival functions of runtime distributions of instances of model B $\langle 20, 8, 60, t\rangle$, for different levels of constrainedness, solved with BT-random. Fig.5 (bottom) shows the survival functions of runtime distributions of instances of model B $\langle 50, 10, 167, t\rangle$, for different levels of constrainedness, solved with MAC-random, a considerably more sophisticated search procedure. The top panel of Fig.6 gives the DPLL data. Again, the two different statistical regimes of the runtime distributions are quite clear.

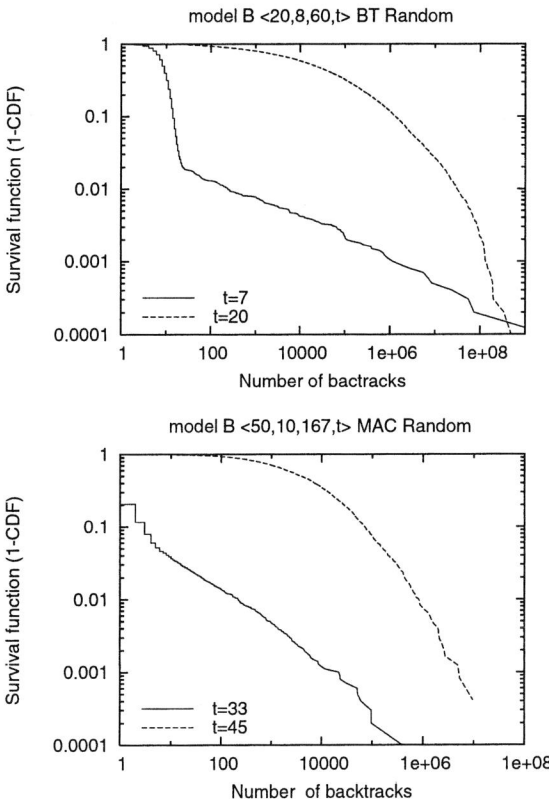

Fig. 5. Heavy-tailed and non-heavy-tailed regimes for instances of model B: (top) $\langle 20, 8, 60, t\rangle$, using BT-random, (bottom) $\langle 50, 10, 167, t\rangle$, using MAC-random.

To summarize our findings:

- For both models (B and E), for CSP and SAT encodings, for each backtrack search strategies, we clearly observe two different statistical regimes – a heavy-tailed and a non-heavy-tailed regime.
- As constrainedness increases (p increases), we move from the heavy-tailed region to the non-heavy-tailed region.
- The transition point from heavy-tailed to non-heavy-tailed regime is dependent on the particular search procedure adopted. As a general observation, we note that as the efficiency (and, in general, propagation strength) of the search method increases, the extension of the heavy-tailed region increases and therefore the heavy-tailed threshold gets closer to the phase transition.
- Exponentially distributed inconsistent sub-tree depth (ISTD) combined with exponential growth of the search space as the tree depth increases implies heavy-tailed runtime distributions. We observe that as the ISTD distributions move away from the exponential distribution, the runtime distributions become non-heavy-tailed.

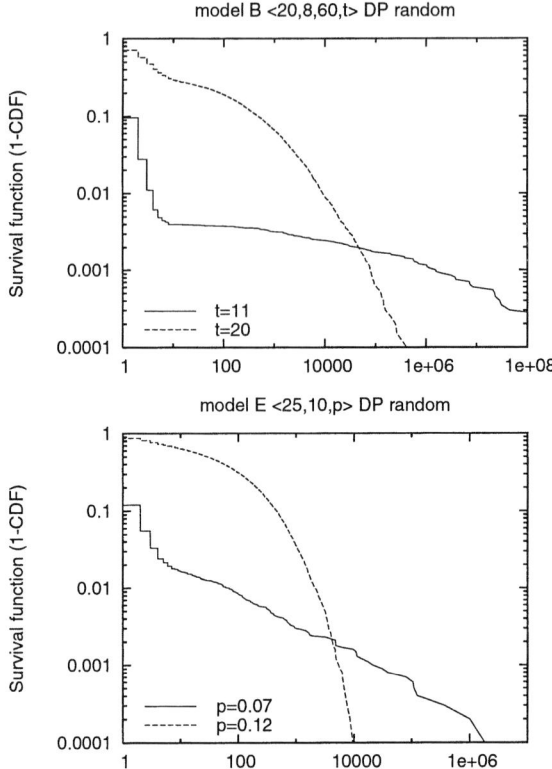

Fig. 6. Heavy-tailed and non-heavy-tailed regimes for instances of (top) model B $\langle 20, 8, 60, t \rangle$, using DP-random (DPLL procedure with static variable ordering and random value selection) and (bottom) model E $\langle 25, 10, p \rangle$ using DP-random.

These results suggest that the existence of heavy-tailed behavior in the cost distributions depends on the efficiency of the search procedure as well as on the level of constrainedness of the problem. Increasing the algorithm efficiency tends to shift the heavy-tail threshold closer to the phase transition.

For both models, B and E, and for the different search strategies, we clearly observed that when the ISTD follows an exponential distribution, the corresponding distribution is heavy-tailed. We refer to the forthcoming long version of this paper for the probability density functions of the corresponding inconsistent sub-tree depth distributions (ISTD) of model B, and for data on the regression fits (see also below) for all curves.

4 Validation

Let X be the search cost of a given backtrack search procedure, $P_{istd}[N]$ be the probability of finding an inconsistent subtree of depth N during search, and $P[X > x|N]$ the probability of having a inconsistent search tree of size larger than x, given a tree of depth N. Assuming that the inconsistent search tree depth follows an exponential distribution in the tail and the search cost inside an inconsistent tree grows exponentially, then the cost distribution of a search method is lower bounded by a Pareto distribution. More formally[4]:

Theoretical Model.

Assumptions:

- $P_{istd}[N]$ is exponentially distributed in the tail, i.e.,

$$P_{istd}[N] = B_1 e^{-B_2 N}, N > n_0 \qquad (1)$$

where B_1, B_2, and n_0 are constants.
- $P[X > x|N]$ is modeled as a complementary Heavyside function, $1 - H(x - k^N)$, where k is a constant and

$$H(x - a) = \begin{cases} 0, x < a \\ 1, x \geq a \end{cases}$$

Then, $P[X > x]$ is Pareto-like distributed

$$P[X > x] \approx \beta x^{-\alpha}$$

for $x > k^{n_0}$, where α and β are constants.

Derivation of result:

Note that $P[X > x]$ is lower bounded as follows

$$P[X > x] \geq \int_{N=0}^{\infty} P_{istd}[N] P[X > x|N] dN \qquad (2)$$

This is a lower bound since we consider only one inconsistent tree contributing to the search cost, when in general there are more inconsistent trees. Given the assumptions above, Eq. (2) results

$$P[X > x] \geq \int_{N=0}^{\infty} P_{istd}[N] (1 - H(x - k^N)) dN = \int_{N=\frac{\ln x}{\ln k}}^{\infty} P_{istd}[N] dN$$

Since $x > k^{n_0}$, we can use Eq.(1) for $P_{istd}[N]$, so Eq.(3) results in:

$$P[X > x] \geq \int_{N=\frac{\ln x}{\ln k}}^{\infty} B_1 e^{-B_2 N} dN = \frac{B_1}{B_2} e^{-B_2 \frac{\ln x}{\ln k}} = \beta x^{-\alpha}; \quad \alpha = \frac{B_2}{\ln k}; \quad \beta = \frac{B_1}{B_2}$$

In order to validate this model empirically we consider an instance of model B $\langle 20, 8, 60, 7 \rangle$, running BT-random, the same instance plotted in Fig. 5(a), for

---

[4] See forthcoming extended version of the paper for further details. A similar analysis goes through using the geometric distribution, the discrete analogue of the exponential.

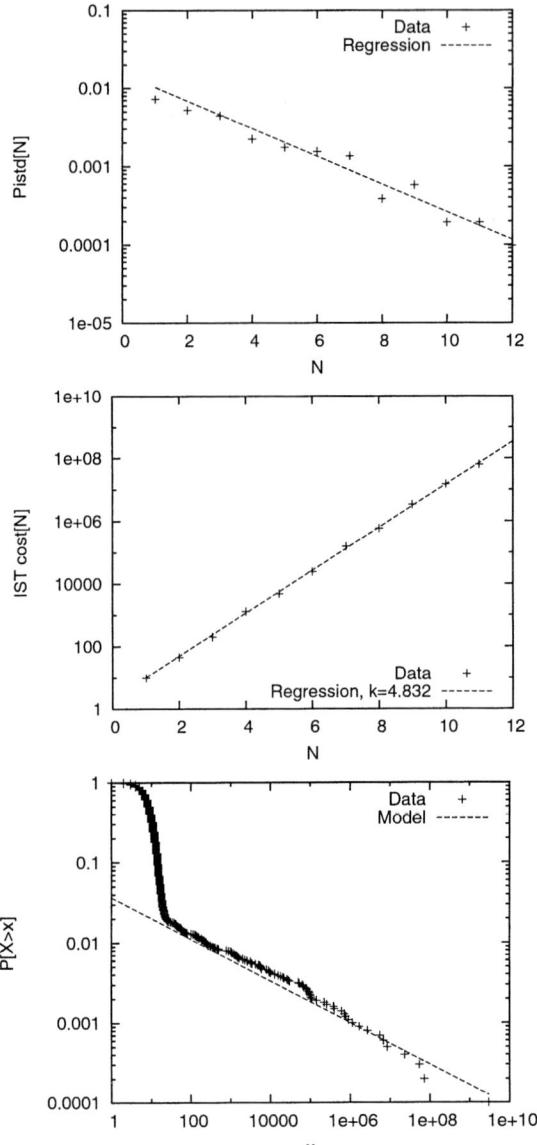

Fig. 7. Regressions for the estimation of B1=0.015, B2=0.408 (top plot; quality of fit $R^2 = 0.88$), and $k = 4.832$ (middle plot; $R^2 = 0.98$) and comparison of lower bound based on the theoretical model with empirical data (bottom plot). We have $\alpha = B_2/\ln(k) = 0.26$ from our model; $\alpha = 0.27$ directly from runtime data. Model B $\langle 20, 8, 60, t \rangle$, using BT-random.

which heavy-tailed behavior was observed ($t = 7$). The plots in Fig. 7 provide the regression data and fitted curves for the parameters B_1, B_2, and k, using $n_0 = 1$. The good quality of the linear regression fit suggests that our assumptions are very reasonable. Based on the estimated values for k, B_1, and B_2, we then compare the lower bound predicted using the formal analysis presented above with the empirical data. As we can see from Fig. 7, the theoretical model provides a good (tight) lower bound for the empirical data.

5 Conclusions and Future Work

We have studied the runtime distributions of complete backtrack search methods on instances of well-known random CSP binary models. Our results reveal different regimes in the runtime distributions of the backtrack search procedures and corresponding distributions of the depth of the inconsistent sub-trees. We see a changeover from heavy-tailed behavior to non-heavy-tailed behavior when we increase the constrainedness of the problem instances. The exact point of changeover depends on the sophistication of the search procedure, with more sophisticated solvers exhibiting a wider range of heavy-tailed behavior. In the non-heavy-tailed region, the instances become harder and harder for the backtrack search algorithm, and the runs become nearly homogeneously long. We have also shown that that there is a clear correlation between the the distributions of the depth of the inconsistent sub-trees encountered by the backtrack search method and the heavy-tailedness of the runtime distributions, with exponentially distributed sub-tree depths leading to heavy-tailed search. To further validate our findings, we compared our theoretical model, which models exponentially distributed subtrees in the search space, with our empirical data: the theoretical model provides a good (tight) lower bound for the empirical data. Our findings about the distribution of inconsistent subtrees in backtrack search give, in effect, information about the inconsistent subproblems that are created during the search. We believe that these results can be exploited in the design of more efficient restart strategies and backtrack solvers.

Acknowledgments

We would like to thank the anonymous reviewers for their comments and suggestions.

References

1. Hogg, T., Huberman, B., Williams, C.: Phase Transitions and Search Problems. Artificial Intelligence **81 (1-2)** (1996) 1–15
2. Gent, I., Walsh, T.: Easy Problems are Sometimes Hard. Artificial Intelligence **70** (1994) 335–345
3. Hogg, T., Williams, C.: The Hardest Constraint Problems: a Double Phase Transition. Artificial Intelligence **69** (1994) 359–377
4. Smith, B., Grant, S.: Sparse Constraint Graphs and Exceptionally Hard Problems. In: Proceedings IJCAI'95, Montréal, Canada (1995) 646–651

5. Selman, B., Kirkpatrick, S.: Finite-Size Scaling of the Computational Cost of Systematic Search. Artificial Intelligence **81** (1996) 273–295
6. Smith, B., Grant, S.: Modelling Exceptionally Hard Constraint Satisfaction Problems. In: Proceedings CP'97, Linz, Austria (1997) 182–195
7. Frost, D., Rish, I., Vila, L.: Summarizing CSP Hardness with Continuous Probability Distributions. In: AAAI-97, Providence RI (1997) 327–333
8. Gomes, C., Selman, B., Crato, N.: Heavy-tailed Distributions in Combinatorial Search. In: Proceedings CP'97, Linz, Austria (1997) 121–135
9. Hoos, H. PhD Thesis,TU Darmstadt (1998)
10. Dechter, R.: Constraint Processing. Morgan Kaufmann (2003)
11. Chen, H., Gomes, C., Selman, B.: Formal Models of Heavy-tailed Behavior in Combinatorial Search. In: Proceedings CP'01, Paphos, Cyprus (2001) 408–421
12. Williams, R., Gomes, C., Selman, B.: Backdoors to Typical Case Complexity. (2003)
13. Walsh, T.: SAT vs CSP. In: Proceedings CP'00, Singapore (2000) 441–456
14. Achlioptas, D., Kirousis, L., Kranakis, E., Krizanc, D., Molloy, M., Stamatiou, Y.: Random Constraint Satisfaction: a More Accurate Picture. In: Proceedings CP'97, Linz, Austria (1997) 107–120
15. Xu, K., Li, W.: Exact Phase Transition in Random Constraint Satisfaction Problems. JAIR **12** (2000) 93–103
16. Bessière, C., Zanuttini, B., Fernández, C.: Measuring Search Trees. In Hnich, B., ed.: Proceedings ECAI'04 Workshop on Modelling and Solving Problems with Constraints, Valencia, Spain (2004)
17. Li, C., Ambulagan: Heuristics Based on Unit Propagation for Satisfiability Problems. In: Proceedings IJCAI'97, Nagoya, Japan (1997) 366–371

Constraint-Based Combinators for Local Search

Pascal Van Hentenryck[1], Laurent Michel[2], and Liyuan Liu[2]

[1] Brown University, Box 1910, Providence, RI 02912
[2] University of Connecticut, Storrs, CT 06269-3155

Abstract. One of the most appealing features of constraint programming is its rich constraint language for expressing combinatorial optimization problems. This paper demonstrates that traditional combinators from constraint programming have natural counterparts for local search, although their underlying computational model is radically different. In particular, the paper shows that constraint combinators, such as logical and cardinality operators, reification, and first-class expressions can all be viewed as differentiable objects. These combinators naturally support elegant and efficient modelings, generic search procedures, and partial constraint satisfaction techniques for local search. Experimental results on a variety of applications demonstrate the expressiveness and the practicability of the combinators.

1 Introduction

Historically, most research on modeling and programming tools for combinatorial optimization has focused on systematic search, which is at the core of branch & bound and constraint satisfaction algorithms. However, in recent years, increased attention has been devoted to the design and implementation of programming tools for local search (e.g., [2, 20, 16, 7, 8, 12, 18]). This is motivated by the orthogonal strengths of the paradigms, the difficulty of obtaining efficient implementations, and the lack of compositionality and reuse in local search.

COMET [9, 17] is a novel, object-oriented, programming language specifically designed to simplify the implementation of local search algorithms. Comet supports a constraint-based architecture for local search organized around two main components: a declarative component which models the application in terms of constraints and functions, and a search component which specifies the search heuristic and meta-heuristic. Constraints and objective functions are natural vehicles to express combinatorial optimization problems and often capture combinatorial substructures arising in many practical applications. But constraints and objective functions have a fundamentally different computational model in COMET as they do not prune the search space. Rather they are *differentiable objects* that maintain a number of properties incrementally and provide algorithms to evaluate the effect of various operations on these properties. The search component then uses these functionalities to guide the local search using selectors and other high-level control structures [17]. The architecture enables local search algorithms to be high-level, compositional, and modular.

However, constraint programming languages and libraries also offer rich languages for combining constraints, including logical and cardinality operators, reification, and expressions over variables. These "combinators" are fundamental in practice, not only because they simplify problem modeling, but also because they lay the foundations for expressing various kinds of ad-hoc constraints that typically arise in complex applications, as well as generic search procedures.

This paper shows that traditional constraint programming combinators bring similar benefits for local search, although their underlying computational model differ significantly. In particular, the paper shows that arithmetic, logical, and cardinality operators, reification, and first-class expressions can all be viewed as differentiable objects, providing high-level and efficient abstractions for composing constraints and objectives in local search. These combinators naturally support very high-level local search models, partial constraint satisfaction techniques, and generic search procedures, which are independent of the application at hand and only rely on generic interfaces for constraints and objective functions. As a consequence, they foster the separation of concerns between modeling and search components, increase modularity, and favor compositionality and reuse. More generally, the paper shows that the rich language of constraint programming is conceptually robust and brings similar benefits to constraint programming and local search, despite their fundamentally different computational models.

The rest of this paper is organized as follows. Sections 2 and 3 discuss how to combine constraints and objective functions in COMET, Section 4 introduces first-class expressions, and Section 5 discusses generic search procedures. Applications and experimental results are presented together with the abstractions in these sections. Section 6 concludes the paper.

2 Constraints

Constraints in COMET are differentiable objects implementing the interface (partially) described in Figure 1. The interface gives access to the constraint variables (method `getVariables`) and to two incremental variables which represent the truth value of the constraint (method `isTrue`) and its violation degree (method `violations`). The violation degree is constraint-dependent and measures how much the constraint is violated. This information is often more useful than the constraint truth value as far as guiding the search is concerned. For instance, the violation degree of an arithmetic constraint $l \geq r$ is given by $\max(0, r - l)$. The violation degree of the combinatorial constraint `allPresent(R,x)`, which holds if all values in range R occur in array x, is given by $\#\{v \in R \mid \neg \exists i : x[i] = v\}$. The method `getViolations` returns the violations which may be attributed to a given variable, which is often useful in selecting local moves. The remaining methods provide the differentiable API of the constraint. They make it possible to evaluate the effect of an assignment, a swap, or multiple assignments on the violation degree. The differentiable API is fundamental in obtaining good performance on many applications, since the quality of local moves can be evalu-

```
Interface Constraint {
   inc{int}[] getVariables();
   inc{boolean} isTrue();
   inc{int} violations();
   int getViolations(inc{int} x);
   int getAssignDelta(inc{int} x,int v);
   int getSwapDelta(inc{int} x1,inc{int} x2);
   int getAssignDelta(inc{int}[] x,int[] v);
}
```

Fig. 1. The Constraint Interface in Comet (Partial Description).

Table 1. The Semantic of Some Constraint Combinators.

Combinator	Violation Degrees
c_1 && c_2	$v(c_1) + v(c_2)$
$c_1 \parallel c_2$	$\min(v(c_1), v(c_2))$
$\tau(c)$	if $v(c) > 0$ then 1 else 0
exactly$(k, [c_1, \ldots, c_n])$	$\text{abs}(\sum_{i=1}^{n} \tau(c_i) - k)$
atmost$(k, [c_1, \ldots, c_n])$	$\max(\sum_{i=1}^{n} \tau(c_i) - k, 0)$
$k \times c$	$k \times v(c)$
satisfactionConstraint(c)	$\tau(c)$

ated quickly. The rest of this section describes modeling abstractions to combine constraints. Table 1 summarizes the violation degrees of the various combinators.

Constraint Systems. Constraint systems, a fundamental modeling abstraction in COMET, are container objects representing a conjunction of constraints. Constraint systems are constraints themselves and implement the Constraint interface. Hence they maintain their truth value and their violation degree, i.e., the sum of the violation degrees of their constraints. They also support the differentiable API. Figure 2 depicts a simple COMET program for the n-queens problem. Lines 1-4 describe the problem variables and data structures, lines 5-9 describe the modeling component, and lines 10-13 specify the search procedure. Line 3 creates a uniform distribution and line 4 declares the decision variables: variable queen[i] represents the row of the queen placed in column i. These incremental variables are initialized randomly using the uniform distribution. Line 5 declares the constraint system and lines 6-8 specify the problem constraints using the ubiquitous allDifferent constraint. More precisely, they specify that the queens cannot be placed on the same row, the same upper diagonal, and the same lower diagonal. Lines 10-13 describe a min-conflict search procedure [11]. Line 11 selects the queen q with the most violations and line 12 chooses a new value v for queen q. Line 13 assigns this new value to the queen, which has the effect of (possibly) updating the violation degree of the subset of affected constraints and of the constraint system. Lines 11-13 are iterated until a solution is found.

```
1.   range Size = 1..1024;
2.   LocalSolver m();
3.   UniformDistribution distr(Size);
4.   inc{int} queen[i in Size](m,Size) := distr.get();

5.   ConstraintSystem S(m);
6.     S.post(allDifferent(queen));
7.     S.post(allDifferent(all(i in Size) queen[i] + i));
8.     S.post(allDifferent(all(i in Size) queen[i] - i));
9.   m.close();

10.  while (S.violations() > 0)
11.    selectMax(q in Size)(S.getViolations(queen[q]))
12.      selectMin(v in Size)(S.getAssignDelta(queen[q],v))
13.        queen[q] := v;
```

Fig. 2. A Comet Program for the Queens Problem.

Constraint systems provide a clean separation between the declarative and search components of a local search. Observe that it is possible to add new constraints to the constraint system without changing the search procedure. Similarly, it is possible to change the search procedure (e.g., adding a tabu list) without modifying the model. It is also important to stress that a single COMET program may use several constraint systems simultaneously. This is useful, for instance, for local search algorithms that maintain the feasibility of a subset of constraints (e.g., the hard constraints), while allowing others to be violated (e.g., the soft constraints).

Logical and Cardinality Operators. One of the appealing features of constraint programming is its ability to combine constraints using logical and cardinality operators. COMET offers similar functionalities for local search. For instance
`Constraint c = ((x != y) || (x != z));`
illustrates a disjunctive constraint in COMET. *The disjunctive constraint is a differentiable object implementing the* `Constraint` *interface.* In particular, the violation degree of a disjunction $c = c_1 \| c_2$ is given by $\min(v(c_1), v(c_2))$, where $v(c)$ denotes the violation degree of c.

COMET also features a variety of cardinality operators. For instance, Figure 3 depicts the use of the cardinality operator $\texttt{exactly}(k, [c_1, \ldots, c_n])$, a differentiable constraint which holds if exactly k constraints hold in $c_1, \ldots, c_n$. The figure depicts a COMET program to solve the magic series problem, a traditional benchmark in constraint programming. A series $(s_0, \ldots, s_n)$ is magic if s_i represents the number of occurrences of i in $(s_0, \ldots, s_n)$. Lines 6-10 in Figure 3 specify the modeling component. Line 8 features the cardinality operator to express that there are `magic[v]` occurrences of v in the magic series and line 9 adds the traditional redundant constraint. Lines 11-19 implement a min-conflict search with a simple tabu-search component. Observe the modeling component in this program which is similar to a traditional constraint programming solution. Interestingly, local search performs reasonably well on this problem as indicated

```
1.   int n = 400;
2.   range Size = 0..n-1;
3.   LocalSolver m();
4.   inc{int} magic[i in Size](m,Size) := 0;
5.   int tabu[i in Size] = -1;

6.   ConstraintSystem S(m);
7.   forall(v in Size)
8.     S.post(exactly(magic[v],all(i in Size) magic[i] == v));
9.   S.post(sum(i in Size) i * magic[i] == n);
10.  m.close();

11.  int it = 0;
12.  while (S.violations() > 0) {
13.    selectMax(s in Size: tabu[s] < it)(S.getViolations(magic[s]))
14.      selectMin(v in Size: magic[s] != v)(S.getAssignDelta(magic[s],v)) {
15.        magic[s] := v;
16.        tabu[s] = it + 3;
17.      }
18.    it = it + 1;
19.  }
```

Fig. 3. A Comet Program for the Magic Series Problem.

Table 2. Performance Results on the Magic Series Program.

n	10	30	50	70	90	110	130	150	170	190	210
$best(T)$	0.00	0.03	0.09	0.21	0.41	0.57	0.84	1.09	1.44	2.09	3.20
$\mu(T)$	0.01	0.09	0.41	1.05	1.78	5.70	13.58	21.70	47.60	67.83	150.41
$worst(T)$	0.02	0.37	1.57	7.35	10.85	30.95	102.63	86.54	347.77	400.20	761.11
$\sigma(T)$	0.01	0.12	0.56	1.73	2.84	9.12	22.87	31.38	81.80	110.71	240.85

in Table 2. The table gives the best, average, and worst times in seconds for 50 runs on a 2.4Ghz Pentium, as well as the standard deviation.

The contributions here are twofold. On the one hand, COMET naturally accommodates logical and cardinality operators as differentiable objects, allowing very similar modelings for constraint programming and local search. On the other hand, implementations of logical/cardinality operators directly exploit incremental algorithms for the constraints they combine, providing compositionality both at the language and implementation level. The implementations can in fact be shown optimal in terms of the input/output incremental model [14], assuming optimality of the incremental algorithms for the composed constraints.

Weighted Constraints. Many local search algorithms (e.g., [15, 4, 19]) use weights to focus the search on some subsets of constraints. Comet supports weight specifications which can be either static or dynamic. (Dynamic weights vary during the search). Weights can be specified with the * operator. For instance the snippet

```
Constraint c = 2 * allDifferent(x)
```

```
1.   LocalSolver m();
2.   UniformDistribution distr(Hosts);
3.   inc{int} boat[Guests,Periods](m,Hosts) := distr.get();
4.   int tabu[Guests,Periods,Hosts] = -1;

5.   ConstraintSystem S(m);
6.   forall(g in Guests)
7.     S.post(2 * allDifferent(all(p in Periods) boat[g,p]));
8.   forall(p in Periods)
9.     S.post(2 * knapsack(all(g in Guests) boat[g,p],crew,cap));
10.  forall(i in Guests, j in Guests : j > i)
11.    S.post(atmost(1,all(p in Periods) boat[i,p] == boat[j,p]));
12.  m.close();
```

Fig. 4. The Modeling Part of a Comet Program for the Progressive Party Problem.

Table 3. Experimental Results for the Progressive Party Problem.

Hosts/Periods	6	7	8	9	10
1-12,16	0.32 (0.30)	0.41 (0.35)	0.60 (0.54)	1.01 (0.69)	3.74 (1.27)
1-13	0.41 (0.34)	0.77 (0.46)	3.15 (0.99)	42.22 (5.80)	
1,3-13,19	0.41 (0.33)	0.79 (0.47)	3.50 (0.92)	28.6 (6.39)	
3-13,25,26	0.44 (0.35)	0.93 (0.50)	4.53 (1.30)	65.32 (7.79)	
1-11,19,21	1.75 (0.54)	36.1 (2.86)			
1-9,16-19	2.81 (1.06)	95.4 (4.81)			

associates a constant weight of 2 to an allDifferent constraint and returns an object implementing the Constraint interface. Its main effect is to modify the violation degree of the constraint and the results of its differentiable API. Weights can also be specified by incremental variables, which is useful in many applications where weights are updated after each local search iterations. This feature is illustrated later in the paper in a frequency allocation application.

Figure 4 depicts the modeling component of a COMET program to solve the progressive party problem. It illustrates both constant weights and the cardinality operator atmost. Line 7 expresses weighted allDifferent constraints to ensure that a party never visits the same boat twice. Line 9 posts weighted knapsack constraints to satisfy the capacity constraint on the boats. Finally, line 11 uses a cardinality constraint to specify that no two parties meet more than once over the course of the event. The cardinality operator makes for a very elegant modeling: it removes the need for the rather specific meetAtmostOnce constraint used in earlier version of the COMET program [9]. It also indicates the ubiquity of cardinality constraints for expressing, concisely and naturally, complex constraints arising in practical applications.

Table 3 describes experimental results for this modeling and the search procedure of [9] augmented with a restarting component that resets the current solution to a random configuration every 100,000 iterations in order to eliminate outlier runs. The table describes results for various configurations of hosts and various numbers of periods. The results report the average running times over

```
1.  SatisfactionSystem S(m);
2.  forall(d in DistanceCtrs)
3.    switch (d.ty) {
4.      case 1: S.post(abs(freq[d.v1]-freq[d.v2]) == d.rhs);break;
5.      case 2: S.post(abs(freq[d.v1]-freq[d.v2]) >  d.rhs);break;
6.      case 3: S.post(abs(freq[d.v1]-freq[d.v2]) <  d.rhs);break;
7.    }
```

Fig. 5. Partial Contraint Satisfaction in Frequency Allocation.

50 runs of the algorithm, as well as the best times in parenthesis. With the addition of a restarting component, the standard deviation for the hard instances is always quite low (e.g., configuration 1-9,16-19 with 7 periods has a mean of 95.4 and a deviation of 4.8) and shows that the algorithm's behavior is quite robust. The results were obtained on a 2.4Ghz Pentium 4 running Linux. The performance of the program is excellent, as the cardinality operator does not impose any significant overhead. Once again, the implementation can be shown incrementally optimal if the underlying constraints support optimal algorithms.

Partial Constraint Satisfaction. Some local search algorithms do not rely on violation degrees; rather they reason on the truth values of the constraints only. This is the case, for instance, in partial constraint satisfaction [3], where the objective is to minimize the (possibly weighted) number of constraint violations. COMET provides an operator to transform an arbitrary constraint into a satisfaction constraint, i.e., a constraint whose violation degree is 0 or 1 only. For instance, the snippet

`Constraint c = satisfactionConstraint(allDifferent(x));`

assigns to c the satisfaction counterpart of the `allDifferent` constraint. The key contribution here is the systematic derivation of the satisfaction implementation in terms of the original constraint interface. The resulting implementation only induces a small constant overhead.

COMET also supports satisfaction systems that systematically apply the satisfaction operator to the constraints posted to them, simplifying the modeling and the declarative reading. Figure 5 illustrates satisfaction systems on an excerpt from a frequency allocation problem, where the objective is to minimize the number of violated constraints. Line 1 declares the satisfaction system S, while lines 4, 5, and 6 post the various types of distance constraints to the system.

3 Objective Functions

We now turn to objective functions, another class of differentiable objects in COMET. Objective functions may be linear, nonlinear, or may capture combinatorial substructures arising in many applications. A typical example is the objective function `MinNbDistinct(x[1],...,x[n])` which minimizes the number of distinct values in `x[1],...,x[n]` and arises in graph coloring, frequency allocation, and other resource allocation problems.

```
Interface Objective {
  inc{int}[] getVariables();
  inc{int} value();
  inc{int} cost();
  int getCost(inc{int} x);
  int getAssignDelta(inc{int} x,int v);
  int getSwapDelta(inc{int} x1,inc{int} x2);
  int getAssignDelta(inc{int}[] x,int[] v);
}
```

Fig. 6. The Objective Interface in Comet (Partial Description).

Table 4. The Semantic of Some Objective Functions.

Objective	Value	Cost
MinNbDistinct(x[E])	$\#\{\ x[e]\ \|\ e \in E\ \}$	$-\sum_i \|\{e \in E \mid x[e] = i\}\|^2$
MinNbDistinct(x[E],w[E])	$\#\{\ x[e]\ \|\ e \in E\ \}$	$\sum_{e \in E} w[x[e]]$
MaxNbDistinct(x[E],w[V])	$\#\{\ x[e]\ \|\ e \in E\ \}$	$\sum_{v \in V : \neg \text{occur}(v,x)} w[v]$
condSum($b[E], c[E]$)	$\sum_{e \in E : b[e]} c[e]$	$\sum_{e \in E : b[e]} c[e]$
minAssignment($b[V], c[E, V]$)	$\sum_{e \in E} \max_{v \in V : b[v]} c[e, v]$	$\sum_{e \in E} \max_{v \in V : b[v]} c[e, v]$
constraintAsObjective(c)	$v(c)$	$v(c)$

This section illustrates how objective functions, like constraints, can be combined naturally to build more complex objectives. Once again, this desirable functionality comes from the Objective interface depicted in Figure 6 and implemented by all objective functions. In particular, the interface gives access to their variables, to two incremental variables, and the differentiable API. The first incremental variable (available through method value) maintains the *value* of the function incrementally. The second variable (available through method cost) maintains the *cost* of the function which may, or may not, differ from its value. The cost is useful to guide the local search more precisely by distinguishing states which have the same objective value. Consider again the objective function nbDistinct. Two solutions may use the same number of values, yet one of them may be closer than the other to a solution with fewer values. To distinguish between these, the cost may favor solutions where some values are heavily used while others have few occurrences. For instance, such a cost is used for graph coloring in [6] and is shown in Table 4 that summarizes the objective functions discussed in this paper. The differentiable API returns the variation of the cost induced by assignments and swaps. The method getCost also returns the contribution of a variable to the cost and is the counterpart of method getViolations for objective functions.

Arithmetic Operators. Objective functions can be combined using traditional arithmetic operators. For instance, the excerpt

`Objective f = condSum(open,fixed) + minAssignment(open,transportionCost);`

illustrates the addition of two objective functions capturing combinatorial substructures expressing the fixed and transportation costs in uncapacitated warehouse location. These functions are useful in a variety of other applications such as k-median and configuration problems. See also [10] for a discussion of efficient incremental algorithms to implement them.

Reification: Constraints as Objective Functions. Some of the most challenging applications in combinatorial optimization feature complex feasibility constraints together with a "global" objective function. Some algorithms approach these problems by relaxing some constraints and integrating them in the objective function. To model such local search algorithms, COMET provides the generic operator `constraintAsObjective` that transforms a constraint into an objective function whose value and cost are the violation degree of the constraint. Moreover, traditional arithmetic operators transparently apply this operator to simplify the declarative reading of the model. The implementation of this combinator, which is also given in Table 4, is in fact trivial, since it only maps one interface in terms of the other.

Frequency Allocation. To illustrate objective functions, consider a frequency allocation problem where feasibility constraints impose some distance constraints on frequencies and where the objective function consists of minimizing the number of frequencies used in the solution. We present an elegant COMET program implementing the Guided Local Search (GLS) algorithm proposed in [19][1]. The key idea underlying the GLS algorithm is to iterate a simple local search where feasibility constraints are integrated inside the objective function. After completion of each local search phase, the weights of the violated constraints are updated to guide the search toward feasible solutions. If the solution is feasible, the weights of some frequencies used in the solutions (e.g., the values that occur the least) are increased to guide the search toward solutions with fewer frequencies.

Figure 7 depicts the modeling part of the GLS algorithm. Line 2 declares the decision variables, while lines 3 and 4 create the incremental variables representing the weights that are associated with constraints and values respectively. Line 5 declares the satisfaction system S and lines 6-18 post the distance constraints in S, as presented earlier in the paper. The only difference is the use of weights which are useful to focus the search on violated constraints. Line 19 declares the objective function `nbFreq` which minimizes the number of distinct frequencies. Note that this function receives, as input, a dynamic weight for each value to guide the search toward solutions with few frequencies. Line 20 is particularly

---

[1] The point is not to present the most efficient algorithm for this application, but to illustrate the concepts introduced herein on an interesting algorithm/application.

```
1.   LocalSolver m();
2.   inc{int} freq[RV](m);
3.   inc{int} w[RC](m) := 0;
4.   inc{int} fw[RF](m): = 0;
5.   SatisfactionSystem S(m);
6.   forall(d in DistanceCtrs)
7.     switch (d.ty) {
8.       case 1:S.post(abs(freq[d.v1]-freq[d.v2]) == d.rhs,w[d.id]);break;
9.       case 2:S.post(abs(freq[d.v1]-freq[d.v2]) >  d.rhs,w[d.id]);break;
10.      case 3:S.post(abs(freq[d.v1]-freq[d.v2]) <  d.rhs,w[d.id]);break;
11.    }
12.  MinNbDistinct nbFreq(freq,fw);
13.  Objective obj = S + nbFreq;
14.  m.close();
```

Fig. 7. The Modeling Part of a Comet Program for Frequency Allocation.

Table 5. Experimental Results for Frequency Allocation.

id	$\mu(S)$	$\sigma(S)$	B(S)	W(S)	$\mu(O)$	$\sigma(O)$	B(O)	W(O)	$\mu(I)$	$\sigma(I)$
1	18.76	2.15	16	24	4.40	2.50	1.84	10.35	778.60	420.02
2	14.00	0.00	14	14	0.69	1.06	0.27	6.20	152.72	257.28
3	15.36	1.23	14	18	2.69	1.96	0.69	9.10	523.40	383.69

interesting: it defines the GLS objective function obj as the sum of the satisfaction system (a constraint viewed as an objective function) and the "actual" objective nbFreq. Of course, the search component uses the objective obj.

Figure 8 depicts the search part of the algorithm. Function GLS iterates two steps for a number of iterations: a local search, depicted in lines 8-20, and the weight adjustment. The weight adjustment is not difficult: it simply increases the weights of violated constraints and, if the solution is feasible, the weights of the frequencies that are used the least in the solution (modulo a normalization factor [19]). The local search considers all variables in a round-robin fashion and applies function moveBest on each of them, until a round does not improve the objective function (lines 8-15). Function moveBest selects, for variable freq[v], the frequency f that minimizes the values of the objective function (ties are broken randomly). It uses the differentiable API to evaluate moves quickly.

It is particularly interesting to observe the simplicity and elegance of the COMET program. The modeling component simply specifies the constraints and the objective function, and combines them to obtain the GLS objective. The search component is expressed at a high level of abstraction as well, only relying on the objective function and the decision variables. Table 5 depicts the experimental results on the first three instances of the Celar benchmarks. It reports quality and efficiency results for 50 runs of the algorithms on a 2.4GHz Pentium IV. In particular, it gives the average, standard deviation, and the best and worst values for the number of frequencies and the time to the best solutions in seconds. It also reports the average number of iterations and its standard deviation. The preliminary results indicate that the resulting COMET program,

```
1.   function void GLS() {
2.     while (it < maxIterations) {
3.       localSearch();
4.       updateWeights();
5.       it++;
6.     }
7.   }
8.   function void localSearch() {
9.     int old;
10.    do {
11.      old = obj.cost();
12.      forall(v in RV) moveBest(v);
13.    } while (old != obj.cost());
14.  }
15.  function void moveBest(int v) {
16.    if (obj.getCost(freq[v]) > 0)
17.      selectMin(f in Domain[v])(obj.getAssignDelta(freq[v],f))
18.        freq[v] := f;
19.  }
```

Fig. 8. The Search Part of a Comet Program for Frequency Allocation.

despite its simplicity and elegance, compares well in quality and efficiency with specialized implementations in [19]. Note that there are many opportunities for improvements to the algorithm.

4 First-Class Expressions

We now turn to first-class expression, another significant abstraction which is also an integral part of constraint programming libraries [5]. First-class expressions are constructed from incremental variables, constants, and arithmetic, logical, and relational operators. In COMET, first-class expressions are differentiable objects which can be evaluated to determine the effect of assignments and swaps on their values. In fact, several examples presented earlier feature first-class expressions. For instance, the COMET code

S.post(allDifferent(all(i in Size) queen[i] + i));

from the n-queens problem can be viewed as a shortcut for

expr{int} d[i in Size] = queen[i] + i;
S.post(allDifferent(d));

The first instruction declares an array of first-class integer expressions, element d[i] being the expression queen[i] + i. The second instruction states the allDifferent constraint on the expression array. As mentioned earlier, expressions are differentiable objects, which can be queried to evaluate the effect of assignments and swaps on their values. For instance, the method call d[i].getAssignDelta(queen[i],5) returns the variation in the value of expression d[i] when queen[i] is assigned the value 5.

```
1.   int n = 40;
2.   range Size = 1..n;
3.   range Domain = 0..n-1;
4.   range SD = 1..n-1;
5.   LocalSolver m();
6.   RandomPermutation perm(Domain);
7.   inc{int} v[Size](m,Domain) := perm.get();
8.   MaxNbDistinct obj(all(k in SD) abs(v[k+1]-v[k]));
9.   m.close();
10.  while (obj.value() < n-1)
11.    select(i in Size: obj.getCost(v[i]) > 0)
12.      selectMax(j in Size: j != i)(obj.getSwapDelta(v[i],v[j]))
13.        v[i] :=: v[j];
```

Fig. 9. A Comet Program for the All-Interval Series Problem.

First-class expressions significantly increase the modeling power of the language, since constraints and objective functions can now be defined over complex expressions, not incremental variables only. Moreover, efficient implementations of these enhanced versions can be obtained systematically by combining the differentiable APIs of constraints, objective functions, and first-class expressions. For instance, in the queens problem, the implementation can be thought of as (1) defining an intermediary set of incremental variables
inc{int} q[i in Size] <- queen[i] + i;
(2) specifying an allDifferent(q) constraint on these variables and (3) implementing the differentiable API as a composition of the differentiable APIs of the expressions queen[i] + i and of the allDifferent constraint.

The all-interval series problem [1] illustrates the richness of first-class expressions in COMET. (The n-queens problem only illustrates a simple use of first-class expressions, since every variable occurs in exactly one expression.) The problem, is a well-known exercise in music composition. It consists of finding a sequence of notes such that all notes in the sequence, as well as tonal intervals between consecutive notes, are different. The all-interval series problem can thus be modeled as the finding of a permutation of the first n integers such that the absolute difference between two consecutive pairs of numbers are all different.

Figure 9 depicts a COMET program solving the all-interval series problem. The basic idea behind the modeling is to maximize the number of different distances in abs(v[2]-v[1]),...,abs(v[n]-v[n-1]). Line 7 declares the variables v[i] in the series, which are initialized to a random permutation of $0..n-1$. This guarantees that all variables have distinct values, a property maintained by the search procedure whose local moves swap the values of two variables. Line 8 specifies the objective function MaxNbDistinct which maximizes the number of distinct distances in abs(v[2]-v[1]),...,abs(v[n]-v[n-1]). It is important to observe that almost all variables occur in two expressions. *As a consequence, it is non-trivial to evaluate the impact of a swap on the objective function, since this may involve up to 4 specific expressions.* The COMET implementation abstracts this tedious and error-prone aspect of the local search through first-class expressions and the combinatorial function MaxNbDistinct.

Table 6. Performance Results on the All-Interval Series Program.

n	μ(Time)	best(Time)	worst(Time)	σ(Time)	μ(Iter)	σ(Iter)
10	0.00	0.00	0.01	0.00	25.18	38.27
15	0.01	0.00	0.06	0.02	203.92	276.25
20	0.04	0.00	0.26	0.07	859.02	1235.77
25	0.07	0.00	0.52	0.10	1183.30	1419.42
30	0.39	0.01	2.41	0.64	6092.78	7985.98
35	0.86	0.03	6.75	1.49	11864.52	16792.77
40	2.62	0.09	18.68	4.05	32669.46	38641.32
45	6.63	0.12	36.79	9.24	78961.70	75349.35
50	34.09	1.27	165.41	52.56	355816.56	416601.45
55	130.05	9.30	278.75	160.56	1277633.38	906189.43

The performance of the algorithm can be improved upon by associating weights to the distances (as suggested in [1]). The justification here is that larger distances are much more difficult to obtain and it is beneficial to bias the search toward them. To accommodate this enhancement, it suffices to replace line 8 by

```
MaxNbDistinct obj(all(k in SD) abs(v[k+1]-v[k]),all(k in SD) k^3);
```

Table 6 gives the experimental results for various values of n and for the COMET program, extended to restart the computation after 1,000 iterations if no solution was found. The resulting COMET significantly outperforms existing programs. The Java implementation from [1] takes an average time of 63 seconds for $n = 30$ on a 733MHz Pentium III (instead of 0.39 seconds for COMET on a 2.4GHz machine). The gain probably comes from the better incrementality of COMET which uses differentiation to evaluate moves quickly. Indeed, our first COMET program for this problem, which did not use first-class expressions and did not support the differentiable API for the objective function, took 10.44 seconds in average over 50 runs for $n = 30$. The incrementality of the COMET program presented here is obtained directly from the composition of differentiable objects, while it is tedious to derive manually.

5 Generic Search Procedures

The combinators presented in this paper have an additional benefit: they provide the foundation for writing generic search procedures in COMET. Indeed, search procedures are now able to interact with declarative components only through the Constraint and Objective interfaces, abstracting away the actual details of constraints and objective functions. These generic search procedures do not depend on the application at hand, yet they exploit the differentiable APIs to implement heuristics and meta-heuristics efficiently. Moreover, these APIs are implemented by efficient incremental algorithms exploiting the structure of the applications. In other words, although the search procedures are generic and do not refer to specificities of the applications, they exploit their underlying structure through the combinators.

```
1.  function void minConflictSearch(ConstraintSystem S) {
2.     inc{int}[] var = S.getVariables();
3.     range Size = var.getRange();
4.     while (S.violations() > 0)
5.        selectMax(i in Size)(S.getViolations(var[i]))
6.           selectMin(v in var[i].getDomain())(S.getAssignDelta(var[i],v))
7.              var[i] := v;
8.  }
```

Fig. 10. A Generic Min-Conflict Search in Comet.

```
1.  function int cdSearch(ConstraintSystem S) {
2.     UniformDistribution noise(0..99);
3.     range C = S.getRange();
4.     Constraint c[i in C] = S.getConstraint(i);
5.     while (S.violations() > 0)
6.        select(i in C: !c[i].isTrue()) {
7.           inc{int}[] var = c[i].getVariables();
8.           range RV = var.getRange();
9.           selectMax(v in RV)(c[i].getViolations(var[v]))
10.             selectMin(val in var[v].getDomain())
                     (c[i].getAssignDelta(var[v],val))
11.                if (S.getAssignDelta(var[v],val) < 0)
12.                   var[v] := val;
13.                else if (noise.get() < 10) {
14.                   var[v] := val;
15.        }
16. }
```

Fig. 11. A Generic Constraint-Directed Search in Comet.

Figure 10 depicts a min-conflict search in COMET. The code is essentially similar to the search procedure in the queens problem: it is only necessary to collect the variable array and its range in lines 2-3, and to use the variable domains in line 6. As a consequence, lines 10-13 in the queens problem can simply be replaced by a call minConflictSearch(S). Similarly, Figure 11 implements a constraint-directed search inspired by search procedures used in WSAT [15, 20] and DRAGONBREATH [13]. The key idea is to select a violated constraint first (line 6) and then a variable to re-assign (line 9). Once again, lines 10-13 in the queens problem can simply be replaced by a call cdSearch(S). Such constraint-oriented local search procedures are particularly effective on a variety of problems, such as the ACC sport-scheduling problem. The actual search procedure in [20] was also successfully implemented in COMET and applied to their integer formulation.

Observe that these search procedures are generic and do not depend on the actual shape of the constraints, which can be propositional, linear, nonlinear, combinatorial, or any combination of these. Moreover, generic search procedures bring another interesting benefit of constraint programming to local search: the ability to provide a variety of (parameterized) default search procedures, while exploiting the specific structure of the application.

6 Conclusion

This paper aimed at demonstrating that constraint-based combinators from constraint programming are natural abstractions for expressing local search algorithms. In particular, it showed that logical and cardinality operators, reification, and first-class expressions can all be viewed as differentiable objects encapsulating efficient incremental algorithms. These combinators, and their counterparts for objective functions, provide high-level ways of expressing complex ad-hoc constraints, generic search procedures, and partial constraint satisfaction. They were also shown to be amenable to efficient implementations. As a consequence, this paper, together with earlier results, indicates that the rich language of constraint programming is a natural vehicle for writing a wide variety of modular, extensible, and efficient local search programs.

References

1. C. Codognet and D. Diaz. Yet Another Local Search Method for Constraint Solving. In *AAAI Fall Symposium on Using Uncertainty within Computation*, 2001.
2. L. Di Gaspero and A. Schaerf. *Optimization Software Class Libraries*, chapter Writing Local Search Algorithms Using EasyLocal++. Kluwer, 2002.
3. E. Freuder. Partial Constraint Satisfaction. Artificial Intelligence, 58, 1992.
4. P. Galinier and J.-K. Hao. A General Approach for Constraint Solving by Local Search. In *CP-AI-OR'00*, Paderborn, Germany, March 2000.
5. Ilog Solver 4.4. Reference Manual. Ilog SA, Gentilly, France, 1998.
6. D. Johnson, C. Aragon, L. McGeoch, and C. Schevon. Optimization by Simulated Annealing: An Experimental Evaluation; Part I, Graph Partitioning. *Operations Research*, 37(6):865–893, 1989.
7. F. Laburthe and Y. Caseau. SALSA: A Language for Search Algorithms. In *CP'98*, Pisa, Italy, October 1998.
8. L. Michel and P. Van Hentenryck. Localizer. *Constraints*, 5:41–82, 2000.
9. L. Michel and P. Van Hentenryck. A constraint-based architecture for local search. In *OOPSLA-02*.
10. L. Michel and P. Van Hentenryck. A Simple Tabu Search for Warehouse Location. *European Journal of Operational Research*, 2004. in press.
11. S. Minton, M.D. Johnston, and A.B. Philips. Solving Large-Scale Constraint Satisfaction and Scheduling Problems using a Heuristic Repair Method. In *AAAI-90*.
12. A. Nareyek. Constraint-Based Agents. Springer Verlag, 1998.
13. A. Nareyek. DragonBreath. www.ai-center.com/projects/dragonbreath/, 2004.
14. G. Ramalingam. *Bounded Incremental Computation*. PhD thesis, University of Wisconsin-Madison, 1993.
15. B. Selman, H. Kautz, and B. Cohen. Noise Strategies for Improving Local Search. In *AAAI-94*, pages 337–343, 1994.
16. P. Shaw, B. De Backer, and V. Furnon. Improved local search for CP toolkits. *Annals of Operations Research*, 115:31–50, 2002.
17. P. Van Hentenryck and L. Michel. Control Abstractions for Local Search. In *CP'03*, Cork, Ireland, 2003. (Best Paper Award).
18. S. Voss and D. Woodruff. *Optimization Software Class Libraries*. Kluwer Academic Publishers, 2002.
19. C. Voudouris and E. Tsang. Partial constraint satisfaction problems and guided local search. In *PACT'96*, pages 337–356, 1996.
20. J. Walser. *Integer Optimization by Local Search*. Springer Verlag, 1998.

Unary Resource Constraint with Optional Activities

Petr Vilím[1], Roman Barták[1], and Ondřej Čepek[1,2]

[1] Charles University
Faculty of Mathematics and Physics
Malostranské náměstí 2/25, Praha 1, Czech Republic
{vilim,bartak}@kti.mff.cuni.cz
[2] Institute of Finance and Administration - VŠFS
ondrej.cepek@mff.cuni.cz

Abstract. Scheduling is one of the most successful application areas of constraint programming mainly thanks to special global constraints designed to model resource restrictions. Among these global constraints, edge-finding filtering algorithm for unary resources is one of the most popular techniques. In this paper we propose a new $O(n \log n)$ version of the edge-finding algorithm that uses a special data structure called Θ-Λ-tree. This data structure is especially designed for "what-if" reasoning about a set of activities so we also propose to use it for handling so called optional activities, i.e. activities which may or may not appear on the resource. In particular, we propose new $O(n \log n)$ variants of filtering algorithms which are able to handle optional activities: overload checking, detectable precedences and not-first/not-last.

1 Introduction

In scheduling, a *unary resource* is an often used generalization of a machine (or a job in openshop). A unary resource models a set of non-interruptible *activities* T which must not overlap in a schedule.

Each activity $i \in T$ has the following requirements:

- earliest possible starting time est_i
- latest possible completion time lct_i
- processing time p_i

A (sub)problem is to find a schedule satisfying all these requirements. One of the most used techniques to solve this problem is *constraint programming*.

In constraint programming, we associate a *unary resource constraint* with each unary resource. A purpose of such a constraint is to reduce a search space by tightening the time bounds est_i and lct_i. This process of elimination of infeasible values is called *propagation*, an actual propagation algorithm is often called a *filtering* algorithm.

Naturally, it is not efficient to remove all infeasible values. Instead, it is customary to use several fast but not complete algorithms which can find only some of impossible assignments. These filtering algorithms are repeated in every node of a search tree, therefore their speed and filtering power are crucial.

Filtering algorithms considered in this paper are:

Edge-finding. Paper [5] presents $O(n \log n)$ version, another two $O(n^2)$ versions of edge-finding can be found in [7, 8].

Not-first/not-last. $O(n \log n)$ version of the algorithm can be found in [10], two older $O(n^2)$ versions are in [2, 9].

Detectable precedences. This $O(n \log n)$ algorithm was introduced in [10].

All these filtering algorithms can be used together to join their filtering powers.

This paper introduces new version of the edge-finding algorithm with time complexity $O(n \log n)$. Experimental results shows that this new edge-finding algorithm is faster than the quadratic algorithms [7, 8] even for $n = 15$. Another asset of the algorithm is the introduction of the Θ-Λ-tree – a data structure which can be used to extend filtering algorithms to handle optional activities.

2 Edge-Finding Using Θ-Λ-Tree

2.1 Basic Notation

Let us establish the basic notation concerning a subset of activities. Let T be a set of all activities on the resource and let $\Theta \subseteq T$ be an arbitrary non-empty subset of activities. An earliest starting time est_Θ, a latest completion time lct_Θ and a processing time p_Θ of the set Θ are defined as:

$$\text{est}_\Theta = \min \{\text{est}_j,\ j \in \Theta\}$$
$$\text{lct}_\Theta = \max \{\text{lct}_j,\ j \in \Theta\}$$
$$p_\Theta = \sum_{j \in \Theta} p_j$$

Often we need to estimate an earliest completion time of a set Θ:

$$\text{ECT}_\Theta = \max \{\text{est}_{\Theta'} + p_{\Theta'},\ \Theta' \subseteq \Theta\} \qquad (1)$$

To extend the definitions also for $\Theta = \emptyset$ let $\text{est}_\emptyset = -\infty$, $\text{lct}_\emptyset = \infty$, $p_\emptyset = 0$ and $\text{ECT}_\emptyset = -\infty$.

2.2 Edge-Finding Rules

Edge-finding is probably the most often used filtering algorithm for a unary resource constraint. Let us recall classical edge-finding rules [2]. Consider a set $\Omega \subseteq T$ and an activity $i \notin \Omega$. If the following condition holds, then the activity i has to be scheduled after all activities from Ω:

$$\forall \Omega \subset T,\ \forall i \in (T \setminus \Omega):$$
$$\text{est}_{\Omega \cup \{i\}} + p_{\Omega \cup \{i\}} = \min \{\text{est}_\Omega,\ \text{est}_i\} + p_\Omega + p_i > \text{lct}_\Omega \quad \Rightarrow \quad \Omega \ll i \qquad (2)$$

Once we know that the activity i must be scheduled after the set Ω, we can adjust est_i:

$$\Omega \ll i \quad \Rightarrow \quad \text{est}_i := \max\{\text{est}_i, \text{ECT}_\Omega\} \tag{3}$$

Edge-finding algorithm propagates according to this rule and its symmetric version. There are several implementations of edge-finding algorithm, two different quadratic algorithms can be found in [7, 8], [5] presents a $O(n \log n)$ algorithm.

Proposition 1. *Let $\Theta(j) = \{k,\ k \in T\ \&\ \text{lct}_k \leq \text{lct}_j\}$. The rules (2), (3) are not stronger than the following rule:*

$$\forall j \in T,\ \forall i \in T \setminus \Theta(j):$$
$$\text{ECT}_{\Theta(j) \cup \{i\}} > \text{lct}_j \quad \Rightarrow \quad \Theta(j) \ll i \quad \Rightarrow \quad \text{est}_i := \max\{\text{est}_i, \text{ECT}_{\Theta(j)}\} \tag{4}$$

Actually, the rules (2) and (3) are equivalent with the rule (4). However, the proof of their equivalence (the reverse implication) is rather technical and therefore it is not included in the main body of this paper. An interested reader can find this proof in the appendix of this paper.

Proof. Let us consider a set $\Omega \subseteq T$ and an activity $i \in T \setminus \Omega$. Let j be one of the activities from Ω for which $\text{lct}_j = \text{lct}_\Omega$. Thanks to this definition of j we have $\Omega \subseteq \Theta(j)$ and so (recall the definition (1) of ECT):

$$\text{est}_{\Omega \cup \{i\}} + p_{\Omega \cup \{i\}} = \min\{\text{est}_\Omega, \text{est}_i\} + p_\Omega + p_i \leq \text{ECT}_{\Theta(j) \cup \{i\}}$$
$$\text{ECT}_\Omega \leq \text{ECT}_{\Theta(j)}$$

Thus: when the original rule (2) holds for Ω and i, then the new rule (4) holds for $\Theta(j)$ and i too, and the change of est_i is at least the same as the change by the rule (3). □

Property 1. The rule (4) has a very useful property. Let us consider an activity i and two different activities j_1 and j_2 for which the rule (4) holds. Moreover let $\text{lct}_{j_1} \leq \text{lct}_{j_2}$. Then $\Theta(j_1) \subseteq \Theta(j_2)$ and so $\text{ECT}_{\Theta(j_1)} \leq \text{ECT}_{\Theta(j_2)}$, therefore j_2 yields better propagation then j_1. Thus for a given activity i it is sufficient to look for the activity j for which (4) holds and lct_j is maximum.

2.3 Θ-Λ-Tree

A Θ-Λ-tree is an extension of a Θ-tree introduced in [10]. Θ-tree is a data structure designed to represent a set of activities $\Theta \subseteq T$ and to quickly compute ECT_Θ. Θ-tree was already successfully used to speed up two filtering algorithms for unary resource: not-first/not-last and detectable precedences [10].

In a Θ-tree, activities are represented as nodes in a balanced binary search tree with respect to est. In the following we will not make a difference between an activity and the tree node which represents that activity. Besides an activity itself, each node k of a Θ-tree holds the following two values:

$$\Sigma P_k = \sum_{j \in \text{Subtree}(k)} p_j$$

$$\text{ECT}_k = \text{ECT}_{\text{Subtree}(k)} = \max \{\text{est}_{\Theta'} + p_{\Theta'}, \Theta' \subseteq \text{Subtree}(k)\}$$

where $\text{Subtree}(k)$ is a set of all activities in a subtree rooted at node k (including activity k itself). The values ΣP_k and ECT_k can be computed recursively from the direct descendants of the node (for more details see [10]):

$$\Sigma P_k = \Sigma P_{\text{left}(k)} + p_k + \Sigma P_{\text{right}(k)} \tag{5}$$

$$\text{ECT}_k = \max \{ \text{ECT}_{\text{right}(k)}, \tag{6}$$
$$\text{est}_k + p_k + \Sigma P_{\text{right}(k)},$$
$$\text{ECT}_{\text{left}(k)} + p_k + \Sigma P_{\text{right}(k)} \}$$

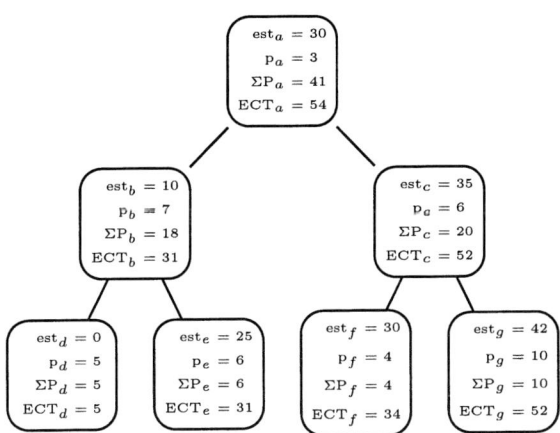

Fig. 1. An example of a Θ-tree for $\Theta = \{a, b, c, d, e, f, g\}$.

Let us now consider alternative edge-finding rule (4). We choose an arbitrary activity j and now we want to check the rule (4) for each applicable activity i, i.e. we would like to find all activities i for which the following condition holds:

$$\text{ECT}_{\Theta(j) \cup \{i\}} > \text{lct}_j$$

Unfortunately, such an algorithm would be too slow: before the check can be performed, each particular activity i must be added into the Θ-tree, and after the check the activity i have to be removed back from the Θ-tree.

The idea how to surpass this problem is to extend the Θ-tree structure the following way: all applicable activities i will be also included in the tree, but as a *gray* nodes. A gray node represents an activity i which is not really in the set Θ. However, we are curious what would happen with ECT_Θ if we are allowed to include **one** of the gray activities into the set Θ. More exactly: let $\Lambda \subseteq T$ be a set of all gray activities, $\Lambda \cap \Theta = \emptyset$. The purpose of the Θ-Λ-tree is to compute the following value:

$$\overline{\mathrm{ECT}}(\Theta, \Lambda) = \max\left\{\{\mathrm{ECT}_\Theta\} \cup \{\mathrm{ECT}_{\Theta \cup \{i\}}, \ i \in \Lambda\}\right\}$$

The meaning of the values ECT and ΣP in the new tree remains the same, however only regular (*white*) nodes are taken into account. Moreover, in order to compute $\overline{\mathrm{ECT}}(\Theta, \Lambda)$ quickly, we add the following two values into each node of the tree:

$$\overline{\Sigma \mathrm{P}}_k = \max\{\mathrm{p}_{\Theta'}, \ \Theta' \subseteq \mathrm{Subtree}(k) \ \& \ |\Theta' \cap \Lambda| \leq 1\}$$
$$= \max\{\{0\} \cup \{\mathrm{p}_i, \ i \in \mathrm{Subtree}(k) \cap \Lambda\}\} + \sum_{i \in \mathrm{Subtree}(k) \cap \Theta} \mathrm{p}_i$$
$$\overline{\mathrm{ECT}}_k = \overline{\mathrm{ECT}}_{\mathrm{Subtree}(k)} = \max\{\mathrm{est}_{\Theta'} + \mathrm{p}_{\Theta'}, \ \Theta' \subseteq \mathrm{Subtree}(k) \ \& \ |\Theta' \cap \Lambda| \leq 1\}$$

$\overline{\Sigma \mathrm{P}}$ is maximum sum of processing activities in a subtree if one of gray activities can be used. Similarly $\overline{\mathrm{ECT}}$ is an earliest completion time of a subtree with at most one gray activity included.

An idea how to compute values $\overline{\Sigma \mathrm{P}}_k$ and $\overline{\mathrm{ECT}}_k$ in node k follows. A gray activity can be used only once. Therefore when computing $\overline{\Sigma \mathrm{P}}_k$ and $\overline{\mathrm{ECT}}_k$, a gray activity can be used only in one of the following places: in the left subtree of k, by the activity k itself (if it is gray), or in the right subtree of k. Note that the gray activity used for $\overline{\Sigma \mathrm{P}}_k$ can be different from the gray activity used for $\overline{\mathrm{ECT}}_k$. The formulae (5) and (6) can be modified to handle gray nodes.

We distinguish two cases: node k is gray or node k is white. When k is white then:

$$\overline{\Sigma \mathrm{P}}_k = \max\left\{\ \overline{\Sigma \mathrm{P}}_{\mathrm{left}(k)} + \mathrm{p}_k + \Sigma \mathrm{P}_{\mathrm{right}(k)}, \right.$$
$$\left. \Sigma \mathrm{P}_{\mathrm{left}(k)} + \mathrm{p}_k + \overline{\Sigma \mathrm{P}}_{\mathrm{right}(k)}\ \right\}$$
$$\overline{\mathrm{ECT}}_k = \max\left\{\ \overline{\mathrm{ECT}}_{\mathrm{right}(k)}, \right. \qquad\qquad\qquad\qquad\qquad (a)$$
$$\mathrm{est}_k + \mathrm{p}_k + \overline{\Sigma \mathrm{P}}_{\mathrm{right}(k)}, \qquad\qquad\qquad (b)$$
$$\mathrm{ECT}_{\mathrm{left}(k)} + \mathrm{p}_k + \overline{\Sigma \mathrm{P}}_{\mathrm{right}(k)}, \qquad\qquad\quad (c)$$
$$\left. \overline{\mathrm{ECT}}_{\mathrm{left}(k)} + \mathrm{p}_k + \Sigma \mathrm{P}_{\mathrm{right}(k)}\ \right\} \qquad\qquad\quad (c)$$

Line (a) considers all sets Θ' such that $\Theta' \subseteq \mathrm{Subtree}(\mathrm{right}(k))$ (see the definition (1) of ECT on page 63). Line (b) considers all sets Θ' such that $\Theta' \subseteq \mathrm{Subtree}(\mathrm{right}(k)) \cup \{k\}$ and $k \in \Theta'$. Finally lines (c) consider sets Θ' such that $\Theta' \cap \mathrm{Subtree}(\mathrm{left}(k)) \neq \emptyset$.

When k is gray then (the meaning of the labels (a), (b) and (c) remains the same):

$$\overline{\Sigma P}_k = \max\{\,\overline{\Sigma P}_{\text{left}(k)} + \Sigma P_{\text{right}(k)},$$
$$\Sigma P_{\text{left}(k)} + p_k + \Sigma P_{\text{right}(k)},$$
$$\Sigma P_{\text{left}(k)} + \overline{\Sigma P}_{\text{right}(k)}\,\}$$

$$\overline{\text{ECT}}_k = \max\{\,\overline{\text{ECT}}_{\text{right}(k)}, \tag{a}$$
$$\text{est}_k + p_k + \Sigma P_{\text{right}(k)}, \tag{b}$$
$$\overline{\text{ECT}}_{\text{left}(k)} + \Sigma P_{\text{right}(k)}, \tag{c}$$
$$\text{ECT}_{\text{left}(k)} + p_k + \Sigma P_{\text{right}(k)}, \tag{c}$$
$$\text{ECT}_{\text{left}(k)} + \overline{\Sigma P}_{\text{right}(k)}\,\} \tag{c}$$

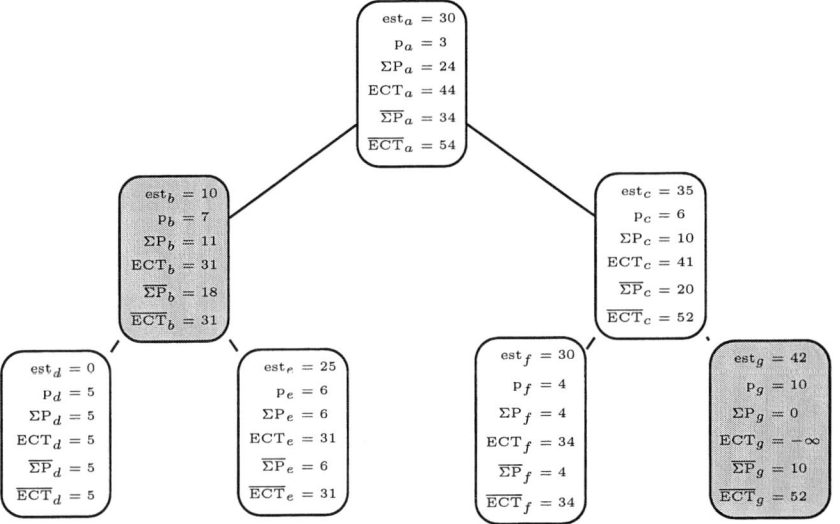

Fig. 2. An example of a Θ-Λ-tree for $\Theta = \{a, c, d, e, f\}$ and $\Lambda = \{b, g\}$.

Thanks to these recursive formulae, $\overline{\text{ECT}}$ and $\overline{\Sigma P}$ can be computed within usual operations with balanced binary trees without changing their time complexities. Note that together with $\overline{\text{ECT}}$ we can compute for each node k the gray activity *responsible* for $\overline{\text{ECT}}_k$. We need to know such responsible gray activity in the following algorithms.

Table 1 shows time complexities of some operations on Θ-Λ-tree.

2.4 Edge-Finding Algorithm

The algorithm starts with $\Theta = T$ and $\Lambda = \emptyset$. Activities are sequentially (in descending order by lct_j) moved from the set Θ into the set Λ, i.e. white nodes are discolored to gray. As soon as $\overline{\text{ECT}}(\Theta, \Lambda) > \text{lct}_\Theta$, a responsible gray activity i is updated. Thanks to the property 1 (page 64) the activity i cannot be updated

Table 1. Time complexities of operations on Θ-Λ-tree.

Operation	Time Complexity
$(\Theta, \Lambda) := (\emptyset, \emptyset)$	$O(1)$
$(\Theta, \Lambda) := (T, \emptyset)$	$O(n \log n)$
$(\Theta, \Lambda) := (\Theta \setminus \{i\}, \Lambda \cup \{i\})$	$O(\log n)$
$\Theta := \Theta \cup \{i\}$	$O(\log n)$
$\Lambda := \Lambda \cup \{i\}$	$O(\log n)$
$\Lambda := \Lambda \setminus \{i\}$	$O(\log n)$
$\overline{\text{ECT}}(\Theta, \Lambda)$	$O(1)$
ECT_Θ	$O(1)$

better, therefore we can remove the activity i from the tree (i.e. remove it from the set Λ).

```
1  for i ∈ T do
2      est'_i := est_i ;
3  (Θ, Λ) := (T, ∅) ;
4  Q := queue of all activities j ∈ T in descending order of lct_j ;
5  j := Q.first ;
6  repeat
7      (Θ, Λ) := (Θ \ {j}, Λ ∪ {j}) ;
8      Q.dequeue ;
9      j := Q.first ;
10     if ECT_Θ > lct_j then
11         fail ; { Resource is overloaded }
12     while ECT(Θ, Λ) > lct_j do begin
13         i := gray activity responsible for ECT(Θ, Λ) ;
14         est'_i := max{est_i, ECT_Θ} ;
15         Λ := Λ \ {i} ;
16     end ;
17 until Q.size = 0 ;
18 for i ∈ T do
19     est_i := est'_i ;
```

Note that at line 13 there have to be some gray activity responsible for $\overline{\text{ECT}}(\Theta, \Lambda)$ because otherwise we would end up by fail on line 11.

During the entire run of the algorithm, maximum number of iterations of the inner while loop is n, because each iteration removes an activity from the set Λ. Similarly, number of iterations of the repeat loop is n, because each time an activity is removed from the queue Q. According to table 1 time complexity of each single line within the loops is $O(\log n)$ maximum. Therefore the time complexity of the whole algorithm is $O(n \log n)$.

Note that at the beginning $\Theta = T$ and $\Lambda = \emptyset$, hence there are no gray activities and therefore $\overline{\text{ECT}}_k = \text{ECT}_k$ and $\overline{\Sigma P}_k = \Sigma P_k$ for each node k. Hence we can save some time by building the initial Θ-Λ-tree as a "normal" Θ-tree.

3 Optional Activities

Nowadays, many practical scheduling problems have to deal with alternatives – activities which can choose their resource, or activities which exist only if a particular alternative of processing is chosen. From the resource point of view, it is not yet decided whether such activities will be processed or not. Therefore we will call such activities *optional*. For an optional activity, we would like to speculate what would happen if the activity actually would be processed by the resource.

Traditionally, resource constraints are not designed to handle optional activities properly. However, several different modifications are used to model them:

Dummy activities. It is basically a workaround for constraint solvers which do not allow to add more activities on the resource during problem solving (i.e. resource constraint is not dynamic [3]). Processing time of activities is turned from constants to domain variables. Several "dummy" activities with processing time domain $\langle 0, \infty)$ are added on the resource as a reserve for possible activity addition. Filtering algorithms work as usual, but they use minimum of possible processing time instead of original constant processing time. Note that dummy activities have no influence on other activities on the resource, because their processing time can be zero. Once an alternative is chosen, a dummy activity is turned into regular activity (i.e. minimum of processing time is no longer zero). In this approach, an impossibility of an alternative cannot be found before that alternative is actually tried.

Filtering of options. The idea is to run a filtering algorithm several times, each time with one of the optional activities added on the resource. When a fail is found, then the optional activity is rejected. Otherwise time bounds of the optional activity can be adjusted. [4] introduces so called PEX-edge-finding with time complexity $O(n^3)$. This is a pretty strong propagation, however rather time consuming.

Modified filtering algorithms. Regular and optional activities are treated differently: optional activities do not influence any other activity on the resource, however regular activities influence other regular activities and also optional activities [6]. Most of the filtering algorithms can be modified this way without changing their time complexities. However, this approach is a little bit weaker than the previous one, because previous approach also checked whether the addition of a optional activity would not cause an immediate fail.

Cumulative resources. If we have a set of similar alternative machines, this set can be modeled as a cumulative resource. This additional (redundant) constraint can improve the propagation before activities are distributed between the machines. There is also a special filtering algorithm [11] designed to handle this type of alternatives.

To handle optional activities we extend each activity i by a variable called existence$_i$ with the domain {true, false}. When existence$_i$ = true then i is a regular activity, when existence$_i \in$ {true, false} then i is an optional activity.

Finally when existence = false we simply exclude this activity from all our considerations.

To make the notation concerning optional activities easy, let R be the set of all regular activities and O the set of all optional activities.

For optional activities, we would like to consider the following issues:

1. If an optional activity should be processed by the resource (i.e. if an optional activity is changed to a regular activity), would the resource be overloaded? The resource is overloaded if there is such a set $\Omega \subseteq R$ that:

$$\text{lct}_\Omega - \text{est}_\Omega < p_\Omega$$

   Certainly, if a resource is overloaded then the problem has no solution. Hence if an addition of a optional activity i results in overloading then we can conclude that existence$_i$ = false.
2. If the addition of an optional activity i does not result in overloading, what is the earliest possible start time and the latest possible completion time of the activity i with respect to regular activities on the resource? We would like to apply usual filtering algorithms for the activity i, however the activity i cannot cause change of any regular activity.
3. If we add an optional activity i, will the first run of a filtering algorithm result in a fail? For example algorithm detectable precedences can increase est$_k$ of some activity k so much that est$_k + p_k >$ lct$_k$. In that case we can also propagate existence$_i$ = false.

We will consider the item 1 in the next section "Overload Checking with Optional Activities". Items 2 and 3 are discussed in section "Filtering with Optional Activities".

4 Overload Checking with Optional Activities

Let us consider an arbitrary set $\Omega \subseteq R$ of regular activities. Overload rule says that if the set Ω cannot be processed within its time bounds then no solution exists:

$$\text{lct}_\Omega - \text{est}_\Omega < p_\Omega \quad \Rightarrow \quad \text{fail}$$

Let us suppose for a while that we are given an activity $i \in T$ and we want to check this rule only for those sets $\Omega \subseteq T$ which have lct$_\Omega =$ lct$_i$. Now consider a set Θ:

$$\Theta = \{j,\ j \in R\ \&\ \text{lct}_j \leq \text{lct}_i\}$$

Overloaded set Ω with lct$_\Omega =$ lct$_i$ exists if and only if ECT$_\Theta >$ lct$_i =$ lct$_\Theta$. The idea of an algorithm is to gradually increase the set Θ by increasing the lct$_\Theta$. For each lct$_\Theta$ we check whether ECT$_\Theta >$ lct$_\Theta$ or not.

But what about optional activities? Let Λ be the following set:

$$\Lambda = \{j,\ j \in O\ \&\ \text{lct}_j \leq \text{lct}_i\}$$

An optional activity can cause overloading if and only if $\overline{\mathrm{ECT}}(\Theta, \Lambda) > \mathrm{lct}_i$. The following algorithm is an extension of the algorithm presented in [10]. Optional activities are represented by gray nodes in the Θ-Λ-tree.

The following algorithm deletes all optional activities k such that an addition of each activity k alone causes an overload. Of course, a combination of several optional activities that are not deleted may still cause an overload!

```
(Θ, Λ) := (∅, ∅);
for i ∈ T in ascending order of lct_i do begin
    if i is a regular activity then begin
        Θ := Θ ∪ {i};
        if ECT_Θ > lct_i then
            fail; { No solution exists}
    end else
        Λ := Λ ∪ {i};
    while ECT(Θ, Λ) > lct_i do begin
        k := optional activity responsible for ECT(Θ, Λ);
        existence_k := false;
        Λ := Λ \ {k};
    end;
end;
```

The complexity of the algorithm is again $O(n \log n)$. The inner while loop is repeated n times maximum because each time an activity is removed from the set Λ. Outer for loop has also n iterations, time complexity of each single line is $O(\log n)$ maximum (see the table 1).

5 Filtering with Optional Activities

The following section is an example how to extend a certain class of filtering algorithms to handle optional activities. The idea is simple: if the original algorithm uses Θ-tree, we will use Θ-Λ-tree instead. The difference is that we represent optional activities by gray nodes. For propagation we still use ECT_Θ, however we can check $\overline{\mathrm{ECT}}(\Theta, \Lambda)$ also. If propagation using $\overline{\mathrm{ECT}}(\Theta, \Lambda)$ would result in an immediate fail we can exclude the optional activity responsible for that.

Let us demonstrate this idea on the detectable precedences algorithm:

```
(Θ, Λ) := ∅;
Q := queue of all activities j ∈ T in ascending order of lct_j − p_j;
for i ∈ T in ascending order of est_i + p_i do begin
    while est_i + p_i > lct_Q.first − p_Q.first do begin
        if i is a regular activity then
            Θ := Θ ∪ {Q.first};
        else
            Λ := Λ ∪ {Q.first};
        Q.dequeue;
```

```
      end;
      est'_i := max {est_i, ECT_{Θ\{i}}};
      if i is a regular activity then
          while ECT(Θ \ {i}, Λ) + p_i > lct_i then begin
              k := an optional activity responsible for ECT(Θ \ {i}, Λ);
              Λ := Λ \ {k};
              existence_k := false;
          end;
  end;
  for i ∈ T do
      est_i := est'_i;
```

The complexity of the algorithm remains the same: $O(n \log n)$.

The same idea can be used to extend the not-first/not-last algorithm presented in [10]. However, extending the edge-finding algorithm is not so easy: edge-finding algorithm already uses Θ-Λ-tree. We will consider this in our future work.

6   Experimental Results

We tested the new edge-finding algorithm on several benchmark jobshop problems taken from OR library [1]. The benchmark problem is to compute a destructive lower bound using the shaving technique. Destructive lower bound is the minimal makespan for which propagation is not able to find conflict without backtracking. Because destructive lower bound is computed too quickly, we use also shaving as suggested in [7]. Shaving is similar to the proof by a contradiction. We choose an activity i, limit its est_i or lct_i and propagate. If an infeasibility is found, then the limitation was invalid and so we can decrease lct_i or increase est_i. Binary search is used to find the best shave. To limit CPU time, shaving was used for each activity only once.

Table 2 shows the results. We measured the CPU[1] time needed to prove the lower bound, i.e. the propagation is done twice: with the upper bound LB and LB-1. Times T1–T3 show running time for different implementations of the edge-finding algorithm: T1 is the new algorithm, T2 is the algorithm [7] and T3 is the algorithm [8]. As can be seen, the new algorithm is quite competitive for $n = 10$ and $n = 15$, for $n \geq 20$ it is faster than the other two edge-finding algorithms.

Optional activities were tested on modified 10x10 jobshop instances. In each job, activities on 5th and 6th place were taken as alternatives. Therefore in each problem there are 20 optional activities and 80 regular activities. Table 3 shows the results. Column LB is the destructive lower bound computed without shaving, column Opt is the optimal makespan. Column CH is the number of choicepoints needed to find the optimal solution and prove the optimality (i.e.

---
[1] Benchmarks were performed on Intel Pentium Centrino 1300MHz.

Table 2. Destructive Lower Bounds.

Prob.	Size	LB	T1	T2	T3
abz5	10 x 10	1196	1.430	1.421	1.466
abz6	10 x 10	941	1.773	1.762	1.815
orb01	10 x 10	1017	1.773	1.783	1.841
orb02	10 x 10	869	1.491	1.486	1.529
ft10	10 x 10	911	1.616	1.618	1.669
la21	15 x 10	1033	0.752	0.784	0.815
la22	15 x 10	925	3.486	3.597	3.763
la36	15 x 15	1267	5.376	5.520	5.768
la37	15 x 15	1397	2.498	2.572	2.667
ta01	15 x 15	1224	9.113	9.304	9.652
ta02	15 x 15	1210	7.097	7.264	7.586
la26	20 x 10	1218	0.749	0.838	0.899
la27	20 x 10	1235	0.908	0.994	1.054
la29	20 x 10	1119	3.357	3.609	3.816
abz7	20 x 15	651	3.283	3.446	3.579
abz8	20 x 15	621	12.00	12.54	13.14
ta11	20 x 15	1295	14.72	15.31	16.03
ta12	20 x 15	1336	17.54	18.30	19.26
ta21	20 x 20	1546	38.43	39.79	41.90
ta22	20 x 20	1501	25.47	26.25	27.37
yn1	20 x 20	816	26.79	27.58	28.91
yn2	20 x 20	842	22.86	23.59	24.69
ta31	30 x 15	1764	4.788	5.485	5.936
ta32	30 x 15	1774	6.515	7.390	7.946
swv11	50 x 10	2983	15.70	19.70	21.62
swv12	50 x 10	2972	19.21	23.43	25.23
ta51	50 x 15	2760	11.68	14.58	15.88
ta52	50 x 15	2756	12.07	15.04	16.32
ta71	100 x 20	5464	131.6	173.6	189.3
ta72	100 x 20	5181	132.0	174.8	190.8

optimal makespan used as the initial upper bound). Finally the column T is the CPU time in seconds.

As can be seen in the table, propagation is strong, all of the problems were solved surprisingly quickly. However more test should be made, especially on real life problem instances.

Acknowledgements

Authors would like to thank all the anonymous referees for their helpful comments and advises. This work has been supported by the Czech Science Foundation under the contract no. 201/04/1102.

Table 3. Alternative activities.

Prob.	Size	LB	Opt	CH	T
abz5-alt	10 x 10	1031	1093	283	0.336
abz6-alt	10 x 10	791	822	17	0.026
orb01-alt	10 x 10	894	947	9784	12.776
orb02-alt	10 x 10	708	747	284	0.328
ft10-alt	10 x 10	780	839	4814	6.298
la16-alt	10 x 10	838	842	27	0.022
la17-alt	10 x 10	673	676	24	0.021
la18-alt	10 x 10	743	750	179	0.200
la19-alt	10 x 10	686	731	84	0.103
la20-alt	10 x 10	809	809	14	0.014

References

[1] OR library. URL http://mscmga.ms.ic.ac.uk/info.html.

[2] Philippe Baptiste and Claude Le Pape. Edge-finding constraint propagation algorithms for disjunctive and cumulative scheduling. In *Proceedings of the Fifteenth Workshop of the U.K. Planning Special Interest Group*, 1996.

[3] Roman Barták. Dynamic global constraints in backtracking based environments. *Annals of Operations Research*, 118:101–118, 2003.

[4] J. Christopher Beck and Mark S. Fox. Scheduling alternative activities. In *AAAI/IAAI*, pages 680–687, 1999.

[5] Jacques Carlier and Eric Pinson. Adjustments of head and tails for the job-shop problem. *European Journal of Operational Research*, 78:146–161, 1994.

[6] F. Focacci, P. Laborie, and W. Nuijten. Solving scheduling problems with setup times and alternative resources. In *Proceedings of the 5th International Conference on Artificial Intelligence Planning and Scheduling*, 2000.

[7] Paul Martin and David B. Shmoys. A new approach to computing optimal schedules for the job-shop scheduling problem. In W. H. Cunningham, S. T. McCormick, and M. Queyranne, editors, *Proceedings of the 5th International Conference on Integer Programming and Combinatorial Optimization, IPCO'96*, pages 389–403, Vancouver, British Columbia, Canada, 1996.

[8] Claude Le Pape Philippe Baptiste and Wim Nuijten. *Constraint-Based Scheduling: Applying Constraint Programming to Scheduling Problems*. Kluwer Academic Publishers, 2001.

[9] Philippe Torres and Pierre Lopez. On not-first/not-last conditions in disjunctive scheduling. *European Journal of Operational Research*, 1999.

[10] Petr Vilím. $O(n \log n)$ filtering algorithms for unary resource constraint. In *Proceedings of CP-AI-OR 2004*. Springer-Verlag, 2004.

[11] Armin Wolf and Hans Schlenker. Realizing the alternative resources constraint problem with single resource constraints. In *To appear in proceedings of the INAP workshop 2004*, 2004.

Appendix

A Equivalence of the Edge-Finding Rules

Let us consider an arbitrary set $\Omega \subseteq T$. Overload rule says that if the set Ω cannot be processed within its time bounds then no solution exists:

$$\text{lct}_\Omega - \text{est}_\Omega < p_\Omega \quad \Rightarrow \quad \text{fail} \tag{7}$$

Note that it is useless to continue filtering when a fail was fired. Therefore in the following we will assume that the resource is not overloaded.

Proposition 2. *The rule (4) is not stronger than the original rules (2) and (3).*

Proof. Let us consider a pair of activities i, j for which the new rule (4) holds. We define a set Ω' as a subset of $\Theta(j) \cup \{i\}$ for which:

$$\text{ECT}_{\Theta(j) \cup \{i\}} = \text{est}_{\Omega'} + p_{\Omega'} \tag{8}$$

Note that thanks to the definition (1) of ECT such a set Ω' must exist.

If $i \notin \Omega'$ then $\Omega' \subseteq \Theta(j)$, therefore

$$\text{est}_{\Omega'} + p_{\Omega'} \stackrel{(8)}{=} \text{ECT}_{\Theta(j) \cup \{i\}} \stackrel{(4)}{>} \text{lct}_j \geq \text{lct}_{\Omega'}$$

So the resource is overloaded (see the overload rule (7)) and fail should have already been fired.

Thus $i \in \Omega'$. Let us define $\Omega = \Omega' \setminus \{i\}$. We will assume that $\Omega \neq \emptyset$, because otherwise $\text{est}_i \geq \text{ECT}_{\Theta(j)}$ and rule (4) changes nothing. For this set Ω we have:

$$\min\{\text{est}_\Omega, \text{est}_i\} + p_\Omega + p_i = \text{est}_{\Omega'} + p_{\Omega'} \stackrel{(8)}{=} \text{ECT}_{\Theta(j) \cup \{i\}} \stackrel{(4)}{>} \text{lct}_j \geq \text{lct}_\Omega$$

Hence the rule (2) holds for the set Ω. To complete the proof we have to show that both rules (3) and (4) adjust est_i equivalently, i.e. $\text{ECT}_\Omega = \text{ECT}_{\Theta(j)}$. We already know that $\text{ECT}_\Omega \leq \text{ECT}_{\Theta(j)}$ because $\Omega \subseteq \Theta(j)$. Suppose now for a contradiction that

$$\text{ECT}_\Omega < \text{ECT}_{\Theta(j)} \tag{9}$$

Let Φ be a set $\Phi \subseteq \Theta(j)$ such that:

$$\text{ECT}_{\Theta(j)} = \text{est}_\Phi + p_\Phi \tag{10}$$

Therefore:

$$\text{est}_\Omega + p_\Omega \leq \text{ECT}_\Omega \stackrel{(9)}{<} \text{ECT}_{\Theta(j)} \stackrel{(10)}{=} \text{est}_\Phi + p_\Phi \tag{11}$$

Because the set $\Omega' = \Omega \cup \{i\}$ defines the value of $\text{ECT}_{\Theta(j) \cup \{i\}}$ (i.e. $\text{est}_{\Omega'} + p_{\Omega'} = \text{ECT}_{\Theta(j) \cup \{i\}}$), it has the following property (see the definition (1) of ECT):

$$\forall k \in \Theta(j) \cup \{i\}: \quad \text{est}_k \geq \text{est}_{\Omega'} \Rightarrow k \in \Omega'$$

And because $\Omega = \Omega' \setminus \{i\}$:

$$\forall k \in \Theta(j): \quad \text{est}_k \geq \text{est}_{\Omega'} \Rightarrow k \in \Omega \tag{12}$$

Similarly, the set Φ defines the value of $\text{ECT}_{\Theta(j)}$:

$$\forall k \in \Theta(j): \quad \text{est}_k \geq \text{est}_\Phi \Rightarrow k \in \Phi \tag{13}$$

Combining properties (12) and (13) together we have that either $\Omega \subseteq \Phi$ (if $\text{est}_{\Omega'} \geq \text{est}_\Phi$) or $\Phi \subseteq \Omega$ (if $\text{est}_{\Omega'} \leq \text{est}_\Phi$). However, $\Phi \subseteq \Omega$ is not possible, because in this case $\text{est}_\Phi + p_\Phi \leq \text{ECT}_\Omega$ what contradicts the inequality (11). The result is that $\Omega \subsetneq \Phi$, and so $p_\Omega < p_\Phi$.

Now we are ready to prove the contradiction:

$$\begin{aligned}
\text{ECT}_{\Theta(j) \cup \{i\}} &\stackrel{(8)}{=} \text{est}_{\Omega'} + p_{\Omega'} \\
&= \min\{\text{est}_\Omega, \text{est}_i\} + p_\Omega + p_i && \text{because } \Omega = \Omega' \setminus \{i\} \\
&= \min\{\text{est}_\Omega + p_\Omega + p_i, \text{est}_i + p_\Omega + p_i\} \\
&< \min\{\text{est}_\Phi + p_\Phi + p_i, \text{est}_i + p_\Phi + p_i\} && \text{by (11) and } p_\Omega < p_\Phi \\
&\leq \text{ECT}_{\Theta(j) \cup \{i\}} && \text{because } \Phi \subseteq \Theta(j)
\end{aligned}$$

$\square$

Constraint Propagation as a Proof System

Albert Atserias[1,*], Phokion G. Kolaitis[2,**], and Moshe Y. Vardi[3,***]

[1] Universitat Politècnica de Catalunya, Barcelona, Spain
[2] University of California, Santa Cruz, USA
[3] Rice University, Houston, USA

Abstract. Refutation proofs can be viewed as a special case of constraint propagation, which is a fundamental technique in solving constraint-satisfaction problems. The generalization lifts, in a uniform way, the concept of refutation from Boolean satisfiability problems to general constraint-satisfaction problems. On the one hand, this enables us to study and characterize basic concepts, such as refutation width, using tools from finite-model theory. On the other hand, this enables us to introduce new proof systems, based on representation classes, that have not been considered up to this point. We consider ordered binary decision diagrams (OBDDs) as a case study of a representation class for refutations, and compare their strength to well-known proof systems, such as resolution, the Gaussian calculus, cutting planes, and Frege systems of bounded alternation-depth. In particular, we show that refutations by ODBBs polynomially simulate resolution and can be exponentially stronger.

1 Introduction

It is well known that the satisfiability problem for Boolean formulas in conjunctive normal form (CNF) can be viewed as a *constraint-satisfaction problem* (CSP). The input to a CSP consists of a set of variables, a set of possible values for the variables, and a set of constraints on the variables. The question is to determine whether there is an assignment of values to the variables that satisfies the given constraints. The study of CSP occupies a prominent place in artificial intelligence and computer science, because many algorithmic problems from a wide spectrum of areas can be modeled as such [Dec03]. These areas include temporal reasoning, belief maintenance, machine vision, scheduling, graph theory, and, of course, propositional logic. Since constraint-satisfaction problems constitute a natural generalization of Boolean satisfiability problems, it is natural to ask for proof systems that generalize the systems for propositional logic to CSP. Such systems would be used to refute the satisfiability of an instance of a constraint-satisfaction problem, much in the same way that resolution is used to refute the satisfiability of a CNF-formula.

---

* Supported in part by CICYT TIC2001-1577-C03-02 and the Future and Emerging Technologies programme of the EU under contract number IST-99-14186 (ALCOM-FT).
** Supported in part by NSF grant IIS-9907419.
*** Supported in part by NSF grants CCR-9988322, CCR-0124077, CCR-0311326, IIS-9908435, IIS-9978135, EIA-0086264, and ANI-0216467, and by BSF grant 9800096.

One of the goals of this paper is to introduce a natural and canonical way of defining a proof system for every constraint-satisfaction problem. In order to achieve this, first we need a unifying framework for representing such problems. This was achieved by Feder and Vardi [FV98], who recognized that essentially all examples of CSPs in the literature can be recast as the following fundamental algebraic problem, called the HOMOMORPHISM PROBLEM: given two finite relational structures **A** and **B**, is there a homomorphism $h : \mathbf{A} \to \mathbf{B}$? Intuitively, the structure **A** represents the variables and the tuples of variables that participate in constraints, the structure **B** represents the domain of values, and the tuples of values that these constrained tuples of variables are allowed to take, and the homomorphisms from **A** to **B** are precisely the assignments of values to variables that satisfy the constraints. For instance, the 3-COLORABILITY problem coincides with the problem of deciding whether there is a homomorphism from a given graph **G** to $\mathbf{K}_3$, where $\mathbf{K}_3$ is the complete graph with three nodes (the triangle). The uniform version of the HOMOMORPHISM PROBLEM, in which both structures **A** and **B** are given as input, is the most general formulation of the constraint-satisfaction problem. Interesting algorithmic problems, however, also arise by fixing the structure **B**, which sometimes is called the *template structure*. Thus, the resulting problem, denoted by $\mathrm{CSP}(\mathbf{B})$, asks: given **A**, is there a homomorphism from **A** to **B**? Note that $\mathrm{CSP}(\mathbf{K}_3)$ is precisely the 3-COLORABILITY problem; more generally, $\mathrm{CSP}(\mathbf{K}_k)$ is the k-COLORABILITY problem, where $\mathbf{K}_k$ is the complete graph with k-nodes, $k \geq 2$.

With constraint-satisfaction problems presented as homomorphism problems in a unifying way, we are closer to our first goal of defining canonical proof systems. The approach we take is via yet another interpretation of CSPs, this time in terms of database theory, building upon the homomorphism framework. As pointed out in [GJC94], every constraint can be thought of as a table of a relational database, and the set of solutions to a CSP can be identified with the tuples in the *join* of all constraints. This fruitful connection between CSPs and database theory is explored further in [KV00a]. Now, a CSP instance is unsatisfiable precisely when the join of the constraints is empty. We adopt this approach and define a $\mathrm{CSP}(\mathbf{B})$ *refutation of an instance* **A** to be a sequence of constraints ending with the empty constraint, such that every constraint in the sequence is an initial constraint, the join of two previous constraints, the projection of some previous constraint, or the weakening of some previous constraint. Projection and weakening are not strictly necessary, but provide a versatile tool for reducing the complexity of the intermediate constraints. Note that the join is a form of constraint propagation, since it allows us to derive new constraints implied by the previous ones. See the work by Freuder [Fre78] for the first theoretical approach to constraint propagation.

The proof systems obtained this way are sound and complete for constraint satisfaction. We embark on the investigation of their general properties by focussing first on the concept of *refutation width*, which is the maximum arity of the constraints in a refutation. Bounding the arity of the constraints generated during the execution of constraint propagation algorithms has already played a crucial role in the development of the theory of CSPs, as a method to achieve tractability [Fre82,Fre90,DP87]. For example, various concepts of consistency popularized by the AI community rely on it [Dec03]. Following the ideas in [FV98,KV00a,AD03], we are able to show that the minimal refutation width of a $\mathrm{CSP}(\mathbf{B})$ instance **A** is characterized by a combinatorial game introduced in the context of finite-model theory. In turn, again following [FV98,KV00a], this leads us naturally to considering the treewidth of the instance as a parameter. As a result, we obtain a deeper understanding and also a purely combinatorial characterization of refutation width.

CSP refutations are perhaps too general to be of practical use. The rules are too general and the constraints, if represented explicitly, may be too large. Hence, we propose a *syntactic* counterpart to general CSP refutations, in which all the constraints are somehow succintly represented. Technically speaking, we consider representation classes for the constraints. Some examples include clauses, linear equalities over a finite field, linear inequalities over the integers, decision trees, decision diagrams, and so on. With this new formalism, CSP proofs become purely syntactical objects, closer to their counterparts in propositional logic. As a case study, we investigate the proof system obtained by using ordered binary decision diagrams (OBDDs) as our representation class for constraints. OBDDs possess many desirable algorithmic properties and have been used successfully in many areas, most notably in formal verification (see [Bry92,BCM+92]). We compare the strength of refutations by OBDDs with other proof systems for propositional logic. We show that OBDD-based refutations polynomially simulate both resolution and the Gaussian calculus; moreover, they are exponentially stronger than either of these systems, even when the weakening rule is not allowed. If we make strong use of weakening, then refutations by OBDDs can polynomially simulate the cutting planes proof system with coefficients written in unary (called CP^* in [BPR97]). In particular, OBDDs provide polynomial-size proofs of the pigeonhole principle. This shows already that refutations by OBDDs can be exponentially stronger than resolution, and even Frege (Hilbert-style) systems with formulas of bounded alternation-depth, because the pigeonhole principle is hard for them [Hak85,Ajt88,BIK+92]. Finally, we observe that for a particular order of the variables, refutations by OBDDs have small communication complexity. By combining this with known techniques about feasible interpolation [IPU94,Kra97], we establish that OBDD-based refutations have polynomial-size monotone interpolants, for a particular order of the variables. This gives exponential lower bounds for a number of examples, including the clique-coloring principle, still for that particular order. Whether the restriction on the order is necessary remains an interesting open problem.

2 Preliminaries

Constraint-Satisfaction Problems. A *relational vocabulary* σ is a collection of *relation symbols* R, each of a specified *arity*. A σ-structure $\mathbf{A}$ consists of a *universe* A, or *domain*, and for each $R \in \sigma$, an *interpretation* $R^\mathbf{A} \subseteq A^r$, where r is the arity of R.

Let $\mathbf{B}$ be a finite σ-structure. We denote by $\mathrm{CSP}(\mathbf{B})$ the class of all finite σ-structures $\mathbf{A}$ such that there is a homomorphism from $\mathbf{A}$ to $\mathbf{B}$. Recall that a homomorphism is a mapping from the universe of $\mathbf{A}$ to the universe of $\mathbf{B}$ that preserves the relations. As mentioned in the introduction, each $\mathrm{CSP}(\mathbf{B})$ is a constraint-satisfaction problem. The structure $\mathbf{B}$ is called the *template structure*. Let us discuss how 3-SAT can be modeled by a particular $\mathrm{CSP}(\mathbf{B})$. This will be of help later in the paper. The relational vocabulary consists of four ternary relation symbols $\{R_0, R_1, R_2, R_3\}$ representing all possible types of 3-clauses: clauses with no negations, clauses with one negation, clauses with two negations, and clauses with three negations. The template structure $\mathbf{T}$ has the truth tables of these types of clauses: $R_0^{\mathbf{T}} = \{0,1\}^3 - \{000\}$, $R_1^{\mathbf{T}} = \{0,1\}^3 - \{100\}$, $R_2^{\mathbf{T}} = \{0,1\}^3 - \{110\}$, and $R_3^{\mathbf{T}} = \{0,1\}^3 - \{111\}$. Every 3-CNF formula φ gives rise to a σ-structure $\mathbf{A}_\varphi$ with universe the set of variables of φ and relations encoding the clauses of φ; for instance, $R_1^{\mathbf{A}_\varphi}$ consists of all triples (x,y,z) of variables of φ such that $(\neg x \vee y \vee z)$ is one of the clauses of φ. Thus, CSP($\mathbf{T}$) is equivalent to 3-SAT, since φ is satisfiable if and only if there is a homomorphism from $\mathbf{A}_\varphi$ to $\mathbf{T}$.

Pebble Games. The *existential k-pebble games* were defined in [KV95,KV00a]. The games are played between two players, the Spoiler and the Duplicator, on two σ-structures $\mathbf{A}$ and $\mathbf{B}$ according to the following rules. Each player has a set of k pebbles numbered $\{1,\ldots,k\}$. In each round of the game, the Spoiler can make one of two different moves: either he places a free pebble on an element of the domain of $\mathbf{A}$, or he removes a pebble from a pebbled element of $\mathbf{A}$. To each move of the Spoiler, the Duplicator must respond by placing her corresponding pebble over an element of $\mathbf{B}$, or removing her corresponding pebble from $\mathbf{B}$, respectively. If the Spoiler reaches a round in which the set of pairs of pebbled elements is not a partial homomorphism between $\mathbf{A}$ and $\mathbf{B}$, then he wins the game. Otherwise, we say that the Duplicator wins the game. The formal definition can be found in [KV95,KV00a], and the close relationship between existential pebble games and constraint-satisfaction problems was discussed at length in [KV00b].

Treewidth. The *treewidth* of a graph can be defined in many different ways [Bod98]. One way is this. The treewidth of a graph $\mathbf{G}$ is the smallest positive integer k such that $\mathbf{G}$ is a subgraph of a k-tree, where a k-tree is defined inductively as follows: the $k+1$-clique $\mathbf{K}_{k+1}$ is a k-tree, and if $\mathbf{G}$ is a k-tree, then the result of adding a new node to $\mathbf{G}$ that is adjacent to exactly the nodes of a k-clique of $\mathbf{G}$ (thus forming a (k+1)-clique) is also a k-tree. The *Gaifman graph* of a structure $\mathbf{A}$ is the graph whose set of nodes is the universe of $\mathbf{A}$, and whose edges relate pairs of elements that appear in some tuple of a relation of $\mathbf{A}$. The *treewidth* of a structure is the treewidth of its Gaifman graph.

3 Proof Systems for CSPs

Notions from Database Theory. A *relation schema* $R(x_1,\ldots,x_k)$ consists of a *relation name* R, and a set of *attribute names* $x_1,\ldots,x_k$. A *database schema* σ is a set of relation schemas. A *relation conforming with* a relation schema $R(x_1,\ldots,x_k)$ is a set of k-tuples. A *database over* a database schema σ is a set of relations conforming with the relation schemas in σ. In other words, a database over σ is a σ-structure, except that the universe of the structure is not made explicit. In the sequel, we often conflate the notation and use the same symbol for both a relation schema and a relation conforming with that schema.

We use $\mathbf{x}$ to denote a tuple of attribute names $(x_1,\ldots,x_k)$ and also to denote the set $\{x_1,\ldots,x_k\}$. It will be clear from context which case it is. Let R be a relation conforming with the relational schema $R(\mathbf{x})$. Let $\mathbf{y} \subseteq \mathbf{x}$ be a subset of the set of attribute names. The *projection* of R with respect to $\mathbf{y}$ is the relation whose attribute names are $\mathbf{y}$, and whose tuples can be extended to tuples in R. We denote it $\pi_\mathbf{y}(R)$. Let R and S be relations conforming with relational schemas $R(\mathbf{x})$ and $S(\mathbf{y})$. The *relational join* of R and S, or simply *join*, is the largest relation T whose attribute names are $\mathbf{x} \cup \mathbf{y}$, and such that $\pi_\mathbf{x}(T) \subseteq R$ and $\pi_\mathbf{y}(T) \subseteq S$. We denote it by $R \bowtie S$. Joins are commutative and associative, and can be extended to an arbitrary number of relations.

Notions from CSPs. Let σ be a relational vocabulary. Let $\mathbf{A}$ and $\mathbf{B}$ be two σ-structures. A k-ary *constraint* is a pair $(\mathbf{x}, R)$, where $\mathbf{x}$ is a k-tuple of distinct elements of the universe of $\mathbf{A}$, and R is a k-ary relation over the universe of $\mathbf{B}$. The constraint $(\mathbf{x}, R)$ can be interpreted as a pair formed by a relation schema $R(\mathbf{x})$ and a relation R conforming with it. Here, $\mathbf{x}$ is the set of attribute names. Thus, it makes sense to talk about joins and projections of constraints. We say that a constraint $(\mathbf{x}, R)$ is a *superset*, or *weakening*, of another constraint $(\mathbf{y}, S)$ if $\mathbf{x} = \mathbf{y}$ and $R \supseteq S$.

If there is a homomorphism from $\mathbf{A}$ to $\mathbf{B}$, then we say that the instance $\mathbf{A}$ of $\mathrm{CSP}(\mathbf{B})$ is *satisfiable*; otherwise, we say that it is *unsatisfiable*. Recall from Section 2 that these definitions generalize Boolean satisfiability and unsatisfiability of 3-CNF formulas. If a CSP instance is unsatisfiable, its satisfiability may be *refuted*. We are interested in *refutations* by means of joins, projections, and weakening. Here, constraints $(\mathbf{x}, R)$ are viewed as relational schemas $R(\mathbf{x})$ with a relation R conforming with it as suggested in the preceding paragraph.

Definition 1 (CSP Refutation). *Let $\mathbf{A}$ and $\mathbf{B}$ be σ-structures. A $\mathrm{CSP}(\mathbf{B})$ proof from $\mathbf{A}$ is a finite sequence of constraints $(\mathbf{x}, R)$ each of which is of one of the following forms:*

1. *Axiom:* $(\mathbf{x}, R^\mathbf{B})$, *where $R \in \sigma$ and $\mathbf{x} \in R^\mathbf{A}$*
2. *Join:* $(\mathbf{x} \cup \mathbf{y}, R \bowtie S)$, *where $(\mathbf{x}, R)$ and $(\mathbf{y}, S)$ are previous constraints.*
3. *Projection:* $(\mathbf{x} - \{x\}, \pi_{\mathbf{x}-\{x\}}(R))$, *where $(\mathbf{x}, R)$ is a previous constraint.*
4. *Weakening:* $(\mathbf{x}, S)$, *where $(\mathbf{x}, R)$ is a previous constraint and $R \subseteq S$.*

A $\mathrm{CSP}(\mathbf{B})$ refutation of $\mathbf{A}$ is a proof whose last constraint has an empty relation.

Note that the projections eliminate one variable at a time. We say that the variable is projected out. The following simple result states that CSP refutations form a sound and complete method for proving that a given instance of a CSP is unsatisfiable. The fact that CSP can be reduced to a join of constraints is mentioned already in [GJC94].

Theorem 1 (Soundness and Completeness). *Let $\mathbf{A}$ and $\mathbf{B}$ be σ-structures. Then, $\mathbf{A}$ has a $\mathrm{CSP}(\mathbf{B})$ refutation if and only if $\mathbf{A}$ is unsatisfiable in $\mathrm{CSP}(\mathbf{B})$. In fact, axioms and joins alone are already enough to refute an unsatisfiable instance.*

Due to space limitations, we need to omit most proofs in this version of the paper. The proof of Theorem 1 shows that refutations need not be any longer than linear in the number of constraints of the CSP instance. However, the critical reader may observe that the intermediate constraints may be arbitrarily complex. On the other hand, the rules of projection and weakening can be used to lower this complexity when necessary. It will become clear later on how this is of any help in applications. At this point, let us introduce a formalism to measure the complexity of the intermediate constraints. A k-ary constraint $(\mathbf{x}, R)$ can be identified with a Boolean-valued function $f : B^k \rightarrow \{0,1\}$ by letting $f(\mathbf{a}) = 1$ if and only if $\mathbf{a} \in R$ (in other words, this is the *characteristic function* of the relation R). Now, functions of this sort can be represented in various ways by means of representation classes.

Definition 2 (**Representation Class**). *Let B be a finite set. A representation class for Boolean-valued functions with domain B^k is a triple $\mathcal{R} = (Q, I, S)$, where Q is a set, called the set of representations, I is a mapping from Q to the set of functions $f : B^k \rightarrow \{0,1\}$ called the interpretation, and S is a mapping from Q to the integers, called the size function.*

To be useful for CSP refutations, representation classes should satisfy certain regularity conditions, such as being closed under joins and projections. In addition, the size function should capture the intuitive notion of *complexity* of a representation. There are many examples of representation classes in the literature, particularly when the domain B is Boolean, that is, $B = \{0, 1\}$.

Examples. Let $B = \{0, 1\}$, and let $A = \{x_1, \ldots, x_n\}$ be a set of propositional variables. Clauses over A form a representation class. The interpretation of a clause is the obvious one, and we may define the size of a clause by the number of literals in it. A clause C can be thought of as a constraint $(\mathbf{x}, R)$, where $\mathbf{x}$ is the set of variables in C (not literals), and R is the set of truth assignments to the variables that satisfy the clause. Unfortunately, clauses are not closed under joins, that is, the join of two clauses is not necessarily a clause. Nonetheless, clauses are closed under the *resolution rule*, which can be seen as a combination of one join and one projection (see also [DvB97]). Indeed, if $C \vee x$ and $D \vee \neg x$ are clauses, then the *resolvent* clause $C \vee D$ is precisely the result of projecting x out of their join. We exploit and elaborate on this connection with resolution in Section 5. Binary decision diagrams (BDDs), a.k.a. branching programs (BPs), also form a representation class (see section 5 for a reminder of the definitions). The interpretation of a BDD is the obvious one, and we may define its size by the number of nodes of its graph. BDDs are closed under joins and projections. In fact, BDDs are closed under all operations, since BDDs can represent all Boolean functions. Moreover, when an order on the variables is imposed, the representation of the join can be obtained in polynomial time. We will discuss these issues in Section 5. Linear inequalities $\sum_i a_i x_i \leq a_0$, for integers a_i, also form a representation class. The interpretation of $\sum_i a_i x_i \leq a_0$ is a k-ary Boolean-valued function $f : B^k \rightarrow \{0,1\}$, where k is the number of variables, defined by $f(b_1, \ldots, b_k) = 1$ if and only if $\sum_i a_i b_i \leq a_0$. The size of a linear inequality may be defined by the number of bits needed to represent the $k+1$ coefficients, or by $a_0 + \sum_i a_i$ if the coefficients are represented in unary. As was the case with clauses, linear inequalities are not closed under joins. Representation classes can also be used to represent functions $f : B^k \rightarrow \{0,1\}$ with non-Boolean domain B. As long as B is finite, BDDs form an appropriate example. The particular case of (non-binary) decision trees is also a good example.

The notion of a representation class suggests a syntactic counterpart of the general notion of CSP refutation. Moreover, it also suggests a way to bound the complexity of the intermediate relations in a CSP refutation. Recall that the width of constraint $(\mathbf{x}, R)$ is the same as its arity, that is, the length of the tuple $\mathbf{x}$.

Definition 3 (Complexity Measures). *Let $\mathbf{B}$ be a σ-structure. Let $\mathcal{R} = (Q, I, S)$ be a representation class for Boolean-valued functions on the universe of $\mathbf{B}$. Let $C_1, \ldots, C_m$ be a $\mathrm{CSP}(\mathbf{B})$ proof, and let $r_i \in Q$ be a representation of the constraint C_i. We say that $r_1, \ldots, r_m$ is an $\mathcal{R}$-proof. Its length is m, its size is $S(r_1) + \cdots + S(r_m)$, and its width is the maximum width of $C_1, \ldots, C_m$.*

It was mentioned already that a representation class should satisfy certain regularity conditions. The actual conditions depend on the application at hand. One particularly useful property is that the representation of a join (projection, weakening) be computable in polynomial time from the representations of the given constraints. In our intended applications, this will indeed be the case.

4 Refutation Width and Treewidth

Characterization of Refutation Width. Width has played a crucial role in the development of the theory of CSPs [DP87]. Part of the interest comes from the fact that a width upper bound translates, for most representations, to a size bound on individual constraints. This is true, for example, for explicit representation and for BDDs. In the proof complexity literature, Ben-Sasson and Wigderson [BSW01] viewed it as a complexity measure for resolution. Here, we adopt the methods for CSP refutations.

Theorem 2. *Let $\mathbf{A}$ and $\mathbf{B}$ be two finite σ-structures. The following are equivalent:*

1. *$\mathbf{A}$ has a $\mathrm{CSP}(\mathbf{B})$ refutation of width k.*
2. *The Spoiler wins the existential k-pebble game on $\mathbf{A}$ and $\mathbf{B}$.*

An intimate connection between pebble games and the notion of strong consistency [Dec92] was established in [KV00b]. This entails an intimate connection between the concepts of refutation width and the concept of strong consistency. Specifically, it follows from the results in [KV00b] and the above theorem that $\mathbf{A}$ has a $\mathrm{CSP}(\mathbf{B})$ refutation of width k precisely when it is impossible to establish strong k-consistency for $\mathbf{A}$ and $\mathbf{B}$.

Next we turn to studying the effect of the treewidth of the instance $\mathbf{A}$ on the width of the CSP refutations. We will need the following result due to Dalmau, Kolaitis and Vardi:

Theorem 3 ([DKV02]). *Let $k \geq 2$, let $\mathbf{A}$ be a finite σ-structure of treewidth less than k, and let $\mathbf{B}$ be a finite σ-structure. Then the following statements are equivalent:*

1. *There is a homomorphism from $\mathbf{A}$ to $\mathbf{B}$.*
2. *The Duplicator wins the existential k-pebble game on $\mathbf{A}$ and $\mathbf{B}$*

It is immediate from Theorems 2 and 3 that if $\mathbf{A}$ is unsatisfiable in $\mathrm{CSP}(\mathbf{B})$ and has treewidth less than k, then $\mathbf{A}$ has a $\mathrm{CSP}(\mathbf{B})$ refutation of width k. In fact, this result remains true in a more general situation. A substructure $\mathbf{C}$ of $\mathbf{A}$ is called a *core* of $\mathbf{A}$ if there is a homomorphism from $\mathbf{A}$ to $\mathbf{C}$, but, for every proper substructure $\mathbf{C}'$ of $\mathbf{C}$, there is no homomorphism from $\mathbf{A}$ to $\mathbf{C}'$. It is known [HN92] that every finite structure $\mathbf{A}$ has a unique core up to isomorphism, denoted by $\mathrm{core}(\mathbf{A})$, and that $\mathbf{A}$ is homomorphically equivalent to $\mathrm{core}(\mathbf{A})$. In the context of database theory, the treewidth of the core of $\mathbf{A}$ captures exactly the smallest number k such that the canonical conjunctive query $Q^{\mathbf{A}}$ can be expressed in the existential positive fragment of first-order logic with k variables [DKV02, Theorem 12]. Now, back to refutations, if $\mathbf{A}$ is an unsatisfiable instance of $\mathrm{CSP}(\mathbf{B})$ and the core of $\mathbf{A}$ has treewidth less than k, then $\mathbf{A}$ also has a $\mathrm{CSP}(\mathbf{B})$ refutation of width k. Indeed, if $\mathbf{A}$ is an unsatisfiable instance of $\mathrm{CSP}(\mathbf{B})$, so is $\mathrm{core}(\mathbf{A})$ because they are homomorphically equivalent; moreover, if $\mathrm{core}(\mathbf{A})$ has treewidth less than k, then $\mathrm{core}(\mathbf{A})$ has a $\mathrm{CSP}(\mathbf{B})$ refutation of width less than k. Since $\mathrm{core}(\mathbf{A})$ is a substructure of $\mathbf{A}$, a $\mathrm{CSP}(\mathbf{B})$ refutation of $\mathrm{core}(\mathbf{A})$ is also a $\mathrm{CSP}(\mathbf{B})$ refutation of $\mathbf{A}$.

One may wonder whether the converse is true. Is the treewidth of the core of $\mathbf{A}$ capturing the width of the refutations of $\mathbf{A}$? Unfortunately, the answer turns out to be negative for rather trivial reasons. Take a $\mathbf{B}$ such that $\mathrm{CSP}(\mathbf{B})$ can be solved by a k-Datalog program for some fixed k. For example, let $\mathbf{B} = \mathbf{K}_2$ so that $\mathrm{CSP}(\mathbf{B})$ becomes 2-COLORABILITY, which is expressible in 3-Datalog. Take a graph $\mathbf{G}$ which is not 2-colorable. Hence, the Spoiler wins the existential 3-pebble game on $\mathbf{G}$ and $\mathbf{K}_2$ [KV00a]. Now just add an arbitrarily large clique to $\mathbf{G}$, that is, let $\mathbf{G}' = \mathbf{G} \cup \mathbf{K}_k$ for some large k. There still exists a $\mathrm{CSP}(\mathbf{B})$ refutation of $\mathbf{G}'$ of width 3, but the core of $\mathbf{G}'$ has treewidth at least $k-1$. This counterexample, however, suggests that something more interesting is going on concerning the relationship between existential k-pebble games and treewidth k.

Theorem 4. *Let $k \geq 2$, let $\mathbf{A}$ and $\mathbf{B}$ be two finite σ-structures. Then the following statements are equivalent:*

1. *The Duplicator wins the existential k-pebble game on $\mathbf{A}$ and $\mathbf{B}$.*
2. *If $\mathbf{A}'$ is a structure of treewidth less than k and such that there is a homomorphism from $\mathbf{A}'$ to $\mathbf{A}$, then the Duplicator wins the existential k-pebble game on $\mathbf{A}'$ and $\mathbf{B}$.*

Proof sketch: (i) $\Rightarrow$ (ii) is easy. (ii) $\Rightarrow$ (i). Let $P_\mathbf{B}$ be the k-Datalog program that expresses the query: "Given $\mathbf{A}$, does the Spoiler win the existential k-pebble game on $\mathbf{A}$ and $\mathbf{B}$?" [KV00a]. Assume that the Spoiler wins the existential k-pebble game on $\mathbf{A}$ and $\mathbf{B}$. Hence $\mathbf{A}$ satisfies $P_\mathbf{B}$, hence it satisfies one of the stages of the k-Datalog program $P_\mathbf{B}$. Each such stage is definable by a union of conjunctive queries, each of which can be written in the existential positive fragment of first-order logic with k variables. Hence $\mathbf{A}$ satisfies $Q^{\mathbf{A}'}$, where $\mathbf{A}'$ is a structure of treewidth less than k. Hence, there is a homomorphism h from $\mathbf{A}'$ to $\mathbf{A}$. But also $\mathbf{A}'$ satisfies $P_\mathbf{B}$, hence the Spoiler wins the existential k-pebble game on $\mathbf{A}'$ and $\mathbf{B}$. □

Now we combine Theorems 2, 3 and 4 to obtain a purely combinatorial characterization of when a structure has a CSP refutation of a certain width.

Corollary 1. *Let $k \geq 2$, let $\mathbf{A}$ and $\mathbf{B}$ be two finite σ-structures. The following are equivalent:*

1. *$\mathbf{A}$ has a $\mathrm{CSP}(\mathbf{B})$ refutation of width k.*
2. *There exists a structure $\mathbf{A}'$ of treewidth less than k and such that there is a homomorphism from $\mathbf{A}'$ to $\mathbf{A}$, and $\mathbf{A}'$ is unsatisfiable in $\mathrm{CSP}(\mathbf{B})$.*

Note that the characterization of refutation width is stated in terms of treewidth and homomorphisms and does not mention refutations at all. Let us add that the structure in (2) can be large, so Corollary 1 does not yield any complexity bound for deciding whether $\mathbf{A}$ has a $\mathrm{CSP}(\mathbf{B})$ refutation of width k. As it turns out, it follows from Theorem 2 and the result in [KP03], that this problem is EXPTIME-complete.

Small-Width Proof-Search Algorithms. Next we study the complexity of finding a satisfying assignment, or refuting the satisfiability, of an instance $\mathbf{A}$ of $\mathrm{CSP}(\mathbf{B})$ when we parameterize by the treewidth k of $\mathbf{A}$. The decision problem has been studied before in certain particular cases. When k is bounded by a constant, the problem can be solved in polynomial time [DP87,Fre90]. When $\mathbf{B}$ is a fixed structure, Courcelle's Theorem [Cou90] implies that the problem can be solved in time $2^{O(k)} n$, where n is the size of $\mathbf{A}$. Indeed, if $\mathbf{B}$ is fixed, then satisfiability in $\mathrm{CSP}(\mathbf{B})$ can be expressed in monadic second-order logic, so Courcelle's Theorem applies. We consider the case in which $\mathbf{B}$ and k are not fixed, and also the problem of finding a satisfying assignment, or a refutation. In the particular case of Boolean $\mathbf{B}$ and resolution refutations, a related problem was studied in [AR02] where branchwidth was used instead of treewidth. Our proof is more general, rather different, and perhaps simpler.

Theorem 5. *The problem of determining whether a structure $\mathbf{A}$ of treewidth k is satisfiable in $\mathrm{CSP}(\mathbf{B})$ can be solved by a deterministic algorithm in time $2^{O(k)} m^{O(k)} n^{O(1)}$, where n is the size of $\mathbf{A}$ and m is the size of $\mathbf{B}$. In particular, the algorithm runs in polynomial time when $k = O(\log n / \log m)$. Moreover, if $\mathbf{A}$ is satisfiable, the algorithm produces a homomorphism $h : \mathbf{A} \to \mathbf{B}$, and if $\mathbf{A}$ is unsatisfiable, it produces a $\mathrm{CSP}(\mathbf{B})$ refutation of width k.*

Proof sketch. The idea is to build an existential positive sentence ψ, with k variables, that is a rewriting of the canonical query $Q^{\mathbf{A}}$. This takes time polynomial in the tree-decomposition of $\mathbf{A}$, which can be found in time $2^{O(k)} n^{O(1)}$. Then we evaluate ψ on $\mathbf{B}$ bottom up, from inner subformulas to the root. Since each subformula involves at most k variables, this takes time $m^{O(k)}$ times the size of the formula, which is time $2^{O(k)} m^{O(k)} n^{O(1)}$ overall. Since $\psi \equiv Q^{\mathbf{A}}$, we have that $\mathbf{B}$ satisfies ψ if and only if there exists a homomorphism from $\mathbf{A}$ to $\mathbf{B}$. □

5 Refutations by OBDDs: A Case Study

Regularity Properties of OBDDs. In this section we study the effect of using *ordered binary decision diagrams* as a representation class for constraints. We focus on the Boolean case $B = \{0, 1\}$.

For the history on the origins of binary decision diagrams, branching programs, and ordered binary decision diagrams we refer the reader to the survey by Bryant [Bry92]. Here are the definitions. Let $x_1, \ldots, x_n$ be n propositional variables. A *binary decision diagram* (BDD), or *branching program* (BP), represents a Boolean function as a rooted, directed acyclic graph $\mathbf{G}$. Each non-terminal node u of $\mathbf{G}$ is labeled by a variable $v(u) \in \{x_1, \ldots, x_n\}$, and has arcs toward two children $t(u)$ and $f(u)$, referred to as the true and the false children respectively. Each terminal node is labeled 0 or 1. For a truth assigment to the variables $x_1, \ldots, x_n$, the value of the function is determined by following the path through the directed graph, from the root to a terminal node, according to the labels of the nodes and the values to the variables. The size of a BDD is the size of the underlying graph $\mathbf{G}$. An *ordered binary decision diagram* (OBDD) is a BDD in which labeled paths are consistent with a specific total order $<$ over the variables. More precisely, for an OBDD we require that the variable labeling a non-terminal node be smaller than the variables labeling its non-terminal children, according to a fixed order over the variables.

The main property of OBDDs is that, in their reduced form, they are *canonical*, meaning that for a given order, two OBDDs for the same function are isomorphic. An immediate consequence is that testing for equivalence of two OBDDs can be solved in time polynomial in their size. Most interesting for us is the fact that representations of joins and projections are computable in polynomial time, and determining whether an OBDD is a weakening of another is decidable in polynomial time.

It follows from this that given a CSP refutation $C_1, \ldots, C_m$ with the constraints represented by OBDDs, the validity of applications of the join rule, the projection rule, and the weakening rule, can be checked in polynomial time. Therefore, refutations by OBDDs when applied to 3-SAT (a particular CSP($\mathbf{B}$), see below) form a proof system in the sense of Cook and Reckhow [CR79].

Strength of Refutations by OBDDs. Let us compare the size of CSP refutations by OBDDs with other well-known proof systems for propositional logic. Recall from Section 2 how 3-SAT is represented as a CSP($\mathbf{B}$) problem. The template structure is $\mathbf{T}$ and its vocabulary consists of four ternary relations $\{R_0, R_1, R_2, R_3\}$, one for each type of 3-clause. Thus, structures for this vocabulary are 3-CNF formulas. A *refutation by OBDDs* of a 3-CNF formula $\mathbf{A}$ is a refutation of $\mathbf{A}$ in CSP($\mathbf{T}$) when constraints are represented by OBDDs for a fixed total order of the variables. Size, length and width of refutations by OBDDs are defined according to Definition 3 in Section 3.

Resolution. The resolution rule is very simple: from $C \vee x$ and $D \vee \neg x$, derive $C \vee D$, where C and D are clauses in which x does not occur. The goal is to derive the empty clause from a given set of initial clauses. The length of a resolution refutation is the number of clauses that are used in it. The size of a resolution refutation is the total number of literals that appear in it. There are two key observations that concern us here. The first is that every clause has a small equivalent OBDD over all orders of the variables. The second observation is that $C \vee D$ can be expressed in terms of one join and one projection from $C \vee x$ and $D \vee \neg x$ (see also [DvB97]). We use both facts for the following result whose proof will be included in the full paper.

Theorem 6. *Let $\mathbf{A}$ be a 3-CNF formula on n variables. If $\mathbf{A}$ has a resolution refutation of length m, then $\mathbf{A}$ has a refutation by OBDDs of length $2m$ and size $O(mn^2)$, even without using the weakening rule and for every order of the variables. Moreover, there is a polynomial-time algorithm that converts the resolution refutation into the refutation by OBDDs.*

We will see below that, in fact, refutations by OBDDs are exponentially stronger than resolution. As an intermediate step we move to a different CSP: systems of equations over $\mathbf{Z}_2$.

Gaussian calculus. One nice feature of OBDDs is that they give a uniform framework for defining all types of constraints. Consider now the CSP defined by systems of linear equations over the two-element field $\mathbf{Z}_2$, with exactly three variables per equation. That is, the vocabulary contains two ternary relation symbols R_0 and R_1 representing the equations $x + y + z = 0$ and $x + y + z = 1$ respectively. The template structure $\mathbf{S}$ contains the truth tables of these equations: that is $R_0^\mathbf{S} = \{000, 011, 110, 101\}$ and $R_1^\mathbf{S} = \{001, 010, 100, 111\}$. Now $\mathrm{CSP}(\mathbf{S})$ coincides with systems of equations over $\mathbf{Z}_2$. The standard method for solving systems of equations is Gaussian elimination. In fact, Gaussian elimination can be used to refute the satisfiability of systems of equations by deriving, for example, $0 = 1$ by means of linear combinations that cancel at least one variable. This has led to proposing the Gaussian calculus as a proof system [BSI99]. Let us see that refutations by OBDDs can polynomially simulate it. Perhaps the most interesting point of the proof is that we actually show that weakening is not required, which is not immediately obvious.

Theorem 7. *Let $\mathbf{A}$ be a system of equations over $\mathbf{Z}_2$ with exactly three variables per equation. If $\mathbf{A}$ has a Gaussian calculus refutation of length m, then $\mathbf{A}$ has a refutation by OBDDs in $\mathrm{CSP}(\mathbf{S})$ of length $2m$ and size $O(mn^2)$, even without using the weakening rule and for every order of the variables. Moreover, there is a polynomial-time algorithm that converts the Gaussian calculus refutation into the refutation by OBDDs.*

We can now use this result to conclude that for 3-CNF formulas, refutations by OBDDs are exponentially stronger than resolution. Consider the standard translation of a linear equation $x + y + z = a$ of $\mathbf{Z}_2$ into a 3-CNF formula. Namely, for $a = 1$ the 3-CNF formula is

$$(x \vee y \vee z) \wedge (x \vee \neg y \vee \neg z) \wedge (\neg x \vee y \vee \neg z) \wedge (\neg x \vee \neg y \vee z),$$

and the formula for $a = 0$ is similar. For a system of equations over $\mathbf{Z}_2$ with three variables per equation $\mathbf{A}$, let $\mathbf{T}(\mathbf{A})$ be its translation to a 3-CNF formula. It is not hard to see that if $\mathbf{A}$ has a refutation by OBDDs in $\mathrm{CSP}(\mathbf{S})$ of length m, then $\mathbf{T}(\mathbf{A})$ has a refutation by OBDDs in $\mathrm{CSP}(\mathbf{T})$ of length $O(m)$. The idea is that the join of the OBDDs for the clauses defining an equation $x + y + z = a$ is precisely an OBDD representing the equation $x + y + z = a$. Therefore, one refutation reduces to the other.

The particular system of equations known as *Tseitin contradictions* [Tse68] is exponentially hard for resolution. This was shown by Urquhart [Urq87] and was later extended by Ben-Sasson [BS02] who showed the same result for every Frege system (Hilbert-style system) restricted to formulas of bounded alternation-depth. This establishes that refutations by OBDDs are exponentially stronger than resolution. For bounded alternation-depth Frege systems, it shows that in some cases refutations by OBDDs might be exponentially stronger. In the next section we see that refutations by OBDDs and bounded alternation-depth Frege systems are incomparable.

Cutting planes. We now show that, in the presence of weakening, refutations by OBDDs polynomially simulate the cutting planes proof system with small coefficients. It is well-known that clauses can be expressed as linear inequalities over the integers. For example the clause $x \vee \neg y \vee z$ can be expressed by $x + (1 - y) + z \geq 1$, or equivalently, $x - y + z \geq 0$. Therefore, a CNF formula translates into a system of inequalities over the integers in a natural way. The cutting planes proof system was introduced in [CCT87]. The lines in the proof are linear inequalities over the integers. There are three rules of inference: addition, scalar multiplication, and integer division. The only rule the requires explanation is the integer division. From $\sum_i (c \cdot a_i) x_i \geq a_0$ derive $\sum_i a_i x_i \geq \lceil a_0/c \rceil$. Intuitively, if all coefficients except the independent term are divisible by c, then we may divide all over, and round-up the independent term. The rule is sound on the integers, meaning that if the x_i's take integer values that satisfy the hypothesis, then the conclusion is also satisfied. The goal of the system is to derive a contradiction $0 \geq 1$ from a given set of linear inequalities. For refuting 3-CNF formulas, each clause is viewed as a linear inequality as described before.

In order to measure the size of a proof we need to specify an encoding for the inequalities. When the coefficients are encoded in unary, the system has been named CP^* and studied in [BPR97]. We see that refutations by OBDDs can polynomially simulate CP^*. As it turns out, the rule of weakening is strongly used here. Whether weakening is strictly necessary remains as an intriguing open problem.

Theorem 8. *Let* **A** *be a 3-CNF. If* **A** *has a CP^* refutation of length m and size s, then* **A** *has a refutation by OBDDs of length $2m$ and size $s^{O(1)}$, for every order of the variables. Moreover, there is a polynomial-time algorithm that converts the CP^* refutation into the refutation by OBDDs.*

One consequence of this is that the *pigeonhole principle*, when encoded propositionally as an unsatisfiable 3-CNF formula, admits polynomial-size OBDD refutations. This follows from the known polynomial-size proofs of the pigeonhole principle in cutting planes [CCT87]. In contrast, the pigeonhole principle requires exponential-size refutations in resolution [Hak85]. It would be good to find a direct construction of the polynomial-size OBDD proof of the pigeonhole principle.

Interpolation. Craig's Interpolation Theorem in the propositional setting is this. Let $A(\mathbf{x}, \mathbf{y})$ and $B(\mathbf{y}, \mathbf{z})$ be propositional formulas for which $\mathbf{x}$, $\mathbf{y}$ and $\mathbf{z}$ are pairwise disjoint. If $A(\mathbf{x}, \mathbf{y}) \wedge B(\mathbf{y}, \mathbf{z})$ is unsatisfiable, then there exists a formula $C(\mathbf{y})$ such that $A(\mathbf{x}, \mathbf{y}) \wedge \neg C(\mathbf{y})$ and $C(\mathbf{y}) \wedge B(\mathbf{y}, \mathbf{z})$ are both unsatisfiable. The promised $C(\mathbf{y})$ is called an *interpolant*.

Interpolation has been used in propositional proof complexity as a method for lower bounds. Following earlier working starting in [IPU94,BPR97], Krajíček [Kra97] suggested the following approach. Suppose we are given a refutation of $A(\mathbf{x}, \mathbf{y}) \wedge B(\mathbf{y}, \mathbf{z})$.

Suppose, further, that we are able to extract an interpolant $C(\mathbf{y})$ by manipulation from the proof. Then, lower bounds for the complexity of the interpolants give lower bounds for the refutations. This idea has been used successfully for a number of proof systems including resolution and cutting planes (see [IPU94,BPR97,Kra97,Pud97]). The feasible interpolation of resolution has been recently used by McMillan [McM03] as an effective abstraction technique in symbolic model checking.

Our aim is to discuss the fact that refutations by OBDDs have feasible interpolation for certain orders of the variables. Following the machinery developed in [IPU94], it is enough to observe that evaluating an OBDD requires small communication complexity for nice orders. We omit further details in this version and state the final result without proof. The *narrowness* of an OBDD is the maximum number of nodes in a level.

Theorem 9. *Let* $\mathbf{F} = A(\mathbf{x},\mathbf{y}) \wedge B(\mathbf{y},\mathbf{z})$ *be an unsatisfiable 3-CNF formula, and let* $n = |\mathbf{y}|$. *If* $\mathbf{F}$ *has an OBDD refutation of length* m *with OBDDs of narrowness bounded by* c, *and with an order that is consistent with* $\mathbf{x} < \mathbf{y} < \mathbf{z}$, *then* $\mathbf{F}$ *has an interpolant circuit of size* $O(c^2(m+n))$. *In particular, if the size of the refutation is* s, *then the size of the interpolant is* $s^{O(1)}$. *In addition, if* $A(\mathbf{x},\mathbf{y})$ *is monotone in* $\mathbf{y}$, *then the interpolant circuit is monotone.*

Let us mention that the monotone feasible interpolation of refutations by OBDDs establishes a separation from Frege systems with formulas of bounded alternation-depth. It is known that monotone interpolants for such systems require exponential-size [Kra97]. This, together with the results of previous sections, establishes that refutations by OBDDs are incomparable in strength with Frege systems of bounded alternation-depth.

6 Concluding Remarks

Viewing constraint propagation as a proof system lifts proof complexity from propositional logic to all constraint-satisfaction problems. There are many questions that remain open from our work.

First, it is necessary to have better understanding of the role of the weakening rule. We know it is not needed to achieve completeness, not even in the case of restricted refutation width in Theorem 2. It remains an open problem to determine whether refutation by OBDDs without weakening can polynomially simulate CP^* refutations. Clarifying the role of weakening is also important for algorithmic applications. Second, the proof complexity of refutations by OBDDs needs further development. One problem that is left open is to find a non-trivial lower bound for the size of refutations by OBDDs that holds for every order of the variables. Another problem that is left open is whether OBDD-based refutations polynomially simulate cutting planes with coefficients written in binary. Are OBDD-based refutations automatizable in the sense of [BPR00]? Can we use the feasible interpolation of OBDD-based refutations in an effective manner analogous to that of McMillan [McM03]?

Finally, it would be good to find practical decision procedures based on CSP proofs, the same way that the DPLL approach is based on resolution. Some progress in this direction is reported in [DR94], which reports on SAT-solving using directional resolution, and in [PV04], which reports on SAT-solving using OBDD-based refutations. This could lead to CSP-solvers that deal directly with the CSP instances, avoiding the need to translate to a propositional formula and using a SAT-solver as it is sometimes done.

References

[AD03]   A. Atserias and V. Dalmau. A combinatorial characterization of resolution width. In *18th IEEE Conference on Computational Complexity*, pages 239–247, 2003.

[Ajt88]   M. Ajtai. The complexity of the pigeonhole principle. In *29th Annual IEEE Symposium on Foundations of Computer Science*, pages 346–355, 1988.

[AR02]   M. Alekhnovich and A. Razborov. Satisfiability, branch-width and Tseitin tautologies. In *43rd Annual IEEE Symposium on Foundations of Computer Science*, pages 593–603, 2002.

[BCM+92]   J.R. Burch, E.M. Clarke, K.L. McMillan, D.L. Dill, and L.J. Hwang. Symbolic model checking: 10^{20} states and beyond. *Information and Computation*, 98(2):142–170, 1992.

[BIK+92]   P. Beame, R. Impagliazzo, J. Krajíček, T. Pitassi, P. Pudlák, and A. Woods. Exponential lower bounds for the pigeonhole principle. In *24th Annual ACM Symposium on the Theory of Computing*, pages 200–220, 1992.

[Bod98]   H. L. Bodlaender. A partial k-arboretum of graphs with bounded treewidth. *Theoretical Computer Science*, 209:1–45, 1998.

[BPR97]   M. L. Bonet, T. Pitassi, and R. Raz. Lower bounds for cutting planes proofs with small coefficients. *Journal of Symbolic Logic*, 62(3):708–728, 1997.

[BPR00]   M. L. Bonet, T. Pitassi, and R. Raz. On interpolation and automatizm for Frege systems. *SIAM Journal of Computing*, 29(6):1939–1967, 2000.

[Bry92]   R. E. Bryant. Symbolic Boolean manipulation with ordered binary-decision diagrams. *ACM Computing Surveys*, 24(3):293–318, 1992.

[BS02]   E. Ben-Sasson. Hard examples for bounded depth frege. In *34th Annual ACM Symposium on the Theory of Computing*, pages 563–572, 2002.

[BSI99]   E. Ben-Sasson and R. Impagliazzo. Random CNF's are hard for the polynomial calculus. In *40th Annual IEEE Symposium on Foundations of Computer Science*, pages 415–421, 1999.

[BSW01]   E. Ben-Sasson and A. Wigderson. Short proofs are narrow–resolution made simple. *Journal of the ACM*, 48(2):149–169, 2001.

[CCT87]   W. Cook, C. R. Coullard, and G. Turán. On the complexity of cutting-plane proofs. *Discrete Applied Mathematics*, 18:25–38, 1987.

[Cou90]   B. Courcelle. Graph rewriting: An algebraic and logic approach. In J. van Leeuwen, editor, *Hankbook of Theoretical Computer Science*, volume 2, pages 194–242. Elsevier Science Publishers, 1990.

[CR79]   S. Cook and R. Reckhow. The relative efficiency of propositional proof systems. *Journal of Symbolic Logic*, 44:36–50, 1979.

[Dec92]   R. Dechter. From local to global consistency. *Artificial Intelligence*, 55(1):87–107, May 1992.

[Dec03]   R. Dechter. *Constraint Processing*. Morgan Kaufmman, 2003.

[DKV02]   V. Dalmau, Ph. G. Kolaitis, and M. Y. Vardi. Constraint satisfaction, bounded treewidth, and finite variable logics. In *8th International Conference on Principles and Practice of Constraint Programming (CP)*, volume 2470 of *Lecture Notes in Computer Science*, pages 310–326. Springer, 2002.

[DP87]   R. Dechter and J. Pearl. Network-based heuristics for constraint-satisfaction problems. *Artificial Intelligence*, 34:1–38, 1987.

[DR94]   R. Dechter and I. Rish. Directional Resolution: The Davis-Putnam Procedure, Revisited. In *4th International Conference on Principles of Knowledge Representation and Reasoning (KR)*, pages 134–145. Morgan Kaufmann, 1994.

[DvB97] R. Dechter and P. van Beek. Local and global relational consistency. *Theoretical Computer Science*, 173(1):283–308, 1997.

[Fre78] E. C. Freuder. Synthesizing constraint expressions. *Communications of the ACM*, 21(11):958–966, 1978.

[Fre82] E. C. Freuder. A sufficient condition for backtrack-free search. *Journal of the Association for Computing Machinery*, 29(1):24–32, 1982.

[Fre90] E. C. Freuder. Complexity of k-tree structured constraint satisfaction problems. In *Proc. AAAI-90*, pages 4–9, 1990.

[FV98]   T. Feder and M. Y. Vardi. The computational structure of monotone monadic SNP and constraint satisfaction: A study through Datalog and group theory. *SIAM Journal of Computing*, 28(1):57–104, 1998.

[GJC94] M. Gyssens, P.G. Jeavons, and D.A. Cohen. Decomposition constraint satisfaction problems using database techniques. *Artificial Intelligence*, 66:57–89, 1994.

[Hak85] A. Haken. The intractability of resolution. *Theoretical Computer Science*, 39:297–308, 1985.

[HN92]   P. Hell and J. Nešetřil. The core of a graph. *Discrete Mathematics*, 109:117–126, 1992.

[IPU94] R. Impagliazzo, T. Pitassi, and A. Urquhart. Upper and lower bounds for tree-like cutting planes proofs. In *9th IEEE Symposium on Logic in Computer Science*, pages 220–228, 1994.

[KP03]   Ph. G. Kolaitis and J. Panttaja. On the complexity of existential pebble games. In *Computer Science Logic '2003, 17th Annual Conference of the EACSL*, volume 2803 of *Lecture Notes in Computer Science*, pages 314–329. Springer, 2003.

[Kra97] J. Krajíček. Interpolation theorems, lower bounds for proof systems, and independence results for bounded arithmetic. *Journal of Symbolic Logic*, 62:457–486, 1997.

[KV95]   Ph. G. Kolaitis and M. Y. Vardi. On the expressive power of Datalog: tools and a case study. *Journal of Computer and System Sciences*, 51:110–134, 1995.

[KV00a] Ph. G. Kolaitis and M. Y. Vardi. Conjunctive-query containment and constraint satisfaction. *Journal of Computer and System Sciences*, 61(2):302–332, 2000.

[KV00b] Ph. G. Kolaitis and M. Y. Vardi. A game-theoretic approach to constraint satisfaction. In *17th National Conference on Artificial Intelligence*, pages 175–181, 2000.

[McM03] K. L. McMillan. Interpolation and SAT-based model checking. In Warren A. Hunt Jr. and Fabio Somenzi, editors, *Proceedings of the 15th International Conference on Computer Aided Verification (CAV)*, volume 2725 of *Lecture Notes in Computer Science*, pages 1–13. Springer, 2003.

[Pud97] P. Pudlák. Lower bounds for resolution and cutting plane proofs and monotone computations. *Journal of Symbolic Logic*, 62(3):981–998, 1997.

[PV04]   G. Pan and M. Y. Vardi. Search vs. symbolic techniques in satisfiability solving. To appear in Proceedings 7th International Conference on Theory and Applications of Satisfiability Testing, 2004.

[Tse68] G. S. Tseitin. *On the complexity of derivation in propositional calculus*, pages 115–125. Consultants Bureau, 1968.

[Urq87] A. Urquhart. Hard examples for resolution. *Journal of the ACM*, 34(1):209–219, 1987.

Backtrack-Free Search for Real-Time Constraint Satisfaction*

J. Christopher Beck, Tom Carchrae, Eugene C. Freuder, and Georg Ringwelski

Cork Constraint Computation Centre
University College Cork, Ireland
{c.beck,t.carchrae,e.freuder,g.ringwelski}@4c.ucc.ie

Abstract. A constraint satisfaction problem (CSP) model can be preprocessed to ensure that any choices made will lead to solutions, without the need to backtrack. This can be especially useful in a real-time process control or online interactive context. The conventional machinery for ensuring backtrack-free search, however, adds additional constraints, which may require an impractical amount of space. A new approach is presented here that achieves a backtrack-free representation by removing values. This may limit the choice of solutions, but we are guaranteed not to eliminate them all. We show that in an interactive context our proposal allows the system designer and the user to collaboratively establish the tradeoff in space complexity, solution loss, and backtracks.

1 Introduction

For some applications of constraint computation, backtracking is highly undesirable or even impossible. Online, interactive configuration requires a fast response given human impatience and unwillingness to undo previous decisions. Backtracking is likely to lead the user to abandon the interaction. In another context, an autonomous spacecraft must make and execute scheduling decisions in real time [10]. Once a decision is executed (e.g., the firing of a rocket) it cannot be undone through backtracking. It may not be practical in real time to explore the implications of each potential decision to ensure that the customer or the spacecraft is not allowed to make a choice that leads to a "dead end". A standard technique in such an application is to compile the constraint problem into some form that allows backtrack-free access to solutions [12]. Except in special cases, the worst-case size of the compiled representation is exponential in the size of the original problem. Therefore, the common view of the dilemma is as a tradeoff between storage space and backtracks: worst-case exponential space requirements can guarantee backtrack-free search while bounding space requirements (e.g., through adaptive consistency [3] techniques with a fixed maximum constraint arity) leave the risk of backtracking. For an application such as the autonomous spacecraft where memory is scarce and backtracking is impossible, the two-way tradeoff provides no solution.

With the above two examples in mind, in this paper, we assert that the two-way tradeoff is too simple to be applicable to all interesting applications. We propose that

---

* This work has received support from Science Foundation Ireland under Grant 00/PI.1/C075 and from the Embark Initiative of the Irish Research Council of Science Engineering and Technology under Grant PD2002/21.

there is a three-way tradeoff: storage space, backtracking, and solution retention. In the extreme, we propose a simple, radical approach to achieving backtrack-free search in a CSP: preprocess the problem to remove values that lead to dead-ends. Consider a coloring problem with variables $\{X, Y, Z\}$ and colors $\{red, blue\}$. Suppose Z must be different from both X and Y and our variable ordering is lexicographic. There is a danger that the assignments $X = red$, $Y = blue$ will be made, resulting in a domain wipeout for Z. A conventional way of fixing this would be to add a new constraint between X and Y specifying that the tuple in question is prohibited. Such a constraint requires additional space, and, in general, such adaptive consistency enforcement may have to add constraints involving as many as $n-1$ variables for an n-variable problem. Our basic insight here is simple, but counter-intuitive. We will "fix" the problem by removing the choice of red for X. One solution, $\{X = red, Y = red, Z = blue\}$, is also removed but another remains, $\{X = blue, Y = blue, Z = red\}$. If we also remove red as a value for Y we are left with a backtrack-free representation for the whole problem. (The representation also leaves us with a single set of values comprising a single solution. In general we will only restrict, not eliminate, choice.)

The core of our proposal is to preprocess a CSP to remove values that lead to a dead-end. This allows us to achieve a "backtrack-free" representation (BFR) where all *remaining* solutions can be enumerated without backtracking and where the space complexity is the same as for the original CSP. We are able to achieve backtrack-free search *and* polynomially bounded storage requirements. The major objection to such an approach is that the BFR will likely only represent a subset of solutions. There are two responses to this objection demonstrating the utility of treating backtracks, space, and solutions together. First, for applications where backtracking is impossible, an extension of the BFR approach provides a tradeoff between space complexity and solution retention. Through the definition of a k-BFR, systems designers can choose a point in this tradeoff. Value removal corresponds to 1-BFR, where space complexity is the same as for the original representation and many solutions may be lost. The value of k is the maximum arity constraint that we add during preprocessing: higher k leads to higher space complexity but fewer lost solutions. The memory capacity can therefore be directly traded off against solution loss. Second, for applications where backtracks are only undesirable, we can allow the user to make the decision about solution loss vs. backtracks by using two representations: the original problem and the BFR. The latter is used to guide value choices by representing the sub-domain for which it is guaranteed that a backtrack-free solution exists. The user can choose between a conservative value assignment that guarantees a backtrack-free solution or a risky approach that does not have such guarantees but allows access to all solutions.

Overall, the quality of a BFR depends on the number and quality of the solutions that are retained. After presenting the basic BFR algorithm and proving its correctness, we turn to these two measures of BFR quality through a series of empirical studies that examine extensions of the basic algorithm to include heuristics, consistency techniques, preferences on solutions, and the representation of multiple BFRs. Each of the empirical studies represents an initial investigation of different aspects of the BFR concept from the perspective of quality. We then present the k-BFR concept, revisit the issue of

Algorithm 1: BFRB - computes a BFR.

BFRB(n):
Obtains a BFR for P_n (maintained as a global variable)

1 **if** *domain of V_n is empty* **then**
2 ⌊ report Failure
3 **if** $n = 1$ **then**
4 ⌊ report Success
5 **foreach** *solution S to the parent subproblem that does not extend to V_n* **do**
6 ⌊ Choose a value v in S and remove it from the domain of its variable.
7 **recursively** seek a BFR for P_{n-1}:
8 If successful, report Success.
9 If not, make one different choice of a value to remove, and recurse again.
10 When there are no more different choices to make, report Failure.

solution loss, and show how our proposal provides a new perspective on a number of dichotomies in constraint computation.

The primary contributions of this paper are the proposal of a three-way tradeoff between space complexity, backtracks, and solution retention, the somewhat counter-intuitive idea of creating backtrack-free representations by value removal, the empirical investigation of a number of variations of this basic idea, and the placing of the idea in the context of a number of important threads of constraint research.

1.1 Related Work

Early work on CSPs guaranteed backtrack-free search for tree-structured problems [4]. This was extended to general CSPs through k-trees [5] and adaptive consistency [3]. These methods have exponential worst-case complexity, but, for preprocessing, time is not a critical factor as we assume we have significant time offline. However, these methods also have exponential worst-case space complexity, which may indeed make them impractical.

Efforts have been made in the past to precompile all solutions in a compact form [1, 8, 9, 11, 12]. These approaches achieved backtrack-free search at the cost of worst-case exponential storage space. While a number of interesting techniques to reduce average space complexity (e.g., meta-CSPs and interchangeability [12]) have been investigated, they do not address the central issue of worst case exponential space complexity. Indeed, as far as we have been able to determine, the need to represent all solutions has not been questioned in existing work. Furthermore, recasting the problem as a three-way tradeoff between space complexity, backtracks, and solution retention appears novel.

2 Algorithm, Alternatives, and Analysis

We describe a basic algorithm for obtaining a BFR by deleting values, prove it correct and examine its complexity. Given a problem P and a variable search order V_1 to V_n, we will refer to the subproblem induced by first k variables as P_k. A variable V_i is a parent of V_k if it shares a constraint and $i < k$. We call the subproblem induced by the parents of V_k the *parent subproblem* of V_k. P_n will be a backtrack-free representation if we can choose values for V_1 to V_n without backtracking. BFRB operates on a problem and produces a backtrack-free representation of the problem, if it is solvable, else reports failure. We will refer to the algorithm's removal of solutions to the parent subproblem of V_k that do not extend to V_k as *processing* of V_k.

The BFRB algorithm is quite straightforward. It works its way upwards through a variable ordering, ensuring that no trouble will be encountered in a search on the way back down, as does adaptive consistency; but here difficulties are avoided by removing values rather than adding (or refining) constraints. (Of course, removing a value can be viewed as adding/refining a unary constraint.)

However, correctness is not as obvious as it might first appear. It is clear that a BFR to a soluble problem must exist; any individual solution provides an existence proof: simply restrict each variable domain to the value in the solution. However, we might worry that BFRB might not notice if the problem is insoluble, or in removing values it might in fact remove all solutions, without noticing it.

Theorem 1 *If P is soluble, BFRB will find a backtrack-free representation.*

Proof: Proof by induction.

Inductive step: If we have a solution s to P_{k-1} we can extend it to a solution to P_k without backtracking. Solution s restricted to the parents of V_k is a solution to the parent subproblem of V_k. There is a value, b, for V_k consistent with this solution, or else this solution would have been eliminated by BFRB. Adding b to s gives us a solution to P_k, since we only need worry about the consistency of b with the parents of V_k.

Base step: P_1 is soluble, i.e. the domain of V_1 is not empty after BFRB. Since P is soluble, let s be one solution, with s_1 as the value for V_1. We will show that if it does not succeed otherwise, BFRB will succeed by providing a representation that includes s_1 in the domain of V_1. We will do this by demonstrating, again by induction, that in removing a solution to a subproblem, s_p, BFRB will always have a choice that does not involve a value of s. Suppose BFRB has proceeded up to V_k without deleting any value in s. It is processing V_k and a solution s_p to the parent subproblem does not extend to V_k. If all the values in s_p are in s, then there is a value in V_k that is consistent with them, namely the value for V_k in s. So one of the values in s_p must not be in s, and BFRB can choose at some point to remove it. (The base step for V_n is trivial.) Now since BFRB tries, if necessary, all choices for removing values, BFRB will choose eventually, if necessary, not to remove any value in s, including s_1. □

Theorem 2 *If P is insoluble, BFRB will report failure.*

Proof: Proof by induction.

$P_n = P$ is given insoluble. We will show that if P_k is insoluble, then after BFRB processes V_k, P_{k-1} is insoluble. Thus eventually BFRB will always backtrack when P_1 becomes insoluble (the domain of V_1 is empty) if not before, and BFRB will eventually run out of choices to try, and report failure.

Suppose P_k is insoluble. We will show that P_{k-1} is insoluble in a proof by contradiction. Suppose s is a solution of P_{k-1}. Then s restricted to the parents of V_k, s_p, is a solution of the parent subproblem of V_k, which is a subproblem of P_{k-1}. There is a value b of V_k consistent with s_p, for otherwise s_p would have been eliminated during processing of V_k. But if b is consistent with s_p, s plus b is a solution to V_k. Contradiction. □

The space complexity of BFRB is polynomial in the number of variables and values, as we are only required to represent the domains of each variable. The worst-case time complexity is, of course, exponential in the number of variables, n. However, as we will see in the next section, by employing a "seed solution", we can recurse without fear of failure, in which case the complexity can easily be seen to be exponential in $(p+1)$, where p is the size of the largest parent subproblem. Of course, $p+1$ may still equal n in the worst case; but when this is not so, we have a tighter bound on the complexity.

3 Extensions and Empirical Analysis

Preliminary empirical analysis showed that the basic BFRB algorithm is ineffective in finding BFRs even for small problems. We therefore created a set of basic extensions that significantly improved the algorithm performance. We then performed further experiments, building on these basic extensions. In this section, we present and empirically analyze these extensions.

3.1 Basic Extensions

A significant part of the running time of BFRB was due to the fallibility of the value pruning decision at line 6. While BFRB is guaranteed to eventually find a BFR for a soluble problem, doing so may require "backtracking" to previous pruning decisions because all solutions had been removed. To remove this thrashing, our first extension to BFRB is to develop a BFR around a "seed" solution. Secondly, no consistency enforcement is present in BFRB. It seems highly likely that such enforcement will reduce the search and increase the quality of the BFRs.

Seed Solutions. In searching for a BFR, we can avoid the need to undo pruning decisions by guaranteeing that at least one solution will not be removed. We do this by first solving the standard CSP (i.e., finding one solution) and then using this solution as a seed during the preprocessing to find a BFR. We modify the BFRB pruning (line 6) to specify that it cannot remove any values in the seed solution. This is sufficient to guarantee that there will never be a need to undo pruning decisions. There is a computational cost to obtaining the seed, and preserving it reduces the flexibility we have in choosing which values to remove; but we avoid thrashing when finding a BFR and thus improve the efficiency of our algorithm. In addition, seed solutions provide a mechanism for guaranteeing that a solution preferred by the system designer is represented in the BFR.

Experiments indicated that not only is using a seed significantly faster, it also tends to produce BFRs which represent more solutions. Given the strength of these results, all subsequent experiments are performed using a seed.

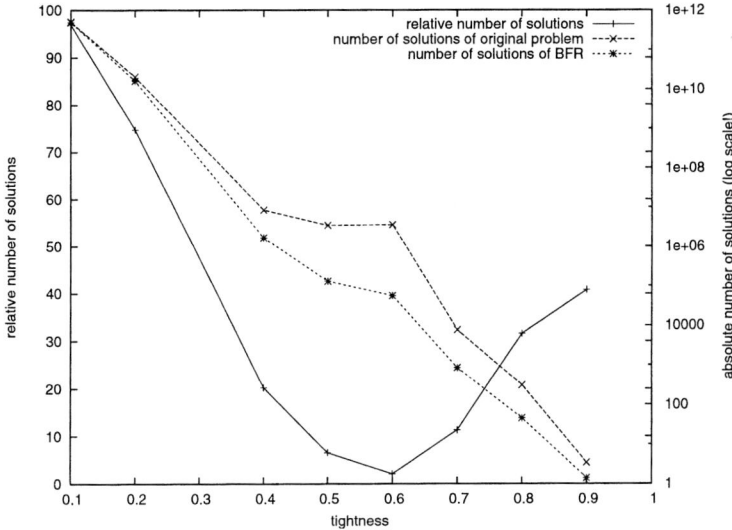

Fig. 1. Absolute and relative number of solutions retained.

Enforcing Consistency. Given the usefulness of consistency enforcement in standard CSP solving, we expect it will both reduce the effort in searching for a BFR and, since non-AC values may lead to dead-ends, reduce the pruning decisions that must be made. We experimented with two uses of arc consistency (AC): establishing AC once in a preprocessing step and establishing AC whenever a value is pruned. The latter variation proved to incur less computational effort as measured in the number of constraint checks to find a BFR and resulted in BFRs which represented more solutions. In our subsequent experiments, we, therefore, establish AC whenever a value is pruned.

Experiments: Solution Coverage. Our first empirical investigation is to assess the number of solutions that the BFR represents. To evaluate our algorithm instantiations, we generated random binary CSPs specified with 4-tuples (n, m, d, t), where n is the number of variables, m the size of their domains, d the density (i.e. the proportion of pairs of variables that have a constraint over them) and t the tightness (i.e. the proportion of inconsistent pairs in each constraint). We generated at least 50 problems for each tested CSP configuration where we could find a solution for at least 30 instances. In the following we refer to the mean of those 30 to 50 instances.

While the absolute number of represented solutions naturally decreases when the problems become harder, the relative number of solutions represented decreases first and then increases. The decreasing lines in Figure 1 represent the absolute number of solutions for the original problem and the BFR for $(15, 10, 0.1, t)$ problems. The numbers for $t \leq 0.4$ are estimated from the portion of solutions on the observed search space and the size of the non-observed search space. Experiment with fewer samples revealed similar patterns for smaller $(10, 5, 0.5, t)$ and larger $(50, 20, 0.07, t)$ problems.

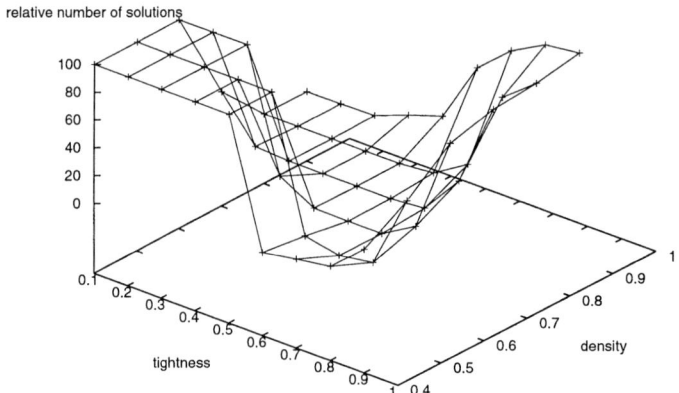

Fig. 2. Percentage of solutions retained by the BFR with differing density and tightness.

The increase in the relative number of solutions retained for very hard problems can be explained by the fact that a BFR always represents at least one solution and that the original problems have only very few solutions for these problem sets. For the very easy problems, there may not be much need to backtrack and thus to prune when creating the BFR. In the extreme case, the original problem is already backtrack-free. In a larger set of experiments we observed the decreasing/increasing behaviour for a range of density and tightness values. In Figure 2, we show the results of this experiment with $(15, 10, d, t)$ problems, where $d \in \{0.4, 1\}$ and $t \in \{0.1, 1\}$ both in steps of 0.1.

Experiments: Computational Effort. Now we consider the computational effort required when using BFRs. Our main interest is the offline computational effort to find a BFR. The online behaviour is also important, however, in a BFR all remaining solutions can be enumerated in linear time (in the number of solutions). As this is optimal, empirical analysis does not seem justified. Similarly, the (exponential) behaviour of finding solutions in a standard CSP is well-known. Figure 3 presents the CPU time for the problems considered in our experiments including the time to compute a seed solution. Times were found using C++ on a 1.8 GHz, 512 MB pentium 4 running Windows 2000.

It can be seen that the time to find BFRs scales well enough to produce them easily for the larger problems of our test set.

Experiments: Solution Quality. The second criteria for a BFR is that it retain good solutions assuming a preference function over solutions. To investigate this, we examine a set of lexicographic CSPs [7] where the solution preference can be expressed via a re-ordering of variables and values such that lexicographically smaller solutions are preferred.

To generate the BFR, a seed solution was found using lexicographic variable and value ordering heuristics that ensures that the first solution found is optimal. The best solution will thus be protected during the creation of the BFR and always be represented by it. For the evaluation of the BFR we used the set of its solutions or a subset of it that

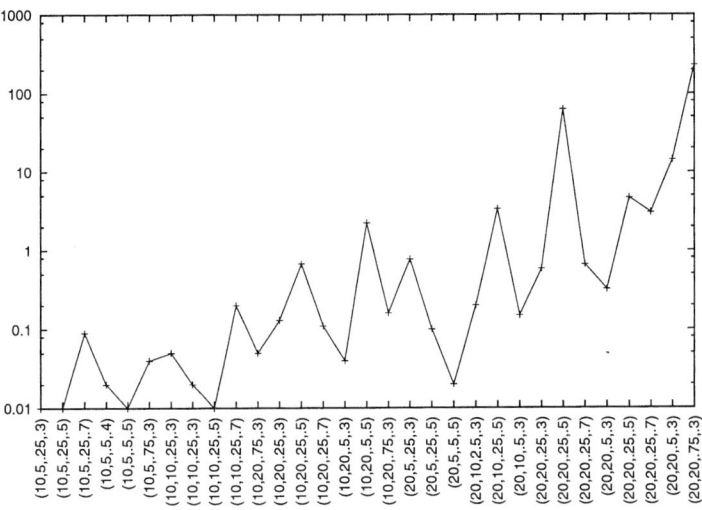

Fig. 3. Average runtime (seconds) to produce BFR.

could be found within a time limit. This set was evaluated with both quantitative and qualitative measure: the number of solutions and their lexicographic rank. In Figure 4 we present such an evaluation for $(10, 5, 0.25, 0.7)$ problems. The problem instances are shown on the x-axis while the solutions are presented on the y-axis with increasing quality. The solid line shows the total number of solutions of the original problem, which we used to sort the different problems to make the graph easier to read. Every 'x' represents a solution retained by the BFR for this problem instance. In the figure we can observe for example, that the instance 35 has 76 solutions and its BFR has a cluster of very high quality (based on the lexicographic preferences) and a smaller cluster of rather poor quality solutions.

3.2 Pruning Heuristics

With the importance of value ordering heuristics for standard CSPs, it seems reasonable that the selection of the value to be pruned in BFRB may benefit from heuristics. It is unclear, however, how the standard CSP heuristics will transfer to BFRB. We examined the following heuristics:

- Domain size: remove a value from the variable with minimum or maximum domain size.
- Degree: remove a value from the variable with maximum or minimum degree.
- Lexicographic: given the lexicographic preference on solutions, remove low values from important variables, in two different ways: (1) prune the value from the lowest variable whose value is greater than its position or (2) prune any value that is not among the best 10% in the most important 20% of all variables.
- Random: remove a value from a randomly chosen variable.

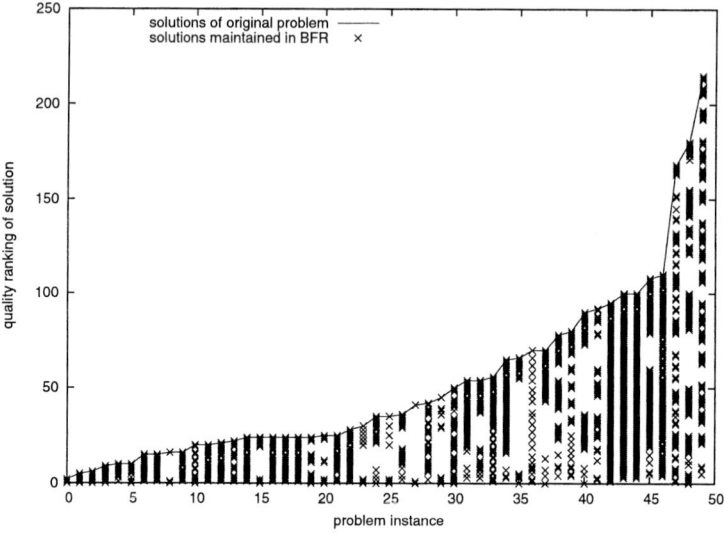

Fig. 4. Solutions maintained by a BFR generated with min-degree heuristic for $(10, 5, 0.25, 0.7)$ problems.

Since we are using a seed solution, if the heuristically preferred value occurs in the seed solution, the next most preferred value is pruned. We are guaranteed that at least one parent will have a value that is not part of the seed solution or else we would not have found a dead-end.

Experiments. BFRs were found with each of the seven pruning heuristics. Using a set of 1600 problems with varying tightness and density, we observed little difference among the heuristics: none performed significantly better than random on either number or quality of solutions retained. Apparently, our intuitions from standard CSP heuristics are not directly applicable to finding good BFRs. Further work is necessary to understand the behaviour of these heuristics and to determine if other heuristics can be applied to significantly improve the solution retention and quality of the BFRs.

3.3 Probing

Since we want BFRs to represent as many solutions as possible, it is useful to model the finding of BFRs as an optimization problem rather than as a satisfaction problem. There are a number of ways to search for a good BFR, for example, by performing a branch-and-bound to find the BFR with the maximal number of solutions. A simple technique investigated here is blind probing. Because we generate BFRs starting with a seed solution, we can iteratively generate seed solutions and corresponding BFRs and keep the BFR that retains the most solutions. This process is continued until no improving BFR is found in 1000 consecutive iterations. Probing is incomplete in the sense that it is not guaranteed to find the BFR with maximal coverage. However, not only does such a technique provide significantly better BFRs based on solution retention, it also provides a baseline against which to compare our satisfaction-based BFRs.

Experiments. Table 1 presents the number of solutions using random pruning with and without probing on seven different problem sets each with 50 problem instances. Probing is almost always able to find BFRs with higher solution coverage. On average, the probing based BFRs retain more that twice as many solutions as the BFRs produced without probing.

Table 1. Average number of solutions with and without probing.

Problem	No Probing	Probing
(10, 10, 0.75, 0.3)	41.36	274.90
(10, 20, 0.5, 0.3)	774.26	3524.22
(10, 5, 0.25, 0.3)	121463.08	134494.04
(10, 5, 0.25, 0.7)	27.84	31.14
(10, 5, 0.5, 0.3)	587.42	2204.08
(10, 5, 0.5, 0.5)	4.10	4.28
(10, 5, 0.75, 0.3)	8.35	25.04

3.4 Representing Multiple BFRs

Another way to improve the solution coverage of BFRs is to maintain more than one BFR. Given multiple BFRs for a single problem, we span more of the solution space and therefore retain more solutions. Multiple BFRs can be easily incorporated into the original CSP by adding an auxiliary variable (whose domain consists of identifier values representing each unique BFR) and n constraints. Each constraint restricts the domain of a variable to the backtrack-free values for each particular BFR identifier. Provided that we only represent a fixed number of BFRs, such a representation only adds a constant factor to the space complexity. Online, all variables are assigned in order except the new auxiliary variable and arc consistency allows the "BFR constraints" to remove values when they are no longer consistent with at least one BFR.

Experiments. To investigate the feasibility of multiple BFRs, we found 10, 50 and 100 differing BFRs for each $(15, 10, 0.7, t)$ problem. The result of applying this technique is shown in Figure 5 in the relation to the solutions of the original problem, the number of solutions of the best BFR that could be found using probing (Iter1000rand), and the number of solutions in a single BFR using random pruning (Random). Representing multiple BFRs clearly increases the solution coverage over the best single BFRs we were able to find with probing.

4 Discussion

In this section we discuss a number of additional issues arise in terms of extensions that we have not yet empirically investigated, the central issue that BFRs do not retain all solutions, the role of online consistency enforcement, and a broader perspective that the BFR concepts allows to a number of aspects of constraint research.

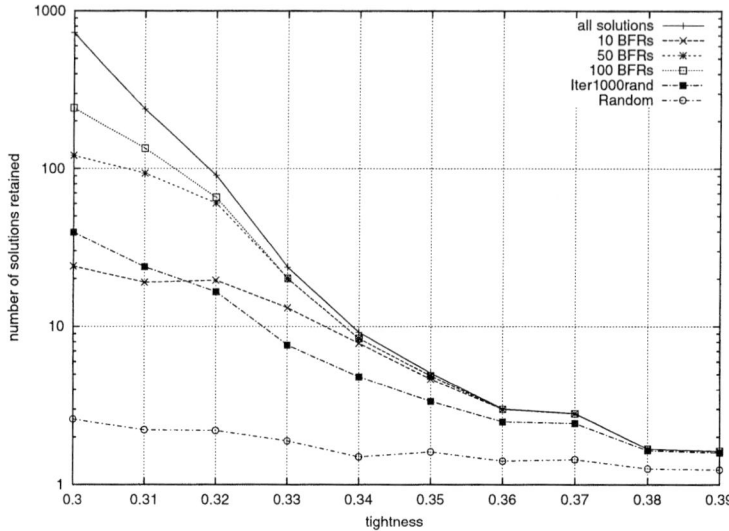

Fig. 5. Solutions represented by multiple BFRs and one BFR found with probing.

4.1 k-BFR and Restricted k-BFR

Instead of pruning values from variable domains, we could add new constraints restricting the allowed tuples. In fact, from this perspective BFRB implements 1-BFR: value removal corresponds to adding unary constraints. This is one end of a spectrum with the other end being adaptive consistency. Between, we can define a range of algorithms in which we can add constraints of arity up to k. For an n-variable problem, when k is 1 we have the a value-removal algorithm, when k is $n-1$ we have full adaptive consistency. As k increases the space complexity of our BFR increases but so does the solution retention.

A further variation (called *restricted k-BFR*) addresses the space increase. Rather than adding constraints, we only tighten existing constraints. For example, assume that partial assignment, $X_1 = v_1, ..., X_m = v_m$, does not extend to a solution and a constraint c over $X_1, ..., X_m$ exists. Restricted k-BFR will simply remove the tuple $(v_1, ..., v_m)$ from c. In general, constraint c will not exist and therefore the algorithm has to consider constraints over subsets of the variables $\{X_1, ..., X_m\}$. Given binary constraints between some pairs of the variables, we can remove the tuple (v_i, v_j) from any constraint where X_i and X_j are involved in the dead-end. A reasonable approach is to identify the highest arity constraint involved in a dead-end and remove a single tuple. This algorithm will always be applicable, since in the extreme no constraints among the parent variables exist and therefore pruning a "tuple" from a unary constraint is equivalent to BFRB. A drawback of restricted k-BFR is that it requires extensional constraint representations.

k-BFR and restricted k-BFR suggest a number of research questions. What is the increase in solution coverage and quality that can be achieved without extra space consumption? If we allow new constraints to be added, how do we choose an appropriate k value? How does a good k relate to the arity of the constraints in the original CSP? Given the spectrum that exists between 1-BFR and adaptive consistency, we believe that future empirical work on these and related questions can be of significant use in making adaptive consistency-like techniques more practically applicable.

4.2 Coming to Terms with Solution Loss

The central challenge to the BFR concept is that solutions are lost: perfectly good solutions to the original CSP are not represented in its BFR. A problem transformation that loses solutions is a radical, perhaps heretical, concept. To revisit one of our motivating examples, failing to represent solutions in an online configuration application means that some valid product configurations cannot be achieved. This appears to be a high price to pay to remove the need to undo previous decisions.

There are three characteristics of problem representations that are relevant here: space complexity, potential number of backtracks, and solution loss. Simultaneously achieving polynomial space complexity, a guarantee of backtrack-free search, and zero solution loss implies that $P = NP$. Therefore, we need to reason about the tradeoffs among these characteristics. Precisely how we make these tradeoffs depends on the application requirements. BFRs allow us to achieve tradeoffs that are appropriate for the application.

In the autonomous space vehicle application example, backtracking is impossible and memory is extremely limited. The tradeoff clearly lies on the side of allowing solution loss: any solution is better than spending too much time or memory in finding the best solution. Therefore, a small number of BFRs that represent a reasonable set of solutions is probably the best approach.

In the interactive configuration application example, space complexity is less of a problem and avoiding backtracks is important. Using BFRs, we can create a system that allows the system designer and user to collaboratively make the three-way tradeoff in two steps. First, the system designer can decide on the space complexity by choosing the arity, k, in a k-BFR approach. In the extreme, a single $n-1$-BFR achieves full adaptive consistency and so, if the memory space is available, a zero backtrack, zero solution loss BFR can be achieved. The system designer, therefore, makes the decision about the tradeoff between the number of solutions that can be found without backtracking and the space complexity. Furthermore, the use of seed solutions means that each BFR can be built around a solution preferred by the system designer: guaranteeing a minimal set of desirable solutions. Second, the BFRs together with the original CSP can be used online to allow the user to make the tradeoff between solution loss and backtracks. The BFRs create a partition of the domain of each variable: those values that are guaranteed to lead to a solution without backtracking and those for which no such guarantee is known. These partitions can be presented to the user by identifying the set of "safe" and "risky" options for a particular decision. If the user chooses to make safe decisions, the BFRs guarantee the existence of a solution. If the user decides to make a risky decision, the system can (transparently) transition to standard CSP techniques without solution guarantees. This allows the user to decide about the tradeoff between backtracks and solution loss: if the user has definite ideas about the desired configuration, more effort in terms of undoing previous decisions may be necessary. If the user prefers less effort and has weaker preferences, a solution existing in one of the BFRs can be found.

The basic BFR concept encompasses solution loss because it allows backtrack-free search with no space complexity penalty for those applications where zero backtracks and limited memory are hard constraints. When solution loss may be more important, the k-BFR concept together with online solving using both the BFR and the original representation allow the system designer and the user to collaboratively decide on the tradeoff among space complexity, backtrack-free search, and solution loss.

4.3 Online Consistency Enforcement

By changing our assumptions about the on-line processing, we can also expand the set of techniques applied in finding the BFR. As noted, we are enforcing arc-consistency during the creation of a BFR: whenever a value is pruned to remove a dead-end, we enforce arc-consistency. When solving a problem online, however, we do no propagation as we are guaranteed that the possible values are (globally) consistent with the previous assignments. If, instead, we use forward checking or MAC online, we can remove fewer dead-ends offline and retain more solutions in a BFR. In creating a BFR, we need to remove dead-ends that may be encountered by the online algorithm. If the online algorithm itself can to avoid some dead-ends (i.e., through use of propagation), they do not need to be dealt with in the BFR. This means, in fact, that a backtrack-free representation is backtrack-free with respect to the online algorithm: a BFR built for MAC will not be a BFR for simple backtracking (though the converse is true). BFRB can be easily modified to ensure that only those dead-ends that exist for a specific online algorithm will be pruned.

4.4 Context

The work on BFRs presents a perspective on a number of fundamental dichotomies in constraint processing.

Inference vs. Search. As in many aspects of constraint computation, the axis that runs from inference to search is relevant for BFRs. The basic BFR algorithm allows us to perform pure search online without fear of failure. BFRs for online algorithms that use some level of inference require more online computation while still ensuring no backtracks and preserving more solutions. It would be interesting to study the characteristics of BFRs as we increase the level of online consistency processing.

Implicit vs. Explicit Solutions. BFR models can be viewed along a spectrum of implicit versus explicit solution representation, where the original problem lies at one end, and the set of explicit solutions at the other. The work on "bundling" solutions provides compact representations of sets of solutions. Hubbe & Freuder [8] and Lesaint [9] represent sets of solutions as Cartesian products, each one of which might be regarded as an extreme form of backtrack-free representation. If we restrict the variable domains to one of these Cartesian products, every combination of choices is a solution. All the solutions can be represented as a union of these Cartesian products, which suggests that we might represent all solutions by a set of distinct BFRs. As we move toward explicit representation, the preprocessing cost rises. Usually the space cost does as well, but 1-BFR and restricted k-BFR are an exception that lets us "have our cake and eat it too".

Removing Values vs. Search. Removing values is related in spirit to work on domain filtering consistencies [2] though these do not lose solutions. Another spectrum in which BFRs play a part therefore is based on the number of values removed. We could envision BFRB variations that remove fewer values, allowing more solutions, but also accepting some backtracking. Freuder & Hubbe [6] remove solutions in another manner, though not for preprocessing, but simply in attempting to search more efficiently. Of course, a large body of work on symmetry and interchangeability does this.

Offline vs. Online Effort. BFRs lie at one end of an axis that increasingly incorporates offline preprocessing or precompilation to avoid online execution effort. These issues are especially relevant to interactive constraint satisfaction, where human choices alternate with computer inference, and the same problem representation may be accessed repeatedly by different users seeking different solutions. They may also prove increasingly relevant as decision making fragments among software agents and web services. Amilhastre et al. [1] have recently explored interactive constraint solving for configuration, compiling the CSP offline into an automaton representing the set of solutions.

"Customer-Centric" vs. "Vendor-Centric" Preferences. As constraints are increasingly applied to online applications, the preferences of the different participants in a transaction will come to the fore. It will be important to bring soft constraints, preferences and priorities, to bear on BFR construction to address the axis that lies between "customer-centric" and "vendor-centric" processing. For example, a customer may tell us, or we may learn from experience with the customer, that specific options are more important to retain. Alternatively, a vendor might prefer to retain an overstocked option, or to remove a less profitable one.

5 Conclusion

In this paper we identify, for the first time, the three-way tradeoff between space complexity, backtrack-free search, and solution loss. We presented an approach to obtaining a backtrack-free CSP representation that does not require additional space and investigated a number of variations on the basic algorithm including the use of seed solutions, arc-consistency, and a variety of pruning heuristics. We have evaluated experimentally the cost of obtaining a BFR and the solution loss for different problem parameters. Overall, our results indicate that a significant proportion of the solutions to the original problem can be retained especially when an optimization algorithm that specifically searches for such "good" BFRs is used. We have seen how multiple BFRs can cover more of the solution space. Furthermore, we have argued that BFRs are an approach that allows the system designer and the user to collaboratively control the tradeoff between the space complexity of the problem representation, the backtracks that might be necessary to find a solution, and the loss of solutions.

Our approach should prove valuable in real-time process control and online interactive problem solving where backtracking is either impossible or impractical. We observed further that the BFR concept provides an interesting perspective on a number of theoretical and practical dichotomies within the field of of constraint programming, suggesting directions for future research.

References

1. Jérôme Amilhastre, Hélène Fargier, and Pierre Marquis. Consistency restoration and explanations in dynamic csps – application to configuration. *Artificial Intelligence*, 135:199–234, 2002.
2. Romuald Debruyne and Christian Bessière. Domain filtering consistencies. *Journal of Artificial Intelligence Research*, (14):205–230, may 2001.
3. R. Dechter and J. Pearl. Network-based heuristics for constraint-satisfaction problems. *Artificial Intelligence*, 14:205–230, 1987.
4. E.C. Freuder. A sufficient condition for backtrack-free search. *Journal of ACM*, 29(1):24–32, 1982.
5. E.C. Freuder. Complexity of k-tree structured constraint-satisfaction problems. In *Proceedings of the Eigth National Conference on Artificial Intelligence (AAAI-90)*, pages 4–9, 1990.
6. E.C. Freuder and P.D. Hubbe. Using inferred disjunctive constraints to decompose constraint satisfaction problems. In *Proceedings of the Thirteenth International Joint Conference on Artificial Intelligence (IJCAI-93)*, pages 254–261, 1993.
7. Eugene C. Freuder, Richard J. Wallace, and Robert Heffernan. Ordinal constraint satisfaction. In *5th International Workshop on Soft Constraints-Soft 2003*, 2003.
8. P.D. Hubbe and E.C. Freuder. An efficient cross-product representation of the constraint satisfaction problem search space. In *Proceedings of the Tenth National Conference on Artificial Intelligence (AAAI-92)*, pages 421–427, 1992.
9. D. Lesaint. Maximal sets of solutions for constraint satisfaction problems. In *Proceedings of the Eleventh European Conference on Artificial Intelligence*, pages 110–114, 1994.
10. Nicola Muscettola, Paul Morris, and Ioannis Tsamardinos. Reformulating temporal plans for efficient execution. In *Principles of Knowledge Representation and Reasoning*, pages 444–452, 1998.
11. N. R. Vempaty. Solving constraint satisfaction problems using finite satate automata. In *Proceedings of the Tenth National Conference on Artificial Intelligence (AAAI-92)*, pages 453–457, 1992.
12. Rainer Weigel and Boi Faltings. Compiling constraint satisfaction problems. *Artificial Intelligence*, 115(2):257–287, 1999.

Deriving Filtering Algorithms from Constraint Checkers

Nicolas Beldiceanu[1], Mats Carlsson[2], and Thierry Petit[1]

[1] LINA FRE CNRS 2729, École des Mines de Nantes, FR-44307 Nantes Cedex 3, France
{Nicolas.Beldiceanu,Thierry.Petit}@emn.fr
[2] SICS, P.O. Box 1263, SE-164 29 Kista, Sweden
Mats.Carlsson@sics.se

Abstract. This article deals with global constraints for which the set of solutions can be recognized by an extended finite automaton whose size is bounded by a polynomial in n, where n is the number of variables of the corresponding global constraint. By reformulating the automaton as a conjunction of signature and transition constraints we show how to systematically obtain a filtering algorithm. Under some restrictions on the signature and transition constraints this filtering algorithm achieves arc-consistency. An implementation based on some constraints as well as on the metaprogramming facilities of SICStus Prolog is available. For a restricted class of automata we provide a filtering algorithm for the relaxed case, where the violation cost is the minimum number of variables to unassign in order to get back to a solution.

1 Introduction

Deriving filtering algorithms for global constraints is usually far from obvious and requires a lot of energy. As a first step toward a methodology for semi-automatic development of filtering algorithms for global constraints, Carlsson and Beldiceanu have introduced [12] an approach to design filtering algorithms by derivation from a finite automaton. As quoted in their discussion, constructing the automaton was far from obvious since it was mainly done as a rational reconstruction of an emerging understanding of the necessary case analysis related to the required pruning. However, it is commonly admitted that coming up with a checker which tests whether a ground instance is a solution or not is usually straightforward. This was for instance done for constraints defined in extension first by Vempaty [29] and later on by Amilhastre et al. [1]. This was also done for arithmetic constraints by Boigelot and Wolper [10]. Within the context of global constraints on a finite sequence of variables, the recent work of Pesant [25] uses also a finite automaton for constructing a filtering algorithm. This article focuses on those global constraints that can be checked by scanning once through their variables without using any extra data structure.

As a second step toward a methodology for semi-automatic development of filtering algorithms, we introduce a new approach which only requires defining a finite automaton that checks a ground instance. We extend traditional finite automata in order not to be limited only to regular expressions. Our first contribution is to show how to reformulate the automaton associated with a global constraint as a conjunction of signature and transition constraints. We characterize some restrictions on the signature and transition constraints under which the filtering algorithm induced by this reformulation achieves arc-consistency and apply this new methodology to the two following problems: 1. The design of filtering algorithms for a fairly large set of global constraints. 2. The design of filtering algorithms for handling the conjunction of several global constraints. While the works of Amilhastre et al. and Pesant both rely on simple automata and use an ad-hoc filtering algorithm, our approach is based on automata with counters and reformulation. As a consequence we can model a larger class of global constraints and prove properties on the consistency by reasoning directly on the constraint hypergraph.

Our second contribution is to provide for a restricted class of automata a filtering algorithm for the relaxed case. This technique relies on the variable based violation cost introduced in [26, 23]. This cost was advocated as a generic way for expressing the violation of a global constraint. However, algorithms were only provided for the soft_alldifferent constraint [26]. We come up with an algorithm for computing a sharp bound of the minimum violation cost and with a filtering algorithm for pruning in order to avoid to exceed a given maximum violation cost.

Section 2 describes the kind of finite automaton used for recognizing the set of solutions associated with a global constraint. Section 3 shows how to come up with a filtering algorithm which exploits the previously introduced automaton. Section 4 describes typical applications of this technique. Finally, for a restricted class of automata, Section 5 provides a filtering algorithm for the relaxed case.

2 Description of the Automaton Used for Checking Ground Instances

We first discuss the main issues behind the task of selecting what kind of automaton to consider for expressing in a concise way the set of solutions associated with a global constraint. We consider global constraints for which any ground instance can be checked in linear time by scanning once through their variables without using any data structure. In order to concretely illustrate this point we first select a set of global constraints and write down a checker for each of them. Finally, we give for each checker a sketch of the corresponding automaton. Based on these observations, we define the type of automaton we will use.

Selecting an Appropriate Description. As we previously said, we focus on those global constraints that can be checked by scanning once through their variables. This is for instance the case of element [19], minimum [3], pattern [11], global_contiguity [22], lexicographic ordering [17], among [6] and inflection [2]. Since they illustrate key points needed for characterizing the set of solutions associated with a global constraint, our discussion will be based on the last four constraints for which we now recall the definition:

- The global_contiguity($vars$) constraint enforces for the sequence of 0-1 variables $vars$ to have at most one group of consecutive 1. For instance, the constraint global_contiguity($[0, 1, 1, 0]$) holds since we have only one group of consecutive 1.

- The lexicographic ordering constraint $\overrightarrow{x} \leq_{lex} \overrightarrow{y}$ over two vectors of variables $\overrightarrow{x} = \langle x_0, \ldots, x_{n-1} \rangle$ and $\overrightarrow{y} = \langle y_0, \ldots, y_{n-1} \rangle$ holds iff $n = 0$ or $x_0 < y_0$ or $x_0 = y_0$ and $\langle x_1, \ldots, x_{n-1} \rangle \leq_{lex} \langle y_1, \ldots, y_{n-1} \rangle$.
- The among(*nvar, vars, values*) constraint restricts the number of variables of the sequence of variables *vars*, which take their value in a given set *values*, to be equal to the variable *nvar*. For instance, among$(3, [4, 5, 5, 4, 1], [1, 5, 8])$ holds since exactly 3 values of the sequence 45541 are located in $\{1, 5, 8\}$.
- The inflection(*ninf, vars*) constraint enforces the number of inflections of the sequence of variables *vars* to be equal to the variable *ninf*. An inflection is described by one of the following patterns: a strict increase followed by a strict decrease or, conversely, a strict decrease followed by a strict increase. For instance, inflection$(4, [3, 3, 1, 4, 5, 5, 6, 5, 5, 6, 3])$ holds since we can extract from the sequence 33145565563 the four subsequences 314, 565, 6556 and 563, which all follow one of these two patterns.

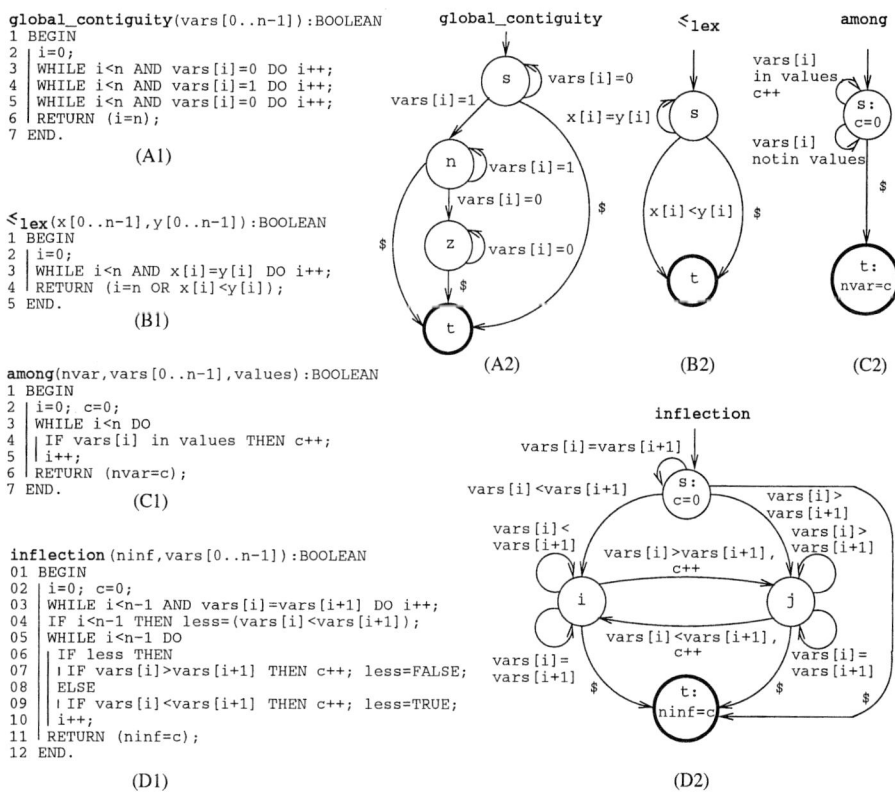

Fig. 1. Four checkers and their corresponding automata.

Parts (A1), (B1), (C1) and (D1) of Fig. 1 depict the four checkers respectively associated with global_contiguity, with $\leq_{lex}$, with among and with inflection. For each checker we observe the following facts:

- Within the checker depicted by part (A1) of Fig. 1, the values of the sequence $vars[0], \ldots, vars[n-1]$ are successively compared against 0 and 1 in order to check that we have at most one group of consecutive 1. This can be translated to the automaton depicted by part (A2) of Fig. 1. The automaton takes as input the sequence $vars[0], \ldots, vars[n-1]$, and triggers successively a transition for each term of this sequence. Transitions labeled by 0, 1 and $ are respectively associated with the conditions $vars[i] = 0$, $vars[i] = 1$ and $i = n$. Transitions leading to failure are systematically skipped. This is why no transition labeled with a 1 starts from state z.

- Within the checker given by part (B1) of Fig. 1, the components of vectors $\vec{x}$ and $\vec{y}$ are scanned in parallel. We first skip all the components that are equal and then perform a final check. This is represented by the automaton depicted by part (B2) of Fig. 1. The automaton takes as input the sequence $\langle x[0], y[0] \rangle, \ldots, \langle x[n-1], y[n-1] \rangle$ and triggers a transition for each term of this sequence. Unlike the global_contiguity constraint, some transitions now correspond to a condition (e.g. $x[i] = y[i]$, $x[i] < y[i]$) between two variables of the $\leq_{\text{lex}}$ constraint.

- Observe that the among($nvar, vars, values$) constraint involves a variable $nvar$ whose value is computed from a given collection of variables $vars$. The checker depicted by part (C1) of Fig. 1 counts the number of variables of $vars[0], \ldots, vars[n-1]$ that take their value in $values$. For this purpose it uses a counter c, which is eventually tested against the value of $nvar$. This convinced us to allow the use of counters in an automaton. Each counter has an initial value which can be updated while triggering certain transitions. The final state of an automaton can enforce a variable of the constraint to be equal to a given counter. Part (C2) of Fig. 1 describes the automaton corresponding to the code given in part (C1) of the same figure. The automaton uses the counter c initially set to 0 and takes as input the sequence $vars[0], \ldots, vars[n-1]$. It triggers a transition for each variable of this sequence and increments c when the corresponding variable takes its value in $values$. The final state returns a success when the value of c is equal to $nvar$. At this point we want to stress the following fact: It would have been possible to use an automaton which avoids the use of counters. However, this automaton would depend on the effective value of the parameter $nvar$. In addition, it would require more states than the automaton of part (C2) of Fig. 1. This is typically a problem if we want to have a fixed number of states in order to save memory as well as time.

- As the among constraint, the inflection($ninf, vars$) constraint involves a variable $ninf$ whose value is computed from a given sequence of variables $vars[0], \ldots, vars[n-1]$. Therefore, the checker depicted in part (D1) of Fig. 1 uses also a counter c for counting the number of inflections, and compares its final value to the $ninf$ parameter. This program is represented by the automaton depicted by part (D2) of Fig. 1. It takes as input the sequence of pairs $\langle vars[0], vars[1] \rangle$, $\langle vars[1], vars[2] \rangle, \ldots, \langle vars[n-2], vars[n-1] \rangle$ and triggers a transition for each pair. Observe that a given variable may occur in more than one pair. Each transition compares the respective values of two consecutive variables of $vars[0..n-1]$ and increments the counter c when a new inflection is detected. The final state returns a success when the value of c is equal to $ninf$.

Synthesizing all the observations we got from these examples leads to the following remarks and definitions for a given global constraint $\mathcal{C}$:

- For a given state, no transition can be triggered indicates that the constraint $\mathcal{C}$ does not hold.
- Since all transitions starting from a given state are mutually incompatible all automata are deterministic. Let $\mathcal{M}$ denote the set of mutually incompatible conditions associated with the different transitions of an automaton.
- Let $\Delta_0, \ldots, \Delta_{m-1}$ denote the sequence of subsets of variables of $\mathcal{C}$ on which the transitions are successively triggered. All these subsets contain the same number of elements and refer to some variables of $\mathcal{C}$. Since these subsets typically depend on the constraint, we leave the computation of $\Delta_0, \ldots, \Delta_{m-1}$ outside the automaton. To each subset Δ_i of this sequence corresponds a variable S_i with an initial domain ranging over $[min, min + |\mathcal{M}| - 1]$, where min is a fixed integer. To each integer of this range corresponds one of the mutually incompatible conditions of $\mathcal{M}$. The sequences $S_0, \ldots, S_{m-1}$ and $\Delta_0, \ldots, \Delta_{m-1}$ are respectively called the *signature* and the *signature argument* of the constraint. The constraint between S_i and the variables of Δ_i is called the *signature constraint* and is denoted by $\Psi_\mathcal{C}(S_i, \Delta_i)$.
- From a pragmatic point the view, the task of writing a constraint checker is naturally done by writing down an imperative program where local variables (i.e., counters), assignment statements and control structures are used. This suggested us to consider deterministic finite automata augmented with counters and assignment statements on these counters. Regarding control structures, we did not introduce any extra feature since the deterministic choice of which transition to trigger next seemed to be good enough.
- Many global constraints involve a variable whose value is computed from a given collection of variables. This convinced us to allow the final state of an automaton to optionally return a result. In practice, this result corresponds to the value of a counter of the automaton in the final state.

Defining an Automaton. An automaton $\mathcal{A}$ of a constraint $\mathcal{C}$ is defined by a sextuple

$$\langle Signature, SignatureDomain, SignatureArg, Counters, States, Transitions \rangle$$

where:

- $Signature$ is the sequence of variables $S_0, \ldots, S_{m-1}$ corresponding to the signature of the constraint $\mathcal{C}$.
- $SignatureDomain$ is an interval which defines the range of possible values of the variables of $Signature$.
- $SignatureArg$ is the signature argument $\Delta_0, \ldots, \Delta_{m-1}$ of the constraint $\mathcal{C}$. The link between the variables of Δ_i and the variable S_i ($0 \leq i < m$) is done by writing down the signature constraint $\Psi_\mathcal{C}(S_i, \Delta_i)$ in such a way that arc-consistency is achieved. In our context this is done by using standard features of the CLP(FD) solver of SICStus Prolog [13] such as arithmetic constraints between two variables, propositional combinators or the global constraints programming interface.

- *Counters* is the, possibly empty, list of all counters used in the automaton $\mathcal{A}$. Each counter is described by a term t(*Counter*, *InitialValue*, *FinalVariable*) where *Counter* is a symbolic name representing the counter, *InitialValue* is an integer giving the value of the counter in the initial state of $\mathcal{A}$, and *FinalVariable* gives the variable that should be unified with the value of the counter in the final state of $\mathcal{A}$.
- *States* is the list of states of $\mathcal{A}$, where each state has the form source(id), sink(id) or node(id). id is a unique identifier associated with each state. Finally, source(id) and sink(id) respectively denote the initial and the final state of $\mathcal{A}$.
- *Transitions* is the list of transitions of $\mathcal{A}$. Each transition t has the form arc(id_1, *label*, id_2) or arc(id_1, *label*, id_2, *counters*). id_1 and id_2 respectively correspond to the state just before and just after t, while *label* depicts the value that the signature variable should have in order to trigger t. When used, *counters* gives for each counter of *Counters* its value after firing the corresponding transition. This value is specified by an arithmetic expression involving counters, constants, as well as usual arithmetic functions such as $+$, $-$, min or max. The order used in the *counters* list is identical to the order used in *Counters*.

Example 1. As an illustrative example we give the description of the automaton associated with the inflection($ninf$, $vars$) constraint. We have:

- *Signature* $= S_0, S_1, \ldots, S_{n-2}$,
- *SignatureDomain* $= 0..2$,
- *SignatureArg* $= \langle vars[0], vars[1]\rangle, \ldots, \langle vars[n-2], vars[n-1]\rangle$,
- *Counters* $=$ t($c, 0, ninf$),
- *States* $= [\text{source}(s), \text{node}(i), \text{node}(j), \text{sink}(t)]$,
- *Transitions* $= [\text{arc}(s, 1, s), \text{arc}(s, 2, i), \text{arc}(s, 0, j), \text{arc}(s, \$, t), \text{arc}(i, 1, i), \text{arc}(i, 2, i),$ $\text{arc}(i, 0, j, [c+1]), \text{arc}(i, \$, t), \text{arc}(j, 1, j), \text{arc}(j, 0, j), \text{arc}(j, 2, i, [c+1]), \text{arc}(j, \$, t)]$.

The signature constraint relating each pair of variables $\langle vars[i], vars[i+1]\rangle$ to the signature variable S_i is defined as follows: $\Psi_{\text{inflection}}(S_i, vars[i], vars[i+1]) \equiv vars[i] > vars[i+1] \Leftrightarrow S_i = 0 \land vars[i] = vars[i+1] \Leftrightarrow S_i = 1 \land vars[i] < vars[i+1] \Leftrightarrow S_i = 2$. The sequence of transitions triggered on the ground instance inflection(4, [3, 3, 1, 4, 5, 5, 6, 5, 5, 6, 3]) is $\xrightarrow[c=0]{s}$ s $\xrightarrow{3=3 \Leftrightarrow S_0=1}$ s $\xrightarrow{3>1 \Leftrightarrow S_1=0}$ j $\xrightarrow[c=1]{1<4 \Leftrightarrow S_2=2}$ i $\xrightarrow{4<5 \Leftrightarrow S_3=2}$ i $\xrightarrow{5=5 \Leftrightarrow S_4=1}$ i $\xrightarrow{5<6 \Leftrightarrow S_5=2}$ i $\xrightarrow[c=2]{6>5 \Leftrightarrow S_6=0}$ j $\xrightarrow{5=5 \Leftrightarrow S_7=1}$ j $\xrightarrow[c=3]{5<6 \Leftrightarrow S_8=2}$ i $\xrightarrow[c=4]{6>3 \Leftrightarrow S_9=0}$ j $\xrightarrow{\$}$ $\xrightarrow{t}{ninf=4}$. Each transition gives the corresponding condition and, eventually, the value of the counter c just after firing that transition.

3 Filtering Algorithm

The filtering algorithm is based on the following idea. For a given global constraint $\mathcal{C}$, one can think of its automaton as a procedure that repeatedly maps a current state Q_i and counter vector $\vec{K}_i$, given a signature variable S_i, to a new state Q_{i+1} and counter vector $\vec{K}_{i+1}$, until a terminal state is reached. We then convert this procedure into a *transition* constraint $\Phi_C(Q_i, \vec{K}_i, S_i, Q_{i+1}, \vec{K}_{i+1})$ as follows. Q_i is a variable whose values correspond to the states that can be reached at step i. Similarly, $\vec{K}_i$ is a vector of variables whose values correspond to the potential values of the counters at step i. Assuming that the automaton associated with C has na arcs $\text{arc}(q_1, s_1, q'_1, \vec{f_1}(\vec{K})), \ldots, \text{arc}(q_{na}, s_{na}, q'_{na}, \vec{f_{na}}(\vec{K}))$, the transition constraint has the following form, implemented in SICStus Prolog[1] with arithmetic, case [2], and element constraints [13]:

$$\bigvee \begin{cases} (Q_i = q_1) \wedge (S_i = s_1) \wedge (Q_{i+1} = q'_1) \wedge (\vec{K}_{i+1} = \vec{f_1}(\vec{K}_i)) \\ \vdots \\ (Q_i = q_{na}) \wedge (S_i = s_{na}) \wedge (Q_{i+1} = q'_{na}) \wedge (\vec{K}_{i+1} = \vec{f_{na}}(\vec{K}_i)) \end{cases}$$

We can then arrive at a filtering algorithm for C by decomposing it into a conjunction of Φ_C constraints, "threading" the state and counter variables through the conjunction. In addition to this, we need the signature constraints $\Psi_C(S_i, \Delta_i)$ ($0 \leq i < m$) that relate each signature variables S_i to the variables of its corresponding signature argument Δ_i. Filtering for the constraint C is provided by the conjunction of all signature and transitions constraints, (s being the start state and t being the end state):

$$\Psi_C(S_0, \Delta_0) \quad \wedge \Phi_C(s, \vec{K}_0, S_0, Q_1, \vec{K}_1) \wedge$$
$$\Psi_C(S_1, \Delta_1) \quad \wedge \Phi_C(Q_1, \vec{K}_1, S_1, Q_2, \vec{K}_2) \wedge$$
$$\vdots$$
$$\Psi_C(S_{m-1}, \Delta_{m-1}) \wedge \Phi_C(Q_{m-1}, \vec{K}_{m-1}, S_{m-1}, Q_m, \vec{K}_m) \wedge$$
$$\Phi_C(Q_m, \vec{K}_m, \$, t, \vec{K}_{m+1})$$

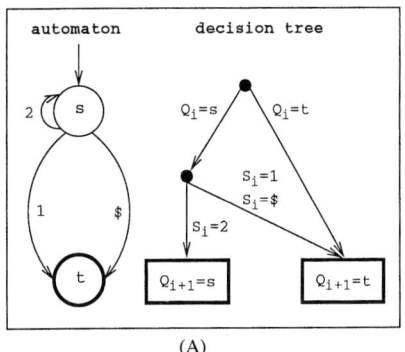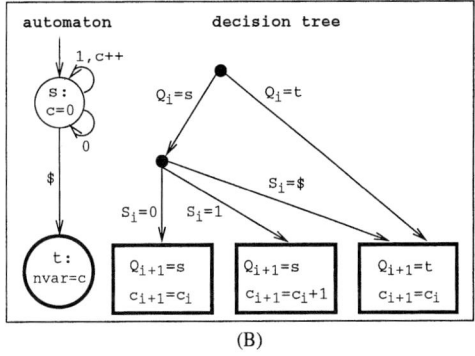

Fig. 2. Automata and decision trees for (A) $\leq_{\text{lex}}$ and (B) among.

A couple of examples will help clarify this idea. Note that the decision tree needs to correctly handle the case when the terminal state has already been reached.

---

[1] In ECLiPSe one could typically use Propia [27], a library supporting generalized propagation, for encoding the transition constraint.

[2] When no counter is used we only need a single case constraint to encode the disjunction expressed by the transition constraint. This disjunction is expressed as a decision tree as illustrated by Fig. 2. Since the case constraint [13, page 463] achieves arc-consistency, it follows that, in this context, the transition constraint achieves arc-consistency.

Example 2. Consider a $\vec{x} \leq_{lex} \vec{y}$ constraint over vectors of length n. First, we need a signature constraint $\Psi_{\leq_{lex}}$ relating each pair of arguments $x[i], y[i]$ to a signature variable S_i. This can be done as follows: $\Psi_{\leq_{lex}}(S_i, x[i], y[i]) \equiv (x[i] < y[i] \Leftrightarrow S_i = 1) \wedge (x[i] = y[i] \Leftrightarrow S_i = 2) \wedge (x[i] > y[i] \Leftrightarrow S_i = 3)$. The automaton of $\leq_{lex}$ and the decision tree corresponding to the transition constraint $\Phi_{\leq_{lex}}$ are shown in part (A) of Fig. 2.

Example 3. Consider an among($nvar, vars, values$) constraint. First, we need a signature constraint Ψ_{among} relating each argument $vars[i]$ to a signature letter S_i. This can be done as follows: $\Psi_{among}(S_i, vars[i], values) \equiv (vars[i] \in values \Leftrightarrow S_i = 1) \wedge (vars[i] \notin values \Leftrightarrow S_i = 0)$. The automaton of among and the decision tree corresponding to the transition constraint Φ_{among} are shown in part (B) of Fig. 2.

Consistency. We consider automata where all subsets of variables in $SignatureArg$ are pairwise disjoint, and that do not involve counters. Many constraints can be encoded by such automata, for instance the global_contiguity and lex_lesseq constraints presented in Fig. 1. For this kind of automata the filtering algorithm achieves arc-consistency, provided that the filtering algorithms of signature and transition constraints achieve also arc-consistency. To prove this property, consider the constraint hypergraph that represents the conjunction of all signature and transition constraints (see Fig. 3). It has two particular properties: there is no cycle in the corresponding intersection graph[3], and for any pair of constraints the two sets of involved variables share at most one variable. Such an hypergraph is so-called *Berge-acyclic* [9]. Berge-acyclic constraint

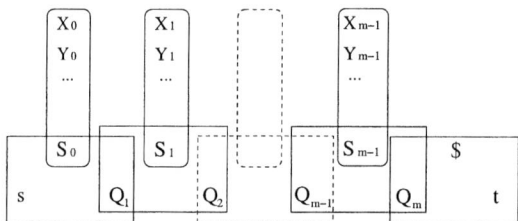

Fig. 3. Constraint hypergraph of the conjunction of transition and signature constraints in the case of disjoint $SignatureArg$ sets. The i-th $SignatureArg$ set Δ_i is denoted by $\{X_i, Y_i, \ldots\}$.

networks were proved to be solvable polynomially by achieving arc-consistency [20, 21]. Therefore, if all signature and transition constraints achieve arc-consistency then we obtain a complete filtering for our global constraint.

Performance. It is reasonable to ask the question whether the filtering algorithm described herein performs anywhere near the performance delivered by a hard-coded implementation of a given constraint. To this end, we have compared a version of the Balanced Incomplete Block Design problem [18, prob028] that uses a built-in $\leq_{lex}$ constraint to break column symmetries with a version using our filtering based on a

---

[3] In this graph each vertex corresponds to a constraint and there is an edge between two vertices iff the sets of variables involved in the two corresponding constraints intersect.

Table 1. Time in milliseconds for finding (A) the first solution of BIBD instances using built-in vs. simulated $\leq_{lex}$ (BCS denotes time spent for breaking column symmetries: with respect to the first column, BCS corresponds to the time spent in the built-in $\leq_{lex}$ constraint), and (B) all solutions to a single built-in vs. simulated $\leq_{lex}$ constraint.

(A)

Problem v, b, r, k, λ	Built-in $\leq_{lex}$ BCS/Other	Simulated $\leq_{lex}$ BCS/Other
6, 50, 25, 3, 10	70/170	250/170
6, 60, 30, 3, 12	120/110	50/110
8, 14, 7, 4, 3	10/80	50/80
9, 120, 40, 3, 10	480/1090	440/1090
10, 90, 27, 3, 6	550/90	1010/90
10, 120, 36, 3, 8	1400/2070	1040/2070
12, 88, 22, 3, 4	450/970	530/970
13, 104, 24, 3, 4	540/1230	540/1230
15, 70, 14, 3, 2	220/910	520/910

(B)

$x_i \in [0, m-1], y_i = m - i$
$|\vec{x}| = |\vec{y}| = m$

m	Built-in $\leq_{lex}$	Simulated $\leq_{lex}$
4	10	20
5	110	170
6	1640	2300
7	29530	39100

finite automaton for the same constraint. In a second experiment, we measured the time to find all solutions to a single $\leq_{lex}$ constraint. The experiments were run in SICStus Prolog 3.11 on a 600MHz Pentium III. The results are shown in Table 1.

4 Applications of This Technique

Designing Filtering Algorithm for Global Constraints. We apply this new methodology for designing filtering algorithms for the following fairly large set of global constraints. We came up with an automaton[4] for the following constraints: **1.** Unary constraints specifying a domain like in [14] or not_in [16]. **2.** Channeling constraints like domain_constraint [28]. **3.** Counting constraints for constraining the number of occurrences of a given set of values like among [6], atleast [16], atmost [16] or count [14]. **4.** Sliding sequence constraints like change [4], longest_change or smooth [2]. longest_change(*size*, *vars*, *ctr*) restricts the variable *size* to the maximum number of consecutive variables of *vars* for which the binary constraint *ctr* holds. **5.** Variations around the element constraint [19] like element_greatereq [24], element_lesseq [24] or element_sparse [16]. **6.** Variations around the maximum constraint [3] like max_index(*vars*, *index*). max_index enforces the variable *index* to be equal to one of the positions of variables corresponding to the maximum value of the variables of *vars*. **7.** Constraints on words like global_contiguity [22], group [16], group_skip_isolated_item [2] or pattern [11]. **8.** Constraints between vectors of variables like between [12], $\leq_{lex}$ [17], lex_different or differ_from_at_least_k_pos. Given two vectors $\vec{x}$ and $\vec{y}$ which have the same number of components, the constraints lex_different($\vec{x}$, $\vec{y}$) and differ_from_at_least_k_pos(k, $\vec{x}$, $\vec{y}$) respectively enforce the vectors $\vec{x}$ and $\vec{y}$ to differ from at least 1 and k components. **9.** Constraints between n-dimensional boxes like

---

[4] These automata are available in the technical report [5]. All signature constraints are encoded in order to achieve arc-consistency.

two_quad_are_in_contact [16] or two_quad_do_not_overlap [7]. **10.** Constraints on the shape of a sequence of variables like inflection [2], top [8] or valley [8]. **11.** Various constraints like in_same_partition(var_1, var_2, *partitions*), not_all_equal(*vars*) or sliding_card_skip0(*atleast, atmost, vars, values*). in_same_partition enforces variables var_1 and var_2 to be respectively assigned to two values that both belong to a same sublist of values of *partitions*. not_all_equal enforces the variables of *vars* to take more than a single value. sliding_card_skip0 enforces that each maximum non-zero subsequence of consecutive variables of *vars* contains at least *atleast* and *atmost* values from the set of values *values*.

Filtering Algorithm for a Conjunction of Global Constraints. Another typical use of our new methodology is to come up with a filtering algorithm for the conjunction of several global constraints. This is usually not easy since this implies analyzing a lot of special cases showing up from the interaction of the different considered constraints. We illustrate this point on the conjunction of the between($\vec{a}, \vec{x}, \vec{b}$) [12] and the exactly_one($\vec{x}$, *values*) constraints for which we come with a filtering algorithm, which maintains arc-consistency. The between constraint holds iff $\vec{a} \leq_{\text{lex}} \vec{x}$ and $\vec{x} \leq_{\text{lex}} \vec{b}$, while the exactly_one constraint holds if exactly one component of $\vec{x}$ takes its value in the set of values *values*.

The left-hand part of Fig. 4 depicts the two automata $\mathcal{A}_1$ and $\mathcal{A}_2$ respectively associated with the between and the exactly_one constraints, while the right-hand part gives the automaton $\mathcal{A}_3$ associated with the conjunction of these two constraints. $\mathcal{A}_3$ corresponds to the product of $\mathcal{A}_1$ and $\mathcal{A}_2$. States of $\mathcal{A}_3$ are labeled by the two states of $\mathcal{A}_1$ and $\mathcal{A}_2$ they were issued. Transitions of $\mathcal{A}_3$ are labeled by the end symbol $ or by a conjunction of elementary conditions, where each condition is taken in one of the following set of conditions $\{a_i < x_i, a_i = x_i, a_i > x_i\}$, $\{b_i > x_i, b_i = x_i, b_i < x_i\}$, $\{x_i \in values, x_i \notin values\}$. This makes up to $3 \cdot 3 \cdot 2 = 18$ possible combinations and leads to the signature constraint $\Psi_{\text{between} \wedge \text{exactly\_one}}(S_i, a_i, x_i, b_i, values)$ between the signature variable S_i and the i-th component of vectors $\vec{a}, \vec{x}$ and $\vec{b}$:

$$S_i = \begin{cases} 0 & \text{if } a_i < x_i \wedge b_i > x_i \wedge x_i \notin values, \quad 9 \text{ if } a_i < x_i \wedge b_i > x_i \wedge x_i \in values, \\ 1 & \text{if } a_i < x_i \wedge b_i = x_i \wedge x_i \notin values, \quad 10 \text{ if } a_i < x_i \wedge b_i = x_i \wedge x_i \in values, \\ 2 & \text{if } a_i < x_i \wedge b_i < x_i \wedge x_i \notin values, \quad 11 \text{ if } a_i < x_i \wedge b_i < x_i \wedge x_i \in values, \\ 3 & \text{if } a_i = x_i \wedge b_i > x_i \wedge x_i \notin values, \quad 12 \text{ if } a_i = x_i \wedge b_i > x_i \wedge x_i \in values, \\ 4 & \text{if } a_i = x_i \wedge b_i = x_i \wedge x_i \notin values, \quad 13 \text{ if } a_i = x_i \wedge b_i = x_i \wedge x_i \in values, \\ 5 & \text{if } a_i = x_i \wedge b_i < x_i \wedge x_i \notin values, \quad 14 \text{ if } a_i = x_i \wedge b_i < x_i \wedge x_i \in values, \\ 6 & \text{if } a_i > x_i \wedge b_i > x_i \wedge x_i \notin values, \quad 15 \text{ if } a_i > x_i \wedge b_i > x_i \wedge x_i \in values, \\ 7 & \text{if } a_i > x_i \wedge b_i = x_i \wedge x_i \notin values, \quad 16 \text{ if } a_i > x_i \wedge b_i = x_i \wedge x_i \in values, \\ 8 & \text{if } a_i > x_i \wedge b_i < x_i \wedge x_i \notin values, \quad 17 \text{ if } a_i > x_i \wedge b_i < x_i \wedge x_i \in values. \end{cases}$$

In order to achieve arc-consistency on the conjunction of the between($\vec{a}, \vec{x}, \vec{b}$) and the exactly_one($\vec{x}$, *values*) constraints we need to have arc-consistency on $\Psi_{\text{between} \wedge \text{exactly\_one}}(S_i, a_i, x_i, b_i, values)$. In our context this is done by using the global constraint programming facilities of SICStus Prolog [14][5].

---

[5] The corresponding code is available in the technical report [5].

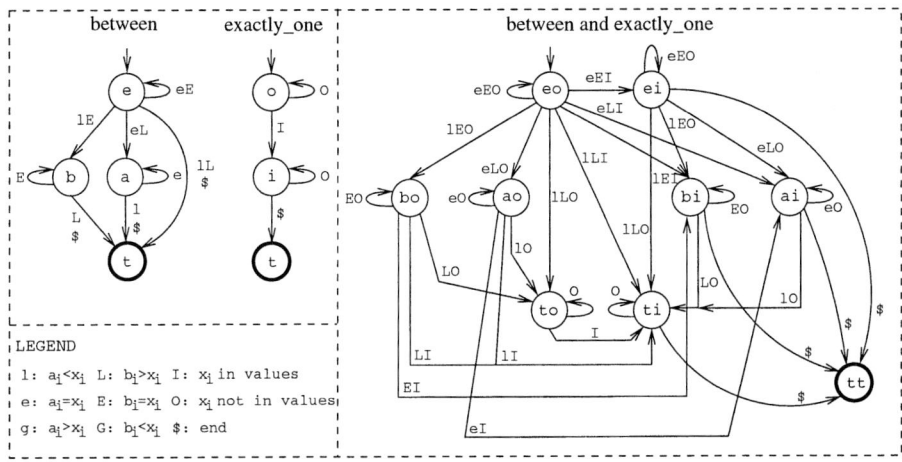

Fig. 4. Automata associated with between and exactly_one and the automaton associated with their conjunction.

Example 4. Consider three variables $x \in \{0,1\}, y \in \{0,3\}, z \in \{0,1,2,3\}$ subject to the conjunction of constraints between($\langle 0,3,1\rangle, \langle x,y,z\rangle, \langle 1,0,2\rangle$) $\wedge$ exactly_one ($\langle x,y,z\rangle, \{0\}$). Even if both the between and the exactly_one constraints achieve arc-consistency, we need the automaton associated with their conjunction to find out that $z \neq 0$. This can be seen as follows: after two transitions, the automaton $\mathcal{A}_3$ will be either in state ai or in state bi. However, in either state, a 0 must already have been seen, and so there is no support for $z = 0$.

5 Handling Relaxation for a Counter-Free Automaton

This section presents a filtering algorithm for handling constraint relaxation under the hypothesis that we don't use any counter in our automaton. It can be seen as a generalization of the algorithm used for the regular constraint [25].

Definition 1. *The* violation cost *of a global constraint is the minimum number of subsets of its signature argument for which it is necessary to change at least one variable in order to get back to a solution.*

When these subsets form a partition over the variables of the constraint and when they consist of a single element, this cost is in fact the minimum number of variables to unassign in order to get back to a solution. As in [26], we add a cost variable *cost* as an extra argument of the constraint. Our filtering algorithm first evaluates the minimum cost value $\mathcal{M}in$. Then, according to max(*cost*), it prunes values that cannot belong to a solution.

Example 5. Consider the constraint global_contiguity($[V_0, V_1, V_2, V_3, V_4, V_5, V_6]$) with the following current domains for variables V_i: $[\{0,1\}, \{1\}, \{1\}, \{0\}, \{1\}, \{0,1\}, \{1\}]$. The constraint is violated because there are necessarily at least two distinct sequences of consecutive 1. To get back to a state that can lead to a solution, it is enough to turn the fourth value to 1. One can deduce $\mathcal{M}in = 1$. Consider now the relaxed form soft_global_contiguity($[V_0, V_1, V_2, V_3, V_4, V_5, V_6]$, $cost$) and assume $\max(cost) = 1$. The filtering algorithm should remove value 0 from V_5. Indeed, selecting value 0 for variable V_5 entails a minimum violation cost of 2. Observe that for this constraint the signature variables $S_0, S_1, S_2, S_3, S_4, S_5, S_6$ are $V_0, V_1, V_2, V_3, V_4, V_5, V_6$.

As in the algorithm of Pesant [25], our consistency algorithm builds a layered acyclic directed multigraph $\mathcal{G}$. Each layer of $\mathcal{G}$ contains a different node for each state of our automaton. Arcs only appear between consecutive layers. Given two nodes n_1 and n_2 of two consecutive layers, q_1 and q_2 denote their respective associated state. There is an arc a from n_1 to n_2 iff, in the automaton, there is an arc $arc(q_1, v, q_2)$ from q_1 to q_2. The arc a is labeled with the value v. Arcs corresponding to transitions that cannot be triggered according to the current domain of the signature variables $S_0, \ldots, S_{m-1}$ are marked as *infeasible*. All other arcs are marked as *feasible*. Finally, we discard isolated nodes from our layered multigraph. Since our automaton has a single initial state and a single final state, $\mathcal{G}$ has one source and one sink, denoted by *source* and *sink*.

Example 5 continued. Part (A) of Fig. 5 recalls the automaton of the global_contiguity constraint, while part (B) gives the multigraph $\mathcal{G}$ associated with the soft_global_contiguity constraint previously introduced. Each arc is labeled by the condition associated to its corresponding transition. Each node contains the name of the corresponding automaton state. Numbers in a node will be explained later on. Infeasible arcs are represented with a dotted line.

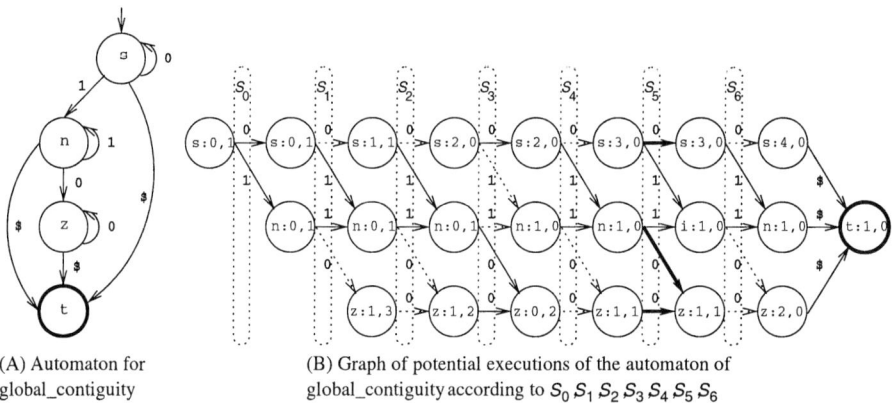

(A) Automaton for global_contiguity

(B) Graph of potential executions of the automaton of global_contiguity according to $S_0\, S_1\, S_2\, S_3\, S_4\, S_5\, S_6$

Fig. 5. Relaxing the global_contiguity constraint.

We now explain how to use the multigraph $\mathcal{G}$ to evaluate the minimum violation cost $\mathcal{M}in$ and to prune the signature variables according to the maximum allowed violation cost $\max(cost)$. Evaluating the minimum violation cost $\mathcal{M}in$ can be seen as finding the path from the source to the sink of $\mathcal{G}$ that contains the smallest number of infeasible arcs. This can be done by performing a topological sort starting from the source of $\mathcal{G}$. While performing the topological sort, we compute for each node n_k of $\mathcal{G}$ the minimum number of infeasible arcs from the source of $\mathcal{G}$ to n_k. This number is recorded in $before[n_k]$. At the end of the topological sort, the minimum violation cost $\mathcal{M}in$ we search for, is equal to $before[sink]$.

Notation 1 *Let i be assignable to a signature variable S_l. $\mathcal{M}in_l^i$ denotes the minimum violation cost value according to the hypothesis that we assign i to S_l.*

To prune domains of signature variables we need to compute the quantity $\mathcal{M}in_l^i$. In order to do so, we introduce the quantity $after[n_k]$ for a node n_k of $\mathcal{G}$: $after[n_k]$ is the minimum number of infeasible arcs on all paths from n_k to $sink$. It is computed by performing a second topological sort starting from the sink of $\mathcal{G}$. Let $\mathcal{A}_l^i$ denote the set of arcs of $\mathcal{G}$, labeled by i, for which the origin has a rank of l. The quantity $\min_{a \to b \in \mathcal{A}_l^i} (before[a] + after[b])$ represents the minimum violation cost under the hypothesis that S_l remains assigned to i. If that quantity is greater than $\mathcal{M}in$ then there is no path from $source$ to $sink$ which uses an arc of $\mathcal{A}_l^i$ and which has a number of infeasible arcs equal to $\mathcal{M}in$. In that case the smallest cost we can achieve is $\mathcal{M}in + 1$. Therefore we have:

$$\mathcal{M}in_l^i = \min(\min_{a \to b \in \mathcal{A}_l^i} (before[a] + after[b]), \mathcal{M}in + 1)$$

The filtering algorithm is then based on the following theorem:

Theorem 1. *Let i be a value from the domain of a signature variable S_l. If $\mathcal{M}in_l^i >$ $\max(cost)$ then i can be removed from S_l.*

The cost of the filtering algorithm is dominated by the two topological sorts. They have a cost proportional to the number of arcs of $\mathcal{G}$ which is bounded by the number of signature variables times the number of arcs of the automaton.

Example 5 continued. Let us come back to the instance of Fig. 5. Beside the state's name, each node n_k of part (B) of Fig. 5 gives the values of $before[n_k]$ and of $after[n_k]$. Since $before[sink] = 1$ we have that the minimum cost violation is equal to 1. Pruning can be potentially done only for signature variables having more than one value. In our example this corresponds to variables V_0 and V_5. So we evaluate the four quantities $\mathcal{M}in_0^0 = \min(0+1, 2) = 1$, $\mathcal{M}in_0^1 = \min(0+1, 2) = 1$, $\mathcal{M}in_5^0 = \min(\min(3+0, 1+1, 1+1), 2) = 2$, $\mathcal{M}in_5^1 = \min(\min(3+0, 1+0), 2) = 1$. If $\max(cost)$ is equal to 1 we can remove value 0 from V_5. The corresponding arcs are depicted with a thick line in Fig. 5.

6 Conclusion and Perspectives

The automaton description introduced in this article can be seen as a restricted programming language. This language is used for writing down a constraint checker, which verifies whether a ground instance of a constraint is satisfied or not. This checker allows pruning the variables of a non-ground instance of a constraint by simulating all potential executions of the corresponding program according to the current domain of the variables of the relevant constraint. This simulation is achieved by encoding all potential executions of the automaton as a conjunction of signature and transition constraints and by letting the usual constraint propagation deducing all the relevant information. We want to stress the key points and the different perspectives of this approach:

- Within the context of global constraints, it was implicitly assumed that providing a constraint checker is a much easier task than coming up with a filtering algorithm. It was also commonly admitted that the design of filtering algorithms is a difficult task which involves creativity and which cannot be automatized. We have shown that this is not the case any more if one can afford to provide a constraint checker.
- Non-determinism has played a key role by augmenting programming languages with backtracking facilities [15], which was the origin of logic programming. Non-determinism also has a key role to play in the systematic design of filtering algorithms: finding a filtering algorithm can be seen as the task of executing in a non-deterministic way the deterministic program corresponding to a constraint checker and to extract the relevant information which for sure occurs under any circumstances. This can indeed be achieved by using constraint programming.
- A natural continuation would be to extend the automaton description in order to get closer to a classical imperative programming language. This would allow reusing directly available checkers in order to systematically get a filtering algorithm.
- Other structural conditions on the signature and transition constraints could be identified to guarantee arc-consistency for the original global constraint.
- An extension of our approach may give a systematic way to get an algorithm (not necessarily polynomial) for decision problems for which one can provide a polynomial certificate. From [30] the decision version of every problem in NP can be formulated as follows: Given x, decide whether there exists y so that $|y| \leq m(x)$ and $R(x, y)$. x is an instance of the problem; y is a short YES-certificate for this instance; $R(x, y)$ is a polynomial time decidable relation that verifies certificate y for instance x; and $m(x)$ is a computable and polynomially bounded complexity parameter that bounds the length of the certificate y. In our context, if $|y|$ is fixed and known, x is a global constraint and its $|y|$ variables with their domains; y is a solution to that global constraint; $R(x, y)$ is an automaton which encodes a checker for that global constraint.

Acknowledgments

We are grateful to I. Katriel for suggesting us the use of topological sort for the relaxation part, and to C. Bessière for his helpful comments w.r.t. Berge-acyclic CSP's.

References

1. J. Amilhastre, H. Fargier, and P. Marquis. Consistency restoration and explanations in dynamic CSPs – application to configuration. *Artificial Intelligence*, 135:199–234, 2002.
2. N. Beldiceanu. Global constraints as graph properties on structured network of elementary constraints of the same type. In R. Dechter, editor, *CP'2000, Principles and Practice of Constraint Programming*, volume 1894 of *LNCS*, pages 52–66. Springer-Verlag, 2000.
3. N. Beldiceanu. Pruning for the minimum constraint family and for the number of distinct values constraint family. In T. Walsh, editor, *CP'2001, Int. Conf. on Principles and Practice of Constraint Programming*, volume 2239 of *LNCS*, pages 211–224. Springer-Verlag, 2001.

4. N. Beldiceanu and M. Carlsson. Revisiting the cardinality operator and introducing the cardinality-path constraint family. In P. Codognet, editor, *ICLP'2001, Int. Conf. on Logic Programming*, volume 2237 of *LNCS*, pages 59–73. Springer-Verlag, 2001.
5. N. Beldiceanu, M. Carlsson, and T. Petit. Deriving filtering algorithms from constraint checkers. Technical Report T2004-08, Swedish Institute of Computer Science, 2004.
6. N. Beldiceanu and E. Contejean. Introducing global constraints in CHIP. *Mathl. Comput. Modelling*, 20(12):97–123, 1994.
7. N. Beldiceanu, Q. Guo, and S. Thiel. Non-overlapping constraints between convex polytopes. In T. Walsh, editor, *Principles and Practice of Constraint Programming (CP'2001)*, volume 2239 of *LNCS*, pages 392–407. Springer-Verlag, 2001.
8. N. Beldiceanu and E. Poder. Cumulated profiles of minimum and maximum resource utilisation. In *Ninth Int. Conf. on Project Management and Scheduling*, pages 96–99, 2004.
9. C. Berge. Graphs and hypergraphs. *Dunod, Paris*, 1970.
10. B. Boigelot and P. Wolper. Representing arithmetic constraints with finite automata: An overview. In Peter J. Stuckey, editor, *ICLP'2002, Int. Conf. on Logic Programming*, volume 2401 of *LNCS*, pages 1–19. Springer-Verlag, 2002.
11. S. Bourdais, P. Galinier, and G. Pesant. HIBISCUS: A constraint programming application to staff scheduling in health care. In F. Rossi, editor, *CP'2003, Principles and Practice of Constraint Programming*, volume 2833 of *LNCS*, pages 153–167. Springer-Verlag, 2003.
12. M. Carlsson and N. Beldiceanu. From constraints to finite automata to filtering algorithms. In D. Schmidt, editor, *Proc. ESOP2004*, volume 2986 of *LNCS*, pages 94–108. Springer-Verlag, 2004.
13. M. Carlsson et al. *SICStus Prolog User's Manual*. Swedish Institute of Computer Science, 3.11 edition, January 2004. http://www.sics.se/sicstus/.
14. M. Carlsson, G. Ottosson, and B. Carlson. An open-ended finite domain constraint solver. In H. Glaser, P. Hartel, and H. Kuchen, editors, *Programming Languages: Implementations, Logics, and Programming*, volume 1292 of *LNCS*, pages 191–206. Springer-Verlag, 1997.
15. J. Cohen. Non-deterministic algorithms. *ACM Computing Surveys*, 11(2):79–94, 1979.
16. COSYTEC. *CHIP Reference Manual*, v5 edition, 2003.
17. A. Frisch, B. Hnich, Z. Kızıltan, I. Miguel, and T. Walsh. Global constraints for lexicographic orderings. In Pascal Van Hentenryck, editor, *Principles and Practice of Constraint Programming (CP'2002)*, volume 2470 of *LNCS*, pages 93–108. Springer-Verlag, 2002.
18. I.P. Gent and T. Walsh. CSPLib: a benchmark library for constraints. Technical Report APES-09-1999, APES, 1999. http://www.csplib.org.
19. P. Van Hentenryck and J.-P. Carillon. Generality vs. specificity: an experience with AI and OR techniques. In *National Conference on Artificial Intelligence (AAAI-88)*, 1988.
20. P. Janssen and M-C. Vilarem. Problèmes de satisfaction de contraintes: techniques de résolution et application à la synthèse de peptides. *Research Report C.R.I.M.*, 54, 1988.
21. P. Jégou. Contribution à l'étude des problèmes de satisfaction de contraintes: algorithmes de propagation et de résolution. Propagation de contraintes dans les réseaux dynamiques. *PhD Thesis*, 1991.
22. M. Maher. Analysis of a global contiguity constraint. In *Workshop on Rule-Based Constraint Reasoning and Programming*, 2002. held along CP-2002.
23. M. Milano. *Constraint and integer programming*. Kluwer Academic Publishers, 2004. ISBN 1-4020-7583-9.
24. G. Ottosson, E. Thorsteinsson, and J. N. Hooker. Mixed global constraints and inference in hybrid IP-CLP solvers. In *CP'99 Post-Conference Workshop on Large-Scale Combinatorial Optimization and Constraints*, pages 57–78, 1999.
25. G. Pesant. A regular language membership constraint for sequence of variables. In *Workshop on Modelling and Reformulation Constraint Satisfaction Problems*, pages 110–119, 2003.

26. T. Petit, J.-C. Régin, and C. Bessière. Specific filtering algorithms for over-constrained problems. In T. Walsh, editor, *Principles and Practice of Constraint Programming (CP'2001)*, volume 2239 of *LNCS*, pages 451–463. Springer-Verlag, 2001.
27. T. Le Provost and M. Wallace. Domain-independent propagation. In *Proc. of the International Conference on Fifth Generation Computer Systems*, pages 1004–1011, 1992.
28. P. Refalo. Linear formulation of constraint programming models and hybrid solvers. In R. Dechter, editor, *Principles and Practice of Constraint Programming (CP'2000)*, volume 1894 of *LNCS*, pages 369–383. Springer-Verlag, 2000.
29. N. R. Vempaty. Solving constraint satisfaction problems using finite state automata. In *National Conference on Artificial Intelligence (AAAI-92)*, pages 453–458. AAAI Press, 1992.
30. G. J. Woeginger. Exact algorithms for NP-hard problems: A survey. In M. Juenger, G. Reinelt, and G. Rinaldi, editors, *Combinatorial Optimization - Eureka! You shrink!*, volume 2570 of *LNCS*, pages 185–207. Springer-Verlag, 2003.

Leveraging the Learning Power of Examples in Automated Constraint Acquisition[*]

Christian Bessiere[1], Remi Coletta[1], Eugene C. Freuder[2], and Barry O'Sullivan[2]

[1] LIRMM-CNRS (UMR 5506), 161 rue Ada 34392 Montpellier Cedex 5, France
{bessiere,coletta}@lirmm.fr
[2] Cork Constraint Computation Centre
Department of Computer Science, University College Cork, Ireland
{e.freuder,b.osullivan}@4c.ucc.ie

Abstract. Constraint programming is rapidly becoming the technology of choice for modeling and solving complex combinatorial problems. However, users of constraint programming technology need significant expertise in order to model their problem appropriately. The lack of availability of such expertise can be a significant bottleneck to the broader uptake of constraint technology in the real world. In this paper we are concerned with automating the formulation of constraint satisfaction problems from examples of solutions and non-solutions. We combine techniques from the fields of machine learning and constraint programming. In particular we present a portfolio of approaches to exploiting the semantics of the constraints that we acquire to improve the efficiency of the acquisition process. We demonstrate how inference and search can be used to extract useful information that would otherwise be hidden in the set of examples from which we learn the target constraint satisfaction problem. We demonstrate the utility of the approaches in a case-study domain.

1 Introduction

Constraint programming is rapidly becoming the technology of choice for modelling and solving complex combinatorial problems. However, users of constraint programming technology need significant expertise in order to model their problem appropriately. The ability to assist users to model a problem in the constraint satisfaction paradigm is of crucial importance in making constraint programming accessible to non-experts. However, there are many obstacles which must be overcome. For example, in some situations users are not capable of fully articulating the set of constraints they wish to model. Instead users can only present us with example solutions and non-solutions of the target constraint satisfaction problem (CSP) they wish to articulate. This situation arises in many real-world scenarios. In purchasing, a human customer may not be able to provide the sales agent with a precise specification of his set of constraints because he is unfamiliar with the technical terms that are required to specify each constraint.

---

[*] The collaboration between LIRMM and the Cork Constraint Computation Centre is supported by a Ulysses Travel Grant from Enterprise Ireland, the Royal Irish Academy and CNRS (Grant Number FR/2003/022). This work has also received support from Science Foundation Ireland under Grant 00/PI.1/C075.

Alternatively, in a data-mining context we may have access to a large source of data in the form of positive and negative examples, and we have been set the task of generating a declarative specification of that data. Earlier work in this area has focused on the generalization problem, inspired by work from the field of Inductive Logic Programming [8]. Here we focus on combining techniques from constraint processing and machine learning to develop a novel approach to constraint acquisition.

We have proposed an algorithm, CONACQ, that is capable of acquiring a model of a CSP from a set of examples [2]. The algorithm is based on version space learning [6]. Version spaces are a standard machine learning approach to concept learning. A version space can be regarded as a set of hypotheses for a concept that correctly classify the training data received; in Section 2 we shall present an example which will serve both a pedagogical role and demonstrate the problem we address in this paper.

However, the CONACQ algorithm suffers from a serious malady that has significant consequences for its ability to acquire constraint networks efficiently. In particular, this malady arises because we are acquiring networks of constraints, some of which may be *redundant* [1, 3, 10]. Informally, for now, we can regard a constraint as being redundant if it can be removed from a constraint network without affecting the set of solutions. While redundant constraints have no effect on the set of solutions to a CSP, they can have a negative effect on the acquisition process. In particular, when using version spaces to represent the set of consistent hypotheses for each constraint, redundancy can prevent us from converging on the most specific hypotheses for the target network, even though the set of training examples is sufficient for this to occur. As a consequence, for a given constraint in the network, its version space may not be sufficiently explicit, but rather contain constraints that are far too general. This is a significant problem since the size of each version space has a multiplicative effect on the number of possible CSPs that correctly classify the training examples. Furthermore, not having the most explicit constraints everywhere in the network can have a negative effect on the performance of some constraint propagation algorithms.

In this paper we present a portfolio of approaches to handling redundant constraints in constraint acquisition. In particular, we address the issue of how to make each constraint as explicit as possible based on the examples given. We shall present an approach based on the notion of *redundancy rules*, which can be regarded as a special-case of relational consistency [4]. We shall show that these rules can deal with some, but not all, forms of redundancy. We shall then present a second approach, based on the notion of *backbone detection* [7], which is far more powerful.

The remainder of this paper is organized as follows. Section 2 presents a simple example of how acquiring redundant constraints can have an adverse effect on the constraint acquisition process. Section 3 presents some formal definitions of the concepts that underpin our approach. We formalize the notion of redundancy in constraint networks, and show how the problem identified in Section 2 can be easily addressed. Section 4 presents a more powerful approach to dealing with redundancy due to disjunctions of constraints. Section 5 presents an empirical evaluation of the various approaches presented in the paper and presents a detailed discussion of our results. A number of concluding remarks are made in Section 6.

2 An Illustrative Example

We demonstrate the potential problems that can arise due to redundancy during an interactive acquisition session using CONACQ in an example scenario. Consider the hypothesis space of constraints presented in Figure 1(a). We assume in our example that all constraints in our target problem can be expressed using this hypothesis space. These constraints are arranged in a lattice, e.g. $\leq$ includes both $<$ and $=$ and so appears above $<$ and $=$, such that more general constraints are placed higher in the hypothesis space. The constraint $\top$ is the universal constraint – all tuples are accepted. The constraint $\bot$ is the null constraint – no tuples are accepted. Positive examples (solutions) and negative examples (non-solutions) enable us to prune away portions of these spaces until, ideally, we have completely identified the user's problem by reducing the version space for each constraint to a single element. The term version space refers to the subset of the hypothesis space that remains as we prune away possibilities after each example is considered. The distinction will become clear as we consider an example below.

The CONACQ algorithm maintains a separate version space for each potential constraint in the CSP. A solution to the target CSP (positive example) provides examples for each constraint in the problem, since *all* constraints must be satisfied in order for an example to be classified as positive. However, negative examples are more problematic to process, since violating at least *one* constraint is sufficient for an example to be classified as negative. Therefore, a negative example provides a disjunction of possible examples. It is only when the algorithm can deduce which constraints must have been violated by the example, causing it to be classified as negative, that the appropriate version spaces can be updated.

For the purposes of this example, we wish to acquire a CSP involving 3 variables, x_1, x_2 and x_3, with domains $D(x_1) = D(x_2) = D(x_3) = \{1, 2, 3, 4\}$. The set of constraints in the target network is $\{x_1 > x_2, x_1 > x_3, x_2 > x_3\}$. In Table 1 the set of examples that will be provided to the acquisition system is presented. The set of examples comprises one positive example (a solution to the target CSP) and two negative examples (non-solutions). Figures 1(b)–1(d) illustrate the effect of each example in turn on the version spaces of the constraints in the network.

Figure 1(b) presents the state of each of the constraint version spaces after the first (and only) positive example, e_1^+, has been processed. We can see that the version space of each constraint now contains four hypotheses: $>, \neq, \geq$ and $\top$. The other hypotheses are eliminated because they are inconsistent with e_1^+. Specifically, if $x_1 = 4 \wedge x_2 = 3$ can be part of a solution, then the constraint between these variables must be *more general than or equal to* $>$. Therefore, we can ignore the possibility that this constraint can be either $=, <, \leq$ or $\bot$. Essentially, we know that any CSP that can be expressed in terms of the constraints presented in Figure 1(a) must comprise constraints that are no more specific than those in the version spaces presented in Figure 1(b). Similar reasoning allows us to reduce the version space for each constraint to that illustrated in Figure 1(b).

Table 1. Examples for Fig. 1.

E	x_1	x_2	x_3
e_1^+	4	3	1
e_2^-	2	3	1
e_3^-	3	1	2

Figure 1(c) presents the effect of processing example e_2^-, the first negative example. Of the three constraints in the problem, e_2^- differs by only one constraint, c_{12}, compared to the constraints implied by the the positive example e_1^+. Therefore, we can further

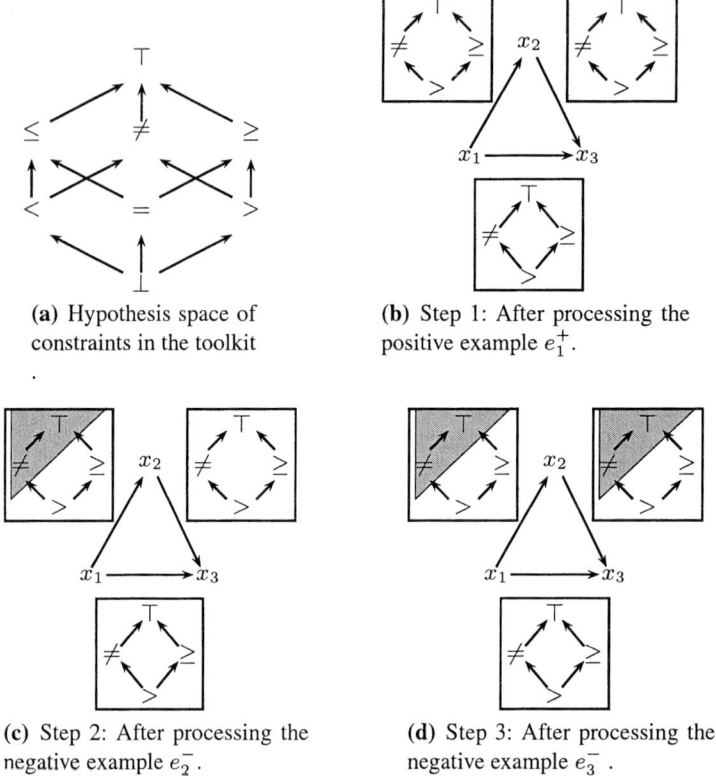

Fig. 1. Acquiring a redundant constraint prevents one version space from converging.

refine the version space of constraint c_{12} by removing both $\neq$ and $\top$. We illustrate this by using a colored shading over those hypotheses that are removed from the version space. Similarly, the reason why e_3^- is classified as negative is due to a single constraint: namely c_{23}. Figure 1(d) illustrates the result of processing negative example e_3^-.

After processing the negative examples e_2^-, e_3^-, the version spaces for the constraint between variables x_1 and x_2 and between variables x_2 and x_3 are reduced to the set of hypotheses $\{>, \geq\}$. However, the version space for the constraint between variables x_1 and x_3 has not. Instead, this version space contains four possible hypotheses: $\{>, \geq, \neq, \top\}$.

This is unfortunate since we cannot now find a set of negative examples which will help this version space to reduce any closer to the target constraint. For example, to eliminate the hypothesis $\neq$, we need a negative example with $x_1 < x_3$ but necessarily satisfying all other acquired constraints, i.e., satisfying their most specific possible alternative: $x_1 > x_2$ and $x_2 > x_3$, so that the only possible reason to reject it is $x_1 < x_3$. Clearly no such example exists. As a consequence, the version spaces in this scenario cannot converge any further. However, it should be pointed out that it was not due to a deficiency in our set of examples, as we shall see in Example 2 later in this paper, that precluded convergence in this case, but as a result of attempting to acquire redundant constraints using the CONACQ algorithm. Specifically, in our example the constraint between x_1 and x_3 is redundant.

Therefore, it is clear that acquiring redundant constraints can prevent us from converging on the most specific hypotheses consistent with a set of examples. However, by exploiting the fact that we are acquiring constraint networks, we can rely on various search and inference techniques to help us leverage the learning power of the examples that have been provided to us. In the ideal, we can exploit redundancy to help us to converge on the target hypothesis much more quickly. In the next section we present an approach exploiting redundant constraints that overcomes the problem we have experienced in this example.

3 Redundancy Rules

In this section, we introduce formal definitions of the basic concepts used in this paper. We then propose definitions of redundancy and redundancy rules, before presenting an approach to dealing with redundant constraints in the CONACQ acquisition process.

3.1 Basic Definitions

A finite *constraint network* N consists of a finite set of variables $X = \{x_1, \ldots, x_n\}$, a set of domains $D = \{D(x_1), \ldots, D(x_n)\}$, where the domain $D(x_i)$ is the finite set of values that variable x_i can take, and a set of constraints $C = \{c_1, \ldots, c_m\}$. Each constraint c_i is defined by the ordered set $var(c_i)$ of the variables it involves, and a set $sol(c_i)$ of allowed combinations of values. An assignment of values to the variables in $var(c_i)$ satisfies c_i if it belongs to $sol(c_i)$. A *solution* to a constraint network is an assignment of a value from its domain to each variable such that every constraint in the network is satisfied. When all the constraints in C involve exactly 2 variables, we say that the constraints and the network are *binary*. This is the case we will study in the rest of the paper since it greatly simplifies notation. We will use $c(x_i, x_j)$ and c_{ij} interchangeably to refer to $sol(c)$ where $var(c) = (x_i, x_j)$. However, all the results are essentially the same for constraints of any arity.

As seen in the previous section, redundancy is a crucial notion that we need to tackle if we want to speed up version space convergence during the constraint acquisition process.

Definition 1 (Redundancy) *Given a constraint network $N = (X, D, C)$, we say that a constraint $c \in C$ is **redundant** wrt N iff the set of solutions of N is the same as the set of solutions of $N_{-c} = (X, D, C \setminus \{c\})$. We note $N_{-c} \models c$.*

3.2 Redundancy in CONACQ

The CONACQ algorithm has been proposed in [2]. Its inputs are a set X of variables with their domains, a set of examples $E = E^+ \cup E^-$, and a bias B. An example $e \in E$ is an assignment of values to variables from X that must be a solution of the target constraint network (if $e \in E^+$) or non solution (if $e \in E^-$).

The bias is composed of constraint scopes (sets of variables on which a constraint c has to be guessed), associated with a set of constraint types that are the different possibilities for $sol(c)$. In the simplest case, where we guess a complete network of binary constraints, the bias contains all pairs of variables from X as possible scopes, associated with all the binary constraint types available in the toolkit. The set of possible constraints on (x_i, x_j) is denoted by its bias, B_{ij}.

The output of CONACQ is any constraint network that has the same set X of variables with their domains, and a set of constraints chosen from the bias such that every element of E^+ is solution and none from E^-. Since the number of constraint networks satisfying these criteria during the acquisition process can be huge (exponential), CONACQ uses version space techniques and maintains only a most specific bound S_{ij} and a most general bound G_{ij} for each pair of variables (x_i, x_j) belonging to the bias. Any constraint in the toolkit subsumed by G_{ij} and subsuming S_{ij} is a candidate for c_{ij} (namely, belongs to the version space).

Theorem 1. *Let X, D, B, E be the input of CONACQ . Let $c_{ij} \in B_{ij}$. If there exists $\{c_{ik}, c_{kj}\} \in B_{ik} \times B_{kj}$ such that $E \models \{c_{ik}, c_{kj}\}$ and c_{ij} is redundant wrt $(X, D, \{c_{ik}, c_{kj}\})$ then the version space cannot shrink its bounds on (x_i, x_j) more than $S_{ij} = c_{ij}$ and $G_{ij} = \top$.*

Proof. Let $c'_{ij} \in B_{ij}$ a constraint subsumed by c_{ij}. Suppose there exists $e \in E^-$ such that e violates c'_{ij}. (This is the only way to remove c'_{ij} from the version space.) We can decrease the local general bound G_{ij} under c'_{ij} only if no other constraint in the version space can reject e. Now, we know that $E \models \{c_{ik}, c_{kj}\}$. Hence, when e is presented, we are guaranteed that c_{ik} and c_{kj} are still higher than their respective lower bounds S_{ik} and S_{kj} (otherwise E would cause some version spaces to collapse, and we could infer what we want on S_{ij} and G_{ij}). If e violates c'_{ij}, it also violates c_{ij} since c'_{ij} is subsumed by c_{ij}. It thus violates $\{c_{ik}, c_{kj}\}$ since c_{ij} is redundant wrt $(X, D, \{c_{ik}, c_{kj}\})$. As a result, we cannot decide that c'_{ij} is the necessary culprit for e's rejection since there exist constraints between S_{ik} and c_{ik}, and between S_{kj} and c_{kj}, which are both in the version space, and could reject e. So, G_{ij} cannot decrease under $\top$.

Regarding S_{ij}, it will increase higher than c_{ij} if and only if there exists $e \in E^+$ that violates c_{ij}. However, if e violates c_{ij}, it also violates $\{c_{ik}, c_{kj}\}$ (see above), which contradicts the assumption that $E \models \{c_{ik}, c_{kj}\}$. □

3.3 Formal Definition of Redundancy Rules

A constraint in a constraint network can be seen as a *constraint type* (or first order predicate) in which we substitute network variables for variables in the predicate. For example, the generic predicate $P(s,t) =$ '$s < t$' of arity $n(P) = 2$ can produce the constraint $x_1 < x_2$ in a constraint network involving x_1 and x_2, or the constraint $y_3 < y_5$ in another constraint network.

Since the process of modeling a problem is usually done using a given constraint toolkit, it seems reasonable to study the concept of redundancy with respect to the set of constraint types available in that toolkit. Let us first define the concept of redundancy rule for general constraint types.

Definition 2 (Redundancy rule) *Let T be a set of constraint types. The Horn clause*

$$\forall t_1, \ldots t_n \bigwedge_i P_i(t_{i_1} \ldots t_{i_{n(P_i)}}) \models Q(t_{j_1} \ldots t_{j_{n(Q)}})$$

*with $P_i \in T \ \forall i$, and $Q \in T$, is a **redundancy rule** wrt T iff there is at least one variable t_{j_h} in Q that appears in some P_i, and for any constraint network N for which a substitution[1] θ maps the rule into N, we have*

$$N_{-\theta(Q)} \models \theta(Q).$$

If $|\{P_i\}| = k$, we say that the rule is a k-redundancy rule.

We immediately focus our attention on redundancy rules in a binary constraints setting where, if in addition we work on a complete network of binary constraints, it is sufficient to deal with 2-redundancy rules [5].

Definition 3 (Binary redundancy rule) *Let T be a set of constraint types of arity 2. A **binary redundancy rule** is a redundancy rule wrt T of the form:*

$$\forall t_1, t_2, t_3, P_1(t_1, t_2) \wedge P_2(t_2, t_3) \models Q(t_1, t_3).$$

Example 1 The Horn clause $\forall x, y, z. (x \geq y) \wedge (y \geq z) \models (x \geq z)$ is a binary redundancy rule since any constraint network in which we have two constraints '$\geq$' such that the second argument of the first constraint is equal to the first argument of the second constraint subsumes the '$\geq$' constraint between the first argument of the first constraint and the second argument of the second constraint.

Given the set T of constraint types available in a toolkit, redundancy rules can be built for the toolkit independently of the problem we will acquire. Thus, redundancy rules can be included as part of the constraint toolkit, in much the same way as propagators are often included in constraint toolkits, at least for the most common constraints.

3.4 Redundancy Rules in CONACQ

We saw in Theorem 1 that it can sometimes occur that the local version space for the constraint between a pair of variables (x_i, x_j) can reach a state where it becomes impossible to make its general bound more specific (thus reducing its size) because it contains a constraint that is redundant with respect to the other constraints already learned by CONACQ. To avoid this problem, we can simply trigger the relevant redundancy rule from the toolkit each time its left-hand side is true, namely the rule becomes "*active*" in a version space.

Definition 4 (Active Redundancy Rule) *Given a binary rule $R = P_1(t_1, t_2) \wedge P_2(t_2, t_3) \models Q(t_1, t_3)$, a version space V, and a mapping θ substituting variables of V for variables in R, we say that R is **active** in V wrt θ if $P_1(\theta(t_1), \theta(t_2))$ is subsumed by $G(\theta(t_1), \theta(t_2))$, and $P_2(\theta(t_2), \theta(t_3))$ is subsumed by $G(\theta(t_2), \theta(t_3))$.*

---

[1] As in most toolkits, we require that θ is 'locally' injective, namely two different t_{i_h}'s in the same P_i cannot map on the same network variable.

Definition 5 (Satisfying a Redundancy Rule) *Let θ be a mapping substituting variables of a version space V for variables in a rule $R = P_1(t_1, t_2) \wedge P_2(t_2, t_3) \models Q(t_1, t_3)$. We say that R is satisfied on V wrt θ if $Q(\theta(t_1), \theta(t_3))$ is subsumed by $G(\theta(t_1), \theta(t_3))$.*

Thus, when a rule R is active with respect to a mapping θ, we can force it to be satisfied (or *apply* it) by modifying the general bound of the constraint on which θ maps its right hand side. This modification does not affect the set of possible networks admitted by the version space. We state this more formally in Definition 6 and Theorem 2.

Definition 6 (Version Space Equivalence) *Let V and V' be two version spaces defined on the same variables and bias. We say that V and V' are **equivalent** iff for any constraint network N obtained by picking a constraint between S_{ij} and G_{ij} for each (x_i, x_j) in V there exists a constraint network N' obtained the same way from V' such that N and N' have the same solutions.*

Theorem 2. *Let V be a version space. Let V' be the version space obtained after a rule R has been applied to V. If R was active on V, then V' and V are equivalent.*

Proof. Suppose there exists a constraint network N in V for which none of the constraint networks in V' have the same set of solutions. This means that the constraint r_{ij} added by the rule R has decreased the general bound G'_{ij} in V'. The constraints allowed by G'_{ij} all reject some solution of N (by assumption). This is necessarily due to r_{ij}. Thus, r_{ij} cannot be redundant wrt N. By definition of what an active redundancy rule is, we deduce that R cannot be active in V, which contradicts the assumption. □

This property guarantees that we can safely apply all the redundancy rules that are active, reducing the size of the version space while its semantics is not affected.

The complexity of applying all the binary rules in a version space is in $O(m \times |\mathcal{B}|^2)$, with $|\mathcal{B}|$ the number of constraint scopes in the bias and m the number of binary rules in the toolkit. For k-redundancy rules this is in $O(m \times |\mathcal{B}|^k)$. Applying k-redundancy rules to a constraint network is a relaxation of relational k-consistency [4]. However, relational k-consistency requires space exponential in the number of variables in the redundant constraint while in our approach we only generate constraints from the toolkit, thus keeping constant space for each constraint.

Example 2 We now apply the method above to example of Figure 1. After processing the examples $\{e_1^+, e_2^-, e_3^-\}$, we know that even in the loosest constraint network still possible, we have $x_1 \geq x_2$ and $x_2 \geq x_3$. Therefore, the rule described in Example 1 is active. By applying it, we can reduce the possible constraint types between x_1 and x_3 to $\{>, \geq\}$.

4 Higher-Order Redundancy

While redundancy rules can handle a particular type of redundancy, there are cases where applying these rules on the version space is not sufficient to find all redundancies. Redundancy rules are well-suited to discovering constraints that are redundant because of conjunctions of other constraints. However, as we shall show in Section 4.1, a constraint can be redundant because of a conjunction of *disjunctions* of constraints. We refer to this as higher-order redundancy. Since our redundancy rules are in the form of Horn clauses, they cannot tackle such redundancies. After a brief description of the way CONACQ stores the information about negative examples, we will show how to tackle these complex redundancies.

4.1 Another Example

In the scenario illustrated in Figure 2, we use the same set of variables and domains as those used in the example presented in Section 2. However, in this case the target network comprises the set of constraints $\{x_1 = x_2, x_1 = x_3, x_2 = x_3\}$. Furthermore, in this example all negative instances differ from e_1^+ by *at least* two constraints (see the table in Figure 2).

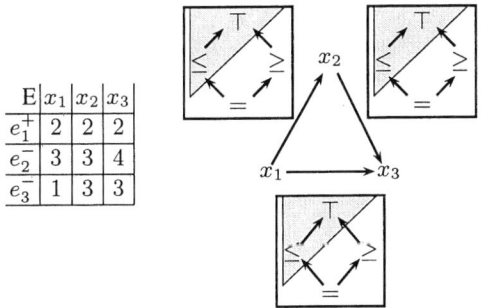

E	x_1	x_2	x_3
e_1^+	2	2	2
e_2^-	3	3	4
e_3^-	1	3	3

Fig. 2. None of the version spaces have converged.

After processing the positive example e_1^+, each version space contains four consistent hypotheses, the most specific hypothesis in each being $=$. The version spaces are depicted in Figure 2. However, each of the negative examples does not contain enough information to immediately eliminate any additional hypotheses from the version spaces for our constraints. For example, negative example e_2^- may be negative because of either constraint c_{12} or c_{23}, or indeed both. Therefore, none of the version spaces of the constraints in our example can be reduced further (indicated with light shading in Figure 2, as opposed to the darker shade used earlier to depict hypotheses being removed from a version space). The version spaces in this example each contain 4 hypotheses due to the disjunction of possible reasons that would classify the negative examples correctly.

Without any further information, particularly negative examples which differ from the positive example by one constraint, no further restrictions can be made on the version spaces of the constraints in our problem. Consequently, none of the version spaces converge. Simply applying redundancy rules also does not help. An alternative approach is required, which will be presented next.

4.2 Storing Negative Examples in CONACQ

As briefly described above, when a negative example e^- is presented to CONACQ it is encoded as a clause $cl_e = l_{ij}^{U_{ij}} \vee \ldots \vee l_{km}^{U_{km}}$ where U_{ij} is the set of most general constraint types available for c_{ij} that reject e^- (i.e., that are violated by e^-). The literal $l_{ij}^{U_{ij}}$ is true if any possible constraint type for c_{ij} in its local version space is at least as specific as the given bound U_{ij}. This is the case if any constraint type r in the general bound G_{ij} of c_{ij} is at least as specific as a constraint type in U_{ij}. This is the condition for c_{ij} to reject e^-. Hence, the clause cl_e means that at least one of the constraints c_{ij} having a literal $l_{ij}^{U_{ij}}$ in cl_e has to be at least as specific as its U_{ij} to reject e^-.

We should point out that a clause does not necessarily contain a literal for each constraint we have to find in the bias. Each constraint c_{ij} for which the specific bound S_{ij} is already more general than U_{ij} will not reject e^-. It is then useless to put a literal for it in the clause since this literal will be forced to be false. For example, if $e_k^- = \{x_1 = 1; x_2 = 1; x_3 = 3\}$ and $S_{12} = \{\geq\}$, c_{12} cannot reject e_k^-. In addition, not all elements of E^- have a stored clause in CONACQ. It can indeed appear that an example is already definitively rejected by some constraint in the version space. For example, take again the e_k^- above and imagine $G_{23} = \{\geq\}$. e_k^- cannot satisfy c_{23}. Hence, it is useless to add a clause in CONACQ to express that e_k^- should be rejected.

The set of all the clauses containing the necessary information about E^- is denoted by $\mathcal{K}$. Since a constraint network assigns a single constraint c_{ij} to each pair of variables (x_i, x_j), it leads to an interpretation for every literal $l_{ij}^{U_{ij}}$ in $\mathcal{K}$. By construction, it is guaranteed that for any constraint network leading to a satisfying interpretation for $\mathcal{K}$, all $e^- \in E^-$ are non-solutions. (See [2] for more details.)

4.3 Finding Higher-Order Redundancies

In the example in Section 4.1 we have seen a case where a constraint is implied by the set of negative examples received by CONACQ but redundancy rules are not able to detect this by themselves. However, all the information necessary to deduce this constraint is contained in the set of redundancy rules and the set $\mathcal{K}$ of clauses encoding the negative examples. The reason for their inability to detect it is that rules are in the form of Horn clauses that we apply only when *all* predicates in the left-hand side are true (i.e., we apply unit propagation on these clauses). To tackle this issue we can build the set $\mathcal{R}$ of all possible substitutions on the given bias for available rules. For each rule $R = P_1(t_1, t_2) \wedge P_2(t_2, t_3) \models Q(t_1, t_3)$, for each substitution θ that maps P_i's and Q on possible constraints in the bias, a clause $\neg l_{\theta(t_1),\theta(t_2)}^{P_1} \vee \neg l_{\theta(t_2),\theta(t_3)}^{P_2} \vee l_{\theta(t_1),\theta(t_3)}^{Q}$ is added to the set $\mathcal{R}$. This process can be done as soon as the bias is given, before the beginning of the acquisition process.

In addition, since the semantics of a literal l_{ij}^U is: 'c_{ij} is at least as specific as U', we need also to link literals involving the same constraint scope. For example, if we have $l_{ij}^>$ true, then a literal $l_{ij}^{\geq}$ should not be able to take the value false. Hence, we need a third set of clauses, the set $\mathcal{L}$ containing $\neg l_{ij}^U \vee l_{ij}^{U'}$ for each pair (x_i, x_j) such that U subsumes U'. These subsumption clauses between two literals l_{ij}^U and $l_{ij}^{U'}$ need only to be included if l_{ij}^U appears in $\mathcal{K}$ and subsumes $l_{ij}^{U'}$ that appears in $\mathcal{R}$. Adding subsumption clauses between two literals in $\mathcal{K}$ would not activate any more rules. This is an important property since the fact that $l_{ij}^{U'}$ comes from $\mathcal{R}$ implies that $|U'| = 1$, which ensures polynomial space for $\mathcal{L}$.

We now have a base of ground clauses, $\mathcal{K} \cup \mathcal{R} \cup \mathcal{L}$, that contains all available information about rules and negative examples. If a literal l_{ij}^{U} in $\mathcal{K} \cup \mathcal{R} \cup \mathcal{L}$ appears positively in all models of $\mathcal{K} \cup \mathcal{R} \cup \mathcal{L}$ (i.e., it belongs to the backbone [7]), we can reduce the local version space of c_{ij} to constraints at least as specific as U. By construction of $\mathcal{K} \cup \mathcal{R} \cup \mathcal{L}$, it is indeed impossible to assign c_{ij} to a constraint more general than U and at the same time reject all negative instances in E^-.

Therefore, after the presentation of a new negative instance e from E^-, we have to build the corresponding clause cl_e, add it to $\mathcal{K}$, update $\mathcal{L}$ if necessary, and test if the addition of cl_e causes some literal[2] to enter the backbone of $\mathcal{K} \cup \mathcal{R} \cup \mathcal{L}$.

The process that we described above guarantees that all the possible redundancies will be detected.

Theorem 3. *Given a version space V, a set $E = E^+ \cup E^-$ of examples, a constraint type r, and the sets $\mathcal{K}, \mathcal{R}, \mathcal{L}$ built as described above, if r is a possible constraint on (x_i, x_j) and r can be inferred from V, the set of rules of the toolkit, and E^-, then the literal l_{ij}^r is a member of the backbone of $\mathcal{K} \cup \mathcal{R} \cup \mathcal{L}$.*

Proof. Let r be a (most specific) possible constraint on (x_i, x_j) that can be inferred from V, the set of rules of the toolkit, and E^-. Suppose l_{ij}^r does not belong to the backbone of $\mathcal{K} \cup \mathcal{R} \cup \mathcal{L}$. By assumption, r is the head of some rules in the toolkit (otherwise CONACQ by itself can learn r on (x_i, x_j)). Then, l_{ij}^r is the head of a subset $\mathcal{R}'$ of the rules in $\mathcal{R}$. Then there exists a model M of $\mathcal{K} \cup \mathcal{R} \cup \mathcal{L}$ for which none of the rules $R \in \mathcal{R}'$ has all the literals of its tail set to true. There are two cases. Either none of the networks N_M built from M allow a solution violating r on (x_i, x_j), which means that a rule that would infer l_{ij}^r from M is missing in $\mathcal{R}$, or some N_M allows solutions violating r on (x_i, x_j), which means that r cannot be inferred since there exists a network rejecting all E^- (by construction of N_M), and allowing solutions rejected by r on (x_i, x_j). Both cases contradict the assumption. Finally, if r was not the most specific constraint that could be learned on (x_i, x_j) (for example $r = '\leq'$ while $l_{ij}^<$ was inferred) the proof holds for the most specific constraint r', and the clauses added to $\mathcal{L}$ permit to infer l_{ij}^r from $l_{ij}^{r'}$. □

However, this process is quite expensive from a computational point of view, since testing if a literal belongs to the backbone of a formula is a coNP-complete problem. This prevents the use of such a technique on big formulae, but as we are concerned with an interactive acquisition process, it is reasonable to assume that the version spaces we need to handle will be small enough to permit a human user to deal with them, and consequently we expect that the speed-of-response for backbone detection will be acceptable. The experimental section will discuss this feature more deeply.

---

[2] Note that a literal is a candidate to enter the backbone only if it appears in the right-hand side of a Horn clause from $\mathcal{R}$ (or it belongs to a unary clause, obviously). Furthermore, the backbone cannot contain negative literals since $\mathcal{R}$ and $\mathcal{L}$ are Horn bases and $\mathcal{K}$ contains only positive clauses.

Example 3 We now apply the above method to the example presented in Section 4.1. The set $\mathcal{R}$ of redundancy rules used in this example is presented in Table 2. It provides a subset of possible binary rules associated with the bias in Figure 1(a). As presented previously, the set $\mathcal{L}$ is built dynamically only when required by $\mathcal{K}$ and $\mathcal{R}$, so we initialize it to $\emptyset$.

Table 2. Binary redundancy rules for the sample problem.

r_1	$l_{12}^{\geq} \wedge l_{23}^{\geq} \models l_{13}^{\geq}$
r_2	$l_{13}^{\geq} \wedge l_{23}^{\leq} \models l_{12}^{\geq}$
r_3	$l_{13}^{\leq} \wedge l_{23}^{\geq} \models l_{12}^{\leq}$
r_4	$l_{12}^{\leq} \wedge l_{23}^{\leq} \models l_{13}^{\leq}$
r_5	$l_{12}^{\leq} \wedge l_{13}^{\geq} \models l_{23}^{\geq}$
r_6	$l_{12}^{\geq} \wedge l_{13}^{\leq} \models l_{23}^{\leq}$

After receiving e_2^-, $\mathcal{K} = \{(l_{13}^{\geq} \vee l_{23}^{\geq})\}$, to apply the technique presented in Section 4.3, we test if either $l_{13}^{\geq}$ or $l_{23}^{\geq}$ belong to the backbone of $\mathcal{K} \cup \mathcal{R} \cup \mathcal{L}$. However, running a SAT solver allows us to determine that both $\mathcal{K} \cup \mathcal{R} \cup \mathcal{L} \cup \{\neg l_{13}^{\geq}\}$ and $\mathcal{K} \cup \mathcal{R} \cup \mathcal{L} \cup \{\neg l_{23}^{\geq}\}$ have solutions. Since the backbone detection did not find any literal, at this stage, we cannot deduce anything more than using previous methods.

However, after receiving e_3^-, $\mathcal{K} = \{(l_{13}^{\geq} \vee l_{23}^{\geq}), (l_{12}^{\geq} \vee l_{13}^{\geq})\}$ we detect the new backbone. We run a SAT solver on $\mathcal{R} \cup \mathcal{K} \cup \mathcal{L} \cup \{\neg l_{13}^{\geq}\}$ and because of the minimal conflict set $\mathcal{K} \cup \{r_1\} \cup \{\neg l_{13}^{\geq}\}$, it fails. Therefore, $l_{13}^{\geq}$ belongs to the backbone and we can use this to refine the version space of constraint c_{13}, removing from it the constraint types $\leq$ and $\top$.

In this example, it is clear that the backbone detection on $\mathcal{K} \cup \mathcal{R} \cup \mathcal{L}$ has permitted us to detect (and learn) a redundant constraint that redundancy rules alone did not.

5 Empirical Study

To compare the approaches to exploiting redundancy to improve the quality of the acquired CSP that we have proposed in this paper, we studied their effects on a sample class of CSP. The bias used in this experiment is the same as that presented in Figure 1(a). Our experiments involved generating target CSPs, which we then attempted to acquire by presenting examples of solutions and non-solutions of them to an acquisition system based on either: (a) CONACQ on its own (CONACQ *standard*); (b) CONACQ using redundancy rules only (CONACQ + *rules*); (c) CONACQ using both redundancy rules and backbone detection (CONACQ +*rules* + *backbone*). These form the columns in Table 3.

In each case we randomly computed a representable set of solutions (non-solutions) to the target CSP which were used as a source of positive (respectively, negative) examples for the acquisition system. We generated target CSPs with 12 variables, 12 values in each domain, 30 constraints and varied the degree of redundancy in them. Clearly, during the acquisition process it is not known between which variables there are constraints so we must assume a complete graph comprising 66 constraints, giving us 66 local version spaces.

The number of examples used in each experiment was equal to the number required for CONACQ $+rules + backbone$ to converge. However, we set a maximum number of examples at 1000 after which we would terminate the acquisition process.

For each acquisition system setup (the 3 different configurations of CONACQ), we recorded the total time (in seconds, *secs*) required to process the set of examples and the final size of the version space, denoted by $|VS|$. The number of examples used is denoted by $\#Exs$ in the last column. We present averages of 10 runs of the experiment.

We have studied the effects of controlling the redundancy in each CSP in two ways (giving us the rows in Table 3). Firstly, we introduced patterns of constraints in the target network of various lengths. In the experiment we used lengths based on the number of variables in the problem: specifically, we use lengths n, $n/2$ and $n/3$ (*Length* column). Secondly, for each length of pattern we selected a pattern of constraints with controlled characteristics and introduced these into the target network. In the experiment we selected patterns of the same constraint selected either from the set $\{\leq, \geq\}$ (looser constraints) or $\{<, =, >\}$ (tighter constraints). For example, a path of length n based on $\{<, =, >\}$ is $x_1 > x_2 > \ldots > x_{12}$, while a path of length $n/2$ based on $\{\leq, \geq\}$ is $x_1 \leq x_2 \leq \ldots \leq x_6$ (see $\{constraints\}$ column). As a "straw-man" we also present results for a target CSP where no pattern was introduced into the network. Our results are presented in Table 3.

It can be clearly seen from Table 3 that, in terms of the size of the resultant version spaces, exploiting redundancy rules with CONACQ improves upon CONACQ alone in all situations. However, exploiting redundancy rules leads to an increase in the amount of time required by the the acquisition to process the set of examples since it relies on the construction of $\mathcal{R}$, derived from the set of negative examples. Combining backbone detection and redundancy rules with CONACQ improves upon CONACQ with redundancy rules, in terms of version space size, but offers a considerably slower response time due to the use of the SAT solver[3].

Furthermore, we can see that as the level of redundancy in the target problem increases, from $n/3$ to n, regardless of the constraints involved in the redundant pattern, the ability of standard CONACQ to converge deteriorates dramatically. It is also interesting to note that CONACQ with redundancy rules also does progressively worse on these networks. This is most clearly noticeable if one compares the top-line of the table, where no redundant pattern was enforced, with the last line in the table, where a pattern of length n was present, keeping the number of examples constant in both cases.

Simply combining redundancy rules with CONACQ is sufficient to detect much of the redundancy that is completely discovered by backbone detection. Specifically, comparing the standard CONACQ column with the CONACQ $+ rules$ column, we can see that there are orders-of-magnitude differences in the size of the version spaces, with a very minor increase in processing time (approximately double in most cases). Note that CONACQ $+rules + backbone$ requires and order of magnitude more time, but achieves convergence.

---

[3] The SAT solver used for backbone detection is zchaff, version 2003.12.04, http://ee.princeton.edu/~chaff/zchaff.php.

Table 3. Comparison of the capability of each acquisition system to exploit redundancy in the larger problem studied (12 variables, 12 values, 30 constraints).

Redundant Pattern Length {constraints}		CONACQ standard $\|VS\|$ (secs)	CONACQ +rules $\|VS\|$ (secs)	CONACQ +rules +backbone $\|VS\|$ (secs)	#Exs
none		4.29×10^9 (<1)	6.71×10^7 (3)	1.68×10^7 (46)	1000
n/3	$\{\leq, \geq\}$	4.10×10^3 (<1)	64 (2)	1 (29)	360
n/2	$\{\leq, \geq\}$	1.72×10^{10} (<1)	4.10×10^3 (2)	1 (23)	190
n	$\{\leq, \geq\}$	1.44×10^{17} (<1)	2.62×10^5 (2)	1 (21)	90
n/3	$\{=, <, >\}$	2.68×10^8 (<1)	1.02×10^3 (2)	1 (27)	280
n/2	$\{=, <, >\}$	7.38×10^{19} (<1)	4.19×10^7 (2)	1 (23)	170
n	$\{=, <, >\}$	2.08×10^{34} (<1)	6.87×10^{10} (2)	1 (21)	70
n	$\{=, <, >\}$	5.07×10^{30} (<1)	1.07×10^9 (3)	1 (40)	1000

Finally, the effect of the tightness of the redundancy pattern introduced into the problem has interesting consequences. On a target network involving looser redundant patterns, those from $\{\leq, \geq\}$, positive instances play a central role in the acquisition of the problem. Specifically, more of them are required for convergence. Furthermore, after receiving positive instances, each local version space is smaller than would be the case if the redundant patterns were made up of the tighter constraints from $\{=, <, >\}$. For example, when $\geq$ is the target, $\{\geq, \top\}$ is the largest possible version space, while for $>$ it is $\{>, \neq, \geq, \top\}$. This explains the exponential difference in version space size between tighter and looser target networks presented in Table 3.

In summary, this experimental evaluation demonstrates that CONACQ on its own is insufficient to fully exploit redundancy during the acquisition process and that convergence may not be possible. The more sophisticated approaches that we propose based on redundancy rules and backbone detection are far superior. However, there is a trade-off to be considered between the need to find the tightest specification on the target network versus the response time of the acquisition system.

We have seen that adding backbone detection and redundancy rules together to enhance CONACQ is best in terms of convergence, but has a high response time cost. Just exploiting redundancy rules with CONACQ offers a very fast response time, with the abilities to converge quite significantly also. Obviously, it is an application-specific and/or problem-specific issue how this tradeoff should be dealt with. For example, in an interactive context, speed-of-response is a critical factor and, therefore, simply relying on redundancy rules may be a reasonable compromise. In such an application backbone detection could be run as a background process, further refining the version spaces that represent the target CSP.

6 Conclusions and Future Work

In this paper we were concerned with automating the formulation of constraint satisfaction problems from examples of solutions and non-solutions. We have combined techniques from the fields of machine learning and constraint programming. In particular we have presented a portfolio of approaches to exploiting the semantics of the constraints that we acquire to improve the efficiency of the acquisition process.

We have demonstrated that the CONACQ algorithm on its own is insufficient to fully handle redundancy during the acquisition process. The more sophisticated approaches that we propose based on redundancy rules and backbone detection are far superior. However, there is a tradeoff to be considered between the need to find the tightest specification on the target network versus the response time of the acquisition system. We have seen that adding backbone detection and redundancy rules together to enhance CONACQ is best but has a high response time cost, while just exploiting redundancy rules with CONACQ offers a very fast response time, with the abilities to converge quite significantly towards the target CSP.

Our future work in this area will look at a number of important issues that must be addressed in real-world acquisition contexts. For example, techniques for handling noise and errors in the process are of critical importance, particularly if human users are providing the training examples [9].

References

1. C.W. Choi, J.H.M. Lee, and P.J. Stuckey. Propagation redundancy in redundant modelling. In *Proceedings of CP-2003*, volume LNCS 2833, pages 229–243. Springer, September 2003.
2. R. Coletta, C. Bessiere, B. O'Sullivan, E.C. Freuder, S. O'Connell, and J. Quinqueton. Constraint acquisition as semi-automatic modeling. In *Proceedings of AI'03*, pages 111–124.
3. A. Dechter and R. Dechter. Removing redundancies in constraint networks. In *Proceedings of AAAI-87*, pages 105–109, 1987.
4. R. Dechter and P. van Beek. Local and global relational consistency. *Theoretical Computer Science*, 173(1):283–308, 1997.
5. A. Mackworth. Consistency in networks of relations. *Artificial Intelligence*, 8:99–118, 1977.
6. T. Mitchell. Generalization as search. *Artificial Intelligence*, 18(2):203–226, 1982.
7. R. Monasson, R. Zecchina, S. Kirkpatrick, B. Selman, and L. Ttroyansky. Determining computational complexity from characteristic 'phase transition'. *Nature*, 400:133–137, 1999.
8. C.D. Page and A.M. Frisch. Generalization and learnability: A study of constrained atoms. In S.H.. Muggleton, editor, *Inductive Logic Programming*, pages 29–61. 1992.
9. M. Sebag. Delaying the choice of bias: A disjunctive version space approach. In *Proceedings of ICML-1996*, pages 444–452, 1996.
10. B.M. Smith. Succeed-first or fail-first: A case study in variable and value ordering. In *Proceedings of PACT-1997*, pages 321–330, 1997.

Disjoint, Partition and Intersection Constraints for Set and Multiset Variables*

Christian Bessiere[1], Emmanuel Hebrard[2], Brahim Hnich[2], and Toby Walsh[2]

[1] LIRMM, Montpelier, France
bessiere@lirmm.fr
[2] Cork Constraint Computation Centre, University College Cork, Ireland
{e.hebrard,b.hnich,tw}@4c.ucc.ie

Abstract. We have started a systematic study of global constraints on set and multiset variables. We consider here disjoint, partition, and intersection constraints in conjunction with cardinality constraints. These global constraints fall into one of three classes. In the first class, we show that we can decompose the constraint without hindering bound consistency. No new algorithms therefore need be developed for such constraints. In the second class, we show that decomposition hinders bound consistency but we can present efficient polynomial algorithms for enforcing bound consistency. Many of these algorithms exploit a dual viewpoint, and call upon existing global constraints for finite-domain variables like the global cardinality constraint. In the third class, we show that enforcing bound consistency is NP-hard. We have little choice therefore but to enforce a lesser level of local consistency when the size of such constraints grows.

1 Introduction

Global (or non-binary) constraints are one of the factors central to the success of constraint programming [7, 8, 1]. Global constraints permit the user to model a problem easily (by compactly specifying common patterns that occur in many problems) and solve it efficiently (by calling fast and effective constraint propagation algorithms). Many problems naturally involve sets and multisets. For example, the social golfers problem (prob010 at CSPLib.org) partitions a set of golfers into foursomes. Set or multiset variables have therefore been incorporated into most of the major constraint solvers (see, for example, [3, 6, 5, 11] for sets, [4] for multisets – under the name *bags*). In a recent report, Sadler and Gervet describe a propagator for a global disjoint constraint on set variables with a fixed cardinality [10]. The aim of this paper is to study other such global constraints on set and multiset variables. Using the techniques proposed in [2], we have proved that some of these global constraints are NP-hard to propagate. For example, both the atmost1-incommon and distinct constraints on sets of fixed cardinality proposed in [9] are NP-hard to propagate. We prove that others are polynomial but not decomposable without hindering propagation. We therefore give efficient algorithms for enforcing bound consistency on such constraints.

---

* The last three authors are supported by Science Foundation Ireland and an ILOG software grant. We wish to thank Zeynep Kiziltan for useful comments.

2 Formal Background

A multiset is an unordered list of elements in which repetition is allowed. We assume that the elements of sets and multisets are integers. Basic operations on sets generalize to multisets. We let $occ(m, X)$ be the number of occurrences of m in the multiset X. Multiset union and intersection are defined by the identities $occ(m, X \cup Y) = max(occ(m, X), occ(m, Y))$ and $occ(m, X \cap Y) = min(occ(m, X), occ(m, Y))$. Finally, we write $|X|$ for the cardinality of the set or multiset X, and use lower case to denote constants and upper case to denote variables.

An integer variable N is a variable whose domain is a set of integers, $dom(N)$. The minimum (maximum) element of N is denoted by $min(N)$ ($max(N)$). A set (resp. multiset) variable X is a variable whose domain is a set of sets (resp. multisets) of integers, given by an upper bound $ub(X)$ and a lower bound $lb(X)$ (i.e., $lb(X) \subseteq X \subseteq ub(X)$). We define bound consistency for integer, set and multiset variables. We can therefore reason about constraints which simultaneously involve integer, set and multiset variables. An assignment is bound valid if the value given to each set or multiset variable is within these bounds, and the value given to each integer variable is between the minimum and maximum integers in its domain. A constraint is bound consistent (denoted by $BC(C)$) iff for each set or multiset variable X, $ub(X)$ (resp. $lb(X)$) is the union (resp. intersection) of all the values for X that belong to a bound valid assignment satisfying the constraint, and for each integer variable N, there is a bound valid assignment that satisfies the constraint for the maximum and minimum values in the domain of X. An alternative definition of BC for set and multiset variables is that the characteristic function (a vector of 0/1 variables) for each set variable, or the occurrence representation (a vector of integer variables) for each multiset variable is bound consistent [12]. We say that a constraint is "decomposable" if there exists a decomposition into a polynomial number of bounded arity constraints, and this decomposition does not hinder bound consistency. We will also use generalized arc consistency (GAC). A constraint is GAC iff every value for every variable can be extended to a solution of the constraint.

3 Taxonomy of Global Constraints

Global constraints over set and multiset variables can be composed from the following (more primitive) constraints:

Cardinality constraints: Many problems involve constraints on the cardinality of a set or multiset. For example, each shift must contain at least five nurses.
Intersection constraints: Many problems involve constraints on the intersection between any pair of sets or multisets. For example, shifts must have at least one person in common.
Partition constraints: Many problems involve partitioning a set or multiset. For example, orders must be partitioned to slabs in the steel mill slab design problem.
Ordering constraints: Many problems involve sets or multisets which are indistinguishable. For example, if each group in the social golfers problem is represented by a set then, as groups are symmetric, these sets can be permuted. We can break this symmetry by ordering the set variables.

Counting constraints: We often wish to model situations when there are constraints on the number of resources (values) used in a solution. For example, we might have set variables for the nurses on each shift and want to count the number of times each nurse has a shift during the monthly roster.

Weight and colour constraints: Many problems involve sets in which there is a weight or colour associated with each element of a set and there are constraints on the weights or colours in each set. For example, the weight of the set of orders assigned to a slab should be less than the slab capacity.

Tables 1 and 2 summarize some of the results presented in this paper. Given a collection of set or multiset variables, Table 1 shows different combinations of restrictions on the cardinality of the intersection of any pair of set or multiset variables (rows) with constraints restricting the cardinality of each set or multiset variable (columns). For instance, the top left corner is the Disjoint constraint, in which where all pairs of set or multiset variables are disjoint (i.e., their intersection is empty) and there is no restriction on the cardinality of the individual sets or multisets. On the other hand, the NEDisjoint also ensures that each set or multiset is non-empty. Table 2 is similar to Table 1, except that we also ensure that the set or multiset variables form a partition. Constraints like Disjoint, Partition, and FCDisjoint on set variables have already appeared in the literature [3, 5, 9, 10, 4].

All results apply to set or multiset variables unless otherwise indicated. In each entry, we name the resulting global constraint, state whether it is tractable to enforce BC on it and whether it is decomposable. For example, the FCPartition constraint over set variables (see Table 2) is not decomposable but we can maintain BC on it in polynomial time. Over multiset variables, the constraint becomes intractable.

Table 1. Intersection × Cardinality.

$\forall k \ldots$		$\forall i < j \ldots$			
		$\|X_i \cap X_j\| = 0$	$\|X_i \cap X_j\| \leq k$	$\|X_i \cap X_j\| \geq k$	$\|X_i \cap X_j\| = k$
-		Disjoint	Intersect$_\leq$	Intersect$_\geq$	Intersect$_=$
		polynomial	polynomial	polynomial	NP-hard
		decomposable	decomposable	decomposable	not decomposable
$\|X_k\| > 0$		NEDisjoint	NEIntersect$_\leq$	NEIntersect$_\geq$	FCIntersect$_=$
		polynomial	polynomial	polynomial	NP-hard
		not decomposable	decomposable	decomposable	not decomposable
$\|X_k\| = m_k$		FCDisjoint	FCIntersect$_\leq$	FCIntersect$_\geq$	NEIntersect$_=$
		poly on sets, NP-hard on multisets	NP-hard	NP-hard	NP-hard
		not decomposable	not decomposable	not decomposable	not decomposable

Table 2. Partition + Intersection × Cardinality.

$\forall k \ldots$		$\bigcup_i X_i = X \wedge \forall i < j \ldots$			
		$\|X_i \cap X_j\| = 0$	$\|X_i \cap X_j\| \leq k$	$\|X_i \cap X_j\| \geq k$	$\|X_i \cap X_j\| = k$
-		Partition: polynomial	?	?	?
		decomposable			
$\|X_k\| > 0$		NEPartition: polynomial	?	?	?
		not decomposable			
$\|X_k\| = m_k$		FCPartition	?	?	?
		polynomial on sets, NP-hard on multisets			
		not decomposable			

4 Disjoint Constraints

The Disjoint constraint on set or multiset variables is decomposable into binary empty intersection constraints without hindering bound consistency [12]. When it is over sets, it appears in a number of constraint solvers such as ILOG Solver (under the name IlcAllNullIntersect) and ECLiPSe. On multisets, the binary version of Disjoint appears in ILOG Configurator [4].

We now study bound consistency on the NEDisjoint and FCDisjoint constraints over set and multiset variables. These constraints are not decomposable so we present algorithms for enforcing BC on them or we prove intractability.

4.1 FCDisjoint

A filtering algorithm for FCDisjoint over set variables was independently proposed in [10]. We give here an alternative polynomial algorithm that uses a dual encoding with integer variables (also briefly described at the end of [10]). J.F. Puget has pointed out to us that this algorithm is very similar to the propagation algorithm used in ILOG Solver for the IlcAllNullIntersect constraint when cardinalities are specified for the set variables involved, and when the "extended" propagation mode is activated. We further show that bound consistency on FCDisjoint is NP-hard on multisets.

When $X_1, \ldots, X_n$ are set variables and $k_1, \ldots, k_n$ are given constants, we can achieve BC on a FCDisjoint$(X_1, \ldots, X_n, k_1, \ldots, k_n)$ constraint as follows:

Algorithm BC-FCD-Sets

1. For all $v \in \bigcup ub(X_i)$, introduce an integer variable Y_v with $dom(Y_v) = \{\}$
2. Initialize the domain of each Y_v as follows:
   (a) $dom(Y_v) \leftarrow \{i \mid v \in lb(X_i)\}$
   (b) if $|dom(Y_v)| > 1$ then **fail**
   (c) if $|dom(Y_v)| = 0$ then $dom(Y_v) \leftarrow \{i \mid v \in ub(X_i)\} \cup \{n+1\}$ /* $n+1$ is a dummy */
3. Maintain GAC on gcc$(Y, \{1..n+1\}, B)$ where Y is the array of Y_v's, and B is the array of the corresponding bounds of the i's where for all $i \leq n$ we have $B[i] = k_i..k_i$ and $B[n+1] = 0..\infty$
4. Maintain the following channelling constraints, for all $i \leq n$ and for all v:
   (a) $i \in dom(Y_v) \leftrightarrow v \in ub(X_i)$
   (b) $dom(Y_v) = \{i\} \leftrightarrow v \in lb(X_i)$

Remark. gcc$(Y, \{1..n+1\}, B)$ is the global cardinality constraint that imposes that in any assignment S of the variables Y, the value i from $\{1..n+1\}$ appears a number of times in the range $B[i]$. The dummy value $n+1$ is necessary to prevent a failure of the gcc when an Y_v cannot take any value in $1..n$ (i.e., value v cannot be used by any X_i).

We first prove the following lemma.

Lemma 1. *Define the one-to-one mapping between assignments S of the dual variables Y and assignments S' of the original set variables X_i by: $v \in S'[X_i]$ iff $S[Y_v] = i$. Then S is consistent with gcc in step (3) of BC-FCD-Sets iff S' is consistent for FCDisjoint.*

Proof. ($\Rightarrow$) We prove that S' is:

Disjoint: Each dual variable Y_v has a unique value, say i. Therefore in S' a value v cannot appear in more than one of the variables $X_1 \ldots X_n$. In the case where $Y_v = n+1$, v does not belong to any set variable assignment.

Fixed Cardinality: gcc ensures that the values i are used by exactly k_i dual variables Y_{v_j}. Hence, $|S'[X_i]| = k_i$.

($\Leftarrow$) We prove that S is:

Consistent with gcc: By construction of Y, if $|S'[X_i]| = k_i$ for each $i \in 1..n$, each i will appear exactly k_i times in S, thus satisfying the gcc. (The dummy value $n+1$ has no restriction on its number of occurrences in Y.)

Consistent with Y *domains:* By construction. □

In the algorithm BC-FCD-Sets, let d be the number of Y_v variables introduced, where each Y_v has domain of size at most $n+1$.

Theorem 1. *BC-FCD-Sets is a sound and complete algorithm for enforcing bound consistency on FCDisjoint with set variables, that runs in $O(nd^2)$ time.*

Proof. Soundness. A value v is pruned from $ub(X_i)$ in step (4) of BC-FCD-Sets either because i was not put in $dom(Y_v)$ in step (2) or because the gcc has removed i from $dom(Y_v)$ in step (3). Lemma 1 tells us that both cases imply that v cannot belong to X_i in a satisfying tuple for FCDisjoint. A value v is added to $lb(X_i)$ in step (4) if $dom(Y_v) = \{i\}$ after applying GAC on the gcc. From Lemma 1 we deduce that any satisfying tuple for FCDisjoint necessarily contains v in X_i. We must also show that the algorithm does not fail if FCDisjoint can be made bound consistent. BC-FCD-Sets can fail in only two different ways. First, it fails in step (2) if a value belongs to two different lower bounds. Clearly, FCDisjoint cannot then be made bound consistent. Second, it fails in step (3) if the gcc cannot be made GAC. In this case, we know by Lemma 1 that FCDisjoint cannot then be made bound consistent.

Completeness. Let $v \in ub(X_i)$ after step (4). Then, $i \in dom(Y_v)$ after step (3). The gcc being GAC, there exists an assignment S satisfying gcc, with $S[Y_v] = i$. Lemma 1 guarantees there exists an assignment S' with $\{v\} \subseteq S'[X_i]$. In addition, let $v \notin lb(X_i)$ after step (4). Then, there exists $j \in dom(Y_v), j \neq i$, after step (3). Thus, there is an assignment S satisfying gcc with $S[Y_v] = j$. Lemma 1 tells us that there is a satisfying assignment S' of FCDisjoint with v not in $S'[X_i]$.

Complexity. Step (1) is in $O(d)$, and step (2) in $O(nd)$. Step (3) has the complexity of the gcc, namely $O(nd^2)$ since we have d variables with domains of size at most $n+1$. Step (4) is in $O(nd)$. Thus, BC-FCD-Sets is in $O(nd^2)$. □

Theorem 2. *Enforcing bound consistency on FCDisjoint with multiset variables is NP-hard.*

Proof. We transform 3SAT into the problem of the existence of a satisfying assignment for FCDisjoint. Let $F = \{c_1, \ldots, c_m\}$ be a 3CNF on the Boolean variables $x_1, \ldots, x_n$. We build the constraint FCDisjoint$(X_1, \ldots, X_{3n+m}, k_1, \ldots, k_{3n+m})$ as follows. Each time a Boolean variable x_i appears positively (resp. negatively) in a clause c_j, we create a value v_i^j (resp. w_i^j). For each Boolean variable x_i, we create two values p_i and n_i. Then, we build the $3n + m$ multiset variables as follows.

1. $\forall i \in 1..n$, /* X_i will take the p_i's iff $x_i = 1$ */
   (a) k_i = number of occurrences of x_i in a clause
   (b) $\{\} \subseteq X_i \subseteq \{v_i^j \mid x_i \in c_j\} \cup \{p_i, \ldots, p_i\}$ /*k_i copies of p_i*/
2. $\forall i \in n+1..2n$, /* X_i will take the n_i's iff $x_i = 0$ */
   (a) k_i = number of occurrences of $\neg x_i$ in a clause
   (b) $\{\} \subseteq X_i \subseteq \{w_i^j \mid \neg x_i \in c_j\} \cup \{n_i, \ldots, n_i\}$ /*k_i copies of n_i*/
3. $\forall i \in 2n+1..3n$, /* X_i forces X_{i-n} and X_{i-2n} to be consistent */
   (a) $k_i = 1$
   (b) $\{\} \subseteq X_i \subseteq \{n_i, p_i\}$
4. $\forall j \in 1..m$, /* X_{3n+j} represents the clause c_j */
   (a) $k_{3n+j} = 1$
   (b) $\{\} \subseteq X_{3n+j} \subseteq \{v_{i_1}^j, w_{i_2}^j, v_{i_3}^j\}$ if $c_j = x_{i_1} \vee \neg x_{i_2} \vee x_{i_3}$

Let M be a model of F. We build the assignment S on the X_i's such that $\forall i \in 1..n$, if $M[x_i] = 1$ then $S[X_i] = \{p_i, \ldots, p_i\}$, $S[X_{i+n}] = \{w_i^j \in ub(X_{i+n})\}$, $S[X_{i+2n}] = \{n_i\}$, else $S[X_i] = \{v_i^j \in ub(X_i)\}$, $S[X_{i+n}] = \{n_i, \ldots, n_i\}$, $S[X_{i+2n}] = \{p_i\}$.

By construction, the cardinalities k_i are satisfied and the disjointness are satisfied on $X_1 \ldots, X_{3n}$. In addition, the construction ensures that if a Boolean variable x_i is true in M (resp. false in M) none of the v_i^j (resp. w_i^j) are used and all the w_i^j (resp. v_i^j) are already taken by $X_1 \ldots, X_{3n}$. Thus, $\forall j \in 1..m$, $S[X_{3n+j}]$ is assigned one of the values v_i^j or w_i^j representing a true literal x_i or $\neg x_i$ in M. And M being a 3SAT model, we are sure that there exists such values not already taken by $X_1 \ldots, X_{3n}$. Therefore, S satisfies FCDisjoint.

Consider now an assignment S of the X_i's consistent with FCDisjoint. Build the interpretation M such that $M[x_i] = 1$ iff $S[X_{i+2n}] = \{n_i\}$. Thanks to the disjointness and cardinalities among $X_1 \ldots, X_{3n}$, we guarantee that if $S[X_{i+2n}] = \{n_i\}$ all the w_i^j are already taken by X_{i+n}, and if $S[X_{i+2n}] = \{p_i\}$ all the v_i^j are already taken by X_i, so that they cannot belong to any X_{3n+j}. But S satisfying FCDisjoint, we know that for each $j \in 1..m$, X_{3n+j} is assigned a value consistent with $X_1 \ldots, X_{3n}$. Therefore, M is a model of F.

As a result, deciding the existence of a satisfying assignment for FCDisjoint with multiset variables is NP-complete. Then, deciding whether GAC finds a wipe out on the occurrence representation is coNP-complete. In addition, on the transformation we use, if GAC detects a wipe then BC does[1] (because of the way p_i and n_i values are set). So, deciding whether BC detects a wipe out is coNP-complete, and enforcing bound consistency on FCDisjoint with multiset variables is NP-hard. □

4.2 NEDisjoint

The constraint NEDisjoint($X_1, \ldots, X_n$) on set variables can be seen as a particular case of constraint FCDisjoint in which the cardinality of the variables X_i can vary

---

[1] GAC on the occurrence representation of multisets is in general not equivalent to BC (whilst on sets it is). If $ub(X_1) = ub(X_2) = \{1, 1, 2, 2\}$, and $k_1 = k_2 = 2$, GAC on the occurrence representation of FCDisjoint removes the possibility for X_1 to have 1 occurrence of 1. BC does not remove anything since the bounds 0 and 2 for $occ(1, X_1)$ are consistent.

from 1 to ∞ instead of being fixed to k_i. Since the way the algorithm BC-FCD-Sets is written permits to express such an interval of values for the cardinality of the set variables X_i, the algorithm BC-NED-Sets is a very simple modification of it. In step (3) of BC-FCD-Sets it is indeed sufficient to assign $B[i]$ to $1..\infty$ instead of $k_i..k_i$, for $1 \leq i \leq n$. J.F. Puget has pointed out to us that the IlcAllNullIntersect constraint in "extended" mode will also achieve BC on non-empty set variables.

When NEDisjoint involves multiset variables, BC remains polynomial. In fact, it is sufficient to transform the multisets in sets and to use BC-NED-Sets on the obtained sets. Once BC achieved on these sets, we just have to restore the initial number of occurrences, noted init-occ, for each remaining value. The cardinality of the multisets are not bounded above, so that if one value has support, any number of occurrences of the same value have support also.

Algorithm BC-NED-Msets

1. for each $i \in 1..n$, v occurring in $ub(X_i)$ do
   init-occ$_{ub}(X_i, v) \leftarrow occ(v, ub(X_i))$; $occ(v, ub(X_i)) \leftarrow 1$
   init-occ$_{lb}(X_i, v) \leftarrow occ(v, lb(X_i))$; $occ(v, lb(X_i)) \leftarrow min(1, \text{init-occ}_{lb}(X_i, v))$
2. BC-NED-Sets$(X_1, \ldots, X_n)$
3. for each $i \in 1..n$, $v \in ub(X_i)$ do
   $occ(v, ub(X_i)) \leftarrow$ init-occ$_{ub}(X_i, v)$
   if $v \in lb(X_i)$ then $occ(v, lb(X_i)) \leftarrow max(1, \text{init-occ}_{lb}(X_i, v))$

5 Partition Constraints

The Partition constraint is decomposable into binary empty intersection constraints and ternary union constraints involving n additional variables without hindering bound consistency [12]. It appears in a number of constraint solvers such as ILOG Solver (under the name IlcPartition) and ECLiPSe when it is over sets. On the other hand, the non-empty and fixed cardinality partition constraints are not decomposable. We therefore present algorithms for enforcing BC on them or we prove intractability.

5.1 FCPartition

It is polynomial to enforce BC on the FCPartition constraint on set variables, but NP-hard on multisets. On set variables, enforcing BC on FCPartition is very similar to enforcing BC on FCDisjoint. Indeed, if the set X being partitioned is fixed, then we can simply decompose a fixed cardinality partition constraint into a fixed cardinality disjoint, union and cardinality constraints without hindering bound consistency.[2] If X is not fixed, we need to do slightly more reasoning to ensure that the X_i's are a partition of X. We present here the additional lines necessary to deal with this.

Line numbers with a prime represent lines modified wrt BC-FCD-Sets. The others are additional lines.

---

[2] As in the FCDisjoint case, J.F. Puget tells us that the filtering algorithm of the IlcPartition constraint in [5] uses a similar approach when the "extended" mode is set.

Algorithm BC-FCP-Sets

1'. For all $v \in ub(X)$, introduce an integer variable Y_v with $dom(Y_v) = \{\}$
2. Initialize the domain of each Y_v as follows:

...

    (c') if $|dom(Y_v)| = 0$ then $dom(Y_v) \leftarrow \{i \mid v \in ub(X_i)\}$
    (d) if $v \notin lb(X)$ then $dom(Y_v) \leftarrow dom(Y_v) \cup \{n+1\}$
    (e) if $|dom(Y_v)| = 0$ then **fail**

...

4. Maintain the following channelling constraints, for all $i \leq n$ and for all v:

...

    (c) $n+1 \notin dom(Y_v) \leftrightarrow v \in lb(X)$
    (d) $ub(X) \subseteq \bigcup ub(X_i)$

Lemma 2. *Define the one-to-one mapping between assignments S of the dual variables Y and assignments S' of the original set variables X_i and X by: $S'[X] = \bigcup S'[X_i]$ and $v \in S'[X_i]$ iff $S[Y_v] = i$. Then S is consistent with* gcc *in step (3) of* BC-FCP-Sets *iff S' is consistent for* FCPartition.

Proof. ($\Rightarrow$) We prove that S' is:

Disjoint and Fixed Cardinality: See Lemma 1.
Partition: Lines (2.c'-d) guarantee that for a value $v \in lb(X)$, Y_v cannot be assigned the dummy value $n+1$ in S. Hence, S' necessarily has an X_i with $v \in S'[X_i]$. Because of line (1'), none of the Y_v represent a value $v \notin ub(X)$. Hence, for all i, $S'[X_i] \subseteq ub(X)$, then $S'[X] \subseteq ub(X)$.

($\Leftarrow$) We prove that S is:

Consistent with gcc: See Lemma 1.
Consistent with Y: If S' is a satisfying assignment for FCPartition, $S'[X_i] \subseteq S'[X], \forall i$. Since $S'[X] \subseteq ub(X)$, we know that any value v appearing in S' has a corresponding variable Y_v. And by construction (lines 2.a, 2.c, 2.d, we know that S is consistent with Y domains. □

Theorem 3. BC-FCP-Sets *is a sound and complete algorithm for enforcing bound consistency on* FCPartition *with set variables that runs in $O(nd^2)$ time.*

Proof. Soundness. A value v is pruned from $ub(X_i)$ in step (4) of BC-FCP-Sets for one of the reasons that already held in FCDisjoint or because Y_v has not been created in line (1'). Lemma 2 tells us that all cases imply that v cannot belong to X_i in a satisfying tuple for FCPartition. Soundness of $lb(X_i)$ comes from Lemma 2 as it came from Lemma 1 on FCDisjoint. We must also show that the algorithm does not fail if FCPartition can be made bound consistent. BC-FCP-Sets can fail in line (2.e) if a value v that belongs to $lb(X)$ cannot belong to any X_i. Clearly, FCPartition cannot then be made bound consistent. The other cases of failure are the same as for FCDisjoint. A value v is pruned from $ub(X)$ in step (4.d) because none of the X_i contains v in its upper bound. This means that this value cannot belong to any satisfying assignment S' (Lemma 2). A value v is added to $lb(X)$ in line (4.c) if no assignment S satisfying the gcc verifies $S[Y_v] = n+1$. This means that v is assigned to a variable X_i in all assignments satisfying FCPartition.

Completeness. Let $v \in ub(X)$ after step (4). Then, there exists X_i with $v \in ub(X_i)$, and so $i \in dom(Y_v)$ after step (3). gcc being GAC, there exists an assignment S satisfying gcc, with $S[Y_v] = i$. Lemma 2 guarantees there exists an assignment S' with $\{v\} \subseteq S'[X]$. Thus, v is in $ub(X)$. In addition, let $v \notin lb(X)$ after step (4). Then, $n+1 \in dom(Y_v)$ after step (3). Thus, there is an assignment S satisfying gcc with $S[Y_v] = n+1$. Lemma 2 tells us that there is a satisfying assignment S' of FCPartition with v not in $S'[X]$.

Complexity. See proof of BC-FCD-Sets. □

Theorem 4. *Enforcing BC on* FCPartition$(X_1, \ldots, X_n, X, k_1, \ldots, k_n)$ *with multiset variables is NP-hard.*

Proof. We know that deciding the existence of a satisfying assignment is NP-complete for FCDisjoint$(X_1, \ldots, X_n, k_1, \ldots, k_n)$ with multiset variables. If we build a multiset variable X with $lb(X) = \emptyset$ and $ub(X) = \bigcup_i ub(X_i)$, then FCPartition$(X_1, \ldots, X_n, X, k_1, \ldots, k_n)$ has a satisfying assignment if and only if FCDisjoint$(X_1, \ldots, X_n, k_1, \ldots, k_n)$ has one. Thus, enforcing bound consistency on FCPartition is NP-hard. □

5.2 NEPartition

The constraint NEDisjoint$(X_1, \ldots, X_n)$ on set variables was a particular case of FCDisjoint in which the cardinality of the variables X_i can vary from 1 to ∞ instead of being fixed to k_i. This is exactly the same for NEPartition on set variables, which is a particular case of FCPartition. Replacing "$B[i] \leftarrow k_i..k_i$" by "$B[i] \leftarrow 1..\infty$" in BC-FCP-Sets, we obtain BC-NEP-Sets.

When NEPartition involves multiset variables, BC remains polynomial. As for BC-NED-Msets, the trick is to transform multisets in sets and to use BC-NEP-Sets on the obtained sets. We just need to be careful with the compatibility of the occurrences of values in X_i variables and the X being partitioned. Once BC is achieved on these sets, we have to restore the initial number of occurrences and check again compatibility with X.

Algorithm BC-NEP-Msets

1. **if** $\bigcup_i lb(X_i) \not\subseteq ub(X)$ **or** $lb(X) \not\subseteq \bigcup_i ub(X_i)$ **then** failure
2. **for each** $i \in 1..n$, v occurring in $ub(X_i)$ **do**
   2.1. **if** $occ(v, ub(X_i)) < occ(v, lb(X))$ **then** $occ(v, ub(X_i)) \leftarrow 0$
   2.2. **if** $occ(v, ub(X_i)) > occ(v, ub(X))$ **then** $occ(v, ub(X_i)) \leftarrow occ(v, ub(X))$
   2.3. init-$occ_{ub}(X_i, v) \leftarrow occ(v, ub(X_i))$; $occ(v, ub(X_i)) \leftarrow 1$
   2.4. init-$occ_{lb}(X_i, v) \leftarrow occ(v, lb(X_i))$; $occ(v, lb(X_i)) \leftarrow min(1, \text{init-}occ_{lb}(X_i, v))$
3. store $lb(X)$; $lb(X) \leftarrow$ set-of$(lb(X))$; $ub(X) \leftarrow$ set-of$(ub(X))$
4. BC-NEP-Sets$(X_1, \ldots, X_n, X)$
5. restore $lb(X)$
6. **for each** $i \in 1..n, v \in ub(X_i)$ **do**
   6.1. $occ(v, ub(X_i)) \leftarrow$ init-$occ_{ub}(X_i, v)$
   6.2. **if** $v \in lb(X_i)$ **then** $occ(v, lb(X_i)) \leftarrow max(1, \text{init-}occ_{lb}(X_i, v), occ(v, lb(X)))$
7. $lb(X) \leftarrow lb(X) \cup \bigcup_i lb(X_i)$; $ub(X) \leftarrow \bigcup_i ub(X_i)$

Theorem 5. BC-NEP-Msets *is a sound and complete algorithm for enforcing bound consistency on* NEPartition *with multiset variables, that runs in* $O(nd^2)$ *time.*

Proof. (Sketch.) As for NEDisjoint on multiset variables, enforcing bound consistency on NEPartition after having transformed the multisets in sets (i.e., we keep only one occurrence of each value in the lower and upper bounds), the removal of a value v from an upper bound by BC-NEP-Sets is a sufficient condition for the removal of all occurrences of v in the original multiset upper bound. The addition v to a lower bound is a sufficient condition for the addition of some occurrences of v in the lower bound (the right number depends on the number of occurrences of v in $lb(X)$ and in the lower bound of the X_i holding v. It is then sufficient to ensure consistency between the number of occurrences in the X_i and X (lines 1, 2.1, 2.2, and 7), to transform multisets in sets (lines 2.3, 2.4, and 3), to call BC-NEP-Sets (line 4), and to restore appropriate numbers of occurrences (lines 5 and 6). Line 1 guarantees that $ub(X)$ can cover all the X_i's lower bounds and that $lb(X)$ can be covered by the X_i's upper bounds. A value v can be assigned in X_i if and only if it can cover the occurrences of v in $lb(X)$ (line 2.1), and it cannot occur more than in $ub(X)$ (line 2.2). Finally, a value v occurs in $lb(X)$ at least as many times as it occurs in some $lb(X_i)$, and occurs in $ub(X)$ exactly as many times as in the $ub(X_i)$ having its greatest number of occurrences (line 7). The complexity is dominated by line 4, with the call to BC-NEP-Sets which is $O(nd^2)$. □

6 Intersection Constraints

The Disjoint constraint restricts the pair-wise intersection of any two set or multiset variables to the empty set. We now consider the cases where the cardinality of the pair-wise intersection is either bounded or equal to a given constant or integer variable (lower case characters denote constants while upper case denote variables):

Intersect$_\leq(X_1,\ldots,X_n,K)$ iff $|X_i \cap X_j| \leq K$ for any $i \neq j$.
Intersect$_\geq(X_1,\ldots,X_n,K)$ iff $|X_i \cap X_j| \geq K$ for any $i \neq j$.
Intersect$_=(X_1,\ldots,X_n,K)$ iff $|X_i \cap X_j| = K$ for any $i \neq j$.

As usual, we can also add non-emptiness and fixed cardinality constraints to the set or multiset variables. For example, FCIntersect$_\leq(X_1,\ldots,X_n,K,C)$ iff $|X_i \cap X_j| \leq K$ for any $i \neq j$ and $|X_i| = C$ for all i. If $K = 0$, Intersect$_\leq$ and Intersect$_=$ are equivalent to Disjoint.

6.1 At Most Intersection Constraints

We show that Intersect$_\leq$ and NEIntersect$_\leq$ can be decomposed without hindering bound consistency, but that it is NP-hard to enforce BC on FCIntersect$_\leq$.

Theorem 6. $BC(\text{Intersect}_\leq(X_1,\ldots,X_n,K))$ *is equivalent to* $BC(|X_i \cap X_j| \leq K)$ *for all* $i < j$.

Proof. Suppose $BC(|X_i \cap X_j| \leq K)$ for all $i < j$. We will show that $BC(\forall i < j.|X_i \cap X_j| \leq K)$. Consider the occurrence representation of the set or multiset variables. Let

X_{il} be the number of occurrences of the value l in X_i. Consider the upper bound on X_{il}. We will construct a support for this value for X_{il} that simultaneously satisfies $|X_i \cap X_j| \leq K$ for all $i < j$. The same support will work for the lower bound on X_{il}. First, we assign K with its upper bound. Then we pick any j with $i \neq j$. As $BC(|X_i \cap X_j| \leq K)$, there is some assignment for X_{jn} and X_{im} ($l \neq m$) within their bounds that satisfies $|X_i \cap X_j| \leq K$. We now extend these assignments to get a complete assignment for every other set or multiset variable as follows. Every other X_{pq} ($p \neq i$ and $p \neq j$) is assigned its lower bound. This can only help satisfy $|X_i \cap X_j| \leq K$ for all $i < j$. This assignment is therefore support for X_{il}. We can also construct support for the upper of lower bound of K in a similar way. Maximality of the bound consistent domains is easy. Consider any value for X_{il} smaller than the lower bound or larger than the upper bound. As this cannot be extended to satisfy $|X_i \cap X_j| \leq K$ for some j, it clearly cannot be extended to satisfy $|X_i \cap X_j| \leq K$ for all $i < j$. A similar argument holds for any value for K smaller than the lower bound or larger than the upper bound. Hence, $BC(\forall i < j.|X_i \cap X_j| \leq K)$. □

Given a set of set or multiset variables, the non-empty intersection constraint NEIntersect$_\leq(X_1,\ldots,X_n,K)$ ensures that $|X_i \cap X_j| \leq K$ for $i \neq j$ and $|X_i| > 0$ for all i. If $K = 0$, this is the NEDisjoint constraint which is not decomposable. If $K > 0$, the constraint is decomposable.

Theorem 7. *If $K > 0$ then $BC(\text{NEIntersect}_\leq(X_1,\ldots,X_n,K))$ is equivalent to $BC(|X_i \cap X_j| \leq K)$ for all $i < j$ and $BC(|X_i| > 0)$ for all i.*

Proof. Suppose $BC(|X_i \cap X_j| \leq K)$ for all $i < j$ and $BC(|X_i| > 0)$ for all i. Then $|lb(X_i) \cap lb(X_j)| \leq max(K)$ for all $i < j$. And if $|ub(X_i)| = 1$ for any i then $lb(X_i) = ub(X_i)$. Consider some variable X_i and any value $a \in ub(X_i) - lb(X_i)$. We will find support in the global constraint for X_i to take the value $\{a\} \cup lb(X_i)$. Consider any other variable X_j. If $|lb(X_j)| = 0$ then we pick any value $b \in ub(X_j)$ and set X_j to $\{b\}$. This will ensure we satisfy the non-emptiness constraint on X_j. As $k > 0$ and $|X_j| = 1$, we will satisfy the intersection constraint between X_j and any other variable. If $|lb(X_j)| > 0$ then we set X_j to $lb(X_j)$. This again satisfy the non-emptiness constraint on X_j. Since $|lb(X_i) \cap lb(X_j)| \leq max(K)$ for all $i < j$, we will also satisfy the intersection constraints. Support can be found in a similar way for X_i to take the value $lb(X_i)$ if this is non-empty. Finally, $min(K)$ has support since $BC(|X_i \cap X_j| \leq K)$ for all $i < j$. Hence NEIntersect$_\leq(X_1,\ldots,X_n,K)$ is BC. □

Enforcing BC on FCIntersect$_\leq$ is intractable.

Theorem 8. *Enforcing BC on FCIntersect$_\leq(X_1,\ldots,X_n,k,c)$ for $c > k > 0$ is NP-hard.*

Proof. Immediate from Theorem 5 in [2]. □

Sadler and Gervet introduce the atmost1-incommon and distinct constraints for set variables with a fixed cardinality [9]. The atmost1-incommon constraint is FCIntersect$_\leq(X_1,\ldots,X_n,1,c)$. Similarly, the distinct constraint on sets of fixed cardinality is is FCIntersect$_\leq(X_1,\ldots,X_n,c-1,c)$. The reduction used in Theorem 5 in [2] works with all these parameters. Hence, all are NP-hard to propagate.

6.2 At Least Intersection Constraints

Similar to the at most intersection constraint, Intersect$_\geq$ and NEIntersect$_\geq$ can be decomposed without hindering bound consistency. However, it is NP-hard to enforce BC on FCIntersect$_\geq$.

Theorem 9. $BC(\text{Intersect}_\geq(X_1, \ldots, X_n, K))$ *is equivalent to* $BC(|X_i \cap X_j| \geq K)$ *for all* $i < j$.

Proof. The proof is analogous to that of Theorem 6 except we extend a partial assignment to a complete assignment that is interval support by assigning each of the additional X_{pq} with the upper bound and (where appropriate) K with its lower bound. □

Two sets cannot have an intersection unless they are non-empty. Hence this result also shows that $BC(\text{NEIntersect}_\geq(X_1, \ldots, X_n, K))$ for $K > 0$ is equivalent to BC on the decomposition. By comparison, enforcing BC on FCIntersect$_\geq$ is intractable.

Theorem 10. *Enforcing BC on* FCIntersect$_\geq(X_1, \ldots, X_n, k, c)$ *for* $c > k > 0$ *is NP-hard.*

Proof. We let $k = 1$. We can reduce the $k = 1$ case to the $k > 1$ case by adding $k - 1$ additional common values to each set variable. The proof again uses a reduction of a 3SAT problem in n variables. The same reduction is used for set or multiset variables. We let $c = n$ and introduce a set variable, S with domain $\{\} \subseteq S \subseteq \{1, \neg 1, \ldots, n, \neg n\}$. This will be set of literals assigned true in a satisfying assignment. For each clause, φ we introduce a set variable, X_φ. Suppose $\varphi = x_i \vee \neg x_j \vee x_k$, then X_φ has domain $\{d_1^\varphi, \ldots, d_{n-1}^\varphi\} \subseteq X_\varphi \subseteq \{i, \neg j, k, d_1^\varphi, \ldots, d_{n-1}^\varphi\}$, where $d_1^\varphi, \ldots, d_{n-1}^\varphi$ are dummy values. To satisfy the intersection and cardinality constraint, S must take at least one of the literals which satisfy φ. Finally, we introduce n set variables, X_i to ensure that one and only one of i and $\neg i$ is in S. Each X_i has domain $\{f_1^i, \ldots, f_{n-1}^i\} \subseteq X_i \subseteq \{f_1^i, \ldots, f_{n-1}^i, i, \neg i\}$. The constructed set variables then have a solution which satisfies the intersection and cardinality constraints iff the original 3SAT problem is satisfiable. Hence enforcing bound consistency is NP-hard. □

6.3 Equal Intersection Constraints

Unlike the at most or at least intersection constraints, enforcing BC on Intersect$_=$ is intractable even without cardinality constraints on the set or multiset variables.

Theorem 11. *Enforcing BC on* Intersect$_=(X_1, \ldots, X_n, k)$ *is NP-hard for* $k > 0$.

Proof. Immediate from Theorem 6 in [2]. □

The same reduction can also be used with the constraint that each set or multiset has a non-empty or fixed cardinality.

Lemma 3. *Enforcing BC on* FCIntersect$_=(X_1, \ldots, X_n, k)$ *is NP-hard for* $k > 0$.

Lemma 4. *Enforcing BC on* NEIntersect$_=(X_1, \ldots, X_n, k, c)$ *is NP-hard for* $k > 0$.

7 Experimental Results

To show the benefits of these global constraints, we ran some experiments using ILOG's Solver toolkit with a popular benchmark involving set variables. The social golfers problem $\langle p, m, n, t \rangle$ is to schedule t golfers into m groups of size n for p weeks, such that no golfer plays in the same group as any other golfer twice. To model this problem, we introduce a set variable of fixed cardinality to represent every group in each week. Each week is then a partition of the set of golfers. Between any two groups, their intersection must contain at most one golfer. We also consider a generalization of the problem in which there is an excess of golfers and some golfers rest each week. When there is no excess of golfers, FCPartition shows no improvement upon its decomposition into ILOG's IlcPartition and cardinality constraints. When there is an excess of golfers, the partitioning constraint is replaced by a disjointness constraint.

We compare the same model using the FCDisjoint constraint and its decomposition into ILOG's IlcAllNullIntersect constraint and cardinality constraints on groups. In the latter case, the filtering level is fixed either to "Default" or "Extended". We understand from conversations with Ilog that "Default" implements the decomposition whilst "Extended" enforces BC on the global constraint. We ran experiments with a time limit of 10 minutes, and five settings for m and n. For each, we present the results for all numbers p of weeks such that at least one strategy needs at least one fail, and at least one strategy can solve the problem within the time limit. We solved each problem using five different variable ordering strategies:

- **static golfer:** picks each golfer in turn, and assigns him to the first possible group of every week.
- **static week:** picks each golfer in turn, and assigns him to one group in the first incomplete week.
- **min domain:** picks a pair (golfer, week) such that the total number of groups in which the golfer can participate in during the given week is minimum, then assigns this golfer to one group.
- **default (group):** ILOG Solver's default strategy for set variables ordered by groups; this picks an element $v \in ub(S)$ and adds it to the lower bound ($v \in S$).
- **default (week):** ILOG Solver's default strategy for set variables ordered by weeks.

We observe that, in terms of fails, FCDisjoint and IlcAllNullIntersect-Extended are equivalent, with two exceptions[3]. Both outperform the decomposition model or are the same. The runtimes follow a similar behaviour, although the decomposition model can be faster when the number of fails are equal. The speed-up obtained by reasoning on the global constraint rather than on disjointness and cardinality separately can be of several orders of magnitude in some cases. With the two default heuristics (last two columns in the table), we notice no difference between our global constraint and the decomposition. These heuristics are not, however, always the best. The min domain heuristic can be superior, but sometimes needs the pruning provided by the global constraint to prevent poor performance.

---

[3] We do not understand these two exceptions but suspect there may be some complex interaction with the dynamic branching heuristic.

problem	model	static golfer	static week	min domain	group (set)	week (set)
⟨6, 8, 4, 36⟩	FCDisjoint	10 / 0.15	-	52 / 0.14	183 / 0.11	-
	IlcAllNullIntersect (Extended)	10 / 0.13	-	52 / 0.11	183 / 0.11	-
	IlcAllNullIntersect (Default)	-	-	190 / 0.13	183 / **0.08**	-
⟨3, 6, 6, 37⟩	FCDisjoint	-	548 / 0.21	0 / 0.02	27 / 0.02	22232 / 2.36
	IlcAllNullIntersect (Extended)	-	548 / 0.2	0 / 0.02	27 / 0.03	22232 / 1.6
	IlcAllNullIntersect (Default)	-	-	0 / **0.01**	27 / 0.02	22232 / 1.3
⟨3, 6, 6, 38⟩	FCDisjoint	-	67 / 0.03	0 / 0.03	4 / 0.02	3446 / 0.39
	IlcAllNullIntersect (Extended)	-	67 / 0.04	0 / 0.02	4 / 0.03	3446 / 0.26
	IlcAllNullIntersect (Default)	-	-	0 / **0.01**	4 / 0.02	3446 / 0.2
⟨3, 6, 6, 39⟩	FCDisjoint	-	1261 / 0.3	0 / **0.02**	7 / 0.03	171574 / 16.52
	IlcAllNullIntersect (Extended)	-	1261 / 0.27	0 / **0.02**	7 / 0.02	171574 / 11.39
	IlcAllNullIntersect (Default)	-	-	0 / **0.02**	7 / **0.02**	171574 / 8.85
⟨3, 6, 6, 40⟩	FCDisjoint	12 / **0.02**	48 / 0.03	0 / **0.02**	0 / **0.02**	8767 / 0.79
	IlcAllNullIntersect (Extended)	12 / 0.03	48 / 0.03	0 / **0.02**	0 / 0.03	8767 / 0.6
	IlcAllNullIntersect (Default)	-	-	0 / **0.02**	0 / **0.02**	8767 / 0.46
⟨3, 5, 5, 26⟩	FCDisjoint	-	44 / 0.03	0 / 0.01	2 / 0	813 / 0.08
	IlcAllNullIntersect (Extended)	-	44 / 0.02	0 / 0.01	2 / 0.01	813 / 0.07
	IlcAllNullIntersect (Default)	-	177880 / 9.62	0 / 0.01	2 / 0	813 / 0.05
⟨3, 5, 5, 27⟩	FCDisjoint	967161 / 160.92	5 / 0.01	0 / 0.01	1 / 0.01	62 / 0.01
	IlcAllNullIntersect (Extended)	967161 / 96.94	5 / 0.01	0 / 0.02	1 / 0.01	62 / 0.01
	IlcAllNullIntersect (Default)	-	1106 / 0.09	0 / 0	1 / 0.01	62 / 0.02
⟨3, 5, 5, 28⟩	FCDisjoint	9 / **0.01**	32 / 0.03	0 / **0.01**	19 / **0.01**	661 / 0.08
	IlcAllNullIntersect (Extended)	9 / **0.01**	32 / **0.01**	0 / **0.01**	19 / **0.01**	661 / 0.06
	IlcAllNullIntersect (Default)	58218 / 3.65	22860 / 1.23	0 / **0.01**	19 / **0.01**	661 / 0.05
⟨3, 5, 5, 29⟩	FCDisjoint	6 / 0.02	2 / 0.01	0 / 0.01	0 / 0.01	18 / 0.01
	IlcAllNullIntersect (Extended)	6 / 0.01	2 / 0.01	0 / 0.01	0 / 0.01	18 / 0.01
	IlcAllNullIntersect (Default)	37208 / 2.25	209 / 0.02	0 / 0.01	0 / 0	18 / 0.01
⟨3, 9, 9, 83⟩	FCDisjoint	-	-	0 / 0.12	453 / 0.17	-
	IlcAllNullIntersect (Extended)	-	-	-	453 / 0.13	-
	IlcAllNullIntersect (Default)	-	-	-	453 / **0.11**	-
⟨3, 9, 9, 84⟩	FCDisjoint	-	-	0 / 0.12	5 / 0.09	-
	IlcAllNullIntersect (Extended)	-	-	5 / 0.13	5 / 0.1	-
	IlcAllNullIntersect (Default)	-	-	-	5 / **0.08**	-
⟨3, 9, 9, 85⟩	FCDisjoint	-	-	0 / 0.13	30 / 0.09	-
	IlcAllNullIntersect (Extended)	-	-	0 / 0.13	30 / 0.1	-
	IlcAllNullIntersect (Default)	-	-	1442064 / 159.75	30 / **0.08**	-
⟨10, 9, 3, 30⟩	FCDisjoint	464 / 0.84	264 / 0.45	-	16055 / 3.75	**15 / 0.26**
	IlcAllNullIntersect (Extended)	464 / 0.56	264 / 0.32	-	16055 / 2.2	**15 / 0.23**
	IlcAllNullIntersect (Default)	-	-	-	16055 / 1.99	**15 / 0.22**
⟨10, 9, 3, 31⟩	FCDisjoint	37 / 0.46	1 / 0.25	0 / 0.39	2 / 0.28	113 / 0.29
	IlcAllNullIntersect (Extended)	37 / 0.41	1 / 0.24	0 / 0.32	2 / 0.26	113 / 0.24
	IlcAllNullIntersect (Default)	-	51223 / 10.45	0 / 0.32	2 / 0.25	113 / **0.23**

8 Conclusions

We have begun a systematic study of global constraints on set and multiset variables. We have studied here a wide range of disjoint, partition, and intersection constraints. The disjoint constraint on set or multiset variables is decomposable (and hence polynomial). On the other hand, the non-empty and fixed cardinality disjoint constraints are not decomposable without hindering bound consistency. We therefore present polynomial algorithms for enforcing bound consistency on the non-empty disjoint constraints for set or multiset variables, for enforcing BC on the fixed cardinality disjoint constraint for set variables, and prove that enforcing BC on the fixed cardinality disjoint constraint on multiset variables is NP-hard. We give very similar results for the partition, non-empty and fixed cardinality partition constraints. We also identify those non-empty intersection constraints which are decomposable, those which are not decomposable but polynomial, and those that are NP-hard. Many of the propagation algorithms we propose here exploit a dual viewpoint, and call upon existing global constraints for finite-domain variables like the global cardinality constraint. We are currently extending this study to counting constraints on set and multiset variables. Propagation algorithms for such constraints also appear to exploit dual viewpoints extensively.

References

1. N. Beldiceanu. Global constraints as graph properties on a structured network of elementary constraints of the same type. In *Proc. CP'00*, pages 52–66. Springer, 2000.
2. C. Bessiere, E. Hebrard, B. Hnich, and T. Walsh. The complexity of global constraints. In *Proc. AAAI'04*, 2004.
3. C. Gervet. Conjunto: constraint logic programming with finite set domains. *Proc. of the 1994 Int. Symp. on Logic Programming*, pages 339–358. MIT Press, 1994.
4. Ilog. User's manual. ILOG Configurator 2.3. 2004.
5. Ilog. User's manual. ILOG Solver 6.0. Sept. 2003.
6. T. Müller and M. Müller. Finite set constraints in Oz. *13th Logic Programming Workshop*, pages 104–115, Technische Universität München, 1997.
7. J-C. Régin. A filtering algorithm for constraints of difference in CSPs. In *Proc. AAAI'94*, pages 362–367. AAAI, 1994.
8. J-C. Ré gin. Generalized arc consistency for global cardinality constraints. In *Proc. AAAI'96*, pages 209–215. AAAI Press/The MIT Press, 1996.
9. A. Sadler and C. Gervet. Global reasoning on sets. In *Proc. of Workshop on Modelling and Problem Formulation (FORMUL'01)*, 2001. Held alongside CP 01.
10. A. Sadler and C. Gervet. Global Filtering for the Disjointness Constraint on Fixed Cardinality Sets. In Technical report IC-PARC-04-02, Imperial College London, March 2001.
11. J. Schimpf, A. Cheadle, W. Harvey, A. Sadler, K. Shen, and M. Wallace. ECLiPSe. In Technical report IC-PARC-03-01, Imperial College London, 2003.
12. T. Walsh. Consistency and propagation with multiset constraints: A formal viewpoint. In *Proc. CP'03*. Springer, 2003.

Decomposition and Learning for a Hard Real Time Task Allocation Problem

Hadrien Cambazard[1], Pierre-Emmanuel Hladik[2], Anne-Marie Déplanche[2], Narendra Jussien[1], and Yvon Trinquet[2]

[1] École des Mines de Nantes, LINA CNRS
4 rue Alfred Kastler – BP 20722 - F-44307 Nantes Cedex 3, France
{hcambaza,jussien}@emn.fr
[2] IRCCyN, UMR CNRS 6597
1 rue de la Noë – BP 92101 - F-44321 Nantes Cedex 3, France
{hladik,deplanche,trinquet}@irccyn.ec-nantes.fr

Abstract. We present a cooperation technique using an accurate management of nogoods to solve a hard real-time problem which consists in assigning periodic tasks to processors in the context of fixed priorities preemptive scheduling. The problem is to be solved off-line and our solving strategy is related to the logic based Benders decomposition. A master problem is solved using constraint programming whereas subproblems are solved with schedulability analysis techniques coupled with an *ad hoc* nogood computation algorithm. Constraints and nogoods are learnt during the process and play a role close to Benders cuts.

1 Introduction

Real-time systems are at the heart of embedded systems and have applications in many industrial areas: telecommunication, automotive, aircraft and robotics systems, etc. Today, applications (*e.g.* cars) involve many processors to serve different demands (cruise control, ABS, engine management, etc.). These systems are made of specialized and distributed processors (interconnected through a network) which receive data from sensors, process appropriate answers and send it to actuators. Their main characteristics lie in functional as well as non-functional requirements like physical distribution of the resources and timing constraints. Timing constraints are usually specified as deadlines for tasks which have to be executed. Serious damage can occur if deadlines are not met. In this case, the system is called a *hard* real-time system and timing predictability is required. In this field, some related works are based on off-line analysis techniques that compute the response time of the constrained tasks. Such techniques have been initiated by Liu and al. [15] and consist in computing the worst-case scenario of execution. Extensions have been introduced later to take into account shared resources, distributed systems [23] or precedence constraints [7].

Our problem consists in assigning periodic and preemptive tasks with fixed priorities (a task is periodically activated and can be preempted by a higher priority task) to distributed processors. A solution is an allocation of the tasks on the processors which meets the schedulability requirements. The problem of assigning a set of hard preemptive real-time tasks in a distributed system is NP-Hard [14]. It has been tackled with heuristic methods [6, 17], simulated annealing [22, 4] and genetic algorithms [6, 19]. However, these techniques are often incomplete and can fail in finding any feasible assignment even after a large computation time. New practical approaches are still needed.

We propose here a decomposition based method which separates the allocation problem itself from the scheduling one. It is related to the Benders decomposition and especially to the logic Benders based decomposition. On the one hand, constraint programming offers competitive tools to solve the assignment problem, on the other hand, real-time scheduling techniques are able to achieve an accurate analysis of the schedulability. Our method uses Benders decomposition as a way of generating precise nogoods in constraint programming.

This paper is organized as follows: Section 2 introduces the problem. Related work and solving strategies are discussed in Section 3. The logical Benders decomposition scheme is briefly introduced and the links with our approach are put forward. Section 4 is dedicated to the master/subproblems and communication between them thanks to nogoods. Experimental results are presented in Section 5 and finally, a discussion of the technique is made in Section 6.

2 Problem Description

2.1 The Real-Time System Architecture

The hard real-time system we consider can be modeled with a software architecture (the set of tasks) and a hardware architecture (the physical execution platform for the tasks). Such a model is used by Tindell [22].

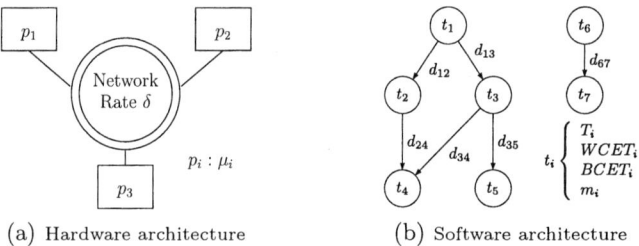

(a) Hardware architecture   (b) Software architecture

Fig. 1. Main parameters of the problem.

Hardware Architecture. The hardware architecture is made of a set $\mathcal{P} = \{p_1, \ldots, p_k, \ldots, p_m\}$ of m identical processors with a fixed memory capacity μ_k, connected to a network. All the processors from $\mathcal{P}$ have the same processing speed. They are connected to a network with a transit rate of δ and a token ring protocol. A token travels around the ring allowing processors to send data only if they hold the token. It stays at the same place during a fixed maximum period of time large enough to ensure all messages waiting on processors are sent.

Software Architecture. To model the software architecture, we consider a valued, oriented and acyclic graph $(\mathcal{T}, \mathcal{C})$. The set of nodes $\mathcal{T} = \{t_1, ..., t_n\}$ corresponds to the tasks whereas the set of edges $\mathcal{C} \subseteq \mathcal{T} \times \mathcal{T}$ refers to message sending between tasks.

A task t_i is defined by its temporal characteristics and resource needs: its period, T_i (a task is periodically activated); its worst-case execution time without preemption, $WCET_i$ and its memory need, m_i. Edges $c_{ij} = (t_i, t_j) \in \mathcal{C}$ are valued with the amount of exchanged data: d_{ij}. Communicating tasks have the same activation period. Moreover, they are able to communicate in two ways: a local communication with no delay using the memory of the processor (requiring the tasks to be located on the same processor) and a distant communication using the network. In any case, we do not consider precedence constraints. Tasks are periodically activated in an independent way, they read and write data at the beginning and the end of their execution.

Finally, each processor is scheduled with a fixed priority strategy. A priority, $prio_i = i$ is given to each task. t_j has priority over t_i if and only if $prio_j < prio_i$ and a task execution may be pre-empted by higher priority tasks.

2.2 The Allocation Problem

An allocation is an application $A : \mathcal{T} \to \mathcal{P}$ mapping a task t_i to a processor p_k:

$$t_i \mapsto A(t_i) = p_k \qquad (1)$$

The allocation problem consists in finding the application A which respects the constraints described below.

Timing Constraints. They are expressed by the means of deadlines for the tasks. Timing constraints enforces the duration between the activation date of any instance of the task t_i and its completion time to be bounded by its deadline D_i (the constraint on D_i is detailed in 4.2).

Resource Constraints. Three kinds of constraints are considered:

- **Memory capacity**: The memory use of a processor p_k cannot not exceed its capacity (μ_k):

$$\forall k = 1..m, \sum_{A(t_i)=p_k} m_i \leqslant \mu_k \qquad (2)$$

- **Utilization factor**: The utilization factor of a processor cannot exceed its processing capacity. The ratio $r_i = WCET_i/T_i$ means that a processor is used $r_i\%$ of the time by the task t_i. The following inequality is a simple necessary condition of schedulability:

$$\forall k = 1..m, \sum_{A(t_i)=p_k} WCET_i/T_i \leqslant 1 \qquad (3)$$

– **Network use**: To avoid overload, the amount of data carried along the network per unit of time cannot exceed the network capacity:

$$\sum_{\substack{c_{ij} = (t_i, t_j) \\ A(t_i) \neq A(t_j)}} d_{ij}/T_i \leq \delta \qquad (4)$$

Allocation Constraints. Allocation constraints are due to the system architecture. We distinguish three kinds of constraints: residence, co-residence and exclusion.

– **Residence**: A task sometimes needs a specific hardware or software resource which is only available on specific processors (*e.g.* a task monitoring a sensor has to run on a processor connected to the input peripheral). It is a couple (t_i, α) where $t_i \in \mathcal{T}$ is a task and $\alpha \subseteq \mathcal{P}$ is the set of available processors for the task. A given allocation A must respect:

$$A(t_i) \in \alpha \qquad (5)$$

– **Co-residence**: This constraint enforces several tasks to be placed on the same processor (they share a common resource). Such a constraint is defined by a set of tasks $\beta \subseteq \mathcal{T}$ and any allocation A has to fulfil:

$$\forall (t_i, t_j) \in \beta^2, A(t_i) = A(t_j) \qquad (6)$$

– **Exclusion**: Some tasks may be replicated for fault tolerance and therefore cannot be assigned to the same processor. It corresponds to a set $\gamma \subseteq \mathcal{T}$ of tasks which cannot be placed together. An allocation A must satisfy:

$$\forall (t_i, t_j) \in \gamma^2, A(t_i) \neq A(t_j) \qquad (7)$$

An allocation is said to be *valid* if it satisfies allocation and resource constraints. It is said to be *schedulable* if it satisfies timing constraints. A solution for our problem is a valid and schedulable allocation of the tasks.

3 About Related Decomposition Approaches

Our approach is based to a certain extent on a Benders decomposition [2] scheme. We will therefore introduce it to highlight the underlying concepts. Benders decomposition can be seen as a form of *learning from mistakes*. It is a solving strategy that uses a partition of the problem among its variables: x, y. The strategy can be applied to a problem of this general form:

$$P : \text{Min } f(x) + cy$$
$$\text{s.t } : g(x) + Ay \geq a \text{ with } : x \in D, y \geq 0$$

A master problem considers only a subset of variables x (often integer variables, D is a discrete domain). A subproblem (SP) tries to complete the assignment on y and produces a Benders cut added to the master problem. This cut has the form $z \geq h(x)$ and constitutes the key point of the method, it is inferred by the dual of the subproblem. Let us consider an assignment x^* given by the master, the subproblem (SP) and its dual (DSP) can be written as follows:

$$\text{SP : Min } cy \qquad\qquad \text{DSP : Max } u(a - g(x^*))$$
$$\text{s.t } Ay \geq a - g(x^*) \text{ with : } y \geq 0 \qquad \text{s.t } uA \leq c \text{ with : } u \geq 0$$

Duality theory ensures that $cy \geq u(a - g(x^*))$. As feasibility of the dual is independent of x^*, $cy \geq u(a - g(x))$ and the following inequality is valid: $f(x) + cy \geq f(x) + u(a - g(x))$. Moreover, according to duality, the optimal value of u^* maximizing $u(a - g(x^*))$ corresponds to the same optimal value of cy. Even if the cut is derived from a particular x^*, it is valid for all x and excludes a large class of assignments which share common characteristics that make them inconsistent. The number of solutions to explore is reduced and the master problem can be written at the Ith iteration:

$$\text{PM : Min } z$$
$$\text{s.t : } z \geq f(x) + u_i^*(a - g(x)) \qquad \forall i < I$$

From all of this, it can be noticed that dual variables need to be defined to apply the decomposition. However, [8] proposes to overcome this limit and to enlarge the classical notion of *dual* by introducing an *inference dual* available for all kinds of subproblems. He refers to a more general scheme and suggests a different way of thinking about duality: a Benders decomposition based on *logic*. Duality now means to be able to produce a proof, the logical proof of optimality of the subproblem and the correctness of inferred cuts. In the original Benders decomposition, this proof is established thanks to duality theorems.

For a discrete satisfaction problem, the resolution of the dual consists in computing the infeasibility proof of the subproblem and determining under what conditions the proof remains valid. It therefore infers valid cuts.

The success of the decomposition depends on both the degree to which decomposition can exploit structures and the quality of the cuts inferred. [8] suggests to identify classes of structured problems that exhibit useful characteristics for the Benders decomposition. Off-line scheduling problems fall into such classes and [10] demonstrates the efficiency of such an approach on a scheduling problem with dissimilar parallel machines.

Our approach is strongly connected to Benders decomposition and the related concepts. It is inspired from methods used to integrate constraint programming into a Benders scheme [21, 3]. The allocation and ressource problem will be considered on one side and schedulability on the other side. The subproblem checks the schedulability of an allocation, finds out why it is unschedulable and design a set of constraints (both symbolic and arithmetic) which rule out all assignments that are unschedulable for the same reason. Our approach concurs therefore the Benders decomposition on this central element: the Benders cut. The proof proposed here is based on off-line analysis techniques from real-time scheduling. One might think that a fast analytic proof could not provide enough relevant information on the inconsistency. As the speed of convergence and the success of the technique greatly depends on the quality of the cut, a conflict detection algorithm will be coupled with analytic techniques: QuickXplain [11]. Moreover, the master problem will be considered as a dynamic problem to avoid redundant computations as much as possible.

4 Solving Strategy

The solving process requires a tight cooperation between master and subproblem(s). Both problems share a common model introduced in the next section in order to easily exchange nogoods. They will be presented before examining the cooperation mechanisms and the incremental resolution of the master.

4.1 Master Problem

The master problem is solved using constraint programming techniques. The model is based on a redundant formulation using three kinds of variables: x, y, w. At first, let us consider n integer variables x (our decision variables) corresponding to each task and representing the processor selected to process the task: $\forall i \in \{1..n\}$, $x_i \in [1..m]$. Secondly, boolean variables y indicate the presence of a task onto a processor: $\forall i \in \{1..n\}, \forall p \in \{1..m\}$, $y_{ip} \in \{0,1\}$. Finally, boolean variables w are introduced to express the fact that a pair of tasks exchanging a message are located on the same processor or not: $\forall c_{ij} = (t_i, t_j) \in C$, $w_{ij} \in \{0,1\}$. Integrity constraints (*channeling constraints*) are used to enforce the consistency of the redundant model. Links between x, y and w are made using *element* constraints. One of the main objectives of the master problem is to efficiently solve the assignment part. It handles two kinds of constraints: allocation and resources.

- **Residence (*cf.* eq (5)):** it consists of forbidden values for x. A constraint is added for each forbidden processor p of t_i: $x_i \neq p$
- **Co-residence (*cf.* eq (6)):** $\forall (t_i, t_j) \in \beta^2, x_i = x_j$
- **Exclusion (*cf.* eq (7)):** $alldifferent(x_i | t_i \in \gamma)$
- **Memory capacity (*cf.* eq (2)):** $\forall p \in \{1..m\}$, $\sum_{i \in \{1..n\}} y_{ip} \times m_i \leq \mu_p$
- **Utilization factor (*cf.* eq (3)):** Let $lcm(T)$ be the least common multiple of periods of the tasks. The constraint can be written as follows:

$$\forall p \in \{1..m\}, \sum_{i \in \{1..n\}} lcm(T) \times WCET_i \times y_{ip}/T_i \leq lcm(T)$$

- **Network use (*cf.* eq (4)):** The network capacity is bounded by δ. Therefore, the size of the set of messages carried on the network cannot exceed this limit:

$$\sum_{i \in \{1..n\}} lcm(T) \times d_{ij} \times w_{ij}/T_i \leq lcm(T) \times \delta$$

Utilization factor and network use are reformulated with the lcm of tasks periods because our constraint solver cannot currently handle constraints with real coefficients and integer variables.

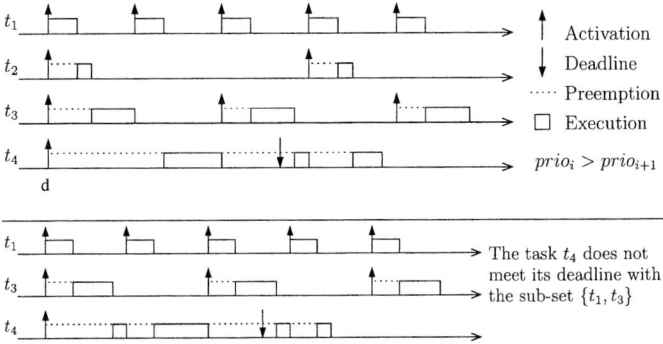

Fig. 2. Illustration of a schedulability analysis. The task t_4 does not meet its deadline. The sub-set $\{t_1, t_3, t_4\}$ is identified to explain the unschedulability of the system.

4.2 Subproblem(s)

An assignment provided by the master problem is a valid allocation of tasks. The problem is here to rule on its schedulability to determine why it may be unschedulable.

Independent Tasks. The first schedulability analysis has been initiated by Liu and Layland [15] for mono-processor real-time systems with independent and fixed priority tasks. The analysis consists in computing for each task t_i its worst response time, $WCRT_i$. The aim is to build the worst execution scenario which penalizes as much as possible the execution of t_i.

For independent tasks, it has been proved that the worst execution scenario for a task t_i happens when all tasks with a higher priority are awoken simultaneously (date d on Figure 2). The worst-case response time of t_i is:

$$WCRT_i = WCET_i + \sum_{t_j \in hp(A, t_i)} \lceil WCRT_i / T_j \rceil WCET_j \qquad (8)$$

$hp(A, t_i)$ corresponds to the set of tasks with a higher priority than t_i and located on the processor $A(t_i)$ for a given allocation A. $WCRT_i$ is easily obtained by looking for the fix-point of equation (8). Then, it is sufficient to compare for each task its worst case response time with its deadline D_i to know if the system is schedulable. In this case, the deadline of a task is equal to its period ($D_i = T_i$).

Communicating Tasks on a Token Ring. The result computed by a task must be made available before its next period to ensure regular data refreshment between tasks. The messages must reach their destination within the time allowed. With the token ring protocol, the maximum delay of transmission on the network is bounded and the TRT is proved to be an upper bound. This duration is computed by taking into account all the messages to be sent on the network:

$$TRT = \sum_{\substack{\{c_{ij} = (t_i, t_j) | \\ A(t_i) \neq A(t_j)\}}} d_{ij} / \delta \qquad (9)$$

The deadline for tasks sending data to non co-located tasks becomes $D_i = T_i - TRT$. A sufficient condition of scheduling is written:

$$\forall i = 1..n, WCET_i + \sum_{t_j \in hp(A, t_i)} \lceil D_i/T_j \rceil WCET_j \leq D_i \qquad (10)$$

4.3 Cooperation Between Master and Subproblem(s)

A complete or partial assignment of variables x, y, w will be now considered. The key point is to find an accurate explanation that encompasses all values of x for which the infeasibility proof (obtained for particular values of x) remains valid. We know at least that the current assignment is contradictory, in other words, a *nogood* is identified. The links between the concept of *nogood* [20] introduced in constraint programming and the Benders cut are underlined in [9].

Independent Tasks. m independent subproblems for each processor are solved. The schedulability of a processor k is established by applying equation (8) to each task t_i located on k ($x_i = k$) in a descendent order of priority until a contradiction occurs. For instance, in Figure 2, the set (t_1, t_2, t_3, t_4) is unschedulable. It explains the inconsistency but is not minimal. However the set (t_1, t_3, t_4) is sufficient to justify the contradiction. In order to compute more precise explanations (*i.e.* achieve a more relevant learning), a conflict algorithm, *QuickXplain* [11], has been used to determine the minimal involved set of tasks (*w.r.t.* inclusion). The *propagation* algorithm considered here is equation (8). Tasks are added from t_1 until a contradiction occurs on t_c, the last added task t_c belongs to the minimal conflict c. The algorithm re-starts by initially adding the tasks involved in c. When c is inconsistent, it represents the minimal conflict among the initial set $(t_1, \ldots, t_c)$. The subset of tasks $\mathcal{T} \subset T$ corresponds to a *NotAllEqual*[1] on x:

$$NotAllEqual(x_i | t_i \in \mathcal{T})$$

It is worth noting that the constraint could be expressed as a linear combination of variables y. However, *NotAllEqual(x_1, x_3, x_4)* excludes the solutions that contain the tasks 1,2,3 gathered on *any* processor.

Communicating Tasks on a Token Ring. The difficulty is to avoid incriminating the whole system:

1. At first, the network is simply not considered. If a processor is unschedulable without taking additional latency times due to the exchange of messages, it is still true in the general case. We can again infer: $NotAllEqual(x_i | t_i \in \mathcal{T})$.
2. Secondly, we only consider the network. When the sending tasks have a period less than TRT, the token does not come back early enough to allow

---

[1] A *NotAllEqual* on a set V of variables ensures that at least two variables among V take distinct values.

the end of their execution. In this case, equation (10) will never be satisfied. A set of inconsistent messages $M \subset \mathcal{C}$ is obtained:

$$\sum_{c_{ij} \in M} w_{ij} < |M|$$

3. The last test consists in checking equation (10). A failure returns a set $T \subseteq \mathcal{T}$ of tasks which is inconsistent with a set of messages $M \subseteq \mathcal{C}$. It corresponds to a *nogood*. We use a specific constraint to take advantage of symmetries and to forbid this assignment as well as permutations of tasks among processors. It can be written as a disjunction between the two previous cuts:

$$nogood(x_i | t_i \in T, w_{ij} | c_{ij} \in M) =$$

$$NotAllEqual(x_i | t_i \in T) \bigvee \sum_{c_{ij} \in M} w_{ij} < |M|$$

QuickXplain has been used again to refine information given in point 2 and 3. Let us now continue with the question of how information learnt from the previous failures can be integrated efficiently ? [21] outlines this problem and notices a possible significant overhead with redundant calculations. To address this issue, we considered the master problem as a dynamic problem.

Incremental Resolution. Solving dynamic constraint problems has led to different approaches. Two main classes of methods can be distinguished: proactive and reactive methods. On the one hand, proactive methods propose to build robust solutions that remain solutions even if changes occur. On the other hand, reactive methods try to reuse as much as possible previous reasonings and solutions found in the past. They avoid restarting from scratch and can be seen as a form of learning. One of the main methods currently used to perform such learning is a justification technique that keeps trace of inferences made by the solver during the search. Such an extension of constraint programming has been recently introduced [12]: explanation-based constraint programming (*e-constraints*).

Definition 1 *An explanation records information to justify a decision of the solver as a reduction of domain or a contradiction. It is made of a set of constraints C' (a subset of the original constraints of the problem) and a set of decisions dc_1, ..., dc_n taken during search. An explanation of the removal of value a from variable v will be written: $C' \wedge dc_1 \wedge dc_2 \wedge \cdots \wedge dc_n \Rightarrow v \neq a$.*

When a domain is emptied, a contradiction is identified. An explanation for this contradiction is computed by uniting each explanation of each removal of value of the variable concerned. At this point, dynamic backtracking algorithms that only question a relevant decision appearing in the conflict are conceivable. By keeping in memory a relevant part of the explanations involved in conflicts, a learning mechanism can be implemented [13].

Here, explanations allow us to perform an incremental resolution of the master problem. At each iteration, the constraints added by the subproblem generate a contradiction. Instead of backtracking to the last choice point as usual, the current solution of the master problem is *repaired* by removing the decisions that occur in the contradiction as done by the MAC-DBT algorithm [12]. Tasks assigned at the beginning of the search can be moved without disturbing the whole allocation. In addition, the model reinforcement phase tries to transform a learnt set of elementary constraints that have been added at previous iterations into higher level constraints. Explanations offer facilities to easily dynamically add or remove a constraint from the constraint network [12].

Notice that the master problem is never re-started. It is solved only once but is gradually *repaired* using the dynamic abilities of the explanation-based solver.

Model Reinforcement. Pattern recognition among a set of constraints that expresses specific subproblems is a critical aspect of the modelisation step. Constraint learning deals with the problem of automatically recognizing such patterns. We would like to perform a similar process in order to extract global constraints among a set of elementary constraints. For instance, a set of difference constraints can be formulated as an all-different constraint by looking for a maximal clique in the induced constraint graph. It is a well-known issue to this question in constraint programming and a version of the Bron/Kerbosh algorithm [5] has been implemented to this end (difference constraints occur when $NotAllEquals$ involve only two tasks). In a similar way, a set of $NotAllEqual$ constraints can be expressed by a *global cardinality constraint* (gcc) [18]. It corresponds now to a maximal clique in a hypergraph (where hyperarcs between tasks are $NotAllEquals$). However, it is still for us an open question that could significantly improve performances.

5 First Experimental Results

For the allocation problem, specific benchmarks are not provided in real-time scheduling. Experiments are usually done on didactic examples [22,1] or randomly generated configurations [17,16]. We opted for this last solution. Our generator takes several parameters into account:

- n, m, mes: the number of tasks, processors (experiments have been done on a fixed size: $n = 40$ and $m = 7$) and messages;
- $\%_{global}$: the global utilization factor of processors;
- $\%_{mem}$: the over-capacity memory, *i.e.* the amount of additionnal memory avalaible on processors with respect to the memory needs of all tasks;
- $\%_{res}$: the percentage of tasks included in residence constraints;
- $\%_{co-res}$: the percentage of tasks included in co-residence constraints;
- $\%_{exc}$: the percentage of tasks included in exclusion constraints;
- $\%_{msize}$: the size of a message is evaluated as a percentage of the period of the tasks exchanging it.

Task periods and priorities are randomly generated. However, worst-case execution time are initially randomly chosen and evaluated again to respect:

$\sum_{i=1}^{n} WCET_i/T_i = m\%_{global}$. The memory need of a task is proportional to its worst-case execution time. Memory capacities are randomly generated but must satisfy: $\sum_{k=1}^{m} \mu_k = (1 + \%_{mem}) \sum_{i=1}^{n} m_i$.

The number of tasks involved in allocation constraints is given by the parameters $\%_{res}$, $\%_{co-res}$, $\%_{exc}$. Tasks are randomly chosen and their number (involved in co-residence and exclusion constraints) can be set through specific levels. Several classes of problems have been defined depending on the difficulty of both allocation and schedulability problems. The difficulty of schedulability is evaluated using the global usage factor $\%_{global}$ which varies from 40 to 90 %. Allocation difficulty is based on the number of tasks included in residence, co-residence and exclusion constraints ($\%_{res}$, $\%_{co-res}$, $\%_{exc}$). Moreover, the memory over-capacity, $\%_{mem}$ has a significant impact (a very low capacity can lead to solve a *packing* problem, sometimes very difficult). The presence of messages impacts on both problems and the difficulty has been characterized by the ratios mes/n and $\%_{msize}$. As we consider precedence chains, we can not have more than one message per task and the ratio mes/n is always less than 1. $\%_{msize}$ reflects the impact of messages on schedulability analysis by linking periods and message sizes.

The table 1 describes the parameters and difficulty class of the considered problems. For instance, a class 2-1-4 indicates a problem with an allocation difficulty in class 2, a schedulability difficulty in class 1 and a network difficulty in class 4.

Table 1. Details on classes of difficulty.

Alloc.	$\%_{mem}$	$\%_{res}$	$\%_{co-res}$	$\%_{exc}$	Sched.	$\%_{global}$	Mes.	mes/n	$\%_{msize}$
1	80	0	0	0	1	40	1	0.5	40
2	40	15	15	15	2	60	2	0.5	70
3	30	25	25	25	3	75	3	0.75	70
4	15	35	35	35	4	90	4	0.875	150

5.1 Independent Tasks

Table 2 summarizes the results of our experiments. *Iter* is the number of iterations between master and subproblems, *NotAllEq* and *Diff* are the number of *NotAllEqual* and difference constraints inferred. *CPU* is the resolution time in seconds and *Xplain* expresses if the QuickXplain algorithm has been used. Finally % Success gives the number of instances successfully solved (a schedulable solution has been found or the proof of inconsistency has been done) within the time limit of 10 minutes per instance. The data are obtained in average (on instances solved within the required time) on 100 instances per class of difficulty with a pentium 4, 3 GigaHz and the Java version of PaLM [12].

The class 1-4 represents the hardest class of problem. Without the allocation problem, the initial search space is complete and everything has to be learnt. Moreover, these problems are close to inconsistency due to the hardness of the schedulability. Limits of our approach seem to be reached in such a case without

Table 2. Average results on 100 instances randomly generated into classes of problems.

Cat(Alloc/Sched)	Xplain	Iter	NotAllEq	Diff	CPU (s)	% Success
1-1	N	46,35	91,29	4,45	0,58	100%
1-1	Y	10,59	39,79	12,41	0,28	100%
1-2	Y	26,75	96,93	28,50	3,46	99%
1-3	Y	65,23	213,87	39,21	28,70	94%
1-4	**Y**	**100,88**	**373,08**	**57,82**	**93,40**	**40%**
2-2	Y	46,00	168,27	23,13	34,51	91%
2-3	Y	58,89	233,63	37,06	71,18	81%
3-4	Y	138,29	131,22	40,65	62,12	91%

an efficient re-modeling of *NotAllEquals* constraints into *gcc* (see 4.3). The cuts generated seem actually quite efficient. A relevant learning can be made in the case of independent tasks by solving m independent subproblems. Of course, if the symetry of the processors does not hold, this could be questionnable.

The execution of a particular and hard instance of class 2-3 is outlined on Figure 3. Resolution time and learnt constraints at each iteration are detailed. The master problem adapts the current solution to the cuts due to its dynamic abilities and the learning process is very quick at the beginning. The number of cuts decreases until a hard satisfaction problem is formulated (*a-b* in Fig. 3). The master is then forced to question a lot of choices to provide a valid allocation (*b*). The process starts again with a quick learning of nogoods (*b-c, c-d*).

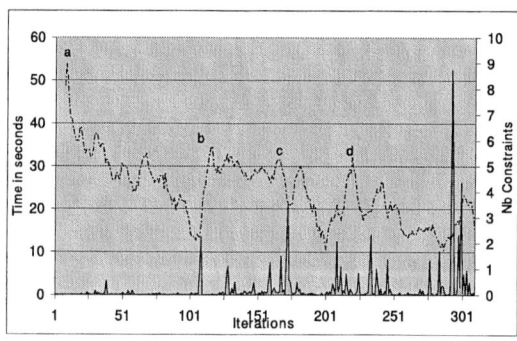

Fig. 3. Execution of a hard instance of class 2-3. Resolution time and a floating average of step 10 of the number of cuts (in dotlines) inferred at each iteration are shown. (310 iterations, 1192 *NotAllEqual*, 75 *differences* partially re-modeled into 12 *alldifferent*).

5.2 Communicating Tasks on a Token Ring

We chose to experiment the technique on a well-known instance of real-time scheduling: the Tindell instance [22], solved thanks to simulated annealing. This instance exhibits a particular structure: the network plays a critical part and feasible solutions have a network utilization almost minimal. We were forced to

Table 3. Average results on 100 instances randomly generated into classes of problems.

Cat(A/S/M)	Iter	NotAllEq	Diff	NetCuts	Nogoods	CPU (s)	%Succ
2-1-1	34,7	47,7	24	23,5	8,6	24,7	98%
2-1-2	40,1	56,9	25,4	36,2	8,4	18,6	93%
2-1-3	**91,9**	**64,2**	**23,5**	**134,3**	**27,2**	**106,6**	**56%**
2-2-1	58,9	118,4	47,5	11,2	2,7	72,7	82%
2-2-2	55,3	116,5	46,9	45,2	9,2	60,5	74%
2-2-3	**77,6**	**97,3**	**39,1**	**96,2**	**43,1**	**142,1**	**38%**

specialize our generic approach on this particular point through the use of an allocation heuristic that try to gather tasks exchanging messages. One can obtain the solution of Tindell very quickly (less than 10 seconds) if minimizing the network at each iteration. Moreover, we experimented our approach on random problems involving messages:

One can see on the table 3 that when several hardness aspects compete on the problem, the difficulty increases (2-2-3 compared to 1-1-3). The presence of messages make the problem much more complex for our approach because independency of subproblems (a key point of Benders) is lost and the network cut is a weak one. Determining what tasks should be or not together becomes a difficult question when a tigth overall memory is combined to a difficult schedulability and a lot of medium size messages. However, simple heuristics approachs have received a lot of attention from the real-time community and could be used to guide the search efficiently in CP. We hope to achieve better results with a more efficient heuristic inspired from the best one designed in real-time systems and coupled with the learnt information of the cuts. More experiments have to be carried out to clearly establish the difficulty frontier.

6 Discussion on the Approach

Our approach tries to use logic based Benders as a mean of generating relevant nogoods. It is not far from the hybrid framework *Branch and Check* of [21] which consists in checking the feasibility of a delayed part of the problem in a subproblem. In our case, the schedulability problem is gradually converted into the assignment problematic. The idea is that the first problem could be dealt with efficiently with constraint programming, and especially, with an efficient re-modeling process. In addition, it avoids thrashing on schedulability inconsistencies. As with explanation based algorithms (MAC-DBT or Decision-repair [13]), it tries to learn from its mistakes.

The technique is actually complete but it could be interesting to relax its completeness (from this point, we step back from Benders). One current problem is the overload of the propagation mechanism because of the accumulation of low power filtering constraints. We could use a tabu list of benders cuts and decide to keep permanently in memory the most accurate nogoods or only those contributing to a stronger model (a fine management of memory can be implemented due to dynamic abilities of the master problem).

One could also think building a filtering algorithm on equation (8). However, the objective is to show how precise nogoods could be used and to validate an approach we intend to implement on complex scheduling models. As analysis techniques quickly become very complex, a contradiction raised by a constraint encapsulating such an analysis seems to be less relevant than a precise explanation of failure.

The idea is to take advantage of the know-how of real-time scheduling community in a decomposition scheme such as the Benders one where constraint programming could efficiently solve the allocation problem.

7 Conclusion and Future Work

We propose in this paper, a decomposition method built to a certain extent on a logic Benders decomposition as a way of generating nogoods. It implements a *logical* duality to infer nogoods, tries to enforce the constraint model and finally performs an incremental resolution of the master problem. It is also strongly related to a class of algorithms which intends to learn from mistakes in a systematic way by managing nogoods.

For independent tasks, the use of QuickXplain is critical to speed up the convergence but the limits seem to be reached for highly constrained and inconsistent problems. Nevertheless, we believe that the difficulty can be overcome through an efficient re-modeling process. The use of an efficient heuristic to guide the CP search is needed on communicating tasks when several hardness aspect compete on the problem. As lot of traditionnal approaches in real time systems are based on heuristics, we hope to benefit from them and more experiments have to be carried out on this point.

Our next step would be to compare our approach with other methods such as traditional constraint and linear programming. We believe it should be also interesting to extend our study to other kinds of network protocols (CAN, TDMA, etc.) and precedence constraints. Moreover, another kind of constraints sometimes occur: disjunction between set of tasks. The disjunction global constraint has not been studied a lot and it could provide accurate modeling and solving tools to tackle the assignment problem with more complex allocation constraints.

Our approach gives a new answer to the problematic of real-time task allocation. It opens new perspectives on integrating techniques coming from a broader horizon than optimization, within CP in a Benders scheme.

References

1. Peter Altenbernd and Hans Hansson. The Slack Method: A New Method for Static Allocation of Hard Real-Time Tasks. *Real-Time Systems*, 15:103–130, 1998.
2. J. F. Benders. Partitionning procedures for solving mixed-variables programming problems. *Numerische Mathematik*, 4:238–252, 1962.
3. T. Benoist, E. Gaudin, and B. Rottembourg. Constraint programming contribution to benders decomposition: A case study. In *CP'02*, pages 603–617, 2002.

4. G. Borriello and D. Miles. Task Scheduling for Real-Time Multiprocessor Simulations. *11th Workshop on RTOSS*, pages 70–73, 1994.
5. Coen Bron and Joep Kerbosch. Algorithm 457: finding all cliques of an undirected graph. *Commun. ACM*, 16(9):575–577, 1973.
6. E. Ferro, R. Cayssials, and J. Orozco. Tuning the Cost Function in a Genetic/Heuristic Approach to the Hard Real-Time Multitask-Multiprocessor Assignment Problem. *Proceeding of the Third World Multiconference on Systemics Cybernetics and Informatics*, pages 143–147, 1999.
7. M. González Harbour, M.H. Klein, and J.P. Lehoczky. Fixed Priority Scheduling of Periodic Tasks with Varying Execution Priority. *Proceeding of the IEEE Real-Time Systelms Symposium*, pages 116–128, December 1991.
8. J.N. Hooker and G. Ottosson. Logic-based benders decomposition. *Mathematical Programming*, 96:33–60, 2003.
9. J.N. Hooker, G. Ottosson, E. S. Thorsteinsson, and H. Kim. A scheme for unifying optimization and constraint satisfaction methods. *Knowledge Engineering Review, special issue on AI/OR*, 15(1):11–30, 2000.
10. Vipul Jain and I. E. Grossmann. Algorithms for hybrid milp/cp models for a class of optimization problems. *INFORMS Journal on Computing*, 13:258–276, 2001.
11. Ulrich Junker. Quickxplain: Conflict detection for arbitrary constraint propagation algorithms. In *IJCAI'01 Workshop on Modelling and Solving problems with constraints (CONS-1)*, Seattle, WA, USA, August 2001.
12. Narendra Jussien. The versatility of using explanations within constraint programming. RR 03-04-INFO, École des Mines de Nantes, France, 2003.
13. Narendra Jussien and Olivier Lhomme. Local search with constraint propagation and conflict-based heuristics. *Artificial Intelligence*, 139(1):21–45, July 2002.
14. E. L. Lawler. Recent Results in the Theory of Machine Scheduling. *Mathematical Programming: The State of the Art*, pages 202–233, 1983.
15. C. L. Liu and J. W. Layland. Scheduling Algorithms for Multiprogramming in a Hard-Real Time Environment. *Journal ACM*, 20(1):46–61, 1973.
16. Y. Monnier, J.-P. Beauvais, and A.-M. Déplanche. A Genetic Algorithm for Scheduling Tasks in a Real-Time Distributed System. *24th Euromicro Conference*, 2, 1998.
17. K. Ramamritham. Allocation and Scheduling of Complex Periodic Tasks. *10th International Conference on Distributed Computing Systems*, pages 108–115, 1990.
18. J.C. Régin. Generalized arc consistency for global cardinality constraint. *AAAI / IAAI*, pages 209–215, 1996.
19. F. E. Sandnes. A hybrid genetic algorithm applied to automatic parallel controller code generation. *8th IEEE Euromicro Workshop on Real-Time Systems*, 1996.
20. Thomas Schiex and Gérard Verfaillie. Nogood recording for static and dynamic constraint satisfaction problem. *IJAIT*, 3(2):187–207, 1994.
21. Erlendur S. Thorsteinsson. Branch-and-check: A hybrid framework integrating mixed integer programming and constraint logic programming. In *CP'01*, 2001.
22. K. Tindell, A. Burns, and A. Wellings. Allocation Hard Real-Time tasks: An NP-Hard Problem Made Easy. *The Journal of Real-Time Systems*, 4(2):145–165, 1992.
23. K. Tindell and J. Clark. Holistic scheduling Analysis for Distributed Hard Real-Time Systems. *Euromicro Journal*, pages 40–117, 1994.

Quantified Constraint Satisfaction and 2-Semilattice Polymorphisms

Hubie Chen

Department of Computer Science
Cornell University
Ithaca, NY 14853, USA
hubes@cs.cornell.edu

Abstract. The quantified constraint satisfaction problem (QCSP) is a natural and useful generalization of the constraint satisfaction problem (CSP) in which both universal and existential quantification of variables is permitted. Because the CSP and QCSP are in general intractable, much effort has been directed towards identifying restricted cases of these problems that are tractable in polynomial time. In this paper, we investigate restricted cases of the QCSP having 2-semilattice polymorphisms. We prove a complete classification of 2-semilattice polymorphisms, demonstrating that each gives rise to a case of the QCSP that is either tractable in polynomial time, or coNP-hard.

1 Introduction

The constraint satisfaction problem (CSP) is widely acknowledged as a convenient framework for modelling search problems. An instance of the CSP consists of a set of variables, a domain, and a set of constraints; each constraint consists of a tuple of variables paired with a relation (over the domain) which contains permitted values for the variable tuple. The question is to decide whether or not there is an assignment mapping each variable to a domain element that satisfies all of the constraints.

All of the variables in a CSP can be thought of as being implicitly existentially quantified. A natural generalization of the CSP is the quantified constraint satisfaction problem (QCSP), where variables may be both existentially and universally quantified. Whereas the CSP concerns deciding the existence of a *static* object, a satisfying assignment, the QCSP concerns deciding the existence of a *dynamic* object: a strategy telling how to set the existentially quantified variables in reaction to an arbitrary setting of the universally quantified variables, so that the constraints are satisfied. The generality of the QCSP framework permits the modelling of a variety of artificial intelligence problems that cannot be expressed using the CSP, for instance, problems from the areas of planning, game playing, and non-monotonic reasoning. Of course, the relatively higher expressiveness of the QCSP comes at the price of higher complexity: whereas the CSP is in general NP-complete, the QCSP is in general complete for the complexity class PSPACE, which is believed to be much larger than NP.

The general intractability of the CSP and QCSP motivates the search for cases of these problems that are tractable in polynomial time. A particularly useful way to restrict the CSP and QCSP in order to obtain tractable cases is to restrict the types of relations that may appear in constraints. Formally, this is done by defining a *constraint language* to be a set of relations and then defining, for each constraint language Γ, the problem $\mathsf{CSP}(\Gamma)$ ($\mathsf{QCSP}(\Gamma)$) to be the restricted version of the CSP (QCSP) where only relations from the set Γ may be present. This form of restriction can capture and place into a unified framework many particular cases of the CSP that have been independently investigated, such as HORN SATISFIABILITY and 2-SATISFIABILITY, as well as their corresponding QCSP generalizations, QUANTIFIED HORN SATISFIABILITY and QUANTIFIED 2-SATISFIABILITY.

The class of problems $\mathsf{CSP}(\Gamma)$ was first considered by Schaefer; he proved a now classic classification theorem which states that for every constraint language Γ over a two-element domain, the problem $\mathsf{CSP}(\Gamma)$ is either in P or is NP-complete [25]. The non-trivial tractable cases of $\mathsf{CSP}(\Gamma)$ given by this result are the HORN SATISFIABILITY, 2-SATISFIABILITY, and XOR-SATISFIABILITY problems. Over the past decade, many more complexity classification theorems in the spirit of Schaefer's have been established for different variants and generalizations of the CSP (see for example the book [15]), including a classification theorem for the problems $\mathsf{QCSP}(\Gamma)$ in domain size two [15,16]. This classification theorem demonstrates that, when Γ is a constraint language over a two-element domain, the only tractable problems of the form $\mathsf{QCSP}(\Gamma)$ are QUANTIFIED HORN SATISFIABILITY [12], QUANTIFIED 2-SATISFIABILITY [1], and QUANTIFIED XOR-SATISFIABILITY [15], reflecting exactly the non-trivial tractable constraint languages provided by Schaefer's theorem; for all other constraint languages Γ, the problem $\mathsf{QCSP}(\Gamma)$ is PSPACE-complete.

In recent years, much effort has been directed towards the program of classifying the complexity of $\mathsf{CSP}(\Gamma)$ for all constraint languages Γ over a finite domain of *arbitrary* size. While this appears to be a particularly challenging research problem, impressive progress has been made, including the papers [18, 21, 19, 20, 17, 23, 22, 8, 4–6, 9, 3]. Many of these papers make use of an intimate connection between CSP complexity and universal algebra that has been developed [21, 19, 8]. The central notion used to establish this connection is that of *polymorphism*; a constraint language has an operation as polymorphism, roughly speaking, if each relation of the constraint language satisfies a certain closure property defined in terms of the operation. There are many results in the literature which demonstrate that if a constraint language Γ has a polymorphism of a certain type, then the problem $\mathsf{CSP}(\Gamma)$ is tractable.

Very recently, the study of QCSP complexity based on constraint languages in domains of arbitrary size was initiated [2, 13, 14]. It has been shown that the same polymorphism-based algebraic approach used to study CSP complexity can also be used to study QCSP complexity [2]. In the papers [2, 13, 14], general sufficient conditions for QCSP tractability have been identified, which, as with many of the CSP tractability results, demonstrate that the presence of a certain type of polymorphism guarantees tractability of a constraint language.

In this paper, we continue the study of QCSP complexity by investigating constraint languages that have a *2-semilattice operation* as polymorphism. A 2-semilattice operation is a binary operation $\star$ that satisfies the semilattice identities restricted to two variables, namely, the identities $x \star x = x$ (idempotence), $x \star y = y \star x$ (commutativity), and $(x \star x) \star y = x \star (x \star y)$ (restricted associativity). 2-semilattices constitute a natural generalization of semilattices, one of the initial classes of polymorphisms shown to guarantee CSP tractability [21], and have been shown to imply CSP tractability via a consistency-based algorithm [3]. We prove a full classification of 2-semilattice polymorphisms for QCSPs, showing that some such polymorphisms guarantee tractability, while others do not. We would like to highlight three reasons as to why we believe our study of 2-semilattice polymorphisms in the QCSP setting is interesting.

First, as pointed out previously in [3], 2-semilattice polymorphisms play an important role in the investigation of *maximal constraint languages*, which are constraint languages that can express any relation when augmented with any relation not expressible by the language. Because a constraint language that can express all relations is intractable, maximal constraint languages are the largest constraint languages that could possibly be tractable (in either the CSP or QCSP setting); hence, studying maximal constraint languages allows one to obtain the most general tractability results possible. (It is worth noting here that all of the tractability results identified by Schaefer's theorem apply to maximal constraint languages.) It follows from a theorem of Rosenberg [24] that maximal constraint languages can be classified into five types; for four of these types of constraint languages, QCSP tractability or QCSP intractability can be derived using established results. For the remaining type – constraint languages having a non-projection binary idempotent operation as polymorphism – a complexity classification has not yet been established. The present work constitutes a step towards understanding this remaining type. We mention that in the CSP setting, the tractability of 2-semilattices has been leveraged to give complete complexity classifications of maximal constraint languages for domains of size three and four [7, 3].

Second, our tractability proofs make use of and validate new machinery for proving QCSP tractability that was developed in [14]. In particular, a key idea from [14] that we make use of here is that of *collapsibility*; roughly speaking, a problem QCSP(Γ) is *j-collapsible* if any problem instance can be reduced to deciding the truth of a conjunction of QCSPs, each of which has a constant number of universal quantifiers and is derived from the original instance by collapsing together universally quantified variables. In [14], it was demonstrated that many constraint languages Γ are such that (1) CSP(Γ) is tractable and (2) the problem QCSP(Γ) is *j*-collapsible; it was also demonstrated that these two properties can be used together to derive the tractability of QCSP(Γ). We give another class of constraint languages having these properties, by showing that QCSP problems having tractable 2-semilattice polymorphisms are 1-collapsible.

This provides further evidence that collapsibility is a fruitful and useful tool for studying QCSP complexity. Moreover, we believe our proof of 1-collapsibility to be the most non-trivial collapsibility proof to date.

Third, although all 2-semilattice polymorphisms are tractable in the CSP setting, 2-semilattice polymorphisms intriguingly yield two modes of behavior in the QCSP setting: some 2-semilattice polymorphisms guarantee tractability, while others do not. This is surprising in light of the fact that for all other types of polymorphisms (of non-trivial constraint languages) that have been investigated, polymorphisms that guarantee CSP tractability also guarantee QCSP tractability. In fact, our results imply the first and only known examples of non-trivial constraint languages that are CSP tractable, but QCSP intractable[1]. The existence of such constraint languages implies that the boundary between tractability and intractability in the QCSP context is genuinely different from the corresponding boundary in the CSP context.

The contents of this paper are as follows. We present the basic terminology and concepts to be used throughout the paper in a preliminaries section (Section 2). We prove a classification theorem which shows that every 2-semilattice polymorphism gives rise to a case of the QCSP that is either tractable in polynomial time, or is coNP-hard; and, we derive some consequences of this theorem (Section 3). We then demonstrate, for the QCSPs having a tractable 2-semilattice polymorphism, a result significantly stronger than mere polynomial time tractability: we show that such QCSPs are 1-collapsible, the strongest possible statement one can show concerning collapsibility (Section 4).

2 Preliminaries

We use $[n]$ to denote the set containing the first n positive integers, that is, $\{1, \ldots, n\}$.

2.1 Quantified Constraint Satisfaction

Quantified formulas. A *domain* is a nonempty set of finite size. A *tuple* (over domain D) is an element of D^k for some $k \geq 1$, and is said to have arity k. The ith coordinate of a tuple $\bar{t}$ is denoted by t_i. A *relation* (over domain D) is a subset of D^k for some $k \geq 1$, and is said to have arity k.

A *constraint* is an expression of the form $R(\bar{v})$, where R is a relation and $\bar{v}$ is a tuple of variables such that R and $\bar{v}$ have the same arity. A *constraint network* is a finite set of constraints, all of which have relation over the same domain, and is said to be over the variable set V if all of its constraints have variables from V. Throughout, we let D denote the domain of our constraints and constraint networks.

---

[1] Here, by a non-trivial constraint language, we mean a constraint language that includes each constant as a relation.

Definition 1. *A quantified formula is an expression of the form $Q_1 v_1 \ldots Q_n v_n \mathcal{C}$, where each Q_i is a quantifier from the set $\{\forall, \exists\}$, and $\mathcal{C}$ is a constraint network over the variable set $\{v_1, \ldots, v_n\}$.*

The quantified formula $Q_1 v_1 \ldots Q_n v_n \mathcal{C}$ is said to have $Q_1 v_1 \ldots Q_n v_n$ as its *quantifier prefix*. We say that the variable v_i comes (strictly) before the variable v_j if $i \leq j$ ($i < j$). We let V_ϕ, Y_ϕ, and X_ϕ denote the variables, universally quantified variables, and existentially quantified variables of a quantified formula ϕ, respectively; we drop the ϕ subscript when it is understood from the context. We generally assume that the universally quantified variables (of a quantified formula) are denoted $y_1, \ldots, y_{|Y|}$, where y_i comes strictly before y_j for $i < j$; similarly, we generally assume that the existentially quantified variables (of a quantified formula) are denoted $x_1, \ldots, x_{|X|}$, where x_i comes strictly before x_j for $i < j$. When W is a non-empty subset of the variable set V_ϕ (of a quantified formula ϕ), we use $\mathsf{first}_\phi(W)$ to denote the unique variable in W coming before all of the other variables in W. For a subset W of the variable set V (of a quantified formula) and a variable v of V, we let $W[\leq v]$ ($W[< v]$) denote the set of variables in W coming (strictly) before v.

Strategies and truth. A constraint $R(v_1, \ldots, v_k)$ is *satisfied* by an assignment f defined on $\{v_1, \ldots, v_k\}$ if $(f(v_1), \ldots, f(v_k)) \in R$. A constraint network $\mathcal{C}$ (over the variable set V) is *satisfied* by an assignment $f : V \to D$ if each constraint C in $\mathcal{C}$ is satisfied by f.

Definition 2. *A strategy σ is a sequence of mappings*

$$\{\sigma_i : D^{\mathsf{rank}(\sigma_i)} \to D\}_{i \in [n]}$$

where the ith mapping σ_i is a function over D having rank $\mathsf{rank}(\sigma_i) \geq 0$.

Note that when σ_i is a mapping of a strategy such that $\mathsf{rank}(\sigma_i) = 0$, we consider σ_i to be a constant, that is, an element of D.

A *strategy for the quantified formula* ϕ is a strategy $\sigma_1, \ldots, \sigma_{|X_\phi|}$ where for $i \in [|X_\phi|]$, the mapping σ_i has rank $|Y_\phi[< x_i]|$. An *adversary for the quantified formula* ϕ is a function $\tau : Y_\phi \to D$. When σ is a strategy and τ is an adversary for the quantified formula ϕ, the *outcome* of σ and τ, denoted by $\mathsf{outcome}(\sigma, \tau) : V_\phi \to D$, is the assignment defined by $\mathsf{outcome}(\sigma, \tau)(x_i) = \sigma_i(\tau(y_1), \ldots, \tau(y_{|Y[< x_i]|}))$ for $x_i \in X_\phi$ and $\mathsf{outcome}(\sigma, \tau)(y_i) = \tau(y_i)$ for $y_i \in Y_\phi$.

A strategy σ for the quantified formula ϕ is said to be *winning* if for all adversaries τ for ϕ, the assignment $\mathsf{outcome}(\sigma, \tau) : V_\phi \to D$ satisfies the constraint network $\mathcal{C}$ of ϕ. We consider a quantified formula ϕ to be *true* if there exists a winning strategy for ϕ. (This is one of many equivalent ways to define truth of a quantified formula.)

Problem formulation. In this paper, we focus on restricted versions of the QCSP where all relations must come from a *constraint language*. A constraint *language* is defined to be a set of relations (not necessarily of the same arity), all of which are over the same domain.

Definition 3. *Let Γ be a constraint language. The* QCSP(Γ) *problem is to decide, given as input a quantified formula ϕ with constraints having relations from Γ, whether or not ϕ is true.*

We define the CSP(Γ) problem to be the restriction of the QCSP(Γ) problem to instances where all quantifiers are existential.

Polymorphisms. A powerful algebraic theory for studying the complexity of CSP(Γ) problems was introduced in [21, 19]; it can also be applied to study the complexity of QCSP(Γ) problems [2]. (We refer the reader to those papers for more information.) An operation $\mu : D^k \to D$ is a *polymorphism* of a relation $R \subseteq D^m$ if for all tuples $\overline{t_1}, \ldots, \overline{t_k} \in R$, the tuple

$$(\mu(t_{11}, \ldots, t_{k1}), \ldots, \mu(t_{1m}, \ldots, t_{km}))$$

is in R. An operation $\mu : D^k \to D$ is a polymorphism of a constraint language Γ if μ is a polymorphism of all relations $R \in \Gamma$. It has been shown that the complexity of CSP(Γ) (and QCSP(Γ)) is tightly connected to the polymorphisms of Γ; in particular, if two finite constraint languages Γ_1, Γ_2 share exactly the same polymorphisms, then CSP(Γ_1) and CSP(Γ_2) are reducible to each other via many-one polynomial time reductions (and likewise for QCSP(Γ_1) and QCSP(Γ_2)). When $\mu : D^k \to D$ is an operation, we use Inv(μ) to denote the set of all relations having μ as polymorphism.

Definition 4. *Let $\mu : D^k \to D$ be an operation. The* QCSP(μ) *problem is to decide, given as input a quantified formula ϕ with constraints having relations from* Inv(μ), *whether or not ϕ is true.*

In other words, the QCSP(μ) problem is that of deciding the truth of a quantified formula where all of the relations have μ as a polymorphism.

2.2 Collapsibility

In this paper, we will make use of machinery developed in [14] (on which the material in this subsection is based) to prove tractability results for the QCSP.

Collapsings of formulas. Define a quantified formula ϕ' to be a *j-collapsing* of a quantified formula ϕ if there exists a subset Y' of Y_ϕ such that $|Y'| = \min(j, |Y_\phi|)$ and ϕ' can be obtained from ϕ by first eliminating, from the quantifier prefix of ϕ, all variables in $Y_\phi \setminus Y'$ except for first$_\phi(Y_\phi \setminus Y')$; and then replacing, in the constraint network of ϕ, all variables in $Y_\phi \setminus Y'$ with first$_\phi(Y_\phi \setminus Y')$. For example, the quantified formula

$$\forall y_1 \exists x_1 \forall y_2 \forall y_3 \exists x_2 \{R_1(y_1, x_1), R_2(y_3, x_2), R_3(y_2, y_3, x_2)\}$$

has the following three 1-collapsings:

$$\forall y_1 \exists x_1 \forall y_2 \exists x_2 \{R_1(y_1, x_1), R_2(y_2, x_2), R_3(y_2, y_2, x_2)\}$$

$$\forall y_1 \exists x_1 \forall y_2 \exists x_2 \{R_1(y_1, x_1), R_2(y_1, x_2), R_3(y_2, y_1, x_2)\}$$
$$\forall y_1 \exists x_1 \forall y_3 \exists x_2 \{R_1(y_1, x_1), R_2(y_3, x_2), R_3(y_1, y_3, x_2)\}.$$

Note that if a quantified formula ϕ is true, then for any $j \geq 1$ and any j-collapsing ϕ' of ϕ, the quantified formula ϕ' is true.

Define a set of functions F of the form $\tau : Y \to D$ to be a j-adversary set for Y if there exists a subset $Y' \subseteq Y$ of size $\min(j, |Y|)$ such that F contains exactly those functions τ having the property that $\tau(y_1) = \tau(y_2)$ for all $y_1, y_2 \in Y \setminus Y'$. When ϕ is a quantified formula and F is a set of adversaries $\tau : Y_\phi \to D$, we say that the formula ϕ is F-winnable if there exists a strategy σ for ϕ such that for all $\tau \in F$, the assignment outcome(σ, τ) satisfies the constraint network of ϕ. As an alternative to saying that the formula ϕ is F-winnable, we will say that F is winnable when ϕ is understood from the context.

It is straightforward to verify that the j-collapsing of a quantified formula corresponding to a subset Y' is true, if and only if the formula is F-winnable, where F is the j-adversary set corresponding to Y'. Hence, we have the following proposition.

Proposition 5. *Let ϕ be a quantified formula. The j-collapsings ϕ' of ϕ are all true if and only if for each j-adversary set F for Y_ϕ, the formula ϕ is F-winnable.*

Collapsibility of problems. We say that a problem of the form QCSP(μ) is j-collapsible if for every quantified formula ϕ that is an instance of QCSP(μ), the following property holds: if all j-collapsings of ϕ are true, then ϕ is true. We say that a problem QCSP(μ) has *bounded collapsibility* if there exists a $j \geq 1$ such that QCSP(μ) is j-collapsible. The following notion of composability is useful for identifying problems of the form QCSP(μ) that have bounded collapsibility.

When $\mu : D^k \to D$ is a function, and $F, F_1, \ldots, F_k$ are sets of functions of the form $\tau : \{y_1, \ldots, y_n\} \to D$, we say that F is μ-composable in one step from $F_1, \ldots, F_k$ if there exist strategies $\pi^1 = \{\pi_i^1 : D^i \to D\}_{i \in [n]}, \ldots, \pi^k = \{\pi_i^k : D^i \to D\}_{i \in [n]}$ such that for all $\tau \in F$, the following two properties hold: (1) for all $i \in [k]$, the mapping $\tau^i : \{y_1, \ldots, y_n\} \to D$ defined by $\tau^i(y_j) = \pi_j^i(\tau(y_1), \ldots, \tau(y_j))$ (for all $j \in [n]$) is contained in F_i, and (2) it holds that $\tau(y_j) = \mu(\tau^1(y_j), \ldots, \tau^k(y_j))$ (for all $j \in [n]$). The key feature of this definition is the following lemma.

Lemma 6. *Let ϕ be a quantified formula with $\{y_1, \ldots, y_n\}$ as its universally quantified variables and with relations invariant under μ, and suppose that F is μ-composable in one step from $F_1, \ldots, F_k$. If ϕ is F_i-winnable for all $i \in [k]$, then ϕ is F-winnable.*

The condition of bounded collapsibility can be combined with CSP tractability to infer QCSP tractability results. Recall that an operation $\mu : D^k \to D$ is *idempotent* when $\mu(d, \ldots, d) = d$ for all $d \in D$.

Theorem 7. *Suppose that μ is an idempotent operation such that QCSP(μ) has bounded collapsibility and CSP(μ) is decidable in polynomial time. Then, QCSP(μ) is decidable in polynomial time.*

3 Classification of 2-Semilattices

In this section, we present a complete complexity classification of 2-semilattice operations in quantified constraint satisfaction. We first formally state the classification theorem (Theorem 8) and discuss some of its implications; then, we prove the theorem in two parts.

3.1 Statement of Classification Theorem and Implications

A 2-semilattice operation is a binary operation $\star : D^2 \to D$ such that for all $x, y \in D$ it holds that $x \star x = x$ (idempotence), $x \star y = y \star x$ (commutativity), and $(x \star x) \star y = x \star (x \star y)$ (restricted associativity). Every 2-semilattice operation $\star : D^2 \to D$ induces a directed graph $\mathcal{G}^\star = (D, E)$ with edge set $E = \{(a, b) \in D \times D : a \star b = b\}$. We use $\mathcal{C}^\star$ to denote the set of strongly connected components (or components, for short) of $\mathcal{G}^\star$, and let $\leq$ be the binary relation on $\mathcal{C}^\star$ where for $C_1, C_2 \in \mathcal{C}^\star$, it holds that $C_1 \leq C_2$ if and only if there exist vertices $v_1 \in C_1$, $v_2 \in C_2$ such that there is a path (in $\mathcal{G}^\star$) from v_1 to v_2. It is straightforward to verify that $\leq$ is a partial order. We say that $C \in \mathcal{C}^\star$ is a *minimal component* if it is minimal with respect to $\leq$, that is, for all $C' \in \mathcal{C}^\star$, $C' \leq C$ implies $C' = C$.

Our classification theorem demonstrates that 2-semilattice operations give rise to two modes of behavior in QCSP complexity, depending on the structure of the graph $\mathcal{G}^\star$.

Theorem 8. *Let $\star : D^2 \to D$ be a 2-semilattice operation. If there is a unique minimal component in $\mathcal{C}^\star$, then QCSP($\star$) is decidable in polynomial time. Otherwise, QCSP($\star$) is coNP-hard.*

One implication of this classification theorem is a complete classification of semilattice operations in QCSP complexity. Recall that a semilattice operation is a binary operation that is associative, commutative, and idempotent. We say that a semilattice operation $\star : D^2 \to D$ has a unit element if there exists an element $u \in D$ such that for all $d \in D$, $d \star u = u \star d = d$.

Corollary 9. *Let $\star : D^2 \to D$ be a semilattice operation. If $\star$ has a unit element, then QCSP($\star$) is decidable in polynomial time. Otherwise, QCSP($\star$) is coNP-hard.*

Proof. When $\star$ is a semilattice operation, it is straightforward to verify that each component in $\mathcal{C}^\star$ is of size one. Hence, $\mathcal{C}^\star$ has a unique minimal component if and only if $\star$ has a unit element. □

We note that the tractability of semilattice operations with unit has been previously derived [14].

Another implication of our classification theorem is the tractability of all *commutative conservative operations*. A commutative conservative operation is a binary operation $\star : D^2 \to D$ that is commutative and conservative. (We say that $\star$ is conservative if for all $x, y \in D$ it holds that $x \star y \in \{x, y\}$.) Such operations were studied in the context of the CSP by Bulatov and Jeavons [11].

Corollary 10. *Let $\star : D^2 \to D$ be a commutative conservative operation. The problem $\mathsf{QCSP}(\star)$ is decidable in polynomial time.*

Proof. It is straightforward to verify that when $\star$ is a commutative conservative operation, the relation $\leq$ on $\mathcal{C}^\star$ is a total ordering, and hence has a unique minimal component. □

The proof of Theorem 8 can be generalized to a multi-sorted version of the QCSP. We refer the reader to [9] for the definition and a study of the multi-sorted CSP; the definition of the multi-sorted QCSP is analogous to this definition.

Theorem 11. *Let $\star$ be a multi-sorted binary operation over a finite collection of domains $\mathcal{D}$, such that the interpretation $\star^D$ of $\star$ on any domain $D \in \mathcal{D}$ is a 2-semilattice operation. If for every domain $D \in \mathcal{D}$ there is a unique minimal component in $\mathcal{C}^{\star^D}$, then $\mathsf{QCSP}(\star)$ is decidable in polynomial time. Otherwise, $\mathsf{QCSP}(\star)$ is coNP-hard.*

3.2 Proof

We prove Theorem 8 in two parts: the tractable cases are established in Theorem 12, and the intractable cases are established in Theorem 13.

Theorem 12. *Let $\star : D^2 \to D$ be a 2-semilattice operation. If there is a unique minimal component in $\mathcal{C}^\star$, then $\mathsf{QCSP}(\star)$ is decidable in polynomial time.*

Proof. First, fix an element b in the minimal component of $\mathcal{C}^\star$. For every element $d \in D$, there exists a path from b to d in $\mathcal{G}^\star$. (This is because for every component C of $\mathcal{C}^\star$ it holds that $B \leq C$, where B denotes the minimal component of $\mathcal{C}^\star$.) Let k be a sufficiently large integer so that for every $d \in D$, there is a path from b to d of length less than or equal to k.

We show that $\mathsf{QCSP}(\star)$ is $(2^k - 1)$-collapsible; the result then follows from Theorem 7 along with the tractability of $\mathsf{CSP}(\star)$ (see [3]). Let ϕ be an instance of $\mathsf{QCSP}(\star)$ where all $(2^k - 1)$-collapsings of ϕ are true. Then, we have that for each $(2^k - 1)$-adversary set F for Y, the set F is winnable. For $W \subseteq Y$ and $d \in D$, define the set $F_{(W,d)}$ to be the set of adversaries $\tau : Y \to D$ such that $\tau(y) = d$ for all $y \in Y \setminus W$. We prove that for every universal variable subset $W \subseteq Y$ with $|W| \geq 2^k - 1$, the set $F_{(W,b)}$ is winnable. This suffices, as it implies that the set $F_{(Y,b)}$, which is the set of all adversaries $\tau : Y \to D$, is winnable.

The proof is by induction on $|W|$. When $|W| = 2^k - 1$, the claim is immediate from the assumption that that each $(2^k - 1)$-adversary set (for Y) is winnable, along with the fact that any subset of a winnable adversary set is winnable. For the induction, assume that $|W| > 2^k - 1$ and let W_0 be a subset of W having size 2^k. Let $\{w_1, \ldots, w_{2^k}\}$ denote the elements of W_0. Let F_i denote $F_{(W \setminus \{w_i\}, b)}$ (for all $i \in [2^k]$). We may assume by induction that F_i is winnable (for all $i \in [2^k]$).

We claim that there are strategies $\pi^1 = \{\pi_i^1 : D^i \to D\}_{i \in [n]}, \ldots, \pi^{2^k} = \{\pi_i^{2^k} : D^i \to D\}_{i \in [n]}$ such that for all $\tau \in F$, the following two properties hold:

(1) for all $i \in [2^k]$, the mapping $\tau^i : \{y_1, \ldots, y_n\} \to D$ defined by $\tau^i(y_j) = \pi_j^i(\tau(y_1), \ldots, \tau(y_j))$ (for all $j \in [n]$) is contained in F_i, and
(2) for all $j \in [n]$, it holds that

$$\tau(y_j) = ((\tau^1(y_j) \star \tau^2(y_j)) \star (\tau^3(y_j) \star \tau^4(y_j))) \star \cdots$$

where the right hand side of the above expression is a balanced binary tree of depth k with leaves $\tau^1(y_j), \ldots, \tau^{2^k}(y_j)$.

By appeal to Lemma 6, establishing this claim entails that $F_{(W,b)}$ is winnable. We consider two cases:

– For universal variables $y_j \in Y \setminus W_0$, we let π_j^i be the projection onto the last coordinate (for all i), so that $\tau^i(y_j) = \tau(y_j)$ and property (2) holds by the idempotence of $\star$. Note that since $\tau(y_j) = b$ when $y_j \in Y \setminus W$, we have that $\tau^i(y_j) = b$ for such y_j (for all i).
– For universal variables $y_j \in W_0$, it suffices by symmetry to show that the polynomial

$$(((b \star x_2) \star (x_3 \star x_4)) \star \cdots)$$

that is a balanced binary tree of depth k with leaves $b, x_2, \ldots, x_{2^k}$, is surjective. Identifying the variables $x_{2^i+1}, \ldots, x_{2^{i+1}}$ to be equivalent (for i ranging from 0 to $k-1$), it suffices to show that the polynomial

$$(\cdots ((b \star x_0') \star x_1') \star \cdots \star x_{k-1}')$$

is surjective. This follows immediately from our choice of k: for any element $d \in D$, there is a path from b to d in $\mathcal{G}^\star$ of length k. (Note that every vertex in $\mathcal{G}^\star$ has a self-loop, so as long as there is a path from b to d with length less than or equal to k, there is a path from b to d with length equal to k.) □

We complete the classification of 2-semilattices by proving a complement to Theorem 12, namely, that the remaining 2-semilattices give rise to QCSPs that are intractable.

Theorem 13. *Let $\star : D^2 \to D$ be a 2-semilattice operation. If there are two or more minimal components in $\mathcal{C}^\star$, then $\mathsf{QCSP}(\star)$ is coNP-hard (even when restricted to $\forall\exists$-formulas).*

Proof. We show coNP-hardness by reducing from the propositional tautology problem. Let $C(y_1, \ldots, y_n)$ be an instance of this problem, where C is a circuit with input gates having labels $y_1, \ldots, y_n$. We assume without loss of generality that all non-input gates of C are either AND or NOT gates, and assign all non-input gates labels $x_1, \ldots, x_m$. The quantifier prefix of the resulting quantified formula is $\forall y_1 \ldots \forall y_n \exists x_1 \ldots \exists x_m$. Let B_0 and B_1 be distinct minimal components in $\mathcal{C}^\star$, and let b_0 and b_1 be elements of B_0 and B_1, respectively. The constraint network of the resulting quantified formula is constructed as follows.

For each AND gate x_i with inputs $v, v' \in \{y_1, \ldots, y_n\} \cup \{x_1, \ldots, x_m\}$, include the four constraints:

- $(v \in B_1) \wedge (v' \in B_1) \Rightarrow (x_i = b_1)$
- $(v \in B_0) \wedge (v' \in B_1) \Rightarrow (x_i = b_0)$
- $(v \in B_1) \wedge (v' \in B_0) \Rightarrow (x_i = b_0)$
- $(v \in B_0) \wedge (v' \in B_0) \Rightarrow (x_i = b_0)$

For each NOT gate x_i with input $v \in \{y_1, \ldots, y_n\} \cup \{x_1, \ldots, x_m\}$, include the two constraints:

- $(v \in B_0) \Rightarrow (x_i = b_1)$
- $(v \in B_1) \Rightarrow (x_i = b_0)$

For the output gate x_o, include the constraint:

- $(x_o \in B_0) \Rightarrow$ FALSE

It is fairly straightforward to verify that each of the given constraints has the $\star$ operation as polymorphism; the key fact is that (for $i \in \{0,1\}$) multiplying any element of D by an element c outside of B_i yields an element c' outside of B_i. (If not, there is an edge from c to c' by restricted associativity of $\star$; this edge gives a contradiction to the minimality of B_i).

We verify the reduction to be correct as follows.

Suppose that the original circuit was a tautology. Let $f : \{y_1, \ldots, y_n\} \to D$ be any assignment to the $\forall$-variables of the quantified formula. Define $f' : \{y_1, \ldots, y_n\} \to (B_0 \cup B_1)$ by $f'(y_i) = f(y_i)$ if $f(y_i) \in B_0 \cup B_1$, and as an arbitrary element of $B_0 \cup B_1$ otherwise. The AND and NOT gate constraints force each x_i to have either the value b_0 or b_1 under f'; it can be verified that the assignment taking x_i to its forced value and y_i to $f(y_i)$ satisfies all of the constraints.

Suppose that the original circuit was not a tautology. Let $g : \{y_1, \ldots, y_n\} \to \{0,1\}$ be an assignment making the circuit C false. Let $g' : \{y_1, \ldots, y_n\} \to D$ be an assignment to the $\forall$-variables of the quantified formula such that $g'(y_i) \in B_{g(y_i)}$ (for all $i \in [n]$). Under the assignment g', the only assignment to the $\exists$-variables x_i satisfying the AND and NOT gate constraints is the mapping taking x_i to b_0 if the gate with label x_i has value 0 under g, and b_1 if the gate with label x_i has value 1 under g. Hence, if all of these constraints are satisfied, then the output gate constraint must be falsified. We conclude that no assignment to the $\exists$-variables x_i satisfies all of the constraints under the assignment g', and so the quantified formula is false. □

4 Tractable 2-Semilattices Are 1-Collapsible

In the previous section, it was shown that for certain 2-semilattice operations $\star$, the problem QCSP($\star$) is polynomial-time tractable. For these operations, it was proved that QCSP($\star$) is j-collapsible for *some* constant j. However, the given proof demonstrated j-collapsibility for constants j that could be arbitrarily large, depending on the operation $\star$. In this section, we refine this result by proving the strongest possible statement concerning the collapsibility of QCSP($\star$): the problem QCSP($\star$) is 1-collapsible whenever QCSP($\star$) is tractable.

Theorem 14. *Let $\star : D^2 \to D$ be a 2-semilattice operation. If there is a unique minimal component in $\mathcal{C}^\star$, then $\mathsf{QCSP}(\star)$ is 1-collapsible.*

In the proof of this theorem, we write adversaries (and sets of adversaries) using tuple notation. We also use the notation $F \triangleleft F_1 \star F_2$ to denote that F is $\star$-composable in one step from F_1 and F_2.

Proof. Fix d_0 to be any element of the unique minimal component of $\mathcal{C}^\star$. For every element $d \in D$, there exists a path from d_0 to d in $\mathcal{G}^\star$. Hence, it is possible to select sufficiently large integers K and L and elements $\{d_i^j\}_{i \in [L], j \in [K]}$ so that:

— each of the sets
$$P^1 = \{d_0^1, d_1^1, \ldots, d_L^1\}$$
$$\vdots$$
$$P^K = \{d_0^K, d_1^K, \ldots, d_L^K\}$$

is a path in the sense that, for all $j \in [K]$, all of the pairs
$$(d_0^j, d_1^j), (d_1^j, d_2^j), \ldots, (d_{L-1}^j, d_L^j)$$
are edges in $\mathcal{G}^\star$; and,

— all elements of D lie on one of these paths, that is, $D = \bigcup_{j=1}^{K} P^j$.

Here, we use $d_0^1, \ldots, d_0^K$ as alternative notation for d_0, that is,
$$d_0 = d_0^1 = \cdots = d_0^K$$

For $i = 0, \ldots, L$ we define
$$D_i \overset{\text{def}}{=} \{d_i^1, \ldots, d_i^k\},$$
and we define
$$E_i \overset{\text{def}}{=} D_0 \cup \cdots \cup D_i.$$

Notice that $E_L = D$.

To prove 1-collapsibility, we fix a problem instance, and assume that each 1-adversary set is winnable. In particular, we assume that each of the sets
$$D \times \{d_0\} \times \cdots \times \{d_0\}$$
$$\vdots$$
$$\{d_0\} \times \cdots \times \{d_0\} \times D$$

is winnable. Our goal is to prove that $D \times \cdots \times D$ is winnable.

We prove by induction that for all $i = 0, \ldots, L$ the set $E_i \times \cdots \times E_i$ is winnable. The base case $i = 0$ holds by assumption. For the induction, assume that $E_i \times \cdots \times E_i$ is winnable (where $i \geq 0$); we show that $E_{i+1} \times \cdots \times E_{i+1}$ is winnable.

We first show that $E_{i+1} \times E_i \times \cdots \times E_i$ is winnable. We have

$$(E_{i+1} \times E_0 \times \cdots \times E_0) \triangleleft (E_i \times E_i \times \cdots \times E_i) \star (D \times \{d_0\} \times \cdots \times \{d_0\}).$$

Then, we have

$$(E_{i+1} \times E_1 \times \cdots \times E_1) \triangleleft (E_i \times E_i \times \cdots \times E_i) \star (E_{i+1} \times E_0 \times \cdots \times E_0)$$

and

$$(E_{i+1} \times E_2 \times \cdots \times E_2) \triangleleft (E_i \times E_i \times \cdots \times E_i) \star (E_{i+1} \times E_1 \times \cdots \times E_1).$$

Continuing in this manner, we can show that $E_{i+1} \times E_i \times \cdots \times E_i$ is winnable. By symmetric arguments, we can show the winnability of the sets

$$(E_i \times E_{i+1} \times E_i \times \cdots \times E_i)$$

$$\vdots$$

$$(E_i \times E_i \times \cdots \times E_i \times E_{i+1}).$$

We have the winnability of $E_{i+1} \times E_{i+1} \times E_i \times \cdots E_i$ by

$$(E_{i+1} \times E_{i+1} \times E_i \times \cdots E_i) \triangleleft (E_{i+1} \times E_i \times E_i \times \cdots \times E_i) \star (E_i \times E_{i+1} \times E_i \times \cdots \times E_i)$$

and we have the winnability of $E_{i+1}^3 \times E_i \times \cdots \times E_i$ by

$$(E_{i+1}^3 \times E_i \times \cdots \times E_i) \triangleleft (E_{i+1}^2 \times E_i \times E_i \times \cdots \times E_i) \star (E_i^2 \times E_{i+1} \times E_i \times \cdots \times E_i).$$

Proceeding in this fashion, we have the winnability of $E_{i+1} \times \cdots \times E_{i+1}$, as desired. □

References

1. Bengt Aspvall, Michael F. Plass, and Robert Endre Tarjan. A Linear-Time Algorithm for Testing the Truth of Certain Quantified Boolean Formulas. Inf. Process. Lett. 8(3): 121-123 (1979).
2. F. Börner, A. Bulatov, A. Krokhin, and P. Jeavons. Quantified Constraints: Algorithms and Complexity. Computer Science Logic 2003.
3. A. Bulatov. Combinatorial problems raised from 2-semilattices. Manuscript.
4. Andrei A. Bulatov. A Dichotomy Theorem for Constraints on a Three-Element Set. FOCS 2002.
5. A. Bulatov. Malt'sev constraints are tractable. Technical report PRG-RR-02-05, Oxford University, 2002.
6. Andrei A. Bulatov. Tractable conservative Constraint Satisfaction Problems. LICS 2003.
7. Andrei A. Bulatov and Andrei A. Krokhin and Peter Jeavons. The complexity of maximal constraint languages. STOC 2001.
8. Andrei A. Bulatov, Andrei A. Krokhin, and Peter Jeavons. Constraint Satisfaction Problems and Finite Algebras. ICALP 2000.

9. A. Bulatov and P. Jeavons. An Algebraic Approach to Multi-sorted Constraints Proceedings of 9th International Conference on Principles and Practice of Constraint Programming, 2003.
10. A. Bulatov, and P. Jeavons. Algebraic structures in combinatorial problems. Technical report MATH-AL-4-2001, Technische Universitat Dresden, 2001.
11. A. Bulatov, and P. Jeavons. Tractable constraints closed under a binary operation. Technical report PRG-TR-12-00, Oxford University, 2000.
12. Hans Kleine Büning, Marek Karpinski, and Andreas Flögel. Resolution for Quantified Boolean Formulas. Information and Computation 117(1): 12-18 (1995).
13. Hubie Chen. Quantified Constraint Satisfaction Problems: Closure Properties, Complexity, and Algorithms. Cornell technical report, 2003.
14. Hubie Chen. Collapsibility and Consistency in Quantified Constraint Satisfaction. AAAI 2004.
15. Nadia Creignou, Sanjeev Khanna, and Madhu Sudan. Complexity Classifications of Boolean Constraint Satisfaction Problems. SIAM Monographs on Discrete Mathematics and Applications 7, 2001.
16. Victor Dalmau. Some Dichotomy Theorems on Constant-free Quantified Boolean Formulas. Technical report LSI-97-43-R, Llenguatges i Sistemes Informàtics - Universitat Politècnica de Catalunya, 1997.
17. Victor Dalmau and Justin Pearson. Set Functions and Width 1. Constraint Programming '99.
18. Tomás Feder and Moshe Y. Vardi. The Computational Structure of Monotone Monadic SNP and Constraint Satisfaction: A Study through Datalog and Group Theory. SIAM J. Comput. 28(1): 57-104, 1998.
19. Peter Jeavons. On the Algebraic Structure of Combinatorial Problems. Theor. Comput. Sci. 200(1-2): 185-204, 1998.
20. P.G.Jeavons, D.A.Cohen and M.Cooper. Constraints, Consistency and Closure. Artificial Intelligence, 1998, 101(1-2), pages 251-265.
21. Peter Jeavons, David A. Cohen, and Marc Gyssens. Closure properties of constraints. J. ACM 44(4): 527-548 (1997).
22. Phokion G. Kolaitis, Moshe Y. Vardi. Conjunctive-Query Containment and Constraint Satisfaction. J. Comput. Syst. Sci. 61(2): 302-332 (2000)
23. Phokion G. Kolaitis and Moshe Y. Vardi. A Game-Theoretic Approach to Constraint Satisfaction. AAAI 2000.
24. I.G. Rosenberg. Minimal Clones I: the five types. Lectures in Universal Algebra (Proc. Conf. Szeged 1983), Colloq. Math. Soc. Janos Bolyai. 1986.
25. T. Schaefer. The complexity of satisfiability problems. Proceedings of the 10th Annual Symposium on Theory of Computing, ACM, 1978.

(Smart) Look-Ahead Arc Consistency and the Pursuit of CSP Tractability

Hubie Chen[1] and Víctor Dalmau[2]

[1] Department of Computer Science
Cornell University
Ithaca, NY 14853, USA
hubes@cs.cornell.edu
[2] Departament de Tecnologia
Universitat Pompeu Fabra
Barcelona, Spain
victor.dalmau@upf.edu

Abstract. The constraint satisfaction problem (CSP) can be formulated as the problem of deciding, given a pair $(\mathbf{A}, \mathbf{B})$ of relational structures, whether or not there is a homomorphism from $\mathbf{A}$ to $\mathbf{B}$. Although the CSP is in general intractable, it may be restricted by requiring the "target structure" $\mathbf{B}$ to be fixed; denote this restriction by $\mathsf{CSP}(\mathbf{B})$. In recent years, much effort has been directed towards classifying the complexity of all problems $\mathsf{CSP}(\mathbf{B})$. The acquisition of $\mathsf{CSP}(\mathbf{B})$ tractability results has generally proceeded by isolating a class of relational structures $\mathbf{B}$ believed to be tractable, and then demonstrating a polynomial-time algorithm for the class. In this paper, we introduce a new approach to obtaining $\mathsf{CSP}(\mathbf{B})$ tractability results: instead of starting with a class of structures, we start with an algorithm called *look-ahead arc consistency*, and give an algebraic characterization of the structures solvable by our algorithm. This characterization is used both to identify new tractable structures and to give new proofs of known tractable structures.

1 Introduction

1.1 Background

Constraint satisfaction problems arise in a wide variety of domains, such as combinatorics, logic, algebra, and artificial intelligence. An instance of the constraint satisfaction problem (CSP) consists of a set of variables and a set of constraints on those variables; the goal is to decide whether or not there is an assignment to the variables satisfying all of the constraints. It is often convenient to cast the CSP as a relational homomorphism problem, namely, the problem of deciding, given a pair $(\mathbf{A}, \mathbf{B})$ of relational structures, whether or not there is a homomorphism from $\mathbf{A}$ to $\mathbf{B}$. In this formalization, each relation of $\mathbf{A}$ contains tuples of variables that are constrained together, and the corresponding relation of $\mathbf{B}$ contains the allowable tuples of values that the variable tuples may take.

The CSP is NP-complete in general, motivating the search for polynomial-time tractable cases of the CSP. A particularly useful way to restrict the CSP in order to obtain tractable cases is to restrict the types of constraints that may be expressed, by requiring the "target structure" **B** to be fixed; denote this restriction by CSP(**B**). This form of restriction can capture and place into a unified framework many particular cases of the CSP that have been independently investigated – for instance, the HORN SATISFIABILITY, 2-SATISFIABILITY, and GRAPH H-COLORABILITY problems. Schaefer was the first to consider the class of problems CSP(**B**); he proved a now famous dichotomy theorem, showing that for all relational structures **B** over a two-element universe, CSP(**B**) is either tractable in polynomial time, or is NP-complete [17]. In recent years, much effort has been directed towards the program of classifying the complexity of CSP(**B**) for all relational structures **B** over a finite universe; impressive progress has been made along these lines, including the papers [11,14,12,13,9,16,15,5,2–4,6,1]. This research program has developed a rich set of tools for studying CSP complexity, which draws on and establishes connections to a diversity of areas, including artificial intelligence, universal algebra, database theory, logic, and group theory. The connection between CSP complexity and universal algebra [14,12,5] has been particularly fruitful and has been used heavily to obtain many of the recent results on CSP(**B**) complexity. A notion used to establish this connection is that of *invariance of a relational structure under an operation*; roughly speaking, a relational structure is invariant under an operation if the relations of the structure satisfy a certain closure property defined in terms of the operation.

A central component of the CSP(**B**) classification program is to identify those structures **B** such that CSP(**B**) is tractable. Indeed, Bulatov and Jeavons [7] have identified a plausible conjecture as to which structures **B** are tractable; in particular, they conjecture that a known necessary condition for tractability is also sufficient. This conjecture has been verified for some large classes of structures **B**; see [2] and [4].

The acquisition of CSP(**B**) tractability results has, almost exclusively, proceeded by isolating an easily describable condition believed to imply tractability, and then demonstrating an algorithm that decides CSP(**B**) for all **B** satisfying the condition [11,14,13,9,5,8,2–4,6,1][1]. As an example, in [8], the class of relational structures invariant under a *commutative conservative* operation is demonstrated to be tractable by an algorithm known as *3-minimality*. A simple algorithm can be given for deciding whether or not a relational structure is invariant under a commutative conservative operation; on the other hand, the meta-question of deciding, given a relational structure **B**, whether or not 3-minimality is a solution procedure for CSP(**B**), is not known to be decidable. Put succinctly, this result (and many others) demonstrate that a well-characterized class of relational structures is tractable, via an algorithm that is *not* well-characterized.

---

[1] A notable exception is the paper [9], which gives an algebraic characterization of those relational structures for which *establishing arc consistency* is a solution procedure.

1.2 Contributions of This Paper

In this paper, we introduce a radically different approach to the acquisition of CSP(**B**) tractability results. Instead of taking as our starting point a well-characterized class of relational structures, we begin with an algorithm for constraint satisfaction, and prove that this algorithm is well-characterized. In particular, we introduce a polynomial-time algorithm which we call *look-ahead arc consistency* (LAAC), and show that those structures **B** for which LAAC decides CSP(**B**) are exactly those structures satisfying a simple algebraic criterion; this algebraic characterization can be readily translated to a decision procedure for the meta-question of deciding whether or not LAAC is a solution procedure for a given relational structure[2]. We then use this algebraic characterization to give a new class of tractable relational structures that is described using the algebraic notion of invariance under an operation. We hope that our work will inspire further research devoted to giving algebraic characterizations of algorithms similar to our characterization, and that such research will stimulate an interplay between our new approach of studying well-characterized algorithms, and the classical approach of studying well-characterized problem restrictions.

In addition to containing relational structures that have not been previously observed to be tractable, the new class of relational structures that we identify also contains structures that can be shown to be tractable by known results. The fact that these latter structures are contained in our new class does not yield any new information from the standpoint of classifying CSP(**B**) problems as either tractable or NP-complete; nonetheless, we believe this fact to be interesting for two reasons. First, it implies that these relational structures can be solved using a new algorithm (namely, LAAC) which we believe to be conceptually simpler than previously given algorithms for the structures; second, it gives an alternative proof of the tractability of such structures. We mention that the LAAC algorithm is a solution method for the well-known 2-SATISFIABILITY problem; this was, in fact, observed first in [10] for a specialization of the LAAC algorithm to inputs that are boolean formulas in conjunctive normal form.

We study both LAAC and an extension of LAAC which we call *smart look-ahead arc consistency* (SLAAC); like LAAC, the SLAAC algorithm runs in polynomial time. We show that there is an algebraic characterization, similar to that for LAAC, of the relational structures for which SLAAC is a solution procedure. We also demonstrate that SLAAC is a solution procedure for a fragment of the class of relational structures invariant under a commutative conservative operation. As mentioned, this class of structures has previously been shown to be tractable [8]; however, we believe our new demonstration of tractability to be interesting for the same two reasons (given above) that our rederivation of known tractability results via LAAC is interesting.

We wish to emphasize that, from our viewpoint, the novelty of this paper lies in our ability to provide, for each of the two algorithms, an exact characterization

---

[2] Amusingly and intriguingly, LAAC is itself a decision procedure for this meta-question: the algebraic criterion concerns the existence of a relational homomorphism to **B**, and can be cast as an instance of CSP(**B**).

of the problems CSP(**B**) for which the algorithm is a solution procedure–and not in the sophistication of the algorithms, which are actually quite simple. Such exact characterizations of algorithms are not in general known, and we regard the ideas in this paper as a starting point for developing exact characterizations for algorithms of higher sophistication.

In what remains of this section, we give a brief overview of the LAAC and SLAAC algorithms. Both of these algorithms make use of *arc consistency*, a localized inference mechanism studied heavily in constraint satisfaction. Arc consistency generalizes *unit propagation*, the process of removing unit clauses from boolean formulas. Any instance of the CSP can be efficiently "tightened" into an equivalent instance (that is, an instance having the same satisfying homomorphisms) that is arc consistent. This tightening provides a sort of one-sided satisfiability check: if the second instance has an empty constraint, then the original instance is unsatisfiable; however, the converse does not hold in general. When the second instance does not have any empty constraints, we say that *arc consistency can be established* on the original instance. The *look-ahead arc consistency* algorithm is the following:

- Arbitrarily pick a variable a, and set E to be the empty set.
- For all values b of the target structure **B**, substitute b for a, and attempt to establish arc consistency; if arc consistency can be established, place b into the set E.
- If E is empty, then output "unsatisfiable"; otherwise, arbitrarily pick a value $b \in E$ and set the variable a to b.
- Repeat.

It can be seen that the algorithm proceeds by picking a variable a, and then constructing a "filtered" set E of possible values for a; it then commits a to any one of the values inside the filtered set (presuming that it is non-empty), and continues. Notice that it never makes sense to set the variable a to a value outside of its "filtered" set E, since if arc consistency cannot be established after value b is substituted for a, then there is no satisfying assignment mapping a to b. This algorithm is quite simple: indeed, up to two arbitrary choices (choice of variable and choice of value) can be made in each iteration, and the only conceptual primitive used other than picking and setting variables is arc consistency. In the "smart" version of look-ahead arc consistency, one of these arbitrary choices is eliminated: the value for a variable a is picked from the set E by applying a set function to E. Despite the simplicity of LAAC and SLAAC, the class of relational structures that are tractable via these algorithms is surprisingly rich.

Note that, due to space limitations, some proofs are omitted.

2 Preliminaries

Our definitions and notation are fairly standard, and similar to those used in other papers on constraint satisfaction. A *relation* over a set A is a subset of A^k (for some $k \geq 1$), and is said to have *arity* k. When R is a relation of arity k and $i_1, \ldots, i_l \in \{1, \ldots, k\}$, we use $\mathrm{pr}_{i_1,\ldots,i_l} R$ to denote the arity l relation $\{(a_{i_1}, \ldots, a_{i_l}) : (a_1, \ldots, a_k) \in R\}$.

Relational structures. A *vocabulary* σ is a finite set of relation symbols, each of which has an associated arity. A *relational structure* $\mathbf{A}$ (over vocabulary σ) consists of a universe A and a relation $R^{\mathbf{A}}$ over A for each relation symbol R of σ, such that the arity of $R^{\mathbf{A}}$ matches the arity associated to R by σ. In this paper, we will only be concerned with relational structures having finite universe. Throughout, we will use bold capital letters $\mathbf{A}, \mathbf{B}, \ldots$ to denote relational structures, and the corresponding non-bold capital letters $A, B, \ldots$ to denote their universes.

When $\mathbf{A}$ and $\mathbf{B}$ are relational structures over the same vocabulary σ, we define $\mathbf{A} \times \mathbf{B}$ to be the relational structure with universe $A \times B$ such that for each relation symbol R of σ, it holds that $R^{\mathbf{A} \times \mathbf{B}} = \{((a_1, b_1), \ldots, (a_k, b_k)) : (a_1, \ldots, a_k) \in R^{\mathbf{A}}, (b_1, \ldots, b_k) \in R^{\mathbf{B}}\}$, where k denotes the arity of R. When $\mathbf{A}$ and $\mathbf{B}$ are relational structures over the same vocabulary σ, we define $\mathbf{A} \cup \mathbf{B}$ to be the relational structure with universe $A \cup B$ such that for each relation symbol R of σ, $R^{\mathbf{A} \cup \mathbf{B}} = R^{\mathbf{A}} \cup R^{\mathbf{B}}$.

When $\mathbf{A}$ and $\mathbf{B}$ are relational structures over the same vocabulary σ, a *homomorphism* from $\mathbf{A}$ to $\mathbf{B}$ is a mapping $h : A \to B$ from the universe A of $\mathbf{A}$ to the universe B of $\mathbf{B}$ such that for every relation symbol R of σ and every tuple $(a_1, \ldots, a_k) \in R^{\mathbf{A}}$, it holds that $(h(a_1), \ldots, h(a_k)) \in R^{\mathbf{B}}$.

Constraint satisfaction. The constraint satisfaction problem, denoted by CSP, is defined to be the problem of deciding, given as input a pair of relational structures $(\mathbf{A}, \mathbf{B})$ over the same vocabulary, whether or not there exists a homomorphism from the *source structure* $\mathbf{A}$ to the *target structure* $\mathbf{B}$. When $(\mathbf{A}, \mathbf{B})$ is a CSP instance, we will say that $(\mathbf{A}, \mathbf{B})$ is *satisfiable* if there is a homomorphism from $\mathbf{A}$ to $\mathbf{B}$; and, we will at times refer to elements of the universe of the source structure $\mathbf{A}$ as *variables*. The CSP($\mathbf{B}$) problem is the restriction of the CSP problem where the target structure must be $\mathbf{B}$.

When $(\mathbf{A}, \mathbf{B})$ is a CSP instance over the vocabulary σ, $a \in A$, and $b \in B$, we let $(\mathbf{A}, \mathbf{B})[a = b]$ denote the CSP instance obtained from $(\mathbf{A}, \mathbf{B})$ in the following way: for each relation symbol R of σ, remove each tuple $(a_1, \ldots, a_k) \in R^{\mathbf{A}}$ such that $a \in \{a_1, \ldots, a_k\}$ and add the tuple $(a_{i_1}, \ldots, a_{i_l})$, where $i_1 < \cdots < i_l$ and $\{i_1, \ldots, i_l\} = \{i : a_i \neq a\}$, to $S^{\mathbf{A}}$, where S a relation symbol such that $S^{\mathbf{B}} = \mathrm{pr}_{i_1, \ldots, i_l}\{(b_1, \ldots, b_k) \in R^{\mathbf{B}} : \forall i \in \{i : a_i = a\}, b_i = b\}$; if necessary, extend the vocabulary σ and the relational structure $\mathbf{B}$ so that there is such a relation symbol S. Intuitively, $(\mathbf{A}, \mathbf{B})[a = b]$ is the CSP instance obtained by setting the variable a to the value b; a mapping h is a homomorphism for $(\mathbf{A}, \mathbf{B})$ sending a to b if and only if the restriction of h to $A \setminus \{a\}$ is a homomorphism for $(\mathbf{A}, \mathbf{B})[a = b]$. We say that a relational structure $\mathbf{B}$ over vocabulary σ *permits constant instantiation for* C if $C \subseteq B$ and the following two properties hold: (1) for every $b \in C$, there exists a relation symbol R_b of σ such that $R_b^{\mathbf{B}} = \{(b)\}$; and, (2) for every relation symbol R of σ, index subset $\{i_1, \ldots, i_l\} \subseteq \{1, \ldots, k\}$ (where k denotes the arity of R and $i_1 < \cdots < i_l$), and $b \in C$, there exists a relation symbol S such that $S^{\mathbf{B}} = \mathrm{pr}_{i_1, \ldots, i_l}\{(b_1, \ldots, b_k) : \forall i \notin \{i_1, \ldots, i_l\}, b_i = b\}$. The key feature of this notion is that if $(\mathbf{A}, \mathbf{B})$ is an instance of CSP($\mathbf{B}$) and $\mathbf{B}$ permits constant instantiation for C, then for any $a \in A$ and $b \in C$, the instance $(\mathbf{A}, \mathbf{B})[a = b]$ is an instance of $\mathsf{CSP}(\mathbf{B})$. If the relational structure $\mathbf{B}$ permits constant instantiation for its entire universe, we simply say that $\mathbf{B}$ *permits constant instantiation*.

An equivalent way of formulating the constraint satisfaction problem is as follows. Define a *constraint* to be an expression of the form $R(a_1, \ldots, a_k)$ where R is a relation of arity k over a finite set B, and each a_i is a variable taken from a finite variable set A. Let us say that an assignment $h : A \to B$ satisfies the constraint $R(a_1, \ldots, a_k)$ if $(h(a_1), \ldots, h(a_k)) \in R$. With these definitions in hand, we can provide a constraint-based formulation of the CSP: given a finite set of constraints – all of which have relations over the same set B, and variables from the variable set A – decide whether or not there is an assignment $h : A \to B$ satisfying all of the constraints. When $\mathbf{A}$ and $\mathbf{B}$ are relational structures over the same vocabulary σ, the instance $(\mathbf{A}, \mathbf{B})$ of the CSP problem as formulated above can be translated into this formulation by creating, for each relation R of σ and for each tuple $(a_1, \ldots, a_k)$ of $R^\mathbf{A}$, a constraint $R^\mathbf{B}(a_1, \ldots, a_k)$. It is straightforward to verify that an assignment $h : A \to B$ satisfies all such constraints if and only if it is a homomorphism from $\mathbf{A}$ to $\mathbf{B}$.

Arc consistency. Suppose that $\mathcal{C}$ is a set of constraints, that is, an instance of the constraint-based CSP. We say that $\mathcal{C}$ is *arc consistent* if for any two constraints $R(a_1, \ldots, a_k)$, $R'(a'_1, \ldots, a'_{k'})$ in $\mathcal{C}$, if $a_i = a'_j$, then $\mathsf{pr}_i R = \mathsf{pr}_j R'$. Any CSP instance $\mathcal{C}$ can be transformed, in polynomial time, into an arc consistent CSP instance that is equivalent in that it has exactly the same satisfying assignments. This is done by continually looking for constraints $R(a_1, \ldots, a_k)$, $R'(a'_1, \ldots, a'_{k'})$ and i, j such that $a_i = a'_j$ and $\mathsf{pr}_i R \neq \mathsf{pr}_j R'$, and replacing R by $\{(a_1, \ldots, a_k) \in R : a_i \in \mathsf{pr}_j R'\}$, and R' by $\{(a'_1, \ldots, a'_{k'}) \in R' : a_j \in \mathsf{pr}_i R\}$.

The procedure of transforming a CSP instance $\mathcal{C}$ into an equivalent arc consistent instance $\mathcal{C}'$ gives a sort of one-sided satisfiability check. Specifically, if the second instance $\mathcal{C}'$ has an empty relation, we can immediately conclude that the original instance $\mathcal{C}$ is unsatisfiable. (This is because no assignment can satisfy a constraint having empty relation.) Note, however, that the converse does not hold: if an instance $\mathcal{C}$ is unsatisfiable, it does not (in general) follow that an equivalent arc-consistent instance $\mathcal{C}'$ contains an empty relation.

When $\mathbf{B}$ is a relational structure over vocabulary σ, define $\mathcal{P}(\mathbf{B})$ to be the relational structure over σ having universe $\wp(B) \setminus \{\emptyset\}$ and such that for every relation symbol R of σ, $R^{\mathcal{P}(\mathbf{B})} = \{(\mathsf{pr}_1 R', \ldots, \mathsf{pr}_k R') : R' \subseteq R^\mathbf{B}, R' \neq \emptyset\}$, where k denotes the arity of R. (By $\wp(B)$, we denote the power set of B.) Let $(\mathbf{A}, \mathbf{B})$ be an instance of the CSP, and let $\mathcal{C}$ be the corresponding equivalent instance in the constraint-based CSP formulation. When the above arc consistency procedure can be applied to the instance $\mathcal{C}$ to obtain an equivalent arc consistent instance $\mathcal{C}'$ that does not have an empty relation, there exists a homomorphism from $\mathbf{A}$ to $\mathcal{P}(\mathbf{B})$. (We can define a homomorphism $h : \mathbf{A} \to \mathcal{P}(\mathbf{B})$ as follows. For any element a of A, let $R'(a_1, \ldots, a_{k'})$ be any constraint in $\mathcal{C}'$ such that $a'_i = a$, and define $h(a) = \mathsf{pr}_i R'$. By the definition of arc consistency, the definition of h on a is independent of the choice of constraint. It is straightforward to verify that h is a homomorphism from $\mathbf{A}$ to $\mathcal{P}(\mathbf{B})$.) Moreover, when there is a homomorphism from **A** to $\mathcal{P}(\mathbf{B})$, the above arc consistency procedure terminates without introducing an empty relation. In light of these facts, when $(\mathbf{A}, \mathbf{B})$ is a CSP instance, we say that *arc consistency can be established on* $(\mathbf{A}, \mathbf{B})$ if there exists a homomorphism from **A** to $\mathcal{P}(\mathbf{B})$.

Invariance. A powerful algebraic theory for studying the complexity of CSP(**B**) problems was introduced in [14, 12]. We briefly recall the key definitions of this theory that will be used in this paper, referring the reader to [14, 12] for a detailed treatment. To every relational structure **B**, we can associate a class of functions, called the *polymorphisms* of **B**, and denoted by Pol(**B**). A function $f : B^k \to B$ is a polymorphism of **B** if f is a homomorphism from $\mathbf{B}^k$ to **B**; when this holds, we also say that **B** is *invariant* under f. An important fact concerning the polymorphisms of a relational structure is that the complexity of CSP(**B**) depends only on Pol(**B**). Precisely, if $\mathbf{B}_1$ and $\mathbf{B}_2$ are relational structures with the same universe such that Pol($\mathbf{B}_1$) = Pol($\mathbf{B}_2$), then CSP($\mathbf{B}_1$) and CSP($\mathbf{B}_2$) are reducible to each other via polynomial-time many-one reductions [12]. This tight connection between the polymorphisms of **B** and the complexity of CSP(**B**) permits the use of sophisticated algebraic tools in the quest to understand the complexity of CSP(**B**), for all relational structures **B** [14, 12, 5].

3 Algorithms

In this section, we present the look-ahead arc consistency algorithm and the smart look-ahead arc consistency algorithm; and, we give purely algebraic characterizations of the class of relational structures solvable by each of the algorithms.

We begin by giving a formal description of look-ahead arc consistency.

Algorithm 1 *Look-Ahead Arc Consistency (LAAC).*
  Input: a CSP *instance* $(\mathbf{A}, \mathbf{B})$.

- *Initialize h to be an empty mapping, that is, a mapping with empty set as domain.*
- *While the universe of* **A** *is non-empty:*
  - *Arbitrarily pick a variable a from the universe of* **A**.
  - *Compute the set E of values b (from the universe of* **B***) such that arc consistency can be established on* $(\mathbf{A}, \mathbf{B})[a = b]$.
  - *If the set E is empty:*
    * *Output "unsatisfiable" and terminate.*
  - *Else:*
    * *Arbitrarily pick a value b from E, and extend h to map a to b.*
    * *Replace* $(\mathbf{A}, \mathbf{B})$ *with* $(\mathbf{A}, \mathbf{B})[a = b]$.
- *Output the mapping h and terminate.*

When **B** is a relational structure, we will say that LAAC is a solution procedure for CSP(**B**) if for every instance (**A**, **B**) of CSP(**B**), when there is a homomorphism from **A** to **B**, the LAAC algorithm outputs such a homomorphism. Notice that if there is no homomorphism from **A** to **B**, the LAAC algorithm will always output "unsatisfiable" on the CSP instance (**A**, **B**).

We now give an algebraic characterization of those relational structures **B** for which LAAC solves CSP(**B**). Our algebraic characterization has a particularly simple form, namely, it concerns the existence of a homomorphism from $\mathcal{L}(\mathbf{B})$, a relational structure derivable from **B**, to **B** itself.

The relational structure $\mathcal{L}(\mathbf{B})$ is defined as follows. For a relational structure **B** with universe B, let $L(B)$ to be the set

$$(\{S \in \wp(B) : |S| > 1\} \times B) \cup \{(\{s\}, \star) : s \in B\}$$

where $\star$ is assumed to not be an element of B.

Define $\mathbf{c_B} : (\wp(B) \setminus \{\emptyset\}) \times B \to L(B)$ to be the (surjective) mapping such that $\mathbf{c_B}(S, b) = (S, \star)$ if $|S| = 1$, and $\mathbf{c_B}(S, b) = (S, b)$ if $|S| > 1$. Intuitively, the mapping $\mathbf{c_B}$ "collapses" together elements of $\mathcal{P}(\mathbf{B}) \times \mathbf{B}$ that share the same singleton set in their first coordinate. Define $\mathcal{L}(\mathbf{B})$ to be the relational structure, over the same vocabulary σ as **B**, having universe $L(B)$ and such that for all relation symbols R of σ, $R^{\mathcal{L}(\mathbf{B})} = \{(\mathbf{c_B}(t_1), \ldots, \mathbf{c_B}(t_k)) : (t_1, \ldots, t_k) \in R^{\mathcal{P}(\mathbf{B}) \times \mathbf{B}}\}$, where k denotes the arity of R. Clearly, $\mathbf{c_B}$ is a homomorphism from $\mathcal{P}(\mathbf{B}) \times \mathbf{B}$ to $\mathcal{L}(\mathbf{B})$; one can think of $\mathcal{L}(\mathbf{B})$ as a "collapsed" version of $\mathcal{P}(\mathbf{B}) \times \mathbf{B}$.

Theorem 1. *Let **B** be a relational structure (with universe B). The LAAC algorithm is a solution procedure for CSP(**B**) if and only if there exists a homomorphism $l : \mathcal{L}(\mathbf{B}) \to \mathbf{B}$ such that $l(\{b\}, \star) = b$ for all $b \in B$.*

Proof. Suppose that there exists a homomorphism l of the described form. We assume that **B** permits constant instantiation; if it does not, it may be expanded to a relational structure which does and still possesses the homomorphism l. It suffices to show that each time a variable is set by LAAC, satisfiability is preserved. Precisely, we show that when **A** is a relational structure such that (**A**, **B**) is satisfiable (via the homomorphism $h : \mathbf{A} \to \mathbf{B}$), then for any $a \in A$, $b \in B$, if arc consistency can be established on (**A**, **B**)$[a = b]$, then (**A**, **B**)$[a = b]$ is satisfiable. When arc consistency can be established on (**A**, **B**)$[a = b]$, it follows (by the definitions of (**A**, **B**)$[a = b]$ and $\mathcal{P}(\mathbf{B})$) that there is a homomorphism $p : \mathbf{A} \to \mathcal{P}(\mathbf{B})$ such that $p(a) = \{b\}$. Composing the homomorphisms $(p, h) : \mathbf{A} \to \mathcal{P}(\mathbf{B}) \times \mathbf{B}$, $\mathbf{c_B} : \mathcal{P}(\mathbf{B}) \times \mathbf{B} \to \mathcal{L}(\mathbf{B})$, and $l : \mathcal{L}(\mathbf{B}) \to \mathbf{B}$, we obtain a homomorphism from **A** to **B** sending a to b, as desired.

Suppose that the LAAC algorithm is a solution procedure for CSP(**B**). It suffices to show that there is a homomorphism $h : \mathcal{P}(\mathbf{B}) \times \mathbf{B} \to \mathbf{B}$ such that $h(\{b_1\}, b_2) = b_1$ for all $b_1, b_2 \in B$, as such a homomorphism can be viewed as the composition of $\mathbf{c_B}$ and l, for some homomorphism l of the described form. We assume for ease of presentation that **B** permits constant instantiation; the same ideas apply when **B** does not permit constant instantiation. For every $b \in B$, let R_b be a relation symbol such that $R_b^\mathbf{B} = \{(b)\}$. Let $\mathbf{C}_{b_1, b_2}$ be the relational structure over the same vocabulary as $\mathbf{B}$ with universe $(\wp(B) \setminus \{\emptyset\}) \times B$ such that $R_{b_1}^{\mathbf{C}_{b_1,b_2}} = \{(\{b_1\}, b_2)\}$, and $R^{\mathbf{C}_{b_1,b_2}} = \emptyset$ for all other relation symbols R. Let C denote the set $\{\mathbf{C}_{b_1,b_2} : b_1, b_2 \in B\}$. We prove that for every subset $C' \subseteq C$, there is a homomorphism from $(\mathcal{P}(\mathbf{B}) \times \mathbf{B}) \cup (\bigcup_{\mathbf{C} \in C'} \mathbf{C})$ to $\mathbf{B}$; this suffices, as such a homomorphism is precisely a homomorphism h of the form desired. (The presence of a structure $\mathbf{C}_{b_1,b_2}$ as part of the source structure ensures that any homomorphism maps $(\{b_1\}, b_2)$ to b_1.)

The proof is by induction on $|C'|$. Suppose $C' = \emptyset$. The mapping from $(\wp(B) \setminus \{\emptyset\}) \times B$ to B that projects onto the second coordinate is a homomorphism from $\mathcal{P}(\mathbf{B}) \times \mathbf{B}$ to $\mathbf{B}$. Now suppose $|C'| \geq 1$. Let $C'' \subseteq C$ and $b_1, b_2 \in B$ be such that $C' = C'' \cup \{\mathbf{C}_{b_1,b_2}\}$ and $|C''| + 1 = |C'|$. The mapping from $(\wp(B) \setminus \{\emptyset\}) \times B$ to $\wp(B) \setminus \{\emptyset\}$ that projects onto the first coordinate is a homomorphism from $(\mathcal{P}(\mathbf{B}) \times \mathbf{B}) \cup (\bigcup_{\mathbf{C} \in C'} \mathbf{C})$ to $\mathcal{P}(\mathbf{B})$, so arc consistency can be established on $((\mathcal{P}(\mathbf{B}) \times \mathbf{B}) \cup (\bigcup_{\mathbf{C} \in C''} \mathbf{C}), B)[(\{b_1\}, b_2), b_1]$. Moreover, the instance $((\mathcal{P}(\mathbf{B}) \times \mathbf{B}) \cup (\bigcup_{\mathbf{C} \in C''} \mathbf{C}), B)$ is satisfiable by induction, so by the assumption that LAAC is an algorithm for $\mathsf{CSP}(\mathbf{B})$, the instance $((\mathcal{P}(\mathbf{B}) \times \mathbf{B}) \cup (\bigcup_{\mathbf{C} \in C'} \mathbf{C}), B)$ is satisfiable. □

Corollary 2. *The class of relational structures $\mathbf{B}$, having the property that the LAAC algorithm is a solution procedure for $\mathsf{CSP}(\mathbf{B})$, is decidable.*

We now turn to the *smart look-ahead arc consistency* (SLAAC) algorithm. The difference between the LAAC and SLAAC algorithms is that the SLAAC algorithm takes as a parameter a set function $f : \wp(B) \setminus \{\emptyset\} \to B$, and when setting a variable, instead of arbitrarily picking from the set E of candidate values, directly sets the variable to $f(E)$. Note that for any relational structure $\mathbf{B}$, if LAAC is a solution procedure for $\mathbf{B}$, then SLAAC is also a solution procedure for $\mathbf{B}$, when parameterized with any set function that is conservative in the sense that $f(S) \in S$, for all non-empty $S \subseteq B$.

The algebraic characterization for the SLAAC algorithm, as with that for the LAAC algorithm, concerns the existence of certain homomorphisms. Before giving this characterization, it is necessary to introduce the following auxiliary notion. For a relational structure $\mathbf{B}$, we define a pair (U, b), where $U \subseteq B$ and $b \in U$, to be *usable* if there exists a satisfiable CSP instance $(\mathbf{A}, \mathbf{B})$ and there exists a variable $a \in A$ such that

$$U = \{u \in B : \text{arc consistency can be established on } (\mathbf{A}, \mathbf{B})[a = u]\}$$

and there is a homomorphism from $\mathbf{A}$ to $\mathbf{B}$ sending a to b.

Theorem 3. *Let $f : \wp(B) \setminus \{\emptyset\} \to B$ be a set function on the set B, and let $\mathbf{B}$ be a relational structure with universe B permitting constant instantiation for the image of f. The SLAAC algorithm, parameterized with f, is a solution procedure for $\mathsf{CSP}(\mathbf{B})$ if and only if for every usable pair (U, b) (of $\mathbf{B}$), there exists a homomorphism $h_{U,b} : \mathcal{P}(\mathbf{B})^k \times \mathbf{B} \to \mathbf{B}$ such that $h_{U,b}(\{b_1\}, \ldots, \{b_k\}, b) = f(U)$, where $b_1, \ldots, b_k$ denote the elements of U.*

Proof. Suppose that there exist homomorphisms $h_{U,b}$ of the described form. As in the proof of Theorem 1, it suffices to show that each time a variable is set by SLAAC, satisfiability is preserved. Precisely, we show that when $\mathbf{A}$ is a relational structure such that $a \in A$, $(\mathbf{A}, \mathbf{B})$ is satisfiable via a homomorphism $h : \mathbf{A} \to \mathbf{B}$ mapping a to b, and $U \subseteq B$ contains exactly those values $c \in B$ such that arc consistency can be established on $(\mathbf{A}, \mathbf{B})[a = c]$, then $(\mathbf{A}, \mathbf{B})[a = f(U)]$ is satisfiable. Note that given these assumptions, the pair (U, b) must be usable. Let $b_1, \ldots, b_k$ be the elements of U; since (for each i) arc consistency can be established on $(\mathbf{A}, \mathbf{B})[a = b_i]$, there is a homomorphism $p_i : \mathbf{A} \to \mathcal{P}(\mathbf{B})$ such that $p(a) = \{b_i\}$. Composing the homomorphisms $(p_1, \ldots, p_k, h) : A \to \mathcal{P}(\mathbf{B})^k \times \mathbf{B}$ and $h_{U,b} : \mathcal{P}(\mathbf{B})^k \times \mathbf{B} \to \mathbf{B}$, we obtain a homomorphism from $\mathbf{A}$ to $\mathbf{B}$ sending a to $f(U)$, as desired.

Suppose that the SLAAC algorithm is a solution procedure for $\mathsf{CSP}(\mathbf{B})$. Let (U, b) be a usable pair, and let $b_1, \ldots, b_k$ denote the elements of U. We show that there exists a homomorphism $h : \mathcal{P}(\mathbf{B}) \times \mathbf{B} \to \mathbf{B}$ such that $h(\{b_1\}, \ldots, \{b_k\}, b) = f(U)$. Let $\mathbf{A}$ denote the structure $\mathcal{P}(\mathbf{B})^k \times \mathbf{B}$, and let a denote the element $(\{b_1\}, \ldots, \{b_k\}, b)$ of $\mathbf{A}$. By the homomorphism from $\mathbf{A}$ to $\mathbf{B}$ that projects onto the ith coordinate, there is a homomorphism from $\mathbf{A}$ to $\mathcal{P}(\mathbf{B})$ such that a is mapped to b_i, implying that arc consistency can be established on $(\mathbf{A}, \mathbf{B})[a = b_i]$ for all $b_i \in U$. Also, by the homomorphism from $\mathbf{A}$ to $\mathbf{B}$ that projects onto the last coordinate, there is a homomorphism from $\mathbf{A}$ to $\mathbf{B}$ such that a is mapped to b.

We extend $\mathbf{A}$ so that the values in U are *exactly* those values c such that arc consistency can be established on $(\mathbf{A}, \mathbf{B})[a = c]$, in the following way. Let $(\mathbf{A}_0, \mathbf{B})$ be a satisfiable CSP instance with a variable $u_0 \in A_0$ such that $U - \{c \in B : \text{arc consistency can be established on } (\mathbf{A}, \mathbf{B})[a_0 = c]\}$, and there is a homomorphism from $\mathbf{A}$ to $\mathbf{B}$ sending a_0 to b. (Such a CSP instance exists by the definition of usable pair.) Identify the variable a_0 with a, assume that $A_0 \setminus \{a_0\}$ and $A \setminus \{a\}$ are disjoint, and consider the CSP instance $(\mathbf{A} \cup \mathbf{A}_0, \mathbf{B})$. The values c in U are exactly those values such that arc consistency can be established on $(\mathbf{A} \cup \mathbf{A}_0, \mathbf{B})[a = c]$. Moreover, $(\mathbf{A} \cup \mathbf{A}_0, \mathbf{B})$ is satisfiable via a homomorphism sending a to b. By the hypothesis that SLAAC solves $\mathsf{CSP}(\mathbf{B})$, the instance $(\mathbf{A} \cup \mathbf{A}_0, \mathbf{B})$ is satisfiable via a homomorphism h' sending a to $f(U)$. The restriction of h' to A gives the desired homomorphism. □

As for LAAC, we can show that the class of structures that are solvable by SLAAC is decidable. This follows from the algebraic characterization given in the previous theorem, along with the following theorem.

Theorem 4. *Let $\mathbf{B}$ be a relational structure, and let (U, b) be a pair where $U \subseteq B$ and $b \in U$. The problem of determining whether or not (U, b) is usable, is decidable.*

Proof. Let (U, b) be a pair where $U \subseteq B$ and $b \in U$, and let $b_1, \ldots, b_k$ denote the elements of U. We show that (U, b) is usable if and only if for all homomorphisms $h : \mathcal{P}(\mathbf{B})^k \times \mathbf{B} \to \mathcal{P}(\mathbf{B})$ such that $|h(\{b_1\}, \ldots, \{b_k\}, b)| = 1$, it holds that $h(\{b_1\}, \ldots, \{b_k\}, b) \in U$. This suffices to establish the theorem: there are finitely many homomorphisms from $\mathcal{P}(\mathbf{B})^k \times \mathbf{B}$ to $\mathcal{P}(\mathbf{B})$, so the condition can be effectively checked.

Suppose that the given homomorphism condition holds. Set $\mathbf{A} = \mathcal{P}(\mathbf{B})^k \times \mathbf{B}$ and $a = (\{b_1\}, \ldots, \{b_k\}, b)$. We claim that the instance $(\mathbf{A}, \mathbf{B})$ and the variable a are witness to the usability of (U, b). Observe that arc consistency can be established on $(\mathbf{A}, \mathbf{B})[a = u]$ if and only if there is a homomorphism from $\mathbf{A}$ to $\mathcal{P}(\mathbf{B})$ sending a to $\{u\}$. Hence, by assumption, we cannot establish arc consistency on $(\mathbf{A}, \mathbf{B})[a = u]$ when $u \notin B$. But, we can establish arc consistency on $(\mathbf{A}, \mathbf{B})[a = b_i]$ for any $b_i \in U$, since the projection onto the ith coordinate is a homomorphism from $\mathcal{P}(\mathbf{B})^k \times \mathbf{B}$ to $\mathcal{P}(\mathbf{B})$ sending a to $\{b_i\}$.

Now suppose that the given homomorphism condition fails. We prove that (U, b) is not usable, by contradiction. Suppose that (U, b) is usable. Let $\mathbf{A}$ and $a \in A$ be witness to the usability of (U, b). It follows that there is a homomorphism $h : \mathbf{A} \to \mathcal{P}(\mathbf{B})^k \times \mathbf{B}$ sending a to $(\{b_1\}, \ldots, \{b_k\}, b)$. Since the homomorphism condition fails, there is a homomorphism $h' : \mathcal{P}(\mathbf{B})^k \times \mathbf{B} \to \mathcal{P}(\mathbf{B})$ such that $h'(\{b_1\}, \ldots, \{b_k\}, b) = c$, where $c \notin U$. Composing h and h', we obtain a homomorphism from $\mathbf{A}$ to $\mathcal{P}(\mathbf{B})$ sending a to c; this implies that arc consistency can be established on $(\mathbf{A}, \mathbf{B})[a = c]$, contradicting that $\mathbf{A}$ and a are witness to the usability of (U, b). □

Corollary 5. *The class of relational structures $\mathbf{B}$, having the property that the SLAAC algorithm is a solution procedure for $\mathsf{CSP}(\mathbf{B})$, is decidable.*

We can employ Theorem 3 to demonstrate that the SLAAC algorithm solves $\mathsf{CSP}(\mathbf{B})$ when the relational structure $\mathbf{B}$ is invariant under a set function. Set functions were studied in the context of CSP complexity in [9]; we say that a relational structure $\mathbf{B}$ is invariant under a set function $f : (\wp(B) \setminus \{\emptyset\}) \to B$ if f is a homomorphism from $\mathcal{P}(\mathbf{B})$ to $\mathbf{B}$; or, equivalently, if it is invariant under all of the functions $f_k : B^k \to B$ defined by $f_k(b_1, \ldots, b_k) = f(\{b_1, \ldots, b_k\})$, for $k \geq 1$.

Theorem 6. *Suppose that the relational structure $\mathbf{B}$ (with universe B) is invariant under a set function $f : (\wp(B) \setminus \{\emptyset\}) \to B$. Then, the SLAAC algorithm is a solution procedure for $\mathsf{CSP}(\mathbf{B})$.*

Proof. We first demonstrate that $\mathbf{B}$ is invariant under a set function h such that the map $b \to h(\{b\})$ acts as the identity on all elements in $\text{im}(h)$. (We use im to denote the image of a function.) Let $c \geq 1$ be sufficiently large so that for all $n > c$, $\text{im}(f_1^c) = \text{im}(f_1^n)$. Define g to be the set function on B such that $g(S) = f_1^c(f(S))$. We have $\text{im}(g_1) = \text{im}(g) = \text{im}(f_1^c)$. Let $d > 1$ be sufficiently high so that g_1^d acts as the identity on all elements in its image, and define h to be the set function on B such that $h(S) = g_1^{d-1}(g(S))$. The map $b \to h(\{b\})$ acts as the identity on all elements in $\text{im}(g_1)$, and hence on all elements in $\text{im}(h)$ (which is a subset of $\text{im}(g_1)$). Moreover, it is straightforward to verify that $\mathbf{B}$ is invariant under all of the functions discussed, in particular, h.

We can assume that the structure $\mathbf{B}$ permits constant instantiation on all elements of $\text{im}(h)$; if it does not, we can enlargen $\mathbf{B}$ so that it does, while preserving the invariance of $\mathbf{B}$ under h.

We claim that the SLAAC algorithm, parameterized with h, solves CSP(**B**). This follows from Theorem 3: for each usable pair (U, b) with $|U| = k$, we have a homomorphism $h_{U,b} : \mathcal{P}(\mathbf{B})^k \times \mathbf{B} \to \mathbf{B}$ of the desired form, given by $h_{U,b}(S_1, \ldots, S_k, b) = h(\bigcup_{i=1}^{k} S_i)$. □

4 Tractability

In this section, we present our primary tractability result, which shows that those relational structures invariant under a certain type of ternary function are tractable via the LAAC algorithm. We also demonstrate that the relational structures for which LAAC is a solution procedure can be combined in certain ways.

Theorem 7. *Suppose that* $t : B^3 \to B$ *is a ternary function satisfying the three identities* $t(x, x, y) = x$, $t(x, y, z) = t(y, x, z)$, *and* $t(t(x, y, w), z, w) = t(x, t(y, z, w), w)$. *For any relational structure* **B** *(with universe* B*) invariant under* t, *the* LAAC *algorithm is a solution procedure for* CSP(**B**).

Proof. We have that, for each fixed $b \in B$, the binary operation $g_b : B^2 \to B$ defined by $g_b(x, y) = g(x, y, b)$ is a semilattice operation. Define $h : (\wp(B) \setminus \{\emptyset\}) \to B$ to be the mapping defined by

$$h(\{s_1, \ldots, s_k\}, b) = g_b(s_1, g_b(s_2, \ldots, g_b(s_{k-1}, s_k) \ldots)).$$

Note that the right-hand side is well-defined, since g_b is a semilattice operation. It can be verified that h is a homomorphism from $\mathcal{P}(\mathbf{B}) \times \mathbf{B}$ to **B** sending any element of the form $(\{s\}, b)$ to s; hence, h can be factored as the composition of the homomorphism $c_\mathbf{B} : \mathcal{P}(\mathbf{B}) \times \mathbf{B} \to \mathcal{L}(\mathbf{B})$ and a homomorphism $l : \mathcal{L}(\mathbf{B}) \to \mathbf{B}$ such that $l(\{s\}, \star) = s$ (for all $s \in B$). It follows from Theorem 1 that the LAAC algorithm is a solution procedure for CSP(**B**). □

One way to view the three identities given in the statement of Theorem 7 is that they require, for each fixed $b \in B$, that the binary operation $g_b : B^2 \to B$ defined by $g_b(x, y) = g(x, y, b)$ is a semilattice operation. The proof of Theorem 7 uses the algebraic characterization of LAAC given by Theorem 1. The relational structures identified by Theorem 7 constitute a new tractable class, described using the notion of invariance, that has not been previously observed.

We can derive the following corollaries from Theorem 7.

Corollary 8. *Let* $d : B^3 \to B$ *be the* dual discriminator *on* B, *that is, the function such that* $d(x, y, z)$ *is equal to* x *if* $x = y$, *and* z *otherwise. For any relational structure* **B** *(with universe* B*) invariant under* d, *the* LAAC *algorithm is a solution procedure for* CSP(**B**).

The dual discriminator is an example of a *near-unanimity operation*; invariance under a near-unanimity operation has previously been demonstrated to imply CSP(**B**) tractability [13]. Another example of a near-unanimity operation that can be shown to imply tractability by Theorem 7 is as follows.

Corollary 9. *Let $B = \{1, \ldots, k\}$, and let* median $: B^3 \to B$ *be the ternary function on B which returns the median of its arguments. For any relational structure $\mathbf{B}$ (with universe B) invariant under* median, *the* LAAC *algorithm is a solution procedure for* CSP($\mathbf{B}$).

The next theorem demonstrates that relational structures for which LAAC is a decision procedure can be combined together to give further relational structures also solvable by LAAC.

Theorem 10. *Suppose that $B_1, \ldots, B_k$ are sets, none of which contain $\top$ as an element, and suppose that $l_1 : L(B_1) \to B_1, \ldots, l_k : L(B_k) \to B_k$ are functions such that (for all $i = 1, \ldots, k$) it holds that (1) $l_i(\{b_i\}, \star) = b_i$, for all $b_i \in B_i$, and (2) if $B_i \cap B_j \neq \emptyset$, then the restrictions of l_i and l_j to $L(B_i \cap B_j)$ are equal, for all $j = 1, \ldots, k$. Define B to be the set $(\bigcup_{i=1}^{k} B_i) \cup \{\top\}$, and let $l : L(B) \to B$ be the function defined by*

- $l(S, b) = s$ *if* $(S, b) = (\{s\}, \star)$,
- $l(S, b) = l_i(S, b)$ *if* $|S| > 1$ *and* $S \cup \{b\} \subseteq B_i$ *for some i, and*
- $l(S, b) = \top$ *otherwise.*

For any relational structure $\mathbf{B}$ (with universe B) such that l is a homomorphism from $\mathcal{L}(\mathbf{B})$ to $\mathbf{B}$, the LAAC *algorithm is a solution procedure for* CSP($\mathbf{B}$). *Moreover, for any relational structure $\mathbf{B}_i$ (with universe B_i) such that l_i is a homomorphism from $\mathcal{L}(\mathbf{B}_i)$ to $\mathbf{B}_i$, l is also a homomorphism from $\mathcal{L}(\mathbf{B}_i)$ to $\mathbf{B}_i$.*

5 Commutative Conservative Operations

We say that a binary operation $\bullet$ over the set B is *commutative conservative* if for all $a, b \in B$, it holds that $a \bullet b = b \bullet a$; and, for all $a, b \in B$, it holds that $a \bullet b \in \{a, b\}$. As mentioned in the introduction, relational structures invariant under a commutative conservative operation have been demonstrated to be tractable [8], via an algorithm that is not well-characterized (in the sense discussed in the introduction). In this final section, we utilize the algebraic technology developed in Section 3 to give a precise classification of those commutative conservative operations whose invariant structures are tractable by the SLAAC algorithm, which as we have shown, is well-characterized.

Our classification is stated in terms of a "forbidden configuration". In particular, we show that the commutative conservative groupoids $(B, \bullet)$ tractable via SLAAC are precisely those that do not contain a forbidden subalgebra F^3. Define F to be the commutative conservative groupoid having universe $\{0, 1, 2, 3\}$ and the following Cayley table.

	0	1	2	3
0	0	1	2	3
1	1	1	2	1
2	2	2	2	3
3	3	1	3	3

---

[3] In this paper, a commutative conservative groupoid is simply a set endowed with a commutative conservative binary operation.

The groupoid F can be regarded as the so-called stone-scissors-paper algebra with a bottom element adjoined.

Theorem 11. *Let $(B, \bullet)$ be a commutative conservative groupoid. The following two statements are equivalent:*

- *The groupoid $(B, \bullet)$ does not have a subalgebra isomorphic to F.*
- *For every relational structure $\mathbf{B}$ (with universe B) invariant under $\bullet$, the SLAAC algorithm is a solution procedure for $\mathsf{CSP}(\mathbf{B})$.*

Acknowledgements

Víctor Dalmau was partially supported by MCyT grants TIC2002-04470-C03 and TIC2002-04019-C03.

References

1. A. Bulatov. Combinatorial problems raised from 2-semilattices. Manuscript.
2. Andrei A. Bulatov. A Dichotomy Theorem for Constraints on a Three-Element Set. FOCS 2002.
3. A. Bulatov. Malt'sev constraints are tractable. Technical report PRG-RR-02-05, Oxford University, 2002.
4. Andrei A. Bulatov. Tractable conservative Constraint Satisfaction Problems. LICS 2003.
5. Andrei A. Bulatov, Andrei A. Krokhin, and Peter Jeavons. Constraint Satisfaction Problems and Finite Algebras. ICALP 2000.
6. A. Bulatov and P. Jeavons. An Algebraic Approach to Multi-sorted Constraints Proceedings of 9th International Conference on Principles and Practice of Constraint Programming, 2003.
7. A. Bulatov, and P. Jeavons. Algebraic structures in combinatorial problems. Technical report MATH-AL-4-2001, Technische Universitat Dresden, 2001.
8. A. Bulatov, and P. Jeavons. Tractable constraints closed under a binary operation. Technical report PRG-TR-12-00, Oxford University, 2000.
9. Victor Dalmau and Justin Pearson. Set Functions and Width 1. Constraint Programming '99.
10. Alvaro del Val. On 2SAT and Renamable Horn. In AAAI'00, Proceedings of the Seventeenth (U.S.) National Conference on Artificial Intelligence, 279-284. Austin, Texas, 2000.
11. Tomás Feder and Moshe Y. Vardi. The Computational Structure of Monotone Monadic SNP and Constraint Satisfaction: A Study through Datalog and Group Theory. SIAM J. Comput. 28(1): 57-104, 1998.
12. Peter Jeavons. On the Algebraic Structure of Combinatorial Problems. Theor. Comput. Sci. 200(1-2): 185-204, 1998.
13. P.G.Jeavons, D.A.Cohen and M.Cooper. Constraints, Consistency and Closure. Artificial Intelligence, 1998, 101(1-2), pages 251-265.
14. Peter Jeavons, David A. Cohen, and Marc Gyssens. Closure properties of constraints. J. ACM 44(4): 527-548 (1997).

15. Phokion G. Kolaitis, Moshe Y. Vardi. Conjunctive-Query Containment and Constraint Satisfaction. J. Comput. Syst. Sci. 61(2): 302-332 (2000)
16. Phokion G. Kolaitis and Moshe Y. Vardi. A Game-Theoretic Approach to Constraint Satisfaction. AAAI 2000.
17. T. Schaefer. The complexity of satisfiability problems. Proceedings of the 10th Annual Symposium on Theory of Computing, ACM, 1978.

Heuristic Selection for Stochastic Search Optimization: Modeling Solution Quality by Extreme Value Theory

Vincent A. Cicirello[1] and Stephen F. Smith[2]

[1] Department of Computer Science, College of Engineering
Drexel University, 3141 Chestnut Street, Philadelphia, PA 19104
cicirello@cs.drexel.edu
[2] The Robotics Institute, Carnegie Mellon University
5000 Forbes Avenue, Pittsburgh, PA 15213
sfs@cs.cmu.edu

Abstract. The success of stochastic algorithms is often due to their ability to effectively amplify the performance of search heuristics. This is certainly the case with stochastic sampling algorithms such as heuristic-biased stochastic sampling (HBSS) and value-biased stochastic sampling (VBSS), wherein a heuristic is used to bias a stochastic policy for choosing among alternative branches in the search tree. One complication in getting the most out of algorithms like HBSS and VBSS in a given problem domain is the need to identify the most effective search heuristic. In many domains, the relative performance of various heuristics tends to vary across different problem instances and no single heuristic dominates. In such cases, the choice of any given heuristic will be limiting and it would be advantageous to gain the collective power of several heuristics. Toward this goal, this paper describes a framework for integrating multiple heuristics within a stochastic sampling search algorithm. In its essence, the framework uses online-generated statistical models of the search performance of different base heuristics to select which to employ on each subsequent iteration of the search. To estimate the solution quality distribution resulting from repeated application of a strong heuristic within a stochastic search, we propose the use of models from extreme value theory (EVT). Our EVT-motivated approach is validated on the NP-Hard problem of resource-constrained project scheduling with time windows (RCPSP/max). Using VBSS as a base stochastic sampling algorithm, the integrated use of a set of project scheduling heuristics is shown to be competitive with the current best known heuristic algorithm for RCPSP/max and in some cases even improves upon best known solutions to difficult benchmark instances.

1 Introduction

The success of stochastic sampling algorithms such as Heuristic-Biased Stochastic Sampling (HBSS) [1] and Value-Biased Stochastic Sampling (VBSS) [2,3] stems from their ability to amplify the performance of search heuristics. The essential idea underlying these algorithms is to use the heuristic's valuation of various choices at a given search node to bias a stochastic decision, and, in doing so, to randomly perturb the heuristic's prescribed (deterministic) trajectory through the search space. In the case of HBSS, a rank-ordering of possible choices is used as heuristic bias; in VBSS, alternatively, the actual heuristic value attributed to each choice is used. This stochastic choice process enables generation of different solutions on successive iterations (or restarts), and effectively results in a broader search in the "neighborhood" defined by the deterministic heuristic. HBSS has been shown to significantly improve the performance of a heuristic for scheduling telescope observations [1]. VBSS has shown similar ability to improve search performance in weighted-tardiness scheduling [2, 3], resource-constrained project scheduling [3], and in a multi-rover exploration domain [4].

The drawback to stochastic sampling algorithms such as HBSS and VBSS is that they require identification of an appropriate domain heuristic, and search performance is ultimately tied to the power of the heuristic that is selected. Heuristics, however, are not infallible, and in most domains there does not exist a single dominating heuristic. Instead different heuristics tend to perform better or worse on different problem instances. In such cases, the choice of any single heuristic will ultimately be limiting and it would be advantageous to gain the collective power of several heuristics. The idea of exploiting a collection of heuristics to boost overall performance has been explored in other search contexts. Allen and Minton use secondary performance characteristics as indicators for which heuristic algorithm is performing more effectively for a given CSP instance [5]. Others have been applying relatively simple learning algorithms to the problem of selecting from among alternative local search operators [6, 7]. Work on algorithm portfolios [8] and the related A-Teams framework [9] take a more aggressive approach, executing several different heuristic search algorithms in parallel.

In this paper, we consider the problem of integrating multiple search heuristics within a stochastic sampling algorithm. Rather than carefully customizing a variant to use a composite heuristic, the approach taken here is to instead design a search control framework capable of accepting several search heuristics and self-customizing a hybrid algorithm on a per problem instance basis. Generally speaking, our approach views each solution constructed by the stochastic sampling algorithm as a sample of the expected solution quality of the base heuristic. Over multiple restarts on a given problem instance, we construct *solution quality distributions* for each heuristic, and use this information to bias the selection of heuristic on subsequent iterations. Gomes et al.'s analysis and use of runtime distributions has led to much success in constraint satisfaction domains [10]. In a similar way, a hypothesis of this paper is that solution quality distributions can provide an analagous basis for understanding and enhancing the performance of stochastic sampling procedures in solving optimization problems.

As suggested above, the search control framework developed in this paper uses online-generated statistical models of search performance to effectively combine multiple search heuristics. Consider that a stochastic search algorithm samples a solution space, guided by a strong domain heuristic. Our conjecture is that the solutions found by this algorithm on individual iterations are generally "good" (with respect to the overall solution space) and that these "good" solutions are rare events. This leads us to the body of work on extreme value theory (EVT). EVT is the statistical study of rare or uncommon events, rather than the usual (e.g., study of what happens at the extreme of a distribution in the tail). With our conjecture stated and with respect to EVT, we can view the distribution of solution qualities found by a stochastic heuristic search algorithm as a sort of snapshot of the tail of the distribution of solution qualities of the overall search space. We specifically employ a distribution called the Generalized Extreme Value (GEV) distribution to model the solution qualities given by individual iterations of the search algorithm. We implement this EVT-motivated approach in two ways: 1) using a well-known, but numerically intensive computation of a maximum likelihood estimation of the GEV; and 2) using kernel density estimation tuned assuming a GEV.

Using VBSS as a base stochastic sampling procedure, we validate this EVT-motivated heuristic performance modeling and heuristic selection policy on the NP-Hard problem of resource-constrained project scheduling with time windows (RCPSP/max). As a baseline and to validate our EVT assumptions, we compare the performance of the approach with one that makes the naive assumption that the solution qualities are normally distributed. We further benchmark the approach against several well-known heuristic algorithms, finding that our EVT-motivated algorithm is competitive with the current best known heuristic algorithm for RCPSP/max; and in some cases even improves upon current best known solutions to difficult problem instances.

2 Modeling a Solution Quality Distribution

2.1 Extreme Value Theory Motivation

Consider that the solutions to a hard combinatorial optimization problem computed on each iteration of a stochastic sampling algorithm are in fact at the extreme when the overall solution-space is considered. If one were to sample solutions uniformly at random, the probability is very low that any of the solutions generated by a stochastic search that is guided by a strong heuristic would be found. In other words, good solutions to any given problem instance from the class of problems of greatest interest to us are, in a sense, rare phenomena within the space of feasible solutions.

For example, using Bresina's concept of a quality density function (QDF) [11], we examined several problem instances of a weighted tardiness scheduling problem. A QDF is the distribution of solution qualities that one would obtain by sampling uniformly from the space of possible solutions to a problem instance. For easy problem instances from our problem set, we found that the optimal solution was on average over 6.4 standard deviations better than the average feasible solution to the problem; the value of the average solution given by a stochastic sampler guided by a strong domain heuristic was also over 6.4 standard deviations better than the average solution in the problem space [3]. Further, for hard problem instances, we found that the average solution given by a single iteration of the stochastic search was over 9.1 standard deviations better than the average random solution; the best known solution was on average 9.4 standard deviations better than the average solution in the problem space [3].

2.2 Generalized Extreme Value Distribution

With this noted, we turn to the field of extreme value theory, which deals with "techniques and models for describing the unusual rather than the usual" [12]. Consider an extreme value analog to the central limit theory. Let $M_n = \max\{X_1, \ldots, X_n\}$ where $X_1, \ldots, X_n$ is a sequence of independent random variables having a common distribution function F. For example, perhaps the X_i are the mean temperatures for each of the

365 days in the year, then M_n would correspond to the annual maximum temperature. To model M_n, extreme value theorists turn to the *extremal types theorem* [12]:

Theorem 1. *If there exists sequences of constants $\{a_n > 0\}$ and $\{b_n\}$ such that $P((M_n - b_n)/a_n \leq z) \to G(z)$ as $n \to \infty$, where G is a non-degenerate distribution function, then G belongs to one of the following families:*

I: $G(z) = \exp(-\exp(-(\frac{z-b}{a})))$, $-\infty < z < \infty$
II: $G(z) = \exp(-(\frac{z-b}{a})^{-\alpha})$ *if* $z > b$ *and otherwise* $G(z) = 0$
III: $G(z) = \exp((\frac{z-b}{a})^{\alpha})$ *if* $z < b$ *and otherwise* $G(z) = 1$

for parameters $a > 0$, b and in the latter two cases $\alpha > 0$.

These are known as the extreme value distributions, types I (Gumbel), II (Fréchet), and III (Weibull). The types II and III distributions are heavy-tailed – one bounded on the left and the other on the right. The Gumbel distribution is medium-tailed and unbounded. These distributions are commonly reformulated into the generalization known as the generalized extreme value distribution (GEV):

$$G(z) = \exp(-(1 + \xi(\frac{z-b}{a}))^{-1/\xi}) \quad (1)$$

where $\{z : 1 + \xi(\frac{z-b}{a}) > 0\}$, $-\infty < b < \infty$, $a > 0$, and $-\infty < \xi < \infty$. The case where $\xi = 0$ is treated as the limit of $G(z)$ as ξ approaches 0 to arrive at the Gumbel distribution. Under the assumption of Theorem 1, $P((M_n - b_n)/a_n \leq z) \approx G(z)$ for large enough n which is equivalent to $P(M_n \leq z) \approx G((z - b_n)/a_n) = G^*(z)$ where $G^*(z)$ is some other member of the generalized extreme value distribution family.

The main point here is that to model the distribution of the maximum element of a fixed-length sequence (or block) of identically distributed random variables (i.e., the distribution of "block maxima"), one needs simply to turn to the GEV distribution regardless of the underlying distribution of the individual elements of the sequence.

2.3 Modeling Solution Quality via the GEV

Theorem 1 only explicitly applies to modeling the distribution of "block maxima". The assumption we now make is that the quality distribution for a stochastic sampling algorithm using a strong heuristic to sample from the solution space behaves the same as (or at least similar to) the distribution of "block maxima" and thus its cumulative distribution function can be modeled by the GEV distribution.

To use the GEV as our model, we must first recognize that we have been assuming throughout that our objective function must be minimized so we need a "block minima" analog to Equation 1. Let $M'_n = \min\{X_1, \ldots, X_n\}$. We want $P(M'_n < z)$. Let $M''_n = \max\{-X_1, \ldots, -X_n\}$. Therefore, $M'_n = -M''_n$ and $P(M'_n < z) = P(-M''_n < z) = P(M''_n > -z) = 1 - P(M''_n \leq -z)$. Therefore, assuming that the distribution function behaves according to a GEV distribution, the probability P_i of finding a better solution than the best found so far (B) using heuristic i can be defined as:

$$P_i = 1 - G_i(-B) = 1 - \exp(-(1 + \xi_i(\frac{-B - b_i}{a_i}))^{-1/\xi_i}) \quad (2)$$

where the b_i, a_i, and ξ_i are estimated from the negative of the sample values. To compute these parameters, we use Hosking's maximum-likelihood estimator of the GEV parameters [13]. In estimating the GEV parameters, Hosking's algorithm is called multiple times, if necessary. The first call uses initial estimates of the parameters as recommended by Hosking (set assuming a Gumbel distribution). If Hosking's algorithm fails to converge, then a fixed number of additional calls are made with random initial values of the parameters. If convergence still fails, we use the values of the parameters as estimated by assuming a type I extreme value distribution (the Gumbel distribution)[1].

2.4 Modeling Solution Quality Using Kernel Density Estimation

A second possibility for estimating the quality distribution is Kernel Density Estimation (see [14]). A kernel density estimator makes little, if any, assumptions regarding the underlying distribution it models. It provides a non-parametric framework for estimating arbitrary probability densities. The advantage of this approach is that it should be possible to more closely estimate arbitrary solution quality distributions. Kernel density estimation takes local averages to estimate a density function by placing smoothed out quantities of mass at each data point. The kernel density estimator is defined as:

$$\hat{f}(x) = \frac{1}{nh} \sum_{i=1}^{n} K(\frac{x - X_i}{h}). \quad (3)$$

$K(\cdot)$ is a kernel function and h is called the bandwidth (also sometimes called the scale parameter or spreading coefficient). The X_i are the n sample values (objective function value of the solutions generated by the n iterations of the stochastic search algorithm). The kernel function we have chosen is the Epanechnikov kernel [15]:

$$K(x) = \frac{3}{4\sqrt{5}}(1 - \frac{x^2}{5}) \text{ for } |x| < \sqrt{5} \text{ and otherwise } 0. \quad (4)$$

Epanechnikov showed that this is the risk optimal kernel, but estimates using other smooth kernels are usually numerically indistinguishable. Thus, the form of the kernel can be chosen to best address computational efficiency concerns. In our case, the Epanechnikov kernel is a clear winner computationally for the following reasons:

- We are most interested in ultimately computing the probability of finding a better solution than the best found so far. This kernel function allows us to easily compute the cumulative probability distribution for arbitrary solution quality distributions.
- Due to the condition $|x| < \sqrt{5}$, only a limited number of sample values must be considered, reducing the computational overhead.

Although the choice of kernel function is not critical in terms of numerical results, the choice of bandwidth can be very crucial. Epanechnikov showed that the optimal choice of bandwidth is $h = (\frac{L}{nM})^{1/5}$, where $L = \int_{-\infty}^{\infty} K(x)^2 \, dx$ where $M = \int_{-\infty}^{\infty} (f''(x))^2 \, dx$, and where n is the number of samples [15]. Unfortunately, this

---
[1] It should be noted that this fallback condition appears to rarely occur, if ever, in our experiments.

computation depends on knowing the true distribution (M depends on $f(x)$). We assume that the underlying distribution is the Gumbel distribution. The reasoning behind this assumption follows our EVT motivation. Given the Gumbel distribution assumption, $M = \frac{1}{4a^5}$, where a is the scale parameter of the Gumbel. Note that the standard deviation of the Gumbel distribution is $\sigma = \frac{\pi a}{\sqrt{6}}$ [16]. From this, we have $a = \frac{\sigma\sqrt{6}}{\pi}$. We can now write M in terms of the sample standard deviation: $M = \frac{\pi^5}{4\sqrt{6}^5 \sigma^5}$. We are using the Epanechnikov kernel so $L = \frac{3}{5\sqrt{5}}$. This results in a value of h computed as: $h = 0.79sn^{-1/5}$ where $s = \min\{\sigma, Q/1.34\}$ and where Q is the interquartile range.

We are interested in the cumulative distribution function for the purpose of computing the probability of finding a better solution than the best found so far. This can be obtained from integrating the kernel density estimator. Thus, we have the probability P_i of finding a solution better than the best found so far, B, given heuristic i[2]:

$$P_i = \int_0^B \frac{1}{n_i h_i} \sum_{j=1}^{n_i} K(\frac{x - S_{i,j}}{h_i}) dx. \tag{5}$$

Given our choice of the Epanechnikov kernel, this evaluates to:

$$P_i = \frac{3}{4n_i h_i \sqrt{5}} \sum_{j, |\frac{B-S_{i,j}}{h_i}| < \sqrt{5}}$$

$$((B - \frac{1}{5h_i^2}(\frac{B^3}{3} - B^2 S_{i,j} + BS_{i,j}^2)) -$$

$$(S_{i,j} - h_i\sqrt{5} - \frac{1}{5h_i^2}(\frac{(S_{i,j} - h_i\sqrt{5})^3}{3} -$$

$$(S_{i,j} - h_i\sqrt{5})^2 S_{i,j} + (S_{i,j} - h_i\sqrt{5})S_{i,j}^2))) \tag{6}$$

It should be noted, that if we maintain the samples in sorted order, then given that B must be less than or equal to the smallest value in this list[3], we compute this sum until we reach a sample $S_{i,j}$ such that $|\frac{B-S_{i,j}}{h_i}| \geq \sqrt{5}$. Once a sample for which this condition holds is reached in the list, the summation can end. Actually, rather than in a sorted list, we maintain the samples in a sorted histogram, maintaining counts of the number of samples with given discrete values.

2.5 Selecting a Search Heuristic

A method is needed for balancing the tradeoff between exploiting the current estimates of the solution quality distributions given by the algorithm's choices and the need for exploration to improve these estimates. The k-armed bandit focuses on optimizing the expected total sum of rewards from sampling from a multiarmed slot machine. At any point during an iterative stochastic sampling search, there is a current best found solution. Future iterations have the objective of finding a solution that is better than the

---

[2] This assumes a minimization problem with lower bound of 0 on the objective function.
[3] Assuming we are minimizing an objective function.

current best. From this perspective, a better analogy than the k-armed bandit would be to consider a multiarmed slot machine in which the objective is to sample the arms to optimize the expected best single sample – what we have termed the "Max k-Armed Bandit Problem" [3]. Elsewhere, we showed that the optimal sampling strategy samples the observed best arm at a rate that increases approximately double exponentially relative to the other arms [3].

Specific to our problem, this means sampling with the observed best heuristic with frequency increasing double exponentially relative to the number of samples given the other heuristics. Consider, as the exploration strategy, Boltzmann exploration as commonly used in reinforcement learning [17] and simulated annealing [18]. With a Boltzmann exploration strategy, we would choose to use heuristic h_i with probability $P(h_i)$:

$$P(h_i) = \frac{\exp((P_i F_i)/T)}{\sum_{j=1}^{H} \exp((P_j F_j)/T)}, \quad (7)$$

where P_i is the probability of finding a solution better than the best found so far, where F_i is the ratio of the number of feasible solutions used in estimating P_i to the total number of samples with i, where there are H heuristics to choose from, and where T is a temperature parameter. To get the double exponential sampling increase, we need to decrease T exponentially. For example, let $T = \exp(-N')$ where N' is the number of samples already taken and sample h_i with probability:

$$P(h_i) = \frac{\exp((P_i F_i)/\exp(-N'))}{\sum_{j=1}^{H} \exp((P_j F_j)/\exp(-N'))}. \quad (8)$$

3 Experimental Design

In this Section, consider the resource constrained project scheduling problem with time windows (RCPSP/max). RCPSP/max is the RCPSP with generalized precedence relations between start times of activities. It is a difficult makespan minimization problem well studied by the Operations Research community. Finding feasible solutions to instances of the RCPSP/max is NP-Hard, making the optimization problem very difficult.

RCPSP/max Formalization. The RCPSP/max problem can be defined formally as follows. Define $P = <A, \Delta, R>$ as an instance of RCPSP/max. Let A be the set of activities $A = \{a_0, a_1, a_2, \ldots, a_n, a_{n+1}\}$. Activity a_0 is a dummy activity representing the start of the project and a_{n+1} is similarly the project end. Each activity a_j has a fixed duration p_j, a start-time S_j, and a completion-time C_j which satisfy the constraint $S_j + p_j = C_j$. Let Δ be a set of temporal constraints between activity pairs $<a_i, a_j>$ of the form $S_j - S_i \in [T_{i,j}^{\min}, T_{i,j}^{\max}]$. The Δ are generalized precedence relations between activities. The $T_{i,j}^{\min}$ and $T_{i,j}^{\max}$ are minimum and maximum time-lags between the start times of pairs of activities. Let R be the set of renewable resources $R = \{r_1, r_2, \ldots r_m\}$. Each resource r_k has an integer capacity $c_k \geq 1$. Execution of an activity a_j requires one or more resources. For each resource r_k, the activity a_j requires an integer capacity $rc_{j,k}$ for the duration of its execution. An assignment of start-times to the activities in A is time-feasible if all temporal constraints are satisfied and is resource-feasible if all resource constraints are satisfied. A schedule is feasible if both sets of constraints are satisfied. The problem is then to find a feasible schedule with minimum makespan M where $M(S) = \max\{C_i\}$. That is we wish to find a set of assignments to S such that $S_{\text{sol}} = \arg\min_S M(S)$. The maximum time-lag constraints are what makes this problem especially difficult. Particularly, due to the maximum time-lag constraints, finding feasible solutions alone to this problem is NP-Hard.

Branch-and-Bound Approaches. There are many branch-and-bound approaches for the RCPSP/max problem. Though for many problem instances it is too costly to execute a branch-and-bound long enough to prove optimality, good solutions are often obtained in a reasonable amount of computation time through truncation (i.e., not allowing the search to run to completion). The current (known) best performing branch-and-bound approach is that of Dorndorf et al. [19] (referred to later as B&B$_{DPP98}$).

Priority-Rule Methods. It should be noted that a priority rule method, as referred to here, is not the same as a dispatch policy. It actually refers to a backtracking CSP search that uses one or more priority-rules (dispatch heuristics) to choose an activity to schedule next, fixing its start time variable. The RCPSP/max is both an optimization problem and a CSP. When a start time becomes fixed, constraint propagation then takes place, further constraining the domains of the start time variables. The specific priority-rule method that we consider here is referred to as the "direct method" with "serial schedule generation scheme" [20, 21]. Franck et al. found the direct method with serial generation scheme to perform better in general as compared to other priority-rule methods.

The serial schedule generation scheme requires a priority-rule or activity selection heuristic. There are a wide variety of such heuristics available in the literature. Neumann et al. recommend five in particular. These five heuristics are those that we later randomize and combine within a single stochastic search:

- LST: smallest "latest start time" first: $\text{LST}_i = \frac{1}{1+LS_i}$.
- MST: "minimum slack time" first: $\text{MST}_i = \frac{1}{1+LS_i-ES_i}$.
- MTS: "most total successors" first: $\text{MTS}_i = |\text{Successors}_i|$, where Successors_i is the set of not necessarily immediate successors of a_i in the project network.
- LPF: "longest path following" first: $\text{LPF}_i = \text{lpath}(i, n+1)$, where $\text{lpath}(i, n+1)$ is the length of the longest path from a_i to a_{n+1}.
- RSM: "resource scheduling method":
  $\text{RSM}_i = \frac{1}{1+\max(0,\max_{g \in \text{eligible set}, g \neq i}(ES_i+p_i-LS_g))}$.

LS_i and ES_i in these heuristics refers to the latest and earliest start times of the activities. Note that we have rephrased a few of these heuristics from Neumann et al.'s definitions so that for each, the eligible activity with the highest heuristic value is chosen. The eligible set of activities are those that can be time-feasibly scheduled given constraints involving already scheduled activities.

Truncating the search when a threshold number of backtracks has been reached and restarting with a different heuristic each restart has been proposed as an efficient and effective heuristic solution procedure. Later, we refer to the following multiple run truncated priority methods:

- PR_{FNS5}: Executing the direct method with serial generation scheme 5 times, once with each of the heuristics described above, and taking the best solution of the 5 as originally suggested by Frank et al. [20, 21]. Results shown later are of our implementation.
- PR_{FN10}: Similarly, this is a best of 10 heuristics. The results shown later are as reported by Dorndorf et al. [19] and Cesta et al. [22] of Franck and Neumann's best of 10 heuristics method [23][4].

Iterative Sampling Earliest Solutions. Cesta et al. present an algorithm for RCPSP/max that they call *Iterative Sampling Earliest Solutions (ISES)* [22]. ISES begins by finding a time feasible solution with a maximum horizon (initially very large) on the project's makespan, assuming one exists. The resulting time-feasible solution, for any interesting problem instance, is generally not resource-feasible. ISES proceeds by iteratively "leveling" resource-constraint conflicts. That is, it first detects sets of activities that temporally overlap and whose total resource requirement exceeds the resource capacity. Given the set of resource-constraint conflicts, it chooses one of the conflicts using heuristic-equivalency (i.e., chooses randomly from among all resource-conflicts within an "acceptance band" in heuristic value from the heuristically preferred choice). It then levels the chosen conflict by posting a precedence constraint between two of the activities in the conflicted set. It continues until a time-feasible and resource-feasible solution is found or until some resource-conflict cannot be leveled. This is then iterated some fixed number of times within a stochastic sampling framework. Then, given the best solution found during the the stochastic sampling process, the entire algorithm is repeated iteratively for smaller and smaller horizons. Specifically, the horizon is repeatedly set to the makespan of the best solution found so far until no further improvement is possible. Cesta et al. show ISES to perform better than the previous best heuristic algorithm for the RCPSP/max problem (namely PR_{FN10}).

Performance Criteria. The set of benchmark problem instances that we use in the experimental study of this Section is that of Schwindt[5]. There are 1080 problem instances in this problem set. Of these, 1059 have feasible solutions and the other 21 are provably infeasible. Each instance has 100 activities and 5 renewable resources. In the experiments that follow, we use the following performance criteria which have been used by several others to compare the performance of algorithms for the RCPSP/max problem:

- Δ_{LB}: the average relative deviation from the known lower bound, averaged across all problem instances for which a feasible solution was found. Note that this is based on the number of problem instances for which the given algorithm was able to find a feasible solution and thus might be based on a different number of problem instances for each algorithm compared. This criteria, as defined, is exactly as used by all of the other approaches to the problem available in the literature.

---

[4] Franck and Neumann's technical report describing this best of 10 strategy is no longer available according to both the library at their institution as well as the secretary of their lab. We have been unable to find out what the 10 heuristics are that produce these results.

[5] http://www.wior.uni-karlsruhe.de/
LS_Neumann/Forschung/ProGenMax/rcpspmax.html

- NO: the number of optimal solutions found. Currently, there are known optimal solutions for 789 of the 1080 problem instances.
- NF: the number of feasible solutions found. Of the 1080 problem instances, 1059 possess at least one feasible solution. The other 21 can be proven infeasible (e.g., by the preprocessing step of the priority-rule method).
- TIME: CPU time in seconds.

For all stochastic algorithms, values shown are averages across 10 runs. Values in parentheses are best of the 10 runs. In the results, as an added comparison point, we list the above criteria for the current best known solutions as BEST. Note that BEST is the best known prior to the algorithms presented in this paper. We further improve upon the best known solutions to some of the problem instances, but this is not considered in BEST.

Value-Biased Stochastic Sampling (VBSS). The first part of our approach uses an algorithm called VBSS [3, 2] to randomize the priority-rule method. Rather than following a priority rule deterministically during the course of the search, we bias a stochastic selection process by a function of the heuristic values. The backtracking priority-rule method is truncated as before when a threshold number of backtracks has been reached; and then restarted some number of times. The best feasible solution found of these restarts is chosen. In the results that follow, we refer to using the stochastic sampling framework VBSS within the priority-rule method for N iterations by: LST[N]; MST[N]; MTS[N]; LPF[N]; and RSM[N]. The bias functions used within VBSS are in each case polynomial: degree 10 for each of LST and MST; degree 2 for MTS; degree 3 for LPF; and degree 4 for RSM. These were chosen during a small number of exploratory solution runs for a small sample of problem instances. NAIVE[N] refers to randomly sampling an equal number of times with each of the five heuristics (N iterations total).

Generating and Using Models of Solution Qualities. Further, using the methods of modeling the distribution of solution qualities presented in this paper, we enhance the performance of the VBSS priority-rule method, effectively combining multiple heuristics within a single multistart stochastic search. We refer to this approach using the above five heuristics for N iterations according to the estimation method as follows: NORM[N] using Normal distribution estimates; KDE[N] using kernel density estimates; and GEV[N] using GEV distribution estimates.

4 Experimental Results

Table 1 shows a summary of the results of using VBSS with the priority-rule method and Table 2 shows a summary of the results of generating and using models of solution quality to enhance the search. We can make a number of observations:

- For any number of iterations of the VBSS enhanced priority-rule method, the best single heuristic to use in terms of finding optimal solutions is the "longest-path following first" (LPF) heuristic. However, we can also observe that the VBSS method using LPF is worst in terms of the number of feasible solutions found. Using LPF and VBSS appears to perform very well on the problem instances for which it can

Table 1. Summary of the results of using VBSS with the priority-rule method.

Algorithm	Δ_{LB}	NO	NF	TIME
LPF[20]	4.4 (4.2)	616 (628)	942 (956)	0.4
LST[20]	6.1 (5.7)	600.7 (612)	1041 (1043)	0.2
MTS[20]	4.6 (4.4)	600 (617)	953.3 (965)	0.4
MST[20]	6.6 (6.1)	598.3 (606)	1038.7 (1041)	0.3
RSM[20]	8.5 (7.7)	447.7 (494)	1027.3 (1031)	0.2
LPF[100]	4.2 (4.0)	632.3 (642)	959.7 (969)	1.1
MTS[100]	4.4 (4.3)	626 (638)	970 (981)	1.1
LST[100]	5.5 (5.2)	617.3 (625)	1044 (1044)	0.6
MST[100]	5.9 (5.6)	609 (614)	1042 (1043)	0.8
RSM[100]	7.4 (6.9)	510.3 (536)	1033.3 (1035)	0.6
LPF[200]	4.1 (4.0)	638.7 (647)	965 (974)	2.1
MTS[200]	4.3 (4.2)	634 (648)	979 (986)	2.0
LST[200]	5.3 (5.1)	625.3 (633)	1044.3 (1045)	1.1
MST[200]	5.7 (5.5)	614.3 (623)	1043.3 (1044)	1.5
RSM[200]	7.1 (6.5)	529.7 (555)	1034.7 (1036)	1.0
LPF[400]	4.1 (4.0)	643.3 (650)	972.3 (980)	4.0
MTS[400]	4.3 (4.2)	641.7 (654)	983.7 (989)	3.7
LST[400]	5.2 (4.9)	631 (638)	1044.7 (1045)	1.9
MST[400]	5.5 (5.3)	619 (629)	1043.7 (1045)	2.8
RSM[400]	6.7 (6.3)	544 (564)	1035.7 (1037)	1.7

find feasible solutions, while at the same time having difficulties finding any feasible solution for a large number of other problem instances.
- We observe similar behavior when the second best heuristic in terms of number of optimal solutions found (VBSS using the "most total successors" (MTS)) is considered. However, like VBSS using LPF, VBSS using MTS performs poorly in terms of finding feasible solutions to the problems of the benchmark set.
- Although VBSS using any of the other three heuristics does not perform as well in terms of finding optimal solutions as compared to using LPF or MTS, using these other heuristics allows the search to find feasible solutions for many more of the problem instances as compared to using only LPF or MTS. Thus, we can see that by combining the five heuristics either by the naive strategy or by using quality models, that we can find feasible solutions to nearly all of the 1059 problem instances on average; while at the same time combining the strengths of the individual heuristics in terms of finding optimal, or near-optimal, solutions.
- Comparing the use of quality models to guide the choice of search heuristic to the naive strategy of giving an equal number of iterations to each of the heuristics, we see that the naive strategy is always the worst in terms of finding optimal solutions. Somewhat more interestingly, it is also always worst in terms of CPU time. Despite the overhead required for estimating the solution quality models, the naive strategy appears to be generally slower – as much as 2.5 seconds slower in the 2000 iteration case. The reason for this is that although there is extra computational overhead in the modeling, using the models gives less iterations to heuristics that appear less likely to find feasible solutions. The naive strategy results in more iterations that do

Table 2. Summary of the results of using VBSS and models of solution quality to enhance the priority-rule method.

Algorithm	Δ_{LB}	NO	NF	TIME
GEV[100]	5.3 (4.9)	650.7 (667)	1050.7 (1053)	0.8
KDE[100]	5.3 (4.9)	649.7 (662)	1050.7 (1053)	0.8
NORM[100]	5.3 (4.9)	648.7 (661)	1050.7 (1053)	0.8
NAIVE[100]	5.3 (5.0)	646.3 (650)	1050 (1052)	0.9
KDE[500]	4.8 (4.6)	665.7 (680)	1053 (1055)	3.1
NORM[500]	4.9 (4.6)	662.3 (673)	1053 (1055)	3.0
GEV[500]	4.9 (4.6)	660 (677)	1053 (1055)	3.2
NAIVE[500]	4.8 (4.6)	658.3 (666)	1052.7 (1055)	3.7
KDE[1000]	4.7 (4.5)	670.3 (683)	1054.7 (1057)	5.8
GEV[1000]	4.8 (4.5)	667 (682)	1054.7 (1057)	6.5
NORM[1000]	4.8 (4.5)	666.7 (678)	1054.7 (1057)	5.8
NAIVE[1000]	4.7 (4.5)	664.7 (673)	1054.7 (1057)	7.0
KDE[2000]	4.6 (4.4)	675.7 (689)	1057 (1059)	11.2
NORM[2000]	4.7 (4.4)	672.3 (685)	1057 (1059)	11.0
GEV[2000]	4.7 (4.4)	672.3 (685)	1057 (1059)	13.0
NAIVE[2000]	4.6 (4.4)	669.7 (678)	1057 (1059)	13.5

not find a feasible solution, thus performing the maximum number of backtracking steps allowed by the serial generation scheme for such infeasible iterations.
- Of the three methods for estimation, kernel density estimation performs best for the RCPSP/max problem. Except for $N = 100$, KDE[N] finds more optimal solutions than the other considered methods. Furthermore, KDE[N] requires significantly less CPU time than does GEV[N] (at least for the particular estimation procedure of the GEV distribution employed here). Also, the additional overhead of KDE[N] compared to NORM[N] appears to be negligible given the CPU timing results.

Table 3 lists the results of a comparison of the enhanced priority-rule method and other algorithms, including branch-and-bound approaches and stochastic search algorithms. We can make the following observations:

- The best performing heuristic method is clearly KDE[N]. In approximately 1/6 of the CPU time used by the previous best performing heuristic method – ISES – KDE[1000] finds as many optimal solutions with a significantly lower average deviation from the known lower bounds. In less than 1/3 of the CPU time required by ISES, KDE[2000] consistently finds as many feasible solutions as ISES; KDE[2000] consistently finds more optimal solutions than ISES; and KDE[2000] on average finds solutions that deviate significantly less from the known lower bounds as compared to ISES.
- In approximately 1/6 of the CPU time, KDE[2000] on average performs as well as the current best branch-and-bound algorithm – $B\&B_{DPP98}$ – in terms of deviation from lower bounds (and better than $B\&B_{DPP98}$ for the best run of KDE[2000]). However, $B\&B_{DPP98}$ finds more optimal solutions than KDE[2000]. KDE[2000] is a competitive alternative to truncated branch-and-bound if one requires good solutions but not necessarily optimal solutions in a highly limited amount of time.

Table 3. Comparison of the enhanced priority-rule method with other algorithms for the RCPSP/max problem.

Algorithm	Δ_{LB}	NO	NF	TIME
BEST	3.3	789	1059	–
B&B$_{DPP98}$	4.6	774	1059	66.7[a]
PR$_{FNS5}$	6.5	603	991	0.2
PR$_{FN10}$	7.7	601	1053	n/a[c]
ISES	8.0 (7.3)	669.8 (683)	1057 (1059)	35.7[b]
KDE[1000]	4.7 (4.5)	670.3 (683)	1054.7 (1057)	5.8
KDE[2000]	4.6 (4.4)	675.7 (689)	1057 (1059)	11.2

[a] Adjusted from original publication by a factor of $\frac{200}{300}$. The branch-and-bound algorithm was implemented on a 200 Mhz Pentium, while we used for our algorithms a Sun Ultra 10 / 300MHz.

[b] Adjusted from original publication by a factor of $\frac{266}{300}$. ISES was originally implemented on a Sun UltraSparc 30 / 266 MHz, while we used for our algorithms a Sun Ultra 10 / 300MHz.

[c] Timing results were not available in some cases. This is indicated by "n/a".

Table 4. New best known solutions found by the algorithms of this paper. LB is the lower bound for the makespan. Old is the previous best known. New is the new best known.

Instance	LB	Old	New	Algorithm(s)
C364	341	372	365	MTS[100]
D65	440	539	521	KDE[2000], GEV[2000]
D96	434	450	445	LPF[20]
D127	428	445	434	LPF[200]
D277	558	575	569	KDE[2000], GEV[2000]

Table 4 lists the problem instances for which we were able to improve upon the current best known solutions. VBSS using the LPF heuristic is able to improve upon the best known solutions to a couple of problem instances. The same is true of VBSS using MTS. KDE[2000] and GEV[2000] also improve upon a couple additional best known solutions.

5 Summary and Conclusions

In this paper, we introduced a general framework for combining multiple search heuristics within a single stochastic search. The stochastic search algorithm that the study focused on was that of VBSS which is a non-systematic tree-based iterative search that uses randomization to expand the search around a heuristic's prescribed search-space region. The approach recommended by this paper, however, can be applied to other search algorithms that rely on the advice of a search heuristic and for any problem for which there is no one heuristic that is obviously better than others.

In developing the approach to combining multiple search heuristics, we have conjectured that the distribution of the quality of solutions produced by a stochastic search algorithm that is guided by a strong domain heuristic can best be modelled by a family of distributions motivated by extreme value theory. This leads to the use of the GEV distribution within our framework. Two methods of implementing the GEV have been considered: 1) maximum likelihood estimates computed by potentially costly numerical methods; and 2) kernel density estimation using a bandwidth parameter tuned under the assumption of a GEV distribution.

The effectiveness of this approach was validated using the NP-Hard constrained optimization problem known as RCPSP/max. On standard benchmark RCPSP/max problems, our EVT-motivated approach was shown to be competitive with the current best known heuristic algorithms for the problem. The best available truncated branch-and-bound approach is capable of finding a greater number of optimal solutions, but at a much greater computational cost. Our EVT-motivated approach is, however, able to find more optimal solutions than ISES (the previous best known heuristic algorithm for RCPSP/max) and with less deviation than ISES from the known lower bounds on solution quality. The approach we have taken in this paper has also improved upon current best known solutions to difficult benchmark instances.

One potentially interesting future direction to explore is whether or not there is any connection between the heavy-tailed nature of runtime distributions of CSP search algorithms noted by Gomes et al. [10] and the heavy-tailed nature of the solution quality distributions observed in our own work – the extreme value distributions type II & III are both heavy-tailed. Are the runtime and solution quality distributions in constrained optimization domains at all correlated, and if so can this be used to enhance search? This is a direction that will be worth exploring.

References

1. Bresina, J.L.: Heuristic-biased stochastic sampling. In: Proceedings of the Thirteenth National Conference on Artificial Intelligence and the Eighth Innovative Applications of Artificial Intelligence Conference, Volume One, AAAI Press (1996) 271–278
2. Cicirello, V.A., Smith, S.F.: Amplification of search performance through randomization of heuristics. In Van Hentenryck, P., ed.: Principles and Practice of Constraint Programming – CP 2002: 8th International Conference, Proceedings. Volume LNCS 2470 of Lecture Notes in Computer Science., Springer-Verlag (2002) 124–138 Ithaca, NY.
3. Cicirello, V.A.: Boosting Stochastic Problem Solvers Through Online Self-Analysis of Performance. PhD thesis, The Robotics Institute, School of Computer Science, Carnegie Mellon University, Pittsburgh, PA (2003) Also available as technical report CMU-RI-TR-03-27.
4. Goldberg, D., Cicirello, V., Dias, M.B., Simmons, R., Smith, S., Stentz, A.: Market-based multi-robot planning in a distributed layered architecture. In: Multi-Robot Systems: From Swarms to Intelligent Automata: Proceedings of the 2003 International Workshop on Multi-Robot Systems. Volume 2., Kluwer Academic Publishers (2003) 27–38 Washington, DC.
5. Allen, J.A., Minton, S.: Selecting the right heuristic algorithm: Runtime performance predictors. In: Proceedings of the Canadian AI Conference. (1996)
6. Cowling, P., Kendall, G., Soubeiga, E.: Hyperheuristics: A tool for rapid prototyping in scheduling and optimisation. In Cagnoni, S., Gottlieb, J., Hart, E., Middendorf, M., Raidl, G.R., eds.: Applications of Evolutionary Computing: EvoWorkshops 2002 Proceedings. Number LNCS 2279 in Lecture Notes in Computer Science, Springer-Verlag (2002) 1–10

7. Nareyek, A.: Choosing search heuristics by non-stationary reinforcement learning. In Resende, M.G.C., de Sousa, J.P., eds.: Metaheuristics: Computer Decision Making. Kluwer Academic Publishers (2003)
8. Gomes, C.P., Selman, B.: Algorithm portfolios. Artificial Intelligence **126** (2001) 43–62
9. Talukdar, S., Baerentzen, L., Gove, A., de Souza, P.: Asynchronous teams: Cooperation schemes for autonomous agents. Journal of Heuristics **4** (1998) 295–321
10. Gomes, C.P., Selman, B., Crato, N.: Heavy-tailed distributions in combinatorial search. In: Principles and Practices of Constraint Programming (CP-97). Lecture Notes in Computer Science, Springer-Verlag (1997) 121–135
11. Bresina, J., Drummond, M., Swanson, K.: Expected solution quality. In: Proceedings of the Fourteenth International Joint Conference on Artificial Intelligence, Morgan Kaufmann (1995) 1583–1590
12. Coles, S.: An Introduction to Statistical Modeling of Extreme Values. Springer-Verlag (2001)
13. Hosking, J.R.M.: Algorithm AS 215: Maximum-likelihood estimation of the paramaters of the generalized extreme-value distribution. Applied Statistics **34** (1985) 301–310
14. Silverman, B.W.: Density Estimation for Statistics and Data Analysis. Monographs on Statistics and Applied Probability. Chapman and Hall (1986)
15. Epanechnikov, V.A.: Non-parametric estimation of a multivariate probability density. Theory of Probability and Its Applications **14** (1969) 153–158
16. NIST/SEMATECH: e-Handbook of Statistical Methods. NIST/SEMATECH (2003) http://www.itl.nist.gov/div898/handbook/.
17. Kaelbling, L.P., Littman, M.L., Moore, A.W.: Reinforcement learning: A survey. Journal of Artificial Intelligence Research **4** (1996) 237–285
18. Kirkpatrick, S., Gelatt, C.D., Vecchi, M.P.: Optimization by simulated annealing. Science **220** (1983) 671–680
19. Dorndorf, U., Pesch, E., Phan-Huy, T.: A time-oriented branch-and-bound algorithm for resource-constrained project scheduling with generalised precedence constraints. Management Science **46** (2000) 1365–1384
20. Franck, B., Neumann, K., Schwindt, C.: Truncated branch-and-bound, schedule-construction, and schedule-improvement procedures for resource-constrained project scheduling. OR Spektrum **23** (2001) 297–324
21. Neumann, K., Schwindt, C., Zimmermann, J.: Project Scheduling with Time Windows and Scarce Resources: Temporal and Resource-Constrained Project Scheduling with Regular and Nonregular Objective Functions. Lecture Notes in Economics and Mathematical Systems. Springer-Verlag (2002)
22. Cesta, A., Oddi, A., Smith, S.F.: A constraint-based method for project scheduling with time windows. Journal of Heuristics **8** (2002) 109–136
23. Franck, B., Neumann, K.: Resource-constrained project scheduling with time windows: Structural questions and priority-rule methods. Technical Report WIOR-492, Universität Karlsruhe, Karlsruhe, Germany (1998)

A Complete Characterization of Complexity for Boolean Constraint Optimization Problems

David Cohen[1], Martin Cooper[2], and Peter Jeavons[3]

[1] Department of Computer Science, Royal Holloway, University of London, UK
d.cohen@rhul.ac.uk
[2] IRIT, University of Toulouse III, France
cooper@irit.fr
[3] Computing Laboratory, University of Oxford, UK
peter.jeavons@comlab.ox.ac.uk

Abstract. We analyze the complexity of optimization problems expressed using valued constraints. This very general framework includes a number of well-known optimization problems such as MAX-SAT, and WEIGHTED MAX-SAT, as well as properly generalizing the classical CSP framework by allowing the expression of preferences. We focus on valued constraints over Boolean variables, and we establish a dichotomy theorem which characterizes the complexity of any problem involving a fixed set of constraints of this kind.

1 Introduction

In the classical constraint satisfaction framework each constraint allows some combinations of values and disallows others. A number of authors have suggested that the usefulness of this framework can be greatly enhanced by extending the definition of a constraint to assign different costs to different assignments, rather than simply allowing some and disallowing others [1]. Problems involving constraints of this form deal with *optimization* as well as feasibility: we seek an assignment of values to all of the variables having the least possible overall combined cost.

In this extended framework a constraint can be seen as a *cost function*, mapping each possible combination of values to a measure of undesirability. Several alternative mathematical frameworks for such cost functions have been proposed in the literature, including the very general frameworks of 'semi-ring based constraints' and 'valued constraints' [1]. For simplicity, we shall adopt the valued constraint framework here (although our results can easily be adapted to the semi-ring framework, for appropriate semi-ring structures). This very general framework includes a number of well-known optimization problems such as MAX-CSP, MAX-SAT, and WEIGHTED MAX-SAT, as well as properly generalizing the classical CSP framework by allowing the expression of preferences.

In general, optimization problems in this framework are NP-hard, so it is natural to investigate what restrictions can be imposed to make them tractable. One way to achieve this is to restrict the form of the cost functions which are allowed in problem instances. Such a restricted set of cost functions is called a **valued constraint language**. In this paper we investigate the complexity of problems involving different kinds of valued constraint languages. We focus on the Boolean case, where each variable can take just two different values, and we obtain a complete characterization of the complexity for all possible valued constraint languages over Boolean variables.

Our results generalize a number of earlier results for particular forms of optimization problem involving Boolean constraints. For example, Creignou et al obtained a complete characterization of the complexity of different constraint languages for the WEIGHTED MAX-SAT problem [2], where all costs are finite, and a cost is associated with each individual constraint (rather than with each individual combination of values for that constraint, as we allow here).

2 Definitions

In the valued constraint framework, a constraint is specified by a function which assigns a *cost* to each possible assignment of values for the variables it is constraining. In general, costs may be chosen from any *valuation structure*, satisfying the following definition.

Definition 1. *A **valuation structure**, χ, is a totally ordered set, with a minimum and a maximum element (denoted 0 and ∞), together with a commutative, associative binary **aggregation operator** (denoted $+$), such that for all $\alpha, \beta, \gamma \in \chi$*

$$\alpha + 0 = \alpha \tag{1}$$
$$\alpha + \gamma \geq \beta + \gamma \quad \text{whenever} \quad \alpha \geq \beta. \tag{2}$$

In this paper we shall use the valuation structure $\overline{\mathbb{N}}$, consisting of the natural numbers together with infinity, with the usual ordering and the usual addition operation.

Definition 2. *An instance of the valued constraint satisfaction problem, VCSP, is a tuple $\mathcal{P} = \langle V, D, C, \chi \rangle$ where:*

- *V is a finite set of **variables**;*
- *D is a finite set of possible **values** for these variables;*
- *χ is a valuation structure representing possible **costs**;*
- *C is a set of **constraints**.*
  *Each element of C is a pair $c = \langle \sigma, \phi \rangle$, where σ is a tuple of variables called the **scope** of c, and ϕ is a mapping from $D^{|\sigma|}$ to χ, called the **cost function** of c.*

Throughout the paper, the ith component of a tuple t will be denoted $t[i]$, and the length of t will be denoted $|t|$. For any two k-tuples u, v we will say that $u \leq v$ if and only if $u[i] \leq v[i]$ for $i = 1, 2, \ldots, k$.

Definition 3. *For any VCSP instance $\mathcal{P} = \langle V, D, C, \chi \rangle$, an **assignment** for $\mathcal{P}$ is a mapping s from V to D. The **cost** of an assignment s, denoted $Cost_{\mathcal{P}}(s)$, is given by the sum (i.e., aggregation) of the costs for the restrictions of s onto each constraint scope, that is,*

$$Cost_{\mathcal{P}}(s) = \sum_{\langle\langle v_1, v_2, \ldots, v_m\rangle, \phi\rangle \in C} \phi(s(v_1), s(v_2), \ldots, s(v_m)).$$

*A **solution** to $\mathcal{P}$ is an assignment with minimal cost, and the goal is to find a solution.*

*Example 1 (**SAT**).* For any instance $\mathcal{P}$ of the standard propositional satisfiability problem, SAT, we can define a corresponding valued constraint satisfaction problem instance $\widehat{\mathcal{P}}$ in which the range of the cost functions of all the constraints is the set $\{0, \infty\}$. For each clause c of $\mathcal{P}$, we define a corresponding constraint $\widehat{c}$ of $\widehat{\mathcal{P}}$ with the same scope; the cost function of $\widehat{c}$ maps each tuple of values allowed by c to 0, and each tuple disallowed by c to ∞.

In this case the cost of an assignment s for $\widehat{\mathcal{P}}$ equals the minimal possible cost, 0, if and only if s satisfies all of the clauses of $\mathcal{P}$.

*Example 2 (**MAX-SAT**).* In the standard MAX-SAT problem the aim is to find an assignment to the variables which maximizes the number of satisfied clauses. For any instance $\mathcal{P}$ of MAX-SAT, we can define a corresponding valued constraint satisfaction problem instance $\mathcal{P}^{\#}$ in which the range of the cost functions of all the constraints is the set $\{0, 1\}$. For each clause c of $\mathcal{P}$, we define a corresponding constraint $c^{\#}$ of $\mathcal{P}^{\#}$ with the same scope; the cost function of $c^{\#}$ maps each tuple of values allowed by c to 0, and each tuple disallowed by c to 1.

In this case the cost of an assignment s for $\mathcal{P}^{\#}$ equals the total number of clauses of $\mathcal{P}$ which are violated by s. Hence a solution to $\mathcal{P}^{\#}$ corresponds to an assignment of $\mathcal{P}$ which violates the minimum number of clauses, and hence satisfies the maximum number of clauses.

A similar construction can be carried out for the weighted version of the MAX-SAT problem.

The problem of finding a solution to a valued constraint satisfaction problem is an NP optimization problem, that is, it lies in the complexity class NPO (see [2] for a formal definition of this class). It follows from Examples 1 and 2 that there is a polynomial-time reduction from some known NP-hard problems to the general VCSP. To achieve more tractable versions of VCSP, we will now consider the effect of restricting the forms of cost function allowed in the constraints.

Definition 4. *Let χ be a valuation structure. A **valued Boolean constraint language** with costs in χ is defined to be a set of functions, Γ, such that each $\phi \in \Gamma$ is a function from $\{0,1\}^m$ to χ, for some natural number m, where m is called the arity of ϕ.*

The class $\mathrm{VCSP}(\Gamma)$ is defined to be the class of all VCSP instances where the cost functions of all constraints lie in Γ.

For any valued Boolean constraint language Γ, if every instance in VCSP(Γ) can be solved in polynomial time then we will say that Γ is **tractable**. On the other hand, if there is a polynomial-time reduction from some NP-hard problem to VCSP(Γ), then we shall say that Γ is **NP-hard**.

*Example 3 (**SAT and MAX-SAT**).* Let Γ be any valued Boolean constraint language.

If we restrict Γ by only allowing functions with range $\{0, \infty\}$, as in Example 1, then each problem VCSP(Γ) corresponds precisely to a classical Boolean constraint satisfaction problem. Such problems are sometimes known as GENERALIZED SATISFIABILITY problems [3]. The complexity of VCSP(Γ) for such restricted sets Γ has been completely characterized, and the six tractable cases have been identified [3, 2].

Alternatively, if we restrict Γ by only allowing functions whose range has exactly two finite values including 0, as in Example 2, then each VCSP(Γ) corresponds precisely to a standard WEIGHTED MAX-SAT problem [2], in which the aim is to find an assignment in which the total weight of satisfied clauses is maximized. The complexity of VCSP(Γ) for such restricted sets Γ has been completely characterized, and the three tractable cases have been identified (see Theorem 7.6 of [2]).

We note, in particular, that when Γ contains just the single binary function ϕ_{XOR} defined by

$$\phi_{XOR}(x,y) = \begin{cases} 0 & \text{if } x \neq y \\ 1 & \text{otherwise} \end{cases}$$

then VCSP(Γ) corresponds to the MAX-SAT problem for the exclusive-or predicate, which is known to be NP-hard (see Lemma 7.4 of [2]).

In an earlier paper [4], we introduced the idea of *expressing* a desired cost function by using a combination of available functions. The next two definitions formalize this idea.

Definition 5. *For any VCSP instance $\mathcal{P} = \langle V, D, C, \chi \rangle$, and any tuple of distinct variables $W = \langle v_1, \ldots, v_k \rangle$, the **cost function for** $\mathcal{P}$ **on** W, denoted $\Phi_\mathcal{P}^W$, is defined as follows:*

$$\Phi_\mathcal{P}^W(d_1, \ldots, d_k) = \min\{Cost_\mathcal{P}(s) \mid s : V \to D, \langle s(v_1), \ldots, s(v_k)\rangle = \langle d_1, \ldots, d_k\rangle\}$$

Definition 6. *A function ϕ is **expressible** over a valued constraint language Γ if there exists an instance $\mathcal{P} = \langle V, D, C, \chi\rangle$ in VCSP(Γ) and a list W of variables from V such that $\phi = \Phi_\mathcal{P}^W$.*

The set of all functions expressible over a valued constraint language Γ is denoted Γ^*.

The notion of expressibility has already been shown to be a key tool in analyzing the complexity of valued constraint languages, as the next result indicates.

Proposition 1 ([4]). *Let Γ and Γ' be valued constraint languages, with Γ' finite. If $\Gamma' \subseteq \Gamma^*$, then VCSP($\Gamma'$) is polynomial-time reducible to VCSP(Γ).*

The next result shows how Proposition 1 can be used to establish NP-hardness of a valued Boolean constraint language.

Corollary 1. *Let Γ be a valued Boolean constraint language, with costs in χ. If Γ^* contains a binary function ϕ_{XOR+} defined by*

$$\phi_{XOR+}(x,y) = \begin{cases} \alpha \text{ if } x \neq y \\ \beta \text{ if } x = y \end{cases}$$

for some $\alpha < \beta < \infty$, then VCSP(Γ) is NP-hard.

Proof. Lemma 7.4 of [2] states that the Boolean problem VCSP($\{\phi_{XOR}\}$) is NP-hard, where ϕ_{XOR} is the Boolean exclusive-or function, as defined in Example 3. Since adding a constant to all cost functions, and scaling all costs by a constant factor, does not affect the difficulty of solving a VCSP instance, we conclude that VCSP($\{\phi_{XOR+}\}$) is also NP-hard. □

A similar notion of expressibility has been used extensively for classical constraints, which are specified using relations, rather than cost functions [5–7]. It has been shown that the relations expressible by a given set of relations are determined by certain algebraic invariance properties of those relations, known as *polymorphisms* [5, 6, 8]. A **polymorphism** of R, as defined in [5, 8], is a function $f : D^k \to D$, for some k, with the property that whenever $t_1, \ldots, t_k$ are in R then so is $\langle f(t_1[1], \ldots, t_k[1]), \ldots, f(t_1[m], \ldots, t_k[m]) \rangle$.

The concept of a polymorphism is specific to *relations*, and cannot be applied directly to the *functions* in a valued constraint language. However, we now define a more general notion, introduced in [4], which we call a **multimorphism**, and which does apply directly to functions.

Definition 7. *Let D be a set, χ a valuation structure, and $\phi : D^m \to \chi$ a function.*

We extend the definition of ϕ in the following way: for any positive integer k, and any list of k-tuples, $t_1, t_2, \ldots, t_m$, over D, we define

$$\phi(t_1, t_2, \ldots, t_m) = \sum_{i=1}^{k} \phi(t_1[i], t_2[i], \ldots, t_m[i])$$

*We say that $F : D^k \to D^k$ is a **multimorphism** of ϕ if, for any list of k-tuples $t_1, t_2 \ldots, t_m$ over D we have*

$$\phi(F(t_1), F(t_2), \ldots, F(t_m)) \leq \phi(t_1, t_2, \ldots, t_m).$$

For any valued constraint language Γ we will say that Γ has a multimorphism F if and only if F is a multimorphism of ϕ for each $\phi \in \Gamma$.

The following result establishes that multimorphisms have the key property that they extend to all functions expressible over a given language.

Theorem 1 ([4]). *Every multimorphism of a valued constraint language Γ is also a multimorphism of Γ^*.*

In the rest of the paper we will usually denote a multimorphism $F : D^k \to D^k$ by listing explicitly the k separate *component* functions $F_i : D^k \to D$, given by $F_i(x_1, x_2, \ldots, x_k) = F(x_1, x_2, \ldots, x_k)[i]$.

It is shown in [4] that if $F : D^k \to D^k$ is a multimorphism of a function ϕ, then each of the component functions, F_i, is a polymorphism of the corresponding *feasibility relation*, Feas(ϕ), which is defined as follows:

Definition 8. *For any function ϕ, with arity m, we define a relation known as the **feasibility relation** of ϕ, and denoted Feas(ϕ), as follows:*

$$\langle x_1, x_2, \ldots, x_m \rangle \in \text{Feas}(\phi) \Leftrightarrow \phi(x_1, x_2, \ldots, x_m) < \infty.$$

3 Dichotomy Theorem

In this section we will show that in the Boolean case all the *tractable* valued constraint languages are precisely characterized by the presence of certain forms of multimorphism. In fact we establish a dichotomy result: if a valued constraint language has one of eight types of multimorphism then it is tractable, otherwise it is NP-hard.

Theorem 2. *For any valued Boolean constraint language Γ, if Γ has one of the following multimorphisms then VCSP(Γ) is tractable:*

1. $\langle \mathbf{0} \rangle$, *where $\mathbf{0}$ is the constant unary function returning the value 0;*
2. $\langle \mathbf{1} \rangle$, *where $\mathbf{1}$ is the constant unary function returning the value 1;*
3. $\langle \max, \max \rangle$, *where max is the binary function returning the maximum of its arguments (i.e., $\max(x, y) = x \vee y$);*
4. $\langle \min, \min \rangle$, *where min is the binary function returning the minimum of its arguments (i.e., $\min(x, y) = x \wedge y$);*
5. $\langle \min, \max \rangle$;
6. $\langle \text{Mjty}, \text{Mjty}, \text{Mjty} \rangle$, *where Mjty is the ternary majority function, (i.e., it satisfies the identity $\text{Mjty}(x, x, y) = \text{Mjty}(x, y, x) = \text{Mjty}(y, x, x) = x$);*
7. $\langle \text{Mnty}, \text{Mnty}, \text{Mnty} \rangle$, *where Mnty is the ternary minority function, (i.e., it satisfies the identity $\text{Mnty}(x, x, y) = \text{Mnty}(x, y, x) = \text{Mnty}(y, x, x) = y$);*
8. $\langle \text{Mjty}, \text{Mjty}, \text{Mnty} \rangle$;

In all other cases VCSP(Γ) is NP-hard.

We shall prove this result using a series of lemmas in Sections 3.1 and 3.2.

A cost function ϕ will be called **essentially classical** if ϕ takes at most one finite value, that is, there is some value α such that $\phi(x) = \beta < \infty \Rightarrow \beta = \alpha$. Any valued constraint language Γ containing essentially classical cost functions only will be called an **essentially classical language**. Note that when Γ is an essentially classical language any assignment with finite cost has the same cost as any other assignment with finite cost. Hence we can solve any instance of VCSP(Γ) for such languages by solving the corresponding classical constraint satisfaction problem in which each valued constraint $\langle \sigma, \phi \rangle$ is replaced by the classical constraint $\langle \sigma, \text{Feas}(\phi) \rangle$ (see Definition 8). Hence the complexity of any essentially classical valued Boolean constraint language can be determined using Schaefer's Dichotomy Theorem for classical Boolean constraints [3, 6]. We will use this observation a number of times in the course of the proof.

3.1 Tractable Cases

To establish the first part of Theorem 2, we must show that a valued Boolean constraint language which has one of the eight types of multimorphisms listed in the theorem is tractable.

We first note that the tractability of any valued constraint language (not necessarily Boolean) which has a multimorphism of one of the first two types listed in Theorem 2 was established in Theorem 2 of [4]. Furthermore, the tractability of any valued constraint language (not necessarily Boolean) which has a multimorphism of the third type listed in Theorem 2 was established in Theorem 4 of [4], and a symmetric argument (with the ordering reversed) establishes the tractability of any valued constraint language with a polymorphism of the fourth type. Finally, the tractability of any valued Boolean constraint language which has a multimorphism of the last type listed in Theorem 2 follows immediately from Theorem 5 of [4].

Hence, for the first part of the proof we only need to establish the tractability of valued constraint languages having one of the remaining three types of multimorphisms listed in Theorem 2. This is done in the next three lemmas.

Lemma 1. *Any valued Boolean constraint language which has the multimorphism $\langle \text{Mjty}, \text{Mjty}, \text{Mjty} \rangle$ is essentially classical, and tractable.*

Proof. Let ϕ be a k-ary cost function which has the multimorphism $\langle \text{Mjty}, \text{Mjty}, \text{Mjty} \rangle$. It follows from the definition of the Mjty function and the definition of a multimorphism that for all $x, y \in D^k$, $3\phi(x) \leq \phi(x) + \phi(x) + \phi(y)$ and $3\phi(y) \leq \phi(y) + \phi(y) + \phi(x)$. Hence, if both $\phi(x)$ and $\phi(y)$ are finite, then we have $\phi(x) \leq \phi(y)$ and $\phi(y) \leq \phi(x)$, so they must be equal. Hence ϕ is essentially classical, so Γ is essentially classical.

Furthermore, since for each $\phi \in \Gamma$, $\text{Feas}(\phi)$ has the polymorphism Mjty, it follows from Schaefer's Dichotomy Theorem [3, 6] that VCSP(Γ) is tractable. □

Lemma 2. *Any valued Boolean constraint language which has the multimorphism $\langle \text{Mnty}, \text{Mnty}, \text{Mnty} \rangle$ is essentially classical, and tractable.*

Proof. Let ϕ be a k-ary cost function which has the multimorphism $\langle \text{Mnty}, \text{Mnty}, \text{Mnty} \rangle$. It follows from the definition of the Mnty function and the definition of a multimorphism that for all $x, y \in D^k$, $3\phi(x) \leq \phi(x) + \phi(y) + \phi(y)$ and $3\phi(y) \leq \phi(y) + \phi(x) + \phi(x)$. Hence, if both $\phi(x)$ and $\phi(y)$ are finite, then we have $\phi(x) \leq \phi(y)$ and $\phi(y) \leq \phi(x)$, so they must be equal. Hence ϕ is essentially classical, so Γ is essentially classical.

Furthermore, since for each $\phi \in \Gamma$, $\text{Feas}(\phi)$ has the polymorphism Mnty, and the Mnty operation is the affine operation over the field with 2 elements, it follows from Schaefer's Dichotomy Theorem [3, 6] that VCSP(Γ) is tractable. □

The only remaining case for which we need to establish tractability is for valued Boolean constraint languages which have the multimorphism $\langle \min, \max \rangle$. It was shown in [4] that valued constraint languages with this multimorphism are closely connected with the submodular set functions used in economics and operations research [9]. Because of this connection, we shall refer to valued constraint languages with the multimorphism $\langle \min, \max \rangle$ as **submodular** languages.

It was established in Theorem 3 of [4] that finite-valued submodular languages are tractable. We now generalize this result in the Boolean case to include all submodular languages, including those where the cost functions take infinite values.

Lemma 3. *Any submodular valued Boolean constraint language is tractable.*

Proof. Let Γ be a submodular valued Boolean constraint language, and let $\mathcal{P}$ be any instance of VCSP(Γ).

Every cost function in $\mathcal{P}$ has the multimorphism $\langle \min, \max \rangle$, and so the corresponding feasibility relation has the polymorphisms min and max. Since the polymorphism Mjty can be obtained by composition from min and max, it follows that each of these feasibility relations has the polymorphism Mjty, and hence is decomposable into *binary* relations [10]. Hence we can determine whether or not $\mathcal{P}$ has a solution with finite cost by solving a corresponding instance of 2-SAT, which can be solved in polynomial-time.

If $\mathcal{P}$ has any finite cost solution, then we can find a solution with minimal cost by solving a submodular minimisation problem over the set of all solutions allowed by the feasibility relations of the constraints of $\mathcal{P}$. This set has the polymorphisms min and max, and hence forms a distributive lattice. A polynomial-time algorithm for minimising a submodular function over a distributive lattice is given in [11]. □

3.2 Intractable Cases

To establish the remaining part of Theorem 2, we must show that a valued Boolean constraint language which does not have any of the types of multimorphisms listed in the theorem is NP-hard. We first deal with essentially classical languages.

Lemma 4. *Any valued Boolean constraint language which is essentially classical and does not have any of the multimorphisms listed in Theorem 2 is NP-hard.*

Proof. If we replace each cost function ϕ in Γ with the relation Feas(ϕ) then we obtain a classical Boolean constraint language Γ' which does not have any of the polymorphisms $\mathbf{0}, \mathbf{1}, \min, \max, \text{Mjty}$ or Mnty.

By Schaefer's Dichotomy Theorem [3,6], Γ' is NP-complete, and hence Γ is NP-hard. □

For the remaining languages, our strategy will be to show that any language which does not have one of the multimorphisms listed in Theorem 2 can express certain special functions, which we now define.

Definition 9. *A unary cost function σ is a **0-selector** if $\sigma(0) < \sigma(1)$ and it is a **finite 0-selector** if, in addition, $\sigma(1) < \infty$. A **(finite) 1-selector** is defined analogously. A **selector** is either a 1-selector or a 0-selector.*

- *A binary cost function ϕ is a **NEQ** function if*

$$\phi(0,1) = \phi(1,0) < \phi(1,1) = \phi(0,0) = \infty.$$

- *A binary cost function ϕ is an **XOR** function if*

$$\phi(0,1) = \phi(1,0) < \phi(1,1) = \phi(0,0) < \infty.$$

Lemma 5. *Let Γ be a valued Boolean constraint language which is not essentially classical.*

If Γ^* contains a NEQ function, then either Γ^* contains both a finite 0-selector and a finite 1-selector, or else Γ^* contains an XOR function.

Proof. Let $\nu \in \Gamma^*$ be a NEQ function.

First we show that if Γ^* contains a finite 0-selector σ_0, then it also contains a finite 1-selector. To see this simply construct the instance $\mathcal{P}_0$ with variables $\{x,y\}$ and constraints $\{\langle\langle x\rangle, \sigma_0\rangle, \langle\langle x,y\rangle, \nu\rangle\}$, and note that $\Phi_{\mathcal{P}_0}^{\langle y\rangle}$ is a finite 1-selector. Similarly, if Γ^* contains a finite 1-selector, then it also contains a finite 0-selector.

Now let $\zeta \in \Gamma$ be a cost function of arity m which is not essentially classical. Choose tuples u, v such that $\zeta(u)$ and $\zeta(v)$ are as small as possible with $\zeta(u) < \zeta(v) < \infty$. Let $\mathcal{P}$ be the VCSP instance with four variables: $\{x_{00}, x_{01}, x_{10}, x_{11}\}$, and three constraints:

$$\langle\langle x_{u[1]v[1]}, \ldots, x_{u[m]v[m]}\rangle, \zeta\rangle, \quad \langle\langle x_{00}, x_{11}\rangle, \nu\rangle, \quad \langle\langle x_{01}, x_{10}\rangle, \nu\rangle.$$

Let $W = \langle x_{01}, x_{11}\rangle$, and $\psi = \Phi_{\mathcal{P}}^W$.

Note that $\psi(0,1) = \zeta(u) + 2\nu(0,1)$ and $\psi(1,1) = \zeta(v) + 2\nu(0,1)$. If $\psi(0,1) \neq \psi(1,0)$, then, by the choice of u, $\psi(0,1) < \psi(1,0)$, and $\psi(0,1) < \psi(1,1) < \infty$, so $\Phi_{\mathcal{P}}^{\langle x_{01}\rangle}$ is a finite 0-selector.

Hence we may assume that $\psi(0,1) = \psi(1,0)$. If $\psi(0,0) \neq \psi(1,1)$, then if $\psi(0,0) < \infty$ the function $\psi(x,x)$ is a finite selector, and hence Γ^* contains both a finite 0-selector and a finite 1-selector. On the other hand, if $\psi(0,0) = \infty$ then construct the instance $\mathcal{P}_2$ with variables $\{x,y\}$ and constraints $\{\langle\langle x,x\rangle, \psi\rangle, \langle\langle x,y\rangle, \psi\rangle\}$. In this case $\Phi_{\mathcal{P}_2}^{\langle y\rangle}$ is a finite 0-selector, and hence Γ^* again contains both a finite 0-selector and a finite 1-selector.

Otherwise we may assume that $\psi(0,1) = \psi(1,0)$ and $\psi(0,0) = \psi(1,1)$. By construction, we have $\psi(0,1) = \zeta(u) + 2\nu(0,1) < \zeta(v) + 2\nu(0,1) = \psi(1,1) < \infty$. So in this case ψ is an XOR function. □

Lemma 6. *Let Γ be a valued Boolean constraint language which is not essentially classical, and does not have either of the multimorphisms $\langle \mathbf{0}\rangle$ or $\langle \mathbf{1}\rangle$.*

Either Γ^* contains a 0-selector and a 1-selector, or else Γ^* contains an XOR function.

Proof. Let $\phi_0 \in \Gamma$ be a cost function which does not have the multimorphism $\langle \mathbf{0} \rangle$, and $\phi_1 \in \Gamma$ be a cost function which does not have the multimorphism $\langle \mathbf{1} \rangle$, and let m be the arity of ϕ_0. Choose a tuple r such that $\phi_0(r)$ is the minimal value of ϕ_0. By the choice of ϕ_0, we have $\phi_0(r) < \phi_0(0, 0, \ldots, 0)$.

Suppose first that Γ^* contains a 0-selector σ_0. Let M be a finite natural number which is larger than all finite costs in the range of ϕ_0. We construct the instance $\mathcal{P} \in \text{VCSP}(\Gamma)$ with two variables $\{x_0, x_1\}$, and two constraints $\langle \langle x_{r[1]}, \ldots, x_{r[m]} \rangle, \phi_0 \rangle$ and $\langle \langle x_0 \rangle, M\sigma_0 \rangle$. It is straightforward to check that $\Phi_\mathcal{P}^{\langle x_1 \rangle}(1) < \Phi_\mathcal{P}^{\langle x_1 \rangle}(0)$, and so in this case Γ^* contains a 1-selector. A similar argument, using ϕ_1, shows that if Γ^* contains a 1-selector, then it also contains a 0-selector.

Hence, we need to show that either Γ^* contains a selector, or it contains an XOR function. If $\phi_0(0, \ldots, 0) \neq \phi_0(1, \ldots, 1)$ then the unary cost function $\sigma(x) = \phi_0(x, \ldots, x)$ in Γ^* is clearly a selector, and the result holds.

Otherwise, we construct the instance $\mathcal{P}' \in \text{VCSP}(\Gamma)$ with two variables $\{x_0, x_1\}$ and the single constraint $\langle \langle x_{r[1]}, \ldots, x_{r[m]} \rangle, \phi_0 \rangle$. Now, by considering the costs of all four possible assignments, we can verify that either $\Phi_{\mathcal{P}'}^{\langle x_0 \rangle}$ or $\Phi_{\mathcal{P}'}^{\langle x_1 \rangle}$ is a selector, or else $\nu = \Phi_{\mathcal{P}'}^{\langle x_0, x_1 \rangle}$ is either an XOR function, or a NEQ function.

If ν is an XOR function we are done, otherwise we appeal to Lemma 5 to complete the proof. □

Many of the remaining lemmas in this Section use the following construction which combines a given cost function ϕ of arbitrary arity with a pair of selectors, in order to express a *binary* cost function with some similar properties.

Construction 1. *Let ϕ be any m-ary cost function which is not identically infinite, and let σ_0 be a 0-selector and σ_1 a 1-selector. Let u, v be two m-tuples, and let M be a natural number larger than all finite costs in the range of ϕ.*

Let $\mathcal{P}$ be a VCSP instance with variables $\{x_{00}, x_{01}, x_{10}, x_{11}\}$, and constraints:

$$\langle \langle x_{u[1]v[1]}, \ldots, x_{u[m]v[m]} \rangle, \phi \rangle, \quad \langle \langle x_{00} \rangle, M\sigma_0 \rangle, \quad \langle \langle x_{11} \rangle, M\sigma_1 \rangle.$$

*The binary cost function $\phi_2 \stackrel{\text{def}}{=} \Phi_\mathcal{P}^{\langle x_{01}, x_{10} \rangle}$ will be called a **compression** of ϕ by u and v.*

Lemma 7. *A function ϕ has a $\langle \max, \max \rangle$ multimorphism if and only if*

- *ϕ is **finitely antitone**, that is, for all tuples u, v with $\phi(u), \phi(v) < \infty$,*

$$u < v \Rightarrow \phi(u) \geq \phi(v).$$

- *Feas(ϕ) has the polymorphism max.*

Proof. If ϕ has a $\langle \max, \max \rangle$ multimorphism, then for all tuples u, v we have $\phi(u) + \phi(v) \geq 2\phi(\max(u, v))$, so both conditions hold.

Conversely, if ϕ does not have a $\langle \max, \max \rangle$ multimorphism, then there exist tuples u, w such that $\phi(u) + \phi(w) < 2\phi(\max(u, w))$. Hence, without loss of generality, we may assume that $\phi(u) < \phi(\max(u, w))$. Setting $v = \max(u, w)$ we get $u < v$ and $\phi(u) < \phi(v)$. If $\phi(v) < \infty$ then the first condition does not hold, and if $\phi(v) = \infty$, then the second condition fails to hold. □

Lemma 8. *Let Γ be a valued Boolean constraint language which is not essentially classical, and does not have any of the multimorphisms $\langle \mathbf{0} \rangle$ or $\langle \mathbf{1} \rangle$ or $\langle \max, \max \rangle$ or $\langle \min, \min \rangle$.*

Either Γ^* contains a finite 0-selector and a finite 1-selector, or else Γ^* contains an XOR function.

Proof. Let ϕ be a cost function in Γ which does not have a $\langle \max, \max \rangle$ multimorphism, and let ψ be a cost function in Γ which does not have a $\langle \min, \min \rangle$ multimorphism.

By Lemma 6, either Γ^* contains an XOR function and we have nothing to prove, or else Γ^* contains a 0-selector, σ_0, and a 1-selector, σ_1.

Since ϕ does not have a $\langle \max, \max \rangle$ multimorphism, it follows from Lemma 7 that either ϕ is not finitely antitone, or else the relation $\operatorname{Feas}(\phi)$ does not have the polymorphism max.

For the first case, choose two tuples u and v, with $u < v$ with $\phi(u) < \phi(v) < \infty$, and let ϕ_2 be a compression of ϕ by u and v (see Construction 1). It is straightforward to check that $\phi_2(0, 0) < \phi_2(1, 1) < \infty$, which means that $\phi_2(x, x)$ is a finite 0-selector belonging to Γ^*.

On the other hand suppose that ϕ is finitely antitone, and that Γ^* contains a finite 1-selector τ. In this case we know that $\operatorname{Feas}(\phi)$ does not have the polymorphism max, so we can choose u, v such that $\phi(u), \phi(v) < \infty$ and $\phi(\max(u, v)) = \infty$. Let ϕ_2 be a compression of ϕ by u and v, and construct the instance $\mathcal{P} \in \operatorname{VCSP}(\Gamma^*)$ with variables $\{x, y\}$, and constraints:

$$\langle \langle x, y \rangle, \phi_2 \rangle, \qquad \langle \langle y, x \rangle, \phi_2 \rangle, \qquad \langle \langle y \rangle, \tau \rangle.$$

The fact that ϕ is finitely antitone gives $\phi(u), \phi(v) \leq \phi(\min(u, v))$. This, together with the fact that $\phi(u)$ and $\phi(v)$ are finite whilst $\phi(\max(u, v))$ is infinite, is enough to show that $\Phi_{\mathcal{P}}^{\langle x \rangle}$ is a finite 0-selector.

So, we have shown that if Γ^* contains a finite 1-selector, then it contains a finite 0-selector whether or not ϕ is finitely antitone. A symmetric argument, exchanging 0 and 1, max and min, and ϕ and ψ, shows that if Γ^* contains a finite 0-selector, then it contains a finite 1-selector.

Hence, to complete the proof we may assume that Γ^* contains no finite selectors. In this case we know that $\operatorname{Feas}(\phi)$ does not have the polymorphism max and $\operatorname{Feas}(\psi)$ does not have the polymorphism min, so we may choose tuples u, v, w, z such that $\phi(u), \phi(v), \psi(w)$ and $\psi(z)$ are all finite, but $\phi(\max(u, v))$ and $\psi(\min(w, z))$ are both infinite. Now let ϕ_2 be a compression of ϕ by u and v, and ψ_2 a compression of ψ by w and z (see Construction 1). We then have that $\rho(x, y) \stackrel{\text{def}}{=} \phi_2(x, y) + \phi_2(y, x) + \psi_2(x, y) + \psi_2(y, x)$ is a NEQ function which is contained in Γ^*. We can now appeal to Lemma 5 to show that Γ^* contains an XOR function, and we are done. □

Lemma 9. *Let Γ be a valued Boolean constraint language which does not have the multimorphism $\langle \min, \max \rangle$.*

If Γ contains both a finite 0-selector and a finite 1-selector, then Γ^* contains a NEQ function or an XOR function.

Proof. Suppose that $\sigma_0 \in \Gamma^*$ is a finite 0-selector, $\sigma_1 \in \Gamma^*$ is a finite 1-selector, and $\phi \in \Gamma$ is non-submodular (i.e., ϕ does not have the multimorphism $\langle \min, \max \rangle$).

Set $\lambda = \sigma_0(1) - \sigma_0(0)$ and $\mu = \sigma_1(0) - \sigma_1(1)$.

Choose u, v such that $\phi(u) + \phi(v) < \phi(\max(u,v)) + \phi(\min(u,v))$. Let ϕ_2 be a compression of ϕ by u and v. It is straightforward to check that ϕ_2 is also not submodular.

There are three cases to consider:

Case (1): $\phi_2(0,0), \phi_2(1,1) < \infty$.

Construct the instance $\mathcal{P} \in \text{VCSP}(\Gamma^*)$ with variables $\{x, y\}$, and constraints

$$\langle \langle x, y \rangle, 2\lambda\mu\phi_2 \rangle,$$
$$\langle \langle x \rangle, \lambda(\phi_2(1,0) + \phi_2(1,1))\sigma_1 \rangle, \quad \langle \langle x \rangle, \mu(\phi_2(0,0) + \phi_2(0,1))\sigma_0 \rangle,$$
$$\langle \langle y \rangle, \lambda(\phi_2(0,1) + \phi_2(1,1))\sigma_1 \rangle, \quad \langle \langle y \rangle, \mu(\phi_2(0,0) + \phi_2(1,0))\sigma_0 \rangle.$$

If we set $W = \langle x, y \rangle$, then it is straightforward to check that $\Phi_\mathcal{P}^W$ is an XOR function.

Case (2): *Exactly* one of $\phi_2(0,0)$ and $\phi_2(1,1)$ is finite.

First suppose that $\phi_2(0,0) = \infty > \phi_2(1,1)$. Let $\alpha = \max\{\phi_2(0,1) + \phi_2(1,0) - 2\phi_2(1,1) + 1, 0\}$, and construct an instance $\mathcal{P}_2 \in \text{VCSP}(\Gamma^*)$ with variables $\{x, u, v, y\}$, and constraints

$$\langle \langle x, u \rangle, \mu\phi_2 \rangle, \quad \langle \langle u, x \rangle, \mu\phi_2 \rangle,$$
$$\langle \langle u, v \rangle, \mu\phi_2 \rangle, \quad \langle \langle v, u \rangle, \mu\phi_2 \rangle,$$
$$\langle \langle v, y \rangle, \mu\phi_2 \rangle, \quad \langle \langle y, v \rangle, \mu\phi_2 \rangle,$$
$$\langle \langle x \rangle, \alpha\sigma_1 \rangle, \quad \langle \langle u \rangle, 2\alpha\sigma_1 \rangle,$$
$$\langle \langle v \rangle, 2\alpha\sigma_1 \rangle, \quad \langle \langle y \rangle, \alpha\sigma_1 \rangle.$$

If we set $W = \langle x, y \rangle$, and $\eta = \Phi_{\mathcal{P}_2}^W$, then it is straightforward to verify that $\eta(0,1) = \eta(1,0)$, $\eta(0,0) = \eta(1,1)$, and

$$\eta(0,0) = \eta(0,1) + \mu(\alpha + 2\phi_2(1,1) - \phi_2(0,1) - \phi_2(1,0)),$$

and hence that η is an XOR function.

A symmetric argument clearly works when $\phi_2(1,1) = \infty > \phi_2(0,0)$.

Case (3): $\phi_2(0,0) = \phi_2(1,1) = \infty$.

In this case the function $\phi_2(x,y) + \phi_2(y,x)$ is a NEQ function which is clearly contained in Γ^*. □

Lemma 10. *A Boolean function ϕ has a $\langle \text{Mjty}, \text{Mjty}, \text{Mnty} \rangle$ multimorphism if and only if:*

- ϕ is **finitely modular**, that is, for all tuples u, v with $\phi(u), \phi(v), \phi(\max(u, v)), \phi(\min(u, v)) < \infty$,

$$\phi(u) + \phi(v) = \phi(\max(u, v)) + \phi(\min(u, v)).$$

- Feas(ϕ) has the polymorphisms Mjty and Mnty.

Proof. Follows immediately from the characterization of valued Boolean constraint languages with a $\langle$Mjty, Mjty, Mnty$\rangle$ multimorphism given in Theorem 4.17 of [12]. □

Lemma 11. *Let Γ be a valued Boolean constraint language which does not have the multimorphism $\langle$Mjty, Mjty, Mnty$\rangle$.*

If Γ^* contains a finite 0-selector, a finite 1-selector, and a NEQ function, then Γ^* contains an XOR function.

Proof. Suppose that $\sigma_0 \in \Gamma^*$ is a finite 0-selector, $\sigma_1 \in \Gamma^*$ is a finite 1-selector, $\nu \in \Gamma^*$ is a NEQ function, and $\phi \in \Gamma$ does not have the multimorphism $\langle$Mjty, Mjty, Mnty$\rangle$. We have to show that Γ^* also contains an XOR function.

By Lemma 10 there are 2 cases: either ϕ is not finitely modular, or Feas(ϕ) does not have both polymorphisms Mjty and Mnty.

In the first case, choose tuples u, v such that $\phi(u) + \phi(v) \neq \phi(\min(u, v)) + \phi(\max(u, v))$. Let ϕ_2 be a compression of ϕ by u and v. It is straightforward to check that ϕ_2 is also not finitely modular. Now construct the instance $\mathcal{P}$ with variables $\{w, x, y, z\}$, and constraints

$$\langle\langle x, w\rangle, \nu\rangle, \quad \langle\langle z, y\rangle, \nu\rangle, \quad \langle\langle x, z\rangle, \phi_2\rangle, \quad \langle\langle w, y\rangle, \phi_2\rangle.$$

It is straightforward to check that either $\Phi_\mathcal{P}^{\langle x, y\rangle}$ or $\Phi_\mathcal{P}^{\langle w, y\rangle}$ is an XOR function.

Next, suppose that Feas(ϕ) has the polymorphism Mjty but not Mnty. In this case, by Theorem 3.5 of [10], Feas(ϕ) is decomposable into binary relations (in other words, it is equal to the relational join of its binary projections). Since Feas(ϕ) does not have the Mnty polymorphism, this implies that one of its binary projections does not have the Mnty polymorphism. The only binary Boolean relations which do not have the Mnty polymorphism have exactly three tuples. Therefore, by projection, it is possible to construct from ϕ a binary cost function ψ such that exactly three of $\psi(0, 0), \psi(0, 1), \psi(1, 0), \psi(1, 1)$ are finite. If $\psi(0, 1)$ or $\psi(1, 0)$ is infinite, then let η be the projection onto variables x, y of $\psi(x, v) + \nu(v, y)$, otherwise let $\eta = \psi$. The cost function η is non-submodular and exactly one of $\eta(0, 0)$ and $\eta(1, 1)$ are infinite, and so, by Case 2 of Lemma 9, Γ^* contains an XOR function.

Suppose now that Feas(ϕ) has the polymorphism Mnty but not Mjty. Since Feas(ϕ) has the polymorphism Mnty, it is an *affine* relation [2] over the finite field with 2 elements, GF(2), and can be expressed as a system of linear equations over GF(2). Creignou et al. define a Boolean relation to be *affine with width 2* if it can be expressed as a system of linear equations over GF(2), with at most two variables per equation [2]. In fact, linear equations over GF(2) with one variable correspond to the unary relations, and linear equations over GF(2) with two variables correspond to the binary equality and disequality relations. The unary relations, and the binary equality and disequality relations all have both the Mjty and Mnty polymorphisms. Thus Feas(ϕ) is affine but not of width 2. Hence, by Lemma 5.34 of [2], Feas(ϕ) can be used to construct the 4-ary affine constraint $w + x + y + z = 0$. In other words, there is some $\psi \in \Gamma^*$ such that $\psi(w, x, y, z) < \infty$ iff $w + x + y + z = 0$.

Now set $\lambda = \psi(0, 0, 1, 1) + \psi(0, 1, 0, 1) + 1$ and construct the VCSP instance $\mathcal{P}$ with variables $\{w, x, y, z\}$, and constraints

$$\langle\langle w, x, y, z\rangle, \psi\rangle, \qquad \langle\langle w\rangle, 3M\sigma_0\rangle, \qquad \langle\langle z\rangle, \lambda\sigma_1\rangle$$

where M is a natural number larger than the square of any finite cost in the range of ψ or σ_1. Let $\eta = \Phi_{\mathcal{P}}^{\langle x, y\rangle}$. It is straightforward to verify that η is a binary non-submodular function where both $\eta(0, 0)$ and $\eta(1, 1)$ are finite. Hence, by Case 1 of Lemma 9, the result follows in this case also.

Finally, if Feas(ϕ) has neither the polymorphism Mnty nor Mjty, then the set of Boolean relations $\{\text{Feas}(\phi), \text{Feas}(\nu)\}$ can be shown to have essentially unary polymorphisms only (see Theorem 4.12 of [7]). By Theorem 4.10 of [7], this implies that in this case Feas(ϕ) can again be used to construct the 4-ary affine constraint $w + x + y + z = 0$, and we can proceed as above. □

Lemma 12. *Let Γ be a valued Boolean constraint language which does not have any of the multimorphisms listed in Theorem 2.*
Either Γ is essentially classical, or else Γ^* contains an XOR function.

Proof. Suppose that Γ is not essentially classical and has none of the multimorphisms listed in Theorem 2. By Lemmas 9 and 8, either Γ^* contains an XOR function, or else Γ^* contains a NEQ function and a finite 0-selector and a finite 1-selector. In the latter case, by Lemma 11 we know that Γ^* contains an XOR function. □

Combining Lemmas 4 and 12, together with Corollary 1, establishes the NP-hardness of any valued Boolean constraint language having none of the multimorphisms listed in Theorem 2, and so completes the proof of Theorem 2.

4 Some Special Cases

Corollary 2. *Let Γ be a valued Boolean constraint language Γ where all costs are finite. If Γ has one of the multimorphisms $\langle \mathbf{0}\rangle$, $\langle \mathbf{1}\rangle$, or $\langle \min, \max\rangle$, then VCSP($\Gamma$) is tractable. In all other cases VCSP(Γ) is NP-hard.*

Proof. Let ϕ be a cost function taking *finite values only*. By Lemma 7, if ϕ has the multimorphism $\langle \max, \max\rangle$, then ϕ is antitone, and hence has the multimorphism $\langle \mathbf{1}\rangle$. By a symmetric argument, if ϕ has the multimorphism $\langle \min, \min\rangle$, then ϕ is monotone, and hence has the multimorphism $\langle \mathbf{0}\rangle$. By Lemma 1, if ϕ has the multimorphism ⟨Mjty, Mjty, Mjty⟩, then ϕ is constant, and hence has the multimorphism ⟨**0**⟩. By Lemma 2, if ϕ has the multimorphism ⟨Mnty, Mnty, Mnty⟩, then ϕ is again constant, and hence has the multimorphism ⟨**0**⟩. By Lemma 10, if ϕ has the multimorphism ⟨Mjty, Mjty, Mnty⟩, then ϕ is modular, and hence submodular, that is, it has the multimorphism ⟨min, max⟩.

The result now follows from Theorem 2. □

Using the construction given in Example 2, this immediately gives a dichotomy theorem for the MAX-SAT problem for any Γ corresponding to a set of relations.

Corollary 3. *If Γ has one of the multimorphisms ⟨**0**⟩, ⟨**1**⟩, or ⟨min, max⟩, then MAX-SAT(Γ) is tractable. In all other cases MAX-SAT(Γ) is NP-hard.*

This result gives an alternative description to the one given in Theorem 7.6 of [2] for the three tractable cases of MAX-SAT.

References

1. Bistarelli, S., Fargier, H., Montanari, U., Rossi, F., Schiex, T., Verfaillie, G.: Semiring-based CSPs and valued CSPs: Frameworks, properties, and comparison. Constraints **4** (1999) 199–240
2. Creignou, N., Khanna, S., Sudan, M.: Complexity Classification of Boolean Constraint Satisfaction Problems. Volume 7 of SIAM Monographs on Discrete Mathematics and Applications. Society for Industrial and Applied Mathematics (2001)
3. Schaefer, T.: The complexity of satisfiability problems. In: Proceedings 10th ACM Symposium on Theory of Computing, STOC'78. (1978) 216–226
4. Cohen, D., Cooper, M., Jeavons, P., Krokhin, A.: Soft constraints: complexity and multimorphisms. In: Proceedings of 9th International Conference on Principles and Practice of Constraint Programming (CP'03). Volume 2833 of Lecture Notes in Computer Science., Springer-Verlag (2003) 244–258
5. Bulatov, A., Krokhin, A., Jeavons, P.: Constraint satisfaction problems and Finite algebras. In: Proceedings ICALP'00. Volume 1853 of Lecture Notes in Computer Science., Springer-Verlag (2000) 272–282
6. Jeavons, P., Cohen, D., Gyssens, M.: Closure properties of constraints. Journal of the ACM **44** (1997) 527–548
7. Jeavons, P.: On the algebraic structure of combinatorial problems. Theoretical Computer Science **200** (1998) 185–204
8. Pöschel, R., Kalužnin, L.: Funktionen- und Relationenalgebren. DVW, Berlin (1979)
9. Nemhauser, G., Wolsey, L.: Integer and Combinatorial Optimization. John Wiley & Sons (1988)
10. Jeavons, P., Cohen, D., Cooper, M.: Constraints, consistency and closure. Artificial Intelligence **101** (1998) 251–265
11. Iwata, S.: A faster scaling algorithm for minimizing submodular functions. SIAM Journal on Computing **32** (2003) 833–840
12. Cohen, D., Cooper, M., Jeavons, P., Krokhin, A.: An investigation of the multimorphisms of tractable and intractable classes of valued constraints. Technical Report CSD-TR-03-03, CS department, Royal Holloway, University of London (2003)

Financial Portfolio Optimisation

Pierre Flener[1], Justin Pearson[1], and Luis G. Reyna[2]

[1] Department of Information Technology, Uppsala University
Box 337, 751 05 Uppsala, Sweden
{Pierre.Flener,Justin.Pearson}@it.uu.se
[2] Global Private Investment Advisory Group, Merrill Lynch
New York, NY 10281-1307, USA
Luis_Reyna@ml.com

Abstract. We give an approximate and often extremely fast method of solving a portfolio optimisation (PO) problem in financial mathematics, which has applications in the credit derivatives market. Its corresponding satisfaction problem is closely related to the balanced incomplete block design (BIBD) problem. However, typical PO instances are an order of magnitude larger than the largest BIBDs solved so far by global search. Our method is based on embedding sub-instances into the original instance. Their determination is itself a CSP. This allows us to solve a typical PO instance, with over 10^{746} symmetries. The high quality of our approximate solutions can be assessed by comparison with a tight lower bound on the cost. Also, our solutions sufficiently improve the currently best ones so as to often make the difference between having or not having a feasible transaction due to investor and rating-agency constraints.

1 Introduction

The structured credit market has seen two new products over the last decade: credit derivatives and credit default obligations (CDOs). These new products have created the ability to leverage and transform credit risk in ways not possible through the traditional bond and loan markets.

CDOs typically consist of a special purpose vehicle that has credit exposure to around one hundred different issuers. Such vehicles purchase bonds and loans and other financial assets through the issuance of notes or obligations with varying levels of risk. In a typical structure, credit losses in the underlying pool are allocated to the most subordinated obligations or notes first. A natural progression of the market has been to use notes from existing CDOs as assets into a new generation of CDOs, called CDO Squared or CDO of CDO [9].

The credit derivatives market has allowed a more efficient mechanism for creating CDO Squared. The idea is to use sub-pools of credit default swaps instead of notes. The sub-pools are chosen from a collection of credits with the level of liquidity and risk adequate to the potential investors. These transactions are sometimes labelled synthetic CDO Squared.

In the creation of a synthetic CDO, the natural question arises on how to maximise the diversification of the sub-pools given a limited universe of previously chosen credits. In a typical CDO Squared, the number of available credits ranges from 250 to 500 and the number of sub-pools from 4 to as many as 25. The investment banker arranging for a CDO Squared usually seeks to maximise the return of the subordinated notes under the constraints imposed by the rating agencies and the investors. This is a challenge that typically is only partially addressed, in part due to the difficulty of pricing the underlying assets [5][1].

In this paper, we analyse the already financially relevant abstracted problem of selecting the credits comprising each of the sub-pools with a minimal overlap, or maximum diversification. The minimisation of the overlap usually results in better ratings for the notes, typically resulting in more efficient structures.

The remainder of this paper is organised as follows. In Section 2, we discuss the well-known problem of balanced incomplete block design (BIBD), which is related to portfolio optimisation. In Section 3, we formulate the portfolio optimisation (PO) problem, which is an optimisation problem, and show its relationship to the BIBD problem, which is a satisfaction problem. Since the known methods of solving BIBD instances by global search do not scale for the solution of typical instances of the satisfaction version of the PO problem, we introduce in Section 4 a method of approximately solving the PO problem, using a notion of embedding small occurrences of an instance in a larger one. Finally, in Section 5, we conclude, discuss related work, and outline future work.

2 Balanced Incomplete Block Designs

Let V be any set of v elements, called *varieties*. Let $B = \{1, \ldots, b\}$. A *balanced incomplete block design* (BIBD) is a bag of b subsets $B_j \subseteq V$, called *blocks*, each of size k:

$$\forall j \in B : |B_j| = k \qquad (1)$$

with $2 \leq k < v$,[2] such that each pair of distinct varieties occurs together in exactly λ blocks. Let V_i be the set of the identifiers of the blocks in which variety i occurs: $V_i = \{j \in B \mid i \in B_j\}$. The V_i are here called *co-blocks*. The previous *balancing condition* can now be formulated by requiring that any two distinct co-blocks intersect over exactly λ elements:

$$\forall\, i_1 \neq i_2 \in V : |V_{i_1} \cap V_{i_2}| = \lambda \qquad (2)$$

An implied constraint is that each co-block has the *same* number r of elements, whose value can be determined:

$$\forall i \in V : |V_i| = r = \frac{\lambda \cdot (v-1)}{k-1} \qquad (3)$$

This constraint and the already mentioned $2 \leq k < v$ imply that none of the co-blocks can be equal:

$$\lambda < r \qquad (4)$$

---

[1] There are very few publicly accessible papers we can cite in this introduction, as most are confidential due to the potential financial value of their results.
[2] If $k = v$, then it is a *complete* block design.

A further implied constraint is that the co-blocks and blocks have together the same number of elements:
$$v \cdot r = b \cdot k \tag{5}$$
These implied constraints are insufficient *existence conditions* for a BIBD.

A BIBD is thus parameterised by a 5-tuple $\langle v, b, r, k, \lambda \rangle$ of parameters, any three of which are independent. Originally intended for the design of statistical experiments, BIBDs also have applications in cryptography and other domains. See [1], or http://mathworld.wolfram.com/BlockDesign.html, or Problem 28 at http://www.csplib.org/ for more information.

Blocks and co-blocks are dual: an alternative formulation is that a BIBD is a *set* of v subsets $V_i \subseteq B$, each of size r, such that the preceding constraints (1) to (5) hold, where block B_j is then the set of varieties comprising it, that is $B_j = \{i \in V \mid j \in V_i\}$.

One way of modelling a BIBD is in terms of its *incidence matrix*, which is a $v \times b$ matrix, such that the entry at the intersection of row i and column j is 1 if $i \in B_j$ (that is $j \in V_i$) and 0 otherwise. The first three constraints are then modelled by requiring, respectively, that there are exactly k ones (that is a sum of k) for each column, a scalar product of exactly λ for any pair of distinct rows, and exactly r ones (that is a sum of r) for each row.

Since the varieties and blocks are indistinguishable, any two rows or columns of the incidence matrix can be freely permuted. Breaking all the resulting $v! \cdot b!$ symmetries can in theory be performed, for instance by $v! \cdot b! - 1$ (anti-) lexicographical ordering constraints between vectors extracted from the incidence matrix [4, 8]. In practice, strictly anti-lexicographically ordering (denoted by $>_{lex}$) the rows (since co-blocks cannot be repeated) as well as anti-lexicographically ordering (denoted by $\geq_{lex}$) the columns (since blocks can be repeated) works quite fine, due to the balancing constraint (2) [7], especially when labelling in a row-wise fashion and trying the value 1 before the value 0. This much improves the best previously reported results under global search and allows the solution of previously unsolved instances. By simultaneously performing symmetry-breaking during search in the SBDD style [6], but augmenting it with group-theoretical insights and some heuristics, improvements of another order of magnitude can be achieved, but only when computing all the solutions [12]. The instances solved in [12] with $4 \leq v \leq 25$, which is the range of interest to us, have values of b up to 50, which is an order of magnitude below our range of interest.

3 Portfolio Optimisation

After precisely formulating the portfolio optimisation (PO) problem of the introduction and exhibiting its relationship to the BIBD problem, we derive an important implied constraint for the PO problem, before showing how to model it and how to exactly solve sub-real-life-scale instances thereof.

3.1 Formulation

The *portfolio optimisation* (PO) problem is formulated as follows. Let $V = \{1, \ldots, v\}$ and let $B = \{1, \ldots, b\}$ be a set of credits. A *portfolio* is a set of v subsets $V_i \subseteq B$, called *sub-pools*, each of size r:

$$\forall i \in V : |V_i| = r \tag{6}$$

such that the maximum intersection size of any two distinct sub-pools is minimised. A portfolio is thus parameterised by a 3-tuple $\langle v, b, r \rangle$ of independent parameters. By abuse of language, $\langle v, b, r \rangle$ denotes even sub-optimal solutions.

There is a universe of about $250 \leq b \leq 500$ credits. A typical portfolio contains about $4 \leq v \leq 25$ sub-pools, each of size $r \approx 100$.

Note that we have formulated the PO problem using the same notation as for the BIBD problem. The relationship with the (co-block formulation of the) BIBD problem is indeed striking, with credits taking the role of the block identifiers, sub-pools taking the role of the co-blocks, and the co-block size being fixed, as per the related constraints (3) and (6). But the similarity ends there, as the BIBD balancing condition (2) refers to a constant λ as the co-block intersection size, while the maximum co-block intersection size is to be minimised in a portfolio. In other words, the BIBD problem is a constraint satisfaction problem (CSP), while the PO problem is a constraint optimisation problem (COP). Also, the typical value of b for a portfolio is an order of magnitude larger than what has been tried so far with global search for BIBDs [12].

For syntactic continuity, let us call λ the maximum of the intersection sizes in a portfolio. This gives us the following PO constraint, related to the BIBD constraint (2):

$$\forall\ i_1 \neq i_2 \in V : |V_{i_1} \cap V_{i_2}| \leq \lambda \tag{7}$$

where λ is then the cost expression that is to be minimised:

$$\text{minimise } \lambda \tag{8}$$

with $\lambda \leq r$ (note the difference with the BIBD implied constraint (4)).

We parameterise a PO CSP by a 4-tuple $\langle v, b, r, \lambda \rangle$ of independent parameters, where λ need not be the minimal value. Note that PO CSPs with $\lambda = r$ are trivial to construct, as it suffices to make all co-blocks equal.

3.2 An Implied Constraint

We now show how to derive a tight lower bound on λ for the PO problem, and argue why the PO problem does not (seem to) have a counterpart of the BIBD constraint (1) on the block sizes, and hence not a counterpart of the BIBD implied constraint (5). The following theorem exactly fits the requirements of the PO problem, provided *all* the credits are used in the portfolio, which is often a realistic assumption:

Theorem 1 (Corrádi [2,10]). *Let $V_1,\ldots,V_v$ be r-element sets and B be their union. If $|V_{i_1} \cap V_{i_2}| \le \lambda$ for all $i_1 \ne i_2$, then*

$$|B| \ge \frac{r^2 \cdot v}{r + (v-1) \cdot \lambda}$$

Since $|B| = b$ here, we get as a PO implied constraint a tight lower bound on λ by rearranging the previous formula and rounding up so that λ is a natural number[3]:

$$\lambda \ge \left\lceil \frac{r \cdot (r \cdot v - b)}{b \cdot (v-1)} \right\rceil \;\land\; \lambda \ge 0 \tag{9}$$

The lower bound predicted by this constraint is not always exact, as shown in the following example.

Example 1. For $\langle 10, 8, 3 \rangle$, we obtain $\lambda \ge \lceil \frac{11}{12} \rceil$, hence $\lambda \ge 1$. For $\langle 9, 8, 3 \rangle$, we obtain $\lambda \ge \lceil \frac{57}{64} \rceil$, hence $\lambda \ge 1$. However, it is not difficult to show (with the method to be shown in Section 3.3) that there are no 10 or even 9 subsets of size 3 in an 8-element set such that they intersect pairwisely over at most $\lambda = 1$ element. In fact, these two instances are at best solved with $\lambda = 2$; some of the sets of such optimal solutions pairwisely intersect over only 1 element. (This example will be continued in Example 2.)

It is tempting to think that tight bounds can be similarly obtained on the block sizes. Indeed, a portfolio $\langle v, b, r \rangle$ becomes a BIBD if b divides $v \cdot r$ and if all the sub-pools must have pairwise intersections of *exactly* (rather than at most) λ elements: the integer value $k = \frac{v \cdot r}{b}$ is then obtained via the BIBD implied constraint (5). In case b does not divide $v \cdot r$, one may be tempted to adjust the portfolio parameters first. However, BIBDs of the size considered here, namely for $250 \le b \le 500$ blocks, are about one order of magnitude larger than what has been tried so far in global search, and our experiments suggest that those methods do not scale to BIBDs of that size, especially that the BIBD existence conditions are very weak. Also, no PO constraint forces the credits to spread in some manner over the sub-pools, so that neither $\lceil \frac{v \cdot r}{b} \rceil$ is an upper bound on k, nor $\lfloor \frac{v \cdot r}{b} \rfloor$ is a lower bound on k. Indeed, we have designed portfolios where the block sizes are distributed over the entire $1, \ldots, v$ range (see Example 2).

It is also tempting to think that it is sufficient (and easier) to find sub-pools whose pairwise intersections are of size exactly λ, rather than upper bounded by λ. However, there is no solution to $\langle 10, 8, 3 \rangle$ where the pairwise intersection sizes are all equal to $\lambda = 2$, whereas Example 1 establishes the existence of a solution where the pairwise intersection sizes are upper bounded by $\lambda = 2$.

3.3 Modelling and Exact Solution

One way of modelling a portfolio is in terms of its *incidence matrix*, which is a $v \times b$ matrix, such that the entry at the intersection of row i and column j is

---

[3] The same bound can be obtained by injecting the resolution of the BIBD implied constraint (5) for k into the BIBD implied constraint (3) and then resolving for λ.

Table 1. An optimal solution to $\langle 10, 8, 3 \rangle$, with cost $\lambda = 2$. The rows correspond to the co-blocks (sub-pools).

	blocks/credits							
1	1	1	1	0	0	0	0	0
2	1	1	0	1	0	0	0	0
3	1	1	0	0	1	0	0	0
4	1	1	0	0	0	1	0	0
5	1	1	0	0	0	0	1	0
6	1	1	0	0	0	0	0	1
7	1	0	1	1	0	0	0	0
8	1	0	1	0	1	0	0	0
9	1	0	1	0	0	1	0	0
10	1	0	1	0	0	0	1	0

1 if $j \in V_i$ and 0 otherwise. The PO constraints (6) and (7) are then modelled by requiring, respectively, that there are exactly r ones (that is a sum of r) for each row and a scalar product of at most λ for any pair of distinct rows.

The following example gives an optimal portfolio under this model, and uses it to show that the PO problem does not enjoy the optimal sub-structure property.

Example 2. (Continuation of Example 1.) An optimal solution to $\langle 10, 8, 3 \rangle$, with cost $\lambda = 2$, is given in Table 1.

Note that the block sizes are distributed over the entire $1, \ldots, v$ range, namely one block each of sizes 1, 5, 6, 10, and four blocks of size 2. Now, for $\langle 8, 8, 3 \rangle$, we obtain $\lambda \geq \lceil \frac{6}{7} \rceil$, hence $\lambda \geq 1$, and it turns out that there *are* 8 subsets of size 3 in an 8-element set such that they intersect pairwise over at most 1 element. We can now see why the PO problem does not enjoy the optimal sub-structure property, namely that an optimal solution to an instance does not necessarily contain optimal solutions to sub-instances. Indeed, the optimal solution to $\langle 10, 8, 3 \rangle$ in Table 1, with cost 2, contains no 8 subsets of size 3 in the 8-element set such that they intersect pairwise over at most 1 element. Note that the last 4 sets each have pairwise intersections of size 1 with 4 of the first 6 sets, while all other pairwise intersections are of size 2.

The tight lower bound on the cost expression λ suggests a (naive) method of exactly solving (small instances of) the PO COP as a sequence of PO CSPs: set λ to some value "comfortably" above that tight lower bound, and lower it by 1 each time that CSP has a solution.

The sub-pools are indistinguishable, and we assume (in a first approximation) that all the credits are indistinguishable. Hence any two rows or columns of the incidence matrix can be freely permuted. Breaking all the resulting $v! \cdot b!$ symmetries can in theory be performed, for instance by $v! \cdot b! - 1$ (anti-)lexicographical ordering constraints [4]. In practice, in the CSP version of the PO problem (where a value for λ is given), strictly anti-lexicographically ordering the rows (since sub-pools cannot be repeated in portfolios with $\lambda < r$) as well as anti-lexicographically ordering the columns (since credits can appear in the same sub-pools) works quite fine for values of b up to about 36, due to the constraint (7), especially when labelling in a row-wise fashion and trying the value 1 before the value 0. However, this is one order of magnitude below the typical value for b in a portfolio. Also, the absence of a constraint on the block sizes makes $\langle v, b, r, \lambda \rangle$ much harder to solve than $\langle v, b, r, k, \lambda \rangle$, if such a k exists. Hence another method than this BIBD-style approach is necessary, or we need to design approximately optimal portfolios, as discussed next.

4 Approximate Solution to Portfolio Optimisation

Our method of efficiently finding possibly approximate solutions to the portfolio optimisation (PO) problem rests on two key insights, explained first.

4.1 Underconstrainedness

The first insight comes from observing that the typical values of v (the number of sub-pools) are quite small for the typical values of b (the number of credits) and r (the size of the sub-pools), as shown in the following example.

Example 3. The first three columns of Table 2 chart how the lower bound on λ evolves with $v \geq 2$ according to the PO implied constraint (9) when $b = 350$ and $r = 100$.

The lower bound on λ initially grows from 0 for $v = 2$, to between 5 and 26 for the typical values of v (which are between 4 and 25), but does not grow much after that; in fact, it never exceeds 29, which it reaches for $v = 127$. This effect is exacerbated for smaller values of b and r, as shown in the fourth and fifth columns of Table 2.

While this example illustrates a prediction weakness of Theorem 1 for large values of v, the main lesson is that there is a range for v in which the lower bound on λ does not change quickly for fixed values of b and r. For the ranges of values of v, b, and r that are of interest here, v is within that zone.

The consequence is that the PO problem instances of interest here seem underconstrained in the sense that one may get (many) more than the intended v sub-pools of the same size r from the same universe of b credits, without seeing the maximum intersection size of the sub-pools increase. Dually, one may draw the intended v sub-pools of the same size r from a (much) smaller universe than the available b credits, without seeing the maximum intersection size of the sub-pools increase. For instance, Theorem 1 predicts that $v = 10$ sub-pools of $r = 100$ credits each may be drawn with a maximum intersection size of 21 from a universe of $347 \leq b \leq 357$ credits. Again, this effect is exacerbated for smaller values of b and r. This underconstrainedness may lead to considerable combinatorial explosion. In fact, we have been unable to solve any PO CSP instances of the magnitude considered here with the BIBD-style method outlined in Section 3.3, even when setting a quite high value for λ and allocating an entire CPU week. Labelling just one row of the incidence matrix already tends to take a lot of time after the first few rows.

Table 2. Unrounded and rounded lower bounds on the maximum intersection size λ for $v \geq 2$ co-blocks and b blocks of size r, as given by the PO implied constraint (9).

	$b = 350$ and $r = 100$		$b = 35$ and $r = 10$			
	unrounded	rounded	unrounded	rounded	time	backtracks
	lower bound	lower bound	lower bound	lower bound	to first	to first
v	on λ	on λ	on λ	on λ	solution	solution
2	-42.86	0	-4.286	0	0.01	0
3	-7.14	0	-0.714	0	0.04	0
4	4.76	5	0.476	1	0.09	1
5	10.71	11	1.071	2	0.26	184
6	14.28	15	1.428	2	0.74	658
7	16.67	17	1.667	2	1.23	921
8	18.37	19	1.837	2	4.89	8872
9	19.64	20	1.964	2	? + 0.85	? + 566
10	20.63	21	2.063	3	1.40	567
11	21.43	22	2.143	3	1.62	567
12	22.08	23	2.208	3	2.07	663
13	22.62	23	2.262	3	3.01	1878
14	23.08	24	2.308	3	3.80	2038
15	23.47	24	2.347	3	4.82	2245
16	23.81	24	2.381	3	9.94	9331
17	24.11	25	2.411	3	12.97	10221
...		25		3		
22	25.17	26	2.517	3	39.59	16078
...		26		3		
29	26.02	27	2.602	3	117.72	35305
...		27		3		
47	27.02	28	2.702	3	?	?
...		28		3		
127	28.01	29	2.801	3	?	?
...		29		3		

4.2 Embeddings

The second insight is that computing optimal solutions is not always practical. As shown below, we can often very efficiently solve real-life PO problem instances with values for λ that are within 5% of, if not identical to, the lower bound given by the PO implied constraint (9). Since that lower bound is not always exact, and since there is currently no better or faster way of solving real-life PO problem instances, our results are sufficient. Some may even turn out to be optimal. So we investigate the approximate solution of real-life PO problem instances. The idea is to embed small PO problem instances within a large, real-life one, as illustrated in the following example.

Example 4. We can embed 10 occurrences of $\langle 10, 35, 10 \rangle$ within $\langle 10, 350, 100 \rangle$. A not necessarily optimal solution to the PO COP $\langle 10, 350, 100 \rangle$ can be built by making 10 copies of each column in any possibly optimal solution to the PO

COP $\langle 10, 35, 10\rangle$. The fifth column of Table 2 gives $\lambda \geq 3$ for the PO COP $\langle 10, 35, 10\rangle$. Solving the PO CSP $\langle 10, 35, 10, 3\rangle$ with the BIBD-style method outlined in Section 3.3 is a matter of about one CPU second and 567 backtracks, and such a portfolio does exist. Since $10 \cdot 3 = 30$, this means that we can build from it a solution to the PO CSP $\langle 10, 350, 100, 30\rangle$. Since the third column of Table 2 gives $\lambda \geq 21$ for the PO COP $\langle 10, 350, 100\rangle$, the built solution with cost $\lambda = 30$ is quite far above that lower bound and may thus be sub-optimal. (This example will be continued in Example 6.)

This kind of embedding is a standard concept for BIBDs. Indeed, a BIBD $\langle v, b, r, k, \lambda\rangle$ is said to be an *m-multiple BIBD* if $\langle v, \frac{b}{m}, \frac{r}{m}, k, \frac{\lambda}{m}\rangle$ parameterises a BIBD under the constraints (1) to (5) [1]. In other words, shrinking the number of blocks by a factor m shrinks the sizes of the co-blocks and their intersections by the same factor m (provided they all divide m). Since there are no existence conditions for portfolios, whose design is a COP rather than a CSP, the corresponding concept for portfolios has an easier definition, given next.

Definition 1. *A portfolio $\langle v, b, r\rangle$ is an m-multiple portfolio if m divides both b and r. We denote this by $\langle v, b, r\rangle = m \cdot \langle v, \frac{b}{m}, \frac{r}{m}\rangle$.*

For the same reason, we can only compare the predicted lower bounds on the maximum sub-pool intersection sizes, rather than the actual intersection sizes as for BIBDs. The following property establishes that the same ratio holds between those lower bounds for portfolios and their multiples.

Property 1. The PO implied constraint (9) predicts $\lambda \geq \lceil \mu \rceil$ for $\langle v, b, r\rangle$ if and only if it predicts $\lambda \geq \lceil \frac{\mu}{m} \rceil$ for $\langle v, \frac{b}{m}, \frac{r}{m}\rangle$.

Example 5. We have $\langle 10, 350, 100\rangle = 10 \cdot \langle 10, 35, 10\rangle$. Table 2 confirms the ratio of 10 between the unrounded lower bounds on λ for the two involved instances.

However, a portfolio is not always an exact multiple of another portfolio. Rather than adjusting the size of a desired portfolio so that it becomes a multiple of another portfolio, we advocate generalising the notion of multiples of a design and here do so for portfolios. Let us first show the intuition on an example.

Example 6. (Continuation of Example 4.) Reconsider the $\langle 10, 350, 100\rangle$ portfolio. It is not a 12-multiple of any portfolio as 12 does not divide both 350 and 100. Since $350 = 12 \cdot 27 + 26$ and $100 = 12 \cdot 8 + 4$, a not necessarily optimal solution to the PO COP $\langle 10, 350, 100\rangle$ can be built by making 12 copies of each column in any possibly optimal solution to the PO COP $\langle 10, 27, 8\rangle$ and appending any possibly optimal solution to the PO COP $\langle 10, 26, 4\rangle$. The PO implied constraint (9) gives $\lambda \geq 2$ for the PO COP $\langle 10, 27, 8\rangle$ and $\lambda \geq 1$ for the PO COP $\langle 10, 26, 4\rangle$. Solving the PO CSPs $\langle 10, 27, 8, 2\rangle$ and $\langle 10, 26, 4, 1\rangle$ with the BIBD-style method outlined in Section 3.3 is a matter of about 1 CPU second and 69 backtracks total, and such portfolios do exist. Since $12 \cdot 2 + 1 = 25$, this means that we can build from them a solution to the PO CSP $\langle 10, 350, 100, 25\rangle$. Since the third column of Table 2 gives $\lambda \geq 21$ for the PO COP $\langle 10, 350, 100\rangle$, the built solution with cost $\lambda = 25$ is still a bit above that lower bound and may thus be sub-optimal. (This example will be continued in Example 7.)

Let us now formalise all the intuitions from this example.

Definition 2. *A portfolio $\langle v, b, r \rangle$ embeds m occurrences of a portfolio $\langle v, b_1, r_1 \rangle$ and 1 occurrence of a portfolio $\langle v, b_2, r_2 \rangle$, which is denoted by $\langle v, b, r \rangle = m \cdot \langle v, b_1, r_1 \rangle + \langle v, b_2, r_2 \rangle$, if the following three constraints hold:*

$$b = m \cdot b_1 + b_2 \tag{10}$$

$$r = m \cdot r_1 + r_2 \tag{11}$$

$$0 \le r_i \le b_i \ge 1 \quad \text{for } i = 1, 2 \tag{12}$$

The constraints (10) and (11) ensure that the embedding is exact. The constraint (12) ensures that the sub-pools can be subsets of the set of credits, for each of the two embedded portfolios. It also eliminates the two cases ($b_i = 0$) where the PO implied constraint (9) cannot be evaluated.

Note that this embedding by vertical division of the incidence matrix is possible because of the full column symmetry of the latter and because no PO constraint works against it. However, an embedding by horizontal division of the incidence matrix will lead to identical rows, that is worst-case solutions ($\lambda = r$).

An upper bound on the cost of an embedding portfolio can be computed from the costs of its embedded portfolios, as shown next.

Property 2. The cost λ of a portfolio embedding m occurrences of a portfolio $\langle v, b_1, r_1 \rangle$ of cost λ_1 and one occurrence of a portfolio $\langle v, b_2, r_2 \rangle$ of cost λ_2 satisfies the inequality $\lambda \le m \cdot \lambda_1 + \lambda_2$.

The reason why there may be a strict inequality is that the cost of a portfolio is the maximum of its sub-pool intersection sizes. Consider $v = 3$ and $m = 1$: the first embedded portfolio may have $1, 1, 2$ as intersection sizes, and the second embedded portfolio may have $1, 2, 1$ as intersection sizes, both with a maximum of 2, giving $1 + 1, 1 + 2, 2 + 1$ as intersection sizes for the embedding portfolio, with a maximum of $3 < 1 \cdot 2 + 2 = 4$. For this reason, the calculated cost 25 of the embedding portfolio in Example 6 is in fact an upper bound, rather than the exact cost as stated there. Hence it is in general better to observe the actual cost of the embedding portfolio than to use the upper bound given by Property 2. In this case, observation establishes that the cost is 25.

4.3 Approximate Solution

The issue now becomes how to construct suitable portfolio embeddings, so that near-optimal, if not optimal, real-life-scale portfolios can be designed. We advocate solving the CSP versions of the two embedded instances, setting as λ the rounded lower bound given by the PO implied constraint (9).

Our method takes as additional input a cost Λ that we are trying to undercut, say because it is the cost of the currently best portfolio (or the upper bound on that cost, as determined by Property 2).

Two heuristic constraints on $m, v, b, r, b_1, r_1, b_2, r_2$ in addition to the three constraints of Definition 2 become necessary in order to make the method pragmatic. Let λ_i be the rounded lower bounds given for the two embedded portfolios

$\langle v, b_i, r_i \rangle$ by the PO implied constraint (9). The additional constraints are justified and given in the following.

First, we must restrict the focus to the pairs of embedded portfolios that have a chance of leading to a portfolio whose combined cost is lower than Λ:

$$m \cdot \lambda_1 + \lambda_2 < \Lambda \tag{13}$$

Indeed, the left-hand side is by Property 2 the upper bound on the cost of the embedding portfolio built from solutions, if they exist, to the two $\langle v, b_i, r_i, \lambda_i \rangle$ PO CSPs. In practice, it is usually equal to the cost of such an embedding portfolio, hence this constraint. Note that this constraint implies that $m < \Lambda$.

Second, knowing that PO CSPs with values of b up to about 36 can often be solved (quite quickly) using the BIBD-style method outlined in Section 3.3, the objective in choosing the parameters of the embedding is to have *both* embedded instances within that range for b:

$$b_i \leq 36 \quad \text{for } i = 1, 2 \tag{14}$$

Note that the determination of candidate embeddings, which are pairs of CSPs, is thus itself a CSP.

There is no guarantee that all PO CSPs with $b \leq 36$ can be solved sufficiently quickly. For instance, the sixth and seventh columns of Table 2 chart the CPU times in seconds and backtracks for $\langle v, 35, 10, \lambda \rangle$ for $v \geq 2$ and λ equal to the rounded lower bound in the fifth column. The experiments were conducted on a Sun SPARC Ultra Station 10 in our SICStus Prolog 3.10.1 implementation of the BIBD-style method outlined in Section 3.3. A question mark means that we stopped the solution process after a CPU hour. The entry in the row $v = 9$ means that $\langle 9, 35, 10, 2 \rangle$ timed out (in fact, it takes about 25 CPU hours and about $537 \cdot 10^6$ backtracks to fail[4]), while $\langle 9, 35, 10, 3 \rangle$ takes only 0.85 CPU seconds and 566 backtracks to succeed. We observe that for the range of values of v where the rounded lower bound on λ remains the same, the runtimes increase with v. In other words, they increase when the rounding distance for the lower bound on λ decreases. This may not always be the case. The same pattern can be observed for the number of backtracks. The rounding distance seems to be a good indicator of the constrainedness of a PO CSP. A good heuristic then seems to be that we should favour embeddings where both embedded instances have not too small rounding distances. In our observation, for the typical values of v, instances with rounding distances below 0.15 are often problematic. Hence we also advocate ordering the embedded instance pairs that satisfy the constraints (10) to (14) by decreasing rounding distance for λ_1, so that the apparently easier pairs are attempted first. Setting a time-limit on each attempt is another useful refinement.

Let us now illustrate this method.

---

[4] Amazingly, these figures were obtained on the same hardware in our OPL implementation under OPL Studio 3.0.2, which performs *no* symmetry breaking for lack of a lexicographical ordering constraint! We aborted our SICStus Prolog 3.10.1 implementation after several CPU days, both with and without symmetry breaking.

Table 3. Embeddings of $\langle 10, 350, 100 \rangle$ satisfying the constraints (10) to (14) for $\Lambda = 25$, ordered by decreasing rounding distance for λ_1.

m	$\langle v, b_1, r_1, \lambda_1 \rangle$	unrounded λ_1	$\langle v, b_2, r_2, \lambda_2 \rangle$	unrounded λ_2	$m \cdot \lambda_1 + \lambda_2$
10	$\langle 10, 32, 09, 2 \rangle$	1.812	$\langle 10, 30, 10, 3 \rangle$	2.592	23
11	$\langle 10, 31, 09, 2 \rangle$	1.903	$\langle 10, 09, 01, 1 \rangle$	0.012	23
9	$\langle 10, 36, 10, 2 \rangle$	1.975	$\langle 10, 26, 10, 4 \rangle$	3.162	22
18	$\langle 10, 18, 05, 1 \rangle$	0.988	$\langle 10, 26, 10, 4 \rangle$	3.162	22
19	$\langle 10, 18, 05, 1 \rangle$	0.988	$\langle 10, 08, 05, 3 \rangle$	2.917	22
11	$\langle 10, 30, 09, 2 \rangle$	2.000	$\langle 10, 20, 01, 0 \rangle$	-0.056	22

Example 7. (Continuation of Example 6.) Let us try and improve the portfolio with cost $\Lambda = 25$ previously obtained for $\langle 10, 350, 100 \rangle = 12 \cdot \langle 10, 27, 8 \rangle + \langle 10, 26, 4 \rangle$. The embeddings satisfying the constraints (10) to (14) are given in Table 3, ordered by decreasing rounding distance for λ_1.

Note that none of these embeddings has a combined cost of $\lambda = 21$, which is the lower bound given by the PO implied constraint (9) for $\langle 10, 350, 100 \rangle$. This may be an artifact of the way we define embeddings or of the way we heuristically constrain the embeddings. Setting a time limit of one CPU hour, we attempt to solve the PO CSPs in the second and fourth columns, proceeding row by row.

The first embedding only takes about 13 CPU seconds and $13,152$ backtracks total to solve its two PO CSPs. Hence we can build a solution to $\langle 10, 350, 100 \rangle$ from 10 copies of the optimal solution (with $\lambda = 2$) to $\langle 10, 32, 9 \rangle$ and one copy of the optimal solution (with $\lambda = 3$) to $\langle 10, 30, 10 \rangle$; it has an observed cost of exactly $\lambda = 10 \cdot 2 + 3 = 23 > 21$.

The second embedding takes about 47 CPU minutes and about $4 \cdot 10^6$ backtracks (mostly because of the first embedded instance, as the second one has $\lambda_2 = r_2$ and is thus trivial to solve). We get another solution of (predicted and observed) cost $23 = 11 \cdot 2 + 1$.

The third embedding has a first embedded PO CSP that times out, hence we ignore it and move on.

The fourth and fifth embeddings both contain $\langle 10, 18, 5, 1 \rangle$, which fails in about 6 CPU minutes and $345,595$ backtracks. Hence $\lambda_1 \geq 2$, and $m \cdot \lambda_1 + \lambda_2$ is at least 40 for the fourth embedding and at least 41 for the fifth embedding, which are both much worse costs than in the currently best solution.

The sixth embedding is very interesting. Its first embedded PO CSP can be solved as a BIBD with blocks of fixed size $k = 3$, as the unrounded λ_1 is a natural number and as b_1 divides $v \cdot r_1$. This additional constraint (1) on the block sizes gives very good propagation, and the BIBD method outlined at the end of Section 2 can solve this instance in about 0.39 CPU seconds and 23 backtracks, whereas the BIBD-style method outlined in Section 3.3 timed out on the corresponding PO CSP, which does not have that constraint. The second embedded PO CSP is trivial (in the sense that there at least as many credits as in the union of the requested sub-pools) since $v \cdot r_2 \leq b_2$ and is solved in about 0.21 CPU seconds and 0 backtracks.

Hence we can build a solution, given in Table 4, to $\langle 10, 350, 100 \rangle$ from 11 copies of the optimal solution (with $\lambda = 2$) to $\langle 10, 30, 9 \rangle$ and one copy of the

Table 4. Our currently best solution to $\langle 10, 350, 100 \rangle$, built from $11 \cdot \langle 10, 30, 9 \rangle + \langle 10, 20, 1 \rangle$, and of cost $11 \cdot 2 + 0 = 22 > 21$.

11 copies of each column of	1 copy of each column of
1111111110000000000000000000	1000000000000000000
1100000001111111000000000000	0100000000000000000
1100000000000001111111000000	0010000000000000000
0011000001100000110000011110000	0001000000000000000
0011000000011000001100000011110	0000100000000000000
0000110001100000000011000011101	0000010000000000000
0000110000000110001000111000010	0000001000000000000
0000001100011000000001011010001	0000000100000000000
0000001010000101110000000001011	0000000010000000000
0000000110000011000101000110100	0000000001000000000

optimal solution (with $\lambda = 0$) to $\langle 10, 20, 1 \rangle$; it has an observed cost of exactly $\lambda = 11 \cdot 2 + 0 = 22 > 21$. Note that the last 10 credits are not used in this solution. This solution may actually turn out to be optimal, considering the prediction weakness of Theorem 1.

5 Conclusions

Summary. We have given an approximate and often extremely fast method of solving a new portfolio optimisation (PO) problem in financial mathematics. Its corresponding satisfaction problem is closely related to the balanced incomplete block design (BIBD) problem. However, typical PO instances are an order of magnitude larger than the largest BIBDs solved so far by global search, and the PO problem lacks a counterpart of a crucial BIBD constraint. Hence current BIBD-style solving methods are not suitable for real-life PO instances. Our method is based on embedding (multiple copies of) independent sub-instances into the original instance. Their determination is itself a constraint satisfaction problem. The high quality of our approximate solutions can be assessed by comparison with a tight lower bound on the cost.

Generalisation. The generalisation of the main idea is as follows, in the context of a large constraint optimisation problem where a (tight) lower bound on its cost can be somehow calculated. The idea is to embed several independent small problem instances P_i within the given large problem instance P. A feasible solution S to P can then be built from possibly optimal feasible solutions S_i to the P_i. The quality of S can be assessed against the lower bound on the cost of the optimal solution to P. If there is a relationship between the costs of S and the S_i, then this relationship can be used to determine the P_i via a CSP, using the lower bounds on their costs. For PO, this relationship is given by Property 2.

Related Work. The idea of exploiting *independent* sub-problems also underlies Tree-Based Russian Doll Search [11]. The idea of embedding (multiple copies of) sub-problem instances into a larger problem instance is related to the concept of abstract local search [3], where a concrete solution is built from a solution to an abstraction of the original problem instance and then analysed for flaws so as to infer a new abstract solution. This works well if the concretisation and analysis steps are tractable and if the abstraction is optimality preserving, in the sense that optimal concrete solutions can be built from abstract solutions. Our embedded problem instances can indeed be jointly seen as an *abstraction* of the original problem instance. For instance, entire bundles of credits are here abstracted into single super-credits. We have been unable so far to prove *optimality preservation* of such portfolio abstractions, or to find conditions for it. As also observed in [3], this is not problematic for hard problem instances, such as the typical PO problem instances considered here, where the utility of abstractions can only be assessed by comparison with other techniques. In any case, we have seen that our portfolio abstractions lead to solutions that are extremely close to a tight lower bound on the cost.

Also, we have found only one paper taking a constraint programming approach to portfolio selection [13], but the tackled problem there is actually different from ours and is limited to portfolios consisting of just one sub-pool.

Future Work. Our notion of embeddings can be generalised to any linear combination of several sub-instances. Indeed, Definition 2 is restricted to embeddings of always *two* sub-instances, with coefficients m and 1, respectively. The price to pay for this restriction may have been that a solution of cost 21 eluded us in Example 7, though it may also be that no such solution exists and that our solution of cost 22 is in fact optimal.

Some additional abstraction may reduce the $1, \ldots, v$ range of observed block sizes. Indeed, a counterpart of the BIBD constraint (1) might enormously speed up the solution process. The facts that some PO instances (such as $\langle 9, 35, 10, 2 \rangle$) take CPU days to fail while increasing their λ (to obtain $\langle 9, 35, 10, 3 \rangle$ here) then leads to quasi instantaneous success, and that other PO instances (such as $\langle 10, 30, 9, 2 \rangle$) take CPU hours to succeed while the corresponding BIBD instances, if any ($\langle 10, 30, 9, 3, 2 \rangle$ here), quasi instantaneously succeed, show that there is still much space for improving our method. Such an additional abstraction might only come at the price of losing optimal solutions, though.

The run-times and backtrack counts of our implementation of the BIBD-style method outlined in Section 4 can be improved with the additional symmetry-breaking techniques of STAB [12].

Finally, it would be interesting to compare our results with those obtained by other complete-search techniques as well as by local-search techniques.

Conclusion and Financial Relevance. Our optimisation has eliminated the need for ad hoc manual permutations. On average, we have found that the overlap in a given portfolio can be decreased anywhere from 2% to 4% by using the current formulation. Even though this may not sound like a dramatic improvement, the ability to reduce the maximum overlap from 25% to 22%, say, may make the difference between having or not having a feasible transaction due to investor and rating-agency constraints.

It should be pointed out that it is easy to reduce the overlap by increasing the number of available credits. However, such new credits tend to be less known and thus more difficult to analyse, resulting in less than efficient portfolios.

In practice, the credits are not all indistinguishable. A client might have personal preferences for or against some credits, declare some credits as mutually exclusive, and so on. The advantage of our deployment of constraint technology is that such specific needs can be neatly added without having to devise new portfolio optimisation algorithms from scratch each time. However, such side constraints may break some of the full column symmetry, so partial symmetry breaking has to be deployed instead. Work in this direction has begun.

Challenge. We challenge the reader to answer the open question whether a $\langle 10, 350, 100 \rangle$ portfolio with optimal cost 21 exists or not.

Acknowledgements

We thank the referees for their useful comments.

References

1. C. J. Colbourn and J. H. Dinitz, editors. *The CRC Handbook of Combinatorial Designs*. CRC Press, 1996.
2. K. Corrádi. Problem at Schweitzer competition. *Mat. Lapok*, 20:159–162, 1969.
3. J. M. Crawford, M. Dalal, and J. P. Walser. Abstract local search. In *Proceedings of the AIPS'98 Workshop on Planning as Combinatorial Search*, 1998.
4. J. M. Crawford, M. Ginsberg, E. Luks, and A. Roy. Symmetry-breaking predicates for search problems. In *Proceedings of KR'96*, pages 148–159, 1996.
5. S. Das and G. Geng. Correlated default processes: A criterion-based copula approach. *Journal of Investment Management*, forthcoming.
6. T. Fahle, S. Schamberger, and M. Sellmann. Symmetry breaking. In T. Walsh, editor, *Proc. of CP'01*, volume 2293 of *LNCS*, pages 93–107. Springer-Verlag, 2001.
7. P. Flener, A. M. Frisch, B. Hnich, Z. Kızıltan, I. Miguel, J. Pearson, and T. Walsh. Breaking row and column symmetries in matrix models. In P. Van Hentenryck, editor, *Proc. of CP'02*, vol. 2470 of *LNCS*, pages 462–476. Springer-Verlag, 2002.
8. P. Flener and J. Pearson. Breaking all the symmetries in matrix models: Results, conjectures, and directions. In *Proceedings of SymCon'02*, 2002. Available at http://www.it.uu.se/research/group/astra/SymCon02/.
9. K. Gilkes and M. Drexler. Drill-down approach for synthetic CDO Squared transactions. Standard and Poor's Publication, December 2003.
10. S. Jukna. *Extremal Combinatorics*. Springer-Verlag, 2001.
11. P. Meseguer and M. Sànchez. Tree-based Russian Doll Search: Preliminary results. In F. Rossi, editor, *Proceedings of the CP'00 Workshop on Soft Constraints*, 2000.
12. J.-F. Puget. Symmetry breaking using stabilizers. In F. Rossi, editor, *Proceedings of CP'03*, volume 2833 of *LNCS*, pages 585–599. Springer-Verlag, 2003.
13. G. Wetzel and F. Zabatta. A constraint programming approach to portfolio selection. In *Proceedings of ECAI'98*, pages 263–264, 1998.

Bounding the Resource Availability of Partially Ordered Events with Constant Resource Impact

Jeremy Frank

Computational Sciences Division
NASA Ames Research Center, MS 269-3
Moffett Field, CA 94035
frank@email.arc.nasa.gov

Abstract. We describe a resource bounding technique called the *Flow Balance Constraint* (FBC) to tightly bound the amount of available resource for a set of partially ordered events with piecewise constant resource impact. We provide an efficient algorithm for calculating FBC and bound its complexity. We compare this technique with two existing resource bounding techniques, the Balance Constraint (BC) due to Laborie and the Resource Envelope (E_t) due to Muscettola. We prove that using FBC to halt search under chronological search with a static variable and value order generates smaller search trees than either BC or E_t. We also show that E_t and BC are not strictly comparable in terms of the size of the search trees generated under chronological search with a static variable and value order. We then show how to generalize FBC to construct tighter resource bounds but at increased computational cost.

1 Introduction

Scheduling requires ordering tasks while simultaneously satisfying temporal and resource constraints. Finding and maintaining *temporally flexible* schedules has numerous advantages over finding a fixed-time schedule. Usually, scheduling is performed assuming that the problem's characteristics are known in advance, do not change, and that the execution of the schedule is deterministic. However, these assumptions are often violated in practice. For example, if events do not take place exactly when they are scheduled, it may be costly to find a new schedule consistent with the actual event execution times [4]. Techniques such as that described in [5] make it possible to efficiently update the flexible schedule once the precise timing of events are known. A second advantage is that it can be less expensive to find flexible schedules because fewer decisions need to be made; thus, less search is necessary. This is true for simple temporal constraints, but the presence of resource constraints requires *efficient tight resource bounding techniques* to determine that the resource constraint is always or never satisfied.

It is straightforward to calculate the resource bounds of events whose execution time are fixed. The task becomes more difficult when activities or events are not fixed in time or are unordered, and more difficult still when events can have arbitrary impact on resources. In the context of constructive search, early detection of success or failure is often important to achieving good search performance. In this paper we focus on the ability of resource bounding techniques to reduce the cost of constructive search algorithms by means of detecting success or failure.

Following Muscettola [1], Laborie [2] has provided a simple but expressive formalism for scheduling problems called *Resource Temporal Networks* (RTNs). In this paper we study RTNs consisting of a *Simple Temporal Network* (STN) as described in [3], constant resource impacts (either production or consumption) for events, and piecewise constant resource bounds; Laborie [2] refers to this subclass as $\langle \mathcal{R}, \mathcal{L}_\mathcal{Q}, STN^{\neq} \rangle$. There are two existing techniques for bounding resource availability in such RTNs; the Balance Constraint (BC) [6] due to Laborie, and the Resource Envelope (E_t) [1] due to Muscettola. These techniques are described in more detail in Section 2. BC features an efficient but loosely bounding approximation, while E_t is more costly but provides a tight bound (in all cases a schedule justifying the bound is proved to exist). Somewhat surprisingly, these techniques are not strictly comparable in terms of the size of the search trees generated under chronological search. We provide examples demonstrating this in Section 3. In Section 4 we describe the *Flow Balance Constraint* (FBC), a novel synthesis of these two approaches. In Section 5 we prove that FBC generates smaller proof trees than either BC or E_t under chronological search. In Section 6 we describe the complexity of a naive algorithm to calculate FBC. We then show how to calculate FBC incrementally, thereby reducing its computational cost. In Section 7 we then generalize FBC in order to construct even tighter resource bounds but at increased computational cost. Finally, in Section 8 we conclude and describe future work.

2 Previous Work

In this paper we will assume that time is represented using integers[1]. We will also assume that the resource impact of each event is known when solving begins. We will assume each RTN has only one resource, that there is one constraint $\leq r$, and one constraint ≥ 0 on the resource. We also assume that the lower bound of the scheduling horizon is 0, and that r units of resource are available at time 0.

The techniques we study are aimed at establishing *Halting Criteria* (HC) for chronological backtracking search algorithms schedulers that maintain temporal flexibility. By "halt" we mean identifying a leaf node in the chronological search tree. A scheduler can halt if the *Necessary Truth Criterion* [2,8] (NTC), is satisfied, namely, if *all* feasible solutions of the STN also satisfy the resource constraints. The NTC is satisfied if the upper bound on the available resource is always below the maximum available resource r, and the lower bound on the available resource is always above 0. Schedulers can also halt if *no* feasible solution of the STN can satisfy the resource constraint [2]. This is true if the upper bound on the available resource is ever below 0, or the lower bound on the available resource is ever above r. Otherwise, the scheduler must continue search, i.e. the current state is an interior node of the search tree.

---
[1] This assumption can be relaxed, but leads to resource bounds holding over half-open intervals of time.
[2] One could refer to this as the Necessary Falsity Criteria (NFC).

We will use the following notation: Let $\mathcal{N}$ be the set of all events of an RTN and $n = |\mathcal{N}|$. Let $X \in \mathcal{N}$; $c(X)$ denotes the resource impact of X. If $c(X) < 0$ X is said to be a *consumer*; if $c(X) > 0$ then X is said to be a *producer*. As defined in [1], X *anti-precedes* Y if X must occurs at or after Y (i.e. $Y \leq X$). A *predecessor set* of a set of events $\mathcal{S}$ has the property that if $X \in \mathcal{S}$ then every event Y such that $Y \leq X$ is also in $\mathcal{S}$. A *successor set* of a set $\mathcal{T}$ has the property that if $X \in \mathcal{T}$ then every event Y such that $Y \geq X$ is also in $\mathcal{T}$. Let R be an RTN and let $A(R)$ be any procedure for evaluating the HC. If $A(R) = T$ then the HC is true and R has a solution. If $A(R) = F$, the HC is true and R has no solution. If $A(R) =?$ the HC is false and it is unknown whether R has a solution.

2.1 The Balance Constraint

Laborie's *Balance Constraint* (BC) [6] calculates bounds on the maximum and minimum amount of a resource immediately prior to and immediately following the execution of an event X. The STN is partitioned relative to X into the following sets: Before $B(X)$, Before or Equal $BS(X)$, Equal $S(X)$, Equal or After $AS(X)$, After $A(X)$, and Unordered $U(X)$. Note that the predecessor set of X is $\{B(X) \cup BS(X) \cup S(X)\}$ and the successor set of X is $\{A(X) \cup AS(X) \cup S(X)\}$ These sets are then used to calculate the following quantities: $L_{min}^<(X)$ for the minimum available resource before X occurs, $L_{max}^<(X)$ for the maximum available resource before X occurs, $L_{min}^>(X)$, for the minimum available resource after X has occurred, and $L_{max}^>(X)$ for the maximum available resource after X has occurred. A sample calculation: let $P_{min}^>(X) = \{B(X) \cup BS(X) \cup \{V \in AS(X) \cup U(X) | c(V) < 0\}\}$ Then $\sum_{Z \in P_{min}^>(X)} c(Z)$. is a lower bound on $L_{min}^>(X)$. The other bounds can be constructed in a similar manner. There may be no schedule consistent with the temporal constraints resulting in these calculated resource availabilities. The computational complexity of BC is dominated by the maintenance of arc-consistency of the STN.

2.2 The Resource Envelope

The *Envelope Algorithm* E_t [1] finds the *envelope* of an RTN, that is, the functions from time to the maximum $L_{max}(t)$ and minimum $L_{min}(t)$ available resource. Events are partitioned into $C(t)$, those that must have occurred by t; $P(t)$, those that are permitted to occur at t, and $O(t)$, those that can't occur until after t. The maximum available resource at a time t, $L_{max}(t)$, corresponds to a schedule in which the events in $P_{max}(t) \subset \{P(t) \cup C(t)\}$ all occur before t. To find the set $\Delta P_{max}(t) \subset P(t)$ that contributes to $P_{max}(t)$, a maximum flow problem is constructed using all anti-precedence links derived from the arc-consistent STN. The rules for building the flow problem to find $L_{max}(t)$ are as follows: all events in $P(t)$ are represented by nodes of the flow problem. If $Y \geq X$ then the flow problem contains an arc $X \to Y$ with infinite capacity. If $c(X) > 0$ then the problem contains an arc $\sigma \to X$ with capacity $c(X)$. If $c(X) < 0$ then the problem contains an arc $X \to \tau$ with capacity $|c(X)|$. To construct the flow problem to find $L_{min}(t)$, if $c(X) > 0$ then the problem contains an arc $X \to \tau$ with capacity $c(X)$, and if $c(X) < 0$ then the problem contains an arc

$\sigma \to X$ with capacity $|c(X)|$. Examples of the flow problem construction are shown in Figure 1. The maximum flow of this flow network matches all possible production with all possible consumption in a manner consistent with the precedence constraints. The predecessor set of those events reachable in the residual flow is $\Delta P_{max}(t)$, and $\Delta P_{max}^C(t) = \{P(t) - \Delta P_{max}(t)\}$. The tightness of the bound is guaranteed by proving that adding the constraints $\{X_{ub} \leq t\} \forall X \in \Delta P_{max}(t)$ and $\{Y_{lb} > t\} \forall Y \in \Delta P_{max}^C(t)$ is consistent with the original STN.

It turns out that $\Delta P_{max}(t)$ need only be computed at $\leq 2n$ distinct times. The complexity of the algorithm described in [1] is $O(n * MaxFlow(n, m) + n^2)$, where $n = |\mathcal{N}|$ and m is the number of anti-precedence relationships in the arc-consistent STN. In [7] this is reduced to $O(MaxFlow(n, m) + n^2)$ by taking advantage of the order in which edges are added to and removed from a single maximum flow problem. The crucial observation is that when computing E_t an event always move from open to pending to closed and stays closed. As shown in Figure 1 (b) and (c), this guarantees that events topologically "late" in the flow problem are removed, while topologically "early" events are added to the flow problem. The insight is that the flow problem need not be solved anew; the previous flow calculation can be reused, thereby saving a factor of n. As an aside, a more general incremental maximum flow algorithm is given in [9], but it doesn't assume any particular order of flow arc additions and deletions.

3 Examples of Non-domination

Muscettola previously demonstrated that E_t can prove the HC is satisfied in cases where BC cannot. In this section we provide an example where E_t fails to prove the HC is satisfied in cases where BC can. The consequence of this is that neither algorithm "dominates" the other when used solely to halt search. Since E_t provides the tightest possible mapping from time to minimum and maximum resource availability, it is somewhat surprising that E_t fails to dominate BC.

3.1 BC Doesn't Dominate E_t

Muscettola [1] describes an RTN for which BC cannot not prove the HC is satisfied but E_t can. This example is modified and reproduced in Figure 1. Initially the resource has 2 units available. BC will calculate $L_{min}^>(A)$ as follows: $U(A) = \{W, X, Y, Z\}$ and $A(A) = \{B, C, D\}$. It assumes W and Y occur before A, and that X and Z occur after A. Since $L_{min}^>(A) = -1$, BC concludes that more decisions are needed. Clearly, this schedule is not consistent with the original STN, so the bound calculated by BC is "loose". The E_t algorithm is able to prove that the HC is satisfied in this case by determining $L_{min}(t) \geq 0$ and $L_{max}(t) \leq 2$ over the scheduling horizon. As a case in point, consider $L_{min}(10)$. The pending set $P(10) = \{B, C, D, X, Y, Z\}$ and the resulting flow problem is shown in Figure 1 (c). The maximum flow for this network saturates the arcs to C and Y. No events are reachable in the residual graph, so $P_{max}^<(10) = \emptyset$. We see that $L_{min}(10) = 0$ since A and W are closed at 10.

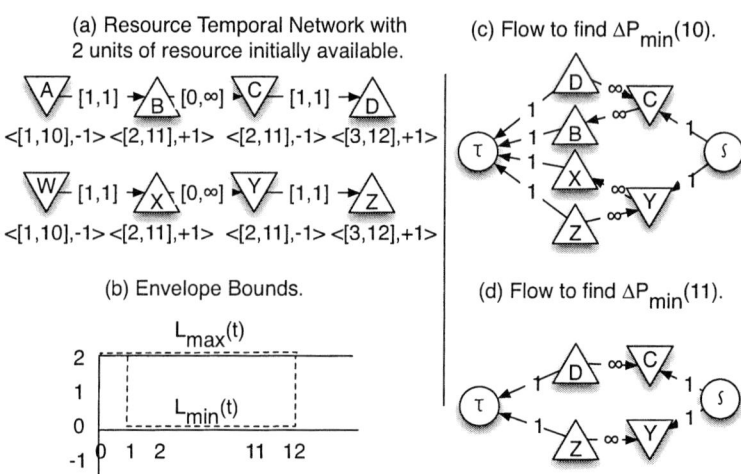

Fig. 1. An RTN for which BC fails to detect that the HC is true because a solution exists.

3.2 E_t Doesn't Dominate BC

Figure 2 describes an RTN for which BC can show that the HC is satisfied. Again, initially the resource has 2 units available. In this case, since $B(D) = \{A, B, C\}$ and $\{BS(D) \cup U(D)\} = \emptyset$, BC will find $L_{max}^{\leq}(D) = -5$. This proves that, no matter what additional constraints are imposed, the resource bound will be violated. By contrast, E_t cannot conclude that the HC is satisfied. We see that B and C can be postponed until time 10, and A can be scheduled as early as 1, leading to $L_{max}(1) = 3$. At time 2, D could occur, but maximizing resource availability would then require scheduling everything before 2 with a resource availability of 0 being the result. At time 2 we can still find a schedule in which A occurs before all other events, with resource availability 3; so $L_{max}(2) = 3$. At time 10, however, both consumption events B and C must have taken place; in order to maximize the available resource, D must occur, leading to $L_{max}(10) = 0$. Furthermore, $L_{min}(t)$ provides no assistance in proving the HC is true. Not only does E_t fail to show that the HC is true, there are non-trivial ordering decisions that can be made; in the worst case, schedulers could spend a considerable amount of time fruitlessly continuing the search from states like the one shown in Figure 2.

4 A Better Check for the Halting Criteria

In order to halt search more effectively than either E_t or BC, we adopt a synthesis of both strategies. We use the same partition of events used by Laborie [6]. Like Laborie, we then find bounds on $L_{max}^{\leq}(X), L_{min}^{\leq}(X), L_{max}^{>}(X)$, and $L_{min}^{>}(X)$. Like Muscettola, we build a maximum flow problem whose residual graph is used to construct the supporting sets $P_{max}^{\leq}(X), P_{min}^{\leq}(X), P_{max}^{>}(X)$, and $P_{min}^{>}(X)$. The rules for constructing the flow problem are identical to those for calculating E_t; only the set of events defining the flow problems are different. To find $\Delta P_{max}^{\leq}(X)$ and $\Delta P_{min}^{\leq}(X)$, we solve a flow problem over the set of events $BS(X) \cup U(X)$. In these cases, $P_{max}^{\leq}(X) =$

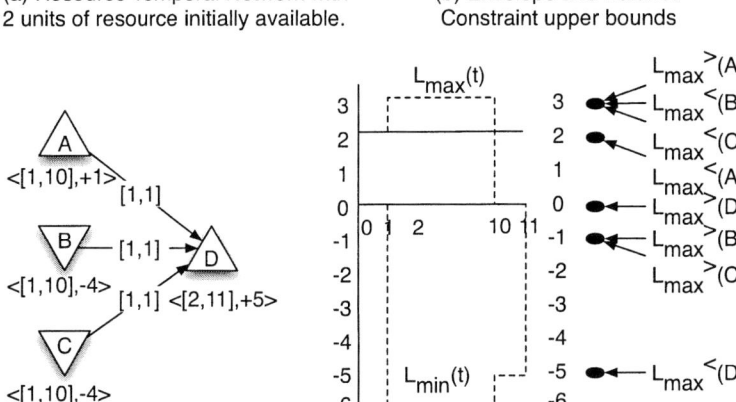

Fig. 2. An RTN for which E_t fails to detect that the HC is true because no solution exists.

$\{\Delta P_{max}^<(X) \cup B(X)\}$ and $P_{min}^<(X) = \{\Delta P_{min}^<(X) \cup B(X)\}$. We define $\Delta P_{max}^{<C}(X) = \{\{BS(X) \cup U(X)\} - \Delta P_{max}^<(X)\}$ and $\Delta P_{min}^{<C}(X) = \{\{BS(X) \cup U(X)\} - \Delta P_{min}^<(X)\}$ To find $\Delta P_{max}^>(X)$ and $\Delta P_{min}^>(X)$, we solve a flow problem over the set of events $AS(X) \cup U(X)$. In these cases, $P_{max}^>(X) = \{\Delta P_{max}^>(X) \cup S(X) \cup B(X) \cup BS(X)\}$ and $P_{min}^>(X) = \{\Delta P_{min}^>(X) \cup S(X) \cup B(X) \cup BS(X)\}$. We define $\Delta P_{max}^{>C}(X) = \{\{AS(X) \cup U(X)\} - \Delta P_{max}^>(X)\}$ and $\Delta P_{min}^{>C}(X) = \{\{AS(X) \cup U(X)\} - \Delta P_{min}^>(X)\}$. These supporting sets define schedules that prove the bounds are tight. For example, the resulting set $P_{max}^<(X)$ defines an STN constructed by adding the constraints $\forall V \in P_{max}^<(X)\{V < X\}$ and $\forall V \in P_{max}^{<C}(X)\{X \leq V\}$. We call the new procedure the *Flow Balance Constraint (FBC)*, since it combines the features of the Balance Constraint with the flow-based approach. For each event X we must calculate 4 bounds; however, the actual number of bounds calculations is $\leq 4n$, since we observe that the same bounds apply $\forall V \in S(X)$. The algorithm for FBC is described in Figure 3. As is done in [6], we maintain the partition of the STN relative to each event X during the arc-consistency enforcement phase.

We now prove that the resulting bounds on quantities like $L_{max}^<(X)$ are tight. To do so, we first show that there is at least one schedule justifying the bound, and then show that there is no better bound than that found using the flow problem.

Theorem 1. *Let R be an RTN and X be an event in R. Suppose $\Delta P_{max}^<(X) \neq \emptyset$. Let R' be the STN formed by adding the following constraints to R: $\{V < X\}$ for all $V \in \Delta P_{max}^<(X)$ and $\{X \leq W\}$ for all $W \in \Delta P_{max}^{<C}(X)$. Then R' has at least one temporally consistent solution.*

Proof. Since $V \in \{BS(X) \cup U(X)\}$ the imposition of a single constraint alone doesn't make the STN inconsistent. Imposing a constraint $V < X$ can only decrease V_{ub} or increase X_{lb}. Since $\Delta P_{max}^<(X)$ is a predecessor set, all $\{V < X\}$ can be imposed simultaneously without impacting consistency. Imposing a constraint $X \leq W$ can only decrease X_{ub} or increase V_{lb}. Since $\Delta P_{max}^{<C}(X)$ is a successor set, all $\{X \leq W\}$ can

FBC($\mathcal{R}$)
    Enforce Arc Consistency on $\mathcal{R}$
    for each event $X \in \mathcal{N}$
        Set up flow problems
        Bound(X)
    end for
end

Bound(X)
    Find $\Delta P^<_{max}(X) \subset BS(X) \cup U(X)$
    $L^<_{max}(X) = \sum_{V \in \{\Delta P^<_{max}(X) \cup B(X)\}} c(V)$
    Find $\Delta P^<_{min}(X) \subset \{BS(X) \cup U(X)\}$
    $L^<_{min}(X) = \sum_{V \in \{\Delta P^<_{min}(X) \cup B(X)\}} c(V)$
    Find $\Delta P^>_{max}(X) \subset \{AS(X) \cup U(X)\}$
    $L^>_{max}(X) = \sum_{V \in \{\Delta P^>_{max}(X) \cup B(X) \cup BS(X) \cup S(X)\}} c(V)$
    Find $\Delta P^>_{min}(X) \subset \{AS(X) \cup U(X)\}$
    $L^>_{min}(X) = \sum_{V \in \{\Delta P^>_{min}(X) \cup B(X) \cup BS(X) \cup S(X)\}} c(V)$
end

Fig. 3. A sketch of the Flow Balance Constraint.

also be imposed simultaneously without impacting consistency. Finally, X is the only event whose bounds are acted on by both classes of constraint. Consider two events A, B. Since $A \in \Delta P^<_{max}(X)$ and $B \in \Delta P^{<C}_{max}(X)$ we know it can't be the case that $B < A$. But then either $A \leq B$ or A and B can be ordered in any way, and we already know X can be ordered any way with respect to A or B. Thus, $A < X \leq B$ is possible and no such ordering prevents other linearizations with respect to X. □

Theorem 2. *Let R be an RTN and X be an event in R. Suppose $\Delta P^<_{max}(X) \neq \emptyset$. Then $\sum_{V \in \Delta P^<_{max}(X) \cup B(X)} c(V)$ is the maximum possible value of $L^<_{max}(X)$.*

Proof. Since we construct the flow problems in exactly the same way as [1], we state this as a corollary of Theorem 1 of [1]. □

The proofs for the tightness of the bounds on $L^>_{max}(X), L^<_{min}(X)$ and $L^>_{min}(X)$, are similar.

4.1 Discovering Constraints with FBC

The calculation of FBC allows the inference of new bounds on temporal constraints and new precedence constraints on events in a manner similar to BC [6]. We know that $L^<_{max}(X) = \sum_{V \in \{\Delta P^<_{max}(X) \cup B(X)\}} c(V)$. Suppose $L^<_{max}(X) > 0, r + \sum_{V \in B(X)} c(V) = d < 0$ and that there is a predecessor set $P \subset \Delta P^<_{max}(X)$ such that $\sum_{V \in P} c(V) < |d|$. If X occurs before or at the same time P ends, then the resource constraint will be violated. Let t be the earliest end time of all such sets. Then $t + 1$ is a valid new lower bound for X, i.e. $X_{lb} > t$. If $|\Delta P^<_{max}(X)| = k$, calculating $\sum_{V \in P} c(V)$ and the earliest end time t for every predecessor set of every event requires $O(k^2)$ since we already store the precedences to create the flow graphs. We can also tighten the bound on X_{ub}.

Suppose there is a predecessor set P such that $\Delta P_{max}^<(X) \subset P \subset \{BS(X) \cup U(X)\}$ and $\sum_{V \in P} c(V) < |d|$. If X occurs at the same time or after P ends then the resource constraint will be violated. Let t be the latest ending time of all such sets. Then $t - 1$ is a valid upper bound on X, i.e. $X_{ub} < t$. If $|\Delta P_{max}^{<C}(X)| = k$, calculating $\sum_{V \in P} c(V)$ and the earliest end time t for every predecessor set of every event requires $O(k^2)$. Similar arguments allow bounding X using $\Delta P_{max}^<(X)$ when $\sum_{V \in B(X)} c(V) > r$ as well as $\Delta P_{min}^>(X)$ and $\Delta P_{max}^>(X)$.

Inferring precedence constraints is a little trickier. Again, suppose $r + \sum_{V \in B(X)} c(V) = d < 0$. Imposing the constraint $X < Y$ doesn't impact $B(X)$ but may lead to a new set defining the maximum available resource, denoted $\Delta P_{max}^{'<}(X)$. Suppose that $\exists Y \in BS(X) \cup U(X)$ such that $X < Y \Rightarrow r + \sum_{V \in \{\Delta P_{max}^{'<}(X) \cup B(X)\}} c(V) < 0$. Then we can safely impose the precedence constraint $X \geq Y$. It is sufficient to find $Y \in \Delta P_{max}^<(X)$ such that its successor set $S \subset \Delta P_{max}^<(X)$ has the property that $\sum_{V \in \{\Delta P_{max}^<(X) - S\}} c(V) < |d|$. Under these circumstances, if X occurs before Y, then the remaining events in $\Delta P_{max}^<(X)$ cannot offset the events in $B(X)$.

Imposing the constraint $Y < X$ may lead to a new $B'(X)$. Suppose that $\exists Y \in \{BS(X) \cup U(X) - \Delta P_{max}^<(X)\}$ such that $Y < X \Rightarrow r + \sum_{V \in \{\Delta P_{max}^{'<}(X) \cup B'(X)\}} c(V) < 0$. Then we can safely impose the constraint $Y \geq X$. It is sufficient to find Y such that its predecessor set $S \subset \{BS(X) \cup U(X)\}$ has the property that $r + \sum_{V \in \{B(X) \cup S\}} c(V) = e < 0$ and $\sum_{V \in \{\Delta P_{max}^<(X) \cap S\}} c(V) < |e|$.

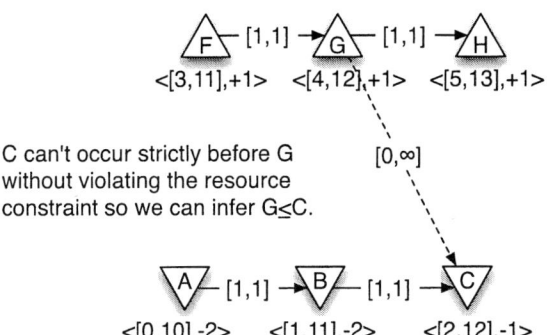

Fig. 4. Inferring new precedence constraints with FBC.

If $|\Delta P_{max}^<(X)| = k$ calculating $\sum_{V \in \Delta P_{max}^<(X) - S} c(V)$ for every successor or predecessor set requires $O(k^2)$ since we already store the precedences to create the flow graphs. Similar implied precedences can be discovered using the other bounds. To see how this works, consider Figure 4. In this case $\Delta P_{max}^<(C) = \{F, G, H\}$. The successor set of G is $\{G, H\}$ and $r + \sum_{V \in \{B(C)\}} = -2$. We see that allowing C to occur before G would lead to a resource constraint violation, since the only event remaining in $\Delta P_{max}^<(C)$ is F; it produces 1, which is not enough to offset $r+\sum_{V\in\{B(C)\}} = -2$. In this case we can infer a new precedence constraint $G \leq C$.

Note that if we relax the assumption that event resource impacts are known and allow schedulers to choose resource impacts, we can also infer restrictions on resource impacts as BC does [6].

4.2 Relating E_t and FBC

In this section, we formally establish the relationship between the intervals over which the FBC and E_t bounds hold. Suppose we find a set $P_{max}^<(X)$ that supports $L_{max}^<(X)$. What is the interval of time over which this value holds? $L_{max}^<(X)$ is the maximum available resource before X occurs assuming that we impose the constraints $\forall V \in P_{max}^<(X)\{V < X\}$ and $\forall V \in P_{max}^{<C}(X)\{X \leq V\}$ to get a new RTN $\mathcal{R}'$. Note that the new unordered set $U'(X) = \emptyset$, and $BS'(X) = \emptyset$, and the new closed set $B'(X) = \{P_{max}^<(X) \cup B(X)\}$. $L_{max}^<(X)$ can be the resource availability no earlier than $V_{lb}^* = \max_{V \in B'(X)} V_{lb}$. Forcing events to precede X does not change their earliest start times. However, forcing events to follow X may lead to a new upper bound for X, $X_{ub'}$. Thus, $L_{max}^<(X) = L_{max'}(t)$ over the interval $[V_{lb}^*, X_{ub'} - 1]$. An example is shown in Figure 5.

Now suppose we find a set $P_{max}^>(X)$ that supports $L_{max}^>(X)$. This bound assumes that we impose the constraints $\forall V \in P_{max}^>(X)\{V \leq X\}$ and $\forall V \in P_{max}^{>C}(X)\{X < V\}$ to get a new RTN $\mathcal{R}'$. Note that the new pending set $U'(X) = \emptyset$, and $\{B'(X) \cup S'(X) \cup BS'(X)\} = P_{max}^>(X)$. $L_{max}^>(X)$ can be the resource availability no later than $W_{ub}^* = \min_{W \in P_{max}^{>C}(X)} W_{ub}$. Forcing events to follow X does not change their upper bounds. However, forcing events to precede X may lead to a new lower bound $X_{lb'}$. that $L_{max}^>(X)$ holds. Thus, $L_{max}^>(X) = L_{max'}(t)$ over the interval $[X_{lb'}, W_{ub}^* - 1]$.

We now can demonstrate the precise relationship between $L_{max}(t)$ and the bounds $L_{max}^<(X), L_{max}^>(X)$ and $L_{min}(t)$ and the bounds $L_{min}^<(X), L_{min}^>(X)$ and

Theorem 3. Let $E_{max}^<(t) = X|L_{max}^<(X)$ holds at t and $E_{max}^>(t) = X|L_{max}^>(X)$ holds at t. Then $L_{max}(t) = \max(\max_{X \in \{E_{max}^<(t) \cup E_{max}^>(t)\}} L_{max}^>(X))$. Let $E_{min}^<(t) = X|L_{min}^<(X)$ holds at t and $E_{min}^>(t) = X|L_{min}^>(X)$ holds at t. Then $L_{min}(t) = \min(\min_{X \in E_{min}^<(t)} L_{min}^<(X), \min_{X \in E_{min}^>(t)} L_{min}^>(X))$.

Proof. The paragraph above describes the intervals over which $L_{max}^<(X)$ and $L_{max}^>(X)$ hold. The rest follows immediately from the definitions. □

5 Dominance

In this section we will describe our dominance criteria and show that FBC dominates E_t and BC; we do not formally show that BC and E_t do not dominate each other, relying on the intuition of Section 3 to adequately demonstrate this. In order to motivate our definition of dominance, suppose that some procedure A is used to check the HC in a chronological search framework with a static variable and value ordering heuristic. Then we would like A to dominate B if A leads to smaller search trees than using B.

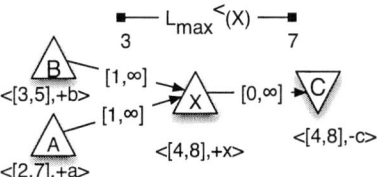

Fig. 5. Deriving the time intervals over which resource availability bounds hold. The example shows the calculation for $L_{max}^<(X)$.

Definition 1. *Let R be an RTN. Let $T(R)$ be the set of all temporally consistent RTNs that can be formed from R by adding temporal constraints to R. Let $A, B : T(R) \rightarrow \{T, F, ?\}$ Let $U_A(R) = \{S \in T(R) | A(S) =?\}$. Then A dominates B on R if $U_A(R) \subset U_B(R)$. A dominates B if $\exists R$ such that A dominates B on R and there exists no S such that B dominates A on S. We write $A \prec_R B$ or $A \prec B$ as appropriate.*

Theorem 4. $FBC \prec BC$.

Proof. Theorems 1 and 2 show that the flow construction guarantees the tightest possible bounds on $L_{max}^<(X), L_{max}^>(X), L_{min}^<(X)$ and $L_{min}^>(X)$ for *any* RTN. Thus there can be no S such that $BC \prec_S FBC$. The example shown in Figure 1 shows at least one RTN R for which $FBC \prec_R BC$. This completes the proof. □

Theorem 5. $FBC \prec E_t$

Proof. Theorems 1, 2 and 3 shows that there is no RTN S for which $E_t \prec_S FBC$. The example in Figure 2 shows that there is at least one RTN R for which $FBC \prec_R E_t$. This completes the proof. □

6 Complexity of Calculating FBC

A naive algorithm for calculating FBC builds a new flow network for each event $X \in \mathcal{N}$. An equally naive analysis of the complexity of this algorithm is $O(n * MaxFlow(n, m) + n^2)$, where m is the number of anti-precedence relationships in the RTN. However, this analysis is unsatisfactory for a number of reasons. Consider the RTN in Figure 1. The flow networks required to calculate FBC are *identical* for A, B, C, D because $S(A) = S(B) = S(C) = S(D)$. Additionally, the flow networks include only a small fraction of the n nodes in the RTN; strict precedences and equalities among events will generally reduce the size of the flow problems. These observations suggest it might be possible to improve upon the bound of $O(n*MaxFlow(n,m)+n^2)$ to calculate FBC.

6.1 A Nontrivial Lower Complexity Bound

In this section we provide a *lower* bound on the complexity of the naive approach to calculating FBC. We do so by constructing an RTN such that the flow problem to solve for each event is both non-trivial and distinct. The RTN is a "square" graph with $\sqrt{n}$ events per side. We index events by row and column in the square. The RTN has the following strict precedences: $(i,j) < (i+1,j)$, and $(i,j) < (i,j+1)$ (obviously omitting those links for which the indices are outside the bounds $[0,\sqrt{n}]$. By construction, $P((i,j)) = ((x,y)|x > i \wedge y < j) \cup ((u,v)|u < i \wedge v > j)$. Thus, all of the flow graphs are distinct and nontrivial. Notice that we can assign $c(X)$ arbitrarily to the events of the RTN, as long as they are all non-zero and there is a mix of consumers and producers. This RTN is shown in Figure 6.

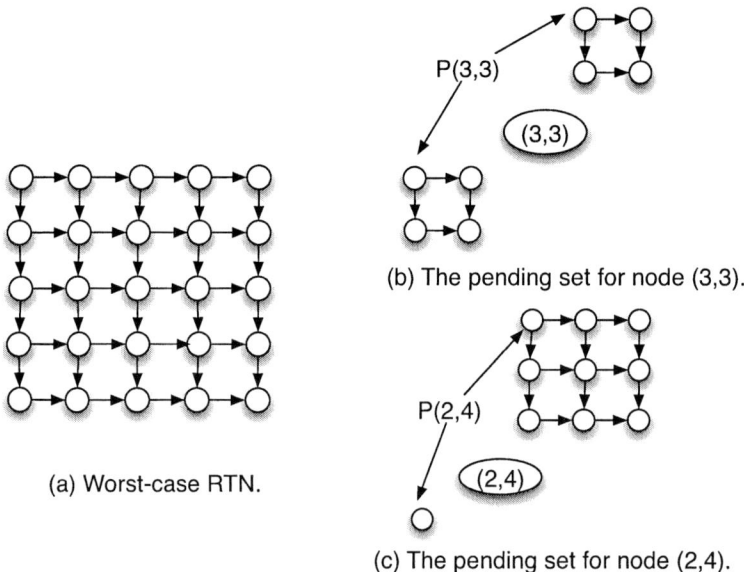

Fig. 6. A perverse RTN providing a worst-case lower bound for calculating FBC.

We now proceed to construct a lower bound on the complexity of the naive approach for calculating FBC on this RTN. By construction we have guaranteed that no "quick fixes" can be used to decrease the complexity. The larger of the two induced flow problem for event (i,j) contains $\max((i-1)(\sqrt{n}-j-1),(j-1)(\sqrt{n}-i-1))$ events, and at least this many flow arcs (we could do an exact count but it isn't necessary since we're providing a lower bound.) Let us now assume we are using a FIFO preflow-push algorithm to solve each flow problem [10]; this ignores any efficiency gained from analyzing the pushable flow, but is also suitable for our purposes. If v is the number of nodes in the flow problem, there are at least v edges, and so the complexity of solving the flow problem is $\Omega(v^{2.5})$. Using these assumptions the total complexity of solving all the flow problems is

$$\leq \sum_{j=1}^{\sqrt{n}} \sum_{i=1}^{\sqrt{n}} \max((i-1)(\sqrt{n}-j-1), (j-1)(\sqrt{n}-i-1))^{2.5}$$

First, we simplify the sum to get a lower bound:

$$\leq \sum_{j=0}^{\sqrt{n}-1} \sum_{i=0}^{\sqrt{n}-1} (i(\sqrt{n}-j))^{2.5}$$

We next approximate the sum with the integral (which, while bounding above, is close enough for our purposes):

$$\approx \int_{j=0}^{\sqrt{n}-1} \left(\int_{i=0}^{\sqrt{n}-1} (i(\sqrt{n}-j))^{2.5} \, di \right) dj$$

The first integral with respect to i is trivial. For the second integral we have

$$\int (\sqrt{n}-j)^{2.5} dj = (\sqrt{n}-j)^{2.5} \left(\frac{j-\sqrt{n}}{3.5} \right)$$

Collecting terms we have

$$\sum_{j=1}^{\sqrt{n}} \sum_{i=1}^{\sqrt{n}} \max((i-1)(\sqrt{n}-j-1), (j-1)(\sqrt{n}-i-1))^{2.5}$$

$$\leq \left(\frac{(\sqrt{n}-1)^{3.5}}{3.5} \right) \left(\frac{\sqrt{n}^{3.5}}{3.5} - \frac{1}{3.5} \right)$$

Collecting the high order positive powers of $\sqrt{n}$ we see that the naive algorithm has a lower bound $\Omega(n^{3.5})$. Thus, for preflow-push flow algorithms using FIFO queues, the naive algorithm for FBC requires $\Omega(n * MaxFlow(n, m))$ for solving the flows.

6.2 Incrementally Calculating FBC

As stated previously, the incremental technique described in [7] shaves a factor of n off the cost of calculating E_t. To do so, the incremental approach relies on restricted modifications of the flow problem. If A is in the flow problem, it may be removed if it has no successors other than the sink remaining in the flow problem; if B is not in the flow problem, it may be added if it has no predecessors other than the source in the flow problem. This provides some hope that we can find a way to eliminate the factor of n "extra" cost for calculating FBC that we described in the previous section. Unfortunately, this is not the case. The crucial element of the complexity analysis in [7] requires that an event always move from open to pending to closed. We show that naively applying the incremental algorithm may result in a non-trivial number of events moving from closed to pending, thereby defeating the cost-savings measures. Consider the RTN described in Figure 6. The longest chain of events is $O(\sqrt{n})$, and there are $O(\sqrt{n})$ chains of events we must solve for which the incremental approach cannot save any computation. Each of these induces a total complexity of $O(MaxFlow(n,m))$. Thus, for this problem, even the incremental approach to solving flow problems customized for the E_t algorithm cannot reduce the complexity of FBC below $\Omega(\sqrt{n} * MaxFlow(n,m) + n^2)$.

We can take advantage of the incremental flow calculation by judicious ordering of the bounds we calculate for an event X. For example, to find $\Delta P_{max}^<(X)$ we solve a flow problem over $\{BS(X) \cup U(X)\}$. To find $\Delta P_{max}^>(X)$ we solve a flow problem over $\{AS(X) \cup U(X)\}$. The change in the flow problem to be solved allows the incremental approach to be used; thus, we can use the solution of the flow that gives us $\Delta P_{max}^<(X)$ in order to find $\Delta P_{max}^>(X)$. The total complexity of solving both flow problems is $O(MaxFlow(n,m))$ where n and m are derived from the anti-precedence graph on $\{BS(X) \cup U(X) \cup AS(X)\}$; this is cheaper than solving both flows separately as long as $U(X) \neq \emptyset$.

We can also take advantage of the incremental flow calculation by storing and reusing flow calculations and ordering the bounds calculations for different events. Suppose $Z \in \{BS(X) \cup S(X)\}$, we are calculating the bounds for X and Z's bounds were previously calculated. Then $A \in BS(Z)$ must be either in $B(X)$ or $BS(X)$ and $B \in U(Z)$ must be either in $B(X), BS(X)$ or $U(X)$. This fits the conditions required to use the incremental approach by reusing the solution to the flow problem on $\{U(Z) \cup BS(Z)\}$. If we had *cached* this solution, we could then retrieve it and reuse it in time proportional to the number of previously stored flow calculations. We can generate an event order $\Pi(X)$ using a Depth-First Search through the anti-precedence graph on all of the events to ensure that we can take advantage of incremental calculations. We call the resulting algorithm $FBC - DFS$, and it is described in Figure 7 below. As before, we need to calculate bounds for only one event $X \in S(Y)$.

Obviously, the cost of $FBC - DFS$ depends on the DFS traversal used to order the bounds calculations, as described in the next result.

Theorem 6. *Let $\mathcal{R}$ be an RTN with m induced anti-precedence constraints in its STN $\mathcal{S}$. Let Π be an ordering induced by a DFS traversal of the anti-precedence graph on $\mathcal{S}$, let w be the number of leaves of the traversal and let l be longest path in the traversal. Then Algorithm $FBC - DFS$ takes $O(w * MaxFlow(n,m)) + n^2$ time, and takes $O(lm)$ space.*

Proof. Each leaf corresponds to a sequence such that $X_{i-1} \in \{B(X_i) \cup BS(X_i) \cup S(X_i)\}$. Then, for each sequence, we can reuse the flow solutions from $top(F_{max})$ and $top(F_{min})$ to solve each X_i; each chain costs $O(MaxFlow(n,m))$. Since there are w such chains, we're done with this part of the proof. Since the longest chain is of length l, we store at most l copies of a flow problem on at most n nodes and m edges.

FBC-DFS$(\mathcal{R}, \Pi(X))$
  Enforce Arc-Consistency on $\mathcal{R}$
  $F_{max} = F_{min} = \emptyset$
  for each event $X_i \in \Pi(X)$
    Find the latest $X_j \in \Pi(X)$ such that $j < i, X_j \in B(X_i) \cup BS(X_i) \cup S(X_i)$
    if $X_j \neq X_{i-1}$ Pop F_{max} and F_{min} to X_j
    Inc-Bound(X_i)
  end for
end

Inc-Bound(X)
  Build flow problems for $L_{max}^<(X)$ from $top(F_{max})$ and $L_{min}^<(X)$ from $top(F_{min})$
  Find $\Delta P_{max}^<(X) \subset \{BS(X) \cup U(X)\}$
  $L_{max}^<(X) = \sum_{V \in \{\Delta P_{max}^<(X) \cup B(X)\}} c(V)$
  Find $\Delta P_{min}^<(X) \subset \{BS(X) \cup U(X)\}$
  $L_{min}^<(X) = \sum_{V \in \{\Delta P_{min}^<(X) \cup B(X)\}} c(V)$
  Build flow problems for $L_{max}^>(X), L_{min}^>(X)$
  Find $\Delta P_{max}^>(X) \subset \{AS(X) \cup U(X)\}$
  $L_{max}^>(X) = \sum_{V \in \{\Delta P_{max}^>(X) \cup B(X) \cup BS(X) \cup S(X)\}} c(V)$
  Find $\Delta P_{min}^>(X) \subset \{AS(X) \cup U(X)\}$
  $L_{min}^>(X) = \sum_{V \in \{\Delta P_{min}^>(X) \cup B(X) \cup BS(X) \cup S(X)\}} c(V)$
  Push the flow solutions for $L_{max}^<(X)$ onto F_{max} and $L_{min}^<(X)$ onto F_{min}
end

Fig. 7. A sketch of the Flow Balance Constraint implemented by using a Depth-First search through the precedence graph and using an incremental approach to reduce computation time for constructing the bounds.

The theory of partially ordered sets gives some bounds on w and l; Let W be the partial order width and L be the partial order length of the partially ordered set induced by the anti-precedence graph. For any DFS traversal, $w \geq W$ and $l \leq L$. However, it is not obvious in general how to efficiently find a good event ordering.

7 Higher Order Balance Constraint

The quantities $L_{max}^<(X), L_{max}^>(X), L_{min}^<(X)$ and $L_{min}^>(X)$ can be thought of as *first order* bounds on resource availability, in that they represent resource bounds before and after one event. In this section we generalize these techniques in order to calculate higher-order resource availability checks after k events. To see why this is valuable, consider Figure 8. Initially there are 2 units of resource available. We see that no first order bound calculated by FBC proves that this RTN is impossible to solve. However, notice that we can show that the *maximum* available resource after both A and B have occurred, which we denote $L_{max}^>(A \wedge B)$, is -1. This corresponds to one of two schedules: it is possible to either schedule $D \leq B$ or $C \leq A$, but not both simultaneously. Thus, without further search, we can prove that the HC is satisfied because no solution exists.

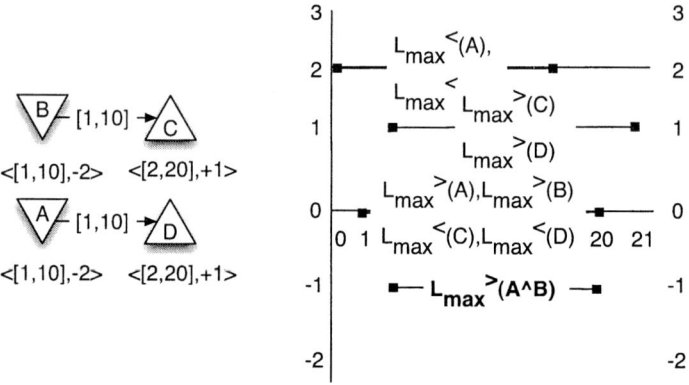

Fig. 8. An RTN for which FBC fails to prove that the HC is unsatisfied.

This example shows that it may be valuable to perform 2^d-order checks on resource availability by determining resource availability immediately before and after sets of 2 events. We assume without loss of generality that $X \in U(Y)$. In order to do this for $L^<_{max}(X \wedge Y)$ we must account for the following possibilities: neither X nor Y have occurred, X has occurred but Y has not, and vice versa. To find the maximum availability strictly before both X and Y we solve the flow problem over the events of $\{\{BS(X) \cup U(X)\} \cap \{BS(Y) \cup U(Y)\}\}$. We call the resulting set of events $\Delta P^<_{max}(X * Y)$. To find the maximum availability strictly before Y assuming $X < Y$ requires adding the constraint and recalculating the partitions of the anti-precedence graph relative to Y. We then solve the flow problem defined by $BS'(Y) \cup U'(Y)$ and call the resulting set $\Delta P^<_{max}(X < Y)$. To find the maximum availability strictly before X assuming $Y < X$ proceeds similarly, and the resulting set is called $\Delta P^<_{max}(Y < X)$. We define $L^<_{max}(X \wedge Y)$ as

$$\max(\sum_{V \in \{\Delta P^<_{max}(X*Y) \cup B(X) \cap B(Y)\}} c(V)$$

$$\sum_{V \in \{B'(Y) \cup \Delta P^<_{max}(X<Y)\}} c(V)$$

$$\sum_{V \in \{B'(X) \cup \Delta P^<_{max}(Y<X)\}} c(V)$$

and $\Delta P^<_{max}(X \wedge Y)$ is the set of events defining the maximum.

For $L^>_{max}(X \wedge Y)$ we we must account for the following possibilities: X and Y occurred at the same time, X occurred before Y, and vice versa. These options account for the possibility that, for example, events in $A(X) \cap U(Y)$ contribute to $L^>_{max}(X \wedge Y)$. To find the maximum assuming $X = Y$, we first solve the flow problem over the events of $\{\{AS(X)\cup U(X)\}\cap\{AS(Y)\cup U(Y)\}\}$. We call the resulting set $\Delta P^>_{max}(X=Y)$. To find the maximum assuming $X < Y$ requires adding the constraint and recalculating the partitions of the anti-precedence graph relative to Y. We solve the flow problem over $\{AS'(Y) \cup U'(Y)\}$, and call the resulting set $\Delta P^>_{max}(X<Y)$. and $\Delta P^>_{max}(X>Y)$ is defined similarly. We define $L^>_{max}(X \wedge Y)$ as

$$\max(\sum_{V\in(\Delta P^>_{max}(X=Y)\cup B(X)\cup BS(X)\cup S(X)\cup B(Y)\cup BS(Y)\cup S(Y)} c(V)$$

$$\sum_{V\in B'(Y)\cup BS'(Y)\cup S'(Y)\cup \Delta P^>_{max}(X<Y)} c(V)$$

$$\sum_{V\in B'(X)\cup BS'(X)\cup S'(X)\cup \Delta P^>_{max}(Y<X)} c(V)$$

and $\Delta P^>_{max}(X \wedge Y)$ is the set of events defining the maximum. The lower bounds are calculated in a similar manner.

Let us see how this works in Figure 8. To find $L^<_{max}(A \wedge B)$, note $\{\{BS(A) \cup U(A)\} \cap \{BS(B) \cup U(B)\}\} = \emptyset$ and $\{B(A) \cap B(B)\} = \emptyset$. Thus, $L^<_{max}(A * B) = 2$, which is achieved by assuming no event has taken place. To find $L^<_{max}(A < B)$, we see that $U'(B) = D$; the best schedule here is A, D for an availability of 1. Similarly, to find $L^<_{max}(B < A)$, we see that $U'(A) = C$; the best schedule here is B, C for an availability of 1. Thus, $L^<_{max}(X \wedge Y) = 2$. To calculate $L^>_{max}(A \wedge B)$ we see that $\Delta P^>_{max}(A = B) = \emptyset$, leading to $L^>_{max}(A = B) = -2$. However, $\Delta P^>_{max}(A < B) = D$; this corresponds to the schedule A, D, B, with the result that $L^>_{max}(A < B) = -1$, and symmetrically $L^>_{max}(B < A) = -1$. Thus, $L^>_{max}(A \wedge B) = -1$.

The total complexity of the resulting naive algorithm for calculating *Second order Flow Balance Constraint* (FBC^2) is $\Omega((n^2) * (MaxFlow(n, m) + n^2))$. The n^2 term comes from the fact that $n(n-1)$ pairs of bounds must be calculated. The complexity bounds obscure the fact that 6 flow problems must be solved per pair of events, and also hides the fact that the precedence constraints must be recalculated for each constraint imposed to set up the flow problems. Note, however, that n^2 is a very crude estimate of the total number of bounds to compute. If A strictly precedes B then $P^<_{max}(A \wedge B) = P^<_{max}(B)$. Thus, the induced precedences vastly reduce the number of bounds to calculate. Additionally, the sizes of the flow problems will generally be larger as the number of events involved climbs. These factors make a more precise complexity analysis difficult. Finally, it is likely that the incremental flow algorithm described in [7] can be used to further reduce the complexity. It is sufficient for our purposes to demonstrate that even tighter inferred constraints can be calculated in time polynomial in the number of events considered. While we can generalize further to higher order bounds, the apparent complexity even of the second order bounds makes it likely that these higher order bounds will not be practical to compute.

8 Conclusions and Future Work

In this paper we have also shown how to exploit the features of BC and E_t to construct FBC, a tighter bound on the availability of resources for RTNs than either of the previous approaches. We have shown that FBC dominates both E_t and BC in terms of the size of search trees generated under chronological backtracking search with a static variable ordering, and that contrary to expectations, BC and E_t do not strictly dominate each other. We have described an incremental algorithm, $FBC - DFS$ that takes advantage of incremental flow calculations by using a depth-first search traversal of the anti-precedence graph. If w is the number of leaves of the traversal and l is longest path in the traversal, algorithm $FBC - DFS$ takes $O(w * MaxFlow(n, m))$ time, and takes $O(lm)$ space. The technique generalize for calculating FBC leads to even tighter bounds, but at sharply increased computational cost.

While we have proven dominance of FBC, an empirical study will be necessary to determine the relative value of E_t, BC and FBC for speeding up the solving of scheduling problems. In particular, it is necessary to determine how to generate good orderings to optimize the performance of $FBC - DFS$. A second, equally important empirical study will be necessary to shed light on how to integrate heuristics that make use of the various bounds. Laborie [6] has built numerous such heuristics for BC. However, such heuristics have complex interactions with the pruning power of the envelopes. It will likely be necessary to trade off between the pruning power and heuristic predictiveness of the resource bounds to craft the best scheduling algorithm.

Changes to dominance criteria that we use are worth contemplating. A dominance criteria for dynamic variable ordering based search would be handy but is complicated due to the interaction of pruning techniques and heuristics. Dominance criteria for local search based algorithms are also desirable. On the one hand, requiring that A dominates B on R if $U_A(R) \subset U_B(R)$ is rather strong, and could be weakened, say, to $|U_A(R))| < |U_B(R))|$. On the other hand, requiring that A dominates B if $\exists R$ such that A dominates B on R and there exists no S such that B dominates A on S is somewhat weak, and perhaps could be strengthened.

Acknowledgments

I would like to thank Ari Jónsson for numerous discussions on this topic. This work was funded by the NASA Intelligent Systems Program.

References

1. Muscettola, N.: Computing the envelope for stepwise-constant resource allocations. In: Proceedings of the 8th International Conference on the Principles and Practices of Constraint Programming. (2002) 139 –154
2. Laborie, P.: Resource temporal networks: Definition and complexity. In: Proceedings of the 18th International Joint Conference on Artificial Intelligence. (2003) 948 – 953
3. Dechter, R., Meiri, I., Pearl, J.: Temporal constraint networks. Artificial Intelligence **49** (1991) 61–94
4. Jónsson, A., Morris, P., Muscettola, N., Rajan, K., Smith, B.: Planning in interplanetary space: Theory and practice. In: Proceedings of the Fifth International Conference on Artificial Intelligence Planning and Scheduling. (2000)
5. Morris, P., Muscettola, N., Tsamardinos, I.: Reformulating temporal plans for efficient execution. In: Proceedings of the 15th National Conference on Artificial Intelligence. (1998)

6. Laborie, P.: Algorithms for propagating resource constraints in ai planning and scheduling: Existing approaches and new results. Artificial Intelligence **143** (2003) 151–188
7. Muscettola, N.: Incremental maximum flows for fast envelope computation. In: Proceedings of the 14th International Conference on Automated Planning and Scheduling. (2004)
8. Chapman, D.: Planning for conjunctive goals. Artificial Intelligence **32** (1987) 333 – 377
9. Kumar, T.K.S.: Incremental computation of resource-envelopes in producer-consumer models. In: Proceedings of the 9th International Conference on the Principles and Practices of Constraint Programming. (2003) 664 – 678
10. Ahuja, R., Magnanti, T., Orlin, J.: Network Flows. Prentice Hall (1993)

Monotone Literals and Learning in QBF Reasoning

Enrico Giunchiglia, Massimo Narizzano, and Armando Tacchella

DIST, Università di Genova, Viale Causa, 13 – 16145 Genova, Italy
{enrico,mox,tac}@dist.unige.it

Abstract. Monotone literal fixing (MLF) and learning are well-known lookahead and lookback mechanisms in propositional satisfiability (SAT). When considering Quantified Boolean Formulas (QBFs), their separate implementation leads to significant speed-ups in state-of-the-art DPLL-based solvers.
This paper is dedicated to the efficient implementation of MLF in a QBF solver with learning. The interaction between MLF and learning is far from being obvious, and it poses some nontrivial questions about both the detection and the propagation of monotone literals. Complications arise from the presence of learned constraints, and are related to the question about whether learned constraints have to be considered or not during the detection and/or propagation of monotone literals. In the paper we answer to this question both from a theoretical and from a practical point of view. We discuss the advantages and the disadvantages of various solutions, and show that our solution of choice, implemented in our solver QUBE, produces significant speed-ups in most cases. Finally, we show that MLF can be fundamental also for solving some SAT instances, taken from the 2002 SAT solvers competition.

1 Introduction and Motivations

Monotone literal fixing (MLF) and learning are well-known lookahead and lookback mechanisms in propositional satisfiability (SAT). When considering Quantified Boolean Formulas (QBFs), their separate implementation leads to significant speed-ups in state-of-the-art DPLL-based solvers (see, e.g., [1,2]). This is witnessed by the plots in Figure 1, which show the performances of our solver QUBE-BJ running with/without MLF (Figure 1, left), and with/without learning (Figure 1, right). The test set used for the plots is the same selection of 450 real-world instances from the 2003 QBF solvers evaluation [3] where QUBE-BJ, a version of QUBE [4] with conflict and solution backjumping [5], was one of the top performers. In Figure 1, each solid-fill dot represents an instance, QUBE-BJ solving time is on the x-axis (seconds, log scale), QUBE-BJ(P) (Figure 1, left), and QUBE-LRN (Figure 1, right) solving times are on the y-axes (seconds, log scale). The diagonal (outlined boxes) represents the solving time of QUBE-BJ against itself and serves the purpose of reference: the dots above the diagonal are instances where QUBE-BJ performs better than the version with MLF (QUBE-BJ(P)) or the version with learning (QUBE-LRN), while the dots below are the instances where QUBE-BJ performances are worse than its siblings. By looking at Figure 1, we can see that both QUBE-BJ(P) and QUBE-LRN outperform QUBE-BJ. Considering the number of instances solved both by QUBE-BJ and each of its siblings, on 228/346

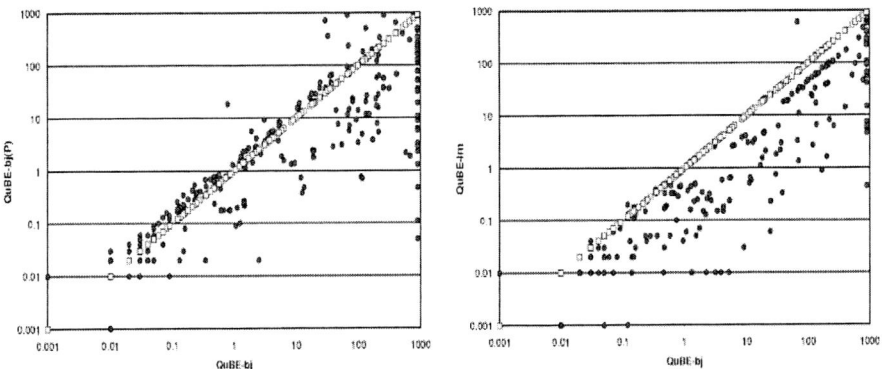

Fig. 1. Effectiveness of MLF and learning in a QBF solver.

(resp. 331/345) instances QUBE-BJ(P) (resp. QUBE-LRN) is as fast as or faster than QUBE-BJ: QUBE-BJ(P) (resp. QUBE-LRN) is at least one order of magnitude faster than QUBE-BJ on 37 (resp. 63) problems, while it is at least one order of magnitude slower on 10 (resp. 6) problems only.

This paper is dedicated to the efficient implementation of MLF in a QBF solver with learning. The interaction between MLF and learning is far from being obvious, and it poses some nontrivial questions about both the detection and the propagation of monotone literals. Indeed, the constraints introduced by learning during the search are redundant, i.e., they could be ignored without affecting the satisfiability of the formula and the correctness of the procedure, but they can substantially speed up the search. The main issue with MLF is that – similarly to what happens in SAT – in QBF solvers learned constraints can greatly outnumber the constraints in the input formula, and this may result in efficiency losses: given a set S of constraints, the detection of a monotone literal l has a cost which is at least linear in the number of occurrences of l in S. If, as in the case of learning, the number of constraints under consideration is increased (substantially), the performances of MLF decrease (significantly). This opens up to the question about whether it is necessary or not to consider learned constraints during the detection and/or propagation of monotone literals. In the paper we answer to this question both from a theoretical and from a practical point of view. We discuss the advantages and the disadvantages of the various solutions, and show that our solution of choice, implemented in our solver QUBE, produces significant speed-ups in most cases. Finally, we show that MLF can be fundamental also for solving a subset of the SAT instances used in the 2002 SAT solvers competition.

The paper is structured as follows. We first review the basics of QBF satisfiability and DPLL based solvers with learning (Section 2). We then discuss the issues related to the implementation of MLF in such solvers (Section 3), and present the possible solutions (Section 4). We end the paper with the experimental analysis (Section 5), the conclusions and the related work (Section 6).

2 Formal Preliminaries

Consider a set P of symbols. A *variable* is an element of P. A *literal* is a variable or the negation of a variable. In the following, for any literal l, $|l|$ is the variable occurring in l; and $\bar{l}$ is the negation of l if l is a variable, and is $|l|$ otherwise. For the sake of simplicity, we consider only formulas in negation normal form (NNF). Thus, for us, a *propositional formula* is a combination of literals using the k-ary ($k \geq 0$) connectives $\wedge$ (for conjunctions) and $\vee$ (for disjunctions). In the following, we use TRUE and FALSE as abbreviations for the empty conjunction and the empty disjunction respectively.

A *QBF* is an expression of the form

$$\varphi = Q_1 z_1 Q_2 z_2 \ldots Q_n z_n \Phi \qquad (n \geq 0) \qquad (1)$$

where every Q_i ($1 \leq i \leq n$) is a quantifier, either existential $\exists$ or universal $\forall$, $z_1, \ldots, z_n$ are distinct variables, and Φ is a propositional formula in $z_1, \ldots, z_n$. For example,

$$\exists x_1 \forall y \exists x_2 \{\{\bar{x}_1 \vee \bar{y} \vee x_2\} \wedge \{\bar{y} \vee \bar{x}_2\} \wedge \{x_2 \vee \{\{x_1 \vee \bar{y}\} \wedge \{y \vee x_2\}\}\}\} \qquad (2)$$

is a QBF. In (1), $Q_1 z_1 \ldots Q_n z_n$ is the *prefix* and Φ is the *matrix*. We say that a literal l is *existential* if $\exists |l|$ belongs to the prefix of (1), and that it is *universal* otherwise. We say that (1) is in *Conjunctive Normal Form* (CNF) when Φ is a conjunction of *clauses*, where each clause is a disjunction of literals; we say that (1) is in *Disjunctive Normal Form* (DNF) when Φ is a disjunction of *terms*, where each term is a conjunction of literals. We use *constraints* when we refer to clauses and terms indistinctly. Finally, in (1), we define

- the *level of a variable* z_i, to be 1 + the number of expressions $Q_j z_j Q_{j+1} z_{j+1}$ in the prefix with $j \geq i$ and $Q_j \neq Q_{j+1}$;
- the *level of a literal* l, to be the level of $|l|$.

For example, in (2) x_2 is existential and has level 1, y is universal and has level 2, x_1 is existential and has level 3.

The semantics of a QBF φ can be defined recursively as follows. If the prefix is empty, then φ's satisfiability is defined according to the truth tables of propositional logic; if φ is $\exists x \psi$, φ is satisfiable if and only if φ_x or $\varphi_{\bar{x}}$ are satisfiable; if φ is $\forall y \psi$, φ is satisfiable if and only if φ_y and $\varphi_{\bar{y}}$ are satisfiable. If φ is (1) and l is a literal with $|l| = z_i$, φ_l is the QBF whose matrix is obtained from Φ by substituting l with TRUE and $\bar{l}$ with FALSE, and whose prefix is $Q_1 z_1 Q_2 z_2 \ldots Q_{i-1} z_{i-1} Q_{i+1} z_{i+1} \ldots Q_n z_n$. Two QBFs are *equivalent* if they are either both satisfiable or both unsatisfiable.

2.1 Basic QBF Solver

Following the terminology of [2], we call *Extended QBF* (EQBF) an expression of the form:

$$Q_1 z_1 \ldots Q_n z_n \langle \Psi, \Phi, \Theta \rangle \qquad (n \geq 0) \qquad (3)$$

where $Q_1 z_1 \ldots Q_n z_n \Phi$ is a QBF, Ψ is a conjunction of clauses, Θ is a disjunction of terms, and such that, given any sequence of literals $l_1; \ldots; l_m$ with $m \leq n$ and $|l_i| = z_i$, the following three formulas are equi-satisfiable:

```
bool SOLVE(Q, Φ, Ψ, Θ, S)                          set SIMPLIFY(Q, Φ, Ψ, Θ, S)
1  ⟨Q, Φ, Ψ, Θ, S⟩ ← SIMPLIFY(Q, Φ, Ψ, Θ, S)       11 while {l}∃ ∈ Φ ∪ Ψ or {l̄}∀ ∈ Θ do
2  if Φ is empty or ∅∀ ∈ Θ then                   12    S ← S ∪ {l}
3     return TRUE                                  13    Q ← REMOVE(Q, |l|)
4  if ∅∃ ∈ Φ ∪ Ψ then                             14    for each c ∈ Φ ∪ Ψ s.t. l ∈ c do
5     return FALSE                                 15       Φ ← Φ \ {c}
6  l ← CHOOSE-LITERAL(Q, Φ, Ψ, Θ)                  16       Ψ ← Ψ \ {c}
7  if l is existential then                        17    for each t ∈ Θ s.t. l̄ ∈ t do
8     return SOLVE(Q, Φ, Ψ ∪ {l}, Θ, S) or         18       Θ ← Θ \ {t}
              SOLVE(Q, Φ, Ψ ∪ {l̄}, Θ, S)           19    for each c ∈ Φ s.t. l̄ ∈ c do
9  else                                            20       Φ ← (Φ \ {c}) ∪ {c \ {l̄}}
10    return SOLVE(Q, Φ, Ψ, Θ ∪ {l̄}, S) and        21    for each c ∈ Ψ s.t. l̄ ∈ c do
              SOLVE(Q, Φ, Ψ, Θ ∪ {l}, S)           22       Ψ ← (Ψ \ {c}) ∪ {c \ {l̄}}
                                                   23    for each t ∈ Θ s.t. l ∈ t do
                                                   24       Θ ← (Θ \ {t}) ∪ {t \ {l}}
                                                   25 return ⟨Q, Φ, Ψ, Θ, S⟩
```

Fig. 2. Basic algorithm of a QBF solver.

$$\{\ldots\{\{Q_1 z_1 Q_2 z_2 \ldots Q_n z_n (\wedge_{c \in \Phi} \vee_{l \in c} l)\}_{l_1}\}_{l_2} \ldots\}_{l_m},$$
$$\{\ldots\{\{Q_1 z_1 Q_2 z_2 \ldots Q_n z_n ((\wedge_{c \in \Phi} \vee_{l \in c} l) \wedge (\wedge_{c \in \Psi} \vee_{l \in c} l))\}_{l_1}\}_{l_2} \ldots\}_{l_m},$$
$$\{\ldots\{\{Q_1 z_1 Q_2 z_2 \ldots Q_n z_n ((\wedge_{c \in \Phi} \vee_{l \in c} l) \vee (\vee_{t \in \Theta} \wedge_{l \in t} l))\}_{l_1}\}_{l_2} \ldots\}_{l_m}.$$

In Figure 2 we present the basic algorithm of a QBF solver. The main function SOLVE takes five parameters: Q is a list and Φ is a set of clauses corresponding, respectively, to the prefix and the matrix of the input QBF, Ψ (resp. Θ) is a set of clauses (resp. terms), and S is a set of literals called *assignment*; initially $S = \emptyset$, $\Psi = \emptyset$, and $\Theta = \emptyset$. SOLVE returns TRUE if the input QBF is satisfiable and FALSE otherwise. SOLVE requires the input QBF to be in CNF, and, as customary in search algorithms, it deals with CNF instances as if they were *sets* of clauses and with clauses as if they were *sets* of literals. SOLVE works in four steps (line numbers refer to Figure 2):

1. Simplify the input instance with SIMPLIFY (line 1).
2. Check if the *termination condition* is met, i.e., if we are done with the current search path and backtracking is needed (lines 2-5): if the test in line 2 is true, then S is a *solution*, while if the test in line 4 is true, then S is a *conflict*; $\emptyset_\exists$ (resp. $\emptyset_\forall$) stands for an *empty clause* (resp. *empty term*), i.e., a constraint comprised of universal (resp. existential) literals only.
3. Choose heuristically a literal l (line 6) such that (i) $|l|$ is in Q, and (ii) there is no other literal l' in Q whose level is greater than the level of l; the literal returned by CHOOSE-LITERAL is called *branching literal*.
4. Branch on the chosen literal: if the literal is existential, then an *OR node* is explored (line 8), otherwise an *AND node* is explored (line 10).

Consider the quadruple $\langle Q, \Phi, \Psi, \Theta \rangle$. In the following we say that a literal l is:

- *open* if $|l|$ is in Q, and *assigned* otherwise;
- *unit* if there exists a clause $c \in \Phi \cup \Psi$ (resp. a term $t \in \Theta$) such that l is the only existential in c (resp. universal in t) and there is no universal (resp. existential) literal $l' \in c$ (resp. $l' \in t$) such that the level of $|l'|$ is greater than the level of $|l|$.

Now consider the simplification routine SIMPLIFY in Figure 2: $\{l\}_\exists$ (resp. $\{l\}_\forall$) denotes a constraint which is unit in l, and REMOVE(Q,z_i) returns the prefix obtained from Q by removing $Q_i z_i$. The function SIMPLIFY has the task of finding and assigning all unit literals at every node of the search tree. SIMPLIFY loops until either $\Phi \cup \Psi$ or Θ contain a unit literal (line 11). Each unit literal l is added to the current assignment (line 12), removed from Q (line 13), and then it is assigned by:

- removing all the clauses (resp. terms) to which l (resp. $\bar{l}$) pertains (lines 14-18), and
- removing $\bar{l}$ (resp. l) from all the clauses (resp. terms) to which $\bar{l}$ (resp. l) pertains (lines 19-24).

We say that an assigned literal l (i) *eliminates* a clause (resp. a term) when l (resp. $\bar{l}$) is in the constraint, and (ii) *simplifies* a clause (resp. a term) when $\bar{l}$ (resp. l) is in the constraint.

2.2 Learning in QBF

The algorithm presented in Figure 2 uses standard chronological backtracking (CB) to visit an implicit AND-OR search tree induced by the input QBF. The main problem with CB is that it may lead to the fruitless exploration of possibly large subtrees where all the leaves are either conflicts (in the case of subtrees rooted at OR nodes) or solutions (in the case of subtrees rooted at AND nodes). This is indeed the case when the conflicts/solutions are caused by some choices done way up in the search tree. Learning, as introduced for QBFs by [2], improves on CB by recording the information which is unveiled during the search, so that it can be reused later to avoid useless exploration of the search space. Adding a learning mechanism to the basic algorithm of Figure 2 amounts to:

- storing in Ψ the clauses corresponding to the *nogoods* determined while backtracking from a contradiction, and
- storing in Θ the terms corresponding to the *goods* determined while backtracking from a solution

in such a way that the EQBF invariants (1) and (2) introduced in Section 2.1 are fulfilled.

In the following, we call *left branch* the first branch explored in a node, and *right branch* the second branch which is possibly explored. Learning is implemented by associating a *reason* to each assignment resulting from a deduction, be it a unit, or a right branch. Assignments resulting from a choice, i.e., left branches, do not have a corresponding reason. The reason of a unit literal is simply a constraint where the literal is unit, and the reason of a right branch is calculated by the learning process as sketched in the following. Each time a contradiction is found, an empty clause c is in $\Phi \cup \Psi$, and it can be used as (initial) *working reason*. While backtracking from a conflict on an existential literal l:

- if $\bar{l}$ is not in the working reason, then l is not responsible for the current conflict and it can be skipped;
- if $\bar{l}$ is in the working reason and l is a unit or a right branch, then a new working reason is obtained by resolving the reason of l with the old working reason;
- if $\bar{l}$ is in the working reason and l is a left branch, then the current working reason is the reason of the right branch on $\bar{l}$.

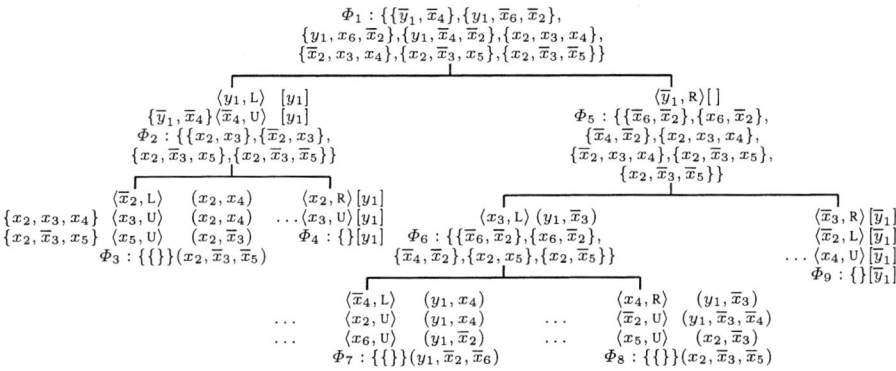

Fig. 3. Search tree of a QBF solver with learning. The prefix is $\forall y_1 \exists x_2 \exists x_3 \exists x_4 \exists x_5 \exists x_6$.

Learning works almost symmetrically for solutions and universal literals, except that the initial working reasons are computed differently. Notice that the procedure outlined above is just a sketch (see [2, 6, 7] for more details). For our purposes, it is sufficient to say that the working reasons are exactly the clauses (resp. the terms) that correspond to nogoods (resp. goods) and that can be stored in Ψ (resp. Θ).

Now consider the following QBF:

$$\forall y_1 \exists x_2 \exists x_3 \exists x_4 \exists x_5 \exists x_6 \{\ \{\overline{y}_1, \overline{x}_4\}, \{y_1, \overline{x}_6, \overline{x}_2\}, \{y_1, x_6, \overline{x}_2\}, \{y_1, \overline{x}_4, \overline{x}_2\},$$
$$\{x_2, x_3, x_4\}, \{\overline{x}_2, x_3, x_4\}, \{x_2, \overline{x}_3, x_5\}, \{x_2, \overline{x}_3, \overline{x}_5\}\ \} \quad (4)$$

In Figure 3 we present a search tree induced by (4) and possibly explored by the QBF solver shown in Figure 2 augmented with learning as described above. In the Figure:

- Φ_1 is the matrix of the input instance (4), and for each $i > 1$, Φ_i is the matrix of (4) after the assignments performed along the path to that node; the numbering of the Φ_i's reflects the depth-first nature of the exploration and we abuse notation by speaking of "node Φ_i" to refer to the node where Φ_i is the result of the applied simplifications.
- Each bifurcation in the search tree corresponds to a node, and the branching literal is indicated immediately below the bifurcation; we tag with "L" the left branch, and with "R" the right branch (the reasons of right branches are not indicated).
- Each unit literal is tagged with "U", and the corresponding reason is indicated at its left, e.g., $\{\overline{y}_1, \overline{x}_4\}$ is the reason of $\overline{x}_4$ at node Φ_2.
- the working reasons computed for conflicts (resp. solutions) during backtracking are indicated at the right of each assignment enclosed by "(" and ")" (resp. "[" and "]"), e.g., $(x_2, \overline{x}_3, \overline{x}_5)$ is the initial working reason of the conflict at node Φ_3, and $[y_1]$ is the initial working reason of the solution at node Φ_4.
- Finally, "..." indicate information that we omitted for the sake of compactness.

The search represented in Figure 3 proceeds as follows. Branching left on y_1 causes $\overline{x}_4$ to be propagated as unit and Φ_1 is simplified into Φ_2. Then, branching on $\overline{x}_2$ causes x_3

and x_5 to be propagated as unit and a contradiction to be found (Φ_3 contains an empty clause). The initial working reason $r_1 = (x_2, \overline{x}_3, \overline{x}_5)$ is the clause that became empty in Φ_3. Resolving r_1 with the reason of x_5 we obtain $r_2 = (x_2, \overline{x}_3)$. Backtracking stops at the left branch $\overline{x}_2$, since x_2 is in the working reason at that point, and we must branch right on x_2 with reason (x_2, x_4). This time a solution is found (Φ_4 is the empty set), and the corresponding working reason $[y_1]$ is calculated. Backtracking now goes up to the left branch on y_1 and the search continues by branching right on $\overline{y}_1$ with reason $[y_1]$, and so on. Notice that right branches can be propagated as unit literals, as long as their reasons are learned. Notice also that the unit on x_2 at node Φ_7, rests on the assumption that the reason of x_2 computed while backtracking from node Φ_3 has been learned.

3 Monotone Literals and Learning: Issues

As we have seen in section 1, MLF turns out to be a very effective pruning technique for QBF solvers. The introduction of MLF in QBF is due to Cadoli et al. [1]. Following their terminology, given a QBF φ a literal l is *monotone* (or *pure*) if $\overline{l}$ does not appear in the matrix of φ. In the presence of learning, the input instance is augmented by the constraints stored while backtracking, so our first question is:

Question 1. What is the definition of pure literal in the presence of learned constraints?

The straightforward answer is the following

Definition 1. *Given an EQBF $\varphi = Q_1 z_1 \ldots Q_n z_n \langle \Psi, \Phi, \Theta \rangle$, a literal l is monotone in φ iff there is no constraint k such that $\overline{l} \in k$ and $k \in \Psi \cup \Phi \cup \Theta$.*

In theory, the argument is closed: detecting monotone literals in the presence of learned constraints amounts to considering the matrix Φ, as well as the learned constraints in Ψ and Θ. However, in practice, we are left with the problem of detecting monotone literals as soon as they arise. It turns out that monotone literal detection algorithms must keep track of the eliminated constraints, while this is unnecessary when unit literal propagation is the only lookahead technique. Indeed, the most efficient algorithms for unit propagation like, e.g., two/three literal watching [8], take into account simplifications only. Thus, introducing MLF is bound to increase the time needed to assign a literal l, and the increase is proportional to the number of constraints that contain l. Moreover, even using a lazy data structure to detect monotone literals like, e.g., clause watching [8], for each variable z in Φ we have to maintain an index to *all* the constraints that contain either z or its negation. Such an index must be (i) updated each time a new constraint is learned, (ii) scanned each time we must search for new constraints to watch, and (optionally) (iii) scanned each time we want to forget a learned constraint. Therefore, under the assumptions of Def. 1, even the best known algorithms for monotone literals detection suffer an overhead proportional to the cardinality of the set $\Phi \cup \Psi \cup \Theta$, which, in practice, tends to be substantially bigger than the cardinality of Φ (in theory it may become exponentially bigger).

Given the above considerations, a pragmatical approach would be to keep the original definition of monotone literals unchanged, i.e., use the following

Definition 2. *Given an EQBF $\varphi = Q_1 z_1 \ldots Q_n z_n \langle \Psi, \Phi, \Theta \rangle$, a literal l is monotone in φ iff there is no constraint k such that $\bar{l} \in k$ and $k \in \Phi$.*

According to this definition, the impact of Ψ and Θ growth is not an issue anymore. The correctness of Def. 2 follows from the fact that Ψ and Θ can be safely discarded without altering the satisfiability of the input QBF or the correctness of the solver. This alternative definition brings us to the second question:

Question 2. Are Def. 1 and Def. 2 equivalent, i.e., do they result in exactly the same sets of monotone literals?

If the answer was positive, then we could rely on Def. 2 for an efficient implementation of monotone literals detection, and we would have an easy integration with learning: if an existential (resp. universal) literal is monotone according to Def. 1, it is always possible to compute the working reason wr of a conflict (resp. solution) in order to avoid $\bar{l} \in wr$ as reported, e.g., in [5][1]. Unfortunately, the answer is negative, as a brief tour of the example in Figure 3 can clarify. Looking at Figure 3, we can see that at node Φ_7, the literal $\bar{x}_4$ is assigned as left branch. According to Def. 2, $\bar{x}_4$ is a monotone literal since there is no constraint in Φ_6 containing x_4. Assuming that all the working reasons are to be learned, the clause (x_2, x_4) has been added to Ψ while backtracking on $\bar{x}_2$ in the leftmost path of the search tree. Therefore, according to Def. 1, $\bar{x}_4$ is not monotone since there is a constraint in $\Phi_6 \cup \Psi_6$ which contains x_4.

Even if Def. 2 captures a different set of monotone literals, still it might be the case that using it does not produce undesired effects, i.e., that the following question admits a positive answer:

Question 3. Is it possible that a working reason obtained from a conflict (resp. a solution) contains a monotone existential (resp. universal) literal detected according to Def. 2?

Notice that the converse situation, i.e., monotone existential (resp. universal) literals appearing in the working reasons obtained from solutions (resp. conflicts) is not an issue, but the normal and expected behavior of the algorithm. Looking at Figure 3 we can see that the answer to our last question is positive. Indeed, if we are to consider x_4 as monotone at node Φ_6, we see that the working reason obtained from the contradiction found at node Φ_7 contains x_4. Notice that the "simple" solutions of discarding x_4 from the working reason (y_1, x_4), is bound to fail: the resulting reason would be (y_1), and it would cause the solver to incorrectly report that (4) is unsatisfiable. As we explain in the next section, computing a suitable reason for $\bar{x}_4$ would involve extra time and more subtle issues that we discuss in some detail. Summing up, we have established that Def. 1 and Def. 2 result in different sets of monotone literals, so they cannot be used indistinctly. In particular, while Def. 2 makes the detection of monotone literals more efficient in the presence of learned constraints, it also introduces complications in the learning algorithm which cannot be easily dismissed.

---

[1] Notice that this property would be preserved even if we considered monotone an existential (resp. universal) literal l when there is no constraint k in $\Phi \cup \Psi$ (resp. $\Phi \cup \Theta$) such that $\bar{l} \in k$; although less restrictive than Def. 1, this alternative characterization of monotone literals has exactly the same drawbacks.

4 Monotone Literals and Learning: Solutions

As discussed in the previous section, if we assume an efficient implementation of monotone literals detection according to Def. 2, we are left with the problem that an existential (resp. universal) monotone literal may appear in the working reason obtained from a conflict (resp. a solution), and there is no easy way to get rid of it. In the following we call these monotone literals *spurious*. If we want to keep Def. 2, then we have two possible solutions: (i) compute reasons for spurious monotone literals, or (ii) forbid simplifications caused by monotone literals in learned constraints. The first solution works *a posteriori*: we let spurious monotone literals arise in the working reason, and then we take care of them. The second one works *a priori*: we prevent spurious literals from appearing in the working reasons. Each solution has its own advantages and disadvantages, which are discussed in the next two subsections. We anticipate that the second solution is the one of our choice, because of its simplicity of implementation combined with its effectiveness.

4.1 Computing Reasons for Monotone Literals

As we have seen in Section 2.2 every deduction in a search algorithm with learning must be supported by a reason, either readily available (as in the case of unit literals), or computed by the learning algorithm (as in the case of right branches). Monotone literals share some similarities with unit literals: they can be propagated as soon as they are detected regardless of their level, and they are the result of a deduction, as opposed to branching literals which result from a choice and must be assigned following the prefix order. However, while the reason of a unit literal can be localized in the constraints that force the literal to be unit, monotone literals are deduced by considering the input instance as a whole. More precisely, a literal l is monotone when all the constraints where $\bar{l}$ occurs are eliminated from at least another literal assigned before l. For instance, looking at Φ_1 in Figure 3, we see that x_4 occurs in $\{x_2, x_3, x_4\}$ and $\{\bar{x}_2, x_3, x_4\}$: whenever x_3 is assigned, both clauses are eliminated and $\bar{x}_4$ becomes monotone, i.e., given Φ_1, once we assign x_3, $\bar{x}_4$ can be assigned as monotone. In this example, a natural choice for the reason of $\bar{x}_4$ to be assigned as monotone at node Φ_6 would be exactly $r = \{\bar{x}_3, \bar{x}_4\}$. However, r cannot be obtained by applying resolution to some of the constraints in Φ_1. Intuitively, adding r to the set of constraints under consideration reduces the set of assignments S satisfying the input formula, but it does not alter the satisfiability of the input QBF. More precisely, let φ be a QBF in CNF, $S = \{l_1, l_2, \ldots, l_n\}$ ($n \geq 0$) be a set of literals, and φ_S be the QBF obtained from φ by assigning the literals in S and then performing unit propagation. The following property holds:

Proposition 3. *Given a QBF φ in CNF, and an existential literal l in φ, let S be a set of literals such that the level of each literal in S is greater than or equal to the level of l. If l is monotone in φ_S, then φ is equivalent to the QBF obtained by adding $(\vee_{l' \in S} \bar{l'} \vee l)$ to the matrix Φ of φ.*

In the hypotheses of the proposition, we can add a new constraint (r in our example) which does not change the satisfiability of the input QBF (and thus of the EQBFs computed during the search), and which enables l (x_4 in our example) to be assigned as a unit literal. Proposition 3 is general enough: during the search, if S is the current assignment, and l is a monotone existential literal, then we can always reconstruct a set S' satisfying the hypotheses of Proposition 3 by

1. considering the set $S' = \{l' \mid l' \in c \cap S, \bar{l} \in c, c \in \Phi\}$. S' contains at least one literal (eliminating the clause) for each clause $c \in \Phi$ with $\bar{l} \in c$.
2. If the level of each literal in S' is greater than the level of l, we are done.
3. Otherwise, let l' one literal in S' with level smaller than the level of l. Then, l' has been assigned as a unit with a reason r. Assign $(S' \setminus \{l'\}) \cup (\{l'' \mid \overline{l''} \in r\} \setminus \{\overline{l'}\})$ to S' and go to step 2.

The procedure is guaranteed to terminate: Indeed, all the branching literals in S have a level greater or equal to the level of l.

In Proposition 3, the assumption that φ is in CNF allows us to define φ_S easily, but it is not essential: if φ is not in CNF, then the clause can be added conjunctively to its matrix. If φ is in CNF, then the clause can be added to the matrix in a seemingly straightforward way. However, this solution has some drawbacks. First, exponentially many monotone existential literals can be detected during the search, and each one may cause the addition of a new clause to Φ with a resulting blow up in space: in such a situation, even restricting monotone literal detection to Φ might cause a substantial increase in the search time. Second, since the reason of a monotone literal l is not readily available, for each spurious monotone literal we should also pay the overhead associated to the computation of its reason.

Things become practically unfeasible when considering universal monotone literals. For these literals, we can state the following proposition, in which we assume that φ_S is defined analogously to the above.

Proposition 4. *Given a QBF φ in DNF, and a universal literal l in φ, let S be a set of literals such that the level of each literal in S is greater than or equal to the level of l. If l is monotone in φ_S, then φ is equivalent to the QBF obtained by adding $(\wedge_{l' \in S} l' \wedge l)$ to its set of terms.*

As before, the assumption that φ is in DNF is not essential. The proposition can be stated for an arbitrary QBF, and the term has to be added disjunctively to its matrix. So far, it is obvious that the treatment of universal monotone literals outlined in this section cannot be easily integrated in DLL-based QBF solvers. As we said in section 2, these solvers work with a CNF representation of the input instance, and this property is lost as soon as we start adding reasons for monotone universal literals. Absorbing the impact of this structural change would involve a complete redesign of the algorithms to deal with non-CNF QBF instances. If the input QBF is in DNF, a symmetrical argument applies to the computation of reasons for monotone existential literals.

4.2 Avoiding Simplifications on Monotone Literals

In the following, we describe how to use Def. 2 for the detection of monotone literals and, at the same time, to avoid the intricacies outlined in the previous subsection. The basic idea is to prevent spurious monotone literals from appearing in the working

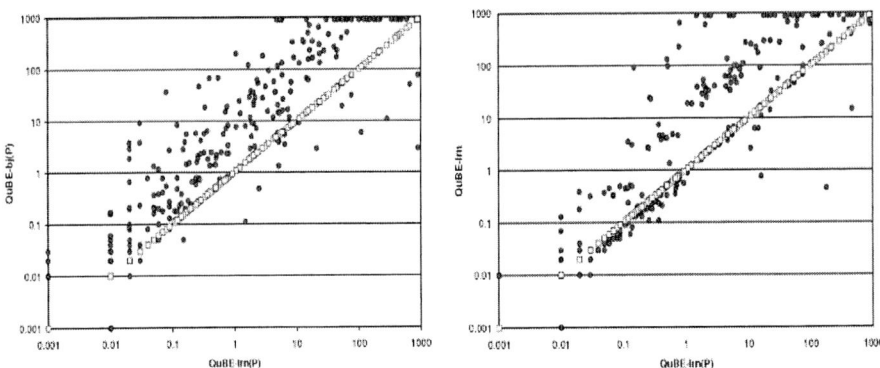

Fig. 4. Effectiveness of MLF in a QBF solver with learning.

reason by skipping the simplifications which involve a monotone literal and a learned constraint. Indeed, the reason why Def. 2 causes spurious monotone literals is that it conveniently disregards the learned constraints in the *detection* phase. Pushing this philosophy further, we can solve the problem by (partially) disregarding learned constraints also during the *propagation* phase. The major (and only) drawback of this approach is that we impact negatively on the effectiveness of learning by preventing some pruning to occur. However, this seems a small price to pay when compared to the implications of computing reasons for spurious monotone literals.

To see that the above solution is indeed effective, assume that an existential (resp. universal) literal l is monotone according to Def. 2, i.e., there is no constraint k in Φ such that $\bar{l} \in k$, but l is not monotone according to Def. 1, i.e., there is at least a clause c in Ψ (resp. a term t in Θ) such that $\bar{l} \in c$ (resp. $\bar{l} \in t$). Let l be an existential literal. If we simplify c when assigning l then, if all the remaining literals of c are simplified, a contradiction is found, and the corresponding working reason will contain l as a spurious monotone literal. If we disregard c when assigning l then c will never be a conflict even if all its remaining literals are simplified, so the working reason wr of a possible conflict can be calculated with $l \notin wr$. Analogously, let l be a universal literal. If we simplify t when assigning $\bar{l}$ then, if all the remaining literals of t are simplified, a solution is found, and the corresponding working reason will contain $\bar{l}$ as a spurious monotone literal. As before, disregarding t when assigning $\bar{l}$ solves the issue. The approach is sound since it is equivalent to temporarily forgetting the learned constraints, and we know from Section 2.2 that this can be done without affecting the correctness of the procedure.

5 Experimental Analysis

As shown in Section 1, both MLF and learning can separately improve the performances of a QBF solver. The question that we address in the following is whether our solution of choice for the integration of MLF with learning is effective, and, in particular, if a QBF solver with MLF and learning can be more effective than the same solver without one of the two optimizations. To answer this question, we consider the systems

Table 1. QUBE-LRN(P), QUBE-LRN, and ZCHAFF performances on FPGA routing instances.

test	ZCHAFF	QUBE-LRN	QUBE-LRN(P)	test	ZCHAFF	QUBE-LRN	QUBE-LRN(P)
bart10	34881	31295	144	bart20	–	–	270
bart11	1399736	2145767	162	bart21	–	–	293
bart12	3993454	–	180	bart22	–	–	288
bart13	176	176	176	bart23	–	–	312
bart14	–	6241121	195	bart24	–	–	336
bart15	–	–	215	bart25	–	–	378
bart16	–	–	210	bart27	–	–	432
bart17	–	–	231	bart26	–	–	405
bart18	–	–	252	bart28	–	–	514
bart19	–	–	248	bart29	–	–	466

QUBE-BJ(P) and QUBE-LRN described in Section 1, and the system QUBE-LRN(P), a version of QUBE that integrates MLF and learning using the techniques described in Section 4.2. Since QUBE is designed with the purpose of being effective on real-world instances, our experiments use the same set of 450 verification and planning benchmarks that constituted part of the 2003 QBF evaluation [3]: 25% of these instances are from verification problems [9, 10], and the remaining are from planning domains [11, 12]. All the experiments where run on a farm of PCs, each one equipped with a PIV 2.4GHz processor, 1GB of RAM, and running Linux RedHat 7.2. For practical reasons, the time limit for each benchmark is set to 900s.

The results of our experiments are reported in the plots of Figure 4. In the plots, each solid-fill dot represents an instance, QUBE-LRN(P) solving time is on the x-axis (seconds, log scale), QUBE-BJ(P) (Figure 4 left), QUBE-LRN (Figure 4 right) solving times are on the y-axes (seconds, log scale). The diagonal (outlined boxes) represents the solving time of QUBE-LRN(P) against itself: similarly to the plots of Figure 1 described in Section 1, the relative position of the solid-fill and the outlined dots gives us an instance-wise comparison between QUBE-LRN(P) and its siblings. The plots of Figure 4 show that, all other things being equal, QUBE-LRN(P) substantially outperforms both QUBE-BJ(P) and QUBE-LRN. Focusing on QUBE-LRN(P) vs. QUBE-BJ(P), we see that both solvers exceed the time limit on 74 instances. On the remaining 376, QUBE-LRN(P) is as fast as, or faster than QUBE-BJ(P) on 345 instances, and it is at least one order of magnitude faster than QUBE-BJ(P) on 79 problems (the converse is true on 10 problems only). These numbers witness that adding MLF does not impact on the performance gap between backjumping and learning. Focusing on QUBE-LRN(P) vs. QUBE-LRN, we see that both solvers exceed the time limit on 75 instances. On the remaining 375, QUBE-LRN(P) is as fast as, or faster than QUBE-LRN on 260 instances, and it is at least one order of magnitude faster than QUBE-LRN on 66 problems (the converse is true on 17 problems only). Therefore, using the techniques described in Section 4.2 we have managed to exploit the pruning power of MLF, without incurring into the possible inefficiencies due to learning. Overall, QUBE-LRN(P) is the best among the four versions of QUBE that we analyzed in our experiments.

In Table 1 we present some of the results obtained running QUBE on a collection of challenging real-world SAT instances described in [13]. The original motivation for this experiment was to assess the performances of QUBE with respect to state-of-the-art SAT solvers. While selecting the solvers to compare with QUBE, we observed that many of the recent ones (e.g., ZCHAFF [14], and BERKMIN [15]) implement some kind of learning mechanism, but most of them do not implement MLF. The reason of this, apart from the intricacies that we have explored in this paper, can also be traced back to the common belief that MLF is not an effective technique in SAT. In the words of Freeman [16]: "... [MLF] only helps for a few classes of SAT problems, and even when it does help, it does not result in a substantial reduction in search tree size.". Indeed, a comparative analysis between QUBE-LRN(P) and QUBE-LRN on our SAT test set, reveals that the overall performances of QUBE-LRN are better than those of QUBE-LRN(P). However, the results on the subset comprised of the "bart"[2] FPGA routing instances reported in Table 1, witness that MLF, combined with learning and an efficient implementation, can dramatically improve the performances also in SAT. Each line of the table reports the label of the instance (first column), the number of *tries*, i.e., the total number of assignments, performed by ZCHAFF (second column), and our solvers QUBE-LRN (third column) and QUBE-LRN(P) (fourth column). We used tries instead of CPU times in order to give a precise account about the size of the search space explored by the solvers. The dash "–" indicates that the number of tries could not be assessed because the solver exceeded the CPU time limit of 20 minutes. As we can see from Table 1, with the only exception of "bart13", the search space of QUBE-LRN(P) is substantially smaller than that of QUBE-LRN and ZCHAFF, and, on most instances, the performance gap is at least three orders of magnitude. We conjecture that the reason of such an improvement lies in the favorable interaction between MLF and the specific CNF conversion used by the authors of the benchmarks series. We are currently investigating the relationships of this result with some recent advancements in non-CNF SAT (see, e.g., [17])

6 Conclusions and Related Work

We have considered the problem of the efficient implementation of MLF in a QBF solver with learning. As we have seen, various solutions are possible, and we discussed the advantages and the disadvantages of each one. Implementing our solution of choice in our state-of-the-art solver QUBE produces positive effects on its performances.

About the related work, MLF has been first defined for QBFs in [18], and since then it has been considered also by many other authors (see, e.g., [5, 19, 2]. Some of these works present also learning schemes (see also [20]), but none of them discusses in any detail whether MLF has been integrated in the corresponding QBF solver, how, and the problems faced in practice.

References

1. M. Cadoli, M. Schaerf, A. Giovanardi, and M. Giovanardi. An algorithm to evaluate quantified boolean formulae and its experimental evaluation. *Journal of Automated Reasoning*, 28(2):101–142, 2002.

---

[2] This is the original nickname given to the instances when they appeared for the first time in the context of the 2002 SAT solvers competition.

2. E. Giunchiglia, M. Narizzano, and A. Tacchella. Learning for Quantified Boolean Logic Satisfiability. In *18th National Conference on Artificial Intelligence (AAAI 2002)*. AAAI Press/MIT Press, 2002.
3. D. Le Berre, L. Simon, and A. Tacchella. Challenges in the QBF arena: the SAT'03 evaluation of QBF solvers. In *Sixth International Conference on Theory and Applications of Satisfiability Testing (SAT 2003)*, volume 2919 of *Lecture Notes in Computer Science*. Springer Verlag, 2003.
4. E. Giunchiglia, M. Narizzano, and A. Tacchella. QuBE: A system for deciding Quantified Boolean Formulas satisfiability. In *First International Joint Conference on Automated Reasoning (IJCAR 2001)*, volume 2083 of *Lecture Notes in Artificial Intelligence*. Springer Verlag, 2001.
5. E. Giunchiglia, M. Narizzano, and A. Tacchella. Backjumping for Quantified Boolean Logic Satisfiability. In *Seventeenth International Joint Conference on Artificial Intelligence (IJCAI 2001)*. Morgan Kaufmann, 2001.
6. E. Giunchiglia, M. Narizzano, and A. Tacchella. Backjumping for Quantified Boolean Logic satisfiability. *Artificial Intelligence*, 145:99–120, 2003.
7. E. Giunchiglia, M. Narizzano, and A. Tacchella. QBF reasoning on real-world instances. In *7th International Conference on Theory and Applications of Satisfiability Testing (SAT 2004)*, 2004. Accepted, final version pending.
8. I.P. Gent, E. Giunchiglia, M. Narizzano, A. Rowley, and A. Tacchella. Watched Data Structures for QBF Solvers. In *Sixth International Conference on Theory and Applications of Satisfiability Testing (SAT 2003)*, volume 2919 of *Lecture Notes in Computer Science*. Springer Verlag, 2003.
9. C. Scholl and B. Becker. Checking equivalence for partial implementations. In *38th Design Automation Conference (DAC'01)*, 2001.
10. Abdelwaheb Ayari and David Basin. Bounded model construction for monadic second-order logics. In *12th International Conference on Computer-Aided Verification (CAV'00)*, number 1855 in LNCS, pages 99–113. Springer-Verlag, 2000.
11. J. Rintanen. Constructing conditional plans by a theorem prover. *Journal of Artificial Intelligence Research*, 10:323–352, 1999.
12. C. Castellini, E. Giunchiglia, and A. Tacchella. Sat-based planning in complex domains: Concurrency, constraints and nondeterminism. *Artificial Intelligence*, 147(1):85–117, 2003.
13. E. Giunchiglia, M. Maratea, and A. Tacchella. (In)Effectiveness of Look-Ahead Techniques in a Modern SAT Solver. In *9th Conference on Principles and Practice of Constraint Programming (CP 2003)*, volume 2833 of *Lecture Notes in Computer Science*. Springer Verlag, 2003.
14. M. W. Moskewicz, C. F. Madigan, Y. Zhao, L. Zhang, and S. Malik. Chaff: Engineering an efficient SAT solver. In *Proceedings of the 38th Design Automation Conference (DAC'01)*, pages 530–535, 2001.
15. E. Goldberg and Y. Novikov. BerkMin: A fast and robust SAT-solver. In *Design, Automation, and Test in Europe (DATE '02)*, pages 142–149, March 2002.
16. J. W. Freeman. *Improvements to propositional satisfiability search algorithms*. PhD thesis, University of Pennsylvania, 1995.
17. A. Kuehlmann, M. K. Ganai, V. Paruthi. Circuit-based Boolean Reasoning. In *38th Design Automation Conference*, 2001.
18. M. Cadoli, M. Schaerf, A. Giovanardi, and M. Giovanardi. An Algorithm to Evaluate Quantified Boolean Formulae and its Experimental Evaluation. In *Highlights of Satisfiability Research in the Year 2000*. IOS Press, 2000.
19. R. Letz. Lemma and model caching in decision procedures for quantified boolean formulas. In *Proceedings of Tableaux 2002*, LNAI 2381, pages 160–175. Springer, 2002.
20. L. Zhang and S. Malik. Conflict driven learning in a quantified boolean satisfiability solver. In *Proceedings of International Conference on Computer Aided Design (ICCAD'02)*, 2002.

Streamlined Constraint Reasoning*

Carla Gomes and Meinolf Sellmann

Cornell University
Department of Computer Science
4130 Upson Hall
Ithaca, NY 14853
{gomes,sello}@cs.cornell.edu

Abstract. We introduce a new approach for focusing constraint reasoning using so-called *streamlining constraints*. Such constraints partition the solution space to drive the search first towards a small and structured combinatorial subspace. The streamlining constraints capture regularities observed in a subset of the solutions to smaller problem instances. We demonstrate the effectiveness of our approach by solving a number of hard combinatorial design problems. Our experiments show that streamlining scales significantly beyond previous approaches.

Keywords: constraint reasoning, search, branching strategies

1 Introduction

In recent years there has been tremendous progress in the design of ever more efficient constraint-based reasoning methods. Backtrack search, the underlying solution method of complete solvers, has been enhanced with a range of techniques. Current state-of-the-art complete solvers use a combination of strong search heuristics, highly specialized constraint propagators, symmetry breaking strategies, non-chronological backtracking, nogood learning, and randomization and restarts.

In this paper, we propose a novel reasoning strategy based on *streamlining constraints*. This work has been inspired by our desire to solve very hard problems from combinatorial design. Combinatorial design is a large and active research area where one studies combinatorial objects with a series of sophisticated global properties [5]. For many combinatorial design problems it is not known whether the combinatorial objects under consideration even exist. As a concrete example, we have been studying an application in statistical experimental design. The application involves the design of experiments in such a way that the outcomes are minimally correlated. Mathematically, the task can be formulated as the problem of generating totally spatially balanced Latin squares. To give the reader a feel for the intricacy of the global constraints of this problem, we first give a brief description.

---
* This work was supported in part by the Intelligent Information Systems Institute, Cornell University (AFOSR grant F49620-01-1-0076).

A Latin square of order N is an N by N matrix, where each cell has one of N symbols, such that each symbol occurs exactly once in each row and column. (Each symbol corresponds to a "treatment" in experimental design.) In a given row, we define the distance between two symbols by the difference between the column indices of the cells in which the symbols occur. Note that each symbol occurs exactly once in each row. So, in a given row, all possible pairs of symbols occur, and for each pair of symbols, we have a well-defined distance between the symbols. For each pair of symbols, we define the total distance over the Latin square as the sum of the distances between the symbols over all rows. A totally spatially balanced Latin square is now defined as a Latin square in which all pairs of symbols have the same total distance [9]. Given the complexity of the total balancing constraint, finding spatially balanced Latin squares is computationally very hard, and, in fact, the very existence of spatially-balanced Latin squares for all but the smallest values of N is an open question in combinatorics.

We performed a series of experiments with both a highly tailored local search method and a state-of-the-art constraint programming approach (ILOG implementation using AllDiff constraints, symmetry breaking, randomization, restarts, and other enhancements). Both our local search method and our CSP-based method could find solutions only up to size $N = 9$. Using the approach introduced in this paper, called streamlining, we can solve considerably larger instances, namely up to size $N = 18$. This is a significant advance given the size of the search space and the complexity of the constraints. To the best of our knowledge, no other method can solve instances of this size.

We will discuss a similar advance in terms of generating diagonally ordered Magic Squares [11,18]. A Magic Square of order N is an N by N matrix with entries from 1 to N^2, such that the sum of the entries in each column, row, and the main diagonals is the same. In a diagonally ordered Magic Square the entries on the main diagonals are strictly ordered. By using streamlined constraints, we could boost the performance of a CSP-based method from $N = 8$ to order $N = 19$. Again, we do not know of any other CSP approach that can handle instances of this size. It is worth noting though, that local search approaches perform very well for the magic square problem [4].

The key idea underlying "streamlining constraints" is to dramatically boost the effectiveness of the propagation mechanisms. In the standard use of propagation methods there is a hard limit placed on their effectiveness because it is required that no feasible solutions are eliminated during propagation: Streamlining is a somewhat radical departure from this idea, since we explicitly partition the solution and search space into sections with different global properties. For example, in searching for totally balanced Latin squares, one can start by searching for solutions that are symmetric. We will extend this idea much further by introducing a range of more sophisticated streamlining properties – such as composability – that are well-aligned with our propagation mechanisms, and allow us to scale up solutions dramatically.

Our approach was inspired by the observations that for certain combinatorial design problems there are constructive methods for generating a solution. Such solutions contain an incredible amount of structure[1]. Our conjecture is that for many other intricate combinatorial problems – if solutions exists – there will often also be highly regular ones. Of course, we do not know the full details of the regularities in advance. The properties we introduce using the streamlining constraints capture regularities at a high-level. In effect, search and propagation is used to fill in the remaining necessary detail.

By imposing additional structural properties in advance we are steering the search first towards a small and highly structured area of the search space. Since our streamlining constraints express properties consistent with solutions of smaller problem instances, we expect these subspaces to still contain solutions. Moreover, by selecting properties that match well with advanced propagation techniques, while allowing for compact representations, our propagation becomes much more effective with the added constraints. In fact, there appears to be a clear limit to the effectiveness of constraint propagation when one insists on maintaining all solutions. The reason for this is that the set of all solutions of a combinatorial problem often does not have a compact representation, neither in theory nor in practice. For example, in the area of Boolean satisfiability testing, it has been found that binary decision diagrams (BDDs), which, in effect, provide an encoding of all satisfying assignments, often grow exponentially large even on moderate size problem instances. So, there may be a hard practical limit on the effectiveness of constraint propagation methods, if one insists on maintaining the full solution set. Streamlining constraints provide an effective mechanism to circumvent this problem.

The paper is organized as follows: In the next section, we introduce the idea of streamlining constraints. In section 3, we present our streamlining results for the diagonally ordered magic squares. In section 4, we discuss a streamlining approach for totally spatially balanced Latin squares. Finally, we conclude in Section 5.

2 Streamlining

In *streamlining*, we partition the search space of a problem P into disjoint sub-problems with respect to a specific set ($\mathcal{S}$) of solution properties that are computationally interesting: Sub-problem P_1 that corresponds to problem P with the additional constraint that $\mathcal{S}$ holds; and sub-problem P_2, the complement of the sub-problem P_1, with respect to the property $\mathcal{S}$. Since the addition of the constraints enforcing S shapes the problem in a favorable way, we name them

---

[1] Note that such constructions are far from "straightforward". For example, the great Euler extensively studied Latin squares and considered a special case, so-called orthogonal Latin squares (OLS). He conjectured that there did not exist solution for orthogonal Latin squares for an infinite number of orders. It took more than a century until a construction for all orders (except 2 and 6 for which it was proven that no solution exists [14]) was developed [3]. Until today, for the mutually orthogonal Latin square problem (MOLS), which is a generalization of OLS, no construction is known – despite the valiant efforts undertaken by mathematicians in combinatorial design theory.

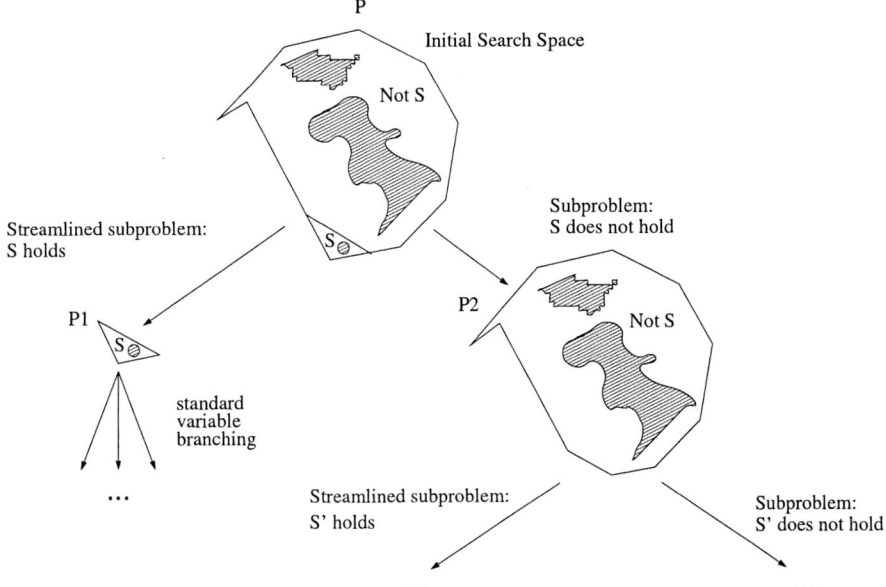

Fig. 1. Streamlining to focus the search on a small, structured part of the search space with hopefully high solution density.

streamlining constraints (or *streamliners*) and the resulting sub-problem P_1 the *streamlined sub-problem*. We can further streamline the resulting sub-problems by considering additional solution properties (see Fig.1).

In general, the search space for problem P_1 will be substantially smaller than that of its complement P_2. However, more importantly, we look for sub-spaces where our constraint propagation methods are highly effective.

Instead of a description in terms of a partitioning of the solution space, one can also describe the effect of streamlining constraints directly in terms of search. For backtrack search, streamlining constraints can be viewed as a strong branching mechanism, used at high levels of the search tree: Streamlining constraints steer the search toward portions of the search space for which streamlined properties hold. As a general global search algorithm, the process can be described as a tree search in which a node represents a portion of the search space and an arc represents the splitting of the search space by enforcing a given property. The top node of the tree represents the entire search space, containing all the solutions to the given problem instance. At the top level(s) of the search tree, we split the search space into sub-sets by enforcing streamlining constraints. For a given node, the branching based on a streamlining constraint originates two nodes: the left node, the first to be explored by the search procedure, corresponds to a streamlined sub-problem for which the streamlining constraint is enforced; the right node corresponds to the complement of the left node with respect to the parent node and the property enforced by the streamlining constraint. Once the search reaches a streamlined sub-problem, further branching decisions may be done based on additional streamlining constraints or using standard branching strategies. If the portion of the search space that corresponds to the streamlined sub-problem P_1 (resulting from enforcing property S) is searched exhaustively without finding a solution, backtracking occurs to the node that is the complement of the streamlined sub-problem, *i.e.*, P_2, for which property S does not hold.

The selection of streamlining constraints is based on the identification of properties of the solution space. Note that we can view redundant constraints as a particular case of streamlining constraints, in which the streamlining property considered holds for all the solutions. However, redundant constraints, while effective since they eliminate portions of the search space that do not contain any solution, are a very conservative example of streamlining constraint reasoning: they do not partition the solution space. In general, streamlining constraints do partition the solution space into disjoints subsets.

The goal of streamlined reasoning is to focus the search on a subspace that is relatively small, highly structured, and that has a good probability of containing a solution. In our current approach, we manually analyze the set of solutions of small problem instances and try to identify properties that hold for a good part of the solutions – without necessarily holding for all the solutions – but that will structure and reduce the remaining search space in this branch considerably. For example, in the case of the problem of generating totally balanced Latin squares, we observed that for instances of small orders, several of the solutions were highly symmetric. So, our streamlining constraint steers the search toward a region of symmetric totally balanced Latin squares. An exciting direction for future work is to develop statistical methods to automatically generate potential streamlining constraints from the solutions of small example instances.

In the selection of streamlining properties there are several tradeoffs to consider that emerge from the conflicting goals of increasing solution density, reducing the search space drastically, and enforcing a structure that can easily be checked: On the one hand, it would be desirable to select properties that hold for most of the solutions (or even for all the solutions, as in redundant constraints) to ensure that many solutions are in the streamlined subproblem. However, the aim to preserve a larger part of the solutions will usually conflict with the goal of structuring and significantly reducing the remaining search space. As we will see later in the paper, more aggressive streamlining strategies, based on selecting properties that hold only for a very small subset of solutions, can in fact be much more effective in steering the search toward a solution in a drastically reduced search space. Another aspect that is important to consider is how well a streamlining constraint propagates: good candidates for streamlining constraints should propagate easily. Finally, we consider the power of a streamlining constraints based on the compactness of the representation of the induced streamlined subproblem. For example, for the problem of totally balanced Latin squares, by choosing a very strong streamliner, we go from a representation that requires N^2 variables to a much more compact representation that requires only N variables.

3 Streamlining Diagonally Ordered Magic Squares

To provide a first illustration of our streamlining approach, we consider the problem of constructing a special class of magic squares. In the next section, we consider the more practically relevant, but also more complex, case of constructing spatially balanced Latin squares.

Definition 1. Diagonally Ordered Magic Squares (DOMS)
Given a natural number n, let us set $S = \frac{n(n^2+1)}{2}$.

- *A square $M = (m_{ij})_{1 \leq i,j \leq n}$ with n^2 pairwise disjoint entries $1 \leq m_{ij} \leq n^2$ is called a* magic square of order n *iff*
  1. *For all rows, the sum of all entries in that row adds up to S, i.e. $\sum_j m_{ij} = S$ for all $1 \leq i \leq n$.*
  2. *For all columns, the sum of all entries in that column adds up to S, i.e. $\sum_i m_{ij} = S$ for all $1 \leq j \leq n$.*
  3. *The sum of all entries in each of the two main diagonals adds up to S, i.e. $\sum_i m_{ii} = S$ and $\sum_i m_{n+1-i,i} = S$.*
- *A magic square is called* diagonally ordered *iff both main diagonals, when traversed from left to right, have strictly increasing values, i.e. $m_{ii} < m_{i+1,i+1}$ and $m_{n+1-i,i} < m_{n-i,i+1}$ for all $1 \leq i < n$.*
- *Given a natural number n, the* Diagonally Ordered Magic Squares Problem (DOMS) *consists in the construction of a diagonally ordered magic square.*

While there exist polynomial-time construction methods for standard magic squares, i.e. without the diagonality constraints, no such construction is know for DOMS. We start out by using a standard constraint programming model, similar to the one used [10]. For details, see the experimental section below. Our experiments show that even small instances are already quite difficult. In particular, we did not find any solutions for order nine or higher. By studying solutions of small order, we found that, for a large number of solutions, the largest entries $(n^2 - n, \ldots, n^2)$ and the smallest entries $(1, \ldots, n)$ are fairly evenly distributed over the square – which makes perfect sense, since one cannot have too many large or too many small numbers clustered together in one row or column (see Fig.2). The question arises: how could one formalize this observation?

(M)				(D)	(L)			
6	9	3	16	*	2	3	1	4
12	7	13	2	*	3	2	4	1
15	4	10	5	*	4	1	3	2
1	14	8	11	*	1	4	2	3

Fig. 2. Structure of solutions: Square M shows a typical diagonally ordered magic square of order 4. In D, we can see how the n largest numbers are distributed very nicely over the square. By associating symbol 1 with numbers $1, \ldots, 4$, symbol 2 with numbers $5, \ldots, 8$, symbol 3 with numbers $9, \ldots, 12$ and finally symbol 4 with numbers $13, \ldots, 16$, we get the square L. We observe: L is a Latin square!

Given a DOMS M of order n, let us define $L = (l_{ij})$ with $l_{ij} = \lfloor (m_{i,j} - 1)/n \rfloor + 1$. In effect, we associate the numbers $kn+1, \ldots, (k+1)n$ with symbol $k \in [1, \ldots, n]$. If no two numbers of any interval $[kn+1, \ldots, (k+1)n]$ occur in the same row or column of M, one can expect that the numbers are quite evenly distributed over the square, which is exactly what we need to do in a magic square[2]. And if this is the case, then L is a Latin square. Now, in order to boost our search, we use "Latin squareness" as a streamliner: By adding the corresponding constraints on the first level of our backtrack search, we focus on squares that are hiding a Latin square structure[3].

Although we observed Latin square structure in many solutions of diagonally ordered magic squares of small orders, it is of course not guaranteed that there exist such magic squares for all orders. However, given that the number of magic squares grows quite rapidly with the order, it appears likely that magic squares with hidden Latin square structure exist for all orders. Moreover, we also do not know in advance whether the additional constraints will actually facilitate the search for magic squares. However, as we will see below, our empirical results show that the constraints dramatically boost our ability to find higher order magic squares.

3.1 Experimental Results

For our base constraint programming model, we used an approach similar to the one described in [10]. Each entry of the square is represented by a variable taking values in $\{1, \ldots, n^2\}$. We add an All-Different constraint [12] on all variables and also add the sum-constraints and diagonal constraints as given by Definition 1. For the branching variable selection, we use a randomized min-domain strategy with restarts.

In the streamlined approach, we also need to provide a structure for the hidden Latin square structure. We add the usual variables and constraints, combined with a dual model defined by the column conjugate[4]. Channeling constraints between the Latin square structure and the magic square are of the form:

$$m_{ij} > (k-1)n \Leftrightarrow l_{ij} \geq k \quad \forall\, 1 \leq k \leq n$$
$$m_{ij} \leq kn \Leftrightarrow l_{ij} \leq k \quad \forall\, 1 \leq k \leq n$$

The Latin square streamliner comes with additional variables, so we have to take them into account in the subsequent tree search. In the branch of the tree where we impose the streamliner, we first assign the Latin square variables and only then search over the original variables. We follow a randomized min-domain strategy for both types of variables with restarts.

---

[2] Note that other, less balanced, solutions do exists. However, the whole idea of streamlining is to focus in on a well-structured subset of the solution space.

[3] Since these magic squares have such beautiful hidden structure, we informally call these *Dumbledore Squares*, in reference of the idea of hiding one magic item within another, as the Sorcerer's Stone in the Mirror of Erised [13].

[4] The notion of row conjugate is defined in our description of spatially balanced Latin squares (Section 4).

Table 1. Solution times in seconds for finding the first diagonally ordered Magic square using the pure and the streamlined CP approach (– means not solved after 10 hours).

order	3	4	5	6	7	8	9	10
pure	0.01	0.01	0.03	1.19	5.05	5391	–	–
streamlined	0.03	0.03	0.03	0.11	0.12	0.42	0.55	0.72

Table 2. Detailed results for higher order streamlined Magic squares. We give the CPU times in seconds that are required to find the first solution, the number of fails on the final restart, the total number of choice points, and the number of restarts.

order	11	12	13	14	15	16	17
time	37.67	112	140	3432	7419	28.6K	61K
last fails	1430	2380	5017	6879	8494	1162	11.6K
total cps	24K	47K	59K	726K	1.9M	4.2M	9.1M
restarts	5	9	10	106	222	399	663

Tables 1 and 2 summarize the results of our experimentation. All experiments in this paper were implemented using ILOG Solver 5.1 and the gnu g++ compiler version 2.91 and run on an Intel Pentium III 550 MHz CPU and 4.0 GB RAM.

Table 1 shows how the streamlining constraint leads to much smaller solution times compared to running on only the original set of constraints (two or more orders of magnitude speedup). We also solve a number instances that were out of reach before. Table 2 summarizes the statistics on those runs. We can see clearly that streamlining significantly boosts performance. Since it took a couple of days to compute them, we do not report details on our experiments with orders 18 and 19 here, but we still want to mention that we were able to compute Dumbledore Squares (i.e. diagonally ordered magic squares with a hidden Latin square structure) of those sizes.

4 Streamlining Spatially Balanced Experiment Design

We now discuss an example of streamlining on a combinatorial design problem of significantly higher practical value. In particular, we consider computing spatially balanced Latin squares. As mention in the introduction, these special Latin squares are used in the design of practical agronomics and other treatment experiments where it is important to minimize overall correlations.

Definition 2. [**Latin square and conjugates**] *Given a natural number* $n \in \mathbb{N}$, *a Latin square* L *on* n *symbols is an* $n \times n$ *matrix in which each of the* n *symbols occurs exactly once in each row and in each column. We denote each element of* L *by* l_{ij}, $i, j \in \{1, 2, \cdots, n\}$. n *is the order of the Latin square.*
[**Row (column) conjugate of a given Latin square**] *Given a Latin square* L *of order* n, *its row (column) conjugate* R *(C) is also a Latin square of order* n, *with symbols*, $1, 2, \cdots, n$. *Each element* r_{ij} (c_{ij}) *of* R *(C) corresponds to the row (column) index of* L *in which the symbol* j *occurs in column (row)* i.

[**Row distance of a pair of symbols**] *Given a Latin square L, the distance of a pair of symbols (k,l) in row i, denoted by $d_i(k,l)$, is the absolute difference of the column indices in which the symbols k and l appear in row i.*

[**Average distance of a pair of symbols in a Latin square**] *Given a Latin square L, the average distance of a pair of symbols (k,l) in L is $\bar{d}(k,l) = \sum_{i=1}^{n} d_i(k,l)/n$.*

It can be shown that for a given Latin square L of order $n \in \mathbb{N}$, the expected distance of any pair in any row is $\frac{n+1}{3}$ [16]. Therefore, a square is totally spatially balanced iff every pair of symbols $1 \leq k < l \leq n$ has an average distance $\bar{d}(k,l) = \frac{n+1}{3}$. (Note that in the introduction we slightly simplified our description by considering the total row distance for each pair without dividing by n, the number of rows.) We define:

Definition 3. [**Totally spatially balanced Latin square**] *Given a natural number $n \in \mathbb{N}$, a totally spatially balanced Latin square (TBLS) is a Latin square of order n in which $\bar{d}(k,l) = \frac{n+1}{3} \ \forall \ 1 \leq k < l \leq n$.*

Fig.3 provides an example illustrating our definitions. In [9] we developed two different approaches for TBLS, one based on local search, the other based on constraint programming. Neither of the two pure approaches is able to compute solutions for orders larger than 9, and only by using a specialized composition technique that works for orders that are multiples of 6, we were able to compute a solution for orders

(L)	(C)	(R)
1 2 3 4 5	1 2 3 4 5	1 5 4 3 2
5 1 2 3 4	2 3 4 5 1	2 1 5 4 3
4 5 1 2 3	3 4 5 1 2	3 2 1 5 4
3 4 5 1 2	4 5 1 2 3	4 3 2 1 5
2 3 4 5 1	5 1 2 3 4	5 4 3 2 1

Fig. 3. A Latin square L, its row conjugate R, and its column conjugate C. The distance of pair $(1,5)$ in row 1 is $d_1(1,5) = 4$, in row 2 it is $d_2(1,5) = 1$, and the average distance for this pair is $\bar{d}(1,5) = \frac{8}{5}$.

12 and 18. We will describe this technique in Section 4.3 as another example of streamlining.

When working on the CP approach, we first tried to use symmetry breaking by dominance detection (SBDD [6,7]) to avoid that equivalent search regions are investigated multiple times. We were surprised to find that a partially symmetry breaking initialization of the first row and the first column yielded far better computation times than our SBDD approach.

We investigated the matter by analyzing the solutions that are found after the initial setting of the first row and column. We found that most solutions exhibited a diagonal symmetry. That is, for a large number of solutions (around 50% when fixing the first column and row) it is the case that $l_{ij} = l_{ji}$. This gave rise to the idea to "streamline" our problem by adding the additional constraint that the solutions we look for should be diagonally symmetric, and then to analyze the set of solutions found in that manner again.

First, we observed that the computation time in the presence of the additional constraint went down considerably. When we then analyzed the newly found set of solutions, we found that all solutions computed were unique in the following sense: not a single pair of solutions to the diagonally symmetric TBLS was symmetric to one another. The question arises: Could we use this fact to streamline our search further?

4.1 Analyzing Solutions to Small TBLS Instances

Before we can formulate the streamlining constraints that evolved out of the observation that all observed solutions to the diagonally symmetric TBLS are unique, let us discuss the inherent symmetries of the problem.

Clearly, any permutation of the rows has no effect on the "Latin square-ness" nor does it affect the spatial balance of the square. The same holds when renaming the symbols. Thus, applying any combination of row and symbol permutations to a feasible solution yields a (possibly new) square that we call "symmetric" to the original one.

Now, by enforcing diagonal symmetry of the squares and initializing both the first row and the first column with $1, \ldots, n$, we found that all solutions computed were *self-symmetric*. (Note that this is an empirical observations based on small order instances.) With the term self-symmetric we denote those squares that are only symmetric to themselves when applying any combination of row and symbol permutations that preserves the initial setting of the first row and column. In some sense, one may want to think of these solutions as located on the "symmetry axis".

An example for a self-symmetric square is given in Figure 4. When we start with solution A and consider a permutation of the rows according to the given permutation ρ_1, we get solution B that is symmetric to A in the sense that B is totally balanced if and only if A is totally balanced. If we want to ensure that our solution preserves the pre-assignments in the first row and the first column, we need to apply unique permutations σ and ρ_2 of symbols and columns next. As a result of this operation, we get square D. For self-symmetric squares, we have that A=D, no matter how we choose the initial row permutation. Note that it is actually enough to consider the permutations ρ_1 and σ only. We chose to allow an additional row permutation ρ_2 so that ρ_1 can be chosen arbitrarily.

(A)			(B)	(C)	(D)
1 2 3 4 5		1 2 3 4 5	3 5 2 1 4	1 2 3 4 5	1 2 3 4 5
2 4 5 3 1	ρ_1	5 4 1 2 3	4 3 1 5 2	5 1 4 2 3	2 4 5 3 1
3 5 2 1 4	σ	4 3 1 5 2	5 1 4 2 3	2 4 5 3 1	3 5 2 1 4
4 3 1 5 2	ρ_2	1 5 2 3 4	2 4 5 3 1	3 5 2 1 4	4 3 1 5 2
5 1 4 2 3			1 2 3 4 5	4 3 1 5 2	5 1 4 2 3

Fig. 4. An example for a self-symmetric solution to diagonally symmetric TBLS. B denotes the square that evolves out of A by applying row permutation ρ_1. C shows the result after applying the symbol-permutation σ that re-establishes the initial setting of the first row. Finally, we get D after applying the row permutation ρ_2 that re-establishes the initial setting of the first column. For self-symmetric squares we observe: A=D, no matter how we choose ρ_1.

For the purpose of streamlining the search for solutions to TBLS, the question arises what constraints we could post to focus our search on self-symmetric squares first. For this purpose, we prove a theorem that allows us to judge easily whether a given square is self-symmetric or not. Let us denote with x_i the permutation of symbols that is defined by row i in some square X. Then:

Theorem 1. *A square A that solves the diagonally symmetric TBLS is self-symmetric iff all permutations defined by A commute with each other, i.e.*

$$a_i \circ a_j = a_j \circ a_i \qquad \forall\, 1 \leq i < j \leq n,$$

whereby a_i denotes the i-th row of A, n denotes the order of the square and $\circ$ denotes the composition of permutations.

For the proof of this theorem, we refer to Appendix A. The proof is based on concepts from permutation group theory. To briefly illustrate the theorem, consider the totally spatially balanced Latin square A in Fig. 4. Consider, for example, permutations defined by the second and the third row of A. We obtain $a_2 \circ a_3 = 5\ 1\ 4\ 2\ 3$ which equals $a_3 \circ a_2$.

4.2 Experimental Results

Our approach is based on constraint programming and can be sketched as follows: Every cell of our square is represented by a variable that takes the symbols as values. We use an All-Different constraint [12] over all cells in the same column as well as all cells in the same row to ensure the Latin square requirement. We also keep a dual model in form of the column conjugate that is connected to the primal model via channeling constraints that were developed for permutation problems [17]. This formulation is particularly advantageous given that by having the dual variables at hand it becomes easier to select a "good" branching variable. In order to enforce the balancedness of the Latin square, we introduce variables for the values $\bar{\mathrm{d}}(k, l)$ and enforce that they are equal to $\frac{(n+1)}{3}$.

With respect to the branching variable selection, for Latin square type problems it has been suggested to use a strategy that minimizes the options both in terms of the position as well as the value that is chosen. In our problem, however, we must also be careful that we can detect unbalancedness very early in the search. Therefore, we traverse the search space symbol by symbol by assigning a whole column in the column conjugate before moving on to the next symbol. For a given symbol, we then choose a row in which the chosen symbol has the fewest possible cells that it can still be assigned to. Finally, we first choose the cell in the chosen row that belongs to the column in which the symbol has the fewest possible cells left.

With Theorem 1, we can now easily streamline this approach by guiding our search towards solutions that are both diagonally symmetric and self-symmetric Latin squares. Based on our experience with smaller problem instances, we conjecture that such solutions will also exist for higher orders. So, following our streamlining approach, at the first two levels of our tree search, before choosing the branching variable as described above, we enforce as branching constraints:

Table 3. Solution times in seconds for finding the first totally spatially balanced Latin square.

order	3	5	6	8	9	11	12	14
pure	0.01	0.02	0.06	16.14	241	–	–	–
streamlined	0.01	0.03	0.05	0.88	0.91	9.84	531	5434

1. $a_{ij} = a_{ji}$ for all $1 \leq i < j \leq n$, and
2. $a_i a_j = a_j a_i$ for all $1 \leq i < j \leq n$.

Table 3 shows the effect of streamlining. We can see clearly how the new method dramatically reduces the runtime, and allows us to solve much larger instances compared to what was possible with the pure model without the streamlining constraints. It is worth noting here that, for all instances, we found diagonally symmetric, self-symmetric solutions, which provides empirical evidence that such solutions exist if the problem is solvable at all. An interesting challenge is to prove this formally. Note, however, that in order to apply streamlining constraints, one need not have such a guarantee.

4.3 Balanced Square Composition

As mentioned earlier, we have also developed a composition technique that builds a balanced square of order $2n$ using as a building block a balanced square of order n. This method is suitable for orders $2n \mod 6 = 0$. Composition is an extreme (and elegant) case of streamlining. Due to space constraints, we describe the method only briefly.

Table 4. Results using composition streamlining. We give CPU times in seconds for finding the first solution, the number of fails on the last restart, the total number of choice points, and the number of restarts.

order	6	12	18
time	0.02	14.36	107K
last fails	1	12K	43K
total cps	2	36K	100M
restarts	0	2	504

The idea works as follows: Given a totally balanced square A of order n such that $2n \mod 6 = 0$, we denote the columns of A by $A_1, \ldots, A_n$. Let us define a shifted copy of A by setting $B = (b_{ij})$ with $b_{ij} = a_{ij} + n$. We denote the columns of B by $B_1, \ldots, B_n$. Now, we would like to compose a solution for order $2n$ out of two copies of each square A and B, whereby a column X_k in the new square $X = (x_{ij})_{1 \leq i,j \leq 2n}$ is forced to equal either $(A_l^T, B_l^T)^T$ or $(B_l^T, A_l^T)^T$ for some $1 \leq l \leq n$. The balancedness constraints are then expressed in terms of the column indices of A and B. Note how this streamliner reduces the size of our problem from n^2 variables to just n variables. See Fig.5 for an illustration.

Table 4 gives our computational results. We see that with streamlining based on composition, we find totally spatially balanced Latin squares of order 18.

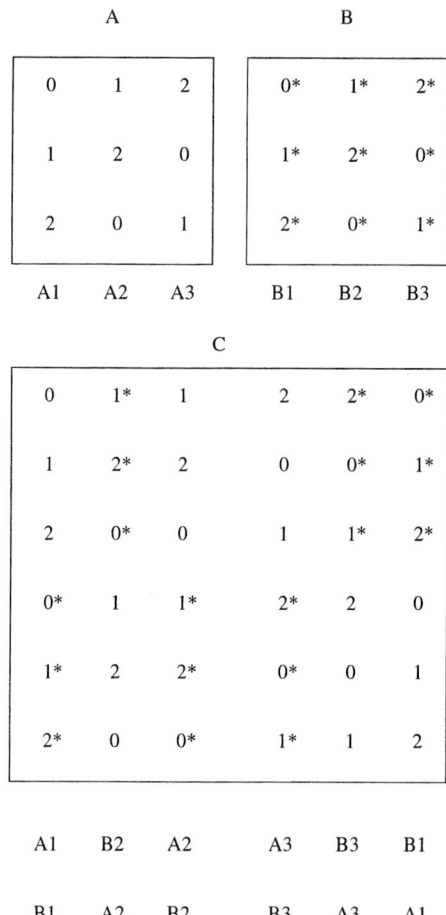

Fig. 5. Illustration of streamlining by composition. A Latin square of order 6 is obtained using as building block a totally balanced Latin square of order 3 (A, left top corner). Latin square A is duplicated with its symbols relabeled, producing Latin square B. The composed Latin square C (order 6) is obtained by selecting entire columns of A and B, such that C is also a totally balanced Latin square of order 6 with the additional property that each of its columns is either of type $(A_i^T, B_i^T)^T$ or $(B_i^T, A_i^T)^T$ ($i = 1, 2$, or 3). By using composition as a streamliner we obtain a much more compact representation for our streamlined problem, with only N variables. The domain of each variable is $\{A_1, A_2, A_3, B_1, B_2, B_3\}$, denoting the column that appears in the column i of the composed Latin square in the top part.

5 Conclusion

We have introduced a new framework for boosting constraint reasoning based on streamlining constraints. The idea consists in adding constraints that partition the set of solutions, thereby focusing the search and propagation mechanism on a small and structured part of the full combinatorial space. We used hard combinatorial design problems to demonstrate that this approach can be very effective. To develop good streamlining constraints, we studied regularities of solutions of small problem instances. A promising area for future work is to use statistical methods to try to discover useful solution regularities automatically.

Acknowledgment

We would like to thank Bart Selman for interesting discussions and very helpful comments regarding the presentation of the streamlining idea.

References

1. R.K. Ahuja, T.L. Magnati, and J.B. Orlin. *Network Flows*. Prentice Hall, 1993.
2. K. R. Apt. The Rough Guide to Constraint Propagation. *5th International Conference on Principles and Practice of Constraint Programming (CP)*, LNCS 1713:1–23, 1999.
3. R.C. Bose, S.S. Shrikhande, and E.T. Parker. Further Results on the Construction of Mutually Orthogonal Latin Squares and the Falsity of Euler's Conjecture. *Canadian Journal of Mathematics*, 12:189–203, 1960.
4. P.Codognet and D.Diaz. An Efficient Library for Solving CSP with Local Search. http://ws.ailab.sztaki.hu/Codognet_Diaz.pdf.
5. C.J. Colbourn and J.H. Dinitz. (Eds.) *The CRC Handbook of Combinatorial Designs*, in CRC Press Series on Discrete Mathematics and its Applications, CRC Press, 1996.
6. T. Fahle, S. Schamberger, and M. Sellmann. Symmetry Breaking. *7th International Conference on Principles and Practice of Constraint Programming (CP)*, LNCS 2239:93–107, 2001.
7. F. Focacci and M. Milano. Global Cut Framework for Removing Symmetries. *7th International Conference on Principles and Practice of Constraint Programming (CP)*, LNCS 2239:77–92, 2001.
8. F. Focacci and P. Shaw. Pruning sub-optimal search branches using local search. CP-AI-OR, pp. 181–189, 2002.
9. C. Gomes, M. Sellmann, H. van Es, and C. van Es. The Challenge of Generating Spatially Balanced Scientific Experiment Designs. Poster CP-AI-OR, 2004. See also www.cs.cornell.edu/gomes/SBLS.htm.
10. ILOG Solver 5.1. User's manual:443–446, 2001.
11. J. Moran. *The Wonders of Magic Squares*. New York: Vintage, 1982.
12. J.-C. Régin. A filtering algorithm for constraints of difference in CSPs. *12th National Conference on Artificial Intelligence*, AAAI, pp. 362–367, 1994.
13. J.K.Rowling. Harry Potter and the Sorcerer's Stone. *Scholastic*, 1998.
14. G. Tarry. Le problème des 36 officiers. *C.R.Assoc. France Av. Science*, 29(2):170–203, 1900.
15. W. Trump. How many magic squares are there? Found at http://www.trump.de/-magic-squares/howmany.html, 2003.
16. H. van Es and C. van Es. The spatial nature of randomization and its effects on outcome of field experiments. *Agron. J*, 85:420–428, 1993.
17. B. Hnich, B.M. Smith, and T. Walsh. Dual Modelling of Permutation and Injection Problems. *Journal of Artificial Intelligence Research*, 21:357–391, 2004
18. E.W. Weisstein. Magic Square. From Mathworld – A Wolfram Web Resource. http://mathworld.worlfram.com/MagicSquare.html, 1999.

Appendix A

Proof (Thm. 1). We use standard permutation group theory for our proof. Denote with S_n the set of bijective functions $\pi : \{1, \ldots, n\} \to \{1, \ldots, n\}$. We call the elements of S_n *permutations*. It is a well know fact that $(S_n, \circ)$ forms a group, whereby the operator $\circ : S_n \times S_n \to S_n$ denotes the standard composition of permutations, i.e. $(\pi_1 \circ \pi_2)(j) = \pi_1(\pi_2(j))$ for all $1 \leq j \leq n$ ($\pi_1 \circ \pi_2$ reads π_1 *after* π_2). For simplicity, when the notation is unambiguous, we leave out the $\circ$-operator sign and simply write $\pi_1 \pi_2$ for the composition of two permutations. With $id \in S_n$ we denote the identity defined by $id(j) = j$ for all $1 \leq j \leq n$. Finally, for all $\pi \in S_n$, the unique function $\phi \in S_n$ with $\phi \pi = id = \pi \phi$ is denoted with π^{-1}. Note that $(S_n, \circ)$ is not abelian, i.e. in general the elements of the group do not commute.

Now, denote with A, B, C, D the subsequent squares that we get by applying permutations ρ_1, σ, and ρ_2. Further, let us set $s = \rho_1^{-1}(1)$ the index of the row that is permuted into the first position by ρ_1. Then, we can identify $\sigma = a_s^{-1}$, since by definition of σ it holds that $\sigma a_s = id$. Similar to σ, also ρ_2 is already determined by the choice of ρ_1. Since the first column of B, when read as a permutation, is equal to ρ_1^{-1}, it follows that $\rho_2 = \sigma \rho_1^{-1} = a_s^{-1} \rho_1^{-1}$, which implies $\rho_2^{-1} = \rho_1 a_s$. Now, let $1 \leq k \leq n$ denote some arbitrary row index. Then:

1. By definition of B, it holds $b_k = a_{\rho_1^{-1}(k)}$.
2. By definition of C, we have $c_k = \sigma b_k = a_s^{-1} a_{\rho_1^{-1}(k)}$.
3. For D, it holds that $d_k = c_{\rho_2^{-1}(k)} = c_{\rho_1 a_s(k)}$.

Equipped with these three facts, let us now prove the desired equivalence:

"$\Rightarrow$" By using our assumption that A is self-symmetric (i.e. A=D), we have:

$$a_k = d_k = c_{\rho_1 a_s(k)} = a_s^{-1} a_{\rho_1^{-1} \rho_1 a_s(k)} = a_s^{-1} a_{a_s(k)}. \tag{1}$$

Next, we exploit that A is diagonally symmetric (i.e. $a_{ij} = a_{ji}$, or, written as permutations, $a_i(j) = a_j(i)$):

$$a_s a_k(j) = a_{a_s(k)}(j) = a_j(a_s(k)) = a_j a_s(k) \quad \forall\, 1 \leq j \leq n. \tag{2}$$

And therefore

$$a_s a_j(k) = a_j a_s(k) \quad \forall\, 1 \leq j \leq n. \tag{3}$$

Note that the above must hold for all $1 \leq s, j, k \leq n$, since $A = D$ for arbitrary choices of ρ_1. Thus, we have

$$a_i a_j = a_j a_i \quad \forall\, 1 \leq i < j \leq n. \tag{4}$$

"$\Leftarrow$" Now let us assume a solution A to the diagonally symmetric TBLS has its first row and column fixed to id (this assumption is important since we will need to use our three facts again in the following). Let us assume further that A contains only commuting permutations. By exploiting the diagonal symmetry of A, we have:

$$a_s a_k(j) = a_s a_j(k) = a_j a_s(k) = a_j(a_s(k)) = a_{a_s(k)}(j) \quad \forall\, 1 \leq k, j \leq n. \tag{5}$$

And thus

$$a_k = a_s^{-1} a_{a_s(k)} = a_s^{-1} a_{\rho_1^{-1} \rho_1 a_s(k)} = c_{\rho_1 a_s(k)} = d_k \quad \forall\, 1 \leq k \leq n. \tag{6}$$

Consequently, A is a self-symmetric square.

□

A Domain Consistency Algorithm for the Stretch Constraint

Lars Hellsten[1], Gilles Pesant[2], and Peter van Beek[1]

[1] University of Waterloo, Waterloo, Canada
{lars,vanbeek}@uwaterloo.ca
[2] École Polytechnique de Montréal, Montreal, Canada
pesant@crt.umontreal.ca

Abstract. The stretch constraint occurs in many rostering problems that arise in the industrial and public service sectors. In this paper we present an efficient algorithm for domain consistency propagation of the stretch constraint. Using benchmark and random instances, we show that this stronger consistency sometimes enables our propagator to solve more difficult problems than a previously proposed propagation algorithm for the stretch constraint. We also discuss variations of the stretch constraint that seem simple and useful, but turn out to be intractable to fully propagate.

1 Introduction

Many rostering and scheduling problems that arise in the industrial and public service sectors involve constraints on stretches of variables, such as limits on the maximum number of shifts a person may work consecutively and limits on the minimum number of days off between two consecutive work stretches. Typical examples arise in automotive assembly plants, hospitals, and fire departments, where both multi-shift rotating schedules and personalized schedules within some scheduling time window are often needed.

Pesant [5] introduced the stretch global constraint and offered a filtering algorithm for the constraint which is capable of providing significant pruning and works well on many realistic problems. In this paper, we present an algorithm based on dynamic programming that achieves a stronger, fully domain consistent level of constraint propagation. This stronger consistency, although more expensive to achieve by a linear factor, enables our algorithm to solve more difficult problems. We also present some natural extensions of the constraint that seem simple and useful, but turn out to be NP-complete to fully propagate.

In Section 2, we provide some background on the stretch constraint. Section 3 presents the main algorithm. A discussion of the algorithm's runtime and correctness is given in Section 4. Section 5 offers some empirical results and discusses some advantages and disadvantages of our algorithm. In Section 6, we examine extensions of the stretch constraint.

2 The Stretch Constraint

The stretch constraint applies to a sequence of n *shift variables*, which we will denote $s_0, s_1, \ldots, s_{n-1}$. We index from 0 to $n-1$ for convenience when performing modular arithmetic for cyclic instances. A stretch formulation also includes a set of m *values* representing *shift types*, $\mathcal{T} = \{\tau_1, \tau_2, \ldots, \tau_m\}$. Each variable s_i has associated with it a set $\text{dom}(s_i) \subseteq \mathcal{T}$ representing values it is allowed to take. An *assignment* of values to variables is an n-tuple from the set $\text{dom}(s_0) \times \cdots \times \text{dom}(s_{n-1})$. We use the notation $\text{value}(s_i)$ to denote the value assigned to s_i when its domain contains exactly one value.

For a given assignment of values to variables, a *stretch* is a maximal sequence of consecutive shift variables that are assigned the same value. Thus, a sequence $s_i, s_{i+1}, \ldots s_{i+k-1}$ is a stretch if $s_i = s_{i+1} = \cdots = s_{i+k-1}$, $i = 0$ or $s_{i-1} \neq s_i$, and $i + k = n$ or $s_{i+k} \neq s_i$. We say that such a stretch *begins* at s_i, has *span* (alternatively, *length*) k, and is of type $\text{value}(s_i)$. We write $\text{span}(s_j) = k$ once the value of s_j has been bound to denote the span of the stretch through s_j.

The following parameters specify a problem instance of stretch. A variable assignment is a solution if it satisfies the requirements specified by these parameters.

- $\Pi \subset \mathcal{T} \times \mathcal{T}$ is a set of ordered pairs, called *patterns*. A stretch of type τ_i is allowed to be followed by a stretch of type τ_j, $\tau_j \neq \tau_i$, if and only if $(\tau_i, \tau_j) \in \Pi$. Note that pairs of the form (τ_k, τ_k) are redundant, since by the definition of a stretch two consecutive stretches do not have the same value.
- $shortest[\tau]$ denotes the minimum length of any stretch of type τ.
- $longest[\tau]$ denotes the maximum length of any stretch of type τ.

We call a stretch of type τ through a variable s_j *feasible* if it satisfies

$$shortest[\tau] \leq \text{span}(s_j) \leq longest[\tau].$$

A *feasible sequence* of stretches is a sequence of feasible stretches which do not overlap, cover a contiguous range of variables, and for which each pair of types of consecutive stretches is in Π.

The kind of rostering problems stretch solves can also be cyclic, in that the roster repeats itself and we assume there is no beginning or end. Such problems are similar enough to the non-cyclic version that only some slight changes to the algorithm and analysis are necessary. Therefore, the discussion in this paper applies to both versions, except where otherwise stated.

3 Propagation Algorithm

Here we present a propagator for stretch that enforces domain consistency. In general, a constraint is said to be domain consistent (also referred to as generalized arc consistent) if for each variable in the constraint, each value in the domain of the variable is part of a solution to the constraint (when the constraint is looked at in isolation). A constraint can be made domain consistent by repeatedly removing values from the domains of the variables that could not be part of a solution to the constraint. Our domain consistency propagation algorithm for the stretch constraint enforces both stretch length constraints and allowed pattern constraints. It is based on a dynamic programming algorithm for the corresponding decision problem, and extended to perform pruning. Initially we will consider only the non-cyclic version.

3.1 Computing Reachability

The main observation we use is that any stretch that appears in a solution is independent of the stretches chosen before and after it, aside from the enforcement of the patterns. Pattern enforcement only depends on the variables adjacent to the stretch. Therefore, a particular stretch appears in a solution if and only if there exists a sequence of stretches ending with a compatible shift type covering the preceding variables, and a sequence of stretches beginning with a compatible shift type covering the subsequent variables.

An alternate way to look at the problem is one of computing reachability in a graph; the nodes in the graph are (variable, type) pairs, and edges correspond to stretches. Our goal is to find all edges that are in some path from some node (s_0, τ_i) to some node (s_{n-1}, τ_j). If the roster needs to be cyclic, then we may have edges between the ending and beginning positions, and will want to find a cycle rather than a path. The set of all edges found will indicate which values are part of some solution, and which values can be safely removed.

The basis of our algorithm is to use dynamic programming to compute, for each variable s_i, and type τ_j, whether there is a feasible sequence of stretches covering the variables $s_0, s_1, \ldots, s_{i-1}$ such that the value of s_{i-1} is compatible with τ_j with respect to Π. The results of this computation are stored in a table of values, *forward* (see Algorithm ComputeForward). Likewise, we compute whether there is a feasible sequence of stretches covering variables $s_{i+1}, s_{i+2}, \ldots, s_{n-1}$ such that the value of s_{i+1} is compatible with τ_j, and store the result in *backward* (see Algorithm ComputeBackward).

Once the reachability information is computed, it is used by a second step that prunes the domains. To make the first step as efficient as possible, we actually store the reachability information in *forward* and *backward* as arrays of prefix sums over the variables. The element $forward[\tau, i]$ indicates the number of variables s_j with $j < i-1$ such that a feasible sequence covers $s_0, s_1, \ldots, s_j$, and ends with a stretch type compatible with τ. The prefix sums allow us to, for a given type, query whether a compatible sequence ends within an arbitrary range in constant time. For example, the difference $forward[\tau, i+1] - forward[\tau, j]$ ($j \leq i$) is greater than zero if and only if there is some feasible sequence of stretches beginning at s_0 and ending between s_{j-1} and s_{i-1} (inclusive) that is compatible with τ.

Another prefix array, *runlength*, is precomputed at the beginning of each stage of the algorithm. For each type τ and variable s_i, it stores the size of the maximal contiguous block of variables whose domains contain τ, up to and including s_i (or including and following s_i for ComputeBackward). This gives an upper bound on the maximum length of a stretch ending (or beginning) at s_i, which may be less than $longest[\tau]$. Note that to make the algorithm concise, we use 1-based indices when looping over variables, rather than the 0-based indices used for shift variables. Indices 0 and $n+1$ correspond to initial values.

Algorithm ComputeForward()
1. $forward[\tau_j, 0] \leftarrow 0$ for all τ_j
2. $forward[\tau_j, 1] \leftarrow 1$ for all τ_j
3. $runlength[\tau_j, i] \leftarrow 0$ for all τ_j, i
4.   **for** $j \leftarrow 1$ **to** m **do**
5.   **for** $i \leftarrow 1$ **to** n **do**
6.   **if** $\tau_j \in \text{dom}(s_{i-1})$ **then** $runlength[\tau_j, i] \leftarrow runlength[\tau_j, i-1] + 1$
7.   **for** $i \leftarrow 1$ **to** n **do**
8.   **for** $j \leftarrow 1$ **to** m **do** $forward[\tau_j, i+1] \leftarrow forward[\tau_j, i]$
9.   **for** $j \leftarrow 1$ **to** m **do**
10. $\text{hi} \leftarrow i - shortest[\tau_j]$
11. $\text{lo} \leftarrow i - \min(longest[\tau_j], runlength[\tau_j, i])$
12.   **if** $\text{hi} \geq \text{lo}$ **and** $forward[\tau_j, \text{hi}+1] - forward[\tau_j, \text{lo}] > 0$ **then**
13.   **for** $k \leftarrow 1$ **to** m **do**
14.   **if** $(\tau_j, \tau_k) \in \Pi$ **then** $forward[\tau_k, i+1] \leftarrow forward[\tau_k, i] + 1$

Algorithm ComputeBackward()
1. $backward[\tau_j, n+1] \leftarrow 0$ for all τ_j
2. $backward[\tau_j, n] \leftarrow 1$ for all τ_j
3. $runlength[\tau_j, i] \leftarrow 0$ for all τ_j, i
4.   **for** $j \leftarrow 1$ **to** m **do**
5.   **for** $i \leftarrow n$ **downto** 1 **do**
6.   **if** $\tau_j \in \text{dom}(s_{i-1})$ **then** $runlength[\tau_j, i] \leftarrow runlength[\tau_j, i+1] + 1$
7.   **for** $i \leftarrow n$ **downto** 1 **do**
8.   **for** $j \leftarrow 1$ **to** m **do** $backward[\tau_j, i-1] \leftarrow backward[\tau_j, i]$
9.   **for** $j \leftarrow 1$ **to** m **do**
10. $\text{lo} \leftarrow i + shortest[\tau_j]$
11. $\text{hi} \leftarrow i + \min(longest[\tau_j], runlength[\tau_j, i])$
12.   **if** $\text{hi} \geq \text{lo}$ **and** $backward[\tau_j, \text{lo}-1] - backward[\tau_j, \text{hi}] > 0$ **then**
13.   **for** $k \leftarrow 1$ **to** m **do**
14.   **if** $(\tau_k, \tau_j) \in \Pi$ **then** $backward[\tau_k, i-1] \leftarrow backward[\tau_k, i] + 1$

The following small example demonstrates how our prefix sums are computed. We consider a roster with three shift types A, B, and C with the bounds on the stretch lengths and initial domains as shown in Table 1 and pattern set $\Pi = \{(A, B), (A, C), (B, A), (C, A)\}$. It is easy to see that the initial configuration is domain consistent. There are five solutions: $\{AAABBBAA$, $AABBBAAA$, $AAACCCCC$, $CCCCCAAA$, $AACCCCAA\}$. Each value present in the domains is used in at least one solution. Now, suppose we assign $s_2 \leftarrow A$ (see Table 5). This has the effect of reducing the set of possible solutions to $\{AAABBBAA$,

Table 1. (left) Bounds on stretch length; (right) Initial domains;

τ_k	$shortest[\tau_k]$	$longest[\tau_k]$
A	2	4
B	3	3
C	4	5

s_0	s_1	s_2	s_3	s_4	s_5	s_6	s_7
A	A				A	A	A
			B	B	B	B	
C	C	C	C	C	C	C	C

$AAACCCCC$}. When we run our algorithm, it should remove the value C from the domains of s_0, s_1, and s_2, and A from s_5.

Table 2 shows a trace of the state after each iteration of the outermost loop in ComputeForward. Table 3 shows the final form of the *backward* table. It is constructed in the same manner as the *forward* table.

Table 2. Building the *forward* table.

$i=0$	0	1	2	3	4	5	6	7	8	9
A	0	1								
B	0	1								
C	0	1								

$i=1$	0	1	2	3	4	5	6	7	8	9
A	0	1	1							
B	0	1	1							
C	0	1	1							

$i=2$	0	1	2	3	4	5	6	7	8	9
A	0	1	1	1						
B	0	1	1	2						
C	0	1	1	2						

$i=3$	0	1	2	3	4	5	6	7	8	9
A	0	1	1	1	1					
B	0	1	1	2	3					
C	0	1	1	2	3					

$i=4$	0	1	2	3	4	5	6	7	8	9
A	0	1	1	1	1	1				
B	0	1	1	2	3	3				
C	0	1	1	2	3	3				

$i=5$	0	1	2	3	4	5	6	7	8	9
A	0	1	1	1	1	1	1			
B	0	1	1	2	3	3	3			
C	0	1	1	2	3	3	3			

$i=6$	0	1	2	3	4	5	6	7	8	9
A	0	1	1	1	1	1	1	2		
B	0	1	1	2	3	3	3	3		
C	0	1	1	2	3	3	3	3		

$i=7$	0	1	2	3	4	5	6	7	8	9
A	0	1	1	1	1	1	1	1	2	3
B	0	1	1	2	3	3	3	3	3	4
C	0	1	1	2	3	3	3	3	3	4

$i=8$	0	1	2	3	4	5	6	7	8	9
A	0	1	1	1	1	1	1	1	2	3	4
B	0	1	1	2	3	3	3	3	4	5
C	0	1	1	2	3	3	3	3	4	5

Table 3. The final *backward* table.

	0	1	2	3	4	5	6	7	8	9
A	3	3	3	3	2	1	1	1	1	0
B	5	4	3	3	3	3	2	1	1	0
C	5	4	3	3	3	3	2	1	1	0

3.2 Pruning Values

Once we have computed the forward and backward reachability information, we are ready to begin pruning values from domains. This process proceeds by considering, for each type, every possible stretch of that type. We check if a stretch is in a solution by examining the *forward* and *backward* tables to see if there are feasible sequences of stretches that can come before and after the one we are considering. If so, we mark the type we are considering, for each of the variables in the stretch. The final pruning step then prunes any value that has not been marked.

In order to make the marking linear in n for each τ_j, we traverse the variables in reverse order, maintaining a queue of possible ending positions. For each position i, we pop any elements from the front of the queue that cannot possibly end a stretch of type τ_j beginning at i. A position $j \geq i$ is not a possible ending position if $j - i + 1 > longest[\tau_j]$, or if there exists some k, $i \leq k \leq j$ such that the variable s_k does not contain τ_j in its domain, i.e. $j - i + 1 > runlength[\tau_j, i]$. Notice that if a position is not a valid ending position for i, it is also not valid for any position smaller than i, so it is always safe to remove invalid positions from the queue.

We also need to ensure that recording the marked intervals is efficient. However, this is easy, since the ending positions we consider are non-increasing. Therefore, each interval we add either extends the previous interval, or is disjoint from the previous interval. We end up with an ordered list of $O(n)$ disjoint intervals which cover a total of $O(n)$ values. We can therefore iterate through the list of intervals and mark all variables within each interval in $O(n)$ time. The details of this part of the algorithm are omitted for clarity.

Algorithm MarkValues()
1. $runlength[\tau_j, i] \leftarrow 0$ for all τ_j, i
2. for $j \leftarrow 1$ to m
3.   for $i \leftarrow 1$ to n do
4.   if $\tau_j \in \text{dom}(s_{i-1})$ then $runlength[\tau_j, i] \leftarrow runlength[\tau_j, i-1] + 1$
5. for $j \leftarrow 1$ to m do
6.   clear queue and list of intervals
7.   for $i \leftarrow n$ downto 0 do
8.   if $i > 0$ and $backward[\tau_j, i] - backward[\tau_j, i+1] > 0$ then
9.   push $i - 1$ onto queue
10.   if $forward[\tau_j, i+1] - forward[\tau_j, i] = 0$ then continue
11.   repeat
12. $e \leftarrow$ front of queue
13.   remove $\leftarrow (longest[\tau_j] < e - i + 1)$ or $(runlength[\tau_j, e] < e - i + 1)$
14.   if remove = true then pop front of queue
15.   until remove = false or queue is empty
16.   if queue is not empty then
17. $e \leftarrow$ front of queue
18.   if $e - i + 1 \geq shortest[\tau_j]$ then
19.   merge $[i, e]$ into the interval list
20.   foreach $(s, e) \in$ the list of intervals do
21.   mark all (i, τ_j) where $s \leq i \leq e$

Table 4 shows an execution trace of MarkValues on the example from the previous section. Finally, Table 5 shows the result, in which domain consistency has been re-established.

Table 4. Trace of MarkValues.

τ_j	i	queue contents	intervals	τ_j	i	queue contents	intervals	τ_j	i	queue contents	intervals
A	8	7	{}	B	8		{}	C	8	7	{}
	7	7	{}		7		{}		7	7	{}
	6	7	{[6,7]}		6	5	{}		6	7,5	{}
	5		{[6,7]}		5	5	{}		5	7,5,4	{}
	4		{[6,7]}		4	5	{}		4	7,5,4	{}
	3	2	{[6,7]}		3	5	{[3,5]}		3	7,5,4	{[3,7]}
	2	2	{[6,7]}		2		{[3,5]}		2		{[3,7]}
	1	2	{[6,7]}		1		{[3,5]}		1	0	{[3,7]}
	0	2	{[0,2],[6,7]}		0		{[3,5]}		0		{[3,7]}

Table 5. (left) Domains after setting $s_2 \leftarrow A$; (right) Domains after re-establishing domain consistency.

s_0	s_1	s_2	s_3	s_4	s_5	s_6	s_7
A	A	A			A	A	A
			B	B	B		
C	C		C	C	C	C	

s_0	s_1	s_2	s_3	s_4	s_5	s_6	s_7
A	A	A				A	A
			B	B	B		
			C	C	C	C	C

4 Analysis of the Algorithm

It is clear that the three stages of the algorithm all terminate, and that each primitive operation in the pseudo-code can be performed in $O(1)$ time. Examining the bounds of the for loops, we see that ComputeForward and ComputeBackward run in $O(nm^2)$ time, where n is the number of shift variables and m is the number of shift types. MarkValues runs in $O(nm)$ time, since we iterate through all variables once for each shift type, building a list of disjoint intervals over $[1, n]$. To achieve domain consistency, we simply need to run these three stages, and remove values which were not marked. The latter step can be performed in $O(nm)$ time, simply by iterating over an $n \times m$ table indicating which variable-value pairs (s_i, τ) are contained in some solution. The overall algorithm therefore runs in $O(nm^2)$ time, and requires $O(nm)$ space. In contrast, Pesant's original stretch propagator runs in $O(m^2 l^2)$ time, where l is the maximum of the maximum lengths of the shift types. In applications of the stretch constraint that have been seen thus far, l is a small value ($6 \leq l \leq 9$). Thus, our algorithm is more expensive to achieve by a linear factor.

One of the limitations of Pesant's algorithm that he discusses is its inability to consider the entire sequence. It is possible for a value in a variable's domain to be inconsistent because it is incompatible with the domain values of a different, far away variable in the sequence of shifts. Even though the domain filtering acts locally, considering variables near a variable that was assigned to, sometimes the changes will cascade throughout the roster. However, this is not always the case, and particularly for large instances can cause Pesant's filtering method to fail where ours succeeds.

The following is a small example that proves our algorithm achieves stronger propagation (see Table 6). We begin with an instance that is initially domain consistent, thus ensuring that any inconsistent values are introduced by incomplete pruning, and were not present to begin with. The problem instance is for a circular roster, with $n = 8$, $m = 3$, and no pattern restrictions (Π contains all ordered pairs of shift types).

Table 6. (left) Bounds on stretch lengths; (right) Initial domains.

τ_k	$shortest[\tau_k]$	$longest[\tau_k]$	s_0	s_1	s_2	s_3	s_4	s_5	s_6	s_7
A	2	4	A	A	A	A			A	A
B	5	5		B	B	B	B	B		
C	2	4	C					C	C	C

It is easy to see that this configuration is domain consistent. There are three solutions: AAAACCCC, ABBBBBAA, and CBBBBBCC. Each value of each variable is used in some solution. We first assign the value C to variable s_7, and then to variable s_0 (see Table 7).

Table 7. (left) Domains after setting $s_7 \leftarrow C$; (right) Domains after setting $s_0 \leftarrow C$.

Algorithm	s_0	s_1	s_2	s_3	s_4	s_5	s_6	s_7	Algorithm	s_0	s_1	s_2	s_3	s_4	s_5	s_6	s_7
Pesant's	A	A	A	A					Pesant's		A	A	A				
Algorithm		B	B	B	B	B			Algorithm		B	B	B	B	B		
	C					C	C	C		C					C	C	C
Domain	A	A	A	A					Domain								
Consistency		B	B	B	B	B			Consistency		B	B	B	B	B		
	C					C	C	C		C						C	C

After the second assignment, since no stretch of B's can be shorter than 5, clearly choosing the value A for s_1, s_2 or s_3 requires a stretch of 5 C's, which is a violation of the maximum stretch of C's. Therefore, after the second assignment, the solution can be determined. Pesant's algorithm observes that it is possible to choose a stretch of A's or B's beginning at s_1 without violating the length constraints for those values, but does not consider the cascading effect of removing values from those domains.

Having shown that our algorithm enforces a stronger level of consistency than Pesant's algorithm, we now show that our algorithm achieves domain consistency. In order to justify that our algorithm achieves domain consistency, we must prove that a value is removed from a variable if and only if that value is not contained in some solution to the constraint. We turn our attention to some facts about the intermediate computations.

Lemma 1. *The prefix sums computed by* ComputeForward *and* Compute Backward *record, for each type τ and position p, the number of previous positions for which some sequence of stretches exists that can be appended with a stretch of type τ. More precisely:*

(a) *The value of $forward[\tau, p]$, $1 \leq p \leq n+1$ as computed by* ComputeForward *is equal to the number of variables s_i with $i < p$ such that some feasible sequence of stretches spans variables $s_0, s_1, \ldots, s_{i-1}$, and is either the empty sequence, or ends with a stretch of type τ' where $(\tau', \tau) \in \Pi$.*

(b) *The value of $backward[\tau, p]$, $0 \leq p \leq n$ as computed by* ComputeBackward *is equal to the number of variables s_i with $i \geq p$ such that some feasible sequence of stretches spans variables $s_i, s_{i+1}, \ldots, s_{n-1}$, and is either the empty sequence, or begins with a stretch of type τ' where $(\tau, \tau') \in \Pi$.*

Proof. We prove (a) by induction on p. Case (b) is analogous and omitted. In the base case, $p = 1$, an empty sequence of stretches is compatible with any type. The algorithm handles this on lines 1-2. For $p > 1$, suppose as our induction hypothesis that the lemma holds for $p' < p$. Clearly this hypothesis implies that if we already know $forward[\tau, p-1]$, it is sufficient to take $forward[\tau, p] = forward[\tau, p-1]$ and then increment this count by one if and only if there is a sequence of stretches compatible with τ spanning $s_0, \ldots, s_{p-2}$. All feasible sequences ending at an earlier shift variable have already been counted. We must show that this is precisely what the algorithm does.

Consider iteration $p-1$ of the outer loop, on lines 7-14. This is the only time a given $forward[\tau, p]$ entry will be modified. Line 8 initializes $forward[\tau, p]$ to the count for the previous variables. All types τ' compatible with τ are considered in the j loop, on lines 9-14. The values lo and hi computed give the range of all possible starting points for a stretch of type τ' ending at s_{p-2}. Moreover, by our induction hypothesis, $forward[\tau', hi+1] - forward[\tau', lo]$ gives the number of variables between $lo-1$ and $hi-1$ (inclusive) where a sequence of stretches compatible with τ' ends. If this value is greater than zero, we can append a stretch of type τ' to one such sequence, and obtain a sequence of stretches spanning $s_0, \ldots, s_{p-2}$, which corresponds to the algorithm setting $forward[\tau, p] = forward[\tau, p-1] + 1$. If there is no such sequence, the count will never be incremented.

Theorem 1 (Correctness of the algorithm). MarkValues *marks a value (p, τ_j) if and only if there is some solution which assigns shift type τ_j to s_p.*

Proof. First, suppose (p, τ_j) is marked. This means that during iteration j of the outer **for** loop, and some iteration $u \leq p$ of the inner **for** loop, the interval $[u, v]$ was recorded, for some $v \geq p$. Thus, $forward[\tau_j, u+1] - forward[\tau_j, u] > 0$. By the lemma, there exists a feasible sequence of stretches spanning variables $s_0, s_1, \ldots, s_{u-1}$, such that the sequence is either empty, or the last stretch is compatible with τ_j. We also know that v was removed from the front of the queue, and must have been pushed onto the queue during some iteration $k \geq u$. Therefore, $backward[\tau_j, k] - backward[\tau_j, k+1] > 0$, so there exists some sequence of stretches spanning variables $s_{k+1}, s_{k+2}, \ldots, s_{n-1}$ such that the sequence is either empty, or the first stretch is compatible with τ_j. Moreover, line 13 removes any positions v' from the front of the queue which are too distant from u to satisfy $longest[\tau_j]$, or for which a stretch from u to v' is impossible. Meanwhile, line 18 ensures e is far enough from u to satisfy $shortest[\tau_j]$. Hence, we can form a feasible stretch of type τ_j covering variables $s_u, s_{u+1}, \ldots, s_v$, prefix this stretch with a sequence of stretches covering all of the preceding variables, and append to it a sequence of stretches covering all of the remaining variables, giving a solution which assigns τ_j to s_p.

Conversely, consider a solution which assigns τ_j to s_p. Let s_u and s_v be the first and last variables in the stretch containing τ_j. We have $backward[\tau_j, v+1] - backward[\tau_j, v+2] > 0$ by the lemma. Therefore, inside the jth iteration of the outermost loop, we will push v onto the queue when $i = v$. When $i = u$, we have $forward[\tau_j, u+1] - forward[\tau_j, u] > 0$, so the **repeat** loop will be entered. Following this loop, v must remain on the queue; the condition on line 13 cannot have been satisfied yet, as we know a stretch of type τ_j can exist spanning $s_u, s_{u+1}, \ldots, s_v$. Therefore, in line 21 $[u, v']$ will be added to the list of intervals, for some $v' \geq v$. It follows that all pairs (i, τ_j) such that $u \leq i \leq v$ will be marked, including (p, τ_j).

4.1 Cyclic Rosters

For the cyclic version of the problem we are not assured that a stretch starts at position 0, and the first and last stretch must differ. These requirements are easy to account for by simply trying all possible starting positions and starting values, and adding a check to ensure that a stretch that ends at position $n - 1$ does not have the same value as the initial stretch. Naively, this adds a factor of $O(nm)$ to the running time. We can improve this by choosing some fixed variable s_i and only considering the possible stretches through s_i. Then the slowdown is at worst $O(m \times \max\{longest[\tau] : \tau \in \mathcal{T}\})$. By always choosing the variable s_i that minimizes the product $|dom(s_i)| \times \max\{longest[\tau] : \tau \in dom(s_i)\}$ we can greatly reduce this slowdown in most typical problems. If s_i is simply the most recently bound variable, we will have $|dom(s_i)| = 1$, giving an upper bound of $O(\max\{longest[\tau] : \tau \in \mathcal{T}\})$ on the slowdown for cyclic instances.

5 Empirical Results

We implemented our new domain consistency algorithm for the stretch constraint (denoted hereafter as DC) using the ILOG Solver C++ library, Version 4.2 [3] and compared it to an existing implementation of Pesant's [5] algorithm which enforces a weaker form of consistency (denoted hereafter as WC; also implemented using ILOG Solver).

We compared the algorithms experimentally on various benchmark and random instances. The experiments on the benchmark instances were run on a 3.0 GHz Pentium 4 with 1 gigabyte of main memory. The experiments on the random instances were run on a 2.40 GHz Pentium 4 with 1 gigabyte of main memory.

We first consider benchmark problems. Our benchmark instances were gathered by Laporte and Pesant [4] and are known to correspond to real-life situations. The problems range from rostering an aluminum smelter to scheduling a large metropolitan police department (see [4] for a description of the individual problems). The constraint models of the benchmark instances combine one or more cyclic stretch constraints with many other constraints including global cardinality constraints [6] and sequencing constraints [7]. The problems are large: the largest stretch constraint has just over 500 variables in the constraint.

Table 8. Number of failed branches and CPU time (sec.) for cyclic rostering problems from the literature. The variable ordering heuristic fills in weekends first, followed by week days chronologically, and within days either (left) chooses the next shift using minimum domain size, or (right) lexicographically. The value ordering is random.

	WC		DC			WC		DC	
	fails	time	fails	time		fails	time	fails	time
atc-1	6	0.01	4	0.00	atc-1	2	0.00	2	0.01
atc-2	11	0.01	0	0.08	atc-2	266	0.04	1	0.06
atc-3	48335	13.02	9	0.06	atc-3	100982	21.86	2	0.04
atc-4	108	0.03	25	0.18	atc-4	2356	0.30	1	0.09
alcan-1	0	0.00	0	0.01	alcan-1	0	0.00	0	0.01
alcan-2	970	0.17	967	0.39	alcan-2	955	0.17	995	0.39
burns	1	0.00	80	0.08	burns	6	0.01	6	0.04
butler	2	0.01	1	0.10	butler	2	0.00	2	0.10
heller	3671	1.34	88	0.27	heller	3259	1.24	88	0.27
horot	0	0.01	0	0.01	horot	1	0.01	0	0.01
hung	22	0.05	0	0.93	hung	3	0.04	0	0.93
laporte	200	0.04	37	0.05	laporte	223	0.04	28	0.04
lau	3	0.01	0	0.09	lau	6	0.01	0	0.09
mot-1	0	0.00	0	0.05	mot-1	3	0.00	3	0.05
mot-2	9	0.01	9	0.05	mot-2	9	0.01	9	0.05
mot-3	3331	0.76	17	0.06	mot-3	2799	0.59	39	0.08
slany1	0	0.00	0	0.00	slany1	0	0.01	0	0.00

On the benchmark problems, our DC propagator offers mixed results over the previously proposed propagator when considering just CPU time (see Table 8). When the number of fails is roughly equal, our stronger consistency can be slower because it is more expensive to enforce. However, our DC propagator also sometimes leads to substantial reductions in number of fails and CPU time. Overall, we conclude that our propagator leads to more robust and predictable performance on these problems. All of the benchmark problems are solved in under one second by our propagator, whereas the propagator based on the weaker form of consistency cannot solve one of the problems in less than twenty seconds.

To systematically study the scaling behavior of the algorithm, we next consider random problems. In our first random model, problems were generated that consisted of a single *cyclic* stretch over n shift variables and each variable

Table 9. Number of failed branches, CPU time (sec.), and number of problems solved within 10 minutes when finding first solution for random cyclic stretch problems. Each fail and time value is the average of only the tests that completed within the time bound of 10 minutes. A total of 50 tests were performed for each combination of n and m.

		WC			DC		
n	m	fails	time	solved	fails	time	solved
50	4	7628.1	0.09	50	0	0.01	50
	6	100089.6	1.21	48	0	0.04	50
	8	138855.7	2.14	50	0	0.08	50
100	4	666002.1	10.17	42	0	0.06	50
	6	281044.4	3.15	38	0	0.15	50
	8	757859.3	11.32	40	0	0.30	50
200	4	246781.2	4.40	19	0	0.26	50
	6	3.5	2.64	24	0	0.59	50
	8	2.9	6.60	22	0	1.09	50
400	4	50653.1	1.19	15	0	1.02	50
	6	90051.8	1.75	17	0	2.40	50
	8	10.2	0.01	14	0	4.25	50

had its initial domain set to include all m shift types. The minimum *shortest*$[\tau]$ and the maximum *longest*$[\tau]$ of the lengths of any stretch of type τ where set equal to a and $a + b$ respectively, where a was chosen uniformly at random from $[1, 4]$ and b was chosen uniformly at random from $[0, 2]$. These particular small constants were chosen to make the generated problems more realistic, but the experimental results appear to be robust for other choices of small values. No pattern restrictions were enforced (all ordered pairs of shift types were allowed). A random variable ordering was used to approximate a realistic context in which fragments of the sequence may be preassigned or fixed through the intervention of other constraints. In such scenarios, there is no guarantee that the chosen variable ordering will be favourable to the stretch propagator. Predictable performance under arbitrary variable orderings indicates that the propagator is robust. In these pure problems nearly all of the run-time is due to the stretch propagators. These problems are trivial for domain consistency, but not so for the weaker form of consistency. We recorded the number of problems that were not solved by WC within a fixed time bound (see Table 9). As n increases, the difference between DC and WC becomes dramatic.

In our second random model, problems were generated that consisted of a single *non-cyclic* stretch. The domain of each variable was set in two steps. First, the initial domain of the variable was set to include all m shift types ($m = 4$, 6, or 8). Second, each of the shift types was removed from the domain with some given probability p, $0.0 \leq p < 0.2$. The minimum and the maximum of the lengths of any stretch of type where set equal to a and $a + b$ respectively, where a was chosen uniformly at random from $[1, 25]$ and b was chosen uniformly at random from $[0, 2]$. No pattern restrictions were enforced and a random variable

Table 10. WC versus DC when finding first solution for random non-cyclic stretch problems: ten best improvements in time (sec.) of WC over DC and ten best improvements in time (sec.) of DC over WC. A total of 1500 tests were performed for each value of n. A blank entry means the problem was not solved within a 10 minute time bound.

	10 best for WC		10 best for DC			10 best for WC		10 best for DC	
n	WC	DC	WC	DC	n	WC	DC	WC	DC
100	0.05	0.13		0.00	200	0.06	0.88		0.06
	0.00	0.06		0.05		0.05	0.77		0.06
	0.00	0.06		0.05		0.05	0.77		0.06
	0.00	0.06	164.69	0.05		0.05	0.55		0.06
	0.00	0.06	145.58	0.05		0.06	0.41		0.06
	0.00	0.06	126.70	0.00		0.13	0.48		0.06
	0.00	0.06	51.64	0.05		0.13	0.42		0.08
	0.00	0.06	38.11	0.05		0.11	0.42		0.11
	0.00	0.06	0.80	0.00		0.17	0.44		0.17
	0.00	0.06	0.69	0.00		0.17	0.42		0.17

ordering was again used. The WC propagator finds these non-cyclic problems much easier than the previous cyclic problems. Nevertheless, on these problems whenever WC is faster than DC the improvement is negligible, whereas our DC propagator can be dramatically faster than WC (see Table 10).

6 Extending Stretch

Now that we have an efficient algorithm for the STRETCH constraint, we turn to the possibility of extending the approach. In this section, we present some variations of the constraint that seem simple and useful, but turn out to be NP-complete to fully propagate.

It is often useful to force a shift of a certain type to occur at least once. For example, there may be a mandatory cleaning shift that we want to include in a daily roster, but we don't care when it occurs. One approach would be to simply schedule the cleaning shift at a fixed time by binding variables ahead of time to create a pre-defined stretch. This has the drawback that it may limit the possible arrangements for the remaining shifts though. It would be better if we were to incorporate this capability directly into the constraint:

$$\text{FORCEDSHIFTSTRETCH}(B_1, \ldots, B_m, s_0, \ldots, s_{n-1})$$

Here $\text{dom}(B_i) = \{0, 1\}$ initially. When $B_i = 1$, a solution includes a stretch of type τ_i, and when it does not, $B_i = 0$. If we want to force a stretch of a certain type to appear, we can set the domain of the corresponding B_i variable accordingly.

Unfortunately, this constraint turns out to be much harder than STRETCH.

Theorem 2. *Deciding whether an instance of* FORCEDSHIFTSTRETCH *has a solution is NP-complete.*

Proof. A witness for the problem is a set of supports, one for each value in each variable's domain. This is polynomial in n and m, which shows that the problem is in NP. To show completeness, we proceed with a reduction from HAMILTONIANPATH.

An instance of HAMILTONIANPATH consists of an undirected graph $G = (V, E)$, and the answer is "yes" if and only if there is a path in G that visits each vertex precisely once. We introduce a shift type τ_v for each vertex $v \in V$, and $|V|$ shift variables. Each shift variable's domain contains all types. For each edge $uv \in E$, we let $\tau_u \tau_v$ be a pattern in Π. Finally, set $B_v = \{1\}$ for each $v \in V$. It is easy to see that by construction, G contains a Hamiltonian path if and only if the corresponding FORCEDSHIFTSTRETCH instance has a solution, and the construction has size $O(|V|^2)$.

Corollary 1. *Enforcing domain consistency for* FORCEDSHIFTSTRETCH *is NP-hard.*

A consequence of this is that any stretch constraint which individually restricts the number of occurrences of each shift type is intractable. Consider the stretch constraint where the minimum length $shortest[\tau_i]$ and the maximum length $longest[\tau_i]$ of every stretch of type τ_i is replaced with a set l_i which contains the lengths of the possible stretches of that type. Unfortunately, it is intractable to enforce domain consistency on such a generalized stretch constraint.

As another example, consider the stretch constraint which is extended to include domain variables c_i, where c_i denotes the number of possible stretches of type τ_i. Such a constraint would prove useful in modeling real-life rostering problems (see [4] for examples). Unfortunately, it is intractable to enforce domain consistency on this extended stretch constraint. One can model restrictions on the number of stretches of a certain type using a combination of a (regular) stretch constraint and a generalized cardinality constraint over auxiliary variables. However, the amount of pruning achieved by enforcing domain consistency on such a decomposition will necessarily be less than on the extended stretch constraint since individually the problems are tractable but the combination is intractable (see [2]).

On a more positive note, we are currently examining a simple extension to the stretch constraint where a single domain variable c is added with domain $[l, u]$, where c denotes the total number of stretches. Such a constraint appears promising as it can be used to model Beldiceanu's [1] change/$\neq$ constraint (and perhaps other constraints in the cardinality-path constraint family; see [1]), yet seems to require only small changes to our algorithm in order to enforce domain consistency on the constraint.

7 Conclusion

We presented an efficient algorithm for domain consistency propagation of the stretch constraint, proved its correctness, and showed its usefulness on a set of benchmark and random problems. We also discussed natural generalizations of the stretch constraint that seemed simple and useful, but turned out to be intractable to fully propagate.

An important problem that we have not addressed in this paper, but one that we are currently working on, is to make our propagator incremental to be more efficient in the case where only a few of the domains have been changed since the most recent previous run of the propagator.

References

1. N. Beldiceanu. Pruning for the cardinality-path constraint family. Technical Report T2001/11A, SICS, 2001.
2. C. Bessière, E. Hebrard, B. Hnich, and T. Walsh. The complexity of global constraints. In *Proceedings of the Nineteenth National Conference on Artificial Intelligence*, San Jose, California, 2004.
3. ILOG S. A. ILOG Solver 4.2 user's manual, 1998.
4. G. Laporte and G. Pesant. A general multi-shift scheduling system. *J. of the Operational Research Society*, 2004. Accepted for publication.
5. G. Pesant. A filtering algorithm for the stretch constraint. In *Proceedings of the Seventh International Conference on Principles and Practice of Constraint Programming*, pages 183–195, Paphos, Cyprus, 2001.
6. J.-C. Régin. Generalized arc consistency for global cardinality constraint. In *Proceedings of the Thirteenth National Conference on Artificial Intelligence*, pages 209–215, Portland, Oregon, 1996.
7. J.-C. Régin and J.-F. Puget. A filtering algorithm for global sequencing constraints. In *Proceedings of the Third International Conference on Principles and Practice of Constraint Programming*, pages 32–46, Linz, Austria, 1997.

A Hybrid Method for Planning and Scheduling

John N. Hooker

Carnegie Mellon University
jh38@andrew.cmu.edu

Abstract. We combine mixed integer linear programming (MILP) and constraint programming (CP) to solve planning and scheduling problems. Tasks are allocated to facilities using MILP and scheduled using CP, and the two are linked via logic-based Benders decomposition. Tasks assigned to a facility may run in parallel subject to resource constraints (cumulative scheduling). We solve minimum cost problems, as well as minimum makespan problems in which all tasks have the same release date and deadline. We obtain computational speedups of several orders of magnitude relative to the state of the art in both MILP and CP.

We address a fundamental class of planning and scheduling problems for manufacturing and supply chain management. Tasks must be assigned to facilities and scheduled subject to release dates and deadlines. Tasks may run in parallel on a given facility provided the total resource consumption at any time remains with limits (cumulative scheduling). In our study the objective is to minimize cost or minimize makespan.

The problem naturally decomposes into an assignment portion and a scheduling portion. We exploit the relative strengths of mixed integer linear programming (MILP) and constraint programming (CP) by applying MILP to the assignment problem and CP to the scheduling problem. We then link the two with a logic-based Benders algorithm.

We obtain speedups of several orders of magnitude relative to the existing state of the art in both mixed integer programming (CPLEX) and constraint programming (ILOG Scheduler). As a result we solve larger instances to optimality than could be solved previously.

1 The Basic Idea

Benders decomposition solves a problem by enumerating values of certain *primary* variables. For each set of values enumerated, it solves the *subproblem* that results from fixing the primary variables to these values. Solution of the subproblem generates a *Benders cut* (a type of nogood) that the primary variables must satisfy in all subsequent solutions enumerated. The next set of values for the primary variables is obtained by solving the *master problem*, which contains all the Benders cuts so far generated.

In this paper, the primary variables define the assignment of tasks to facilities, and the master problem is the assignment problem augmented with Benders cuts. The subproblem is the set of cumulative scheduling problems (one for each facility) that result from a given assignment.

In classical Benders decomposition [1,3], the subproblem is always a continuous linear or nonlinear programming problem, and there is a standard way to obtain Benders cuts. In a logic-based Benders method, the subproblem is an arbitrary optimization problem, and a specific scheme for generating cuts must be devised for each problem class by solving the *inference dual* of the subproblem. In the present context, the Benders cuts must also be linear inequalities, since the master problem is an MILP. It is also important in practice to augment the master problem with a linear relaxation of the subproblem.

The main contribution of this paper is to develop effective linear Benders cuts and subproblem relaxations for (a) minimum cost problems with cumulative scheduling, and (b) minimum makespan problems with cumulative scheduling in which all tasks have the same release date and deadine.

2 Previous Work

Logic-based Benders decomposition was introduced by Hooker and Yan [6] in the context of logic circuit verification. The idea was formally devloped in [4] and applied to 0-1 programming by Hooker and Ottosson [5].

Jain and Grossmann [7] successfully applied logic-based Benders to minimum-cost planning and scheduling problems in which the subproblems are one-machine disjunctive (rather than cumulative) scheduling problems. The Benders cuts are particularly simple in this case because objective function is expressed solely in terms of master problem variables, so that the subproblem is a feasibility problem rather than an optimization problem. Two goals of the present paper are (a) to accommodate cumulative scheduling, and (b) to develop Benders cuts when the objective function involves subproblem variables, and the subproblem is an optimization problem, as in the case of minimum makespan problems.

In related work, we observed in [4] that the master problem need only be solved once by a branching algorithm that accumulates Benders cuts as they are generated. Thorsteinsson [8] showed that this approach, which he called *branch-and-check*, can result in substantially better performance on the Jain and Grossmann problems than standard logic-based Benders. We did not implement branch and check for this study because it would require hand coding of a branch-and-cut algorithm for the master problem. But we obtained substantial speedups without it.

Classical Benders decomposition can also be useful in a CP context, as shown by Eremin and Wallace [2].

3 The Problem

The planning and scheduling problem may be defined as follows. Each task $j \in \{1, \ldots, n\}$ is to be assigned to a facility $i \in \{1, \ldots m\}$, where it consumes processing time p_{ij} and resources at the rate c_{ij}. Each task j has release time

r_j and deadline d_j. The tasks assigned to facility i must be given start times t_j in such a way that the total rate of resource consumption on facility i is never more than C_i at any given time.

We investigate two objective functions. If we let x_j be the facility assigned to task j, the *cost* objective is $g(x,t) = \sum_j f_{x_j j}$, where f_{ij} is the fixed cost of processing task j on facility i. The *makespan* objective is $g(x,t) = \min_j \{t_j + p_{x_j j}\}$.

4 Constraint Programming Formulation

The problem is succintly written using the constraint cumulative(t, p, c, C), which requires that tasks be scheduled at times $t = (t_1, \ldots, t_n)$ so that the total rate of resource consumption at any given time never exceeds C. Thus $\sum_{j \in J_t} c_j \leq C$ for all t, where $J_t = \{j \mid t_j \leq t \leq t_j + p_j\}$ is the set of tasks underway at time t.

The planning and scheduling problem becomes

$$\text{minimize} \quad g(x,t)$$
$$\text{subject to} \quad \text{cumulative}((t_j | x_j = i), (p_{ij} | x_j = i), (c_{ij} | x_j = i), C_i), \text{ all } i \quad (1)$$
$$r_j \leq t_j \leq d_j - p_{x_j j}, \text{ all } j$$

where $g(x,t)$ is the desired objective function and $(t_j | x_j = i)$ denotes the tuple of start times for tasks assigned to facility i. The second constraint enforces the time windows.

5 Mixed Integer Programming Formulation

The most straightforward MILP formulation discretizes time and enforces the resource capacity constraint at each discrete time. Let the 0-1 variable $x_{ijt} = 1$ if task j starts at discrete time t on facility i. The formulation is

$$\min \quad g(x,t)$$
$$\text{subject to} \quad \sum_{it} x_{ijt} = 1, \text{ all } j \quad (a)$$
$$\sum_j \sum_{t' \in T_{ijt}} c_{ij} x_{ijt'} \leq C_i, \text{ all } i, t \quad (b) \quad (2)$$
$$x_{ijt} = 0, \text{ all } j, t \text{ with } d_j - p_{ij} < t \leq r_j \text{ or } t > n - p_{ij} + 1 \quad (c)$$

where $T_{ijt} = \{t' \mid t - p_{ij} < t' \leq t\}$ is the set of discrete times at which a task j in progress on facility i at time t might start processing. Constraint (a) ensures that each task starts once on one facility, (b) enforces the resource limit, and (c) the time windows. The cost objective is $g(x,t) = \sum_{ijt} f_{ij} x_{ijt}$. The makespan objective is $g(x,t) = z$, together with the constraints $z \geq \sum_{it}(t + p_{ij}) x_{ijt}$ for all j.

Due to the size of (2), we also investigated a smaller discrete event model suggested by [9, 10], which uses continuous time. However, it proved to be much harder to solve than (2). We therefore omitted the discrete event model from the computational studies described below.

6 Logic-Based Benders Decomposition

Logic-based Benders decomposition applies to problems of the form

$$\begin{aligned}\text{minimize } & f(x,t) \\ \text{subject to } & C(x,t) \\ & x \in D_x, \; t \in D_t\end{aligned} \qquad (3)$$

where $C(x,t)$ is a set of constraints containing variables x,t. D_x and D_t denote the domains of x and t, respectively. When x is fixed to a given value $\bar{x} \in D_x$, the following *subproblem* results:

$$\begin{aligned}\text{minimize } & f(\bar{x},t) \\ \text{subject to } & C(\bar{x},t) \\ & t \in D_t\end{aligned} \qquad (4)$$

Here $C(\bar{x},t)$ is the constraint that results from fixing $x = \bar{x}$ in $C(x,t)$.

The *inference dual* of (4) is the problem of inferring the tightest possible lower bound on $f(\bar{x},t)$ from $C(\bar{x},t)$. It can be written

$$\begin{aligned}\text{maximize } & v \\ \text{subject to } & C(\bar{x},t) \Longrightarrow f(\bar{x},t) \geq v \\ & v \in \mathbb{R}\end{aligned} \qquad (5)$$

where $\Longrightarrow$ means "implies" (see [4] for details).

The solution of the dual can be viewed as a derivation of the tightest possible bound $\hat{v}$ on $f(x,t)$ when $x = \bar{x}$. For purposes of Benders decomposition, we wish to derive not only a bound when $x = \bar{x}$ but a function $B_{\bar{x}}(x)$ that provides a valid lower bound on $f(x,t)$ for any given $x \in D_x$. In particular, $B_{\bar{x}}(\bar{x}) = \hat{v}$. If z is the objective function value of (3), this bounding function provides the valid inequality $z \geq B_{\bar{x}}(x)$, which we call a *Benders cut*.

In iteration H of the Benders algorithm, we solve a *master problem* whose constraints are the Benders cuts so far generated:

$$\begin{aligned}\text{min } & z \\ \text{subject to } & z \geq B_{x^h}(x), \; h = 1, \ldots, H-1 \\ & z \in \mathbb{R}, \; x \in D_x\end{aligned} \qquad (6)$$

Here $x^1, \ldots, x^{H-1}$ are the solutions of the previous $H-1$ master problems. Then the solution $\bar{x}$ of (6) defines the next subproblem (4).

If we let $v_1^*, \ldots, v_{H-1}^*$ denote the optimal values of the previous $H-1$ subproblems, the algorithm continues until the optimal value z_H^* of the master problem equals $v^* = \min\{v_1^*, \ldots, v_{H-1}^*\}$. It is shown in [4,5] that the algorithm converges finitely to an optimal solution under fairly weak conditions, which hold in the present case. At any point in the algorithm, z_H^* and v^* provide lower and upper bounds on the optimal value of the problem.

In the planning and scheduling problem (1), any assignment $\bar{x}$ of tasks to facilities creates the subproblem:

$$\begin{aligned} \min \quad & g(\bar{x}, t) \\ \text{subject to} \quad & \text{cumulative}((t_j|\bar{x}_j = i), (p_{ij}|\bar{x}_j = i), (c_{ij}|\bar{x}_j = i), C_i), \text{ all } i \\ & r_j \le t_j \le d_j - p_{\bar{x}_j j}, \text{ all } j \end{aligned} \quad (7)$$

which decomposes into a separate scheduling problem for each facility. After solving the subproblem we generate a Benders cut that becomes part of the master problem (6).

The bounding function $B_{\bar{x}}(x)$ is generally obtained by examining the type of reasoning that led to a bound for $x = \bar{x}$ and extending this reasoning to obtain a bound for general x. In the present context, however, only the primal solution (the schedule itself) is available from the commercial CP solver. We therefore design Benders cuts that require only this information.

7 Minimizing Cost

The cost objective presents the simplest case, since cost can be computed in terms of master problem variables, and the subproblem is a feasibility problem. Let $J_{hi} = \{j \mid x_j^h = i\}$ be the set of tasks assigned to facility i in iteration h. If there is no feasible schedule for facility i, the most obvious Benders cut simply rules out assigning this same set J_{hi} of tasks to facility i. In this case $B_{x^h}(x)$ takes the value ∞ when there is an infeasibility and the value $\sum_j f_{x_j j}$ otherwise. The master problem (6), written as a 0-1 programming problem, becomes

$$\begin{aligned} \text{minimize} \quad & \sum_{ij} f_{ij} x_{ij} \\ \text{subject to} \quad & \sum_i x_{ij} = 1, \text{ all } j & (a) \\ & \sum_{j \in J_{hi}} (1 - x_{ij}) \ge 1, \text{ all } i, \; h = 1, \ldots, H-1 & (b) \\ & \text{relaxation of subproblem} & (c) \end{aligned} \quad (8)$$

where $x_{ij} \in \{0, 1\}$, and where constraints (b) are the Benders cuts.

Experience shows that it is important to include a relaxation of the subproblem within the master problem. A straightforward relaxation can be obtained as follows. For any two times t_1, t_2, let $J(t_1, t_2)$ be the set of tasks j whose time windows lie between t_1 and t_2; that is, $t_1 \le r_j$ and $d_j \le t_2$. If the tasks $j \in J \subset J(t_1, t_2)$ are assigned to the same facility i, then clearly the "energy consumption" $\sum_{j \in J} p_{ij} c_{ij}$ of these tasks can be at most $C_i(t_2 - t_1)$ if they are to be scheduled in the time interval $[t_1, t_2]$. This yields the valid inequality

$$\frac{1}{C_i} \sum_{j \in J(t_1, t_2)} p_{ij} c_{ij} x_{ij} \le t_2 - t_1, \quad (9)$$

Let $\mathcal{R}_i = \emptyset$.
For $j = 1, \ldots, p$:
  Set $k' = 0$.
  For $k = 1, \ldots, q$:
    If $r_k \geq r_j$ and $T^i(\bar{r}_j, \bar{d}_k) < T^i(\bar{r}_j, \bar{d}_{k'})$ then
      Remove from $\mathcal{R}_i$ all $R^i(\bar{r}_{j'}, \bar{d}_k)$ for which $T^i(\bar{r}_j, \bar{d}_k) \geq T^i(\bar{r}_{j'}, \bar{d}_k)$.
      Add $R^i(\bar{r}_j, \bar{d}_k)$ to $\mathcal{R}_i$ and set $k' = k$.

Fig. 1. $O(n^3)$ algorithm for generating an inequality set $\mathcal{R}_i$ that relaxes the time window constraints for facility i. By convention $\bar{d}_0 = -\infty$.

Let $\mathcal{R}_i = \emptyset$, and set $j = 0$.
For $k = 1, \ldots, p_d$:
  If $T^i(r_0, \bar{d}_k) > T^i(r_0, \bar{d}_j)$ then add $R^i(r_0, \bar{d}_k)$ to $\mathcal{R}_i$ and set $j = k$.

Fig. 2. $O(n)$ algorithm for generating an inequality set $\mathcal{R}_i$ that relaxes the time window constraints for facility i, where $r_0 = \bar{d}_0 = \min_j\{r_j\}$ and $T^i(r_0, r_0) = 0$.

which we refer to as inequality $R^i(t_1, t_2)$. If we let $\bar{r}_1, \ldots, \bar{r}_{n_r}$ be the distinct elements of $\{r_1, \ldots, r_n\}$ in increasing order, and similarly for $\bar{d}_1, \ldots, \bar{d}_{n_d}$, we have a relaxation consisting of the inequalities

$$R^i(\bar{r}_j, \bar{d}_k), \quad j = 1, \ldots, n_r, \; k = 1, \ldots, n_d \tag{10}$$

for each facility i. These inequalities serve as the relaxation (c) in (8).

Many of these inequalities may be redundant of the others, and if desired they can be omitted from the relaxation. Let

$$T^i(t_1, t_2) = \frac{1}{C_i} \sum_{j \in J(t_1, t_2)} p_{ij} c_{ij} - t_2 + t_1$$

be the *tightness* of $R^i(t_1, t_2)$. It is easily verified that $R^i(t_1, t_2)$ dominates $R^i(u_1, u_2)$ whenever $[t_1, t_2] \subset [u_1, u_2]$ and $T^i(t_1, t_2) \geq T^i(u_1, u_2)$. A set of undominated inequalities can be generated for each facility using the algorithm of Fig. 1. It has $O(n^3)$ complexity in the worst case, since it is possible that none of the inequalities are eliminated. This occurs, for instance, when each $r_j = j - 1$, $d_j = j$, and $p_{ij} = 2$. However, the algorithm need only be run once as a preprocessing routine.

In practice the relaxation can be simplified by supposing that the release times are all $r_0 = \min_j\{r_j\}$. Then the relaxation (c) in (8) consists of

$$R^i(r_0, \bar{d}_k), \quad k = 1, \ldots, n_d$$

for each facility i. The redundant inequalities can be eliminated running the simple $O(n)$ algorithm of Fig. 2 for each facility. Similarly, one can suppose that the deadlines are all $d_0 = \max_j\{d_j\}$ and use the inequalities $R^i(\bar{r}_j, d_0)$.

8 Minimizing Makespan

This case is less straightforward because the subproblem is an optimization problem. However, there are relatively simple linear Benders cuts when all tasks have the same release date, and they simplify further when all deadlines are the same. We also use a linear subproblem relaxation that is valid for any set of time windows.

The Benders cuts are based on the following fact:

Lemma 1. *Consider a minimum makespan problem P in which tasks $1,\ldots,n$ with release time 0 and deadlines $d_1,\ldots,d_n$ are to be scheduled on a single facility i. Let M^* be the minimum makespan for P, and $\hat{M}$ the minimum makespan for the problem $\hat{P}$ that is identical to P except that tasks $1,\ldots,s$ are removed. Then*

$$M^* - \hat{M} \le \Delta + \max_{j \le s}\{d_j\} - \min_{j \le s}\{d_j\} \qquad (11)$$

where $\Delta = \sum_{j=1}^{s} p_{ij}$. In particular, when all the deadlines are the same, $M^* - \hat{M} \le \Delta$.

Proof. Consider any optimal solution of $\hat{P}$ and extend it to a solution S of P by scheduling tasks $1,\ldots,s$ sequentially after $\hat{M}$. That is, for $k=1,\ldots,s$ let task k start at time $\hat{M} + \sum_{j=1}^{k-1} p_{ij}$. The makespan of S is $\hat{M} + \Delta$. If $\hat{M} + \Delta \le \min_{j \le s}\{d_j\}$, then S is clearly feasible for P, so that $M^* \le \hat{M} + \Delta$ and the lemma follows. Now suppose $\hat{M} + \Delta > \min_{j \le s}\{d_j\}$. This implies

$$\hat{M} + \Delta + \max_{j \le s}\{d_j\} - \min_{j \le s}\{d_j\} > \max_{j \le s}\{d_j\} \qquad (12)$$

Since $M^* \le \max_{j \le s}\{d_j\}$, (12) implies (11), and again the lemma follows.

The bound $M^* - \hat{M} \le \Delta$ need not hold when the deadlines differ. Consider for example an instance with three tasks where $(r_1, r_2, r_3) = (0,0,0)$, $(d_1, d_2, d_3) = (2, 1, \infty)$, $(p_{i1}, p_{i2}, p_{i3}) = (1, 1, 2)$, and $(c_{i1}, c_{i2}, c_{i3}) = (2, 1, 1)$. Then if $s=1$, we have $M^* - \hat{M} = 4 - 2 > \Delta = p_{i1} = 1$.

Now consider any given iteration of the Benders algorithm, and suppose for the moment that all the time windows are identical. Let J_{hi} be the set of tasks assigned to facility i in a previous iteration h, and M^*_{hi} the corresponding minimum makespan incurred by facility i. The solution of the current master problem removes task $j \in J_{hi}$ from facility i when $x_{ij} = 0$. Thus by Lemma 1, the resulting minimum makespan for facility i is reduced by at most

$$\sum_{j \in J_{hi}} p_{ij}(1 - x_{ij}) \qquad (13)$$

This yields a bounding function

$$B_{x^h}(x) = M^*_{hi} - \sum_{j \in J_{hi}} p_{ij}(1 - x_{ij})$$

that provides a lower bound on the optimal makespan of each facility i. We can now write Benders cuts (b) in the master problem:

$$
\begin{aligned}
\text{minimize } & M \\
\text{subject to } & \sum_i x_{ij} = 1, \text{ all } j & (a) \\
& M \geq M_{hi}^* - \sum_{j \in J_{hi}} (1 - x_{ij}) p_{ij}, \text{ all } i,\ h = 1, \ldots, H-1 & (b) \\
& M \geq \frac{1}{C_i} \sum_j c_{ij} p_{ij} x_{ij}, \text{ all } i & (c)
\end{aligned} \quad (14)
$$

where $x_{ij} \in \{0, 1\}$. The relaxation (c) is similar to that for the minimum cost problem.

If the deadlines differ (and the release times still the same), the minimum makespan for facility i is at least

$$
M_{hi}^* - \left(\sum_{j \in J_{hi}} p_{ij}(1 - x_{ij}) + \max_{j \in J_{hi}}\{d_j\} - \min_{j \in J_{hi}}\{d_j\} \right)
$$

if one or more tasks are removed, and is M_{hi}^* otherwise. This lower bounding function can be linearized to obtain the Benders cuts

$$
\left.
\begin{aligned}
& M \geq M_{hi}^* - \sum_{j \in J_{hi}} (1 - x_{ij}) p_{ij} - w_{hi} \\
& w_{hi} \leq \left(\max_{j \in J_{hi}}\{d_j\} - \min_{j \in J_{hi}}\{d_j\} \right) \sum_{j \in J_{hi}} (1 - x_{ij}) \\
& w_{hi} \leq \max_{j \in J_{hi}}\{d_j\} - \min_{j \in J_{hi}}\{d_j\}
\end{aligned}
\right\} \text{ all } i,\ h = 1, \ldots, H-1 \quad (15)
$$

Thus (15) replaces (14b) when the deadlines differ and all release times are equal. For purposes of computational testing, however, we focus on the case in which all time windows are the same, since this seems to be the more important case, and it permits simpler and stronger Benders cuts.

9 Computational Results

We solved randomly generated problems with MILP (using CPLEX), CP (using the ILOG Scheduler), and the logic-based Benders method. All three methods were implemented with OPL Studio, using the OPL script language. The CP problems, as well as the CP subproblems of the Benders method, were solved with the assignAlternatives and setTimes options, which result in substantially better performance.

Random instances were generated as follows. The capacity limit was set to $C_i = 10$ for each facility i. For each task j, c_{ij} was assigned the same random value for all facilities i and drawn from a uniform distribution on $[1, 10]$. For instances with n tasks and m facilities, the processing time p_{ij} of each task j on facility i was drawn from a uniform distribution on $[i, 10i]$. Thus facility 1 tends to run about i times faster than facility i for $i = 1, \ldots, m$. Since the average of $10i$ over m facilities is $5(m+1)$, the total processing time of all tasks is roughly proportional to $5n(m+1)$, or about $5n(m+1)/m$ per facility. The release dates were set to zero, and the deadline for every task was set to $5\alpha n(m+1)/m$ (rounded to the nearest integer). We used $\alpha = 1/3$, which results in a deadline that is loose enough to permit feasible solutions but tight enough so that tasks are reasonably well distributed over the facilities in minimum cost solutions. In minimum cost problems, the cost f_{ij} is drawn from a uniform distribution on $[2(m-i+1), 20(m-i+1)]$, so that faster facilities tend to be more expensive.

No precedence constraints were used, which tends to make the scheduling portion of the problem more difficult.

Table 1 displays computational results for 2, 3 and 4 facilities as the number of tasks increases. The CP solver is consistently faster than MILP, and in fact MILP is not shown for the makespan problems due to its relatively poor performance. However, CP is unable to solve most problems with more than 16 tasks within two hours of computation time.

The Benders method is substantially faster than both CP and MILP. Its advantage increases rapidly with problem size, reaching some three orders of magnitude relative to CP for 16 tasks. Presumably the advantage would be greater for larger problems.

As the number of tasks increases into the 20s, the Benders subproblems reach a size at which the computation time for the scheduling subproblem dominates and eventually explodes. This point is reached later when there are more facilities, since the subproblems are smaller when the tasks are spread over more facilities.

In practice, precedence constraints or other side constraints often accelerate the solution of the scheduling subproblems. Easier subproblems could allow the Benders method to deal with larger numbers of tasks. This hypothesis was tested by adding precedence constraints to the problem instances described above; see Table 2. This resulted in fast solution of the scheduling subproblems, except in the three largest makespan instances, which we omit because they do not test the hypothesis. Easier subproblems in fact allow solution of somewhat larger instances. We also obtained good quality bounds on optimal makespan even when computation was terminated early. This approach that can be used for problems that are too large to solve to optimality.

Table 3 investigates how the Benders method scales up to a larger number of facilities, without precedence constraints. The average number of tasks per facility is fixed to 5. The random instances are generated so that the fastest facility is roughly twice as fast as the slowest facility, with the other facility speeds spaced evenly in between.

Since the subproblems remain relatively small as the problem size increases, it is possible to accommodate more tasks than in Table 1. However, the number of iterations tends to increase with the number of facilities. Since each iteration

Table 1. Computation times in seconds for minimum cost and minimum makespan problems, using MILP, CP, and logic-based Benders methods. Each time represents the average of 5 instances. Computation was cut off after two hours (7200 seconds), and a + indicates that this occurred for at least one of the five problems.

Facilities	Tasks	Min cost			Min makespan	
		MILP	CP	Benders	CP	Benders
2	10	1.9	0.14	0.09	0.80	0.08
	12	199	2.2	0.06	4.0	0.39
	14	1441	79	0.04	299	7.8
	16	3604+[a]	1511	1.1	3737	30
	18		7200+	7.0	7200+	461
	20			85		
3	10	0.86	0.13	0.37	0.85	0.06
	12	797	2.6	0.55	7.5	0.3
	14	114	35	0.34	981	0.7
	16	678[a]	1929	4.5	4414	6.5
	18		7200+	14.6	7200+	13.3
	20			2.9		34
	22			23		1509[b]
	24			53		
4	10	2.0	0.10	0.6	0.07	0.09
	12	7.2	1.4	4.0	1.9	0.09
	14	158	72	2.8	524	0.8
	16	906[a]	344	0.8	3898	0.9
	18		6343+	5.2	7200+	13.9
	20			2.6		25
	22			22		472
	24			114		

[a] CPLEX ran out of memory on one or more problems, which are omitted from the average time.
[b] Average over three problems.

adds more Benders cuts to the master problem, the computation time for solving the master problem dominates in larger problems and eventually becomes prohibitive.

10 Conclusions and Future Research

We find that logic-based Benders decomposition can substantially improve on the state of the art when solving minimum-cost and minimum-makespan planning and scheduling problems, in the latter case when all tasks have the same release date and deadline.

In the case of minimum makespan probems, the Benders approach has the additional advantage that it can be terminated early while still yielding both a feasible solution and a lower bound on the optimal makespan. The bound improves steadily as the algorithm runs.

Table 2. Computational results for minimum cost and minimum makespan problems on two facilities with precedence constraints, using the Benders method. Computation time and number of iterations are shown for individual problem instances. Computation was cut off after 600 seconds. Minimum makespans are also given, except when computation is terminated prematurely, in which case lower and upper bounds are shown. In such cases a feasible solution with makespan equal to the upper bound is obtained.

Tasks	Minimum Cost		Minimum Makespan		
	sec	iter.	makespan	sec	iter.
12	0.02	3	17	0.2	14
14	0.05	5	13	0.3	17
16	0.5	24	27	1.6	32
18	0.02	15	27	25	152
20	0.9	39	37	0.7	13
22	0.7	34	26–27	600	480
24	7.7	115	32	13	92
26	2.1	24	37	442	268
28	21	162	35-37	600	351
30	73	261	50-53	600	206
32	>600	>666			
34	>600	>602			
36	235	318			

Table 3. Computation times in seconds and number of iterations for minimum cost and minimum makespan problems, using the Benders method. Each figure represents the average of 5 instances.

Tasks	Facilities	Min cost		Min makespan	
		sec	iterations	sec	iterations
10	2	0.1	9	0.2	10
15	3	0.7	15	1.6	25
20	4	50^a	57	13	37
25	5	2.9	18	213	82
30	6	4.8	26	2075^c	103
35	7	128	62		
40	8	976^b	108		

[a] Includes one outlier that ran for 240 sec and 191 iterations.
[b] One problem was terminated after 3600 sec and 98 iterations.
[c] Average of 2 problems.

Several issues remain for future research:

- Can effective Benders cuts be developed for minimum makespan problems in which tasks have different release dates and deadlines?
- Can a Benders method be applied for other objectives, such as minimum tardiness or minimum number of late tasks?
- Would a branch-and-check approach to the Benders method described here significantly improve performance on planning and scheduling problems?

- Would access to "dual" information from the CP scheduler (results of edge finding, etc.) result in more effective Benders cuts, and how would these cuts be derived?

References

1. Benders, J. F., Partitioning procedures for solving mixed-variables programming problems, *Numerische Mathematik* **4** (1962): 238-252.
2. Eremin, A., and M. Wallace, Hybrid Benders decomposition algorithms in constraint logic programming, in T. Walsh, ed., *Principles and Practice of Constraint Programming (CP 2001), Lecture Notes in Computer Science* **2239**, Springer (2001).
3. Geoffrion, A. M., Generalized Benders decomposition, *Journal of Optimization Theory and Applications* **10** (1972): 237-260.
4. Hooker, J. N., *Logic-based Methods for Optimization: Combining Optimization and Constraint Satisfaction*, John Wiley & Sons (2000).
5. Hooker, J. N. and G. Ottosson. Logic-based Benders decomposition, *Mathematical Programming* **96** (2003) 33-60.
6. Hooker, J. N., and Hong Yan, Logic circuit verification by Benders decomposition, in V. Saraswat and P. Van Hentenryck, eds., *Principles and Practice of Constraint Programming: The Newport Papers*, MIT Press (Cambridge, MA, 1995) 267-288.
7. Jain, V., and I. E. Grossmann, Algorithms for hybrid MILP/CP models for a class of optimization problems, *INFORMS Journal on Computing* **13** (2001) 258–276.
8. Thorsteinsson, E. S., Branch-and-Check: A hybrid framework integrating mixed integer programming and constraint logic programming, *Lecture Notes in Computer Science* **2239** (2001) 16–30.
9. Türkay, M., and I. E. Grossmann, Logic-based MINLP algorithms for the optimal synthesis of process networks, *Computers and Chemical Engineering* **20** (1996) 959–978.
10. Zhang, X., and R. W. H. Sargent, The optimal operation of mixed production facilities, *Computers and Chemical Engineering* (1996) **20** 897–904.

Counting-Based Look-Ahead Schemes for Constraint Satisfaction

Kalev Kask, Rina Dechter, and Vibhav Gogate

Donald Bren School of Information and Computer Science
University of California, Irvine, CA 92967
{kkask,dechter,vgogate}@ics.uci.edu

Abstract. The paper presents a new look-ahead scheme for backtracking search for solving constraint satisfaction problems. This look-ahead scheme computes a heuristic for value ordering and domain pruning. The heuristic is based on approximating the number of solutions extending each partial solution. In particular, we investigate a recent partition-based approximation of tree-clustering algorithms, Iterative Join-Graph Propagation (IJGP), which belongs to the class of belief propagation algorithms that attracted substantial interest due to their success for probabilistic inference. Our empirical evaluation demonstrates that the counting-based heuristic approximated by IJGP yields a scalable, focused search.

1 Introduction

We investigate the power of solution counting as a heuristic for guiding backtracking search for finding a single solution of a constraint problem. Specifically, given a set of instantiated variables (i.e., a partial solution), the task is to compute, for each value a of each uninstantiated variable X, the number of solutions that agree with the given instantiated variables as well as the candidate assignment $X = a$. Clearly, if we could solve this task exactly, it would make solving the CSP task trivial – we can generate a solution in a backtrack free manner by instantiating variables, one at a time, by choosing a value that has a solution count greater than 0, with respect to the previously instantiated variables. Since the counting problem is a #P-complete problem, the complexity of exact algorithms, such as variable elimination algorithms, is too high to be practical and approximations are necessary. Our approach is to approximate solution counting and use it as a heuristic function for guiding a (backtracking) search for solving the CSP problems.

Our approximation idea is motivated by the success of the class of generalized belief propagation, such as Join-Graph Propagation (IJGP) [5, 10] in solving the belief updating problem in Bayesian networks. IJGP(i) is a parameterized iterative propagation scheme controlled by its i-bound. As i grows the algorithm is more accurate but also requires more time and space. When i equals the tree-width of the graph, the algorithm is exact. It was shown that the IJGP(i) scheme is powerful, and superior (provides a superior time-accuracy tradeoff) to competing algorithms on many classes of belief networks. It was shown, in particular, that even the least accurate version of $i = 2$, is often quite good. We therefore adapt the IJGP scheme for the task of solution counting (SC) and use it as a heuristic to guide backtracking search. We compare the resulting backtracking algorithm called IJGP-SC against MAC [11], one of the most powerful lookahead backtracking methods, against Stochastic Local Search (SLS), and against backtracking algorithms equipped with alternative heuristics computed by *mini-clustering/mini-bucket* (a partition-based scheme of tree-decomposition algorithms). We compare the performance of these algorithms on random CSPs, graph coloring problems and Quasi-group completion problems.

Our results are very promising. We show that IJGP-SC yields a very focused search with relatively few deadends, especially when the problems become larger and harder. We compare the algorithms in terms of scalability – how does the relative complexity of an algorithm change as the problem size grows and what is the largest problem size that each of the algorithms can solve in a range of hardness. Our results show that over the problems tried the lowest bound of i=2 was by far the most cost-effective (the time overhead for larger i-bounds did not pay off). We therefore focused much of the subsequent empirical testing on IJGP(i=2)-SC. Our results on random CSPs show that IJGP-SC is more scalable than MAC and SLS. Specifically, while MAC/SLS are better at small problem sizes ($N = 100 - 300$), IJGP-SC improves as N grows, and when $N = 500$, IJGP-SC outperforms other algorithms; at $N = 1000$ IJGP-SC can solve more problem instances faster than competing algorithms and by $N = 2000$ (which is the largest problem size we tried), none of the competing algorithms can solve any problems, while IJGP-SC can still solve about 25% of the solvable problems (given a time-bound of 5 hours). We also compare the performance on hard 3-coloring and Quasi-group completion problems. Our preliminary results show that MAC is the best algorithm on 3-coloring problems (with N up to 200) while IJGP-SC is superior to MAC on Quasi-group completion problems.

We also investigate the impact of the number of iterations, used in IJGP-SC, on the heuristic quality. It can be shown that when IJGP-SC converges, it performs arc-consistency, yielding pruning of domains of variables similar to MAC. However, waiting for convergence (relative to zero counts; general convergence is not guaranteed) may not be cost effective. IJGP-SC with fewer iterations may produce a value ordering that is sufficiently accurate to result in a few deadends. We contrast this with MAC which relies heavily on full arc consistency (domain pruning).

Our results are significant because 1) our base algorithm in IJGP-SC is naive backtracking that is not enhanced by either backjumping or learning 2) our implementation can be further optimized to yield significant speed-up and most significantly, it cannot be matched to the level of hacking invested in MAC, 3) we believe the strength of MAC (pruning domains by arc-consistency) and the strength of IJGP in value ordering are complementary and can be combined in a single algorithm. We plan to investigate the combined approach in the future.

The paper is organized as follows. In Section 2 we provide background information. In Sections 3 we introduce the solution-count heuristic function. The corresponding search algorithm and other competing algorithms are presented in Section 4. In Section 5 we discuss experimental data and finally in Section 6 we provide discussion of related work and concluding remarks.

2 Preliminaries

Definition 1 (constraint satisfaction problem). *A* Constraint Network (CN) *[4] is defined by a triplet* (X, D, C) *where X is a set of variables* $X = \{X_1, ..., X_n\}$, *associated with a set of discrete-valued domains,* $D = \{D_1, ..., D_n\}$, *and a set of constraints* $C = \{C_1, ..., C_m\}$. *Each constraint C_i is a pair* (S_i, R_i), *where R_i is a relation* $R_i \subseteq D_{S_i}$ *defined on a subset of variables* $S_i \subseteq X$ *called the scope of C_i. The relation denotes all compatible tuples of D_{S_i} allowed by the constraint. The primal graph of a constraint network, called a* constraint graph, *has a node for each variable, and an arc between two nodes iff the corresponding variables participate in the same constraint. A* solution *is an assignment of values to variables* $x = (x_1, ..., x_n)$, $x_i \in D_i$, *such that all constraint are satisfied. The Constraint Satisfaction Problem (CSP) is to determine if a constraint network has a solution, and if so, to find a solution. A binary CSP is one where each constraint involves at most two variables. Solution-counting is the task of counting the number of solutions.*

The task of solution counting can be solved when formulating each constraint by a cost function that assigns 1 for allowed tuples and 0 for unallowed tuples. The cost of an assignment is the product of all cost functions and the task is to count the number of assignments with cost 1. This task can be solved exactly by inference algorithms defined over a tree-decomposition of the problem specification. Intuitively, a tree-decomposition takes a collection of functions and partitions them into a tree of clusters. The cluster tree is often called a *join-tree* or a *junction tree*. The clusters in the tree-decomposition have to satisfy the running-intersection property [4]. The subset of variables in the intersection of any two adjacent clusters in the tree is called a separator. The *tree-width* of a tree-decomposition is the maximum number of variables in a cluster minus 1 and the separator width is the maximum number of variables in any separator. The tree-width of a graph is the minimum tree-width over all its tree-decompositions and is identical to another graph parameter called induced-width [3].

Cluster-tree elimination (CTE) [2] is a message-passing algorithm over the clusters of a tree-decomposition, each associated with variable and function subsets. CTE computes two messages for each edge (one in each direction), from each node to its neighbors, in two passes, from the leaves to the root and from the root to the leaves. The message that cluster u sends to cluster v, for the solution-counting task is as follows: The cluster multiplies all its own functions, with all the messages received from its neighbors excluding v and then eliminates, by summation, all variables not in the separator between u and v. The complexity of CTE is time exponential in the tree-width and space exponential

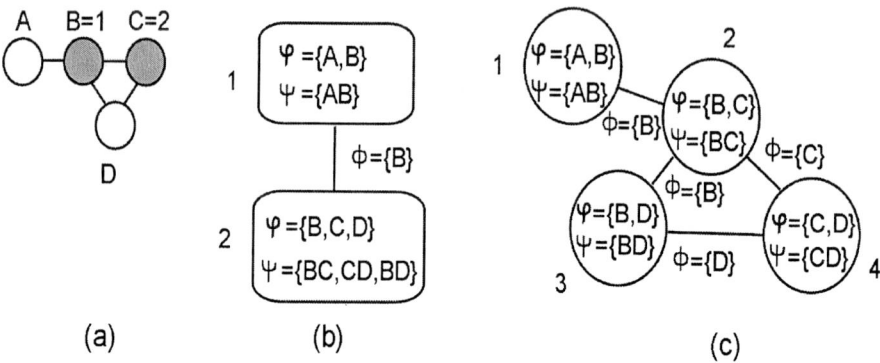

Fig. 1. (a) A graph coloring problem with B=1, C=2; (b) and (c) join-graph decompositions of the problem; (b) is also a tree-decomposition.

in the maximum size of the separator width. CTE can output for each value and each variable the number of solutions extending this variable-value pair. For more details see [4, 2, 5].

Iterative Join-Graph Propagation (IJGP) [5] can be perceived as an iterative version of CTE. It applies the same message-passing to *join-graphs* rather than *join-trees*, iteratively. A join-graph is a decomposition of functions into a graph of clusters (rather than a tree) that satisfies the running intersection property. The IJGP class of algorithms generalizes loopy belief propagation. These algorithms are not guaranteed to converge, nor have bounded accuracies, however they have been demonstrated to be useful approximation methods for various belief networks, especially for probabilistic decoding [5]. While CTE is exact, and requires only 2 iterations, IJGP tends to improve its performance with additional iterations.

The size of clusters in a join-graph can be far smaller than the tree-width and is only restricted by the function's scopes. IJGP can be parameterized by i which controls the cluster size in the join-graph, yielding a class of algorithms (IJGP(i)) whose complexity is exponential in i, that allow a trade-off between accuracy and complexity. As i increases, accuracy generally increases. When i is big enough to allow a tree-structure, IJGP(i) coincides with CTE and becomes exact.

Example 1. Figure 1(a) shows a graph coloring problem with 4 nodes $\{A, B, C, D\}$, each with a domain $\{1, 2, 3\}$, such that $B = 1$ and $C = 2$. In Figures 1(b) and 1(c) we have two join-graph decompositions of this problem, of which Figure 1(b) is also a tree-decomposition. This problem has 2 solutions, $\{A = 2, B = 1, C = 2, D = 3\}$ and $\{A = 3, B = 1, C = 2, D = 3\}$. Therefore, the (exact) solution counts are as follows: $SC(A = 2) = 1$, $SC(A = 3) = 1$, $SC(D = 3) = 2$. In order to compute the solution count for $SC(D = 3)$ based on the join-graph in Figure 1(b), IJGP will compute (using node 2) $\sum_{B,C}(C_{BC} * C_{CD} * C_{BD} * h_{(1,2)}(B))$ where C_{BC}, C_{CD}, C_{BD} are functions stored in node 2 of the join-tree and

$h_{(1,2)}(B)$ is a message that node 1 sends to node 2. Note that this is exact value of $SC(D = 3)$ since Figure 1(b) is a tree-decomposition. In order to compute the solution count for $SC(D = 3)$ based on the join-graph in Figure 1(c), IJGP will compute (using node 3) $\sum_B (C_{BD} * h_{(2,3)}(B) * h_{(4,3)}(D))$ where C_{BD} is a function stored in node 3 of the join-graph and $h_{(2,3)}(B)$, $h_{(4,3)}(D)$ are messages that nodes 2 and 4 send to node 3. Note that this value is an approximation of the exact value. A formal description of the IJGP-SC algorithm is given next.

3 Approximating SC by IJGP

Our application of IJGP for solution counting is technically very similar to the application of IJGP for belief updating in Bayesian networks [5]. We will discuss some technical points here. As input, constraints are modelled by cost functions that assign 1 to combinations of values that are allowed, and 0 to nogoods. IJGP-SC diverges (solution count values computed by IJGP-SC may get arbitrarily large) and thus the solution count values computed by IJGP would be trivial upper bounds on the exact values. To avoid double-point precision overflow we normalize all messages as they are computed. As a result, IJGP(i)-SC will output, for each variable X_i, not solution count absolute values, but their ratios. For example, IJGP(i)-SC($X = a$)=0.4 means that in approximately 40% of the solutions, $X = a$. When the solution count ratio computed by IJGP(i)-SC is 0, the absolute value is 0 as well, and therefore the corresponding value a of X can be pruned. Note, however, that we don't need to know the solution counts very precisely because we use the counts only to create a variable and value ordering during backtracking search. All we want is that the approximated solution counts be sufficiently accurate as to yield a good value-ordering heuristic.

IJGP(i)-SC is presented in Figure 2. As input it takes a join-graph and an activation schedule which specifies the order in which messages are computed. It executes a number of iterations. At the end of iteration j we compute the distance $\Delta(j)$ between messages computed during iteration j and the previous iteration $j-1$. We use this distance to decide whether IJGP(i)-SC is converging. We stop IJGP(i)-SC when either a predefined maximum number of iterations is exceeded (indicating that IJGP(i)-SC is not converging), the distance $\Delta(j)$ is not decreasing (IJGP(i)-SC is diverging), or $\Delta(j)$ is less than some predefined value (0.1) indicating that IJGP(i)-SC has reached a fixed-point.

It is easy to see that solution count values 0 computed by IJGP(i)-SC are correct [6], i.e. whenever IJGP(i)-SC($X = a$)=0, the true solution count $SC(X = a)$=0 as well. Consequently, when running IJGP(i) until convergence the algorithm also accomplishes i-consistency.

4 Algorithms

4.1 Backtracking with IJGP-SC

A formal description of a backtracking algorithm using solution counts computed by IJGP-SC(i) as a heuristic function is given in Figure 3. At each node in the

---

Algorithm IJGP(i)-SC
Input: A join-graph decomposition $< JG, \chi, \psi, \phi >$, $JG = (V, E)$ is a join-graph for $CSP = < X, D, C >$. For every node $v \in V$ and edge $e \in E$, $\chi(v)$ is its set of variables, $\psi(v)$ is its set of functions and $\phi(e)$ is a set of edge labels. Each constraint $C(S_k)$ is represented by a cost function $f(S_k) = 1$ iff $S_k \in R_k$ and 0 otherwise. Instantiated variables I. Activation schedule $d = (u_1, v_1), \ldots, (u_{2*|E|}, v_{2*|E|})$.
Output: A solution count approximation for each singleton assignment $X = a$.

Denote by $h_{(u,v)}$ the message from vertex u to v in JG; $cluster(u) = \psi(u) \cup \{h_{(v,u)} | (v,u) \in E\}$; $cluster_v(u) = cluster(u)$, excluding message from v to u. Let $h_{(u,v)}(j)$ be $h_{(u,v)}$ computed during the j-th iteration of IJGP. $\delta_{h_{(u,v)}}(j) = \sum_{\phi(u,v)} (h_{(u,v)}(j) - h_{(u,v)}(j-1))/|h_{(u,v)}(j)|$, $\Delta(j) = \sum_{d_l \in d} (\delta_{h_{d_l}}(j))/2 * |E|$.

1. **Process instantiated variables**:
   Assign relevant instantiated values to all $R_k \in \psi(u)$, $\chi(u) := \chi(u) - I$, $\forall u \in V$.
2. **Repeat iterations of IJGP** :
   - Along d, for each edge (u_i, v_i) in the ordering,
   - compute $h_{(u_i,v_i)} = \alpha \sum_{elim(u_i,v_i)} \prod_{f \in cluster_{v_i}(u_i)} f$, where α is a normalization constant.
3. **until**:
   - Max number of iterations is exceeded, or
   - Distance $\Delta(j)$ is less than 0.1,
   - $\Delta(j) > \Delta(j-1)$.
4. **Compute solution counts**:
   For every $X_i \in X$ let u be a vertex in JG such that $X_i \in \chi(u)$. Compute $SC(X_i) = \alpha \sum_{\chi(u) - \{X_i\}} (\prod_{f \in cluster(u)} f)$, where α is a normalization constant.

Fig. 2. Algorithm IJGP(i)-SC.

search space it runs IJGP(i)-SC and prunes domains of future variables whose approximated solution count is 0. The algorithm selects as next the variable with the smallest domain, breaking ties in favor of a variable having the largest single (approximated) solution count. The strength of IJGP(i)-SC however is in guiding value ordering. The algorithm chooses a value having the largest approximated solution count (fraction).

We will refer to BB-IJGP-SC as IJGP-SC. In the course of carrying out experiments, we have implemented two versions of BB-IJGP-SC. The first version (called IJGP(i)-SC, where $i = 2, 3, \ldots$), is a simple, general implementation that can be run on a CSP without restrictions on the constraint scope and can use any legal join-graph. i denotes the bound on the cluster size used to generate the join-graph (thus i controls the complexity as well as accuracy of IJGP(i)-SC). Note that processing each node in the join-graph is exponential in i.

We also have a more efficient implementation (called IJGP-SC*) for the special case of $i = 2$. This version assumes binary constraints and uses the problem's dual-graph as its join-graph. The reason for developing this more specialized im-

Procedure BB-IJGP(i)-SC($\mathcal{G},i,I$)
Input: Join-graph $\mathcal{G}$, parameter i, set of instantiated variables I.
Output: A solution, or proof of inconsistency, or timeout.
1. If $I = X$, return 1/0 depending on whether I satisfies all constraints.
2. **Run** IJGP-SC(i); let $\{scX_j\}$ be the set of heuristic values computed by IJGP-SC(i) for each variable $X_j \in X - I$.
3. **Prune** domains of uninstantiated variables, by removing values $x \in D(X_l)$ for which $scX_l(x) = 0$.
4. **Backtrack** If $D(X_l) = \emptyset$ for some variable X_l, return 0.
5. **Otherwise** let X_j be the uninstantiated variable with the smallest domain: $X_j = argmin_{X_k \in X-I}|D(X_k)|$.
6. **Repeat** while $D(X_j) \neq \emptyset$
    i. Let x_k be the value of X_j with the largest heuristic estimate:
    $x_k = argmax_{x_j \in D(X)} scX_j(x_j)$.
    ii. Set $D(X) = D(X) - x_k$.
    iii. Compute $csp = BB - IJGP - SC(\mathcal{G}, i, I \cup \{X_j = x_k\})$.
    iv. If csp=1, return 1.
7. **Return** 0.

Fig. 3. Branch-and-Bound with IJGP(i)-SC.

plementation is to be more competitive with MAC which is restricted to binary constraints, and because IJGP(i=2)-SC (the general version) was superior to higher values of i time-wise.

4.2 The MAC Algorithm

Maintaining arc consistency or the MAC algorithm [11] is one of the best performing algorithms for random binary CSPs that uses arc-consistency lookahead. The performance of the basic MAC algorithm can be improved by using variable and value ordering heuristics during search. In our implementation[1], we have used the *dom/deg* heuristic for variable ordering while the min-conflicts (*MC*) heuristic for value ordering. This combination was shown to perform the best on random binary CSPs [1]. The *dom/deg* heuristic selects the next variable to be instantiated as the variable that has the smallest ratio between the size of the remaining domain and the degree of the variable. The MC heuristic chooses the value that removes the smallest number of values from the domains of the future variables.

4.3 Stochastic Local Search

We also compare against Stochastic Local Search (SLS), which, while incomplete, has been successfully applied to a wide range of automated reasoning problems. The SLS algorithm we use is a basic greedy search algorithm that uses a number of heuristics to improve its performance (see [7] for more details).

---

[1] The implementation is based on Tudor's Hulubei's implementation available at http://www.hulubei.net/tudor/csp

4.4 MBTE-SC/MC

On 100 variable random problems, we will compare IJGP(i)-SC against MBTE (i)-SC and MBTE(i)-MC, using various i-bounds. MBTE(i)-SC and MBTE(i)-MC are backtracking algorithms that use a heuristic computed by the mini-cluster-tree elimination algorithm [2]. In case of MBTE(i)-SC, the heuristic is Solution Counting, whereas in case of MBTE(i)-MC, the heuristic is Min-Conflicts.

5 Experimental Results

We have performed three sets of experiments: (1) Comparison of scalability of IJGP-SC and MAC, (2) The effect of using different i-bounds on the performance of IJGP(i)-SC, and (3) The effect of using different number of iterations.

All experiments use a cpu time bound and if a solution is not found within this time bound, we record a time-out. Note that only those instances that were solved by at least one algorithm within the time bound are considered as soluble instances. All experiments were carried out on a Pentium-2400 MHz PC with 2 GB of RAM running version 9.0 of the red-hat Linux operating system.

5.1 Problem Sets and Terminology

Random CSPs. Random binary CSPs were generated using the parametric model (N, K, C, T) called ModelB [12]. In this model, for a given N and K, we select C constraints uniformly at random from the available $N(N-1)/2$ binary constraints and then for each constraint we select exactly T tuples (called as constraint tightness) as no-goods from the available K^2 tuples. The number of variables was varied between 100 and 2000. The domain size K for all instances was 4 and the constraint tightness T was also 4. This tightness is the same as in $not - equal$ constraints.

We will refer to the set of random CSPs having n variables as the n-variable-set. For each n-variable-set, we tried to systematically (experimentally) locate the phase transition region by varying the number of constraints. However, the phase transition region could not be located for problems sets having more than 500 variables, due to the presence of large number of instances on which the algorithms (including MAC and SLS) did not terminate (in almost 3 days of cpu time). So for such problems, we chose to extrapolate the location of the phase transition region based on the statistics on smaller number of variables. We test the performance of our algorithms in the phase-transition region because the hardest csp instances appear there [12].

Random 3-coloring problems. We generated random 3-coloring problems using Joseph Culberson's flat graph coloring generator. This generator generates graph coloring problems which are guaranteed to be 3-colorable. We experimented with 3-coloring problems having 100 and 200 vertices with 0 flatness.

For these problems, we used a specialized graph coloring solver[2] to locate the settings at which hard problems occur with a high probability.

Balanced Quasi-group completion problems with holes. We also generated random balanced Quasi-group completion problems with holes (balanced QWH) using the generator developed by Henry Kautz et al. [8]. Note that the problems generated by this generator are guaranteed to be consistent. We mapped these problems into a binary csp as follows: (1) The variables in the csp are the holes in a balanced QWH problem (2) The domain of each variable is the initial number of colors minus the colors already assigned to the row and column of the hole (3) The binary constraints in our csp formulation are the $not-equal$ constraints between two variables (or holes) that lie in the same column or row. We experimented with balanced QWH problems of order 18 and 20 respectively. For these problems, we used the results provided in [8] to locate the settings at which hard problems appear with a high probability.

The tables used in this section use the following terminology. The columns T and B give the time in seconds and number of backtracks respectively. Column TB gives the time-bound used while the column #Solved gives the number of instances solved by the algorithm in the given time-bound. Column V gives the number of variables and C gives the number of constraints. Note that an asterisk (∗) indicates that the median time was same as the time-bound used.

5.2 Scalability of IJGP-SC vs. MAC

First we compare IJGP-SC* against MAC in terms of scalability. In Table 1 we have results on random CSPs. For each N, we generated 200 instances at the 50% solubility point. Each row reports the statistics taken over soluble instances.

We observe from Table 1 that IJGP-SC* is superior to MAC in terms of scalability. We see that MAC is better than IJGP-SC* time-wise in the range $100 - 300$. However, as the number of variables increases above 400, MAC is inferior to IJGP-SC*. In particular, when $N \geq 500$, IJGP-SC* can solve many more problems than MAC. Also, IJGP-SC* is by far superior to MAC in terms of number of backtracks. A more detailed comparison between MAC and IJGP-SC* in terms of time and number of backtracks on individual instances in the 500-variable-set is shown in the two scatter plots of Figure 4.

Note that the results are likely based on a subset of the soluble instances that constitute easy instances at the 50% solubility point, because when $N > 1000$ we keep the time bound constant at 5 hours. However, the main point is that: given a time-bound IJGP-SC* solves more problems and faster than MAC as the problem size increases.

In order to test the performance of IJGP(2)-SC and MAC in the underconstrained region, we ran experiments on the 1000-variable-set. The number of constraints was varied between 4000 and 4100. The scatter plots in Figure 5 show the results on individual instances in the 1000-variable-set with a time-out

---

[2] Solver and generator are available at http://www.cs.ualberta.ca/~joe/Coloring/

Table 1. Performance of MAC and IJGP-SC* on random problems.

Statistics	V	C	IJGP-SC* T	IJGP-SC* B	IJGP-SC* #Solved	MAC T	MAC B	MAC #Solved	TB
Average	100	430	2.35	119.76		0.32	62.26		
Median	100	430	0.63	0	117	0.2	46	117	15 min
Average	200	850	104.25	3014.59		1.55	950.5		
Median	200	850	3.496	42	102	0.715	461	102	1hr
Average	300	1280	188.4	7882.2		27.54	12409.4		
Median	300	1280	74.5	352	98	9.1	4428	102	2 hr
Average	400	1710	218.6	2363.7		231.2	87456.7		
Median	400	1710	113.4	360.5	91	143.8	57549	86	3 hr
Average	500	2150	621.7	704.2		1065.2	178921.2		
Median	500	2150	431.62	389	72	653.2	122309	58	4hr
Average	700	2970	1073.2	141.2		*	*		
Median	700	2970	732.5	89	67	*	*	3	5hr
Average	1000	4250	1148.2	87.4		*	*		
Median	1000	4250	1073.6	83	41	*	*	2	5hr
Average	1200	5100	1297.2	98.1		*	*		
Median	1200	5100	881.2	71	23	*	*	4	5hr
Average	1500	6370	712.8	3.4		*	*		
Median	1500	6370	634.6	0	16	*	*	0	5hr
Average	1700	7250	1756.2	145.2		*	*		
Median	1700	7250	1212.4	78	15	*	*	0	5hr
Average	2000	8500	788.2	1.6		*	*		
Median	2000	8500	765.4	0	28	*	*	0	5hr

Table 2. Performance of IJGP-SC* and MAC on 3-coloring problems.

Statistics	V	C	IJGP-SC* T	IJGP-SC* B	IJGP-SC* #Solved	MAC T	MAC B	MAC #Solved	TB
Average	100	239	1.38	279		0.18	40		
Median	100	239	0.74	129	100	0.1	32	100	15min.
Average	200	479	267.14	37763		0.75	876		
Median	200	479	125.34	24273	92	0.54	354	100	1hr.

of 5 hrs. Once again we observe that MAC is superior both time-wise and in number of backtracks.

For the Quasi-group completion problems with holes (balanced QWH), we see that (Table 3) IJGP-SC* is superior to MAC both in terms of time and number of backtracks. The statistics on each row in Table 3 is based on 100 instances. We also observe that IJGP-SC* solves more problems than MAC within the specified time-bound.

On the other hand, our preliminary results on 3-coloring problems (see Table 2), show a contrasting picture in which MAC is superior both in terms of cpu-time and number of backtracks. We currently don't have a good explanation

Table 3. Performance of IJGP-SC* and MAC on balanced QWH problems.

Statistics	Order	Holes	IJGP-SC*			MAC			TB
			T	B	#Solved	T	B	#Solved	
Average	18	150	463.06	17437.8		954.74	1254880		
Median	18	150	10.78	726	100	218.64	269919	91	1800s
Average	18	158	178.22	6453		714.56	975632		
Median	18	158	13.21	934	100	219.45	248212	94	1800s
Average	20	176	1214.5	11712.1		*	*		
Median	20	176	319.1	3326	81	*	*	22	1hr.
Average	20	187	1176.49	9773.49		*	*		
Median	20	187	159.33	768	78	*	*	19	1hr.

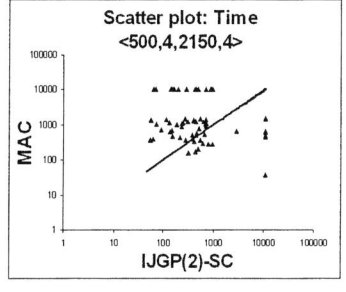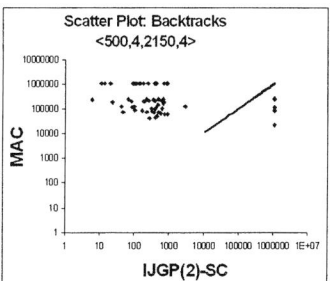

Fig. 4. IJGP-SC* vs. MAC for *soluble 500 variable problems with K=4, T=4, C=2150*.

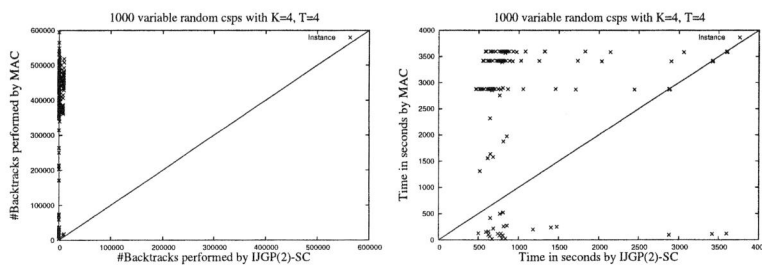

Fig. 5. IJGP(2)-SC vs. MAC for *soluble 1000 variable problems with K=4, T=4*.

for this phenomenon. We will address this question when we compare the effect of using different number of iterations on the performance of IJGP-SC*.

5.3 Effect of Using Different Number of Iterations

In order to determine the effect of iterations, we report results on (1) hard 100 and 200 vertex flat 3-coloring instances, (2) 100 and 200 variable random CSPs and (3) balanced Quasi-group completion problems with holes (balanced QWH) of order 18 and 20. The results are summarized in Tables 4 , 5 and 6. The statistics on each row in these tables is based on 100 random instances.

Table 4. The effect of number of iterations on IJGP-SC* on random csp instances.

Statistics	V	E	MAC T	MAC B	IJGP-SC* 10 iterations T	IJGP-SC* 10 iterations B	IJGP-SC* 100 iterations T	IJGP-SC* 100 iterations B	IJGP-SC* 500 iterations T	IJGP-SC* 500 iterations B	TB
Average	100	430	0.32	62.26	2.35	119.76	5.88	3.23	26.3	2.5	15min.
Median	100	430	0.2	46	0.63	0	5.91	0	28.21	0	
Average	200	850	1.55	950.5	104.25	3014.59	39.91	28.69	131.34	16.35	1hr.
Median	200	850	0.72	461	3.5	42	26.43	0	128.59	0	

Table 5. The effect of number of iterations on IJGP-SC* for balanced QWH.

Statistics	Order	Holes	MAC T	MAC B	IJGP-SC* 10-iterations T	IJGP-SC* 10-iterations B	IJGP-SC* 100-iterations T	IJGP-SC* 100-iterations B	IJGP-SC* 500-iterations T	IJGP-SC* 500-iterations B	TB
Average	18	150	954.74	1254880	463.06	17437.8	432.4	1400	1189.2	724.91	1800s
Median	18	150	218.64	269919	10.78	726	170.53	622	688.92	345	
Average	18	158	714.56	975632	178.22	6453	213.56	744.3	533.4	387	1800s
Median	18	158	219.45	248212	13.21	934	145.67	507	412.56	218	
Average	20	176	*	*	1214.5	11712.1	2080.43	2168.8	2908.4	542.3	1 hr.
Median	20	176	*	*	319.1	3326	2706	1176	1845.2	471	
Average	20	187	*	*	1176.49	9773.49	1682.48	1454.8	2118.38	311.21	1 hr.
Median	20	187	*	*	159.33	768	1058.73	198	1998	47	

Table 6. The effect of number of iterations on IJGP-SC* for 3-coloring problems.

Statistics	V	E	MAC T	MAC B	IJGP-SC* 10 iterations T	IJGP-SC* 10 iterations B	IJGP-SC* 100 iterations T	IJGP-SC* 100 iterations B	IJGP-SC* 500 iterations T	IJGP-SC* 500 iterations B	TB
Average	100	239	0.18	40	1.38	279	2.21	47	10.41	7	15 min.
Median	100	239	0.1	32	0.74	129	1.39	31	7.13	0	
Average	200	479	0.75	876	267.14	37763	27.9	141	53.72	39	1hr.
Median	200	479	0.54	354	125.34	24273	23.99	108	39.85	13	

We can see that as we increase the number of iterations, the number of backtracks decreases. This is to be expected because as the number of iterations is increased the pruning power of IJGP-SC* increases (it becomes closer to full arc-consistency). We believe however that the decrease in backtracks is primarily due to a better value ordering heuristic. Our claim can be supported by comparing the performance of IJGP-SC* with MAC.

Dechter and Mateescu ([6]) proved that the pruning caused by IJGP-SC* is equivalent to arc-consistency when the algorithm is run until convergence. Thus, if we ignore the effect of value-ordering heuristic, MAC should prune better than IJGP-SC*. On the other hand, Tables 4 , 5 and 6 show that the number of backtracks performed by IJGP-SC* with 500 iterations is better than MAC. This suggests that the SC based value ordering heuristic used in IJGP-SC* is more powerful than MAC's min-conflict value-ordering heuristic.

Note that the time taken by IJGP-SC* is dependent on two factors (1) the number of backtracks made and (2) the number of iterations. The tables indicate the trade-off between the two. We see (Tables 4 and 5) that as we increase the number of iterations, the median number of backtracks required by IJGP-SC* for 10, 100 and 500 iterations is almost equal. On the other hand, from Table 6 we can see that IJGP-SC* requires significantly more iterations for 3-coloring problems than random CSPs and balanced QWH problems to obtain comparable level of accuracy (backtracks). This explains the poor performance of IJGP-SC* as compared to MAC for 3-coloring problems.

5.4 Effect of Using Different i-Bounds

To determine the effect of varying the i-bound, we experimented with $N = 100$ random problems and generated 200 instances each with 420, 430, 440 and 450 constraints. We have decomposed our results into two subsets, the first consisting of only the soluble instances while the other consisting of only insoluble instances (Table 7). It is evident that algorithms with i-bound 2 dominate their counterparts with higher i-bounds in terms of cpu time. In general, for a given i-bound, IJGP(i)-SC was better than MBTE(i)-SC which was in turn better than MBTE(i)-MC in terms of cpu time and the number of backtracks. As expected the number of backtracks decreases as i-bound increases.

5.5 Performance of SLS

We ran SLS on random problems from $N = 100$(Table 7) until $N = 1000$. We saw that SLS was competitive with MAC and IJGP-SC at problem sizes $N = 100$-500. However at $N = 1000$ SLS failed to solve any problems. We admit that our implementation of SLS may not be competitive with the best local search algorithms.

6 Related Work and Conclusions

The paper presents a new look-ahead scheme based on the Iterative Join-Graph Propagation (IJGP) approximation of the solution counting task. We compare a simple backtracking algorithm using the IJGP-SC heuristic against MAC and SLS on random CSPs, graph coloring problems and Quasi-group completion problems. We show that the counting heuristic produces a highly focused search that has as much as orders of magnitude fewer backtracks than MAC. In our experiments we use IJGP-SC mostly as a value ordering heuristic, while the strength of MAC lies in domain pruning.

Horsch and Havens [9] have studied the task of computing solution probabilities. Their algorithm, called Probabilistic Arc Consistency (pAC), is a generalization of arc consistency and approximates solution counts for each singleton assignment. We believe our approach of employing IJGP for computing solution

Table 7. Median Time and Backtracks required by various algorithms on the 100-variable-set, $i=i$-bound used. The quantity in the bracket indicates the number of instances on which the results are based on. We have used use IJGP(i)-SC, the non-optimized version.

C	IJGP(i)-SC			MBTE(i)-SC			MBTE(i)-MC			SLS	MAC
	i=2	i=3	i=4	i=2	i=3	i=4	i=2	i=3	i=4		
	Time for soluble instances										
420.0(163)	1.2	1.9	3.9	4.1	5.6	9.9	4.7	4.5	5.9	0.2	0.2
430.0(109)	1.3	2.1	4.2	14.4	15.8	16.1	13.0	7.1	15.8	0.2	0.2
440.0(85)	1.4	2.1	7.0	29.0	30.2	20.9	9.9	20.4	20.7	0.3	0.4
450.0(43)	1.4	2.2	11.2	9.3	38.9	287.2	134.9	57.8	89.5	0.7	0.6
	Backtracks for soluble instances										
420.0(163)	0.0	0.0	0.0	111.0	103.0	115.0	83.0	29.0	10.0		44.0
430.0(109)	2.0	3.0	2.0	261.0	267.0	155.0	243.0	62.0	92.0		40.0
440.0(85)	2.0	39.0	132.0	485.5	331.0	334.5	415.0	48.5	140.0		73.0
450.0(43)	0.0	0.0	69.0	178.0	400.0	1550.0	1673.0	565.0	531.0		58.0
	Time for insoluble instances										
420.0(37)	76.6	139.9	168.7	392.6	327.9	398.2	398.4	223.2	276.4		0.4
430.0(91)	44.0	62.7	107.9	276.6	231.7	306.7	148.0	134.1	171.1		0.7
440.0(115)	26.2	43.4	80.1	211.5	232.6	311.8	164.1	141.4	161.3		0.4
450.0(157)	30.2	38.2	90.4	230.6	231.6	327.3	132.0	124.4	156.5		0.4
	Backtracks for insoluble instances										
420.0(37)	1501.0	1718.5	1415.0	4870.0	2870.0	2211.0	4463.5	2577.0	1764.0		92.5
430.0(91)	944.0	762.5	792.5	2818.5	1829.5	1415.0	2038.0	1599.0	1350.0		61.0
440.0(115)	565.0	549.0	617.0	2332.0	1861.0	1549.0	2068.0	1460.0	1048.0		67.0
450.0(157)	573.0	420.0	481.0	2090.0	1622.0	1429.0	1756.0	1131.0	918.0		52.0

counts is much more general, allowing a tradeoff between accuracy and complexity. Our experimental work is far more extensive; [9] experiments with problems up to 70 variables and finds that while pAC greatly reduces the number of backtracks competing algorithms are often still superior time-wise; we solve problems with up to 2000 variables, and show that often, especially for large problems, IJGP-SC is superior to some of the best competing algorithms.

The main result of the paper is in demonstrating the power of counting approximation by IJGP as a value-ordering heuristic. Specifically, we showed that backtracking with IJGP-SC is superior to MAC in terms of scalability on random CSPs and Quasi-group completion problems, while (based on preliminary results) on graph coloring MAC is superior to IJGP-SC. On random CSPs, MAC is superior to IJGP-SC when the problem size is small. However, as the problem size grows to $N = 500$, IJGP-SC is better than MAC in terms of CPU time. As N grows further, IJGP-SC can solve more problems and in less CPU time.

Acknowledgments

This work was supported in part by the NSF grant IIS-0086529 and the MURI ONR award N00014-00-1-0617.

References

[1] Christian Bessiere and Jean-Charles Regin. MAC and combined heuristics: Two reasons to forsake FC (and CBJ?) on hard problems. In *CP'96*, 1996.
[2] R. Dechter, K. Kask, and J. Larrosa. A general scheme for multiple lower-bound computation in constraint optimization. *CP-2001*, 2001.
[3] R. Dechter and J. Pearl. Tree clustering for constraint networks. *Artificial Intelligence*, pages 353–366, 1989.
[4] Rina Dechter. *Constraint Processing*. Morgan Kaufmann, 2003.
[5] Rina Dechter, Kalev Kask, and Robert Mateescu. Iterative join graph propagation. In *UAI '02*, pages 128–136. Morgan Kaufmann, August 2002.
[6] Rina Dechter and Robert Mateescu. A simple insight into iterative belief propagation's success. *UAI-2003*, 2003.
[7] K. Kask and R. Dechter. Gsat and local consistency. In *IJCAI-95*, 1995.
[8] Henry A. Kautz, Yongshao Ruan, Dimitris Achlioptas, Carla P. Gomes, Bart Selman, and Mark E. Stickel. Balance and filtering in structured satisfiable problems. In *IJCAI*, pages 351–358, 2001.
[9] Horsch Michael and Havens Bill. Probabilistic arc consistency: A connection between constraint reasoning and probabilistic reasoning. In *UAI-2000*, pages 282–290, 2000.
[10] J. Pearl. *Probabilistic Reasoning in Intelligent Systems*. Morgan Kaufmann, 1988.
[11] Daniel Sabin and Eugene C. Freuder. Understanding and improving the MAC algorithm. In *CP (1997)*, pages 167–181, 1997.
[12] Barbara Smith. The phase transition in constraint satisfaction problems: A CLoser look at the mushy region. In *Proceedings ECAI'94*, 1994.

Completable Partial Solutions in Constraint Programming and Constraint-Based Scheduling

András Kovács[1] and József Váncza[2]

[1] Budapest University of Technology and Economics
Magyar tudósok körútja 2/d, 1117 Budapest, Hungary
akovacs@mit.bme.hu
[2] Computer and Automation Research Institute
Kende utca 13-17, 1111 Budapest, Hungary
vancza@sztaki.hu

Abstract. The paper introduces the notion of freely completable partial solutions to characterize constraint satisfaction problems that have components which are relatively easy to solve and are only loosely connected to the remaining parts of the problem. Discovering such partial solutions during the solution process can result in strongly pruned search trees. We give a general definition of freely completable partial solutions, and then apply it to resource-constrained project scheduling. In this domain, we suggest a heuristic algorithm that is able to construct freely completable partial schedules. The method – together with symmetry breaking applied before search – has been successfully tested on real-life resource-constrained project scheduling problems containing up to 2000 tasks.

1 Introduction

In this paper we address the problem of exploiting certain structural properties of constraint satisfaction problems in the course of the solution process. We suggest a method that looks for such a binding of a subset of the variables, which does not constrain the domain of the remaining variables in any way. This kind of bindings is called a *freely completable partial solution*.

Broadly speaking, freely completable partial solutions are traits of such constraint satisfaction problems (CSPs) that have some components which are relatively easy to solve and are only loosely connected to the remaining parts of the problem. Once detected, these partial solutions can be exploited well during the search for solutions: decisions in the easy-to-solve component of the problem can be eliminated, and search can be focused to making the relevant decisions only.

With pruning the search tree, the method may exclude even all but one solutions. In this way, it is closely related to *symmetry breaking*, except that our approach treats *all* solutions equivalent and does not necessitate the explicit declaration of symmetry functions. It can be applied in satisfiability problems and optimization problems which are solved as a series of satisfiability problems.

Our particular motivation was to improve the efficiency of *constraint-based scheduling* methods. By now, constraint programming provides attractive representation and solution methods for solving complex, real-life scheduling problems. However, even the most advanced systems are often unable to solve large problems – which may include an order of magnitude more tasks than typical benchmarks – to an acceptable range of the optimum. Industrial scheduling problems require rich and large-size models, but, at the same time, they can be simple in the sense that they have a loosely connected structure of easy and hard sub-problems. In a real factory, projects visit resources in sequences more or less determined by the manufacturing technology applied. There are product families, members of which are produced in a similar way, using common resources in the same order, while, on the other way around, different product families often use basically different (though not disjoint) sets of resources. Typically, there are many non-bottleneck resources and non-critical projects as well. Some of these properties (e.g., symmetries) can be detected even at the time of model building, but the problem structure remains hidden and can be discovered only at solution time.

In what follows we first discuss equivalence and consistency preserving transformations of CSPs. After summing up related works, a general definition of freely completable partial solutions is given in Sect. 3. Then we shortly present our approach to solving resource-constrained scheduling problems, give a problem-specific definition of freely completable partial schedules and propose a heuristic algorithm to construct partial solutions with such a property. Next we describe how we break symmetries in scheduling problems. Sect. 6. evaluates computational experiments and gives a comparative analysis of constraint-based scheduling algorithms that run on industrial, large-size problem instances without and with the suggested extensions. Finally, conclusions are drawn.

2 Transformations of Constraint Problems

Let there be given a constraint satisfaction problem Π as follows. $X = \{x_i\}$ denotes a finite set of *variables*. Each variable x_i can take a value from its *domain* D_i. There is a set of *constraints* C defined on the variables. The set of variables present in the N-ary constraint $c(x_{i_1}, \ldots, x_{i_N}) \in C$, or briefly c, is denoted by $X_c = \{x_{i_1}, \ldots, x_{i_N}\}$. The solution of a constraint program is a binding S of the variables, i.e., $\forall x_i \in X : x_i = v_i^S \in D_i$ such that all the constraints are satisfied, $\forall c \in C : c(v_{i_1}^S, \ldots, v_{i_N}^S) = true$.

The solution process of a constraint satisfaction problem generally consists of a tree search. Constraint programming earns its efficiency from the *transformations* of the constraint problem, such as domain reductions and addition of inferred constraints, performed within the search nodes.

2.1 Preserving Equivalence vs. Consistency

According to the definitions in [1], a transformation $\Pi \Rightarrow \Pi'$ is called *equivalence preserving* if for every binding S of the variables, S is a solution of Π iff it is also a solution of Π'. For example, constraint propagation and shaving preserve equivalence.

However, a wider set of transformations, i.e., the so-called *consistency preserving* transformations are eligible to solve problems when one has to decide only whether Π has a solution or not. A transformation $\Pi \Rightarrow \Pi'$ is defined to be consistency preserving, if it holds that Π' has a solution iff Π has a solution.

Current general purpose constraint solvers perform equivalence preserving transformations. The reason for that is rooted in their modular structure. *Local propagation algorithms* are attached to individual constraints, hence do not have a view of the entire model. They remove only such values from the variables' domains that cannot be part of any solution because violate the given constraint. In contrast, transformations which do not preserve equivalence, remove also values which *can* participate in some of the solutions. Without loosing the chance of finding a solution (or proving infeasibility), this is possible only with an overall, global view of the model.

2.2 Related Work

Recently, several efforts have been made to explore consistency preserving techniques. Typical transformations which preserve consistency, but do not retain equivalence, are the applications of *symmetry breaking techniques* and *dominance rules*.

In symmetry breaking two basic approaches compete. The first adds symmetry breaking constraints to the model before search, see e.g., [9]. For instance, row and column symmetries in matrix models can be eliminated by lexicographical ordering constraints. Other methods, such as the Symmetry Breaking During Search [15], Symmetry Breaking via Dominance Detection [13], or the Symmetry Excluding Search [2] algorithms, prune symmetric branches of the search tree during search. All of these general frameworks require an explicit declaration of the symmetries in the form of symmetry functions or a dominance checker.

In constraint-based scheduling, it is a common technique to apply dominance rules to prune the search tree. A dominance rule defines a property that must be satisfied at least by one of the optimal solutions. Hence, also the application of a dominance rule can be regarded as a transformation that preserves the consistency of the original problem. E.g., in the field of resource constrained project scheduling, two similar dominance rules are suggested in [3,11] that bind the start time of a task to the earliest possible value if its predecessors are already processed and the given resource is not required by any other task at that time. Note that this assignment can also be seen as a freely completable solution. A dominance rule to decompose the scheduling problem over time is described in [3]. More complex – and more expensive – dominance rules are discussed by [12]. Several dominance rules as well as rules for the insertion of redundant precedence constraints are proposed for the problem of minimizing the number of late jobs on a single machine, see [5].

Early *solution synthesis* techniques of constraint solving can be regarded as precursors of our proposed method [20]. For example, [14] presents a synthesis algorithm that incrementally builds lattices representing partial solutions for one, two, etc. variables, until a complete solution is found. However, synthesis methods were aimed at finding complete solutions of the problem by themselves whereas we are content with constructing partial solutions that are freely completable.

A basically different approach to exploiting problem structure is by using branching strategies which identify and resolve the most critical subproblems in a CSP. In [7], various search heuristics are presented that extract information from the constraint-based model of job-shop scheduling problems (hence, they are referred to as *textures*) to drive the search heuristic. Similar, so-called *profile-based* analysis methods are suggested in [8] that are tailored to cumulative resource models. Alternatively, a clique-based approach is proposed by [18] to find those subsets of connected activities whose resource requirements can produce a conflict. The above approaches are in common that they point out – resembling the decision method of human schedulers – the most critical resources and/or activities time and again during the solution process.

3 Freely Completable Partial Solutions

In what follows we suggest a framework which performs consistency preserving transformations on structured constraint satisfaction problems by binding a subset of the variables. This binding is selected so that it does not constrain in any way the domains of the remaining variables. We call this kind of partial solutions freely completable, and characterize them formally as follows.

A partial solution PS is a binding of a subset $X^{PS} \subseteq X$ of the variables, $\forall x_i \in X^{PS} : x_i = v_i^{PS}$. We define PS freely completable, iff for each constraint $c \in C$:

- If $X_c \subseteq X^{PS}$, then $c(v_{i_1}^{PS}, \ldots, v_{i_N}^{PS}) = true$, i.e., c is satisfied.
- If $X_c \not\subseteq X^{PS} \land X_c \cap X^{PS} \neq \emptyset$, then let $D'_{i_k} = \{v_{i_k}^{PS}\}$ for $x_{i_k} \in X^{PS}$, and $D'_{i_k} = D_{i_k}$ for $x_{i_k} \notin X^{PS}$. Then, $\forall (u_{i_1}, \ldots, u_{i_N}) \in D'_{i_1} \times \ldots \times D'_{i_N} :$ $c(u_{i_1}, \ldots, u_{i_N}) = true$. Note that this means that *all the possible* bindings of the variables not included in PS lead to the satisfaction of c.
- If $X_c \cap X^{PS} = \emptyset$, then we make no restrictions.

Proposition 1: If PS is a freely completable partial solution, then binding the variables $x_i \in X^{PS}$ to the values v_i^{PS}, respectively, is a consistency preserving transformation.

Proof: Suppose that there exists a solution S of the constraint program. Then, the preconditions in the above definition prescribe that the binding $x_i \in X^{PS} :$ $x_i = v_i^{PS}, x_i \notin X^{PS} : x_i = v_i^S$ is also solution, because every constraint is satisfied in it. On the other hand, it is trivial that any solution of the transformed problem is a solution of the original problem, too. □

Note that whether a partial solution is freely completable or not, depends on *all* the constraints present in the model. In case of an optimization problem, this includes the constraints posted on the objective value as well. Thus, this transformation can not be applied e.g., within a branch and bound search, where such constraints are added during the search process.

A freely completable partial solution PS, apart from the trivial $X^{PS} = \emptyset$ case, does not necessary exist for constraint satisfaction problems, or it can be difficult to find. Notwithstanding, we claim that in structured, practical problems, fast and simple heuristics are often capable to generate such a PS. In what follows, this will be demonstrated for the case of constraint-based scheduling.

4 An Application in Constraint-Based Scheduling

We applied the above framework to solve *resource constrained project scheduling* problems. For that purpose, a commercial constraint-based scheduler [16] was extended by a heuristic algorithm for finding freely completable partial solutions during the search process. In addition, potential symmetries of similar projects were excluded by adding symmetry breaking constraints *before* search.

4.1 Problem Statement and Solution Approach

The scheduling problems are defined as follows. There is a set of tasks T to be processed on a set of cumulative resources R. Capacity of the resource $r \in R$ is denoted by $q(r) \in \mathbb{Z}^+$. Each task $t \in T$ has a fixed duration $d(t)$ and requires one unit of resource $r(t)$ during the whole length of its execution, without preemption. Tasks can be arbitrarily connected by end-to-start and start-to-start precedence constraints. These will be denoted by $(t_1 \rightarrow t_2)$ and $(t_1 \dashrightarrow t_2)$, respectively, and determine a directed acyclic graph of the tasks together. The objective is to find start times $start(t)$ for the tasks such that all the precedence and resource capacity constraints are observed and the makespan, i.e., the maximum of the tasks' end times, $end(t) = start(t) + d(t)$ is minimal.

We solve this constrained optimization problem as a series of satisfiability problems in the course of a *dichotomic search*. In successive search runs, the feasibility of the problem is checked for different trial values of the makespan. If UB is the smallest value of the makespan for which a solution is known and LB is the lowest value for which infeasibility has not been proven, then the trial value $\lfloor (UB + LB)/2 \rfloor$ is probed next. Then, depending on the outcome of the trial, either the value of UB or LB is updated. This step is iterated until the time limit is hit or $UB = LB$ is reached, which means that an optimal solution has been found.

Within each search run, the initial time window of each task $t \in T$, limited by its earliest start time $est(t)$ and latest finish time $lft(t)$, equals the interval from time 0 to the trial value of the makespan. In the constraint-based representation of the problem, one variable $start(t)$ stands for the start time of each task $t \in T$. The initial domain of $start(t)$ is the interval $[est(t), lft(t) - d(t)]$. These domains are later tightened by the propagators of the precedence and resource capacity constraints. For propagating precedence constraints, an *arc-B-consistency* algorithm, while for resource capacity constraints the *edge-finding* algorithm is applied [4].

During the search, we build schedules chronologically using the so-called *settimes* strategy [16]. This relies on the LFT priority rule [10], which works as follows. It selects the earliest time instant τ for which there exists a non-empty set $T_\tau \subseteq T$ of unscheduled tasks that can be started at time τ. A task $t \in T$ belongs to T_τ iff all its end-to-start predecessors have ended and all its start-to-start predecessors have started by τ, and there is at least one unit of resource $r(t)$ free in the interval $[\tau, \tau + d(t)]$. From T_τ, the task t^* with the smallest latest finish time $lft(t^*)$ is selected. The settimes branching algorithm then generates two sons of the current search node, according to the decisions whether $start(t^*)$ is bound to $est(t^*)$, or t^* is postponed.

4.2 Freely Completable Partial Schedules

A partial solution PS of a scheduling problem, i.e., a *partial schedule*, is a binding of the start time variables $start(t)$ of a subset of the tasks, which will be denoted by $T^{PS} \subseteq T$. According to the previous definitions, PS is called freely completable, if the following conditions hold for each constraint of the model.

For end-to-start precedence constraints $c : (t_1 \rightarrow t_2)$,

- $t_1, t_2 \in T^{PS}$ and $end(t_1) \leq start(t_2)$, i.e., c is satisfied, or
- $t_1 \in T^{PS}, t_2 \notin T^{PS}$ and $end(t_1) \leq est(t_2)$, i.e., c is satisfied irrespective of the value of $start(t_2)$, or
- $t_1 \notin T^{PS}, t_2 \in T^{PS}$ and $lft(t_1) \leq start(t_2)$, i.e., c is satisfied irrespective of the value of $start(t_1)$, or
- $t_1, t_2 \notin T^{PS}$, i.e., PS does not make any commitments on the start times of t_1 and t_2.

This definition can be extended to start-to-start precedence constraints $c : (t_1 \dashrightarrow t_2)$ likewise:

- $t_1, t_2 \in T^{PS}$ and $start(t_1) \leq start(t_2)$, or
- $t_1 \in T^{PS}, t_2 \notin T^{PS}$ and $start(t_1) \leq est(t_2)$, or
- $t_1 \notin T^{PS}, t_2 \in T^{PS}$ and $lft(t_1) - d(t_1) \leq start(t_2)$, or
- $t_1, t_2 \notin T^{PS}$.

To check resource capacity constraints, we define $M^+_{r,\tau}$ as the set of tasks $t \in T^{PS}$ which are under execution at time τ on resource r, while $M^-_{r,\tau}$ as the set of tasks $t \notin T^{PS}$ which *might be* under execution at the same time:

$M^+_{r,\tau} = \{t | t \in T^{PS} \wedge r(t) = r \wedge (start(t) \leq \tau \leq end(t))\}$
$M^-_{r,\tau} = \{t | t \notin T^{PS} \wedge r(t) = r \wedge (est(t) \leq \tau \leq lft(t))\}$

Now, one of the followings must hold for every resource $r \in R$ and for every time unit τ:

- $|M^+_{r,\tau}| + |M^-_{r,\tau}| \leq q(r)$, i.e., the constraint is satisfied at time τ irrespective of how PS will be complemented to a complete schedule, or
- $M^+_{r,\tau} = \emptyset$, i.e., PS does not make any commitment on r at time τ.

4.3 A Heuristic Algorithm

We applied the following heuristic algorithm to construct freely completable partial schedules. The algorithm is run once in each search node, with actual task time windows drawn from the constraint solver.

The method is based on the LFT priority rule-based scheduling algorithm, which also serves as the origin of the branching strategy. It was modified so that it generates freely completable partial schedules when it is unable to find a consistent complete schedule. The algorithm assigns start times to tasks in a chronological order, according to the priority rule, and adds the processed tasks to T^{PS}.

```
1  PROCEDURE FindAnyCaseConsistentPS()
2     % Let U be the set of tasks not yet scheduled.
3     U := {t|t ∈ T : start(t) is not bound}
4     WHILE (U ≠ ∅)
5        Choose a task t ∈ U and a start time τ using the LFT rule;
6        Remove t from U;
7        IF τ + d(t) ≤ lft(t) THEN
8           start(t) := τ;
9           Add t to T^PS
10       ELSE
11          FailOnTask(t);

12 PROCEDURE FailOnTask(t)
13    IF t ∈ T^PS THEN
14       Remove t from T^PS;
15    FORALL task t' ∈ T^PS : (t' → t) ∈ C
16       IF end(t') > est(t) THEN
17          FailOnTask(t');
18    FORALL task t' ∈ T^PS : (t' --→ t) ∈ C
19       IF start(t') > est(t) THEN
20          FailOnTask(t');
21    FORALL task t' ∈ T^PS : r(t') = r(t)
22       % Let I be the time interval in which t and t' can be
23       % processed concurrently.
24       I := [start(t'), end(t')] ∩ [est(t), lft(t)];
25       IF ∃τ ∈ I : |M^+_{r(t),τ}| + |M^-_{r(t),τ}| > q(r(t)) THEN
26          FailOnTask(t');
```

Fig. 1. The heuristic algorithm for constructing freely completable partial schedules.

Whenever the heuristic happens to assign an obviously infeasible start time to a task t, i.e., $start(t) > lft(t) - d(t)$, t is removed from T^{PS}. The removal is recursively continued on all tasks t' which are linked to t by a precedence or a resource capacity constraint, and the previously determined start time $start(t')$ of which can be incompatible with any value in the domain of $start(t)$. After having processed all the tasks, the algorithm returns with a freely completable partial schedule PS. In the best case, it produces a complete schedule, $T^{PS} = T$, while in the worst case, PS is an empty schedule, $T^{PS} = \emptyset$. The pseudo-code of the algorithm is presented in Fig. 1.

Certainly, this simple heuristic can be improved in many ways. First of all, we applied a small random perturbation on the LFT priority rule. This leads to slightly different runs in successive search nodes, which allows finding freely completable partial solutions which were missed in the ancestor nodes nodes. In experiments (see Sect. 6.), the modified rule, named LFT^{rand}, resulted in roughly 20 % smaller search trees than LFT.

The time spent for building potentially empty partial schedules can be further decreased by restricting the focus of the heuristic to partial schedules PS which obviate the actual branching in the given search node. Task t^*, whose immediate scheduling or postponement is the next search decision in the constraint-based solver, is already known before running the heuristic. This next branching would be eliminated by PS only if $t^* \in T^{PS}$. Otherwise, finding PS does not immediately contribute to decreasing the size of the search tree, and it is likely that PS will only be easier to find later, deeper in the search tree. Accordingly, when FailOnTask is called on t^*, the heuristic algorithm can be aborted and an empty schedule returned. These improvements can be realized by replacing one line and adding three lines to the pseudo-code of the basic algorithm, as shown in Fig. 2.

```
1  PROCEDURE FindAnyCaseConsistentPS()
...
5      Choose a task t ∈ U and a start time τ using the LFT^rand rule;
...

12 PROCEDURE FailOnTask(t)
12A    IF t is the task on which the branching is anticipated THEN
12B        T^PS := ∅;
12C        EXIT; % The next branching cannot be avoided.
...
```

Fig. 2. Improvements of the heuristic algorithm.

4.4 An Illustrative Example

In the following, an example is presented to demonstrate the working of the heuristic algorithm that constructs freely completable partial schedules. Suppose there are 3 projects, consisting of 8 tasks altogether, to be scheduled on three unary resources. Tasks belonging to the same project are fully ordered by end-to-start precedence constraints. The durations and resource requirements of the tasks are indicated in Fig. 3, together with the time windows received by the heuristic algorithm from the constraint-based solver in the root node of the search tree. The trial value of the makespan is 10.

t	d(t)	est(t)	lft(t)	r(t)
t11	1	0	2	R3
t12	4	1	10	R1
t21	2	0	3	R3
t22	2	2	5	R2
t23	5	4	10	R3
t31	2	0	3	R2
t32	4	2	7	R1
t33	3	6	10	R2

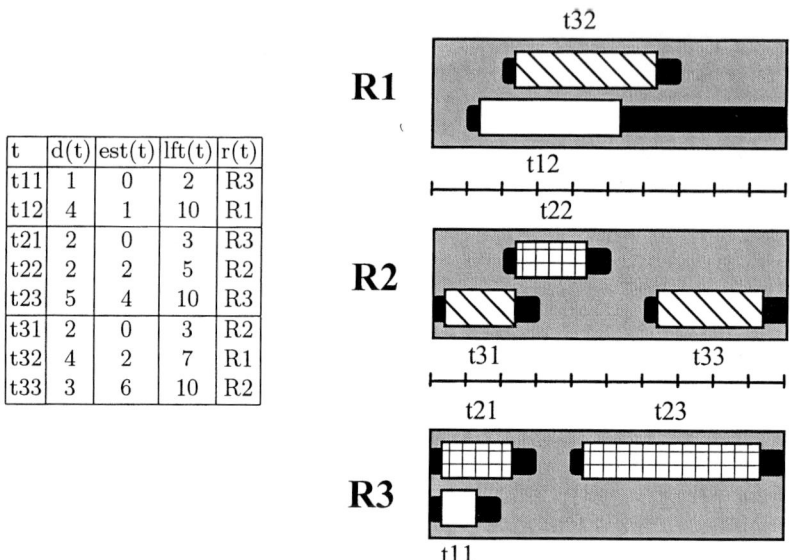

Fig. 3. Parameters of the sample problem.

Note that in order to be able to present a compact but non-trivial example, we switched off the edge-finding resource constraint propagator in the constraint solver engine, and used time-table propagation only.

The algorithm begins by assigning start times to tasks in chronological order, according to the LFT priority rule: $start(t11) = 0$, $start(t31) = 0$, $start(t21) = 1$, $start(t12) = 1$ and $start(t22) = 3$, see Fig. 4.a. All these tasks are added to T^{PS}.

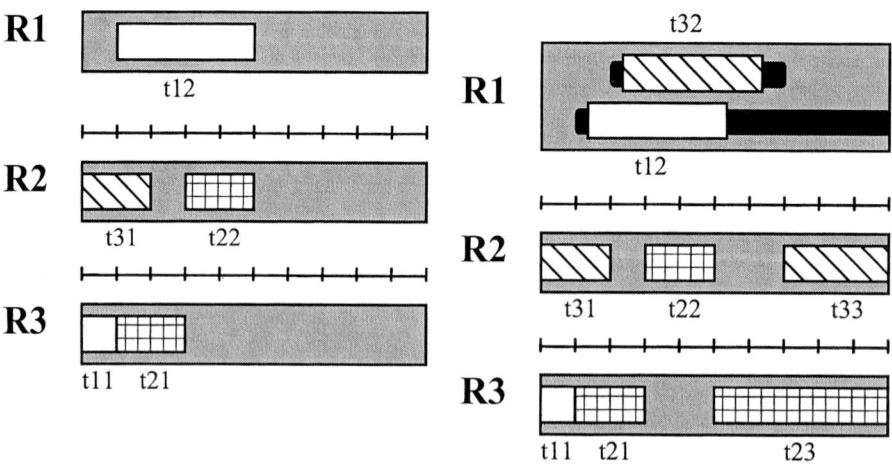

Fig. 4. a.) Building the partial schedule. b.) The freely completable partial schedule.

Now, it is the turn of $t32$. Unfortunately, its execution can start the soonest at time 5, and consequently, it cannot be completed within its time window. Hence, the function FailOnTask is called on $t32$, and recursively on all the tasks which could cause this failure. At this example, it only concerns $t12$ which is removed from T^{PS}. Then, further tasks are scheduled according to the LFT priority rule: start times are assigned to the two remaining tasks, $start(t23) = 5$ and $start(t33) = 7$. The heuristic algorithm stops at this point, and it returns the freely completable partial schedule PS with $T^{PS} = \{t11, t21, t22, t23, t31, t33\}$, see Fig. 4.b.

After having bound the start times of these tasks in the constraint-based solver, the solver continues the search process for the remaining two tasks. In the next search node, it infers the only remaining valid start times for $t12$ and $t32$ by propagation. This leads to an optimal solution for this problem, as shown at Fig. 5.

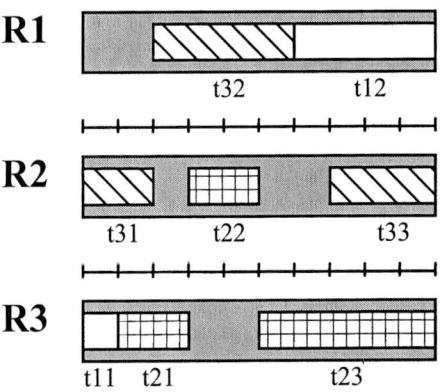

Fig. 5. The final schedule.

5 Breaking the Symmetries Between Similar Projects

In real industrial plants, products can often be ordered into a few number of product families. Members of the same family generally share parts of their routings, which introduces a huge number of symmetries in the scheduling problem. We exclude symmetries of similar projects by adding symmetry breaking constraints to the model *before* search, by using the following method.

Let P and Q denote two *isomorphic* subsets of T. P and Q are considered isomorphic iff their cardinality is the same and their tasks can be indexed such that

$$\forall i \in [1, ..., n] : \quad d(p_i) = d(q_i) \land r(p_i) = r(q_i), \text{ and}$$
$$\forall i, j \in [1, ..., n] : \quad (p_i \rightarrow p_j) \Leftrightarrow (q_i \rightarrow q_j) \land (p_i \dashrightarrow p_j) \Leftrightarrow (q_i \dashrightarrow q_j).$$

Furthermore, suppose that there are no outgoing precedence constraints from P and no incoming precedence constraints to Q.

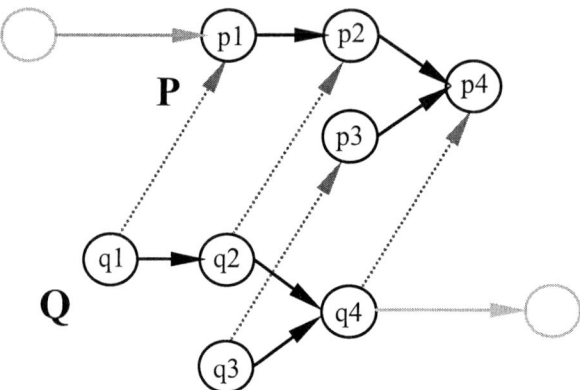

Fig. 6. Symmetry breaking.

Proposition 2: If there exists a solution S of the scheduling problem, then it also has a solution S' which satisfies all the precedence constraints $(q_i \to p_i)$ if resource $r(p_i)$ is unary, and $(q_i \dashrightarrow p_i)$ if resource $r(p_i)$ has a higher capacity.

Proof: Let us construct the desired solution S' departing from S by swapping each pair of tasks p_i, q_i for which the added precedence constraint is not satisfied:

$$\forall i \in [1,...,n]: \quad start(p_i)^{S'} = max(start(p_i)^S, start(q_i)^S),$$
$$start(q_i)^{S'} = min(start(p_i)^S, start(q_i)^S).$$

Now, all resource capacity constraints are satisfied in S', because the durations and resource requirements of p_i and q_i are the same. End-to-start precedence constraints $(p_i \to p_j)$ cannot be violated in S', either, because

- If neither of the ith or jth pairs of tasks were swapped, then the start times of p_i and p_j are unchanged in S' w.r.t S;
- If only the ith pair of tasks was swapped, then
  $end(p_i)^{S'} = end(q_i)^S \leq start(q_j)^S \leq start(p_j)^S = start(p_j)^{S'}$;
- If only the jth pair of tasks was swapped, then
  $end(p_i)^{S'} = end(p_i)^S \leq start(p_j)^S \leq start(q_j)^S = start(p_j)^{S'}$;
- If both of the ith and jth pairs of tasks were swapped, then
  $end(p_i)^{S'} = end(q_i)^S \leq start(q_j)^S = start(p_j)^{S'}$.

For start-to-start precedence constraints, the proof is analogous. □

Note that by the iterative application of this proposition, an arbitrary number of symmetrical subsets can be fully ordered. In our system, we add precedence constraints to the model according to proposition 2. Thus, P and Q stand for the sections of two projects, which fall into the scheduling horizon, and where the project containing Q is in a slightly more advanced state. These symmetries can easily be found with the help of some appropriate task identifiers.

6 Experiments

The above algorithms were developed and implemented as part of the efforts to improve the efficiency of the job-shop level scheduler module of our integrated production planner and scheduler system [17, 19, 21]. This scheduler unfolds medium-term production plans into detailed schedules on a horizon of one week.

The starting point of the implementation was the constraint-based scheduler of Ilog [16]. It was extended by the symmetry breaker as a pre-processor, and the heuristic algorithm for constructing freely completable partial schedules, run once in each search node. Both extensions were encoded in C++. The experiments were run on a 1.6 GHz Pentium IV computer.

The test problem instances originate from an industrial partner that manufactures mechanical parts of high complexity. The products can be ordered into several product families. A project, aimed at the fabrication of an end product, usually contains 50 to 500 machining, assembly and inspection operations. The precedence relations between the tasks of a project form an in-tree. There are cc. 100 different unary and cumulative resources in the plant.

Four systems participated in the test: DS denotes a dichotomic search using only propagation algorithms of the commercial CP solver. First, it was extended by the symmetry breaker (DS+SB), then by the algorithm for building freely completable partial solutions (DS+FC). In the last system, all components were switched on (DS+SB+FC).

Test runs were performed on two sets of data. Problem set 1 consists of 30 instances received from the industrial partner, each containing from 150 up to 990 tasks. The solution time limit was set to 120 seconds. Even the simplest algorithm, DS could find optimal solutions for all but one problem. The symmetry breaker further improved on its results, but the systems exploiting freely completable partial solutions were the definite winners, thanks to an extremely low number of search nodes. In many cases, including those where the first solution proved to be optimal, these two systems could solve the problems without any search. The results are presented in Table 1, with separate rows for instances which could be solved to optimality (+) and those which could not (–). *Search time* and *search nodes* both include finding the solutions and proving optimality. *Error* is measured by the difference of the best known upper and lower bounds, in the percentage of the lower bound.

A set of 18 larger problem instances – with up to 2021 tasks – was generated by merging several problems from problem set 1. 14 of them were solvable with standard methods of DS. Just like on problem set 1, identifying the freely completable partial solutions of the problems significantly reduced the size of the search tree. The complete system could solve all the problem instances within the time limit. The detailed results are presented in Table 2 for each problem instance[1].

---

[1] An extended set of problem instances is available online at
http://www.mit.bme.hu/~akovacs/projects/fcps/instances.html

Table 1. Results on problem set 1.

Method	Number of instances	Avg. search nodes	Avg. search time (sec)	Avg. Error (%)
DS (+)	29	282.5	2.00	-
DS (−)	1	59073.0	120.00	12.0
DS+SB (+)	30	272.1	1.67	-
DS+FC (+)	30	8.0	0.83	-
DS+SB+FC (+)	30	6.6	0.73	-

Table 2. Results on problem set 2.

Instance	Tasks	DS			DS+SB			DS+FC			DS+SB+FC		
		Nodes	Time (sec)	Error (%)	Nodes	Time (sec)	Error (%)	Nodes	Time (sec)	Error (%)	Nodes	Time (sec)	Error (%)
#1	836	836	14	-	836	11	-	0	8	-	0	0	-
#2	1027	1027	21	-	2054	22	-	0	11	-	0	1	-
#3	1138	2280	27	-	2276	27	-	13	11	-	0	10	-
#4	944	18650	120	7.1	12547	120	4.2	30	14	-	9	8	-
#5	1328	10294	120	11.0	9779	120	4.2	382	120	2.0	9	13	-
#6	639	24991	120	12.2	13785	65	-	2083	120	0.8	8	5	-
#7	1141	12334	120	8.9	2283	32	-	730	120	4.2	137	30	-
#8	994	1988	21	-	1988	22	-	0	7	-	0	8	-
#9	1932	3864	101	-	3857	110	-	0	22	-	0	24	-
#10	1876	3745	99	-	3745	106	-	18	28	-	81	55	-
#11	2021	2021	76	-	2021	82	-	0	30	-	0	33	-
#12	1637	1637	46	-	1637	50	-	0	20	-	0	23	-
#13	1771	1771	53	-	1771	59	-	0	24	-	0	24	-
#14	1337	4004	45	-	1337	27	-	794	112	-	212	32	-
#15	1592	3175	52	-	3184	55	-	525	106	-	0	16	-
#16	1098	1098	32	-	1098	40	-	0	18	-	73	29	-
#17	953	953	22	-	953	28	-	0	14	-	6	13	-
#18	819	819	17	-	811	22	-	0	11	-	0	13	-

The systems were also tested on Lawrence's job-shop benchmark problems la01-la20 [6]. Since these benchmarks basically lack the structural properties of industrial problems that our algorithms exploit, we did not expect the complete system to significantly improve on the performance of the commercial constraint-based scheduler. In fact, it turned out that freely completable partial solutions also exist in these benchmark instances, and our algorithms managed to decrease the size of the search tree by a factor of 7.3 on average, but this reduction did not always return the time invested in the construction of freely completable partial schedules.

7 Conclusions

In this paper we suggested general notions and specialized algorithms to treat constraint satisfaction problems that have relatively easy-to-solve and loosely connected sub-problems in their internal structure. We argued that solutions of such components should be discovered and separated as freely completable partial solutions by consistency preserving transformations.

We made this concept operational in the field of resource-constrained project scheduling. The method was validated on large-size practical scheduling problems, where only a few search decisions really matter. Such problems are hard to solve for pure propagation-based solvers because many search decisions produce equivalent choices. However, by constructing freely completable partial solutions we were able to avoid growing the search tree by branchings on irrelevant search decisions, and thus scheduling problems of large size became tractable.

We are currently extending the approach for other application areas of constraint programming, such as graph coloring. This requires the creation of heuristic algorithms that build freely completable partial solutions for the given problem class.

Acknowledgements

The authors wish to thank András Márkus and Tamás Kis for their valuable comments. This research has been supported by the grant OTKA T046509.

References

1. Apt, K.R.: Principles of Constraint Programming. Cambridge Univ. Press. (2003)
2. Backofen, R., Will, S.: Excluding Symmetries in Constraint-based Search, Constraints 7(3), pp. 333-349 (2002)
3. Baptiste, P., Le Pape, C.: Constraint Propagation and Decomposition Techniques for Highly Disjunctive and Highly Cumulative Project Scheduling Problems. Constraints 5(1/2), pp. 119-139. (2000)
4. Baptiste, P., Le Pape, C., Nuijten, W.: Constraint-based Scheduling. Kluwer Academic Publishers. (2001)
5. Baptiste, P., Peridy, L., Pinson, E.: A Branch and Bound to Minimize the Number of Late Jobs on a Single Machine with Release Time Constraints. European Journal of Operational Research 144(1), pp. 1-11. (2003)
6. Beasley, J.E: The OR-Library. http://www.ms.ic.ac.uk/info.html
7. Beck, J.Ch., Fox, M.S.: Dynamic Problem Structure Analysis as a Basis for Constraint-Directed Scheduling Heuristics. Artificial Intelligence 117, pp. 31-81. (2000)
8. Cesta, A., Oddi, A., Smith, S.F.: Profile-Based Algorithms to Solve Multiple Capacitated Metric Scheduling Problems. In Proc. of the 4th International Conference on Artificial Intelligence Planning Systems, pp. 214-223. (1998).
9. Crawford, J., Luks, G., Ginsberg, M., Roy, A.: Symmetry Breaking Predicates for Search Problems. In Proc. of the 5th Int. Conf. on Knowledge Representation and Reasoning, pp. 148-159. (1996)

10. Davis, E., Patterson, J.: A Comparision of Heuristic and Optimum Solutions in Resource-Constrained Project Scheduling. Management Science 21, pp. 944-955. (1975)
11. Demeulemeester, E.L., Herroelen, W.S.: A Branch-and-bound Procedure for the Multiple Resource-Constrained Project Scheduling Problem. Management Science 38(12), pp. 1803-1818. (1992)
12. Demeulemeester, E.L., Herroelen, W.S.: Project Scheduling: A Research Handbook. Kluwer Academic Publishers. (2002)
13. Fahle, T., Schamberger, S., Sellmann, M.: Symmetry Breaking. In Principles and Practice of Constraint Programming – CP2001, pp. 93-107. (2001)
14. Freuder, E.C.: Synthesizing Constraint Expressions. Communications ACM 21(11), pp. 958-966. (1978)
15. Gent, I.P., Smith, B.M.: Symmetry Breaking in Constraint Programming. In Proc. of the 14th European Conference on Artificial Intelligence, pp. 599-603. (2000)
16. Ilog Scheduler 5.1 User's Manual. (2001)
17. Kovács, A.: A Novel Approach to Aggregate Scheduling in Project-Oriented Manufacturing. In Proc. of the 13th Int. Conference on Automated Planning and Scheduling, Doctoral Consortium, pp. 63-67. (2003)
18. Laborie, Ph., Ghallab, M.: Planning with Shareable Resource Constraints. In Proc. of the 14th Int. Joint Conference on Artificial Intelligence, pp. 1643-1649. (1995)
19. Márkus, A., Váncza, J., Kis, T., Kovács, A., Project Scheduling Approach to Production Planning, CIRP Annals - Manuf. Techn. 52(1), pp. 359-362. (2003)
20. Tsang, E.: Foundations of Constraint Satisfaction. Academic Press. (1993)
21. Váncza, J., Kis, T., Kovács, A.: Aggregation – The Key to Integrating Production Planning and Scheduling. CIRP Annals - Manuf. Techn. 53(1), pp. 377-380. (2004)

Set Domain Propagation Using ROBDDs

Vitaly Lagoon and Peter J. Stuckey

Department of Computer Science and Software Engineering
The University of Melbourne, Vic. 3010, Australia
{lagoon,pjs}@cs.mu.oz.au

Abstract. Propagation based solvers typically represent variables by a current *domain* of possible values that may be part of a solution. Finite set variables have been considered impractical to represent as a domain of possible values since, for example, a set variable ranging over subsets of $\{1, \ldots, N\}$ has 2^N possible values. Hence finite set variables are presently represented by a lower bound set and upper bound set, illustrating all values definitely in (and by negation) all values definitely out. Propagators for finite set variables implement *set bounds* propagation where these sets are further constrained. In this paper we show that it is possible to represent the domains of finite set variables using reduced ordered binary decision diagrams (ROBDDs) and furthermore we can build efficient *domain* propagators for set constraints using ROBDDs. We show that set domain propagation is not only feasible, but can solve some problems significantly faster than using set bounds propagation because of the stronger propagation.

1 Introduction

Many constraint satisfaction problems are naturally expressed using set variables and set constraints, where the set variables range over subsets of a given a finite set of integers.

One widely-adopted approach to solving CSPs combines backtracking tree search with constraint propagation. *Constraint propagation*, based on local consistency algorithms, removes infeasible values from the domains of variables to reduce the search space. One of the most successful consistency techniques is *domain consistency* [14] which ensures that for each constraint c, every value in the domain of each variable can be extended to an assignment satisfying c. For simplicity, we refer to constraint propagation based on domain consistency as *domain propagation*. *Propagators* are functions to perform constraint propagation.

Unfortunately domain propagation where the variables range over sets is usually considered infeasible. For example, if a variable must take as a value a subset of $\{1, \ldots, N\}$ there are 2^N possible values. Simply representing the domain of possible values seems to be impractical. For this reason constraint propagation over set variables is always, as far as we are aware, restricted to use *set bounds propagation* [6, 11].

In set bounds propagation, a set variable v has its domain represented by two sets L the least possible set (that is all the values that must be in the set v) and U the greatest possible set (that is the complement of all values that cannot be in set v). Set bounds propagators update the least and greatest possible sets of variables v according to the constraints in which they are involved.

Interestingly set bounds propagation as defined in [6] is equivalent to modelling the problem using Boolean constraints and applying domain propagation to these constraints. That is the set variable v is represented by N Boolean variables $v_1, \ldots, v_N$ which represent the propositions $v_i \Leftrightarrow i \in v$. Refined versions of set bounds propagation, that add a representation of the cardinality of a variable to its domain, such as [1, 10], give stronger propagation.

In this paper we investigate this Boolean modelling approach further. We show it is possible to represent the domains of finite set variables using reduced ordered binary decision diagrams (ROBDDs). We shall show that domains can be represented by very small ROBDDs, even if they represent a large number of possible sets. Furthermore we represent set constraints using ROBDDs, and use this to build efficient *domain* propagators for set constraints. ROBDD representations of simple set constraints are surprisingly compact.

In summary the contributions of this paper are:

– We show how to efficiently representing domains of (finite) set variables using ROBDDs.
– We show that we can build efficient constraint propagators for primitive set constraints using ROBDDs
– We illustrate the wealth of modelling possibilities that arise using ROBDDs to build propagators.
– We give experiments illustrating that set domain propagation is advantageous for (finite) set constraint problems.

2 Preliminaries

In this paper we consider finite set constraint solving (over sets of integers) with constraint propagation and tree search.

Let $\mathcal{V}$ denote the set of all set variables. Each variable is associated with a finite set of possible values (which are themselves sets), defined by the domain of the CSP. A *domain* D is a complete mapping from a fixed (countable) set of variables $\mathcal{V}$ to finite sets of finite sets of integers. The *intersection* of two domains D_1 and D_2, denoted $D_1 \sqcap D_2$, is defined by the domain $D_3(v) = D_1(v) \cap D_2(v)$ for all v. A domain D_1 is *stronger* than a domain D_2, written $D_1 \sqsubseteq D_2$, if $D_1(v) \subseteq D_2(v)$ for all variables v. A domain D_1 is equal to a domain D_2, denoted $D_1 = D_2$, if $D_1(v) = D_2(v)$ for all variables v.

We also use *range* notation whenever possible: $[L \mathrel{..} U]$ denotes the set of sets of integers $\{d \mid L \subseteq d \subseteq U\}$ when L and U are sets of integers.

We shall be interested in the notion of an *initial domain*, which we denote D_{init}. The initial domain gives the initial values possible for each variable. In effect an initial domain allows us to restrict attention to domains D such that

$D \sqsubseteq D_{init}$. For our purposes we shall restrict attention to initial domains D_{init} where $D_{init}(x) = [\emptyset \mathrel{..} \{1,\ldots,N\}]$ for all variables x.

A *valuation* θ is a mapping of variables to sets of integer values, written $\{x_1 \mapsto d_1, \ldots, x_n \mapsto d_n\}$. We extend the valuation θ to map expressions or constraints involving the variables in the natural way.

Let *vars* be the function that returns the set of variables appearing in an expression, constraint or valuation. In an abuse of notation, we define a valuation θ to be an element of a domain D, written $\theta \in D$, if $\theta(v_i) \in D(v_i)$ for all $v_i \in vars(\theta)$.

Constraints. A constraint places restriction on the allowable values for a set of variables and is usually written in well understood mathematical syntax. For our purposes we shall restrict ourselves to the following *primitive set constraints*: (element) $k \in v$, (not element) $k \notin v$, (equality) $v = w$, (constant) $v = d$, (subset) $v \subseteq w$, (union) $u = v \cup w$, (intersection) $u = v \cap w$, (subtraction) $u = v - w$, (complement) $v = \overline{w}$, (disequality) $v \neq w$, (cardinality equals) $|v| = k$, (cardinality lower) $|v| \geq k$, and (cardinality upper) $|v| \leq k$, where u, v, w are set variables, d is a constant finite set and k is a constant integer. A *set constraint* is a (possibly existentially quantified) conjunction of primitive set constraints. Later we shall introduce more complex forms of set constraint.

We define $solns(c) = \{\theta \mid vars(\theta) = vars(c) \land \models_\theta c\}$, that is the set of θ that make the constraint c hold true. We call $solns(c)$ the *solutions* of c.

Propagators and Propagation Solvers. In the context of propagation-based constraint solving, a constraint specifies a propagator, which gives the basic unit of propagation. A *propagator* f is a monotonically decreasing function from domains to domains, i.e. $D_1 \sqsubseteq D_2$ implies that $f(D_1) \sqsubseteq f(D_2)$, and $f(D) \sqsubseteq D$. A propagator f is *correct* for constraint c iff for all domains D

$$\{\theta \mid \theta \in D\} \cap solns(c) = \{\theta \mid \theta \in f(D)\} \cap solns(c)$$

This is a weak restriction since for example, the identity propagator is correct for all constraints c.

Example 1. For the constraint $c \equiv v \subseteq w$ the function $f(D)(v) = \{d_1 \in D(v) \mid d_1 \subseteq \bigcup D(w)\}$, $f(D)(w) = D(w)$, is a correct propagator for c. Let $D_1(v) = \{\{1\}, \{1,3,5\}, \{6\}, \{3,4\}\}$ and $D_1(w) = \{\{1\}, \{3,4,5\}, \{2\}\}$, then $f(D_1) = D_2$ where $D_2(v) = \{\{1\}, \{1,3,5\}, \{3,4\}\}$ and $D_2(w) = D_1(w)$.

A *propagation solver* for a set of propagators F and current domain D, $solv(F, D)$, repeatedly applies all the propagators in F starting from domain D until there is no further change in resulting domain. $solv(F, D)$ is the largest domain $D' \sqsubseteq D$ which is a fixpoint (i.e. $f(D') = D'$) for all $f \in F$. In other words, $solv(F, D)$ returns a new domain defined by

$$iter(F, D) = \bigsqcap_{f \in F} f(D) \quad \text{and} \quad solv(F, D) = \text{gfp}(\lambda d. iter(F, d))(D)$$

where gfp denotes the greatest fixpoint w.r.t $\sqsubseteq$ lifted to functions.

Domain Consistency. A domain D is *domain consistent* for a constraint c if D is the least domain containing all solutions $\theta \in D$ of c, i.e, there does not exist $D' \sqsubset D$ such that $\theta \in D \wedge \theta \in solns(c) \rightarrow \theta \in D'$.

A set of propagators F maintains *domain consistency* for a constraint c, if $solv(F, D)$ is always domain consistent for c.

Define the *domain propagator* for a constraint c as

$$dom(c)(D)(v) = \{\theta(v) \mid \theta \in D \wedge \theta \in solns(c)\} \text{ where } v \in vars(c)$$
$$dom(c)(D)(v) = D(v) \text{ otherwise}$$

Example 2. For the constraint $c \equiv v \subseteq w$ and let $D_3 = dom(c)(D_1)$ where $D_1(v) = \{\{1\}, \{1,3,5\}, \{6\}, \{3,4\}\}$ and $D_1(w) = \{\{1\}, \{3,4,5\}, \{2\}\}$, then $D_3(v) = \{\{1\}, \{3,4\}\}$ and $D_3(w) = \{\{1\}, \{3,4,5\}\}$. Now D_3 is domain consistent with respect to c.

Set Bounds Consistency. Domain consistency has been considered prohibitive to compute for constraints involving set variables. For that reason, set bounds propagation [6, 10] is typically used where a domain maps a set variable to a lower bound set of integers and an upper bound set of integers.

We shall enforce this by treating the domain $D(x)$ of a set variable x as if it were the range $[\cap D(x) .. \cup D(x)]$. In practice if only set bounds propagators are used, all domains will be of this form in any case. Define $ran(D)$ as the domain D' where $D'(x) = [\cap D(x) .. \cup D(x)]$. The set bounds propagator returns the smallest set range which includes the result returned by the domain propagator.

Define the *set bounds propagator* for a constraint c as

$$sb(c)(D)(v) = \frac{D(v) \cap}{[\cap dom(c)(ran(D))(v) .. \cup dom(c)(ran(D))(v)]} \quad v \in vars(c)$$
$$sb(c)(D)(v) = D(v) \text{ otherwise}$$

Example 3. Given constraint $c \equiv v \subseteq w$ and $D_4 = sb(c)(D_1)$, where D_1 is defined in Example 2. Then $ran(D_1)(v) = [\emptyset .. \{1,3,4,5,6\}]$, $ran(D_1)(w) = [\emptyset .. \{1,2,3,4,5\}]$, $D_4(v) = \{\{1\}, \{1,3,5\}, \{3,4\}\}$ and $D_4(w) = \{\{1\}, \{3,4,5\}, \{2\}\}$.

Boolean Formulae and Binary Decision Diagrams. We make use of the following Boolean operations: $\wedge$ (conjunction), $\vee$ (disjunction), $\neg$ (negation), $\rightarrow$ (implication), $\leftrightarrow$ (bi-implication) and $\exists$ (existential quantification). We denote by $\exists_V F$ the formula $\exists x_1 \cdots \exists x_n F$ where $V = \{x_1, \ldots, x_n\}$, , and by $\bar{\exists}_V F$ we mean $\exists_{V'} F$ where $V' = vars(F) - V$.

The *Reduced Ordered Binary Decision Diagram* (ROBDD) [3] is a canonical representation of Boolean function. An ROBDD is a directed acyclic graph. There are two terminal nodes are labeled with the Boolean constants 0 (false) and 1 (true). Each non-terminal node is labelled by a variable and has two branches, a 1-branch and a 0-branch, corresponding respectively to the two possible values of the variable. Thus, the value of a Boolean function for a given assignment of variables can be computed as a terminal reached from the root by following the corresponding 1- or 0-branches. An ROBDD obeys the following restrictions:

- Variables are totally ordered by some ordering $\prec$ and each child node (with label w) of a node labelled v is such that $v \prec w$.
 - There are no duplicate subgraphs (nodes with the same variable label and 1- and 0-branches).
 - There are no redundant tests (each non-terminal node has different 1- and 0-branches).

Example 4. The ROBDD for the formula $(v_1 \rightarrow w_1) \wedge (v_2 \rightarrow w_2)$ with the ordering of variables $v_1 \prec v_2 \prec w_1 \prec w_2$ is shown in Figure 2(a). The ROBDD is read as follows. Each non-leaf node has a decision variable. If the variable is false (0) we take the left 0-branch (dashed), if the variable is true (1) we take the right 1-branch (solid). One can verify that for example a valuation that make the formula true, e.g. $\{v_1 \mapsto 1, v_2 \mapsto 0, w_1 \mapsto 1, w_2 \mapsto 1\}$, give a path to the node 1, while valuations that make the formula false, e.g. $\{v_1 \mapsto 0, v_2 \mapsto 1, w_1 \mapsto 1, w_2 \mapsto 0\}$, give a path to the node 0.

The ROBDD-based representations of Boolean functions are *canonical* meaning that for a fixed order of variables two Boolean functions are equivalent if and only if their respective ROBDDs are identical.

There are efficient algorithms for many Boolean operations applied to ROBDDs. Let $|r|$ be the number of internal nodes in ROBDD r then the complexity of the basic operations for constructing new ROBDDs is $O(|r_1||r_2|)$ for $r_1 \wedge r_2$, $r_1 \vee r_2$ and $r_1 \leftrightarrow r_2$, $O(|r|)$ for $\neg r$, and $O(|r|^2)$ for $\exists x.r$. Note however that we can test whether two ROBDDs are identical, whether $r_1 \leftrightarrow r_2$ is equivalent to true (1), in $O(1)$.

Although in theory the number of nodes in an ROBDDs can be exponential in the number of variables in the represented Boolean function, in practice ROBDDs are often very compact and computationally efficient. This is due to the fact that ROBDDs exploit to a very high-degree the symmetry of models of a Boolean formula.

3 Basic Set Domain Propagation

3.1 Modelling Set Domains Using ROBDDs

The key step in building set domain propagation using ROBDDs is to realise that we can represent a finite set domain using an ROBDD.

Let x be a set variable taking a value A subset of $\{1, \ldots, N\}$, then we can represent A using a valuation θ_A of the vector of Boolean variables $V(x) = \langle x_1, \ldots, x_N \rangle$, where $\theta_A = \{x_i \mapsto 1 \mid i \in A\} \cup \{x_i \mapsto 0 \mid i \notin A\}$. We can represent an arbitrary set of subsets S of $\{1, \ldots, N\}$ by a Boolean formula ϕ which has exactly the solutions $\{\theta_A \mid A \in S\}$. We will order the variables $x_1 \prec x_2 \cdots \prec x_N$. For example the set of sets $S = \{\{1, 2\}, \{\}, \{2, 3\}\}$ where $N = 3$ is represented by the formula $(x_1 \wedge x_2 \wedge \neg x_3) \vee (\neg x_2 \wedge \neg x_2 \wedge \neg x_3) \vee (\neg x_1 \wedge x_2 \wedge x_3)$.

An ROBDD allows us to represent (some) subsets of $2^{\{1,\ldots,N\}}$ efficiently. The initial domain for x, $D_{init}(x) = [\emptyset \mathrel{..} \{1, \ldots, N\}]$, is represented by the $O(1)$ sized ROBDD 1, independent of N.

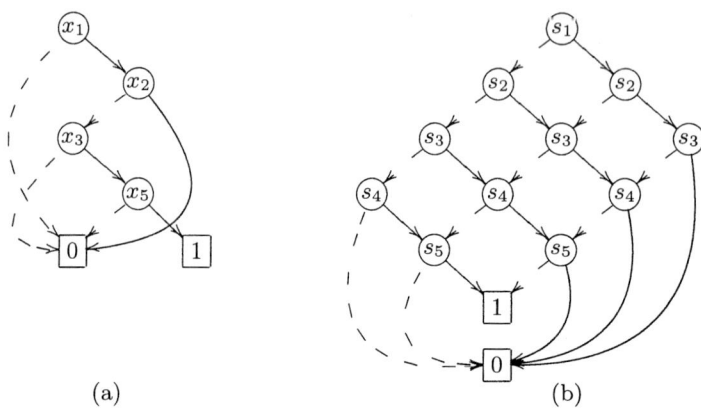

Fig. 1. ROBDDs for (a) $[\{1,3,5\} .. \{1,3,\ldots N\}]$ and (b) $(s \subseteq \{1,2,3,4,5\}, |s| = 2)$.

If $D(x) = [\{1,3,5\} .. \{1,3,\ldots,N\}]$, we can represent these 2^{N-4} sets by the ROBDD shown in Figure 1(a), again independent of N. Indeed any domain $D'(x)$ of the form $[L .. U]$ can be represented in $O(|L| + N - |U|)$.

Even some sets of subsets that may appear difficult to represent are also representable efficiently. Consider representing all the subsets of $\{1,2,3,4,5\}$ of cardinality 2. Then the ROBDD representing this domain is shown in Figure 1(b).

3.2 Modelling Primitive Set Constraints Using ROBDDs

We will convert each primitive set constraint c to an ROBDD $B(c)$ on the Boolean variable representations $V(x)$ of its set variables x. We must be careful in ordering the variables in each ROBDD in order to build small representations of the formula.

Example 5. Consider the two representations of the ROBDD for the constraint representing $v \subseteq w$ where $D_{init}(v) = D_{init}(w) = [\emptyset .. \{1,2\}]$ shown in Figure 2. The first representation with the ordering $v_1 \prec v_2 \prec w_1 \prec w_2$ is much larger than the second with ordering $v_1 \prec w_1 \prec v_2 \prec w_2$. In fact if we generalize for initial domains of size N the ordering $v_1 \prec \cdots \prec v_N \prec w_1 \prec \cdots \prec w_N$ leads to an exponential representation, while the order $v_1 \prec w_1 \prec v_2 \prec w_2 \prec \cdots \prec v_N \prec w_N$ is linear.

By ordering the Boolean variables pointwise we can guarantee linear representations $B(c)$ for each primitive constraint c except those for cardinality. The table of expressions and sizes is shown in Figure 3. The cardinality primitive constraints use a subsidiary Boolean formula defined by the function $card(v, l, u, n)$ which is the cardinality of v restricted to the elements from $n + 1, \ldots, N$ is between l and u. It is defined recursively as follows:

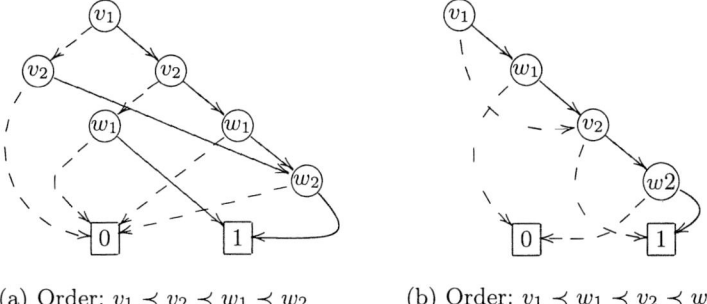

(a) Order: $v_1 \prec v_2 \prec w_1 \prec w_2$ (b) Order: $v_1 \prec w_1 \prec v_2 \prec w_2$

Fig. 2. Two ROBDDs for $v \subseteq w$.

c	Boolean expression $B(c)$	size of ROBDD
$k \in v$	v_k	$O(1)$
$k \notin v$	$\neg v_k$	$O(1)$
$v = w$	$\bigwedge_{1 \leq i \leq N}(v_i \leftrightarrow w_i)$	$O(N)$
$v = d$	$\bigwedge_{i \in d} v_i \wedge \bigwedge_{1 \leq i \leq N, i \notin d} \neg v_i$	$O(N)$
$v \subseteq w$	$\bigwedge_{1 \leq i \leq N}(v_i \to w_i)$	$O(N)$
$u = v \cup w$	$\bigwedge_{1 \leq i \leq N}(u_i \leftrightarrow (v_i \vee w_i))$	$O(N)$
$u = v \cap w$	$\bigwedge_{1 \leq i \leq N}(u_i \leftrightarrow (v_i \wedge w_i))$	$O(N)$
$u = v - w$	$\bigwedge_{1 \leq i \leq N}(u_i \leftrightarrow (v_i \wedge \neg w_i))$	$O(N)$
$v = \overline{w}$	$\bigwedge_{1 \leq i \leq N} \neg(v_i \leftrightarrow w_i)$	$O(N)$
$v \neq w$	$\bigvee_{1 \leq i \leq N} \neg(v_i \leftrightarrow w_i)$	$O(N)$
$|v| = k$	$card(v, k, k, 0))$	$O(k(N-k))$
$|v| \geq k$	$card(v, k, N, 0)$	$O(k(N-k))$
$|v| \leq k$	$card(v, 0, k, 0)$	$O(k(N-k))$

Fig. 3. Boolean representation of set constraints and size of ROBDD.

$$card(v, l, u, n) = \begin{cases} 1 & \text{if } l \leq 0 \wedge N - n \leq u \\ 0 & \text{if } N - n < l \vee u < 0 \\ (\neg v_{n+1} \wedge card(v, l, u, n+1)) \vee & \\ (v_{n+1} \wedge card(v, l-1, u-1, n+1)) & \text{otherwise} \end{cases}$$

This definition also shows why the representation is quadratic since the right hand sides directly represent ROBDD nodes. For any formula $card(v, l, u, n)$ it involves at most a quadratic number of subformulæ.

3.3 Basic Set-Domain Solver

We build a domain propagator $dom(c)$ for constraint c using ROBDDs as follows. Let $vars(c) = \{v_1, \ldots, v_n\}$ then we define

$$dom(c)(D)(v_i) = \exists_{V(v_i)}.B(c) \wedge \bigwedge_{j=1}^{n} D(v_j)$$

This formula directly defines the domain consistency operator. Because each of $B(c)$ and $D(v_j)$ is an ROBDD this is directly implementable using ROBDD operations.

Example 6. Assume $N = 2$ and suppose $D(v) = \{\{1\}, \{1,2\}\}$, and $D(w) = [\emptyset .. \{1,2\}]$, represented by the ROBDDs v_1 and 1. We conjoin these with the ROBDD for $v \subseteq w$ shown in Figure 2(c) (the result is a similar ROBDD with left child of the root 0). We project this ROBDD onto the Boolean variables w_1, w_2 of w obtaining the formula w_1. The new domain of W becomes w_1 representing sets $\{\{1\}, \{1,2\}\}$.

The basic propagation mechanism improves slightly on the mathematical definition by (a) only revisiting propagators when the domain of one of their variables changes (b) ensuring that the last propagator is not re-added by its own changes since it is idempotent. We can also execute unary constraint propagators just once. The code for solv is shown below where for simplicity the first argument is a set of constraints, rather than their domain propagators.

```
solv(C, D)
    Q := C
    while (∃c ∈ Q)
        D' := dom(c)(D)
        V := {v ∈ V | D(v) ≠ D'(v)}
        Q := (Q ∪ {c' ∈ C | vars(c') ∩ V ≠ ∅}) − {c}
        D := D'
    return D
```

Note that detecting the set V of variables changed by the $dom(c)$ is cheap because the equivalence check $D(v) = D'(v)$ for ROBDDs is constant time (the two pointers must be identical).

4 Towards a More Efficient Set Domain Solver

4.1 Removing Intermediate Variables

For many real problems the actual problem constraints will not be primitive set constraints, but rather more complicated set constraints that can be split into primitive set constraints. This means that we introduce new variables and multiple propagators for a single problem constraint.

Example 7. Consider the following constraint $|v \cap w| \leq 1$ which is found in many problems, requiring that v and w have at most one element in common. This can be represented as primitive set constraints by introducing an intermediate variable u as $\exists u.u = v \cap w \wedge |u| \leq 1$. For set bounds propagation this breaking down of the constraint is implicitly performed.

Now the splitting into primitive constraints does not affect the propagation strength of the resulting set of propagators. But it does add a new variable, and complicate the propagation process by making more constraints.

Using an ROBDD representation of the more complex constraint we can avoid splitting the constraint. Instead we construct a Boolean representation directly using ROBDD operations. Essentially we can take the ROBDDs for the individual primitive constraints and project away the intermediate variable.

Example 8. We can build a propagator $dom(c)$ directly for the constraint $c \equiv |v \cap w| \leq 1$, by constructing the ROBDD $\exists_{V(u)}.B(u = v \cap w) \wedge B(|u| \leq 1)$. The resulting ROBDD has size $O(N)$.

This contrasts with set bounds propagation where we must carefully construct a new propagator for each kind of primitive constraint we wish to support. Typically only the given primitive constraints are provided and intermediate variables are silently introduced. This approach is used for instance in set constraint solvers provided by ECL^iPS^e [5].

4.2 Building Global Constraints

Just as we can create more complex ROBDDs for constraints that are typically broken up into primitive sets constraints, we can also build domain propagators for complex conjunctions of constraints using ROBDD operations, so called *global constraints*.

Example 9. Consider the following constraint $\texttt{partition}(v_1, \ldots, v_n)$ which requires that the sets $v_1, \ldots, v_n$ form a partition of $\{1, \ldots, N\}$. The meaning in terms of primitive set constraints is

$$\bigwedge_{i=1}^{n} \bigwedge_{j=i+1}^{n} (\exists u_{ij}.u_{ij} = v_i \cap v_j \wedge u_{ij} = \emptyset) \wedge$$
$$\exists w_1 \ldots w_{n+1}.w_{n+1} = \emptyset \wedge \bigwedge_{i=1}^{n}(w_i = v_i \cup w_{i+1}) \wedge w_1 = \{1, \ldots, N\}$$

Now $dom(\texttt{partition}(v_1, \ldots, v_n))$ is much stronger in propagation than the set of propagators for the primitive constraints in its definition. For example consider $\texttt{partition}(v_1, \ldots, v_3)$ and domain D where $D(v_1) = D(v_2) = \{\{1\}, \{2\}\}$ and $D(v_3) = \{\{2\}, \{3\}\}$ and $N = 3$. While the individual propagators will not modify the domain, the global propagator will revise the domain of v_3 to $\{\{3\}\}$.

We can build a single ROBDD (of size $O(nN)$) representing this formula, and hence we have built a domain constructor for the entire constraint.

Clearly as we build larger and larger global constraint propagators we will build larger and larger ROBDD representations. There is a tradeoff in terms of strength of propagation versus time to propagate using this ROBDD.

Example 10. Consider the constraint $\texttt{atmost}([v_1, \ldots, v_n], k)$ introduced in [12], which requires that each of the n sets of cardinality k should intersect pairwise in at most one element. The meaning in terms of primitive set constraints is

$$\bigwedge_{i=1}^{n} |v_i| = k \quad \wedge \quad \bigwedge_{i=1}^{n} \bigwedge_{j=i+1}^{n} (\exists u_{ij}.u_{ij} = v_i \cap v_j \wedge |u_{ij}| \leq 1)$$

While we can create an ROBDD that represents the entire global constraint the resulting ROBDD is exponential in size. Hence it is not practical to use as a global propagator.

4.3 Breaking Symmetries with Order Constraints

In many problems involving set constraints there will be large numbers of symmetries which can substantially increase the size of the search space. One approach to removing symmetries is to add order constraints $v < w$ among sets. $v < w$ means that the list of Booleans $V(v)$ is lexicographically smaller than the list of Booleans $V(w)$. These order constraints can be straightforwardly represented using ROBDDs of size $O(N)$. We represent $v < w$ by the formula $ltset(v, w, 1)$ where

$$ltset(v, w, n) = \begin{cases} 0 & n > N \\ (\neg v_n \wedge w_n) \vee ((v_n \leftrightarrow w_n) \wedge ltset(v, w, n+1)) & \text{otherwise} \end{cases}$$

5 Experiments

We have implemented a set-domain solver based on the method proposed in this paper. Our implementation written in Mercury [13] integrates a fairly naïve propagation-based mechanism with an ROBDD library. We have chosen the CUDD package [4] as a platform for ROBDD manipulations.

We conducted a series of experiments using our solver and compared the experimental results with the data collected by running the ECL^{i}PS^e [5] ic_sets set bounds propagation solver on the same problems. All experiments were conducted on a machine with Pentium-M 1.5 GHz processor running Linux v2.4.

5.1 Ternary Steiner Systems

A ternary Steiner system of order N is a set of $N(N-1)/6$ triplets of distinct elements taking their values between 1 and N, such that all the pairs included in two different triplets are different. A Steiner triple system of order N exists if and only if $n \equiv 1, 3 \mod 6$, as shown by Kirkman [7]. A ternary Steiner system of order N is naturally modelled using set variables $s_1 \ldots s_m$, where $m = N(N-1)/6$ and constrained by:

$$\bigwedge_{i=1}^{m}(|s_i| = 3) \wedge \bigwedge_{i=1}^{m-1} \bigwedge_{j=i+1}^{m}(|s_i \cap s_j| \leq 1 \wedge (s_i < s_j))$$

where we have added ordering constraints $s_i < s_j$ to remove symmetries.

We conducted a series of experiments finding the first solution for Steiner systems of orders 7,9,13 and 15. We use four labeling strategies given by crosscombinations of two ways of choosing a variable for labeling and two modes of assigning values. The choice of variable is either sequential or "first-fail" i.e., a variable with a smallest domain is chosen at each labeling step. Once a variable is chosen we explore the two possibilities for each possible element of set from

Table 1. ROBDD set domain solver for finding Steiner systems. The simple model with separate constraints and intermediate variables.

Problem	Model size ×10³	"element in set" labeling						"element not in set" labeling					
		sequential			first-fail			sequential			first-fail		
		time sec.	fails	size ×10³	time sec.	fails	size ×10³	time sec.	fails	size ×10³	time sec.	fails	size ×10³
steiner(7)	3	0.1	1	18	0.0	1	18	0.0	0	16	0.0	0	16
steiner(9)	11	4.6	365	324	4.7	370	325	1.3	100	180	1.4	100	180
steiner(13)	47	—	—	—	—	—	—	—	—	—	—	—	—
steiner(15)	140	—	—	—	—	—	—	23.9	0	1,058	24.1	0	1,058

least to greatest. Each element is either a member of the set represented by the variable, or it is not. The alternative (element in set) or (element not in set) we try first induces the two modes of value assignment. This order is significant in practice, as we show in our experiments.

Table 1 summarizes the experimental data produced by our BDD-based solver for the model where each primitive set constraint is represented separately and intermediate variables are introduced (see Example 7). For each problem we provide the size of the corresponding model. The sizes listed in this and the following tables are measured in the number of (thousands of) ROBDD nodes. For each run we count the run-time, the number of fails i.e., the number of times the solver backtracks from its choice of value, and the maximum number of live ROBDD nodes reached during the run. The "—" entries correspond to runs which could not complete in ten minutes.

A better ROBDD model of the constraints for the Steiner problem merges the constraints on each pair s_i and s_j, constructing a single ROBDD for each $\psi_{ij} = (|s_i \cap s_j| \leq 1) \wedge (s_i < s_j)$, and avoiding the intermediate variable. The results using this model are shown in Table 2. While the resulting model can be larger, the search space is reduced since $dom(\psi_{ij})$ propagates more strongly than the set $\{dom(|s_i \cap s_j| \leq 1), dom(s_i < s_j)\}$, and the time and peak size usage is substantially decreased. Hence it is clearly beneficial to eliminate intermediate variables and merge constraints.

Table 2. ROBDD set domain solver for finding Steiner systems. The improved model with merged constraints and no intermediate variables.

Problem	Model size ×10³	"element in set" labeling						"element not in set" labeling					
		sequential			first-fail			sequential			first-fail		
		time sec.	fails	size ×10³	time sec.	fails	size ×10³	time sec.	fails	size ×10³	time sec.	fails	size ×10³
steiner(7)	3	0.0	0	4	0.0	0	4	0.0	0	4	0.0	0	4
steiner(9)	11	0.0	2	17	0.1	798	23	0.1	9	20	0.1	9	20
steiner(13)	76	—	—	—	336.3	21,264	398	160.5	24,723	295	80.2	6,195	288
steiner(15)	92	2.8	0	172	—	—	—	2.2	0	160	2.4	0	160

Table 3. ECL^{i}PS^e set bounds solver for finding Steiner systems.

Problem	"element in set"				"element not in set"			
	sequential		first-fail		sequential		first-fail	
	time	fails	time	fails	time	fails	time	fails
steiner(7)	0.0	9	0.0	9	0.0	10	0.0	10
steiner(9)	1.0	542	1.2	542	4.9	1,394	4.8	1,394
steiner(13)	—	—	—	—	—	—	—	—
steiner(15)	2.4	6	33.9	7,139	2.8	65	3.4	65

Table 4. Finding all solutions of Steiner ternary systems.

Problem	solutions	ECL^{i}PS^e		ROBDD-based solver	
		time	fails	time	fails
steiner(7)	30	3.9	3015	0.1	38
steiner(9)	840	—	—	22.5	8934

We compared the set domain propagation solver against the ECL^{i}PS^e set bounds propagation solver ic_sets using the same model and search strategies. We had to implement a version of $v < w$ for sets using reified constraints. Table 3 shows the corresponding results to Table 2.

Clearly the set domain solver involves far less search than the set bounds solver. It is also able to find solutions to the hardest example steiner(13). The set domain solver is faster than set bounds solving except for steiner(15) with sequential labeling, and when with first-fail labeling it gets stuck in a very unproductive part of the search space. One should note that with first-fail labeling the search spaces explored are quite different, since the variable ordering changes.

In order to better gauge the relationship between the two approaches without being biased by search strategy we ran experiments to find all distinct Steiner systems of orders 7 and 9 modulo the lexicographic ordering. Table 4 summarizes the results of the experiments. We list the best results for the both solvers. The results are in both cases are obtained using the "first-fail" and "element not in set" labeling strategy. The run of the ECL^{i}PS^e solver for $N = 9$ was aborted after one hour. Due to a large number of solutions neither of the two solvers can enumerate all solutions for $N = 13$ and $N = 15$. Clearly the reduced search space for the set domain solver is of substantial benefit in this case.

5.2 The Social Golfers Problem

The problem consists in arranging $N = g \times s$ players into g groups of s players each week, playing for w weeks, so that no two players play in the same group twice. The problem is modeled using an $w \times g$ matrix of set variables v_{ij} where $1 \leq i \leq w$ and $1 \leq j \leq g$ are the week and the group indices respectively. The experiments described in this section are based on the following model.

Table 5. Social golfers.

Problem	Model size ×10³	ROBDD-based solver						ECL^{i}PS^e			
		sequential			first-fail			sequential		first-fail	
		time sec.	fails	size ×10³	time sec.	fails	size ×10³	time sec.	fails	time sec.	fails
2-5-4	12	0.1	0	44	0.1	0	44	5.3	10,468	5.8	10,468
2-6-4	24	0.2	0	136	0.2	0	130	35.5	64,308	38.7	64,308
2-7-4	48	0.7	0	382	0.6	0	346	70.3	114,818	75.4	114,818
2-8-5	131	3.7	0	1,431	3.5	0	1,367	—	—	—	—
3-5-4	23	0.5	0	197	0.4	0	199	9.3	14,092	11.2	14,092
3-6-4	45	2.8	0	1,157	2.2	0	952	59.2	83,815	74.5	83,815
3-7-4	87	18.2	0	2,133	3.5	0	1,504	113.6	146,419	155.7	146,419
4-5-4	38	1.2	0	456	1.2	0	487	10.5	14,369	15.0	14,369
4-6-5	94	302.9	0	6,184	174.9	0	3,341	—	—	—	—
4-7-4	135	—	—	—	22.1	0	1,817	135.8	149,767	221.5	149,767
4-9-4	118	—	—	—	334.1	0	6,815	22.7	19,065	38.1	19,065
5-4-3	20	41.0	5,165	481	32.4	3,812	481	—	—	—	—
5-5-4	56	5.5	41	1,313	3.8	18	1,123	267.3	199,632	317.0	199,632
5-7-4	80	—	—	—	55.0	0	2,789	—	—	—	—
5-8-3	89	21.2	0	1,638	6.6	0	1,514	4.1	2,229	4.4	2,229
6-4-3	28	28.8	2,132	471	20.3	1,504	379	—	—	—	—
6-5-3	56	2.6	82	352	1.8	34	321	—	—	—	—
6-6-3	105	2.7	0	742	2.4	7	602	2.7	1,462	2.9	1,462
7-5-3	75	—	—	—	24.6	528	940	—	—	—	—
7-5-5	80	static fail						—	—	—	—

$$\bigwedge_{i=1}^{w}\left(\texttt{partition}^{<}(v_{i1},\ldots,v_{ig}) \wedge \bigwedge_{j=1}^{g}|v_{ij}| = s\right) \wedge$$
$$\left(\bigwedge_{i,j\in\{1\ldots w\},\, i\neq j} \bigwedge_{k,l\in\{1\ldots g\}} |v_{ik} \cap v_{jl}| \leq 1\right) \wedge \left(\bigwedge_{i=1}^{w-1} \bigwedge_{j=i+1}^{w} v_{i1} \leq v_{j1}\right)$$

The global constraint partition$^<$ is a variant of the partition constraint defined in Section 4.2 imposing a lexicographic order on its arguments i.e., $v_1 < \cdots < v_n$. The corresponding propagator is based on a single ROBDD.

Table 5 summarizes the results of our experiments with social golfers problem. Each instance of the problem shown in the table under "Problem" column is in the form $w - g - s$, where w is a number of weeks in the schedule, g is a number of groups playing each week, and s is a size of each group. We used the same instances of the problem as in [8]. For the ROBDD-based solver we provide model sizes, run times, number of fails and peak numbers of live nodes reached during the computation. For the ECL^{i}PS^e solver we provide the run times and numbers of fails. The experiments in the both solvers were carried out using "element in set" labeling strategy. Entries "—" indicate that the run was aborted after ten minutes.

As we can see from the table the ROBDD-based solver betters the ECL^{i}PS^e solver in all but one case (4-9-4). Note also that the ROBDD-based solver using "first-fail" labeling is able to cope with all twenty instances of the problem, while the ECL^{i}PS^e solver runs out of time in eight cases. The entries for 4-9-4 and 4-6-5 demonstrate that the ROBDD-based approach is sometimes more sensitive to domain sizes than the set-bounds propagation. Set-domain representations may grow rapidly as the number of potential set members grows. The more detailed set-domain information requires more computational resources for its propagation. As a result, in cases like 4-9-4 even a computation not involving backtracking can be less efficient than a search-intensive solution based on a simpler propagation.

There are three instances in the table: 5-4-3, 6-4-3 and 7-5-5 for which the problem has no solution. Reporting that no solution exists for these cases requires a solver to explore the entire search space. Note that neither of the three instances can be solved by the ECL^{i}PS^e solver, while the ROBDD-based solver always completes in under a minute. The case of 7-5-5 is especially interesting emphasizing the strength of set-domain propagation. In this case our solver reports inconsistency of the initial configuration before the actual labeling is started. Thus, the problem is solved quickly (under 0.5 sec) and there is no search involved.

Finally, we compared our experimental results with those collected by Kiziltan [8] for the same instances of the social golfers problem. The experiments reported by Kiziltan are based on four different Boolean models incorporating intricate techniques of symmetry breaking. Comparing the results for the "first-fail" strategy of the ROBDD-based solver with the best results of Kiziltan we could see that our solver improves on the number of fails in all but two cases and in run time in six cases out of the twenty[1]. Given the current naïve implementation of our system we find these results very encouraging.

6 Conclusions and Future Work

We have shown that set domain propagation is practical and advantageous for solving set problems. Set domain propagation using ROBDDs opens up a huge area of exploration: determining which constraints can be efficiently represented using ROBDDs, and determining the best model for individual problems. Clearly not all constraints (such as `atmost`) can be handled solely using ROBDD propagation, which leads us to ask how we can create more efficient global propagators for such constraints. Some avenues of investigation are using size bounded ROBDDs to approximate the global constraints, or building more complicated partial propagation approaches using ROBDD building blocks. Clearly we should incorporate set bounds propagation into our solver, this is straightforward by separating the fixed Boolean variables (L and $\bar{U}$) from the non-fixed Boolean variables in the domain representation. Together with higher priority for set bounds propagators this should increase the efficiency of set domain propagation. Finally, it would be interesting to compare the set domains solver versus a set bounds solver with better cardinality reasoning such as Cardinal [1] and Mozart [10].

---

[1] The timing comparisons are not very meaningful having been carried out on different machines.

References

1. F. Azevedo and P. Barahona. Modelling digital circuits problems with set constraints. In *Proceedings of the 1st International Conference on Computational Logic*, volume 1861 of *LNCS*, pages 414–428. Springer-Verlag, 2000.
2. C. Bessiére and J.-C. Régin. Arc consistency for general constraint networks: preliminary results. In *Proceedings of the 15th International Joint Conference on Artificial Intelligence (IJCAI-97)*, pages 398–404, 1997.
3. R. Bryant. Symbolic Boolean manipulation with ordered binary-decision diagrams. *ACM Computing Surveys*, 24(3):293–318, 1992.
4. http://vlsi.colorado.edu/~fabio/CUDD/.
5. http://www.icparc.ic.ac.uk/eclipse/.
6. C. Gervet. Interval propagation to reason about sets: Definition and implenentation of a practical language. *Constraints*, 1(3):191–244, 1997.
7. T. P. Kirkman. On a problem in combinatorics. *Cambridge and Dublin Math. Journal*, pages 191–204, 1847.
8. Z. Kiziltan. *Symmetry Breaking Ordering Constraints*. PhD thesis, Uppsala University, 2004.
9. K. Marriott and P. J. Stuckey. *Programming with Constraints: an Introduction*. The MIT Press, 1998.
10. T. Müller. *Constraint Propagation in Mozart*. PhD thesis, Universität des Saarlandes, Naturwissenschaftlich-Technische Fakultät I, Fachrichtung Informatik, 2001.
11. J.-F. Puget. PECOS: A high level constraint programming language. In *Proceedings of SPICIS'92*, 1992.
12. A. Sadler and C. Gervet. Global reasoning on sets. In *FORMUL'01 workshop on modelling and problem formulation*, 2001.
13. Z. Somogyi, F. Henderson, and T. Conway. The execution algorithm of Mercury, an efficient purely declarative logic programming language. *JLP*, 29(1–3):17–64, 1996.
14. P. Van Hentenryck, V. Saraswat, and Y. Deville. Design, implementation, and evaluation of the constraint language cc(FD). *JLP*, 37(1–3):139–164, 1998.

Global Constraints for Integer and Set Value Precedence

Yat Chiu Law and Jimmy H.M. Lee

Department of Computer Science and Engineering
The Chinese University of Hong Kong
Shatin, N.T., Hong Kong
{yclaw,jlee}@cse.cuhk.edu.hk

Abstract. The paper introduces *value precedence* on integer and set sequences. A useful application of the notion is in breaking symmetries of indistinguishable values, an important class of symmetries in practice. Although value precedence can be expressed straightforwardly using if-then constraints in existing constraint programming systems, the resulting formulation is inefficient both in terms of size and runtime. We present two propagation algorithms for implementing global constraints on value precedence in the integer and set domains. Besides conducting experiments to verify the feasibility and efficiency of our proposal, we characterize also the propagation level attained by various usages of the global constraints as well as the conditions when the constraints can be used consistently with other types of symmetry breaking constraints.

1 Introduction

Symmetry is a beauty in nature, but a curse to solving algorithms of constraint satisfaction problems (CSPs). This paper concerns an important class of symmetries, namely those induced by indistinguishable values, examples of which include colors in graph coloring problems and personnels of the same rank in many rostering problems. We introduce the notion of *value precedence* on sequences, and explain how imposing value precedence on a sequence of constrained variables can break symmetries of indistinguishable values in both integer and set domains.

The value precedence condition on a sequence of variables is easy to express using if-then constraints, but such a formulation is inefficient both in terms of number of constraints and propagation efficiency. We propose linear time propagation algorithms for maintaining value precedence as the basis of efficient implementation of two global constraints on integer and set variable sequences respectively. Experimental results on three benchmarks confirm the efficiency of our proposal. In addition, we give theoretical results to (a) ensure consistent use of the constraint with other symmetry breaking constraints and (b) characterize the consistency level attained by various usages of the global constraints.

Interchangeable values [5] can be exchanged for a single variable without affecting the satisfaction of constraints, while indistinguishable values in a solution assignment can be swapped to form another solution of the same problem. Gent [9] designs a special constraint which assumes that all the domain values of a set of variables are indistinguishable and breaks the symmetries among them. Our proposed constraint, however, breaks the symmetry of two indistinguishable values. Multiple constraints have to be used to tackle a set of indistinguishable values. This allows breaking symmetries where only part of the domain values of the variables are indistinguishable. Frisch et al. [6, 8] present global constraints for lexicographic ordering and multiset ordering on two sequences of variables, which are useful in breaking row and column symmetries in matrix models [4].

2   Background

A CSP is a triple (X, D, C), where $X = \{x_0, \ldots, x_{n-1}\}$ is a set of variables, D is a function that maps each $x \in X$ to its associated domain $D(x)$, giving the set of possible values for x, and C is a set of constraints. There are two common classes of variables in CSPs. A *constrained integer variable* (or simply *integer variable*) [11] x has an integer domain, i.e., $D(x)$ is an integer set. A *constrained set variable* (or simply *set variable*) [11] x has a set domain, i.e., each element in the domain is a set. In most implementations, the domain of a set variable x is represented by two sets. The *possible set* $PS(x)$ contains elements that belong to at least one of the possible values of x. The *required set* $RS(x)$ contains elements that belong to all the possible values of x. By definition, $RS(x) \subseteq PS(x)$. Domain reduction of a set variable x is done by removing values from $PS(x)$ and adding values to $RS(x)$. If a value being removed from $PS(x)$ is in $RS(x)$, then a fail is triggered. Similarly, adding a value to $RS(x)$ which is not in $PS(x)$ also triggers a fail. When $PS(x) = RS(x)$, the set variable is bound to its required set.

An *assignment* $x \mapsto a$ means that variable $x \in X$ of a CSP is mapped to the value $a \in D(x)$. A *compound assignment* $\langle x_{i_1}, \ldots, x_{i_k} \rangle \mapsto \langle a_1, \ldots, a_k \rangle$ denotes the k assignments $x_{i_j} \mapsto a_j$ for $1 \leq j \leq k$. Note the requirement that no variables can be assigned more than once in a compound assignment. A *complete assignment* is a compound assignment for all variables in a CSP. A *solution* of a CSP (X, D, C) is a complete assignment making all constraints in C true.

An *extension* of an assignment $x \mapsto a$ for a variable x in a constraint c is a compound assignment that includes $x \mapsto a$. A constraint c is *generalized arc consistent* (GAC) [13] if and only if every assignment $x \mapsto a$ for each variable x in c, where $a \in D(x)$, can be extended to a solution of c. GAC is prohibitive to enforce on constraints involving set variables. Instead, set bounds consistency [10] is typically enforced on these constraints. A constraint c on set variables is *set bounds consistent* [10] (SBC) if and only if the $PS(x)$ and $RS(x)$ of each set variable x in c can be extended to a solution of c.

3   Integer and Set Value Precedence

In this section, we define *value precedence* for integer and set sequences, and give its use for symmetry breaking and methods for maintaining such a constraint.

Value precedence of s over t in an integer sequence $\boldsymbol{x} = \langle x_0, \ldots, x_{n-1}\rangle$ means if there exists j such that $x_j = t$, then there must exist $i < j$ such that $x_i = s$. We say that value s is an *antecedent* while value t is a *subsequent*, and that the antecedent s *precedes* the subsequent t in $\boldsymbol{x}$, written as $s \prec_{\boldsymbol{x}} t$. For example, the sequence $\boldsymbol{x} = \langle 0, 2, 2, 1, 0, 1\rangle$ implies $0 \prec_{\boldsymbol{x}} 1$, $0 \prec_{\boldsymbol{x}} 2$, and $2 \prec_{\boldsymbol{x}} 1$. Note that if a value j does not appear in $\boldsymbol{x}$, then $i \prec_{\boldsymbol{x}} j$ is true for any i. In the previous example, $0 \prec_{\boldsymbol{x}} 3$ and $4 \prec_{\boldsymbol{x}} 3$ are thus also true. Note that value precedence is transitive: if $i \prec_{\boldsymbol{x}} j$ and $j \prec_{\boldsymbol{x}} k$, then $i \prec_{\boldsymbol{x}} k$.

The notion of value precedence can be extended to sequences of sets, where antecedents and subsequents are elements of the sets in the sequence. *Value precedence* of s over t in a sequence $\boldsymbol{x}$ of sets means that if there exists j such that $s \notin x_j$ and $t \in x_j$, then there must exist $i < j$ such that $s \in x_i$ and $t \notin x_i$. For example, consider the sequence $\boldsymbol{x} = \langle\{0,2\},\{0,1\},\emptyset,\{1\}\rangle$. We have $0 \prec_{\boldsymbol{x}} 1$ and $2 \prec_{\boldsymbol{x}} 1$. We also have $0 \prec_{\boldsymbol{x}} 2$, because there is no set in $\boldsymbol{x}$ that contains 2 but not 0. Again, if j does not belong to any set in $\boldsymbol{x}$, then $i \prec_{\boldsymbol{x}} j$ is true for any i. Thus, we also have, say, $0 \prec_{\boldsymbol{x}} 4$.

3.1 Application of Value Precedence

Value precedence can be used for breaking symmetries of indistinguishable values. Two values s and t are *indistinguishable* [2,9] under a subset of variables $U \subseteq X$ of a CSP P if and only if for each solution of P, swapping occurrences of s and t in the assigned values of the variables in U obtains another solution of P. For example, let $\boldsymbol{x} = \langle x_0, \ldots, x_4\rangle$ and $\boldsymbol{u} = \langle x_1, x_2, x_3\rangle$ be sequences of X and U respectively. Suppose $\boldsymbol{x} \mapsto \langle\{1,2\},\{0,2\},\{0,1\},\{1,2\},\emptyset\rangle$ is a solution of P, and values 0 and 1 are indistinguishable under U. Then, swapping the occurrences of 0 and 1 in the assignments of U in the solution obtains $\boldsymbol{x} \mapsto \langle\{1,2\},\{1,2\},\{0,1\},\{0,2\},\emptyset\rangle$, which should be another solution of P.

Given two indistinguishable values under U in a CSP, we can break the symmetry of the values by maintaining value precedence for them. We have to construct a sequence $\boldsymbol{u}$ of U, and assume one value to be the antecedent and the other to be the subsequent. Without loss of generality, we usually pick the smaller value as antecedent. In the previous example, we have $\boldsymbol{x} = \langle x_0, \ldots, x_4\rangle$ and $\boldsymbol{u} = \langle x_1, x_2, x_3\rangle$. The symmetry of the indistinguishable values 0 and 1 under U can be broken by maintaining the constraint $0 \prec_{\boldsymbol{u}} 1$ on variables x_1, x_2, and x_3 in $\boldsymbol{u}$. Thus, $\boldsymbol{x} \mapsto \langle\{1,2\},\{0,2\},\{0,1\},\{1,2\},\emptyset\rangle$ remains a solution, but its symmetrical counterpart $\boldsymbol{x} \mapsto \langle\{1,2\},\{1,2\},\{0,1\},\{0,2\},\emptyset\rangle$ would now be rejected because $0 \prec_{\boldsymbol{u}} 1$ is false.

Sometimes there can be more than two indistinguishable values in a CSP. Suppose $V = \{v_0, \ldots, v_{k-1}\}$ is a set of mutually indistinguishable values for variables in U. To break the symmetries induced by V, we can impose an arbitrary value precedence $v_{i_0} \prec_{\boldsymbol{u}} \cdots \prec_{\boldsymbol{u}} v_{i_{k-1}}$ on the values in V for $\boldsymbol{u}$, where $\boldsymbol{u}$ is a sequence of U. Suppose $V = \{0, 1, 2, 3\}$. We can maintain $0 \prec_{\boldsymbol{u}} 1 \prec_{\boldsymbol{u}} 2 \prec_{\boldsymbol{u}} 3$.

Besides symmetries of indistinguishable values, a CSP can have other types of symmetries. A *variable symmetry* of a CSP, for example, is a bijective mapping σ from the set of variables $X = \{x_0, \ldots, x_{n-1}\}$ of the CSP to itself,

$\sigma : X \to X$, such that for each solution $x \mapsto \langle v_0, \ldots, v_{n-1} \rangle$ of the CSP where $x = \langle x_0, \ldots, x_{n-1} \rangle$, there exists another solution $\langle \sigma(x_0), \ldots, \sigma(x_{n-1}) \rangle \mapsto \langle v_0, \ldots, v_{n-1} \rangle$ for the CSP. Variable symmetries can be broken by expressing lexicographic ordering constraints $x \leq_{lex} \langle \sigma(x_0), \ldots, \sigma(x_{n-1}) \rangle$ for each variable symmetry σ in the CSP [3][1]. When tackling both variable symmetries and symmetries of indistinguishable values simultaneously in a CSP, we have to ensure that the two corresponding sets of symmetry breaking constraints are consistent. For example, we have a CSP $P = (\{x, y\}, D, \{x \neq y\})$, where $D(x) = D(y) = \{1, 2\}$. P has (a) the variable symmetry σ such that $\sigma(x) = y$ and $\sigma(y) = x$, and (b) values 1 and 2 are indistinguishable. To break symmetry (a), we can use the constraint $x \leq y$ (which is a degenerated lexicographic ordering); whereas $2 \prec_{\langle x,y \rangle} 1$ can break symmetry (b). These two constraints result in no solution, which is undesirable.

Two sets of symmetry breaking constraints are *consistent* [4] if and only if at least one element in each symmetry class of assignments, defined by the composition of the symmetries under consideration, satisfies both sets of constraints. The following theorem shows when maintaining $s \prec_u t$ is consistent with variable symmetry breaking constraints.

Theorem 1. *Let X be the set of variables of a CSP, and x and u be sequences of X and $U \subseteq X$ respectively. Suppose in the CSP, C_{var} is the set of symmetry breaking constraints $x \leq_{lex} \langle \sigma(x_0), \ldots, \sigma(x_{n-1}) \rangle$ (resp. $\langle \sigma(x_0), \ldots, \sigma(x_{n-1}) \rangle \leq_{lex} x$) for some variable symmetries σ, and s and t are any two integer indistinguishable values under U. Maintaining $s \prec_u t$ (resp. $t \prec_u s$) is consistent with C_{var} if $s < t$ (resp. $t < s$) and u is a subsequence of x, i.e., u can be formed by deleting some elements from x.*

According to Theorem 1, $x \leq y$ and $1 \prec_{\langle x,y \rangle} 2$ (or $y \leq x$ and $2 \prec_{\langle x,y \rangle} 1$) are consistent, resulting in a single solution $\langle x, y \rangle \mapsto \langle 1, 2 \rangle$ (or $\langle x, y \rangle \mapsto \langle 2, 1 \rangle$).

In order for Theorem 1 to apply also to set variables, we need to define an ordering for sets. One possible definition, which is similar to that of multiset ordering [8], is as follows. A set x is *smaller than or equal to* another set y, written as $x \leq_{set} y$, if and only if (1) $y = \emptyset$, or (2) $\min(x) < \min(y)$, or (3) $\min(x) = \min(y) \to (x \setminus \{\min(x)\} \leq_{set} y \setminus \{\min(y)\})$. Note that $\emptyset$ is the largest element in the ordering. For example, $\{1, 2\} \leq_{set} \{1, 3, 4\} \leq_{set} \{1, 3\}$. Using this ordering, lexicographic ordering of set sequences becomes possible.

3.2 Constraints for Maintaining Value Precedence

Constraints to enforce value precedence $s \prec_x t$ for a sequence of constrained variables x can be constructed straightforwardly from its declarative meaning. Suppose x is a sequence of integer variables. Since s must precede t, x_0, the first variable in x, must not be assigned t. The constraints are then

---

[1] Sometimes the lexicographic ordering constraints can be simplified to contain fewer variables. An example is the row ordering and column ordering constraints for row and column symmetries [4].

1. $x_0 \neq t$ and
2. $x_j = t \rightarrow \bigvee_{0 \leq i < j} x_i = s$ for $1 \leq j < n$.

If $\boldsymbol{x}$ is a sequence of set variables, then t must not be in x_0 without being accompanied by s. Hence, the constraints are

1. $s \in x_0 \vee t \notin x_0$ and
2. $(s \notin x_j \wedge t \in x_j) \rightarrow \bigvee_{0 \leq i < j}(s \in x_i \wedge t \notin x_i)$ for $1 \leq j < n$.

Note that for both integer and set variables, we need n constraints, which we collectively call *if-then value precedence constraints*, to maintain value precedence. Among the n constraints, one is a unary constraint, and the remaining $n - 1$ are if-then constraints. The following theorem shows that for integer (*resp.* set) variables, GAC (*resp.* SBC) on the *conjunction* of the n if-then value precedence constraints is equivalent to GAC (*resp.* SBC) on each individual if-then value precedence constraint.

Theorem 2. *Given an integer (resp. set) variable sequence $\boldsymbol{x}$. GAC (resp. SBC) on $s \prec_{\boldsymbol{x}} t$ is equivalent to GAC (resp. SBC) on each individual if-then value precedence constraint for integer (resp. set) variables.*

4 Propagation Algorithms for Value Precedence

We develop two *value precedence global constraints* for maintaining value precedence, one for integer variables and the other for set variables, in ILOG Solver 4.4 [11]. Both constraints use the same prototype $ValuePrecede(\boldsymbol{x}, s, t)$, meaning $s \prec_{\boldsymbol{x}} t$, where $\boldsymbol{x}$ is a variable sequence. Note that s and t are integer constants. In particular, GAC (*resp.* SBC) is enforced on the integer (*resp.* set) value precedence constraint. The integer and set versions of the propagation algorithms, namely **IntValuePrecede** and **SetValuePrecede** respectively, are similar. Their complexity is *linear to the length of the variable sequence*. Both of them make use of three pointers, namely α, β, and γ, which point to different indices of the sequence $\boldsymbol{x}$, but the pointers have different meanings for the integer and set versions. The two algorithms are also similar to that of the lexicographic ordering global constraint [6] in the sense that both maintain pointers running in opposite directions from the two ends of variable sequences. In subsequent discussions, we assume the variable sequence $\boldsymbol{x} = \langle x_0, \ldots, x_{n-1} \rangle$.

4.1 Integer Version

In **IntValuePrecede**, pointer α is the smallest index of $\boldsymbol{x}$ such that s is in the domain of x_α, i.e., $s \in D(x_\alpha)$ and $s \notin D(x_i)$ for $0 \leq i < \alpha$. If no variables in $\boldsymbol{x}$ have value s in their domains, then we define that $\alpha = n$. Pointer β is the second smallest index of $\boldsymbol{x}$ such that s is in the domain of x_β, i.e., $s \in D(x_\beta)$ and $s \notin D(x_i)$ for $\alpha < i < \beta$. If no or only one variable in $\boldsymbol{x}$ contain value s in their domains, then we define that $\beta = n$. Pointer γ is the smallest index of $\boldsymbol{x}$ such that x_γ is bound to t, i.e., $D(x_\gamma) = \{t\}$ and $D(x_i) \neq \{t\}$ for $0 \leq i < \gamma$. If no variables in $\mathbf{x}$ are bound to t, then we define that $\gamma = n$. During propagation, α and β must be increasingly updated, while γ must be decreasingly updated. For example, let $\mathbf{x} = \langle x_0, x_1, x_2, x_3 \rangle$, $s = 1$, and $t = 2$. Suppose we have:

$\mathbf{x}$	x_0	x_1	x_2	x_3
$D(x_i)$	$\{2,3\}$	$\{1,2,3\}$	$\{2\}$	$\{1,3\}$

Then, we have $\alpha = 1$, $\beta = 3$, and $\gamma = 2$.

Recall that the integer if-then value precedence constraints are $x_0 \neq t$ and $x_j = t \rightarrow \bigvee_{0 \leq i < j} x_i = s$ for $1 \leq j < n$. Pointer α tells that $x_i \neq s$ for $0 \leq i < \alpha$. Hence, we must have $x_i \neq t$ for $0 \leq i \leq \alpha$. Our first pruning rule is that:

1. *value t can be removed from the domains of the variables before or at position α in $\mathbf{x}$.*

In the above example, we have $\alpha = 1$. Therefore, we can remove value 2 from the domains of x_0 and x_1 as shown in Fig. 1(a).

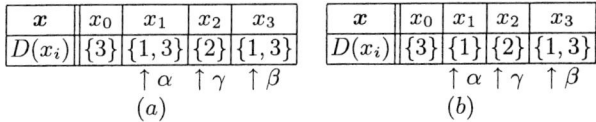

Fig. 1. Illustrating the use of the pointers α, β, and γ in **IntValuePrecede**.

Pointer γ tells the smallest index of $\mathbf{x}$ such that x_γ is bound to t. Therefore, according to the if-then value precedence constraints, $\bigvee_{0 \leq i < \gamma} x_i = s$ must be satisfied. Since $x_i \neq s$ for $0 \leq i < \alpha$, $\bigvee_{0 \leq i < \gamma} x_i = s$ can be refined to $\bigvee_{\alpha \leq i < \gamma} x_i = s$. Furthermore, pointer β tells that $x_i \neq s$ for $\alpha < i < \beta$. Therefore, if $\gamma < \beta$, then $\bigvee_{\alpha \leq i < \gamma} x_i = s$ becomes $x_\alpha = s$. Our second pruning rule is that:

2. *if $\gamma < \beta$, then x_α can be bound to s.*

Note that once x_α is bound to s, $s \prec_\mathbf{x} t$ is satisfied. In the above example, we have $3 = \beta > \gamma = 2$. Therefore, we can bound x_1 (x_α) to 1, as shown in Fig. 1(b), and 1 must precede 2 in $\mathbf{x}$ afterwards.

The propagation algorithm **IntValuePrecede**, shown in Fig. 2, is based on the two pruning rules just described. Procedure *initialize()* is called when a value precedence constraint is posted. It finds initial values for the pointers α, β, and γ. In the procedure, we first search the position for α, starting from position 0. During the search, the first pruning rule is applied. After that, we search a value for γ. Since value t is removed from $D(x_i)$ for $0 \leq i \leq \alpha$, γ must be greater than α and the position search for γ can start from position $\alpha + 1$. Note that the second pruning rule cannot be applied at this point because pointer β is not yet initialized. After fixing γ, procedure *updateBeta()* is invoked to find a value for β. By definition, β must be greater than α. Therefore the search starts from position $\alpha + 1$. After fixing β, the second pruning rule can be applied.

procedure *initialize*()
$\alpha := 0$;
while $\alpha < n \wedge s \notin D(x_\alpha)$ **do** $D(x_\alpha) := D(x_\alpha) \setminus \{t\}; \alpha := \alpha + 1$ **endwhile**
$\beta := \alpha; \gamma := \alpha$;
if $\alpha < n$ **then**
   $D(x_\alpha) := D(x_\alpha) \setminus \{t\}$;
   repeat $\gamma := \gamma + 1$ **until** $\gamma = n \vee D(x_\gamma) = \{t\}$;
   updateBeta()
endif

procedure *propagate*(i)
if $\beta \leq \gamma$ **then**
   if $i = \alpha \wedge s \notin D(x_i)$ **then**
     $\alpha := \alpha + 1$;
     while $\alpha < \beta$ **do** $D(x_\alpha) := D(x_\alpha) \setminus \{t\}; \alpha := \alpha + 1$ **endwhile**
     while $\alpha < n \wedge s \notin D(x_\alpha)$ **do** $D(x_\alpha) := D(x_\alpha) \setminus \{t\}; \alpha := \alpha + 1$ **endwhile**
     if $\alpha < n$ **then** $D(x_\alpha) := D(x_\alpha) \setminus \{t\}$ **endif**
     $\beta := \alpha$;
     if $\alpha < n$ **then** *updateBeta*() **endif**
   else if $i = \beta \wedge s \notin D(x_i)$ **then**
     updateBeta()
   endif
endif

procedure *updateBeta*()
repeat $\beta := \beta + 1$ **until** $\beta = n \vee s \in D(x_\beta)$;
if $\beta > \gamma$ **then** $D(x_\alpha) := D(x_\alpha) \cap \{s\}$ **endif**

procedure *checkGamma*(i)
if $\beta < \gamma \wedge i < \gamma \wedge D(x_i) = \{t\}$ **then**
   $\gamma := i$;
   if $\beta > i$ **then** $D(x_\alpha) := D(x_\alpha) \cap \{s\}$ **endif**
endif

Fig. 2. The **IntValuePrecede** propagation algorithm.

Procedure *propagate*(i) in Fig. 2 is called whenever the domain of x_i is modified. If $\gamma < \beta$, then value precedence is already maintained and we can skip the propagation process. Otherwise, if $i = \alpha$ and $s \notin D(x_i)$, then pointers α and β have to be updated. The search for new position for α starts from position β, because x_β is the original second earliest variable that contains s in its domain. Once value s is removed from $D(x_\alpha)$, β becomes the first potential value for α. However, before the search, value t has to be removed from $D(x_i)$ for $\alpha < i < \beta$. During the search, the first pruning rule is applied. Pointer β is updated after finding a new value for α. The search for new value for β starts from position $\alpha + 1$. The procedure *updateBeta*() is called to update β. In the procedure, once β is updated, the second pruning rule is applied to check whether $\beta > \gamma$.

In procedure *propagate*(i), if $i = \beta$ and $s \notin D(x_i)$, then only pointer β has to be updated. Hence, the procedure *updateBeta*() is called to find a new value for β and to apply the second pruning rule.

We need a procedure to update γ also. Procedure $checkGamma(i)$ in Fig. 2 is called whenever x_i is bound to a value. If $i < \gamma$ and x_i is bound to t, then γ is updated to i, and the second pruning rule is applied to check whether $\beta > \gamma$. The **IntValuePrecede** algorithm enforces GAC on $s \prec_x t$.

Theorem 3. *Given an integer variable sequence x and integers s and t. The **IntValuePrecede** algorithm triggers failure if $s \prec_x t$ is unsatisfiable; otherwise, the algorithm prunes values from domains of variables in x such that GAC on $s \prec_x t$ is enforced and solutions of $s \prec_x t$ are preserved.*

4.2 Set Version

In **SetValuePrecede**, the meanings of the pointers α, β, and γ are different from those in the integer version. Pointer α is the smallest index of x such that s is in the possible set of x_α and t is *not* in the required set of x_α, i.e., $s \in PS(x_\alpha) \wedge t \notin RS(x_\alpha)$ and $s \notin PS(x_i) \vee t \in RS(x_i)$ for $0 \leq i < \alpha$. If $s \notin PS(x_i) \vee t \in RS(x_i)$ for $0 \leq i < n$, then we define that $\alpha = n$. Pointer β is the second smallest index of x such that s is in the possible set of x_β and t is *not* in the required set of x_β, i.e., $s \in PS(x_\beta) \wedge t \notin RS(x_\beta)$ and $s \notin PS(x_i) \vee t \in RS(x_i)$ for $\alpha < i < \beta$. If $\alpha = n$ or $s \notin PS(x_i) \vee t \in RS(x_i)$ for $\alpha < i < n$, then we define that $\beta = n$. Pointer γ is the smallest index of x such that s is *not* in the possible set of x_γ and t is in the required set of x_γ, i.e., $s \notin PS(x_\gamma) \wedge t \in RS(x_\gamma)$ and $s \in PS(x_i) \vee t \notin RS(x_i)$ for $0 \leq i < \gamma$. The definition of γ implies $s \notin x_\gamma \wedge t \in x_\gamma$. If $s \in PS(x_i) \vee t \notin RS(x_i)$ for all $0 \leq i < n$, then we define that $\gamma = n$. As in the integer version, α and β must be updated increasingly, while γ must be updated decreasingly. Let $x = \langle x_0, x_1, x_2, x_3 \rangle$, $s = 1$, and $t = 2$. Suppose we have:

x	x_0	x_1	x_2	x_3	x_4
$PS(x_i)$	$\{2,3\}$	$\{1,2\}$	$\{1,2,3\}$	$\{2,3\}$	$\{1,2\}$
$RS(x_i)$	$\emptyset$	$\{2\}$	$\{3\}$	$\{2,3\}$	$\emptyset$

Then, we have $\alpha = 2$, $\beta = 4$, and $\gamma = 3$.

Pointer α tells that $s \notin x_i \vee t \in x_i$ for $0 \leq i < \alpha$. Hence, according to the set if-then value precedence constraints $s \in x_0 \vee t \notin x_0$ and $(s \notin x_j \wedge t \in x_j) \rightarrow \bigvee_{0 \leq i < j}(s \in x_i \wedge t \notin x_i)$ for $1 \leq j < n$, the constraints $s \in x_i \vee t \notin x_i$ for $0 \leq i \leq \alpha$ must be satisfied. Since $s \in PS(x_\alpha) \wedge t \notin RS(x_\alpha)$ must be true. Therefore $s \in x_\alpha \vee t \notin x_\alpha$ is already consistent. Consequently, our first pruning rule for **SetValuePrecede** is to maintain consistency on $s \in x_i \vee t \notin x_i$ for $0 \leq i < \alpha$.

1. For $0 \leq i < \alpha$, if s is not in $PS(x_i)$, then t can be removed from $PS(x_i)$; otherwise, s can be added to $RS(x_i)$.

In the above example, value 1 is not in $PS(x_0)$ so that we can remove 2 from $PS(x_0)$. Value 2 is in $PS(x_1)$; thus 1 is added to $RS(x_1)$. The resulting domains are shown in Fig. 3(a).

Pointer γ tells that $s \notin x_\gamma \wedge t \in x_\gamma$. According to the if-then value precedence constraints, the constraint $\bigvee_{0 \leq i < \gamma}(s \in x_i \wedge t \notin x_i)$ must be satisfied. By

x	x_0	x_1	x_2	x_3	x_4
$PS(x_i)$	$\{3\}$	$\{1,2\}$	$\{1,2,3\}$	$\{2,3\}$	$\{1,2\}$
$RS(x_i)$	$\emptyset$	$\{1,2\}$	$\{3\}$	$\{2,3\}$	$\emptyset$

                         ↑α   ↑γ   ↑β

(a)

x	x_0	x_1	x_2	x_3	x_4
$PS(x_i)$	$\{3\}$	$\{1,2\}$	$\{1,3\}$	$\{2,3\}$	$\{1,2\}$
$RS(x_i)$	$\emptyset$	$\{1,2\}$	$\{1,3\}$	$\{2,3\}$	$\emptyset$

                         ↑α   ↑γ   ↑β

(b)

Fig. 3. Illustrating the use of the pointers α, β, and γ in **SetValuePrecede**.

the meaning of α, this constraint can be refined to $\bigvee_{\alpha \leq i < \gamma}(s \in x_i \wedge t \notin x_i)$. Furthermore, pointer β tells that $s \notin x_i \vee t \in x_i$ for $\alpha < i < \beta$. Therefore, if $\gamma < \beta$, then $\bigvee_{\alpha \leq i < \gamma}(s \in x_i \wedge t \notin x_i)$ becomes $s \in x_\alpha \wedge t \notin x_\alpha$. Our second pruning rule for **SetValuePrecede** is that:

2. if $\gamma < \beta$, then s can be added to $RS(x_\alpha)$ and t can be removed from $PS(x_\alpha)$.

The constraint $s \prec_x t$ is satisfied once x_α is proved to contain s but not t. In the above example, we have $3 = \gamma < \beta = 4$. Therefore, value 1 can be added to $RS(x_\alpha)$ and 2 can be removed from $PS(x_\alpha)$, as shown in Fig. 3(b).

Like **IntValuePrecede**, the **SetValuePrecede** algorithm in Fig. 4 is based on two pruning rules. It contains four procedures with the same name as the integer version, and with similar structures also. Procedure $initialize()$ is called when $ValuePrecede(x, s, t)$ is posted. It initializes the pointers α, β, and γ. The two pruning rules are applied during initialization. Procedure $propagate(i)$ is called whenever the domain of variable x_i is modified, i.e., either $PS(x_i)$ or $RS(x_i)$ is modified. If $\gamma < \beta$, value precedence is already maintained and no propagation is needed. Otherwise, there are two different cases. In the first case, $i = \alpha \wedge (s \notin PS(x_i) \vee t \in RS(x_i))$, pointers α and β have to be updated. In the second case, $i = \beta \wedge (s \notin PS(x_i) \vee t \in RS(x_i))$, only pointer β has to be updated. After these two cases, procedure $checkGamma(i)$ is called to check whether pointer γ has to be updated. This is different from the integer version, where $checkGamma(i)$ is called only when x_i is bound to a value. This is because, in the set version, pointer γ may need update even when x_i is not bound. The **SetValuePrecede** algorithm enforces SBC on $s \prec_x t$.

Theorem 4. *Given a set variable sequence x and integers s and t. The **SetValuePrecede** algorithm triggers failure if $s \prec_x t$ is unsatisfiable; otherwise, the algorithm prunes values from domains of variables in x such that SBC on $s \prec_x t$ is enforced and solutions of $s \prec_x t$ are preserved.*

5 Multiple Indistinguishable Values

In many circumstances, there are more than two indistinguishable values in the same problem, but our global constraints can deal with only two such values at a time. To break symmetries on a set of variables U induced by a set of indistinguishable values $V = \{v_0, \ldots, v_{k-1}\}$ for $k > 2$, we can impose the $ValuePrecede()$ constraints using *all* pairs of values in V: $v_i \prec_u v_j$ for

procedure *initialize*()
$\alpha := 0$;
while $\alpha < n \land (s \notin PS(x_\alpha) \lor t \in RS(x_\alpha))$ **do**
   if $s \notin PS(x_\alpha)$ **then** $PS(x_\alpha) := PS(x_\alpha) \setminus \{t\}$ **else** $RS(x_\alpha) := RS(x_\alpha) \cup \{s\}$ **endif**
   $\alpha := \alpha + 1$
endwhile
$\beta := \alpha;\ \gamma := \alpha$;
if $\alpha < n$ **then**
   repeat $\gamma := \gamma + 1$ **until** $\gamma = n \lor (s \notin PS(x_\gamma) \land t \in RS(x_\gamma))$;
   updateBeta()
endif

procedure *propagate*(i)
if $\beta \leq \gamma$ **then**
   if $i = \alpha \land (s \notin PS(x_i) \lor t \in RS(x_i))$ **then**
     if $s \notin PS(x_i)$ **then** $PS(x_i) := PS(x_i) \setminus \{t\}$ **else** $RS(x_i) := RS(x_i) \cup \{s\}$ **endif**
     $\alpha := \alpha + 1$;
     while $\alpha < \beta$ **do**
       if $s \notin PS(x_\alpha)$ **then** $PS(x_\alpha) := PS(x_\alpha) \setminus \{t\}$ **else** $RS(x_\alpha) := RS(x_\alpha) \cup \{s\}$ **endif**
       $\alpha := \alpha + 1$
     endwhile
     while $\alpha < n \land (s \notin PS(x_\alpha) \lor t \in RS(x_\alpha))$ **do**
       if $s \notin PS(x_\alpha)$ **then** $PS(x_\alpha) := PS(x_\alpha) \setminus \{t\}$ **else** $RS(x_\alpha) := RS(x_\alpha) \cup \{s\}$ **endif**
       $\alpha := \alpha + 1$
     endwhile
     $\beta := \alpha$;
     if $\alpha < n$ **then** *updateBeta*() **endif**
   else if $i = \beta \land (s \notin PS(x_i) \lor t \in RS(x_i))$ **then**
     updateBeta()
   endif
   checkGamma(i)
endif

procedure *updateBeta*()
repeat $\beta := \beta + 1$ **until** $\beta = n \lor (s \in PS(x_\beta) \land t \notin RS(x_\beta))$;
if $\beta > \gamma$ **then** $PS(x_\alpha) := PS(x_\alpha) \setminus \{t\};\ RS(x_\alpha) := RS(x_\alpha) \cup \{s\}$ **endif**

procedure *checkGamma*(i)
if $\beta < \gamma \land i < \gamma \land s \notin PS(x_i) \land t \in RS(x_i)$ **then**
   $\gamma := i$;
   if $\beta > i$ **then** $PS(x_\alpha) := PS(x_\alpha) \setminus \{t\};\ RS(x_\alpha) := RS(x_\alpha) \cup \{s\}$ **endif**
endif

Fig. 4. The **SetValuePrecede** propagation algorithm.

$0 \leq i < j \leq k - 1$, where $\boldsymbol{u}$ is a sequence of U. By transitivity of value precedence, however, an alternative is to impose constraints using only *adjacent* pairs of values in V: $v_i \prec_{\boldsymbol{u}} v_{i+1}$ for $0 \leq i \leq k - 2$. Although achieving the same value precedence effect, the two approaches differ in the level of propagation.

Theorem 5. *Given an integer (resp. set) variable sequence $\boldsymbol{u}$, and a set of integer indistinguishable values $V = \{v_0, \ldots, v_{k-1}\}$ under U. GAC (resp. SBC) on $v_i \prec_u v_j$ for $0 \leq i < j \leq k-1$ is strictly stronger than GAC (resp. SBC) on $v_i \prec_u v_{i+1}$ for $0 \leq i \leq k-2$.*

For example, consider the variable sequence $\boldsymbol{x} = \langle x_0, \ldots, x_3 \rangle$ with $D(x_0) = \{0, 3\}$, $D(x_1) = \{1, 3\}$, $D(x_2) = \{1, 2, 3\}$, and $D(x_3) = \{2\}$. Suppose $V = \{0, 1, 2\}$ is a set of indistinguishable values under $\{x_0, \ldots, x_3\}$. The constraints $\{0 \prec_x 1, 1 \prec_x 2\}$ are GAC with respect to the current variable domains, but the constraints $\{0 \prec_x 1, 1 \prec_x 2, 0 \prec_x 2\}$ are not, since $x_0 \mapsto 3$ cannot be extended to a solution. Suppose $\boldsymbol{y} = \langle y_0, \ldots, y_3 \rangle$ is a sequence of set variables with $PS(y_0) = \{0\}$, $PS(y_1) = \{1\}$, $PS(y_2) = PS(y_3) = \{1, 2\}$, $RS(y_0) = RS(y_1) = RS(y_2) = \emptyset$, and $RS(y_3) = \{2\}$. The constraints $\{0 \prec_y 1, 1 \prec_y 2\}$ are SBC with respect to the variable domains, but $\{0 \prec_y 1, 1 \prec_y 2, 0 \prec_y 2\}$ are not, since $y_0 \mapsto RS(y_0)$, i.e., $y_0 \mapsto \emptyset$, cannot be extended to a solution.

As we shall see in the experimental results, such difference in propagation level, although theoretically possible, might not show up often in practice.

6 Experiments

To demonstrate the feasibility of our proposal, we test our implementations on the Schur's lemma and the social golfer problem. The experiments aim to compare (a) the effect of all-pair and adjacent-pair posting of the global constraints and (b) our global constraints against the use of if-then value precedence constraints. We report also the results of another of our recently developed approach to maintain value precedence using multiple viewpoints and channeling [12].

All the experiments are run using ILOG Solver 4.4 [11] on a Sun Blade 1000 workstation with 2GB memory. We report the number of fails and CPU time for each instance of each model. The best number of fails and CPU time among the models for each instance are highlighted in bold.

6.1 Schur's Lemma

Schur's lemma, "prob015" in CSPLib[2], is the problem of putting n balls labeled $\{1, \ldots, n\}$ into three boxes such that for any triple of balls (x, y, z) with $x + y = z$, not all are in the same box. This problem has a solution if $n < 14$. We experiment with a variant of this problem, where the triple (x, y, z) must consist of distinct values to relax the unsatisfiability condition. To model the problem into CSPs, we use variables $\boldsymbol{x} = \langle x_1, \ldots, x_n \rangle$ all with domain $\{1, 2, 3\}$, where the variables and domain values represent the balls and the boxes respectively. In this representation, the domain values 1, 2, and 3 are indistinguishable, and we can use the value precedence constraint to break the symmetries. In order to increase the difficulty of the problem, we "glue" two copies of the same instance together to form a larger instance. Suppose $P = (X, D_X, C_X)$ is a Schur's lemma

---
[2] Available at http://www.csplib.org

Table 1. Experimental Results for the Schur's Lemma.

n	adj-pair fails	adj-pair time	all-pair fails	all-pair time	if-then fails	if-then time	int-bool fails	int-bool time	int-set fails	int-set time
7	130	0.11	130	0.11	130	0.18	449	0.24	2232	0.57
8	811	0.52	811	0.54	811	0.91	1489	1.04	5478	2.4
9	8506	1.87	8506	1.97	8506	3.57	9733	3.64	17093	8.4
10	38373	6.13	38373	6.4	38373	12.81	40541	11.76	53663	27.68
11	141150	16.33	141150	17.23	141150	36.65	144546	30.73	165152	73.4
12	419979	35.42	419979	37.73	419979	87.46	424828	65.53	454876	159.41
13	942128	65.93	942128	70.28	942128	174.42	948450	119.92	987858	295.08

problem. We replicate a copy of P and systematically replace all variables in X by variables in Y such that $X \cap Y = \emptyset$, yielding $P' = (Y, D_Y, C_Y)$ which is semantically equivalent to P. We try to solve $(X \cup Y, D, C_X \cup C_Y)$, where $D(x) = D_X(x)$ for $x \in X$ and $D(y) = D_Y(y)$ for $y \in Y$. This gluing operation doubles the number of variables and constraints, and introduces also a variable symmetry σ such that $\sigma(x_i) = y_i$ and $\sigma(y_i) = x_i$. This variable symmetry can be broken by the constraint $x \leq_{lex} y$ as ensured by Theorem 1, where x and y are sequences of X and Y respectively. We test this problem on five models. The experimental results of searching for all solutions are summarized in Table 1. The first and second models use value precedence constraints on adjacent pairs (adj-pair) and all pairs (all-pair) of the values respectively. The third model (if-then) uses the if-then constraints on adjacent pairs of values. The fourth (int-bool) and fifth (int-set) models use multiple viewpoints and channeling constraints [12].

Models using global constraints are substantially more efficient than the other approaches. The all-pair and adj-pair models achieve the same pruning, which is shared also by the if-then model. Therefore, the all-pair model is slightly slower since it has to process more value precedence constraints. Results of the channeling approach (int-bool and int-set) are provided for reference purposes only, since the approach relies on purely modeling techniques and no invention of new propagation algorithms. Its advantage is simplicity of and readiness for use in existing constraint programming systems. Although the channeling approach achieves less propagation, it is more efficient than the if-then model.

We have also experimented on Flener et al.'s version of Schur's lemma [4]. Our global constraints' results are more efficient than those of Gent reported by Flener et al. [4].

6.2 Social Golfer Problem

The social golfer problem, "prob010" in CSPLib, is to find a w-week schedule of g groups, each containing s golfers, such that no two golfers can play together more than once. The total number of golfers is $n = g \times s$. We denote an instance of the problem as (g, s, w). The problem is highly symmetric [1]:

Table 2. Experimental Results for the Social Golfer Problem, using Integer Variables.

g,s,w	adj-pair fails	time	all-pair fails	time	if-then fails	time	int-bool fails	time	int-set fails	time
5,3,5	26429	4.26	26429	4.69	26429	10.92	26577	5.6	26429	8.66
5,3,7	8235	1.94	8235	2.14	8235	5.95	8435	2.68	8235	4.22
5,4,3	51314	13.63	51314	14.66	51314	44.32	51733	17.33	51314	28.28
5,4,4	1127237	351.07	1127237	377.52	1127237	1118.24	1132576	444.62	1127237	728.64
6,2,11	54	0.02	54	0.03	54	0.07	54	0.04	54	0.06
6,3,5	1141372	321.97	1141372	364.2	1141372	919.49	1145472	418.08	1141372	634.68
6,4,3	2226446	651.88	2226446	725.96	2226446	2592.27	2249286	812.3	2226446	1332.83
7,2,13	1039	0.3	1039	0.37	1039	1.08	1081	0.48	1039	0.61
7,3,4	351	0.09	351	0.11	351	0.36	358	0.13	351	0.19
7,4,3	1093376	368.07	1093376	423.14	1093376	1873.08	1116598	454.44	1093376	770.46
7,5,2	48794	22.83	48794	25.64	48794	152.57	50257	27.81	48794	49.56
8,3,5	785865	249.1	785865	302.19	785865	1073.7	791800	321.13	785865	510.85
8,4,9	17	0.09	17	0.09	17	0.73	18	0.11	17	0.17
8,5,2	71463	38.04	71463	43.46	71463	321.33	74679	45.22	71463	82.24
8,8,9	19	0.3	19	0.35	19	3.92	19	0.36	19	0.61
9,5,2	9686	6.35	9686	7.27	9686	71.65	10248	7.51	9686	13.74

1. Players can be permuted among the $n!$ combinations.
2. Weeks of schedule can be exchanged.
3. Groups can be exchanged inside weeks.

In the following, we describe an integer and a set model for the problem, so as to test both the integer and the set versions of the global constraints.

Integer Model. One way to model the social golfer problem is to use variables $g_{i,k}$ for each golfer i in week k with $0 \leq i < n$ and $0 \leq k < w$. The domain of the variables $D(g_{i,k}) = \{0, \ldots, g-1\}$ contains the group numbers that golfer i can play in week k.

In this integer model, symmetries 1 and 2 are variable symmetries, and they can be broken by row ordering and column ordering constraints [4]. Note that these constraints do not completely break the compositions of the row and column symmetries. There are methods [7, 8] to introduce extra constraints to break more of them but they are out of the scope of this paper. Symmetry 3 is an example of symmetries of indistinguishable values. Therefore we can express value precedence constraints to break the symmetries. Theorem 1 ensures the safe posting of both types of symmetry breaking constraints.

Table 2 shows the experimental results of solving for the first solution of various instances using different models respectively. The results are similar to those for the Schur's lemma. Models using global constraints are the fastest among all, confirming the efficiency of our integer propagation algorithm. Again, the all-pair model shows no advantage in pruning over the adj-pair model, and is thus slightly less efficient due to the overhead in maintaining additional constraints. The if-then model, achieving the same amount of propagation as the global constraint approach, performs the worst in runtime among all models. Note that the performance of int-bool model approaches that of the global constraint models.

Table 3. Experimental Results for the Social Golfer Problem, using Set Variables.

g, s, w	no-break fails	no-break time	adj-pair fails	adj-pair time	all-pair fails	all-pair time	if-then fails	if-then time	set-bool fails	set-bool time	set-int fails	set-int time
5,3,5	62	0.03	38	0.02	38	0.02	38	0.26	38	0.04	38	0.04
5,3,7	716851	313.66	716827	329.71	716827	446.65	-	-	716827	496.82	716827	480.04
5,4,3	2602	0.21	107	0.02	107	0.04	107	0.22	107	0.04	107	0.03
5,4,4	2886	0.37	391	0.07	391	0.13	391	0.93	391	0.13	391	0.13
6,2,11	66	0.12	66	0.13	66	0.15	66	2.39	66	0.17	66	0.16
6,3,5	51	0.04	51	0.03	51	0.05	51	0.44	51	0.06	51	0.05
6,4,3	20652	1.89	1011	0.13	1011	0.32	1011	2.1	1011	0.31	1011	0.28
7,2,13	672	0.66	672	0.65	672	0.72	672	34.07	672	0.79	672	0.74
7,3,4	30	0.02	23	0.03	23	0.03	23	0.36	23	0.04	23	0.03
7,4,3	35860	3.85	2827	0.38	2827	1.25	2827	6.58	2827	1	2827	0.91
7,5,2	-	-	10503	0.93	10503	5.11	10503	15.48	10503	2.91	10503	2.38
8,3,5	32216	5.85	32192	6.34	32192	13.58	32192	102.18	32192	12.03	32192	11.64
8,4,9	-	-	-	-	-	-	-	-	-	-	-	-
8,5,2	-	-	20519	2.04	20519	15.81	20519	47.09	20519	6.63	20519	5.67
8,8,9	64	0.42	64	0.44	64	1.94	64	35.95	64	0.76	64	0.68
9,5,2	-	-	4021	0.49	4021	4.25	4021	15.06	4021	1.64	4021	1.49

Set Model. Another way to model the social golfer problem is to use variables $p_{j,k}$ for each group j in week k with $0 \leq j < g$ and $0 \leq k < w$. Since a group in a week can contain multiple golfers, the variables $p_{j,k}$ are set variables and their domains are represented by the possible set $PS(p_{j,k}) = \{0,\ldots,n-1\}$, which is the set of golfers.

In this model, symmetries 2 and 3 are variable symmetries, and they can be broken by constraints $\min(p_{j,k}) < \min(p_{j+1,k})$ for $0 \leq j \leq g-2$ and $0 \leq k < w$ and $\min(p_{0,k} \setminus \{0\}) < \min(p_{0,k+1} \setminus \{0\})$ for $0 \leq k \leq w-2$ respectively [1]. These constraints are the result of simplifying the corresponding lexicographic ordering constraints for breaking the variable symmetries. Symmetry 1 becomes symmetries of indistinguishable values $\{0,\ldots,n-1\}$, which can be tackled by value precedence constraints. Again, Theorem 1 ensures the consistency of the two sets of symmetry breaking constraints.

Table 3 summarizes the experimental results of solving for the first solution of various problem instances using various models. A cell labeled with "-" means that the search does not terminate in one hour of CPU time. In this experiment, we report also the result of a model (no-break) with no indistinguishable value symmetry breaking constraints, since there are instances with few symmetries to break (as indicated by the number of fails) during the search for the first solution. In those cases, the no-break model edges the performance of the adj-pair and all-pair models, but the good news is that the margin is small. This shows that our global constraint implementations incur low overhead. In the cases with substantial pruning of search space by symmetry breaking, the adj-pair and all-pair models perform substantially better in terms of percentage speedup than the other models although the timings are small in general. In this experiment, all models with symmetry breaking achieve the same propagation.

7 Conclusion

The contributions of our work are three-fold. First, the notion of value precedence is introduced. We show how the notion can be used to design constraints for breaking symmetries of indistinguishable values. Second, we present linear time propagation algorithms for implementing global constraints on value precedence. Experiments are conducted to verify the efficiency of our proposal. Results confirm that our implementations incur little overhead and are robust. Third, we give theoretical results to characterize the exact behavior of our proposed algorithms in different usage scenarios.

An interesting line of future research is to generalize the value precedence constraints. First, the antecedent and subsequent can be also constrained integer variables instead of just integer constants. Second, Theorem 5 ensures that more propagation can be achieved if we can maintain value precedence on an arbitrary non-singleton set of values simultaneously.

Acknowledgments

We thank the anonymous referees for their constructive comments which help improve the quality of the paper. We also acknowledge The University of York for providing the source of the lexicographic ordering global constraint for our reference. The work described in this paper was substantially supported by a grant from the Research Grants Council of the Hong Kong Special Administrative Region (Project no. CUHK4219/04E).

References

1. N. Barnier and P. Brisset. Solving the Kirkman's schoolgirl problem in a few seconds. In *Proceedings of CP-02*, pages 477–491, 2002.
2. B. Benhamou. Study of symmetry in constraint satisfaction problems. In *Proceedings of PPCP-94*, 1994.
3. J. Crawford, M. Ginsberg, E. Luks, and A. Roy. Symmetry-breaking predicates for search problems. In *Proceedings of KR-96*, pages 148–159, 1996.
4. P. Flener, A. M. Frisch, B. Hnich, Z. Kiziltan, I. Miguel, J. Pearson, and T. Walsh. Breaking row and column symmetries in matrix models. In *Proceedings of CP-02*, pages 462–476, 2002.
5. E. C. Freuder. Eliminating interchangeable values in constraint satisfaction problems. In *Proceedings of AAAI-91*, pages 227–233, 1991.
6. A. M. Frisch, B. Hnich, Z. Kiziltan, I. Miguel, and T. Walsh. Global constraints for lexicographical orderings. In *Proceedings of CP-02*, pages 93–108, 2002.
7. A. M. Frisch, C. Jefferson, and I. Miguel. Constraints for breaking more row and column symmetries. In *Proceedings of CP-03*, pages 318–332, 2003.
8. A. M. Frisch, I. Miguel, Z. Kiziltan, B. Hnich, and T. Walsh. Multiset ordering constraints. In *Proceedings of IJCAI-03*, pages 221–226, 2003.
9. I.P. Gent. A symmetry breaking constraint for indistinguishable values. In *Proceedings of SymCon-01*, 2001.
10. C. Gervet. Interval propagation to reason about sets: Definition and implementation of a practical language. *Constraints*, 1(3):191–244, 1997.
11. ILOG. *ILOG Solver 4.4 Reference Manual*, 1999.
12. Y. C. Law and J. H. M. Lee. Breaking value symmetries in matrix models using channeling constraints. Technical report, The Chinese Univ. of Hong Kong, 2004.
13. R. Mohr and G. Masini. Good old discrete relaxation. In *Proceedings of ECAI-88*, pages 651–656, 1988.

Quality of LP-Based Approximations for Highly Combinatorial Problems[*]

Lucian Leahu and Carla P. Gomes

Dpt. of Computer Science, Cornell University, Ithaca, NY 14853, USA
{lleahu,gomes}@cs.cornell.edu

Abstract. We study the quality of LP-based approximation methods for pure combinatorial problems. We found that the quality of the LP-relaxation is a direct function of the underlying constrainedness of the combinatorial problem. More specifically, we identify a novel phase transition phenomenon in the solution integrality of the relaxation. The solution quality of approximation schemes degrades substantially near phase transition boundaries. Our findings are consistent over a range of LP-based approximation schemes. We also provide results on the extent to which LP relaxations can provide a global perspective of the search space and therefore be used as a heuristic to guide a complete solver.

Keywords: phase transition, approximations, search heuristics, hybrid LP/CSP

1 Introduction

In recent years we have witnessed an increasing dialogue between the Constraint Programming (CP) and Operations Research (OR) communities in the area of combinatorial optimization. In particular, we see the emergence of a new area involving hybrid solvers integrating CP- and OR-based methods.

OR has a long and rich history of using Linear Programming (LP) based relaxations for (Mixed) Integer Programming problems. In this approach, the LP relaxation provides bounds on overall solution quality and can be used for pruning in a branch-and-bound approach. This is particularly true in domains where we have a combination of linear constraints, well-suited for linear programming (LP) formulations, and discrete constraints, suited for constraint satisfaction problem (CSP) formulations. Nevertheless, in a *purely combinatorial* setting, so far it has been surprisingly difficult to integrate LP-based and CSP-based techniques. For example, despite a significant amount of beautiful LP results for Boolean satisfiability (SAT) problems (see e.g., [1–4]), practical state-of-the-art solvers do not yet incorporate LP relaxation techniques.

In our work we are interested in studying highly combinatorial problems, i.e., problems with integer variables and mainly symbolic constraints, such as sports scheduling, rostering, and timetabling. CP based strategies have been

---

[*] Research supported by the Intelligent Information Systems Institute, Cornell University (AFOSR grant F49620-01-1-0076).

shown to outperform traditional LP/IP based approaches on these problems. As a prototype of a highly combinatorial problem we consider the Latin square (or quasigroup) completion problem [5])[1]. A Latin square is an n by n matrix, where each cell has one of n symbols (or colors), such that each symbol occurs exactly once in each row and column. Given a partial coloring of the n by n cells of a Latin square, determining whether there is a valid completion into a full Latin square is an NP-complete problem [7]. The underlying structure of this problem is similar to that found in a series of real-world applications, such as timetabling, experimental design, and fiber optics routing problems [8, 9].

In this paper, we study the quality of LP based approximations for the problem of completing Latin squares. We start by considering the LP assignment formulation [9], described in detail in section 2. In this formulation, we have n^3 variables, some of them with pre-assigned values. Each variable, x_{ijk} ($i, j, k = 1, 2 \ldots, n$), is a 0/1 variable that takes the value 1 if cell (i, j) is colored with color k. The objective function is to maximize the total number of colored cells in the Latin square. A natural bound for the objective function is therefore the number of cells in the Latin squares, i.e., n^2. In the LP relaxation, we relax the constraint that the variables have to be integer, and therefore each variable can take its value in the interval $[0, 1]$.

We consider a variant of the problem of completing Latin squares, referred to as Latin squares (or quasigroup) with holes. In this problem, one starts with a complete Latin square and randomly deletes some of the values assigned to its n^2 cells, which we refer to as "holes". This problem is guaranteed to have a completion, and therefore we know *a priori* that its optimal value is n^2. This problem is NP-hard and it exhibits an easy-hard-easy pattern in complexity, measured in the runtime (backtracks) to find a completion [10].

In our study we observed an interesting phase transition phenomenon in the *solution integrality* of the LP relaxation. To the best of our knowledge, this is the first time that such a phenomenon is observed. Note that phase transition phenomena have been reported for several combinatorial problems. However, such results generally refer to phase transitions with respect to the solvability of the instances, not with respect to the solution integrality for LP relaxations or more generally with respect to the quality of approximations.

The top plot in figure 1 depicts the easy-hard-easy pattern in computational complexity, measured in number of backtracks, for the problem of Latin squares with holes[2]. The x axis in this plot corresponds to the density of holes in the

---

[1] The multiplication table of a quasigroup is a Latin square. The designation of Quasigroup Completion Problem was inspired by the work done by the theorem proving community on the study of quasigroups as highly structured combinatorial problems. For example, the question of the existence and non-existence of certain quasigroups with intricate mathematical properties gives rise to some of the most challenging search problems [6].

[2] Each data point in this plot was generated by computing the median solution runtime for 100 instances.

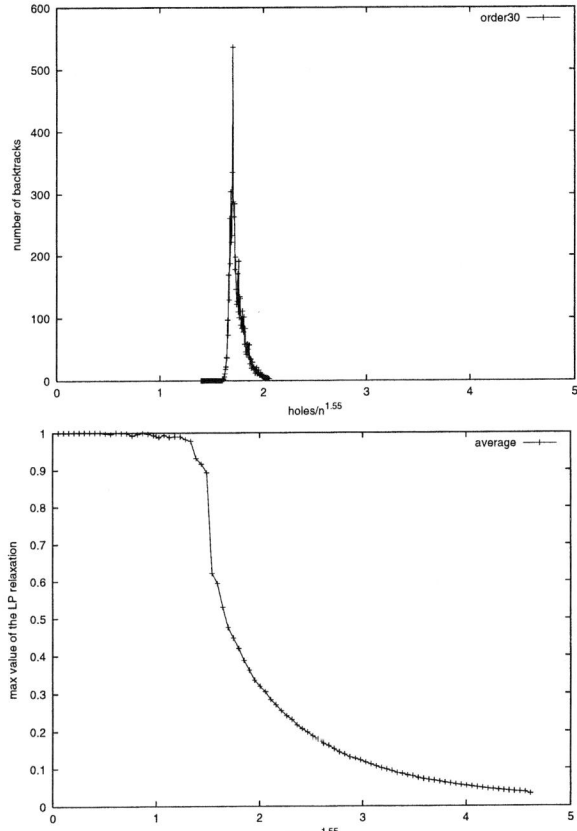

Fig. 1. Easy-hard-easy pattern in complexity for the Latin square with holes problem (top). Phase transition phenomenon in solution integrality for the assignment based LP relaxation (bottom).

Latin square[3]. The left-hand side of the plot corresponds to the over-constrained area – i.e., a region in which instances only have a few holes and therefore lots of pre-assigned values. This is an "easy" region since it is easy for a solver to find a completion, given that only a few holes need to be colored. The right-hand side of the plot corresponds to the under-constrained area – i.e., a region in which instances have lots of holes and therefore only a few pre-assigned colors. This is also an easy region since there are lots of solutions and it is easy to find a solution. The area between the over-constrained and the under-constrained areas is the critically constrained area, where the cost in complexity peaks. In this region, instances have a critical density in holes that makes it difficult for a solver to find a completion: a wrong branching decision at the top of the search tree may steer the search into a very large inconsistent sub-tree. The

---

[3] The density of holes is Number of Holes/$n^{1.55}$. Note that if the denominator were n^2, we could talk about percentage of holes. It turns out that for scaling reasons, the denominator is $n^{1.55}$ [10].

bottom plot of figure 1 shows the phase transition phenomenon in the solution integrality for the LP relaxation of the assignment formulation of the Latin squares with holes problem. Each data point is the average (over 100 instances) of the maximum variable value of the LP relaxation. We observe a drastic change in solution integrality as we enter the critically constrained region (around 1.5 in hole density): in the critically constrained area the average LP relaxation variable solution values become fractional (less than 1), reaching 0.5 in the neighborhood of the peak of the computational complexity. After this point, the average LP relaxation variable solution values continue to become more fractional, but at a slower rate. The intuition is that, in the under-constrained area, there are lots of solutions, several colors can be assigned to the same cell, and therefore the LP relaxation becomes more fractional.

Two interesting research issues are closely related to the quality of the LP relaxation:

- What is the quality of LP based approximations?
- Does the LP relaxation provide a global perspective of the search space? Is it a valuable heuristic to guide a complete solver for finding solutions to hard combinatorial problems?

In order to address the first question, we study the quality of several LP based approximations. In recent years there has been considerably research in the area of approximation algorithms. Approximation algorithms are procedures that provide a feasible solution in polynomial time. Note that in most cases it is not difficult to devise a procedure that finds some solution. However, we are interested in having some guarantee on the quality of the solution, a key aspect that characterizes approximation algorithms. The quality of an approximation algorithm is the "distance" between its solutions and the optimal solutions, evaluated over all the possible instances of the problem. Informally, an algorithm approximately solves an optimization problem if it always returns a feasible solution whose measure is close to optimal, for example within a factor bounded by a constant or by a slowly growing function of the input size. More formally, given a maximization problem Π and a constant α $(0 < \alpha < 1)$, an algorithm $\mathcal{A}$ is an α-approximation algorithm for Π if its solution is at least α times the optimum, considering all the possible instances of problem Π. We remark that approximation guarantees on the quality of solutions are worst-case notions. Quite often the analysis is somewhat "loose", and may not reflect the best possible ratio that can be derived.

We study the quality of LP based approximations from a novel perspective: we consider "typical" case quality, across different areas of constrainedness. We consider different LP based approximations for the problem of Latin squares with holes, including an approximation that uses a "stronger" LP relaxation, so-called packing formulation. Our analysis shows that the quality of the approximations is quite sensitive to the particular approximation scheme considered. Nevertheless, for the approximation schemes that we considered, we observe that as we enter the critically constrained area the quality of the approximations drops dramatically. Moreover, in the under-constrained area, approximation schemes that use the LP relaxation information in a more greedy way (basically setting the highest values suggested by the LP) performed considerably better than non greedy approximations.

To address the second research question, i.e., to what extent the LP relaxation provides a global perspective of the search space and therefore to what extent it can be used as a heuristic to guide a complete solver, we performed the following experiment: set the x highest values suggested by the LP relaxation (we varied x between 1 and 5% of the variables, eliminating obvious conflicts); check if the resulting instance is still completable. Interestingly, most of the instances in the over-constrained *and* under-constrained area remained completable after the setting dictated by the LP relaxation. This suggests that despite the fact that the LP relaxation values are quite fractional in the under-constrained area, the LP still provides global information that captures the multitude of solutions in the under-constrained area. In contrast, in the critically constrained area, the percentage of completable instances drops dramatically, as we set more and more variables based on the LP relaxation.

In summary, our results indicate that LP based approximations go through a drastic phase change in quality as we go from the over-constrained area to the critically constrained area, closely correlated with the inherent hardness of the instances. Overall, LP based approximations provide a global perspective of the search space, though we observe a clear drop in quality in the critically constrained region.

The structure of rest of the paper is as follows: in the next section we describe two different LP formulations for the Latin square problem. In section 3 we provide detailed results on the quality of different LP-based approximations across the different constrainedness regions and in section 4 we study the value of the LP relaxation as a backtrack search heuristic. Finally in section 5 we provide conclusions and future research directions.

2   LP-Based Problem Formulations

2.1   Assignment Formulation

Given a partial Latin square of order n, PLS, with partially assigned values to some of its cells denoted by $PLS_{ij} = k$, the Latin square completion problem can be expressed as an integer program [9]:

$$\max \sum_{i=1}^{n}\sum_{j=1}^{n}\sum_{k=1}^{n} x_{ijk}$$

subject to

$$\sum_{i=1}^{n} x_{ijk} \leq 1, \quad \forall j,k$$

$$\sum_{j=1}^{n} x_{ijk} \leq 1, \quad \forall i,k$$

$$\sum_{k=1}^{n} x_{ijk} \leq 1, \quad \forall i, j$$

x_{ijk} — cell (i,j) takes symbol k $\quad \forall i, j, k$

$x_{ijk} = 1 \quad \forall i, j, k$ such that $PLS_{ij} = k$

$x_{ijk} \in \{0, 1\} \quad \forall i, j, k$

$i, j, k = 1, \ldots, n$

If the PLS is completable, the optimal value of this integer program is n^2, i.e., all cells in the PLS can be legally colored.

2.2 Packing Formulation

An alternate formulation for the Latin square problems is the *packing formulation* [11, 12]. The assignment formulation described in the previous section uses variables x_{ijk} for each cell (i,j) and each color k. Instead, note that the cells having the same color in a PLS form a (possibly partial) matching of the rows and columns of the PLS. Informally, a matching corresponds to a full or partial valid assignment of a given color to the rows (or columns) of the Latin square matrix. For each color k, let $\mathcal{M}_k$ be the set of all matchings of rows and columns that extend the matching corresponding to color k in a PLS. For each color k and for each matching $M \in \mathcal{M}_k$, we introduce a binary variable y_{kM}. Using this notation, we can generate the following IP formulation:

$$\max \sum_{k=1}^{n} \sum_{M \in \mathcal{M}_k} |M| y_{kM}$$

subject to

$$\sum_{M \in \mathcal{M}_k} y_{kM} = 1, \quad \forall k$$

$$\sum_{k=1}^{n} \sum_{M \in \mathcal{M}_k : (i,j) \in M} y_{kM} \leq 1, \quad \forall i, j$$

$$y_{kM} \in \{0, 1\} \quad \forall k, M.$$

Once again, we consider the linear programming relaxation of this formulation by relaxing the integrality constraint, i.e., the binary variables take values in the interval $[0, 1]$. Note that, for any feasible solution y to this linear programming relaxation, one can generate a corresponding feasible solution x to the assignment formulation, by simply computing $x_{ijk} = \sum_{M \in \mathcal{M}_k : (i,j) \in M} y_{kM}$. This construction implies that the value of the linear programming relaxation of the assignment formulation (which provides an upper bound on the desired integer programming formulation) is at least the bound implied by the LP relaxation of the packing formulation; that is, the packing formulation provides a tighter upper bound. Interestingly, from the solution obtained for the assignment formulation one can generate a corresponding solution to the packing formulation, using an algorithm that runs in polynomial time. This results from the fact that the extreme points of each polytope

$$P_k = \{x : \sum_{i=1}^{n} x_{ijk} \leq 1 (j=1,\ldots,n), \sum_{j=1}^{n} x_{ijk} \leq 1 (i=1,\ldots,n), x \geq 0\},$$

for each $k = 1, \ldots, n$ are integer, which is a direct consequence of the Birkhoff-von Neumann Theorem [13]. Furthermore, these extreme points correspond to matchings, i.e., a collection of cells that can receive the same color. Therefore, given the optimal solution to the assignment relaxation, we can write it as a convex combination of extreme points, i.e., matchings, and hence obtain a feasible solution to the packing formulation of the same objective function value. Hence, the optimal value of the packing relaxation is at most the value of the assignment relaxation. It is possible to compute the convex combination of the matchings efficiently. Hence, the most natural view of the algorithm is to solve the assignment relaxation, compute the decomposition into matchings, and then perform randomized rounding to compute the partial completion.

In the next section we study the quality of different randomized LP-based approximations for the Latin square problem based on the assignment and packing formulations.

3 Quality of LP-Based Approximations

We consider LP-based approximation algorithms for which we solve the linear programming relaxation of the corresponding formulation (assignment formulation or packing formulation), and (appropriately) interpret the resulting fractional solution as providing a probability distribution over which to set the variables to 1 (see e.g., [14]).

Consider the generic integer program $\max cz$ subject to $Az = b$, $z \in \{0,1\}^N$, and solve its linear relaxation to obtain z^*. If each variable z_j is then set to 1 with probability z_j^*, then the expected value of the resulting integer solution is equal to the LP optimal value, and, for each constraint, the expected value of the left-hand side is equal to the right-hand side. Of course, we have no guarantee that the resulting solution is feasible, but it provides a powerful intuition for why such a *randomized rounding* is a useful algorithmic tool (see e.g., [14]). This approach has led to striking results in a number of settings (e.g., [15–17]).

3.1 Uniformly at Random

Based on the Assignment Formulation. – This approximation scheme selects an uncolored cell (i, j) uniformly at random, assigning a color k with probability equal to the value of the LP relaxation for the corresponding variable x_{ijk}. Before proceeding to the next uncolored cell, we perform forward checking, by invalidating the color just set for the current row and column.

Algorithm 1   Random LP Assignment
Input: an assignment LP solution x for an order n PLS.
Repeat until all uncolored cells have been considered:
    Randomly choose an uncolored cell (i,j).
    Set $color_{ij} \leftarrow k$ with probability x_{ijk}.
    Invalidate color k for row i and column j:

$$x_{ipk} \leftarrow 0, \forall p \neq j$$

$$x_{qjk} \leftarrow 0, \forall q \neq i$$

Output: the number of colored cells.

Based on the Packing Formulation. – As we mentioned above we can generate a solution for the packing formulation from the assignment formulation in polynomial time. Once we have the packing LP relaxation y, we can proceed to color the cells. In the following we present a randomized rounding scheme. This scheme interprets the solution for a variable y_{kM} as the probability that the matching $M \in \mathcal{M}_k$ is chosen for color k. The scheme selects randomly such a matching for each color k, according to these probabilities. Note that this algorithm can output matchings that overlap. In such cases, we select an arbitrary color from the colors involved in the overlap.

Algorithm 2   Random LP Packing
Input: a packing LP solution $\mathcal{M}$ for an order n PLS.
Repeat for each color k:
    Interpret the values of y_{kM}, $M \in \mathcal{M}_k$, as probabilities.
    Select exactly one matching according to these probabilities.
Output: the number of colored cells.

Figure 2 plots the quality of the approximation using the algorithm Random LP Assignment (left) and the algorithm Random LP Packing (right), as

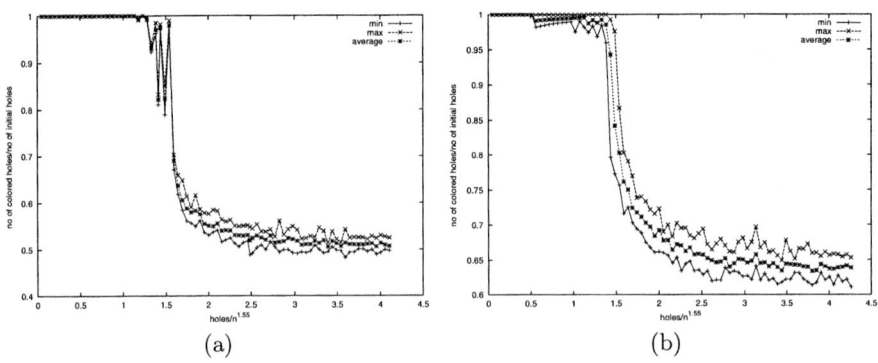

Fig. 2. (a) Random LP Assignment Approximation and (b) Random LP Packing Approximation Quality.

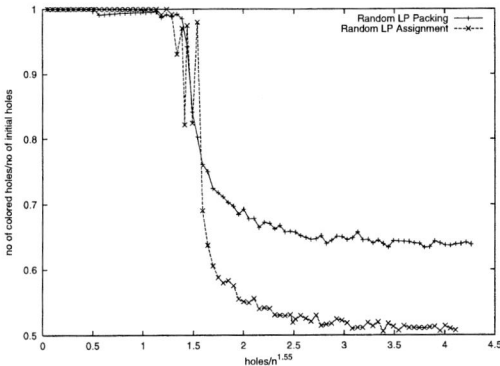

Fig. 3. Random LP Packing vs. Random LP Assignment – Average Case.

a function of the hole density (the quality of the approximation is measured as number of colored holes/number of initial holes). Both plots display a similar qualitative behavior: we see a clear drop in the quality of the approximations as we enter the critically constrained area. The rate at which the quality of the approximation decreases slows down in the under-constrained area. This phenomenon is similar to what we observed for the solution integrality of the LP relaxation. However, the quality of the approximation given by the algorithm Random LP Packing is considerably better, especially in the under-constrained area (note y-axis scales in figure 2). This was expected given that the LP relaxation for the packing formulation is stronger than the relaxation given by the assignment formulation (see figure 3). In fact Random LP Packing is guaranteed to be at most $(1 - \frac{1}{e}) \approx 0.63$ from the optimal solution [11]. For approximations based on the assignment formulation the known formal guarantee is a factor 0.5 from optimal [9].

3.2 Greedy Random Approximations

Based on the Assignment Formulation. – The following rounding scheme takes as input an assignment LP relaxation. It considers all uncolored cells uniformly at random, and assigns to each such cell the color that has the highest value of the LP relaxation. After each assignment, a forward check is performed, by invalidating the color just set for the current row and column.

Algorithm 3   Greedy Random LP Assignment
Input: an assignment LP solution x for an order n PLS.
Repeat until all uncolored cells have been considered:
    Randomly choose an uncolored cell (i, j).
    Find $k < n$ that $\max_k x_{ijk}$.
    If $x_{ijk} > 0$, set $color_{ij} \leftarrow k$, invalidate color k for row i and column j:
$$x_{ipk} \leftarrow 0, \forall p \neq j$$
$$x_{qjk} \leftarrow 0, \forall q \neq i$$
Output the number of colored cells.

Based on the Packing Formulation. – For the LP packing formulation, we also consider a cell based approach. All uncolored cells are considered uniformly at random. For one such cell (i, j), we find a color k corresponding to $M \in \mathcal{M}_k$, $\forall k = 1, \ldots, n$, such that y_{kM} is the highest value of the LP relaxation for all matchings M that match row i to column j. We perform forward checking by invalidating color k for row i and column j (i.e., removing (i, j) from all the matchings $M \in \mathcal{M}_k$).

Algorithm 4 Greedy Random LP Packing
Input: a packing LP solution y for an order n PLS.
Repeat until all uncolored cells have been considered:
 Randomly choose an uncolored cell (i, j).
 Find a matching $M \in \mathcal{M}_k \forall k = 1, \ldots, n$, such that i is matched to j in M, with the highest value of the LP relaxation.
 If such a matching exists, set $color_{ij} \leftarrow k$ and invalidate color k for row i and column j:

$$\forall M' \in \mathcal{M}_k, \forall p \neq j, \text{ remove } (i, p) \text{ from } M'$$

$$\forall M' \in \mathcal{M}_k, \forall q \neq i, \text{ remove } (q, j) \text{ from } M'$$

Output: the number of colored cells.

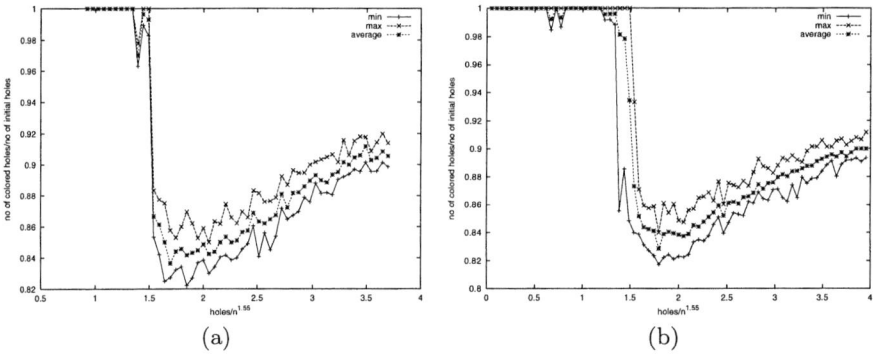

Fig. 4. (a) Greedy Random LP Assignment and (b) Greedy Random LP Packing.

Figure 4 plots the quality of the approximation using the algorithm Greedy Random LP Assignment (left) and the algorithm Greedy Random LP Packing (right). Again, both plots display a similar qualitative behavior: we see a clear drop in the quality of the approximations as we enter the critically constrained area. In addition, and contrarily to the results observed with the random approximations discussed earlier, both plots show that the quality of the approximation increases in the under-constrained area. Recall that these approximations are greedy, picking the next cell to color randomly and then just setting it to the highest value suggested by the LP. This seems to suggest that the information provided by the LP is indeed valuable, which is further enhanced by the fact

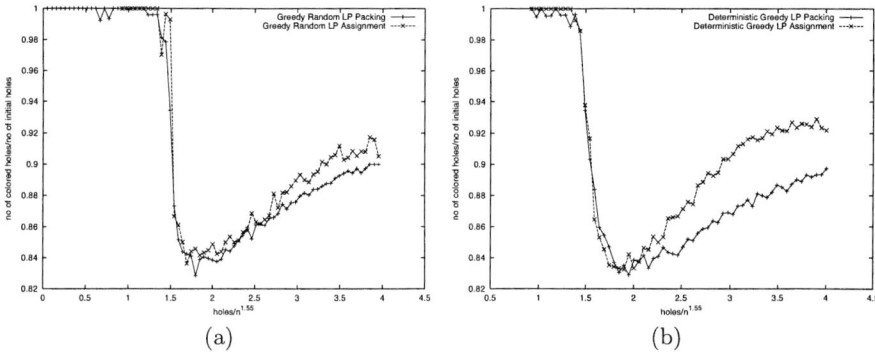

Fig. 5. (a) Greedy Random LP Packing vs. Greedy Random LP Assignment. (b) Deterministic Greedy LP Assignment vs. Deterministic Greedy LP Packing – Average Case.

that forward checking is performed after each color assignment to remove inconsistent colors from unassigned cells. Interestingly, in the under-constrained area, the quality of the Random LP Packing approximation is slightly worse than the the Random LP Assignment approximation. (See figure 5(a).) The intuition is that, because this approximation "optimizes" the entire matchings per color, it is not as greedy as the approximation based on the assignment formulation and therefore it does not take as much advantage of the look-ahead as the Greedy Random LP Assignment does.

3.3 Greedy Deterministic Approximations

We now consider deterministic approximations that are even greedier than the previous ones: they pick the next cell/color to be set by finding the cell/color with the highest LP value.

Based on the Assignment Formulation. – Greedy Deterministic LP Assignment considers the uncolored cell values of the LP relaxation in decreasing order. After each assignment, forward check ensures the validity of the future assignments, so that the end result is a valid extension of the original PLS.

Algorithm 5   Greedy Deterministic LP Assignment
Input: an assignment LP solution x for an order n PLS.
Repeat until all uncolored cells have been considered:
    Find $\max x_{ijk}$ such that (i,j) is an uncolored cell.
    Set $color_{ij} \leftarrow k$.
        Invalidate color k for row i and column j:
$$x_{ipk} \leftarrow 0, \forall p \neq j$$
$$x_{qjk} \leftarrow 0, \forall q \neq i$$
Output: the number of colored cells.

Based on the Packing Formulation. – Now we turn out attention to a deterministic rounding scheme for the packing LP formulation. We describe a greedy rounding scheme. We consider the matchings $M \in \mathcal{M}_k, \forall k = 1, \ldots, n$, in decreasing order of the corresponding y_{kM} values. At each step we set the color for the uncolored cells corresponding to the current matching. For each such cell (i, j), we perform forward checking by invalidating the color k for row i and column j.

Algorithm 6   Greedy Deterministic LP Packing
Input: a packing LP solution y for an order n PLS.
Repeat until no more options (i.e., max = 0) or all cells colored:
    Find the matching $M \in \mathcal{M}_k, \forall k = 1, \ldots, n$, that has the highest value of the LP relaxation.
    If such a matching exists, set $color_{i,j} \leftarrow k, \forall (i, j)$ such that cell (i, j) is not colored and i is matched to j in M. Invalidate color k for row i and column j:

$$\forall M' \in \mathcal{M}_k, \forall p \neq j, \text{ remove } (i, p) \text{ from } M'$$

$$\forall M' \in \mathcal{M}_k, \forall q \neq i, \text{ remove } (q, j) \text{ from } M'$$

Output: the number of colored cells.

Figure 5(b) compares the quality of the approximation Greedy Deterministic LP Assignment against the approximation Greedy Deterministic LP Packing. What we observed before for the case of the greedy random approximations is even more clear for greedy deterministic approximations: in the under-constrained region, Greedy Deterministic LP Assignment clearly outperforms Greedy Deterministic LP Packing. The intuition is that a similar argument as the one mentioned for the random greedy approximations explains this phenomenon. Greedy Deterministic LP Packing sets the color for more cells at the same time (i.e., all the uncolored cells in the considered matching), as opposed to Greedy Deterministic LP Assignment and even Greedy Random LP Packing, which consider just one uncolored cell at each step. Thus, both the Greedy Deterministic LP Assignment and the Greedy Random LP Packing perform forward checking after setting each cell. This is not the case for Greedy Deterministic LP Packing: this approximation performs forward checking only after setting a matching. In figure 6, we compare the performance of the approximations that perform the best in each of the cases considered against a purely blind random strategy. We see that the greedy approximations based on the LP assignment formulation perform better. Overall, all the approximations we have tried outperform the purely blind random strategy. We remark that, the quality of the purely random strategy improves as the problem becomes "really easy" (i.e., the right hand side end of the graph). In this small region, the pure random method slightly outperforms the Random LP approximations: as the problem becomes easier (i.e., many possible solutions), the LP solution becomes more fractional and thus is less likely to provide satisfactory guidance.

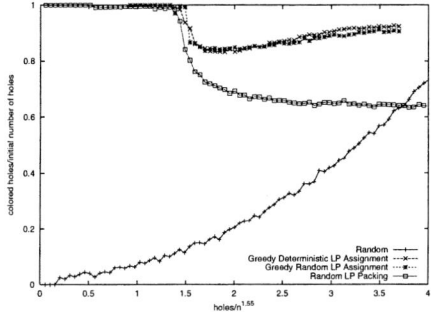

Fig. 6. Random LP Packing vs. Greedy Random LP Assignment vs. Greedy Deterministic LP Assignment vs. Pure Random Approximation – Average Case.

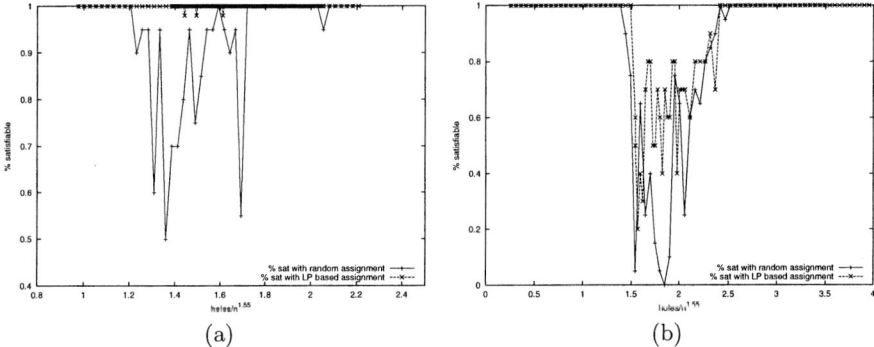

Fig. 7. (a) Percentage of satisfiable instances after setting 1 hole; and (b) 5% of holes for LP based vs. random heuristics.

4 LP as a Global Search Heuristic

Related to the quality of the LP based approximations is the question of whether the LP relaxation provides a good global perspective of the search space and therefore can be used as a heuristic to guide a complete solver for finding solutions to hard combinatorial problems. To address this question we performed the following experiment: set the x highest values suggested by the LP relaxation (we varied x between 1 and 5% of the variables, eliminating obvious conflicts); run a complete solver on the resulting instance and check if it is still completable. In order to evaluate the success of the experiment, we also set x values uniformly at random (avoiding obvious row/column conflicts) and then check if the resulting instance is completable.

Figure 7 displays the percentage of satisfiable instances after setting 1 hole (left) and after setting 5% of the holes (right), based on the highest value of the LP relaxation (assignment formulation) against the purely random strategy. As expected, the percentage of satisfiable instances when using the LP guidance is clearly higher than when using a random strategy.

Interestingly, the information provided by the LP seems quite robust, both in the over-constrained and under-constrained area, with nearly 100% of the instances satisfiable after the setting. On the other hand, in the critically constrained area, the information provided by the LP relaxation is less accurate, even in the case of setting just one hole; in the critically constrained area several instances become unsatisfiable[4]. As we set more and more values based on the LP relaxation, the percentage of unsatisfiable instances in the critically constrained area increases dramatically.

5 Conclusions

We have studied the quality of LP based approximations for purely combinatorial problems. Our first results show that the quality of the approximation is closely correlated to the constrainedness of the underlying constraint satisfaction problem. In fact, we see that solution quality sharply degrades in the critically constrained areas of the problem space. This abrupt change in solution quality directly correlates with a phase transition phenomenon observed in solution integrality of the LP relaxation. At the phase transition boundaries, the LP solutions become highly fractional. The phase transition in LP solution integrality coincides with the peak in search cost complexity.

We considered two different LP formulations for the Latin square problem; an assignment based and a packing based formulation. The packing formulation is provably stronger than the assignment based formulation. This is reflected in terms of the quality of random approximations, i.e., approximations that uniformly at random pick the next cell to be colored and assign it a randomly, weighted according to the LP relaxation values.

There are different ways, however, of interpreting the LP relaxation values. For example, in a more greedy approach, we assign colors to cells starting with the highest LP relaxation values. Such a greedy scheme is beyond formal analysis at this point. However, empirically we found that in this approach the assignment based formulation gives higher quality assignments (more colored cells) than the packing based formulation. So, interestingly, a tighter LP formulation does not necessarily lead to better approximations when constructing solutions incrementally.

Finally, we considered the quality of LP relaxation when used as a global search heuristic. In particular, we considered setting some initial cells based on the LP relaxation (using the highest values in the LP relaxation of the assignment formulation). We then checked whether the partial Latin square could still be completed. We found that outside the critically constraint problem regions the LP relaxation provides good guidance. However, on critically constrained problems, even when just one cell is colored, we see that the relaxation starts making some mistakes. When setting 5% of the cells based on the LP relaxation, the error rate becomes substantial in the critical area. These results show

---

[4] Recall that we are using the Latin square with holes and therefore we know that each instance is completable (satisfiable).

that although LP relaxations can provide useful high-level search guidance, on critically constrained problems, it makes sense to combine LP guidance with a randomized restart strategy to recover from potential incorrect settings at the top of the search tree.

LP relaxations are traditionally used for search space pruning. In this setting, a tighter LP formulation provides more powerful pruning. However, our results indicate that when LP relaxations are used in approximation schemes or as a global search heuristic, the situation is more complex, with the tightest LP bounds not necessarily leading to the best approximations and/or search guidance.

Acknowledgments

We would like to thank the anonymous reviewers for their comments and suggestions.

References

1. Hooker, J.: Resolution vs. cutting plane solution of inference problems: Some computational experience. Operations Research Letter **7** (1988) 1–7
2. Hooker, J.: Resolution and the integrality of satisfiability problems. Mathematical Programming **74** (1996) 1–10
3. Kamath, A., Karmarkar, N.K., Ramakrishnan, K.G., Resende, M.G.C.: A continuous approach to inductive inference. Mathematical Programming **57** (1992) 215–238
4. Warners, J.: Nonlinear approaches to satisfiability problems. PhD thesis, Technische Universiteit Eindhoven (1999)
5. Gomes, C., Selman, B.: Problem Structure in the Presence of Perturbations. In: Proceedings of the Fourteenth National Conference on Artificial Intelligence (AAAI-97), New Providence, RI, AAAI Press (1997) 221–227
6. Slaney, J., Fujita, M., Stickel, M.: Automated reasoning and exhaustive search: Quasigroup existence problems. Computers and Math. with Applications **29** (1995) 115–132
7. Colbourn, C.: The complexity of completing partial latin squares. Discrete Applied Mathematics (1984) 25–30
8. Laywine, C., Mullen, G.: Discrete Mathematics using Latin Squares. Wiley-Interscience Series in Discrete mathematics and Optimization (1998)
9. Kumar, S.R., Russell, A., Sundaram, R.: Approximating latin square extensions. Algorithmica **24** (1999) 128–138
10. Achlioptas, D., Gomes, C., Kautz, H., Selman, B.: Generating Satisfiable Instances. In: Proceedings of the Seventeenth National Conference on Artificial Intelligence (AAAI-00), New Providence, RI, AAAI Press (2000)
11. Gomes, C., Regis, R., Shmoys, D.: An Improved Approximation Algorithm for the Partial Latin Square Extension Problem. In: Proceedings of the Fourteenth Annual ACM-SIAM Symposium on Discrete Algorithms (SODA-03), Baltimore, MD, USA (2003) 832–833
12. Gomes, C., Shmoys, D.: Approximations and Randomization to Boost CSP Techniques. To appear in Annals of Operations Research (2004)

13. von Neumann, J.: A certain zero-sum two-person game equivalent to the optimal assignment problem. In: Contributions to the Theory of Games, vol. 2. Princeton University Press, Princeton (1953)
14. Motwani, R., Naor, J., Raghavan, P.: Randomized approximation algorithms in combinatorial optimization. In Hochbaum, D.S., ed.: Approximation Algorithms for NP-Hard Problems. PWS Publishing Company (1997)
15. Goemans, M.X., Willianson, D.P.: 0.878-approximation algorithms for max-cut and max-sat. In: Proceedings of the 26th Annual ACM-SIAM Symposium on Theory of Computing. (1994) 422–431
16. Chudak, F., Shmoys, D.: Improved approximation algorithms for the uncapacitated facility location problem. In: Submitted for publication. (1999) Preliminary version of this paper (with the same title) appeared in proceedings of the Sixth Conference on Integer Programming and Combinatorial Optimization.
17. Gomes, C., Williams, R.: Approximation algorithms. In: Introduction to Optimization, DecisionSupport and Search Methodologies (to appear). (2004)

Constraint Satisfaction in Semi-structured Data Graphs

Nikos Mamoulis[1] and Kostas Stergiou[2]

[1] Department of Computer Science and Information Systems
University of Hong Kong
nikos@csis.hku.hk
[2] Department of Information and Communication Systems Engineering
University of the Aegean
konsterg@aegean.gr

Abstract. XML data can be modeled as node-labeled graphs and XML queries can be expressed by structural relationships between labeled elements. XML query evaluation has been addressed using mainly database, and in some cases graph search, techniques. We propose an alternative method that models and solves such queries as constraint satisfaction problems (CSPs). We describe common constraint types occurring in XML queries and show how query evaluation can benefit from methods for preprocessing and solving CSPs. We identify an important non-binary constraint that is a common module of XML queries and describe a generalized arc consistency algorithm with low cost that can ensure polynomial query evaluation. Finally, we demonstrate that maintaining the consistency of such non-binary constraints can greatly accelerate search in intractable queries that include referential relationships.

1 Introduction

XML is becoming a standard for information exchange over the Internet. This flexible markup language allows both data content and structure to be described in a single document. XML is very appropriate for describing semi-structured data, which do not comply to a well-defined schema. XML documents can be viewed as rooted, node-labeled graphs, where the intermediate nodes take values from the set of potential element labels and the leaves store textual information. The nodes of XML graphs can be viewed as object instances, whose labels identifies their class. Having stored semi-structured data in a large XML document, we are often interested in the retrieval of object instances which satisfy some *structural constraints* between them. Such requests can be modeled as XML queries, expressed in a language like XPath [19].

Although the evaluation of simple structural queries has received a lot of attention from database research, little has been done to address the evaluation of complex queries where there is a large structure of objects to be retrieved or/and the structural constraints between the objects are complicated. The rapid increase in the use of XML in a wide variety of applications makes the need to address such problems a pressing one.

In this paper we propose the use of the constraint satisfaction paradigm as a new way of handling XML navigational (i.e. path) queries. We demonstrate that the expressiveness of constraint satisfaction allows us to capture in a natural way a wide variety of such queries, from simple to very complex ones. Also, advanced constraint programming algorithms and heuristics allow us to handle complex problems that are otherwise difficult to deal with.

We begin by providing a mapping of all the common structural relationships used in XML navigational queries to a set of unary and binary constraints with well-defined semantics. Evaluation of queries with primitive structural constraints only (e.g. parent, child, sibling, etc.) has been recently shown to be in PTIME [7, 16, 12]. For example, consider the query "find a faculty member who has an RA and a TA", issued in an XML document containing structural information about a university. In other words, we are looking for twigs in an XML graph (e.g., see Figure 1), where the parent element is tagged by faculty and has two children elements tagged by RA and TA. In general, XML navigational queries are instances of the graph containment problem which has been shown to be polynomial for some classes of graphs, like trees. Interestingly, we show that such results can be also derived by constraint programming theory.

In addition, we identify an interesting conjunctive non-binary constraint that is commonly found in XML queries. This *all-different + ancestor-descendant* constraint (ADAD for short) relates a parent (or ancestor in general) with a number of children (or descendants in general) and, in addition, children (descendants) of the same label are related with an all-different constraint. For instance, consider the query "find a faculty member who has at least 3 RAs", which does not allow the instances of the RA variables to take the same value. Such queries fall in a class defined in [8] that can be evaluated in PTIME. We present an alternative efficient way to process XML queries that contain only ADAD and primitive structural constraints. To achieve this, we provide a filtering algorithm of low complexity for ADAD constraints. Finally, we show how queries that also include precedence (i.e., ordering) constraints can be evaluated in PTIME using constraint programming techniques.

Although many classes of XML queries are in PTIME, the general containment problem in XML graphs, where arbitrary *referential* (i.e., IDREF) constraints are included (e.g., see [11]) is intractable. We show how such intractable containment queries can be modeled as CSPs, and make an empirical comparison of various CSP search algorithms. The results show that maintaining specialized non-binary constraints, such as ADAD, can significantly increase pruning and speed-up search.

The rest of the paper is organized as follows. Section 2 provides background about XML query processing in database systems, and constraint satisfaction problems. In Section 3 we describe how simple and complex XML queries can be formulated as CSPs. In Section 4 we discuss the application of constraint programming techniques to preprocess and solve this class of problems. We also elaborate on the complexity of query evaluation for different classes of queries and include an experimental evaluation of search algorithms on intractable XML queries when formulated as CSPs. Finally, Section 5 concludes and discusses future work.

2 Background

In this section, we review work carried out in the database community for XML query processing, focusing on the widely used query language XPath, and also give some basic background on constraint satisfaction.

2.1 XML Databases and Query Processing

XML *elements* in angled braces (i.e., '<' and '>') are used to denote object instances. Each element carries a *label* describing a class the object belongs to (e.g., university, department, faculty). All information related to an object is enclosed between the beginning and ending tag the object.

XML documents can be modeled as rooted node-labeled graphs (or simply trees, in the absence of reference links), where the intermediate nodes take values from the set of potential element labels (or else object classes) and the leaves store textual information. For example, Figure 1 shows the XML tree for a part of an XML document, containing information about a University. XML syntax also allows for reference links (i.e., IDREF) between elements. For instance, a faculty member could refer to the university where he graduated (e.g., 'BigSchool') by a reference link (e.g., IDREF='BigSchool').

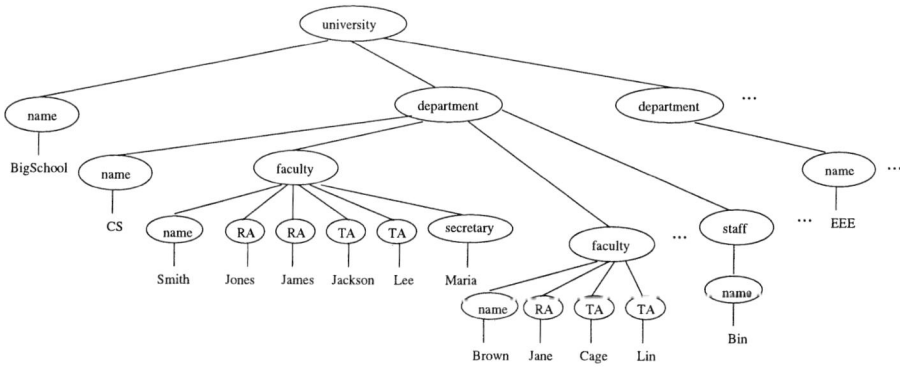

Fig. 1. An XML tree.

The World Wide Web Consortium [19] has been continuously revising the definition of XPath; a query language for XML data. XPath allows for the definition of queries where the problem variables must have some structural relationships. For instance, the XPath expression document("university.xml")//faculty/name refers to all nodes labeled name, which have a parent labeled faculty, in the XML document file "university.xml".

The popularity of XML attracted database researchers to study the efficient management of XML data. As a result, a number of native XML management systems or extensions of relational systems have been developed [15,3]. In addition, new indexing methods and query processing algorithms have been proposed [16]. Some of these methods (e.g., [1,9,10]) consider the documents as labeled trees, ignoring the cycles due to IDREF links. Others (e.g., [11]), are also applicable for path queries in node labeled graphs, which may contain cycles. In general, from a CP perspective, only easy problems (i.e., high selective queries with few variables of large domains) have been considered and the methods aim at minimizing the I/O cost.

Recently is has been proved that all queries that can be expressed by XPath 1.0 can be evaluated in PTIME [7]. Different polynomial worst-case bounds have been provided for several classes of such queries. Interestingly, [7] demonstrates that several commercial XPath 1.0 evaluation engines still use exponential algorithms even for simple, polynomial queries such as the ones discussed in this paper. Our work is related to that of [7, 8] in the sense that we discuss polynomial algorithms for various classes of queries, albeit from a CSP perspective. However, we also discuss the evaluation of generic graph containment queries, beyond XPath 1.0. Such queries can be expressed by the new version (2.0) of XPath, as discussed later.

2.2 Constraint Satisfaction Problems

Constraint satisfaction is a paradigm that can capture a wide variety of problems from AI, engineering, databases, and other disciplines. A constraint satisfaction problem (CSP) consists of a set of variables $X = \{x_1, \ldots x_n\}$, a set of domains $D = \{D(x_1), \ldots, D(x_n)\}$, where $D(x_i)$ is the finite set of possible values for variable x_i, and a set C of constraints over subsets of the variables. A constraint c on variables $x_i, \ldots, x_j$ is a subset of the Cartesian product $D(x_i) \times \ldots \times D(x_j)$ that specifies the allowed combinations of values for variables $x_i, \ldots, x_j$. The operation performed to determine whether a constraint is satisfied is called a *consistency check*. An assignment of a value a to variable x_i is denoted by (x_i, a).

CSPs that contain constraints between at most two variables are called binary. CSPs with constraints between arbitrary numbers of variables are called n-ary (or non-binary). A CSP is usually represented by a constraint graph (or hyper-graph in the case of n-ary problems) where nodes correspond to variables and edges (hyper-edges) correspond to constraints. The basic goal in a CSP is to find one or all assignments of values to variables so that all the constraints are satisfied.

A constraint $c = (x_i, x_j)$ is *arc consistent* (AC) iff for each value a in $D(x_i)$ there exists a value b in $D(x_j)$ so that the assignments (x_i, a) and (x_j, b) satisfy c. In this case we say that b is a *support* for a on constraint c. A binary CSP is AC if all its constraints are arc consistent. These definitions extend to non-binary constraints in a straightforward way. A non-binary constraint is *generalized arc-consistent* (GAC) iff for any variable in the constraint and value that it is assigned, there exist compatible values for all the other variables in the constraint.

3 Formulating XML Queries as CSPs

While evaluating an XML query, we actually search for a set of elements in the XML graph with labels and structural relationships between them that match the labels of the nodes in the query and the relationships between them. We can represent the entities in a query as variables, the elements (nodes) in the XML graph as the possible values of the variables, the labels of the query nodes as unary constraints, and the structural relationships between query nodes as directed binary constraints. Queries expressed in XPath can be transformed into CSPs in a straightforward way. Each variable in the XPath expression becomes a variable in the CSP, the domains are the nodes of the XML graph, and the constraints are the relationships between variables in the query.

Example 1. Consider the query "is there any department which has 3 faculty members with one RA and one TA?". Figure 2a shows how we can express it using XPath 2.0. Observe that the expression already uses similar terminology to CSPs. It asks for instances of nodes labeled department (variable x_1), which are ancestors of three *different* faculty nodes (variables x_2, x_3, x_4), which have children labeled RA and TA. The query can be modeled as a CSP; the corresponding constraint graph is shown in Figure 2b. There are 10 variables with unary constraints (some of the labels are omitted from the graph for the sake of readability). E.g., x_2, x_3, x_4 can take label faculty. There are also binary constraints, denoting ancestor/descendant or parent/child relationships. E.g., x_1 is an ancestor of each one of $x_2, x_3,$ and x_4. Finally, there are inequality constraints between $x_2, x_3,$ and x_4 in order to forbid these variables to take the same value. These constraints could be alternatively modeled as a non-binary *all-different* constraint.

We can represent each element e in the XML data graph with a quadruple $\langle label(e), pre(e), post(e), pre_{parent}(e)\rangle$, where $label(e)$ is the label of the node, and $pre(e)$ and $post(e)$ are the values given to element e by a preorder and postorder traversal of the rooted graph (ignoring IDREF links). We also keep the preorder value of e's parent node. This representation facilitates the fast implementation of various types of constraint checks. [9] uses a similar representation to build an indexing structure on XML data[1].

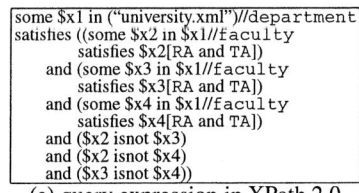

(a) query expression in XPath 2.0

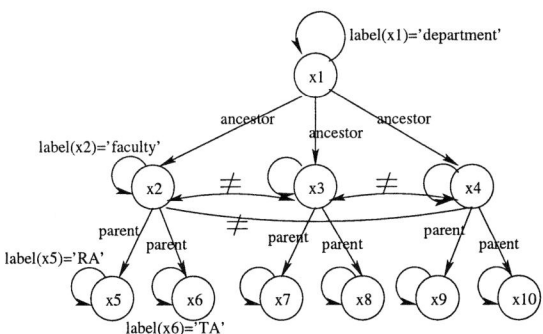

(b) a constraint graph representation

Fig. 2. Two representations of an XML query.

---

[1] Note that the choice of element representation is independent of the CSP formulation; other representations are possible with only slight changes in the definitions of constraints.

The *primitive* structural relationships between nodes in XML graphs are *child, parent, sibling, descendant, ancestor*. These relationships can be expressed as binary directed constraints in the CSP formulation. In Table 1, we define the semantics of the primitive constraints and also the precedence constraints *preceding, following, preceding_sibling, following_sibling*, which will be described shortly. For each constraint c on variables x_i and x_j, a constraint check amounts to checking whether the corresponding conditions of Table 1 hold. This can be done in constant time. Note that for every directed constraint $c(x_1, x_2)$ there is a equivalent inverse constraint $\bar{c}(x_2, x_1)$. For example, the inverse of $parent(x_1, x_2)$ is $child(x_2, x_1)$.

Another useful observation is that the child constraints are functional and the parent constraints are piecewise functional [18]. A binary constraint $c = (x_i, x_j)$ is *functional* if for every value $a \in D(x_i)$, there exists at most one support in $D(x_j)$. Consider a constraint $child(x_i, x_j)$. Each value $a \in D(x_i)$ can only have one parent in the XML graph. Therefore, the constraint is functional. A *piecewise functional* constraint $c = (x_i, x_j)$ is a constraint where the domains of x_j can be partitioned into groups such that each value of $D(x_i)$ is supported by at most one group of $D(x_j)$. Consider a constraint $parent(x_i, x_j)$. We can partition $D(x_j)$ into groups such that each group includes the children of a value $a \in D(x_i)$ in the XML graph. Now each value $a \in D(x_i)$ will be supported by at most one group, and therefore the constraint is piecewise functional.

Table 1. Semantics of primitive and precedence constraints.

$parent(x_1, x_2) \Leftrightarrow pre(x_1) = pre_{parent}(x_2)$
$child(x_1, x_2) \Leftrightarrow pre_{parent}(x_1) = pre(x_2)$
$sibling(x_1, x_2) \Leftrightarrow pre_{parent}(x_1) = pre_{parent}(x_2) \wedge pre(x_1) \neq pre(x_2)$
$descendant(x_1, x_2) \Leftrightarrow pre(x_1) > pre(x_2) \wedge post(x_1) < post(x_2)$
$ancestor(x_1, x_2) \Leftrightarrow pre(x_1) < pre(x_2) \wedge post(x_1) > post(x_2)$
$preceding(x_1, x_2) \Leftrightarrow pre(x_1) < pre(x_2)$
$following(x_1, x_2) \Leftrightarrow pre(x_1) > pre(x_2)$
$preceding\_sibling(x_1, x_2) \Leftrightarrow pre(x_1) < pre(x_2) \wedge sibling(x_1, x_2)$
$following\_sibling(x_1, x_2) \Leftrightarrow pre(x_1) > pre(x_2) \wedge sibling(x_1, x_2)$

The precedence relationships *preceding* and *following* are used to express ordering associations between XML constructs, conventionally based on a preorder traversal of the graph. Note that the preorder traversal is possible if we ignore all relationships among elements except the hierarchical *child, parent* relationships. Other precedence relationships are *preceding_sibling, following_sibling*, with obvious meaning. The primitive and precedence relationships do not capture all structural information contained in any XML document. There could also be *referential relationships* that represent IDREF links. Simply put an IDREF relationship allows one to specify a pointer from one element e to another element e'.

Precedence relationships can be captured in the CSP model using simple constraints on the preorder values of elements, as shown in Table 1. Since IDREF links do not carry any specific semantics they cannot be easily represented by a function (or predicate). We can represent them explicitly by their allowed tuples. That is, a referential constraint c between variables x_i and x_j is encoded as a table, where each row is a 2-tuple $\langle e, e' \rangle$, such that $e \in D(x_i)$, $e' \in D(x_j)$, and there exists a referential constraint between elements e and e' in the XML data graph.

The XML queries that have been investigated in the database literature typically have a few variables (of large domains) connected with primitive structural constraints. Such queries correspond to small and relatively easy CSPs and can be handled more efficiently using database techniques. However, these techniques are not suitable for queries involving large numbers of densely constrained variables, with relatively small domains. In such cases, advanced indexing methods are impractical and evaluation degenerates to the use of simple nested loops joins, corresponding to static chronological backtracking search in CSP terminology. In contrast, constraint programming has more advanced search algorithms combined with powerful heuristics to offer.

4 Query Evaluation as Constraint Satisfaction

In our framework, query evaluation can be simply viewed as constraint satisfaction search. We introduce a simple method for preprocessing CSPs with XML structural constraints that can reduce the search effort by adding implied constraints to the problem. We also discuss search algorithms for such CSPs.

4.1 Constraint Inference

Constraint inference has been shown to be very useful as a preprocessing step in certain classes of CSPs. By "constraint inference" we mean the addition of new constraints to the problem that are implied by existing ones. In temporal CSPs, for example, path consistency algorithms are used to preprocess the given problem, usually resulting in considerable reduction of the search effort [4]. Constraint inference can replace existing constraints with tighter ones and even detect inconsistency in a problem, avoiding unnecessary search. In general CSPs, algorithms like path consistency are not commonly used, but recent studies (e.g., [17, 6]) have demonstrated the benefits of adding implied (sometimes called redundant) constraints in various types of problems.

Constraint inference can also be used for preprocessing in the context of CSPs with structural constraints. Inference operations *inversion*, *intersection* and *composition* defined for (directed) temporal constraints in [4] can be naturally extended for (directed) structural constraints. Inversion of a constraint $c(x_i, x_j)$ (denoted by $\bar{c}(x_i, x_j)$) infers a constraint $c'(x_j, x_i)$. For instance, the inversion $\overline{parent}(x_i, x_j)$ of constraint $parent(x_i, x_j)$ is $child(x_j, x_i)$. Intersection (denoted by $\oplus$) computes the "tightest" constraint on variables x_i and x_j that can be derived from two constraints $c(x_i, x_j)$ and $c'(x_i, x_j)$. For instance, the intersection $ancestor(x_i, x_j) \oplus parent(x_i, x_j)$ is $parent(x_i, x_j)$. Note that not all intersections of primitive constraints give consistent results. For example, the intersection $child(x_i, x_j) \oplus parent(x_i, x_j)$ is inconsistent. The composition of two constraints $c(x_i, x_j)$ and $c'(x_j, x_k)$ (denoted by $c(x_i, x_j) \otimes c'(x_j, x_k)$) derives a new constraint $c''(x_i, x_k)$ by transitivity. For instance, the composition $parent(x_i, x_j) \otimes parent(x_j, x_k)$ is $ancestor(x_i, x_k)$. Inversion, intersection, and composition tables for all combinations of primitive and precedence constraints can be easily derived. In addition, we can adapt path consistency algorithms used in temporal CSPs [4] to minimize the constraint graph of an XML query and/or detect inconsistency. Details are omitted due to space constraints.

4.2 Tractable Queries

Primitive Structural Constraints. An important and very common class of XML queries can be expressed using only the primitive structural relationships *child, parent, sibling, descendant, ancestor*. For example, consider the query "find faculty members with an RA and a TA". Note that their constraint graph corresponds to a tree. As a result, these queries can be processed in PTIME, since according to [5], AC ensures backtrack-free search in acyclic binary constraint graphs[2]. To be precise, AC for CSPs of such queries can be achieved in time $O(ed)$, where e is the number of primitive constraints in the query and d is the domain size of the variables (i.e., the size of the data). This follows directly from [18] where it is proved that AC for functional and piecewise functional constraints is computable in $O(ed)$ time. Then backtrack-free search can be achieved in linear time by visiting each variable x, starting from the root of the constraint graph, in depth-first order, assigning a value a to x and instantiating the children of x by the supports of (x, a) in them, recursively. Note that queries with primitive constraints only are part of a core fragment of XPath 1.0, which was shown to be in time linear to the size of the query and the size of the data in [7]. Here, we have shown how the same result can be derived using constraint programming theory.

All-Different + Ancestor-Descendant Constraints. We now study a special class of non-binary constraints that are commonly found in XML queries. Consider for example the constraint graph of Figure 2b. This graph is a tree of primitive structural constraints plus a set of binary "not-equals" constraints among sibling nodes with the same label. For example, there are three `faculty` nodes linked with binary "not-equals" constraints and connected to their parent in the graph by the *same* ancestor constraint. Alternatively, we could have a common parent/child constraint. We can consider this set of relationships as a special non-binary constraint, which we call *all-different + ancestor-descendant* constraint (ADAD for short).

Definition 1. *An ADAD constraint on variables $x_1, \ldots, x_k$, where variables x_i, $i = 1, \ldots, k-1$ are siblings of the same label and variable x_k is their parent, is defined as $c_{AP}(x_k, x_1) \wedge \ldots \wedge c_{AP}(x_k, x_{k-1}) \wedge$ all-different$(x_1, \ldots x_{k-1})$, where c_{AP} is a single* parent *or* ancestor *constraint.*

For example, the constraints between variables x_1, x_2, x_3, and x_4 in Figure 2b can be replaced by a 4-ary ADAD constraint. This constraint is the conjunction of the all-different constraint between x_2, x_3, and x_4, and the ancestor-descendant constraints between x_1 and each of x_2, x_3, and x_4. We can now model an XML query graph, where the query involves only primitive relationships, as a set of ADAD constraints. Binary constraints like $parent(x_2, x_5)$ can trivially be considered ADAD constraints with a single child. Conjunctive non-binary constraints like ADAD with specialized filtering algorithms are useful in many CSPs (e.g., [14]).

The ADAD constraint can also be used to model aggregation queries with the XPath function *count(node-set)*. This function takes a set of nodes as argument and returns

---

[2] Note that a weaker form of AC, called directional AC, is enough to guarantee backtrack-free search.

the number of nodes in the set, and can be used to select tree patterns with a specific number of elements or restrict the number of elements to be within a specific range. For example, the query //faculty[count(child::lecturer)≥5] selects elements labeled faculty that have 5 or more children labeled lecturer. We can formulate such a query using an ADAD constraint on one variable labeled faculty and five variables labeled lecturer. The use of ADAD constraints is particularly suitable for queries where the count() function is applied on variables that are inner nodes (not leaves) of the query constraint graph. For example, the query "find a faculty member with 5 children labeled lecturer, such that each one of them has a child labeled TA".

In the discussion that follows, when we refer to an ADAD constraint, we use 'parent' to denote the common parent or ancestor in the constraint and 'children' to denote its children or descendants. Note that the term 'parent' is overloaded to denote the parent node of the *query graph*; e.g., in the graph of Figure 2b, the parent of x_2, x_3, x_4 is x_1, however, the relationships on the corresponding edges are *ancestor*.

An XML query with ADAD constraints could alternatively be modeled using only primitive relationships as a binary CSP, or as a CSP involving only binary and non-binary all-different constraints. Summarizing we can consider three models:

binary model – in this model the relationships are captured by (i) binary structural constraints (child, parent, ancestor, descendant) and (ii) binary 'not-equals' constraints between sibling nodes of the same label.
mixed model – in this model the relationships are captured by (i) binary structural constraints (child, parent, ancestor, descendant) and (ii) non-binary all-different constraints between sibling nodes.
non-binary model – in this model the relationships are captured by non-binary ADAD constraints only.

As we will show later, achieving GAC in the non-binary model guarantees that a solution can be found in backtrack-free manner. In Figure 3 we sketch an algorithm of low complexity that computes GAC for an ADAD constraint. The algorithm explicitly verifies the consistency of each value a of the parent variable x_k, by reducing the domains of the children variables according to a and applying GAC for the all-different constraint between them. If a value a of x_k is eliminated, the values of the children variables which are consistent with a are deleted from the corresponding domains.

To prove that the algorithm of Figure 3 achieves GAC for an ADAD constraint we need to show that if a value in the domain of some variable is not GAC then the algorithm will remove it. This divides in two cases. First, assume that value a of variable x_k (i.e. the parent node) is not GAC. This means that there is no supporting tuple $\langle b_1, \ldots, b_{k-1} \rangle$, where $b_i \in D(x_i)$, such that $\forall\ b_i\ parent(a, b_i) = TRUE$ and *all-different*$(b_1, \ldots, b_{k-1}) = TRUE$. In this case, when value a is examined, GAC on the all-different sub-constraint will detect the inconsistency (lines 7, 8) and a will be removed (line 9). Second, assume that value b_j of variable x_j, with $j \neq k$, (i.e. a child node) is not GAC. This means that there is no supporting tuple $\langle b_1, \ldots, b_{j-1}, b_{j+1}, \ldots, b_{k-1}, a \rangle$, where $b_i \in D(x_i), i \neq j$ and $a \in D(x_k)$, such that the ADAD constraint is satisfied. This can happen in two cases; first if the parent of b_j in the XML graph is not in the domain of x_k (e.g., its parent is not labeled department). Such values are eliminated right in the beginning of the algorithm

```
boolean GAC (ADAD constraint c(x_1, x_2, ..., x_k))
1:   for each x_i, i ∈ {1,...,k-1}
2:       for each value b ∈ D(x_i)
3:           if b has no support in D(x_k) remove b from D(x_i)
4:   for each value a ∈ D(x_k) //parent
5:       for each x_i, i ∈ {1,...,k-1}
6:           temporarily remove from D(x_i) all values b
                 such that parent(a,b)=false;
7:       compute GAC for constraint all-different(x_1,...x_{k-1});
8:       if there is a domain wipeout
9:           remove a from D(x_k);
10:      for each x_i, i ∈ {1,...,k-1}
11:          permanently remove all values b from D(x_i)
                 such that parent(a,b)=true;
12:      restore all temporarily removed values;
13:  if D(x_k) is wiped out return false;
14:  return true;
```

Fig. 3. GAC filtering for an ADAD constraint.

(lines 1–3). Now, assume that the parent of b_j in the XML graph is value $a \in D(x_k)$. When a is examined (line 4), the algorithm will compute the set of supporting values of a in each variable $x_1, \ldots x_{k-1}$, temporarily reducing the domain of variables to only values consistent with a. Since value b_j is not GAC, but it has support in x_k, it should be not GAC with the reduced domains of the other children variables and it will be eliminated during GAC of the sub-constraint all-different($b_1, \ldots, b_{k-1}$).

We now discuss the complexity of the algorithm of Figure 3.

Proposition 1. *The worst-case time complexity of applying GAC on one ADPC constraint is $O(d^2k\sqrt{k})$.*

Proof. The preprocessing step (lines 1–3) takes $O(kd)$ time to enforce AC on the $k-1$ ancestor-descendant constraints. At the same time we can build a data structure which for each value a of x_k holds two pointers; one to the first descendant of a (according to the preorder values of the elements in the XML graph) and another to its last descendant. The outer iteration of line 4 is executed at most d times; once for each value a of the ancestor variable x_k. In each iteration we reduce the domains of variables $x_1, \ldots x_{k-1}$ to include only values that are descendants of a in the XML graph. This is done using the data structure built before. Then, we apply a GAC algorithm on the all-different sub-constraint over variables $x_1, \ldots x_{k-1}$, with d domain size each in the worst case. Using the algorithm of [13], this can done in $O(dk\sqrt{k})$ time. For d values of the outer iteration, we get $O(d^2k\sqrt{k})$. The complexity, including the preprocessing step, is $O(kd+d^2k\sqrt{k})$ = $O(d^2k\sqrt{k})$.

In the case where the ADPC constraint consists of parent-child constraints, the complexity of GAC reduces to $O(dk\sqrt{k})$. This can be achieved by taking advantage of the piecewise functionality of parent-child constraints in the following way: The domains of the children are partitioned into g groups, one for each value in the domain of the parent (which has domain size g). Now, the iteration of line 4 in Figure 3 will be executed g times, and in each iteration the cost of GAC on the all-different constraint will be $O(\frac{d}{g}k\sqrt{k})$. Thus, the complexity of GAC on the ADPC constraint will be

$O(g_g^d k\sqrt{k})=O(dk\sqrt{k})$. The same holds for ADPC constraints consisting of ancestor-descendant constraints that are piecewise functional. This occurs when any label in the data graph does not appear more than once along any branch.

If some query contains more than one ADAD constraints then in order to achieve GAC in the constraint graph, we can adapt a standard AC algorithm to use the filtering function of Figure 3 and propagate the consistency of ADAD constraints using a stack. If some query contains e ADPC constraints then GAC can be applied in $O(ed^2k\sqrt{k})$ time in the general case, and $O(edk\sqrt{k})$ time for the special cases discussed above. Realistically, the ADPC constraints in a query do not share more than one variable, which means that $e = n/k$. In this case the complexity of GAC in the general case is $O(nd^2\sqrt{k})$. In the special piecewise functional cases, GAC can be applied in $O(nd\sqrt{k})$ time, which is particularly efficient.

According to [5], GAC ensures backtrack-free search in constraint graphs that are hyper-trees. Therefore achieving GAC in the non-binary model of an XML query, consisting of primitive relationships only, is enough to guarantee backtrack-free search, and thus polynomial query evaluation. In XPath, one expression binds exactly one variable and usually all solutions are required. That is we need to retrieve all the values of the variable that satisfy the query. In the CSP formulation, these values are the arc consistent values in the variable's domain. We can also easily retrieve the whole tree patterns that match the query pattern using the data structure described in the proof of Proposition 1. It is interesting to note that queries with ADAD constraints only belong to a special class called "extended Wadler fragment" in [8]. For queries in this class [8] provide an algorithm of $O(n^2d^2)$ cost, whereas our GAC + backtrack free search approach can solve such problems at a lower complexity.

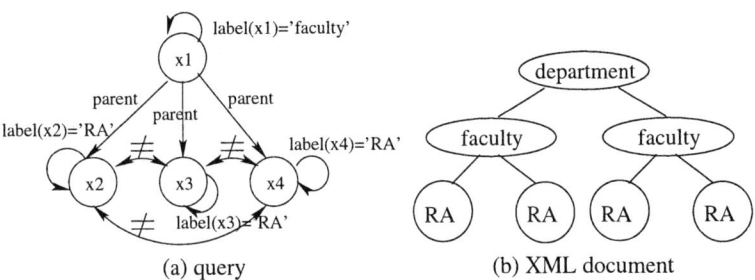

Fig. 4. necessity of non-binary model.

A natural question to ask is if it is necessary to introduce the non-binary model with the ADAD constraints in order to achieve backtrack-free search. As we discussed, there are two alternative models for the problem; the binary model and the mixed model. Can AC (GAC) in these two models guarantee backtrack free search? As the following example shows, the answer to this question is no.

Example 2. Consider the query depicted in Figure 4a and the XML data graph of Figure 4b. If we model this problem as a CSP we will have one variable x_1 for the academic and three variables x_2, x_3, x_4 for the RAs. The domain of x_1 comprises two values, corresponding to the two academics of the XML data graph. Similarly, the domains of x_2, x_3, and x_4 include the four RA nodes of the XML graph. Let us first assume that AC is applied on the binary model (i.e., considering all constraints as binary). Observe that the two possible values for x_1 have supports in the domains of x_2, x_3, and x_4. In addition, the values of each child variable find support in the parent's domain and also in the domains of the sibling variables using the binary "non-equals" constraint. However, it is easy to see that the problem is inconsistent. To discover the inconsistency, we have to search. Similarly, AC on the mixed model leaves the variable domains unchanged; enforcing GAC using the non-binary all-different constraint does not prune any values. This example proves the following proposition.

Proposition 2. Let Q be an XML query, consisting of primitive relationships only, represented in either the binary or the mixed model. Achieving GAC in the constraint graph of Q does not guarantee backtrack-free search.

Precedence Constraints. We now discuss how to deal with precedence constraints (i.e., *preceding, following*) that may be included in a query. Queries with primitive and precedence constraints only form the core fragment of XPath 1.0 [7]. Note that a precedence constraint in a query with only structural constraints may define a cycle, which, in theory, could make the problem intractable. However, we show how to obtain PTIME complexity (as proved in [7]) by changing the constraint model. The key idea is that a precedence constraint between any two nodes x_i, x_j of the query graph can be reduced to a precedence constraint between two of their ancestors $a(x_i), a(x_j)$ which are siblings. If there are no such ancestors, this means that the subgraphs where x_i and x_j belong are only connected by the precedence constraint and thus search complexity is not affected by it. Thus, we only need to consider how precedence constraints between siblings can affect search. In a way similar to the ADAD constraints, we can treat them as ternary constraints defined by $c_{AP}(p, a(x_i)) \wedge c_{AP}(p, a(x_j)) \wedge c_{PR}(x_i, x_j)$, where c_{AP} is a *parent* or *ancestor* constraint and c_{PR} is the original precedence constraint between x_i and x_j. Thus, each arbitrary precedence constraint is either a simple binary constraint connecting otherwise disconnected query subgraphs or can be reduced to a simple, local ternary constraint between a parent and its children. In any case, the constraint graph reduces to a hyper-tree. GAC can be applied on this hyper-tree in PTIME and ensures backtrack-free search. In summary, we have shown that any query with only simple structural, precedence, and ADAD constraints can be solved in PTIME using constraint programming techniques.

4.3 Intractable Queries

Queries that include referential relationships are intractable. Such relationships induce cycles in the constraint graph of the query. As proved in [5], CSPs whose constraint graph contains arbitrary cycles are NP-complete. The same result can be derived for arbitrary graph containment problems [12]. Note that such queries cannot be expressed by XPath 1.0, but only by XPath 2.0, which allows for the definition of variables and links between them via IDREF relationships[3].

For intractable problems, we experimentally studied the effects of considering ADAD constraints in GAC preprocessing and search. First, we generated a large XML graph, which is a hierarchy of nested containments enriched by IDREF links. There are 7 labels (0–6, apart from an unlabeled root), each corresponding to a level of the tree; i.e., nodes with label 0 can only have children with label 1, nodes with label 1 can only have children with label 2, etc. Each generated node has a random number of children between 0 and 6. Finally, from the node pairs (e_i, e_j), which are have no parent/child relationship and do not have the same label, 10% are selected and an IDREF link is generated between e_i and e_j.

Next, we generated a number of XML queries (i.e., CSPs) as follows. Each query class is described by a quadruple $\langle s, e, k, p \rangle$. For each query in the class, there is one variable labeled s. Each variable labeled l, for $s \leq l < e$, has exactly k children labeled $l + 1$. Also, for $p\%$ of the variable pairs (x_i, x_j) with different labels, not linked by a parent/child constraint, an IDREF constraint is generated. For instance, in queries of the class $\langle 2, 4, 3, 10 \rangle$ there is a variable labeled 2, with three children labeled 3, each of which has three children labeled 4. Also 10% of variable pairs of different labels not linked by a parent/child constraint are linked by an IDREF constraint.

We implemented two AC algorithms. The first is the AC2001 algorithm [2] that considers only binary constraints. The second is a GAC algorithm that considers non-binary ADAD constraints and employs the filtering technique of Figure 3. For binary IDREF constraints, GAC operates like AC2001. We also implemented four search algorithms. The first one, denoted by FC, is a version of *forward checking* that treats all constraints as binary. The second one, denoted by MAC, maintains AC on all binary constraints (using AC2001) after each instantiation. The third one, denoted by FC$^+$ is slightly stronger than FC, enforcing GAC on ADAD constraints when parent variables are instantiated. Finally, MGAC is a method that maintains full GAC.

In order to reduce the checks and computational effort of all filtering and search methods, the XML data elements are sorted on $(label(e), pre(e))$. We create a directory index that points for every label to the first and the last position in the elements array that contain this label. Note that this is done only once and used for all XML queries, later on. Before evaluating a query, we apply a preprocessing step that finds for each value e_x of a parent variable x the first consistent value in the domains of its children variables. For the children y labeled α of $x \leftarrow e_x$ we apply binary search on the sorted elements array to find the first value e_{y_f} labeled α with preorder larger than or equal to $pre(e_x)$. During AC or search, we can immediately access all values $e_y \geq e_{y_f}$ of each child y of x variable are consistent with $x \leftarrow e_x$, while $post(e) < post(e_x)$, whenever we need to check the parent/child constraints for $x \leftarrow e_x$. The preprocessing step simulates a database technique (e.g., [9]) that could use an index for the same purpose. Moreover, we immediately eliminate e_x from the domain of x (and its children from the domains

---

[3] A polynomial fragment of queries, called XPattern, that considers IDs is shown to be in PTIME in [7]. However, this fragment only includes queries that explicitly select nodes based on their IDs and therefore such references can be dealt with at a preprocessing step. In a CSP context, we can consider such ID selections as unary (i.e., node) constraints.

of the children variables), if the e_x has less children than k in the data graph (i.e., less than those in the ADAD constraint with x as parent). In this case, the all-different constraint cannot be satisfied among the children (Hall's theorem). Note that this is a cheap (but incomplete) filtering for the non-binary ADAD constraint and enforcing it before binary algorithms actually favors them.

Table 2 compares the efficiency of four filtering and search combinations for several query classes. For instance, AC-FC denotes that binary AC is used for filtering before search and if the problem is arc-consistent, FC is used for search. For each query class, we generated 30 instances and averaged the search time (in seconds) and the number of variable instantiations during search (enclosed in parentheses). Note that the parent-child constraints are the same for each problem in a query class; only the IDREF constraints change between problems. p is tuned so that query classes are in the hard region (i.e., roughly half problems are insoluble). Horizontal lines separate classes with different number of children in their ADAD constraints (i.e., different k).

Table 2. Search performance of algorithms.

query	AC-FC	AC-MAC	GAC-FC$^+$	GAC-MGAC
1. $\langle 2, 6, 2, 3.8 \rangle$	32.9(29K)	3.7(86)	23.1(16.7K)	3.7(86)
2. $\langle 3, 6, 2, 14 \rangle$	2.7(2843)	4.3(87)	1.9(2198)	4.3(87)
3. $\langle 3, 6, 2.5, 3 \rangle$	21.5(6811)	8.9(130)	6.4(2225)	1.3(39)
4. $\langle 4, 6, 3, 25 \rangle$	7.2(2113)	53.2(215)	3.6(937)	16.2(77)
5. $\langle 4, 6, 4, 8 \rangle$	177.1(98K)	228.8(4102)	1.3(292)	3.2(32)
6. $\langle 4, 6, 5, 3 \rangle$	1.6(616)	8.3(183)	0.1(44)	0.8(23)

Algorithms that consider the non-binary constraint (i.e., GAC-FC$^+$ and GAC-MGAC) are up to two orders of magnitude faster than their binary counterparts (i.e., AC-FC and AC-MAC) and the difference, in general, increases with k. Note that when $k = 2$ (i.e., each parent variable has only two children) there is no difference between AC and GAC. For these two classes FC$^+$ performs better than FC; enforcing AC for the children of the instantiated variable pays-off. Full maintenance of arc consistency is not always beneficial; MAC algorithms were found better than their FC counterparts for problem classes 1 and 3 only.

5 Summary

In this paper we presented a new CSP-based way for the processing of XML queries. We identified the most common structural constraints between XML query variables and showed how constraint inference, filtering, and search can be adapted for networks of such constraints. We identified the particularly important *all-different + ancestor-descendant* (ADAD) non-binary constraint and theoretically showed that queries containing only such constraints can be processed efficiently using constraint programming. To achieve this, we described a polynomial filtering algorithm for this constraint. Going one step further, we showed that maintaining this constraint brings significant benefits to search in intractable problems that contain ADAD and IDREF constraints. In the future, we plan to study the coverage of additional XPath constructs (e.g., quantifiers) with constraint programming techniques. In addition, intend to investigate the application of other (apart from *all-different*) specialized non-binary constraints (e.g., the global cardinality constraint) in hard search problems on XML data graphs. We will also perform an empirical comparison of constraint programming and database methods, such as the ones presented in [7].

References

1. S. Al-Khalifa, H. V. Jagadish, J. M. Patel, Y. Wu, N. Koudas, and D. Srivastava. Structural joins: A primitive for efficient XML query pattern matching. In *Proceedings of IEEE ICDE*, 2002.
2. C. Bessière and J. Régin. Refining the basic constraint propagation algorithm. In *Proceedings of IJCAI*, 2001.
3. A. B. Chaudhri, A. Rashid, and R. Zicari. *XML Data Management: Native XML and XML-Enabled Database Systems*. Addison-Wesley, 2003.
4. R. Dechter, I. Meiri, and J. Pearl. Temporal constraint networks. *Artificial Intelligence*, 49:61–95, 1991.
5. E. Freuder. A sufficient condition for backtrack-free search. *Journal of the ACM*, 29(1):24–32, 1982.
6. I. Gent and B. Smith. Symmetry Breaking in Constraint Programming. In *Proceedings of ECAI*, pages 599–603, 2000.
7. G. Gottlob, C. Koch, and R. Pichler. Efficient algorithms for processing XPath queries. In *Proceedings of VLDB*, 2002.
8. G. Gottlob, C. Koch, and R. Pichler. XPath query evaluation: Improving time and space efficiency. In *Proceedings of ICDE*, 2003.
9. T. Grust. Accelerating XPath location steps. In *Proceedings of ACM SIGMOD*, 2002.
10. H. Jiang, H. Lu, and W. Wang. Efficient processing of XML twig queries with or-predicates. In *Proceedings of ACM SIGMOD*, 2004.
11. R. Kaushik, P. Bohannon, J. F. Naughton, and H. F. Korth. Covering indexes for branching path queries. In *Proceedings of ACM SIGMOD*, 2002.
12. G. Miklau and D. Suciu. Containment and equivalence for a fragment of XPath. *J. ACM*, 51(1):2–45, 2004.
13. J. C. Régin. A filtering algorithm for constraints of difference in CSPs. In *Proceedings of AAAI*, 1994.
14. J. C. Régin and M. Rueher. A global constraint combining a sum constraint and difference constraints. In *Proceedings of CP*, 2000.
15. J. Shanmugasundaram, K. Tufte, C. Zhang, G. He, D. J. DeWitt, and J. F. Naughton. Relational databases for querying XML documents: Limitations and opportunities. In *Proceedings of the VLDB Conference*, 1999.
16. D. Shasha, J. T.-L. Wang, and R. Giugno. Algorithmics and applications of tree and graph searching. In *Proceedings of ACM PODS*, 2002.
17. B. Smith, K. Stergiou, and T. Walsh. Using auxiliary variables and implied constraints to model non-binary problems. In *Proceedings of AAAI*, 2000.
18. P. van Hentenryck, Y. Deville, and C.-M. Teng. A generic arc-consistency algorithm and its specializations. *Artificial Intelligence*, 57:291–321, 1992.
19. WWW Consortium. *XML Path Language (XPath) 2.0, W3C Working Draft*, http://www.w3.org/TR/xpath20/, November 2003.

Strategies for Global Optimization of Temporal Preferences

Paul Morris[3], Robert Morris[3], Lina Khatib[1,3],
Sailesh Ramakrishnan[2,3], and Andrew Bachmann[2,3]

[1] Kestrel Technology
[2] QSS Group Inc.
[3] Computational Sciences Division
NASA Ames Research Center
Moffett Field, CA 94035
pmorris@email.arc.nasa.gov

Abstract. A temporal reasoning problem can often be naturally characterized as a collection of constraints with associated local preferences for times that make up the admissible values for those constraints. Globally preferred solutions to such problems emerge as a result of well-defined operations that compose and order temporal assignments. The overall objective of this work is a characterization of different notions of global temporal preference within a temporal constraint reasoning framework, and the identification of tractable sub-classes of temporal reasoning problems incorporating these notions. This paper extends previous results by refining the class of useful notions of global temporal preference that are associated with problems that admit of tractable solution techniques. This paper also resolves the hitherto unanswered question of whether the solutions that are globally preferred from a *utilitarian* criterion for global preference can be found tractably. A technique is described for identifying and representing the entire set of utilitarian-optimal solutions to a temporal problem with preferences.

1 Introduction

Many temporal reasoning problems can be naturally characterized as collections of constraints with associated local preferences for times that make up the admissible values for those constraints. For example, one class of vehicle routing problems [14] consists of constraints on requested service pick-up or delivery that allow flexibility in temporal assignments around a specified fixed time; solutions with assignments that deviate from this time are considered feasible, but may incur a penalty. Similarly, dynamic scheduling problems [12], whose constraints may change over time, thus potentially requiring solution revision, often induce preferences for revised solutions that deviate minimally from the original schedule.

To effectively solve such problems, it is necessary to be able to order the space of assignments to times based on some notion of global preference, and to have a mechanism to guide the search for solutions that are globally preferred. Such a framework arises as a simple generalization of the Simple Temporal Problem (STP) [5], in which temporal constraints are associated with a local preference function that maps admissible times into values; the result is called *Simple Temporal Problem with Preferences (STPP)* [9]. Globally optimal solutions to STPPs emerge as a result of well-defined operations that compose and order partial solutions.

Different concepts of composition and comparison result in different characterizations of global optimality. Past work has introduced three notions of global preference: Weakest Link (maximize the least preferred time), Pareto, and utilitarian. Much of the work to date has been motivated by the overall goal of finding tractable solutions to temporal optimization problems with realistic global preference criteria. In particular, NASA is motivated to create systems that will automatically find optimally preferred solutions to problems in the rover planning domain [3], where the goal is to devise plans for investigating a number of scientifically promising science targets.

In addition to reviewing the STPP framework (section 2), this paper extends previous results motivated by the overall goal of identifying useful notions of global preference that correspond to problems that can be solved tractably. First, we introduce a new category of global optimality called *stratified egalitarian* optimality, and prove that it precisely characterizes the subset of Pareto optimal solutions returned by a tractable technique called WLO+ introduced previously (section 3). Second, we provide an affirmative answer to the question of whether the utilitarian optimal solutions to temporal preference problems can be also found tractably within this framework. A technique is described for identifying and representing the whole set of utilitarian-optimal solutions to a temporal reasoning problem with preferences (section 4). This paper closes with a summary of experiments (section 5) and a discussion of future work.

2 Simple Temporal Problems with Preferences

A *temporal constraint* determines a restriction on the distance between an arbitrary pair of distinct events. In [9], a *soft temporal constraint* between events i and j is defined as a pair $\langle I, f_{ij} \rangle$, where I is a set of intervals $\{[a,b], a \leq b\}$ and f_{ij} is a *local preference function* from $\bigcup I$ to a set A of admissible preference values. For the purposes of this paper, we assume the values in A are totally ordered, and that A contains designated values for minimum and maximum preferences.

When I is a single interval, a set of soft constraints defines a *Simple Temporal Problem with Preferences* (STPP), a generalization of Simple Temporal Problems [5]. An STPP can be depicted as a pair (V, C) where V is a set of variables standing for temporal events or timepoints, and $C = \{\langle [a_{ij}, b_{ij}], f_{ij} \rangle\}$ is a set of soft constraints defined over V. An STPP, like an STP, can be organized as a network of variables representing events, and links labeled with constraint information. A *solution* to an STPP is a complete assignment to all the variables that satisfies the temporal constraints.

A soft temporal constraint $\langle [a_{ij}, b_{ij}], f_{ij} \rangle$ results from defining a preference function f_{ij} over an interval $[a_{ij}, b_{ij}]$. Clearly, removing the preference functions from the set of constraints making up an STPP P results in an STP; we call this the STP *underlying P*.

We define a *preference vector* of all the local preference values associated with a set $F = \{f_{ij}\}$ of local preference functions and a solution S. Formally, let $f_{ij}(S)$ refer to the preference value assigned by f_{ij} to the temporal value that S assigns to the distance between events i and j, and let

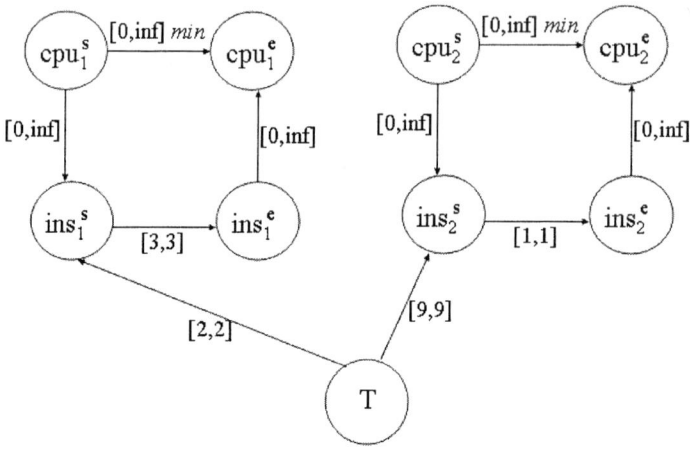

Fig. 1. The STPP for a Rover Science Planning Problem (T is any timepoint).

$$U_{F(S)} = \langle f_{12}(S), f_{13}(S), \ldots f_{1n}(S),$$
$$f_{23}(S), \ldots f_{2n}(S),$$
$$\ddots \quad \vdots$$
$$f_{n-1,n}(S) \rangle$$

be the *preference vector* associated with F and S. In what follows the context will permit us to write U_S instead of $U_{F(S)}$ without ambiguity, and U_S^k will refer to the kth preference value of U_S.

For an example of an STPP, consider a simple Mars rover planning problem, illustrated in Figure 1. The rover has a sensing instrument and a CPU. There are two sensing events, of durations 3 time units and 1 time unit (indicated in the figure by the pairs of nodes labeled ins_1^s, ins_1^e and ins_2^s, ins_2^e respectively). The event T depicts a reference time point (sometimes referred to as "the beginning of time") that allows for constraints to be specified on the start times for events. There is a hard temporal constraint that the CPU be on while the instrument is on, as well as a soft constraint that the CPU should be on as little as possible, to conserve power. This constraint is expressed in the STPP as a function from temporal values indicating the possible durations that the CPU is on, to preference values. For simplicity, we assume that the preference function min on the CPU duration constraints is the negated identity function; i.e., $min_{ij}(t) = -t$; thus higher preference values, i.e. shorter durations, are preferred.

A solution to an STPP has a *global preference value*, obtained by combining the local preference values using operations for composition and comparison. Optimal solutions to an STPP are those solutions which have the best preference value in terms of the ordering induced by the selected comparison operator. Solving STPPs for globally preferred assignments has been shown to be tractable, under certain assumptions about the "shape" of the local preference functions and about the operations used to compose and compare solutions.

For example, first consider a class of local preference functions that includes any function such that if one draws a horizontal line anywhere in the Cartesian plane of

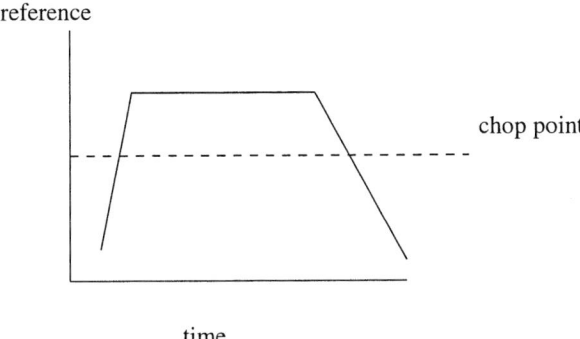

Fig. 2. "Chopping" a semi-convex function.

the graph of the function, the set of X such that $f(X)$ is not below the line forms an interval. This class of *semi-convex* functions includes linear, convex, and also some step functions.

Second, consider an STPP solver based on the notion of *Weakest Link Optimization* (WLO). This framework consists of an operator for composing preference values in A based on the minimal value of the component values. This framework induces an evaluation of solutions based on a single, "weakest link" value. Given preference vectors U_S and $U_{S'}$ corresponding to distinct solutions S and S', we will say that S is *Weakest-Link-Optimal (WLO) -preferred* to S', or S' is *WLO-dominated* by S, if $min(U_{S'}) < min(U_S)$, where $min(U)$ returns the minimum value of vector U. *WLO-optimal solutions* are those to which no other solutions are WLO-preferred.

STPPs with semi-convex preference functions for WLO-optimal solutions can be solved tractably by a process called the *chop method*. This method is based on the act of "chopping" a preference function (Figure 2). Semi-convexity implies that the set of times for which the preference function returns a value above a selected chop point forms a convex interval; call this interval the *chop-induced constraint*. For a set of preference functions in an STPP, chopping all of them at the same preference value induces a Simple Temporal Problem, namely, of finding a set of assignments that satisfies all the chop-induced constraints. A binary search will return the largest preference value v_{opt} for which a solution to the induced STP exists; it can been shown that the solutions at v_{opt} are *WLO-optimal*.

Because the chop method returns the solution to an STP, its output is a *flexible temporal plan*, i.e., a set of solutions that have the same WLO-optimal value. Plan flexibility is often considered important in ensuring robustness in an execution environment that is uncertain [11]. Nonetheless, the WLO criterion for globally preferred solutions has the disadvantage of being "myopic", in the sense that it bases its evaluation on a single value. This feature can be shown to limit its usefulness in solving real temporal planning problems. The rover example in Figure 1 can be used to illustrate this myopia. Because the CPU must be on at least as long as the sensing events, any globally preferred solution using WLO has preference value -3. The set of solutions that have the WLO-optimal value includes solutions in which the CPU duration for the second sensing event varies from 1 to 3 time units (again, since WLO bases its evaluation solely on the least preferred value). The fact that WLO is unable to discriminate between the global values of these solutions, despite the fact that the one with 1 time unit is obviously preferable to the others, can be clearly viewed as a limitation.

Less myopic global preference criteria can be defined. For example, we can say that S' *Pareto-dominates* S if for each j, $U_S^j \leq U_{S'}^j$ and for some k, $U_S^k < U_{S'}^k$. The *Pareto optimal set* of solutions is the set of non-Pareto-dominated solutions. Similarly, we can say that S' *utilitarian-dominates* S if $\sum_j U_S^j < \sum_j U_{S'}^j$, and the *utilitarian optimal set* of solutions is the set of non-utilitarian-dominated solutions.

In a previous result [10], it was shown that a restricted form of Pareto-optimality can be achieved by an iterative application of the chop method. The intuition is that if a constraint solver could "ignore" the links that contribute the weakest link values (i.e. the values that determined the global solution evaluation), then it could eventually recognize solutions that dominate others in the Pareto sense. The links to be ignored are called *weakest link constraints*: formally, they comprise all links in which the optimal value for the preference function associated with the constraint is the same as the WLO value for the global solution. Formalizing the process of "ignoring" weakest link values is a two-step process of committing the flexible solution to consist of the interval of optimal temporal values, and reinforcing this commitment by resetting their preferences to a single, "best" value. Formally, the process consists of:

- squeezing the temporal domain to include all and only those values which are WLO-optimally preferred; and
- replacing the preference function by one that assigns the highest (most preferred) value to each element in the new domain.

The first step ensures that only the best temporal values are part of any solution, and the second step allows WLO to be re-applied to eliminate Pareto-dominated solutions from the remaining solution space. The resulting algorithm, called WLO+ returns, in polynomial time, a Simple Temporal Problem (STP) whose solutions are a nonempty subset of the WLO-optimal, Pareto-optimal solutions to an STPP. The algorithm WLO+ from [10] is reproduced in Figure 3 for completeness. Where C is a set of soft constraints, the STPP (V, C_P) is solved (step 3) using the chop approach. In step 5, we depict the soft constraint that results from the two-step process described above as $\langle [a_{opt}, b_{opt}], f_{best} \rangle$, where $[a_{opt}, b_{opt}]$ is the interval of temporal values that are optimally preferred, and f_{best} is the preference function that returns the most preferred preference value for any

Inputs: an STPP $P = (V, C)$
Output:
An STP (V, C_P) whose solutions are Pareto optimal for P.
(1) $C_P = C$
(2) while there are weakest link soft constraints in C_P do
(3)   Solve (V, C_P)
(4)   Delete all weakest link soft constraints from C_P
(5)   For each deleted constraint $\langle [a, b], f \rangle$,
(6)   add $\langle [a_{opt}, b_{opt}], f_{best} \rangle$ to C_P
(7) Return (V, C_P)

Fig. 3. STPP solver WLO+ returns a solution in the Pareto optimal set of solutions.

input value. Notice that the run time of WLO+ is $O(|C|)$ times the time it takes to execute $Solve(V, C_P)$, which is a polynomial.

WLO+, applied to the rover example in Figure 1, finds a Pareto optimal solution in two iterations of the while loop. In the first iteration, the weakest link is that between the start and end of the first CPU event. WLO+ deletes this link and replaces it with one with the interval $[3, 3]$ and the local preference function f_{best}. This new STPP is then solved on the second iteration, whereby the WLO-optimal solution with the CPU duration of 1 is generated. The solution to this STPP is a Pareto-optimal solution to the original problem.

WLO+ was a positive result in the search for tractable methods for finding globally preferred solutions based on less myopic criteria for global preference than WLO-optimality. We now proceed to refine and expand these results in two ways: first by offering a more concise characterization of the class of solution returned by WLO+, and secondly, by showing how restricted classes of STPP with a utilitarian criterion for global preference can be solved tractably.

3 WLO+ and Stratified Egalitarianism

As noted in the previous section, the set of solutions returned by running WLO+ on an STPP is a subset of the set of Pareto Optimal Solutions for that problem. In this section, we present a concise description of this set. By doing so, it is revealed that WLO+ is based on a useful concept of global preference.

We introduce a concept of global preference called Stratified Egalitarianism (SE). Consider again two preference vectors U_S and $U_{S'}$ associated with solutions S and S'. We will say S' SE-dominates S at preference level (or stratum) x if:

- $U_S^i < x$ implies $U_{S'}^i \geq U_S^i$.
- There exists an i such that $U_S^i < x$ and $U_{S'}^i > U_S^i$.
- $U_S^i \geq x$ implies $U_{S'}^i \geq x$.

We say that S' SE-dominates S (without further qualification) if there is any level x such that S' SE-dominates S at x. It is not hard to see that the SE-dominance relation is antisymmetric and transitive[1], thus inducing a partial ordering of solutions. A solution S' will be said to be SE-optimal if it is not SE-dominated. Note that if a solution S' Pareto-dominates S, then S' SE-dominates S at the "highest" level of the $U_{S'}$ vector. Thus, SE-optimality implies Pareto optimality. Furthermore, if S' dominates S in the WLO ordering, then S' SE-dominates S at the "lowest" level of the $U_{S'}$ vector. Thus, SE-optimality also implies WLO optimality.

Using an economic metaphor to ground intuition, x represents a sort of *poverty line*, and a "policy" S' has a better overall quality than S if some members below the poverty line in S are improved in S', even if some of those above the poverty line in S are made worse off in S' (as long as they do not drop below the poverty line). This metaphor suggests that SE-optimality could be a reasonable criterion for specifying globally preferred solutions.

---

[1] The proof makes use of the requirement that the preference values be totally ordered.

Economists have considered some notions of egalitarian optimality, but have rejected them as being "non-rational" because they do not imply Pareto optimality. Note that SE-optimality does, however, meet this rationality criterion, but we are unaware of any consideration of the SE preference ordering in the economics literature.

We now prove that the WLO+ algorithm finds exactly the SE-optimal solutions.

Theorem 1. *The set of solutions returned by WLO+ is precisely the set of SE-optimal solutions.*

Proof. Consider a solution S not returned by WLO+, i.e., one that is eliminated at some iteration of the WLO+ algorithm; let the optimal value (i.e., value of the weakest link) of the set of solutions be v at that iteration. Let S' be any survivor at that iteration. There must be some link i such that $U_S^i < v$ (otherwise S wouldn't be eliminated). But $U_{S'}^i \geq v$ since S' survives. Thus, $U_{S'}^i > U_S^i$. Note also that $U_{S'}^j \geq v$ for all links j. Thus, for any value k such that $U_S^k \leq v$, we have $U_{S'}^k \geq U_S^k$. It follows that S is dominated at stratum v.

Conversely, suppose S is dominated at some stratum v but, for the sake of contradiction, suppose S is not excluded from the set of solutions returned by WLO+. From the assumption that S is dominated at stratum v, there exists an S' and i such that $v > U_S^i$ and $U_{S'}^i > U_S^i$, and for any j, $U_{S'}^j \leq v$ implies $U_{S'}^j \geq U_S^j$. During the execution of the WLO+ algorithm, an increasing sequence V of preference values $v_1, v_2, \ldots, v_N = 1$ (where 1 is the "best" preference value) is created, representing the WLO optimal values at each iteration. Clearly, $U_S^i < 1$ (where 1 is the "best" preference value), so one of the Vs must exceed U_S^i. Suppose v_K is the smallest element in V such that $v_K > U_S^i$. Note that S would be removed at this iteration, as a result of its being not WLO optimal, unless the preference function for link i had been reset at an iteration $J < K$. But that function would get reset only if i was a weakest link at J. Then $v_J \leq U_S^i$ since $J < K$, and v_K is the smallest V such that $v_K > U_S^i$. Note however, that for all links j, either $U_{S'}^j \geq v > v_J$ or $U_{S'}^j \geq U_S^j$. Thus, S' would have survived to this iteration if S had. However, $U_{S'}^i > U_S^i \geq v_J$, which contradicts the fact that i is a weakest link. □

3.1 SE Versus Leximin

Another global optimality criterion discussed in [8]) is leximin optimality. The leximin ordering compares the minimum value of two preference vectors, then the second lowest and so on, until it finds a difference; the ordering of the first such mismatch determines the leximin ordering of the vectors. It is not difficult to show that SE-dominance implies leximin-dominance, but the converse is not true in general. For example, the preference vector $\langle 5, 1 \rangle$ dominates $\langle 1, 3 \rangle$ in the leximin ordering but not in the SE ordering. (The SE ordering cares about individuals but leximin does not.)

Nevertheless, it is possible to prove a partial converse as follows.

Theorem 2. *If $x > y$ in leximin-order, then $z > y$ in SE-order, where x, y, and z are preference vectors, and $z = (x + y)/2$ is the average of x and y.*

Proof. Note that the coordinate ordering is arbitrary, so we can assume without loss of generality that y is sorted in increasing order. (This simplifies the notation below.)

Suppose $x > y$ in leximin-order. Let $k = \min\{j \mid x_j \neq y_j\}$. Note that for $j \geq k$, we have $x_j \geq y_k$ since otherwise $y > x$ in leximin-order instead of vice versa. Also $y_j \geq y_k$ for $j \geq k$, since y is sorted. Thus, for $j \geq k$, we have $z_j \geq y_k$. It is also easy to see that if x_j and y_j are unequal, which can only happen for $j \geq k$, then one of them must exceed y_k, so $z_j > y_k$ in this case. It follows that either $x_j = y_j$ or $z_j > y_k$. In particular, $z_k > y_k$.

Now let $v = \min\{z_j \mid z_j > y_k\}$. (Note that v is well-defined since $j = k$ satisfies the condition.) We claim that $z >_{\text{SE}} y$ at level v. To see this, note from the previous paragraph that for all j either $x_j = y_j$, in which case $z_j = y_j$, or $z_j > y_k$. In the latter case, $z_j \geq v$ by the definition of v. Since also $z_k > y_k$ and $v > y_k$, this establishes the result. □

It is well-known that the solutions to an STPP form a convex set, so if S and S' are solutions, then $(S + S')/2$ is also a solution. Furthermore, if the preference functions are convex, then $U^j_{(S+S')/2} \geq (U^j_S + U^j_{S'})/2$ for all j. It follows that if a solution S is leximin-dominated by a solution S', then it is SE-dominated by $(S + S')/2$, which is also a solution. Thus, in the setting of an STPP with convex preference functions, leximin-optimality coincides with SE-optimality. (However, our previous remarks show they are not equivalent in a more general setting.)

4 Utilitarian Optimality

Perhaps the most natural criterion for global optimality is *utilitarian*, where the global value of a solution is the sum of the local values. In this section, we consider applying a utilitarian global optimality criterion to the temporal preference problem. We show that determining the set of all utilitarian optimal solutions as an STP is tractable in the case where all the preference functions are convex and piecewise linear. Piecewise linear preference functions characterize soft constraints in many real scheduling problems; for example, in vehicle routing (where the best solutions are close to desired start times) and in dynamic rescheduling (where the goal is to find solutions that minimally perturb the original schedule).

We first consider the problem of finding a *single* utilitarian optimal solution. (Some constructions related to this have previously appeared in the literature [1, 12]. Our main contribution in this respect will be what follows, where the whole set of solutions is determined as an STP.)

Consider an STPP with preferences $F = \{f_{ij}\}$, and assume that the goal is to find a utilitarian optimal solution S, i.e. where $\sum_{ij} f_{ij}(S)$ is optimal. Suppose each f_{ij} is convex and piecewise linear. Thus, there is a sequence of intersecting line segments that make up f_{ij}. We will denote the individual linear functions corresponding to the segments by $f^1_{ij}, f^2_{ij}, \ldots, f^{m_{ij}}_{ij}$, as illustrated in Figure 4.

In this case, we will show that the utilitarian optimization problem can be reduced to a Linear Programming Problem (LPP), which is known to be solvable in polynomial time by Karmarkar's Algorithm [4]. This result generalizes the observation in [9] that STPPs with linear preference functions can be mapped into LPPs.

Since the f's are convex, notice that $y \leq f_{ij}(x)$ if and only if $y \leq f^1_{ij}(x) \wedge y \leq f^2_{ij}(x) \wedge \ldots y \leq f^{m_{ij}}_{ij}(x)$. (See Figure 4.) For the LPP, we introduce an auxiliary variable

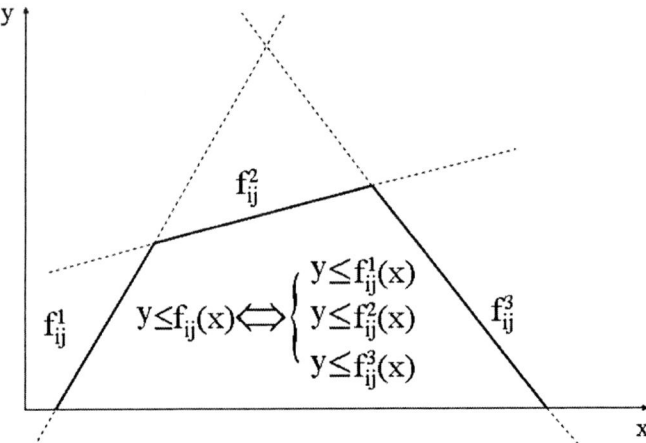

Fig. 4. Convex Piecewise Linear Function.

Z_{ij} for each f_{ij}, together with m_{ij} additional linear constraints of the form

$$Z_{ij} \le f_{ij}^k(S).$$

We also introduce a set of variables $X = \{X_1, X_2, \ldots X_n\}$ for the nodes in the STP. Note that X_i and X_j, respectively, correspond to the start and end points of the edge associated with f_{ij}. An interval $[p_{ij}, q_{ij}]$ denotes the domain of f_{ij}.

The complete LPP can now be formulated as follows. The indices are assumed to range over their available values, which should be clear from the above discussion. Note that ij in $\{f_{ij}\}$ and $\{Z_{ij}\}$ range over the edges associated with preferences. This could be a small subset of the entire edges in real applications. Finally, we introduce a variable S_{ij} for each temporal distance assignment in a solution.

- Variables: $\{X_i\}$, $\{S_{ij}\}$, and $\{Z_{ij}\}$.
- Constraints (conjunctive over all values of the indices):
    1. $S_{ij} = X_j - X_i$
    2. $p_{ij} \le S_{ij} \le q_{ij}$
    3. $Z_{ij} \le f_{ij}^k(S)$
- Objective Function: $\sum_{ij} Z_{ij}$

Theorem 3. *The solution to the LPP as formulated above provides a utilitarian optimal solution to the STPP.*

Proof. Consider the candidate STPP solution S obtained from the values of the $\{X_i\}$ variables in an optimal solution of the LPP. Clearly, the constraints (items 1 and 2) guarantee that S satisfies the STP underlying the STPP. It only remains to show that it is optimal in the utilitarian ordering for the STPP. From the constraints in item 3, we see that $Z_{ij} \le f_{ij}^k(S)$ for each linear component k and hence $Z_{ij} \le f_{ij}(S)$. We claim that $Z_{ij} = f_{ij}(S)$. To see this, note that the Z_{ij} variables can be varied independently without affecting the constraints in items 1 and 2. If $Z_{ij} < f_{ij}(S)$, then the objective function can be increased, without violating any constraints, by increasing Z_{ij} to $f_{ij}(S)$, which contradicts the assumption that the solution is already optimal. Thus, $Z_{ij} = f_{ij}(S)$ for each ij, and so $\sum_{ij} Z_{ij} = \sum_{ij} f_{ij}(S)$.

Suppose now there was a better solution S' for the STPP in terms of the utilitarian ordering. Then $\sum_{ij} f_{ij}(S') > \sum_{ij} f_{ij}(S) = \sum_{ij} Z_{ij}$. Observe that we can now formulate a better solution to the LPP based on S' (where we set $Z'_{ij} = f_{ij}(S')$), which is a contradiction. Thus, the S obtained from the LPP is also optimal for the STPP. □

The previous result shows that, for an STPP with preference functions that are convex and piecewise linear, a single solution can be obtained by mapping the problem into an LPP. An interesting question presents itself: is there a compact representation for the *entire* set of the utilitarian optimal solutions to the STPP? In particular, can the set be represented as the solutions to an STP, as can the corresponding set for SE-optimality?

This question is answered in the affirmative by the theorem that follows. As it turns out, whereas solving a primal LPP problem gives a single solution, solving instead a *dual* LPP problem [13] provides the entire set of solutions. Specifically, the dual solution is used to find additional temporal constraints on the STP that underlies the STPP so that its solutions are all and only the optimal solutions to the STPP.

Theorem 4. *Suppose an STPP P has preference functions that are convex and piecewise linear. Then the set of all utilitarian optimal solutions can be represented as the solutions to an STP that is formed by adding constraints to the STP underlying P.*

Proof. We map the STPP into an LPP in the same way as before. Note that we can apply certain results from linear programming theory [13, page 101]: the set of solutions to an LPP coincides with one of the faces of the (hyper) polyhedron that defines the feasible region[2]. Note also that the faces can be obtained by changing some of the inequalities to equalities. In a well-known result, the indices of the constraints that change to equalities can be obtained by solving the *dual* of the original LPP.

There are two kinds of inequalities in the LPP that are not already equalities: edge bounds and preference value bounds. In the former case, changing an edge bound to an equality instead of an inequality can be accomplished by adding a simple temporal constraint. In the latter case, an inequality of the form $Z_{ij} \leq f_{ij}^k(S)$ is changed to the equality $Z_{ij} = f_{ij}^k(S)$. This change can be accomplished by restricting the solution to be within the bounds of the f_{ij}^k "piece" of the piecewise linear preference function, which can also be performed through adding a simple temporal constraint. Figure 5 demonstrates this process. A piecewise-linear function with three pieces is displayed. One of the pieces, f, has become part of an equality preference constraint $Z = f(X)$ as the result of solving the dual LPP. The consequence of this update is to add the temporal bound $[a, b]$ to the STP underlying the original STPP. This bound limits the duration of the edge to be that of the piece of the original preference function that has become an equality. We make the following claims.

1. No temporal value outside the interval $[a, b]$ can be part of an optimal solution; and
2. Every solution of the restricted STP is an optimal solution of the original STPP.

---

[2] In this context, the term *face* includes vertices, edges, and higher-dimensional bounding surfaces of the polyhedron, as well as the whole polyhedron.

The first claim is obvious from the figure: if there are solutions which contain temporal values outside the bound, they must receive a preference value less than the linear function of the selected piece (by the convexity of the preference function); hence they are not optimal, since this piece is satisfied with equality in all the optimal solutions.

To see that the second claim is true, consider any solution S of the restricted STP. We can extend this to a feasible solution of the (primal) LPP by setting $Z_{ij} = f_{ij}(S)$ for each i and j. Note that $f_{ij}(S) = f_{ij}^k(S)$ for each preference edge that has been restricted to a k piece as discussed above, so $Z_{ij} = f_{ij}^k(S)$ will be satisfied in these cases. Thus, the extended solution is in the optimal face of the LPP, and hence S is optimal for the STPP.

Thus, from the information provided by the dual solution to the LPP, a new STP is formed whose solutions are all and only the utilitarian-optimal solutions of the original STPP. □

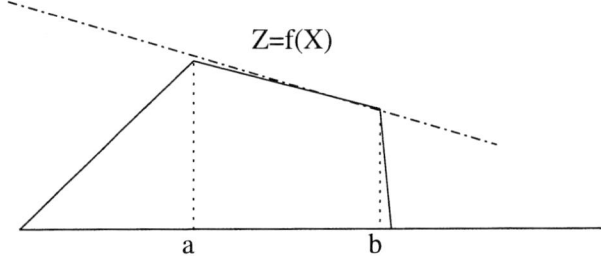

Fig. 5. Squeezing a Temporal Bound by Adding a Preference Equality.

This theorem suggests an approach to transforming an STPP into an STP all of whose solutions are utilitarian-optimal for the original problem. First, formulate an LPP as described in the theorem. Second, solve the dual of the LPP to identify the LPP constraints that change from being inequalities to being equalities. Third, map these changes to the STP that underlies the original STPP, again as described above.

As an example, consider the STPP shown in figure 6 (left) with nodes A, B, and C and edges $x1$, $x2$, and $x3$ for which the domains are $[0, 10]$. The preference function f on both $x1$ and $x2$ is given by

$$f(x) = \begin{cases} x \text{ for } 0 \leq x \leq 6 \\ 6 \text{ for } 6 \leq x \leq 10 \end{cases}$$

Note that this is convex and piecewise-linear with 2 pieces. There is no preference (or constant preference) for $x3$.

We can obtain a single optimal solution to this STPP by solving an LPP:

$$\text{maximize } cX : AX \leq b$$

where $X = (x1, x2, x3, z1, z2)$ and $z1$ and $z2$ are the preferences for $x1$ and $x2$ respectively. This is shown in more detail on the right of figure 6[3]. Each optimal solution

---

[3] For expository reasons, this is simplified from the earlier formulation. In particular, we have eliminated the node variables and consolidated the graph constraints into cycle constraints.

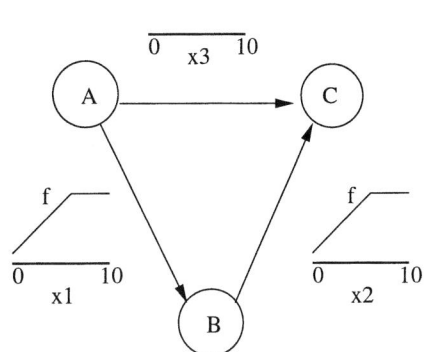

	Primal Variables				
	x1	x2	x3	z1	z2
Dual Variables	Primal Constraints				
y1	x1				≤ 10
y2		x2			≤ 10
y3			x3		≤ 10
y4	-x1			+z1	≤ 0
y5				z1	≤ 6
y6		-x2			+z2 ≤ 0
y7					z2 ≤ 6
y8	x1 +x2 -x3				≤ 0
y9	-x1 -x2 +x3				≤ 0

Fig. 6. STPP to LPP example. The primal objective is max : $(z1 + z2)$ while the dual objective is min : $(10y1 + 10y2 + 10y3 + 6y5 + 6y7)$.

has a value of 10 for the objective. However, our goal is to find the additional constraints needed to define the STP that characterizes *all* the optimal solutions. For this, we need only find a single solution to the dual problem. The dual solution has $\{y3, y4, y6, y8\}$ as the variables with non-zero values. As a consequence of the Duality Theorem, we conclude that the inequalities corresponding to $y3$, $y4$, $y6$, and $y8$, shown in figure 6, are satisfied as equalities. From $(x3 = 10)$ we conclude that $x3$ satisfies $[10,10]$. From $(-x1 + z1 = 0)$ we conclude that $x1$ is restricted to $[0,6]$ (a single piece of the preference function), and similarly for $x2$ using $(-x2 + z2 = 0)$. By computing the minimal STP, we can further restrict $x1$ and $x2$ to $[4, 6]$.

5 Experimental Results

Experiments were conducted comparing the performance of WLO+ with a Simplex LP solver. As noted above, WLO+ generates flexible plans in polynomial (worse-case cubic) time that are SE-optimal. The simplex algorithm applied to temporal planning generates fixed utilitarian-optimal plans and is known to perform well in practice but takes exponential time in the worst case. In these experiments, we were interested in comparing both the run-time performance of the two approaches, as well as the quality of WLO+ solutions with respect to an utilitarian evaluation, on a variety of randomly generated problems. The results summarized in this section are intended to be preliminary in nature.

A random problem generator was constructed to generate an STPP to be solved by WLO+. A convertor routine is applied to the problem to construct the equivalent LP, in the manner discussed above. The random problem is generated from a seed consisting of a grounded solution. All the programs were compiled optimized on a dual processor 3.06 GHz Linux box. All times reported below include the time to solve the problem but exclude the times to convert the inputs. The LP solver utilized was the *lp_solve* free MIP solver.

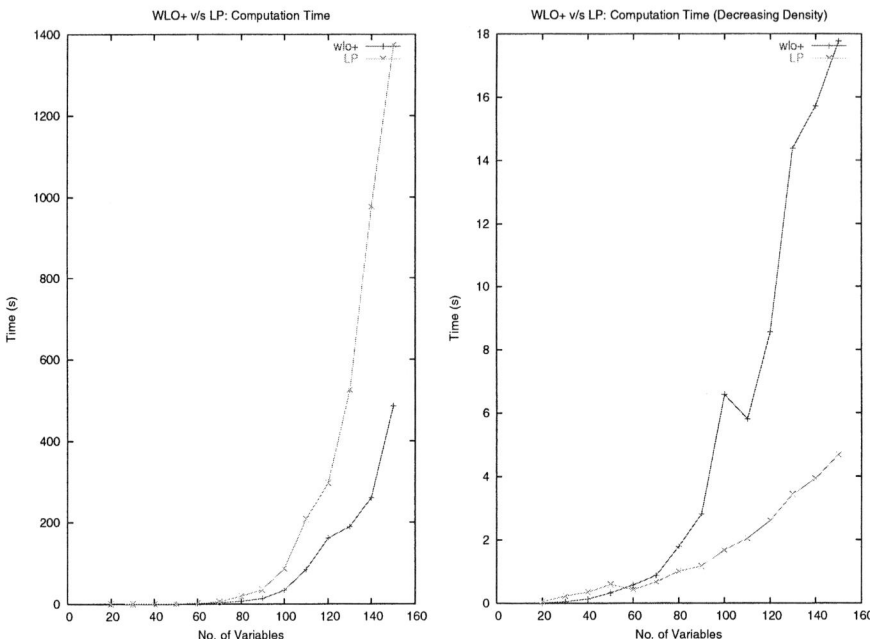

Fig. 7. Simplex vs. WLO+: Time to Solution.

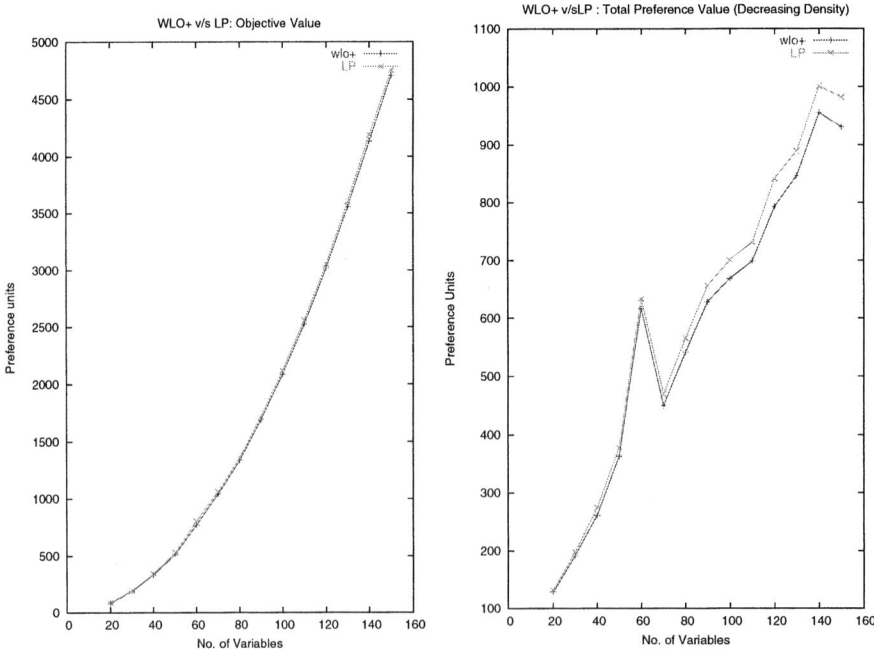

Fig. 8. Simplex vs. WLO+: Solution Quality.

The solvers were tested on problems of varying constraint density. (The density here is determined as the ratio of the number of constraints compared to the number that a complete graph would have.) In one set of experiments, the densities were fixed at 10, 50, or 80%. Five problem instances for each density were generated, and the results were averaged to form a single data point. In another set of experiments, the density varied with the problem size (in order to obtain sparse graphs), using the formula $1600/N$, where N is the number of STP nodes. (This keeps the ratio of constraints to nodes constant.) Problem sizes varied between 20 and 150 variables.

The results are shown in Figures 7 and 8, where the graphs on the left of the page show results where densities do not vary with respect to problem size, and those on the right show results when density varies with size. The top two graphs compare solution times for the two solvers, and the bottom two graphs compare solution quality. WLO+ was shown to be faster than the LP solver, on average, and this improvement seemed to increase with problem size. However, LP tended to out-perform WLO+ on sparse problems. This result is somewhat surprising, given the fact that WLO+ uses the Bellman-Ford shortest-path algorithm to solve the underlying STP. Bellman-Ford is designed to perform well in sparse graphs. Further analysis is required to interpret this result.

With respect to solution quality, the SE-optimal solutions generated by WLO+ were, on average, within 90% of the utilitarian-optimal value. These results suggest that WLO+ offers a feasible alternative to LP-based solution techniques, sacrificing tolerable amounts of solution quality for an increase in speed.

6 Discussion and Conclusion

The work reported here contributes to the overall goal of increasing the adeptness of automated systems for planning and scheduling. The objectives of this work overlap with those of a number of diverse research efforts. First, this work offers an alternative approach for reasoning about preferences to approaches based on multi-objective decision theory [2]. Specifically, the characterizations of optimization problems and their properties resemble those found in [7]. The work in this paper also contributes to, and builds upon, the on-going effort to extend CSP algorithms and representations to solve optimization problems or problems where knowledge is uncertain (for example, [6]). Finally, the focus on solving problems involving piecewise-linear constraints has similarities to other efforts more grounded in Operations Research (for example, [1]).

References

1. F. Ajili and H. El Sakkout. A probe-based algorithm for piecewise linear optimization in scheduling. *Annals of Operations Research*, 118:25–48, 2003.
2. F. Bacchus and A. Grove. Graphical models for preference and utility. In *Proceedings of the Eleventh Conference of Uncertainty in Artificial Intelligence*, pages 3–10. Morgan Kaufmann, 1995.
3. J. Bresina, K. Golden, D. Smith, and R. Washington. Increased flexibility and robustness of mars rovers. In *Proceedings of the 5th International Symposium on Artificial Intelligence, Robotics and Automation for Space, ESTEC*, Noordwijk, Netherlands, 1999.

4. T.H. Cormen, C.E. Leiserson, and R.L. Rivest. *Introduction to Algorithms*. MIT press, 1990.
5. R. Dechter, I. Meiri, and J. Pearl. Temporal constraint networks. *Artificial Intelligence*, 49:61–95, 1991.
6. D. Dubois, H. Fargier, and H. Prade. Possibility theory in constraint satisfaction problems: Handling priority, preference and uncertainty. *Applied Intelligence*, 6(4):287–309, 1996.
7. M. Ehrgott. Discrete decision problems, multiple criteria optimization classes and lexicographic max-ordering. In *Trends in Multicriteria Decision Making, volume 465 of Lecture Notes in Economics and Mathematical Systems*, pages 31–44. Springer, 1998.
8. Ulrich Junker. Preference-based search and multi-criteria optimization. In *Proceedings of AAAI-02*. AAAI Press, 2003.
9. L. Khatib, P. Morris, R. Morris, and F. Rossi. Temporal reasoning about preferences. In *Proceedings of the 17th International Joint Conference on Artificial Intelligence (IJCAI-01)*, Seattle (WA, USA), 2001. Morgan Kaufmann, San Francisco, CA.
10. L. Khatib, P. Morris, R. Morris, and B. Venable. Tractable pareto optimization of temporal preferences. In *Proceedings of the 18th International Joint Conference on Artificial Intelligence (IJCAI-03)*, Acupulco, Mexico, 2003. Morgan Kaufmann, San Francisco, CA.
11. N. Muscettola, P. Morris, and I. Tsamardinos. Reformulating temporal plans for efficient execution. In *Proceedings of Sixth International Conference on Principles of Knowledge Representation and Reasoning (KR'98)*, 1998.
12. H. El Sakkout, M. Wallace, and T. Richards. Minimal perturbance in dynamic scheduling. In *Proceedings of the 13th European Conference on Artificial Intelligence (ECAI-98)*, pages 504–508, 1998.
13. A. Schrijver. *Theory of linear and integer programming*. John Wiley and Sons, NY, 1986.
14. Paolo Toth and Daniele Vigo. *The Vehicle Routing Problem*. SIAM Monographs on Discrete Mathematics and Applications, Philadelphia, PA, 2000.

ID Walk: A Candidate List Strategy with a Simple Diversification Device

Bertrand Neveu[1], Gilles Trombettoni[1], and Fred Glover[2]

[1] Projet COPRIN, CERTIS-I3S-INRIA
Route des lucioles, BP 93, 06902 Sophia Antipolis, France
{Bertrand.Neveu,Gilles.Trombettoni}@sophia.inria.fr
[2] Leeds School of Business, University of Colorado, Boulder
CO 80309-0419, USA
Fred.Glover@colorado.edu

Abstract. This paper presents a new optimization metaheuristic called ID Walk (Intensification/Diversification Walk) that offers advantages for combining simplicity with effectiveness. In addition to the number S of moves, ID Walk uses only one parameter Max which is the maximum number of candidate neighbors studied in every move. This candidate list strategy manages the Max candidates so as to obtain a good tradeoff between intensification and diversification.

A procedure has also been designed to tune the parameters automatically. We made experiments on several hard combinatorial optimization problems, and ID Walk compares favorably with correspondingly simple instances of leading metaheuristics, notably tabu search, simulated annealing and Metropolis. Thus, among algorithmic variants that are designed to be easy to program and implement, ID Walk has the potential to become an interesting alternative to such recognized approaches.

Our automatic tuning tool has also allowed us to compare several variants of ID Walk and tabu search to analyze which devices (parameters) have the greatest impact on the computation time. A surprising result shows that the specific diversification mechanism embedded in ID Walk is very significant, which motivates examination of additional instances in this new class of "dynamic" candidate list strategies.

1 Introduction

Local search is widely used in combinatorial optimization because it often yields a good solution in reasonable time. Among the huge number of metaheuristics that have been designed during the last decades, only a few can obtain a good performance on most problems while managing a small number of parameters.

The goal of our work was to obtain a new computationally effective metaheuristic by performing a study of the most intrinsic phase of the search process, the phase that examines a list of candidates (neighbors) for the next move. This study has led us to design a new, simple and very promising *candidate list strategy (CLS)* to provide a metaheuristic that implements local search devices in the neighborhood exploration phase.

Several CLS procedures have been designed in the past, particularly in connection with tabu search [8]. The ID Walk (Intensification/Diversification Walk)

metaheuristic presented in this paper can be viewed as an extension of the
AspirationPlus CLS approach [8] that is endowed with a simple and efficient
diversification mechanism, called SpareNeighbor below, to exit from local minima.

Roughly, ID Walk performs S moves and returns the best solution found during the walk. Every time ID Walk selects a move, it examines at most Max candidate neighbors by selecting them randomly one by one. If the cost of a neighbor x' is *less than or equal to* the cost of the current solution x, then x' is chosen for the next move (rudimentary intensification effort). If no neighbor has been accepted among the Max examined, then one of these candidates, with a cost worse than the one of x, is chosen for the next move (rudimentary diversification device). Two variants perform this simple diversification process by setting a specific value to a parameter called SpareNeighbor. In the first variant ID(any), where SpareNeighbor is set to any, *any* previously rejected candidate is randomly selected (among the Max visited neighbors). In the second variant ID(best), where SpareNeighbor is set to best, a *best* (or rather less worsening, in terms of cost) previously rejected candidate is selected.

The first part of the paper introduces the ID Walk candidate list strategy. Section 2 gives a detailed description of the two variants of ID Walk. Performed on a large sample of benchmarks, ID Walk compares very favorably with correspondingly simple instances of leading metaheuristics, notably tabu search, simulated annealing [11] and Metropolis [2].

The second part of this paper tries to understand the role of key intensification and diversification parameters in the optimization process. Section 3 uses tabu search, several variants of ID Walk, and our automatic tuning tool to learn more about the impact of parameters on the computation time. Two CLS devices are studied along with the tabu list. This first analysis performed on numerous instances from different problem classes reveals that the SpareNeighbor diversification device used by ID Walk and tabu search has generally a crucial impact on performance.

2 Description of ID Walk and Comparison with Leading Metaheuristics

This section describes the two main variants of ID Walk, introduces a straightforward tool used to tune automatically easy to program metaheuristics and reports the experimental results performed on a large sample of problems.

2.1 Description of ID Walk

Without loss of generality, the following pseudo-code description assumes that ID Walk solves a combinatorial *minimization* problem.

The move selection is the main contribution of ID Walk and Max is a simple parameter for imposing a ratio between intensification and diversification efforts:

– First, the parameter is often useful to limit the number of neighbors visited in problems with large neighborhoods, to avoid an exhaustive search.

```
algorithm IDWalk (S: number of moves, Max: number of neighbors,
SpareNeighbor : type of diversification)
    Start with a configuration x
    BestConfiguration ← x
    for i from 1 to S do
        Candidate ← 1
        RejectedCandidates ← ∅
        Accepted? ← false
        while (Candidate ≤ Max) and (not Accepted?) do
            x' ← Select (Neighborhood(x), any)
            if cost(x') ≤ cost(x) then
                Accepted? ← true
            else
                RejectedCandidates ← RejectedCandidates ∪ {x'}
            end
            Candidate ← Candidate +1
        end
        if Accepted? then
            x ← x'
        else
            x ← Select (RejectedCandidates, SpareNeighbor)
        end
        if cost(x) < cost(BestConfiguration) then BestConfiguration ← x
    end.
    return BestConfiguration
end.
```

- Second, Max must be sufficiently large to allow the search to pursue better solutions in an aggressive way (intensification).
- Third, Max must be sufficiently small to allow the search to exit from local minima (diversification).

We have designed two variants of ID Walk that embedd two different ways for exiting from local minima, and thus two degrees of diversification. These variants differ only on the way a candidate is chosen when none of them has been accepted (in the while loop), that is, they differ on the SpareNeighbor parameter.

The Variant ID(any)
ID(any) (Intensification/Diversification Walk with *Any* "spare" neighbor) corresponds to the algorithm ID Walk called with SpareNeighbor equal to any. In this case, the Select function chooses any neighbor among the Max previously rejected candidates. This neighbor is randomly selected.

The Variant ID(best)
ID(best) (Intensification/Diversification Walk with *Best* "spare" neighbor) corresponds to the algorithm ID Walk called with SpareNeighbor equal to best. In

this case, the Select function chooses a best neighbor (i.e., with a lowest cost for the objective function) among the Max rejected candidates.

Note that a variant of tabu search also uses a parameter SpareNeighbor set to best. The behavior of the TS used in this paper is similar to the one of ID(best) in case all the studied candidates have not been accepted because they are all tabu and do not meet the aspiration criterion: instead of getting stuck, TS and ID(best) move to the best neighbor, in terms of cost. (More common variants of TS select a neighbor that has least recently or least frequently been selected in the past, breaking ties by reference to cost.)

2.2 Automatic Parameter Tuning Procedure

We have implemented a straightforward procedure for tuning the two parameters of IDWalk. In accordance with experimental observations, we have assumed, somewhat naively, that for a given walk length S, there exists one value for Max that maximizes the performance, i.e., that gives the best average cost of the solution. We suspected however that the best value of Max depends on S, so that the implemented procedure for tuning Max is called every time the number of moves is increased. The principle of the automatic tuning procedure is the following:

1. $S \leftarrow S_0$ (the walk length S is initialized)
2. Until a maximum running time is exceeded:
   (a) Tune Max by running the algorithm IDWalk on reduced walk lengths S/K. Let N_i be the value found for the parameter.
   (b) Run the algorithm IDWalk(S, N_i,SpareNeighbor).
   (c) $S \leftarrow F \times S$

In the experiments presented below, $S_0 = 10^6$ moves, $K = 50$, and we have chosen an increasing factor $F = 4$. Note that we restart from scratch (i.e., from a new configuration) when moving from S_j to S_{j+1}. Only the lattest value of Max is reused.

Thus, every phase i, performed with a given walk length S, includes a step (a) tuning Max and a solving step (b) keeping Max constant. Runs in steps (a) and (b) are performed with a given number of trials (e.g., 10 trials). In the tuning step (a), $P = 10$ different parameter values are tried for N_i in a dichotomous way. The number of moves of our tuning procedure is then: $\sum_{i=1}^{maxiter} S_0(1+P/K)F^i$

The tuning step (a) is perfomed as follows. Starting from an initial value for Max (depending on the metaheuristic), Max is divided by 2 or multiplied by 2 until a minimum is reached, in terms of cost. The value of Max is then refined in a dichotomous way.

Our automatic tuning procedure is also applied to other algorithms with one parameter such as Metropolis and simulated annealing with a linear temperature decrease. In this case, the (initial) temperature replaces the parameter Max in the above description.

This tuning procedure has also been extended to tune algorithms with two parameters (in addition to the number S of moves), such as the tabu search and more sophisticated variants of IDWalk that will be introduced in Section 3.

2.3 Experiments and Problems Solved

We have performed experiments on 21 instances issued from 5 categories of problems, generally encoded as weighted MAX-CSPs problems with two different neighborhoods, which yields in fact 35 instances. Graph coloring instances are proposed in the DIMACS challenge [16]. We have also tested CELAR frequency assignment problems [5] [1], a combinatorial game, called Spatially-balanced Latin Square, and random Constraint Satisfaction Problems (CSPs).

Several principles are followed in this paper concerning the experimental part. First, we compare metaheuristics that have at most two parameters. Indeed, the simple versions of the leading metaheuristics have only a few parameters and the procedure described above can tune them automatically. Second, for the sake of simplicity, we have not tested algorithms including restart mechanisms. This would make our automatic tuning procedure more complicated. More important, the restart device, although often useful, is in a sense orthogonal to the CLS mechanisms studied in this article that are applied during the move operation. Third, no clever heuristics have been used for generating the first configuration that is generally randomly produced, or only incorporates straightforward considerations[2]. In addition, for three among the five categories of tested problems, two different neighborhoods with specific degrees of intensification are used.

Random CSPs

We have used the generator of random uniform binary CSPs designed by Bessière [1] to generate 30 CSP instances with two different densities. All are satisfiable instances placed before the complexity peak. Ten (resp. twenty) instances in the first (resp. second) category have 1000 (resp. 500) binary constraints, 1000 variables with a domain size 15, and tightness 50 (resp. 88). A tightness 50 means that 50 tuples over 225 (15×15) do not satisfy the constraints.

These constraint satisfaction instances are handled as optimization MAX-CSPs: the number of violated constraints is minimized during the search and a solution is given by a configuration with cost 0.

The usual definition of neighborhood used for CSPs is chosen here: a new configuration x' is a neighbor of the current configuration x if both have the same values, except for one variable v which takes different values in both configurations. More precisely, we define two different neighborhoods:

- (VarConflict) Configurations x and x' are neighbors iff v belongs to a violated constraint.
- (Minton) Following the Min-conflict heuristics proposed by Minton et al. [15], v belongs to a violated constraint, and the new value of v in configuration x' is different than the old value and produces the lowest number of conflicts.

---

[1] Thanks to the "Centre d'électronique de l'Armement".
[2] For the latin square problem, a line contains the n different symbols (in any order); for the car sequencing, the initial assembly line contains the n cars (in any order).

Graph Coloring Instances

We have selected three graph coloring instances from the two most difficult categories in the catalogue: the le450_15c with 450 nodes and 16680 edges, the le450_25c with 450 nodes and 17425 edges, and the more dense flat300_28 instance with 300 nodes and 21695 edges. All instances are embedded with specially constructed best solutions having, respectively, 15, 25 and 28 colors.

In this paper, graph coloring instances are encoded as MAX-CSP: variables are the vertices in the graph to be colored; the number d of colors with which the graph must be colored yields domains ranging from 1 to d; vertices linked by an edge must be colored with different colors: the corresponding variables must take different values. Coloring a graph in d colors amounts in minimizing the number of violated constraints and finding a solution with cost 0.

The two neighborhoods VarConflict and Minton defined above are used.

CELAR Frequency Assignment Instances

We have also selected the three most difficult instances of radio link frequency assignment [5]: celar6, celar7 and celar8. These instances are realistic since they have all been built from different sub-parts of a real problem. The celar6 has 200 variables and 1322 constraints; the celar7 has 400 variables and 2865 constraints; the celar8 has 916 variables and 5744 constraints.

The variables are the frequencies to be assigned a value which belong to a predefined set of allowed frequencies (domain size about 40). The constraints are of the form $|x_i - x_j| = \delta$ or $|x_i - x_j| > \delta$. Our encoding is standard and creates only the even variables in the CSP along with only the inequalities[3].

The objective function to be minimized is a weighted sum of violated constraints. Note that the weights of the constraints in celar7 belong to the set $\{1, 10^2, 10^4, 10^6\}$, making this instance highly challenging. In addition to these problems, we have solved the celar9 and celar10 instances which have the same type of constraints and also unary soft constraints which assign some variables to given values. All the instances are encoded with the VarConflict neighborhood.

Spatially-Balanced Latin Square

The latin square problem consists in placing r different symbols (values) in each row of a $r \times r$ square (i.e., grid or matrix) such that every value appears only once in each row and in each column. We tried an encoding where the latin square constraint on a row is satisfied and a specific neighborhood: swap in a row two values which take part in a conflict in a latin square column constraint. A simple descent algorithm (with allowed plateaus) can quickly find a solution for a latin square of size 100. This suggests that there are no local minima.

The *spatially-balanced* latin square problem [9] must also solve additional constraints on every value pair: the average distance between the columns of two values in each row must be equal to $(r + 1)/3$. The problem is challenging for both exact and heuristic methods. An exact method can only solve the problem for sizes up to 8 and 9. A simple descent algorithm could not solve them. As shown in the experiments below, TS and ID(best) can solve them easily.

---

[3] A bijection exists between odd and even variables. A simple propagation of the equalities allows us to deduce the values of the odd variables.

Car Sequencing

The car sequencing problem deals with determining a sequence of cars on an assembly line so that predefined constraints are met. We consider here the nine harder instances available in the benchmark library CSPLib [7]. In these instances, every car must be built with predefined options. The permutation of the n cars on the assembly line must respect the following constraints: consider every option o_i; for any sequence of $q(o_i)$ consecutive cars on the line, *at most* $p(o_i)$ of them must require option o_i, where $p(o_i)$ and $q(o_i)$ are two integers associated to o_i. A neighbor is obtained by simply permuting two cars on the assembly line. Two neighborhoods have been implemented:

- (NoConflict) Any two cars can be permuted.
- (``VarConflict'') Two cars c_1 and c_2 are permuted such that c_2 is randomly chosen while c_1 violates the requirement of an option o_i, that is, c_1 belongs to a sub-sequence of length $q(o_i)$ containing more than $p(o_i)$ cars with o_i.

2.4 Compared Optimization Metaheuristics

We have compared ID Walk with correspondingly simple versions of leading optimization metaheuristics that manage only a few parameters. All algorithms have been developed within the same software system [17]. Our platform INCOP is implemented in C++ and the tests have been performed on a PentiumIII 935 Mhz with a Linux operating system. All algorithms belong to a hierarchy of classes that share code, so that sound comparisons can be made between them.

Our Metropolis algorithm is standard. It starts with a random configuration and a walk of length S is performed as follows. A neighbor is accepted if its cost is lower than or equal to the current configuration. A neighbor with a cost higher than the current configuration is accepted with a probability function of a constant temperature. When no neighbor is accepted, the current configuration is not changed. Our simulated annealing SA approach follows the same schema, with a temperature decreasing during the search. It has been implemented with a linear decrease from an initial temperature (given as parameter) to 0.

Our simple TS variant is implemented as follows: a tabu list of recently executed moves avoids coming back to previous configurations. The aspiration criterion is applied when a configuration is found that is better than the current best cost. The two parameters of this algorithm are the tabu list length (which is fixed) and the size of the examined neighborhood. The best neighbor which is not tabu is selected.

2.5 Results

This section reports the comparisons between ID(any), ID(best), simulated annealing (SA), Metropolis and tabu search (TS) on the presented problems. 20 among the 35 instances make no significant difference between the tested algorithms and the corresponding results are thus reported in Appendix A.

Note that the goal of these experiments is to compare simple versions of the leading metaheuristics implemented in the same software architecture. We do not compare with the best metaheuristics on every tested instance. In particular, ad-hoc metaheuristics obtain sometimes better results than our general-purpose algorithms do (see below). However, due to the efficient implementation of our library INCOP and due to the advances provided by ID Walk, very good results are often observed. More precisely:

- As shown below, ID(any) is excellent on CELAR instances and is competitive with state-of-the-art algorithms [12, 20, 13, 3]. The only slightly better general-purpose metaheuristic is GWW_idw, a more sophisticated population-based algorithm with four parameters [18].
- Several ad-hoc algorithms obtain very good results on the 3 tested graph coloring instances [16, 4, 6]. However, the results obtained by ID(best) and TS are impressive on le450_15c. Also, our TS, and our SA with more time [17], can color for the first time flat_300_28_0 in 30 colors.
- ID(best) and TS obtain even better results than the complicated variants of SA used by the designers of the balanced latin square problem [9].
- On car sequencing problems, we obtain competitive results as compared to the local search approach implemented in the COMET library [14] and the ant colony optimization approaches described in [10] (although the lattest seems faster on the easiest car sequencing instances).

CELAR Instances

Table 1. Comparisons between algorithms on CELAR instances. The first column contains the best bound ever found for the instance (not proven for celar7 and celar8). The second column reports the time per trial in minutes. For the other columns, each cell contains the average cost (left) on 10 or 20 trials, and the best cost (right). The numbers are reported minus the value of the best known bound, i.e., 0 means that the bound has been obtained.

	Bound	T	ID(any)		ID(best)		Metropolis		SA		TS	
celar6	3389	14	**58**	**0**	470	304	1659	517	778	150	389	227
celar7	343592	6	**29742**	**406**	$8.6\,10^5$	487406	$5.6\,10^6$	$2.5\,10^6$	$9\,10^5$	113301	$9\,10^5$	376787
celar8	262	50	29	5	131	73	108	38	**19**	**2**	84	38
celar9	15571	3	**0**	**0**	801	671	2188	416	69	0	644	249
celar10	31516	1	**0**	**0**	323	0	59	0	0	0	0	0

The results show that ID(any) is clearly superior to others. The only exception concerns celar8 for which SA is better than ID(any). The following remarks highlight the excellent performance of ID(any):

- ID(any) can reach the best kwown bound for all the instances. With more available time, the best bound 262 is reached for celar8 and bounds less than 343600 can be obtained on the challenging celar7 that has a very chahuted landscape (with constraint violation weights ranging from 1 to 10^6).
- Only a few ad-hoc algorithms can obtain such results on celar6 and celar7 [12, 20], while all the tested algorithms are general-purpose.
- The excellent result on celar9 (10 sucesses on 10 trials) is in fact obtained in 7 s, instead of 3 min for others. The excellent result on celar10 is in fact obtained in 1 s, instead of resp. 47 s and 34 s for SA and TS.

Graph Coloring Instances

Table 2. Comparisons between algorithms on graph coloring instances. For le450_15c, a cell contains the average time required per trial in seconds and the number of times (on 10 trials) the graph can be colored in 15 colors (into parentheses). For le450_25c, a cell contains the average cost (left) and the best cost (right) among the ten trials, obtained in 800 seconds per trial. The numbers are reported minus 25, i.e., 0 means that the graph has been colored in 25 colors.

	Neighborhood	#col	ID(any)	ID(best)	Metropolis	SA	TS
le450_15c	VarConflict	15	99 (10)	151 (8)	220 (0)	82 (3)	112 (10)
le450_15c	Minton	15	27 (10)	8 (10)	108 (10)	74 (6)	3 (10)
le450_25c	VarConflict	25	3.3 2	3.6 2	4.1 3	5.9 2	2.3 0
le450_25c	Minton	25	3.2 3	3.5 2	3.2 2	3.8 2	2.6 1

TS obtains generally the best results, especially on le450_25c. It can even color le450_25c once in 800s with the VarConflict neighborhood.

ID(any) and ID(best) also obtain good results, especially on le450_15c.

Spatially-Balanced Latin Square Instances

Table 3. Comparisons between algorithms on spatially-balanced latin square instances. Each cell contains the average time in seconds per trial (over 10 trials). For blatsq8, all the algorithms always find a solution (10/10). For blatsq9, the number of successes (between 0 to 10) is indicated into parentheses.

	ID(any)	ID(best)	Metrop.	SA	TS
blatsq8	23	1.5	10	15	2.8
blatsq9	998 (6)	5 (10)	26 (10)	46 (10)	9 (10)

These tests show that ID(best) and TS clearly dominate the others.

Car Sequencing Instances

Table 4 collapses the results obtained on the two most difficult instances of car sequencing (in the CSPLib): pb10-93 and pb16-81.

The reader can first notice that the results obtained with the more "aggressive" neighborhood are better for all the metaheuristics. The trend is confirmed on the other instances in appendix, although this is not systematic.

Table 4. Comparisons between algorithms on car sequencing instances. Each cell contains the average time in seconds per trial (over 10 trials) and the number of successes into parentheses (between 0 to 10).

	Neighborhood	ID(any)	ID(best)	Metrop.	SA	TS
pb10-93	NoConflict	759 (0)	1842 (6)	737 (6)	697 (0)	5902 (4)
pb10-93	VarConflict	1330 (1)	442 (10)	509 (7)	709 (4)	1400 (9)
pb16-81	NoConflict	2450 (8)	499 (10)	945 (10)	592 (9)	580 (9)
pb16-81	VarConflict	603 (2)	188 (10)	677 (10)	1039 (9)	99 (10)

On these instances, ID(best) give the best results (twice) or is only twice slower than the best one, that is Metropolis or TS. ID(any) and SA are less effective.

Summary

On the 15 instances tested above (some of them being encoded with two different neighborhoods), we can conclude that:

- ID(any) dominates others on 4 CELAR and 1 graph coloring instances.
- ID(best) dominates others on 1 spatially-balanced latin square instance and 2 car sequencing instances. It is also generally good when TS is the best.
- Metropolis dominates others on only 1 car sequencing instance and is sometimes very bad.
- SA dominates others only on celar8 and is sometimes very bad.
- TS dominates others on 3 graph coloring instances, 1 spatially-balanced latin square instance and 1 car sequencing instance.

As a result, TS gives the best results on these instances, although it is bad on some CELAR problems, especially celar7.

We should highlight the excellent results obtained by the "best" metaheuristic among ID(any) and ID(best) on all the instances: one version of ID Walk is the best for 8 over the 15 tested instances, and is very efficient on 5 others (generally ID(best)). They are only clearly dominated by TS on the graph coloring instance le450_25c (with the 2 implemented neighborhoods).

2.6 Using the Automatic Tuning Tool in Our Experiments

Our tuning tool has allowed us to perform the large number of tests gathered above. The robustness of the tuning process depends on the tested problem and metaheuristic. Car sequencing instances seem more difficult to be tuned automatically. Also, the tool is less reliable when applied with SA and metaheuristics with two parameters (TS and more sophisticated variants of ID Walk), so that a final manual tuning was sometimes necessary to obtain reliable results. The complexity times reported above do not include the tuning time. However, note that more than 80% of them have been obtained automatically. Especially, Table 5 reports the overall time spent to obtain the results of ID(best) and ID(any) on the 15 instances above. This underlines that all the results, except 1, have been obtained automatically.

For readers who wish to investigate ID_Walk on their own, Table 6 gathers the values selected for Max in our experiments.

Table 5. Total time (tuning+solving) in minutes spent on the 15 instances by ID Walk. (N), (V) and (M) denote the different neighborhoods, resp., NoConflict, VarConflict, Minton.

Instance	celar6	celar7	celar8	celar9	celar10	blatsq8	blatsq9	pb10-93(N)
ID(any)	manual	147	666	36	2	7	311	142
ID(best)	414	200	702	45	51	2.5	4.5	524

Instance	pb10-93(V)	pb16-81(N)	pb16-81(V)	le_15c(V)	le_15c(M)	le_25c(V)	le_25c(M)
ID(any)	295	611	164	117	24	429	223
ID(best)	89	374	75	67	4	251	186

Table 6. Values computed for the Max parameter by the automatic tuning tool (except for celar6).

Instance	celar6	celar7	celar8	celar9	celar10	blatsq8	blatsq9	pb10-93(N)
ID(any)	125	125	120	256	225	175	212	2800
ID(best)	15	7	29	45	16	125	71	1110

Instance	pb10-93(V)	pb16-81(N)	pb16-81(V)	1e_15c(V)	1e_15c(M)	1e_25c(V)	1e_25c(M)	
ID(any)	1200	900	562	40	4	100	6	
ID(best)	468	579	179	20	3	93	6	

3 Variants

Several variants of ID Walk have been designed to better understand the role of different devices on performance. Section 3.1 describes these variants and Section 3.2 perform some experiments that lead to significant results.

3.1 Description of Variants

In addition to the number S of moves, the variants ID(a,g) and ID(b,g) have only one parameter (like ID(any) or ID(best)), while ID(a,t) and ID(a,m) have two (like TS).

Variant ID(a,t) (ID(any) with a Tabu List)

ID(a,t) is ID(any) endowed with a tabu list of fixed length. One of the Max neighbor is accepted iff its cost is better than or equal to the current cost and is not tabu.

Variant ID(a,g) ("Greedy" Variant of ID(any))

At every move, ID(a,g) examines the Max candidates: it selects the best neighbor among the Max candidates if one of them improves or keeps the current cost; otherwise it randomly selects *any* of them.

Remark: This variant is allowed by the original move procedure[4] implemented in the INCOP library [17]. More precisely, INCOP allows the user to define a *minimum number* Min *of neighbors* that are visited at every move, among which the best accepted candidate is returned. Without going into details, Min is set to 0 (or 1) in the variants above and is set to Max in the "greedy" variants.

Variant ID(b,g) ("Greedy" Variant of ID(best))

ID(b,g) selects the best neighbor among the Max candidates (Min=Max). ID(b,g) is similar to a TS with no tabu list (or a tabu list of null length).

Other variants could be envisaged. In particular, many well known devices could enrich ID Walk, such as strategic oscillation (i.e., making Max vary with time). However, the aim of the next section is to compare the impact on performance of the following three mechanisms:

- the Min parameter,
- the SpareNeighbor diversification device,
- the tabu list.

---

[4] The Min parameter is also used in the Aspiration Plus strategy.

3.2 First Comparison Between Local Search Devices

There is no need to go into details to discover a significant result in the local search field. The impact of the SpareNeighbor parameter on performance is highly crucial, while it is unused in most metaheuritics and implicit (and fixed to best) in a simple form of tabu search. The result is clear on three categories of problems (among five): CELAR, latin square and car sequencing. Therefore we believe that this diversification device should be studied more carefully in the future and incorporated in more metaheuristics. This surprising result also explains the success of ID(any) and ID(best) (in disjoint cases especially).

On the opposite, we can observe that the impact of Min is very weak.

We can finally observe that the tabu list is very effective for graph coloring instances, but the effect on the other categories of problems is not clear.

Note that all the metaheuristics have a good behavior on the uniform random CSP instances. The results are thus reported in Appendix A.

To sum up, 1 category of problems does not discriminate the tested devices, 1 category takes advantage on the tabu list, and 3 categories are well handled by this new SpareNeighbor diversification device.

Impact of Parameter SpareNeighbor

Table 7 has been arranged so that columns on the left side correspond to metaheuristics with SpareNeighbor=any, while columns on the right side correspond to metaheuristics with SpareNeighbor=best. The impact of parameter SpareNeighbor is very significant on CELAR, latin square and car sequencing problems, for which several orders of magnitude can sometimes be gained by choosing any (for CELAR) or best (for latin square and car sequencing).

Table 7. Measuring the impact of Min, SpareNeighbor and the tabu list on performance. Every cell has the same content as described in the previous tables (only the average cost appears for celar7). The last column p-q gives the length p of the TS tabu list and the length q of the ID(a,t) tabu list.

Instance	Neigh.	ID(a)	ID(a,t)	ID(a,g)	ID(b)	ID(b,g)	TS	p-q
celar6	VarC	58 0	60 0	96 0	470 304	408 308	389 227	1-6
celar7	VarC	$3\,10^4$	$4\,10^4$	$4.8\,10^4$	$8.6\,10^5$	$8\,10^5$	$9\,10^5$	50-48
celar8	VarC	29 5	37 13	38 16	131 73	91 54	84 38	2-45
celar9	VarC	0 0	0 0	0 0	801 671	36 313	644 249	15-12
celar10	VarC	0 0	0 0	0 0	323 0	0 0	0 0	2-5
le_15c	VarC	99 (10)	18 (10)	92 (10)	151 (8)	152 (6)	112 (10)	72-56
le_15c	Mint.	27 (10)	1 (10)	4 (10)	8 (10)	14 (10)	3 (10)	45-10
le_25c	VarC	3.3 2	3.3 2	3.7 3	3.6 2	2.8 1	2.3 0	2-4
le_25c	Mint.	3.2 3	2.4 1	4.1 2	3.5 2	2.8 2	2.6 1	2-4
blatsq8	VarC	99	171	84	2	4	4	0-2
blatsq9	VarC	1410(5)	1581(5)	972(1)	40(10)	16(10)	16(10)	0-3
pb10-93	NoC	759(0)	4301(0)	5979(0)	1842(6)	1698(2)	5902(4)	1-1
pb10-93	VarC	1330(1)	5381(0)	1457(0)	442(10)	1264(10)	1400(9)	1-1
pb16-81	NoC	2450(8)	894(2)	1763(0)	499(10)	1182(10)	580(9)	1-2
pb16-81	VarC	603(2)	890(0)	862(1)	188(10)	236(10)	99(10)	1-4

On car sequencing instances, we can notice that a good performance is obtained by setting `SpareNeighbor` to `best` and by using a `VarConflict` neighborhood. Both trends indicate that the notion of intensification is very significant.

Impact of the Tabu List

The observations are especially based on the comparison between `ID(b,g)` and `TS` since `ID(b,g)` can be viewed as `TS` with a null tabu list. The comparison between `ID(any)` and `ID(a,t)` is informative as well. The interest of the tabu list is not clear on CELAR and car sequencing problems. The impact of the tabu list seems null on latin square when `SpareNeighbor` is set to `best` since the automatic tuning procedure selects a list of length 0. It is even slightly counterproductive when `SpareNeighbor = any`. On the opposite, the gain in performance of the tabu list is quite clear on graph coloring for which `ID(a,t)` and our `TS` variant obtain even better results than `ID(any)` and `ID(b,g)` resp.

Weak Impact of Parameter `Min`

The reader should first understand that the parameter `Min` set to `Max` allows a more aggressive search but is generally more costly since all the neighbors are necessarily examined.

The observations are especially based on the comparison between `ID(any)` (Min=0) and `ID(a,g)` (Min=Max) on one hand, and `ID(best)` and `ID(b,g)` on the other hand. First, the impact on performance of setting `Min` to 0 or `Max` seems negligible, except for 4 instances (among 15+15): `celar7`, `le450_15c` (VarConflict), `pb10-93` (VarConflict) and `pb16-81` (NoConflict). Second, it is generally better to select a null value for `Min`, probably because a large value is more costly. Third, we also made experiments with another variant of `ID(any)` where `Min` can be tuned between 0 and `Max`. This variant did not pay off, so that the results are not reported in the paper.

This analysis suggests to not pay a great attention to this parameter and thus to favor a null value for `Min` in metaheuritics.

4 Conclusion

We have presented a very promising candidate list strategy. Its performance has been highlighted on 3 over the 5 categories of problems tested in this paper. Moreover, a first analysis has underlined the significance of the `SpareNeighbor` diversification device that is ignored by most of the metaheuristics.

All the metaheuristics compared in this paper have two points in common with ID Walk. They are simple and have a limited number of parameters. Moreover, they use a specific mechanism to exit from local minima.

Our study could be extended by analyzing the impact of random restart mechanisms. In particular, it would allow us to compare ID Walk with the `GSAT` and the `WALKSAT` [19] algorithms used for solving the well-known SAT problem (satisfiability of logical propositional formula). Note that `WALKSAT` is equipped with specific intensification and diversification devices.

ID Walk can be viewed as an instance of the `AspirationPlus` strategy, where parameters `Min` and `Plus` (see [8]) are set to 0, and where the aspiration level can be adjusted *dynamically* during the search: the aspiration level (threshold) for IDWalk always begins at the value of the current solution, but when none of the Max candidates qualify, the aspiration level is increased to the value of "any" candidate (SpareNeighbor=any) or of the "best" one (SpareNeighbor=best). Since the value of Min is not important (with "static" aspiration criteria) and since we have exhibited a significant and efficient instance of a dynamic AspirationPlus strategy, this paper strongly suggests the relevance of investigating additional dynamic forms in this novel and promising class of strategies.

In particular, the SpareNeighbor parameter can be generalized to take a value k between 1 (any) and Max (best), thus selecting the "best of k randomly chosen moves". Another variant would select any of the k best candidates.

Acknowledgments

Thanks to Pascal Van Hentenryck for useful discussions on preliminary works.

References

1. C. Bessière. Random Uniform CSP Generators. http://www.lirmm.fr/ bessiere/generator.html.
2. D. T. Connolly. An improved annealing scheme for the qap. *European Journal of Operational Research*, 46:93–100, 1990.
3. S. de Givry, G. Verfaillie, and T. Schiex. Bounding the optimum of constraint optimization problems. In *Proc. CP97*, number 1330 in LNCS, 1997.
4. R. Dorne and J.K. Hao. Tabu search for graph coloring, T-colorings and set T-colorings. In *Meta-heuristics: Advances and Trends in Local Search Paradigms for Optimization*, pages 77–92. Kluwer Academic Publishers, 1998.
5. A. Eisenblätter and A. Koster. FAP web - A website about Frequency Assignment Problems. http://fap.zib.de/.
6. P. Galinier and J.K. Hao. Hybrid evolutionary algorithms for graph coloring. *Journal of Combinatorial Optimization*, 3(4):379–397, 1999.
7. I. Gent and T. Walsh. CSPLib: a benchmark library for constraints. In *Proc. of Constraint Programming CP'99*, 1999.
8. F. Glover and M. Laguna. *Tabu Search*. Kluwer Academic Publishers, 1997.
9. C. Gomes, M. Sellmann, C. van Es, and H. van Es. The challenge of generating spatially balanced scientific experiment designs. In *Proc. of the first CPAIOR conference, LNCS 3011*, pages 387–394, 2004.
10. J. Gottlieb, M. Puchta, and C. Solnon. A study of greedy, local search and ant colony optimization approaches for car sequencing problems. In *Proc. of the Evo-COP conference, LNCS 2611*, pages 246–257, 2003.
11. S. Kirkpatrick, C. Gellat, and M. Vecchi. Optimization by simulated annealing. *Science*, 220:671–680, 1983.
12. A. Kolen. A genetic algorithm for frequency assignment. Technical report, Universiteit Maastricht, 1999.
13. A. Koster, C. Van Hoesel, and A. Kolen. Solving frequency assignment problems via tree-decomposition. Technical Report 99-011, Universiteit Maastricht, 1999.
14. L. Michel and P. Van Hentenryck. A constraint-based architecture for local search. In *Proc. of the OOPSLA conference*, 2002.

15. S. Minton, M. Johnston, A. Philips, and P. Laird. Minimizing conflict: a heuristic repair method for constraint satisfaction and scheduling problems. *Artificial Intelligence*, 58:161–205, 1992.
16. C. Morgenstern. Distributed coloration neighborhood search. In David S. Johnson and Michael A. Trick, editors, *Cliques, Coloring, and Satisfiability: Second DIMACS Implementation Challenge, 1993*, volume 26, pages 335–357. American Mathematical Society, 1996.
17. B. Neveu and G. Trombettoni. INCOP: An Open Library for INcomplete Combinatorial OPtimization. In *Proc. Int. Conference on Constraint Programming, CP'03, LNCS 2833*, pages 909–913, 2003.
18. B. Neveu and G. Trombettoni. When Local Search Goes with the Winners. In *Int. Workshop CPAIOR'2003*, pages 180–194, 2003.
19. B. Selman, H. Kautz, and B. Cohen. Local search strategies for satisfiability testing. In *Cliques, Coloring, and Satisfiability: Second DIMACS Implementation Challenge. Theoretical Computer Science, vol. 26, AMS*, 2003.
20. C. Voudouris and E. Tsang. Solving the radio link frequency assignment problem using guided local search. In *Nato Symposium on Frequency Assignment, Sharing and Conservation in Systems(AEROSPACE)*, 1998.

A Results over Less Discriminating Benchmarks

Table 8. Comparing metaheuristics on the 20 remaining instances: 4 random CSPs, 2 graph coloring instances, and 14 car sequencing instances. Every cell has the same content as described in the previous tables. For random CSPs, the time includes the tuning step (see Section 2.2) and a run is interrupted as soon as a solution is found.

Instance	Neigh.	ID(a)	ID(a,t)	ID(a,g)	ID(a,m)	ID(b)	ID(b,g)	TS	Metr.	SA
csp1	VarC	91	110	228	88	165	–	121	200	105
csp1	Mint.	127	69	197	253	77	–	64	99	172
csp2	VarC	86	61	211	206	115	–	118	101	245
csp2	Mint.	49	76	126	161	98	–	67	42	43
flat_28	VarC	5.1 4	5.7 4	4.7 3	5.7 5	5.4 5	4.7 3	5 3	5.5 3	6.5 5
flat_28	Mint.	4.5 4	4.9 4	5 4	4.4 3	5.3 4	5 4	5.1 0	4.3 3	5.5 4
pb4-72	NoC	49	32	379	49	96	173	130	40	57
pb4-72	VarC	93	118	143	132	15	41	29	30	126
pb6-76	NoC	0.2	0.1	0.7	1.2	0.2	0.5	0.4	0.2	0.4
pb6-76	VarC	0.1	0.4	0.2	0.15	0.1	0.4	0.4	0.3	1.0
pb19-71	NoC	4	11	28	9	6	14	31	5	10
pb19-71	VarC	3	4	9	3	2	4	4	5	7
pb21-90	NoC	12	22	40	12	6	14	13	10	4
pb21-90	VarC	5	4	13	2	2	5	4	3	9
pb26-82	NoC	22	107	466	70	55	290	150	22	25
pb26-82	VarC	177	291	96	57	15	28	22	25	141
pb36-92	NoC	59	107	866	71	51	103	86	76	241
pb36-92	VarC	64	50	146	43	9	18	23	16	30
pb41-66	NoC	4	5	33	4	7	20	24	8	9
pb41-66	VarC	1.4	1.6	7.1	1.4	0.7	3.2	1.7	0.7	0.7

Understanding Random SAT:
Beyond the Clauses-to-Variables Ratio

Eugene Nudelman[1], Kevin Leyton-Brown[2],
Holger H. Hoos[2], Alex Devkar[1], and Yoav Shoham[1]

[1] Computer Science Department, Stanford University, Stanford, CA
{eugnud,avd,shoham}@cs.stanford.edu
[2] Computer Science Department, University of British Columbia, Vancouver, BC
{kevinlb,hoos}@cs.ubc.ca

Abstract. It is well known that the ratio of the number of clauses to the number of variables in a random k-SAT instance is highly correlated with the instance's empirical hardness. We consider the problem of identifying such features of random SAT instances automatically using machine learning. We describe and analyze models for three SAT solvers – kcnfs, oksolver and satz – and for two different distributions of instances: uniform random 3-SAT with varying ratio of clauses-to-variables, and uniform random 3-SAT with fixed ratio of clauses-to-variables. We show that surprisingly accurate models can be built in all cases. Furthermore, we analyze these models to determine which features are most useful in predicting whether an instance will be hard to solve. Finally we discuss the use of our models to build SATzilla, an algorithm portfolio for SAT[1].

1 Introduction

SAT is among the most studied problems in computer science, representing a generic constraint satisfaction problem with binary variables and arbitrary constraints. It is also the prototypical $\mathcal{NP}$-hard problem, and its worst-case complexity has received much attention. Accordingly, it is not surprising that SAT has become a primary platform for the investigation of average-case and empirical complexity. Particular interest has been paid to randomly generated SAT instances. In this paper we concentrate on such instances as they offer both a range of very easy to very hard instances for any given input size and the opportunity to make connections to a wealth of existing work.

Early work [15, 2] considered the empirical performance of DPLL-type solvers running on uniform random k-SAT instances, finding a strong correlation between the instance's hardness and the ratio of the number of clauses to the number of variables in the instance. Further, it was demonstrated that the hardest region (*e.g.*, for random 3-SAT, a clauses-to-variables ratio of roughly 4.26) corresponds exactly to a phase transition in an algorithm-independent property of the instance: the probability that a randomly-generated formula having a given ratio will be satisfiable. This well-publicized finding led to increased enthusiasm for the idea of studying algorithm performance experimentally, using the same tools as are used to study natural phenomena. Over the past decade,

---

[1] We'd like to acknowledge very helpful assistance from Nando de Freitas, and our indebtedness to the authors of the algorithms in the SATzilla portfolio. We also thank the anonymous reviewers for helpful comments.

this approach has complemented worst-case analysis of algorithms, improving our understanding of algorithms' empirical behavior with interesting findings on (*e.g.*) islands of tractability [8], search space topologies for stochastic local search algorithms [5, 4], backbones [13], backdoors [18] and random restarts [3].

Inspired by the success of this work on SAT and related problems, in 2002 we proposed a new methodology for using machine learning to study empirical hardness [11]. We applied this methodology to the combinatorial auction winner determination problem (WDP), an $\mathcal{NP}$-hard combinatorial optimization problem equivalent to weighted set packing. In subsequent papers [10, 9] we extended our methodology, demonstrating techniques for improving empirical algorithm performance through the construction of algorithm portfolios and for automatically generating hard benchmark distributions. In this paper we come full-circle and apply our techniques to uniform random 3-SAT – the problem that originally inspired their development.

The work which is perhaps the most related to our own is [7, 14]. There classification techniques are used to categorize runs of CSP and SAT solvers according to length. In [11, 9] we discuss the relationship between this work and our approach in more detail. It is worth pointing out that, different from ours, their work focuses on understanding the behavior of solvers during the run, as opposed to studying the effect of problem structure on hardness. In addition, as argued in [11], standard classifications techniques can be sometimes inappropriate in this context, for example, because of boundary cases.

Our current work has three goals. First, we aim to show that inexpensively-computable features can be used to make accurate predictions about the empirical hardness of random SAT instances, and to analyze these models in order to identify important features. We consider three different SAT algorithms and two different instance distributions. The first distribution contains random 3-SAT instances with a varying ratio of clauses to variables, allowing us to see whether our techniques automatically select the clauses-to-variables ratio as an important feature, and also what other features are important in this setting. Our second distribution contains random 3-SAT instances with the ratio of clauses-to-variables held constant at the phase transition point. This distribution has received much attention in the past; it gives us the opportunity to explain the orders-of-magnitude runtime variation that persists in this so-called "hard region."

Second, we show that empirical hardness models have other useful applications for SAT. Most importantly, we describe a SAT solver, SATzilla, which uses hardness models to choose among existing SAT solvers on a per-instance basis. We explain some details of its construction and summarize its performance.

Our final goal is to offer a concrete example in support of our abstract claim that empirical hardness models are a useful tool for gaining understanding of the behavior of algorithms for solving $\mathcal{NP}$-hard problems. Thus, while we believe that our SAT results are interesting in their own right, and while studying random 3-SAT is useful because it allows connection to existing theoretical work, we want to emphasize that very few of our techniques are particular to SAT. Indeed, we have achieved equally strong results applying our methodologies to qualitatively different problems[2].

---

[2] WDP, for example, is very different from SAT: while feasible solutions can be identified in constant time, the goal is to find an *optimal* feasible solution, and there is thus no opportunity to terminate the algorithm the moment a solution is found. We also have promising unpublished results for TSP and the computation of Nash equilibria.

2 Methodology

Although the work surveyed above has led to great advances in understanding the empirical hardness of SAT problems, most of these approaches scale poorly to more complicated domains. In particular, most of these methods involve exhaustive exploration of the search and/or distribution parameter spaces, and require considerable human intervention and decision-making. As the space of relevant features grows and instance distributions become more complex, it is increasingly difficult either to characterize the problem theoretically or to explore its degrees of freedom exhaustively. Moreover, most current work focuses on understanding algorithms' performance profiles, rather than trying to characterize the hardness of individual problem instances.

2.1 Empirical Hardness Models

In [11] we proposed a novel experimental approach for predicting the runtime of a given algorithm on individual problem instances:

1. **Select a problem instance distribution.**
   Observe that the choice of distribution is fundamental – different distributions can induce very different algorithm behavior.
2. **Select one or more algorithms.**
3. **Select a set of inexpensive, distribution-independent features.**
   It is important to remember that individual features need not be perfectly predictive of hardness; ultimately, our goal will be to combine features together. Thus, it is possible to take an inclusive approach, adding all features that seem reasonable and then removing those that turned out to be unhelpful (see step 5). Furthermore, many features that proved useful for one constraint satisfaction or optimization problem can carry over into another.
4. **Generate a set of instances and for each one, determine the running time of the selected algorithms and compute the features.**
5. **Eliminate redundant or uninformative features.**
   Much better models tend to be learned when all features are informative. A variety of statistical techniques are available for eliminating or de-emphasizing the effect of such features. The simplest approach is to manually examine pairwise correlations, eliminating features that are highly correlated with what remains. Shrinkage techniques (such as lasso [16] or ridge regression) are another alternative.
6. **Use machine learning to select a function of the features that predicts each algorithm's running time.**
   Since running time is a continuous variable, regression is the natural machine-learning approach to use for building runtime models. For more detail about why we prefer regression to other approaches such as classification, see [11].

2.2 Building Models

There are a wide variety of different regression techniques; the most appropriate for our purposes perform supervised learning[3]. Such techniques choose a function from a given hypothesis space (*i.e.*, a space of candidate mappings from the given features to the running time) in order to minimize a given error metric (a function that scores the quality of a given mapping, based on the difference between predicted and actual running times on training data, and possibly also based on other properties of the mapping). Our task in applying regression to the construction of hardness models thus reduces to choosing a hypothesis space that is able to express the relationship between our features and our response variable (running time), and choosing an error metric that both leads us to select good mappings from this hypothesis space and can be tractably minimized.

The simplest regression technique is linear regression, which learns functions of the form $\sum_i w_i f_i$, where f_i is the ith feature and the w's are free variables, and has as its error metric root mean squared error (RMSE). Linear regression is a computationally appealing procedure because it reduces to the (roughly) cubic-time problem of matrix inversion.

Choosing a Hypothesis Space. Although linear regression seems quite limited, it can actually be extended to a wide range of hypothesis spaces. There are two key tricks. The first is to introduce new features that are functions of the original features. For example, in order to learn a model which is a quadratic function of the features, the feature set can be augmented to include all pairwise products of features. A hyperplane in the resulting much-higher-dimensional space corresponds to a quadratic manifold in the original feature space. The key problem with this approach is that the set of features grows quadratically, which may cause the regression problem to become intractable and can also lead to overfitting. Thus, it can make sense to add only a subset of the pairwise products of features; *e.g.*, only pairwise products of the k most important features in the linear regression model. Of course, we can use the same idea to reduce many other nonlinear hypothesis spaces to linear regression: all hypothesis spaces which can be expressed by $\sum_i w_i g_i(\mathbf{f})$, where the g_i's are arbitrary functions and $\mathbf{f} = \{f_i\}$.

Sometimes we want to consider hypothesis spaces of the form $h\left(\sum_i w_i g_i(\mathbf{f})\right)$. For example, we may want to fit a sigmoid or an exponential curve. When h is a one-to-one function, we can transform this problem to a linear regression problem by replacing our response variable y in our training data by $h^{-1}(y)$, where h^{-1} is the inverse of h, and then training a model of the form $\sum_i w_i g_i(\mathbf{f})$. On test data, we must evaluate the model $h\left(\sum_i w_i g_i(\mathbf{f})\right)$. One caveat about this trick is that it distorts the error metric: the error-minimizing model in the transformed space will not generally be the error-minimizing model in the true space. In many cases this distortion is acceptable, however, making this trick a tractable way of performing many different varieties of nonlinear regression. In this paper we use exponential models ($h(y) = 10^y$; $h^{-1}(y) = \log_{10}(y)$) and logistic models ($h(y) = 1/(1 + e^{-y})$; $h^{-1}(y) = \ln(y)\ln(1-y)$ with values of y first mapped onto the interval $(0, 1)$). Because logistic functions have a finite range, we found them particularly useful for modeling capped runs.

---
[3] Because of our interests in being able to analyze our models and in keeping model sizes small, we avoid model-free approaches such as nearest neighbor.

2.3 Evaluating the Importance of Variables in a Hardness Model

Once we are able to construct an accurate empirical hardness model, it is natural to try to explain why it works. A key question is which features were most important to the success of the model. It is tempting to interpret a linear regression model by comparing the coefficients assigned to the different features, on the principle that larger coefficients indicate greater importance. This can be misleading for two reasons. First, features may have different ranges, though this problem can be mitigated by normalization. More fundamentally, when two or more features are highly correlated then models can include larger-than-necessary coefficients with different signs. A better approach is to force models to contain fewer variables, on the principle that the best low-dimensional model will involve only relatively uncorrelated features. Once such a model has been obtained, we can evaluate the importance of each feature to that model by looking at each feature's *cost of omission*. That is, we can train a model without the given feature and report the resulting increase in (cross-validated) prediction error. To make them easier to compare, we scale the cost of omission of the most important feature to 100 and scale the other costs of omission in proportion.

There are many different "subset selection" techniques for finding good, small models. Ideally, exhaustive enumeration would be used to find the best subset of features of desired size. Unfortunately, this process requires consideration of a binomial number of subsets, making it infeasible unless both the desired subset size and the number of base features are very small. When exhaustive search is impossible, heuristic search can still find good subsets. We considered four heuristic methods: *forward selection*, *backward elimination*, *sequential replacements* and *LAR*. Since none of these four techniques is guaranteed to find the optimal subset, we combine them together by running all four and keeping the model with the smallest cross-validated (or validation-set) error.

3 Hardness Models for SAT

3.1 Features

Figure 1 summarizes the 91 features used by our SAT models. Since not every feature is useful in every distribution, we discard uninformative or highly correlated features after fixing the distribution. For example, while ratio of clauses-to-variables was important for SATzilla, it is not at all useful for the fixed-ratio dataset. In order to keep values to sensible ranges, whenever it makes sense we normalize features by either the number of clauses or the number of variables in the formula.

We divide the features into nine groups. The first group captures problem size, measured by the number of clauses, variables, and the ratio of the two. Because we expect this ratio to be an important feature, we gave it additional expressive power by including squares and cubes of both the ratio and its reciprocal. Also, because we know that features are more powerful in simple regression models when they are directly correlated with the response variable, we include a "linearized" version of the ratio which is defined as the absolute value of the difference between the ratio and the phase transition point, 4.26. It turns out that for variable-ratio data this group of features alone suffices to construct reasonably good models. However, including the rest of our features significantly improves these models. Moreover, in the presence of other features, including

Problem Size Features:
1. **Number of clauses:** denoted c
2. **Number of variables:** denoted v
3-5. **Ratio:** c/v, $(c/v)^2$, $(c/v)^3$
6-8. **Ratio reciprocal:** (v/c), $(v/c)^2$, $(v/c)^3$
9-11. **Linearized ratio:** $|4.26-c/v|$, $|4.26-c/v|^2$, $|4.26-c/v|^3$

Variable-Clause Graph Features:
12-16. **Variable nodes degree statistics:** mean, variation coefficient, min, max and entropy.
17-21. **Clause nodes degree statistics:** mean, variation coefficient, min, max and entropy.

Variable Graph Features:
22-25. **Nodes degree statistics:** mean, variation coefficient, min, and max.

Clause Graph Features:
26-32. **Nodes degree statistics:** mean, variation coefficient, min, max, and entropy.
33-35. **Weighted clustering coefficient statistics:** mean, variation coefficient, min, max, and entropy.

Balance Features:
36-40. **Ratio of positive and negative literals in each clause:** mean, variation coefficient, min, max, and entropy.
41-45. **Ratio of positive and negative occurrences of each variable:** mean, variation coefficient, min, max, and entropy.
46-48. **Fraction of unary, binary, and ternary clauses**

Proximity to Horn Formula
49. **Fraction of Horn clauses**

50-54. **Number of occurrences in a Horn clause for each variable**: mean, variation coefficient, min, max, and entropy.

LP-Based Features:
55. **Objective value of linear programming relaxation**
56. **Fraction of variables set to 0 or 1**
57-60. **Variable integer slack statistics:** mean, variation coefficient, min, max.

DPLL Search Space:
61-65. **Number of unit propagations:** computed at depths 1, 4, 16, 64 and 256
66-67. **Search space size estimate:** mean depth to contradiction, estimate of the log of number of nodes.

Local Search Probes:
68-71. **Minimum fraction of unsat clauses in a run:** mean and variation coefficient for SAPS and GSAT (see [17]).
72-81. **Number of steps to the best local minimum in a run:** mean, median, variation coefficient, 10th and 90th percentiles for SAPS and GSAT.
82-85. **Average improvement to best:** For each run, we calculate the mean improvement per step to best solution. We then compute mean and variation coefficient over all runs for SAPS and GSAT.
86-89. **Fraction of improvement due to first local minimum:** mean and variation coefficient for SAPS and GSAT.
90-91. **Coefficient of variation of the number of unsatisfied clauses in each local minimum:** mean over all runs for SAPS and GSAT.

Fig. 1. SAT instance features used for constructing our predictive models.

higher-order features 4, 5, 7, 8, 10 and 11 does not improve accuracy much and does not qualitatively change the results reported below. Due to space constraints, for the rest of this paper we focus on models that use all of the ratio features.

The next three groups correspond to three different graph representations of a SAT instance. The variable-clause graph (VCG) is a bipartite graph with a node for each variable, a node for each clause, and an edge between them whenever a variable occurs in a clause. The variable graph (VG) has a node for each variable and an edge between variables that occur together in at least one clause. The clause graph (CG) has nodes representing clauses and an edge between two clauses whenever they share a negated literal. Each of these graphs corresponds to a constraint graph for the associated CSP; thus, each encodes aspects of the problem's combinatorial structure. For each graph we compute various node degree statistics. For the CG we also compute statistics of weighted clustering coefficients, which measure the extent to which each node belongs to a clique. For each node the *weighted clustering coefficient* is the number of edges among its neighbors (including the node itself) divided by $k(k+1)/2$, where k is the number of neighbors. Including the node when counting edges has an effect of weighting the classical clustering coefficient by the node degree.

The fifth group measures the balance of a formula in several different senses, while the sixth group measures the proximity of the instance to a Horn formula, motivated by the fact that such formulas are an important SAT subclass. The seventh group of features is obtained by solving a linear programming relaxation of an integer program representing the current SAT instance. Denote the formula $C_1 \wedge \cdots \wedge C_n$ and let x_j denote both boolean and LP variables. Define $v(x_j) = x_j$ and $v(\neg x_j) = 1 - x_j$. Then the program is maximize $\sum_{i=1}^{n} \sum_{l \in C_i} v(l)$ subject to $\forall C_i : \sum_{l \in C_i} v(l) \geq 1, \forall x_j : 0 \leq x_j \leq 1$. The objective function prevents the trivial solution where all variables are set to 0.5. The eighth group involves running DPLL "probes." First, we run a DPLL procedure to an exponentially-increasing sequence of depths, measuring the number of unit propagations done at each depths. We also run depth-first random probes by repeatedly instantiating random variables and performing unit propagation until a contradiction is found. The average depth at which a contradiction occurs is an unbiased estimate of the log size of the search space [12]. Our final group of features probes the search space with two stochastic local search algorithms, GSAT and SAPS. We run both algorithms many times, each time continuing the search trajectory until a plateau cannot be escaped within a given number of steps. We then average statistics collected during each run.

3.2 Experimental Setup

Our first dataset contained 20 000 uniform random 3-SAT instances with 400 variables each. To determine the number of clauses in each instance, we determined the clauses-to-variables ratio by drawing a uniform sample from $[3.26, 5.26]$ (*i.e.*, the number of clauses varied between 1 304 and 2 104) [4]. Our second dataset contained 20 000 uniform random 3-SAT instances with 400 variables and 1 704 clauses each, corresponding to a fixed clauses-to-variables ratio of 4.26. On each dataset we ran three solvers – kcnfs, oksolver and satz– which performed well on random instances in previous years' SAT competitions. Our experiments were executed on 2.4 GHz Xeon processors, under Linux 2.4.20. Our fixed-ratio experiments took about four CPU-months to complete. In contrast, our variable-ratio dataset took only about one CPU-month, since many instances were generated in the easy region away from the phase transition point. Every solver was allowed to run to completion on every instance.

Each dataset was split into 3 parts – training, test and validation sets – in the ratio 70 : 15 : 15. All parameter tuning was performed with the validation set; the test set was used only to generate the graphs shown in this paper. We performed machine learning and statistical analysis with the R and Matlab software packages.

4 Variable-Ratio Random Instances

We had three goals with this distribution. First, we wanted to show that our empirical hardness model training and analysis techniques would be able to sift through all the features provided and "discover" that the clauses-to-variables ratio was important to

---

[4] This range was chosen symmetrically around the phase transition point, 4.26, to ensure that an approximately equal number of satisfiable and unsatisfiable instances would be obtained.

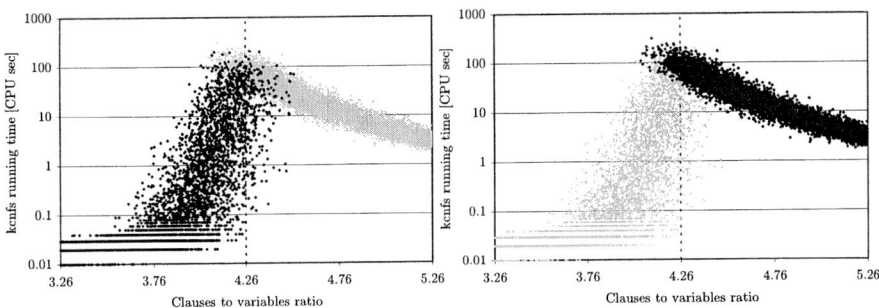

Fig. 2. Runtime of kcnfs on variable-ratio satisfiable (left) and unsatisfiable instances (right).

the empirical hardness of instances from this distribution. Second, having included nine features derived from this ratio among our 91 features we wanted to find out which particular function of these features would be most predictive of hardness. Third, we wanted to find out what *other* features, if any, were important in this setting.

We begin by examining the clauses-to-variables ratio, c/v, in more detail. Figure 2 shows kcnfs runtime (log scale) vs. c/v, for satisfiable and unsatisfiable instances. First observe that, as expected, there is a clear relationship between runtime and c/v. At the same time, c/v is not a very accurate predictor of hardness by itself: particularly near the phase transition point, there are several orders of magnitude of runtime variance across different instances. This is particularly the case for satisfiable instances around the phase transition; while the variation in runtime between unsatisfiable instances is consistently much smaller. (It may be noted that overall, our dataset is balanced in that it consists of 10 011 satisfiable and 9 989 unsatisfiable instances.)

To build models, we first considered linear, logistic and exponential models in our 91 features, evaluating the models on our validation set. Of these, linear were the worst, and logistic and exponential were similar, with logistic being slightly better. Next, we wanted to consider quadratic models under these same three transformations. However, a full quadratic model would have involved 4 277 features, and given that our training data involved 14 000 different problem instances, training the model would have entailed inverting a matrix of nearly sixty million values. In order to concentrate on the most important quadratic features, we first used our variable importance techniques to identify the best 30-feature subset of our 91 features. We computed the full quadratic expansion of these features, then performed forward selection – the only subset selection technique that worked with such a huge number of features – to keep only the most useful features. We ended up with 360 features, some of which were members of our original set of 91 features and the rest of which were products of these original features. Again, we evaluated linear, logistic and exponential models; all three model types were better with the expanded features, and again logistic models were best. Although the actual RMSE values obtained by three different kinds of models were very close to each other, linear models tended to have much higher prediction bias and many more outliers, especially among easy instances.

Figure 3 (left) shows the performance of our logistic models in this quadratic case for kcnfs (evaluated for the first time on our test set). Note that this is a very accurate model: perfect predictions would lie exactly on the line $y = x$, and the vast majority

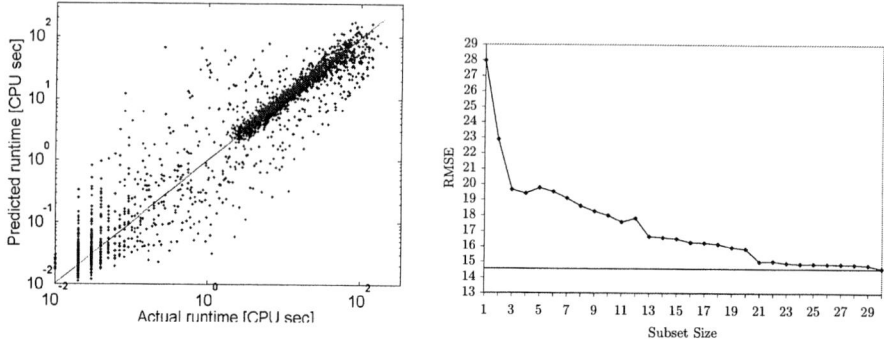

Fig. 3. Actual vs. predicted runtimes for kcnfs on variable-ratio instances (left) and RMSE as a function of model size (right).

Table 1. Variable importance in size 4 model for variable-ratio instances.

Variable	Cost of Omission
$\lceil c/v - 4.26 \rceil$ [9]	100
$\lvert c/v - 4.26 \rvert^2$ [10]	69
$(v/c)^2 \times$ SAPS_BestCoeffVar_Mean [7 × 90]	53
$\lvert (c/v) - 4.26 \rvert \times$ SAPS_BestCoeffVar_Mean [9 × 90]	33

of points lie on or very close to this line, with no significant bias in the residuals[5]. The plots for satz and oksolver look very similar; the RMSE values for the kcnfs, satz and oksolver models are 13.16, 24.09, and 81.32 seconds, respectively.

We now turn to the question of which variables were most important to our models. For the remainder of this paper we focus only on our models for kcnfs; our results with the other two algorithms are comparable. First, we discuss what it means for our techniques to identify a variable as "important." If a set of variables X is identified as the best subset of a given size, and this subset has a RMSE that is close to the RMSE of the complete model, this indicates that the variables in X are *sufficient* to approximate the performance of the full model – useful information, since it means that we can explain an algorithm's empirical hardness in terms of a small number of features. It must be stressed, however, that this does not amount to an argument that choosing the subset X is *necessary* for good performance in a subset of size k. Because variables are very often correlated, there may be other sets that would achieve similar performance; furthermore, since our subset selection techniques are heuristic, we are not even guaranteed that X is the globally best subset of its size. Thus, we can draw conclusions about the variables that are present in small, well-performing subsets, but we must be very careful in drawing conclusions about the variables that are absent.

Figure 3 (right) shows the validation set RMSE of our best subset of each size. Note that our best four-variable model achieves a root-mean-squared error of 19.42 seconds, while our full 360-feature model had an error of about 14.57 seconds. Table 1 lists the four variables in this model along with their normalized costs of omission. Note that the most important feature (by far) is the linearized version of c/v, which also occurs

---

[5] The banding on very small runtimes in this and other scatterplots is a discretization effect due to the low resolution of the operating system's process timer.

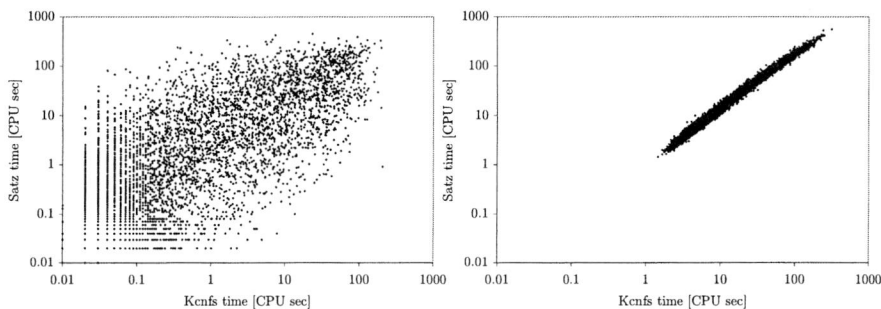

Fig. 4. Runtime correlation between kcnfs and satz for satisfiable (left) and unsatisfiable (right) variable-ratio instances.

(in different forms) in the other three features of this model. Hence, our techniques correctly identified the importance of the clauses-to-variables ratio, which satisfies our first goal. In terms of the second goal, these results indicate that the simple absolute distance of the ratio c/v from the critical value 4.26 appears to be the most informative variant of the nine related features we considered.

The third and fourth features in this model satisfy our third goal: we see that c/v variants are not the only useful features in this model. Interestingly, both of these remaining variables are based on a local search probing feature, the coefficient of variation over the number of clauses unsatisfied in local minima found by SAPS, a high-performance local search algorithm for SAT. It may appear somewhat surprising that such a local search probing feature can convey meaningful information about the runtime behavior of a DPLL algorithm. However, notice that deep local minima in the space searched by a local search algorithm correspond to assignments that leave few clauses unsatisfied. Intuitively, such assignments can cause substantial difficulties for DPLL search, where the respective partial assignments may correspond to large subtrees that do not contain any solutions. However, our current understanding of the impact of the features captured by local search probes on DPLL solver performance is rather limited, and further work is needed to fully explain this phenomenon.

While analyzing our variable-ratio models, we discovered that the weighted clause graph clustering coefficient (33) was one of the most important features. In fact, it was the most important feature if we excluded higher-order c/v and v/c features from models. It turns out, that the WCGCC is almost perfectly correlated with v/c, as illustrated in Figure 6 (left). This is particularly interesting as both the clustering coefficient and the connectivity of the constraint graph have been shown to be important statistics in a wide range of combinatorial problems, such as graph coloring and WDP. This correlation provides very nice new structural insight into the clause-to-variables ratio: it shows explicitly how constraint structure changes as the ratio varies. This discovery demonstrates how our empirical hardness methodology can help to gain new understanding of the nature of $\mathcal{NP}$-Hard problems.

The previously mentioned similar performance of our predictive models for kcnfs, satz and oksolver raises the question of whether the underlying reason simply lies in a strong correlation between the respective runtimes. Figure 4 shows the correlation of kcnfs runtime vs. satz runtime on satisfiable and unsatisfiable instances. Note that

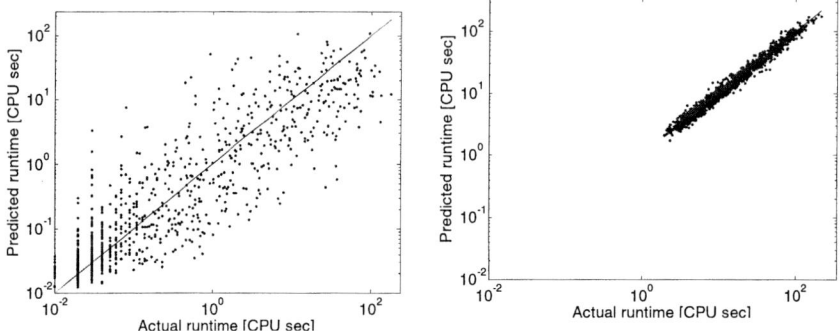

Fig. 5. Actual vs. predicted runtimes for kcnfs on satisfiable (left) and unsatisfiable (right) variable-ratio instances.

there are two qualitatively different patterns in the performance correlation for the two types of instances: runtimes on UNSAT instances are almost perfectly correlated, while runtimes on SAT instances are almost entirely uncorrelated. We conjecture that this is because proving unsatisfiability of an instance essentially requires exploring the entire search tree, which does not differ substantially between the algorithms, while finding a satisfiable assignment depends much more on each algorithm's different heuristics. We can conclude that the similar model accuracy between the algorithms is due jointly to the correlation between their runtimes on UNSAT instances and to the ability of our features to express each algorithm's runtime profile on both SAT and UNSAT instances.

Motivated by qualitative differences between satisfiable and unsatisfiable instances, we studied the subsets of all satisfiable and all unsatisfiable instances from our dataset separately. Analogously to what we did for the full dataset, we trained a separate predictive model for each of these two subsets. Interestingly, as seen in Figure 5, the predictions for unsatisfiable instances are much better than those for satisfiable instances (RMSE 5.3 vs. 13.4). Furthermore, the 'loss curves', which indicate the best RMSE achieved in dependence of model size (cf. Figure 3), are rather different between the two subsets: For the satisfiable instances, seven features are required to get within 10% of full model accuracy (in terms of RMSE), compared to only three for the unsatisfiable instances. While the seven features in the former model are all local search probe features (namely, in order of decreasing importance, features 68^2, 68×70, 90, 70, 70^2, 90×71 and 71), the three features in the latter are DPLL probe and constraint graph features (namely features 66^2, 66 and 26×27).

It must be noted that excluding all local search probe features (68-91 in Figure 1) in the process of model construction leads to models with only moderately worse performance (RMSE 16.6 instead of 13.4 for satisfiable, 5.5 instead of 5.3 for unsatisfiable, and 17.2 instead of 13.2 for all instances). Interestingly, in such models for satisfiable instances, features based on LP relaxation (features 55–60 in Figure 1) become quite important. Even when excluding all probing and LP features (features 55-91), reasonably accurate models can still be obtained (RMSE 14.7, 8.4, and 17.1 for satisfiable, unsatisfiable, and all instances, respectively); this indicates that combinations of the remaining purely structural features still provide a sufficient basis for accurate runtime predictions on the variable-ratio instance distribution.

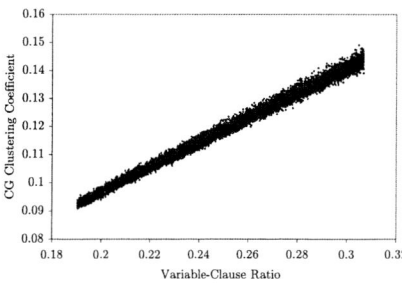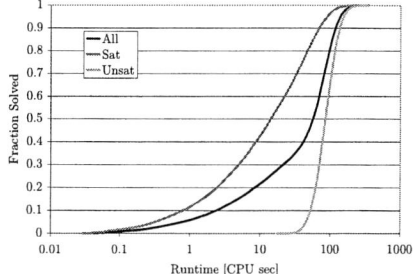

Fig. 6. Left: Correlation between CG weighted clustering coefficient and v/c. Right: Distribution of kcnfs runtimes across fixed-ratio instances.

Table 2. Variable importance in size 4 model for fixed-ratio instances.

Variable	Cost of Omission
SAPS_BestSolution_Mean^2 [68^2]	100
SAPS_BestSolution_Mean × Mean_DPLL_Depth [68 × 66]	74
GSAT_BestSolution_CoeffVar × Mean_DPLL_Depth [71 × 66]	21
VCG_CLAUSE_Mean × GSAT_FirstLMRatio_Mean [17 × 88]	9

5 Fixed-Ratio Random Instances

According to a widely held (yet somewhat simplistic) belief, uniform random 3-SAT is easy when far from the phase-transition point, and hard when close to it. In fact, while the first part of this statement is generally true, the second part is not. Figure 6 (right) shows cumulative distributions of the kcnfs's runtime per instance across our second dataset, comprising 20 000 fixed-ratio uniform random 3-SAT instances with 400 variables at $c/v = 4.26$, indicating substantial variation in runtime between instances in the phase transition region. (Similar observations have been made previously for local search algorithms [6].) Random-3-SAT at the phase transition point is one of the most widely used classes of benchmark instances for SAT; in the context of our study of empirical hardness models this instance distribution is particularly interesting since the most important features for predicting instance hardness for the variable-ratio distribution, namely variants of c/v, are kept constant in this case. Hence, it presents the challenge of identifying other features underlying the observed variation in hardness.

We built models in the same way as described in Section 4, except that all variants of c/v are constant and were hence omitted. Again, we achieved the best (validation set) results with logistic models on a (partial) quadratic expansion of the features; Fig. 7 (left) shows the performance of our logistic model for kcnfs on test data (RMSE = 35.23); similar results were obtained for oksolver and satz (RMSE = 220.43 and 60.71, respectively; note that particularly for oksolver, the higher RMSE values are partly due to overall higher runtimes). The shape of the scatter plots can be visually misleading: although it appears to be not tight, there are many more points that lie along the diagonal than outliers (this becomes evident when plotting the data on a heat map).

Figure 7 (right) shows the validation set RMSE of the best model we found at each subset size. Here, a 4-variable model obtains RMSE 39.02 on the validation set, which is within 10% on the RMSE of the full model. The variables in the model, along with their costs of omission, are given in Table 2. Note that this model is dominated by local

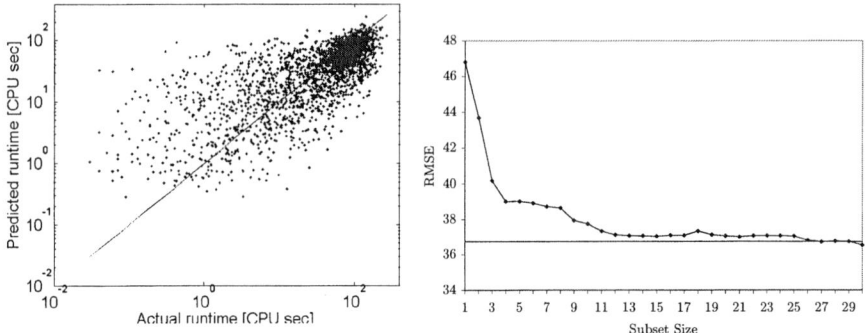

Fig. 7. Actual vs. predicted runtimes for kcnfs on fixed-ratio instances (left) and RMSE as a function of model size (right).

search and DPLL probing features, and the most important feature is the deepest local minimum reached on a SAPS trajectory (BestSolution), which intuitively captures the degree to which a given instance has "almost" satisfying assignments.

As for the variable-ratio set, we studied the subsets of all satisfiable and all unsatisfiable instances from our fixed-ratio data set separately and trained separate models for each of these subsets. Analogous to our results for the variable-ratio sets, we found that our model for the former subset gave significantly better predictions than that for the latter (RMSE 15.6 vs. 30.2). Surprisingly, in both cases, only a single feature is required to get within 10% of full model accuracy (in terms of RMSE on the training set): the product of the two SAPS probing features 69 and 82 in the case of satisfiable instances, and the square of DPLL probing feature 66 in the case of unsatisfiable instances.

We also constructed models that do not use local search features and/or probing features and obtained results that are qualitatively the same as those for the variable-ratio data set. Furthermore, we have observed results on the correlation of runtimes between solvers that are analogous to those reported in Section 4.

6 SATzilla and Other Applications of Hardness Models

While so far, we have argued that accurate empirical hardness models are useful because of the insight they give into problem structure, these models also have other applications [9]. For example, it is very easy to combine accurate hardness models with an existing instance generator to create a new generator that makes harder instances, through the use of rejection sampling techniques. Within the next few months, we intend to make available a new generator of harder random 3-SAT formulas. This generator will work by generating an instance from the phase transition region and then rejecting it in inverse proportion to the log time of the minimum of our three algorithms' predicted runtimes.

A second application of hardness models is the construction of algorithm portfolios. It is well known that for SAT different algorithms often perform very differently on the same instances (cf. left side of Figure 4). On distributions for which this sort of uncorrelation holds, selecting among algorithms on a per-instance basis offers the potential for substantial improvements over per-distribution algorithm selection. Empirical hardness models allow us to choose algorithms based on predicted runtimes. Interestingly, fairly inaccurate models often suffice to build good portfolios: if algorithms' performances are close to each other, picking the wrong one is not very costly, while if algorithms' behaviors differ significantly, the discrimination task is relatively easy.

We can offer concrete evidence for the utility of the latter application of hardness models: SATzilla, an algorithm portfolio that we built for the 2003 SAT competition. This portfolio consisted of 2clseq, eqSatz, HeerHugo, JeruSat, Limmat, oksolver, Relsat, Sato, Satz-rand and zChaff. The 2004 version dropped HeerHugo, but added Satzoo, kcnfs, and BerkMin.

To construct SATzilla we gathered from various public websites a library of about 5 000 SAT instances, for which we computed runtimes and the features described in Section 3.1. We built models using ridge regression. To yield better models, we dropped from our dataset all instances that were solved by all or none of the algorithms, or as a side-effect of feature computation. Upon execution, SATzilla begins by running a UBCSAT [17] implementation of WalkSAT to filter out easy satisfiable instances. Next, it runs the Hypre preprocessor [1] to clean up instances, allowing features to better reflect the problem's "combinatorial core." Third, SATzilla computes its features, terminating if any feature (*e.g.*, probing or LP relaxation) solves the problem. Some features can take inordinate amounts of time, particularly with very large inputs. To prevent feature computation from consuming all of our allotted time, certain features run only until a timeout is reached, at which point SATzilla gives up on them. Fourth, SATzilla evaluates a hardness model for each algorithm. If some of the features have timed out, it uses a different model which does not involve the missing feature. Finally, SATzilla executes the algorithm with the best predicted runtime.

SATzilla performed very well both in 2003 and 2004. In 2003, it was the only complete solver that did well both on random and on structured instances. It finished second and third in different categories, loosing only to new-generation solvers. In 2004, it was leading among complete solvers in the first round, but didn't advance to the final round due to complicated new competition rules.

7 Conclusion and Future Work

We have shown that empirical hardness models are a valuable tool for the study of the empirical behavior of complex algorithms such as SAT solvers. We were able to build accurate models of runtime on test distributions of fixed- and variable-ratio uniform random-3-SAT instances. On the variable-ratio dataset, our techniques were able to automatically "discover" the importance of the c/v ratio. Analysis in this case provided insight into the structural variations in uniform random 3-SAT formulas at the phase transition point that correlate with the dramatic variation in empirical hardness. Finally, we argued that our empirical hardness models offer practical benefit in less well-controlled domains by presenting SATzilla, our algorithm portfolio for SAT.

The results presented suggest a number of avenues for future research. One issue that clearly deserves further investigation is the degree to which our methodology can be used to predict and explain the performance of stochastic local search algorithms for SAT, which have recently been shown to outperform the best systematic solvers on various classes of random SAT instances. Another obvious and very relevant direction is the extension of our work to more structured types of SAT instances. Also, our results for the satisfiable and unsatisfiable subsets suggest that hierarchical models could give even better results. Such models may use some features to predict the satisfiability (or more generally, the type) of a given instance, and a subsidiary model for predicting the runtime. And finally, we believe that by studying in more detail *how* some of the features identified through the use of predictive statistical models cause instances to be easy or hard for certain types of algorithms, our understanding of how to solve SAT most efficiently will be further advanced.

References

1. Fahiem Bacchus and Jonathan Winter. Effective preprocessing with hyper-resolution and equality reduction. In *Proc. SAT-2003*, pages 341–355, 2003.
2. P. Cheeseman, B. Kanefsky, and W. M. Taylor. Where the Really Hard Problems Are. In *Proc. IJCAI-1991*, pages 331–337, 1991.
3. C. Gomes, B. Selman, N. Crato, and H. Kautz. Heavy-tailed phenomena in satisfiability and constraint satisfaction problems. *J. of Automated Reasoning*, 24(1):67–100, 2000.
4. H. H. Hoos and T. Stützle. *Stochastic Local Search – Foundations and Applications*. Morgan Kaufmann, 2004 (to appear).
5. H.H. Hoos. SAT-encodings, search space structure, and local search performance. In *Proc. IJCAI-99*, pages 296–302. Morgan Kaufmann, 1999.
6. H.H. Hoos and T. Stützle. Towards a characterisation of the behaviour of stochastic local search algorithms for sat. *Artificial Intelligence*, 112:213–232, 1999.
7. E. Horvitz, Y. Ruan, C. Gomes, H. Kautz, B. Selman, and M. Chickering. A Bayesian approach to tackling hard computational problems. In *Proc. UAI-2001*, pages 235–244, 2001.
8. Phokion Kolaitis. Constraint satisfaction, databases and logic. In *Proc. IJCAI-2003*, pages 1587–1595, 2003.
9. K. Leyton-Brown, E. Nudelman, G. Andrew, J. McFadden, and Y. Shoham. Boosting as a metaphor for algorithm design. In *Proc. CP-2003*, pages 899–903, 2003.
10. K. Leyton-Brown, E. Nudelman, G. Andrew, J. McFadden, and Y. Shoham. A portfolio approach to algorithm selection. In *Proc. IJCAI-2003*, pages 1542–1542, 2003.
11. K. Leyton-Brown, E. Nudelman, and Y. Shoham. Learning the empirical hardness of optimization problems: The case of combinatorial auctions. In *Proc. CP-2002*, pages 556–572, 2002.
12. L. Lobjois and M. Lemaître. Branch and bound algorithm selection by performance prediction. In *Proc. AAAI-1998*, pages 353–358, 1998.
13. R. Monasson, R. Zecchina, S. Kirkpatrick, B. Selman, and L. Troyansky. Determining computational complexity from characteristic 'phase transitions'. *Nature*, 400:133–137, 1999.
14. Y. Ruan, E. Horvitz, and H. Kautz. Restart policies with dependence among runs: A dynamic programming approach. In *Proc CP2-2002*, pages 573–586, 2002.
15. B. Selman, D. G. Mitchell, and H. J. Levesque. Generating hard satisfiability problems. *Artificial Intelligence*, 81(1-2):17–29, 1996.
16. R. Tibshirani. Regression shrinkage and selection via the lasso. *J. Royal Statist. Soc B*, 58(1):267–288, 1996.
17. D. Tompkins and H. Hoos. UBCSAT: An implementation and experimentation environment for SLS algorithms for SAT and MAX-SAT. In *Proc. SAT-2004*, pages 37–46, 2004.
18. R. Williams, C. Gomes, and B. Selman. Backdoors to typical case complexity. In *Proc. IJCAI-2003*, pages 1173–1178, 2003.

Symbolic Decision Procedures for QBF[*]

Guoqiang Pan and Moshe Y. Vardi

Dept. of Computer Science, Rice University
{gqpan,vardi}@cs.rice.edu

Abstract. Much recent work has gone into adapting techniques that were originally developed for SAT solving to QBF solving. In particular, QBF solvers are often based on SAT solvers. Most competitive QBF solvers are search-based. In this work we explore an alternative approach to QBF solving, based on symbolic quantifier elimination. We extend some recent symbolic approaches for SAT solving to symbolic QBF solving, using various decision-diagram formalisms such as OBDDs and ZDDs. In both approaches, QBF formulas are solved by eliminating all their quantifiers. Our first solver, QMRES, maintains a set of clauses represented by a ZDD and eliminates quantifiers via multi-resolution. Our second solver, QBDD, maintains a set of OBDDs, and eliminate quantifier by applying them to the underlying OBDDs. We compare our symbolic solvers to several competitive search-based solvers. We show that QBDD is not competitive, but QMRES compares favorably with search-based solvers on various benchmarks consisting of non-random formulas.

1 Introduction

Propositional satisfiability (known as *SAT*) testing is one of the central problem in computer science; it is a fundamental problem in automated reasoning [44] and a key problem in computational complexity [16]. More recently, SAT solving has also shown to be effective in providing a generic problem-solving framework, with applications to planning [37], scheduling [18], bounded model checking [6], and more. Starting with the seminal papers [21,22] in the early 1960s, the field has seen tremendous progress. Most SAT solvers today are based on the basic search-based approach of [21], rather than the resolution-based approach of [22]. Recently, highly tuned search-based SAT solvers [32,57] have been developed, combining intelligent branching, efficient Boolean constraint propagation, backjumping, and conflict-driven learning. These solvers have shown to be quite effective in solving industrial-scale problems [17].

Quantified propositional satisfiability (known as *QBF*) captures problems of higher complexity (PSPACE vs NP), including temporal reasoning [51], planning [49], and modal satisfiability [46]. Much recent work has gone into adapting techniques that were originally developed for SAT solving to QBF solving, cf. [9,41]. In particular, QBF solvers are often based on SAT solvers; for example, QuBE [31] is based on SIM [30], while Quaffle [58] is based on ZChaff [57]. Essentially all competitive QBF solvers are search-based [40]. In spite of the growing sophistication of QBF solvers, it is fair to say that they have shown nowhere near the effectiveness of SAT solvers [40].

---
[*] Supported in part by NSF grants CCR-9988322, CCR-0124077, CCR-0311326, IIS-9908435, IIS-9978135, EIA-0086264, ANI-0216467, and by BSF grant 9800096.

Our goal in this paper is to explore an alternative approach to QBF solving, based on symbolic quantifier elimination. The underlying motivation is the success of symbolic techniques based on *binary decision diagrams* (BDDs) [8] and their variants in various automated-reasoning applications, such as model checking [10], planning [14], and modal satisfiability testing [45, 46]. Early attempts to apply symbolic techniques to SAT solving simply used the capacity of BDDs to represent the set of all satisfying assignments and were not too effective [56]. More recent efforts focused on SAT solving using quantifier elimination, which, in essence, goes back to the original approach of [22], since resolution as used there can be viewed as a variable-elimination technique, ala Fourier-Motzkin. (Resolution is typically thought of as a constraint-propagation technique [24], but since a variable can be eliminated once all resolutions on it have been performed [22], it can also be thought as a quantifier-elimination technique.) In [13] it is shown how *zero-suppressed decision diagrams* (ZDDs) [42] can offer a compact representation for sets of clauses and can support symbolic resolution (called there *multiresolution*). In [47, 50] it is shown how *ordered Boolean decision diagrams* (OBDDs) can support symbolic quantifier elimination. In both [13] and [47] the symbolic approach is compared to search-based approaches, showing that, search-based techniques seem to be generally superior, but the symbolic techniques are superior for certain classes of formulas[1].

While the case for symbolic techniques in SAT solving cannot be said to be too strong, they are intriguing enough to justify investigating their applicability to QBF. On one hand, extending search-based technique to QBF has not, as we noted, been too successful. On the other hand, symbolic quantifier elimination handles universal quantifiers just as easily (and sometimes more easily) as it handles existential quantifiers, so extending symbolic techniques to QBF is quite natural. (Symbolic techniques have already been used to address conformant-planning problems [14], which can be expressed as QBF instances of low alternation depth.) In this work we investigate the two symbolic techniques to QBF. We extend the ZDD-based multi-resolution approach of [13] and the OBDD-based approach of symbolic quantifier elimination of [47]. We call the two approaches *QMRES* and *QBDD*. We compare these two approaches with three leading search-based QBF solvers: Quaffle and QuBE, which were mentioned earlier, and Semprop [49]. Unlike other comparative works [40], we decided to split our benchmark suite according to the provenance of the benchmarks, as our goal is to identify classes of problems for which the symbolic approaches are suited. We use a benchmark suite generated by Rintanen [49], which consists of a variety of constructed formulas (we omitted the random formulas), a second generated by Ayari [3], which consists of scalable formulas converted from circuit descriptions and protocol descriptions, and those generated by Pan [46], which consist of QBF formulas translated from modal logic formulas. Our experiments reveal that QMRES is significantly superior to QBDD. In fact, QBDD does not seem to be a competitive solver. (Though we return to this point at our concluding discussion.) In contrast, QMRES is quite competitive. While it is comparable to search-based method on Rintanen's formulas, QMRES outperforms them on Ayari's and Pan's formulas. At the same time, QMRES performs abysmally on random formulas. This suggests that symbolic techniques ought to be considered as comple-

---

[1] See www.cs.rice.edu/~vardi/papers/

mentary to search-based techniques and should belong in the standard tool kit of QBF solver implementors.

We start this paper with a description of current symbolic algorithms and the semantics of QBF in Section 2. We then describe our two symbolic QBF decision procedures in Section 3. We compare these solvers to search-based solvers in Section 4. We conclude with a discussion in Section 5.

2 Background

2.1 Symbolic Approaches to SAT

A *binary decision diagram* (BDD) is a rooted directed acyclic graph that has only two terminal nodes labeled **0** and **1**. Every non-terminal node is labeled with a Boolean variable and has two outgoing edges labeled 0 and 1. An *ordered* binary decision diagram (OBDD) is a BDD with the constraint that the input variables are ordered and every path in the OBDD visits the variables in ascending order. We assume that all OBDDs are *reduced*, which means that every node represents a distinct logic function. OBDDs constitute an efficient way to represent and manipulate Boolean functions [8], in particular, for a given variable order, OBDDs offer a canonical representation. Checking whether an OBDD is satisfiable is also easy; it requires checking that it differs from the predefined constant **0** (the empty OBDD). The *support set* of an OBDD is the set of variables labeling its internal nodes.

In [56, 15], OBDDs are used to construct a compact representation of the set of all satisfying truth assignments of CNF formulas. The input formula φ is a conjunction $c_1 \wedge \ldots \wedge c_m$ of clauses. The algorithm constructs an OBDD A_i for each clause c_i. (Since a clause excludes only one assignment to its variables, A_i is of linear size.) An OBDD for the set of satisfying truth assignments is then constructed incrementally; B_1 is A_1, while B_{i+1} is the result of APPLY$(B_i, A_i, \wedge)$, where APPLY$(A, B, \circ)$ is the result of applying a Boolean operator $\circ$ to two OBDDs A and B. Finally, the resulting OBDD B_m represents all satisfying assignments of the input formula.

We can apply existential quantification to an OBDD B:

$$(\exists x)B = \text{APPLY}(B|_{x \leftarrow 1}, B|_{x \leftarrow 0}, \vee),$$

where $B|_{x \leftarrow c}$ restricts B to truth assignments that assign the value c to the variable x. Note that quantifying x existentially eliminates it from the support set of B. The satisfiability problem is to determine whether a given formula $c_1 \wedge \ldots \wedge c_m$ is satisfiable. In other words, the problem is to determine whether the existential formula $(\exists x_1) \ldots (\exists x_n)(c_1 \wedge \ldots \wedge c_m)$ is true. Since checking whether the final OBDD B_m is equal to **0** can be done in constant time, it makes little sense, however, to apply existential quantification to B_m. Suppose that a variable x_j does not occur in the clauses $c_{i+1}, \ldots, c_m$. Then the existential formula can be rewritten as

$$(\exists x_1) \ldots (\exists x_{j-1})(\exists x_{j+1}) \ldots (\exists x_n)((\exists x_j)(c_1 \wedge \ldots \wedge c_i) \wedge (c_{i+1} \wedge \ldots \wedge c_m)).$$

This means that after constructing the OBDD B_i, we can existentially quantify x_j before conjuncting B_i with $A_{i+1}, \ldots, A_m$.

This motivates the following change in the earlier OBDD-based satisfying-solving algorithm [50]: after constructing the OBDD B_i, quantify existentially variables that do not occur in the clauses $c_{i+1}, \ldots, c_m$. In this case we say that the quantifier $\exists x$ has been *eliminated*. The computational advantage of quantifier elimination stems from the fact that reducing the size of the support set of an OBDD typically (though not necessarily) results in a reduction of its size; that is, the size of $(\exists x)B$ is typically smaller than that of B. In a nutshell, this method, which we describe as *symbolic quantifier elimination*, eliminates all quantifiers until we are left with the constant OBDD 1 or 0. Symbolic quantifier elimination was first applied to SAT solving in [33] (under the name of *hiding functions*) and tried on random 3-SAT instances. The work in [50, 47] studied this method further, and considered various optimizations[2].

So far we processed the clauses of the input formula in a linear fashion. Since the main point of quantifier elimination is to eliminate variables as early as possible, reordering the clauses may enable us to do more aggressive quantification. That is, instead of processing the clauses in the order $c_1, \ldots, c_m$, we can apply a permutation π and process the clauses in the order $c_{\pi(1)}, \ldots, c_{\pi(m)}$. The permutation π should be chosen so as to minimize the number of variables in the support sets of the intermediate OBDDs. This observation was first made in the context of symbolic model checking, cf. [11, 29, 36, 7]. Unfortunately, finding an optimal permutation π is by itself a difficult optimization problem, motivating heuristic approaches.

A particular heuristic that was proposed in the context of symbolic model checking in [48] is that of *clustering*. In this approach, the clauses are not processed one at a time, but several clauses are first partitioned into several clusters. For each cluster C we first apply conjunction to all the OBDDs of the clauses in the C to obtain an OBDD B_C. The clusters are then combined, together with quantifier elimination, as described earlier. Heuristics are required both for clustering the clauses and ordering the clusters. A particular clustering heuristic was proposed in [25] in the context of constraint satisfaction. Consider some order of the variables. Let the *rank* (from 1 to n) of a variable x be $rank(x)$, let the rank $rank(\ell)$ of a literal ℓ be the rank of its underlying variable, and let the rank $rank(c)$ of a clause c be the minimum rank of its literals. The clusters are the equivalence classes of the relation $\sim$ defined by: $c \sim c'$ iff $rank(c) = rank(c')$. The rank of a cluster is the rank of its clauses. The clusters are then processed in order of increasing rank. This approach is referred to as *bucket elimination* (BE) [23] (each cluster is thought as a "bucket") or as *adaptive consistency* [24]. An equivalent way of viewing this is to say that variable are eliminated in order of increasing rank, where eliminating a variable x requires conjoining of all OBDDs with x in their support set and then quantifying this variable existentially.

A good variable order for bucket elimination is an order that would minimize the size of the support set of intermediate OBDDs. The goal is to approach the *induced width*, which is the maximal support set under the optimal elimination order. Induced width is known to be equal to the *treewidth* [25, 28]. The treewidth of the formula is defined with respect to its *Gaifman graph*, whose vertices are the set of variables in the

---

[2] Note that symbolic quantifier elimination provides *pure* satisfiability solving; the algorithm returns 0 or 1. To find a satisfying truth assignment when the formula is satisfiable, the technique of self-reducibility can be used, cf. [4].

formula and its edges connect variables that co-occur in a clause. (We use vertices and variables interchangeably.) Treewidth measures how close the graph is to being a tree; the treewidth of a tree is 1 [27]. BE, with respect to an optimal order, yields the optimal reduction of support set size [19] and is guaranteed to have polynomial running time for input instances of logarithmic treewidth, since this guarantees a polynomial upper bound on OBDD size.

Finding an optimal variable order for BE is known to be NP-hard, since computing the treewidth of a graph is NP-hard [2], so one has to resort to various heuristics, cf. [38]. An order that is often used in constraint satisfaction [24] and works quite well in the context of symbolic satisfiability solving [47] is the "maximum cardinality search" (MCS) order of [55], which is based on the graph-theoretic structure of the formula, i.e., the Gaifman graph. MCS ranks the vertices from n to 1 in the following way: as the next vertex to number, select the vertex adjacent to the largest number of previously numbered vertices (ties can be broken in various ways).

If constraints are represented by clauses rather than by OBDDs, then variables can be eliminated via resolution. Given a set C of clauses and a variable x, the variable can be eliminated by adding to C all resolvents on x and then eliminating all clauses where x occurs. Formally $(\exists x)C$ is logically equivalent to $Resolve_x(C)$, where $Resolve_x(C)$ is the set of clauses obtained from C by adding all resolvents on x and then deleting all clauses containing x. In fact, completeness of resolution is shown by eliminating all variables one by one, each time replacing a set C of clauses by $Resolve_x(C)$ [22]. (Eliminating variables in such a fashion is reminiscent of Fourier-Motzkin variable elimination for systems of linear inequalities and of Gaussian variable elimination for systems of linear equalities.) This approach is also referred to as *directional resolution* [26] (see report there on experimental comparison of directional resolution to search-based techniques).

Rather than represent clauses explicitly as in [22,26], multi-resolution [13] takes a symbolic approach to directional resolution, where clause sets are represented by ZDDs [42]. Each propositional literal ℓ is represented by a ZDD variable v_ℓ, and clause sets are represented as follows:

- The empty clause ϵ is represented by the terminal node 1.
- The empty set $\emptyset$ is represented by the terminal node 0.
- Given a set C of clauses and a literal ℓ whose ZDD variable v_ℓ is lowest in a given variable order, we can split C into two subsets: $C_\ell = \{c \mid c \in C, \ell \in c\}$ and $C' = C - C_\ell$. Given ZDDs representing $C'' = \{c \mid c \vee \ell \in C_\ell\}$ and C', a ZDD representing C would be rooted at v_ℓ and have ZDDs for C'' and C' as its left and right children.

This representation is the dual of using ZDDs to represent Irredundant Sum of Products (ISOPs) of Boolean functions [42].

We use two set operations on sets of clauses: (1) $\times$ is the crossproduct operator, where for two clause sets C and D, $C \times D = \{c \mid \exists c' \in C, \exists c'' \in D, c = c' \cup c''\}$, and (2) $+$ is subsumption-free union, so if both C and D are subsumption free, and $c \in C + D$, then there is no $c' \subset c$, where $c' \in C + D$. Multi-resolution can be easily implemented using $\times$ on cofactors: given a ZDD f, f_{x+} and f_{x-} is used to represent the ZDDs corresponding to the positive cofactor on the ZDD variable corresponding to the literal $x/\neg x$, so $f_{x^+} = \{a \mid a \vee x \in f\}$ and $f_{x^-} = \{a \mid a \vee \neg x \in f\}$. Now $f_{x^+} \times f_{x^-}$ (after removing tautologies) represents the set of all resolvents of f on x, which has to be combined with $f_{x'}$, which is the ZDD for the clauses not containing x.

2.2 QBF

Quantified Boolean Formulas (QBF) extend propositional logic by adding propositional quantifiers to propositions. In QBF terms, propositional satisfiability is the special case where all variables are quantified existentially. The addition of alternating quantifiers pushes the complexity of the problem from NP-complete for propositional satisfiability to PSPACE-complete for QBF [53].

We consider QBF formulas in prenex clausal normal form (CNF):

$$\varphi = Q_1 X_1 Q_2 X_2 \ldots Q_n X_n \varphi',$$

where each Q_j is $\forall$ or $\exists$, the X_is are disjoint sets of propositional variables, and φ' is a propositional formula in CNF. We refer to $Q_1 X_1 \ldots Q_n X_n$ as the *prefix* of φ and to φ' as the *matrix* of φ. We define A_φ as the set of universally quantified variables and, correspondingly, define E_φ as the set of existentially quantified variables. The *alternation depth* $alt(x)$ of a variable x is the index i where $x \in X_i$. All QBF formulas can be converted to prenex normal form with only a linear blow-up. We assume without loss of generality that all variables are quantified.

The semantics for QBF can be defined in terms of the semantics of propositional logic. If φ is quantifier free, then satisfaction ($\models$) is defined as for propositional logic. Otherwise, given an assignment α, we have that $\alpha \models \exists x \varphi$ iff $\alpha[x \mapsto \top] \models \varphi$ or $\alpha[x \mapsto \bot] \models \varphi$, and $\alpha \models \forall x \varphi$ iff $\alpha[x \mapsto \top] \models \varphi$ and $\alpha[x \mapsto \bot] \models \varphi$. If every variable in φ is quantified, then either for all assignments α, we have $\alpha \models \varphi$, or for all assignments α, we have $\alpha \not\models \varphi$. Thus, we can write $\models \varphi$ or $\not\models \varphi$; that is, satisfiability and validity coincide.

Most SAT solvers are search-based, following the ideas of [21]. QBF solvers build upon search techniques developed for SAT, forcing backtracking on universal variables and branching on variables according to alternation order [12]. A decision procedure based on an extension of resolution to QBF (called *Q-resolution*) is described in [9], but, to the best of our knowledge has not been implemented. We comment later on the difference between Q-resolution and our multi-resolution approach to QBF.

3 Symbolic Quantifier Elimination for QBF

The basic idea of our approach is to extend symbolic quantifier elimination from SAT to QBF. Given a QBF formula $\varphi = Q_1 X_1 Q_2 X_2 \ldots Q_n X_n \varphi'$, we eliminate the quantifiers from *inside out*, that is, in order of decreasing alternating depth, starting with the variables in X_n. At each stage, we maintain a set of constraints, represented symbolically either as a ZDD (expressing a set of clauses) or as a set of OBDDs. To eliminate an existential variable from a set of clauses we perform multi-resolution, while universal variables can be eliminated by simply deleting them [9]. To eliminate an existential variable x from a set of OBDDs we conjoin the OBDDs in whose support set x occurs and then quantify it existentially, while to eliminate a universal variable we quantify it universally. (We can apply universal quantification to an OBDD B: $(\forall x)B = \text{APPLY}(B|_{x \leftarrow 1}, B|_{x \leftarrow 0}, \wedge)$.) The variables within a quantifier block $Q_i X_i$ are unordered and can be eliminated in any order. Here we apply the heuristics described in Section 2.1.

We note that our resolution approach to QBF is different than that of [9]. We require that quantifiers be eliminated from the inside out; thus, resolution can be performed only on the existential variables in the innermost quantifier block. In contrast, Q-resolution [9] allows resolution on non-innermost existential variables. The difference stems from the fact that the focus in Q-resolution is on generating resolvents, while the focus here is on quantifier elimination. For Q-resolution to be complete, *all* resolvents need to be kept. In contrast, once we have performed multi-resolution on a variable x, all clauses containing it are deleted.

First, we describe QMRES, a multi-resolution QBF solver. We provide pseudocode in Algorithm 1.

Algorithm 1 Multi-resolution for QBF.

Q-Multi-Res(φ, S, v)
Require: S is the set of clauses forming matrix of φ, and $v = \langle v_1 \ldots v_n \rangle$ is an order of variables where $alt(v_i) \geq alt(v_{i+1})$
Ensure: returns **true** if φ is valid and **false** otherwise
  for i=1..n **do**
    if v_i is existential **then**
      $S \Leftarrow (S_{v_i^+} \times S_{v_i^-}) + S_{v_i'}$
    else
      $S \Leftarrow S_{v_i^+} + S_{v_i^-} + S_{v_i'}$
    end if
    $S \Leftarrow Unitprop(S)$ {Apply unit propagation}
  end for
  return $S \neq \{\phi\}$

Note that in addition to multi-resolution the algorithm applies a naive form of unit propagation (weaker then what is described in [58]). When the clause set is represented using ZDDs, clauses with only a single literal can be easily enumerated without traversing the whole ZDD, since such clauses are represented by a path of length 2 in the ZDD. Existential unit literals can then be resolved on without regard to their alternation depth. (If a universal literal becomes unit, the formula is false.) The overhead of such a check are negligible so we applied it in all cases.

We now describe QBDD, an OBDD-based QBF solver. We provide pseudocode in Algorithm 2[3]:

In Section 2.1 we described the MCS heuristics for variable ordering. MCS is only one of many variable-ordering heuristics that are used to approximate treewidth [38]. We explored several other variable-ordering heuristics in [47]. MCS came out as the

---

[3] We used $choose\_bucket(R_i) = i + 1$, which avoided the overhead of traversing the BDD R_i and finding the lowest ordered variable according to v.

Algorithm 2 Bucket Elimination for QBF.

QBDD(φ, S, v)
Require: S, v as in Q-Multi-Res
Ensure: returns true if φ is valid and false otherwise
  Build BDD clusters $S_1 \ldots S_n$, where a clause $c \in S$ is in cluster S_i if v_i is the lowest ordered variable in c
  for i=1..n **do**
    if v_i is existential **then**
      $R_i = \exists x_i \bigwedge_{c \in S_i} c$
    else
      $R_i = \forall x_i \bigwedge_{c \in S_i} c$
    end if
    if $R_i = 0$ **then**
      return false
    end if
    $j = choose\_bucket(R_i)$
    $S_j = S_j \cup \{R_i\}$
  end for
  return true
---

overall best performers across a wide variety of benchmarks. It is interesting to note that MCS is not necessarily the best performer in terms of induced width. Other heuristics, such as *min-fill* [24] yield better induced width. One has to remember, however, that variable order impacts not only the induced width but also decision-diagram size. In turns out that a variable that reduce the size of the support set of decision diagram does not necessarily reduces its size. While these effects may be less marked for ZDD-based clause representation, we chose to use MCS for both of our algorithms.

As described earlier, however, MCS is computed from the matrix of the QBF formula, ignoring completely the quantifier prefix. Since quantifier elimination proceed from the inside out, we need to adapt MCS to take into account alternation depth. We first perform MCS on the matrix only, ignoring alternation. Then, variable order for quantifier elimination is generated, where at each step we choose a variable from those with the highest alternation depth that has the lowest MCS rank.

4 Experimental Results

We compare the symbolic approaches with three search-based solvers: QuBE [31], Quaffle [58], and Semprop [41]. These solvers use sophisticted heuristics for branch-variable selection and lemma/conflict caching. For both symbolic solvers, we used CUDD [52] as the underlying decision diagram engine, and for QMRES, we used the multi-resolution engine implemented by Chatalic and Simon [13].

We use three classes of benchmarks from the QBFLIB benchmark suites[43], those generated by Rintanen [49], from which we omitted the random formulas but kept a variety of hand constructed formulas, those generated by Ayari [3], which consist of scalable formulas converted from circuit descriptions and protocol descriptions, and those generated by Pan [46], which consist of formulas translated from modal logic.

4.1 Symbolic vs. Search

A first observation, consistent with propositional logic, is that symbolic approaches typically performs very badly on random problems. For example, symbolic approaches are orders of magnitude slower for uniform propositional 3-CNF problems [47]. (In our QBF experiments, the symbolic approaches completed none of the uniform random formulas in the Rintanen's benchmarks within the 1000s timeout limit.) In the following, we compare the symbolic and search approaches only on constructed formulas, ignoring the results for random problems. (In general, QBF solvers typically behave quite differently on random vs. non-random formulas, which is why comparative studies separate the two cases [40].)

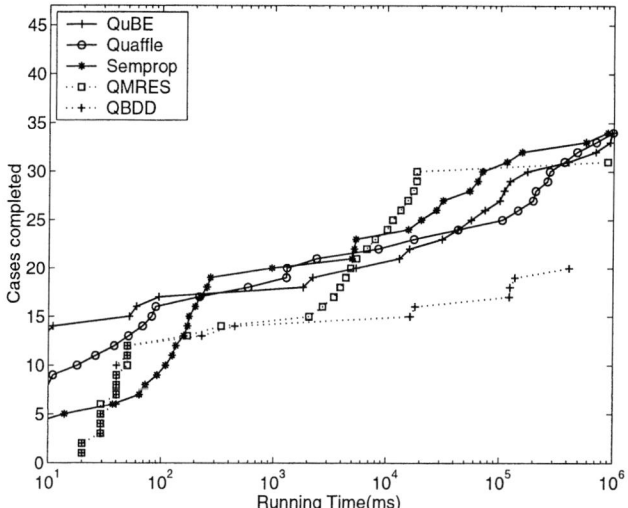

Fig. 1. Rintanen's Benchmarks (Non-random).

First we evaluated our solvers on Rintanen's and Ayari's benchmark suites [49, 3]. Rintanen's benchmark suite is one of the first benchmark suite for QBF, including formulas constructed from planning problems, hand-constructed formulas, and randomly generated formulas covering a wide range of difficulty and alternation depth. Ayari's benchmark suite is one of the first to encode bounded-model-construction problems in QBF through M2L-STR, a monadic second-order logic on finite words [3], with typically quite low alternation depth.

The results for Rintanen's benchmarks are plotted in Figure 1 and the results for Ayari's Benchmarks are plotted in Figure 2. We used the plotting style presented in [30, 54], which plotted the number of completed cases against the time taken to run each case. A solver with a higher curve dominates one with a lower curve since it solved more cases in the same amount of time.

Our first observation is that QMRES clearly dominates QBDD. This is somewhat surprising, since similar experiments we performed on propositional formulas showed that with the same variable order, the OBDD-based approach dominates the ZDD-based

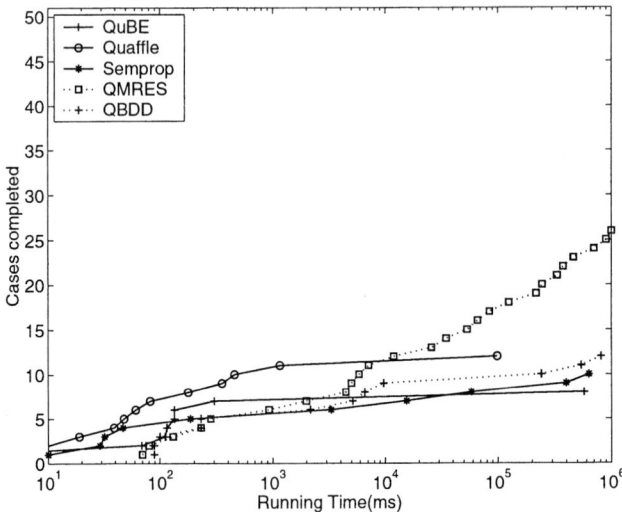

Fig. 2. Ayari's Benchmarks.

in most cases, falling behind only for highly under-constrained problems, where the compression of ZDD-based clause set representation is greater. In contrast, ZDD-based clause sets seems to be getting better compression across the range of the QBF problems, resulting in node usage that are orders of magnitude smaller then that of QBDD.

Comparing symbolic solvers against search-based solvers, the picture is somewhat mixed. For Rintanen's benchmarks, there is no clear winner, but for Ayari's benchmarks, QMRES showed a clear edge. Some of the formulas in the Rintanen's benchmarks, for example, blocks problems, only have a low alternation depth and small number of universal variables, allowing search to perform effectively. In essence, such problems are closer to SAT, where search-based approach typically outperform symbolic solvers [47]. On the other hand, Ayari's problems are derived from circuit and protocol problems, whose symmetry favors the compression of the symbolic approach. It is interesting to note that the advantage of QMRES shows only when more difficult problems are considered. On easier problems search-based methods are faster.

Next, we come to formulas obtained by translation to QBF from modal formulas in the logic $\mathcal{K}$ [46]. The original modal formulas are scalable classes constructed by Heuerding and Schwendimann [35], where modal properties are nested to construct successively harder formulas. The resulting QBF formulas are grouped in the same 18 classes as the modal formulas, half satisfiable and half unsatisfiable, and each class contains 21 cases of which alternation depth scales linearly. Using translation from modal logic allowed construction of high alternation-depth problems that are both non-trivial and tractable. The formulas span a large range of difficulty and sizes, from hundreds to tens of thousands of variables. All the original modal formulas can be solved using modal solvers. We plotted time vs. cases solved in Figure 3. We see that QMRES clearly dominates the search-based methods. (This is consistent with the results described in [46], where symbolic modal solvers dominate search-based solvers.)

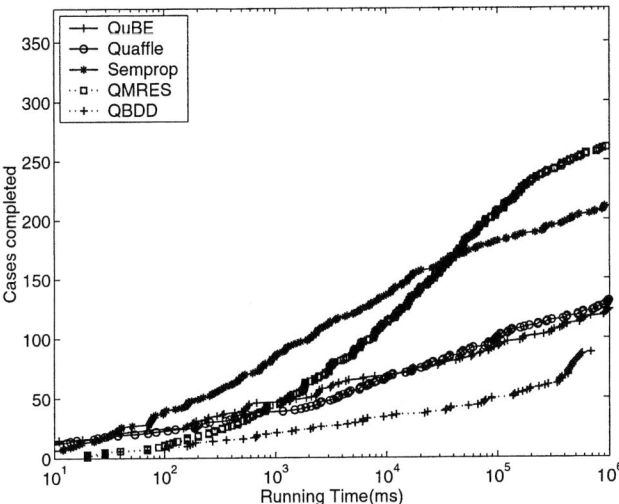

Fig. 3. Modal Logic Benchmarks.

A fundamental question is why a symbolic method outperforms search-based method for QBF, while the situation is reversed for SAT [47]. A possible explanation is that propositional satisfiability is in essence a search for a satisfying assignment. SAT solvers excel in quickly eliminating unsuccessful search branches, combining backjumping and conflict-based learning. In contrast, search-based QBF solvers have to deal with backtracking forced by the universal quantifers, which seems to nullify many of the advanced search heuristics of SAT solvers. Since QBF solving requires dealing with the whole space of possible assignments, symbolic methods benefit from the compression provided by decision diagrams.

4.2 QMRES vs QBDD

To better understand the disappointing performance of the BDD-based approach, we take a deeper look at Pan's formulas, which are generated from the modal formulas of [35] through two different translation steps, first from ML to non-CNF QBF, then from non-CNF QBF to QBF. In addition to running QMRES and QBDD on the final QBF formulas, we run KBDD, an OBDD-based modal solver [46], on the original modal formulas. We also run an ad-hoc OBDD-based solver on the intermediate non-CNF QBF formulas, where we translate propositional formulas to OBDDs without going through the CNF step and then apply quantifier elimination.

In Figure 4, we plotted the performance of the corresponding solvers. We see that the native solver KBDD performs best, with QMRES and QBDD-non-CNF very close to each other and not far behind the native solver. There is a much larger gap between these two and the performance of QBDD, resulting from the CNF translation. The gap between the performance of KBDD and QBDD-non-CNF can be attributed to the conversion of conjunction in modal formulas to universal quantification in the QBF translation. The gap between the performance of QMRES and QBDD-non-CNF to that of QBDD can be attributed to the the cost incurred by the OBDD-based solver in handling

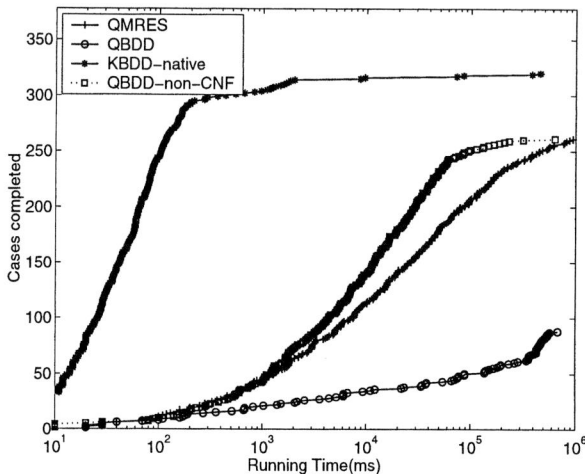

Fig. 4. Study of overhead on ML benchmarks.

the additional variables generated in the conversion to CNF and the difficulty in implementing certain optimizations under the BDD representation, for example, unit propagation. suggests that the OBDD-based approach might be more effective for problems whose natural encoding is not in CNF.

5 Discussion

QBF, as a straightforward extension of propositional logic, shares much with SAT in the implementation of decision procedures. Nevertheless, alternation in QBF causes significant overhead to search-based solvers, requiring them to cover the whole search space. This greatly reduces the efficiency of the typical heuristics used for search-based solvers, whose optimization is usually focused toward minimizing the number of backtracks. For symbolic techniques, on the other hand, the addition of alternating quantifiers does not introduce analogous difficulties. Our results show that for difficult non-random QBF problems, symbolic quantifier elimination approaches are very competitive and belong in the standard tool kit of QBF solver implementors.

Recently, another quantifier elimination based solver (Quantor) was developed by Biere [5]. In addition to eliminating existential variables by resolution, universal variables can be eliminated using skolemization and expansion. His approach used a explicit representation of clauses instead of the symbolic representation used here. 38 previously unsolved constructed problems in the second QBF solver evaluation [39] have been solved using QMRES and Quantor. This bolsters support in arguing that quantifier elimination is an important addition to the pool of techniques of solver implementors.

Much further work is needed in this area, both to investigate various optimization techniques for symbolic solvers (e.g., variable order, non-CNF approaches, and representation beyond decision diagrams, for example, BEDs [1] or DNNFs [20]) as well as to investigate the trade-off between symbolic and search-based techniques. In particular, it would be interesting to investigate hybrid approaches, extending some work done in the context of model checking [34].

Acknowledgement

We would like to thank Laurent Simon for making available to us his ZRes package, which served as the basis for QMRES.

References

1. H. R. Anderson and H. Hulgaard. Boolean expression diagrams. *Informaton and Computation*, 179(2):194–212, 2002.
2. S. Arnborg, D.G. Corneil, and A. Proskurowski. Complexity of finding embeddings in a k-tree. *SIAM J. Alg. Disc. Math*, 8:277–284, 1987.
3. A. Ayari and D. Basin. Bounded model construction for monadic second-order logics. In *Proceedings of CAV'00*, 2000.
4. J. Balcazar. Self-reducibility. *Journal of Computer and System Sciences*, 41(3):367–388, 1990.
5. A. Biere. Resolve and expand. In *SAT 2004*, 2004.
6. A. Biere, Cimatti A, E.M. Clarke, M. Fujita, and Y. Zhu. Symbolic model checking using SAT procedures instead of BDD. In *Proc. 36th Conf. on Design Automation*, pages 317–320, 1999.
7. M. Block, C. Gröpl, H. Preuß, H. L. Proömel, and A. Srivastav. Efficient ordering of state variables and transition relation partitions in symbolic model checking. Technical report, Institute of Informatics, Humboldt University of Berlin, 1997.
8. R.E. Bryant. Graph-based algorithms for Boolean function manipulation. *IEEE Trans. on Comp.*, Vol. C-35(8):677–691, August 1986.
9. H.K. Buning, M. Karpinski, and A. Flogel. Resolution for quantified Boolean formulas. *Inf. and Comp.*, 117(1):12–18, 1995.
10. J. Burch, E. Clarke, K. McMillan, D. Dill, and L. Hwang. Symbolic model checking: 10^{20} states and beyond. *Infomation and Computation*, 98(2):142–170, 1992.
11. J.R. Burch, E.M. Clarke, and D.E. Long. Symbolic model checking with partitioned transition relations. In *Int. Conf. on Very Large Scale Integration*, 1991.
12. M. Cadoli, M. Schaerf, A. Giovanardi, and M. Giovanardi. An algorithm to evaluate quantified Boolean formulae and its experimental evaluation. *Journal of Automated Reasoning*, 28(2):101–142, 2002.
13. P. Chatalic and L. Simon. Multi-Resolution on compressed sets of clauses. In *Twelfth International Conference on Tools with Artificial Intelligence (ICTAI'00)*, pages 2–10, 2000.
14. A. Cimatti and M. Roveri. Conformant planning via symbolic model checking. *J. of AI Research*, 13:305–338, 2000.
15. C. Coarfa, D. D. Demopoulos, A. San Miguel Aguirre, D. Subramanian, and M.Y. Vardi. Random 3-SAT: The plot thickens. *Constraints*, pages 243–261, 2003.
16. S. A. Cook. The complexity of theorem proving procedures. In *Proc. 3rd ACM Symp. on Theory of Computing*, pages 151–158, 1971.
17. F. Copty, L. Fix, R. Fraer, E. Giunchiglia, G. Kamhi, A. Tacchella, and M.Y. Vardi. Benefits of bounded model checking at an industrial setting. In *Computer Aided Verification, Proc. 13th International Conference*, volume 2102 of *Lecture Notes in Computer Science*, pages 436–453. Springer-Verlag, 2001.
18. J.M. Crawford and A.B. Baker. Experimental results on the application of satisfiability algorithms to scheduling problems. In *AAAI*, volume 2, pages 1092–1097, 1994.
19. V. Dalmau, P.G. Kolaitis, and M.Y. Vardi. Constraint satisfaction, bounded treewidth, and finite-variable logics. In *CP'02*, pages 310–326, 2002.
20. A. Darwiche. Decomposable negation normal form. *J. ACM*, 48(4):608–647, 2001.

21. M. Davis, G. Logemann, and D. Loveland. A machine program for theorem proving. *Journal of the ACM*, 5:394–397, 1962.
22. S. Davis and M. Putnam. A computing procedure for quantification theory. *Journal of ACM*, 7:201–215, 1960.
23. R. Dechter. *Learning in graphical models*, chapter Bucket elimination: a unifying framework for probabilistic inference, pages 75–104. 1999.
24. R. Dechter. *Constraint Processing*. Morgan Kaufmann, 2003.
25. R. Dechter and J. Pearl. Network-based heuristics for constraint-satisfaction problems. *Artificial Intelligence*, 34:1–38, 1987.
26. R. Dechter and I. Rish. Directional resolution: The Davis-Putnam procedure, revisited. In *KR'94: Principles of Knowledge Representation and Reasoning*, pages 134–145. 1994.
27. R.G. Downey and M.R. Fellows. *Parametrized Complexity*. Springer-Verlag, 1999.
28. E.C Freuder. Complexity of k-tree structured constraint satisfaction problems. In *Proc. AAAI-90*, pages 4–9, 1990.
29. D. Geist and H. Beer. Efficient model checking by automated ordering of transition relation partitions. In *CAV 1994*, pages 299–310, 1994.
30. E. Giunchiglia, M. Maratea, A. Tacchella, and D. Zambonin. Evaluating search heuristics and optimization techniques in propositional satisfiability. *Lecture Notes in Computer Science*, 2083, 2001.
31. E. Giunchiglia, M. Narizzano, and A. Tacchella. QuBE, a system for deciding quantified Boolean formulae satisfiability. In *IJCAR'01*, 2001.
32. E. Goldberg and Y. Novikov. BerkMin: A fast and robust SAT solver, 2002.
33. J. F. Groote. Hiding propositional constants in BDDs. *FMSD*, 8:91–96, 1996.
34. A. Gupta, Z. Yang, P. Ashar, L. Zhang, and S. Malik. Partition-based decision heuristics for image computation using SAT and BDDs. In *ICCAD*, 2001.
35. A. Heuerding and S. Schwendimann. A benchmark method for the propositional modal logics K, KT, S4. Technical report, Universität Bern, Switzerland, 1996.
36. R. Hojati, S. C. Krishnan, and R. K. Brayton. Early quantification and partitioned transition relations. pages 12–19, 1996.
37. H. Kautz and B. Selman. Planning as satisfiability. In *Proc. Eur. Conf. on AI*, pages 359–379, 1992.
38. A.M.C.A. Koster, H.L. Bodlaender, and S.P.M. van Hoesel. Treewidth: Computational experiments. Technical report, 2001.
39. D. Le Berre, L. Simon, M. Narizzano, and A. Tacchella. QBF evaluation 2004. http://satlive.org/QBFEvaluation/2004/, 2004.
40. D. Le Berre, L. Simon, and A. Tacchella. Challenges in the qbf arena: the sat'03 evaluation of qbf solvers. In *In Sixth International Conference on Theory and Applications of Satisfiability Testing (SAT 2003)*, 2003.
41. R. Letz. Lemma and model caching in decision procedures for quantified Boolean formulas. In *TABLEAUX 2002*, pages 160–175, 2002.
42. S. Minato. *Binary Decision Diagrams and Applications to VLSI CAD*. Kluwer, 1996.
43. M. Narizzano. QBFLIB, the quantified Boolean formulas satisfiability library. http://www.qbflib.org.
44. A. Newell and H. A. Simon. The logic theory machine: A complex information processing system. *IRE Trans. Inf. Theory*, IT-2:61–79, 1956.
45. G. Pan, U. Sattler, and M.Y. Vardi. BDD-based decision procedures for K. In *Proc. of CADE 2002*, volume 2392 of *LNAI*, pages 16–30, 2002.
46. G. Pan and M.Y. Vardi. Optimizing a symbolic modal solver. In *Proc. of CADE 2003*, 2003.
47. G. Pan and M.Y. Vardi. Search vs. symbolic techniques in satisfiability solving. In *SAT 2004*, 2004.

48. R. Ranjan, A. Aziz, R. Brayton, B. Plessier, and C. Pixley. Efficient BDD algorithms for FSM synthesis and verification. In *Proc. of IEEE/ACM Int. Workshop on Logic Synthesis*, 1995.
49. J. Rintanen. Constructing conditional plans by a theorem-prover. *J. of A. I. Res.*, 10:323–352, 1999.
50. A. San Miguel Aguirre and M. Y. Vardi. Random 3-SAT and BDDs: The plot thickens further. In *Principles and Practice of Constraint Programming*, pages 121–136, 2001.
51. A.P. Sistla and E.M. Clarke. The complexity of propositional linear temporal logic. *J. ACM*, 32:733–749, 1985.
52. F. Somenzi. CUDD: CU decision diagram package, 1998.
53. L.J. Stockmeyer. The polynomial-time hierarchy. *Theo. Comp. Sci.*, 3:1–22, 1977.
54. G. Sutcliffe and C. Suttner. Evaluating general purpose automated theorem proving systems. *Artificial intelligence*, 131:39–54, 2001.
55. R. E. Tarjan and M. Yannakakis. Simple linear-time algorithms to tests chordality of graphs, tests acyclicity of hypergraphs, and selectively reduce acyclic hypergraphs. *SIAM Journal on Computing*, 13(3):566–579, 1984.
56. T. E. Uribe and M. E. Stickel. Ordered binary decision diagrams and the Davis-Putnam procedure. In *1st Int. Conf. on Constraints in Computational Logics*, pages 34–49, 1994.
57. L. Zhang and S. Malik. The quest for efficient Boolean satisfiability solvers. In *CAV 2002*, pages 17–36, 2002.
58. L. Zhang and S. Malik. Towards symmetric treatment of conflicts and satisfaction in quantified Boolean satisfiability solver. In *CP'02*, 2002.

Propagation Guided Large Neighborhood Search

Laurent Perron, Paul Shaw, and Vincent Furnon

ILOG SA
9, rue de Verdun, 94253 Gentilly Cedex, France
{lperron,pshaw,vfurnon}@ilog.fr

Abstract. In this article, we explore how neighborhoods for the Large Neighborhood Search (LNS) framework can be automatically defined by the volume of propagation of our Constraint Programming (CP) solver. Thus we can build non trivial neighborhoods which will not be reduced to zero by propagation and whose size will be close to a parameter of the search. Furthermore, by looking at the history of domain reductions, we are able to deduce even better neighborhoods. This idea is validated by numerous experiments with the car sequencing problem. The result is a powerful and completely automatic method that is able to beat our hand-written neighborhoods both in term of performance and of stability. This is in fact the first time for us that a completely generic code is better than a hand-written one.

1 Introduction

Large Neighborhood Search (LNS) methods have proved to be successful on a variety of hard combinatorial problems, *e.g.*, vehicle routing [1, 2], scheduling (job-shop: shuffle [3], shifting bottleneck [4], forget-and-extend [5]; RCPSP: block neighborhood [6]), network design [7], frequency allocation [8]. Over the years, LNS has proved to be competitive with other local search techniques. It complements the Constraint Programming framework as LNS benefits from improved propagation while Constraint Programming benefits from this efficient, while simple, search framework.

For all the problems mentioned above, success was made possible through the writing of highly specialized dedicated neighborhoods that took advantage of specific knowledge and properties of the problem at hand. For instance, on jobshop problems, the neighborhoods usually involve the critical path of the schedule. On routing problems, they use the insertion technique and the notion of trips. On frequency allocation problems, they rely on geometric properties or on frequency closeness. In fact, we could conjecture, and rightly so, that neighborhood design is the most crucial part of a Large Neighborhood Search solver.

Unfortunately, while the LNS framework is very simple, easy to code (a complete code is less than 200 lines of code in our case), and quite natural in the CP context, writing such finely crafted neighborhoods is difficult and time consuming. It requires deep knowledge of the problem, as well as a lot of experiments, and thus running time, for effective tuning.

This difficulty stems from many factors: the nature itself of the neighborhoods and their link to the main problem, the adequacy of these neighborhoods with regard to the difficult part of the problem, the choice of the size of the neighborhoods, the interleaving of neighborhoods in cases where multiple neighborhoods are needed, and, in general, the whole architecture of the LNS-based solver.

From these remarks, we can conclude that Large Neighborhood Search is a powerful tool when used by optimization specialists. It allows one to reuse the knowledge of the problem expert in the definition of specific neighborhoods and thus allows those specialists to achieve good results.

While satisfactory from the point of view of problem solving, we would like to reuse the LNS framework on a broader scale. In fact, we believe that the biggest challenge in the CP community is to provide a default search mechanism as is available in Math Programming solvers like ILOG CPLEX[9]. To meet this challenge, we believe that LNS could be part of the solution when we have an optimization problem. The problem then becomes how neighborhoods for LNS could be automatically generated from the model as we would like the default search mechanism to adapt itself to the problem and not to require any special input.

We investigated an original idea that will use the propagation of the Constraint Programming solver itself to define the neighborhoods. We hope to build structured neighborhoods simply by looking at which variables are affected through propagation when one variable is frozen. We call this strategy Propagation Guided Large Neighborhood Search.

This idea is loosely related to the work on impact of search[10]. This paper is based on a subset of Philippe Refalo's work, which provides a much richer framework for understanding the relations created between variables by propagation.

This idea will then be improved by *reversing* the technique and by building neighborhoods by expansion instead of by reduction.

Finally, we will test these ideas on the car sequencing problem. We have already tackled this problem[11] and would like to compare these automatic neighborhoods with our own hand-written specific neighborhoods.

In particular, we would like to conduct four kinds of experiments. First, we will compare both implementations of random neighborhoods (with and without Propagation Guided LNS). Second, we would like to compare the best pure LNS approaches (from [11]) with the Propagation Guided large neighborhoods. Third, we will compare the interleaving of the two kinds of neighborhoods. And finally, we will throw in our best automatic neighborhoods, namely adaptative reversed propagation guided large neighborhoods.

2 The Car Sequencing Problem

This section presents the car sequencing problem. It explains how it was first formulated as a Constraint Satisfaction Problem (CSP) and then how we transformed it into an optimization problem.

2.1 An Industrial Problem

The car sequencing problem is concerned with ordering the set of cars to be fed along a production line so that various options on the cars can be installed without over-burdening the production line. Options on the cars are things like air conditioning, sunroof, DVD player, and so on. Each option is installed by a different working bay. Each of these bays has a different capacity which is specified as the proportion of cars on which the option can be installed.

2.2 The Original Formulation

The original car sequencing problem is stated as follows: We are given a set of options O and a set of configurations $K = \{k | k \subseteq O\}$. For each configuration $k \in K$, we associate a demand d_k which is the number of cars to be built with that configuration. We denote by n the total number of cars to be built: $n = \sum_{k \in K} d_k$. For each option $o \in O$ we define a *sequence length* l_o and a *capacity* c_o which states that no more than c_o cars in any sequence of l_o cars can have option o installed. The throughput of an option o is given as a fraction c_o/l_o. Given a sequence of configurations on the production line $s = < s_1, \ldots, s_n >$, we can state that:

$$\forall o \in O, \forall x \in \{1 \ldots n - l_o + 1\} \sum_{i=x}^{x+l_o-1} U_o(s_i) \leq c_o$$

where $U_o(k) = 1$ if $o \in k$ and 0 otherwise.

This statement of the problem seeks to produce a sequence s of cars which violates none of the capacity restrictions of the installation bays; it is a decision problem.

2.3 From a Decision Problem to an Optimization Problem

In this paper, we wish to apply local search techniques to the car sequencing problem. As such, we need a notion of the quality of a sequence, even if it does not satisfy all the capacity constraints. Approaches in the past have softened the capacity constraints and added a cost when the capacity of any installation bay is exceeded; for example, see [15, 16]. Such an approach then seeks a solution of violation zero by a process of improvement (or reduction) of this violation.

However, when Constraint Programming is used, this violation-based representation can be undesirable as it results in little propagation until the violation of the partial sequence closely approaches or meets its upper bound. (This upper bound could be imposed by a local search, indicating that a solution better than a certain quality should be found.) Only at this point does any propagation into the sequence variables begin to occur.

We instead investigated an alternative model which keeps the capacity constraints as hard constraints but relaxes the problem by adding some additional cars of a single new configuration. This additional configuration is an 'empty' configuration: it requires no options and can be thought of as a stall in the production line. Such configurations can be inserted into a sequence when no 'real' configurations are possible. This allows capacity restrictions to be respected by lengthening the sequence of real configurations. The idea, then, is to process all the original cars in the least possible number of slots. If all empty configurations come at the end of the sequence, then a solution to the original decision problem has been found. We introduce a cost variable c which is defined to be the number of slots required to install all cars minus n. So, when $c = 0$, no empty configurations are interspersed with real ones, and a solution to the original decision problem has been found.

3 Large Neighborhood Search

In this section, we define the Large Neighborhood Search framework (LNS).

3.1 The Large Neighborhood Framework

Large Neighborhood Search (LNS) is a technique which is based upon a combination of local and tree-based search methods. As such, it is an ideal candidate to be used when one wishes to perform local search in a Constraint Programming environment. The basic idea is that one iteratively relaxes a part of the problem, and then re-optimizes that part, hoping to find better solutions at each iteration. Constraint Programming can be used to add bounds on the search variable to ensure that the new solution found is not worse than the current one.

Large Neighborhood Search has its roots in the shuffling procedures of [3], but has become more popular of late thanks to its successes [1, 12, 13].

The main challenge in Large Neighborhood Search is knowing which part of the problem should be relaxed and re-optimized. A random choice rarely does as well as a more reasoned one, as was demonstrated in [1], for example.

The architecture of the LNS solver is organized as follows. Given an intermediate solution, we try to improve it with LNS. Thus, we choose one neighborhood and freeze all variables that do not appear in this neighborhood. Then we choose a small search limit (here a fail limit)[1], and we start a search on the unfrozen part of the model with a search goal (usually the one used to build the first solution). At each iteration, we select the first acceptable solution (strictly better or equal in the case of walking) if there is one (which is rare). This is described in algorithm 1.

3.2 The Need for Good Neighborhoods

Over the past three years, we have investigated the application of Large Neighborhood Search on different difficult optimization problems. These include network planning[12], jobshop with earliness and tardiness costs[14], and car sequencing[11].

---

[1] See [13] to see the effect of the search limit on the performance of the search.

Algorithm 1 LNS Architecture.

Produce initial solution
while Optimal solution not found *and* time limit not crossed **do**
  Choose fragment
  Freeze remaining variables
  if Search for improving solution **then**
    Update current solution
  end if
end while

On the network design problem, we learned that neighborhoods that exploit the structure of the problem are vastly superior to random neighborhoods. This is consistent with [1]. In practice, we experienced a 6% improvement on the average cost over 1344 problems when switching from tree search to LNS. We saw a 10% improvement when switching from random neighborhoods to problem-specific neighborhoods, while switching from one to eight processors only improved the average cost by 2.5%.

On the jobshop problems, we introduced a new type of neighborhood that directly deals with the objective function. The cost of a solution of a jobshop problem with earliness and tardiness costs is the sum of the individual costs of each job in the problem. Traditionally, the back-propagation[2] is very weak in CP over a sum function. By using the LNS framework, we were able to remedy this weakness by freezing most terms of the sum expression and thus allowing the bound reduction of the cost function introduced by the optimization process to be propagated to a few terms (usually only one) of the big sum expression.

Amazingly, while we were able to get rid of the purely random neighborhood in the network design problem, removing this same random neighborhood on the jobshop problem led to very poor results. This proves that diversity is a key issue in LNS and that all the structured neighborhoods we wrote for this problem lacked the diversity needed to be really robust and efficient. This diversity was provided by a purely random neighborhood that relaxed a few activities randomly.

Finally, on the car sequencing problem, which we will reuse in this article, we stumbled upon the poor performance of our LNS solver. These poor results were explained by two factors. First, the LNS architecture was too naive and could benefit a lot from lessons learned in the local search community – in particular all the methods designed to escape local minima. Second, some efficient transformations of the model cannot be implemented in the LNS framework as they involved most, if not all, the decision variables of the problem. Fortunately, such moves were easily integrated in the LNS architecture using the fast restart policy present in our solver. Please refer to [11] for more details.

4 Propagation Based Large Neighborhood Search

In this section, we define Propagation Guided Large Neighborhood Search, namely PGLNS.

---
[2] The propagation of a reduction on the cost function over the full problem.

4.1 Using Propagation Guided LNS to Determine the Neighborhood

The idea of using propagation to define neighborhoods is very simple. It is in fact two-fold. First, we will use the current size of the domains of the decision variables to control the size of the resulting neighborhood. Second, when a variable is frozen, propagation occurs. By tracing the volume of domain reduction, we can detect which variables are linked to the frozen variable. We will use this information to determine the next variable to freeze. The complete method is described in algorithm 2.

Algorithm 2 Propagation Guided LNS.
---
   while Fragment size greater than desired size **do**
     if Variable list empty **then**
       Choose unbound variable randomly
     else
       Choose variable in variable list
     end if
     Freeze variable and propagate
     Update variable list
   end while

Our approach merges the selection of variables to freeze and the freezing itself of these variables. It maintains a list of candidate variables for freezing. Both the size of this list and the way it is updated are parameters of this algorithm. In our tests, the variable list sorted by the size of the domain reduction that occurred on the variable in the list and the size of the list is ten. We also noticed that the list was never full, meaning that the graph of dependencies is quite loose.

The algorithm loops until the size of the search space is small enough. In our implementation, we sum the logarithm of the domain of all variables. When this sum is below a given constant, we stop the freezing/selection/updating process.

When the list is empty, which is true at the beginning of the freezing process, the algorithm automatically selects an unfrozen variable randomly. After the variable is frozen to the value it had in the previous intermediate solution, we compare the size of the domain of all variables before and after the freezing part. Then for each variable that does exhibit a change in its domain size, we update the list with these variables.

In our implementation, the list keeps the most affected variables; it is thus a sorted list.

4.2 Rationale

The rationale behind this idea is the notion of efficient neighborhoods or efficient freezing. Let us consider two variables in the model X and Y linked by an equality constraint $X = Y$. Creating a neighborhood that will freeze X without freezing Y is absurd as the equality constraint will automatically freeze Y when X is frozen. Unfortunately, the construction of neighborhoods for LNS usually depends on a size parameter. Therefore, if some unfrozen variables are wasted, then the neighborhood is in fact smaller than the desired size. It is thus inefficient.

In fact, by following the effects of propagation, we dynamically discover the closely linked subparts of the problem. Our hope is then to build efficient neighborhoods where we have something to search. This means a neighborhood where not all the variables of the fragments have been fixed by propagation.

Thus, with this method, we hope to build non trivial neighborhoods which size will be within an expected range after the initial propagation.

4.3 Reversing PGLNS

The previous method defines neighborhoods by reduction. It starts from the full set of unbounded variables and start instantiating them until it reaches a desized resulting size. If we look more closely at what happens, we can see than when a variable belonging to a closely linked subset of the problem is instantiated, the PGLNS algorithm will try to bind all variables belonging to this subset.

Unfortunately, chances that this same algorithm builds a neighborhood that will contain exactly this closely linked subset of the problem are very small. As soon as it hits one of the variables belonging to this subset of variables, then it will bind all these variables. This is really a bad property of this method as this subset of ht problem looks like a promising candidate for a neighborhood.

Thus, we decided to *reverse* the PGLNS and build neighborhoods by expansion instead of by reduction.

Algorithm 3 Reverse Propagation Guided LNS.
while Fragment size smaller than desired size **do**
  if Variable list empty **then**
    Choose variable randomly
  else
    Choose variable in variable list
  end if
  Add variable size to the fragment size
  Update variable list with variables close to the selected variable
end while

As described in algorithm 3, we will build the neighborhood iteratively by adding variables to the fragment. This method relies on a **closeness** relation. We decided to define this closeness relation as the average volume of propagation (that was involved on one variable when another was instantiated) other the previous runs of direct PGLNS.

This algorithm is further improved by adding a multiplicative correction factor to the desired fragment size. Instead a requiring a final fragment of size s, we will require a fragment of size $s * \epsilon$. Furthermore, this ϵ will be continuously updated throughout the search process. By looking at the desired size, the desired corrected size and the exact obtained size, we can smoothly update ϵ.

This epsilon in fact measures the volume of reduction that happens during the neighborhood application. Observation shows that this ϵ ranges between 1.2

and 2.0 during the search. Furthermore, it varies with the size of the problem and time as it tends to decrease as the problem becomes tighter.

Experimental results show that this ϵ is a crucial improvement to the PGLNS and the reverse PGLNS technique as only by using this method were we able to beat our hand-written neighborhoods.

5 Experimental Results

5.1 Experimental Context

We have generated three series of twenty problems for the car sequencing problem using the generator described in [11]. These three series consist of problems of size 100 for the first series, 300 for the second series and 500 for the last series.

All tests were run on a Pentium-M 1.4 GHz with 1 GB of RAM. The code was compiled with Microsoft Visual Studio .NET 2003.

All our experiments rely on randomness. To deal with unstable results, we report the average of ten runs for each test case. All tests use a time limit of ten minutes. All figures report the average runs for each configuration.

The x-axis corresponds to the time in seconds (from 0 to 600). The y-axis corresponds to the sum of all stalls obtained on the average for the 20 instances for a series.

5.2 The Contenders

Pure Random Neighborhoods. The first two contenders are the pure random ones. We compare the original random neighborhood we had implemented for [11] with a Propagation Guided neighborhood with a list size of 0 (which always selects the next variable randomly as it does not record listed variables).

We can already point out that these two neighborhood builders select variables randomly in the same way. The only difference lies in the size of the final search space. The number of variables will be fixed in the case of the original neighborhood while the product of the size of all domains will be fixed in the second case.

These contenders are called *Pure Random* and *Random PGLNS*.

Advanced Neighborhoods. Then we compare the original interval-based neighborhoods used in [11] with a Propagation Guided neighborhood. For this last neighborhood, the size of the variable list is ten and when a variable is affected again, the propagation effects (the difference between the logs of the size of the domain before and after propagation) sum themselves. Finally, we always select the most affected variable.

These contenders are called *Interval Neighborhood* and *PGLNS*.

Mixed Advanced and Random Neighborhoods. In our previous experiments, we obtained better results by interleaving purely random neighborhoods with the advanced ones. This interleaving is completely fair as we select one neighborhood type and then the other in sequence.

We have implemented this same idea here. We tested the original random neighborhood mixed with the original interval based neighborhood. This was pitted against the same combination of random Propagation Guided neighborhood and generic Propagation Guided neighborhood.

This gives two more contenders: *Interval + Random Neighborhood* and *Random PGLNS + PGLNS*.

Adding Reverse PGLNS. Finally, we have also implemented and tested reverse PGLNS and adaptative reverse PGLNS. The first one uses a constant ϵ of 1. The second one uses a dynamic ϵ.

This gives the last two contenders: *PGLNS + reverse* and *PGLNS + adaptative reverse PGLNS*. It should be noted that these last two contenders also include the random PGLNS neighborhood. All three neighborhoods are uses fairly, in sequence.

5.3 Experimental Results

We will present results for each group of twenty instances. Figure 1 will show results for instances of size 100, figure 2 will show results for instances of size 300 and figure 3 will show results for instances of size 500.

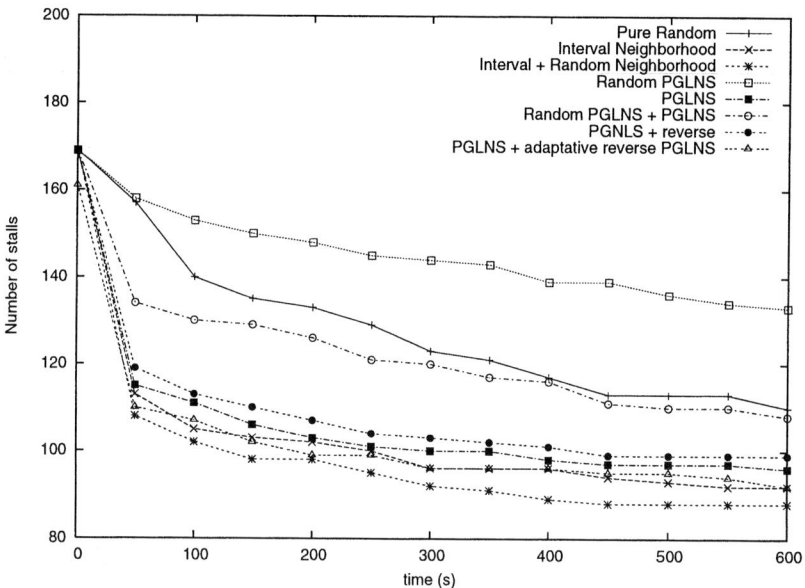

Fig. 1. Results for problems with size 100.

On the Random Contenders. In fact, the "random PGLNS" subsumes "Pure Random" except on the small instances. This hints at inefficient size management for the small instances for the Propagation Guided random neighborhoods and a better size management for the same neighborhood builder for the medium and large scaled instances.

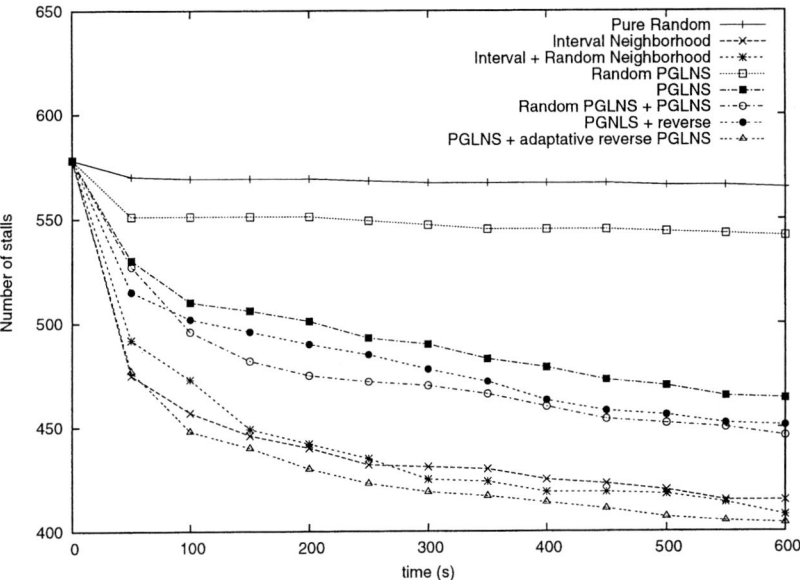

Fig. 2. Results for problems with size 300.

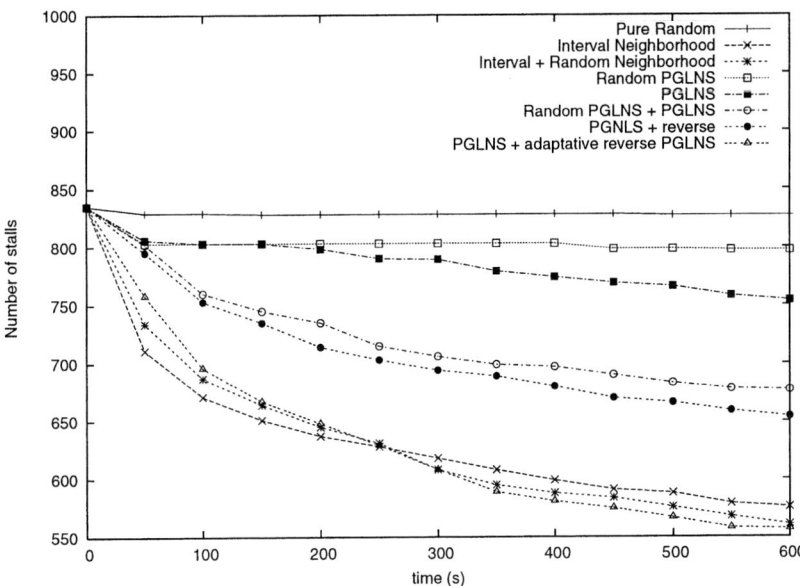

Fig. 3. Results for problems with size 500.

We can also notice that these neighborhoods do not improve the solution on medium size and big size instances. They are in fact quite inefficient.

On the Advanced Contenders. These results we welcomed with mixed feelings. The good news is that "PGLNS" is competitive with "Interval neighborhood" on the small instances.

Unfortunately, this does not scale and the gap between the two methods increases as the size of the instances grows.

This clearly demonstrates the difference in robustness between a tuned neighborhood and an automatically generated one. For instance, the hand-written one knows about the objective structure (the sum of stalls which are not contiguous with the end of the sequence) and knows what is a stall (in our model, a special value that can be assigned to cars, and the neighborhood instantiation will skip cars bound to stalls). This specific knowledge cannot simply be extracted from the model and the decision variables. This lack of information explains the gap between the two neighborhood builders.

On the Mixed Contenders. The gap between the hand written neighborhoods and the automatic neighborhoods is greatly reduced when mixing random and advanced neighborhoods. While this mix benefits both approaches. The improvement is much greater for "Random PGLNS + PGLNS" than for "Random + interval neighborhood".

Unfortunately, this gap still exists and grows with the problem size. On the other hand, we can notice the huge difference in performance between the purely random neighborhoods and the improved ones, even the Propagation Guided generic one.

Thus we can improve the perception we have of these Propagation Guided neighborhoods as they do improve greatly upon the purely random ones, and they do not require extra knowledge or coding from the user of these methods. Thus, we have greatly improved the default behavior of Large Neighborhood Search. This is very promising

When Using Reverse PGLNS. The non-adaptative implementation of reverse PGLNS improves the previous method by a small margin. On the small instances, it is now competitive with the best hand-written algorithms. The gap remains important on instances of medium and big size.

This first method uses a constant ϵ of one (or no ϵ at all as it is a multiplicative factor). If we now use a dynamic ϵ, the landscape is dramatically changed. Adaptative reverse PGLNS is able to beat our hand-written neighborhoods. Careful monitoring of the ϵ values shows that at first it greatly increases from its initial value of one to almost two. Then it starts slowly to decrease. After each new solution, we have observed small surges in value (an increase of 0.2 of its value). Then this ϵ converges towards a value of between 1.2 and 1.4 depending on the instances.

The initial surge can be explained by the fact that the information collected by the PGLNS method is quite innacurate and thus a lot of unexpected propagation occurs during the neighborhood build process. After a while, this information is refined the ϵ decrease towards a stable value that represent the volume of the initial propagation. Furthermore, the topology is changed after each solution as the current solution is updated at this moment. And thus, the stored information is less accurate and ϵ goes up again until its next stabilization.

5.4 Robustness and Stability

In this section, we compare the stability of each method against the effect of randomness. We give the following table showing all mean deviation for each method and by problem sizes.

Method	Size 100	Size 300	Size 500
Pure Random	2.0	1.8	0.4
Interval Neighborhood	2.5	4.0	6.8
Random + Interval Neighborhood	2.0	4.6	7.8
Random PGLNS	1.0	1.6	0.8
PGLNS	0.2	2.2	4.2
Random PGLNS + PGLNS	0.4	3.5	1.3
PGLNS + reverse	2.1	3.8	2.5
PGLNS + adaptative reverse PGLNS	1.1	3.0	4.2
Best value	87	395	545

The first comment is that pure random methods are very stable. They find bad solution with remarquable stability. In fact, poor methods like PGLNS alone tend to be very stable for the same reason.

The second comment is that PGLNS methods are more stable. In fact, they produce lower standart deviation figures, especially on the larger instances. In particular, the best method (PGLNS + adaptative reverse PGLNS) is also the most stable one. This is very good news indeed.

6 Conclusion and Future Work

Finally, we were able to beat our own hand-written neighborhoods using a completely generic approach. And we did beat them both in term of objective value and in term of stability. Although we did not spend a huge amount of time writing those neighborhoods, this is still a very good result.

Unfortunately, there are still parts of the algorithm that we do not master completely and there lie our future directions of research.

Reverse Memory. Managing the memory of direct instantiation to use in the reverse case has a lot of parameter. How should we memorize previous domain reduction, how should we forget them? Both questions are completely open.

Applications. Is there something in the car sequencing problem that, some structure, that allows our PGLNS to be successful? Can this be applied to other problems? We have no clue at the moment and only experiments on other kind of problems will tell us the exact validity of the PGLNS framework.

Learning. In our framework, we use three methods, pure random, PGLNS and reverse PGLNS. Should we implement reinforcement learning and focus on the successful methods or is the stability a direct consequence of the mix of these three methods?

Improved Information. Should we store more in the PGLNS application to use in the reverse case than the volume of domain reduction. Should we distinguish between partial domain reduction and variable bounding? Is there some information that can be extracted from the sequence of neighborhood builds?

Neighborhood Focus. Should we do something special when a particular neighbor is successful? Should we stay close to it? Should we diverge? These questions could be answered in a completely generic way.

In fact, all these questions without answers show how naive we are in this area. Only detailed experiments on a wide variety of problems will improve our understanding of this very promising idea. We will gladly continue this work and try to reach the grail of search, meaning a completely automatic improvement method for CP.

Acknowledgements

We would like to thank Philippe Refalo for his bright work on impact for Constraint Programming. Finally, we would like to thank Stephanie Cook who, once again, transformed this article is something readable.

We also would like to thank the referee for the useful comments and insights.

References

1. Shaw, P.: Using constraint programming and local search methods to solve vehicle routing problems. In Maher, M., Puget, J.F., eds.: Proceeding of CP '98, Springer-Verlag (1998) 417–431
2. Bent, R., Hentenryck, P.V.: A two-stage hybrid local search for the vehicle routing problem with time windows. Technical Report CS-01-06, Brown University (2001)
3. Applegate, D., Cook, W.: A computational study of the job-shop scheduling problem. ORSA Journal on Computing **3** (1991) 149–156
4. J. Adams, E.B., Zawack, D.: The shifting bottleneck procedure for job shop scheduling. Management Science **34** (1988) 391–401
5. Caseau, Y., Laburthe, F.: Effective forget-and-extend heuristics for scheduling problems. In: Proceedings of the First International Workshop on Integration of AI and OR Techniques in Constraint Programming for Combinatorial Optimisation Problems (CP-AI-OR'99). (1999)
6. Palpant, M., Artigues, C., Michelon, P.: Solving the resource-constrained project scheduling problem by integrating exact resolution and local search. In: 8th International Workshop on Project Management and Scheduling PMS 2002. (2002) 289–292

7. Le Pape, C., Perron, L., Régin, J.C., Shaw, P.: Robust and parallel solving of a network design problem. In Hentenryck, P.V., ed.: Proceedings of CP 2002, Ithaca, NY, USA (2002) 633–648
8. Palpant, M., Artigues, C., Michelon, P.: A heuristic for solving the frequency assignment problem. In: XI Latin-Iberian American Congress of Operations Research (CLAIO). (2002)
9. CPLEX: ILOG CPLEX 9.0 User's Manual and Reference Manual. ILOG, S.A. (2003)
10. Refalo, P.: Impact based strategies for constraint programming. Submitted to CP 2004 (2004)
11. Perron, L.: Combining forces to solve the car sequencing problem. In: Proceeding of CP-AI-OR 2004, Springer Verlag (2004)
12. Chabrier, A., Danna, E., Le Pape, C., Perron, L.: Solving a network design problem. To appear in Annals of Operations Research, Special Issue following CP-AI-OR'2002 (2003)
13. Perron, L.: Fast restart policies and large neighborhood search. In: Proceedings of CPAIOR 2003. (2003)
14. Danna, E., Perron, L.: Structured vs. unstructured large neighborhood search: A case study on job-shop scheduling problems with earliness and tardiness costs. In: Proceeding of CP 2003, Springer Verlag (2003)
15. Michel, L., Hentenryck, P.V.: A constraint-based architecture for local search. In: Proceedings of the 17th ACM SIGPLAN conference on Object-oriented programming, systems, languages, and applications, ACM Press (2002) 83–100
16. Gottlieb, J., Puchta, M., Solnon, C.: A study of greedy, local search and ant colony optimization approaches for car sequencing problems. In: Applications of evolutionary computing (EvoCOP 2003), Springer Verlag (2003) 246–257 LNCS 2611.

A Regular Language Membership Constraint for Finite Sequences of Variables

Gilles Pesant[1,2]

[1] École Polytechnique de Montréal, Montreal, Canada
[2] Centre for Research on Transportation (CRT)
Université de Montréal, C.P. 6128, succ. Centre-ville, Montreal, H3C 3J7, Canada
pesant@crt.umontreal.ca

Abstract. This paper describes a global constraint on a fixed-length sequence of finite-domain variables requiring that the corresponding sequence of values taken by these variables belong to a given regular language, thereby generalizing some other known global constraints. We describe and analyze a filtering algorithm achieving generalized arc consistency for this constraint. Some comparative empirical results are also given.

1 Introduction

For constraint programming (CP) to become widely used as a problem modeling and solving methodology, it must be expressive but also powerful. Global constraints are an important step in that direction: they represent substructures commonly found in certain problems; they encapsulate efficient algorithms to reason about these substructures and about the rest of the problem through shared variables. This paper describes a global constraint on a fixed-length sequence of finite-domain variables requiring that the corresponding sequence of values taken by these variables belong to a given regular language[1]. Regular languages are a good compromise between expressiveness and computational efficiency for deciding membership. One finds such a substructure, for example, in rostering and car sequencing problems.

We briefly recall regular expressions, regular languages, and their connection with automata theory (the interested reader may consult, for example, [7]). An alphabet Σ is a finite set of symbols. A string over an alphabet is a finite sequence of symbols from that alphabet. The (infinite) set of all strings over Σ is denoted by $\Sigma^\star$. Any subset of $\Sigma^\star$ is called a language. Deciding whether a particular string belongs to a given language is easier for some languages than for others.

A regular expression over Σ is built from Σ and the symbols "(", ")", "ϵ", "+", and "$\star$", according to the following recursive definition:

- ϵ (the empty string) and each member of Σ is a regular expression;
- if α and β are regular expressions then so is $(\alpha\beta)$;

---

[1] A preliminary version of this paper appeared as [10].

- if α and β are regular expressions then so is $(\alpha + \beta)$;
- if α is a regular expression then so is $\alpha^\star$.

Every regular expression represents a regular language in $\Sigma^\star$, according to the interpretation of "+" and "$\star$" as set union and Kleene star, respectively.

A deterministic finite automaton (DFA) may be described by a 5-tuple $(Q, \Sigma, \delta, q_0, F)$ where Q is a finite set of states, Σ is an alphabet, $\delta : Q \times \Sigma \to Q$ is a partial transition function, $q_0 \in Q$ is the initial state, and $F \subseteq Q$ is the set of final (or accepting) states. Given an input string, the automaton starts in the initial state q_0 and processes the string one symbol at a time, applying the transition function δ at each step to update the current state. The string is accepted if and only if the last state reached belongs to the set of final states F. The languages recognized by DFA's are precisely regular languages.

We define our global constraint using a DFA – equivalently, we could have used a regular expression without any significant impact on computation time [3].

Definition 1 (regular language membership constraint).
Let $M = (Q, \Sigma, \delta, q_0, F)$ denote a deterministic finite automaton and **x** a sequence of finite-domain variables $\langle x_1, x_2, \ldots, x_n \rangle$ with respective domains D_1, D_2, \ldots, $D_n \subseteq \Sigma$. Under a regular language membership constraint regular(**x**, M), any sequence of values taken by the variables of **x** must belong to the regular language recognized by M.

Example 1. Consider a sequence **x** of five variables with $D_i = \Sigma = \{a, b, c\}$, $1 \leq i \leq 5$ and regular expression $aa^\star bb^\star aa^\star + c^\star$, equivalently described by the automaton M of Figure 1. Under constraint regular(**x**, M), assigned sequences $\langle a, a, b, b, a \rangle$ and $\langle c, c, c, c, c \rangle$ are valid but $\langle a, b, b, b, c \rangle$ and $\langle a, a, b, b, b \rangle$ are not.

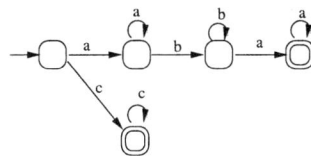

Fig. 1. A DFA corresponding to $aa^\star bb^\star aa^\star + c^\star$. Final states are shown with a double circle.

Such a definition may appear restrictive since it only allows the strings of the regular language that have a given length n. But because that constraint, like most other global constraints, is destined to be integrated into a larger model where other constraints are present, it is a much better choice to use a fixed-length sequence of variables each ranging over a finite alphabet than a single variable ranging over an infinite set of strings of arbitrary length.

In CP, combinatorial problems are typically modeled with several finite-domain variables. Constraints are then expressed on different subsets of these variables and cooperate through shared variables. Consider for example a rostering problem modeled with a two-dimensional array of variables, each taking their value from the set of possible activities (different work shifts, day off, training, and so forth). Each row, made up of seven variables, represents a week and each column, a day of the week. There could be a `regular` constraint on each individual row to indicate valid patterns of activities during a week and another `regular` constraint on the column for Monday to limit the number of Monday evening work shifts in a row. There could also be a cardinality constraint on weekend variables to ensure enough weekends off, and so on. Breaking up the roster into single-day chunks allows us to express the previous constraints directly from the original variables.

The next section presents related work on the integration of regular languages and patterns in CP. Section 3 describes the data structures and the filtering algorithm encapsulated in the regular language membership constraint, analyses the time and space complexity of the algorithm, and shows that it achieves generalized arc consistency. Section 4 discusses an improvement on the algorithm of the previous section. Section 5 shows how some important global constraints are special cases of this one. Finally, Section 6 presents some empirical results.

2 Related Work

In the literature, the study of regular language membership constraints has usually involved variables ranging over an infinite set of strings. We do not insist on such works and only mention them if they are embedded in CP systems. We rather concentrate on membership constraints for sequences of finite-domain variables.

The constraint logic programming language CLP($\Sigma^\star$) [14] introduces membership constraints in regular languages described by regular expressions, of the form "X in ρ", where X is a single variable. One important difference with the work described in this paper is that the domain of a variable is an infinite set, the strings in $\Sigma^\star$, as opposed to a finite set of symbols from Σ in our case. Its constraint solver is based on a flexible constraint scheduling strategy to ensure termination (which is cause for concern with infinite domains) and on a collection of deduction rules to determine the satisfaction of individual constraints. With an application to software project planning in mind, [6] discusses constraint reasoning over infinite sets of strings restricted to belong to regular languages. This allows the sets to be represented by finite automata on which operations such as intersection, concatenation, and negation are efficiently computed. Here again variables have an infinite domain.

Other constraint logic programming languages have offered some support to reason about sequences of symbols. PROLOG III [5] features equations on lists. Lists are built from constants, list variables and a concatenation operator. A length operator is also defined. CLP($\mathcal{S}$) [11] manipulates equations on strings, built very much like PROLOG III's lists except that each string variable has a length parameter associated to it. The constraint solver exploits equalities and inequalities on these lengths to speed up the rule-based unification algorithm used for string equations.

Some constraints enforcing patterns of values have also been defined for finite-domain variables. ILOG Solver's `IlcTableConstraint` [8] takes as main arguments a sequence of n finite-domain variables and a set of n-tuples representing the valid assignments of values to these variables. For sets described by a regular expression, as in our case, the number of n-tuples would usually need to be very large and this possibly reflects on the computational complexity of the constraint. CHIP's `sequence` constraint [4] is a very expressive global constraint on the number of times a certain pattern of length ℓ appears in a sequence of variables. Patterns are expressed as sums and cardinalities of values taken by some of the ℓ variables in the subsequence. The constraint is not designed for (regular) patterns of arbitrary length over the whole sequence.

Finally, there is some work related to the approach used in this paper. In [2], a specific DFA is used to build the filtering algorithm of a lexicographic ordering constraint. Automata provide a more concise representation for a search tree defined over a constraint satisfaction problem in [13, 1]. In a dynamic programming approach to knapsack constraints, [12] builds and updates a graph whose structure is very similar to the one introduced in the next section.

3 The Consistency Algorithm

The idea behind the consistency algorithm for the `regular` constraint is to process the sequence **x** with the automaton M in a two-stage forward-backward manner, collecting for each variable x_i in **x** and each value $v_j \in D_i$ the set of states from Q that support variable-value pair (x_i, v_j). The sets are updated as the domains change and whenever one of these sets becomes empty, a value becomes unsupported and can be removed from a domain.

Let $\Sigma = \{v_1, v_2, \ldots, v_m\}$. The two-stage process is best seen as constructing a layered directed multigraph $(N^1, N^2, \ldots, N^{n+1}, A)$ where each layer $N^i = \{q_0^i, q_1^i, \ldots, q_{|Q|-1}^i\}$ contains a different node for each state of M and arcs only appear between consecutive layers. The graph is acyclic by construction. Arcs are related to variable-value pairs: an arc from q_k^i to q_ℓ^{i+1} is admissible for inclusion in A only if there exists some $v_j \in D_i$ such that $\delta(q_k, v_j) = q_\ell$. The arc is labeled with the value v_j allowing the transition between the two states. In the first layer the only node with outgoing arcs is q_0^1 since q_0 is the only initial state. Observe that it is enough, given a variable-value pair, to store an arc as the origin state: the destination state can be obtained by one application of the transition function. Accordingly, we maintain sets of states Q_{ij} to stand for the arcs related to variable-value pair (x_i, v_j).

Set Q_{ij} also acts as the support for variable x_i taking value v_j. As we will see later, multiset A is built to contain exactly the admissible arcs that belong to a path from q_0 in the first layer to a member of F in the last layer. When this condition is met for some arc related to variable-value pair (x_i, v_j), we can be sure that there is at least one sequence of values taken from the respective current domains of the variables of **x**, and with value v_j for variable x_i in particular, that belongs to the regular language. As long as Q_{ij} is not empty, we know that one such arc exists.

```
procedure initialize():
  {clear the data structures}
  for all i ∈ {1, 2, ..., n} do
    for all j ∈ {1, 2, ..., m} do
      Q_ij := ∅;
    for all k ∈ {0, 1, ..., |Q| − 1} do
      outarcs[i][k] := ∅;
      outdeg[i][k] := 0;
      inarcs[i + 1][k] := ∅;
      indeg[i + 1][k] := 0;
    N_{i+1} := ∅;
  {forward phase: accumulate}
  N_1 := {q_0};
  for i := 1 to n do
    for all v_j ∈ D_i, q_k ∈ N_i do
      if δ(q_k, v_j) is defined then
        add q_k to Q_ij; {state q_k is a candidate for support}
        add δ(q_k, v_j) to N_{i+1};
  {backward phase: validate}
  N_{n+1} := N_{n+1} ∩ F;
  for i := n downto 1 do
    for all q_k ∈ N_i do
      mark[k] := false;
    for all v_j ∈ D_i, q_k ∈ Q_ij do
      if δ(q_k, v_j) ∈ N_{i+1} {state q_k confirmed as support} then
        add (q_k, δ(q_k, v_j)) to outarcs[i][k];
        increment outdeg[i][k];
        add (q_k, δ(q_k, v_j)) to inarcs[i + 1][δ(q_k, v_j)];
        increment indeg[i + 1][δ(q_k, v_j)];
        mark[k] := true;
      else
        remove q_k from Q_ij;
    for all q_k ∈ N_i do
      if mark[k] = false then
        remove q_k from N_i;
  {clean up the domains}
  for all i ∈ {1, 2, ..., n}, j ∈ {1, 2, ..., m} do
    if Q_ij = ∅ then
      remove value v_j from domain D_i;
```

Algorithm 1. Upon the constraint being posted, build the graph to initialize the data structures and filter out inconsistent values.

Given automaton M and sequence **x** of variables (with their respective domains) in the statement of the constraint, Algorithm 1 builds the graph by initializing our main data structure, the Q_{ij} sets. The incoming and outgoing arcs at each node of the graph are stored in $inarcs[i+1][k]$ and $outarcs[i][k]$, $1 \leq i \leq n$, $0 \leq k \leq |Q|-1$ as doubly-linked lists. Each arc in one structure is also linked to its twin in the other structure and to the Q_{ij} sets, to allow constant time updates. In addition, the in- and out-degree of each node is maintained in $indeg[i+1][k]$ and $outdeg[i][k]$, $1 \leq i \leq n$, $0 \leq k \leq |Q|-1$. All of these data structures are restorable upon backtracking. In the first phase, candidate arcs are collected by reaching forward from the initial state q_0 in the first layer using the domains of the x_i's. In the second phase, the arcs collected during the first phase are only kept if they can be reached backward from a state of F in the last layer. Finally, domains are possibly filtered if some Q_{ij}'s are empty.

---

procedure propagate(i, j):
  for all $q_k \in Q_{ij}$ **do**
    remove $(q_k, \delta(q_k, v_j))$ from $outarcs[i][k]$;
    remove $(q_k, \delta(q_k, v_j))$ from $inarcs[i+1][\delta(q_k, v_j)]$;
    decrement_outdeg(i, k);
    decrement_indeg($i+1, \delta(q_k, v_j)$);
  $Q_{ij} := \emptyset$;

Algorithm 2. Upon v_j being removed from D_i in the course of the computation, update the data structures and filter out inconsistent values.

Algorithm 2 is executed whenever some value v_j is removed from the domain of variable x_i in the course of the computation. Removing a value corresponds to removing one or several arcs in the graph (as many as there are supporting states in Q_{ij}). The in- and out-degrees of the corresponding nodes must then be updated accordingly (Algorithms 3 and 4). If some degree reaches zero, the node no longer belongs to a path from q_0 in the first layer to a member of F in the last layer: that information is propagated along such former paths going through that node and other domains are possibly filtered as a result.

---

procedure decrement_outdeg(i, k):
decrement $outdeg[i][k]$;
if $outdeg[i][k] = 0$ **and** $i > 1$ **then**
  for all $(q_\ell, q_k) \in inarcs[i][k]$ **do**
    let v_j be the label of arc (q_ℓ, q_k);
    remove (q_ℓ, q_k) from $outarcs[i-1][\ell]$;
    remove q_ℓ from $Q_{i-1,j}$;
    if $Q_{i-1,j} = \emptyset$ **then**
      remove value v_j from domain D_{i-1};
    decrement_outdeg($i-1, \ell$);
  $inarcs[i][k] := \emptyset$;

Algorithm 3. Decrementing the out-degree of node q_k^i.

Example 2. In rostering problems, the assignment of consecutive shifts must often follow certain patterns. Consider a sequence **x** of five variables with $D_1 = \{a, b, c, o\}$, $D_2 = \{b, o\}$, $D_3 = \{a, c, o\}$, $D_4 = \{a, b, o\}$, and $D_5 = \{a\}$. Consider also the following pattern: between a's and b's, a's and c's, or b's and c's, there should be at least one o; furthermore, a's followed by o's followed by c's is not allowed, and neither are b's followed by o's followed by a's nor c's followed by

```
procedure decrement_indeg(i, k):
  decrement indeg[i][k];
  if indeg[i][k] = 0 and i < n then
    for all (q_k, q_ℓ) ∈ outarcs[i][k] do
      let v_j be the label of arc (q_k, q_ℓ);
      remove (q_k, q_ℓ) from inarcs[i + 1][δ(q_k, v_j)];
      remove q_k from Q_{ij};
      if Q_{ij} = ∅ then
        remove value v_j from domain D_i;
      decrement_indeg(i + 1, δ(q_k, v_j));
    outarcs[i][k] := ∅;
```

Algorithm 4. Decrementing the in-degree of node q_k^i.

o's followed by b's. Figure 2 gives the corresponding DFA. (In the figures, we identify the states as integers, for readability). Algorithm 1 builds the graphs of Fig. 3.

Non-empty support sets are

$Q_{1a} : \{1\}, Q_{1b} : \{1\}, Q_{1c} : \{1\}, Q_{1o} : \{1\}$,
$Q_{2o} : \{1, 2, 3, 4\}$,
$Q_{3a} : \{1, 5, 7\}, Q_{3c} : \{1, 6, 7\}, Q_{3o} : \{1, 5, 7\}$,
$Q_{4a} : \{1, 2, 5, 7\}, Q_{4o} : \{1, 2, 4, 5, 7\}$,
$Q_{5a} : \{1, 2, 5, 7\}$.

As a result, value b is removed from D_2 and D_4. Suppose now that value o is removed from D_4 in the course of the computation. Algorithm 2 updates the graph as shown in Figure 4, causing values b and c to be removed from D_1 and D_3 respectively.

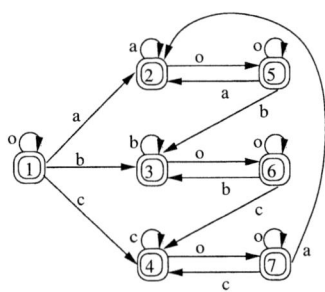

Fig. 2. A deterministic finite automaton for a common pattern in rostering.

We now show that the algorithms achieve domain consistency (i.e. generalized arc consistency). Let $L_\mathbf{x} = \{\langle a_1, a_2, \ldots, a_n \rangle \mid a_k \in D_k, 1 \leq k \leq n\}$ be the set of all sequences of symbols (strings) formed by replacing each variable of $\mathbf{x}$ by a value in its domain, and $L_\mathbf{x}(M) \subseteq L_\mathbf{x}$ the subset of these strings that are accepted by M. For convenience, we extend the definition of the transition function so that it applies to strings as well: $\delta(q_k, \langle a_1, a_2, \ldots, a_\ell \rangle) = \delta(\delta(\ldots \delta(\delta(q_k, a_1), a_2), \ldots), a_\ell)$. At the end of Algorithm 1, the following holds:

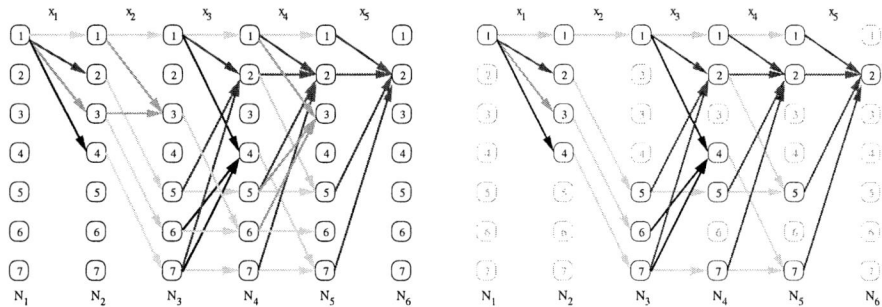

Fig. 3. The layered directed graph at the end of the forward (left) and backward (right) phases.

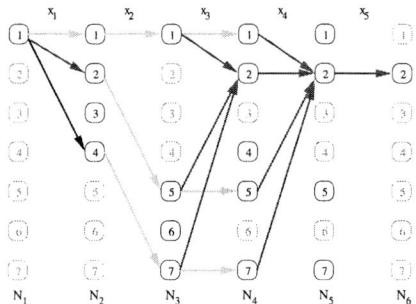

Fig. 4. The layered directed graph after removing value o from the domain of x_4.

Lemma 1. $Q_{ij} = \{q \in Q \mid \exists \langle a_1, \ldots, a_{i-1}, v_j, a_{i+1}, \ldots, a_n \rangle \in L_{\mathbf{x}}(M)$ with $\delta(q_0, \langle a_1, \ldots, a_{i-1} \rangle) = q\}$.

Proof. Considering first the forward phase, it is easy to prove by induction on i that N_i contains all the nodes that may be reached by processing the first i characters of a word in $L_{\mathbf{x}}$. It follows that $Q_{ij} = \{q \in Q \mid \exists \langle a_1, \ldots, a_{i-1}, \ldots \rangle \in L_{\mathbf{x}}$ with $\delta(q_0, \langle a_1, \ldots, a_{i-1} \rangle) = q$ and $\delta(q, v_j)$ defined $\}$ since every possible state (corresponding to a node of N_i) is considered.

Similarly for the backward phase, we can prove by induction on i that N_i contains all the nodes that may reach F by processing the last $n-i+1$ characters of a word in $L_{\mathbf{x}}$. Hence a state q is kept in Q_{ij} during the backward phase if and only if $\exists \langle \ldots, v_j, a_{i+1}, \ldots, a_n \rangle \in L_{\mathbf{x}}$ such that $\delta(q, \langle \ldots, v_j, a_{i+1}, \ldots, a_n \rangle) \in F$.

Putting the two together, we get the result.

Theorem 1. *Constraint* regular($\mathbf{x}, M$) *is domain consistent if and only if* $Q_{ij} \neq \emptyset, \forall 1 \leq i \leq n, j \in D_i$.

Proof. By the previous lemma, if a Q_{ij} set is non-empty then there is at least one sequence of values for variables $\langle x_1, \ldots, x_{i-1}, x_{i+1}, \ldots, x_n \rangle$ supporting the assignment of value v_j to variable x_i. If the sets are non-empty for every variable and every value in its domain then every variable-value pair has a support and the constraint is domain consistent.

If a Q_{ij} set is empty then by the same lemma there is no supporting path for that variable-value pair and the constraint cannot be domain consistent.

Since Algorithm 2 updates the graph throughout the computation in order to mirror changes in the domains, domain consistency is maintained.

We now turn to complexity analysis. The worst-case running time of Algorithm 1, called once, is dominated by the construction of the graph and is in $\mathcal{O}(nm|Q|)$. Its space complexity is in $\mathcal{O}(nm|Q|)$ as well. Each time a domain is modified, Algorithm 2 is called: for each state removed from Q_{ij}, the corresponding arc is removed from the *inarcs* and *outarcs* lists in constant time and Algorithms 3 and 4 are called. If the decremented degrees remains greater than zero, no further arcs are removed and these calls take constant time. Otherwise, for each new arc removed some constant time work is performed plus one recursive call. In all, the initial call of Algorithm 2 therefore takes constant time per arc removed from the graph, which is a good way to evaluate the amount of work performed at each call. It is actually a bounded incremental algorithm whose complexity is linearly related to the number of changes in the data structures.

Because the number of states of the automaton influences both the time and space complexity, it is desirable to use the smallest one possible. Computing a minimum state DFA can be achieved in $\mathcal{O}(|Q|\log|Q|)$ time [15].

4 Cutting Down on Supports

At first, it seems difficult to improve the time complexity of the incremental filtering algorithm since it is optimally efficient for each arc removed. But the numbers of arcs may be reduced. Because we maintain all supports, there may be many arcs stored in our data structures. We only really need one support per variable-value pair. Fewer arcs means less work in maintaining the data structures. Following this idea, we implemented another version of the consistency algorithm which maintains at least one support per variable-value pair and we sketch it below.

Starting from the graph outputted by Algorithm 1, we build a subgraph made up of supporting paths covering every consistent variable-value pair. Pairs obviously share paths and a pair may be covered by several paths. Heuristics help select arcs so that the collection of paths uses as few arcs as possible. Whenever a value is removed from a domain, those of the corresponding arcs from the original graph which belong to supporting paths disappear. Every such path is left broken in two pieces that must each be repaired with other arcs, if possible. Repairing them may involve undoing some of the path.

5 Instances of the regular Constraint

Regular languages allow us to express many non trivial relationships between the variables of a sequence. In particular, a regular language membership constraint generalizes some known global constraints.

Definition 2 (stretch). *A* stretch *is a maximal subsequence of identical values in an assigned sequence* **x**. *The* type *of a stretch is the value v_j taken by its variables and we denote it as v_j-stretch.*

The stretch constraint [9] puts restrictions on the length of stretches in a sequence. This can also be expressed as a regular language and encoded in an automaton using as many states for each value as the maximum length of the corresponding stretch. Minimum and maximum lengths for each type of stretch are expressed by choosing the final states appropriately. For example, the DFA of Fig. 5 enforces a-stretches of length 2 and b-stretches of length 2 or 3.

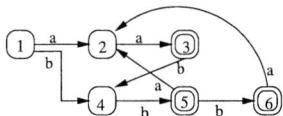

Fig. 5. A deterministic finite automaton for a stretch constraint.

Sometimes the sequence of variables for a stretch constraint is considered circular, i.e. x_1 follows x_n. This could be problematic for our approach. Fortunately, because what must be verified is bounded above (in terms of the number of variables) by the largest maximum length of a stretch, we can model the circular case by duplicating and adding blocks of variables to the original sequence. We sketch this below.

Let ℓ be the largest maximum length among all types of stretches. We duplicate variables $x_1, x_2, \ldots, x_\ell$ (call this block **a**) and concatenate them at the end of the original sequence. Then we create two distinct blocks of $\ell-1$ new variables each (call them **b** and **b'**) whose domains contain every possible value from the original sequence plus an extra dummy value whose stretches are unconstrained. Add one such block at each end of the modified sequence. The resulting sequence looks like **bxab'**. Block **a** allows any stretch begun near the end of **x** to continue from the beginning of **x** and blocks **b** and **b'** ensure that we do not unnecessarily constrain the extremities of **xa**, allowing any first or last stretch to complete and padding with the dummy value.

Definition 3 (pattern). *We call* pattern *two or more consecutive stretches. A pattern made up of p stretches of type $v_1, v_2, \ldots, v_p$, in that order, we call a p-pattern and denote it by $[\![v_1 v_2 \cdots v_p]\!]$. It follows from the definition of a stretch that $v_j \neq v_{j+1}$, $1 \leq j \leq p-1$.*

Patterns are a proper subclass of regular expressions: an a-stretch can be described as aa^*; the 3-pattern $[\![aob]\!]$, as $aa^*oo^*bb^*$ (recall Ex. 2).

A mix of the previous two is sometimes requested in rostering problems: for example, "after three consecutive night shifts, a doctor should be off for at least the next two days". We will call such a constraint a *patterned stretch*. The corresponding regular language is represented by the automaton in Figure 6: any three consecutive a's must be followed by at least two b's.

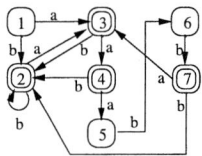

Fig. 6. A deterministic finite automaton for a patterned stretch constraint.

Even the well-known alldifferent constraint could be expressed using regular. Since the alphabet Σ is finite, the language of strings made up of distinct symbols is necessarily finite as well (each string is of length at most $|\Sigma|$) and may be represented by a regular expression which, at the very least, takes the union of the individual strings. For n variables and $m \geq n$ values, we require at least 2^n states, one for each subset of Σ of size at most n. A transition is allowed on symbol v_j from state-subset S (with $v_j \notin S$) to state-subset $S \cup \{v_j\}$, the initial state corresponds to the empty subset, and final states correspond to subsets of size n. However, such an approach clearly suffers from an exponential growth of the automaton and one would quickly run into memory consumption issues.

6 Empirical Results

In this section we wish to compare the computation time of the two implementations proposed for the regular language membership constraint. We also examine the possible trade-off between overall computation time and number of backtracks for these implementations and specialized filtering algorithms for special cases of regular languages.

In our experiments, we vary the number of variables in our sequence and the number of values in the initial domains. The variable and value selection heuristics we use simply choose a variable or value at random. Each line in a table represents an average over 30 runs.

We first compare our two implementations using randomly generated automata with a varying number of states (Table 1). The proportion of undefined transitions in δ was set to 30% and the proportion of final states to 50% (the value of the former has some influence on relative performance but the latter seems to have very little). Our second implementation steadily dominates the other but not spectacularly. There is probably still plenty of room for improvement in the way arcs are selected for supporting paths and such choices should have an impact on performance.

Table 2 reports on instances of circular stretch constraints with randomly generated minimum and maximum stretch lengths. It compares the stretch constraint [9] (Columns 2 and 4) with our two implementations of regular (Columns 5 and 6). For the former, we report the average number of backtracks and the average computation time in seconds. For the latter, we only give the average computation time – there are never any backtracks since our filtering algorithms guarantee that a partial solution can always be completed. Entries

Table 1. Comparing our two versions of `regular` on randomly generated automata.

			regular	
nb of vars	nb of values	nb of states	all supports time(s)	a support time(s)
25	5	10	0.002	0.002
		20	0.005	0.004
		40	0.009	0.008
		80	0.021	0.019
25	10	10	0.005	0.004
		20	0.011	0.007
		40	0.023	0.015
		80	0.045	0.032
25	20	10	0.011	0.008
		20	0.023	0.014
		40	0.045	0.028
		80	0.091	0.060
50	5	10	0.007	0.005
		20	0.012	0.010
		40	0.023	0.021
		80	0.051	0.050
50	10	10	0.013	0.010
		20	0.025	0.018
		40	0.051	0.037
		80	0.100	0.076
50	20	10	0.026	0.018
		20	0.051	0.033
		40	0.098	0.066
		80	0.196	0.133

Table 2. A comparison on stretch constraint instances.

		stretch		regular	
nb of vars	nb of values	backtracks	time(s)	all supports time(s)	a support time(s)
25	3	2	0.002	0.003	0.006
	5	5	0.003	0.007	0.008
	7	40	0.006	0.015	0.013
	9	6	0.003	0.026	0.022
	11	183	0.019	0.039	0.035
50	3	4	0.007	0.007	0.008
	5	93	0.012	0.013	0.015
	7	15773	0.913	0.027	0.023
	9	34695	1.734	0.045	0.041
	11	512945	45.210	0.070	0.057
100	3	418729	62.178	0.014	0.017
	5	-	-	0.029	0.025
	7	-	-	0.051	0.051
	9	-	-	0.082	0.072
	11	-	-	0.129	0.108

Table 3. A comparison on pattern constraint instances.

nb of vars	shiftchange		regular	
			all supports	a support
	backtracks	time(s)	time(s)	time(s)
25	0	0.002	0.003	0.003
50	0	0.004	0.004	0.005
100	0.3	0.005	0.013	0.009

marked '−' indicate that several of the runs could not be solved within one hour of computing time. We observe that in cases where few backtracks are performed with stretch, that implementation is faster. But as soon as the instances become harder, that specialized implementation significantly falls behind in computation time. Comparing the two implementations of regular for stretch constraints, there is no clear dominance on these instances.

Table 3 reports on a few experiments with the pattern described in Example 2. It compares a sophisticated specialized filtering algorithm previously designed by the author to our versions of regular with the automaton of Figure 2. The specialized algorithm performs better on these instances but, as observed in the "backtracks" column, it does not achieve domain consistency. More difficult instances mixed with other constraints would probably provide a more accurate picture.

7 Conclusion

This paper introduced an expressive global constraint that can help model complex sequencing rules present in many problems. A filtering algorithm that achieves generalized arc consistency was described for the constraint. Its theoretical complexity was analyzed and its practical efficiency was demonstrated against other special purpose filtering algorithms. From a user interface point of view, it would probably benefit from front-ends designed for particular contexts (such as stretch or pattern constraints) that would feel more natural than a regular expression to the ordinary user and that would automatically translate it into the appropriate DFA.

Even though regular languages already offer a very rich formalism to express constraints on sequences of variables, as exemplified by the previous global constraints equivalently modeled by regular, we can actually go beyond regular languages with that same constraint. This is because the finiteness of the sequence of variables yields a finite language of finite strings. In the extreme, any finite language, regular or not, is easily given in extension as a regular expression. Hence membership can be enforced with a regular constraint. However the number of states needed in the automaton can become very large, making it inefficient to use that constraint for such a purpose. A natural question is whether membership constraints for richer formal languages, such as context-free grammars, could be efficiently implemented on sequences of finite-domain variable but the usefulness of their additional expressiveness should first be established.

Acknowledgements

The author wishes to thank Geneviève Hernu for implementing part of the constraint and conducting the experiments, and anonymous referees for their comments on an earlier version of this paper. This work was partially supported by the Canadian Natural Sciences and Engineering Research Council under grant OGP0218028.

References

1. J. Amilhastre, H. Fargier, and P. Marquis. Consistency Restoration and Explanations in Dynamic CSPs – Application to Configuration. *Artificial Intelligence*, 135:199–234, 2002.
2. M. Carlsson and N. Beldiceanu. Revisiting the Lexicographic Ordering Constraint. Technical Report T2002:17, SICS, 2002. 13 p.
3. C. Chang and R. Paige. From Regular Expressions to DFA's Using Compressed NFA's. *Theoretical Computer Science*, 178:1–36, 1997.
4. The Sequence Global Constraint of CHIP. Technical Report COSY/SEQ/032, COSYTEC, Orsay, France, 1999.
5. A. Colmerauer. An Introduction to PROLOG III. *Communications of the ACM*, 33(7):69–90, 1990.
6. K. Golden and W. Pang. Constraint Reasoning over Strings. In *Principles and Practice of Constraint Programming – CP 2003: Proceedings of the Ninth International Conference*, pages 377–391. Springer-Verlag LNCS 2833, 2003.
7. J. E. Hopcroft and J. D. Ullman. *Introduction to Automata Theory, Languages and Computation*. Addison Wesley, 1979.
8. ILOG S.A., Gentilly, France. *ILOG Solver Reference Manual, version 4.4*, 1999.
9. G. Pesant. A Filtering Algorithm for the Stretch Constraint. In *Principles and Practice of Constraint Programming – CP 2001: Proceedings of the Seventh International Conference*, pages 183–195. Springer-Verlag LNCS 2239, 2001.
10. G. Pesant. A Regular Language Membership Constraint for Sequences of Variables. In *Proc. Second International Workshop on Modelling and Reformulating Constraint Satisfaction Problems, Principles and Practice of Constraint Programming (CP'03)*, pages 110–119, Kinsale, Ireland, 2003.
11. A. Rajasekar. Applications in Constraint Logic Programming with Strings. In *Principles and Practice of Constraint Programming: Proc. Second International Workshop*, pages 109–122, Rosario, Orcas Island, Washington, USA, 1994. Springer-Verlag LNCS 874.
12. M.A. Trick. A Dynamic Programming Approach for Consistency and Propagation for Knapsack Constraints. *Annals of Operations Research*, 118:73–84, 2003.
13. N.R. Vempaty. Solving Constraint Satisfaction Problems Using Finite State Automata. In *Proc. National Conference on Artificial Intelligence (AAAI-92)*, pages 453–458. AAAI Press, 1992.
14. C. Walinsky. CLP(Σ^*): Constraint Logic Programming with Regular Sets. In *Proceedings of the Sixth International Conference on Logic Programming*, pages 181–196, Lisbon, Portugal, 1989. MIT Press.
15. B.W. Watson. A taxonomy of finite automata minimization algorithms. Technical Report Computing Science Note 93/44, Eindhoven University of Technology, The Netherlands, 1993.

Generating Robust Partial Order Schedules

Nicola Policella[1,*], Angelo Oddi[1], Stephen F. Smith[2], and Amedeo Cesta[1]

[1] Institute for Cognitive Science and Technology
Italian National Research Council
Rome, Italy
{policella,a.oddi,a.cesta}@istc.cnr.it
[2] The Robotics Institute
Carnegie Mellon University
Pittsburgh, PA, USA
sfs@cs.cmu.edu

Abstract. This paper considers the problem of transforming a resource feasible, fixed-times schedule into a *partial order schedule* (POS) to enhance its robustness and stability properties. Whereas a fixed-times schedule is brittle in the face of unpredictable execution dynamics and can quickly become invalidated, a POS retains temporal flexibility whenever problem constraints allow it and can often absorb unexpected deviation from predictive assumptions. We focus specifically on procedures for generating *Chaining Form POS*s, wherein activities competing for the same resources are linked into precedence chains. One interesting property of a Chaining Form POS is that it is "makespan preserving" with respect to its originating fixed-times schedule. Thus, issues of maximizing schedule quality and maximizing schedule robustness can be addressed sequentially in a two-step scheduling procedure. Using this approach, a simple chaining algorithm was recently shown to provide an effective basis for transforming good quality solutions into POSs with good robustness properties. Here, we investigate the possibility of producing POSs with better robustness and stability properties through more extended search in the space of Chaining Form POSs. We define two heuristics which make use of a structural property of chaining form POSs to bias chaining decisions. Experimental results on a resource-constrained project scheduling benchmark confirm the effectiveness of our approach.

1 Introduction

The usefulness of schedules in most practical scheduling domains is limited by their brittleness. Though a schedule offers the potential for a more optimized execution than would otherwise be obtained, it must in fact be executed as planned to achieve this potential. In practice, this is generally made difficult by a dynamic execution environment, where unexpected events quickly invalidate the schedule's predictive assumptions and bring into question the continuing validity of the schedule's prescribed actions. The lifetime of a schedule tends to be very short, and hence its optimizing advantages are generally not realized.

---

[*] Ph.D. student at the Department of Computer and Systems Science, University of Rome "La Sapienza", Italy.

Part of the schedule brittleness problem stems from reliance on a classical, fixed-times formulation of the scheduling problem, which designates the start and end times of activities as decision variables and requires specific assignments to verify resource feasibility. By instead adopting a graph formulation of the scheduling problem, wherein activities competing for the same resources are simply ordered to establish resource feasibility, it is possible to produce schedules that retain temporal flexibility where problem constraints allow. In essence, such a "flexible schedule" encapsulates a set of possible fixed-times schedules, and hence is equipped to accommodate some amount of executional uncertainty.

One important open question, though, is how to generate flexible schedules with good robustness properties. In [1] a two-stage approach to generating a flexible schedule is introduced as one possibility. Under this scheme, a feasible fixed-times schedule is first generated in stage one (in this case, an early start times solution), and then, in the second stage, a procedure referred to as *chaining* is applied to transform this fixed-times schedule into a temporally flexible schedule in so-called *Chaining Form*. Concepts similar to the idea of a *Chaining Form* schedule have also been used elsewhere: for example, the Transportation Network introduced in [2], and the Resource Flow Network described in [3] are based on equivalent structural assumptions. The common thread underlying these particular representations of the schedule is the characteristic that activities which require the same resource units are linked via precedence constraints into precedence chains. Given this structure, each constraint becomes more than just a simple precedence. It also represents a *producer-consumer* relation, allowing each activity to *know* the precise set of predecessors which will *supply* the units of resource it requires for execution. In this way, the resulting network of chains can be interpreted as a flow of resource units through the schedule; each time an activity terminates its execution, it passes its resource unit(s) on to its successors. It is clear that this representation is robust if and only if there is temporal slack that allows chained activities to move "back and forth".

In a recent paper [4], this approach – find a solution then make it flexible – was shown to produce schedules with better robustness properties than a more direct, least-commitment generation procedure. These results establish the basic viability of a chaining approach. At the same time, the procedure used in this work to produce a Chaining Form solution was developed simply to provide a means of transforming a given fixed-times schedule into a temporally flexible one. Although final solutions were evaluated with respect to various robustness properties, no attention was given to the potential influence of the chaining procedure itself on the properties exhibited by the final solution. In this paper, we examine the problem of generating a schedule in Chaining Form from the broader perspective of producing temporally flexible schedules with good robustness properties, and investigate the design of informed chaining procedures that exploit knowledge of these properties to increase the robustness of the final generated solution. We first establish basic properties that indicate the potential of extended search in the space of chaining solutions, and also show that a Chaining Form schedule is "makespan preserving" with respect to its originating fixed-times schedule. Then we define two heuristics explicitly designed to take advantage of *Chaining Form* analysis and to search for solutions with good robustness properties. Experimental results on resource-constrained project scheduling benchmark problems confirm the effectiveness of these search procedures. We begin by establishing a reference scheduling problem and summarizing the basic notion of schedule robustness that underlies our work.

2 Scheduling Problem

We adopt the Resource-Constrained Project Scheduling Problem with minimum and maximum time lags, RCPSP/max, as a reference problem [5]. The basic entities of interest in this problem are *activities*. The set of activities is denoted by $V = \{a_1, a_2, \ldots a_n\}$. Each activity has a fixed *processing time*, or *duration*, d_i. Any given activity must be scheduled without preemption.

A *schedule* is an assignment of start times to activities $a_1, a_2, \ldots a_n$, i.e. a vector $S = (s_1, s_2, \ldots, s_n)$ where s_i denotes the start time of activity a_i. The time at which activity a_i has been completely processed is called its *completion time* and is denoted by e_i. Since we assume that processing times are deterministic and preemption is not permitted, completion times are determined by:

$$e_i = s_i + d_i \tag{1}$$

Schedules are subject to two types of constraints, *temporal constraints* and *resource constraints*. In their most general form temporal constraints designate arbitrary minimum and maximum time lags between the start times of any two activities,

$$l_{ij}^{min} \leq s_j - s_i \leq l_{ij}^{max} \tag{2}$$

where l_{ij}^{min} and l_{ij}^{max} are the minimum and maximum time lag of activity a_j relative to a_i. A schedule $S = (s_1, s_2, \ldots, s_n)$ is *time feasible*, if all inequalities given by the activity precedences/time lags (2) and durations (1) hold for start times s_i.

During their processing, activities require specific resource units from a set $R = \{r_1 \ldots r_m\}$ of resources. Resources are *reusable*, i.e. they are released when no longer required by an activity and are then available for use by another activity. Each activity a_i requires of the use of req_{ik} units of the resource r_k during its processing time d_i. Each resource r_k has a limited capacity of c_k units.

A schedule is *resource feasible* if at each time t the demand for each resource $r_k \in R$ does not exceed its capacity c_k, i.e.

$$\sum_{s_i \leq t < e_i} req_{ik} \leq c_k. \tag{3}$$

A schedule S is called *feasible* if it is both time and resource feasible.

3 Robustness and Flexible Schedules

As indicated above, we are concerned with the generation of schedules that offer some degree of robustness in the face of a dynamic and uncertain execution environment. In any given scheduling domain, there can be different sources of executional uncertainty:

durations may not be exactly known, there may be less resource capacity than expected (e.g., due to machine breakdowns), or new tasks may need to be taken into account.

The concept of robustness has been approached from different perspectives in previous work. Some definitions of robustness have emphasized the ability to preserve some level of solution quality, such as preservation of makespan in [6, 3]. Alternatively, other work has considered robustness to be an execution-oriented quality. For example, in [7] robustness is defined as a property that is dependent on the repair action entailed by a given unexpected event. This view singles out two distinct, co-related aspects of robustness: the ability to keep pace with the execution (implying bounded computational cost) and the ability to keep the *evolving* solution stable (minimizing disruption). In fact a small perturbation to a scheduled event can, in general, cause a large ripple of changes through the current schedule.

Our view of robustness is also execution-oriented. We consider a solution to a scheduling problem to be *robust* if it provides two general features: (1) the ability to absorb external events without loss of consistency, and (2) the ability to keep the pace with execution. Our approach is to focus on generating flexible schedules, i.e., schedules that retain temporal flexibility. We expect a flexible schedule to be easy to change, and the intuition is that the degree of flexibility in such a schedule is indicative of its robustness. More precisely, our approach (see also [4]) adopts a graph formulation of the scheduling problem and focuses on generation of *Partial Order Schedules* ($POSs$). Within a POS, each activity retains a set of feasible start times, and these options provide a basis for responding to unexpected disruptions. An attractive property of a POS is that reactive response to many external changes can be accomplished via simple propagation in an underlying temporal network (a polynomial time calculation); only when an external change exhausts all options for an activity it is necessary to recompute a new schedule from scratch. Given this property and given a predefined horizon H, the *size* of a POS – the number of fixed-times schedules (or possible execution futures) that it "contains" – is suggestive of its overall robustness[1]. In general, the greater the size of a POS the more robust it is. Thus, our challenge is to generate $POSs$ of maximum possible size. Before considering this challenge we first define the notion of a Partial Order Schedule (POS) more precisely.

3.1 Partial Order Schedules

We represent a scheduling problem P as the graph $G_P(V_P, E_P)$, where the set of nodes $V_P = V \cup \{a_0, a_{n+1}\}$ consists of the set of activities specified in P and two dummy activities representing the origin (a_0) and the horizon (a_{n+1}) of the schedule, and the set of edges E_P contains P's temporal constraints between pairs of activities. In particular for each constraint of the form $l_{ij}^{min} \leq s_j - s_i \leq l_{ij}^{max}$, there is an edge $(a_i, a_j) \in E_P$ with label $[l_{ij}^{min}, l_{ij}^{max}]$.

A solution of the scheduling problem can be represented as an extension of G_P, where a set E_R of simple precedence constraints, $a_i \prec a_j$, is added to remove all the possible resource conflicts. In particular, let $F \subseteq V$ be any subset of activities such that there exists a time t where $\sum_{s_i \leq t < e_i} req_{ik} > c_k$. This subset is called a forbidden set

---

[1] The use of an horizon is justified by the need to compare $POSs$ of finite size.

[5] (or contention peak), and a *minimal forbidden set* (or resource conflict or *minimal critical set*) is a set $F_{min} \subseteq F$ such that each of its proper subsets is not a forbidden set. Any minimal forbidden set F_{min} is removed by adding a single precedence constraint between any pair of activities in F_{min}, and these additional constraints become the elements of E_R. Noting these concepts and recalling that a time feasible schedule is a schedule that satisfies all the constraints defined in (1) and (2), and a feasible schedule is a schedule that is both time and resource feasible, we can define a *Partial Order Schedule* as follows:

Given a scheduling problem, $G_P(V_P, E_P)$, a *Partial Order Schedule* is a graph $POS(V_P, E_P \cup E_R)$ such that any *time feasible* schedule is also a *feasible* schedule.

Before concluding, we introduce two further concepts which will be used in the remaining of the paper: the *earliest start schedule* of a POS, $ES(POS)$, is defined as the schedule $S = (s_1, s_2, \ldots, s_n)$ in which each activity is scheduled to start at its earliest start time, $s_i = est(a_i)$ for $1 \le i \le n$. Finally, the makespan of a POS is defined as the makespan of its earliest start schedule, that is, $mk(POS) = max_{a_i \in V}\{est(a_i) + d_i\}$.

4 Partial Order Schedules in Chaining Form: Basic Properties

In our previous work [1] we developed a two-stage procedure for generating a POS, based on generation and subsequent transformation of a "fixed-times" schedule. In this procedure, the second transformation step is accomplished by a *chaining* procedure, so called because fixed-times commitments are converted into sequences (chains) of activities to be executed by various resources. In [4], we showed this approach to be capable of generating POSs more efficiently than a least commitment POS generation procedure while simultaneously producing POSs with better robustness properties. These results indicate the potential of this two-stage approach for generating robust schedules. At the same time, the chaining procedure underlying this work was developed originally to provide a means for efficiently generating POSs.

Our goal in this section is to examine the concept of Chaining Form solutions from the broader perspective of generating robust POSs and to establish properties that can guide the development of chaining procedures capable of generating more robust POSs. We describe a canonical graph form, the Chaining Form POS^{ch}, for representing a POS and show that any given POS is expressible in this form. Thanks to this result we can restrict our attention to the design of procedures that explore the space of partial order schedules in chaining form, POS^{ch}. This will then be accomplished introducing a family of operators for transforming a generic fixed-times schedule into a partial order schedule in chaining form, POS^{ch}.

As introduced in [1], the concept of chaining form refers to a POS in which a *chain* of activities is associated with each unit of each resource. In the case of scheduling problems involving activities which require only a single unit of a resource, a solution is in a *chaining form* if for each unit j of a resource r_k it is possible to identify a set (possibly empty) of activities $\{a_{j,0}, a_{j,1}, \ldots, a_{j,N_j}\}$ such that $a_{j,i-1}$ will be executed before $a_{j,i}, a_{j,i-1} \prec a_{j,i}$ for $i = 1, \ldots, N_j$. This definition can be easily extended to the

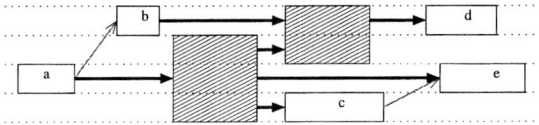

Fig. 1. A partial order schedule in chaining form.

general case where each activity can require one or more units of one or more resources. In such a case, any activity requiring $req_{ik} > 1$ resource units can be replaced with a set of req_{ik} activities (each requiring one unit) that are constrained to execute in parallel. As a consequence, in the general case, an activity will be allocated to as many chains as necessary to fulfill its resource requirements.

Figure 1 represents a partial order schedule in chaining form for a problem with a single resource r_k with capacity $c_k = 4$. The bold arcs represent the set of chains and the thin arcs designate further constraints defined in the problem. The size of each activity reflects both its duration and its resource requirement, respectively, the length represent the duration while the height the request. Hence, the gray activities will require more than one unit of resource. This implies that both of them will be allocated to more than one chain.

By definition, a solution in chaining form is a partial order schedule. It is also possible to prove that any partial order schedule POS admits at least an equivalent POS in chaining form[2].

Theorem 1. *Given a partial order schedule POS there exists a partial order schedule in chaining form, POS^{ch}, that represents at least the same set of solutions.*

Proof. Let $\overline{POS}(V_P, \overline{E})$ be the transitive closure of the graph POS, where $\overline{E} = E_P \cup E_R \cup E_T$ and E_T is the set of simple precedence constraints $a_h \prec a_l$ added to POS, when there is a precedence constraint between a_h and a_l induced by the constraints represented in the set $E_P \cup E_R$. It is always possible to construct a graph $POS^{ch}(V_P, E_P \cup E^{ch})$ with $E^{ch} \subseteq \overline{E}$ such that POS^{ch} represents at least the same set of solutions of POS. In fact, given the set $\overline{E}$, for each resource r_k, we can always select a subset of simple precedence constraints $E_k^{ch} \subseteq \overline{E}$ such that it induces a partition of the set of activities requiring the same resource r_k into a set of chains. In particular, for each resource r_k and unit j of resource r_k, it is possible to identify a set (possibly empty) of activities $\{a_{j,0}, a_{j,1}, \ldots, a_{j,n_j}\}$ such that $(a_{j,i-1}, a_{j,i}) \in E_k^{ch} \subseteq \overline{E}$ with $i = 1, \ldots, n_j$ and $E^{ch} = \bigcup_{k=1}^{m} E_k^{ch}$.

Proof by contradiction: let us assume as not possible the construction of such a POS^{ch}. Then, there is at least one resource r_k for which there is an activity a_k which does not belong to any chain of r_k. This means that there exists at least a set of mutual overlapping activities $\{a_{i1}, a_{i2}, \ldots, a_{ip}\}$, where each activity a_{ij} belongs to a different chain and $p = c_k$, such that the set $\{a_k, a_{i1}, a_{i2}, \ldots, a_{ip}\}$ represents a forbidden set. This last fact contradicts the hypothesis that POS is a partial order schedule. Thus, it is always possible to build a POS^{ch} from a POS with $E^{ch} \subseteq \overline{E}$. □

---

[2] An analogous result is proved in [3].

Chaining(P, S)
Input: A problem P and one of its fixed-times schedules S
Output: A partial order solution POS^{ch}
1. $POS^{ch} \leftarrow P$
2. Sort all the activities according to their start times in S
3. Initialize the all chains empty
4. **for each** resource r_j
5.   **for each** activity a_i
6.   **for** 1 **to** req_{ij}
7. $k \leftarrow SelectChain(a_i, r_j)$
8. $a_k \leftarrow last(k)$
9. $AddConstraint(POS^{ch}, a_k \prec a_i)$
10. $last(k) \leftarrow a_i$
11. **return** POS^{ch}

Fig. 2. Basic Chaining procedure.

Given this result, we can restrict our attention, without loss of generality, to the set of POSs which have a chaining form. Hence, a general operator for transforming a fixed-times schedule into a POS can be defined as follows:

Definition 1 (Chaining operator). *Given a fixed-times schedule S a chaining operator $ch()$ is an operator that applied to S returns a partial order schedule*

$$POS_S^{ch} = ch(S)$$

such that POS_S^{ch} is in chaining form and S is contained in the set of solution it describes.

Figure 2 describes a basic chaining operator. The first step sorts all activities according to their start times in the schedule S. Then the activities are incrementally allocated on the different chains. We note that in case where an activity requires more than one unit of one or more resources, it will be allocated to a number of chains equal to the overall number of resource units it needs. The function $SelectChain(a_i, r_j)$ is the core of the procedure; it can admit different definitions giving different results. A basic implementation chooses, for each activity, the first available chain of r_j. Given an activity a_i, a chain k is *available* if the end time of the last activity allocated on it, $last(k)$, is not greater than the start time of a_i. Note that since the input to a chaining operator is a consistent solution it will always be possible to find the chains that the activity a_i needs.

A chaining operator can be seen as a post-processing step which dispatches (or allocates) tasks to specific resource units once that a resource feasible (fixed-times) solution has been built. Given that a common objective of the first step in many scheduling domains will be to construct a feasible fixed-times solution that minimizes makespan, the following property plays an important role:

Property 1. Given a fixed-times schedule S and its POS_s^{ch}

$$mk(ES(POS_s^{ch})) \leq mk(S).$$

That is, the makespan of the earliest solution of POS_S^{ch} is not greater than the makespan of the input solution S.

By definition S is one of the solutions represented by POS_S^{ch} then $mk(ES(POS_S^{ch})) \leq mk(S)$. Practically, since only simple precedence constraints already contained in the input solution S are added, the makespan of the output solution will not be greater than the original one. Thus, in the case of a makespan objective, the robustness of a schedule can be increased without degradation to its solution quality.

5 Generating More Robust Schedules via Iterative Sampling

The chaining operator introduced in the previous section transforms a feasible fixed-times solution into a POS in chaining form by dispatching activites to specific resource units[3]. In the basic implementation shown in Fig. 2 this dispatching process is carried out in a specific deterministic manner; the $SelectChain(a_i, r_j)$ sub-procedure always dispatches the next activity a_i to the first available resource unit (chain) associated with its required resource r_j. However, since there are generally choices as to how to dispatch activities to resource units, it is possible to generate different POSs from a given initial fixed-times schedule, and these different POSs can be expected to have different robustness properties. In this section, we follow up on this observation, and define a set of procedures for searching this space of possible chaining solutions. The goal in each case is to maximize the size of the final POS produced by the chaining process. Given the results of the previous section, we can search this space of possible POS^{ch} with assurance that the "optimal" solution is reachable.

We adopt an Iterative Sampling search procedure as a basic framework for exploring the space of the possible POSs in chaining form. Specifically, the chaining operator described in Fig. 2 is executed n times starting from the same initial fixed-times solution, and non-determinism is added to the strategy used by $SelectChain(a_i, r_j)$ to obtain different POSs across iterations. Each POS generated is evaluated with respect to some designated measure of robustness, and the best POS found overall is returned at the end of the search. In Section 6.1 we describe the two metrics used in the actual implementation to approximate POS size, and explain why it is not possible to directly analyze the size of a POS.

As a baseline for comparison, we define an initial iterative search procedure in which $SelectChain(a_i, r_j)$ allocates activities to available chains in a completely random manner. Though this completely random iterative procedure will certainly examine a large number of candidate POS^{ch}s, it does so in an undirected way and this is likely to limit overall search effectiveness. A more effective procedure can be obtained by using a heuristic to bias the way in which chains are built.

To design a more informed heuristic for dispatching activities to chains, it is useful to examine the structure of solutions produced by the chaining procedure. Consider the example in Fig. 1. Note that both the activities requiring multiple resource units (the gray activities) and the precedence constraints between activities that are situated in different chains tie together the execution of different chains. These interdependencies, or *synchronization points*, tend to degrade the flexibility of a solution. In fact, if we consider each single chain as being executed as a separate process, each synchronization point will mutually constrain two, otherwise independent processes. When an

---
[3] Note that such a procedure is required to enable schedule execution.

unforeseen event occurs and must be taken into account, the presence of these points will work against the POS's ability to both absorb the event and retain flexibility for future changes. Hence it is desirable to minimize the number of synchronization points where possible.

A synchronization point can originate from one of two different sources:

- a constraint defined in the problem which relate pairs of activities belonging to different chains;
- an activity that requires two or more resource units and/or two or more resources will be part of two or more chains.

In the first case, the synchronzation point is strictly a consequence of the problem. However, in the second case, the synchronization point could follow from the way that the chains are built and might be preventable. For example, consider the POS given in Fig. 3. Here a more flexible solution than the one previously discussed in Fig. 1 is obtained by simply allocating the two gray activities to the same subset of chains. In the POS in Fig. 1 the two gray activities span all four chains. They effectively split the solution into two parts, and the whole execution phase will depend on the execution of these two activities. On the contrary, choosing to allocate these activities to common chains results in at least one chain that can be independently executed.

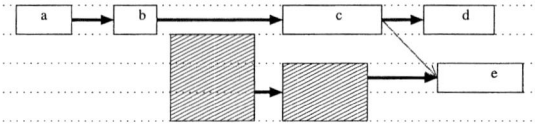

Fig. 3. A more flexible POS.

Based on this observation, we define a first heuristic chain selection procedure that favors allocation of activities to common chains. Under this procedure, allocation of an activity a_i proceeds according to the following four steps: **(1)** an initial chain k is randomly selected from among those available for a_i and the constraint $a_k \prec a_i$ is posted, where a_k is the last activity in chain k. **(2)** If a_i requires more than one resource unit, then the remaining set of available chains is split into two subsets: the set of chains which has a_k as last element, C_{a_k}, and the set of chains which does not, $\bar{C}_{a_k}$. **(3)** To satisfy all remaining resource requirements, a_i is allocated first to chains belonging to the first subset, $k' \in C_{a_k}$ and, **(4)** in case this set is not sufficient, the remaining units of a_i are then randomly allocated to the first available chains, k'', of the second subset, $k'' \in \bar{C}_{a_k}$.

To see the benefits of using this heuristic, let us reconsider once again the example in Fig. 1. As described above, the critical allocation decisions involve the two gray activities, which require 3 and 2 resource units respectively. If the first resource unit selected for the second gray activity happens to coincide with one that is already allocated to the first gray activity, then use of the above heuristic will force selection of a second common chain for the second gray activity. A possible result of using this heuristic chain selection procedure is in fact the POS in Fig. 3.

The example in Figure 3 allows us to show a second anomaly that can be observed in chaining form POSs. Notice the presence of a synchronization point due to the problem constraint between activity c and e. While such problem constraints cannot be eliminated, they can in fact be made redundant if both activities can be allocated to the same chain(s). This observation leads to the definition of a second heuristic chain selection procedure, which augments the first by replacing the random selection of the first chain for a given activity (step (1)) with a more informed choice that takes into account existing ordering relations with those activities already allocated in the chaining process. More precisely, step (1) of our first heuristic is replaced by the the following sequence of steps: **(1a)** the chains k for which their last element, $last(k)$, is already ordered wrt activity a_i, are collected in the set P_{a_i}. Then **(1b)** if $P_{a_i} \neq \emptyset$ a chain $k \in P_{a_i}$ is randomly picked, otherwise **(1c)** a chain k is randomly selected among the available ones. **(1d)** A constraint $a_k \prec a_i$ is posted, where a_k is the last activity of the chain k. At this point the procedure proceeds with the steps **(2)**, **(3)**, and **(4)** described above.

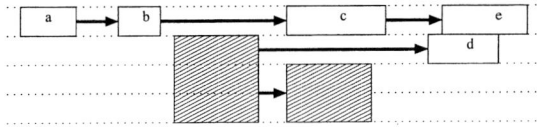

Fig. 4. A even more flexible POS.

Figure 4 shows the result of applying of this second heuristic chain selection procedure to our example. Since both activity c and activity e are dispatched to the same chain the synchronization point present in Fig. 3 is eliminated.

6 Experimental Evaluation

In this section we evaluate the performance of the algorithms proposed in Section 5 with respect to a set of metrics to evaluate both solution's robustness and stability. Our comparison is based on the benchmark $J30$ defined in [8], which consists of 270 problem instances with 30 activities and 5 resources. The remainder of this section is organized as follows. We first present two metrics which characterize robustness by approximating the size of a POS and discuss experimental results obtained relative to these metrics with various proposed algorithms. Next, we introduce a complementary metric that characterizes solution *stability* and additionally evaluate our experimental results with respect to this metric.

6.1 Measuring Robustness

As suggested earlier, a POS represents a set of temporal solutions that are also resource feasible, and this set provides a means for tolerating some amount of executional uncertainty. When an unexpected event occurs (e.g., a start time delay), the temporal propagation mechanism (a polynomial time calculation) can be applied to update the start times of all activities and, if at least one temporal solution remains viable, produces a new POS. Hence, it follows that within the same horizon H, the greater the number of solutions represented in a POS, the greater its robustness. It is worth noting that in order to have a finite number of solutions, we always assume that all activities in a given problem must be completed within a specified finite horizon. In particular, we consider a default horizon H imposed on each problem equal to the sum of all activity durations d_i and the sum of all the minimal time legs l_{ij}^{min}. Unfortunately counting the number of solutions in a POS is a #P-complete problem (e.g., see [9] page 330). For this reason, in the following section we will use two measures which are indirectly related to the number of solutions in a POS.

The first metric is taken from [1] and is defined as the average width, relative to the temporal horizon, of the temporal slack associated with each pair of activities (a_h, a_l):

$$fldt = \sum_{h \neq l} \frac{Slack(a_h, a_l)}{H \times n \times (n-1)} \times 100 \qquad (4)$$

where H is the horizon of the problem, n is the number of activities and $Slack(a_h, a_l)$ is the width of the allowed distance interval between the end time of activity a_h and the start time of activity a_l. This metric characterizes the *fluidity* of a solution, i.e., the ability to use flexibility to absorb temporal variation in the execution of activities. The higher the value of $fldt$, the less the risk of a "domino effect", i.e. the higher the probability of localized changes.

A second measure is taken from [10] and is called $flex$. This measure counts the *number of pairs of activities in the solution which are not reciprocally related by simple precedence constraints*. This metric provides an analysis of the configuration of the solution. The rationale for this measure is that when two activities are not related it is possible to move one without moving the other one. Hence, the higher the value of $flex$ the lower the degree of interaction among the activities.

6.2 Results

Table 1 summarizes the main results[4], in particular we compare the following three sets of chaining methods:

- the basic chaining operator as described in Figure 2, named CHN;
- the iterative sampling procedure which maximizes only the flexibility metric, $flex$. There are three different variants: the pure randomized version, IS_{flex}, the first heuristic biased version aimed at maximizing chain overlap between activities that require multiple resource units, ISH_{flex}, and the enhanced heuristic biased version which adds consideration of extant activity ordering constraints, ISH^2_{flex}.
- same as above with the difference that the optimized parameter is the fluidity, $fldt$. In this case the procedures are named IS_{fldt}, ISH_{fldt} and ISH^2_{fldt}.

---

[4] All algorithms presented in the paper are implemented in C++ on a Pentium 4-1,500 MHz processor under Linux OS.

Table 1. Performance of the algorithms.

	$flex$	$fldt$	cpu	npc	mk
CHN	7.0	27.4	5.4	38.7	107.1
IS_{flex}	7.7	28.8	82.7	44.8	106.8
ISH_{flex}	9.1	29.2	82.4	39.1	106.7
ISH^2_{fldt}	13.3	31.3	79.2	28.3	105.7
IS_{fldt}	7.3	29.3	74.8	44.7	106.1
ISH_{fldt}	8.5	30.3	72.0	39.6	106.4
ISH^2_{fldt}	12.8	32.3	69.1	28.9	105.4

The results shown in Table 1 are the average values obtained over the subset of solved problems in the $J30$ benchmark. For each procedure five parameters value are shown: the flexibility ($flex$), the fluidity ($fldt$), the CPU-time in seconds (cpu), the number of precedence constraints posted (npc) and the makespan (mk). With respect to CPU time, we include both the time to find an initial fixed-times solution and the time required by the chaining procedure. In the case of iterative procedures, the values shown reflect 100 iterations.

Analyzing the results, we first observe that all search procedures outperform the basic chaining procedure, it is clearly worthwhile to explore the space of possible POS^{ch} derivable from a given fixed-times solution S if the goal is to maximize solution robustness. In fact, all search strategies are also seen to produce some amount of improvement in solution makespan, an interesting side benefit. We further observe that the two heuristic strategies based on minimizing the number of synchronization points clearly outperform the basic iterative randomized procedure. The iterative sampling procedure with heuristic bias, ISH_{flex}, is able to improve 30% over the basic chaining results while the version using the enhanced heuristic, ISH^2_{flex}, obtains a gain of about 90% (from 7.0 to 13.3). The informed selection of the first chain thus is clearly a determining factor in achieving good quality solutions. These results are also confirmed by the corresponding procedures for the $fldt$ parameter. In this case, improvement ranges from about 10% for the first heuristic ISH_{fldt}, to about 18%, for ISH^2_{fldt}.

Another discriminating aspect of the performance of the enhanced heuristic ISH^2_{fldt} is its ability to take advantage of pre-existing precedence constraints and reduce the number of posted constraints[5] (see npc column in Table 1). This effect, as might have been predicted, was seen to improve both the fluidity and (especially) the flexibility values. Moreover, use of the enhanced heuristic also yielded the most significant reduction in solution makespan. Intuitively, the lower number of constraints may contribute to compression of the critical path. On the other side of the coin, use of the iterative procedure incurs a non negligible additional computational cost.

Figure 5 highlights a further aspect which differentiates the heuristic biased iterative procedures from the pure randomized procedure. This picture plots the value of the best solution found by each iterative procedure as the search progresses (with respect to the number of iterations). Fig. 5(a) represents the results obtained when the metric

---

[5] Note that in any of the chaining methods a precedence constraint $a_k \prec a_i$ is posted iff a_k and a_i are not ordered already.

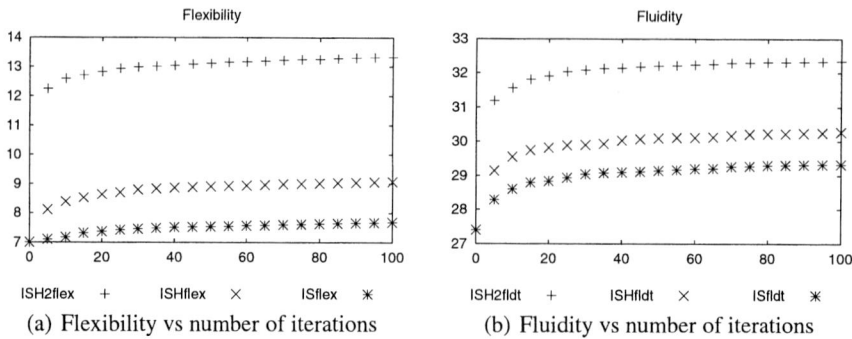

Fig. 5. Iterative sampling's efficiency.

$flex$ is taken into account while in Fig. 5(b) the procedures aim at optimizing the $fldt$ value. The heuristic biased procedures are seen to find better solutions at a much faster rate than the basic randomized procedure, and quickly reach solutions better than the best solutions generated by the basic randomized procedure (as shown in Table 1). For instance the best solution obtained by ISH_{flex} after 10 iterations is higher quality than the solution obtained by IS_{flex} after 100 iterations (see Fig. 5(a)); likewise, ISH^2_{flex} (ISH^2_{fldt}) are able to obtain better solutions that can be obtained by any other procedures in just a few iterations. It is clear that the use of heuristic bias focuses the search on a more significant region of the search space for both robustness metrics, and that this bias both accelerates and enhances generation of better solutions.

6.3 Evaluating Schedule Stability

As introduced in the first part of the work, it is possible to take a different point of view in maximizing the robustness of a POS: we can search for a *stable set of solutions*. That is, we search for a POS that is both (1) capable of finding new start time assignments for all activities consistent with the new constraints imposed by an exogenous event (exhibiting robustness), and (2) capable of *absorbing* the modification (minimizing its broader impact). For example, suppose that the start time s_i of the activity a_i is delayed by Δ_{in}. Then we would like the average delay of other activities Δ_{out} to be much much smaller: $\Delta_{out} \ll \Delta_{in}$. To evaluate the stability of a solution we consider a single type of modification event: the start time s_i of a single activity a_i with *window* of possible start times $[est(a_i), lst(a_i)]$ is increased to a value $s_i + \alpha w_i/100$, where $0 \leq \alpha \leq 100$ and $w_i = lst(a_i) - est(a_i)$. In the following we give a definition of *stability* and reevaluate the same results obtained in the previous section with respect to this metric. Our goal is to understand the correlations with other proposed metrics.

A more operative definition of stability is given by the following formula:

$$stby(\alpha) = \frac{1}{n(n-1)} \sum_{i=1}^{n} \sum_{\substack{j=1 \\ j \neq i}}^{n} \frac{\delta_j(\alpha)}{w_i} \qquad (5)$$

Table 2. Evaluation of the stability (percentage value).

α	CHN	ISH_{fldt}	ISH^2_{fldt}	ISH_{flex}	ISH^2_{flex}	LB
1	0.09	0.08	0.07	0.08	0.07	0.05
2	0.29	0.27	0.24	0.27	0.25	0.15
4	0.89	0.82	0.76	0.82	0.77	0.48
8	2.51	2.34	2.22	2.33	2.21	1.48
16	6.59	6.26	6.01	6.14	5.93	4.33
25	11.78	11.28	10.85	11.00	10.68	8.14
50	27.42	26.43	25.37	25.66	24.92	19.84
75	43.67	42.22	40.43	40.91	39.68	32.06
100	**60.18**	58.24	55.69	56.40	**54.65**	44.42

where the stability $stby(\alpha)$ is defined as the average value $\frac{\delta_j(\alpha)}{w_i}$ over all pairs (a_i, a_j), with $a_i \neq a_j$, when an increase of start time $\alpha w_i/100$ is performed on each activity start time separately. We observe that the single value $\frac{\delta_j(\alpha)}{w_i}$ represents the relative increment of the start time of the activity a_j (the absolute value is $\delta_j(\alpha)$) when the start time of the activity a_i is increased to the value $s_i + \alpha w_i/100$. Note that, by definition, the $stby(\alpha)$ value is included in the interval $[0, 1]$.

Table 2 compares the values of the function $stby(\alpha)$ for different values of α (*disruption*). We compare five sets of data: the stability of the solutions obtained with the application of the chaining operator, CHN, and the stability obtained with the procedures ISH_{fldt}, ISH_{flex}, ISH^2_{fldt}, ISH^2_{flex}. To enable a better evaluation lower bound values are also given. These are calculated using the initial partial order (i.e. the input problem) without any additional resource constraints. As can be seen, the stability of the set of $J30$ solutions improves over the simple chaining results and the best improvement is obtained with the procedure ISH^2_{fldt}: when the disruption α reaches the maximal value ($\alpha = 100$) the value of the stability is reduced from 60% to about 54%. These results indicate that the solutions generated by the iterative procedures, in addition to exhibiting good properties with respect to solution flexibility, also do not exhibit any negative side-effects with respect to solution stability.

7 Conclusion and Future Work

In this paper, we have considered the problem of transforming a resource feasible, fixed-times schedule into a *Partial Order Schedule* (*POS*) to enhance its robustness and stability properties. Unlike other related work in this area [2, 3], we consider a complex problem, RCPSP/max, that is not polynomially solvable, and hence enhances the need for flexible solutions.

We focused specifically on the problem of generating *POS*s in *Chaining Form*, where activities competing for the same resources are linked into precedence chains. The paper pointed out two basic properties: (1) that a given *POS* can always be represented in Chaining Form; and (2) that chaining - the process of constructing a Chaining Form *POS* - is makespan preserving with respect to an input schedule. As a consequence, issues of maximizing schedule makespan and maximizing schedule robustness can be addressed sequentially in a two-step scheduling procedure.

On the basis of the first property, we considered the possibility of producing POSs with better robustness and stability properties through more extended search in the space of Chaining Form POSs. In particular, three iterative sampling procedures for chaining are proposed: the first one simply randomizes the choices made by a simple chaining algorithm; the remaining two take account of structural properties of more robust Chaining Form POSs to heuristically bias chaining decisions. To evaluate these procedures, we developed metrics for assessing the robustness and stability of a generated POS. Experimental results on a set of challenging resource constrained project scheduling benchmarks were shown to confirm the effectiveness of the approach. In general, consideration of Chaining Form POSs emphasizes the presence of synchronization points as obstacles to flexibility, and this fact can be exploited to generate POSs with good robustness properties.

Several directions can be mentioned for future work. One is to study the possibility of further enhancing the flexibility of a Chaining Form solution by dropping the requirement that each chain be totally ordered and instead allow specific subsets of activities allocated to a given chain to remain unordered (and permutable as execution circumstances dictate). The work of [11] provides a starting point for considering this sort of extension. A second possibility for future research is the definition of broader search strategies that use a chaining operator as a core component. In fact, the result obtained by any chaining operator is biased by the initial solution that seeds the chaining procedure. From this perspective, one point to investigate is the relation between the initial solution and the partial order schedule which can be obtained through chaining.

Acknowledgments

Stephen F. Smith's work is supported in part by the Department of Defense Advanced Research Projects Agency and the U.S. Air Force Research Laboratory - Rome, under contracts F30602-00-2-0503 and F30602-02-2-0149, by the National Science Foundation under contract # 9900298 and by the CMU Robotics Institute. Amedeo Cesta, Angelo Oddi, and Nicola Policella's work is partially supported by ASI (Italian Space Agency) under project ARISCOM (Contract I/R/215/02).

We would like to thank an anonymous reviewer for several comments that helped us to improve the presentation.

References

1. Cesta, A., Oddi, A., Smith, S.F.: Profile Based Algorithms to Solve Multiple Capacitated Metric Scheduling Problems. In: Proceedings of AIPS-98. (1998)
2. Artigues, C., Roubellat, F.: A polynomial activity insertion algorithm in a multi-resource schedule with cumulative constraints and multiple modes. European Journal of Operational Research **127** (2000) 297–316
3. Leus, R., Herroelen, W.: Stability and Resource Allocation in Project Planning. IIE Transactions **36** (2004) 667–682
4. Policella, N., Smith, S.F., Cesta, A., Oddi, A.: Generating Robust Schedules through Temporal Flexibility. In: Proceedings of ICAPS'04. (2004)

5. Bartusch, M., Mohring, R.H., Radermacher, F.J.: Scheduling project networks with resource constraints and time windows. Annals of Operations Research **16** (1988) 201–240
6. Leon, V., Wu, S., Storer, R.: Robustness measures and robust scheduling for job shops. IIE Transactions **26** (1994) 32–43
7. Ginsberg, M.L., Parkes, A.J., Roy, A.: Supermodels and Robustness. In: Proceedings of AAAI-98. (1998)
8. Kolisch, R., Schwindt, C., Sprecher, A.: Benchmark instances for project scheduling problems. In Weglarz, J., ed.: Project Scheduling - Recent Models, Algorithms and Applications. Kluwer, Boston (1998) 197–212
9. Motwani, R., Raghavan, P.: Randomized Algorithms. Cambridge University Press (1995)
10. Aloulou, M.A., Portmann, M.C.: An Efficient Proactive Reactive Scheduling Approach to Hedge against Shop Floor Disturbances. In: Proceedings of MISTA 2003. (2003)
11. Artigues, C., Billaut, J., Esswein, C.: Maximization of solution flexibility for robust shop scheduling. European Journal of Operational Research (2004) To appear.

Full Dynamic Substitutability by SAT Encoding

Steven Prestwich

Cork Constraint Computation Centre
Department of Computer Science
University College, Cork, Ireland
s.prestwich@cs.ucc.ie

Abstract. Symmetry in constraint problems can be exploited to greatly improve search performance. A form of symmetry that has been the subject of considerable research is value interchangeability. Automatically detecting full interchangeability is thought to be intractable, so research has focused on either discovery of local interchangeability or programmer knowledge of full interchangeability. This paper shows that full dynamic substitutability can be broken in a CSP by reformulating it as a SAT problem. No analysis is necessary, space requirements are modest, solutions are collected into Cartesian products, and unit propagation enforces forward checking on the CSP. In experiments on unsatisfiable problems, better results are obtained than with standard SAT encodings.

1 Introduction

Many important problems in AI can be formulated as constraint satisfaction problems (CSPs). A CSP is a triple (V, D, C) where V is a set of variables, D the set of their domains, and C a set of constraints on the variables that specify the permitted combinations of assignments of domain values to subsets of the variables, or equivalently the forbidden combinations. CSPs are usually solved by search algorithms that alternate backtracking with some form of constraint propagation, for example forward checking or arc consistency.

Constraint problems often exhibit symmetries, and a great deal of research has recently been devoted to *symmetry breaking* techniques for reducing search space size. The most straightforward approach is to add constraints to the problem formulation, so that each equivalence class of solutions to the original problem corresponds to a single solution in the new problem [28]. Alternatively symmetries may be detected and exploited dynamically during search [2, 14, 17, 18]. Symmetries may also be used to guide search to a solution [24]. A form of symmetry that has received considerable attention is Freuder's notion of *value interchangeability* [15], sometimes called a *syntactic symmetry* [5]:

Definition. *A value a for variable v is fully interchangeable with value b if and only if every solution in which $v = a$ remains a solution when b is substituted for a and vice-versa [15].*

If two values are interchangeable then one of them can be removed from the domain, reducing the size of the problem; alternatively they can be replaced by a single meta-value, or bundled together in a Cartesian product representation of the search space. Each of these approaches avoids revisiting equivalent solutions. However, computing fully interchangeable values is believed to be intractable [8, 13, 15, 34] so local forms such as *neighbourhood interchangeability* are much more commonly used:

Definition. *A value a for variable v is neighbourhood interchangeable with value b if and only if for every constraint on v, the values compatible with $v = a$ are exactly those compatible with $v = b$ [15].*

Freuder further defined a hierarchy of local k-interchangeabilities such that neighbourhood interchangeability is equivalent to 2-interchangeability and full interchangeability to n-interchangeability, where n is the number of variables, and described an algorithm for computing k-interchangeable values that takes time exponential in k. Several further types of interchangeability were defined in [15] and subsequently by other researchers. In particular:

Definition. *A value a for variable v is fully substitutable with value b if and only if every solution in which $v = a$ remains a solution when b is substituted for a (but not necessarily vice-versa) [15].*

Substitutability is weaker than interchangeability. Note that the term *weaker* is used in the interchangeability literature to mean *achieves more problem reduction*; the weakness refers to the preconditions under which interchangeability can be exploited. Again because substitutable values are expensive to compute, *neighbourhood substitutability* (with the obvious definition) is more commonly used. Another variant is:

Definition. *A value a for variable v is dynamically interchangeable for b with respect to a set A of variable assignments if and only if they are fully interchangeable in the subproblem induced by A [15].*

Values may become interchangeable or substitutable during backtrack search after some variables have been instantiated, so even a problem with no interchangeable values may exhibit dynamic interchangeability under some search strategy. We may also define an even weaker variant which is not explicitly mentioned in [15], but is a natural generalisation of full substitutability and dynamic interchangeability:

Definition. *A value a for variable v is dynamically substitutable with value b with respect to a set A of variable assignments if and only if a is fully substitutable for b in the subproblem induced by A.*

The contribution of this paper is to show that (full) dynamic substitutability can be exploited in any CSP without expensive analysis. Surprisingly, this can be done statically for all search trees via a simple automatic reformulation of the CSP. The paper is organised as follows. Section 2 defines the reformulation and analyses its properties. Section 3 evaluates it on colouring benchmarks. Section 4 reviews related work. Section 5 concludes the paper and discusses future work.

2 The Maximal Encoding

This section describes a new reformulation of the CSP to a problem in propositional satisfiability (SAT). The SAT problem is to determine whether a Boolean expression has a satisfying set of truth assignments. The problems are usually expressed in conjunctive normal form: a conjunction of clauses $C_1 \wedge C_2 \wedge \ldots$ where each clause is a disjunction of literals $l_1 \vee l_2 \vee \ldots$ and each literal is either a Boolean variable v or its negation $\neg v$. A Boolean variable can be assigned the value *true* (T) or *false* (F). SAT problems can be viewed as CSPs with binary domains, for example a clause $a \vee b \vee \bar{c}$ is a constraint forbidding the assignments ($a = F$, $b = F$, $c = T$). We first focus on binary CSPs then discuss non-binary problems.

2.1 Three Known Encodings

A binary CSP can be reformulated as a SAT problem (*SAT encoded*) in a variety of ways. The most natural and widely-used encoding is the *direct encoding* [33]. A SAT variable x_{vi} is defined as true if and only if the CSP variable v is assigned value i, where i and j denote values in the domain $\{1, \ldots, d\}$ of v. The direct encoding consists of three sets of clauses. Each CSP variable must take at least one domain value, expressed by *at-least-one* (ALO) clauses $x_{v1} \vee x_{v2} \vee \ldots \vee x_{vd}$. No CSP variable can take more than one domain value, expressed by *at-most-one* (AMO) clauses $\bar{x}_{vi} \vee \bar{x}_{vj}$. Conflicts ($v = i$, $w = j$) are enumerated by *conflict* (CON) clauses $\bar{x}_{vi} \vee \bar{x}_{wj}$.

A well-known variant of the direct encoding contains no AMO clauses and often improves local search performance. This is also often called the direct encoding, but to avoid ambiguity we shall refer to it as the *multivalued encoding*. In this encoding there is no longer a 1–1 correspondence between SAT and CSP solutions: from a multivalued SAT solution we extract a CSP solution by taking any one of the allowed values for each CSP variable.

The *support encoding* encodes support instead of conflict [16]. It consists of ALO, AMO and *support* (SUP) clauses: if $i_1 \ldots i_k$ are the supporting values in the domain of CSP variable v for value j in the domain of CSP variable w, then there is a support clause $x_{vi_1} \vee \ldots \vee x_{vi_k} \vee \bar{x}_{wj}$. The interest of this encoding is that unit propagation performs arc-consistency in the CSP, whereas on the direct encoding it performs only forward checking (unit propagation is the main or only inference rule in many SAT backtrackers). It has been shown to give better search performance than the direct encoding on some CSPs [16]. It can also be generalised to non-binary CSPs and to other forms of consistency [7].

2.2 The New Encoding

Recall that the direct encoding is the multivalued encoding plus AMO clauses. Our new encoding is the multivalued encoding plus clauses of the form $x_{vi} \lor \bigvee_{(w,j) \in K_{vi}} x_{wj}$ for each variable v and value i, where K_{vi} is the set of pairs (w, j) such that there exists a conflict $(v = i, w = j)$. We call these *maximality* (MAX) clauses because they force a maximal number of assignments to each variable: if no assignment to another variable conflicts with an assignment $v = a$ then $v = a$ is forced to be part of the SAT solution. Whereas AMO clauses prevent two CSP solutions from being part of the same SAT solution, MAX clauses collect them together in the same SAT solution. We call the new encoding consisting of the ALO, CON and MAX clauses the *maximal encoding*. Maximal encoding SAT solutions are Cartesian products of partial domains such that any combination of values is a solution, and no further values can be added to the product. From such a solution we extract a CSP solution in the same way as from the multivalued encoding: take any allowed value for each CSP variable.

As an example consider the vertex colouring problem in Figure 1, used in [15] to illustrate the difference between full and local interchangeability. The boxes represent vertices a, b, c, d and the lines represent the arcs of the graph, while the numbers in the boxes are the available colours for the vertices. Each vertex corresponds to a CSP variable, each arc to a disequality constraint, and the colours to the variable domains. Colours 1, 2 and 3 for vertex a are fully interchangeable: in any solution d must be 1 so b and c cannot be 1, and values 2 and 3 are not in the domains of b and c. However, the colours are not neighbourhood interchangeable because $a = 1$ does not satisfy the constraint $a \neq b$ for all values of b: it conflicts with $b = 1$. Thus neighbourhood interchangeability cannot improve this problem, but our technique should be able to because it exploits full interchangeability (and more). The maximal encoding of the problem is also shown in Figure 1. This SAT problem has exactly one solution, breaking all symmetries: the Cartesian product $\{1, 2, 3\} \times \{4, 5\} \times \{4, 5\} \times \{1\}$ for variables a, b, c, d. A loosely-constrained CSP with 12 solutions has been reformulated to a tightly-constrained SAT problem with 1 solution.

Note that a CSP solution may be contained in more than one SAT solution. For example consider another vertex colouring problem with two adjacent vertices v, w where v has two available colours $\{1, 2\}$ and w has two available colours $\{2, 3\}$. This problem has three colourings: $[v = 1, w = 2]$, $[v = 1, w = 3]$ and $[v = 2, w = 3]$. The maximal encoding of this problem has two SAT solutions $\{1\} \times \{2, 3\}$ and $\{1, 2\} \times \{3\}$ for v, w. Each contains two colourings but $[v = 1, w = 3]$ occurs in both.

2.3 Properties

First we show that the new encoding breaks a very weak form of interchangeability. We use the term "break" from the symmetry literature even though substitutability is not a symmetry but a dominance relation, and though related solutions are collected together into Cartesian products instead of being excluded. The point is that the related solutions are not generated individually.

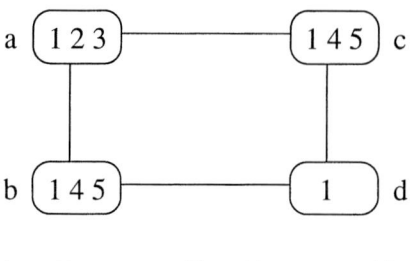

ALO: $x_{a1} \lor x_{a2} \lor x_{a3}$ $x_{b1} \lor x_{b4} \lor x_{b5}$ $x_{c1} \lor x_{c4} \lor x_{c5}$ x_{d1}
CON: $\bar{x}_{a1} \lor \bar{x}_{b1}$ $\bar{x}_{a1} \lor \bar{x}_{c1}$ $\bar{x}_{b1} \lor \bar{x}_{d1}$ $\bar{x}_{c1} \lor \bar{x}_{d1}$
MAX: $x_{a1} \lor x_{b1} \lor x_{c1}$ x_{a2} x_{a3}
         $x_{b1} \lor x_{a1} \lor x_{d1}$ x_{b4} x_{b5}
         $x_{c1} \lor x_{a1} \lor x_{d1}$ x_{c4} x_{c5}
         $x_{d1} \lor x_{c1} \lor x_{b1}$

Fig. 1. A vertex colouring example and its maximal encoding.

Theorem. *The maximal encoding breaks all dynamic substitutabilities.*

Proof. Suppose that, under some partial assignment A, value a is fully substitutable for value b in the domain of variable v. Clearly for any solution S containing assignments $v = a$ and A, no assignment conflicts with $v = a$ (because S is a solution). By substitutability we can replace $v = a$ by $v = b$ to get another solution S', so no S assignment conflicts with $v = b$. Therefore any maximal encoding representation of S also contains the assignment $v = b$, so S and S' are collected together in the same maximal encoding solution. This holds for arbitrary A and thus in any search tree. □

Thus the maximal encoding also breaks all stronger variants including dynamic interchangeability, full substitutability and full interchangeability. The next two theorems establish the correctness and completeness of the encoding.

Theorem. *Taking any of the allowed values for each CSP variable under the maximal encoding yields a CSP solution.*

Proof. In a maximal encoding solution no clause is violated, including the CON and ALO clauses. So each CSP variable is assigned a value and none of the assignments are in conflict. □

Theorem. *Every CSP solution occurs in at least one maximal encoding solution.*

Proof. Given a CSP solution we can construct a maximal encoding solution in which it occurs. We do this in three steps. (i) For each CSP assignment $v = i$ set x_{vi} to true. (ii) Set to true any false x_{vi} such that there is no constraint $(v = i, w = j)$ with x_{wj} true; repeat until no such x_{vi} remain. (iii) Set all other x_{vi} to false. These assignments violate no ALO clause because each v has some

x_{vi} set to true. Assignments (i) violate no CON clause because they derive from a CSP solution, (ii) violate no CON clause by construction, and (iii) violate no CON clauses because they are all false assignments and CON clauses contain only negated literals. Finally, suppose that a MAX clause $x_{vi} \vee \bigvee_{(w,j) \in K_{vi}} x_{wj}$ is violated. Then x_{vi} and the x_{wj} are false. But x_{vi} satisfies the condition in (ii) for setting to true, so it cannot be false. This contradiction shows that all MAX clauses are satisfied, so we have constructed a SAT solution under the maximal encoding. This contains the assignments representing the CSP solution, so the CSP solution is contained in the maximal encoding solution. □

Recall that unit propagation on the direct encoding performs forward checking on the CSP, while on the support encoding it performs arc consistency:

Theorem. *Unit propagation on the maximal encoding performs forward checking on the CSP.*

Proof. Take any partial assignment A on the CSP variables and any domain value a for an unassigned variable v. If forward checking on A prunes a from the domain of v then there must be an assignment $w = b$ in A and a constraint $(v = a, w = b)$, for some variable w and value b. But this constraint must correspond to a CON clause $\bar{x}_{va} \vee \bar{x}_{wb}$. Moreover $w = b$ under A so x_{wb} is true. Then unit propagation on the CON clause forces x_{va} to be false. □

The space complexity of the encoding is as follows. Given a CSP with n variables, d domain values and c constraints. There are n ALO clauses of size d, nd^2 AMO clauses of size 2, cd^2 CON clauses of size 2, nd MAX clauses of size c, and cd SUP clauses of size d. Therefore in terms of the number of literals the direct and support encodings both have space complexity $O(nd^2 + cd^2)$ while the maximal encoding has $O(nd^2 + cdn)$. For problems in which $n \gg d$ (for example vertex 3-colouring) the maximal encoding therefore has higher space complexity, but is otherwise comparable. In our experiments we will present data on encoding sizes.

2.4 Extension to Non-binary Problems

Neighbourhood interchangeability has recently been extended to non-binary CSPs [22]. We now show that the new encoding can also be generalised to handle non-binary constraints (for space reasons we do not provide proofs). An obvious way is first to transform the CSP to binary form, which is always possible [1, 30]. However, performance is sometimes better on non-binary models, so we extend the encoding to non-binary CSPs. CON clauses may now have more than two literals, and the MAX clauses are replaced by expressions of the form $x_{vi} \vee \bigvee_{c \in C_{vi}} \left(\bigwedge_{(w,j) \in A_{vic}} x_{wj} \right)$ for each variable v and value i, where C_{vi} is the set of conflicts c involving $v = i$, and A_{vic} is the set of pairs (w, j) such that there exists an assignment $w = j$ in c (with w and v distinct variables). A generalised SAT solver such as [32] could handle these expressions directly but standard solvers require conjunctive normal form. Expanding the expression to conjunctive normal form yields a number of clauses that is exponential in the constraint arity, so instead we define an auxiliary variable $a_{vic} \leftrightarrow \bigwedge_{(w,j) \in A_{vic}} x_{wj}$ for each variable v, value i and conflict $c \in C_{vi}$, and substitute these definitions in the MAX clauses to obtain $x_{vi} \lor \bigvee_{c \in C_{vi}} a_{vic}$. The encoding consists of CON, ALO and the new MAX clauses, plus clauses derived from the auxiliary variable definitions.

3   Experimental Results

To evaluate the maximal encoding we compare it with the direct and support encodings on a set of binary CSPs. We use vertex colouring problems and a generalisation called *bandwidth colouring*, in which two adjacent vertices i and j cannot be assigned colours that are closer in value than a specified distance d_{ij}. The constraints are conflicting assignments ($v_i = c_i$, $v_j = c_j$) where i and j are adjacent and $|c_i - c_j| < d_{ij}$. In pure vertex colouring all distances are 1. Problems are taken from a recent graph colouring symposium[1], which have the advantages that they are publicly available, were not designed with interchangeability in mind, and are of several types: the DSJC and R graphs are randomly generated, the mulsol and zeroin graphs are based on register allocation for variables in real codes, the miles graphs are geometric and based on distances between US cities, the GEOM graphs are geometric and based on randomly placed points in a square, the queen graphs are derived from the N-queens problem, the myciel graphs are based on the Mycielski transformation and are triangle-free, the school graph is a school timetabling problem, and the "book graphs" anna–jean are derived from the relationships between characters in works of literature.

The search algorithm we use is Chaff [25], the first of the latest generation of fast SAT backtrackers. Chaff is deterministic and does not allow results to be averaged over multiple runs. However, it has been shown [10] that such solvers can vary significantly in performance if SAT problems are randomly transformed, for example by permuting variable names or randomly selecting a variable and flipping all its occurrences in the problem. These transformations do not affect the solvability or intrinsic hardness of a problem, and can be used to find average behaviour of deterministic solvers. They are also used in solver competitions; for details on them see [10]. We applied them and took median results over 100 runs of Chaff.

On satisfiable problems, with the number of colours K set sufficiently high for colourability, results were erratic. Chaff found a first solution for myciel7 a few times more quickly under the maximal than under the direct and support encodings, but this was an exception and it usually took longer. However, this was offset by the fact that the SAT solutions combined several colourings as a Cartesian product. For space reasons we do not present a table of figures but mention some results: under the maximal encoding Chaff took an order of

---

[1] http://mat.gsia.cmu.edu/COLOR04

magnitude longer to find 12 11-colourings for queen9_9gb than it took to find 1 11-colouring under the support or direct encodings; it took an order of magnitude longer to find 200 5-colourings for DSJC125.1gb; slightly longer to find 25,000 5-colourings for R75_1gb; an order of magnitude longer to find 10^{14} 33-colourings for GEOM60; a few times longer to find 10^{24} 8-colourings for miles250; and three orders of magnitude longer to find 10^{67} 11-colouring for anna. These results indicate that the new encoding might be more useful for finding all solutions.

Unfortunately Chaff does not provide all-solution search except in the special case of unsatisfiable problems, so we set K low enough to make each problem unsatisfiable. Figures 2 and 3 compare encodings on uncolourable vertex and bandwidth problems respectively. Note that there is no point in applying the support encoding to pure vertex colouring because arc consistency is no more powerful than forward checking on disequality constraints [7], so only the direct

graph	K	direct			maximal		
		bt	sec	literals	bt	sec	literals
DSJC125.5	7	7368	2.3	60599	**2145**	**0.5**	110698
DSJC125.9	7	**2695**	**0.7**	103579	2574	1.3	196658
DSJC250.9	8	9442	5.7	462352	**7623**	**5.4**	896704
mulsol.i.1	7	5667	1.8	64603	**4119**	**1.9**	112245
mulsol.i.2	7	9055	3.6	63602	**4413**	**1.8**	111307
mulsol.i.3	7	9598	3.9	63840	**5070**	**2.3**	112154
mulsol.i.4	7	8073	3.2	64309	**5241**	**2.3**	113008
mulsol.i.5	7	7388	2.8	64736	**4880**	**2.1**	113778
zeroin.i.1	7	3648	**1.2**	67739	**3067**	1.5	117159
zeroin.i.2	7	5497	2.3	59913	**2414**	**1.0**	101724
zeroin.i.3	7	5337	2.2	59654	**2415**	**1.0**	101661
anna	8	**8196**	**2.8**	**16720**	18714	13	17984
david	8	5616	1.5	**12064**	**4130**	**1.0**	14384
homer	8	**7861**	**3.1**	61952	17709	14	**61032**
huck	8	5947	1.7	**9552**	**3506**	**0.6**	10816
jean	8	**5803**	**1.4**	9184	6285	1.5	**9384**
miles500	7	**2834**	**0.5**	**22652**	7769	6.2	34552
miles750	8	**8484**	**3.8**	**42000**	9076	3.9	69664
miles1000	8	20676	21	59648	**5221**	**2.3**	104960
miles1500	8	33175	44	**91360**	**5875**	**4.7**	168384
queen8_12	8	20785	15.3	**28032**	**9193**	**3.2**	45312
queen9_9	8	12055	5.3	**22080**	**4557**	**0.9**	35088
queen10_10	8	20256	19	**29920**	**6197**	**1.5**	48640
queen11_11	8	14926	8.3	**39424**	**4635**	**0.9**	65296
queen12_12	8	29068	36	**50752**	**6340**	**1.9**	85376
myciel5	4	13152	**1.0**	**2640**	6716	1.1	4152
myciel6	4	26212	**5.1**	**7560**	14148	4.7	12840
myciel7	4	31565	**8.9**	**21936**	18582	10	39288
school	7	4341	**1.3**	**286195**	**3659**	1.4	540050

Fig. 2. Results on unsatisfiable vertex colouring problems.

		direct			support			maximal		
graph	K	bt	sec	literals	bt	sec	literals	bt	sec	literals
GEOM60	32	5390	0.8	**163424**	**2316**	0.7	350176	17711	4.5	207808
GEOM70	35	12970	**3.1**	**250220**	**7278**	5.8	594120	105608	60	333840
GEOM80	32	10118	6.8	**276012**	**3462**	**5.4**	624916	36054	20	393304
GEOM90	31	7250	3.3	**318232**	**2810**	4.2	729692	35324	**15**	469064
GEOM100	31	10194	8.3	**389310**	**2161**	4.3	888138	33144	18	592620
GEOM110	31	9359	5.7	**447482**	**1945**	**4.0**	1029730	32981	15	690364
GEOM120	31	7130	4.9	**526958**	**2021**	5.4	1237314	32654	19	830716
myciel5gb	4	13152	1.0	**2640**	17576	2.7	8304	**6716**	1.1	4152
myciel6gb	4	26212	5.2	**7560**	20679	7.1	25680	**14148**	4.8	12840
myciel7gb	4	31565	9.1	**21936**	18342	21	78576	18582	11	39288
queen8_8gb	7	4435	0.7	**13328**	5743	2.2	74480	**2483**	**0.3**	21280
queen9_9gb	8	12055	5.4	**22080**	15585	11	140352	**4557**	**0.9**	35088
queen10_10gb	8	19814	18	**29920**	25549	25	194560	**6197**	**1.5**	48640
queen11_11gb	8	20710	19	**39424**	24769	26	261184	**6197**	**1.5**	65296
queen12_12gb	8	29846	36	**50755**	41134	63	341507	**6340**	**1.9**	85379
DSJC125.1gb	4	51	0.0	7888	**49**	0.0	25552	78	0.0	**12776**
DSJC125.5gb	8	7829	2.5	**70256**	—	—	506048	**3901**	**1.2**	126512
DSJC125.9gb	8	9442	5.9	**119376**	—	—	899008	**7623**	**5.5**	224752
R75_1gb	3	18	0.0	**2139**	**15**	0.0	5151	19	0.0	3435
R75_5gb	6	991	**0.1**	**19587**	**1121**	1.2	104007	2169	0.3	34671
R75_9gb	7	5695	1.7	**38860**	6224	23	249952	**3160**	**0.9**	71417
R100_1gb	4	2302	0.2	**5672**	**2602**	0.5	17888	3760	0.4	8944
R100_5gb	6	2945	**0.5**	**33072**	**1805**	3.0	180432	8768	2.9	60144
R100_9gb	8	23736	22	**77408**	—	—	574464	**7729**	**5.3**	143616

Fig. 3. Results on unsatisfiable bandwidth colouring problems.

and maximal encodings are compared on the pure problems (in experiments the support encoding gave worse results than the direct encoding on pure vertex colouring). Both figures show CPU time (sec), number of backtracks (bt) and model size (literals). The fastest time, smallest number of backtracks and smallest models for each problem are highlighted in **bold**. An entry "—" means that the median time was over 100 seconds.

In terms of backtracks the support encoding is best on the GEOM graphs, the direct encoding is best on the smaller miles graphs, and the maximal encoding is best on the DSJC (pure and bandwidth), myciel (pure and bandwidth), queens (pure and bandwidth), mulsol, zeroin, school, and larger miles graphs, but worst on the GEOM graphs. In terms of CPU time the direct encoding is best on the school and smaller miles graphs, and the maximal encoding is best on the queens (pure and bandwidth), DSJC (bandwidth), mulsol, zeroin, and the large miles graphs, but worst on the GEOM graphs. So on several problem types the maximal encoding speeds up proofs of unsatisfiability, and the exploitation of interchangeability seems to be more important than the level of consistency. In terms of model sizes the maximal encoding is almost always larger than the maximal encoding (by a factor of less than 2), but the support encoding is larger still (often by a larger factor). The maximal encoding clearly does not use an excessive amount of space on these problems.

Though the first-solution results are disappointing the unsatisfiability results are very encouraging. This agrees in spirit with recent experiments [22] on random CSPs, which showed that using neighbourhood interchangeability to combine solutions during search yields greatest improvement at and beyond the phase transition, where a significant number of problems are unsatisfiable. It appears that interchangeability reasoning has a more significant effect on non-solution search states than on CSP solutions. In fact these results are not very surprising in the light of other work on symmetry breaking. We often transform a problem by reasoning about symmetric solutions, then find that the transformation improves proofs of unsatisfiability. Moreover, it is well-known that symmetry breaking sometimes degrades first-solution search, and some methods are designed to avoid exactly this problem [2, 18]. A final comment on the above experiments. We could obtain better results by adding symmetry breaking clauses to pre-colour a clique before SAT encoding. However, our aim here is not to obtain the best results but simply to use the graphs as a source of CSPs.

4 Related Work

Since Freuder's original interchangeability paper [15] there has been considerable research in this area of symmetry breaking. Benson & Freuder [6] apply neighbourhood interchangeability before search to improve forward checking. Lal, Choueiry & Freuder [22] apply dynamic neighbourhood interchangeability to non-binary CSPs. Haselböck [19] defines a weakened form of neighbourhood interchangeability with respect to certain constraints. Bowen & Likitvivatanavong [9] enhance neighbourhood interchangeability by splitting domain values into sub-values. Chmeiss & Saïs [11] study a generalisation of neighbourhood substitutability and its exploitation by adding constraints to the model. Bellicha et al. [4] study other generalisations and their dynamic exploitation during search. Choueiry & Noubir [13] define *neighbourhood partial interchangeability*, which is weaker than neighbourhood interchangeability and incomparable with full interchangeability. Choueiry & Davis [12] extend this to a dynamic version. Weigel, Faltings & Choueiry [34] define *context dependent interchangeability*, which is weaker than full interchangeability and also intractable to fully compute, then use approximation algorithms to partially exploit it. Beckwith, Choueiry & Zou [3] show that dynamic variable ordering remains an important heuristic when combined with neighbourhood interchangeability. They also design a set of random benchmark problems with a controlled amount of interchangeability, whereas many algorithms are tested on pure random CSPs. Bistarelli, Faltings & Neagu [8] extend neighbourhood interchangeability and substitutability to soft constraint problems.

Weaker forms of interchangeability have also been exploited. van Hentenryck et al. [20] break full interchangeability and two related variants. For example in *wreath-value interchangeability* variables take values from a domain $D_1 \times D_2$ such that values are interchangeable in D_1, and in D_2 for fixed values of D_1; this is a form of dynamic interchangeability in which the assigned set of variables is $\{v_1\}$ where v_1 is the variable with domain D_1. They break these symmetries in constant time and space using dedicated search algorithms. This approach has been generalised to arbitrary value symmetries by Roney-Dougal et al. [29]. However, these approaches assume that the user knows the symmetries of the problem in advance, whereas ours requires no user knowledge and breaks a weak form of substitutability. In recent work [27] this author describes constraints that can be added to any binary CSP in order to exploit dynamic interchangeability and to *partially* exploit dynamic substitutability, by excluding some solutions. That approach has the advantage that it can be combined with other techniques such as arc consistency, whereas the maximal encoding achieves only forward checking. However, it fully exploits dynamic substitutability, and preserves all solutions as Cartesian products.

Cartesian products can be effective on under-constrained problems. Hubbe and Freuder [21] describe backtracking and forward checking algorithms for computing *cross product representations* (CPRs) that contain dynamic neighbourhood interchangeable values, while Silaghi, Sam-Haroud & Faltings [31] describe related algorithms that enforce arc consistency. Our SAT solutions can be viewed as a form of CPR that bundle together values under weaker conditions. More precisely, they correspond to Lesaint's *maximal consistent decisions* (MCDs) [23], which are Cartesian products of partial variable domains that contain only solutions, and are maximal in the sense that adding further values causes inconsistency. Weigel, Bliek & Faltings [35] point out that SAT solutions under the multivalued encoding include MCDs, and our maximality clauses exclude all other SAT solutions. Lesaint describes a version of the forward checking algorithm (GFC) for finding MCDs, so GFC also exploits dynamic substitutability. But Lesaint does not analyse the interchangeability properties of MCDs, except to point out that fully interchangeable values occur in the same set of MCDs. We believe that a SAT backtracker applied to our encoding will be more efficient than GFC: the encoding enforces maximality by extra constraints which can be used for propagation, and improves backtrack performance on unsatisfiable problems, whereas GFC uses generate-and-test to detect maximality and behaves identically to standard forward checking on unsatisfiable problems. Note that we can also apply a SAT local search algorithm to the encoding, giving another way of computing MCDs that may be more successful on large problems.

To place this work in the context of other interchangeability research, Figure 4 shows a directed graph adapted from [13]. The abbreviations are as follows: DS denotes full dynamic substitutability; DSS *dynamic semi-substitutability*, our previous partial exploitation of DS [27]; FI full interchangeability; KI k-interchangeability; NI neighbourhood interchangeability; PI partial interchangeability (see [13, 15] for a definition); NPI neighbourhood PI [13]; NIc Haselböck's weakened NI [19]; CDI context-dependent interchangeability [34]; aCDI approximated CDI [34]; FS full substitutability; and NS neighbourhood substitutability. An arrow from A to B denotes that B is a weaker form of interchangeability than A. The graph illustrates the relative weakness of DS compared to most variants.

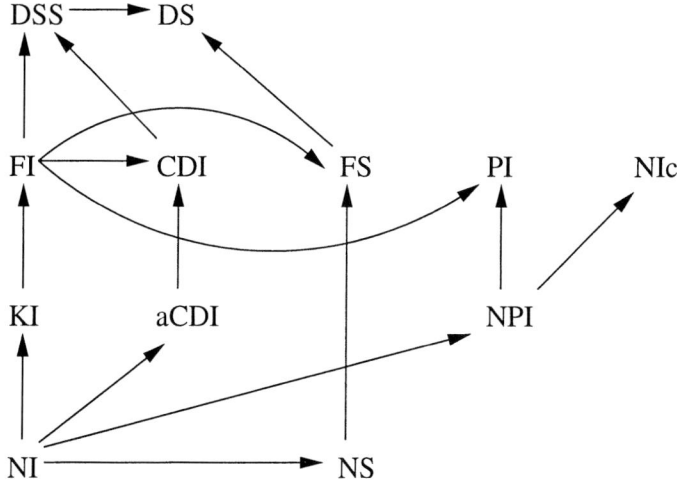

Fig. 4. Relating various forms of interchangeability.

5 Conclusion

The automatic detection of non-local forms of interchangeability is believed to require intractable analysis, so researchers have either used stronger local forms or relied on knowledge provided by the constraint programmer. We showed that a reformulation approach avoids both requirements. The reformulation is a new SAT encoding that induces full dynamic substitutability with forward checking on the CSP, when solved with an off-the-shelf SAT backtracker. Empirical results show that this technique significantly improves proofs of unsolvability. It can also make first-solution search slower, but this is offset by the fact that each solution is a compact representation of a (sometimes very large) set of CSP solutions.

Generating a large set of similar solutions has application to interactive problem solving and explanation [13], and robustness under dynamic situations [12, 13, 22, 34]. Local interchangeability has been applied to this task but weaker forms will obviously generate larger sets. The new encoding is a way of coercing any SAT solver (including backtracking and local search algorithms) to generate *maximal consistent decisions* [23] and (equivalently) *pure clusters* [26], which have application to dynamic and distributed CSPs respectively.

A side benefit of this work is the discovery of an interesting new CSP-to-SAT encoding, with similar space requirements to those of more well-known encodings. Increasing the number of such encodings is of interest to SAT research because it advances the use of SAT techniques on combinatorial problems. A drawback with our approach is that by SAT encoding a CSP we lose much of its structure, though some SAT solvers are able to retain structure [32]. In future work we intend to investigate CSP reformulations combining other forms of interchangeability and consistency, and evaluate them on other binary and non-binary CSPs.

Acknowledgments

This work was supported in part by the Boole Centre for Research in Informatics, University College, Cork, Ireland, and also by Science Foundation Ireland under Grant 00/PI.1/C075. Thanks to Gene Freuder and other 4C members for helpful discussions, and to the anonymous referees for useful comments.

References

1. F. Bacchus, P. van Beek. On the Conversion Between Non-Binary and Binary Constraint Satisfaction Problems Using the Hidden Variable Method. *Fifteenth National Conference on Artificial Intelligence*, Madison, Wisconsin, USA, 1998, pp. 311–318.
2. R. Backofen, S. Will. Excluding Symmetries in Constraint-Based Search. *Fifth International Conference on Principles and Practice of Constraint Programming, Lecture Notes in Computer Science* vol. 1713, Springer-Verlag, 1999, pp. 73–87.
3. A. M. Beckwith, B. Y. Choueiry, H. Zou. How the Level of Interchangeability Embedded in a Finite Constraint Satisfaction Problem Affects the Performance of Search. *Fourteenth Australian Joint Conference on Artificial Intelligence, Lecture Notes in Artificial Intelligence* vol. 2256, Springer-Verlag, 2001, pp. 50–61,
4. A. Bellicha, M. Habib, M. C. Vilarem, C. Capelle, T. Kokeny. CSP Techniques Using Partial Orders on Domain Values. *ECAI'94 Workshop on Constraint Satisfaction Issues raised by Practical Applications*, T. Schiex and C. Bessière (eds.), Amsterdam, 1994.
5. B. Benhamou. Study of Symmetry in Constraint Satisfaction Problems. *Principles and Practice of Constraint Programming*, 1994.
6. B. W. Benson, E. C. Freuder. Interchangeability Preprocessing Can Improve Forward Checking. *Tenth European Conference on Artificial Intelligence*, Vienna, Austria, 1992, pp. 28–30.
7. C. Bèssiere, E. Hebrard, T. Walsh. Local Consistencies in SAT. *Sixth International Conference on Theory and Applications of Satisfiability Testing*, Santa Margherita Ligure, Italy, 2003, pp. 400–407.
8. S. Bistarelli, B. V. Faltings, N. Neagu. Interchangeability in Soft CSPs. *Joint ERCIM / CoLogNet International Workshop on Constraint Solving and Constraint Logic Programming, Lecture Notes in Artificial Intelligence* vol. 2627, Springer Verlag, 2002, pp. 31–46.
9. J. Bowen, C. Likitvivatanavong. Splitting the Atom: a New Approach to Neighbourhood Interchangeability in Constraint Satisfaction Problems. Poster, *Eighteenth International Joint Conference on Artificial Intelligence*, Acapulco, Mexico, 2003.
10. F. Brglez, X. Y. Li, M. F. Stallman. The Role of a Skeptic Agent in Testing and Benchmarking of SAT Algorithms. *Fifth International Symposium on the Theory and Applications of Satisfiability Testing*, University of Cincinnati, 2002, pp. 354–361.
11. A. Chmeiss, L. Saïs. About Neighborhood Substitutability in CSPs. *Third International Workshop on Symmetry in Constraint Satisfaction Problems*, Kinsale, Ireland, 2003, pp. 41–45.
12. B. Y. Choueiry, A. M. Davis. Dynamic Bundling: Less Effort for More Solutions. *Fifth International Symposium on Abstraction, Reformulation and Approximation, Lecture Notes in Computer Science* vol. 2371, Springer-Verlag, 2002, pp. 64–82.

13. B. Y. Choueiry, G. Noubir. On the Computation of Local Interchangeability in Discrete Constraint Satisfaction Problems. *Fifteenth National Conference on Artificial Intelligence*, Madison, WI, USA, 1998, pp. 326–333.
14. T. Fahle, S. Schamberger, M. Sellman. Symmetry Breaking. *Seventh International Conference on Principles and Practices of Constraint Programming, Lecture Notes in Computer Science* vol. 2239, Springer-Verlag, 2001, pp. 93–107.
15. E. C. Freuder. Eliminating Interchangeable Values in Constraint Satisfaction Problems. *Ninth National Conference on Artificial Intelligence*, Anaheim, CA, 1991, pp. 227–233.
16. I. P. Gent. Arc Consistency in SAT. *Fifteenth European Conference on Artificial Intelligence*, Lyons, France, 2002, pp. 121–125.
17. I. P. Gent, W. Harvey, T. Kelsey. Groups and Constraints: Symmetry Breaking During Search. *Eighth International Conference on Principles and Practice of Constraint Programming, Lecture Notes in Computer Science* vol. 2470, Springer-Verlag, 2002, pp. 415–430.
18. I. P. Gent, B. Smith. Symmetry Breaking During Search in Constraint Programming. *Fourteenth European Conference on Artificial Intelligence*, 2000, pp. 599–603.
19. A. Haselböck. Exploiting Interchangeabilities in Constraint Satisfaction Problems. *Thirteenth International Joint Conference on Artificial Intelligence*, Chambéry, France, 1993, pp. 282–287.
20. P. van Hentenryck, M. Ågren, P. Flener, J. Pearson. Tractable Symmetry Breaking for CSPs with Interchangeable Values. *Eighteenth International Joint Conference on Artificial Intelligence*, Acapulco, Mexico, August 2003, pp. 277–282.
21. P. D. Hubbe, E. C. Freuder. An Efficient Cross Product Representation of the Constraint Satisfaction Problem Search Space. *Tenth National Conference on Artificial Intelligence*, San Jose, California, USA, 1992, pp. 421–427.
22. A. Lal, B. Y. Choueiry, E. C. Freuder. Neighborhood Interchangeability and Dynamic Bundling for Non-Binary Finite CSPs. *Joint Annual Workshop of ERCIM / CoLogNet on Constraint Solving and Constraint Logic Programming*, Lausanne, Switzerland, 2004 (to appear).
23. D. Lesaint. Maximal Sets of Solutions for Constraint Satisfaction Problems. *Eleventh European Conference on Artificial Intelligence*, Amsterdam, The Netherlands, 1994, pp. 110–114.
24. P. Meseguer, C. Torras. Exploiting Symmetries Within Constraint Satisfaction Search. *Artificial Intelligence* vol. 129 nos. 1–2, 2001, pp. 133–163.
25. M. Moskewicz, C. Madigan, Y. Zhao, L. Zhang, S. Malik. Chaff: Engineering an Efficient SAT Solver. *Thirty Eighth Design Automation Conference*, Las Vegas, 2001, pp. 530–535.
26. A. J. Parkes. Exploiting Solution Clusters for Coarse-Grained Distributed Search. *IJCAI'01 Workshop on Distributed Constraint Reasoning*, Seattle, Washington, USA, 2001.
27. S. D. Prestwich. Full Dynamic Interchangeability with Forward Checking and Arc Consistency. *ECAI'04 Workshop on Modeling and Solving Problems With Constraints*, Valencia, Spain, 2004.
28. J.-F. Puget. On the Satisfiability of Symmetrical Constrained Satisfaction Problems. J. Komorowski, Z. W. Ras (eds.), Methodologies for Intelligent Systems, *International Symposium on Methodologies for Intelligent Systems, Lecture Notes in Computer Science* vol. 689, Springer-Verlag, 1993, pp. 350–361.

29. C. M. Roney-Dougal, I. P. Gent, T. W. Kelsey, S. A. Linton. Tractable Symmetry Breaking using Restricted Search Trees. *Sixteenth European Conference on Artificial Intelligence*, Valencia, Spain, 2004 (to appear).
30. F. Rossi, C. Petrie, V. Dhar. On the Equivalence of Constraint Satisfaction Problems. *Nineteenth European Conference on Artificial Intelligence*, Stockholm, Sweden, 1990, pp. 550–556.
31. M.-C. Silaghi, D. Sam-Haroud, B. V. Faltings. Ways of Maintaining Arc Consistency in Search Using the Cartesian Representation. *New Trends in Constraints, Joint ERCIM / Compulog Net Workshop, Lecture Notes in Computer Science* vol. 1865, Springer-Verlag, 2000, p. 173–187.
32. C. Thiffault, F. Bacchus, T. Walsh. Solving Non-Clausal Formulas with DPLL Search. *Seventh International Conference on Theory and Applications of Satisfiability Testing*, Vancouver, Canada, 2004, pp. 147–156.
33. T. Walsh. SAT v CSP. *Sixth International Conference on Principles and Practice of Constraint Programming, Lecture Notes in Computer Science* vol. 1894, Springer-Verlag, 2000, pp. 441–456.
34. R. Weigel, B. V. Faltings, B. Y. Choueiry. Context in Discrete Constraint Satisfaction Problems. *Twelfth European Conference on Artificial Intelligence*, Budapest, Hungary, 1996, pp. 205–209.
35. R. Weigel, C. Bliek, B. V. Faltings. On Reformulation of Constraint Satisfaction Problems. *Thirteenth European Conference on Artificial Intelligence*, Brighton, United Kingdom, 1998, pp. 254–258.

Improved Bound Computation in Presence of Several Clique Constraints

Jean-Francois Puget

ILOG, 9 avenue de Verdun, 94253 Gentilly, France
puget@ilog.fr

Abstract. Bound consistency can easily and efficiently be enforced on linear constraint. However, bound consistency techniques deal with every constraint separately. We show that in some cases much stronger bounds can be computed by looking globally at the set of linear constraints. A simple algorithm for computing such bounds is derived from a new decomposition scheme. We prove that these bounds can be as tight as possible. In some cases this can be better than the standard reduced cost fixings. This algorithm has been implemented within a global constraint. Experimental results on balanced incomplete block design (BIBD) show its effectiveness: we were able to significantly improve over the best published results for this class of problems.

1 Introduction

We are looking at the following problem. Given a linear constraint which is covered by a set of clique constraints (a sum of binary variables equal to 1), we want to compute bounds on the general constraint.

For instance, let us look at the following constraints. All the binary variables x_j appear in at least one clique constraint.

$$\begin{aligned} x_1 + x_2 + x_3 + x_4 &= z \\ x_1 + x_2 + x_3 &= 1 \\ x_1 + x_3 + x_4 &= 1 \\ x_2 + x_3 + x_4 &= 1 \end{aligned}$$

Bound consistency deduces nothing more than what can be deduced using the first constraint alone:
$$0 \leq z \leq 4$$

The technique described in this paper enables to deduce :
$$x_1 = 0, x_2 = 0, x_3 = 1, z = 1$$

The general setting of the problem is the following. Let I be the interval $[1, m]$, J be the interval $[1, n]$, and J_i be non empty sets subject to $\bigcup_i J_i = J$.

We are given n binary variables x_j, m numbers c_j, and one general integer variable z subject to the following constraints.

$$\sum_{j \in J} c_j x_j = z$$
$$\sum_{j \in J_i} x_j = 1, \quad \forall i \in I$$
$$z \geq 0$$
$$x_j = 0 \vee 1, \forall j \in J$$

The problem is to compute tight bounds for z, and to set as many x_j as possible given bounds for z.

Such sets of linear constraint occur as a sub problem in the MAX CSP approach described in [5]. In this work, each variable x_j represents the possible violation of a constraint, and each clique constraint represents a conflict set. The variable z is the number of constraint violations (every c_j is equal to 1). The problem is then cast into a graph theoretic problem which is **NP**-complete. On the contrary, we chose to cast the problem into a **P** problem (linear programming), as we shall see.

Linear constraints are ubiquitous in combinatorial optimization. This has been recognized since the early days of constraint programming, as witnessed by the linear solvers available in most CP systems. Moreover, linear solvers have been linked to constraint propagation algorithms after the seminal work of De Backer and Beringer [1]. Their idea was to use the linear solver as a global constraint able to check the satisfiability of a set of linear constraints. This global constraint is fed with the bounds computed by the constraint propagation algorithm. However, this global constraint does not provide bounds for all the variables appearing in the linear constraints. Fortunately, such bounds can be easily computed using each linear constraint separately. Indeed, it is quite easy and efficient to enforce bound consistency on linear constraints, see [4] for instance. However, for the problem described above, much better bounds can be computed by looking at the set of linear constraints.

The special case where there is one clique constraint can be solved easily, as we shall see in section 2. The general case can be decomposed into m instances of this special case. This yields a simple and efficient bound computation algorithm which is described in section 3. Using a linear programming approach, we prove in section 4 that this decomposition scheme can yield tight bounds on z. Our approach can be further generalized, as explained in section 5. In section 6 we give some hints about our implementation and we report some experimental results for balanced incomplete block design (BIBD).

2 The One Clique Problem

We are given two constraints.

$$\sum_{j \in J} c_j x_j = z$$

$$\sum_{j \in J} x_j = 1$$

$$x_j = 0 \vee 1, \forall j \in J$$

Two special cases are easy to deal with. First, if a given x_k is fixed to zero, we delete x_k from the equations, if there is more than one binary variable left, otherwise the problem is not feasible. Second, if a given x_k is fixed to 1, then $z = c_k$, and $x_i = 0$ for all $i \neq k$. We therefore assume that the x_i are not fixed to 0 or 1 in the reminder of this section. In such case, the bounds for z and the x_j are given by the following equations. We note $\overline{z}$ the upper bound for z and we note $\underline{z}$ its lower bound.

$$z \geq min(c_j)_{j \in J} \tag{1}$$
$$z \leq max(c_j)_{j \in J} \tag{2}$$
$$x_j = 0, \; if \; c_j < \underline{z} \tag{3}$$
$$x_j = 0, \; if \; c_j > \overline{z} \tag{4}$$

These equations are stronger than what bound consistency would give on each constraint.

Note that the above can also be applied to the case where the clique constraint is an inequality

$$\sum_{j \in J} x_j \leq 1$$

In such case equations (2), (3), and (4) are valid. Similarly, if the clique constraint is an inequality

$$\sum_{j \in J} x_j \geq 1$$

then equations (1), (3), and (4) are valid.

In the rest of this article we will assume that all clique constraints are equalities. However, most of the results we will derive are partly valid for inequalities, as discussed above.

3 The Multi-clique Problem

The general case can be decomposed into m instances of the one clique problem. Let us introduce our approach on the example before describing the general case.

3.1 An Example

Let us repeat here our example for the sake of clarity.

$$\text{Ex1} \begin{cases} x_1 + x_2 + x_3 + x_4 = z \\ x_1 + x_2 + x_3 \quad\quad = 1 \\ x_1 + \quad\quad x_3 + x_4 = 1 \\ \quad\; x_2 + x_3 + x_4 = 1 \end{cases}$$

Note that z must be integer by the first constraint. We introduce a floating point variable z_i for each of the clique constraint and m constraints as follows.

$$\mathbf{Ex2} \begin{cases} x_1 + x_2 + x_3 + x_4 = z \\ z_1 + z_2 + z_3 = z \\ \frac{1}{2}x_1 + \frac{1}{2}x_2 + \frac{1}{3}x_3 = z_1 \\ x_1 + x_2 + x_3 = 1 \\ \frac{1}{2}x_1 + \frac{1}{3}x_3 + \frac{1}{2}x_4 = z_2 \\ x_1 + x_3 + x_4 = 1 \\ \frac{1}{2}x_2 + \frac{1}{3}x_3 + \frac{1}{2}x_4 = z_3 \\ x_2 + x_3 + x_4 = 1 \end{cases}$$

Note that the sum of the constraints of **Ex2** involving the variables z_i is equal to the first constraint of **Ex2**. Note also that we now have 3 instances of the one clique problem, one for each of the variables z_i. Using (1) and (2) for each instance, we have

$$\frac{1}{3} \leq z_i \leq \frac{1}{2} \quad \forall i = 1\ldots 3$$

This in turn gives by summation

$$1 \leq z \leq 3/2$$

Since z is integer, we get $z = 1$. Bound consistency on the second constraint then implies

$$z_i = \frac{1}{3} \quad \forall i = 1\ldots 3$$

Then, using (4) on the last two constraints, we get

$$x_1 = 0, x_2 = 0$$

and finally using bound consistency on the last constraint

$$x_3 = 1$$

3.2 The General Case

The general setting is easily derived from the example. We are given a problem

$$\mathbf{P} \begin{cases} \sum_{j \in J} c_j x_j = z \\ \sum_{j \in J_i} x_j = 1, \quad \forall i \in I \\ z \geq 0 \\ x_j = 0 \vee 1, \forall j \in J \end{cases}$$

We transform the problem into an extended set of constraints with m additional variables z_i, and with additional numbers a_{ij} such that

$$\mathbf{EP} \begin{cases} \sum_{i \in I} z_i = z \\ \sum_{j \in J_i} a_{ij} x_j = z_i, & \forall i \in I \\ \sum_{j \in J_i} x_j = 1, & \forall i \in I \\ \sum_{i \in I} a_{ij} = c_j, & \forall j \in J \\ a_{ij} = 0, & \text{if } j \notin J_i \\ z \geq 0 \\ x_j = 0 \vee 1, & \forall j \in J \end{cases}$$

The coefficients a_{ij} can be chosen as follows:

$$a_{ij} = \frac{\xi_{ij} c_j}{\sum_{k \in I} \xi_{kj}} \tag{5}$$

where $\xi_{ij} = 1$ if $j \in J_i$, 0 otherwise.

This is what we have used in the example above. It is easy to check that these values satisfy the above equations. We'll see in the next section how to chose a_{ij} in order to get the tightest possible bounds for z in general.

This transformation preserves solutions in the following way.

Assume that we have a solution of **P**, given by the values x_j^* and z^* for the variables x_j and z respectively. Let us define z_i^* as follows. $z_i^* = \sum_{j \in J_i} a_{ij} x_j^*$. It is easy to check that the values x_j^*, z^*, and z_i^* are a solution for **EP**.

Conversely, assume we are given a solution of **EP**, given by the values x_j^*, z^*, and z_i^*, for the variables x_j, z, and z_i respectively. It is easy to check that the values x_j^* and z^* are a solution for **P**.

The problem **EP** contains m instances of the one clique problem, one for each of the variables z_i. Each instance is given by

$$\sum_{j \in J_i} a_{ij} x_j = z_i$$
$$\sum_{j \in J_i} x_j = 1$$

Using (1) and (2) we then get the following

$$z_i \geq l_i$$
$$z_i \leq u_i$$

where

$$l_i = min(a_{ij})_{j \in J_i}$$
$$u_i = max(a_{ij})_{j \in J_i}$$

Then, by summation

$$z \geq \sum_{i \in I} l_i$$
$$z \leq \sum_{i \in I} u_i$$

Let us see what happens if one of the variables x_i is fixed to 0 or to 1. Let L_j (resp. U_j) be the set of constraints where a_{ij} is the minimum (resp. maximum):

$$L_j = \{i | a_{ij} \neq 0 \wedge \forall k < j, a_{kj} = 0\}$$
$$U_j = \{i | a_{ij} \neq 0 \wedge \forall k > j, a_{kj} = 0\}$$

If x_j is set to 1, then the bounds of the variables z_i are modified as follows. If a_{ij} is not equal to 0 then we get $l_i = u_i = a_{ij}$. Note that if $i \in L_i$, the lower bound for z_i is not modified. Similarly, if $i \in U_i$, the upper bound for z_i is not modified. By summation, we get:

$$z \geq \sum_{i \in I} l_i + \sum_{i \in J_i, i \notin L_i} (a_{ij} - l_i)$$
$$z \leq \sum_{i \in I} u_i + \sum_{i \in J_i, i \notin U_i} (a_{ij} - u_i)$$

Hence, x_i cannot be equal to 1 if one of the following holds:

$$\sum_{i \in J_i, i \notin U_i} (a_{ij} - u_i) < \underline{z} - \sum_{i \in I} l_i$$
$$\sum_{i \in J_i, i \notin L_i} (a_{ij} - l_i) > \overline{z} - \sum_{i \in I} u_i$$

Let us see what happens if x_i is set to 0. Let min_i (resp. max_i) be the second smallest (resp. largest) coefficient in the ith constraint. If x_j is set to 0, then the bounds of the variables z_i are modified as follows. If i belongs to L_i, then :

$$z_i \geq l_i + min_i - a_{ij}$$

If i belongs to U_i, then :

$$z_i \leq u_i + max_i - a_{ij}$$

By summation, we get

$$z \geq \sum_{i \in I} l_i + \sum_{i \in L_i} (min_i - a_{ij})$$
$$z \leq \sum_{i \in I} u_i + \sum_{i \in U_i} (max_i - a_{ij})$$

Hence, x_j cannot be equal to 0 if one of the following holds:

$$\sum_{i \in L_i} (min_i - a_{ij}) > \overline{z} - \sum_{i \in I} l_i$$
$$\sum_{i \in U_i} (max_i - a_{ij}) < \underline{z} - \sum_{i \in I} u_i$$

We just proved the following result.

Theorem 1. *With the above notations, given variables x_i and z satisfying* **P**, *and a set of values* $(a_{ij})_{i \in I, j \in J}$ *subject to*

$$\sum_{i \in I} a_{ij} = c_j, \quad \forall j \in J \qquad (6)$$

$$a_{ij} = 0, \; if \; j \notin J_i \qquad (7)$$

the following conditions hold.

$$z \geq \sum_{i \in I} l_i \qquad (8)$$

$$z \leq \sum_{i \in I} u_i \qquad (9)$$

$$x_j = 0, \; if \sum_{i \in J_i, i \notin U_i} (a_{ij} - u_i) < \underline{z} - \sum_{i \in I} l_i \qquad (10)$$

$$x_j = 0, \; if \sum_{i \in J_i, i \notin L_i} (a_{ij} - l_i) > \overline{z} - \sum_{i \in I} u_i \qquad (11)$$

$$x_j = 1, \text{ if } \sum_{i \in L_i}(min_i - a_{ij}) > \overline{z} - \sum_{i \in I} l_i \qquad (12)$$

$$x_j = 1, \text{ if } \sum_{i \in U_i}(max_i - a_{ij}) < \underline{z} - \sum_{i \in I} u_i \qquad (13)$$

Note that these bounds can be computed without explicitly introducing the variables z_i.

4 Getting Tight Bounds

The best bounds for z can be computed using a linear programming approach. Indeed, the best upper bound for z is the optimal value uz of the linear program

$$\mathbf{LP1} \begin{cases} Maximize \\ \quad \sum_{j \in J} c_j x_j \\ subject\ to \\ \quad \sum_{j \in J} \xi_{ij} x_j = 1, \forall i \in I \\ \quad x_j \geq 0, \forall j \in J \end{cases}$$

and the best lower bound for z is the optimal value lz of the linear program

$$\mathbf{LP2} \begin{cases} Minimize \\ \quad \sum_{j \in J} c_j y_j \\ subject\ to \\ \quad \sum_{j \in J} \xi_{ij} y_j = 1, \forall i \in I \\ \quad y_j \geq 0, \forall j \in J \end{cases}$$

The optimal value for **LP2** is the same as the optimal of its dual which is:

$$\mathbf{LP2'} \begin{cases} Maximize \\ \quad \sum_{i \in I} l_i \\ subject\ to \\ \quad \sum_{i \in I} \xi_{ij} l_i \leq c_j, \forall j \in J \end{cases}$$

Intuitively, l_i represents the lower bound on the variables z_i we have introduced in the previous section. Note that we do not have $l_i \geq 0$. We have the following result.

Lemma 2. *With the above notations, let l_i^* be the optimal values for problem* **LP2'**. *There exists values $(a_{ij})_{i \in I, j \in J}$ satisfying equations (6) and (7) such that*

$$\xi_{ij} l_i^* \leq a_{ij} \qquad (14)$$

Proof. Let us introduce the sets J_j defined by $J_j = \{i | \xi_{ij} = 1\}$
The values l_i^* satisfy **LP2'**, therefore for each j we have $\sum_{i \in I} \xi_{ij} l_i^* \leq c_j$
Let us define the reduced cost s_i : $s_j = c_j - \sum_{i \in I} \xi_{ij} l_i^*$
Let then define $a_{ij} = \begin{cases} \xi_{ij} l_i^* + s_j & if\ i = min(J_j) \\ \xi_{ij} l_i^* & otherwise \end{cases}$

By construction $\xi_{ij}l_i^* \leq a_{ij}$. Moreover these a_{ij} satisfy conditions (6) and (7). □

Lemma 3. *With the above notations, let a_{ij} be any set of values satisfying (6), (7), and (14). We have*

$$l_i^* = min(a_{ij})_{j \in J_i} \qquad (15)$$

Proof. Given a_{ij} satisfying conditions (6), (7) and (14), let us prove that (15) holds. We define $l_i' = min(a_{ij})_{j \in J_i}$, $\forall i \in I$
Then $\xi_{ij}l_i' \leq a_{ij}$, $\forall i \in I$, $\forall j \in J$
By summation over i we get $\sum_{i \in I} \xi_{ij}l_i' \leq \sum_{i \in I} a_{ij}$, $\forall j \in J$
Therefore l' is a solution of **LP2'**. From (14), we have $l_i^* \leq l_i'$, $\forall i \in I$
If this inequality was strict for at least one i, then by summation we would get $\sum_{i \in I} l_i^* < \sum_{i \in I} l_i'$
This would mean that l' is a better solution for **LP2'** than l^*, which contradicts the fact that l^* is an optimal solution. Therefore, $l_i^* = l_i'$, $\forall i \in I$. □

Theorem 4. *With the above notations, let lz be the optimal value for **LP**. There exists $(a_{ij})_{i \in I, j \in J}$ satisfying equations (6) and (7) such that*

$$lz = \sum_{i \in I} min(a_{ij})_{j \in J_i}$$

Proof. Let lz be the best lower bound for z. This bound is the optimal value for the linear program **LP**. This is also the optimal value for its dual problem **LP2'**, i.e. $lz = \sum_{i \in I} l_i^*$
From lemma 2 we have that there exists a_{ij} satisfying (6), (7) and (14). By lemma 3, we have that each l_i^* satisfies condition (15). By summation we get $\sum_{i \in I} l_i^* = \sum_{i \in I} min(a_{ij})_{j \in J_i}$. □

The proof of this result gives a way to compute the a_{ij}. Indeed, solving **LP2** gives the dual values l_i^*. Then a_{ij} can be constructed as in the proof of the lemma 1. In such case, the bounds we get for the variables x_j are what is called reduced cost fixings.

Similarly, a tight upper bound can be computed with the linear program **LP1**. This yields the following result.

Theorem 5. *With the above notations, let uz be the optimal value for **LP1**. There exists $(a_{ij})_{i \in I, j \in J}$ satisfying equations (6) and (7) such that*

$$uz = \sum_{i \in I} max(a_{ij})_{j \in J_i}$$

In what precedes, the bounds we compute for the variables x_i are simply reduced cost fixings. We will see in the next section that for a generalized version of our problem we can get stronger bounds than reduced cost fixings.

5 Generalized Problem

We examine in this section how the decomposition approach we have developed so far could be extended to cope with more general forms of **P**. We first generalize the one clique problem, then we look at the multiple clique problem.

5.1 The Generalized Bound Case

An immediate generalization of the multi clique problem is to allow for any right hand side term for the clique constraint. More precisely, we are given the following problem, where b is an arbitrary integer.

$$\sum_{j \in J} c_j x_j = z$$
$$\sum_{j \in J} x_j = b$$

The lower (resp. upper) bound on z is then given by the sum of the b smallest (resp. largest) c_j. More precisely, let us define $min^k S$ (resp. $max^k S$) to be the sum of the k smallest (resp. largest) elements of the list S.

Theorem 6. *With the above notations, the following conditions hold*

$$z \geq min^b(c_j)_{j \in J} \tag{16}$$
$$z \leq max^b(c_j)_{i \in J} \tag{17}$$
$$x_j = 0, \text{ if } c_j < \underline{z} - max^{b-1}(c_k)_{k \in J, k \neq j} \tag{18}$$
$$x_j = 0, \text{ if } c_j > \overline{z} - min^{b-1}(c_k)_{k \in J, k \neq j} \tag{19}$$
$$x_j = 1, \text{ if } max^b(c_k)_{k \in J, k \neq j} < \underline{z} \tag{20}$$
$$x_j = 1, \text{ if } min^b(c_k)_{k \in J, k \neq j} > \overline{z} \tag{21}$$

Proof. Let us prove that (19) is valid. The proof for (18) is similar. Assume that $c_j > \overline{z} - min^{b-1}(c_k)_{k \in J}$ for a given j. Let us introduce $z' = z - c_j x_j$. We then have
$$\sum_{k \in J, k \neq j} c_k x_k = z'$$
$$\sum_{k \in J, k \neq j} x_k = b - 1$$
From (17) applied to the above 2 equations, we get $min^{b-1}(c_k)_{k \in J, k \neq j} \leq z'$
We then have
$c_j x_j = z - z'$
$\quad \leq \overline{z} - min^{b-1}(c_k)_{k \in J, k \neq j}$
$\quad < c_j$
Therefore $x_j = 1$ would lead to a contradiction.

Let us prove that (20) is valid. The proof for (21) is similar. Assume that $x_j = 0$ for a given j. Then, $max^b(c_k)_{k \in J} = max^b(c_k)_{k \in J, k \neq j}$.
Assume further that $max^b(c_k)_{k \in J, k \neq j} < \underline{z}$.
Then $max^b(c_k)_{k \in J} < \underline{z}$
This contradicts (17). □

5.2 The General Case

Let us look at a slightly more general problem where the right hand side of clique constraints can be any integer b_i, instead of 1. We are given a problem defined by

$$\mathbf{P'} \begin{cases} \sum_{j \in J} c_j x_j = z \\ \sum_{j \in J_i} x_j = b_i, & \forall i \in I \\ z \geq 0 \\ x_j = 0 \vee 1, \forall j \in J \end{cases}$$

We transform the problem into an extended set of constraints with m additional variables z_i, and additional coefficients a_{ij} such that

$$\mathbf{EP'} \begin{cases} \sum_{i \in I} z_i = z \\ \sum_{j \in J_i} a_{ij} x_j = z_i, & \forall i \in I \\ \sum_{j \in J_i} x_j = b_i, & \forall i \in I \\ \sum_{i \in I} a_{ij} = c_j, & \forall j \in J \\ a_{ij} = 0, & if\ j \notin J_i \\ z \geq 0 \\ x_j = 0 \vee 1, & \forall j \in J \end{cases}$$

The problem **EP'** contains m instances of the generalized bound problem, one for each of the variables z_i. Using (16) and (17), we then get bounds for each variable z_i, and by summation:

$$z \geq \sum_{i \in I} min^{b_i}(a_{ij})_{j \in J_i}$$

$$z \leq \sum_{i \in I} max^{b_i}(a_{ij})_{j \in J_i}$$

These equations enable the computation of bounds for z. Conversely, given some bounds for z, new bounds can be computed for the variables x_j. In order to express them, let us generalize the definitions of the previous section. L_i^k (resp. U_i^k) is the set of constraints where a_{ij} is one of the k smallest (resp. largest) coefficients. Then, by similar arguments than for theorem 1, we have

Theorem 7. *With the above notations, given variables x_i and z satisfying* **P'***, and a set of values $(a_{ij})_{i \in I, j \in J}$ subject to*

$$\sum_{i \in I} a_{ij} = c_j, \quad \forall j \in J \qquad (22)$$

$$a_{ij} = 0,\ if\ j \notin J_i \qquad (23)$$

the following conditions hold.

$$z \geq \sum_{i \in I} l_i \qquad (24)$$

$$z \le \sum_{i \in I} u_i \qquad (25)$$

$$x_j = 0, \; if \sum_{i \in J_i, i \notin U_i}(a_{ij} + max_i^{b_i-1} - u_i) < \underline{z} - \sum_{i \in I} l_i \qquad (26)$$

$$x_j = 0, \; if \sum_{i \in J_i, i \notin L_i}(a_{ij} + min_i^{b_i-1} - l_i) > \overline{z} - \sum_{i \in I} u_i \qquad (27)$$

$$x_j = 1, \; if \sum_{i \in L_i}(min_i^{b_i+1} - a_{ij} - l_i) > \overline{z} - \sum_{i \in I} l_i \qquad (28)$$

$$x_j = 1, \; if \sum_{i \in U_i}(max_i^{b_i+1} - a_{ij}) - u_i) < \underline{z} - \sum_{i \in I} u_i \qquad (29)$$

where

$$min_i^k = min^k(a_{ij})_{j \in J_i}$$
$$max_i^k = max^{b_i}(a_{ij})_{j \in J_i}$$
$$l_i = min_i^{b_i}$$
$$u_i = max_i^{b_i}$$

Note that these bounds can be computed without explicitly introducing the variables z_i. As before, the bounds may depend on the values of the a_{ij}. Unfortunately, it is not possible to devise a linear program to compute the best possible values for these coefficients unless we do some approximations of the functions min^k and max^k. If we replace these functions by $k * min$ and $k * max$, then a linear programming approach as in the previous section can be used. However, this means that the sum of the k smallest (resp. largest) elements is replaced by k times the smallest (resp. largest) element. This yields less tight bounds. This shows that bounds computed using reduced costs are less tight than then one using the functions min^k and max^k. Another possibility is to use the values defined in (5). However, this will not yield the best possible bounds.

6 Experimental Results

We have implemented the bound computations of section 5 into a global constraint that takes a set of linear constraints as input. This global constraint is added in addition to the original linear constraints. We describe briefly its implementation before giving some experimental results.

6.1 Implementation Hints

In order to efficiently compute bounds, the c_j are sorted in ascending order. Then, equations (16) and (17) are easy to maintain incrementally. it is sufficient to maintain indices for the first and last b_i smallest and largest coefficients in each constraint. This ensures an amortized complexity of $O(n)$ over one branch in the search tree. A similar approach can be used for equations (26), (27), (28), and (29).

We have implemented the above using (5) as values for the coefficients a_{ij}. Although this does not provide the tightest bounds, it does improve a lot bound propagation as shown by our first example. Moreover, these bounds can be computed efficiently because there is no need to invoke a linear solver.

6.2 Balanced Incomplete Block Designs

In order to evaluate this technique, we have selected problems where multi clique problems occur very often, namely balanced incomplete block designs (BIBD). A BIBD is defined as an arrangement of v points into b blocks such that each block contains exactly k distinct points, each point occurs in exactly r different blocks, and every two distinct points occur together in exactly λ blocks. An other way of defining a BIBD is in term of it's *incidence matrix*, which is a binary matrix with v rows, b columns, r ones per row, k ones per column, and scalar product λ between any pair of distinct rows. A BIBD is fully specified by its parameters (v, k, λ), the other parameters can be computed using

$$r = \frac{\lambda(v-1)}{(k-1)}, \ b = \frac{\lambda v(v-1)}{k(k-1)}$$

A BIBD can be represented as a CSP with a v by b matrix model. Each variable in the matrix is a binary variable y_{ij} with domain $\{0, 1\}$. There are three sets of constraints :

$$\sum_{j=1}^{b} y_{i,j} = r, \ \forall i = 1 \ldots v \tag{30}$$

$$\sum_{i=1}^{v} y_{i,j} = k, \ \forall j = 1 \ldots b \tag{31}$$

$$\sum_{j=1}^{b} y_{i',j} y_{i,j} = \lambda, \ \forall ii', \ 1 \leq i' < i \leq v \tag{32}$$

We use a static variable ordering : variables are selected row by row, then column by column. The value ordering is also fixed : 1 is tried first, then we try 0. This generates possible designs in a decreasing lexicographic ordering.

These problems have a lot of symmetries. Those symmetries can be partially removed by adding lexicographic constraints on rows and columns[2]. Additional constraints can then be derived as shown by[3]. We have added those constraints to the problem.

6.3 Using Linear Constraints

Let us assume that the first m rows are already bound. We now try to assign values to the variables in the $m+1$ row. Let us define the sets J_i to be the set of indices of the variables in row i that are bound to 1. Then equations (32) and (30) for $i = m + 1$ yield

$$\sum_{j=1}^{b} x_j = r \tag{33}$$

$$\sum_{j \in J_i} x_j = \lambda, \ \forall i = 1 \ldots m \tag{34}$$

where $x_j = y_{m+1,j}$.

This set of constraints is an instance of the problem **P'** studied in section 5.2. Therefore it is valid to add an instance of our global constraint every time a row is completed. In other words we dynamically add instances of our new global constraint during search.

6.4 Computing One Solution

We report in table 1 the running times (in seconds) needed to compute one solution for various instances of the BIBD problem taken from [3]. All running times are obtained on a laptop PC at 1.4 GHz, using ILOG Solver. We also report the number of nodes of the search tree. The model A is the model described in the section 6.2. The model B is A plus the addition of our global constraint during the search, as explained in section 6.3. The model C is the model A using the symmetry breaking method STAB[6][7]. Last, the model D is C plus the addition of our global constraints during search.

Table 1. Results for computing one solution.

BIBD	A		B		C		D		A/B		C/D	
$v\ k\ \lambda$	nodes	time	nodes	time	nodes	time	nodes	time	nodes	time	nodes	time
6 3 4	39	0.01	19	0.01	31	0.01	15	0.01	2.6	2	2.1	1
7 3 5	29	0.01	29	0.01	29	0.01	29	0.01	1.6	2	1	1
6 3 10	219	0.03	64	0.02	159	0.04	39	0.02	3.8	2.5	4.1	2
12 6 5	1772	0.16	68	0.03	448	0.08	66	0.04	26.3	6	6.8	2
10 3 2	75	0.02	52	0.03	64	0.03	52	0.03	1.6	1	1.2	1
14 7 6	10100	0.57	111	0.06	2276	0.29	107	0.07	91	10	21	4.1
7 3 20	119	0.04	119	0.05	119	0.05	119	0.06	1.5	1.6	1	0.8
8 4 12	118826	0.6	78	0.03	918	0.14	78	0.03	1520	22	12	4.7
8 4 21	187073	9.1	138	0.04	6406	0.63	138	0.06	1356	262	46	10.5
7 2 10	230	0.07	230	0.08	230	0.08	230	0.09	0	1.3	1	0.9
9 3 5	104	0.03	74	0.03	104	0.05	74	0.05	1.7	1.7	1.4	1
9 4 15	398437	18.6	2781	0.30	6476	0.65	2781	0.37	143	72	2.3	2.2

The last 4 columns give the Improvement between A and B, and between C and D. These improvements are negligible for the easiest problems, and then go up to a factor of 15020 with the difficulty of the problem. To our knowledge, the model D is the fastest published way to compute one solution for BIBD.

6.5 Computing Canonical Solutions

Another interesting problem is to compute all the solutions of BIBD. One of the best published method is the STAB method. By lack of space we do not report detailed results here, but the STAB method is also improved by the addition of our global constraints during search. On a comprehensive set of problems taken from[7] the reduction in the number of nodes range from 0 to 4, while the speedup ranges from 1 to 2.

Table 2. Results for computing all canonical solutions.

BIBD $v\ k\ \lambda$	sol	E nodes	E time	F nodes	F time	E/F node	E/F time
7 3 2	4	50	0.14	44	0.09	1.1	1.6
8 4 3	4	57	0.37	38	0.24	1.5	1.5
6 3 4	4	86	0.31	60	0.06	1.4	5.2
10 4 2	3	59	0.41	40	0.31	1.5	1.3
13 3 1	2	157	1.6	126	0.7	1.2	2.3
7 3 3	10	214	0.9	186	0.43	1.2	2.1
6 3 6	6	285	1.24	184	0.32	1.5	3.9
16 4 1	1	17	1.24	10	2.1	1.7	0.6
15 5 2	0	1069	6.7	403	1.2	2.7	5.6
9 4 3	11	485	6.72	232	1.8	2.1	3.7
15 7 3	5	275	7.6	200	3.4	1.4	2.2
22 7 2	0	670	4.2	355	1.6	1.9	2.6
6 3 8	13	770	5.9	492	0.86	1.6	6.9
7 3 4	35	1062	9.9	979	2.9	1.1	3.4
9 3 2	36	1080	12.7	925	6.9	1.2	1.8
6 3 10	19	1756	23.5	1131	2.2	1.6	10.7
10 5 4	21	2807	58	1036	7.7	2.7	7.5
25 5 1	1	65	49	45	48	1.4	1.0
7 3 5	109	4306	83	3993	17.2	1	4.8
15 3 1	80	14362	871	9835	530	1.5	1.6

A related problem is to find all the unique solutions up to symmetries. These solutions are called canonical solutions. This is a very challenging problem. For instance, there are only 80 such solutions for the 15 3 1 BIBD, whereas model A of the previous section has more than 32 millions solutions for it. For each BIBD instance we report the number of solutions, the number of nodes and the running times for two models. The model E is the model C of the previous section combined together with the symmetry breaking method SBDD as shown in [6]. The model F is the model D of the previous section together with the same SBDD method. The last two columns give the improvements between the two models. On this set of problems, the reduction in the number of nodes range from 1.1 to 2.7, while the speedup ranges from 0.6% to 10.7%. To our knowledge, the model F is the fastest published method for computing all canonical solutions for BIBDs.

7 Conclusion

We have studied how to improve over bound consistency for linear constraints. By looking at a set of constraints at once, we were able to derive much stronger bounds than what can be obtained by bound consistency. When the right hand side of the clique constraints are equal to 1 we proved that these bounds could be the best possible bounds. in this case the bounds computed for the variables x_j are equivalent to the reduced cost fixings known in linear programming approach.

However, we have shown that stronger bounds could be derived when the right hand sides were greater than 1. We have implemented these improved bound computations into a global constraints. Experimental results on a comprehensive set of problem instances show the effectiveness of our approach. As a side result we were able to improve over the best published results for BIBDs.

Several research avenues are now open for future work. First of all, we could use our technique in the MAX CSP setting of [5]. It would be interesting to see if we could get some improvements there. Second, we should experimentally compare our approach to the use of a global linear constraint. Indeed, the global linear constraint would not compute the same bounds, but it could detect some infeasibilities earlier. It remains to be seen if the result would be competitive with ours. Last, we plan to study the generalization of our decomposition approach when the variables x_i are not binary variables. We conjecture that this could yield better variable fixings than reduced cost fixings.

Acknowledgements

The author would like to thank Jean-Charles Regin, Ed Rothberg and Marie Puget for their useful remarks on previous drafts of this article.

References

1. Bruno De Backer, Henri Beringer A CLP Language Handling Disjunctions of Linear Constraints. Proceedings of ICLP 1993 : 550-563
2. P. Flener, A. M. Frisch, B. Hnich, Z. Kiziltan, I. Miguel, J. Pearson, T. Walsh. Breaking Row and Column Symmetries in Matrix Models. Proceedings of CP'02, pages 462-476, 2002
3. A.M. Frisch, C. Jefferson, I. Miguel, Symmetry-breaking as a Prelude to Implied Constraints : A Constraint Modeling Pattern Technical report APES-74-2004, December 2003
4. W. Harvey and P. J. Stuckey. Improving Linear Constraint Propagation by Changing Constraint Representation. Constraints : An International Journal, 8(2) :173-207, 2003.
5. T. Petit, C. Bessiere et J.-C. Regin. Detection de conflits pour la resolution de problemes sur-contraints, JNPC'03 , 2003, pp. 293-307 (in French)
6. Puget, J.-F. : Symmetry Breaking Using Stabilizers. In proceedings of CP'03, pp 585-589.
7. Puget, J.-F. : Using Constraint Programming to Compute Symmetries. In proceedings of SymCon 03, a CP'03 workshop.

Improved Algorithms for the Global Cardinality Constraint

Claude-Guy Quimper, Alejandro López-Ortiz,
Peter van Beek, and Alexander Golynski

University of Waterloo, Waterloo, Canada

Abstract. We study the global cardinality constraint (gcc) and propose an $O(n^{1.5}d)$ algorithm for domain consistency and an $O(cn + dn)$ algorithm for range consistency where n is the number of variables, d the number of values in the domain, and c an output dependent variable smaller than or equal to n. We show how to prune the cardinality variables in $O(n^2 d + n^{2.66})$ steps, detect if gcc is universal in constant time and prove that it is NP-Hard to maintain domain consistency on extended-GCC.

1 Introduction

Previous studies have demonstrated that designing special purpose constraint propagators for commonly occurring constraints can significantly improve the efficiency of a constraint programming approach (e.g., [8, 11]). In this paper we study constraint propagators for the global cardinality constraint (gcc). A gcc over a set of variables and values states that the number of variables instantiating to a value must be between a given upper and lower bound, where the bounds can be different for each value. This type of constraint commonly occurs in rostering, timetabling, sequencing, and scheduling applications (e.g., [4, 10, 13]).

Several pruning algorithms have been designed for the gcc. Van Hentenryck et al. [14] express the gcc as a collection of "atleast" and "atmost" constraints and prunes the domain on each individual constraint. Régin [9] gives an $O(n^2 d)$ algorithm for domain consistency of the gcc (where n is the number of variables and d is the number of values), Puget [15], Quimper et al. [5], and Katriel and Thiel [6] respectively give an $O(n \log n)$, $O(n)$ and $O(n + d)$ algorithm for bounds consistency, and Leconte [7] gives an $\Theta(n^2)$ algorithm for range consistency of the all-different constraint, a specialization of gcc. In addition to pruning the variable domains, Katriel and Thiel's algorithm determines the maximum and the minimum number of variables that can be assigned to a specific value for the case where the variable domains are intervals.

We improve over Régin's algorithm and give an $O(n^{1.5}d)$ algorithm for domain consistency. In addition, we compute the maximum and the minimum number of variables that can be assigned to a value in respectively $O(n^2 d)$ and $O(n^{2.66})$ steps for the case where the variable domains are not necessarily intervals (i.e., the domains can contain holes) as often arises when domain consistency is enforced on the variables. We present a new algorithm for range consistency with running time $O(cn + dn)$ ($O(cn)$ under certain conditions) where c is an output dependent variable between 1 and n. This new algorithm improves over Leconte's algorithm for the all-different constraint that is distributed as part of ILOG Solver [4]. We detect in constant time if a branch in a search tree only leads to solutions that satisfy the *gcc*. This efficient test avoids useless calls to a propagator. Finally, we study a generalized version of *gcc* called extended-*gcc* and prove that it is NP-Hard to maintain domain consistency on this constraint.

2 Problem Definition

A *constraint satisfaction problem* (CSP) consists of a set of n *variables*, $X = \{x_1, \ldots, x_n\}$; a set of values D; a finite domain $dom(x_i) \subseteq D$ of possible *values* for each variable x_i, $1 \leq i \leq n$; and a collection of m *constraints*, $\{C_1, \ldots, C_m\}$. Each constraint C_i is a constraint over some set of variables, denoted by $vars(C_i)$, that specifies the allowed combinations of values for the variables in $vars(C_i)$. Given a constraint C, we use the notation $t \in C$ to denote a tuple t – an assignment of a value to each of the variables in $vars(C)$ – that satisfies the constraint C. We use the notation $t[x]$ to denote the value assigned to variable x by the tuple t. A *solution* to a CSP is an assignment of a value to each variable that satisfies all of the constraints.

We assume in this paper that the domains are totally ordered. The minimum and maximum values in the domain $dom(x)$ of a variable x are denoted by $\min(dom(x))$ and $\max(dom(x))$, and the interval notation $[a, b]$ is used as a shorthand for the set of values $\{a, a+1, \ldots, b\}$.

CSPs are usually solved by interleaving a backtracking search with a series of constraint propagation phases. A CSP can be made locally consistent by repeatedly removing unsupported values from the domains of its variables. This allows us to reduce the domain of a variable after an assignment has been made in the backtracking search phase.

Definition 1 (Support). *Given a constraint C, a value $v \in dom(x)$ for a variable $x \in vars(C)$ is said to have:*

(i) *a domain support in C if there exists a $t \in C$ such that $v = t[x]$ and $t[y] \in dom(y)$, for every $y \in vars(C)$;*
(ii) *an interval support in C if there exists a $t \in C$ such that $v = t[x]$ and $t[y] \in [\min(dom(y)), \max(dom(y))]$, for every $y \in vars(C)$.*

Definition 2 (Local Consistency). *A constraint problem C is said to be:*

(i) *bounds consistent if for each $x \in vars(C)$, each of the values $\min(dom(x))$ and $\max(dom(x))$ has an interval support in C.*
(ii) *range consistent if for each $x \in vars(C)$, each value $v \in dom(x)$ has an interval support in C.*
(iii) *domain consistent if for each $x \in vars(C)$, each value $v \in dom(x)$ has a domain support in C.*

When testing for bounds consistency, we assume, without loss of generality, that all variable domains are intervals.

The global cardinality constraint problem (*gcc*) considers a matching between the variables in X with the values in D. A variable $x \in X$ can only be assigned to a value that belongs to its domain $dom(x)$ which is a subset of D. An assignment satisfies the constraint if and only if all values $v \in D$ are assigned by at least l_v variables and at most u_v variables. The all-different constraint is a *gcc* such that $l_v = 0$ and $u_v = 1$ for all values v in D.

The *gcc* problem can be divided in two different constraint problems. The **lower bound constraint problem** (*lbc*) which ensures that all values $v \in D$ are assigned by at least l_v variables and the **upper bound constraint problem** (*ubc*) which ensures that all values $v \in D$ are assigned by at most u_v variables.

3 Domain Consistency

Régin [9] showed how to enforce domain consistency on *gcc* in $O(|X|^2|D|)$ steps. For the special case of the all-different constraint, domain consistency can be enforced in $O(|X|^{1.5}|D|)$. An alternative, presented in [5], runs in $O(u|X|^{1.5}|D| + l^{1.5}|X||D|^{1.5})$ where u and l are respectively the maximum u_v and the maximum l_v. The latter algorithm offers a better complexity for certain values of l and u. Our result consists of an algorithm that runs in $O(|X|^{1.5}|D|)$ and therefore is as efficient as the algorithm for the all-different constraint.

Our approach is similar to the one used by Régin [8] for propagating the *all-different* constraint except that our algorithm proceeds in two passes. The first one makes the *ubc* domain consistent and the second pass makes the *lbc* domain consistent. Quimper et al. [5] have previously formally shown that this suffices to make the *gcc* domain consistent.

3.1 Matching in a Graph

For the *ubc* and *lbc* problems, we will need to construct a special graph. Following Régin [8], let $G(\langle X, D \rangle, E)$ be an undirected bipartite graph such that nodes at the left represent variables and nodes at the right represent values. There is an edge (x_i, v) in E iff the value v is in the domain $dom(x_i)$ of the variable. Let $c(n)$ be the capacity associated to node n such that $c(x_i) = 1$ for all variable-nodes $x_i \in X$ and $c(v)$ is an arbitrary non-negative value for all value-nodes v in D. A matching M in graph G is a subset of the edges E such that no more than $c(n)$ edges in M are adjacent to node n. We are interested in finding a matching M with maximal cardinality.

The following concepts from flow and matching theory (see [1]) will be useful in this context. Consider a graph G and a matching M. The residual graph G_M of G is the directed version of graph G such that edges in M are oriented from values to variables and edges in $E - M$ are oriented from variables to values. A node n is *free* if the number of edges adjacent to n in M is strictly less than the capacity $c(n)$ of node n. An augmenting path in G_M is a path with an odd number of links that connects two free nodes together. If there is an augmenting path p in G_M, then there exists a matching M' of cardinality $|M'| = |M| + 1$ that is obtained by inverting all edges in G_M that belongs to the augmenting path p. A matching M is maximal iff there is no augmenting path in the graph G_M.

Hopcroft and Karp [3] describe an algorithm with running time $O(|X|^{1.5}|D|)$ that finds a maximum matching in a bipartite graph when the capacities $c(n)$ are equal to 1 for all nodes. We generalize the algorithm to obtain the same complexity when $c(v) \geq 0$ for the value-nodes and $c(x_i) = 1$ for variable-nodes.

The Hopcroft-Karp algorithm starts with an initial empty matching $M = \emptyset$ which is improved at each iteration by finding a set of disjoint shortest augmenting paths. An iteration that finds a set of augmenting paths proceeds in two steps.

The first step consists of performing a breath-first search (BFS) on the residual graph G_M starting with the free variable-nodes. The breath-first search generates a forest of nodes such that nodes at level i are at distance i from a free node. This distance is minimal by property of BFS. Let m be the smallest level that contains a free value-node. For each node n at level $i < m$, we assign a list $L(n)$ of nodes adjacent to node n that are at level $i + 1$. We set $L(n) = \emptyset$ for every node at level m or higher.

The second step of the algorithm uses a stack to perform a depth-first search (DFS). The DFS starts from a free variable-node and is only allowed to branch from a node n to a node in $L(n)$. When the algorithm branches from node n_1 to n_2, it deletes n_2 from $L(n_1)$. If the DFS reaches a free value-node, the algorithm marks this node as non-free, clears the stack, and pushes a new free variable-node that has not been visited onto the stack. This DFS generates a forest of trees whose roots are free variable-nodes. If a tree also contains a free value-node, then the path from the root to this free-value node is an augmenting path. Changing the orientation of all edges that lie on the augmenting paths generates a matching of greater cardinality.

In our case, to find a matching when capacities of value-nodes $c(v)$ are non-negative, we construct the duplicated graph G' where value-nodes v are duplicated $c(v)$ times and the capacity of each node is set to 1. Clearly, a matching in G' corresponds to a matching in G and can be found by the Hopcroft-Karp algorithm. We can simulate a trace of the Hopcroft-Karp algorithm run on graph G' by directly using graph G. We simply let the DFS visit $c(n) - \deg_M(n)$ times a free-node n where $\deg_M(n)$ is the number of edges in M adjacent to node n. This simulates the visit of the free duplicated nodes of node n in G. Even if we allow multiple visits of a same node, we maintain the constraint that an edge cannot be traversed more than once in the DFS. The running time complexity for a DFS is still bounded by the number of edges $O(|X||D|)$.

Hopcroft and Karp proved that if s is the cardinality of a maximum cardinality matching, then $O(\sqrt{s})$ iterations are sufficient to find this maximum cardinality matching. In our case, s is bounded by $|X|$ and the complexity of each BFS and DFS is bounded by the number of edges in G_M i.e. $O(|X||D|)$.

The total complexity is therefore $O(|X|^{1.5}|D|)$. We will run this algorithm twice, first with $c(v) = u_v$ to obtain a matching M_u and then with $c(v) = l_v$ to obtain a matching M_l.

3.2 Pruning the Domains

Using the algorithm described in the previous section, we compute a matching M_u in graph G such that capacities of variable-nodes are set to $c(x_i) = 1$ and capacities of value-nodes are set to $c(v) = u_v$. A matching M_u clearly corresponds to an assignment that satisfies the *ubc* if it has cardinality $|X|$ i.e. if each variable is assigned to a value.

Consider now the same graph G where capacities of variable-nodes are $c(x_i) = 1$ but capacities of value-nodes are set to $c(v) = l_v$. A maximum matching M_l of cardinality $|M_l| = \sum l_v$ represents a partial solution that satisfies the *lbc*. Variables that are not assigned to a value can in fact be assigned to any value in their domain and still satisfy the *lbc*.

Pruning the domains consists of finding the edges that cannot be part of a matching. From flow theory, we know that an edge can be part of a matching iff it belongs to a strongly connected component or it lies on a path starting from or leading to a free node.

Régin's algorithm prunes the domains by finding all strongly connected components and flagging all edges that lie on a path starting or finishing at a free node. This can be done in $O(|X||D|)$ using DFS as described in [12]. Finally, Quimper et al. [5] proved that pruning the domains for the *ubc* and then pruning the domains for the *lbc* is sufficient to prune the domains for the *gcc*.

3.3 Dynamic Case

If during the propagation process another constraint removes a value from a domain, we would like to efficiently reintroduce domain consistency over *ubc* and *lbc*. Régin [8] describes how to maintain a maximum matching under edge deletion and maintain domain consistency in $O(\delta|X||D|)$ where δ is the number of deleted edges. His algorithm can also be applied to ours.

4 Pruning the Cardinality Variables

Pruning the cardinality variables l_v and u_v seems like a natural operation to apply to *gcc*. To give a simple example, if variable u_v constrains the value v to be assigned to at most 100 variables while there are less than 50 variables involved in the problem, it is clear that the u_v can be reduced to a lower value. We will show in the next two sections how to shrink the cardinality lower bounds l_v and cardinality upper bounds u_v.

In general, the pruned bounds on the cardinality variables obtained by our algorithm are at least as tight as those obtained by Katriel and Thiel's algorithm [6], and can be strictly tighter in the case where domain consistency has been enforced on the (ordinary) variables.

4.1 Growing the Lower Bounds

Let G be the value graph where node capacities are set to $c(x_i) = 1$ for variable-nodes and $c(a) = u_a$ for value-nodes. For a specific value v, we want to find the smallest value l_v such that there exists a matching M of cardinality $|X|$ that satisfies the capacity constraints such that $\deg_M(v) = l_v$.

We construct a maximum cardinality matching M_u that satisfies the capacity constraints of G. For each matched value v (i.e. $\deg_{M_u}(v) > 0$), we create a graph G^v and M_u^v that are respectively a copy of graph G and matching M_u^v to which we removed all edges adjacent to value-node v. The partial matching M_u^v can be transformed into a maximum cardinality matching by repeatedly finding an augmenting path using a DFS and applying this path to M_u^v. This is done in $O(\deg_{M_u}(v)|X||D|)$ steps. Let C_v be the cardinality of the maximum matching.

Lemma 1. *Any matching M_u in G of cardinality $|X|$ requires $\deg_{M_u}(v)$ to be at least $|M_u| - C_v$.*

Proof. If by removing all edges connected to value-node v the cardinality of a maximum matching in a graph drops from $|M|$ to C_v then at least $|M| - C_v$ edges in M were adjacent to value-node v and could not be replaced by other edges. Therefore value-node v is required to be adjacent to $|M| - C_v$ edges in M in order to obtain a matching of cardinality $|X|$. □

Since M_u is a maximum matching, we have $\sum_v \deg_{M_u}(v) = |X|$ and therefore the time required to prune all cardinality lower bounds for all values is $O(\sum_v \deg_{M_u}(v)|X||D|) = O(|X|^2|D|)$.

4.2 Pruning Upper Bounds

We want to know what is the maximum number of variables that can be assigned to a value v without violating the *lbc*; i.e. how many variables can be assigned to value v while other values $w \in D$ are still assigned to at least l_w variables. We consider the residual graph G_{M_l}. If there exists a path from a free variable-node to the value-node v then there exists a matching M_l' that has one more variable assigned to v than matching M_l and that still satisfies the *lbc*.

Lemma 2. *The number of edge-disjoint paths from free variable-nodes to value-node v can be computed in $O(|X|^{2.66})$ steps.*

Proof. We first observe that a value-node in G_{M_l} that is not adjacent to any edge in M_l cannot reach a variable-node (by definition of a residual graph). These nodes, with the exception of node v, cannot lead to a path from a free variable-node to node v. We therefore create a graph $G_{M_l}^v$ by removing from G_{M_l} all nodes that are not adjacent to an edge in M_l except for node v. To the graph $G_{M_l}^v$, we add a special node s called the source node and we add edges from s to all free-variable nodes. Since there are at most $|X|$ matched variable-nodes, we obtain a graph of at most $2|X| + 1$ nodes and $O(|X|^2)$ edges.

The number of edge-disjoint paths from the free variable-nodes to value-node v is equal to the maximum flow between s and v. A maximum flow in a directed bipartite graph where edge capacities are all 1 can be computed in $O(n^{1.5}m)$ where n is the number of nodes and m the number of edges (see Theorem 8.1 in [1]). In our case, we obtain a complexity of $O(|X|^{2.66})$. □

The maximum number of variables that can be assigned to value v is equal to the number of edges adjacent to v in M_l plus the number of edge-disjoint paths between the free-nodes and node v. We compute a flow problem for computing the new upper bounds u_v of each value and prune the upper bound variables in $O(|D||X|^{2.66})$ steps.

5 Range Consistency

Enforcing range consistency consists of removing values in variable domains that do not have an interval support. Since we are only interested in interval support, we assume without loss of generality that variable domains are represented by intervals $dom(x_i) = [a, b]$.

Using notation from [7, 5], we let $C(S)$ represent the number of variables whose domain is fully contained in set S and $I(S)$ represent the number of variables whose domains intersect set S.

Maximal (Minimal) Capacity. The *maximal (minimal) capacity* $\lceil S \rceil$ ($\lfloor S \rfloor$) of set S is the maximal (minimal) number of variables that can be assigned to the values in S. We have $\lceil S \rceil = \sum_{v \in S} u_v$ and $\lfloor S \rfloor = \sum_{v \in S} l_v$.

Hall Interval. A *Hall interval* is an interval $H \subseteq D$ such that the number of variables whose domain is contained in H is equal to the maximal capacity of H. More formally, H is a Hall interval iff $C(H) = \lceil H \rceil$.

Failure Set. A failure set is a set $F \subseteq D$ such that there are fewer variables whose domains intersect F than its minimal capacity; i.e., F is a failure set iff $I(F) < \lfloor F \rfloor$.

Unstable Set. An *Unstable set* is a set $U \subseteq D$ such that the number of variables whose domain intersects U is equal to the minimal capacity of U. The set U is unstable iff $I(U) = \lfloor U \rfloor$.

Stable Interval. A *Stable interval* is an interval that contains more variable domains than its lower capacity and that does not intersect any unstable or failure set, i.e. S is a stable interval iff $C(S) > \lfloor S \rfloor$, $S \cap U = \emptyset$ and $S \cap F = \emptyset$ for all unstable sets U and failure sets F. A stable interval S is *maximal* if there is no stable interval S' such that $F \subset F'$.

A *basic Hall interval* is a Hall interval that cannot be expressed as the union of two or more Hall intervals. We use the following lemmas taken from [7, 5].

Lemma 3 ([7]). *A variable cannot be assigned to a value in a Hall interval if its whole domain is not contained in this Hall interval.*

Lemma 4 ([5]). *A variable whose domain intersects an unstable set cannot be instantiated to a value outside of this set.*

Lemma 5 ([5]). *A variable whose domain is contained in a stable interval can be assigned to any value in its domain.*

We show that achieving range consistency is reduced to the problem of finding the Hall intervals and the unstable sets and pruning the domains according to Lemma 3 and Lemma 4. Leconte's $\Theta(|X|^2)$ algorithm (implemented in ILOG) enforces range consistency for the all-different constraint ($l_v = 0$ and $u_v = 1$). Leconte proves the optimality of his algorithm with the following example.

Example 1 (Leconte 96 page 24 [7]). Let $x_1, \ldots, x_n$ be n variables whose domains contain distinct odd numbers ranging from 1 to $2n - 1$ and let $x_{n+1}, \ldots, x_{2n}$ be n variables whose domains are $[1, 2n - 1]$. An algorithm maintaining range consistency needs to remove the n odd numbers from n variable domains which is done in $\Theta(n^2)$.

We introduce an algorithm that achieves range consistency in $O(t + C|X|)$ where $C \leq |X|$ and t is the time required to sort $|X|$ variables by lower and upper bounds. If $C = |X|$ then we obtain an $O(|X|^2)$ algorithm but we can also obtain an algorithm that is as fast as sorting the variables in the absence of Hall intervals and unstable sets.

The first step of our algorithm is to make the variables bounds consistent using already existing algorithms [5, 6]. We then study basic Hall intervals and basic unstable sets in bounds consistent problems.

In order to better understand the distribution of Hall intervals, unstable sets, and stable intervals over the domain D, we introduce the notion of a *characteristic interval*. A characteristic interval I is an interval in D iff for all variable domains, both bounds of the domain are either in I or outside of I.

A *basic characteristic* interval is a characteristic interval that cannot be expressed as the union of two or more characteristic intervals. A characteristic interval can always be expressed as the union of basic characteristic intervals.

Lemma 6. *In a bounds consistent problem, a basic Hall interval is a basic characteristic interval.*

Proof. In a bounds consistent problem, no variables have a bound within a Hall interval and the other bound outside of the Hall interval. Therefore every basic Hall interval is a basic characteristic interval. □

Lemma 7. *In a bounds consistent problem, a maximum stable interval is a characteristic interval.*

Proof. Quimper et al. [5] proved that in a bounds consistent problem, stable intervals and unstable sets form a partition of the domain D. Therefore, either a variable domain intersects an unstable set and has both bounds in this unstable set or it does not intersect an unstable set and is fully contain in a stable interval. Consequently, a maximum stable interval is a characteristic interval. □

Lemma 8. *Any unstable set can be expressed by the union and the exclusion of basic characteristic intervals.*

Proof. Let U be an unstable set and I be the smallest interval that covers U. Since any variable domain that intersects U has both bounds in U, then I is a characteristic interval. Moreover, $I - U$ forms a series of intervals that are in I but not in U. A variable domain contained in I must have either both bounds in an interval of $I - U$ such that it does not intersect U or either have both bounds in U. Therefore the intervals of $I' = I - U$ are characteristic intervals and U can be expressed as $U = I - I'$. □

5.1 Finding the Basic Characteristic Intervals

Using the properties of basic characteristic intervals, we suggest a new algorithm that makes a problem range consistent and has a time complexity of $O(t + cH)$ where t is the time complexity for sorting n variables and H is the number of basic characteristic intervals. This algorithm proceeds in four steps:

1. Make the problem bounds consistent in $O(t + |X|)$ steps (see [5]).
2. Sort the variables by increasing lower bounds in $O(t)$ steps.
3. Find the basic characteristic intervals in $O(|X|)$ steps.
4. Prune the variable domains in $O(c|X|)$ steps.

Step 1 and Step 2 are trivial since we can use existing algorithms. We focus our attention on Steps 3 and 4.

Step 3 of our algorithm finds the basic characteristic intervals. In order to discover these intervals, we maintain a stack S of intervals that are the potential basic characteristic intervals. We initialize the stack by pushing the infinite interval $[-\infty, \infty]$. We then process each variable domain in ascending order of lower bound. Let I be the current variable domain and I' the interval on top of the stack. If the variable domain is contained in the interval on top of the stack ($I \subseteq I'$), then the variable domain could potentially be a characteristic interval and we push it on the stack. If the variable domain I has its lower bound in the interval I' on top of the stack and its upper bound outside of this interval, then neither I or I' can be characteristic intervals, although the interval $I \cup I'$ could potentially be a characteristic interval. In this case, we pop I' off the stack and we assign I to be $I \cup I'$. We repeat the operation until I is contained in I'. Note that at any time, the stack contains a set of nested intervals.

If we process a variable domain whose lower bound is greater than the upper bound of the interval I' on the stack, then by construction of the stack, I' is a basic characteristic interval that we print and pop off of the stack. We repeat the operation until the current variable domain intersects the interval on the stack.

Algorithm 1 processes all variables and prints the basic characteristic intervals in increasing order of upper bounds. In addition to this task, it also identifies which kind of characteristic intervals the algorithm prints: a Hall interval, a Stable interval or an interval that could contain values of an unstable set. This is done by maintaining a counter c_1 that keeps track of how many variable domains are contained in an interval on the stack. Counter c_2 is similar but only counts the first $\lfloor A \rfloor$ variables contained in each sub-characteristic interval A. A characteristic interval I is a stable interval if c_2 is greater than $\lfloor I \rfloor$ and might contain values of an unstable set if c_2 is equal to $\lfloor I \rfloor$. We ignore characteristic intervals with $c_2 < \lfloor I \rfloor$ since those intervals are not used to define Hall intervals, stable intervals or unstable sets.

Input : X are the variable domains sorted by non decreasing lower bounds
Result : Prints the basic characteristic intervals and specifies if they are Hall intervals, stable intervals or contain values of an unstable set
$S \leftarrow$ empty stack
$\text{push}(S, \langle [-\infty, \infty], 0, 0 \rangle)$
Add a dummy variable that forces all elements to be popped off of the stack on termination
$X \leftarrow X \cup [\max(D) + 1, \max(D) + 3]$
for $x \in X$ **do**
$\quad$ **while** $\max(top(S).interval) < \min(dom(x))$ **do**
$\quad\quad \langle I, c_1, c_2 \rangle \leftarrow pop(S)$
$\quad\quad$ **if** $\lceil I \rceil = c_1$ **then** print "Hall Interval": I
$\quad\quad$ **else if** $\lfloor I \rfloor < c_2$ **then** print "Stable Interval": I
$\quad\quad$ **else if** $\lfloor I \rfloor = c_2$ **then** print "Might Contain Values from Unstable Sets": I
$\quad\quad \langle I', c_1', c_2' \rangle \leftarrow pop(S)$
$\quad\quad \text{push}(\langle I', c_1 + c_1', c_2' + \min(c_2, \lfloor I \rfloor) \rangle)$
$\quad I \leftarrow dom(x), c_1 \leftarrow 1, c_2 \leftarrow 1$
$\quad$ **while** $\max(top(S).interval) \leq \max(I)$ **do**
$\quad\quad \langle I', c_1', c_2' \rangle \leftarrow pop(S)$
$\quad\quad I \leftarrow I \cup I'$
$\quad\quad c_1 \leftarrow c_1 + c_1'$
$\quad\quad c_2 \leftarrow c_2 + c_2'$
$\quad \text{push}(S, \langle I, c_1, c_2 \rangle)$

Algorithm 1: Prints the basic characteristic intervals in a bounds consistent problem.

Algorithm 1 runs in $O(|X|)$ steps since a variable domain can be pushed on the stack, popped off the stack, and merged with another interval only once.

Once the basic characteristic intervals are listed in non-decreasing order of upper bounds, we can easily enforce range consistency on the variable domains. We simultaneously iterate through the variable domains and the characteristic intervals both sorted by non-increasing order of upper bounds. If a variable x_i is only contained in characteristic intervals that contain values of an unstable set, then we remove all characteristic intervals strictly contained in the variable domain. We also remove from the domain of x_i the values whose lower capacity l_v is null. In order to enforce the ubc, we remove a Hall interval H from all variable domains that is not contained in H.

Removing the characteristic intervals from the variable domains requires at most $O(c|X|)$ steps where $c \leq |X|$ is the number of characteristic intervals. Removing the values whith null lower capacities requires at most $O(|X||D|)$ instructions but can require no work at all if lower capacities l_v are all null or all positive. If lower capacities are all positive, no values need to be removed from the variable domains. If they are all null, the problem does not have unstable sets and only Hall intervals need to be considered. The final running time complexity is either $O(c|X|)$ or $O(c|X| + |D||X|)$ depending if lower capacities are all null, all positive, or mixed.

Example: Consider the following bounds consistent problem where $D = [1, 6]$, $l_v = 1$, and $u_v = 2$ for all $v \in D$. Let the variable domains be $dom(x_i) = [2, 3]$ for $1 \leq i \leq 4$, $dom(x_5) = [1, 6]$, $dom(x_6) = [1, 4]$, $dom(x_7) = [4, 6]$, and $dom(x_8) = [5, 5]$. Algorithm 1 identifies the Hall interval $[2, 3]$ and the two characteristic intervals $[5, 5]$ and $[1, 6]$ that contain values of an unstable set. Variable domains $dom(x_5)$ to $dom(x_8)$ are only contained in characteristic intervals that might contain values of unstable sets. We therefore remove the characteristic intervals $[2, 3]$ and $[5, 5]$ that are stricly contained in the domains of x_5, x_6, and x_7. The Hall interval $[2, 3]$ must be removed from the variable domains that strictly contain it, i.e. the value 2 and 3 must be removed from the domain of variables x_6 and x_8. After removing the values, we obtain a range consistent problem.

5.2 Dynamic Case

We want to maintain range consistency when a variable domain $dom(x_i)$ is modified by the propagation of other constraints. Notice that if the bounds of $dom(x_i)$ change, new Hall intervals or unstable sets can appear in the problems requiring other variable domains to be pruned. We only need to prune the domains according to these new Hall intervals and unstable sets.

We make the variable domains bounds consistent and find the characteristic intervals as before in $O(t + |X|)$ steps. We compare the characteristic intervals with those found in the previous computation and perform a linear scan to mark all new characteristic intervals. We perform the pruning as explained in Section 5.1. Since we know which characteristic intervals were already present during last computation, we can avoid pruning domains that have already been pruned.

If no new Hall intervals or unstable sets are created, the algorithm runs in $O(t + |X|)$ steps. If variable domains need to be pruned, the algorithm runs in $O(t + c|X|)$ which is proportional to the number of values removed from the domains.

6 Universality

A constraint C is universal for a problem if any tuple t such that $t[x] \in dom(x)$ satisfies the constraint C. We study under what conditions a given *gcc* behaves like the universal constraint. We show an algorithm that tests in constant time if the *lbc* or the *ubc* are universal. If both the *lbc* and the *ubc* accept any variable assignment then the *gcc* is universal. This implies there is no need to run a propagator on the *gcc* since we know that all values have a support. Our result holds for domain, range, and bounds consistency.

6.1 Universality of the Lower Bound Constraint

Lemma 9. *The lbc is universal for a problem if and only if for each value $v \in D$ there exists at least l_v variables x such that $dom(x) = \{v\}$.*

Proof. $\Longleftarrow$ If for each value $v \in D$ there are l_v variables x such that $dom(x) = \{v\}$ then it is clear that any variable assignment satisfies the *lbc*.
$\Longrightarrow$ Suppose for a *lbc* problem there is a value $v \in D$ such that there are less than l_v variables whose domain only contains value v. Therefore, an assignment where all variables that are not bounded to v are assigned to a value other than v would not satisfy the *lbc*. This proves that *lbc* is not universal under this assumption. $\square$

The following algorithm verifies if the *lbc* is universal in $O(|X| + |D|)$ steps.

1. Create a vector t such that $t[v] = l_v$ for all $v \in D$.
2. For all domains that contain only one value v, decrement $t[v]$ by one.
3. The *lbc* is universal if and only if no components in t are positive.

We can easily make the algorithm dynamic under the modification of variable domains. We keep a counter c that indicates the number of positive components in vector t. Each time a variable gets bound to a single value v, we decrement $t[v]$ by one. If $t[v]$ reaches the value zero, we decrement c by one. The *lbc* becomes universal when c reaches zero. Using this strategy, each time a variable domain is pruned, we can check in constant time if the *lbc* becomes universal.

6.2 Universality of the Upper Bound Constraint

Lemma 10. *The ubc is universal for a problem if and only if for each value $v \in D$ there exists at most u_v variable domains that contain v.*

Proof. $\Longleftarrow$ Trivially, if for each value $v \in D$ there are u_v or fewer variable domains that contain v, there is no assignment that could violate the *ubc* and therefore the *ubc* is universal.
$\Longrightarrow$ Suppose there is a value v such that more than u_v variable domains contain v. If we assign all these variables to the value v, we obtain an assignment that does not satisfy the *ubc*. $\square$

To test the universality of the *ubc*, we could create a vector a such that $a[v] = I(\{v\}) - u_v$. The *ubc* is universal iff no components of a are positive. In order to perform faster update operations, we represent the vector a by a vector t that we initialize as follows: $t[\min(D)] \leftarrow -u_{\min(D)}$ and $t[v] \leftarrow u_{v-1} - u_v$ for $\min(D) < v \leq \max(D)$. Assuming variable domains are initially intervals, for each variable $x_i \in X$, we increment the value of $t[\min(dom(x_i))]$ by one and decrement $t[\max(dom(x_i)) + 1]$ by one. Let i be an index initialized to value $\min(D)$. The following identity can be proven by induction.

$$a[v] = I(\{v\}) - u_v = \sum_{j=i}^{v} t[j] \tag{1}$$

Index i divides the domain of values D in two sets: the values v smaller than i are not contained in more than u_v variable domains while other values can be contained in any number of variable domains. We maintain index i to be the highest possible value. If index i reaches a value greater than $\max(D)$ then all values v in D are contained in less than u_v variable domains and therefore the *ubc* is universal. Algorithm 2 increases index i to the first value v that is contained in more than u_v domains. The algorithm also updates vector t such that Equation 1 is verified for all values greater than or equal to i.

while $(i \leq \max(D))$ *and* $(t[i] \leq 0)$ **do**
$\quad i \leftarrow i + 1$;
$\quad$ **if** $i \leq \max(D)$ **then**
$\quad\quad t[i] \leftarrow t[i] + t[i-1]$;

Algorithm 2: Algorithm used for testing the universality of the *ubc* that increases index i to the smallest value $v \in D$ contained in more than u_v domains. The algorithm also modifies vector t to validate Equation 1 when $v \geq i$.

Suppose a variable domain gets pruned such that all values in interval $[a, b]$ are removed. To maintain the invariant given by Equation 1 for values greater than or equal to i, we update our vector t by removing 1 from component $t[\max(a, i)]$ and adding one to component $t[\max(b+1, i)]$. We then run Algorithm 2 to increase index i. If $i > \max(D)$ then the *ubc* is universal since no value is contained in more domains than its maximal capacity.

Initializing vector t and increasing iterator i until $i > \max(D)$ requires $O(|X| + |D|)$ steps. Therefore, checking universality each time an interval of values is removed from a variable domain is achieved in amortized constant time.

7 NP-Completeness of Extended-GCC

We now consider a generalized version of *gcc* that we call extended-*gcc*. For each value $v \in D$, we consider a set of cardinalities $K(v)$. We want to find a solution where value v is assigned to k variables such that $k \in K(v)$. We prove that it is NP-Complete to determine if there is an assignment that satisfies this constraint and therefore that it is NP-Hard to enforce domain consistency on extended-*gcc*.

Consider a CNF formula consisting of n clauses $\wedge_{i=1}^{n} \vee_j C_i^j$, where each literal C_i^j is either a variable x_k or its negation $\overline{x_k}$. We construct the corresponding bipartite graph G as follows. On the left side, we put a set of vertices named x_k for each boolean variable occurring in the formula, and set of vertices named C_i^j for each literal. On the right side, we put a set of vertices named x_k and $\overline{x_k}$ (for each variable x_k on the left side), and a set of vertices named C_i for each of n clauses in the formula. We connect variables x_k on the left side with both literals x_k and $\overline{x_k}$ on the right side, connect C_i^j with the corresponding literal on the right side, and connect C_i^j with the clause C_i where it occurs. Define the sets $K(l)$ as $\{0, \deg_G(l)\}$ for each literal l and $K(C_i)$ as $[0, \deg_G(C_i)-1]$ for each clause C_i.

For example, the CNF formula $(x_1 \vee x_2) \wedge (\overline{x_1} \vee x_2)$ is represented as the graph in Figure 1.

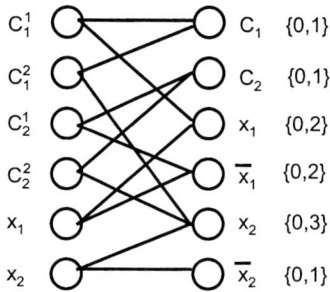

Fig. 1. Graph for $(x_1 \vee x_2) \wedge (\overline{x_1} \vee x_2)$

Let A be some assignment of boolean variables, the corresponding matching M can be constructed as follows. Match each vertex x_k on the left side with literal x_k if $A[x_k]$ is true and with $\overline{x_k}$ otherwise. The vertex C_i^j is matched with its literal if the logical value of this literal is true and with the clause C_i otherwise. In this matching, all the true literals l are matched with all possible $\deg(l)$ vertices on the left side and all the false ones are matched to none. The clause C_i is satisfied by A iff at least one of its literals C_i^j is true and hence is not matched with C_i. So the $deg_M(C_i) \in K(C_i)$ iff C_i is satisfied by A. On the other hand, the constraints $K(l)$ ensure that there are no other possible matchings in this graph. Namely, exactly one of $\deg_M(x_k) = 0$ or $\deg_M(\overline{x_k}) = 0$ can be true. These conditions determine the mates of all variables x_k as well as the mates of all literals C_i^j. Thus, the matchings and satisfying assignments are in one to one correspondence and we proved the following.

Lemma 11. *SAT is satisfiable if and only if there exists a generalized matching M in graph G.*

This shows that determining the satisfiability of extended-GCC is NP-complete and enforcing domain consistency on the extended-GCC is NP-hard.

8 Conclusions

We presented faster algorithms to maintain domain and range consistency for the *gcc*. We showed how to efficiently prune the cardinality variables and test *gcc* for universality. We finally showed that extended-*gcc* is NP-Hard.

References

1. R. K. Ahuja, T. L. Magnanti, and J. B. Orlin Network Flows: Theory, Algorithms, and Applications. Prentice Hall, first edition, 1993.
2. P. Hall. On representatives of subsets. *J. of the London Mathematical Society*, pages 26–30, 1935.
3. J. Hopcroft and R. Karp $n^{\frac{5}{2}}$ algorithm for maximum matchings in bipartite graphs *SIAM Journal of Computing* 2:225-231
4. ILOG S. A. ILOG Solver 4.2 user's manual, 1998.
5. C.-G. Quimper, P. van Beek, A. López-Ortiz, A. Golynski, and S. B. Sadjad. An efficient bounds consistency algorithm for the global cardinality constraint. *CP-2003 and Extended Report CS-2003-10*, 2003.
6. I. Katriel, and S. Thiel. Fast Bound Consistency for the Global Cardinality Constraint *CP-2003*, 2003.
7. M. Leconte. A bounds-based reduction scheme for constraints of difference. In *the Constraint-96 Int'l Workshop on Constraint-Based Reasoning.* 19–28, 1996.
8. J.-C. Régin. A filtering algorithm for constraints of difference in CSPs. In *AAAI-1994*, pages 362–367.
9. J.-C. Régin. Generalized arc consistency for global cardinality constraint. In *AAAI-1996*, pages 209–215.
10. J.-C. Régin and J.-F. Puget. A filtering algorithm for global sequencing constraints. In *CP-1997*, pages 32–46.
11. K. Stergiou and T. Walsh. The difference all-difference makes. In *IJCAI-1999*, pages 414–419.
12. R. Tarjan Depth-first search and linear graph algorithms. *SIAM Journal of Computing* 1:146-160.
13. P. Van Hentenryck, L. Michel, L. Perron, and J.-C. Régin. Constraint programming in OPL. In *PPDP-1999*, pages 98–116.
14. P. Van Hentenryck, H. Simonis, and M. Dincbas. Constraint satisfaction using constraint logic programming. *Artificial Intelligence*, 58:113–159, 1992.
15. J.-C. Régin and J.-F. Puget. A filtering algorithm for global sequencing constraints. In *CP-1997*, pages 32–46.

Impact-Based Search Strategies for Constraint Programming

Philippe Refalo

ILOG, Les Taissounieres, 1681, route des Dolines
06560 Sophia Antipolis, France
refalo@ilog.fr

Abstract. A key feature of constraint programming is the ability to design specific search strategies to solve problems. On the contrary, integer programming solvers have used efficient general-purpose strategies since their earliest implementations. We present a new general purpose search strategy for constraint programming inspired from integer programming techniques and based on the concept of the *impact* of a variable. The impact measures the importance of a variable for the reduction of the search space. Impacts are learned from the observation of domain reduction during search and we show how restarting search can dramatically improve performance. Using impacts for solving multiknapsack, magic square, and Latin square completion problems shows that this new criteria for choosing variables and values can outperform classical general-purpose strategies.

1 Introduction

One of the key features of constraint programming is the ability to exploit the structure of a problem to design an adapted search strategy to solve it. Since the earliest constraint logic programming systems based on Prolog, facilities were available to design sophisticated search procedures. As a consequence, not much use is made of general-purpose strategies in constraint programming. The most popular ones are based on first selecting variables having the minimum domain size [11]. Ties can be broken with the dynamic degree of variables [6]. Other variations include the ratio between the size of the domain and the degree of the variable [4] or looking at the neighborhood structure of the variable [15,3].

On the other hand, in integer programming solvers, it is considered that designing a search strategy is complex. It is true that the underlying concepts of integer programming that need to be understood (i.e., relaxed optimal solution, dual values, reduced costs) are not very intuitive. In comparison, the constraint programming concept of domain reduction is easier to understand and to use for the design of a search strategy.

As a consequence, a class of techniques for efficient general-purpose strategies in integer programming has emerged. The emphasis of integer programming being optimization, these techniques are based on estimating the importance of a variable with respect to the variation of the objective function value. The criteria used is called a *pseudo-cost* [7]. These techniques are so efficient that it has become rare that someone can compete with them by designing his or her own strategy.

In the following we propose new general-purpose strategies for constraint programming inspired by the notion of pseudo-cost. These strategies are based on the concept of *impact*. An impact measures the importance of an assignment $x = a$ for the search space reduction. Impacts are obtained from the domain reduction involved by assignments made during search.

In this context, probing on some variables at a node to get the true impacts can improve performance. This is analogous to *strong branching* [5] which is an efficient technique for solving hard integer programming problems. Furthermore, restarting search permits the solver to use the impacts learned during search in order to start a new, and hopefully smaller, search tree by making more relevant choices at the beginning.

Our goal is to provide better performance than the general strategies based on the domain size or on the degree. Experiments illustrate the benefits of this new approach on multiknapsack, magic square and Latin square completion problems. Before going into details, let us review basic facts about search strategies.

2 Search Strategies

The problem considered is to rapidly find a solution of a set of constraints $S = \{c_1, \ldots, c_m\}$ over a set of variables $V = \{x_1, \ldots, x_n\}$ having domains $D_{x_1}, \ldots, D_{x_n}$ or to prove that none exists. A solution is a set of assignments $\{x_1 = a_1, \ldots, x_n = a_n\}$ such that $a_i \in D_{x_i}$ and such that each constraint is satisfied when each variable x_i is replaced by the value a_i. Optimization problems are not considered here but only satisfaction problems.

To solve this problem, a common approach is *backtrack search*. At each step (or node), backtrack search chooses a non-assigned variable x_i and a subset $E \subset D_{x_i}$ and states the choice point

$$x_i \in E \text{ or } x_i \in D_{x_i} - E$$

In general, the subset E contains a single value. The constraint $x_i \in E$ is added to the current problem (the node problem) and variable domains are reduced with constraint propagation. When a constraint is violated or when a domain is empty, the search procedure backtracks to the last choice point by undoing constraint additions and tries the first unexplored branch encountered. When the domain of all variables contains a single value and no constraint is violated, a solution is found.

The performance of backtrack search (or the number of nodes it traverses) varies dramatically depending on the strategy used to choose a variable and the value for this variable. Searching for a solution to a problem involves facing two objectives that can be contradictory:

1. If the problem has a solution, find one quickly.
2. If the problem has no solution, create a small search tree to prove it.

In Case 1., using the structure of the problem can be very helpful. However, general-purpose strategies ignore the overall problem structure. These strategies assume that the problem is Case 2., with the hope that reducing the size of the whole search tree will also reduce the size of the search tree needed to reach a first solution.

In this context, there are principles for reducing the search effort that are worth mentioning here:

First principle. Since all variables have to be instantiated, first choosing the variable that maximally constrains the rest of the search space reduces the search effort. This principle is popular and widely applied. It is often implemented by choosing the variable having the smallest domain first or the one that participates in the largest number of constraints (the variable degree) first or a combination of both. Updating the domains and degrees at each node permits the solver to make better choices [11].

Second principle. This concerns the choice of a value. It is not that useful if the problem has no solution. However, if the problem has solutions, a solution can be reached more quickly if one chooses a value that maximizes the number of possibilities for future assignments.

Third principle. Make good choices at the top of the search tree. Choices made at the top of the search tree have a huge impact on its size and a bad choice can have disastrous effects. Applying this principle means that some effort must be made *before* starting the search to make good choices from the beginning.

The two first principles have been used in constraint programming for a long time but the last one is not always applied.

It is interesting to see that the integer programming community has applied these three principles since the early seventies but in a different context (see next section). In integer programming, the emphasis is on finding optimal solutions. An estimation of the objective function improvement is associated to a variable. According to these principles, the variable chosen first is the one involving the largest improvement; then the branch chosen first is the one that involves the least improvement.

Inspired by the integer programming strategies, we introduce the concept of *impact* in constraint programming. An impact associates a value with each assignment $x_i = a_j$, $a_j \in D_{x_i}$ to measure the importance of this assignment for the search space reduction. Here also, to reduce the search tree, a variable with the greatest impact should be chosen first and a value with the smallest impact should be used first.

3 Pseudo-costs in Integer Programming

Pseudo-costs are widely used in integer programming solvers such as CPLEX [1]. They have been introduced briefly in [2] and fully described in [7]. They have been successfully used for the default search strategies of modern integer programming solvers. Even if it is possible to redesign the search strategy in these solvers, pseudo-cost based strategies are so effective that it has become rare for someone to obtain a speedup by designing a dedicated strategy.

In integer programming problems, constraints are linear, and the domain of a variable is an interval of real or integer values. In addition, there is a linear cost function to be minimized (the maximization case is ignored, as it is similar). Integer programming solvers maintain a relaxed optimal solution at each node. This solution is given by a linear solver (such as the simplex method) applied to the node problem where integrality conditions on integer variables have been removed. This relaxed solution on a variable x is noted x^*. The value of the objective function in this solution is z^*. It is a lower bound on the optimal value of the problem. The value z^* increases as variables are instantiated during search. It is the amount of that increase that is used to select variables.

3.1 Variable and Value Selection

Consider a variable x whose non-integer value is $x^* = \lfloor x^* \rfloor + f$ where $0 < f < 1$. Forcing x to be an integer is done by creating the choice point

$$x \leq \lfloor x^* \rfloor \text{ or } x \geq \lceil x^* \rceil$$

Let z^* be the objective function value before the choice point. Let Δ_{down} be the increase of the objective value when adding the constraint $x \leq \lfloor x^* \rfloor$ and Δ_{up} be the increase of the objective value when adding the constraint $x \geq \lceil x^* \rceil$.

The values Δ_{down} and Δ_{up} can be computed for each variable having a non-integer value by solving two linear programs. From the first principle above, the variable to be chosen is the one having a maximum impact on the objective. In practice, it is the one that maximizes the weighted sum

$$v(x) = \alpha \min(\Delta_{down}, \Delta_{up}) + \beta \max(\Delta_{down}, \Delta_{up})$$

Usually more importance is given to the maximum of Δ_{down} and Δ_{up}. For $\alpha = 1$, choosing β greater than 3 gives good results (see [12]).

From the second principle above, the first branch to explore is the one that creates the smallest improvement in the objective function value with the hope of getting solutions with a low objective value earlier.

3.2 Pseudo-costs

The pseudo-costs of a variable x measure the increase of the objective function value per unit of change of x when adding the constraint $x \leq \lfloor x^* \rfloor$ or $x \geq \lceil x^* \rceil$. The *down pseudo cost* $PC_{down}(x) = \Delta_{down} / f$ corresponds to the decrease of x^* and the *up pseudo-cost* $PC_{up}(x) = \Delta_{up} / (1-f)$ corresponds to the increase of x^*.

A fundamental observation about pseudo-costs is that experiments reveal that the pseudo-costs of a variable tend to be the same from one node to another (see [7] and [12]). As a consequence we can avoid solving two linear programs (one for Δ_{down} and one for Δ_{up}) for each non-integer variable at each node, which is computationally very heavy. We can estimate that the up and down pseudo-costs of a variable x at a node are likely to be the average of the ones observed so far when choices are made on x. This averaged pseudo-cost (PC^e) is used to compute an estimation of $v(x)$ from an estimation of the objective function variation:

$$\Delta^e_{down} = f * PC^e_{down}(x) \text{ if } x \leq \lfloor x^* \rfloor \text{ is added}$$
$$\Delta^e_{up} = (1-f) * PC^e_{up}(x) \text{ if } x \geq \lceil x^* \rceil \text{ is added}$$

3.3 Strong Branching

On some problems the pseudo-costs may vary between nodes and it may be worth computing the estimation by solving a linear program. As it is costly to perform this operation on every non-integer variable, this is done only for some of them. In particular, this is done for breaking ties between variables that have similar estimations. This process has been introduced in [5] and is called *strong branching*.

More precisely, strong branching consists of performing a limited number of dual simplex iterations on a subset of variables having a non-integer value. Dual simplex tries to recover optimality that was destroyed by the addition of the constraint $x \leq \lfloor x^* \rfloor$ or $x \geq \lceil x^* \rceil$. After a certain number of iterations, the simplex iterations are stopped. The current (maybe still non-integer) value x^* and the current objective value z^* are used to compute an approximated pseudo-cost. It is used to differentiate variables instead of the averaged pseudo-cost. Although strong branching can create a significant overhead at each node, it can pay off on hard integer programs by dramatically reducing the number of nodes [1].

3.4 Pseudo-costs Initialization

At the beginning of search, pseudo-costs are unknown. Having pseudo-costs at this time is extremely important since choices made high in the tree are crucial. Computing explicit pseudo-costs by bounding up and down variables that have a non-integer value can degrade performance significantly [2]. As for strong branching, a trade-off consists of performing a limited number of dual simplex iterations [12]. The approximated pseudo-cost computed in this way is usually replaced by the first observed one.

4 Impacts in Constraint Programming

As with pseudo-costs, the basic idea of impacts is intuitive. In constraint programming, when a value is assigned to a variable, constraint propagation reduces the domains of other variables. We consider that the number of all possible combinations of values for the variables (the Cartesian product) is an estimation of the search size. Therefore, an estimation of the size of the search tree is the product of every variable domain size:

$$P = |D_{x_1}| \times \ldots \times |D_{x_n}|$$

4.1 Impact of an Assignment

If we look at this product before (P_{before}) and after (P_{after}) an assignment $x_i = a$ we have an estimation of the importance of this assignment for reducing the search space. This reduction rate is called the *impact* of the assignment

$$I(x_i = a) = 1 - \frac{P_{after}}{P_{before}}$$

The higher the impact, the greater the search space reduction. From this definition, an assignment that fails has an impact of 1.

The impact of assignments can be computed for every value of all non-instantiated variables, but this can create a huge overhead. From the experiments we have made, impacts, like pseudo-costs, do not vary much from node to node. The impact value distribution of a given assignment almost always presents a sharp and unique peak centered on the average value. An important consequence is that the impact of an assignment at a given node can be the average of the observed impacts of this assignment up to this point. If K is the index set of impacts observed so far for assignment $x_i = a$, $\bar{I}$ is the averaged impact:

$$\bar{I}(x_i = a) = \frac{\sum\limits_{k \in K} I^k(x_i = a)}{|K|}$$

A nice consequence is that impacts do not need to be computed explicitly at each node but are available almost for free.

4.2 Impact of a Variable

The impact of a variable x_i can be the average of impacts $\bar{I}(x_i = a)$ for $a \in D_{x_i}$. A more accurate measure would use only the values remaining in its domain. Thus, if the current domain of x_i at a node is D'_{x_i} we have

$$\tilde{I}(x_i) = \frac{\sum\limits_{a \in D'_{x_i}} \bar{I}(x_i = a)}{|D'_{x_i}|}$$

This approach is not accurate enough. The goal is to choose a variable having the largest impact when assigning to it one of the values remaining in its domain. Since it is assumed that each value will be tried (the hypothesis is that the problem is infeasible as mentioned above) we need to consider the search reduction if *every* value of the domain is tried. Let P be the product of the domain sizes at a node and consider a variable x_i. The estimation of the size of the search space when trying $x_i = a$ with $a \in D'_{x_i}$ is

$$P \times (1 - \bar{I}(x_i = a))$$

This is an estimation of the size of the search tree for $x_i = a_j$. If we were to try every value, an estimation of the search tree is the *sum* of the estimation for each value remaining in the domain:

$$\sum_{a \in D'_{x_i}} P \times (1 - \bar{I}(x_i = a))$$

The value P is a constant at a node and it is not relevant to compare the impact of several variables at the same node. Finally, the impact of a variable that depends on its current domain is defined as

$$\mathcal{I}(x_i) = \sum_{a \in D'_{x_i}} 1 - \bar{I}(x_i = a)$$

Experiments we have made comparing the use of the average impact $\tilde{I}(x)$ and the use of the sum of impacts on values $\mathcal{I}(x)$ show that using $\mathcal{I}(x)$ is much more efficient over all the problems we have tested.

4.3 Initialization of Impacts

As we said previously, some effort must be made before starting search to compute impacts. This helps to differentiate variables at the root node and to make better choices at the beginning of the search where this is crucial. One approach is to try every value for every variable. However on problems where domains are large this can be more costly than solving the problem itself. Impacts can be approximated before search in order to be efficiently computed.

The basic idea is to divide the domain D_{x_i} of a variable x_i into distinct subdomains $D_{x_i} = D^1_{x_i} \cup \ldots \cup D^k_{x_i}$ and compute the impact of $x_i \in D^w_{x_i}$. The impact of a value of a subdomain is then

$$I(x_i = a) = 1 - \frac{1 - I(x_i \in D^w_{x_i})}{|D^w_{x_i}|} \text{ for } a \in D^w_{x_i}$$

This formula assumes that the overall impact of x_i is shared equally between its values. The advantage is that when two domain reductions $x_i \in D^u_{x_i}$ and $x_i \in D^v_{x_i}$ have the same impact, the values in the largest domain have an impact greater than the one of the smallest domain since in one case there are more values to achieve the same reduction.

It is not realistic to decide to split a domain by imposing a maximal size on the $D^j_{x_i}$ because variables with a small domain, such as binary variables, will never be considered in an approximation and large domains will require more computation than smaller ones. Instead we recursively split a domain into two parts a certain number of times s (the splitting value) in order to ensure that small domains will be approximated and to bound the effort for large ones. Domains are then divided into at most 2^s subdomains. Here also, an approximated impact is replaced by the first truly observed impact.

4.4 Node Impacts

To get accurate impact values, one can compute the impact of a set of variables at a node by trying all possible assignments for each variable from the set. This is a costly technique similar to strong branching. It should be used to break ties in a subset of variables that have equivalent impacts. However, it can pay off if there are many ties to break. It can also be relevant when impacts appear to vary more than expected from one node to another.

Additionally, removing those of the tried values that fail from the domains leads to a weaker form of singleton arc-consistency [13] that helps to further reduce the search tree.

In order to reduce the time spent on computing node impacts, they can be approximated the same way that initial impacts can.

4.5 Restarts

Restarting the search (i.e., stopping the search process and restarting it from scratch) is an effective technique when using randomized strategies [8]. Restart has been used to solve Boolean satisfaction problems. In particular it is used in the SAT solver Chaff [14] where variable and value choices at the top of the tree are made randomly until a certain depth.

The basic idea behind the association of restart and randomization is to give equal chances to all parts of the search space to be explored at the beginning of the search.

Concerning impacts, as the search progresses we get more and more accurate impacts. We learn in this way what are the important assignments and variables. Consequently, we may discover that variables assigned high in the search tree are not as important as they seemed at the beginning. Therefore, as with any strategy that learns during search, it is useful to restart search from time to time in order to use the most recent information with the hope that the new search tree will be smaller. Section 5.5 give more details about the automatic restart procedure and some experimental results.

5 Experiments

The experiments in this section aim to show the relevance of impacts with regards to classical strategies. We also demonstrate the importance of impact initialization, of computing node impacts and of restart by comparing these approaches all together. For this purpose we have studied multiknapsack and magic square problems. Additional results on Latin square completion problems are also given in the last subsection as we tried to solve the instance in many different ways.

5.1 Problems and Hardware

Two sets of problems are considered. The first one is a set of multiknapsack problems where only a solution needs to be found (there is no cost function). These problems are modeled by a set of linear constraints over binary variables. They are usually hard for constraint programming solvers. Five problems come from the smaller set of the operations research library[1] where the cost function is constrained to take its optimal value (problems mknap1-*). These problems have between 6 and 11 constraints and from 15 to 50 variables. Four other problems are isolated subproblems of a real-life configuration problem (problems mc*). These subproblems have 2 constraints and 31 variables.

The second set of problems is magic square problems. The problem consists of filling in a matrix $n \times n$ by a set of all different values such that the sum of values in each row, in each column, and in the two diagonals is the same. The model we use contains one *alldifferent* constraint over all variables and $2n + 2$ linear constraints to constrain the sum of values.

All experiments in this section were made on a Pentium 4 / 2.8Gz machine using ILOG Solver 6.0. The time is given in seconds and the time limit is 1500s. The number of choice points is shown as a measure of the size of the search tree.

5.2 Classical Strategies

We compare our strategy with the minimum domain strategy, which is the classical strategy. We have tried variations around this strategy. In particular the Brelaz method to break ties has been tested [6], as well as the ratio between domain size and variable degree presented in [4]. None of the approaches improved the minimum size domain significantly on the problems considered. Therefore only the minimum size domain results are given in the comparisons. We also compare with a random strategy (i.e. it chooses variables and values randomly). This permits us to avoid biasing the comparison with the exceptionally bad results of the minimum size domain strategy due to its dependence on the order of variables.

5.3 Impacts and Initialization

To show the relevance of impact-based strategies and of impact initialization, this test compares

- a random search strategy (variables and values are chosen randomly);
- the minimum domain size strategy, that chooses first the variable with the minimum domain size and the smallest available value for this variable;
- a strategy using impacts where the best variable x_i is the one that maximizes $\mathcal{I}(x_i)$ and the best value a is the one that minimizes $\bar{I}(x_i = a)$;
- the same strategy with initialization of impacts before search.

---

[1] Problems are available at
http://mscmga.ms.ic.ac.uk/jeb/orlib/mdmkpinfo.html

	Random		Min. domain size		Impact w/o init.		Impact + init.	
Problems	Time	Ch.pts.	Time	Ch.pts.	Time	Ch.pts.	Time	Ch.pts.
mknap1-0	0.02	2	0.01	2	0.02	2	0.03	2
mknap1-2	0.02	10	0.02	37	0.05	15	0.03	26
mknap1-3	0.03	408	0.03	384	0.06	304	0.05	186
mknap1-4	0.55	11485	0.66	16946	0.24	3230	0.05	434
mknap1-5	48.91	1031516	3.33	99002	1.7	29418	0.22	4247
mknap1-6	>1500		716.75	21532775	>1500		50.46	902319
mc3923	14.67	491445	867.24	42328413	197.65	5862508	0.38	11768
mc3800	2.28	75270	131.22	6396644	248.81	7348618	0.06	1769
mc3888	53.40	1784812	722.73	35242940	33.93	1007735	1.36	44682
mc3914	26.91	899114	895.10	43631272	305.56	9084462	0.44	14390

Fig. 1. Initialization of impacts on multiknapsack problems.

	Random		Min. domain size		Impact w/o init.		Impact + init.	
Size	Time	Ch.pts.	Time	Ch.pts.	Time	Ch.pts.	Time	Ch.pts.
5	0.08	258	0.02	632	0.05	148	0.13	3486
6	12.20	458023	1.78	125789	52.62	1067734	0.16	3458
7	301.17	9756428	>1500		2.30	40310	0.11	1594
8	>1500		>1500		48.68	748758	9.70	134031
9	>1500		>1500		>1500		1.47	15244
10	>1500		>1500		>1500		10.13	67581
11	>1500		>1500		>1500		>1500	

Fig. 2. Initialization of impacts on magic square problems.

The initialization of impacts before search is not approximated. The overhead of this full initialization is negligible for both types of problem. In impact strategies, remaining ties are broken with a random variable and value choice.

The results are shown in Figure 1 and 2.

Concerning multiknapsack problems, the minimum domain size strategy does not perform well except for smaller instances. This is due to the binary variables. A free variable always has a domain size of 2. As a consequence, this strategy only depends on the order of variables. It chooses the first free variable and then the value 0 before the value 1. Choosing randomly can improve performance on the configuration multiknapsack problems.

Using impacts outperforms both minimum domain size and random strategies. It is interesting to note that without initialization the results are much worse (even worse than the random strategy sometimes) and the instance mknap1-6 cannot be solved. This shows the high importance of impact initialization for this problem. Moreover the cost of computing these initial impacts (that are not approximated for this test) is negligible here.

Magic square problems also benefit from impacts. Without initialization, problems of size 8 can be solved but initialization of impacts permits the solver to go up to size 10. Here again the cost of computing initial impacts before search is negligible with respect to the solving time.

	Impacts		Node Impacts	
Problems	Time	Ch.pts	Time	Ch.pts
mknap1-0	0.03	2	0.03	0
mknap1-2	0.03	26	0.03	29
mknap1-3	0.05	186	0.05	79
mknap1-4	0.05	434	0.13	1321
mknap1-5	0.22	4247	0.17	2154
mknap1-6	50.46	902319	20.34	98805
mc3923	0.38	11768	3.03	24890
mc3800	0.06	1769	0.22	2897
mc3888	1.36	44682	1.31	12571
mc3914	0.44	14390	0.59	6415

Fig. 3. Node impacts on multiknapsack problems.

	Impacts		Node Impacts	
Size	Time	Ch.pts	Time	Ch.pts
5	0.13	3486	0.08	439
6	0.16	3458	0.19	2353
7	0.11	1594	0.25	259
8	9.70	134031	2.16	17535
9	1.47	15244	2.00	1844
10	10.13	67581	>1500	
11	>1500		38.01	90483
12	>1500		55.76	92650
13	>1500		42.50	7471
14	>1500		187.83	106258
15	>1500		>1500	
16	>1500		587.23	189884
17	>1500		>1500	

Fig. 4. Node impacts on magic square problems.

5.4 Node Impacts

Note that node impacts can be approximated the same way that initial impacts can. However this does not greatly improve performance on the magic square and multiknapsack problems. Therefore full impacts are computed at a node.

The experiments done with the computation of node impacts compare

- an impact strategy with initialization;
- and impact strategy with initialization where ties are broken with node impacts and remaining ties are broken randomly.

The results go beyond expectations (see Figure 3 and 4). For most problems, the use of node impacts reduces the size of the search tree up to a factor of 10.

For the multiknapsack problem it does not increase the overall running time in general (except for mc3923 which is significantly slower) and even helps to reduce the solving time for the hardest instance (mknap1-6).

For the magic square problem node impacts permit the solver to solve much larger instances, although the problem of size 10 cannot be solved within the time limit. However, instances 11, 12, 13, 14 and 16 can be solved within the time limit.

5.5 Restart

We have tried various strategies for doing automatic restarts. A very simple approach proved to be quite effective. Before the first run we imposed a maximum number of failures of $3n$ where n is the number of variables. This value is called the *cutoff*. Then at each restart we increase this value by multiplying it by a value $e > 1$. The increase of the cutoff permits us to guarantee that the search process is complete. The cutoff will always reach a value that is sufficiently large enough to explore the whole search tree in a single run. Setting e to 2 theoretically increases the size of the search tree by a factor of 2 (if we consider that restart is useless). However this increases the cutoff too quickly and better results were obtained with $e = \sqrt{2}$ which theoretically increases the cumulative size by a factor of $2\sqrt{2}$.

Size	Impacts Time	Impacts Ch.pts.	Random + MDS Time	Random + MDS Ch.pts.	Impacts + restart Time	Impacts + restart Ch.pts.
5	0.13	3486	0.03	306	0.05	840
6	0.16	3458	0.05	324	0.03	454
7	0.11	1594	0.06	572	0.05	320
8	9.70	134031	1.69	21604	1.31	29107
9	1.47	15244	294.49	3413789	0.25	3206
10	10.13	67581	187.14	2111256	2.19	35796
11	>1500		>1500		0.67	5227
12	>1500		>1500		14.89	182392
13	>1500		>1500		13.22	108501
14	>1500		>1500		21.25	83047
15	>1500		>1500		38.64	95769
16	>1500		>1500		1354.64	975655
17	>1500		>1500		>1500	

Fig. 5. Restart on magic square problems.

The experiments using restarts compare

- an impact strategy with initialization;
- random choices until depth 5 and minimum domain size (MDS) strategy below using restart;
- an impact strategy with initialization using restart.

The second strategy permits us to measure the importance of restart.

Results on the magic square problem are presented in Figure 5. Restarting search using random choices until depth 5 improves the minimum domain size strategy (see figure 2) but it does not give better results than using impacts without restart. When using impacts, restart improves the performance of the instances solved by using the impacts alone and solves all instances within the time limit up to size 16.

The results for the multiknapsack problems are not presented here. Using restarts is ineffective on these problems. The time to find a solution increases by a factor between 2 and 3 on average (close to $2\sqrt{2}$). This means that initial impacts are good enough to avoid bad choices at the beginning on these instances.

5.6 Latin Square Completion Problems

The third set of problems tested is the Latin square completion problem. The Latin square problem consists of filling an $n \times n$ matrix with values from the set $\{1, \ldots, n\}$ such that values on each line and on each column are all different. The problem is simply formulated by one *alldifferent* constraint for each row and each column. The Latin square completion problem has, in addition, some variables already instantiated in the matrix. The set of problems considered is a selection of hard instances generated randomly [10].

The experiments using restarts compare

- the minimum domain size strategy;
- random choices until depth 5 and minimum domain size (MDS) strategy below using restarts;
- an impact strategy with initialization;
- and impact strategy with initialization using restarts.

In these problems, variables have a large domain and initialization without approximation can be costly (up to 300s on some problems) and therefore we have used approximations with a splitting value $s = 4$. The domains are then divided in at most 16 subdomains and the maximum time for initialization goes down to 7 seconds.

		min. domain size		Random + MDS		Impacts		Impacts + restart	
order	holes	Time	Ch. pts	Time	Ch. pts	Time	Ch.pts	Time	Ch.pts
18	120	0.06	2	0.05	4	0.05	1	0.05	2
30	316	8.81	18627	15.89	23545	0.07	30	0.06	31
30	320	0.47	856	0.52	552	0.17	277	0.15	278
33	381	>1500		>1500		>1500		>1500	
35	405	>1500		>1500		9.84	16367	453.04	752779
40	528	>1500		>1500		>1500		>1500	
40	544	>1500		>1500		>1500		>1500	
40	560	>1500		>1500		>1500		225.34	289686
50	2000	2.95	225	8.42	1728	13.52	1734	13.53	1735
50	825	>1500		>1500		>1500		>1500	
60	1440	>1500		>1500		>1500		>1500	
60	1620	>1500		>1500		>1500		115.91	56050
60	1692	410.63	193687	>1500		41.40	21746	299.23	164048
60	1728	>1500		>1500		7.95	2332	8.02	2333
60	1764	849.78	486639	>1500		639.82	334699	99.32	48485
60	1800	>1500		865.86	197549	7.81	1933	7.78	1934
70	2450	>1500		>1500		>1500	382745	175.94	43831
70	2940	10.17	1463	138.53	22585	32.39	3731	32.51	3732
70	3430	9.92	1252	53.67	7659	51.39	3072	51.03	3073

Fig. 6. Results on Latin square completion problems.

The results are presented in Figure 6. These instances are hard for the minimum domain size strategy which cannot solve 11 over 19 instances. The addition of restart with random choices until depth 5 does not improve it. Using impacts permits the solver to solve 3 more instances. Using restart in addition to impacts permits the solver to solve another 3 instances. Thus 5 instances out of 19 remain unsolved with the new strategy with restarts.

It is worth mentioning that using node impacts to break ties without restart as presented in Section 4.4 solves the instance 60/1440 in 14.5 seconds and 2583 choice points. However the instance 70/2450 cannot be solved with node impacts.

Additionally, we have tried a stronger propagation by using the alldifferent constraint on a matrix [9]. It improves computation times in several cases but not all of them. However, it permits the solver to solve the instance 33/381 which can only be solved by SAT solvers (see [10]). It is solved in 1357s and 1128390 choice points. Thus 3 instances remain unsolved for our search strategy.

6 Conclusion

The new general-purpose strategy based on impacts presented in this paper is inspired from integer programming techniques where default search strategies are extensively used. Impacts permit us to benefit from the search effort made up to a certain node by storing the observed importance of variables. As we have seen, impact initialization, search restart and computation of node impacts are central techniques for improving performance. These techniques permit us to solve instances that remain unsolved with standard strategies. The significant improvement over the minimum size domain strategy on multiknapsack, magic square and Latin square completion problems and the negligible overhead created by the update of impacts make us believe that this class of strategies is a candidate for becoming the basis of a default search goal for constraint programming.

Acknowledgments

The author thanks Oliver Lhomme, Jean-Charles Régin and Paul Shaw for animated discussions about search strategies.

References

1. ILOG CPLEX 9.0. User Manual. ILOG, S.A., Gentilly, France, September 2003.
2. M. Benichou, J.M. Gauthier, P. Girodet, G. Hentges, G. Ribiere, and O. Vincent. Experiments in mixed-integer linear programming. Mathematical Programming, (1):76–94, 1971.
3. C. Bessiere, A. Chmeiss, and L. Sais. Neighborhood-based variable ordering heuristics for the constraint satisfaction problem. In Proceedings of CP 2001, pages 565–569, 2001.

4. C. Bessière and J-C. Régin. MAC and combined heuristics: Two reasons to forsake FC (and CBJ?) on hard problems. In CP96, Second International Conference on Principles and Practice of Constraint Programming, pages 61–75, Cambridge, MA, USA, 1996.
5. R.E. Bixby, W. Cook, A. Cox, and E.K. Lee. Parallel mixed integer programming. Technical Report Research Monograph CRPC-TR95554, Center for Research on Parallel Computation, 1995.
6. D. Brélaz. New methods to color the vertices of a graph. Communication of the ACM, (22):251–256, 1979.
7. J.-M. Gauthier and G. Ribiere. Experiments in mixed-integer linear programming using pseudo-costs. Mathematical Programming, (12):26–47, 1977.
8. C. Gomes. Complete randomized backtrack search (survey). In M. Milano, editor, Constraint and Integer Programming: Toward a Unified Methodology, pages 233–283. Kluwer, 2003.
9. C. Gomes and J.-C. Regin. Modelling alldi. matrix models in constraint programming. In Optimization days, Montreal, Canada, 2003.
10. C. Gomes and D. Shmoys. Completing quasigroups or latin squares: A structured graph coloring problem. In Proceedings of the Computational Symposium on Graph Coloring and Extensions, 2002.
11. R. Haralick and G. Elliot. Increasing tree search efficiency for constraint satisfaction problems. Artificial Intelligence, (14):263–313, 1980.
12. J. Linderoth and M. Savelsberg. A computational study of search strategies for mixed integer programming. INFORMS Journal on Computing, 11(2):173–187, 1999.
13. J.J. McGregor. Relational consistency algorithms and their application in finding subgraph and graph isomorphisms. Information Science, 19:229-250, 1979.
14. M.W. Moskewicz, C.F. Madigan, and S. Malik. Chaff: Engineering an efficient SAT solver. In Design Automation Conference, 2001.
15. B. Smith. The Brelaz heuristic and optimal static ordering. In Proceedings of CP'99, pages 405–418, (Alexandria, VA), 1999.

The Cardinality Matrix Constraint*

Jean-Charles Régin[1] and Carla P. Gomes[2]

[1] ILOG, 1681, route des Dolines, 06560 Valbonne, France
regin@ilog.fr
[2] Computing and Information Science, Cornell University, Ithaca NY 14850 USA
gomes@cs.cornell.edu

Abstract. Cardinality matrix problems are the underlying structure of several real world problems such as rostering, sports scheduling , and timetabling. These are hard computational problems given their inherent combinatorial structure. Constraint based approaches have been shown to outperform other approaches for solving these problems. In this paper we propose the cardinality matrix constraint, a specialized global constraint for cardinality matrix problems. The cardinality matrix constraint takes advantage of the intrinsic structure of the cardinality matrix problems. It uses a global cardinality constraint per row and per column and one cardinality (0,1)-matrix constraint per symbol. This latter constraint corresponds to solving a special case of a network flow problem, the transportation problem, which effectively captures the interactions between rows, columns, and symbols of cardinality matrix problems. Our results show that the cardinality matrix constraint outperforms standard constraint based formulations of cardinality matrix problems.

1 Introduction

In recent years Constraint Programming (CP) techniques have been shown to effectively solve hard combinatorial problems. In fact, constraint based methods excel at solving problems that are inherently combinatorial, clearly outperforming traditional Operations Research (OR) techniques. Sports scheduling and rostering problems are good examples of highly combinatorial problems, for which CP based techniques have been shown to be very successful (see e.g., [11,15]).

In a rostering problem, given a set of workers, a set of tasks, and a set of days (typically a week), the goal is to assign the tasks per person and per day satisfying various constraints. Among them, typical constraints require the workload per day to be constrained by the number of times each task has to be performed, and the schedule of each person to be constrained by the number of times each task has to be performed.

Sports scheduling problems and rostering problems are particular cases of what we refer to as *cardinality matrix problems*. Cardinality matrix problems are expressed by a matrix of variables where each row and each column are constrained by cardinality constraints, that is by constraints that define the

---

* Supported by the Intelligent Information Systems Institute, Cornell University (AFOSR grant F49620-01-1-0076) and EOARD grant FA8655-03-1-3022.

number of times each value in a row or in a column has to be assigned to variables. We can model the rostering problem as a cardinality matrix problem in which each row of the matrix corresponds to a worker and each column of the matrix corresponds to a day of the week. The values in the matrix correspond to tasks. The cardinality constraints on the rows constrain the number of tasks to be assigned per worker and the cardinality constraints on the columns constrain the number of task to be assigned daily.

A straightforward model for representing cardinality matrix problems, e.g., rostering problems, consists of:

- a matrix of variables, in which each variable corresponds to a cell that takes as value the task to be performed on a given day by a given person. The variable domains are the set of tasks that can be performed by a given person for a given day.
- a global cardinality constraint (GCC) for every row, which constrains the number of times each task has to be performed by the person corresponding to the row.
- a global cardinality constraint for every column, which constrains the number of times each task has to be performed for the day corresponding to the column.

This formulation uses several global constraints and can give good results in practice. However, it suffers from some major drawbacks, namely:

1. There is poor communication between the variables constraining the number of times a value has to be taken, called cardinality variables.
2. The communication between the rows and the columns is poor. In fact, any GCC defined on a row and any GCC defined on a column have only one variable in common. This means that we have an efficient way to deal with all the variables of a row (or a column) as a whole, but we are not able to really deal with the notion of a matrix.
3. The GCCs deal with a set of predefined intervals constraining for each value the number of times the value has to be assigned. In real-life problems, variables defining these intervals are more often used. Even if it is easy to deduce intervals from these variables, because it corresponds to the boundaries of these variables, we do not have filtering algorithms to reduce their ranges in the general case (such a filtering algorithm has been proposed when the domains of the variables on which the GCCs are defined are ranges [9]).

The communication between constraints mentioned in (1) and (2) can be improved by adding implied constraints. An implied constraint for a given CSP is a constraint that can be deduced from the other constraints of the CSP, but which introduces a filtering algorithm that can reveal inconsistencies which are not discovered by the combination of the filtering algorithms of the other constraints. So the introduction of implied constraints can lead to a reduction of the number of backtracks needed to find one solution or to prove that there is none. The introduction of implied constraints can improve dramatically the efficiency of search since it allows for the detection of inconsistencies earlier than it would be possible if such constraints were not stated explicitly (see e.g., [3]).

The limitation stated in point (2) deserves a more careful study. Consider a restricted form of the cardinality matrix problems: the alldiff matrix problem [8]. In this case, each value has to be assigned at most once in each row and each column. The alldiff matrix characterizes the structure of several real world problems, such as design of scientific experiments or fiber optics routing. Consider the following example: a 6x6 matrix has to be filled with numbers ranging from 1 to 6 (this is a latin square problem). A classical model in CP consists of defining one variable per cell, each variable can take a value from 1 to 6, and one alldiff constraint per row and one alldiff constraint per column. Now, consider the following situation:

		1	2		
		2	1		
		3	4		
		4	5		
•	•			•	•
•	•			•	•

In this case, the alldiff constraints are only able to deduce that:
- only the values 5 and 6 can be assigned to the cells $(5,3)$ and $(6,3)$
- only the values 3 and 6 can be assigned to the cells $(5,4)$ and $(6,4)$.

However, with a careful study we can see that the value 6 will be assigned either to $(5,3)$ and $(6,4)$ or to $(5,4)$ and $(6,3)$ this means that the other columns of rows 5 and 6 cannot take these values and therefore we can remove the value 6 from the domains of the corresponding variables (the ones with a • in the figure). We will show how our approach, using what we refer to as the cardinality (0,1)-matrix, automatically performs these inferences.

One of the key successful approaches in CP has been the identification of typical constraints that arise in several real-world problems and associate with them very specialized and efficient filtering algorithms, so-called *global constraints*. In recent years several global constraints have been proposed and shown to boost dramatically the performance of CP based techniques.

We propose the *cardinality matrix constraint* to capture the structure of cardinality matrix problems such as the rostering problem. A cardinality matrix constraint (cardMatrix) C is specified in terms of an $n \times m$ matrix M of variables which take their values from a set of s symbols, and two sets (*rowCard* and *colCard*) of cardinality variables that specify the number of times each symbol has to appear in a row (*rowCard*) and the number of times each symbol has to appear in a column (*colCard*). More specifically, the set of cardinality variables *rowCard* constrains the number of variables of a row i of M instantiated to a symbol p to be equal to $rowCard[i,p]$ and the set of cardinality variables *colCard* constrains the number of variables of a column j of M instantiated to a symbol q to be equal to $colCard[j,q]$. In order to take advantage of the structure underlying the *cardinality matrix constraint* we introduce a constraint named cardinality (0,1)-matrix. The cardinality (0,1)-matrix is a particular case of a network flow problem, the transportation problem. This constraint effectively captures the interactions between rows, columns, and symbols in a cardinality matrix problem. We also develop a simple filtering algorithm for the cardinality matrix constraint with a low complexity that enables us to reduce the ranges of the cardinality variables. As we show in our experimental section, we obtain very promising results which allow us to solve problems that could not be solved before with constraint programming techniques. We also compare the performance of our approach against standard formulations of a cardinality matrix problems. We obtain dramatic speed ups with our approach.

The rest of the paper is organized as follows: In the next section we define our notation and present definitions concerning constraint programming and graph theory. We then roughly present the cardinality matrix constraint and propose a simple filtering algorithm for reducing the ranges of cardinality variables of a GCC. Next, we introduce the Cardinality (0,1)-Matrix Constraint followed by the description of a filtering algorithm for the Cardinality Matrix Constraint. We present experimental results in section 7, followed by conclusions.

2 Preliminaries

$\mathcal{D}_0 = \{D_0(x_1), \ldots, D_0(x_n)\}$ to represent the set of initial domains of $\mathcal{N}$. Indeed, we consider that any constraint network $\mathcal{N}$ can be associated with an initial domain $\mathcal{D}_0$ (containing $\mathcal{D}$), on which constraint definitions were stated.

A **constraint** C on the ordered set of variables $X(C) = (x_{i_1}, \ldots, x_{i_r})$ is a subset $T(C)$ of the Cartesian product $D_0(x_{i_1}) \times \cdots \times D_0(x_{i_r})$ that specifies the **allowed** combinations of values for the variables $x_1, \ldots, x_r$. An element of $D_0(x_1) \times \cdots \times D_0(x_r)$ is called a **tuple** on $X(C)$. $\tau[x]$ denotes the value of x in the tuple τ.

Let C be a constraint. A tuple τ on $X(C)$ is **valid** if $\forall x \in X(C), \tau[x] \in D(x)$. C is **consistent** iff there exists a tuple τ of $T(C)$ which is valid. A value $a \in D(x)$ is **consistent with** C iff $x \notin X(C)$ or there exists a valid tuple τ of $T(C)$ with $a = \tau[x]$. A constraint is **arc consistent** iff $\forall x_i \in X(C), D(x_i) \neq \emptyset$ and $\forall a \in D(x_i)$, a is consistent with C.

The **value graph** of a set of variables X is the bipartite graph $GV(X) = (X, \cup_{x_i \in X} D(x_i), E)$ where $(x, a) \in E$ iff $a \in D(x)$.

We recall the formal definition of a global cardinality constraint:

Definition 1 *A global cardinality constraint C defined on X and associated with a set of values V with $D(X) \subseteq V$ is a constraint in which each value $a_i \in V$ is associated with two positive integers l_i and u_i with $l_i \leq u_i$ and*
$T(C) = \{\, \tau \text{ s.t. } \tau \text{ is a tuple on } X(C)$
$\qquad \text{and } \forall a_i \in V : l_i \leq \#(a_i, \tau) \leq u_i \}$
It is denoted by $gcc(X, V, l, u)$.

Note that an alldiff constraint can be defined by a GCC in which all lower bound are equals to 0 and all upper bounds are equal to 1.

An instantiation of all variables that satisfies all the constraints is called a solution of a CN. Constraint Programming (CP) proposes to search for a solution by associating with each constraint a filtering algorithm that removes some values of variables that cannot belong to any solution. These filtering algorithms are repeatedly called until no new deduction can be made. Then, CP uses a search procedure (like a backtracking algorithm) where filtering algorithms are systematically applied when the domain of a variable is modified.

2.1 Graph Theory

These definitions are based on books of [2,16,1].

A **directed graph** or **digraph** $G = (X, U)$ consists of a **node set** X and an **arc set** U, where every arc (u, v) is an ordered pair of distinct nodes. We will denote by $X(G)$ the node set of G and by $U(G)$ the arc set of G.

A **path** from node v_1 to node v_k in G is a list of nodes $[v_1, ..., v_k]$ such that (v_i, v_{i+1}) is an arc for $i \in [1..k-1]$. The path **contains** node v_i for $i \in [1..k]$ and arc (v_i, v_{i+1}) for $i \in [1..k-1]$. The path is **simple** if all its nodes are distinct. The path is a **cycle** if $k > 1$ and $v_1 = v_k$. An undirected graph is **connected** if there is a path between every pair of nodes. The maximal connected subgraphs of G are its **connected components**. A directed graph is **strongly connected** if there is a path between every pair of nodes. The maximal strongly connected subgraphs of G are its strongly connected components. A **bridge** is an edge whose removal increases the number of connected components.

Let G be a graph for which each arc (i, j) is associated with two integers l_{ij} and u_{ij}, respectively called the **lower bound capacity** and the **upper bound capacity** of the arc. A **flow** in G is a function f satisfying the following two conditions[1]:

- For any arc (i, j), f_{ij} represents the amount of some commodity that can "flow" through the arc. Such a flow is permitted only in the indicated direction of the arc, i.e., from i to j. For convenience, we assume $f_{ij} = 0$ if $(i, j) \notin U(G)$.
- A **conservation law** is observed at each node: $\forall j \in X(G) : \sum_i f_{ij} = \sum_k f_{jk}$.

A **feasible flow** is a flow in G that satisfies the **capacity constraint**, that is, such that $\forall (i, j) \in U(G)\ l_{ij} \leq f_{ij} \leq u_{ij}$.

Definition 2 *The **residual graph** for a given flow f, denoted by $R(f)$, is the digraph with the same node set as in G. The arc set of $R(f)$ is defined as follows: $\forall (i, j) \in U(G)$:*

- $f_{ij} < u_{ij} \Leftrightarrow (i, j) \in U(R(f))$ *and upper bound capacity* $r_{ij} = u_{ij} - f_{ij}$.
- $f_{ij} > l_{ij} \Leftrightarrow (j, i) \in U(R(f))$ *and upper bound capacity* $r_{ji} = f_{ij} - l_{ij}$.

All the lower bound capacities are equal to 0.

2.2 Notation

- $max(x)$ (resp. $min(x)$) denotes the maximum (resp. minimum) value of $D(x)$.
- $D(X)$ denotes the union of domains of variables of X (i.e. $D(X) = \cup_{x_i \in X} D(x_i)$). • $\#(a, \tau)$ is the number of occurrences of the value a in the tuple τ.

---

[1] Without loss of generality (see p.45 and p.297 in [1]), and to overcome notation difficulties, we will consider that if (i, j) is an arc of G then (j, i) is not an arc of G, and that all boundaries of capacities are nonnegative integers.

- $\#(a, X)$ is the number of variables of X such that $a \in D(x)$.
- $Row(M)$ (resp. $Col(M)$) is the set of indices of the rows (resp. columns) of the matrix M.
- If X is a $n \times m$ array, that is X=x[i,j]), then $vars(i, *, X) = \{x[i,j], j = 1..m\}$ and $vars(*, j, X) = \{x[i,j], i = 1..n\}$.

3 Cardinality Matrix Constraint: Presentation

Definition 3 *A* **cardinality matrix** *constraint is a constraint C defined on a Matrix $M = x[i,j]$ of variable s taking their values in a set V, and on two sets of cardinality variables $rowCard[i,j]$ and $colCard[i,j]$ and*
$T(C) = \{\ \tau\ s.t.\ \tau\ is\ a\ tuple\ on\ X(C)$
    $and\ \forall a_k \in V, \forall i \in Row(M) : \#(a_k, vars(i, *, M)) = rowCard[i, k]$
    $and\ \forall a_k \in V, \forall j \in Col(M) : \#(a_k, vars(i, *, M)) = colCard[j, k]$
It is denoted by card-Matrix$(M, V, rowCard, colCard)$.

In order to show how a cardinality matrix constraint is represented we need first to introduce cardinality variables. The GCCs consider that the lower and the upper bounds are integer. There is no problem to use variables instead of integers. In this case, the lower bound is the minimal value of the domain of the variable and the upper bound is the maximal value of the domain. We will call such variables **cardinality variables**. Thus, we can define a global cardinality constraint involving cardinality variables (abbreviated cardVar-GCC):

Definition 4 *A* **global cardinality constraint involving cardinality variables** *defined on X and card and associated with a set of values V with $D(X) \subseteq V$ is a constraint C in which each value $a_i \in V$ is associated with a cardinality variable card[i] and*
$T(C) = \{\ \tau\ s.t.\ \tau\ is\ a\ tuple\ on\ X(C)$
    $and\ \forall a_i \in V : card[i] = \#(a_i, \tau)\}$
It is denoted by $gcc(X, V, card)$.

We propose to represent a cardinality matrix constraint by:
- one cardVar-GCC per row and one cardVar-GCC per column;
- a sum constraint involving the previous cardinality variables stating that the number of symbols taken by all the rows (resp. all the columns) is the size of the matrix;
- one cardinality (0,1)-matrix constraint involving cardinality variables per symbol. Such a constraint involves boolean variables corresponding to the presence or the absence of the symbol for a cell of the matrix, and combines the rows and the columns for the symbol.

Thus, with such a representation the communication is improved in two ways:
- by the presence of cardinality variables
- by the introduction of a new constraint combining the rows and the columns for each symbol.

This communication will be efficent if some powerful filtering algorithms are available to reduce the domains of the cardinality variables and the domains of the boolean variables on which cardinality (0,1)-matrix constraints are defined. This is what we study in the next sections.

4 Filtering Algorithm for costVar-GCC

A GCC C is consistent iff there is a flow in the the value network of C [12]. The consistency of $gcc(X, V, card)$ is equivalent to the consistency of the constraint $gcc(X, V, l, u)$ where for every $a_i \in V$ $l[i] = min(card[i])$ and $u[i] = max(card[i])$. When the minimum or the maximum value of the domain of a cardinality variable is modified then C is modified and so the consistency of the constraint must be established again. Since the flow algorithms are incremental, a new feasible flow can be computed in $O(m)$, where m is the number of arcs of the network.

Arc consistency for cardVar-GCC can be established for the variables of X by using the method of GCCs, because the problem remains the same for these variables. For the cardinality variables we are more interested in the validity of the minimum and the maximum value of the domains. Bound consistency can be established by searching for the minimum and the maximum value such that a feasible flow exists. However, the cost of this method is high and its practical advantage has not been proved in general. Therefore, we propose a simple filtering algorithm whose cost is low and which is worthwhile in practice:

Property 1 *Let $C = gcc(X, V, card)$ be a cardVar-GCC. Then, we have:*
- $\forall a_i \in V$ $card[i] \leq \#(a_i, X)$
- $\sum_{a_i \in V} card[i] = |X|$

The second point is a classical sum constraint and bound consistency can be established in $O(|V|)$. Then, we immediately have the property:

Property 2 *Let $C = gcc(X, V, card)$ be a cardVar-GCC, $GV(X)$ be the value graph of X. Then for every connected component CC of $GV(X)$ we have:*
$\sum_{a_i \in vals(CC))} card[i] = |vars(CC)|$,
where $vals(CC)$ denotes the values of V belonging to CC and $vars$ denotes the variables of X belonging to CC.

Proof: All the connected components are disjoint by definition, thus the problem is equivalent to a disjunction of GCCs, each of them corresponding to a connected component. Then, Property 1 can be independently applied on each GCC. ⊙

The filtering algorithm associated with cardinality variables is defined by Property 1 and by Property 2. Its complexity is in $O(|V|)$ for all the sum constraints that can be defined and $O(m)$ for the search for connected components, where m is the number of edges of the value graph of X [15].

At first glance, Property 2 seems weak, but in fact this is not true, as shown by the following property:

Property 3 *Let $C = gcc(X, V, card)$ be a cardVar-GCC, cy be a cardinality variable, and k be an integer. If $cy = k$ in every solution of C then the domain of cy is set to k after establishing arc consistency of the X variables and after establishing bound consistency of sum constraints defined by Property 2*

In order to prove this property we need first to introduce a theorem which is a generalization of a property used to establish arc consistency for a GCC, because it deals with any kind of lower and upper bound capacities, and not only (0,1).

Theorem 1 *Let f be a feasible flow in N, and (x, a) be an arc of N. Then, for every feasible flow f' in N: $f_{xa} = f'_{xa}$ if and only if one of the following property is satisfied:*

(i) $(x, a) \notin R(f)$ and $(a, x) \notin R(f)$

(ii) $R(f)$ contains (x, a) or (a, x) but not both and x and a belong to two different strongly connected components of $R(f)$

(iii) $(x, a) \in R(f)$ and $(a, x) \in R(f)$ and (x, a) is a bridge of $ud(scc(R(f), x))$, where $ud(scc(R(f), x))$ is the undirected version of the strongly connected component of $R(f)$ containing x.

Proof: *(i)* From definition of $R(f)$, this means that $l(x, a) = u(a, x)$, so the flow value cannot be changed in any feasible flow.

(ii) The flow theory claims that:

• the flow value of (x, a) can be increased if and only if $(x, a) \in R(f)$ and there is path from a to x in $R(f) - \{(a, x)\}$, that is in $R(f)$ in this case because we have $(x, a) \in R(f) \Rightarrow (a, x) \notin R(f)$.

• the flow value of (x, a) can be decreased if and only if $(a, x) \in R(f)$ and there is path from x to a in $R(f) - \{(x, a)\}$, that is in $R(f)$ in this case because we have $(a, x) \in R(f) \Rightarrow (x, a) \notin R(f)$.

So in this case, a flow value is constant if and only if a and x belong to two different strongly connected components.

(iii) We will call non trivial (u, v) cycle, a directed cycle which contains (u, v) but not (v, u). There are two possibilities:

1) there is a non trivial (x, a) cycle or a non trivial (a, x) cycle. This means that the flow can be increased or decreased, therefore it has not the same value for every feasible flow. Moreover, there exists a directed cycle which is non trivial, so this cycle is also a cycle in the undirected version and the arc (x, a) is not a bridge and conversely.

2) there does not exist a non trivial (x, a) cycle and there does not exist a non trivial (a, x) cycle. Let $X(x)$ be the set of nodes of $scc(R(f) - \{a\}, x)$, and $X(a)$ be the set of nodes of $scc(R(f) - \{x\}, a)$. Then $\forall p \in X(x), p \neq x$ and $\forall q \in X(a), q \neq a$, we can prove that the arcs (p, q), (q, p), (x, q), (q, x), (a, p), (p, a) do not exist. Suppose that (p, q) exists. Then, there is a path from x to p which does not contain a and an arc (p, q) and a path from q to a which does not contain x, therefore this means that we identify a non trivial (a, x) cycle, which contradicts the hypothesis. A similar reasoning is valid for all the arcs. Hence, if (x, a) and (a, x) are removed from $R(f)$ then x and a will belong to two different connected component of the undirected version of $R(f)$. This is equivalent to saying, that (x, a) is a bridge.⊙

Now, we can give a **proof of Property 3**: Let a be the value whose cardinality is cy, and f be a feasible flow of $N(C)$, the value network of C. For convenience we will use $USCC = ud(scc(R(f), a))$, $SCC = scc(R(f), a)$, $CC = cc(GV(X), a)$, $X_S = vars(SCC)$, and $V_S = vals(SCC)$. If the flow value of (a, t) is the same for every feasible flow, then from Theorem 1 either a and t belong to different connected components or (a, t) is a bridge of $USCC$.

In the first case, this means that all the arcs between a value of SCC and t have the same direction. In other words, the flow value of these arcs is either equal to the lower bound capacity or is equal to the upper bound capacity. So we have either $|X_S| = \sum_{a_i \in V_S} min(card[i])$ or $|X_S| = \sum_{a_i \in V_S} max(card[i])$. In both cases the bound consistency of the constraint $|X_S| = \sum_{a_i \in V_S} card[i]$ will instantiate all these cardinality variables to the current flow value of their corresponding arc.

In the second case, (a, t) is a bridge of $USCC$ and the value graph does not contain t, so CC is a subgraph of $USCC$. If SCC contains t and if (a, t) is a bridge of $USCC$ then (a, t) and (t, a) exist in $R(f)$ and there is no other arc between $vals(CC)$ and t. Thus, the lower and the upper bound capacities are equal for every value of $vals(CC)$ which is not equal to a. In this case, the bound consistency of the sum constraint involving cy will instantiate cy to the current flow value of its corresponding arc. ⊙

5 Cardinality (0,1)-Matrix Constraint

5.1 Absence of Cardinality Variables

Definition 5 *Let $M = x[i, j]$ be a matrix of (0,1)-variables. A **Cardinality (0,1)-Matrix** constraint is a constraint C defined on M in which*
- *every row i is associated with two positive integers $lr[i]$ and $ur[i]$ with $lr[i] \leq ur[i]$*
- *every column j is associated with two positive integers $lc[i]$ and $uc[i]$ with $lc[i] \leq uc[i]$, and*
$T(C) = \{\tau \text{ s.t. } \tau \text{ is a tuple on } X(C)$
$\text{and } \forall i \in Row(M) : lr[i] \leq \sum_{j \in Col(M)} x[i, j] \leq ur[i]$
$\text{and } \forall j \in Col(M) : lc[j] \leq \sum_{i \in Row(M)} x[i, j] \leq uc[j]\}$
It is denoted by card-(0,1)-Matrix(M, lr, ur, lc, uc).

This constraint corresponds to a generalization of a well known problem named "Matrices composed of 0's and 1's" by Ford and Fulkerson [6]. In this latter problem, there is no lower bound for the rows and no upper bound for the columns. Both Ryser [14] and Gale [7] independently showed that this problem can be solved by using a flow. The introduction of lower bounds on rows and upper bounds on columns only slightly modified the flow:

Definition 6 *Given $M = x[i, j]$ a matrix of (0,1)-variables and $C = $ card-(0,1)-Matrix(M, lr, ur, lc, uc) a cardinality (0,1)-matrix constraint; the bipartite network of C, denoted by $N(C)$, consists of a node set defined by:*

- a set of nodes $SR = \{r_1, ..., r_n\}$ corresponding to the rows of M.
- a set of nodes $SC = \{c_1, ..., c_m\}$ corresponding to the columns of M.
- a source node s and a sink t

and an arc set A defined by:
- $\forall r_i \in SR$ $(s, r_i) \in A$ with a lower bound capacity equal to $lr[i]$ and an upper bound capacity equal to $ur[i]$.
- $\forall c_j \in SC$ $(c_j, t) \in A$ with a lower bound capacity equal to $lc[j]$ and an upper bound capacity equal to $uc[j]$.
- $\forall r_i \in SR, \forall c_j \in SC$ $(r_i, c_j) \in A$ with a capacity equal to $x[i, j]$, that is the lower bound capacity is equal to $min(x[i, j])$ and the upper bound capacity is equal to $max(x[i, j])$.
- an arc (t, s) without capacity constraint.

Note that the (0,1)-variables define the capacity constraints of the arcs between nodes corresponding to rows and nodes corresponding to columns.

Proposition 1 *C is consistent if and only if there is a feasible flow in the bipartite network of C.*

We can establish arc consistency of the card-(0,1)-Matrix constraint by a similar method to the one used for GCCs[2]:

Proposition 2 *Let C be a consistent cardinality (0,1)-Matrix constraint and f be a feasible flow in the bipartite network of C. Then we have:*
$\forall r_i \in SR, \forall c_j \in SC$: r_i and c_j do not belong to the same strongly connected component in $R(f)$ if and only if $x[i, j] = f_{r_i c_j}$.

Proof: Immediate from Properties (i) and (ii) of Theorem 1 (Property (iii) cannot be applied because the capacity of the arcs between rows and columns are 0 or 1). ⊙

Thus, arc consistency can be established by only one identification of the strongly connected components in $R(f)$, that is in $O(|M|)$.

The advantage of the cardinality (0,1)-matrix constraint is emphasized by the following theorem:

Theorem 2 *Consider $C = \text{card-}(0,1)\text{-matrix}(M, lr, ur, lc, uc)$ a cardinality (0, 1)-matrix constraint. Establishing arc consistency for C ensures that for every $p \times q$ rectangle, denoted by T we simultaneously have:*

$$\sum_{(i,j) \in T} x[i,j] \geq \sum_{i \in Row(T)} lr[i] - \sum_{j \in (Col(M) - Col(T))} uc[j] \quad (1)$$

$$\sum_{(i,j) \in T} x[i,j] \geq \sum_{i \in Col(T)} lc[i] - \sum_{j \in (Row(M) - Row(T))} ur[j] \quad (2)$$

---

[2] A similar constraint, althrough expressed in a quite different way, with the same kind of algorithm to establish arc consistency, is given in [10].

Proof: C is consistent. Consider Q the rectangle containing the same rows as T and the columns that are not contained in T. Every feasible flow of $N(C)$ satisfied the constraints on the rows: $\sum_{(i,j)\in(T\cup Q)} x[i,j] \geq \sum_{i\in Row(T)} lr[i]$. We have $\sum_{(i,j)\in(T\cup Q)} x[i,j] = \sum_{(i,j)\in T} x[i,j] + \sum_{(i,j)\in Q} x[i,j]$, so $\sum_{(i,j)\in T} x[i,j] + \sum_{(i,j)\in Q} x[i,j] \geq \sum_{i\in Row(T)} lr[i]$. Moreover $\sum_{(i,j)\in Q} x[i,j] \leq \sum_{j\in(Col(M)-Col(T))} uc[j]$, because the constraints on the columns of Q are satisfied. So, Equation 1 is satisfied.

Similarly, consider Q the rectangle containing the same columns as T and the rows that are not contained in T. Every feasible flow of $N(C)$ satisfies the constraints on the columns: $\sum_{(i,j)\in(T\cup Q)} x[i,j] \geq \sum_{i\in Col(T)} lc[i]$. We have $\sum_{(i,j)\in(T\cup Q)} x[i,j] = \sum_{(i,j)\in T} x[i,j] + \sum_{(i,j)\in Q} x[i,j]$, so $\sum_{(i,j)\in T} x[i,j] + \sum_{(i,j)\in Q} x[i,j] \geq \sum_{i\in Col(T)} lc[i,k]$. Moreover $\sum_{(i,j)\in Q} x[i,j] \leq \sum_{j\in(Row(M)-Row(T))} ur[j]$, because the constraints on the rows of Q are satisfied. So, Equation 2 is satisfied. ⊙

A corollary of this theorem is close to a necessary condition of a theorem proposed for latin square by Ryser [13]:

Corollary 1 *If $\forall i \in Row(M)$ $lr[i] = ur[i] = 1$, and $\forall j \in Col(M)$ $lc[j] = uc[j] = 1$, then $\sum_{(i,j)\in T} x[i,j] \geq p - (n-q)$*

Thus, with only one cardinality (0,1)-matrix constraint we are able to take into account a property which is available for all $p \times q$ rectangles involved in the constraint. Instead of having an exponential number of cardinality constraints (because every row and column can be permuted) we have only one cardinality (0,1)-matrix constraint.

5.2 Introduction of Cardinality Variables

In a way similar as the one used for GCCs we propose to introduce cardinality variables in Cardinality (0,1)-Matrix constraint.

Definition 7 *Let $M = x[i,j]$ be a matrix of (0,1)-variables. A **Cardinality (0,1)-Matrix constraint involving cardinality variables** is a constraint C defined on M and rowCard and colCard in which*
- *every row i is associated with a cardinality variable $rowCard[i]$*
- *every column j is associated with a cardinality variable $colCard[j]$, and*

$T(C) = \{ \tau$ s.t. τ *is a tuple on* $X(C)$
and $\forall i \in Row(M) : \sum_{j\in Col(M)} x[i,j] = rowCard[i]$
and $\forall j \in Col(M) : \sum_{i\in Row(M)} x[i,j] = colCard[j]\}$
It is denoted by card-(0,1)-Matrix$(M, rowCard, colCard)$.

The consistency of $C = card$-$(0,1)$-$matrix(M, lr, ur, lc, uc)$ is equivalent to the consistency of the constraint $card$-$(0,1)$-$matrix(M, rowCard, colCard)$ where $\forall i \in Row(M)$ $lr[i] = min(rowCard[i])$ and $ur[i] = max(rowCard[i])$ and $\forall j \in Col(M)$ $lc[i] = min(colCard[i])$ and $uc[i] = max(colCard[i])$. When the minimum or the maximum value of the domain of a cardinality variable is modified then C is modified and so the consistency of the constraint must be established again. Since the flow algorithms are incremental, a new feasible flow can be computed in $O(m)$.

Arc consistency can be established for the variables of M, because the problem remains the same for these variables. For the cardinality variables we have similar properties as for cardVar-GCCs:

Property 4 *Let $C = gcc(X, V, card)$ be a cardinality (0,1)-Matrix constraint involving cardinality variables. Then, we have:*
$\sum_{i \in Row(M)} rowCard[i] = \sum_{j \in Col(M)} colCard[j]$

Bound consistency of a sum constraint involving n variables can be established in $O(n)$. As for cardVar-GCCs, we have the property:

Property 5 *Let C be a cardinality (0,1)-matrix constraint involving cardinality variables, $ud(N(C) - \{s,t\})$ be the undirected version of the network of C in which the node s and t have been removed. Then for every connected component CC of $ud(N(C) - \{s,t\})$ we have:*
$\sum_{i \in Row(CC)} rowCard[i] = \sum_{j \in Col(CC)} colCard[j]$,
where $Row(CC)$ denotes the rows of M belonging to CC and $Col(CC)$ denotes the columns of M belonging to CC.

Proof: All the connected components are disjoint by definition, thus the problem is equivalent to a disjunction of cardinality (0,1)-matrix constraint, each of them corresponding to a connected component. Then, Property 1 can be independently applied on each constraint. ⊙

The filtering algorithm associated with cardinality variables is defined by Property 4 and by Property 5. Its complexity is $O(|Row(M)| + |Col(M)|)$ for all the sum constraints that can be defined and $O(m)$ for the search for connected components, where m is the number of edges of $ud(N(C) - \{s,t\})$.

6 Filtering Algorithm for the Cardinality Matrix Constraint

A cardinality matrix constraint is modeled by a cardVar-GCC on every row, a cardVar-GCC on every column, a constraint between the sum of cardinality variables, and a cardinality (0,1)-matrix constraint per symbol:

Definition 8 *Let $C = card\text{-}Matrix(M, V, rowCard, colCard)$ be a cardinality matrix constraint involving n rows, m columns and s symbols. Then,*

- *for every row i we define $Cr_i = gcc(vars(i, *, M), V, vars(i, *, rowCard))$*
- *for every column j we define $Cc_j = gcc(vars(*, j, M), V, vars(j, *, colCard))$*
- *for every value $a_k \in V$ we define the cardinality (0,1)-matrix $Cm_k = card\text{-}(0,1)\text{-}matrix(B_k, vars(*, k, rowCard), vars(*, k, colCard))$*

- for every value $a_k \in V$ and for every variables $x[i,j], i = 1..n, j = 1..m$ we define the (0,1)-variable $b[i,j,k]$ and the constraint $b[i,j,k] = 1 \Leftrightarrow a_k \in D(x[i,j])$. We will denote by B_k all the (0,1)-variables defined from a_k, and by Cb_k the set of constraints defined from a_k.
- we define the constraints: $Cgr : \sum_{i=1..n} \sum_{k=1..s} rowCard[i,k] = nm$ and $Cgc : \sum_{j=1..m} \sum_{k=1..s} colCard[j,k] = nm$

Given

$$X_Q = M \cup rowCard \cup colCard \cup (\bigcup_{k=1..s} B_k)$$
$$\mathcal{D}(X_Q) \text{ the set of domains of the variables } X_Q$$

$$C_Q = \bigcup_{i=1..n} Cr_i \cup \bigcup_{j=1..m} Cc_i \cup \bigcup_{k=1..s} Cb_k \cup \bigcup_{k=1..s} Cm_k \cup Cgr \cup Cgc$$

The constraint network $\mathcal{Q} = (X_Q, \mathcal{D}(X_Q), C_Q)$ is called **the constraint network associated with a card-matrix constraint**.

Proposition 3 *Given $C = card\text{-}matrix(M, V, rowCard, colCard)$, and $\Pi = (M, \mathcal{D}(M), \{C\})$ be a constraint network and $\mathcal{Q}$ the constraint network associated with C then, Π is satisfiable iff $\mathcal{Q}$ is satisfiable.*

Proof: When the M variables of Π are instantiated, the Cb constraint s of $\mathcal{Q}$ instantiated the (0,1)-variables of $\mathcal{Q}$ and since a solution satisfied the cardinality constraint for all the symbols then a solution of Π is a solution of $\mathcal{Q}$. Conversely, a solution of $\mathcal{Q}$ is obviously a solution of Π because the M and the cardinality variables of $\mathcal{Q}$ are the variables of Π, and the constraints of Π are satisfied by any solution of $\mathcal{Q}$.⊙

So, a card-matrix constraint can be filtered by applying arc consistency to the constraint network associated with it.

7 Experiments

In order to perform comparisons with other approaches for which there are results reported in the literature we performed our empirical analysis for the particular case of the cardinality matrix constraint in which each value has to be assigned at most once in each row and column (alldiff matrix constraint). We used hard Latin square instances. (The benchmark instances are available from: http://mat.gsia.cmu.edu/COLOR02 or from gomes@cs.cornell.edu.)

A new strategy to select the next variable and the value to branch on for Latin square problems was proposed in [4]. This strategy clearly outperforms all the previous ones that have been tested. It consists of selecting the variable with the minimum domain size and then select the value which occurs the fewest times in the domains of the variables of the rows and the columns of the selected variable. We will denote it by dom-lessO. This strategy is a kind of minimum conflict strategy. We have improved this strategy by breaking the tie of variables. When two variables have the same size of domain we select the one for which the number of instantiated variables of the row and of the column is maximum. We tested several combinations (like the minimum number of already instantiated variables), and it appears that our variant is the most robust one. Breaking ties is interesting, but the ways we break the ties seem almost equivalent. We will denote our new strategy by dom-maxB-lessO.

	2alldiff-AC dom-lessO		3alldiff-AC dom-lessO		2alldiff-GAC dom-lessO		alldiff-matrix dom-lessO	
	time	#fails	time	#fails	time	#fails	time	#fails
qwh.order30.holes316		> 50,000		> 50,000	0.33	10	0.33	3
qwh.order30.holes320		> 50,000		> 50,000	1.16	1334	0.34	22
qwh.order50.holes2000		> 50,000	1.45	230	4.6	0	5.8	0
qwh.order60.holes1440		> 50,000		> 50,000		> 50,000		> 50,000
qwh.order60.holes1620		> 50,000		> 50,000		> 50,000	66.9	24,604
qwh.order60.holes1692		> 50,000		> 50,000	15.96	7,084	7.57	7,917
qwh.order60.holes1728		> 50,000		> 50,000		> 50,000	3.16	14
qwh.order60.holes1764		> 50,000		> 50,000	3.4	277	3.68	150
qwh.order60.holes1800		> 50,000		> 50,000	3.9	554	3.4	3
qwh.order70.holes2450		> 50,000		> 50,000	5.77	24	6.5	1
qwh.order70.holes2940		> 50,000		> 50,000	9.7	398	10.8	74
qwh.order70.holes3430		> 50,000		> 50,000	14.4	0	17	0

	2alldiff-GAC dom-lessO		2alldiff-GAC dom-maxB-lessO		alldiff-matrix dom-lessO		alldiff-matrix dom-maxB-lessO	
	time	#fails	time	#fails	time	#fails	time	#fails
qwh.order30.holes316	0.33	10	0.62	476	0.33	3	0.37	44
qwh.order30.holes320	1.16	1334	0.33	21	0.34	22	0.35	32
qwh.order50.holes2000	4.6	0	4.57	1	5.8	0	5.7	1
qwh.order60.holes1440		> 50,000		> 50,000		> 50,000	2.32	18
qwh.order60.holes1620		> 50,000		> 50,000	66.9	24,604	6.54	1,439
qwh.order60.holes1692	15.96	7,084	2.75	54	7.57	7,917	3.15	47
qwh.order60.holes1728		> 50,000	2.7	4	3.16	14	3.16	9
qwh.order60.holes1764	3.4	277	2.82	1	3.68	150	3.28	12
qwh.order60.holes1800	3.9	554	15.28	1,369	3.4	3	4.0	261
qwh.order70.holes2450	5.77	24	5.7	1	6.5	1	6.6	35
qwh.order70.holes2940	9.7	398	9.5	145	10.8	74	11.1	130
qwh.order70.holes3430	14.4	0	14.2	0	17	0	17.2	2

We present two sets of results. The first one is a comparison of our method with the approach of [4], the most competitive CP based strategy. We will see that our approach, using the alldiff matrix constraint, outperforms the approach reported in [4]. The second one is a comparison of the branching strategies when the alldiff matrix constraint is used.

The "2alldiff-GAC" method is the classical model using 2 alldiff constraints associated with the filtering algorithm establishing arc consistency. The "3alldiff-AC" method is the model in which 3 alldiff constraints have been used but the global constraints are not used, and "2alldiff-AC" method uses only 2 alldiff constraints. This latter method has been used by [4]. All the experiments have been performed on a Pentium IV M, 2Mhz running under Windows XP Professional, and ILOG Solver 6.0. The code is available upon request from the authors. Thus, these experiments are reproducible.

These results clearly show that:
- difficult instances cannot be solved without efficient filtering algorithms
- the alldiff-matrix clearly outperforms 2alldiff models
- the branching strategy we propose is better than the previous ones.

Several instances remain open for a CP approach: qwh.order40.holes528, qwh.order40.holes544, qwh.order40.holes560, qwh.order33.holes.381.bal, qwh.order50.holrd825.bal. The instance qwh.order35.holes405 is solved with our approach in 9,900 s and 6,322,742 backtracks.

8 Conclusion

We present the Cardinality Matrix Constraint to efficiently model cardinality matrix problems. We also propose a simple filtering algorithm of low cost to reduce the ranges of the cardinality variables. The cardinality (0,1)-matrix constraint is a particular case of the transportation problem, a well-studied network flow problem, and it provides a good representation to capture the interactions between rows, columns, and symbols. We report results for the Alldiff Matrix constraint, a particular case of the Cardinality Matrix Constraint. Our results show that the Alldiff Matrix constraint clearly outperforms standard formulations of Alldiff Matrix problems.

References

1. R. Ahuja, T. Magnanti, and J. Orlin. *Network Flows*. Prentice Hall, 1993.
2. C. Berge. *Graphe et Hypergraphes*. Dunod, Paris, 1970.
3. M. Dincbas, H. Simonis, and P. Van Hentenryck. Solving the car-sequencing problem in constraint logic programming. In *ECAI'88, proceedings of the European Conference on Artificial Intelligence*, pages 290–295, 1988.
4. I. Dotu, A. del Val, and M. Cebrian. Redundant modeling for the quasigroup completion problem. In *Proceedings of CP'03*, pages 288–302, 2003.
5. K. Easton, G. Nemhauser, and M. Trick. Sports scheduling. In J. Leung, editor, *Handbook of Scheduling: Models, Algorithms and Performance Analysis*. CRC Press, 2004.
6. L. Ford and D. Fulkerson. *Flows in Networks*. Princeton University Press, 1962.
7. D. Gale. A theorem on flows in networks. *Pacific J. Math*, 7:1073–1082, 1957.
8. C. Gomes and J.-C. Regin. The alldiff matrix. Technical report, Intelligent Information Institute - Cornell University, 2003.
9. I. Katriel and S. Thiel. Fast bound consistency for the global cardinality constraint. In *Proceedings CP'03*, pages 437–451, Kinsale, Ireland, 2003.
10. W. Kocjan and P. Kreuger. Filtering methods for symmetric cardinality constraints. In *First International Conference, CPAIOR 2004*, pages 200–208, Nice, France, 2004.
11. M. Milano (ed.). *Constraint and Integer Programming: Toward a Unified Methodology*. Kluwer, 2003.

12. J.-C. Régin. Generalized arc consistency for global cardinality constraint. In *Proceedings AAAI-96*, pages 209–215, Portland, Oregon, 1996.
13. H. Ryser. A combinatorial theorem with application to latin rectangles. *Proc. Amec. Math. Soc.*, 2:550–552, 1951.
14. H. Ryser. Combinatorial properties of matrices of zeros and ones. *Canad. J. Math*, 9:371–377, 1957.
15. R. Tarjan. Depth-first search and linear graph algorithms. *SIAM Journal of Computing*, 1:146–160, 1972.
16. R. Tarjan. *Data Structures and Network Algorithms*. CBMS-NSF Regional Conference Series in Applied Mathematics, 1983.

Controllability of Soft Temporal Constraint Problems

Francesca Rossi[1], Kristen Brent Venable[1], and Neil Yorke-Smith[2]

[1] University of Padova, Italy
{frossi,kvenable}@math.unipd.it
[2] IC–Parc, Imperial College, London, UK
nys@icparc.ic.ac.uk

Abstract. In real-life temporal scenarios, uncertainty and preferences are often essential, coexisting aspects. We present a formalism where temporal constraints with both preferences and uncertainty can be defined. We show how three classical notions of controllability (strong, weak and dynamic), which have been developed for uncertain temporal problems, can be generalised to handle also preferences. We then propose algorithms that check the presence of these properties and we prove that, in general, dealing simultaneously with preferences and uncertainty does not increase the complexity beyond that of the separate cases. In particular, we develop a dynamic execution algorithm, of polynomial complexity, that produces plans under uncertainty that are optimal w.r.t. preference.

1 Motivation

Research on temporal reasoning, once exposed to the difficulties of real-life problems, can be found lacking both expressiveness and flexibility. To address the lack of expressiveness, preferences can be added to the temporal framework; to address the lack of flexibility to contingency, reasoning about uncertainty can be added. In this paper we introduce a framework to handle both preferences and uncertainty in temporal problems. This is done by merging the two pre-existing models of *Simple Temporal Problems with Preferences* (STPPs) [5] and *Simple Temporal Problems under Uncertainty* (STPUs). [12]. We adopt the notion of controllability of STPUs, to be used instead of consistency because of the presence of uncertainty, and we adapt it to handle preferences.

The proposed framework, *Simple Temporal Problems with Preferences and Uncertainty* (STPPUs), represents temporal problems with preferences and uncertainty via a set of variables, which represent the starting or ending times of events (which may be controllable or not), and a set of soft temporal constraints over the variables. Each constraint includes an interval containing the allowed durations of the event or the allowed interleaving times between events, and a preference function associating each element of the interval with a value corresponding to how much its preferred. Such soft constraints can be defined on both controllable and uncontrollable events.

Examples of real-life problems with temporal constraints, preferences, and uncertainty can easily be found in several application domains (e.g. [7]). Here we describe in detail one such problem, arising in an aerospace application domain. The problem refers to planning for fleets of *Earth Observing Satellites* (EOS) [4]. This planning problem involves multiple satellites, hundreds of requests, constraints on when and how to service each request, and multiple resources. Scientists place requests to receive earth images from space. After the image data is acquired by an EOS, it can either be downlinked in real time or recorded on board for playback at a later time. Ground stations or other satellites are available to receive downlinked images. Each satellite can communicate only with a subset of other satellites and/or ground stations, and transmission rates differ. Further, there may be different costs associated with using different communication resources. In [4], the EOS scheduling problem is dealt with through a constraint-based interval representation. Candidate plans are represented by variables and constraints which reflect the temporal relationships and ordering decisions between actions.

This problem contains all the aspects we address in this paper. It has temporal constraints which include duration and ordering constraints associated with the data collecting, recording, and downlinking tasks. Moreover, solutions are preferred based on objectives such maximising the number of high priority requests serviced, maximising the expected quality of the observations, and minimising the cost of downlink operations (notice that most of these preferences can be directly translated into preferences on durations of tasks). Finally, there is uncertainty due to weather: specifically to the duration and persistence of cloud cover, since image quality is reduced by the amount of cloud cover over the target. In the rest of the paper, we will use EOS as a running example to illustrate our STPPU framework.

The specific contributions of this paper are: a way to model simple temporal problems with both uncertainty and preferences; definitions of strong, weak, and dynamic controllability for such problems; an overall view of the logical relationship among these notions; algorithms to check controllability, complexity results, and a general scheme which guides in the use of the algorithms. In particular, we show that checking dynamic controllability of a Simple Temporal Problem with Preferences and Uncertainty can be done in polynomial time. Thus we prove that adding preferences does not make the problem more difficult, given that uncontrollable events may occur.

Most proofs have been omitted for lack of space. This paper is a revised and updated version of [15], a poster paper focused mainly on strong controllability.

2 Background

In a *Temporal Constraint Problem* [2], variables denote timepoints and constraints represent the possible temporal relations between them. The constraints are quantitative, describing restrictions either on durations of events or on distances (interleaving times) between events, in terms of intervals over the timeline. In general such problems are **NP**-complete. However, if each temporal constraint has just one interval – hence the constraints have form $l_{ij} \leq x_j - x_i \leq u_{ij}$, where the x denote timepoints – then we have a *Simple Temporal Problem* (STP) that can be solved in polynomial time by enforcing path consistency. An STP is said to be *path consistent* iff any consistent assignment to two variables can be extended to a consistent assignment to three variables. Path consistency in the context of STPs is enforced by performing two operation on temporal intervals: *intersection* ($\oplus$) and *composition* ($\otimes$). Intersection is defined as the usual interval intersection. Composition is defined as: $I_1 \otimes I_2 = \{t = a + b \mid a \in I_1, b \in I_2\}$. Given an STP and a constraint c_{ij} on variables x_i and x_j with interval I_{ij}, it is possible to show that the STP is path consistent iff $\forall i, j, I_{ij} \subseteq I_{ij} \oplus (I_{ik} \otimes I_{kj}) \; \forall k$ [10].

To address the lack of flexibility in execution of standard STPs, the *Simple Temporal Problem under Uncertainty* (STPU) framework [12] divides the timepoints into two classes: *executable* (or requirement) and *contingent* (or uncontrollable). The former, as in an STP, are decided by the agent, but the latter are decided by 'Nature': the agent has no control over when the activity will end; it observes rather than executes. The only information known prior to observation is that Nature will respect the interval on the duration. Durations of contingent links are assumed independent.

Controllability of an STPU is the analogue of consistency of an STP. Controllable implies the agent has a means to execute the timepoints under its control, subject to all constraints. Three notions have been proposed in [12]. Firstly, an STPU is *Strongly Controllable* (SC) if there is a fixed execution strategy that works in all *situations* (an observation of all contingent timepoints). Checking strong controllability is in **P** [12]. Secondly, an STPU is *Dynamically Controllable* (DC) if there is an online execution strategy that depends only on observed timepoints in the past and that can always be extended to a complete schedule whatever may happen in the future. Checking dynamic controllability is also in **P**; and we will call the algorithm proposed in [8] to test this property CHECK-DC. Thirdly, an STPU is *Weakly Controllable* (WC) if there exists at least one execution strategy for every situation. Checking weak controllability is co-**NP** [12]. The three notions are ordered by their strength: Strong $\Rightarrow$ Dynamic $\Rightarrow$ Weak.

Separately, to address the lack of expressiveness in standard STPs, the *Simple Temporal Problem with Preferences* (STPP) framework [5] merges STPs with semiring-based soft constraints. Soft temporal constraints are specified by means of a *preference function* on the constraint interval, $f : [l, u] \to A$, where A is a set of preference values. The set A is part of a semiring. Recall that a *semiring* is a tuple $\langle A, +, \times, \mathbf{0}, \mathbf{1} \rangle$ such that: A is a set and $\mathbf{0}, \mathbf{1} \in A$; $+$ is commutative, associative and $\mathbf{0}$ is its unit element; $\times$ is associative, distributes over $+$, $\mathbf{1}$ is its unit element and $\mathbf{0}$ is its absorbing element. Further, in a *c-semiring* $+$ is idempotent, $\mathbf{1}$ is its absorbing element and $\times$ is commutative. In [1] semiring-based soft constraints are presented as a unifying, expressive framework since they can model various types of preferences and different ways of aggregating them. In this paper we will use, as underlying structure for handling preference, the *fuzzy* semiring $S_{\text{FCSP}} = \langle [0, 1], \max, \min, 0, 1 \rangle$.

In general, STPPs are **NP**-complete. However, under certain restrictions – if preference functions are semi-convex (i.e. having at most one peak), constraints are combined via an idempotent operation (like min), and preference values are totally ordered (like $[0, 1]$) – then finding an optimal solution of an STPP is a polynomial problem [5].

Two solvers for STPPs with these restrictions are presented by [9]. We now outline CHOP-SOLVER, since some of the algorithms we propose here employ a similar *chopping procedure*. This procedure takes an STPP satisfying the above conditions, and a preference level β, and returns an STP (i.e. a problem without preferences). For each soft constraint of the STPP, $c = \langle [l, u], f \rangle$, there is a hard constraint on the same variables in the STP, $c' = [l', u'] = \{t : t \in [l, u], f(t) \geq \beta\}$. The consistency of the STP obtained can be tested, e.g. by enforcing path consistency. We recall that path consistency applied to an STP leaves the problem (if consistent) in its *minimal* form: its intervals contain only elements that belong to at least one solution. CHOP-SOLVER takes as input an STPP and searches for the highest preference level, *opt*, at which chopping the STPP gives a consistent STP; *opt* can be found performing a binary search in the preference interval $[0, 1]$. It can be easily proven that all and only the solutions of the STP obtained chopping at *opt* are optimal solutions of the input STPP (i.e. it has no solution with preference $> opt$). Thus the minimal problem obtained by enforcing path consistency at level *opt* is minimal also with respect to the optimal solutions of the STPP. Summarising, CHOP-SOLVER takes an STPP and returns the optimal level *opt* and an STP in minimal form containing all and only the optimal solutions of the given STPP.

3 Simple Temporal Problems with Preferences and Uncertainty

An intuitive definition of an STPPU is an STPP for which the timepoints are partitioned into two classes, executable and contingent, just as in an STPU. Symmetrically an STPPU can be viewed as an STPU to which preference functions are added. Contingent constraints become *soft contingent constraints* and requirement constraints become *soft requirement constraints*.

Both soft contingent and requirement constraints are defined as a pair $\langle I, f \rangle$, where (as before) the interval $I = [l, u]$ contains the possible durations or distances between the two constrained timepoints, and $f_{ij} : I \rightarrow A$ is a *preference function* mapping each element of the interval into an element of the preference set of the semiring $S = \langle A, +, \times, \mathbf{0}, \mathbf{1} \rangle$. Since we are assuming the fuzzy semiring as a underlying structure, the optimisation criterion in this paper is to maximise the minimum preference obtained by an assignment on any constraint. Although it may appear conservative, this 'weakest link' criterion applies in many cases and it is attractive computationally because of the idempotency of the multiplicative operator min. Further, without loss of generality, and following the assumptions made for STPUs [8], we may assume no two contingent constraints end at the same timepoint.

In both types of constraints, the preference function represents the preference of the agent on the duration of an event or on the distance between two events. The difference is that, while for soft requirement constraints the agent has control and can be guided by the preferences in choosing values for the timepoints, for soft contingent constraints the preference represents merely a desire of the agent on the possible outcomes of Nature; there is no control on the outcomes. We will illustrate shortly.

We can now state formally the definition of an STPPU:

Definition 1 (STPPU). *A* Simple Temporal Problem with Preferences and Uncertainty (STPPU) *P is a tuple* $P = (N_e, N_c, L_r, L_c, S)$ *where: N_e is the set of executable points; N_c is the set of contingent points; L_r is the set of soft requirement constraints over semiring S; L_c is the set of soft contingent constraints over semiring S; and $S = \langle A, +, \times, \mathbf{0}, \mathbf{1} \rangle$ is a c-semiring.*

Once we have a complete assignment to all timepoints we can compute its global preference. This is done according to the semiring-based soft constraint schema: first we project the assignment on all soft constraints, obtaining an element of the interval and the preference associated to that element; then we combine all the preferences obtained with the multiplicative operator of the semiring (min in this paper). Given two assignments with their preference, the best is chosen using the additive operator (max in this paper). An assignment is *optimal* if there is no other with a higher preference.

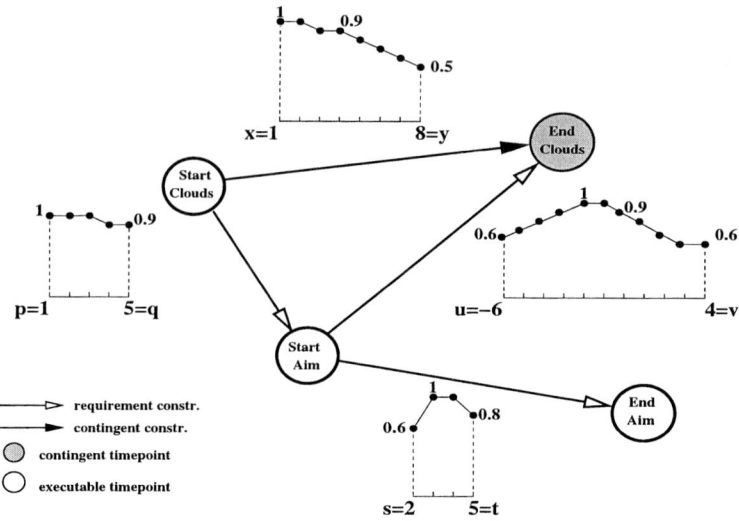

Fig. 1. Example STPPU from the Earth Observing Satellites domain.

A solution of an STPPU, a *schedule*, is a complete assignment of values (times) to all the timepoints, executable and contingent, that satisfies the constraints with preference ≥ 0. We can distinguish two parts of a schedule: a *situation* ω, the duration of all contingent events, and a *control sequence* δ, the set of assignments to all executable timepoints. One the one hand, ω represents the assignments made by Nature; on the other hand, δ represents the decisions made by the agent. We define $Sol(P)$ to be the set of all schedules. Given a situation ω, the *projection* P_ω of an STPPU P is the STPP obtained by replacing in P the contingent events with their values in ω and the associated preferences. We indicate with $opt(P_\omega)$ the preference value of an optimal solution of P_ω. We define $Proj(P)$ to be the set of all projections. Then a *strategy* is a map S: $Proj(P) \rightarrow Sol(P)$ such that for every projection P_ω, $S(P_\omega)$ is a schedule which includes ω. Regarding notation, given an executable timepoint x, we will write $[S(P_\omega)]_x$ to indicate the value assigned to x in $S(P_\omega)$, and $[S(P_\omega)]_{<x}$ to indicate the durations of the contingent events that finish prior to x in $S(P_\omega)$.

Example 1. Consider as an example the following scenario from the Earth Observing Satellites domain [4] described in Sect. 1. Suppose a request for observing a region of interest has been received and accepted. To collect the data, the instrument must be aimed at the target before images can be taken. It might be, however, that for a certain period during the time window allocated for this observation, the region of interest is covered by clouds. The earlier the cloud coverage ends the better, since it will maximise both the quality and the quantity of retrieved data; but coverage is not controllable.

Suppose the time window reserved for an observation is from 1 to 8 units of time and that we start counting time when the cloud occlusion on the region of interest is observable. Suppose, in order for the observation to succeed, the aiming procedure must start before 5 units after the starting time, ideally before 3 units, and it actually can only begin after at least 1 time unit after the weather becomes observable. Ideally the aiming procedure should start slightly before the cloud coverage will end. If it starts too early then, since the instrument is activated immediately after it is aimed, clouds might still occlude the region and the image quality will be poor. On the other hand, if it waits until the clouds have disappeared then precious time during which there is no occlusion will be wasted aiming the instrument instead of taking images. The aiming procedure can be controlled by the mission manager and it can take anywhere between 2 and 5 units of time. An ideal duration is 3 or 4 units, since a short time of 2 units would put the instrument under pressure, while a long duration, like 5 units, would waste energy.

This scenario, rather tedious to describe in words, can be compactly represented by the STPPU shown in Fig. 1 with the following features: (1) a set of executable timepoints SC, SA, EA; (2) a contingent timepoint EC; (3) a set of soft requirement constraints on {SC → SA, SA → EC, SA → EA}; (4) a soft contingent constraint {SC → EC}; and (5) the fuzzy semiring $S_{\text{FCSP}} = \langle [0, 1], \max, \min, 0, 1 \rangle$.

A solution of the STPPU in Fig. 1 is the schedule $s = \{\text{SC} = 0, \text{SA} = 2, \text{EC} = 5, \text{EA} = 7\}$. The situation associated with s is the projection on the only contingent constraint, SC → EC, i.e. $\omega_s = 5$, while the control sequence is the assignment to the executable timepoints, i.e. $\delta_s = \{\text{SC} = 0, \text{SA} = 2, \text{EA} = 7\}$. The global preference is obtained considering the preferences associated with the projections on all constraints, that is $\text{pref}(2) = 1$ on SC → SA, $\text{pref}(3) = 0.6$ on SA → EC, $\text{pref}(5) = 0.9$ on SA → EA and $\text{pref}(5) = 0.8$ on SC → EC. The preferences must then be combined using the multiplicative operator of the semiring, which is min, so the global preference of s is 0.6. Another solution $s' = \{\text{SC} = 0, \text{SA} = 4, \text{EC} = 5, \text{EA} = 9\}$ has global preference 0.8. Thus s' is a better solution than s according to the semiring ordering since $\max(0.6, 0.8) = 0.8$. □

4 Strong and Weak Controllability with Preferences

We now consider how it is possible to extend the notion of controllability to accommodate preferences. In general we are interested in the ability of the agent to execute the timepoints under its control not only subject to all constraints but also in the best possible way w.r.t. preferences. It transpires the meaning of 'best possible way' depends on the types of controllability we introduced earlier.

Definition 2 (Optimal Strong Controllability). *An STPPU P is Optimally Strongly Controllable (OSC) iff there is an execution strategy S s.t.* $\forall P_\omega \in Proj(P)$, $S(P_\omega)$ *is an optimal solution of* P_ω, *and* $[S(P_1)]_x = [S(P_2)]_x$, $\forall P_1, P_2$ *projections and for every executable timepoint x.*

In other words, an STPPU is OSC if there is a fixed control sequence that works in all possible situations and is optimal in each of them. In the definition, 'optimal' means that there is no other assignment the agent can choose for the executable timepoints that could yield a higher preference in any situation. Since this is a powerful restriction, we can instead look at just reaching a certain quality threshold:

Definition 3 (α-Strong Controllability). *An STPPU P is α-Strongly Controllable (α-SC), with $\alpha \in A$ a preference, iff there is a strategy S s.t.:*

1. $\forall P_\omega \in Proj(P)$, $S(P_\omega)$ is a solution of P_ω such that $[S(P_1)]_x = [S(P_2)]_x$, $\forall P_1, P_2$ projections and for every executable timepoint x; and
2. the global preference of $S(P_\omega)$ is at least preference $opt(P_\omega)$ if $opt(P_\omega) \leq \alpha$.

In other words, an STPPU is α-SC if there is a fixed control sequence that works in all situations and results in optimal schedules for those situation where the optimal preference level of the projection is $\leq \alpha$. Clearly, OSC implies α-SC $\forall \alpha$.

It is possible to check whether an STPPU is Optimally Strongly Controllable or α-Strongly Controllable in polynomial time [15]. To check if an STPPU is OSC we chop it at every preference level, starting from the minimum preference. At each level we obtain a different STPU; the SC of each STPU is checked using the algorithm proposed in [12], which reduces the problem to checking the consistency of an STP only on the executable timepoints. The original STPPU is OSC iff at each preference level the STP obtained is consistent and, considering each constraint of the STPs, the intersection of its intervals across all preference values is non-empty.

Notice, however, that it is very unlikely for an STPPU to be OSC, since OSC is opt-SC where opt is the optimal preference value of the STPPU considered as an STPP. The algorithm proposed for checking OSC can be easily modified to check, given a certain preference α, if the STPPU is α-SC; or even to find the highest α such that this property is satisfied. For example, the STPPU in Fig. 1 is not OSC since there is no choice for SA that will be optimal whatever happens on the contingent constraint SC $\rightarrow$ EC. However the strategy that assigns a time to SA that is 4 units after that assigned to SC works in all possible situations and is optimal for all those situations that have an optimal value of their projection ≤ 0.9. Hence the STPPU in Fig. 1 is 0.9-SC.

Secondly, we extend similarly Weak Controllability:

Definition 4 (Optimal Weak Controllability). *An STPPU is* Optimally Weakly Controllable *(OWC) iff* $\forall P_\omega \in Proj(P)$ *there is a strategy* S_ω *s.t.* $S_\omega(P_\omega)$ *is an optimal solution of* P_ω.

In other words, an STPPU is OWC if, for every situation, there is a fixed control sequence that results in an optimal schedule for that situation.

Optimal Weak Controllability of an STPPU is equivalent to Weak Controllability of the corresponding STPU obtained by ignoring preferences. The reason is that if a projection P_ω has at least one solution then it must have an optimal solution (i.e. one with the highest preference $opt(P_\omega)$). This also implies that an STPPU is such that its underlying STPU is either WC or not. Hence it does not make sense to define a notion of α-Weak Controllability. To check OWC, it is enough to apply the algorithm proposed in [13] to the underlying STPU.

It is easy to see that α-SC for any α implies OWC. In Sect. 8 we discuss the relations between the properties defined in this and the next section. For instance, in Example 1, from the fact that the STPPU is 0.9-SC we can derive that it is also OWC.

5 Dynamic Controllability with Preferences

Dynamic Controllability is seen as the more useful notion of controllability in practice. It addresses the ability of the agent to execute a schedule by choosing incrementally the values to be assigned to executable timepoints, looking only at the past. When preferences are available, it is desirable that the agent acts not only in a way that is guaranteed to be consistent with any possible future outcome but also in a way that ensures the absence of regrets w.r.t preferences.

Definition 5 (Optimal Dynamic Controllability). *An STPPU P is Optimal Dynamic Controllable (ODC) iff there is a strategy S such that $\forall P_1, P_2$ in $Proj(P)$ and for any executable timepoint x:*

1. *if $[S(P_1)]_{<x} = [S(P_2)]_{<x}$ then $[S(P_1)]_x = [S(P_2)]_x$;*
2. *$S(P_1)$ is a consistent complete assignment for P_1 and $S(P_2)$ is a consistent complete assignment for P_2;*
3. *$\text{pref}(S(P_1))$ is optimal in P_1 and $\text{pref}(S(P_2))$ is optimal in P_2.*

In other words, an STPPU is ODC is there exists a means of extending any current partial control sequence to a complete control sequence in the future in such a way that the resulting schedule will be optimal. As before, we also soften the optimality requirement to having a preference reaching a certain threshold.

Definition 6 (α-Dynamic Controllability). *An STPPU P is α-Dynamic Controllable (α-DC) iff there is a strategy S such that $\forall P_1, P_2$ in $Proj(P)$ such that $opt(P_1) \leq \alpha$ and $opt(P_2) \leq \alpha$, and for any executable x, the three conditions of Definition 5 hold.*

In other words, an STPPU is α-DC if there is a means of extending any current partial control sequence to a complete sequence; but optimality is guaranteed only for situations with preference less or equal to α.

6 Checking Optimal Dynamic Controllability

In this section we describe an algorithm that tests whether an STPPU is ODC, and we prove that the test is performed in polynomial time. The idea is to chop the STPPU at different preference levels, in the same way as CHOP-SOLVER does (recall Sect. 2), except now the output of this chopping procedure is an STPU. Starting from the lowest preference and moving up in the preference ordering, at each step the STPPU is chopped and the Dynamic Controllability of the STPU obtained is checked.

We next give more details on how Dynamic Controllability of an STPU can be checked in polynomial time using the algorithm proposed in [8]. We call the algorithm CHECK-DC. It works locally on triangles of simple temporal constraints (with no preferences), on two executable timepoints A and B and a contingent timepoint C. Without loss of generality, let the intervals be $[x, y]$ on the contingent constraint AC, $[p, q]$ on the requirement constraint AB, and $[u, v]$ on the other requirement constraint BC. For example, in Fig. 1, $A = \text{SC}$, $B = \text{SA}$, and $C = \text{EC}$. The idea is to consider how executable C can be ordered w.r.t. the ending time of the contingent event represented by AC. This is determined by looking at interval $[u, v]$ of constraint BC, which contains the allowed interleaving times that can occur between B and C. Based on the signs of u and v, three different cases arise.

In the *Follow case* ($v < 0$), executable B will always follow C. If the STPU is path consistent then it is also DC since, given the time at which C occurs after A, it is always possible to find a consistent value for B. In the *Precede case* ($u \geq 0$), B will always precede or happen simultaneously with C. Then the STPU is DC if $y - v \leq x - u$ since, if so, any assignment to B, v_B, such that $v_B - v_A$, where v_A is the assignment to A, is in $[y - v, x - u] \subseteq [p, q]$, and so is consistent with any assignment to C, v_C (i.e. $v_C - v_B \in [u, v]$). In this case, interval $[p, q]$ on AB should be replaced by $[y-v, x-u]$. Lastly, in the *Unordered case* ($u < 0$ and $v \geq 0$), B can either follow or precede C. To ensure DC, B must wait either for C to occur first, or for $t = y - v$ units of time to pass after A. In other words, either C occurs and B can be activated at the first value consistent with C's time, or B can safely be executed t units of time after A's execution. This can be described by an additional constraint which is expressed as a *wait* on AB and is written $\langle C, t \rangle$. Of course if $x \geq y - v$ then we can raise the lower bound of AB to $y - v$ (*unconditional Unordered reduction*), and in any case we can raise it to x if $x > p$ (*general Unordered reduction*). Waits can be propagated, or *regressed*, from one constraint to another. For example, a wait on AB may induce a wait on other constraints involving A, e.g. AD, depending on the type of constraint DB.

Algorithm CHECK-DC [8] applies these rules to all triangles in the STPU and propagates all possible waits. This propagation is based on the intuition that a wait that must be respected by some executable, B, can (1) affect the allowed execution times of another related (via some constraint path) executable, say B'; or (2) can impose a new, possibly, longer wait on B'. The actual rules that guide such propagation are rather complex and cannot be thoroughly described here due lack of space; we refer to [8].

If no inconsistency is found – no requirement interval becomes empty and no contingent interval is squeezed (i.e. removing possible uncontrollable outcomes) – then the STPU is DC. In that case, the algorithm returns an STPU where some constraints may have waits to satisfy, and the intervals contain only the elements that appear in at least one possible dynamic strategy, i.e. the minimal form of the STPU.

Returning now to the algorithm we propose for testing ODC, the basic idea is to move, bottom up, in the preference set chopping the STPPU and testing the DC of each STPU obtained. If at a given level the STPU is DC then its minimal form is saved. Once a preference level is found, say γ, such that the corresponding STPU is not DC, then the STPPU will not be β-DC for all $\beta \geq \gamma$; thus we can stop the chopping procedure. At this point, the intuitive idea is too keep only elements that guarantee DC at all preference levels lower than γ, performing an 'intersection' of the minimal STPUs obtained up to $\gamma - 1$. If such intersection is non-empty then the STPPU is $(\gamma - 1)$-DC. Applying CHOP-SOLVER to the STPPU will give the highest preference, opt, of any complete assignment. If $\gamma - 1 = opt$ then the STPPU is also ODC.

We now define formally what we have sketched above.

Theorem 1. *Consider an STPPU P and the STPU Q^α obtained chopping P at level α and applying path consistency. Let $[p_{AB}^\alpha, q_{AB}^\alpha]$ be the interval obtained on any requirement constraint AB, by applying CHECK-DC to Q^α, and let $\langle C, t^\alpha \rangle$ be its wait, if any. Then P is ODC iff the following conditions hold: (1) for every α, Q^α is DC; (2) for each requirement constraint AB, the intersection $I = \bigcap_\alpha [t_{AB}^\alpha, q_{AB}^\alpha]$ is not empty.* □

Table 1. First column: preference level α. Next three columns: intervals obtained chopping at all preference levels the constraint triangle on variables SC, SA, and EC shown in Fig. 1. Last column: subintervals obtained on constraint SC $\rightarrow$ SA by applying CHECK-DC and considering only elements following the wait.

preference	(SC $\rightarrow$ EC)$^\alpha$	(SC $\rightarrow$ SA)$^\alpha$	(SA $\rightarrow$ EC)$^\alpha$	$[t^\alpha_{\text{SC,SA}}, q^\alpha_{\text{SC,SA}}]$
0.5	[1, 8]	[1, 5]	[−6, 4]	[4, 5]
0.6	[1, 7]	[1, 5]	[−6, 4]	[3, 5]
0.7	[1, 6]	[1, 5]	[−5, 2]	[4, 5]
0.8	[1, 5]	[1, 5]	[−4, 1]	[4, 5]
0.9	[1, 4]	[1, 5]	[−3, 0]	[4, 5]
1	[1, 2]	[1, 3]	[−2, −1]	[3, 3]

We refer to the two conditions in the theorem as property **M**. It is not hard to see why **M** is necessary for ODC. First, assume the first condition **M1** does not hold. Since $Proj(Q^\alpha) \subseteq Proj(P)$, and since $Proj(Q^\alpha)$ contains all the projections that have optimum preference at least α, then, since Q^α is not DC, there is no global strategy S for P such that $S(P_1)$ has optimal preference in P_1 and $S(P_2)$ in P_2, $\forall P_1, P_2$ with preference at least α. This allows us to conclude that P is not ODC. Secondly, assume instead that **M1** holds but **M2** does not. Each requirement constraint AB might, at different preference levels α, be squeezed in different ways and have different waits t^α_{AB}. At each level α the sub interval $[t^\alpha_{AB}, q^\alpha_{AB}]$ contains the assignments for B that are consistent with all future values of any contingent timepoint and that guarantee a preference $\geq \alpha$. If intersecting these sub-intervals across all preference levels gives an empty interval, then there is no unique value for B that satisfies the properties mentioned above (consistency and optimality) for every preference level. Thus, P is not ODC.

Example 1 is not ODC. Consider the triangle of constraints on variables SC, SA, EC where EC is the only contingent timepoint. Table 1 shows the intervals obtained on each of the constraints chopped at all preference levels. In the last column we show intervals $[t^\alpha_{AB}, q^\alpha_{AB}]$ where constraint AB is SC $\rightarrow$ SA.

It is easy to see that chopping the problem at any preference level gives a STPU that is Dynamically Controllable. At preference level 1 we have an instance of the Follow case, so consistency is equivalent to controllability. At levels 0.5 and 0.7–0.9, SA will either have to wait for the cloud coverage to end or wait for at least 4 units of time after the clouds have been observed at first (i.e. after SC). At preference level 0.6, SA must wait only for 3 time units. However the STPPU is not ODC since the intersection of the intervals in the last column is empty. Consider the scenario in which the clouds coverage lasts for 2 units of time. Since this is consistent with SA occurring 3 unit after SC and this gives a solution with preference value 1, the optimal preference of the projection of situation $\omega = 2$ on contingent constraint SC $\rightarrow$ EC is 1. However if we execute SA at 3 time units after SC and EC happens, say, at 4 units after SC, then the solution obtained has preference 0.8, which is not optimal for the STPP corresponding to situation $\omega = 4$ on contingent constraint SC $\rightarrow$ EC (which has 0.9 as optimal preference value, the preference of the solution obtained in which SA is executed 5 units of time after SC). This shows that there is no way of dynamically assigning values to the executables to guarantee optimality in every possible situation.

CHECK-ODC(triangular STPPU P)
1 STPU $Q \leftarrow IP(P)$
2 **if** CHECK-DC(Q) returns 'not DC'
3   **then return** 'not ODC'
4 CHOP-SOLVER($IU(P)$)
5 **for** $\alpha \leftarrow \alpha_{min}$ **to** opt
6   **do** STPP $Q^\alpha \leftarrow$ PC-2(CHOP(P, α))
7   **if** CHECK-DC(Q^α) returns 'not DC'
8   **then return** 'not ODC'
9   save $DC(Q^\alpha)$
10 **for** requirement links AB s.t. $\exists \alpha : t^\alpha_{AB} < q^\alpha_{AB}$
11   **do** $I \leftarrow \bigcap_\alpha [t^\alpha_{AB}, q^\alpha_{AB}]$
12   **if** $I = \emptyset$
13   **then return** 'not ODC'
14      $I_{AB} \leftarrow [\min_\alpha \{p^\alpha_{AB}\}, \min_\alpha \{q^\alpha_{AB}\}]$
15   wait $t_{AB} \leftarrow \max_\alpha \{t^\alpha_{AB}\}$
16 PC-2($IP(IU(P))$)

Fig. 2. Algorithm for checking ODC of an STPPU by determining whether **M** holds.

6.1 Determining ODC by Checking Property M

We have just informally shown that property **M** is necessary for ODC. To see that it is also sufficient for ODC, we present the pseudocode of an algorithm that, given as input an STPPU P, checks if **M** is satisfied. We then show that if the algorithm reports success then P is ODC. Fig. 6.1 shows the pseudocode of the algorithm that checks **M**.

Algorithm CHECK-ODC takes as input an STPPU P. It checks whether the STPU Q obtained ignoring the preference functions, $IP(P)$ (line 1), is DC, by applying CHECK-DC (line 2). If it is not the case, there is no chance for the original STPPU to be ODC. Otherwise, CHOP-SOLVER is applied to $IU(P)$, i.e. to P considered as an STPP (line 4). This allows us to find the global optimal preference opt. At this point the algorithm checks if the STPUs obtained by chopping P and applying path consistency with PC-2 at different preference levels are DC (lines 5–9). It starts bottom-up from preference α_{min} up to opt, where α_{min} is the minimum preference on any constraint[1]. If at any level the DC test fails, the algorithm stops and returns failure (line 8). The dynamically controllable versions of the STPUs at each the preference level are saved (line 9).

Now, for every preference level α, each requirement constraint AB will have interval $I^\alpha_{AB} = [p^\alpha_{AB}, q^\alpha_{AB}]$ and a wait t^α_{AB} which is the maximum wait that B must satisfy for any related contingent timepoint C, for the subproblem at preference level α. CHECK-ODC thus considers each requirement constraint and checks if it is in an Unordered or Precede case with at least one contingent timepoint at some preference level (line 10). If so, the algorithm computes the intersection of the sub-intervals $[t^\alpha_{AB}, q^\alpha_{AB}]$

---
[1] In general the minimum preference, α_{min}, will be assigned to an element of a contingent constraint, since it is reasonable to leave in the requirement constraints only elements with a preference higher than that of the worst possible uncontrollable outcome.

(line 11). If this intersection is empty then the algorithm again stops and returns failure (line 13). While checking this property, the algorithm updates P, replacing the interval on AB with $I_{AB} = [\min_\alpha\{p^\alpha_{AB}\}, \min_\alpha\{q^\alpha_{AB}\}]$, the preference function with its restriction to this interval, and imposing wait $t_{AB} = \max_\alpha\{t^\alpha_{AB}\}$ (lines 14 and 15).

The last step is to apply path consistency to the STP obtained ignoring preferences and uncertainty (line 16). This reduces the intervals by leaving out the elements that are not in any solution of the STP. Running path consistency in line 16 does not squeeze any contingent interval since it is possible to show that no element of a contingent interval loses its support, because of the reductions in line 14.

6.2 Executing an ODC STPPU

We now reconsider the execution algorithm, EXECUTE, presented in [8], in light of preferences. Adapting it, we show that if given as input an STPPU which has passed CHECK-ODC, it produces dynamically an optimal execution strategy. After initial propagation from the start timepoint, EXECUTE performs iteratively the following steps until the execution is completed. First, it immediately executes any executable timepoints that have reached their upper bounds. Then it arbitrarily picks and executes any executable timepoint x such that (1) the current time is within its bounds; (2) all the timepoints, y, that must be executed before x have been executed; and (3) all waits on x have been satisfied. The effect of the execution is propagated. The current time is advanced, propagating the effect of any contingent timepoints that occur. For an STPPU, the only difference is that the propagation now involves also preferences. Propagating the effect of an execution implies chopping the problem at the minimum preference level obtained by that execution on any constraint up to the current time. We denote EXECUTE equipped with this new type of propagation as EXECUTE-ODC.

Assuming that an STPPU P has passed CHECK-ODC, then the corresponding STPU obtained ignoring preferences, $Q = IP(P)$, is DC. Let P' be the STPPU returned by running CHECK-ODC on P, and Q' be the STPU returned by procedure CHECK-DC on Q. Observe that the contingent intervals in $IP(P')$ and Q' are exactly the same (in fact they are those of P and Q respectively); both algorithms CHECK-ODC and CHECK-DC leave contingent intervals unchanged, as required by the definitions of ODC and DC. Further, given a requirement constraint AB and and a contingent timepoint C, if $\langle C, t \rangle$ is the wait in P' and $\langle C, t' \rangle$ is the wait in Q', then $t \geq t'$ (intuitively: the wait necessary to be optimal may be longer than the one necessary to be only consistent). These relationships allow us to inherit directly from [8] that running EXECUTE-ODC on STPPU P' cannot fail due to any of the following events: a deadlock caused by a wait that never expires, an un-respected wait, or a squeezed contingent interval.

At this point we know that a dynamic schedule is completed by the execution algorithm, so it only remains to prove that it is optimal.

Theorem 2. *If STPPU P has successfully passed* CHECK-ODC *then the dynamic schedule produced by* EXECUTE-ODC *is optimal.* □

Since all waits have been respected, it must be $([S(P)]_B - [S(P)]_A) \geq t_{AB}$, for any requirement constraint AB. This means that $([S(P)]_B - [S(P)]_A) \in \bigcap_\alpha [t^\alpha_{AB}, q^\alpha_{AB}]$. But hence $f_{AB}([S(P)]_B - [S(P)]_A) \geq \alpha = opt_P$ since P has passed CHECK-ODC.

We now consider the complexity of CHECK-ODC. Assuming there is a maximum number of points R in an interval, in [8] it is shown that checking DC of an STPU can be done in time $O(n^2 R)$. If there are a finite number ℓ of different preference levels, we can state the following result for CHECK-ODC, since the complexity of applying CHOP-SOLVER in line 5 of algorithm, $O(n^3 \ell R)$, dominates that of all other steps.

Theorem 3. *The complexity of determining ODC of an STPPU with n variables, ℓ preference levels, and intervals of maximum size R is $O(n^3 \ell R)$.* □

7 Checking α-Dynamic Controllability

Optimal Dynamic Controllability is a strong property. Instead, one may be satisfied by knowing, for a given preference value α, whether the STPPU is α-Dynamically Controllable. As stated earlier, this implies that a control sequence can be incrementally created only on the basis of past assignments. It is guaranteed to be optimal if the 'partial' preference obtained by combining the preferences on contingent constraints is smaller or equal to α. In other words, what is guaranteed is that, up to preference level α, there is always a choice for the executables that will not worsen the overall complexity; for preferences above α this might not be the case.

We can state a theorem analogous to that presented for ODC. The two conditions in Theorem 1 now must hold only for all $\beta \leq \alpha$, rather than for all α. In fact, an STPPU is ODC iff it is opt-DC, where opt is the optimal preference value of STPPU P considered as an STPP. Consequently, the algorithm used to test α-DC is exactly the same as CHECK-ODC, except for line 4, which is no longer necessary (since we do not need to compute value opt), and for line 5, where the **for** loop need only go up to preference level α and not opt. Thus the worst case complexity of checking α-DC is the same as that of checking ODC.

A further query we might ask is: what is the highest level α at which P is α-DC? This query can be answered by modifying CHECK-ODC in order to find the highest preference level at which a dynamic schedule exists. We will call this algorithm MAX-α-DC. The only change needed is in line 12. Assuming the intersection proceeds bottom-up from the lowest preference α_{min}, if a preference level β is found such that the intersection becomes empty, the algorithm does not stop; instead it saves β and continues until it has considered all the requirement constraints. It then returns the minimum of all such β preferences found, β_{min}. It is easy to see that β_{min} is the highest preference α_{max} level for which there exists a dynamic schedule. Again the complexity of this algorithm is the same as that of checking ODC and hence is polynomial.

Consider now our Example 1 and the results in Table 1. It is easy to see that the STPPU shown is, for example 0.7-DC and 0.8-DC. The highest preference α such that it is α-DC is 0.9. In fact, if we choose to assign to SA either 4 or 5 units of time (i.e. any element in the intersection of intervals $[t^\alpha_{SC,SA}, q^\alpha_{SC,SA}]$ for α from 0.5 to 0.9), the preference of the complete solution is at least greater or equal to that of the corresponding projection, for those projections that have optimal preference ≤ 0.9. We obtain the set of solutions represented in Table 2, according to the value assigned by Nature to EC.

Table 2. Solutions of the STPPU in Fig. 1. First four rows: assignments to the variables. Fifth row: global preference of the solution. Last row: optimal preference level of the STPP that is the projection of the corresponding situation.

SC	0	0	0	0	0	0	0	0
EC	1	2	3	4	5	6	7	8
SA	4	4	4	4	4	4	4	4
EA	7	7	7	7	7	7	7	7
pref	0.9	0.9	0.9	0.9	0.8	0.7	0.6	0.5
opt	1	1	0.9	0.9	0.8	0.7	0.6	0.5

$$\text{OSC} \longleftrightarrow \text{opt-SC} \to \alpha\text{-SC} \to \alpha_{min}\text{-SC} \to 0\text{-SC} \to \text{SC}$$
$$\downarrow \qquad \downarrow \qquad \downarrow \qquad \downarrow \qquad \downarrow \qquad \downarrow$$
$$\text{ODC} \longleftrightarrow \text{opt-DC} \to \alpha\text{-DC} \to \alpha_{min}\text{-DC} \to 0\text{-DC} \to \text{DC} \to \text{WC} \longleftrightarrow \text{OWC}$$

Fig. 3. Comparison of controllability notions. α_{min} is the smallest preference over any constraint; $opt \geq \alpha \geq \alpha_{min}$.

8 Comparing and Using Controllability

In all, we have introduced five new notions of controllability. In Fig. 3 we show the relations between them. The proofs of such relations, while omitted for lack of space, are rather immediate.

As a general strategy given an STPPU, the first property to check is OSC. This can be done in polynomial time. If the problem is OSC, the solution obtained is valid and optimal in all possible situations. However, OSC is a strong property and holds infrequently. If the problem is not OSC, the highest preference level α for which α-SC holds can be found in polynomial time by using the algorithm described in Sect. 4. If such preference level is not satisfactory (for it can be very low), then we can turn to checking ODC or β-DC for $\beta > \alpha$. Both these things can be done in polynomial time.

If the problem is not even Dynamically Controllable, but the situation can be known (just) before execution, then the last possibility is to check WC, which is equivalent to OWC. This will at least allow the agent to know in advance if there is a way to cope with every situation. However, checking WC is not necessarily in **P** [12].

9 Related Work

Temporal reasoning is a diverse area, dividing roughly into qualitative and quantitative approaches. For the Temporal Constraint Problem (TCP), a survey is [10], which also discusses some of the hybrid qualitative/quantitative approaches. The Simple Temporal Problem under Uncertainty, which the STPPU builds on, introduces uncertainty due to contingent events. Besides STPUs, uncertainty has been introduced into the TCP with possibilistic reasoning; [14] is one framework for *Fuzzy Temporal Constraint Problems*. In principle, vagueness due to soft preferences can also be accommodated with fuzzy constraints. Closer to STPPUs, contingent events can be ascribed an explicit probability distribution (rather than the implicit uniform distribution of a STPU), to yield *Probabilistic STPs* [11]; preferences are not part of this framework. Note, in contrast to STPPUs, the complexity of solving both Fuzzy TCP and Probabilistic STPs is not polynomial in general. Probabilistic temporal reasoning is found outside the TCP, for instance in temporal synthesis [6], where the amount of memory required for a dynamic solving strategy is also considered. Separately, for the general CSP, [3] introduced the distinction between controllable and uncontrollable variables, to yield *mixed CSP*. Many authors have introduced preferences, to yield soft CSP frameworks: for instance the unifying semiring-based soft CSPs [1] which the STPPU builds on.

10 Summary

Temporal constraint problems in the real world feature both preferences and uncertainty. In this paper we have introduced the Simple Temporal Problem with Preferences and Uncertainty and defined five levels of controllability. We have provided algorithms to determine whether the different levels hold, and shown that the complexity of checking controllability in a STPPU is the same as that for the equivalent notion in a STPU. In particular, the key notion of Dynamic Controllability can be tractably extended to account for preferences.

We have implemented and tested the algorithms for OSC and ODC on randomly generated problems. The experimental results show that, as expected, the time needed to check OSC and ODC grows with the size of the problem. ODC is slower than OSC on Strongly Controllable problems. However, in both cases controllability checking can be performed in reasonable time (less than 3 minutes for 500 variables). Future work is to apply the algorithms to the Earth Observing Satellites and other real-world problem domains. We are also investigating the use of probabilities over contingent constraints and their combination with preferences and uncertainty.

Acknowledgements

We thank Robert Morris and Carmen Gervet for conversations on STPPUs, the participants of the Online'03 workshop for their discussions, and the reviewers for their constructive comments. This work is partially supported by ASI (Italian Space Agency) under project ARISCOM (Contract I/R/215/02), and by the EPSRC under grant GR/N64373/01.

References

1. S. Bistarelli, U. Montanari, and F. Rossi. Semiring-based constraint solving and optimization. *Journal of the ACM*, 44(2):201–236, 1997.
2. R. Dechter, I. Meiri, and J. Pearl. Temporal constraint networks. *Artificial Intelligence*, 49:61–95, 1991.
3. H. Fargier, J. Lang, and T. Schiex. Mixed constraint satisfaction: A framework for decision problems under incomplete knowledge. In *AAAI-96*, pages 175–180, 1996.

4. J. Frank, A. Jonsson, R. Morris, and D. Smith. Planning and scheduling for fleets of earth observing satelliets. In *Proc. of 6th i-SAIRAS*, 2001.
5. L. Khatib, P. Morris, R. A. Morris, and F. Rossi. Temporal constraint reasoning with preferences. In *IJCAI'01*, pages 322–327, 2001.
6. O. Kupferman, P. Madhusudan, P. S. Thiagarajan, and M. Y. Vardi. Open systems in reactive environments: Control and synthesis. *LNCS 1877*, 2000.
7. N. Layaida, L. Sabry-Ismail, and C. Roisin. Dealing with uncertain durations in synchronized multimedia presentations. *Multimedia Tools and Applications*, 18(3):213–231, 2002.
8. P. Morris, N. Muscettola, and T. Vidal. Dynamic control of plans with temporal uncertainty. In *IJCAI'01*, pages 494–502, 2001.
9. F. Rossi, A. Sperduti, K. Venable, L. Khatib, P. Morris, and R. Morris. Learning and solving soft temporal constraints: An experimental study. In *CP'02*, pages 249–263, 2002.
10. E. Schwalb and L. Vila. Temporal constraints: A survey. *Constraints*, 3(2/3):129–149, 1998.
11. I. Tsamardinos. A probabilistic approach to robust execution of temporal plans with uncertainty. In *Second Hellenic Conference on AI (SETN'02)*, pages 97–108, 2002.
12. T. Vidal and H. Fargier. Handling contingency in temporal constraint networks. *J. Experimental and Theoretical Artificial Intelligence*, 11(1):23–45, 1999.
13. T. Vidal and M. Ghallab. Dealing with uncertain durations in temporal constraint networks dedicated to planning. In *ECAI-96*, pages 48–52, 1996.
14. L. Vila and L. Godo. On fuzzy temporal constraint networks. *Mathware and Soft Computing*, 1(3):315–334, 1994.
15. N. Yorke-Smith, K. B. Venable, and F. Rossi. Temporal reasoning with preferences and uncertainty. In *Poster paper in IJCAI-03*, pages 1385–1386, 2003.

Hybrid Set Domains to Strengthen Constraint Propagation and Reduce Symmetries

Andrew Sadler and Carmen Gervet

IC–Parc, Imperial College London, SW7 2AZ, UK
{ajs2,cg6}@icparc.ic.ac.uk

Abstract. In CP literature combinatorial design problems such as sport scheduling, Steiner systems, error-correcting codes and more, are typically solved using Finite Domain (FD) models despite often being more naturally expressed as Finite Set (FS) models. Existing FS solvers have difficulty with such problems as they do not make strong use of the ubiquitous set cardinality information. We investigate a new approach to strengthen the propagation of FS constraints in a tractable way: extending the domain representation to more closely approximate the true domain of a set variable. We show how this approach allows us to reach a stronger level of consistency, compared to standard FS solvers, for arbitrary constraints as well as providing a mechanism for implementing certain symmetry breaking constraints. By experiments on Steiner Systems and error correcting codes, we demonstrate that our approach is not only an improvement over standard FS solvers but also an improvement on recently published results using FD 0/1 matrix models as well.

1 Introduction

Combinatorial designs have applications in areas as diverse as error-correcting codes, sport scheduling, Steiner systems and more recently networking and cryptography (e.g. see [1] for a survey). While a combinatorial design problem is defined in terms of discrete points, or sets, in the CLP framework it is modeled as a constraint satisfaction problem (CSP) with variables representing the points or sets and having a domain of values. Conceptually these domains are sets of possible instantiations but in practice it is often a requirement that the domains be approximated for efficiency reasons. A common approach to approximating variable domains is to use upper and lower bounds (where "upper" and "lower" are defined by some appropriate ordering on domain elements) which are known to enclose the actual domain. Finite Set (FS) domains are ordered by inclusion (the subset ($\subseteq$) order) and have bounds which are ground sets e.g. $X \in [\{1\}, \{1,2,3\}]$. The lower bound, denoted $glb(X)$, contains the definite elements of the set $\{1\}$ while the upper bound $lub(X)$, contains in addition the potential elements $\{2,3\}$. The constraint reasoning is based on local bound consistency techniques extended to handle set constraints [2] and solvers of this sort have been embedded in a growing number of CP languages (e.g. ECL^{i}PS^e, ILOG, CHOCO, Facile, BProlog). The bounds representation is compact and benefits from interval reasoning techniques which allow us to remove at a minimal cost set values that can never be part of any solution. However it does not guarantee in general, that all the values from a domain are locally consistent (true for the set cardinality constraint) and it does not provide any form of global reasoning.

Because of these weaknesses, many of the recent proposals to tackle combinatorial design problems efficiently assume a FD model where the domain elements are naturally ordered ($\leq$) and the bounds are the min/max value. Extensive research towards improving the efficiency of FD consistency algorithms (e.g. global constraints [3,4]) and search (e.g. symmetry breaking approaches) [5,6] has made this a powerful and general scheme. However many combinatorial design problems are more naturally expressed in FS models, we investigated ways to achieve better efficiency for such models.

In this paper we discuss briefly our work on global filtering for n-ary set constraints over fixed cardinality sets and present in much more detail a new domain representation for set variables. Experimental results are shown on Steiner systems and error-correcting code problems.

The paper is structured as follows. In Sect. 2, we give background on consistency notions for finite set constraint systems. Section 3 addresses the problem of global set constraints. Section 4 introduces the new set interval representation. Section 5 defines the hybrid domain and in Sect. 6 we experimentally evaluate our approach.

2 Background

The solving of a CSP is handled by interleaving constraint propagation (domain reduction) and search. The constraint propagation can be formally defined by the level of consistency enforced for each constraint or system of constraints. We recall the different consistency notions used in this paper.

Given a finite domain representation, we say that a constraint is Generalized Arc Consistent (GAC) iff any value assigned to a variable from its domain can be extended to a complete assignment to the constraint [7]. GAC generalizes arc consistency (AC) defined for binary constraints.

Maintaining GAC can be costly however and so when dealing with domains which are approximated by bounds it is often easier/more efficient to only ensure that the bounds of the domain, when assigned to the variable, can be extended to a complete assignment. This notion of "bounds consistency" is used in many FD solvers where bounds are the min/max domain elements mentioned above.

When dealing with FS domains represented as bounds ordered by the $\subseteq$ relation, the bounds (glb/lub) cannot, in general, be extended to a complete assignment in the problems that we consider because of the presence of cardinality restrictions. e.g. $X \subseteq \{1,2,3,4\}, |X| = 2$, not all subsets of $\{1,2,3,4\}$ have 2 elements. [2] introduces a local consistency notion for various binary and ternary set relations that ensures the ordering and depending on the constraint relation a certain level of consistency is reached (e.g. AC for the set inclusion). [8] extends the consistency notions of [2] to multi-sets (sets where an element may occur more than once) and combines them with the standard bounds consistency notions for FD into a level of consistency called BC which can be applied to constraints involving all the three types of variables. For FD variables the definition is exactly that of standard FD "bounds consistency" and for (multi-)set variables the "bounds" which are required to be "consistent" (i.e. extendable to complete assignment) are *not* the glb/lub but correspond to the bounds on the number of times any given element may occur within a set. For simple sets these bounds are always 0..1.

3 Global Set Constraints

To strengthen set constraint propagation in the presence of set cardinality information we first investigated global set constraints, seeking tractable and effective global filtering algorithms for n-ary set constraint over fixed cardinality sets. For practical modelling reasons FS solvers provide a number of n-ary constraints like `all_disjoint`, `all_union` which are syntactic abstractions for a collection of respectively binary and ternary constraints ($X_1 \cap X_2 = \emptyset$, $X_1 \cup X_2 = X_{12}$). The constraint reasoning is based on local bounds consistency.

[8] shows that BC on n-ary `all_disjoint` is equivalent to BC on the decomposition. This holds because any set can be assigned the empty set. However, when the set cardinalities are constrained (and not zero), which is ubiquitous in combinatorial design problems, the equivalence no longer holds.

Using some standard results from design theory we derived four global conditions which must hold for disjoint sets of fixed cardinality. Using an extension of Hall's theorem[9] we proved that these conditions, if satisfied, were sufficient to ensure BC, and were able to convert the proof procedure into an efficient polynomial time algorithm[1] to enforce said consistency level. Interestingly this implementation corresponds closely to the GAC algorithm for the Global Cardinality Constraint of Régin[10]. Owing to space restrictions we refer the reader to [11] for details.

Other Global Constraints. Despite the existence of a polynomial filtering algorithm for the global disjoint constraint, we believe it unlikely that such BC algorithm exist for the more general case of global cardinality-intersection constraints, like the `atmost1` constraint of [12]. Despite large amount of work being done on the problem, to date, it is not known whether some relatively small instance of Steiner systems (which the `atmost1` constraint models) exist or not, e.g. $S(4,5,17)$ and $S(5,6,17)$[2]. These open instances lend weight to our belief.

Another approach is thus necessary to make active use of the cardinality information for arbitrary set constraints in an efficient and effective manner.

---

[1] $O(ncv\sqrt{nc})$ where n=num vars, c=cardinality and v=size of largest lub.
[2] See Sect. 6 for explanation of notation.

4 Lexicographic Bounds – The FD Analogy

The motivation that lead us to consider lexicographic bounds to represent set variables is two fold: 1) to keep a compact representation for set variables, 2) to build upon the analogy with bounds reasoning for integer variables and its efficient and effective constraint propagation, e.g. [13].

If we think of a FD variable as a FS variable constrained to have exactly 1 element, then the domain of the FD variable corresponds directly to the lub of the FS variable. The min/max bounds of the FD domain are the smallest/largest elements in the lub. Extending the idea of min/max bounds to FS variables with arbitrary (and non fixed) cardinalities will require a suitable total order on the FS domain elements (as $\leq$ totally orders the FD domain elements).

We propose a new bounds representation for set domains based on an ordering different from the set inclusion (subset order). The ordering is lexicographic and we define *lexicographic bounds* denoted $\langle \inf, \sup \rangle$. This ordering relation defines a *total* order on sets of natural numbers, in contrast to the *partial* order $\subseteq$. We use the symbols $\prec$ (and $\preceq$) to denote a total strict (respectively non-strict) lexicographic order.

Definition 1. *Let $\preceq$ be a total order on sets of integers defined as follows*

$$X \preceq Y \text{ iff } X = \emptyset \vee x < y \vee (x = y \wedge X \setminus \{x\} \preceq Y \setminus \{y\})$$
$$\text{where } x = max(X) \text{ and } y = max(Y) \quad (1)$$

Example 1. Consider the sets $\{1,2,3\}, \{1,3,4\}, \{1,2\}, \{3\}$, the list that orders these sets w.r.t. $\preceq$ is $[\{1,2\}, \{3\}, \{1,2,3\}, \{1,3,4\}]$.

This lexicographic ordering for sets is not the only possible definition, nor is it, perhaps, the most common when talking about sets. We use this definition for two reasons: 1) for sets of cardinality 1 it is equivalent to the $\leq$ ordering of FD variables and 2) usefully, it extends the $\subseteq$ ordering and we have:

Theorem 1. $\forall X, Y \in \mathcal{P}(\mathbb{N}) : X \subseteq Y \Rightarrow X \preceq Y$

Proof. If $X \subseteq Y$ then either $X = \emptyset$ in which case $X \preceq Y$ for all Y, or $\emptyset \subset X \subseteq Y$ in which case consider the max elements of X and Y (namely $x = max(X)$ and $y = max(Y)$ resp.). Since $X \subseteq Y$ we have that $x \leq y$ because X contains no elements greater than those in Y, so if $x < y$ then clearly by definition $X \leq Y$ and we are done. If $x = y$ then we consider the next largest elements in each set and our arguments hold recursively (since sets are finite). □

Theorem 1 will be used in the hybrid domain to make inferences between the two bounds representations for set variables (we also use this equivalent implication with the direction reversed $\forall X, Y \in \mathcal{P}(\mathbb{N}) : X \nsubseteq Y \Leftarrow X \not\preceq Y$).

This ordering defined on ground sets of integers is not new; it is simply the standard arithmetic ordering ($\leq$) on the natural numbers written in binary, where the binary number corresponds to the 0/1 characteristic vector representation of the ground set. More explicitly, for any two ground sets of integers

X and Y, and their corresponding characteristic binary numbers $\boldsymbol{X}$ and $\boldsymbol{Y}$, we have the following equivalence

$$X \preceq Y \text{ iff } \boldsymbol{X} \leq \boldsymbol{Y} \qquad (2)$$

Example 2. Consider $X = \{4, 2\}$ and $Y = \{4, 3, 2\}$, equiv $\boldsymbol{X} = [0, 1, 0, 1, 0]$ and $\boldsymbol{Y} = [0, 1, 1, 1, 0]$.

Clearly we have $X \preceq Y$ and $\boldsymbol{X} \leq \boldsymbol{Y}$.

A common use of this ordering is in search problems to break symmetries (e.g. [14] on SAT clauses or [5, 6] on vectors of FD variables). It is important to understand that this is *not* the use to which we put the ordering here. We use this order on *ground* sets as a means to approximate the domain of a Finite Set variable by upper and lower bounds w.r.t. this order. We will show in a later section how we can implement a constraint to enforce the order between FS vars.

Figure 1 shows the relationship between the partial inclusion order and our total lexicographic order.

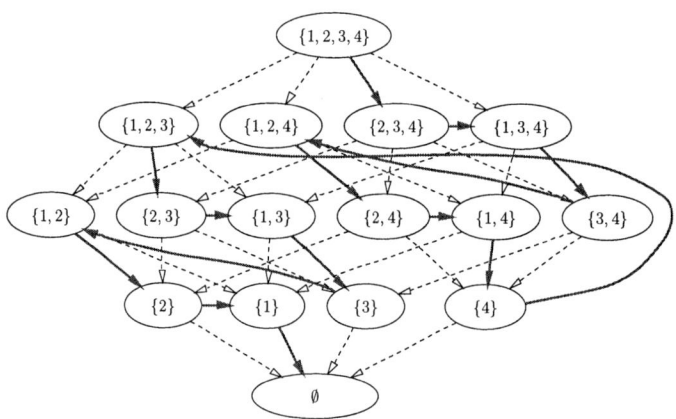

Fig. 1. A graph showing the $\preceq$ order (solid) superimposed onto the standard $\subset$ lattice (dashed).

Intuitively, the relationship between the two ordering relations is best viewed by moving downwards from the top of the lattice. Each horizontal line represents sets incomparable with $\subset$ relation. On the other hand, one can follow the directed arc in bold starting from $\{1, 2, 3, 4\}$ to create the totally ordered list of sets under $\preceq$ from the greatest to the smallest:$[\{4, 3, 2, 1\}, \{4, 3, 2\}, \{4, 3, 1\}, \{4, 3\}, \{4, 2, 1\}, \{4, 2\}, \{4, 1\}, \{4\}, \{3, 2, 1\}, \{3, 2\}, \{3, 1\}, \{3\}, \{2, 1\}, \{2\}, \{1\}, \emptyset]$.

Note that the sets above have been written with their elements in arithmetic *de*creasing order and observe that all sets "beginning" with a common sequence (e.g. all sets beginning with $\{4, 3\}$) are to be found together. Similarly all beginning with $\{3\}$ are together, though not all the sets *containing* $\{3\}$. It is this *grouping* property of the lex order, combined with its extension of the $\subseteq$ order (Theorem 1) that will form the basis of the hybrid inference rules in the next section.

The following table summarizes, the different domain approximations at hand. We use $[glb, lub]$ to denote the set of all sets which contain glb and are contained in lub. We use $\langle inf, sup \rangle$ to represent the set of all sets which come after inf and before sup in the $\preceq$ order.

type	domain	order	minimal	maximal
FD	$\mathbb{N}$	$\leq$ (total)	min	max
FS	$\mathcal{P}(\mathbb{N})$	$\subseteq$ (partial)	glb	lub
FS (lex)	$\mathcal{P}(\mathbb{N})$	$\preceq$ (total)	inf	sup

Given that the lexicographic order embeds the partial inclusion order (Theorem 1), one could wonder whether it can replace it altogether.

Pros. The lex bound domain overcomes one major weakness of the subset bound domain, in that it allows us to make more active use of the cardinality constraint. Since the lex bounds are valid instantiations of the set variable, then any condition which must hold for the set variable (e.g. constraints on the set variable, like the cardinality constraint) can be enforced on the lex bounds.

Example 3. A set X is known to take two or three elements from $\{5, 4, 3, 2, 1\}$. The subset bounds representation can not yield tighter bounds when considering the cardinality constraint, i.e. $X \in [\emptyset, \{5, 4, 3, 2, 1\}]$. However, with the lex bound representation, we can prune the bounds. Let the initial bounds describe the same initial domain $X \in \langle \emptyset, \{5, 4, 3, 2, 1\} \rangle$ ($2^5 = 32$ unique sets). When propagating the cardinality constraints, we are able to tighten the domain to $\langle \{2, 1\}, \{5, 4, 3\} \rangle$, (26 unique sets). If now cardinality is bound to be exactly 2 then we have bounds $\langle \{2, 1\}, \{5, 4\} \rangle$ which corresponds to only $\binom{5}{2} = 10$ sets.

Cons. Despite its success allowing cardinality constraint to filter the domain more actively, the lex bound representation is unable to always represent certain critical constraints. Primary amongst these constraints is the inclusion or exclusion of a single element. Such constraints are not always representable in the domain because the lex bounds represent possible set *instances* and not *definite* and *potential* elements of a set.

Example 4. Consider the bound constraint $X \in \langle \emptyset, \{4, 3, 2, 1\} \rangle$. The constraint $1 \in X$ yields new bounds of $X \in \langle \{1\}, \{4, 3, 2, 1\} \rangle$, unfortunately not all sets which lie in this range contain the element 1 (eg. $\{3, 2\}$). Note however that the constraint $4 \in X$ allows us to prune the bounds to $X \in \langle \{4\}, \{4, 3, 2, 1\} \rangle$ where all the sets in the range *do* contain 4 (see Fig. 1 for a visual proof).

It is the inability to capture such fundamental constraints efficiently in the domain which lead us to consider a hybrid domain of both subset and lexicographic bounds.

5 Hybrid Domain

In this section we extend the subset domain representation with extra bounds representing the lexicographically smallest and largest instantiations of the set, as well as bounds for the cardinality. We give extra rules to be used in addition to those given for subset domains in [15]. Taken together these rules are necessary and sufficient to maintain consistent hybrid domains w.r.t. the constraint store[3].

We represent the bounds which constitute the domain of a variable as $X \in [a_X, b_X] | c_X, d_X | \langle e_X, f_X \rangle$, where: a_X, b_X are lower,upper bound w.r.t. $\subseteq$, c_X, d_X are lower,upper bound w.r.t. $|X|$ (cardinality), e_X, f_X are lower,upper bound w.r.t. $\preceq$. We will in fact for the sake of brevity, overload the $\in$ symbol further and use $X \in [a_X, b_X] | c_X, d_X |$ to indicate that the variable X lies within the lattice $[a_X, b_X]$ and has cardinality in the range $c_X..d_X$.

We use the above naming convention, where the letters a, b, c, d, e, f are suffixed by the set variable names (which will be one of X, Y, Z). When we refer to numeric elements of the domain we use the lowercase letter x, when we refer to set values from the domain we use the lowercase letter s. We adopt the operational semantics style of [16] and present our inferences as rewrite rules operating on a constraint store. The rewrite rules have the form

$$\frac{\text{inference}}{\{\text{Old store}\} \longmapsto \{\text{New store}\}}$$

however to save space we may omit the domain constraints from the stores (e.g. $X \in [a_X, b_X] | c_X, d_X | \langle e_X, f_X \rangle$) and adopt the notation that any "primed" bound (e.g. a'_X) appearing in the inference indicates the new value of that bound in the new store. Furthermore when the old and new stores contain the same constraints we will give only the inference, with the common store being shown in the section heading. Finally, the special constraint $tell(\ldots)$ is used to indicate the addition of a new constraint, allowing special actions to be performed when constraints are setup.

5.1 Intra-domain Consistency – $\{X \in [a_X, b_X] | c_X, d_X | \langle e_X, f_X \rangle\}$

There follows a number of inference rules designed to keep the various bounds of our hybrid domain mutually consistent. There will be one rule associated with each of the six bounds, followed by one rule indicating failure[4].

IR 1. $a'_X = a_X \cup \{x | x \in e_X \cap f_X \wedge \forall_{x' \in (e_X \cup f_X) \setminus (e_X \cap f_X)} \ x' < x\}$

IR 1 states, in essence, that any elements which form a common "beginning" to both lex bounds (see Sect. 4), should be part of the glb.

IR 2. $b'_X = b_X \setminus \{x | \{x\} \cup a_X \succ f_X \vee (d_X - |a_X| = 1 \wedge \{x\} \cup a_X \prec e_X)\}$

---
[3] Note that the way the new bounds are actually computed is not presented here. This depends on ones choice of data structures and generic fixed point algorithm.
[4] Instantiation when $e_X = f_X$ is guaranteed by IR 1, IR 2 and the rules of [15].

IR 2 tells us when elements can never be part of the set because their inclusion would violate the lex bounds. There are two such cases, indicated by the disjunction in the definition of the set of elements to exclude.

- Firstly, no element can be included, which if added to the glb would cause it to be greater than ($\succ$) the lex upper bound f_X. This follows from Theorem 1.
- The second case arises when there is at most one more element which *could* be added to the set (i.e. when $d_X - |a_X| = 1$), in such a situation any potential element if added to the glb must not cause it to be less than ($\prec$) the lex lower bound e_X.

IR 3. $c'_X = \begin{cases} max(|a_X|, c_X) & \text{if } a_X = e_X \\ max(|a_X| + 1, c_X) & \text{otherwise} \end{cases}$

When e_X and a_X coincide (are equal), then the cardinality is at least the number of elements in a_X. When they do not, then we know that X must contain a_X, but cannot be exactly a_X (since $a_X \prec e_X$), hence the cardinality is at least the number of elements in $a_X + 1$.

IR 4. $d'_X = \begin{cases} min(|b_X|, d_X) & \text{if } b_X = f_X \\ min(|b_X| - 1, d_X) & \text{otherwise} \end{cases}$

A similar argument holds for IR 4 as holds for IR 3.

IR 5. $e'_X = \inf\left(\{s | s \in [a_X, b_X] | c_X, d_X| \wedge s \succeq e_X\}\right)$

IR 6. $f'_X = \sup\left(\{s | s \in [a_X, b_X] | c_X, d_X| \wedge s \preceq f_X\}\right)$

Together, IR 5 and IR 6 ensure that the lex bounds of the domain can only undergo monotonic reduction.

IR 7. $\dfrac{e_X \succ f_X \vee e_X = \inf(\emptyset) \vee f_X = \inf(\emptyset)}{\{X \in [a_X, b_X] | c_X, d_X | \langle e_X, f_X \rangle\} \longmapsto \{\texttt{fail}\}}$

If the domain becomes empty, or no values exist for the new lex bounds then clearly we should fail.

5.2 Constraints

Inclusion – $\{X \subseteq Y\}$. Strict inclusion ($\subset$) requires strict total orders ($\prec$ and $<$).

IR 8. $\dfrac{}{\{tell(X \subseteq Y)\} \longmapsto \{X \subseteq Y, X \preceq Y, c_X \leq c_Y, d_X \leq d_Y\}}$

Intersection – $\{Z = X \cap Y\}$. Similar rules exist for the variable Y.

IR 9. $\dfrac{}{\{tell(Z = X \cap Y)\} \longmapsto \{Z = X \cap Y, tell(Z \subseteq X), tell(Z \subseteq Y)\}}$

IR 10. $e'_X = \inf(\{s | s \in [a_X, b_X] | c_X, d_X| \wedge |s \cap a_Y| \leq d_Z \wedge |s \cap b_Y| \geq c_Z\})$

IR 11. $f'_X = \sup(\{s | s \in [a_X, b_X] | c_X, d_X| \wedge |s \cap a_Y| \leq d_Z \wedge |s \cap b_Y| \geq c_Z\})$

Union – $\{Z = X \cup Y\}$. Similar rules exist for the variable Y.

IR 12. $$\overline{\{\,tell(Z = X \cup Y)\,\} \longmapsto \{\,Z = X \cup Y, tell(X \subseteq Z), tell(Y \subseteq Z)\,\}}$$

IR 13. $e'_X = \inf(\{s | s \in [a_X, b_X] | c_X, d_X | \wedge |s \cup a_Y| \leq d_Z \wedge |s \cup b_Y| \geq c_Z\})$

IR 14. $f'_X = \sup(\{s | s \in [a_X, b_X] | c_X, d_X | \wedge |s \cup a_Y| \leq d_Z \wedge |s \cup b_Y| \geq c_Z\})$

Difference – $\{Z = X \setminus Y\}$.

IR 15. $$\overline{\{\,tell(Z = X \setminus Y)\,\} \longmapsto \{\,Z = X \setminus Y, tell(Z \subseteq X)\,\}}$$

IR 16. $e'_X = \inf(\{s | s \in [a_X, b_X] | c_X, d_X | \wedge |s \setminus b_Y| \leq d_Z \wedge |s \setminus a_Y| \geq c_Z\})$

IR 17. $f'_X = \sup(\{s | s \in [a_X, b_X] | c_X, d_X | \wedge |s \setminus b_Y| \leq d_Z \wedge |s \setminus a_Y| \geq c_Z\})$

IR 18. $e'_Y = \inf(\{s | s \in [a_Y, b_Y] | c_Y, d_Y | \wedge |a_X \setminus s| \leq d_Z \wedge |b_Y \setminus s| \geq c_Z\})$

IR 19. $f'_Y = \sup(\{s | s \in [a_Y, b_Y] | c_Y, d_Y | \wedge |a_X \setminus s| \leq d_Z \wedge |b_Y \setminus s| \geq c_Z\})$

Ordering Constraint – $\{X \preceq Y\}$.

IR 20. $e'_Y = inf(\{s | s \in [a_Y, b_Y] | c_Y, d_Y | \langle e_Y, f_Y \rangle \wedge s \succeq e_X\})$

IR 21. $f'_X = sup(\{s | s \in [a_X, b_X] | c_X, d_X | \langle e_X, f_X \rangle \wedge s \preceq f_Y\})$

6 Experiments and Comparisons

We implemented our lex bound inferences atop the `ic_sets` library in ECL^{i}PS^e[17], using a list of integers in decreasing order to represent each lex bound. This allows all required new bounds to be calculated in $O(|b_X|)$ time which we believe is close to optimal given the nature of our lex ordering and the presence of cardinality bounds[5]. To illustrate the benefits of our hybrid domain over the conventional subset domain for reasoning about set problems in the presence of cardinality information, we look at error correcting codes and the commonly referenced problem of finding Steiner systems. A 2GHz Pentium 4 with 1GB of RAM was used for all experiments.

Unless otherwise stated the search procedure used in the following problems is the following: Each set variable is fully instantiated before moving to the next, in a fixed order. Each set is instantiated by first trying to include, then on backtracking, exclude the largest unassigned element from its domain.

Definition 2 (Binary error correcting codes). *A binary error correcting code is a collection of bit-strings (vectors of 0s and 1s of length (n)), called codewords, with the property that the distance between any two codewords is at least some number (d). The distance between two codewords is defined to be the number of positions in which the two bit-strings vary. This distance function is called the* Hamming *distance.*

---

[5] Note that subset bounds alone can be updated in $O(1)$ time, e.g. in `ic_sets`.

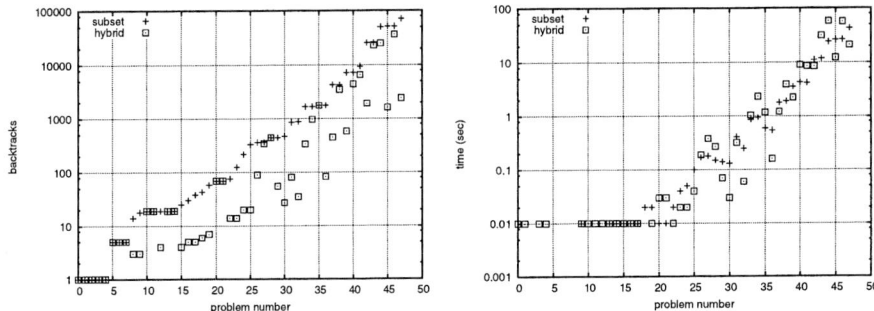

Fig. 2. Backtracks and runtimes for solved fixed weight binary error correcting codes.

A variant of this problem is to find codes which have a fixed weight (w), where the weight of a code is defined as the number of 1s that each codeword contains. Each codeword must contain the same number of 1s.

We can model this problem using set variables (S_i) to represent the codewords (C_i), with the correspondence that the codeword represents the characteristic function of the set (i.e. the element x is in the set S_i iff the code C_i has a 1 at position x). Using the set model, the distance between two codewords can be defined as the cardinality of the symmetric difference of the two sets. From the basic set constraints presented in this paper (and present in most set solvers), we can define the symmetric difference in a number of ways, but in keeping with [18] we define the distance between two sets as

$$distance(S_i, S_j) = n - |S_i \cap S_j| - |\{1 \ldots n\} \setminus (S_i \cup S_j)|$$

As an optimization problem then, the task is to find (and prove) the maximum size (number of codewords = $a(n, d, w)$) for a binary error correcting code with given parameters (n, d) and optionally fixed weight (w).

We solve the optimization problem by simply trying to find increasingly larger codes, and proving optimality by failing to find one larger. We increase the code size by one codeword each iteration.

Figure 2 shows the backtracks and runtimes required to find and prove the optimal code size for non-trivial (i.e. non-zero size) instances of the constant weight error correcting codes optimization problem with parameters $n \in \{6, 7, 8, 9, 10\}$, $d \in \{4, 6, 8, 10, 12\}$ and $w \in \{3, 4, 5, 6, 7, 8\}$. The graphs show those 48 problems which were proved to optimality in under 240 seconds by both subset and hybrid solvers. The results were ordered by the number of backtracks required using the subset domain, thus the problems exhibit a general trend of greater difficulty as the problem number increases.

We observe that the backtracks for our hybrid domain, though occasionally the same as the subset domain in the easier problems, are in general significantly lower[6]. Whilst the runtimes can be seen to be comparable overall, they show

---

[6] Note the logarithmic scale used on both graphs.

fluctuations whereby in some instances our approach is slower, and in others it is faster. The former occurs when the reduction in backtracks is insufficient to outweigh the overheads associated with maintaining the stronger consistency, and is entirely expected. The point is well illustrated by the final two pairs of data points on each graph. The final two points on the backtrack graph represent a 96.6% reduction in the number of backtracks, whereas the previous two represent a "mere" 29.2% reduction. The corresponding runtime changes are 50.9% faster and 1114.5% slower. Better CPU times can be expected by investigating different data structures for the hybrid domain bounds and an integrated solver for the whole hybrid domain.

Not shown in the graphs are the optimality proofs that only our hybrid domain solver was able to find in the 240 second time limit. $a(9,4,7) = 4$ was found with 21779 backtracks in 201.71 seconds and $a(10,6,7) = 3$ was found with 14619 backtracks in 111.14 seconds.

Definition 3 (Steiner Systems). *A steiner system $S(t, k, v)$ is a set A of v points and a family of subsets of size k of A (called blocks) such that any t points in A appear in exactly one block.*

To demonstrate the benefits of our approach on existing models we adopt the common Steiner system set model of $\binom{v}{t}/\binom{k}{t}$ set variables representing the blocks of the design, constrained such that the pairwise intersection contains *at most* 1 element. We call this the *primal* model.

Another way to model Steiner systems, and design problems in general using set variables is to employ what we call a *dual* model. Instead of modelling the blocks themselves as set variables, we instead number the blocks 1..b and have a set variable corresponding to each point of the base set, which contains the block numbers in which the element occurs. In [12] a global constraint atmost1 is proposed which does strictly more than just constraining the size of the dual-sets. We find however that the full inferences of this constraint are costly to attain and instead, in our experiments, we settle for a simple redundant constraint that constrains the number of times an element may appear in the design to be exactly r. This second model we refer to as the *+dual sum* model as it can be easily implemented by summing vectors of reified inclusion Booleans.

Table 1 clearly shows the benefit that our hybrid domain brings in reducing the size of the search space. In many cases removing backtracks altogether and in others reducing the number by as much as 159 times.

Table 2 shows the computational cost of maintaining this higher level of consistency. In many cases the time taken to find the solution actually increases. This is especially pronounced when the search space is large and solutions are relatively easy to find. Consider the $S(2, 3, 31)$ system which contains 155 blocks, each of which can be instantiated to one of $\binom{31}{3} = 4495$ values, this constitutes quite a large search space out of which 930 backtracks is a relatively small number. With the "+dual sum" model this instance can be solved without backtracks using the simple subset domain representation and so the extra mechanism for reasoning with the hybrid domain can only add overhead.

Table 1. Backtracks to find first soln.

	backtracks			
	primal		+dual sum	
$S(t,k,v)$	subset	hybrid	subset	hybrid
$S(2,3,07)$	6	0	0	0
$S(2,3,09)$	4521	384	2398	15
$S(2,3,15)$	90	0	0	0
$S(2,3,31)$	930	0	0	0
$S(2,4,13)$	19	0	1	0
$S(2,5,21)$	40	0	0	0
$S(3,4,08)$	60	2	8	2
$S(3,4,16)$	4136	132	240	132
$S(3,6,22)$	3048	42	92	42

Table 2. Time to find first soln.

	time (s)			
	primal		+dual sum	
$S(t,k,v)$	subset	hybrid	subset	hybrid
$S(2,3,07)$	0.01	0.01	0.01	0.01
$S(2,3,09)$	2.95	1.63	3.23	0.13
$S(2,3,15)$	0.41	1.01	0.18	1.06
$S(2,3,31)$	31.3	100.9	6.83	99.63
$S(2,4,13)$	0.04	0.14	0.02	0.14
$S(2,5,21)$	0.16	2.97	0.1	2.83
$S(3,4,08)$	0.05	0.07	0.03	0.08
$S(3,4,16)$	41.59	59.7	7.11	54.69
$S(3,6,22)$	15.29	77.48	2.47	54.98

Table 3. Time and backtracks taken to find all 151200 solutions of $S(2,3,7)$.

domain	model	time(s)	backtracks	bt/sol
subset	primal	609	1557048	10.30
hybrid	primal	594	200507	1.33
subset	+dual sum	378	410479	2.71
hybrid	+dual sum	462	195349	1.29

However, when considering *harder* problems such as the $S(2,3,09)$ instance, 12 blocks each with $\binom{9}{3} = 84$ possible values, the 4521 backtracks is a more significant proportion of the search space. The reduction of this number to 384 by the hybrid domain results in a 44.7% reduction in the runtime. With the "+dual sum" model, the reduction of the backtracks by 99.3% results in runtime reduction of 96.0%.

To investigate whether we had simply been "lucky" or "unlucky" to find (resp. not find) solutions quickly we ran experiments to find *all* solutions to the various designs. Due to the large numbers of (symmetric) solutions that exist for steiner systems, we were only able to find all solutions to the $S(2,3,7)$ in a reasonable time. Table 3 shows, for the primal model, that the overheads associated with our hybrid domains is almost exactly balanced by the reduced search space (87.1% fewer backtracks and 2.5% less runtime). For the "+dual sum" model we observe a 52.4% reduction in backtracks which, given the current implementation, does not come with a reduction in runtime. However, the results are promising.

6.1 Symmetry

Much work has been done recently to improve the efficiency of searching for solutions of highly symmetric problems. In this section we compare our work with developments in one particular family of symmetry breaking techniques, the lex-ordered symmetry breaking constraint in matrix models.

In [19] the authors show how existing symmetry breaking techniques like lex[5, 6] can be combined with more conventional constraint like the sum constraint to both increase the amount of pruning and (in some instances) reduce the time taken to solve problems. The authors demonstrate their technique on finding and proving the in-existence of a number of small Steiner systems.

The model they choose is a 2D matrix of 0/1 FD variables where rows correspond to the characteristic function of a block, and columns therefore correspond to the dual sets mentioned earlier. A constraint on the magnitude of the scalar product between any two rows, corresponds to the restriction that two sets may intersect in at most 1 element. They compare the effect of posting lex constraints on both the rows and the columns ($>_{lex} R \geq_{lex} C$), with posting lex on the columns ($\geq_{lex} C$) and a specialized constraint called LexGreaterAndSum on the rows, we will denote this specialized constraint which combines the lex ordering with the sum constraint as ($>_{lex}^{\Sigma} R$) for brevity.

For comparison, our model is the same as that presented in the previous section where set variables correspond to rows, with the addition of dual sets (corresponding to the columns). Simple channelling constraints maintain the correspondence between the sets. The lex constraints are enforced locally between adjacent rows and adjacent columns using the inference rules IR 20 and IR 21. The dual sets are not constrained to have a fixed cardinality since no such constraints existed on the columns in the matrix model. We implement the exact same labelling strategies, row-wise and column-wise, as used in [19] by channelling to a matrix of reified inclusion Booleans.

In tables 4 and 5 we duplicate and extend the results of [19], adding for comparison the final column showing how our model performs. Note that the third column contains the backtrack values from the original paper, with the runtimes being scaled by the same factor as the runtimes for the previous column for which we were able to duplicate backtrack counts. From these results our hybrid domain model not only out performs the plain double-lex constrained matrix model in terms of search space reduction and runtimes, but also outperforms the specialized LexGreaterAndSum constrained model as well; providing, in the hardest of the problems, a 95.0% backtrack reduction compared to the double-lex model and further 48.5% compared to the specialized LexGreaterAndSum model. Runtimes drop by 85.2% and 23.8% respectively as well.

Table 4. Comparison with table 1 of [19]. Row-wise labelling.

Prob $S(t,k,v)$	No sym breaking btracks	$>_{lex} R \geq_{lex} C$ btracks	time(s)	$>_{lex}^{\Sigma} R \geq_{lex} C$ btracks	est time(s)	$\succ R \succeq C$ btracks	time(s)
$S(2,3,6)$	6194	13	0.0	11	0.0	7	0.0
$S(2,3,7)$	6	2	0.0	1	0.0	0	0.0
$S(2,3,8)$	-	>16hr	740	0.7	390	0.7	58	0.3
$S(2,3,9)$	4521	336	0.5	250	0.5	12	0.2
$S(2,3,10)$	-	>16hr	723209	1339.8	433388	1136.4	12346	167.8

Table 5. Comparison with table 3 of [19]. Column-wise labelling.

Prob $S(t,k,v)$	No sym breaking btracks	time(s)	$>_{lex} R \geq_{lex} C$ btracks	time(s)	$>_{lex}^{\Sigma} R \geq_{lex} C$ btracks est	time(s)	$\succ R \succeq C$ btracks	time(s)
$S(2,3,6)$	26351	9.8	46	0.0	27	0.0	22	0.0
$S(2,3,7)$	585469	340.6	151	0.1	52	0.1	42	0.2
$S(2,3,8)$	-	>16hr	6837	5.5	1962	3.1	1314	3.7
$S(2,3,9)$	-	>16hr	90561	98.0	8971	14.0	5232	18.0
$S(2,3,10)$	-	>16hr	37861490	48789.8	3701480	9478.1	1906918	7226.4

Conclusion. The hybrid domain provides a natural data structure for the lex ordering constraints ($\prec$ and $\preceq$) and the set constraints of the problem ($\cap$ and $|\ |$) to interact effectively. By keeping the set based model, but enhancing the domain representation and local inferences, we can reason at least as strongly and efficiently as less intuitive FD matrix models and without the need to identify and invent specialized global constraint propagation algorithms.

7 Related Work

The most closely related work to ours is that of [16], which extended the inference rules of [15] with extra rules operating on set cardinalities. In our framework we are clearly free to implement all the extra inferences of [16] and hence can reach at least the same degree of pruning. We can however make important inferences that cannot be made in [16].

Example 5. $Z = X \cap Y$, $X \in [\emptyset, \{5,4,3,2,1\}] |3,3|$, $Y \in [\emptyset, \{4,3,2,1\}] |3,4|$, $Z \in [\emptyset, \{4,3,2,1\}] |3,3|$. These domains are a fixed point for both traditional set solvers and [16]. However with our lex bounds added (i.e. for X, we have $\langle\{3,2,1\},\{5,4,3\}\rangle$), IR 11 reduces this to $\langle\{3,2,1\},\{4,3,2\}\rangle$ and IR 2 gives us $X \in [\emptyset, \{4,3,2,1\}]$.

8 Conclusion

We have analysed Finite Sets solvers in the light of modern techniques and advances in efficiently modeling and solving combinatorial design problems. We presented a new and novel hybrid domain for FS variables which allows us to strengthen the level of consistency that we reach in a tractable and efficient manner. It is clearly stronger than BC achieved by standard set solvers since we prune more but defining the level of consistency reached for such multi-bounded domains is an open problem.

We showed how our implementation prototype is able to improve not only the state of the art in FS solving for a class of combinatorial design problems, but also improves on recently published results that use FD 0/1 matrix models and specialized global constraints. Though sometimes slower than existing FS techniques, our approach is typically faster at solving problems with cardinality constraints especially when there are no (or few) solutions as well as at proving optimality. Furthermore we believe that the CPU times can be improved further for all cases by considering a fully integrated set solver built specifically for hybrid domains (i.e. not atop an existing solver).

References

1. Colbourn, Dinitz, Stinson: Applications of combinatorial designs to communications, cryptography, and networking. In: Surveys in Combinatorics London Mathematical Society Lecture Note Series 187. Cambridge University Press (1999)
2. Gervet, C.: Interval Propagation to Reason about Sets: Definition and Implementation of a Practical Language. CONSTRAINTS journal **1(3)** (1997) 191–244
3. Beldiceanu, N., Contejean, E.: Introducing Global Constraints in CHIP. In: Mathematical Computation Modelling. Volume 20(12). (1994)
4. Régin, J.C.: A filtering algorithm for constraints of difference in csps. In: Proc. AAAI-94. (1994)
5. Flener, P., Frisch, A., Hnich, B., Kiziltan, Z., Miguel, I., Pearson, J., Walsh, T.: Breaking row and column symmetries in matrix models. In: Proc. CP'02. LNCS, Springer (2002)
6. Gent, I.P., Prosser, P., Smith, B.M.: A 0/1 encoding of the gaclex for pairs of vectors. In: ECAI/W9 Modelling and Solving Problems with Constraints. (2002)
7. Mackworth, A.: On reading sketch maps. In: IJCAI'77. (1977) 598–606
8. Walsh, T.: Consistency and propagation with multiset constraints: A formal viewpoint. In: Proc. CP-2003. (2003)
9. Hall, P.: On Representatives of Subsets. J. of London Math. Soc. **10** (1935) 26–30
10. Régin, J.C.: Generalized arc consistency for global cardinality constraint. In: Proc. AAAI-96. (1996)
11. Sadler, A., Gervet, C.: Global filtering for the disjoint constraint on fixed cardinality sets. Technical Report IC-PARC-04-2, Imperial College, London (2004)
12. Sadler, A., Gervet, C.: Global reasoning on sets. In: FORMUL'01 workshop in conjunction with CP-01. (2001)
13. Puget, J.F.: A fast algorithm for the bound consistency of alldiff constraints. AAAI (1998)
14. Crawford, J., Ginsberg, M., Luks, E.M., Roy, A.: Symmetry breaking predicates for search problems. In: Fifth Int. Conf. on Knowledge Rep. and Reasoning. (1996)
15. Gervet, C.: Conjunto: constraint logic programming with finite set domains. In: Proc. ILPS-94. (1994)
16. Azevedo, F.: Cardinal: an extended set solver. Computational Logic (2000)
17. Schimpf, J., Cheadle, A.M., Harvey, W., Sadler, A., Shen, K., Wallace, M.: ECL^{i}PS^e. Technical Report 03-1, IC-Parc, Imperial College London (2003)
18. Müller, T., Müller, M.: Finite set constraints in Oz. In: 13. Workshop Logische Programmierung. (1997)
19. Hnich, B., Kiziltan, Z., Walsh, T.: Combining symmetry breaking with other constraints: lexicographic ordering with sums. In: Proc. SymCon. (2003)

Speeding Up Constraint Propagation

Christian Schulte[1] and Peter J. Stuckey[2]

[1] IMIT, KTH – Royal Institute of Technology, Sweden
schulte@imit.kth.se
[2] Dept. of Comp. Sci. & Soft. Eng., Univ. of Melbourne, Australia
pjs@cs.mu.oz.au

Abstract. This paper presents a model and implementation techniques for speeding up constraint propagation. Two fundamental approaches to improving constraint propagation are explored: keeping track of which propagators are at fixpoint, and choosing which propagator to apply next. We show how idempotence reasoning and events help track fixpoints more accurately. We improve these methods by using them dynamically (taking into account current domains to improve accuracy). We define priority-based approaches to choosing a next propagator and show that dynamic priorities can improve propagation. We illustrate that the use of multiple propagators for the same constraint can be advantageous with priorities, and introduce staged propagators which combine the effects of multiple propagators with priorities for greater efficiency.

1 Introduction

At the core of a finite domain constraint programming system is a constraint propagation engine that repeatedly executes propagators for the constraints of a problem. Propagators discover and remove values from the domains of variables which can no longer take part in a solution of the constraints.

There are two important decisions the engine must make: which propagators should execute, and in which order should they execute. In this paper we investigate how to make a propagation engine as efficient as possible.

In order to make constraint propagation efficient, it is clear that the engine needs to take the following issues into account: avoid unnecessary propagator execution, restrict propagation to relevant variables, and choose the cheapest possible method for propagation. In this paper we show how propagation can be speeded up if the engine takes these issues into account.

The contributions of the paper are as follows. We give a formal definition of propagation systems including idempotent and event-based optimizations used in current propagation systems. We extend event-based propagation systems to use dynamically changing event sets. We introduce multiple propagators and staged propagators for use with propagation queues with priority. We give experimental results that clarify the impact of idempotent and event-based optimizations and show that dynamic event sets and staged propagators can be advantageous.

Plan of the Paper. The next section introduces propagation-based constraint solving, followed by a model for constraint propagation systems in Sect. 3. Section 4 presents how to optimize propagation by taking idempotence and events into account. Which propagator should be executed next and how propagation can be organized is discussed in Sect. 5. The following section evaluates the different variants of constraint propagation discussed. Section 7 concludes.

2 Propagation-Based Constraint Solving

This section defines terminology and the basic components of a constraint propagation engine. In this paper we restrict ourselves to integer constraint solving.

Domains. A *domain* D is a complete mapping from a fixed (countable) set of variables $\mathcal{V}$ to finite sets of integers. A *false domain* D is a domain with $D(x) = \emptyset$ for some $x \in \mathcal{V}$. Let $D_\bot(x) = \emptyset$ for all $x \in \mathcal{V}$. A variable $x \in \mathcal{V}$ is *fixed* by a domain D, if $|D(x)| = 1$. The *intersection* of domains D_1 and D_2, denoted $D_1 \sqcap D_2$, is defined by the domain $D(x) = D_1(x) \cap D_2(x)$ for all $x \in \mathcal{V}$.

A domain D_1 is *stronger* than a domain D_2, written $D_1 \sqsubseteq D_2$, if $D_1(x) \subseteq D_2(x)$ for all $x \in \mathcal{V}$. A domain D_1 is stronger than (equal to) a domain D_2 w.r.t. variables V, denoted $D_1 \sqsubseteq_V D_2$ (resp. $D_1 =_V D_2$), if $D_1(x) \subseteq D_2(x)$ (resp. $D_1(x) = D_2(x)$) for all $x \in V$.

We shall use range notation $[l\,..\,u]$ to define the set of integers $\{d \mid l \leq d \leq u\}$.

Valuations and Constraints. An *integer valuation* θ is a mapping of variables to integer values, written $\{x_1 \mapsto d_1, \ldots, x_n \mapsto d_n\}$. We extend the valuation θ to map expressions and constraints involving the variables in the natural way.

Let *vars* be the function that returns the set of variables appearing in a valuation. In an abuse of notation, we define a valuation θ to be an element of a domain D, written $\theta \in D$, if $\theta(x_i) \in D(x_i)$ for all $x_i \in vars(\theta)$.

The *infimum* and *supremum* of an expression e with respect to a domain D are defined as $\inf_D e = \inf \{\theta(e) | \theta \in D\}$ and $\sup_D e = \sup \{\theta(e)|\theta \in D\}$.

A *constraint* c over variables $x_1, \ldots, x_n$ is a set of valuations θ such that $vars(\theta) = \{x_1, \ldots, x_n\}$. We also define $vars(c) = \{x_1, \ldots, x_n\}$.

Propagators. We will *implement* a constraint c by a set of propagators $prop(c)$ which map domains to domains. A *propagator* f is a monotonically decreasing function from domains to domains: $f(D) \sqsubseteq D$, and $f(D_1) \sqsubseteq f(D_2)$ whenever $D_1 \sqsubseteq D_2$. A propagator f is *correct* for a constraint c iff for all domains D

$$\{\theta \in D\} \cap c = \{\theta \in f(D)\} \cap c$$

This is a very weak restriction, for example the identity propagator is correct for all constraints c.

A set of propagators F is *checking* for a constraint c, if for domains D where all variables $vars(c)$ are fixed the following holds: $f(D) = D$ for all $f \in F$, iff the unique valuation $\theta \in D$ where $vars(\theta) = vars(c)$ is a solution of c ($\theta \in c$). We assume that $prop(c)$ is a set of propagators that are correct and checking for c.

The *output* variables $output(f) \subseteq \mathcal{V}$ of a propagator f are the variables changed by the propagator: $x \in output(f)$ if there exists a domain D such that $f(D)(x) \neq D(x)$. The *input* variables $input(f) \subseteq \mathcal{V}$ of a propagator f is the smallest subset $V \subseteq \mathcal{V}$ such that for each domain D: $D =_V D'$ implies that $D' \sqcap f(D) =_{output(f)} f(D') \sqcap D$. Only the input variables are useful in computing the application of the propagator to the domain.

Example 1. For the constraint $c \equiv x_1 \leq x_2 + 1$ the function f_A defined by $f_A(D)(x_1) = \{d \in D(x_1) \mid d \leq \sup_D x_2 + 1\}$ and $f_A(D)(v) = D(v), v \neq x_1$ is a correct propagator for c. Its output variables are $\{x_1\}$ and its input variables are $\{x_2\}$. Let $D_1(x_1) = \{1, 5, 8\}$ and $D_1(x_2) = \{1, 5\}$, then $f(D_1) = D_2$ where $D_2(x_1) = D_2(x_2) = \{1, 5\}$.

The propagator f_B defined as $f_B(D)(x_2) = \{d \in D(x_2) \mid d \geq \inf_D x_1 - 1\}$ and $f_B(D)(v) = D(v), v \neq x_2$ is another correct propagator for c. Its output variables are $\{x_2\}$ and input variables $\{x_1\}$.

The set $\{f_A, f_B\}$ is checking for c. The domain $D(x_1) = D(x_2) = \{2\}$ corresponding to a solution of c is a fixpoint of both propagators. The non-solution domain $D(x_1) = \{2\}, D(x_2) = \{0\}$ is not a fixpoint (of either propagator).

A *propagation solver* for a set of propagators F and an initial domain D, $solv(F, D)$, finds the greatest mutual fixpoint of all the propagators $f \in F$. In other words, $solv(F, D)$ returns a new domain defined by

$$solv(F, D) = \text{gfp}(\lambda d.iter(F, d))(D) \qquad iter(F, D) = \bigsqcap_{f \in F} f(D)$$

where gfp denotes the greatest fixpoint w.r.t $\sqsubseteq$ lifted to functions.

3 Constraint Propagation Systems

A constraint propagation system evaluates the function $solv(F, D)$ during backtracking search. We assume an execution model for solving a constraint problem with a set of constraints C and an initial domain D_0 as follows. We execute the procedure $\text{search}(\emptyset, F, D_0)$ for an initial set of propagators $F = \cup_{c \in C} prop(c)$. This procedure is used to make precise the optimizations presented in the remainder of the paper.

```
search(F_o, F_n, D)
    D := isolv(F_o, F_n, D)                              % propagation
    if (D is a false domain) return false
    if (∃x ∈ V.|D(v)| > 1)
        choose {c_1, ..., c_m} where C ∧ D ⊨ c_1 ∨ ··· ∨ c_m   % search strategy
        for i ∈ [1 .. m]
            if (search(F_o ∪ F_n, prop(c_i), D)) return true
    return false
```

Note that the propagators are partitioned into two sets, the old propagators F_o and the new propagators F_n. The *incremental* propagation solver $isolv(F_o, F_n, D)$ (to be presented later) takes advantage of the fact that D is guaranteed to be a fixpoint of the old propagators.

The somewhat unusual definition of search is quite general. The default search strategy for many problems is to choose a variable x such that $|D(x)| > 1$ and explore $x = \inf_D x$ or $x \geq \inf_D x + 1$. This is commonly thought of as changing the domain D for x to either $\{\inf_D x\}$ or $\{d \in D(x) \mid d > \inf_D x\}$. This framework allows more general strategies, for example $x_1 \leq x_2$ or $x_1 > x_2$.

The basic incremental propagation solver algorithm is as follows:

$\mathsf{isolv}(F_o, F_n, D)$
    $F := F_o \cup F_n;\ Q := F_n$
    while $(Q \neq \emptyset)$
        $f := \mathsf{choose}(Q)$ % select next propagator to apply
        $Q := Q - \{f\};\ D' := f(D)$
        $Q := Q \cup \mathsf{new}(f, F, D, D')$ % add propagators $f' \in F$
        $D := D'$ % not necessarily at fixpoint at D'
    return D

The algorithm uses a queue of propagators to apply Q. Initially, Q contains the new propagators. Each time the while loop is executed, a propagator f is deleted from the queue, f is applied, and then all propagators that may no longer be at a fixpoint at the new domain D' are added to the queue. An invariant of the algorithm is that at the while statement $f(D) = D$ for all $f \in F - Q$.

isolv leaves two components undefined: $\mathsf{choose}(Q)$ chooses the propagator $f \in Q$ to be applied next; $\mathsf{new}(f, F, D, D')$ determines the set of propagators $f' \in F$ which are not guaranteed to be at their fixpoint at the domain D'. The remainder of the paper investigates how to best implement these two components.

4 Fixpoint Reasoning

The core aim of the constraint propagation solver $\mathsf{solv}(F, D)$ is to find a domain that is a mutual fixpoint of all $f \in F$. The incremental solver $\mathsf{isolv}(F_o, F_n, D)$ already takes into account that initially D is a fixpoint of propagators $f \in F_o$. The role of new is (generally) to return *as few* propagators $f \in F$ as possible.

A basic definition of new is as follows

$$\mathsf{new}_{input}(f, F, D, D') = \{f' \in F \mid input(f') \cap \{x \in \mathcal{V} \mid D(x) \neq D'(x)\} \neq \emptyset\}$$

Here all propagators f' are added whose input variables domain have changed. By the definition of input variables, if none of them have changed for f', then $f'(D') = D'$ since $f(D) = D$ if $f' \in F - Q$.

isolv with this definition of new (assuming $F_o = \emptyset$) is more or less equivalent to the propagation algorithm of Apt ([1] page 267).

4.1 Idempotence

A propagator f is *idempotent* if $f(D) = f(f(D))$ for all domains D. That is, applying f to any domain D yields a fixpoint of f.

Example 2. The propagator f_C defined by $f_C(D)(x_1) = \{d \in D(x_1) \mid \frac{3}{2}d \in D(x_2)\}$, $f_C(D)(x_2) = \{d \in D(x_2) \mid \frac{2}{3}d \in D(x_1)\}$, and $f_C(D)(x) = D(x), x \notin \{x_1, x_2\}$ is the domain propagator for the constraint $3x_1 = 2x_2$. The propagator f_C is idempotent.

Example 3. While many propagators are idempotent, some widely used ones are *not* idempotent. Consider the constraint $3x_1 = 2x_2$ and the propagator f_G:

$$f_G(D)(x_1) = D(x_1) \cap [\lceil (2\inf_D x_2)/3 \rceil \mathrel{..} \lfloor (2\sup_D x_2)/3 \rfloor]$$
$$f_G(D)(x_2) = D(x_2) \cap [\lceil (3\inf_D x_1)/2 \rceil \mathrel{..} \lfloor (3\sup_D x_1)/2 \rfloor]$$
$$f_G(D)(x) = D(x) \quad x \notin \{x_1, x_2\}$$

Then $prop(3x_1 = 2x_2) = \{f_G\}$ in almost all constraint programming systems. f_G is the the bounds propagator (considering solutions over the real numbers) for for $3x_1 = 2x_2$. Now f_G is not idempotent. Consider $D(x_1) = [0 .. 3]$ and $D(x_2) = [0 .. 5]$. Then $D' = f_G(D)$ is defined by $D'(x_1) = [0 .. 3] \cap [0 .. \lfloor 10/3 \rfloor] = [0 .. 3]$ and $D'(x_2) = [0 .. 5] \cap [0 .. \lfloor 9/2 \rfloor] = [0 .. 4]$. Now $D'' = f_G(D')$ is defined by $D''(x_1) = [0 .. 3] \cap [0 .. \lfloor 8/3 \rfloor] = [0 .. 2]$ and $D''(x_2) = [0 .. 4] \cap [0 .. \lfloor 9/2 \rfloor] = [0 .. 4]$. Hence $f_G(f_G(D)) = D'' \neq D' = f_G(D)$.

We can always create an idempotent propagator f' from a propagator f by defining $f'(D) = solv(\{f\}, D)$. Indeed, in some implementations (for example [8]) $prop(3x_1 = 2x_2)$ is defined as the fixpoint of applying f_G.

Static Idempotence. Assume that $idem(f) = \{f\}$ if f is an idempotent propagator and $idem(f) = \emptyset$ otherwise. The definition of new is improved by taking idempotence into account

$$\mathsf{new}_{sidem}(f, F, D, D') = \mathsf{new}_{input}(f, F, D, D') - idem(f)$$

An idempotent propagator is never put into the queue after application.

Note that this is an important optimization. Otherwise each propagator f that changes the domain is likely to be executed again to check it is at fixpoint. Almost all constraint propagation solvers take into account static idempotence (for example ILOG Solver [9], Choco [11], and SICStus [10]). Some systems even only allow idempotent propagators (for example Mozart [13]).

Dynamic Idempotence. Even if a propagator is not idempotent we can often determine that $f(D)$ is a fixpoint of f for a specific domain D.

We can make use of dynamic idempotence by extending a propagator f to return a new domain D' and an indication whether D' is a fixpoint. For simplicity we assume a function $idem(f, D)$ that returns $\{f\}$ if it can show that $f(D)$ is a fixpoint for f and $\emptyset$ otherwise (of course without calculating $f(f(D))$, otherwise we gain nothing). In practice this will be included in the code for f.

$$\mathsf{new}_{didem}(f, F, D, D') = \mathsf{new}_{input}(f, F, D, D') - idem(f, D)$$

Note that the dynamic case extends the static case since for idempotent f it holds that $idem(f, D) = \{f\}$ for all domains D.

Example 4. Consider applying f_G from Example 3 to the domain D'' from the same example. Now $D''' = f_G(D'')$ is defined by $D'''(x_1) = [0 .. 2] \cap [0 .. \lfloor 8/3 \rfloor] = [0 .. 2]$ and $D'''(x_2) = [0 .. 4] \cap [0 .. \lfloor 6/2 \rfloor] = [0 .. 3]$. Notice that the new bound $x_2 \leq 3$ is obtained without rounding $\lfloor 6/2 \rfloor = 6/2$. In this case we are guaranteed that the propagator is at a fixpoint ([8] Theorem 8).

4.2 Events

The next improvement for avoiding propagators to be put in the queue is to consider what changes in domains of input variables can cause the propagator to no longer be at a fixpoint. An *event* is a change in the domain of a variable.

Assume that the domain D changes to the domain $D' \sqsubseteq D$. The usual events defined in a constraint propagation system are:

- $\mathit{fix}(x)$: the variable x becomes fixed, that is $|D'(x)| = 1$ and $|D(x)| > 1$.
- $\mathit{lbc}(x)$: the lower bound of variable x changes, that is $\inf_{D'} x > \inf_D x$.
- $\mathit{ubc}(x)$: the upper bound of variable x changes, that is $\sup_{D'} x < \sup_D x$.
- $\mathit{dmc}(x)$: the domain of variable x changes, that is. $D'(x) \subset D(x)$.

Clearly the events overlap. Whenever a $\mathit{fix}(x)$ event occurs then a $\mathit{lbc}(x)$ event, a $\mathit{ubc}(x)$ event, or both events must also occur. If any of the first three events occur then a $\mathit{dmc}(x)$ event occurs. These events satisfy the following property.

Definition 1. *An event ϕ is a change in domain defined by an event condition $\phi(D, D')$ which states that event ϕ occurs when the domain changes from D to $D' \sqsubseteq D$. The event condition must satisfy the following property*

$$\phi(D, D'') = \phi(D, D') \vee \phi(D', D'')$$

where $D'' \sqsubseteq D' \sqsubseteq D$. So an event occurs on a change from D to D'' iff it occurs in either the change from D to D' or from D' to D''.

Given a domain D and a stronger domain $D' \sqsubseteq D$, then $\mathit{events}(D, D')$ is the set of events ϕ where $\phi(D, D')$. Suppose $D'' \sqsubseteq D' \sqsubseteq D$, then clearly $\mathit{events}(D, D'') = \mathit{events}(D, D') \cup \mathit{events}(D', D'')$.

Most integer propagation solvers use the events defined above, although some systems collapse $\mathit{ubc}(x)$ and $\mathit{lbc}(x)$ into a single event (for example, SICStus [10] and ILOG Solver [9]). Choco [11] maintains an event queue and interleaves propagator execution with events causing more propagators to be added to the queue.

Static Event Sets. Re-execution of certain propagators can be avoided since they require certain events to generate new information.

Definition 2. *A propagator f is dependent on a set of events $es(f)$ iff (a) for all domains D if $f(D) \neq f(f(D))$ then $\mathit{events}(D, f(D)) \cap es(f) \neq \emptyset$, and (b) for all domains D and D' where $f(D) = D$, $D' \sqsubseteq D$ and $f(D') \neq D'$ then $\mathit{events}(D, D') \cap es(f) \neq \emptyset$.*

The definition captures the following. If f is not at a fixpoint then one of the events in its event set occurs. If f is at a fixpoint D then any change to a domain which is not a fixpoint D' involves an occurrence of one of the events in its set. Note that for idempotent propagators the case (a) never occurs.

For convenience later we will store the event set chosen for a propagator f in an array $evset[f] = es(f)$.

Clearly if we keep track of the events since the last invocation of a propagator, we do not need to apply a propagator if it is not dependent on any of these events.

Example 5. An event set for f_A is $\{ubc(x_2)\}$. An event set for f_B is $\{lbc(x_1)\}$. An event set for f_C is $\{dmc(x_1), dmc(x_2)\}$. An event set for f_G is $\{lbc(x_1), ubc(x_1), lbc(x_2), ubc(x_2)\}$. This is easy to see from the definitions of these propagators. If they use $\inf_D x$ then $lbc(x)$ is in the event set, similarly if they use $\sup_D x$ then $ubc(x)$ is in the event set. If they use the entire domain $D(x)$ then $dmc(x)$ is in the event set.

Indexical propagation solvers [17,5,4] are based on such reasoning. They define propagators in the form $f(D)(x) = D(x) \cap e(D)$ where e is an indexical expression. The event set for such propagators is automatically defined by the domain access terms that occur in the expression e.

Using events we can define a much more accurate version of new that only adds propagators for which one of the events in its event set has occurred.

$$\mathsf{new}_{events}(f, F, D, D') = \{f' \in F \mid evset[f'] \cap events(D, D')\} - idem(f, D)$$

This version of new (without dynamic idempotence) roughly corresponds with what most constraint propagation systems currently implement.

Dynamic Events Sets. Events help to improve the efficiency of a propagation-based solver. Just as we can improve the use of idempotence by examining the dynamic case, we can also consider dynamically updating event sets as more information is known about the variables in the propagator.

Definition 3. *A propagator f is dependent on a set of events $es(f, D)$ in the context of domain D iff for all domains $D_0 \sqsubseteq D$ if $f(D_0) \neq f(f(D_0))$ then $events(D_0, f(D_0)) \cap es(f) \neq \emptyset$, and for domains D_0 and D_1 where $D_0 \sqsubseteq D$, $f(D_0) = D_0$, $D_1 \sqsubseteq D_0$ and $f(D_1) \neq D_1$ then $events(D_0, D_1) \cap es(f) \neq \emptyset$.*

Clearly given this definition $es(f, D)$ is monotonically decreasing with D. The simplest kind of event reduction occurs by entailment.

Definition 4. *A propagator f is entailed for domain D, if for each domain $D' \sqsubseteq D$ we have $f(D') = D'$.*

An entailed propagator makes no future contribution. If f is entailed by D then $es(f, D) = \emptyset$ and f is never re-applied. Most current constraint propagation systems take into account entailment.

Example 6. Consider the propagator f_A and the domain D with $D(x_1) = [1 \mathrel{..} 3]$ and $D(x_2) = [3 \mathrel{..} 7]$. Then the constraint holds for all $D' \sqsubseteq D$ and $es(f, D) = \emptyset$.

Changing event sets can occur in cases other than entailment.

Example 7. Consider the propagator f_H for $x_0 = \min(x_1, x_2)$ defined by

$$\begin{aligned}
f_H(D)(x_0) &= D(x_0) \cap [\min(\inf_D x_1, \inf_D x_2) \mathrel{..} \min(\sup_D x_1, \sup_D x_2)] \\
f_H(D)(x_i) &= D(x_i) \cap [\inf_D x_0 \mathrel{..} +\infty] & i \in \{1, 2\} \\
f_H(D)(x) &= D(x) & x \notin \{x_0, x_1, x_2\}
\end{aligned}$$

The static event set $es(f_H)$ is $\{lbc(x_0), lbc(x_1), ubc(x_1), lbc(x_2), ubc(x_2)\}$. Note that this propagator is idempotent. But given domain D where $D(x_0) = [1 \mathrel{..} 3]$ and $D(x_2) = [5 \mathrel{..} 7]$ we know that modifying the value of x_2 will never cause propagation. A minimal definition of $es(f_H, D)$ is $\{lbc(x_0), lbc(x_1), ubc(x_1)\}$.

Another example is a propagator for the exactly constraint [18]: exactly m out of the variables $x_1, \ldots, x_n$ are equal to a value k. As soon as one of the x_i becomes different from k, all events for x_i can be ignored.

Using dynamic event sets we can refine our definition of new as follows.

$\mathsf{new}_{devents}(f, F, D, D')$
$\quad F' := \{f' \in F \mid evset[f'] \cap events(D, D')\} - idem(f, D)$
$\quad evset[f] := es(f, D')$
$\quad$ **return** F'

Every time a propagator f is applied its event set is updated to take into account newly available information.

A related idea is the "type reduction" of [16] where propagators are improved as more knowledge on domains (here called types) becomes available. For example, the implementation of $x_0 = x_1 \times x_2$ will be replaced by a more efficient one, when all elements in $D(x_1)$ and $D(x_2)$ are non-negative.

5 Which Propagator to Execute Next

We now address how to define which propagator f in the queue Q should execute first, that is how to define the choose function.

The simplest policy is implemented as a FIFO queue of propagators. Propagators are added to the queue, if they are not already present, and choose selects the oldest propagator in the queue. The FIFO policy ensures fairness so that computation is not dominated by a single group of propagators, while possibly not discovering failure (a false domain) from other propagators quickly.

5.1 Priorities

Static Priorities. A statically prioritized queue associates with each propagator a fixed priority, we will assume an integer in the range $[1 \mathrel{..} k]$. In effect the queue

Q is split into k queues, $Q[1], \ldots Q[k]$ where each $Q[i]$ is a FIFO queue for the propagators with priority i. Selection always chooses the oldest propagator in the lowest numbered queue $Q[i]$ which is non-empty. Static prioritization allows to ensure that quick propagators are executed before slow propagators.

Example 8. We will assume 7 static priorities, and give names to the integer priorities as follows: UNARY=1 BINARY=2, TERNARY=3 LINEAR=4, QUADRATIC=5, CUBIC=6, and VERYSLOW=7.

For example the propagator f_I for $x_1 \leq 4$ defined by $f_I(D)(x_1) = D(x_1) \cap [-\infty \,..\, 4]$ and $f_I(D)(x) = D(x)$ when $x \neq x_1$ might be given priority UNARY, while f_C and f_G might be given priority BINARY. The domain propagator defined by Régin [15] for the `alldifferent` constraint $\wedge_{i=1}^n \wedge_{j=i+1}^n x_i \neq x_j$ (with complexity $O(n^{2.5})$) might be given priority QUADRATIC. The `alldifferent` bounds propagator defined by Puget [14] (with complexity $O(n \log n)$) might be given priority LINEAR.

Another model for priorities in constraint propagation based on composition operators is [6]. The model, however, runs all propagators of lower priority before switching propagation back to propagators of higher priority.

Most systems have some form of static priorities, typically using two priority levels (for example, SICStus [10], Mozart [13]). The two levels are often not entirely based on cost: in SICStus all indexicals have high priority and all other lower priority. While ECL^{i}PS^e [19, 7] supports 12 priority levels, its finite domain solver also uses only two priority levels where another level is used to support constraint debugging. A similar, but more powerful approach is used by Choco [11] using seven priority levels allowing both LIFO and FIFO traversal.

Prioritizing particular operations during constraint propagation is important in general. For (binary) arc consistency algorithms, ordering heuristics for the operations performed during propagation can reduce the total number of operations required [20]. For interval narrowing, prioritizing constraints can avoid slow convergence, see for example [12].

Dynamic Priorities. As evaluation proceeds, variables become fixed and propagators can be replaced by more specialized versions. If a propagator is replaced by a more specialized version, also its priority should change.

Example 9. Consider the propagator f_J for updating x_1 in the constraint $x_1 = x_2 + x_3$ defined by

$$f_J(D)(x_1) = D(x_1) \cap [\inf_D(x_2) + \inf_D(x_3) \,..\, \sup_D(x_2) + \sup_D(x_3)]$$
$$f_J(D)(x) = D(x) \qquad x \neq x_1$$

might have initial priority TERNARY. When the variable x_2 becomes fixed to d_2 say, then the implementation for x_1 can change to

$$f_J(D)(x_1) = D(x_1) \cap [d_2 + \inf_D(x_3) \,..\, d_2 + \sup_D(x_3)]$$

and the priority can change to BINARY.

Changing priorities is also relevant when a propagator with $n > 3$ variables with priority LINEAR (or worse) reduces to a binary or ternary propagator.

5.2 Combining Propagation

Multiple Propagators. Once we have a prioritized propagation queue it makes sense to have multiple propagators, say f_1 and f_2, in $prop(c)$ where f_1 is strictly stronger than the f_2 ($f_1(D) \sqsubseteq f_2(D)$). Usually we should just run f_1. But with priorities it makes sense to run the weaker (and presumably faster) propagator f_2 with a higher priority than f_1. This makes information available earlier to other propagators. When the stronger propagator f_1 is eventually run, it is able to take advantage from propagation provided by other cheaper propagators.

Example 10. Consider the propagator $f_K(D)$ for the `alldifferent` constraint.

$E := \emptyset$
for $i \in [1 .. n]$
   if $(\exists d.D(x_i) = \{d\})$
      if $(d \in E)$ **return** $D_\bot$ **else** $E := E \cup \{d\}$
for $i \in [1 .. n]$
   if $(|D(x_i)| > 1)$ $D(x_i) := D(x_i) - E$
return D

The propagator does a linear number of set operations in each invocation and is checking. It can be made idempotent by testing that no variable becomes fixed.

Another propagator for the same constraint is the domain propagator f_L by Régin [15]. We can use both propagators: f_K with priority LINEAR, and f_L with priority QUADRATIC. This means that we will not invoke f_L until we have reached a fixpoint of f_K and all LINEAR and higher priority propagators.

If we just use f_L then we need to invoke the more expensive f_L to obtain the same domain changes as f_K, and then fail.

Staged Propagators. Once we are willing to use multiple propagators for a single constraint it becomes worth considering how to more efficiently manage them. Instead of using two (or more) distinct propagators we can combine the several propagators into a single propagator with more effective behavior.

We assume that a propagator has an internal state variable, called its stage. When it is invoked, the stage determines what form of propagation applies.

Example 11. Consider the `alldifferent` constraint with implementations f_K and f_L discussed in Example 10. We combine them into a staged propagator:

- On a $fix(x)$ event, the propagator is moved to stage A, and placed in the queue with priority LINEAR.
- On a $dmc(x)$ event, unless the propagator is in stage A already, the propagator is put in stage B, and placed in the queue with priority QUADRATIC.
- Execution in stage A uses f_K, the propagator is put in stage B, and placed in the queue with priority QUADRATIC, unless it is entailed.
- Execution in stage B uses f_L, afterwards the propagator is removed from all queues (stage NONE).

The behavior of the staged propagator is identical to the multiple propagators for the sample execution of Example 10. In addition to the obvious advantage of having a single staged propagator, the advantage comes from avoiding the execution of f_L when the constraint is entailed.

Example 12. Consider the unit coefficient linear equation $\Sigma_{i=1}^{n} a_i x_i = d$ constraint where $|a_i| = 1, 1 \leq i \leq n$. We have two implementations, f_M which implements bounds consistency (considering real solutions, with linear complexity) for the constraint, and f_N which implements domain consistency (with exponential complexity).

We combine them into a staged propagator as follows:

- On a $lbc(x)$ or $ubc(x)$ event, the propagator is moved to stage A, and placed in the queue with priority LINEAR.
- On a $dmc(x)$ event, unless the propagator is in stage A already, the propagator is put in stage B, and is placed in the queue with priority VERYSLOW.
- Execution in stage A uses f_M, afterwards the propagator is put in stage B, and placed in the queue with priority VERYSLOW, unless each x_i has a range domain in which case it is removed from all queues (stage NONE).
- Execution in stage B uses f_N, afterwards the propagator is removed from all queues (stage NONE).

The staged propagator is advantageous since the "fast" propagator f_M can more often determine that its result $D' = f_M(D)$ is also a fixpoint for f_N.

Staged propagators can be used similarly for the bounds version of the alldifferent constraint. Another area where staged propagators can be used is constraint-based scheduling, where typically different propagation methods with different strength and efficiency are available [2].

6 Evaluation

Evaluating dynamic idempotence, modifying event sets, or calculating priorities, for example, might take more time than the time saved by reduced evaluation of propagators. Hence it is important to experimentally verify the benefits of these improvements to propagation solvers.

All experiments use Gecode, a C++-based constraint programming library currently under development.[1] Gecode is a successor to the constraint programming support in Mozart [13]. Its current performance is considerably better than Mozart. All examples have been run on a Dell Laptop with a 1.5 GHz Pentium M CPU and 512 MB main memory running Windows XP. Runtimes are the average of 25 runs with a coefficient of deviation less than 2.5% for all benchmarks.

Table 1 gives the number of propagation steps and Table 2 the runtime for the different fixpoint reasoning approaches. Propagation steps and runtimes are given as absolute values for the base solver (*input*) and relative to the base solver for all other solvers.

---

[1] The library is available upon request from the first author.

Table 1. Propagation steps for different fixpoint reasoning.

Benchmark	input steps	sidem	didem	events	devents
		relative %			
cars	12 018	100.0	100.0	99.7	99.7
golomb-10-d	7 210 956	79.5	79.5	77.3	77.3
partition	147 739	81.7	81.7	81.2	81.2
photo	480 778	99.3	96.8	73.4	73.4
queens-100	505 670	100.0	100.0	3.2	3.2
alpha	262 499	95.7	94.4	73.0	73.0
golomb-10-b	7 159 721	79.0	79.3	77.1	77.1
knights-16	170 376	94.3	129.9	43.7	43.7
queens-100-a	885	100.0	87.7	58.3	58.3
m-seq-500	116 451	100.0	99.9	100.0	56.0
minsort	55 638	81.1	81.1	84.7	54.5

Fixpoint Reasoning. The examples used are standard benchmarks but minsort which sorts 100 numbers by using 100 min constraints involving 100 variables each together with binary linear inequalities. A -d (resp. -b) at the end of the name means that domain (resp. bounds) propagation is used for all occurring alldifferent and linear equation constraints. queens-100-a uses three naive (as in Example 10) alldifferent-propagators, while queens-100 uses quadratically many binary disequality propagators. For clarity, the examples have been run without using priorities and without multiple or staged propagators.

Table 2. Runtime for different fixpoint reasoning.

Benchmark	input milliseconds	sidem	didem	events	devents
		relative %			
cars	7.72	100.4	100.4	100.2	101.3
golomb-10-d	10 107.72	99.9	99.8	102.4	102.4
partition	136.04	90.3	90.4	90.9	90.8
photo	200.69	99.0	98.4	93.9	94.0
queens-100	139.04	102.5	102.6	74.2	72.7
alpha	179.98	99.0	99.4	90.1	90.4
golomb-10-b	6 897.52	104.3	100.7	102.3	102.5
knights-16	313.53	99.5	101.4	98.0	98.1
queens-100-a	6.97	99.7	101.0	101.6	101.6
m-seq-500	634.51	101.9	99.7	101.8	28.1
minsort	142.08	97.3	97.4	98.7	55.0

The benchmarks show that static idempotence (*sidem*) reduces the number of propagation steps, in particular for examples using domain-consistent alldifferent propagators (golomb-10-d, ortho-latin-5). This can also be true for cheap propagators (minsort). However, the effect on runtime is less noticeable (one reason is that useless execution of a domain-consistent alldifferent propagator is cheap due to its incrementality).

Benchmarks that profit from events are in particular those with propagators that depend on $fix(x)$ events (such as the disequality propagators in queens-100 and reified propagators in photo and knights).

The second group (separate box in the tables) of examples use propagators that can take advantage of dynamic idempotence (*didem*). Dynamic idempotence appears to be not beneficial, while it can both increase (knights-16) and decrease (queens-100-a) propagation steps, the runtime shows no improvement.

The third group of examples stress the importance of using dynamic event sets. For both examples, where minsort uses min propagators as described in Example 7 and m-seq-500 uses exactly propagators, the propagation steps reduce by almost a factor of two with a considerable reduction in runtime.

Table 3. Propagation steps for different priority and multiple propagator approaches.

Benchmark	no priority			static priority			dynamic priority		
	none		multi stage	none		multi stage	none		multi stage
	steps			relative %					
alpha	190 042	100.0	100.0	100.9	100.9	100.9	**54.2**	**54.2**	**54.2**
cars	11 981	100.0	100.0	102.9	102.9	102.9	**72.1**	**72.1**	**72.1**
knights-16	134 727	100.0	100.0	**45.8**	**45.8**	**45.8**	**45.8**	**45.8**	**45.8**
m-seq-500	65 227	100.2	100.2	**68.3**	**68.3**	**68.3**	94.6	94.6	94.6
photo	352 897	100.0	100.0	**89.1**	**89.1**	89.2	90.9	90.9	90.9
color-1-d	4 117 534	148.5	102.4	**98.7**	125.4	101.6	108.9	157.6	112.7
color-2-d	4 705 953	143.9	102.6	**102.9**	133.1	105.2	116.0	160.9	120.0
donald-b	340	120.9	105.3	100.0	109.1	105.3	100.0	109.1	105.3
donald-d	34	197.1	105.9	**108.8**	217.6	214.7	**108.8**	217.6	217.6
golomb-10-b	5 520 302	260.1	114.2	**132.5**	140.4	140.4	**132.5**	140.4	140.4
golomb-10-d	5 571 319	101.0	113.4	**130.7**	138.4	138.4	**130.7**	138.4	138.4
ortho-latin-5-d	547 872	140.3	108.4	143.8	**94.4**	139.4	146.9	104.0	137.4
partition-d	119 893	104.7	101.6	88.5	89.4	88.4	**84.5**	85.3	**84.5**
square-5-b	71 609	105.1	108.3	129.5	133.8	133.8	**106.7**	110.9	110.9
square-5-d	56 632	158.5	111.4	**125.1**	166.6	211.1	116.7	144.1	208.4

Priorities. Table 3 shows the number of propagation steps required to solve each benchmark, relative to the base solver. Table 4 shows the relative execution times. Important additional benchmarks are color-1 and color-2 implementing graph coloring on large graphs (50 nodes) with large cliques (for each clique a domain-consistent alldifferent propagator is used). The first group of benchmarks (the upper box in the tables) does not use multiple or staged propagators. The second group uses multiple and staged propagators (bounds-consistent alldifferent for the -b variants, domain-consistent alldifferent and linear equalities for the -d variants).

The addition of static or dynamic priorities can substantially decrease the number of propagations required. It can, more rarely, also increase the number of propagations required. Once we examine timing we see that dynamic priorities are slightly advantageous over static priorities in most cases since they run cheaper propagators.

Table 4. Runtime for different priority and multiple propagator approaches.

Benchmark	No priority		Static priority		Dynamic priority	
	none	multi stage	none	multi stage	none	multi stage
	millisecs		relative %			
alpha	165.04	99.7 100.2	95.9	95.8 96.5	71.8	71.7 **71.6**
cars	7.66	99.9 100.0	104.5	104.8 104.7	86.6	86.6 **86.1**
knights-16	306.48	99.9 100.0	**97.3**	97.4 97.4	97.4	97.4 97.5
m-seq-500	175.66	99.9 **99.0**	113.2	114.0 114.1	108.0	107.3 108.8
photo	188.35	99.5 100.4	**96.8**	97.7 97.7	98.3	98.9 98.9
color-1-d	10 137.76	116.6 76.9	95.9	103.0 **76.6**	104.6	123.3 83.2
color-2-d	12 036.52	108.3 80.0	99.4	99.9 **79.1**	107.5	117.4 89.1
donald-b	0.87	101.5 **85.5**	101.2	92.2 87.8	101.7	91.6 87.8
donald-d	46.80	94.0 96.3	93.6	95.5 **90.8**	96.5	91.2 96.3
golomb-10-b	7 022.12	256.2 82.0	53.1	**50.5** 50.9	52.9	50.8 51.1
golomb-10-d	10 281.96	101.9 84.7	51.8	50.5 **50.1**	51.8	50.9 50.2
ortho-latin-5-d	2 075.58	104.1 92.2	125.5	63.8 **58.1**	124.8	70.1 65.3
partition-d	123.46	103.7 96.9	80.6	79.2 78.2	78.5	77.4 **76.1**
square-5-b	143.64	102.5 82.6	82.0	78.4 77.2	78.6	75.2 **73.5**
square-5-d	2 830.28	83.9 99.6	120.5	54.0 **46.4**	112.2	54.0 51.2

The addition of multiple or staged propagators unsurprisingly increases the number of propagations required, since we are increasing the number of propagators in the model, occasionally quite badly (for example, square-5-d). For large examples, both approaches offer considerable faster runtimes, where staged propagators are unsurprisingly always better than using multiple propagators. It is important to note that staged propagation is always best when using priorities.

7 Conclusion and Future Work

We have given a formal definition of propagation systems including idempotence, events, and priorities used in current propagation systems and have evaluated their impact. We have introduced dynamically changing event sets which are shown to improve efficiency considerably. The paper has introduced multiple and staged propagators which are shown to be an important optimization in particular for improving the efficiency of costly global constraints.

While the improvements to an engine of a propagation based constraint solver have been discussed for integer constraints, the techniques readily carry over to arbitrary constraint domains such as finite sets.

A rather obvious way to further speed up constraint propagation is to consider not only cost but also estimated impact for a propagator. However, while computing cost is straightforward it is currently not clear to us how to accurately predict propagation impact.

References

1. K. Apt. *Principles of Constraint Programming*. Cambridge University Press, 2003.
2. P. Baptiste, C. Le Pape, and W. Nuijten. *Constraint-based Scheduling*. Kluwer Academic Publishers, 2001.
3. N. Beldiceanu, W. Harvey, M. Henz, F. Laburthe, E. Monfroy, T. Müller, L. Perron, and C. Schulte. TRICS 2000. Technical Report TRA9/00, School of Computing, National University of Singapore, Sept. 2000.
4. M. Carlsson, G. Ottosson, and B. Carlson. An open-ended finite domain constraint solver. In *PLILP'97*, volume 1292 of *LNCS*, pages 191–206. Springer-Verlag, 1997.
5. P. Codognet and D. Diaz. Compiling constraints in clp(FD). *The Journal of Logic Programming*, 27(3):185–226, June 1996.
6. L. Granvilliers and E. Monfroy. Implementing constraint propagation by composition of reductions. In *ICLP'03*, volume 2916 of *LNCS*, pages 300–314. Springer-Verlag, 2003.
7. W. Harvey. Personal communication, Apr. 2004.
8. W. Harvey and P. J. Stuckey. Constraint representation for propagation. In *CP'98*, volume 1520 of *LNCS*, pages 235–249. Springer-Verlag, 1998.
9. ILOG S.A. *ILOG Solver 5.0: Reference Manual*. Gentilly, France, 2000.
10. Intelligent Systems Laboratory. SICStus Prolog user's manual, 3.11.1. Technical report, Swedish Institute of Computer Science, 2004.
11. F. Laburthe. CHOCO: implementing a CP kernel. In Beldiceanu et al. [3], pages 71–85.
12. O. Lhomme, A. Gotlieb, and M. Rueher. Dynamic optimization of interval narrowing algorithms. *The Journal of Logic Programming*, 37(1–3):165–183, 1998.
13. T. Müller. The Mozart constraint extensions reference, 1999. Available from www.mozart-oz.org.
14. J.-F. Puget. A fast algorithm for the bound consistency of alldiff constraints. In *Proceedings of the 15th National Conference on Artificial Intelligence (AAAI-98)*, pages 359–366, Madison, WI, USA, July 1998. AAAI Press/The MIT Press.
15. J.-C. Régin. A filtering algorithm for constraints of difference in CSPs. In *Proceedings of the Twelfth National Conference on Artificial Intelligence*, volume 1, pages 362–367, Seattle, WA, USA, 1994. AAAI Press.
16. P. Savéant. Constraint reduction at the type level. In Beldiceanu et al. [3], pages 16–29.
17. P. Van Hentenryck, V. Saraswat, and Y. Deville. Design, implementation and evaluation of the constraint language cc(FD). *Journal of Logic Programming*, 37(1–3):139–164, 1998.
18. P. Van Hentenryck, H. Simonis, and M. Dincbas. Constraint satisfaction using constraint logic programming. *Artificial Intelligence*, 58:113–159, 1992.
19. M. Wallace, S. Novello, and J. Schimpf. Eclipse: A platform for constraint logic programming. Technical report, IC-Parc, Imperial College, London, UK, 1997.
20. R. J. Wallace and E. C. Freuder. Ordering heuristics for arc consistency algorithms. In *Ninth Canadian Conference on Artificial Intelligence*, pages 163–169, Vancouver, Canada, 1992.

Theoretical Foundations of CP-Based Lagrangian Relaxation*

Meinolf Sellmann

Cornell University, Department of Computer Science
4130 Upson Hall, Ithaca, NY 14853
sello@cs.cornell.edu

Abstract. CP-based Lagrangian Relaxation allows us to reason on local substructures while maintaining a global view on an entire optimization problem. While the idea of cost-based filtering with respect to systematically changing objective functions has been around for more than three years now, so far some important observations have not been explained. In this paper, we prove a simple theorem that explains a variety of effects that are encountered in practice, the most counter-intuitive being the fact that suboptimal Lagrangian multipliers can have stronger filtering abilities than optimal ones.

Keywords: cost-based filtering, optimization constraints, relaxed consistency

1 Introduction

When analyzing and modeling real-world optimization problems, we often find that they consist in a conglomerate of much simpler substructures. These substructures often exhibit special properties that do not hold for the overall problem, frequently they have been studied before, and efficient algorithms for their optimization exist. When solving a composed problem, we would like to exploit our knowledge of the substructures that constitute the problem as a whole. In constraint programming (CP), the core idea is to encapsulate each substructure in a constraint, whereby traditionally we treat the objective function independently of the other constraints (we formulate our search for an improving solution as a feasibility problem).

In order to improve the filtering abilities of our constraint program, we may wish to follow the successful trend to develop rather strong global constraints and consider to combine the objective function with the corresponding constraints that define each substructure. That is, for each substructure we formulate an *optimization constraint* [9] that expresses our wish that we are looking for improving solutions that are at least feasible when we ignore all other substructures. Then, by exploiting our knowledge on the individual substructures, we can develop efficient *cost-based filtering* algorithms [9] that we use for domain filtering in each choice point. That is, by locally reasoning about one optimization substructure at a time, we try to simplify the overall problem by eliminating all

---

* This work was supported by the Intelligent Information Systems Institute, Cornell University (AFOSR grant F49620-01-1-0076).

variable assignments that will not yield to feasible and improving solutions with respect to that optimization constraint. As it is standard in CP, this process is iterated until we reach a fix point where no optimization constraint alone is able to shrink the domain of the variables further.

There is one problem with this procedure though: By looking at only one substructure at a time, we will usually vastly underestimate the objective costs (that we try to minimize) that can still be achieved. Consequently, cost-based filtering will be rather ineffective since most often we will assume that it is still possible to improve the objective even when this is not the case. In order to obtain a good estimate on the best objective performance that is still achievable, we simply cannot afford to ignore the other substructures completely. Instead, we need to introduce some kind of global view on the entire problem that allows us to compute a more accurate bound estimate.

At first, it sounds as if this necessity stood in contradiction with the idea of arguing locally about one substructure at a time. As it turns out, though, for linear problems there is an easy way to take the other constraints into account while still reasoning about individual substructures only. The simple idea consists in softening the other constraints and placing them in the objective function. Via a penalty term we increase the objective's cost, the more violated the other constraints are the higher the price that has to be paid. In mathematical programming, this softening and penalizing of constraints is known as *Lagrangian relaxation*.

For the purpose of cost-based filtering, Lagrangian relaxation allows us to consider a global bound on the overall problem while exploiting local structure. Following the work in [8] where local reasoning was combined with strengthened lower bounds by adding cuts in a Lagrangian fashion, the idea of CP-based Lagrangian Relaxation was first formalized in [23] and later used in [24, 22, 25] for the automatic recording problem that consists in a conjunction of a Knapsack and a weighted stable set problem. While numerous practical applications of this procedure have shown that CP-based Lagrangian Relaxation can boost the practical performance of solution approaches (see [25, 26, 19] for examples), there are many outstanding theoretical questions: Why should one perform filtering for sub-optimal Lagrangian multipliers? What are the best penalties for filtering? Do we need filtering algorithms for all substructures, or can filtering be as effective when we only use one filtering algorithm for just one substructure? And how effective can CP-based Lagrangian Relaxation be in the best case?

In this paper, we prove a simple but central theorem that answers these questions. Our hope is, that the knowledge of the underlying theory of CP-based Lagrangian Relaxation will help to focus on the important issues when working on practical solution approaches. The paper is organized as follows: In the next section, we briefly review the concept of CP-based Lagrangian Relaxation. After giving an example in Section 3, we investigate the theoretical properties of the method in Section 4. A practical experiment presented in Section 5 shows the behavior of CP-based Lagrangian relaxation for a real-world problem instance. Finally, we conclude in Section 6.

2 What Is CP-Based Lagrangian Relaxation?

Given a natural number n and vectors $l, u \in \mathbb{N}^n$, we consider an integer linear optimization problem (IP) consisting of the two constraint families $\mathcal{A}$: $Ax \leq b$, $x_i \in \{l_i, \ldots, u_i\}$, and $\mathcal{B}$: $Bx \leq d$, $x_i \in \{l_i, \ldots, u_i\}$:

$$\begin{aligned}
\text{Minimize} \quad & L = c^T x \\
\text{subject to} \quad & Ax \leq b \\
& Bx \leq d \\
& x_i \in \{l_i, \ldots, u_i\}.
\end{aligned}$$

There exist many examples of real-world problems that can be decomposed naturally in that way. To mention just three: The well known traveling salesman problem for example can be viewed as a combination of an assignment problem and a special spanning tree problem [13, 14]. The automatic recording problem [24] consists in a combination of a Knapsack and a weighted stable set problem. And the network design problem consists in a shortest path problem combined with a special continuous Knapsack problem [26].

2.1 Pruning

A common way to achieve a global lower bound $\bar{L}$ on such a problem is to drop the integrality constraints $x_i \in \{l_i, \ldots, u_i\}$ and to replace them by $l_i \leq x_i \leq u_i$ instead. We get

$$\begin{aligned}
\text{Minimize} \quad & \bar{L} = c^T x \\
\text{subject to} \quad & Ax \leq b \\
& Bx \leq d \\
& l \leq x \leq u.
\end{aligned}$$

In mathematical programming, this or a similar bound would be used to identify parts of the search space that do not contain improving solutions, an idea that is called pruning: If we find that all solutions that could potentially be found in the subtree rooted at the current choice point are non-improving, we can backtrack immediately. Of course, our algorithm works the better the more accurate our bound estimate is. The trade-off here consists in finding a rather accurate bound that can still be computed quickly.

2.2 Filtering

In CP, we want to do more than pruning and that is: We would like to be able to identify those variable assignments that will not yield to feasible improving solutions. The process of removing values from variable domains because of such considerations is called *cost-based filtering* [9].

The strongest form of cost-based filtering for an optimization constraint would be to require that *all* variable assignments be identified that will not yield to improving and feasible solutions with respect to the given constraint. This corresponds to achieving generalized arc-consistency for an optimization constraint.

However, even for very elementary constraints such as Knapsack constraints or shorter path constraints this turns out to be an NP-hard problem [21], which is why the idea of *relaxed consistency* was introduced in [7].

The idea of relaxed consistency is the following: Considering the $\bar{L}$-bound, we could use that bound for cost-based filtering by solving a series of LPs $\bar{L}[x_i = v]$ where we set some variable x_i, $1 \leq i \leq n$, to some value $v \in \{l_i, \ldots, u_i\}$. Then, given an upper bound B (an upper bound is usually given by the value of the best know solution computed so far, but in some approaches, like for instance in the context of CP-based column generation, it can also reflect our search for negative reduced costs), we can eliminate v from the domain of x_i if $\bar{L}[x_i = v] \geq B$ [1]. After filtering in this fashion, we are sure that all potential variable assignments are eliminated from the problem that would cause the bound $\bar{L}$ to exceed the current best known solution value. Then, we say that this procedure achieves a state of relaxed-$\bar{L}$-consistency [7]. With respect to the lower bound that we have chosen, this is the strongest form of consistency that can be achieved for an optimization constraint.

The problem with the previous probing procedure is that it requires to reoptimize a dual feasible LP many times (and that is the case even if we used a more sophisticated binary search to compute the new bounds on the variables), which is usually unattractive with respect to the required computation time. Therefore, it has been suggested to estimate the loss in performance by carrying out exactly one dual reoptimization step. This method is known as *reduced-cost filtering* [18]. It is computationally cheap, but since it only indirectly exploits the structure of the problem it has a tendency to be rather ineffective.

2.3 How to Maintain a Global View While Reasoning Locally

To improve the inherent trade-off between computational effort and effectivity, next we may try to decompose the problem so as to be able to reason about the well-shaped substructures that we identified in the problem. Assume that efficient cost-based filtering algorithms Prop($\mathcal{A}$) and Prop($\mathcal{B}$) exist for the constraint families $\mathcal{A}$ and $\mathcal{B}$, respectively. The obvious approach to solve problem L exactly is to apply a branch-and-bound algorithm using linear relaxation bounds for pruning and the existing filtering algorithms Prop($\mathcal{A}$) and Prop($\mathcal{B}$) for tightening the problem formulation in every choice point. That is, we can easily use a global bound for pruning with respect to the objective function, and we know how to use local structure for filtering with respect to local feasibility and optimization improvement.

However, even though Prop($\mathcal{A}$) and Prop($\mathcal{B}$) may be effective for the substructures they have been designed for, their application to the combined problem is usually not. This is because tight bounds on the objective cannot be

---

[1] Note that, due to $\bar{L}[x_i \leq v] \geq \bar{L}[x_i \leq w]$ for all $w \geq v$ (the lower bound constraints follow analogously), this procedure will not split the domains of the variables x. That is, after the filtering the domains of the variables x_i can again be represented as closed intervals: $x_i \in \{\hat{l}_i, \ldots, \hat{u}_i\}$ for some $\hat{l}_i \geq l_i$ and $\hat{u}_i \leq u_i$, $1 \leq i \leq n$.

obtained by taking only a subset of the restrictions into account. An accurate bound on the overall problem can only be computed by looking at the entire problem, but it cannot be achieved by looking at either one constraint family only. The core challenge here is to bring together the merits of reasoning about one well-shaped and well-understood substructure at a time while still maintaining a global view on the overall problem.

A standard method from mathematical programming allows us to do exactly that: Lagrangian relaxation permits us to bring together the advantages of a tight global bound and the existing filtering algorithms that exploit the special structure of their respective constraint families[2]. The idea of Lagrangian relaxation is simple: we soften some of the constraints by removing them as hard constraints and penalizing their violation in the objective function. For this purpose, we introduce a vector of Lagrangian multipliers $\lambda \leq 0$ (which are our penalty factors) and define the *Lagrangian subproblem*

$$\begin{aligned} \text{Minimize} \quad & L_\mathcal{B}(\lambda) = c^T x - \lambda^T(Ax - b) \\ \text{subject to} \quad & Bx \leq d \\ & x_i \in \{l_i, \ldots, u_i\}. \end{aligned}$$

For every choice of $\lambda \leq 0$, linear programming theory tells us that $L_\mathcal{B}(\lambda)$ is a lower bound on L. Therefore, we can use this lower bound (for all choices of $\lambda \leq 0$!) and filter with respect to every objective function that is generated in that way. This is the core idea of CP-based Lagrangian Relaxation. In order to achieve good lower bounds, we embed this filtering in a search for good penalties: The Lagrangian multiplier problem or *Lagrangian dual* consists in finding the best set of penalties that will maximize the lower bound:

$$\begin{aligned} \text{Maximize} \quad & G = L_\mathcal{B}(\lambda) \\ \text{subject to} \quad & \lambda \leq 0. \end{aligned}$$

There exist a variety of iterative algorithms for optimizing the Lagrangian dual which gives rise to a piece-wise linear, concave function. Standard algorithms used in the literature are subgradient algorithms, bundle methods, and the volume algorithm [1, 3, 5, 11, 12]: we start by choosing a set of multipliers $\lambda \leq 0$, solve the Lagrangian subproblem $L_\mathcal{B}(\lambda)$ and update the multipliers guided by the solutions of the Lagrangian subproblems that were solved. This process is iterated until the process converges or until we are satisfied with the solution quality.

In summary, CP-based Lagrangian Relaxation consists in the following procedure: Assume we are given a linear optimization problem that consists in the conjunction of two constraint families $\mathcal{A}$ and $\mathcal{B}$ for which an efficient filtering algorithm Prop($\mathcal{B}$) is known. We try to optimize Lagrangian multipliers for $\mathcal{A}$ and use Prop($\mathcal{B}$) for filtering in each Lagrangian subproblem $L_\mathcal{B}(\lambda)$. That is, in each Lagrangian subproblem we use the current lower bound that we obtain to perform cost-based filtering with respect to substructure $\mathcal{B}$.

---

[2] The idea of Lagrangian relaxation was first presented in [6] for resource allocation problems. Held and Karp used it for the TSP [13, 14], and it has been applied in many different areas since then. For a general introduction we refer the reader to [1].

3 A Disturbing Example

To make the discussion less abstract, consider the following example that is an instance of the two-dimensional Knapsack problem [17]:

$$\begin{array}{ll} \text{Minimize} & -3x_1 - 3x_2 - 3x_3 \\ \text{subject to} & 9x_2 - 3x_3 \leq 6 \\ & 9x_1 + 6x_2 - 3x_3 \leq 6 \\ & x_i \in \{0, 1\}. \end{array}$$

We view the problem as composed of two Knapsack substructures, $\mathcal{A}$:

$$\begin{array}{ll} \text{Minimize} & -3x_1 - 3x_2 - 3x_3 \\ \text{subject to} & 9x_2 - 3x_3 \leq 6 \\ & x_i \in \{0, 1\}, \end{array}$$

and $\mathcal{B}$:

$$\begin{array}{ll} \text{Minimize} & -3x_1 - 3x_2 - 3x_3 \\ \text{subject to} & 9x_1 + 6x_2 - 3x_3 \leq 6 \\ & x_i \in \{0, 1\}. \end{array}$$

We assume that a Knapsack filtering algorithm for $\mathcal{B}$ exists. For our example it makes no difference whether this filtering algorithm actually achieves generalized arc-consistency for the Knapsack constraint [20, 27], or whether it achieves a state of relaxed consistency only [7, 20]. We will present the effect of both types of filtering algorithms. To make the description of our example complete, let us assume that we are looking for solutions with an objective cost lower or equal -3 only.

We observe: Neither with respect to substructure $\mathcal{A}$ nor with respect to substructure $\mathcal{B}$ is it possible to filter any value from the variables' domains!

Therefore, following the idea of CP-based Lagrangian Relaxation, we choose a multiplier $\lambda \leq 0$, say $\lambda := -1/2$, and we relax the substructure $\mathcal{A}$ into the objective function. We achieve $L_{\mathcal{B}}(-\frac{1}{2})$:

$$\begin{array}{ll} \text{Minimize} & -3x_1 + \frac{3}{2}x_2 - \frac{9}{2}x_3 - 3 \\ \text{subject to} & 9x_1 + 6x_2 - 3x_3 \leq 6 \\ & x_i \in \{0, 1\}. \end{array}$$

An optimal integer and fractional solution to this problem is $x^T = (1, 0, 1)$ with an objective cost of -21/2 which is clearly lower or equal -3. Thus, this lower bound does not allow us to prune the current node. Moreover, we can see also that cost-based filtering again has no effect (even if we use an arc-consistency filtering algorithm for the Knapsack constraint). However, we are still in the process of finding a good Lagrangian multiplier, so we keep our hopes high and continue with $\lambda := -1/7$. We get $L_{\mathcal{B}}(-\frac{1}{7})$:

$$\begin{array}{ll} \text{Minimize} & -3x_1 - \frac{12}{7}x_2 - \frac{24}{7}x_3 - \frac{6}{7} \\ \text{subject to} & 9x_1 + 6x_2 - 3x_3 \leq 6 \\ & x_i \in \{0, 1\}. \end{array}$$

The optimal integer and fractional solution to this problem is $x^T = (1,0,1)$ with an objective cost of -51/7 which is also lower or equal -3. So again, we cannot prune the search at this stage. However, no matter whether we use an arc-consistency filtering routine or whether we only achieve relaxed consistency, now we can infer that $x_3 = 1$: The arc-consistency algorithm infers that if $x_3 = 0$ then the best we can do is to set $x_2 = 1$ and $x_1 = 0$ which results in an objective cost of -18/7 which is not lower or equal -3 anymore. In case that we use a filtering routine based on relaxed continuous consistency, the best we can do after setting $x_3 = 0$ is to set $x_1 = 2/3$ and $x_2 = 0$ which results in an objective cost of -20/7 which is also greater than -3.

At this stage, what we would actually like to do is to remove value 0 form the domain of variable x_3. However, we have to be very careful here since we are still in the search for an optimal Lagrangian multiplier λ, and the standard approaches for the optimization of the Lagrangian dual are not guaranteed to be robust enough to permit a change of the underlying problem during the optimization. Therefore, we just note that value 0 is subject to deletion of the domain of x_3 right after the Lagrangian dual has been solved.

We may now consider to set $\lambda = 0$, which results in $L_\mathcal{B}(0)$:

$$\begin{aligned} \text{Minimize} \quad & -3x_1 - 3x_2 - 3x_3 \\ \text{subject to} \quad & 9x_1 + 6x_2 - 3x_3 \leq 6 \\ & x_i \in \{0,1\}. \end{aligned}$$

The best integer solution for this problem is again $x^T = (1,0,1)$ with an objective cost of -6 (the best fractional solution is $x^T = (\frac{1}{3}, 1, 1)$ with an associated cost of -7). But wait: $L_\mathcal{B}(0)$ is the same as $L_\mathcal{B}$, and for $L_\mathcal{B}$ we had found before that we cannot filter any value from the variables' domains. So how can it be that for $L_\mathcal{B}(-\frac{1}{7})$ we find a lower bound of -51/7, but are able to detect that $x_3 \neq 0$, while for $L_\mathcal{B}(0)$ we find an improved (as a matter of fact: optimal) lower bound of -6 (or -7) but cannot filter at all?!

4 Properties of CP-Based Lagrangian Relaxation

4.1 The Theorem of Filtering Penalties

Let us state the situation that we find ourselves in again: We have found an example that shows that there exist Lagrangian multipliers that yield to a worse bound and at the same time to more filtering. We are left with a heap of questions: How can that be when it is the bound estimate that is the basis of our reasoning that a certain variable assignment will not yield to an improving solution? What are good multipliers for filtering if it is not the same set that solves the Lagrangian dual? How effective can CP-based Lagrangian Relaxation be when compared with relaxed-$\bar{L}$-consistency? And wouldn't it strengthen our filtering method if we could also filter with respect to substructure $\mathcal{A}$ by exploiting the cost-based filtering algorithm Prop($\mathcal{A}$) ? In order to answer these questions, we prove the following simple but central *Theorem of Filtering Penalties*:

Theorem 1. *Given $1 \leq j \leq n$, a value $v \in \{l_j, \ldots, u_j\}$, let $L_\mathcal{B}(\lambda)[x_j = v]$ denote the IP that evolves when adding the constraint $x_j = v$ to $L_\mathcal{B}(\lambda)$. Furthermore, let $B \in \mathbb{Q}$ denote an upper bound on the objective of L such that $\bar{L}[x_j = v] \geq B$. Finally, denote the continuous relaxation of $L_\mathcal{B}(\lambda)$ by $\bar{L}_\mathcal{B}(\lambda)$. Then there exists a vector $\lambda \leq 0$ such that $L_\mathcal{B}(\lambda)[x_j = v] \geq \bar{L}_\mathcal{B}(\lambda)[x_j = v] \geq B$.*

Proof. Let $\lambda \leq 0$ denote a vector of optimal dual values of the constraint family $\mathcal{A}$ in $\bar{L}[x_j = v]$. The theory of Lagrangian relaxation shows that the vector λ defines optimal Lagrangian multipliers for $\bar{L}_\mathcal{B}(\lambda)[x_j = v]$, and it holds $\bar{L}_\mathcal{B}(\lambda)[x_j = v] = \bar{L}[x_j = v]$. And therefore,

$$L_\mathcal{B}(\lambda)[x_j = v] \geq \bar{L}_\mathcal{B}(\lambda)[x_j = v] = \bar{L}[x_j = v] \geq B. \qquad (1)$$

□

While this theorem looks rather technical, it has a set of important implications that will answer all our questions above:

Remark 1. The Filtering Penalties Theorem shows that for every variable x_j and value $v \in \{l_j \ldots, u_j\}$ that can be filtered with respect to the relaxation $\bar{L}$, there exists a vector of Lagrangian multipliers that allows us to filter this value with respect to the constraint family $\mathcal{B}$. More precisely, this can already be achieved when the filtering algorithm for $\mathcal{B}$ only achieves a state of relaxed-$\bar{L}_\mathcal{B}(\lambda)$-consistency.

Remark 2. When the filtering algorithm for $\mathcal{B}$ only achieves a state of relaxed-$\bar{L}_\mathcal{B}(\lambda)$-consistency, CP-based Lagrangian Relaxation is at most as effective as a filtering algorithm for the overall problem that achieves relaxed-$\bar{L}$-consistency.

Remark 3. Due to symmetry in the argumentation, we can also deduce that for every variable x_j and value $v \in \{l_j \ldots, u_j\}$ that can be filtered with respect to the relaxation $\bar{L}$, there exists a vector of Lagrangian multipliers that allows us to filter this value with respect to the constraint family $\mathcal{A}$ only. This means that, when we consider the right Lagrangian multipliers, it is completely sufficient to perform cost-based filtering with respect to one substructure only!

Remark 4. The proof of Theorem 1 also tells us what the best filtering penalties are when our cost-based filtering algorithm for substructure $\mathcal{B}$ achieves relaxed-$\bar{L}_\mathcal{B}(\lambda)$-consistency. They are not the best multipliers for the constraints in $\mathcal{A}$ in $\bar{L}$, but the best penalties for $\mathcal{A}$ in $\bar{L}[x_j = v]$! This is the reason why suboptimal multipliers can be more efficient for filtering than the optimal multipliers for the original problem.

Note that it is only the last observation that, for the first time, justifies the procedure of CP-based Lagrangian Relaxation that we proposed first in [23] and that consists in performing domain filtering not just for the optimal multipliers only, but for *all* Lagrangian multipliers that we encounter during the optimization of the Lagrangian dual. However, Remark 4 does not imply that the search for good Lagrangian multipliers should be terminated early, since an efficient tree search approach will always rely on the pruning power of good lower bound estimates. The remark just explains why it makes sense to perform cost-based filtering *during* the optimization of the Lagrangian dual and not just for the final, optimal or near-optimal multipliers only. Moreover, as we will see in the following two subsections, the observation that suboptimal Lagrangian multipliers can have stronger filtering abilities than the optimal penalties has severe consequences for the behavior of the entire method.

Another aspect is worth noting here[3]: The effect that a worse bound could lead to better filtering is actually not specific for Lagrangian relaxation. Suppose that we use a reduced-cost filtering algorithm for bounds L_1 and L_2, i.e., we filter v from the domain of variable x_i iff $L_j + \overline{c_{iv}}^j \geq B$ whereby B is an upper bound, $1 \leq j \leq 2$, and $\overline{c_{iv}}^j$ denotes the reduced costs of setting $x_i = v$ for relaxation j. You may want to think of L_1 and L_2 as emerging from two different, dual feasible solutions. Clearly, it is then possible that $L_1 \geq L_2$ but $\overline{c_{iv}}^1 < \overline{c_{iv}}^2$. Then, it may very well be the case that $L_2 + \overline{c_{iv}}^2 \geq B \geq L_1 + \overline{c_{iv}}^1$, i.e. it may so happen that lower bound L_2, although providing a worse lower bound overall, allows the reduced-cost filtering of v from the domain of x_i, while the better bound L_1 does not. Therefore, when we use for example a dual simplex algorithm to compute a lower bound, it makes perfect sense to apply reduced-cost filtering not only on the optimal simplex tableau, but also in every simplex iteration.

Note that, in the above discussion, we used the term "bound" in a very loose manner. It could really mean both: a specific lower bound that is usually associated with one dual feasible solution, or even a completely different bound, for example as represented by another relaxation. This being said, it is worth noting that, for CP-based Lagrangian Relaxation, also a dominated relaxation could result in more filtering. This stands in contrast to relaxed consistency where a dominant bounding routine (i.e. a bound that is always not worse than another) will always achieve at least as much filtering efficiency as a dominated bound. In that regard, the counter-intuitive effect of worse bounds pruning more is really caused by the heuristic nature of CP-based Lagrangian Relaxation and reduced-cost filtering.

4.2 Solving the Lagrangian Dual and Idempotence

When using CP-based Lagrangian Relaxation, after having shrunk the domain of the variables, the immediate re-application of the filtering algorithm may yield a further reduction of the domains. This effect is a result of Remark 4 and the fact that the algorithms used for the maximization of the Lagrangian dual – such as subgradient algorithms, bundle methods or the volume algorithm [3] – will in general proceed differently when the domains of the variables have changed. As a result, different Lagrangian multipliers and subproblems are investigated, which may very well result in a different filtering behavior. As a consequence, the filtering procedure as described is not idempotent [2].

---

[3] We owe this observation to an anonymous referee – thanks!

Moreover, as mentioned in Section 3, it is not clear whether domain reduction should actually take place during the optimization of the Lagrangian dual. We are safe if we just mark those values that can be deleted from variable domains and postpone the actual reduction until the Lagrangian dual is solved. On the other hand, it may be also favorable to incorporate the new knowledge as early as possible. It is subject to further research to investigate how e.g. a subgradient search can cope with changing problems, and whether convergence can still be proven in such a scenario. A practical evaluation of how subgradient algorithms can cope with changing subproblems (for example by resetting the step-length factor) was published in [26].

4.3 Continuity

Since the filtering behavior of the reduction algorithm based on Lagrangian relaxation relies on the subproblems investigated during the optimization of the Lagrangian dual, we cannot be sure that our cost-based filtering algorithm exhibits a property that we call *continuity*:

Definition 1. *Let B denote an upper bound on the minimization problem L, let $\mathcal{C}$ denote the current choice point and denote with $B_\mathcal{C}$ the best lower bound and with $B_\mathcal{C}[x = v]$ the best bound achieved regarding the removal of v from the domain of x in the current choice point $\mathcal{C}$. Consider some variable x and v in the domain of x that was not removed, i.e. $\delta := B - B_\mathcal{C}[x = v] > 0$. Now assume that a primal heuristic finds a new upper bound $\bar{B} \leq B - \delta$ next. We call a cost-based filtering algorithm continuous, if it is guaranteed that in every child node $\mathcal{D}$ of the current choice point $\mathcal{C}$ it is detected that v can be removed from the domain of x.*

In other words: A cost-based filtering algorithm is called continuous if and only if we can guarantee that a call to the filtering algorithm with smaller domains and improved upper bounds will remove at least all values that could have been deleted on the original domains if the improved upper bound had been known at that time.

As an implication of our discussion in the previous section, despite the fact that $B_\mathcal{D} \geq B_\mathcal{C}$, CP-based Lagrangian Relaxation is not a continuous filtering technique: Let $\lambda \leq 0$ denote Lagrangian multipliers in $\mathcal{C}$ that are optimal for the filtering of v from the domain of x, i.e. $L_\mathcal{B}(\lambda)[x = v] = B_\mathcal{C}[x = v]$. (Note that Remark 4 tells us that in general $L_\mathcal{B}(\lambda) < B_\mathcal{C}$!) Then we cannot be sure that, when performing problem reduction in $\mathcal{D}$, the algorithm optimizing the Lagrangian dual will investigate the Lagrangian multipliers λ. Thus, it may very well be the case that

$$B_\mathcal{D}[x = v] < \bar{B} < B_\mathcal{C}[x = v] < B.$$

There is no obvious way how this problem could be overcome. However, our awareness of the problem can motivate strategies to strengthen the filtering abilities of our method. Assume for example, that the filtering algorithm for $\mathcal{B}$

actually provides the values $B_C[x = v]$, and for every variable-value-pair (x, v) we store the maximal value computed in all previous choice points. Then, as soon as the upper bound value B drops below this value, v can be removed from the domain of x. This procedure may be viewed as generation of local no-goods of the form: $(B > \max_C B_C[x = v]) \vee (x \neq v)$.

5 A Practical Experiment

After having studied the theoretical properties of CP-based Lagrangian Relaxation, we decided to conduct some experiments in order to see how the method behaves in practice. For this purpose, we consider the resource constrained shortest path problem (RCSSP) that consists in the conjunction of two shorter-path constraints [21]. We couple the two optimization constraints by CP-based Lagrangian Relaxation, using a specialized cutting plane algorithm [15] for the optimization of the Lagrangian dual.

In Figure 1 we show the run of the optimality proof for an instance that was taken from $http://www.mpi-sb.mpg.de/\~mark/cnop$. It models the approximation of a one-dimensional curve by a piecewise-linear function with a constraint on the approximation error introduced and the objective to minimize the number of sampling points. The instance contains almost 200K directed edges.

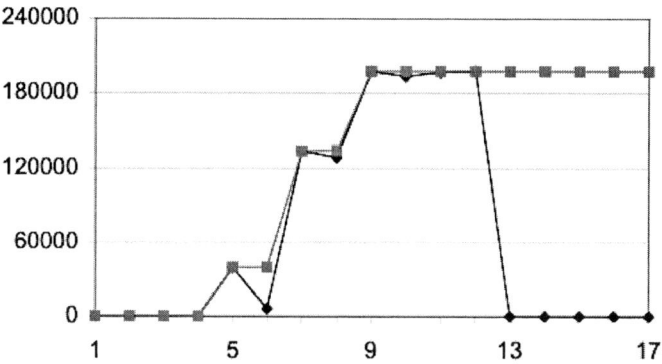

Fig. 1. The graph shows the number of edges filtered over the iterations of the cutting plane algorithm optimizing the Lagrangian dual. The upper curve gives the cardinality of the set of all edges filtered until the current iteration, the lower curve gives the number of edges filtered in the current iteration only. Note that the upper curve is not the integral of the lower, since values can be filtered in multiple iterations; this happens in iterations 7 and 8, for instance.

In the first iterations (1–4), we can see how filtering is ineffective when only the isolated substructures are considered. In general, one would expect to see some slight filtering here, but for all our tests on the RCSSP we found that this is always very marginal when compared to the filtering that can be achieved by CP-based Lagrangian Relaxation. As the quality of the Lagrangian multiplier improves (iterations 5–9), we notice that filtering becomes more and more effective. Then, in iteration 13, we suddenly notice that no filtering can be established anymore, even though we are close to finding the optimal multiplier in iteration 17. This clearly illustrates the fact that optimal multipliers need not have superior filtering abilities - as a matter of fact, the filtering achieved with optimal multipliers can be dramatically less. As we see, this is not an academic detail, but actually an effect that occurs for real-world instances.

While we observe a similar behavior for quite a few other RCSSP instances, of course the effect is not always that drastic. Often, we can also achieve very good filtering for the optimal multipliers. However, it is worth noting here that no one iteration alone is capable of filtering all edges. Iterations 9–12 come close to achieving maximum filtering effectiveness, but, as the exact numbers show, in none of them all edges are filtered that are detected throughout the optimization of the Lagrangian dual. We believe that the fact that these iterations are so effective at all is more an expression of the simple structure of the RCSSP. In general, multipliers for the filtering of different values will certainly differ as well.

6 Conclusion

We investigated the theoretical foundations of CP-based Lagrangian Relaxation. An example showed that suboptimal Lagrangian multipliers can have stronger filtering abilities than optimal penalties. We were able to explain this counter-intuitive observation by proving the simple but central Theorem of Filtering Penalties. It allowed us to derive several properties of CP-based Lagrangian Relaxation: 1. When cost-based filtering for the optimization substructures is based on linear continuous bounds, CP-based Lagrangian Relaxation is at most as effective as a filtering algorithm that achieves relaxed-$\bar{L}$-consistency for the entire problem. 2. If we traverse the right Lagrangian multipliers during the optimization of the Lagrangian dual and filtering is based on linear continuous bounds, then filtering with respect to one substructure alone is as effective as filtering with respect to all substructures. 3. CP-based Lagrangian Relaxation is neither an idempotent nor a continuous propagation technique.

Our hope is that the theoretical understanding of the technique will help to engineer superior solution approaches for composed combinatorial optimization problems. We have seen already that the theoretical discussion can stimulate new ideas such as the addition of local no-goods. An important practical question regards the time when the actual filtering effects are executed and whether this can be done during the optimization of the Lagrangian dual. Some work in the past has focused on improving the lower bounds during the solution of the Lagrangian dual. Our work shows that this does not not necessarily imply an improved filtering behavior, and careful testing is required to evaluate the practical benefits of doing so.

Finally, we have seen that it can be as efficient when filtering with respect to just one substructure only as it is when applying filtering algorithms to all substructures in the problem. Our previous practical experience confirms this theoretical finding. For capacitated network design for example, it did not pay off to filter with respect to both the shortest path and the Knapsack substructures [26]. Moreover, in the context of automatic recording the application of Knapsack filtering on top of weighted stable set filtering only paid off marginally [25]. Note also that for this problem the number of Lagrangian subproblems that had to be investigated to optimize the Lagrangian dual was very low, which decreases our chances to traverse the good filtering penalties. Therefore, attempts to integrate several filtering algorithms in a Lagrangian fashion must be viewed very critically: Filtering more than one substructure may be a pure waste of time, especially when filtering is based on linear bounds and when many Lagrangian subproblems are investigated during the solution of the Lagrangian dual.

Acknowledgment

We would like to thank Robert Wright for conducting many numerical experiments on the RCSSP and for providing Figure 1.

References

1. R.K. Ahuja, T.L. Magnati, and J.B. Orlin. *Network Flows*. Prentice Hall, 1993.
2. K. R. Apt. The Rough Guide to Constraint Propagation. *5th International Conference on Principles and Practice of Constraint Programming (CP)*, LNCS 1713:1–23, 1999.
3. F. Barahona and R. Anbil. The Volume Algorithm: producing primal solutions with a subgradient algorithm. *Mathematical Programming*, 87:385–399, 2000.
4. Y. Caseau and F. Laburthe. Solving Small TSPs with Constraints. *14th International Conference on Logic Programming (ICLP)*, pp. 316–330, The MIT Press, 1997.
5. H. Crowder. Computational improvements for subgradient optimization. *Symposia Mathematica*, XIX:357–372, 1976.
6. H. Everett. Generalized lagrange multiplier method for solving problems of optimum allocation of resource. *Operations Research*, 11:399–417, 1963.
7. T. Fahle and M. Sellmann. Cost-Based Filtering for the Constrained Knapsack Problem. *Annals of Operations Research*, 115:73–93, 2002.
8. F. Focacci, A. Lodi, and M. Milano. Cutting Planes in Constraint Programming: an hybrid approach. *Proceedings of the 6th International Conference on Principles and Practice of Constraint Programming (CP)*, Springer LNCS 1894:187–201, 2000.
9. F. Focacci, A. Lodi, and M. Milano. Cost-Based Domain Filtering. *5th International Conference on Principles and Practice of Constraint Programming (CP)*, LNCS 1713:189–203, 1999.
10. F. Focacci, A. Lodi, and M. Milano. Solving TSP through the Integration of OR and CP Techniques. *Workshop on Large Scale Combinatorial Optimization and Constraints*, Electronic Notes in Discrete Mathematics, 1998.
11. A. Frangioni. A Bundle type Dual-ascent Approach to Linear Multi-Commodity Min Cost Flow Problems. *Technical Report*, Dipartimento di Informatica, Universita di Pisa, TR-96-01, 1996.

12. A. Frangioni. Dual Ascent Methods and Multicommodity Flow Problems. *Doctoral Thesis*, Dipartimento di Informatica, Universita di Pisa, TD-97-05, 1997.
13. M. Held and R.M. Karp. The traveling-salesman problem and minimum spanning trees. *Operations Research*, 18:1138–1162, 1970.
14. M. Held and R.M. Karp. The traveling-salesman problem and minimum spanning trees: Part II. *Mathematical Programming*, 1:6–25, 1971.
15. J.E. Kelley. The Cutting Plane Method for Solving Convex Programs. *Journal of the SIAM*, 8:703–712, 1960.
16. G. Kliewer, M. Sellmann, and A. Koberstein. Solving the capacitated network design problem in parallel. *3rd meeting of the PAREO Euro working group on Parallel Processing in Operations Research (PAREO)*, 2002.
17. S. Martello and P. Toth. An exact algorithm for the Two-Constraint 0-1 Knapsack Problem. *Operations Research*, 51:826–835, 2003.
18. G. Ottosson and E.S. Thorsteinsson. Linear Relaxation and Reduced-Cost Based Propagation of Continuous Variable Subscripts. *2nd International Workshop on Integration of AI and OR Techniques in Constraint Programming for Combinatorial Optimization Problems (CP-AI-OR)*, Paderborn Center for Parallel Computing, Technical Report tr-001-2000:129–138, 2000.
19. M. Sellmann. The Practice of Approximated Consistency for Knapsack Constraints. *National Conference on Artificial Intelligence (AAAI)*, to appear, 2004.
20. M. Sellmann. Approximated Consistency for Knapsack Constraints. *Principles and Practice of Constraint Programming (CP)*, Springer LNCS 2833: 679–693, 2003.
21. M. Sellmann. Cost-Based Filtering for Shorter Path Constraints. *Principles and Practice of Constraint Programming (CP)*, Springer LNCS 2833: 694–708, 2003.
22. M. Sellmann. Pruning Techniques in Constraint Programming and Combinatorial Optimization. *Ph.D. Thesis*, University of Paderborn, 2002.
23. M. Sellmann and T. Fahle. CP-Based Lagrangian Relaxation for a Multimedia Application. *3rd International Workshop on Integration of AI and OR Techniques in Constraint Programming for Combinatorial Optimization Problems (CP-AI-OR)*, pp. 1–14, 2001.
24. M. Sellmann and T. Fahle. Coupling Variable Fixing Algorithms for the Automatic Recording Problem. *9th Annual European Symposium on Algorithms (ESA)*, LNCS 2161:134–145, 2001.
25. M. Sellmann and T. Fahle. Constraint Programming Based Lagrangian Relaxation for the Automatic Recording Problem. *Annals of Operations Research*, 118:17–33, 2003.
26. M. Sellmann, G. Kliewer, and A. Koberstein. Lagrangian Cardinality Cuts and Variable Fixing for Capacitated Network Design. *10th Annual European Symposium on Algorithms (ESA)*, LNCS 2461:845–858, 2002.
27. M. Trick. A Dynamic Programming Approach for Consistency and Propagation for Knapsack Constraints. *3rd International Workshop on Integration of AI and OR Techniques in Constraint Programming for Combinatorial Optimization Problems (CP-AI-OR)*, pp. 113–124, 2001.

A Constraint for Bin Packing

Paul Shaw

ILOG S.A., Les Taissounieres HB2
2681 Route des Dolines, 06560 Valbonne, France
pshaw@ilog.fr

Abstract. We introduce a constraint for one-dimensional bin packing. This constraint uses propagation rules incorporating knapsack-based reasoning, as well as a lower bound on the number of bins needed. We show that this constraint can significantly reduce search on bin packing problems. We also demonstrate that when coupled with a standard bin packing search strategy, our constraint can be a competitive alternative to established operations research bin packing algorithms.

1 Introduction

The one-dimensional bin packing problem is described as follows: Given n indivisible items, each of a known non-negative size s_i, and m bins, each of capacity C, can we pack all n items into the m bins such that the sum of the sizes of the items in any bin is not greater than C? This problem is an important NP-complete problem having various applications (a good review paper [2] cites stock cutting and television commercial break scheduling as well as the obvious application of physical packing).

In recent years, good exact algorithms for the bin packing problem have been put forward (for example, see [10, 11, 15]), so why examine a constraint-based approach? The main reason is that most real bin packing problems are not pure ones, but form a component of a larger system. For example, almost all resource allocation problems have a bin packing component; this set includes timetabling, rostering, scheduling, facility location, line balancing, and so on. When problems become less pure, standard algorithms often become inapplicable, making constraint programming more attractive. Additionally, the use of a dedicated constraint (in place of a collection of constraints defining the same solution set) normally allows for a significant increase in constraint propagation, the all-different constraint [14] being the classic example.

In this paper, we introduce a dedicated constraint $\mathcal{P}$ for the one-dimensional bin packing problem. Section 2 introduces some notation as well as a typical bin packing model. Section 3 describes new pruning and propagation rules based on reasoning over single bins. Section 4 then introduces a lower bounding method on the number of bins used. Section 5 describes experiments on the new constraint. Finally, section 6 describes the most relevant work and section 7 concludes.

2 Preliminaries

2.1 General Notation

All constrained variables we consider in this paper are non-negative integer. Associated with each variable x is an initial domain $D_0(x) \subset \{0\ldots\infty\}$. The goal is to assign each variable an element from its domain without violating any constraints: such an assignment is referred to as a *solution*. We assume that this assignment procedure proceeds constructively, building the solution one piece at a time. At each point in this construction, we have a *partial assignment* which we define to be the set of *current domains* of all variables. The current domain $D(x)$ of variable x is always a (non-strict) subset of its initial domain $D_0(x)$. We also denote the minimum and maximum of the domain of x in the current partial assignment as $\underline{x}$ and $\overline{x}$ respectively.

When performing a domain reduction on a variable x, assume that $D'(x)$ is the domain of x after the reduction. We use $x \leftarrow a$ to denote $D'(x) = D(x) \cap a$, $\underline{x} \leftarrow a$ to denote $D'(x) = D(x) \cap \{a\ldots\infty\}$, $\overline{x} \leftarrow a$ to denote $D'(x) = D(x) \cap \{0\ldots a\}$, and $x \not\leftarrow a$ to denote $D'(x) = D(x)\setminus a$.

If at any time, for any variable x, $D(x) = \emptyset$, then the constraint system prunes the search. What happens then depends on the search strategy employed, but normally the search will backtrack to a previous choice point (if one exists), changing an earlier decision.

2.2 Bin Packing Problem

Any instance of the packing constraint $\mathcal{P}$ takes three parameters which are a vector of m constrained variables $l = \langle l_1 \ldots l_m \rangle$ representing the *load* of each bin, a vector of n constrained variables $b = \langle b_1 \ldots b_n \rangle$ indicating, for each item, the index of the bin into which it will be placed, and a vector of n non-negative integers $s = \langle s_1 \ldots s_n \rangle$ representing the size of each item to be packed. Without loss of generality, we assume that the sizes are sorted according to $s_i \geq s_{i+1}$. The total size to be packed is denoted by $S = \sum_{i=1}^{n} s_i$. The set of item indices is represented by $I = \{1\ldots n\}$ and the set of bin indices by $B = \{1\ldots m\}$.

Note that, because variables in b and l can have arbitrary domains when given to the constraint, problems more general that pure bin packing problems can be specified. These include variable-sized bin packing [4], problems where bins have a minimum load requirement, and those where not all items can be packed in all bins.

The semantics of the bin packing problem dictate that $\mathcal{P}$ must ensure for each bin $j \in B$ that $l_j = \sum_{\{i \mid i \in I \wedge b_i = j\}} s_i$ and for each item $i \in I$ that $b_i \in B$.

2.3 Bin Packing Notation

We introduce some notation to specify the states of bins in partial assignments. We define as the *possible set* P_j of a bin j as the set of items that are packed or may potentially be packed in it: $P_j = \{i \mid i \in I \wedge j \in D(b_i)\}$. We define the *required set* R_j of bin j as the set of items packed in the bin: $R_j = \{i \mid i \in P_j \wedge |D(b_i)| = 1\}$. We refer to $C_j = P_j - R_j$ as the *candidate set* of bin j. We refer to the total size of items packed in bin j as $p_j = \sum_{i \in R_j} s_i$, and to the set of unpacked items as $U = \{i \mid i \in I \wedge |D(b_i)| > 1\}$.

2.4 Typical Bin Packing Model

We present what we consider to be a typical constraint programming model of the bin packing problem, which will be referred to as a comparison base in the rest of the paper. We introduce intermediate 0–1 variables $x_{i,j}$ that determine if item i has been placed in bin j. These variables are maintained by nm constraints as below. We have, for each item i:

$$\forall j \in B \; x_{i,j} = 1 \Leftrightarrow b_i = j$$

Alternatively, we could remove the b variables from the model and add n constraints of the form $\sum_{j \in B} x_{i,j} = 1$. The x variables would then become the decision variables.

The loads on the bins are maintained by m scalar products. For bin j we have:

$$l_j = \sum_{i \in I} w_i x_{i,j}$$

All items must be packed, and for each item i:

$$b_i \in B$$

Finally, it is often useful to add the redundant constraint specifying that the sum of the bin loads is equal to the sum of the item sizes.

$$\sum_{j \in B} l_j = S$$

2.5 Propagations Performed Both by the Typical Model and by $\mathcal{P}$

When the typical model in the previous section is implemented in ILOG Solver [7] it carries out certain "basic" constraint propagations. These propagations are also carried out by $\mathcal{P}$, and each one of them is detailed in this section.

Pack All. All items must be packed. This is enforced for each item $i \in I$ via:

$$\underline{b_i} \leftarrow 1 \qquad\qquad \overline{b_i} \leftarrow m$$

Load Maintenance. The minimum and maximum load of each bin is maintained according to the domains of the bin assignment variables b. For brevity, we denote $\text{SUM}(X) = \sum_{i \in X} s_i$, where $X \subseteq I$ is any set of items under consideration. For each bin $j \in B$:

$$\underline{l_j} \leftarrow \text{SUM}(R_j) \qquad\qquad \overline{l_j} \leftarrow \text{SUM}(P_j)$$

Load and Size Coherence. We perform the following propagations which are derived from the fact that the sum of the items sizes must be equal to the sum of bin loads. This means that for any bin $j \in B$, its load is equal to the total size to be packed, minus the loads of all other bins. This translates into the following propagation rules:

$$\underline{l_j} \leftarrow S - \sum_{k \in B \setminus j} \overline{l_k} \qquad \overline{l_j} \leftarrow S - \sum_{k \in B \setminus j} \underline{l_k}$$

This propagation rule is very important as it is only rule which communicates information between different bins (aside from the implicit rule disallowing item i from all bins other than j when item i is packed in bin j.) Especially important is that it can increase the *lower bound* of the bin load. This property is analogous to the notion of spare capacity used in [5]. The spare capacity sc in a bin packing problem is $sc = mC - S$ (the capacity available less the total size to be packed). In any solution, each bin must be filled to at least a level of $C - sc$, otherwise more space would be wasted than spare capacity available. The above propagation rules dynamically maintain this information, propagating bounds on load and implicitly reducing spare capacity when a bin is packed to less than its full capacity.

The commitment rule below makes use of the lower bound on bin load, as do the additional pruning and propagation rules introduced in section 3.

Single Item Elimination and Commitment. An item is eliminated as a candidate for packing in a bin if it cannot be added to the bin without the maximum load being exceeded. For bin j:

$$\text{if } \exists i \ i \in C_j \land p_j + s_i > \overline{l_j} \text{ then } b_i \not\leftarrow j$$

An item is committed to a bin if packing all candidates into the bin except that item would not increase the packed quantity to the required minimum load of the bin. For bin j:

$$\text{if } \exists i \ i \in C_j \land \text{SUM}(P_j) - s_i < \underline{l_j} \text{ then } b_i \leftarrow j$$

3 Additional Propagation Rules

The idea of constraint propagation is to eliminate domain values when it can be ascertained that these values can never appear in a solution to the constraint. (A solution to a constraint is an assignment of all variables involved in the constraint which does not violate the constraint.) Constraint propagation algorithms often try to achieve generalized arc consistency (GAC) which means that *all* values which cannot be involved in a solution to the constraint are removed. Unfortunately, for the packing constraint $\mathcal{P}$, achieving GAC is NP-complete. So, instead of trying to achieve GAC, we set ourselves the more humble goal of increasing propagation strength over that of the typical model.

The additional constraint propagation rules that we introduce are all based upon treating the simpler problem of packing a single bin. That is, given a bin j, can we find a subset of C_j that when packed in the bin would bring the load the range $[l_j, \overline{l_j}]$? This problem is a type of knapsack or subset sum problem [9]. Proving that there is no solution to this problem for any bin j would mean that search could be pruned. However, as shown by Trick [17], we can go further and even achieve GAC for this reduced single-bin problem.

For bin j we define $M_j = \{m \mid m \subseteq C_j \wedge \underline{l_j} \leq p_j + \text{Sum}(m) \leq \overline{l_j}\}$. M_j is the set of sets of additional items which can be packed while respecting the constraints on load. If M_j is empty, there is no legal packing of bin j, and we can prune search. For $M_j \neq \emptyset$, we make deductions on the candidate items:

$$\text{if } \forall m \in M_j \ i \in m \text{ then } b_i \leftarrow j \qquad \text{if } \forall m \in M_j \ i \notin m \text{ then } b_i \nleftarrow j$$

That is, if an item appears in every set of items that can be placed in the bin, we can commit it to the bin. Conversely, if the item never appears in such a set, we can eliminate it as a candidate item. Trick did not treat the case where the load was a variable, but it is nevertheless possible to deduce illegal bin loads:

$$\text{if } \exists v \in D(l_j) \ \forall m \in M_j \ v \notin m \text{ then } l_j \nleftarrow v$$

So, if no legal packing can attain load v, v cannot be a legal load for the bin.

In [17], a pseudo-polynomial dynamic programming algorithm is used to achieve consistency. The time complexity of the algorithm is $O(|C_j|\overline{l_j}^2)$, meaning that it can become inefficient when items are large or many items can be packed in a bin. Sellmann [16] proposes an approach where efficiency can be traded for propagation strength by dividing down values; in our case, item sizes and bin capacities. By selecting an appropriate divisor, the resulting algorithm can produce a trade-off between propagation strength and time invested. Here, we take a different approach, using efficient algorithms which do not depend on item size or bin capacity, but which like [16], do not in general achieve GAC on the subset sum subproblem.

3.1 Detecting Non-packable Bins

Here, we describe a method which can detect non-packable bins in time $O(|C_j|)$. The advantage of the method is its efficiency; the drawback is that it is not complete, and some non-packable bins may not be identified as such.

We try to find a proof that $\forall m \subseteq C_j \ p_j + \text{Sum}(m) < \underline{l_j} \vee p_j + \text{Sum}(m) > \overline{l_j}$. That is, there is no subset of candidate items whose sizes – together with the already packed items – sum to a legal load. We search for this proof in a particular way based on identifying what we refer to as *neighboring subsets*[1] of C_j. Assume two sets $C_j^1, C_j^2 \subseteq C_j$. These sets are neighboring if there is no other subset of C_j whose items sum to a value strictly between $\text{Sum}(C_j^1)$ and $\text{Sum}(C_j^2)$. (This

---

[1] The author has found no pre-existing definition of the proposed notion in the literature.

implies that C_j^1 and C_j^2 are neighboring if $|\text{SUM}(C_j^2) - \text{SUM}(C_j^1)| \leq 1$.) We describe a neighboring predicate $N(j, C_j^1, C_j^2)$ as follows:

$$N(C_j^1, C_j^2) \Leftrightarrow N(C_j^2, C_j^1)$$

$$\text{SUM}(C_j^1) \leq \text{SUM}(C_j^2) \Rightarrow (N(C_j^1, C_j^2) \vee \text{BETWEEN}(j, C_j^1, C_j^2))$$

$$\text{BETWEEN}(j, C_j^1, C_j^2) \Leftrightarrow \exists m \subseteq C_j \ \text{SUM}(C_j^1) < \text{SUM}(m) < \text{SUM}(C_j^2)$$

Generation of Neighboring Subsets. Neighboring subsets are generated which conform to a particular structure. We use the terms *low-set* and *high-set* for two subsets which we consider as candidates for being neighbors. The understanding is that when the low-set has a sum not greater than the high-set, then the two subsets are neighbors. This will become clearer in what follows.

Figure 1 shows a set of candidate items X sorted by non-increasing size, and three subsets marked A, B and C. Subset A comprises the k largest candidate items. Subset C comprises the k' smallest candidate items. Subset B comprises the $k + 1$ smallest items outside subset C. Subsets A and B may contain the same item, but subset C is disjoint from the other two. We choose the low-set L_k to be the union of subsets A and C and the high-set H_k to be the subset B.

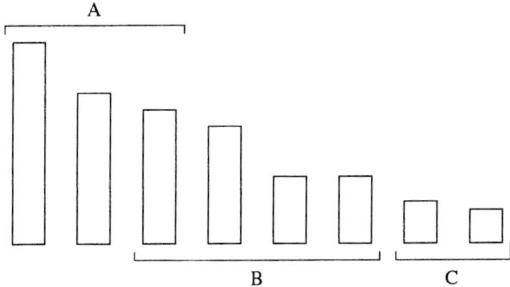

Fig. 1. Structure of neighboring subsets

We now show that for this particular structure, if $\text{SUM}(L_k) \leq \text{SUM}(H_k)$, then L_k and H_k are neighboring. When $\text{SUM}(L_k) = \text{SUM}(H_k)$, the proof is trivial. We therefore concentrate on the case where $\text{SUM}(L_k) < \text{SUM}(H_k)$. L_k is formed from the k largest items and the k' smallest items. We can see that for any $m \subseteq X$ for which $\text{SUM}(m) > \text{SUM}(L_k)$, $|m| \geq k + 1$. This must be the case as L_k already contains the k largest items. Moreover m cannot contain any of the k' smallest items as then $\text{SUM}(L_k) \geq \text{SUM}(H_k)$ in contradiction to our initial assumption. To see this, imagine $i \in m$ and that i is one of the smallest k' items in X. In this case m is composed of k items not in the smallest k' and item i, while L_k is composed of the largest k items, plus item i (and possibly some other items). Since the largest k items must have a total size not less than k items chosen more freely, it follows that if m contains one of the k' smallest items then

boolean function NoSum(X, α, β)
  if $\alpha \leq 0 \vee \beta \geq$ Sum(X) **then**
    return false
  $\Sigma_A, \Sigma_B, \Sigma_C := 0$ {See figure 1 for meaning of A, B, C}
  $k, k' := 0$ {k largest items, k' smallest items}
  while $\Sigma_C + s_{|X|-k'} < \alpha$ **do**
    $\Sigma_C := \Sigma_C + s_{|X|-k'}$
    $k' := k' + 1$
  end while
  $\Sigma_B := s_{|X|-k'}$
  while $\Sigma_A < \alpha \wedge \Sigma_B \leq \beta$ **do**
    $k := k + 1$
    $\Sigma_A := \Sigma_A + s_k$
    if $\Sigma_A < \alpha$ **then**
      $k' := k' - 1$
      $\Sigma_B := \Sigma_B + s_{|X|-k'}$
      $\Sigma_C := \Sigma_C - s_{|X|-k'}$
      while $\Sigma_A + \Sigma_C \geq \alpha$ **do**
        $k' := k' - 1$
        $\Sigma_C := \Sigma_C - s_{|X|-k'}$
        $\Sigma_B := \Sigma_B + s_{|X|-k'} - s_{|X|-k'-k-1}$
      end while
    end if
  end while
  return $\Sigma_A < \alpha$
end function

Fig. 2. Procedure for detecting non-existence of sums in $[\alpha, \beta]$

Sum$(m) \leq$ Sum(L_k). Having now discounted the smallest k' items from m, the smallest Sum(m) is then obtained when m is made up of the $k+1$ smallest items outside of the smallest k', i.e. when $m = H_k$.

As an example of this reasoning, we consider a bin j with $p_j = 0$, $l_j = 34$, $\overline{l_j} = 35$ and candidates items of sizes 10, 10, 10, 9, 9, 9, 9, 2, 1. The bin can be shown non-packable by considering the neighboring subsets produced when $k = 3$ and $k' = 2$. In this case, the low-set sums to $10 + 10 + 10 + 2 + 1 = 33$ and the high-set to $9 + 9 + 9 + 9 = 36$.

Implementation. Here we describe a procedure NoSum which determines if a subset of a set of items X cannot sum to a value in the range $[\alpha, \beta]$. Being an incomplete method, NoSum can generate false negatives but this is not problematic as only the positive result is actively used in pruning. We remind the reader that item sizes obey the relation $s_i \geq s_{i+1}$. NoSum is detailed in figure 2.

The method is reasonably simple despite its appearance. The variables Σ_A, Σ_B and Σ_C hold the total sizes of items in the subsets A, B, and C shown in figure 1. The variables k and k' keep their meaning from the previous section.

Essentially, k is increased from 0 until the k largest items are not less than α, the lower bound on the required sum. For each k, k' is chosen such that $\Sigma_A + \Sigma_C$ is maximized while being less than α. This is done initially by adding up the k' smallest item sizes. Thereafter, each time k is increased, k' is reduced again until $\Sigma_A + \Sigma_C < \alpha$. During this reduction phase, Σ_B is maintained by 'sliding' the window of the B subset to the right so that it remains adjacent to subset C (again, see figure 1). If we find that $\Sigma_B > \beta$, then we have found a proof that no subset of the items can sum to a value in $[\alpha, \beta]$.

The time complexity of NoSum is linear in $|X|$, but is usually much better as it is bounded by the value of k' after the initial loop. That is, the maximum number of candidate items that can be added together while maintaining their sum strictly less than α. We refer to this quantity as N_j^α. We assume that $\text{Sum}(X)$ can be computed in constant time by incrementally maintaining the total item size of any candidate set when it is reduced.

3.2 Pruning Rule

Given the function NoSum, it is trivial to derive a pruning rule. The only manipulation needed is to remove the effect of items already packed in the bin from the load target. For any bin j:

$$\text{if NoSum}(C_j, \underline{l_j} - p_j, \overline{l_j} - p_j) \text{ then } \textbf{prune}$$

3.3 Tightening Bounds on Bin Load

The reasoning used for detecting non-packable bins can also be used to tighten bounds on the bin load. For this, NoSum needs slight modification to deliver on return the values of $\alpha' = \Sigma_A + \Sigma_C$ and $\beta' = \Sigma_B$. These are the total sizes of the two neighboring subsets when NoSum answers in the affirmative. We can then specify the tightening rules as:

$$\text{if NoSum}(C_j, \underline{l_j} - p_j, \underline{l_j} - p_j) \text{ then } \underline{l_j} \leftarrow p_j + \beta'$$

$$\text{if NoSum}(C_j, \overline{l_j} - p_j, \overline{l_j} - p_j) \text{ then } \overline{l_j} \leftarrow p_j + \alpha'$$

3.4 Elimination and Commitment of Items

As proposed in [5], we construct from the pruning rule propagation rules to eliminate and commit items. We make a proposition, then ask the pruning rule if this proposition leads to a contradiction; if so, we can assert the negation of the proposition. We commit item i to bin j and then ask if bin j is packable. If it is not, then i can be eliminated from the candidates of bin j. A similar argument holds for committing items; we assume that i is eliminated, then ask if the bin is packable. If not, we can commit the item to the bin. Given a candidate item $i \in C_j$:

$$\text{if NoSum}(C_j \backslash i, \underline{l_j} - p_j - s_i, \overline{l_j} - p_j - s_i) \text{ then } b_i \neq j$$

$$\text{if NoSum}(C_j \backslash i, \underline{l_j} - p_j, \overline{l_j} - p_j) \text{ then } b_i \leftarrow j$$

In both of these rules, item i is eliminated as a candidate, but in the first, the bounds passed to NoSum are reduced to reflect the increased size of the packed items due to the inclusion of i in R_j. In the second rule, the proposition is to eliminate an item and so the packed size does not change.

Examining a bin j for all item eliminations and commitments takes time $O(|C_j|N_j^{l_j})$, which can be up to $O(|C_j|^2)$ but is typically much less as normally $N_j^{l_j} \ll |C_j|$. When the pruning rule is restricted to consider only neighboring subsets for which either $k = 0$ or $k' = 0$, we know of algorithms which run in time $O(|C_j|)$. These algorithms combine the logic of the pruning and propagation in one procedure and are thus more complex than the use of the pruning rule as a subordinate procedure. In this paper, these linear algorithms are not used do to their increased complexity, reduced propagation strength (as the pruning rule used is less general), and marginal reduction in calculation time per search node.

4 Using a Lower Bound

The usual simple lower bound for the fixed capacity bin packing problem is arrived at by relaxing the constraint that each item is indivisible. Given a fixed capacity C, the bound, which we shall term L_1 (following Martello and Toth [13]) is:

$$L_1(C, s) = \left\lceil \frac{1}{C} \sum_{i \in I} s_i \right\rceil$$

Martello and Toth showed L_1 to have an asymptotic performance ratio of $\frac{1}{2}$, which means that the the bound L_1 can be arbitrarily close to one half of the number of bins used in an optimal solution.

However there are better bounds which also are efficient to compute. In [13], Martello and Toth introduced bound L_2 which dominates L_1 and has an asymptotic performance ratio of $\frac{2}{3}$. In their experiments, Martello and Toth show this bound to be typically much tighter than L_1. Korf [10] also found this. In his tests on problems with random sizes from 0 up to the bin capacity, 90 item problems require an average of 47.68 bins. For these problems, the L_1 bound averaged 45.497, whereas the L_2 bound averaged 47.428. The L_2 bound can be calculated in linear time if the item sizes are sorted.

The bound works by splitting the items into four subsets using a parameter K. N_1 contains all items that are strictly larger than $C - K$. N_2 contains all items not in N_1, but which are strictly larger than half the bin capacity. N_3 contains all items not in N_1 or N_2 of size at least K. The items of size strictly less than K are not considered. Now, no items from N_2 or N_3 can be placed with items from N_1, so $|N_1|$ forms a term of the lower bound. Moreover, each item in $|N_2|$ needs a bin of its own and so $|N_2|$ forms another term. Finally, the free space in the bins of N_2 is subtracted from the total size of items in N_3 (as items in N_3 can be placed with those in N_2). If the result is positive, this is an overspill which will consume more bins. The result of this extra bin calculation is added to $|N_1| + |N_2|$ to arrive at the bound for a given K. The maximum of this bound calculation over all $0 \leq K \leq C/2$ is the lower bound L_2.

4.1 Adapting the Lower Bound to Partial Solutions

One simple way to apply the lower bound for a fixed capacity bin packing problem is to do so before search begins. If L_2 returns a value greater than the number of bins available, then we can declare the problem infeasible. However, we would like to benefit from the lower bound test when bins are of different sizes, meaning that it could be applied during search as well as treating problems that have bins of variable sizes from the outset.

The idea is that after each extension of the partial assignment of items to bins, we transform the current partial assignment into one which can be handled by the bounding function L_2. We then prune the search if the lower bound calculated exceeds the number of bins available.

The transformation carried out is relatively straightforward. First, we find the bin with the maximum potential load; this will then become the fixed capacity in the transformed problem: $C = \max_{j \in B} \overline{l_j}$. Then, in order to account for items already packed as well as bin capacities less than C, we create a new vector z of item sizes that contains the sizes of all item in U, the unpacked items, plus one additional item a_j for each bin j. We define:

$$a_j = p_j + C - \overline{l_j}$$

This requires some explanation as it involves two manipulations. First, we are introducing items into the packing problem representing the already packed items. We could just add the items themselves, but that would miss the opportunity to group items that have already been packed together. When we group these items, we have the potential for a better bound. Second, we are introducing items to 'top up' each bin with capacity less than C. That is, we have overestimated the capacity of bin j. So, to emulate the fact that a bin has a lesser capacity, we introduce an item into the transformed packing problem which says that an additional $C - \overline{l_j}$ must be packed. Finally, we take the further opportunity to fuse these two items into one as we know that all the packed items and the 'top up' item must be packed in the same bin.

We denote by a the vector $\langle a_1 \ldots a_m \rangle$ and assume a function SORTDEC(a) which sorts it non-increasing order. Likewise, we assume a function MERGE(x, y) which merges two such sorted vectors x and y, maintaining the ordering property. We now define the vector z of items sizes to be passed to L_2 as $z =$ MERGE($\langle s_i \mid i \in U \rangle$, SORTDEC($a$)). Search is pruned whenever $L_2(C, z) > m$. The time complexity of the bounding procedure is $O(n + m \log m)$.

5 Experiments

We conduct experiments to compare $\mathcal{P}$ to the typical model presented in section 2.4. Throughout these tests we use a machine with a Pentium IV processor running at 2GHz and 1GB of memory. Tests are performed with ILOG Solver.

We compare the typical model, which we call the *basic* level of propagation described in section 2.5, with the enhanced model incorporating the additional rules described in sections 3 and 4. We decompose these extra rules into use of the lower bound described in section 4 (which we term "+LB"), and use of the pruning and propagation rules described in section 3 (which we term "+P"). Use of both of these sets of rules together is indicated by "+LB +P".

We use a standard search procedure, *complete decreasing best fit* (CDBF) [5], which packs items in order of non-increasing size, packing each item in the first bin with least free space that will accommodate it. On backtracking, the search states that the chosen item cannot be placed in the selected bin. A symmetry breaking rule is also used which states that on backtracking, all "equivalent" bins are also eliminated as candidates for the current item and indeed all other unpacked items of the same size. An equivalent bin is one which carries the same load as the one being eliminated from consideration. In addition, no choice point is created if all available bins for a particular item are equivalent: the item is packed into the first of them. Finally, we added the additional dominance rule which states that if an item can fill a partially filled bin to capacity, then it is immediately packed in this bin. This rule subsumes Gent's pair packing preprocessing rule [6], and is the simplest special case of a rule described in [11].

In CDBF, to find the minimal number of bins, we solve a succession of decision problems starting with the maximum number of bins set to the simple lower bound L_1. Each time the packing problem is proven to be insoluble, the number of bins is increased until a solution is found, which is necessarily optimal.

In the first instance, we chose a set of known benchmarks which could be comfortably solved by all models, from *basic* to +LB +P, so that comparisons could be made without extensive CPU times being expended. In this regard, we examined the smallest instances of series 1 of [15]. These problems have 50 items with sizes chosen from $\{[1, 100], [20, 100], [30, 100]\}$ and bin capacities chosen from $\{100, 120, 150\}$. The suite comprises 20 instances for each combination of capacity and size distribution, making 180 instances in total.

Figure 3 plots the number of choice points taken for the 180 benchmarks, where the benchmarks have been sorted according to the number of choice points needed to solve the problem using all additional propagations (+LB +P). In accordance with observations in [5, 10], there is great variation in the effort needed to solve the problems. For some problems, the additional propagation reduces the number of choice points by over three orders of magnitude. One problem took over three million choice points using the *basic* level, but was solved without branching using +LB +P.

Figure 4 plots two different views of the problems where additional propagations (+P) and lower bound pruning (+LB) are activated independently. We can see that the use of the additional propagations (+P) is more important than the use of the lower bound (+LB). In fact, the lower bound often performs no additional pruning over +P. However, on some problems, the search is significantly cut by the used of the lower bound. We argue that the small additional lower bound cost is paid back by increased robustness.

Table 1 shows all instances that were not solved in under 100 choice points. As mentioned, we can see that the lower bound calculation often performs no or

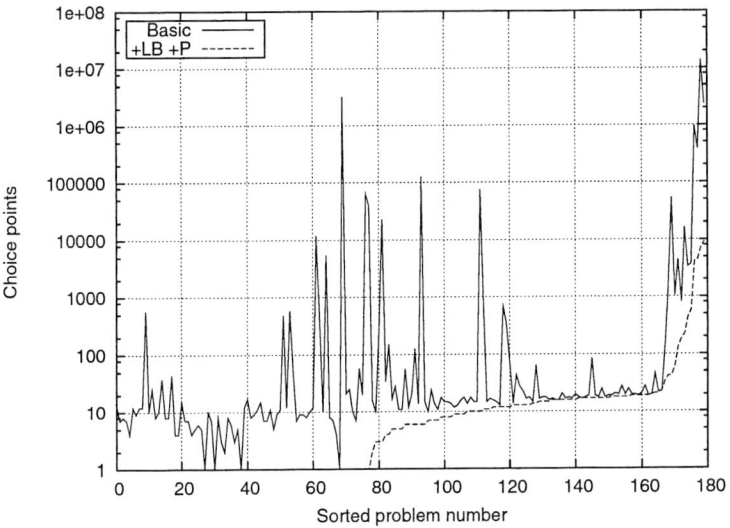

Fig. 3. Sorted 50 item instances

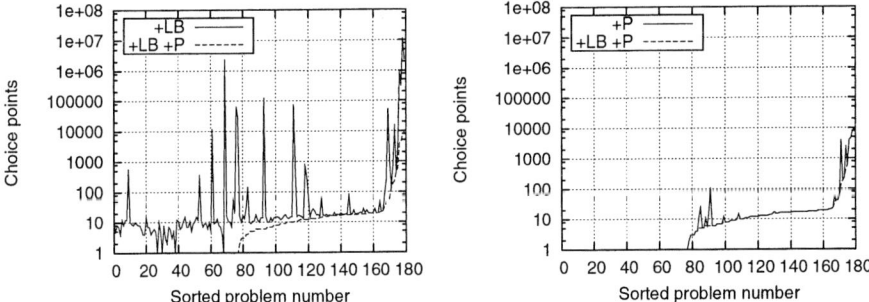

Fig. 4. Sorted 50 item instances, broken down into different propagation types

Table 1. Hardest instances, sorted by choice points needed by +LB +P

Name	Choice Points				Run Time (s)			
	Basic	+LB	+P	+LB +P	Basic	+LB	+P	+LB +P
N1C2W1_G	4485	138	4133	136	0.38	0.02	0.48	0.02
N1C3W2_G	802	742	187	187	0.05	0.05	0.03	0.03
N1C3W2_J	16101	16035	225	225	0.88	0.76	0.04	0.04
N1C2W1_C	3412	435	2639	435	0.22	0.04	0.24	0.05
N1C3W1_R	3756	2902	609	586	0.25	0.18	0.10	0.09
N1C1W2_A	966684	966684	4154	4154	42.29	38.00	0.40	0.44
N1C3W2_H	382812	302637	4562	4562	15.74	10.89	0.62	0.66
N1C3W2_F	13971619	11671895	7491	7491	651.95	483.19	1.45	1.53
N1C3W4_I	2354291	2342765	9281	9281	105.67	92.60	0.74	0.80

little pruning, but it did reduce the number of choice points by over a factor of thirty on one of these problems. The additional propagations (+P) can result in massive speed increases however, reducing run times by orders of magnitude.

We now look at another benchmark set in order to compare $\mathcal{P}$ with other other bin packing algorithms. We examine the benchmarks of Falkenauer [3]. These benchmarks are well-known, but have been criticized by Gent [6] as being too easy. The problems can certainly be solved by simple methods. However, Gent's methods are geared towards consideration of *bins*, and finding items which fill them to completely to capacity; they do not resemble CDBF, which might be applied as a first try at solving a problem with a bin packing component, before exploring less well-known methods. Falkenauer gives the performance of Martello and Toth's branch and bound algorithm [12] on these problems which was, until more recently, the best exact algorithm for bin packing. This method is also based on the decreasing best fit strategy, but makes heavy use of quite complex reduction procedures, lower bounds and dominance criteria.

Table 2 shows the results of runs on the smallest sizes of the "uniform" and "triplets" benchmarks using all propagations (+LB +P). Comparison of run times should be done with care, as the results of Martello and Toth's algorithm (MTP) are reproduced from [3] and are likely to be around one order of magnitude greater than those of $\mathcal{P}$. However, the number of choice points is a fairly reliable measure. Where MTP is marked with a $>$ sign, it means that the optimum solution was not found. All problems are solved fairly easily by the combination of $\mathcal{P}$ and CDBF except for u120_08 and u120_19. The former is solved in under 7 minutes, whereas the latter takes 15 hours. Martello and Toth's procedure falls foul of problems u120_08 and u120_19 as does ours, but performs much worse on the triplets set, finding optima for only 6 of the problems. By contrast, $\mathcal{P}$ plus CDBF solves all of these problems quickly.

Korf [11] also tested his algorithm on these problem sets, finding that his algorithm could solve all problems quickly. However, one interesting phenomenon is that for the two problems that his algorithm found the most difficult, our method found solutions instantly. Conversely, for the two most difficult problems we report, his algorithm found solutions instantly. The fact that MTP and CDBF find uniform problems 08 and 19 difficult, while Korf's algorithm does not, seems to indicate that a change of search strategy could be useful. This is supported by the fact that Gent's methods [6] were quickly successful on these problems. Korf also tested on the triplets set with 120 items and reported finding solutions instantly to all but four of the twenty problems. We do not report our results on these problems for reasons of space, but interestingly, our algorithm found solutions to all of these four troublesome problems instantly.

What is perhaps surprising about these experiments is that although constraint programming is a general technology which is rarely the best method to apply to a pure problem, by a combination of a dedicated constraint and a standard search procedure, we manage to produce a competitive algorithm.

Table 2. Falkenauer's problems solved with +LB +P, comparison with MTP

Name	Choice Points MTP	$\mathcal{P}$	Run Time (s) MTP	$\mathcal{P}$	Name	Choice Points MTP	$\mathcal{P}$	Run Time (s) MTP	$\mathcal{P}$
u120_00	56	39	0.1	0.02	t60_00	36254	62	9.5	0.03
u120_01	0	36	0.1	0.01	t60_01	28451	173	12.6	0.05
u120_02	124935	38	29.0	0.02	t60_02	> 1.5M	116	> 564.2	0.02
u120_03	74	31	0.0	0.02	t60_03	> 1.5M	195	> 444.7	0.04
u120_04	0	38	0.0	0.02	t60_04	> 1.5M	12	> 404.6	0.01
u120_05	43	32	0.1	0.02	t60_05	> 1.5M	176	> 415.2	0.04
u120_06	69	32	0.0	0.04	t60_06	> 1.5M	77	> 485.7	0.02
u120_07	54	38	0.0	0.03	t60_07	> 1.5M	193	> 395.9	0.04
u120_08	> 10M	2.63M	> 3681.4	398.34	t60_08	> 1.5M	359	> 451.6	0.06
u120_09	103	35	0.1	0.03	t60_09	26983	201	9.6	0.06
u120_10	0	34	0.1	0.01	t60_10	1783	16	0.9	0.01
u120_11	64	32	0.1	0.02	t60_11	13325	36	6.3	0.01
u120_12	88	25	0.0	0.03	t60_12	6450	24	1.5	0.01
u120_13	0	34	0.0	0.02	t60_13	> 1.5M	30	> 385.0	0.01
u120_14	0	33	0.0	0.02	t60_14	> 1.5M	14	> 400.8	0.01
u120_15	36	36	0.1	0.02	t60_15	> 1.5M	90	> 537.4	0.02
u120_16	0	33	0.0	0.02	t60_16	> 1.5M	30	> 528.3	0.01
u120_17	48	30	0.0	0.02	t60_17	> 1.5M	50	> 429.9	0.01
u120_18	24	35	0.0	0.01	t60_18	> 1.5M	146	> 385.6	0.03
u120_19	> 7.5M	321.89M	> 3679.4	15H08	t60_19	> 1.5M	140	> 399.5	0.03

6 Related Work

Johnson's initial work [8] brought bin packing algorithms to the fore, but exact algorithms were lacking until the Martello and Toth's reduction and branch and bound procedures [12,13]. However, in the last five years there has been significant interest and progress from the OR community (for example [1,15]) using branch and bound and mathematical programming approaches. Korf's bin completion algorithm [10,11], which makes heavy use of dominance properties, and Gent's work [6] have shown that the AI field has much to offer the domain. Trick [17] has shown that GAC can be achieved for knapsack constraints – a key subproblem of bin packing – using dynamic programming. Sellmann [16] has further proposed approximating this consistency to accelerate solving procedures.

7 Conclusion

This paper has introduced a constraint for bin packing. The constraint uses pruning and propagation rules based on a notion of *neighboring subsets* in subset sum problems as well as a lower bound on the number of bins used. We have demonstrated that this new constraint can cut search by orders of magnitude. Additional comparisons on established benchmarks showed that the new constraint coupled with a simple standard packing algorithm can significantly outperform Martello and Toth's procedure.

The packing constraint $\mathcal{P}$ has been available in ILOG Solver since version 6.0. All propagations described here will be available in Solver 6.1 to be released in autumn 2004.

References

1. J. Valerio de Carvalho. Exact solution of bin-packing problems using column generation and branch-and-bound. *Annals of Operations Research*, 86:629–659, 1999.
2. E. G. Coffman, Jr, M. R. Garey, and D. S. Johnson. Approximation algorithms for bin packing: A survery. In D. Hochbaum, editor, *Appoximation algorithms for NP-Hard Problems*, pages 46–93. PWS Publishing, Boston, 1996.
3. E. Falkenauer. A hybrid grouping genetic algorithm for bin packing. *Journal of Heuristics*, 2:5–30, 1996.
4. D. K. Friesen and M. A. Langston. Variable sized bin packing. *SIAM Journal on Computing*, 15:222–230, 1986.
5. I. Gent and T. Walsh. From approximate to optimal solutions: Constructing pruning and propagation rules. In *Proceedings of the 15th IJCAI*, 1997.
6. I.P. Gent. Heuristic solution of open bin packing problems. *Journal of Heuristics*, 3:299–304, 1998.
7. ILOG S.A., Gentilly, France. *ILOG Solver 6.0. User Manual*, September 2003.
8. D. S. Johnson. Fast algorithms for bin packing. *Journal of Computer and System Sciences*, 8:272–314, 1974.
9. H. Kellerer, U. Pferschy, and D. Pisinger. *Knapsack Problems*. Springer, 2004.
10. R. Korf. A new algorithm for optimal bin packing. In *Proceedings of 18th AAAI*, pages 731–736, 2002.
11. R. Korf. An improved algorithm for optimal bin packing. In *Proceedings of the 18th IJCAI*, pages 1252–1258, 2003.
12. S. Martello and P. Toth. *Knapsack problems*. Wiley, Chichester, 1990.
13. S. Martello and P. Toth. Lower bounds and reduction procedures for the bin packing problem. *Discrete and Applied Mathematics*, 28(1):59–70, 1990.
14. J.-C. Régin. A filtering algorithm for constraints of difference in CSPs. In *Proceedings of the 12th AAAI*, pages 362–367. American Association for Artificial Intelligence, AAAI Press / The MIT Press, 1994.
15. A. Scholl, R. Klein, and C. Jürgens. BISON: A fast hybrid procedure for exactly solving the one-dimensional bin packing problem. *Computers & Operations Research*, 24:627–645, 1997.
16. M. Sellmann. Approximated consistency for knapsack constraints. In *Proceedings of the CP' 03*, pages 679–693. Springer, 2003.
17. M. Trick. A dynamic programming approach for consistency and propagation for knapsack constraints. In *Proceedings of CP-AI-OR '01*, 2001.

Solving Non-clausal Formulas with DPLL Search*

Christian Thiffault[1], Fahiem Bacchus[1,**], and Toby Walsh[2,***]

[1] Department of Computer Science, University of Toronto
Toronto, Ontario, Canada
{cat,fbacchus}@cs.toronto.edu
[2] Cork Constraint Computation Center, University College Cork, Ireland
tw@4c.ucc.ie

Abstract. Great progress has been made on DPLL based SAT solvers operating on CNF encoded SAT theories. However, for most problems CNF is not a very natural representation. Typically these problems are more easily expressed using unrestricted propositional formulae and hence must be converted to CNF before modern SAT solvers can be applied. This conversion entails a considerable loss of information about the problem's structure. In this work we demonstrate that conversion to CNF is both unnecessary and undesirable. In particular, we demonstrate that a SAT solver which operates directly on a propositional formula can achieve the same efficiency as a highly optimized modern CNF solver. Furthermore, since the original formula remains intact, such a solver can exploit the original problem structure to improve over CNF solvers. We present empirical evidence showing that exploiting the original structure can yield considerable benefits.

1 Introduction

State of the art SAT solvers typically solve CNF encoded SAT theories using DPLL based algorithms [1]. However, many problems are more naturally expressed by arbitrary propositional formulas or Boolean circuits. Hence in order to use modern SAT solvers these problems must be converted into CNF. Converting to a simple and uniform representation like CNF provides conceptual and implementational simplicity. Indeed, a number of key techniques for improving the effectiveness and efficiency of DPLL solvers were originally designed to exploit the simple structure of CNF. However, such a conversion also entails considerable loss of information about the problem's structure, information that could be exploited to improve search efficiency.

In this paper, we argue that conversion to CNF is both unnecessary and undesirable. In particular, we have implemented NOCLAUSE, a non-CNF DPLL like solver that achieves a raw efficiency very similar to modern highly optimized CNF solvers by employing techniques very similar to those used in modern CNF solvers. Furthermore, we demonstrate how the additional structure present in the original propositional formula can be exploited to achieve significant gains in solving power, to the point where on various benchmarks NOCLAUSE outperforms the CNF solver it was based on.

---

* An extended abstract on this topic was presented at the SAT-2004 conference.
** Supported by Natural Science and Engineering Research Council of Canada.
*** Supported by Science Foundation Ireland.

The performance of our non-CNF solver is particularly encouraging for two other reasons. First, our implementation, although carefully constructed, does not employ any cache level optimizations. Nevertheless its raw performance is still close to that of the highly optimized CNF solver ZCHAFF [2]. Hence, there does not seem to be any intrinsic reason why a non-CNF solver cannot be as efficient as a CNF solver given equal engineering effort. Second, there are many other potential ways of exploiting the structure of the original propositional formula that we have not yet experimented with. It seems likely that some of these possibilities could yield additional performance improvements.

We begin by discussing CNF based SAT solvers, the way in which CNF encodings are generated, and the inherent disadvantages of CNF encodings. Then we present a method for performing DPLL search with a non-clausal encoding, and discuss the implementation techniques we utilized to obtain efficient inference on the non-clausal encoding. To go beyond mimicking current levels of performance we then present two techniques for exploiting the extra structure present in the non-clausal encoding. Empirical evidence shows that these techniques yield significant increases in performance. There has been some earlier work in the verification and theorem proving communities on formula based (or circuit based) solvers. We discuss this previous work pointing out the differences and similarities with our approach in various sections of the paper. Finally we close with some concluding remarks.

2 SAT Solving Using CNF

Many problems are more naturally described using arbitrary propositional formulas rather than clausal form. For example, hardware verification problems are often initially expressed in non-clausal form. To check the satisfiability of such formulas, the standard technique is to convert them to CNF and utilize a CNF SAT solver. Conversion to CNF is typically achieved using Tseitin encodings [3]. It is useful to review this encoding to better understand the correspondence between a non-clausal solver and a CNF solver.

Tseitin encodings work by adding new variables to the CNF formula, one new variable for every subformula of the original propositional formula, along with clauses to capture the dependence between these new variables and the subformulas. This is best illustrated by an example. Consider the propositional formula $(A \Rightarrow (C \wedge D)) \vee (B \Rightarrow (C \wedge E))$. The Tseitin encoding would introduce the new variable F_1 to represent the subformula $C \wedge D$ and the new clauses $(\neg F_1, C)$, $(\neg F_1, D)$, and $(\neg C, \neg D, F_1)$ to capture the relation $F_1 \equiv (C \wedge D)$. Similarly we would have $F_2 \equiv (C \wedge E)$ and the clauses $(\neg F_2, C)$, $(\neg F_2, E)$, and $(\neg C, \neg E, F_2)$. With these new variables we would now have $A \Rightarrow (C \wedge D) \equiv A \Rightarrow F_1 \equiv \neg A \vee F_1$, and $B \Rightarrow (C \wedge E) \equiv \neg B \vee F_2$. Now two more new variables would be introduced $F_3 \equiv \neg A \vee F_1$ and $F_4 \equiv \neg B \vee F_2$ with the clauses $(\neg F_3, \neg A \vee F_1)$, $(A \vee F_3)$, $(\neg F_1, F_3)$, $(\neg F_4, \neg B \vee F_2)$, $(B \vee F_4)$, and $(\neg F_2, F_4)$. Finally, we introduce one more new variable $F_5 \equiv F_3 \vee F_4$ with the clauses $(\neg F_5, F_3, F_4)$, $(\neg F_3, F_5)$, and $(\neg F_4, F_5)$ [1].

Tseitin CNF encodings are linear in the size of the original formula as long as the Boolean operators that appear in the formula have linear clausal encodings. For ex-

---

[1] It is possible to build a more optimal encoding that only imposes the condition $F_5 \Rightarrow F_3 \vee F_4$ rather than equivalence as long as F_5 is not the descendant of an equivalence operator [4].

ample, the operators *and, or, not, nand, nor*, and *implies* all have linear sized clausal encodings. The k-ary *and* operator $A = A_1 \wedge \cdots \wedge A_k$ can be represented with a set of clauses of length $O(k)$ over the propositional variables A_i. Operators that do not have linear clausal encodings include k-ary biconditionals, k-ary counting operators (e.g., exactly 3 of the k inputs are true), and k-ary parity operators. The CNF encoding also retains some of the structure of the original formula. For example, any truth assignment to the variables of the original formula generates a truth assignment to every subformula; i.e., every subformula evaluates to TRUE or FALSE under this truth assignment. It is not difficult to see that a setting of the original variables will force a corresponding setting of the "subformula" variables in the CNF encoding.

The CNF encoding has two main disadvantages. The first, and most fundamental problem is that a great deal of structural information is lost: the clauses no longer directly reflect the structure of the original circuit. For example, it is not immediately obvious that the F_i variables represent derived signals rather than input signals, that F_4 is upstream of F_2 in the original circuit, or that F_4 encodes an *or* gate while F_1 encodes an *and* gate. In this simple example, some of this information can be computed from the clausal encoding. In general, however, whilst some of this information can be computed from the clausal encoding, some of it is intractable to compute. For example, it is intractable to determine which variables represent derived signals and which represent the original variables in an arbitrary CNF encoded formula [5].

The second problem is that the CNF theory contains more variables, which means that the space of truth assignments from which a solution must be found has been enlarged by an exponential sized factor. This does not necessarily mean that in practice the search for a solution is any harder. Nevertheless, as we shall explain, the difficulty of searching this larger space is exacerbated by the first problem, the lack of structural information.

Loss of Structural Information. A number of works show that the structural information lost in a CNF encoding can be used to give significant performance improvement. For example, the EqSATZ solver [6] achieves significant gains by extracting and exploiting biconditionals from the CNF theory. Until very recently, it was the only solver able to complete the par32 family of problems which contain many biconditionals. More recently, the Lsat solver [7] has shown that extracting even more extensive structural information can allow some problems, that are very hard for clausal solvers, to be solved quite easily. Given that these solvers have to utilize specialized (and incomplete) methods to extract the structural information they need, and given that many problems start off with a structure rich non-clausal encoding, it is natural to see if we can solve the problem more efficiently and effectively in its original non-clausal encoding. In addition to this empirical evidence, recent theoretical results show that on some problems structure can be exploited to derive branching decisions that reduce the size of the search space exponentially [8].

The Added Variables. The second problem, that of additional variables in the CNF encoding, is an issue that has been the subject of some previous work. The main approach taken, e.g., [9, 10, 7], has been to annotate the CNF theory to distinguish between the original variables (the primary inputs) and the derived variables (the internal signals).

It is assumed that either the annotation is supplied with the CNF encoding (thus a small amount of additional structural information is preserved) or is approximated by examining the CNF encoding [7]. Given this annotation, the recommendation is then to restrict the DPLL search from branching on any derived variable: once all of the primary inputs have been set all of the derived signals can be determined by unit propagation. The benefit of this technique is that now the CNF encoding can be solved by searching in the same sized state space: the set of assignments to the original propositional variables.

Unfortunately, there is compelling empirical and theoretical evidence that this simple technique is not robust. For example, the Lsat solver uses this technique of branching only on input variables. It displays impressive performance on a number of problems, but very disappointing performance on an even wider range of problems. The most robust and powerful SAT solvers do not restrict their branching decisions in this manner. From a theoretical point of view it can be shown that restricting the solver to branching only on the input variables entails a reduction in the power of the proof system it implements. A number of results of this form have been given in [11]. These results show that there exist families of Boolean circuits on which a DPLL solver that branches only on the input variables (in the clausal encoding) will always explore an exponentially sized search tree (irrespective of how it chooses which of the input variables it wants to branch on), while a DPLL solver that is allowed to branch on the derived variables can construct a constant sized refutation tree.

Theorem 1. *There exists families of Boolean circuits such that a short resolution proof of unsatisfiability exists if and only if branching on derived variables is allowed [11].*

This result shows that we want to branch on the derived variables, so as not to suffer a loss in power of the proof system. Hence, it is useful to analyze more carefully possible sources of inefficiency that such branching can produce. First, it should be noted that it is not necessarily the case that a DPLL procedure will search a larger space when additional variables are introduced. For example, if we add the new variables $Y_1, \ldots, Y_n$ to a theory containing the variables $X_1, \ldots, X_n$, but also include the clauses $(\neg X_i, Y_i)$ and $(\neg Y_i, X_i)$ making each Y_i equivalent to its corresponding X_i, then there will be no effect on the size of the DPLL search tree: each time Y_i or X_i is set the other variable will be set by unit propagation.

A major source of inefficiency introduced when branching on derived variables arises from subsequent branching on variables that have become *don't care* due to previous decisions. Consider for example a formula of the form $PHP^n \vee (q \wedge p)$, where PHP^n is an unsatisfiable formula requiring an exponentially sized resolution refutation (e.g., the pigeon hole problem with n pigeons), and q and p are propositional variables. The clausal encoding of this formula contains the added variables $B_1 \equiv PHP^n$, $B_2 \equiv (q \wedge p)$, $B_3 \equiv (B_1 \vee B_2)$, and other variables added by the clausal encoding of PHP^n. If the solver first assigns $B_3 = \text{TRUE}$, then $B_2 = \text{TRUE}$ both q and p will be unit propagated to TRUE. This set of assignments satisfies the formula. However, the clausal theory will still contain the clauses encoding the subformula $B_1 \equiv PHP^n$ so the solver's job will not yet be completed. If the solver was then to set the input variables of PHP^n, any such setting would force the setting $B_1 = \text{FALSE}$ and the solver would be finished. Similarly, if the solver was to set $B_1 = \text{FALSE}$ then it could find a setting of the variables in PHP^n that falsifies PHP^n and again it would be finished. However, if it made the wrong decision of first setting $B_1 =$ TRUE, then it would be faced with having to produce an exponentially size refutation of PHP^n in order to backtrack to reset $B_1 =$ FALSE. All of this work is unnecessary, but in the clausal encoding it is difficult to detect that the work is not needed.

In this example, we do not need to branch on any of the variables encoding PHP^n. This part of the formula has become irrelevant and the variables in it have become don't care since their values cannot affect the value of the formula. How often CNF DPLL solvers branch unnecessarily on don't care variables, and how much search is wasted by doing so is an empirical question. We present results which along with previous evidence [12, 13] indicates that the amount of wasted time is significant.

3 DPLL Without Conversions

Our approach is designed to decide if a propositional formula is satisfiable. A propositional formula can be represented as an operator tree, where each internal node is a Boolean operator and its children are subtrees representing its operands. After inputing the formula we first compress it by converting the tree representation into a directed acyclic graph (DAG) in which all duplicates of a sub-formula are merged. For example, in the formula $(A \Rightarrow (C \land D)) \lor (B \Rightarrow (C \land D))$ the DAG would contain only one instance of the subformula $(C \land D)$. Propositional formulas represented as DAGS are often called Boolean circuits. The conversion to a Boolean circuit can be done bottom up using hashing to identify common sub-formulas.

Once the DAG representation is computed we store it in a contiguous section of memory and associate with each node of the DAG (gate) the following data:

1. A unique identifier.
2. A list of parent nodes (in a DAG a node might have many parents).
3. A list of children nodes.
4. The type of the node (e.g., the node might be a propositional variable, an *and* gate, an *or* gate, etc.).
5. A truth value (TRUE, FALSE, *don't care*, or *unknown*.)
6. The decision level at which the node's truth value changed from *unknown*.
7. The reason that a node's truth value changed from *unknown* (either the trigger of a propagation rule or a conflict clause).

Given this representation our task is to consistently label the nodes with truth values such that the top level node (representing the entire formula) is labeled TRUE. A labeling is consistent if it respects the logic of the node types. For example, if an *and* node is labeled TRUE all of its children must be labeled TRUE, if a *not* node is labeled FALSE its child must be labeled TRUE, etc. We try to find a consistent labeling, or prove that one does not exist, using a backtracking tree search (i.e., a DPLL search) on the truth values assigned to each node. Such an approach has been used in previous work on circuit-based solvers, e.g., [14–16].

Our backtracking search procedure chooses an unlabeled node to label, labels it TRUE or FALSE, propagates the consequences of that label, and then recursively tries to label the remaining nodes. If that fails it backtracks and tries the opposite label. Note that the search can choose to label (branch on) any unlabeled node in the DAG.

Choosing an internal node corresponds to branching on the truth value of a subformula of the input, while choosing a leaf node corresponds to branching on the truth value of one of the inputs of the circuit.

Once a node is labeled with a truth value, the consequences of that truth value are propagated through the DAG. Propagation utilizes the node's data to propagate other labels through the DAG, e.g., if a node is labeled FALSE then FALSE is propagated to all of its parents that are *and* gates; if it is labeled TRUE and it is an *and* gate then TRUE is propagated to all of its children, etc. Propagation of labels goes up and down the DAG guided by a simple set of propagation rules. Similar propagation rules were used in the works cited above.

A contradiction is detected when a node gets both a TRUE and a FALSE label. Once we have a contradiction we must backtrack and try a different labeling. It is not difficult to see that setting the truth value of a node corresponds precisely to setting the variables identified with the subformula headed by that node in the Tseitin CNF encoding. Similarly, propagation of labels corresponds to unit propagation in the CNF theory.

Proposition 1. *If assigning a variable v the truth value x in the Tseitin CNF encoding of a circuit causes another variable v' to be assigned the truth value y by unit propagation, then assigning the node corresponding to v the value x will cause the node corresponding to v' to be assigned the value y by applying our propagation rules.*

As in [15], for each propagated label we remember the set of node labels that caused the propagation. For example, if we propagate TRUE to an *and* because all of its children were set to TRUE we would associate the TRUE labels of all of the children as the reason for the TRUE labeling of the *and* node. If the *and* node is subsequently labeled FALSE because of propagation from one of its parents, we would have another set of node labels as the reason for the FALSE label. We can combine these labels to obtain a conflict set. The negation of the labels in the conflict set is a conflict clause just like those constructed by CNF solvers. In fact, by successively replacing the most recently propagated label by its reason until we have only one label at the current decision level, we can implement precisely 1-UIP learning [17]. As in [15], we discover and then store such conflicts in a clausal database. These conflict clauses are then unit propagated using standard techniques (assigning two node labels as the watch labels). Thus nodes in the DAG are labeled by unit propagation from the conflict clauses as well as by propagation in the circuit DAG.

Efficient Propagation in the DAG. The main difference in our implementation and the previous circuit based SAT solvers cited above is that we adopt the watch literal technique from CNF solvers and apply it to our circuit representation. Watches are used wherever they can make a propagation rule more efficient. Propagation through an *and* gate provides a typical example. There are four rules for propagating *and* gates:

1. If the *and* becomes TRUE propagate TRUE to all of its children.
2. If a child becomes FALSE propagate FALSE to the *and* node.
3. If all of the children become TRUE propagate TRUE to the *and* node.
4. If the *and* node is FALSE and all but one of the children are TRUE then propagate FALSE to the unlabeled child.

Watches do not help the first two rules. In fact in the clausal encoding the first two rules would correspond to unit propagation through the binary clauses $(\neg A, C)$, where A is literal corresponding to the *and* node and C is one of its children. Watches do not aid in the efficiency of binary clauses either. To make the second rule efficient we divide the parent list of a node into separate lists based on the parent's type. So we would have a separate list of *and* parents, another list of *or* parents, etc. Thus when a node is labeled FALSE we can efficiently propagate FALSE to all of its *and* parents.

Watches offer significant improvement for the third and fourth rules. For every *and* node we assign two children to be TRUE watches, and for every node we maintain a list of parents it serves as a TRUE watch for (the node might also be a FALSE watch for some *or* nodes). We maintain the invariant that neither watch should be assigned TRUE unless we have no other choice, or the other watch is already FALSE. When a node is assigned TRUE we examine each of the parents for which it is a TRUE watch. For each parent we first look at the other watch child, if that child is already FALSE we do not need to do anything. If it is TRUE then we know that every child of the parent is now true, and we can activate the third rule propagating TRUE to the parent. Otherwise we look to see if we can find another child of the parent that is currently unassigned or FALSE and make that the new watch. If we cannot find an alternative watch we leave the current watch intact, obtaining one TRUE watch and one unassigned watch, and check the *and* node to see if it is currently FALSE. If it is then we activate rule four and propagate FALSE to the sole unassigned watch child. Finally, whenever we label an *and* node FALSE, we look at its two watch children. If one of these is TRUE we know that the other is the only remaining unassigned child, and we activate rule four propagating FALSE to that child.

Previous circuit based solvers (e.g., [14, 15]) have restricted themselves to binary Boolean operators and have used tables to perform label propagation in the DAG. Although table lookup is fast, to propagate TRUE to an *and* node containing thousands of children (and then converted to a tree of binary *and* nodes) requires a table lookup every time one of the children is labeled. With the watch child technique, we only need to perform some computation when a watch child is labeled. One of the suites we experimented with (VLIW-SAT.1.1 due to M. Velev) contained *and* nodes with an average of 15.9 children, and had some *and* nodes with over 100,000 children. The other suites also contained some *and* nodes with thousands of children. As a result we found that implementing the watch child technique for triggering propagation in the DAG yielded very significant gains in efficiency. Besides watches for the *and* propagation rules we were able to use an analogous set of watches for the *or*, *iff*, and *xor* propagation rules. Watches were also used in don't care propagation.

As a result, conversion to CNF does not seem to be necessary. A non-clausal DPLL SAT solver can duplicate the search performed by a CNF solver: labeling nodes corresponds to making literals in the CNF encoding TRUE, propagation in the DAG corresponds to unit propagation in the CNF encoding, conflicting labels corresponds to conflicting assignments to a variable in the CNF encoding, and conflicts consisting of sets of labels correspond to conflict clauses in the clausal encoding. Furthermore, propagation in the DAG can be made just as efficient as unit propagation in the CNF encoding by using watched children. Besides being able to duplicate the behavior of CNF solvers, non-CNF solvers also have the advantage of being able to exploit additional structural information not present in a CNF encoding. In the next section we present some simple techniques for exploiting this structure.

4 Exploiting Structure

4.1 Complex Gates

It is well known that every DPLL search tree for an UNSAT problem can be converted to a similarly sized resolution refutation of the problem. Hence, a clausal DPLL solver is inherently limited by the power of resolution. Non-clausal DPLL solvers on the other hand can employ complex gates and special purpose propagators for those gates that in certain cases, can circumvent the limitations imposed by resolution. In fact, any subcircuit can be encoded as a single gate and propagation through that subcircuit realized by a specialized propagation algorithm.

For example, the SAT problem might be an encoding of a CSP problem containing an all-different constraint. In general, reasoning with all-different requires exponentially sized resolution proofs (e.g., the pigeon hole problem can be encoded with a single all-different constraint over a set of multi-valued variables). Hence, the causal encoding to SAT will suffer an exponential loss of efficiency over polytime all-different propagators. In a non-clausal solver, on the other hand, a single gate can be used to encode an all-different constraint and a polytime propagator can be used to propagate truth values through the gate.

4.2 Don't Care Propagation

The problem described earlier where a clausal solver might branch on a don't care variable is easily addressed using the circuit structure. Two techniques have previously been described in the literature for exploiting don't cares. Gupta et al. tag each variable with fanin and fanout information from the original circuit [13]. Using this information they are able to detect when a clause encodes part of the circuit that no longer influences the output, given the variable assignments we have already made. Such clauses are tagged as being inactive and are restored to active status when backtracking makes them relevant again. The detection of inactive clauses requires a sweep through all of the active clauses in the theory. This sweep must be performed at every node in the search tree.

Safarpour et al. use a different technique [12]. They maintain the original circuit and use it to mark variables that dynamically become don't cares (*lazy* in their notation). Then they prohibit the CNF solver from branching on don't care variables. They scan the entire circuit to detect don't care variables at every node of the search tree.

Like Safarpour et al. we also use a variable marking technique. However, we have gained efficiency by using watches and by not having to maintain both a CNF encoding as well as a circuit description. To understand how watches improve efficiency consider a typical example when a node is the child of an *and* node that has been labeled FALSE. The node's label is then irrelevant with respect to its impact on this particular *and* parent. However, the node might still be relevant to the label of its other parents. Hence, a node's value becomes irrelevant to the circuit as a whole only when for each of its parents it is either irrelevant to that parent's value, or that parent has itself become irrelevant to the circuit's output.

To perform efficient propagation of don't care values through the DAG we use a single don't care watch parent for each node. The invariant for a don't care watch parent is that the parent should not be a don't care and that the child it is watching should not be irrelevant to its value. Whenever a node is assigned at truth value that makes its watched children irrelevant, or when a don't care value is propagated to it we search for a new don't care watch parent for each watched child. If we fail to find one we can propagate a don't care to the child and then perhaps subsequently to the child's children, etc. Our use of watches means that computation is required only when the watch parent is modified, changes to the other parents do not require any computation. In the approaches described above a node will be checked every time one of its parents is modified.

Some of the problems we experimented with contained nodes with over 8,000 parents, and an average of 23 parents per node. Many other problems contained nodes with over a 1,000 parents. Hence our watch technique yielded significant gains. As described below, on some problems we obtained a speedup of 38 times using don't care propagation. The above cited works report speedups from don't care propagation in the order of only 3 to 7 times. This also provides evidence that CNF solvers are wasting a significant amount of time by branching on don't care variables, and are thus suffering from the loss of structural information in the CNF encoding.

4.3 Conflict Clause Reduction

Another structure based technique we have implemented is conflict clause reduction. To the best of our knowledge this technique is new to this work. The idea is simple. When we learn a conflict clause it will contain some set of node labels. We examine these labels to see if any of them are "locally" redundant given the circuit structure, and if they are we remove them. We say that label ℓ makes label ℓ' *redundant* if one of the DAG propagation rules generates ℓ' from ℓ. For example, if n is an *and* node and n' is one of its children, then $n =$ FALSE makes $n' =$ FALSE redundant. In a conflict clause we can remove any redundant labeling. For example, if we have the conflict clause $(n =$ FALSE$, n' =$ FALSE$, x =$ TRUE$, \ldots)$ we can reduce this clause to $(n =$ FALSE$, x =$ TRUE$, \ldots)$. This corresponds to a resolution step: we have that $n' =$ FALSE $\Rightarrow n =$ FALSE $\equiv (n' =$ TRUE$, n =$ FALSE$)$, which resolved against the conflict clause yields the reduced clause. In addition to removing any label made redundant by another label, we can transitively remove all labels made redundant by the redundant label. Since redundancies are defined with respect to local DAG propagation rules, all redundancies can be efficiently checked by examining the parents and children of the node in the label.

The above resolution of $(n' =$ TRUE$, n =$ FALSE$)$ and $(n =$ FALSE$, n' =$ FALSE$, x =$ TRUE$, \ldots)$ is known as Krom Subsumption. Krom subsumption has been utilized before in clausal SAT solvers [18]. The difficulty lies in detecting that the binary clause $(n' =$ TRUE$, n =$ FALSE$)$ holds. van Gelder and Tsuji [18] utilized extensive binary clause reasoning to discover a large number of binary clauses at each stage of the search. These binary clauses were then used to perform Krom subsumption (however their solver did not generate new learned clauses). The advantage of the non-clausal representation is that a very local test can be performed (running the local propagation rules) to effectively circumscribe the computation required to detect the needed binary clauses.

We experimented with various uses of conflict clause reduction and found empirically that the most effective use was to employ reduction on shorter conflict clauses, length 100 or less. For longer conflict clauses, the clause remained long even after reduction, whereas on the shorter clauses the reduction produced more useful clauses. It should also be noted that conflict clause reduction has a cumulative effect: conflict clauses produce new conflict clauses, so shorter conflict clauses produce new conflict clauses that are themselves shorter.

5 Empirical Results

Our non-clausal DPLL solver NOCLAUSE uses the ideas described above. We represent the input as a propositional formula in ISCAS format, convert it to a non-redundant Boolean circuit, perform 1-UIP clause learning at failures, use ZCHAFF's VSIDS heuristic to guide branching, perform don't care propagation, and use the circuit structure to reduce all learned clauses of size 100 or less.

We designed our solver to perform a carefully controlled experimental comparison with the ZCHAFF solver. ZCHAFF is no longer the fastest SAT solver, but its source code is available. Hence, we were able to have better control over the differences between our solver and ZCHAFF. In particular, we duplicated as much as possible ZCHAFF's branching heuristic, clause learning, and clause database management techniques by careful examination of the ZCHAFF code. Hence we were able to build NOCLAUSE so that the differences with ZCHAFF are mainly dependent on NOCLAUSE's use of the circuit structure. This allows us to assess more accurately the benefits of using a non-CNF representation.

For this reason we compare only with the ZCHAFF solver. Our aim is to demonstrate the specific benefits of a non-CNF representation. Other more recent solvers, e.g., BerkMin and Siege, employ different branching heuristics from ZCHAFF and to some extent different clause learning techniques, and are often able to outperform ZCHAFF with these new techniques. However, as explained in Sec. 3 a non-CNF solver can be made to duplicate the search performed by a CNF solver. Thus it should be possible to implement the same branching and clause learning techniques employed in these other solvers with a commensurate gain in efficiency. It seems plausible that at least some of the gains we obtain from exploiting structural information would be preserved under these alternate branching and clause learning strategies. Unfortunately, the exact nature of the strategies employed in many of these solvers remains undisclosed so it is difficult to test such a conjecture.

Another restriction in our experimental results is that our solver requires non-CNF input. It was quite difficult to obtain non-CNF test problems, and the only ones that were able to obtain had already suffered some loss of structural information by been encoded into ISCAS format which contains only *and*, *or*, and *not* gates. We expect to see even

Table 1. Comparison between ZCHAFF and NoClause on 4 benchmark suites. Time: CPU seconds to solve all problem in suite. Decision: number of branches in the search tree. Impl/s: number of unit implications per second during search. Size: average size of a learned conflict clause.

Benchmark	ZCHAFF				NOCLAUSE			
	Time	Decisions	Impl/s	Size	Time	Decisions	Impl/s	Size
sss-sat-1.0 (100)	128	2,970,794	728,144	70	225	1,532,843	616,705	39
vliw-sat-1.1 (100)	3,284	154,742,779	302,302	82	1,033	4,455,378	260,779	55
fvp-unsat-1.0 (4)	245	3,620,014	322,587	326	172	554,100	402,621	100
fvp-unsat-2.0 (22)	20,903	26,113,810	327,590	651	4,104	5,537,711	267,858	240

better performance on problems which have not been so transformed. All experiments were run on a 2.4GHz Pentium IV machine with 3GB of RAM.

Table 1 shows the performance of ZCHAFF and NOCLAUSE on four different benchmark suites containing a total of 226 problems. These suites were the only difficult problems we found that were available in both CNF and non-CNF formats. The table shows the total run time (all times in CPU seconds) to solve the suite, the total number of decisions (branches) over all of the search trees explored, and the rate of unit propagations per second achieved. It also shows the average size of the conflict clauses learned over the suite. We see that NOCLAUSE is faster on all but the easiest of suites (sss-sat-1.0, where each problem took ZCHAFF an average of 1.3 seconds to solve). NOCLAUSE is significantly faster on the hardest of the suite fvp-unsat-2.0. We also see that it makes far fewer decisions and learns shorter conflict clauses. Furthermore, its raw performance, measured in terms of implications per seconds is comparable with ZCHAFF.

Table 2 shows the runtimes of ZCHAFF and NOCLAUSE in more detail on the fvp-unsat.2.0 suite. On the larger problems, ZCHAFF is learning very long conflict clauses, much longer than those learned by NOCLAUSE. We also see that NOCLAUSE displays more uniform scaling behavior.

Table 3 shows the effect of don't care propagation on NOCLAUSE's performance. We see that don't care propagation is a major contributor to its performance. Without don't care propagation NOCLAUSE for the most part has inferior performance to ZCHAFF being slower on two of the benchmarks and slightly faster on the other two. The table also shows the average number of don't care implications per second on these suites, and the average number of backjump levels on detecting a conflict. We see that without don't cares the solver will jump back further on average. This is because the solver is able to jump back over decision levels where don't care variables were branched on. Nevertheless, despite the ability of conflict clauses to jump back over don't care decisions, don't care decisions still have a significant negative impact on performance.

Table 4 shows in more detail the results of don't care propagation on the non-trivial problems in the fvp-unsat-2.0 suite. We see that don't care propagation has its largest impact on the hardest problems. For example, we obtain a speed up factor 34 on the 6pipe instance. We also see that the total number of propagations per second (implications plus don't cares indicated in the Total/s column) remains fairly similar with

Table 2. Comparison between ZCHAFF and NOCLAUSE on the complete fvp-unsat-2.0 benchmark suite. #Vars: number of variables in problem instance. Other columns as in Table 1.

Problem	# Vars.	ZCHAFF Time	Decisions	Impl/s	Cls Size	NOCLAUSE Time	Decisions	Impl/s	Cls Size
2pipe	892	0.14	6,362	1,156,271	35	0.27	4,880	1,133,000	17
2pipe_1	834	0.17	5,254	1,075,924	32	0.13	3,323	925,923	13
2pipe_2	925	0.25	6,664	1,042,740	38	0.31	5,697	828,923	18
3pipe	2,468	2.74	39,102	865,566	88	1.45	14,898	702,202	24
3pipe_1	2,223	2.43	25,939	724,459	87	7.93	39,859	419,688	48
3pipe_2	2,400	3.80	35,031	723,537	93	5.99	31,622	414,157	36
3pipe_3	2,577	6.94	53,806	653,575	105	7.10	37,258	427,852	53
4pipe	5,237	188.89	541,195	467,001	253	9.87	41,637	509,433	40
4pipe_1	4,647	26.55	131,223	512,108	158	35.52	114,512	327,098	77
4pipe_2	4,941	49.76	210,169	482,896	186	36.50	112,720	327,298	84
4pipe_3	5,233	144.34	392,564	424,551	254	62.03	169,117	316,049	108
4pipe_4	5,525	93.83	295,841	470,936	228	42.26	122,497	326,186	112
5pipe	9,471	54.68	334,761	526,457	258	33.34	102,077	409,154	93
5pipe_1	8,441	126.11	381,921	425,921	273	116.18	255,894	280,758	140
5pipe_2	8,851	138.62	397,550	437,166	276	177.24	362,840	279,298	165
5pipe_3	9,267	137.70	385,239	441,319	271	134.08	292,802	295,976	165
5pipe_4	9,764	873.81	1,393,529	370,906	406	284.62	503,128	270,234	208
5pipe_5	10,113	249.11	578,432	456,400	324	137.09	283,554	298,903	172
6pipe	15,800	4,550.92	5,232,321	322,039	619	297.13	435,781	288,855	232
6pipe_6	17,064	1,406.18	2,153,346	402,301	469	1,056.56	1,326,371	267,207	309
7pipe	23,910	12,717.00	12,437,654	306,433	900	1,657.70	1,276,763	244,343	336
7pipe_bug	24,065	128.90	1,075,907	266,901	393	0.29	481	403,148	10

Table 3. Analysis of DON'T CARE propagations in NOCLAUSE on 4 benchmark suites. DC/s: number of don't care implications per second. Step: average number of levels backtracked over on backtrack.

Benchmark	NOCLAUSE Time	Decisions	Step	Impl/s	DC/s	NOCLAUSE without DON'T CARES Time	Decisions	Step	Impl/s
sss-sat-1.0 (100)	225	1,532,843	4.20	411,760	204,945	272	3,095,245	6.75	652,927
vliw-sat-1.1 (100)	1,033	4,455,378	6.32	175,995	84,784	2,120	13,208,363	10.86	381,188
fvp-unsat-1.0 (4)	172	554,100	3.95	212,012	190,609	494	3,442,123	12.42	295,179
fvp-unsat-2.0 (22)	4,104	5,537,711	3.03	186,603	81,255	30,934	20,382,047	3.18	335,242

the addition of don't care propagation. However, some of that raw speed must now be used to perform don't care propagation which results in a lower rate of implications per second. Nevertheless, this more than pays for itself in the reduced number of decisions.

Table 5 shows the effect of conflict clause reduction on performance. The size column shows the average size of a conflict clause learned. We see that without reduction the conflicts are significantly larger. Note that the size of the clause was measured prior to being reduced. The table also shows the percentage of clauses that are examined for reduction (only clauses of length 100 or less are reduced) and for these the percentage reduction achieved. We see that for the easier suites, sss-sat-1.0, and vliw-sat-1.1, clause

Table 4. Analysis of the DON'T CARE propagations in NOCLAUSE on the non-trivial problems from the fvp-unsat-2.0 benchmark. Total/s: number of implications per second plus the number of don't care propagations per second.

Problem	NOCLAUSE					NOCLAUSE without DON'T CARES		
	Time	Decisions	Impl/s	DC/s	Total/s	Time	Decisions	Impl/s
4pipe	9.87	41,637	337,405	172,028	509,433	57.68	198,828	526,014
4pipe_1	35.52	114,512	236,336	90,762	327,098	62.65	159,049	413,037
4pipe_2	36.50	112,720	234,174	93,124	327,298	94.46	212,986	438,386
4pipe_3	62.03	169,117	233,951	82,098	316,049	213.27	365,007	404,224
4pipe_4	42.26	122,497	244,725	81,460	326,186	318.64	525,623	412,208
5pipe	33.34	102,077	281,338	127,816	409,154	246.93	650,312	559,266
5pipe_1	116.18	255,894	194,417	86,341	280,758	300.59	489,825	380,509
5pipe_2	177.24	362,840	190,681	88,617	279,298	360.67	585,133	392,928
5pipe_3	134.08	292,802	206,226	89,750	295,976	387.65	593,815	405,352
5pipe_4	284.62	503,128	198,872	71,362	270,234	2097.31	1,842,074	360,270
5pipe_5	137.09	283,554	212,402	86,501	298,903	379.19	543,535	448,226
6pipe	297.13	435,781	194,494	94,361	288,855	10,241.64	4,726,470	283,592
6pipe_6	1,056.56	1,326,371	192,991	74,216	267,207	3,455.35	2,615,479	374,503
7pipe	1,657.70	1,276,763	163,934	80,409	244,343	12,685.59	6,687,186	343,710
7pipe_bug	0.29	481	345,986	57,162	403,148	1.00	2,006	481,415

Table 5. Analysis of clause reductions in NOCLAUSE on 4 benchmark suites. Exam: percentage of conflict clauses examined. Rem: percentage of literals removed from the examined clauses.

Benchmark	NOCLAUSE						NOCLAUSE without reductions			
	Time	Decisions	Impl/s	Size	Exam	Rem	Time	Decisions	Impl/s	Size
sss-sat-1.0	225	1,532,843	616,705	39	90%	12%	228	1,624,312	628,953	52
vliw-sat-1.1	1,033	4,455,378	260,779	55	88%	11%	984	4,322,679	281,017	90
fvp-unsat-1.0	172	554,100	402,621	100	73%	11%	402	820,582	311,127	119
fvp-unsat-2.0	4,104	5,537,711	267,858	240	33%	16%	5,675	7,614,898	246,498	418

reduction does not help – the clauses are already quite short. For the two harder suites clause reduction does provide useful performance gains, although the gain is less significant that that achieved with don't cares. We also see that as the problems get harder, the conflict clauses get longer and a smaller percentage of them are examined for reduction (the examined column). However, despite only reducing 33% of the conflicts in the fvp-unsat-2.0 suite, we still cut the average size of the conflicts by almost half. This shows that reducing only some of the conflicts can still have a significant impact on the other learned conflicts.

Table 6 shows in more detail the results of conflict clause reduction on the non-trivial problems in the fvp-unsat-2.0 suite. We see that clause reduction does not always improve performance, e.g., 5pipe and 5pipe_2. However, overall it appears to offer a useful performance enhancement. Clause reduction also influences the branching heuristic (as mentioned above we use ZCHAFF's VSIDS heuristic which counts how many times a literal appears in recent conflict clauses, see [2] for details), and we see

Table 6. Analysis of clause reductions in NOCLAUSE on the non-trivial problems from the fvp-unsat-2.0 benchmark. Exam: percentage of NoGoods examined; Rem: percentage of literals removed from the examined clauses.

Problem	NOCLAUSE						NOCLAUSE without reductions			
	Time	Decisions	Impl/s	Size	Exam	Rem	Time	Decisions	Impl/s	Size
4pipe	9.87	41,637	509,433	40	90%	18%	30.50	105,543	384,022	148
4pipe_1	35.52	114,512	327,098	77	73%	16%	45.13	146,250	324,710	132
4pipe_2	36.50	112,720	327,298	84	71%	16%	54.97	160,462	311,666	132
4pipe_3	62.03	169,117	316,049	108	55%	15%	69.70	189,004	320,735	162
4pipe_4	42.26	122,497	326,186	112	59%	15%	80.13	204,747	303,505	157
5pipe	33.34	102,077	409,154	93	63%	17%	16.29	67,868	437,006	113
5pipe_1	116.18	255,894	280,758	140	42%	14%	195.81	410,159	289,525	204
5pipe_2	177.24	362,840	279,298	165	33%	15%	159.45	348,772	297,682	199
5pipe_3	134.08	292,802	295,976	165	32%	13%	154.02	331,226	294,891	218
5pipe_4	284.62	503,128	270,234	208	30%	13%	504.27	806,083	269,251	264
5pipe_5	137.09	283,554	298,903	172	32%	11%	216.11	424,870	305,280	237
6pipe	297.13	435,781	288,855	232	37%	16%	647.78	834,635	251,934	540
6pipe_6	1,056.56	1,326,371	267,207	309	14%	10%	1,421.42	1,648,993	253,759	380
7pipe	1,657.70	1,276,763	244,343	336	28%	22%	2,053.92	1,778,995	201,923	761
7pipe_bug	0.29	481	403,148	10	100%	0%	0.29	481	403,148	10

that on the fvp-unsat-2.0 suite performance improvement is correlated with the number of decisions. Further analysis of the interaction between the branching heuristic and clause reduction is a topic for future investigation.

6 Conclusion

Our results demonstrate that conversion to CNF is unnecessary. A DPLL like solver can reason with Boolean circuits just as easily as with a clausal theory. We have implemented NOCLAUSE, a non-CNF DPLL like solver with similar raw efficiency to highly optimized clausal DPLL solvers. Reasoning with Boolean circuits offers a number of advantages. For example, we can support much more complex inference like formula rewriting, as well as propagation rules for complex gates like counting gates. We can also use the circuit structure to simplify learned clauses, and to inform branching heuristics. NOCLAUSE is related to a number of previous works on circuit based Boolean solvers. Its main innovations are (a) greater efficiency through adaptation of the watch literal technique and (b) its new technique of conflict clause reduction. It is also the first circuit based solver that performs don't care propagation (previous uses of don't care reasoning have built on top of CNF solvers). We have demonstrated empirically that don't care propagation has a very significant impact on performance, and that conflict clause reduction can offer useful performance improvements.

Our experimental results are very promising. We often outperform a highly optimized solver like ZCHAFF. We expect that the results would be even more favorable if the benchmarks available to us had not already lost some of their structure. As we explained before, the ISCAS format only contains *and*, *or*, and *not* gates. There are many other ways in which we expect performance could be further improved. For example, more complex preprocessing of the input circuit, as in BCSat [16], is likely to offer major efficiency gains. Most interesting, however, is that we have only scratched the surface with respect to using structure to perform more sophisticated clause learning, branching, and non-chronological backtracking. Future work on these topics has the potential to deliver significant performance improvements.

References

1. Davis, M., Logemann, G., Loveland, D.: A machine program for theorem-proving. Communications of the ACM **4** (1962) 394–397
2. Moskewicz, M., Madigan, C., Zhao, Y., Zhang, L., Malik, S.: Chaff: Engineering an efficient sat solver. In: Proc. of the Design Automation Conference (DAC). (2001)
3. Tseitin, G.: On the complexity of proofs in poropositional logics. In Siekmann, J., Wrightson, G., eds.: Automation of Reasoning: Classical Papers in Computational Logic 1967–1970. Volume 2. Springer-Verlag (1983) Originally published 1970.
4. Plaisted, D.A., Greenbaum, S.: A structure-preserving clause form translation. Journal of Symbolic Computation **2** (1986) 293–304
5. Lang, J., Marquis, P.: Complexity results for independence and definability in propositional logic. In: Proceedings of the International Conference on Principles of Knowledge Representation and Reasoning. (1998) 356–367
6. Li, C.M.: Integrating equivalence reasoning into Davis-Putnam procedure. In: Proceedings of the AAAI National Conference (AAAI). (2000) 291–296
7. Ostrowski, R., Grégoire, E., Mazure, B., Sais, L.: Recovering and exploiting structural knowledge from CNF formulas. In: Principles and Practice of Constraint Programming. Number 2470 in Lecture Notes in Computer Science, Springer-Verlag, New York (2002) 185–199
8. Beame, P., Kautz, H., Sabharwal, A.: Using problem structure for efficient clause learning. In: Sixth International Conference on Theory and Applications of Satisfiability Testing (SAT 2003). Number 2919 in Lecture Notes In Computer Science, Springer (2003) 242–256
9. Giunchiglia, E., Sebastiani, R.: Applying the Davis-Putnam procedure to non-clausal formulas. In: AI*IA 99: Advances in Artificial Intelligence: 6th Congress of the Italian Association for Artificial Intelligence. Volume 1792 of Lecture Notes in Computer Science., Springer (2000) 84–95
10. Giunchiglia, E., Maratea, M., Tacchella, A.: Dependent and independent variables for propositional satisfiability. In: Proceedings of the 8th European Conference on Logics in Artificial Intelligence (JELIA). Volume 2424 of Lecture Notes in Computer Science., Springer (2002) 23–26
11. Järvisalo, M., Junttila, T., Niemelä, I.: Unrestricted vs restricted cut in a tableu method for Boolean circuits. In: AI&M 2004, 8th International Symposium on Artificial Intelligence and Mathematics. (2004) Available on-line at http://rutcor.rutgers.edu/ amai/aimath04/.
12. Safarpour, S., Veneris, A., Drechsler, R., Lee, J.: Managing don't cares in Boolean satisfiability. In: Proceedings of the Design, Automation and Test in Europe Conference and Exhibition Volume I (DATE'04), IEEE Computer Society (2004) 10260
13. Gupta, A., Gupta, A., Yang, Z., Ashar, P.: Dynamic detection and removal of inactive clauses in SAT with application in image computation. In: Proceedings of the 38th conference on Design automation, ACM Press (2001) 536–541

14. Circuit-based Boolean Reasoning. In: Proceedings of the 38th conference on Design automation, ACM Press (2001)
15. Ganai, M.K., Ashar, P., Gupta, A., Zhang, L., Malik, S.: Combining strengths of circuit-based and cnf-based algorithms for a high-performance SAT solver. In: Proceedings of the 39th conference on Design automation, ACM Press (2002) 747–750
16. Junttila, T., Niemelä, I.: Towards an efficient tableau method for Boolean circuit satisfiability checking. In: Computational Logic - CL 2000; First International Conference. Volume 1861 of Lecture Notes in Computer Science., Springer (2000) 553–567
17. Zhang, L., Madigan, C.F., Moskewicz, M.H., Malik, S.: Efficient conflict driven learning in a Boolean satisfiability solver. In: Proceedings of the 2001 IEEE/ACM international conference on Computer-aided design, IEEE Press (2001) 279–285
18. Van Gelder, A., Tsuji, Y.K.: Satisfiability testing with more reasoning and less guessing. In Johnson, D., Trick, M., eds.: Cliques, Coloring and Satisfiability. Volume 26 of DIMACS Series in Discrete Mathematics and Theoretical Computer Science. American Mathematical Society (1996) 559–586

A Hyper-arc Consistency Algorithm for the Soft Alldifferent Constraint

Willem Jan van Hoeve

CWI, P.O. Box 94079, 1090 GB Amsterdam, The Netherlands
W.J.van.Hoeve@cwi.nl
http://homepages.cwi.nl/~wjvh/

Abstract. This paper presents an algorithm that achieves hyper-arc consistency for the soft alldifferent constraint. To this end, we prove and exploit the equivalence with a minimum-cost flow problem. Consistency of the constraint can be checked in $O(nm)$ time, and hyper-arc consistency is achieved in $O(m)$ time, where n is the number of variables involved and m is the sum of the cardinalities of the domains. It improves a previous method that did not ensure hyper-arc consistency.

1 Introduction

If a constraint satisfaction problem (CSP) is over-constrained, i.e. has no solution satisfying all constraints, it is natural to allow certain constraints, the soft constraints, to be violated and search for solutions that violate as few soft constraints as possible. Constraints that are not decided to be soft are hard constraints, and should always be satisfied.

Several methods have been proposed to handle over-constrained CSPs, see for instance [6, 2, 4]. In this paper, we follow the scheme proposed by Régin, Petit, Bessière and Puget [11], that is particularly useful for non-binary constraints. The idea is as follows. A cost function is assigned to each soft constraint, measuring the violation. Then the soft CSP is transformed into a constraint optimization problem (COP), where all constraints are hard, and the (weighted) sum of cost functions is minimized. This approach allows one to use specialized filtering algorithms for soft constraints, as shown by Petit, Régin and Bessière [7].

For the soft alldifferent constraint, an algorithm is presented in [7] that removes inconsistent values in $O(m^2 n \sqrt{n})$ time, where n is the number of variables and m the sum of the cardinalities of their domains. However, that algorithm does not ensure hyper-arc consistency. In this paper, we propose an algorithm that does ensure hyper-arc consistency and runs in $O(nm)$ time. In principle, we consider the soft alldifferent constraint as a minimum-cost flow problem in a particular graph. Checking the consistency can then be done in $O(nm)$ time. Thereafter, domain values are checked for consistency by an efficient shortest path computation, which takes in total $O(m)$ time.

The outline of the paper is as follows. Section 2 presents definitions related to constraint satisfaction problems. Section 3 shows a graph-theoretic analysis of the soft alldifferent constraint, using flow theory. In Section 4 the filtering algorithm is presented. We conclude with a discussion in Section 5.

2 Background

We assume familiarity with the basic concepts of constraint programming. For a thorough explanation of constraint programming, see [1].

A constraint satisfaction problem (CSP) consists of a finite set of variables $\mathcal{V} = \{v_1, \ldots, v_r\}$ with finite domains $\mathcal{D} = \{D_1, \ldots, D_r\}$ such that $v_i \in D_i$ for all i, together with a finite set of constraints $\mathcal{C}$, each on a subset of $\mathcal{V}$. A constraint $C \in \mathcal{C}$ is defined as a subset of the Cartesian product of the domains of the variables that are in C. A tuple $(d_1, \ldots, d_r) \in D_1 \times \cdots \times D_r$ is a solution to a CSP if for every constraint $C \in \mathcal{C}$ on the variables $v_{i_1}, \ldots, v_{i_k}$ we have $(d_{i_1}, \ldots, d_{i_k}) \in C$. A constraint optimization problem (COP) is a CSP together with an objective function to be optimized. A solution to a COP is a solution to the corresponding CSP, that has an optimal objective function value.

Definition 1 (Hyper-arc consistency). *A constraint C on the variables $x_1, \ldots, x_k$ is called hyper-arc consistent if for each variable x_i and value $d_i \in D_i$, there exist values $d_1, \ldots, d_{i-1}, d_{i+1}, \ldots, d_k$ in $D_1, \ldots, D_{i-1}, D_{i+1}, \ldots, D_k$, such that $(d_1, \ldots, d_k) \in C$.*

Definition 2 (Consistent CSP). *A CSP is hyper-arc consistent if all its constraints are hyper-arc consistent. A CSP is inconsistent if it has no solution. Similarly for a COP.*

Definition 3 (Pairwise difference). *Let $x_1, \ldots, x_n$ be variables with respective finite domains $D_1, \ldots, D_n$. Then*

$$\texttt{alldifferent}(x_1, \ldots, x_n) = \{(d_1, \ldots, d_n) \mid d_i \in D_i, d_j \neq d_k \text{ for } j \neq k\}.$$

In [7], two different measures of violation for a soft constraint are presented. The first is the minimum number of variables that need to change their value in order to satisfy the constraint. For this measure, applied to the alldifferent constraint, [7] also contains a hyper-arc consistency algorithm. The second measure is the number of violated constraints in the binary decomposition of the constraint, if this decomposition exists. For the alldifferent constraint, such a decomposition does exist, namely $x_i \neq x_j$ for $i \in \{1, \ldots, n-1\}, j \in \{i+1, \ldots, n\}$. We follow this second, more refined, measure and present it in terms of the soft alldifferent constraint. For $\texttt{alldifferent}(x_1, \ldots, x_n)$, let the cost of violation be defined as

$$\text{violation}(x_1, \ldots, x_n) = |\{(i, j) \mid x_i = x_j, \text{ for } i < j\}|. \tag{1}$$

Definition 4 (Soft pairwise difference). *Let $x_1, \ldots, x_n, z$ be variables with respective finite domains $D_1, \ldots, D_n, D_z$. Then*

$$\texttt{soft\_alldifferent}(x_1, \ldots, x_n, z) =$$
$$\{(d_1, \ldots, d_n, \tilde{d}) \mid d_i \in D_i, \tilde{d} \in D_z, \text{violation}(d_1, \ldots, d_n) \leq \tilde{d}\}.$$

The variable z in Definition 4 will serve as a so-called cost variable, which will be minimized during the solution process. This means that admissible tuples in Definition 4 are those instantiations of variables, such that the number of violated dis-equality constraints $d_i \neq d_j$ is not more than that of the currently best found solution, represented by $\max D_z$. At the same time, $\min D_z$ should not be less than the currently lowest possible value of $\text{violation}(x_1, \ldots, x_n)$.

An over-constrained CSP with an alldifferent constraint is transformed into a COP by introducing z, replacing alldifferent with soft_alldifferent, and minimizing z. This is illustrated in the following example.

Example 1. Consider the following over-constrained CSP

$$x_1 \in \{a, b\}, x_2 \in \{a, b\}, x_3 \in \{a, b\}, x_4 \in \{b, c\},$$
$$\text{alldifferent}(x_1, x_2, x_3, x_4).$$

We transform this CSP into

$$z \in \{0, \ldots, 6\},$$
$$x_1 \in \{a, b\}, x_2 \in \{a, b\}, x_3 \in \{a, b\}, x_4 \in \{b, c\},$$
$$\text{soft\_alldifferent}(x_1, x_2, x_3, x_4, z),$$
$$\text{minimize } z.$$

This COP is not hyper-arc consistent, as there is no support for $z < 1$. If we remove 0 from D_z, the COP is hyper-arc consistent, because there are at most 6 simultaneously violated dis-equalities. Suppose now that during the search for a solution, we have found the tuple $(x_1, x_2, x_3, x_4, z) = (a, a, b, c, 1)$, that has one violated dis-equality. Then $z \in \{1\}$ in the remaining search. As the assignment $x_4 = b$ always leads to a solution with $z \geq 2$, b can be removed from D_4. The resulting COP is hyper-arc consistent again.

One should take into account that a simplified CSP is considered in Example 1. In general, a CSP can consist of many more constraints, and also more cost-variables that together with z form an objective function to be minimized.

Throughout this paper, let $m = \sum_{i \in \{1, \ldots, n\}} |D_i|$ for variables $x_1, \ldots, x_n$.

3 Graph-Theoretic Analysis

A directed graph is a pair $G = (V, A)$ where V is a finite set of vertices V and A is a family[1] of ordered pairs from V, called arcs. A pair occurring more than once in A is called a multiple arc. For $v \in V$, let $\delta^{\text{in}}(v)$ and $\delta^{\text{out}}(v)$ denote the family of arcs entering and leaving v respectively.

A (directed) walk in G is a sequence $P = v_0, a_1, v_1, \ldots, a_k, v_k$ where $k \geq 0$, $v_0, v_1, \ldots, v_k \in V$, $a_1, \ldots, a_k \in A$ and $a_i = (v_{i-1}, v_i)$ for $i = 1, \ldots, k$. If there is no confusion, P may be denoted as $P = v_0, v_1, \ldots, v_k$. A (directed) walk is called a (directed) path if $v_0, \ldots, v_k$ are distinct. A closed (directed) walk, i.e. $v_0 = v_k$, is called a (directed) circuit if $v_1, \ldots, v_k$ are distinct.

---

[1] A family is a set in which elements may occur more than once.

3.1 Minimum-Cost Flow Problem

First, we introduce the concept of a flow, following Schrijver [12, pp. 148–150].

Let $G = (V, A)$ be a directed graph and let $s, t \in V$. A function $f : A \to \mathbb{R}$ is called a flow from s to t, or an $s-t$ flow, if

$$\begin{aligned}(i) \ & f(a) \geq 0 & \text{for each } a \in A, \\ (ii) \ & f(\delta^{\text{out}}(v)) = f(\delta^{\text{in}}(v)) \text{ for each } v \in V \setminus \{s, t\},\end{aligned} \quad (2)$$

where $f(S) = \sum_{a \in S} f(a)$ for all $S \subseteq A$. Property $(2)(ii)$ ensures flow conservation, i.e. for a vertex $v \neq s, t$, the amount of flow entering v is equal to the amount of flow leaving v.

The value of an $s-t$ flow f is defined as

$$\text{value}(f) = f(\delta^{\text{out}}(s)) - f(\delta^{\text{in}}(s)).$$

In other words, the value of a flow is the net amount of flow leaving s, which can be shown to be equal to the net amount of flow entering t.

When we study flows we typically endow capacity constraints, via a "capacity" function $c : A \to \mathbb{R}_+$. We say that a flow f is under c if $f(a) \leq c(a)$ for each $a \in A$. A feasible flow is a flow under c.

We also assign costs to flows via a "cost" function $w : A \to \mathbb{R}_+$. Doing so the cost of a flow f is defined as

$$\text{cost}(f) = \sum_{a \in A} w(a) f(a).$$

A minimum-cost flow is an $s-t$ flow under c of maximum value and minimum cost. The minimum-cost flow problem is the problem of finding such a minimum-cost flow.

A minimum-cost flow can be computed using an algorithm originally due to Ford and Fulkerson [5] (we follow the description given by Schrijver [12, pp. 183–185]). It consists of successively finding shortest (with respect to the cost function) $s-t$ paths in the so-called residual graph, while maintaining an optimal flow.

Define the residual graph $G_f = (V, A_f)$ of f (with respect to c), where

$$A_f = \{a \mid a \in A, f(a) < c(a)\} \cup \{a^{-1} \mid a \in A, f(a) > 0\}.$$

Here $a^{-1} = (v, u)$ if $a = (u, v)$. We extend w to $A^{-1} = \{a^{-1} \mid a \in A\}$ by defining

$$w(a^{-1}) = -w(a)$$

for each $a \in A$.

Any directed path P in G_f gives an undirected path in $G = (V, A)$. We define $\chi^P \in \mathbb{R}^A$ by

$$\chi^P(a) = \begin{cases} 1 & \text{if } P \text{ traverses } a, \\ -1 & \text{if } P \text{ traverses } a^{-1}, \\ 0 & \text{if } P \text{ traverses neither } a \text{ nor } a^{-1}, \end{cases}$$

Algorithm 1 Minimum-cost $s-t$ flow.

set $f = \mathbf{0}$
while termination criterion not satisfied **do**
    compute minimum-cost $s-t$ path P in G_f
    if no $s-t$ path in G_f exists **then**
        terminate
    else
        set ε maximal, such that $\mathbf{0} \leq f + \varepsilon\chi^P \leq c$
        reset $f = f + \varepsilon\chi^P$
    end if
end while

---

for $a \in A$. Define the cost of a path P as $\text{cost}(P) = \sum_{a \in P} w(a)$.

Call a feasible flow extreme when it has minimum cost among all feasible flows with the same value. Then the following holds (cf. [12, Theorem 12.3 and 12.4]). Let $\mathbf{0}$ denote the all-zero vector of appropriate size.

Theorem 1. *A flow f is extreme if and only if each directed circuit of G_f has nonnegative cost.*

Theorem 2. *Let f be an extreme flow in $G = (V, A)$. Let P be a minimum-cost $s - t$ path in G_f, for some $s, t \in V$, and let $\varepsilon > 0$ be such that $f' = f + \varepsilon\chi^P$ satisfies $\mathbf{0} \leq f' \leq c$. Then f' is an extreme flow again.*

In fact, for f, P, ε and f' in Theorem 2 holds

$$\text{value}(f') = \text{value}(f) + \varepsilon,$$
$$\text{cost}(f') = \text{cost}(f) + \varepsilon \cdot \text{cost}(P).$$

This means that we can find a minimum-cost $s - t$ flow in G by successively computing minimum-cost $s - t$ paths in G_f. Along such a path we increase the amount of flow to the maximum possible value ε. By Theorem 2, the last flow (of maximum value) we obtain must be extreme, and hence optimal. This is presented as Algorithm 1. Note that the cost of minimum-cost $s - t$ paths in G_f is bounded, because there are no directed circuits of negative cost in G_f. For rational capacities, Algorithm 1 terminates with a feasible $s - t$ flow of maximum value and minimum cost. Although faster algorithms exist for general minimum-cost flow problems, Algorithm 1 suffices when applied to our problem. This is because in our particular graph Algorithm 1 is faster than the algorithms for general minimum-cost flow problems.

3.2 From soft_alldifferent to Minimum-Cost Flow

We transform the problem of finding a solution to the soft_alldifferent constraint into a minimum-cost flow problem.

Construct the directed graph $G = (V, A)$ with

$$V = \{s, t\} \cup X \cup D_X$$

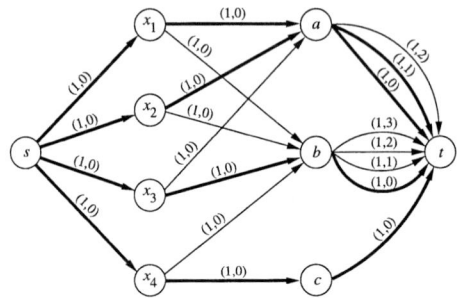

Fig. 1. Graph G for the soft_alldifferent constraint of Example 1. For each arc a, $(c(a), w(a))$ is given. Bold arcs indicate an optimal $s - t$ flow with cost 1.

and
$$A = A_X \cup A_s \cup A_t$$

where
$$X = \{x_1, \ldots, x_n\},$$
$$D_X = \bigcup_{i \in \{1,\ldots,n\}} D_i,$$

and
$$A_X = \{(x_i, d) \mid d \in D_i\},$$
$$A_s = \{(s, x_i) \mid i \in \{1, \ldots, n\}\},$$
$$A_t = \{(d, t) \mid d \in D_i, i \in \{1, \ldots, n\}\}.$$

Note that A_t contains parallel arcs if two or more variables share a domain value. If there are k parallel arcs (d, t) between some $d \in D_X$ and t, we distinguish them by numbering the arcs as $(d, t)_0, (d, t)_1, \ldots, (d, t)_{k-1}$ in a fixed but arbitrary way.

To each arc $a \in A$, we assign a capacity $c(a) = 1$ and a cost $w(a)$. If $a \in A_s \cup A_X$, then $w(a) = 0$. If $a \in A_t$, so $a = (d, t)_i$ for some $d \in D_X$ and integer i, the value of $w(a) = i$.

In Figure 1, the graph G for the soft_alldifferent constraint in Example 1 is depicted. For each arc a, $(c(a), w(a))$ is given.

Theorem 3. *An integer flow f that is a solution to the minimum-cost flow problem in G corresponds to an instantiation of variables $x_1, \ldots, x_n$ in soft_alldifferent$(x_1, \ldots, x_n, z)$, minimizing violation$(x_1, \ldots, x_n)$.*

Proof. For an integer flow f in G, $f(a) = 1$ if arc a is used, and $f(a) = 0$ otherwise. An arc $a = (x_i, d) \in A_X$ with $f(a) = 1$ corresponds to the instantiation $x_i = d$. By construction, every solution f to the minimum-cost flow problem in G has value$(f) = n$. Thus a solution corresponds to assigning a value to each variable x_i, $i \in \{1, \ldots, n\}$.

The cost function $w(a_i) = i$ for k parallel arcs $a_0, \ldots, a_{k-1} \in A_t$ corresponds to counting the number of violations caused by assigning $i + 1$ variables to a particular value. Namely, for these parallel arcs, a minimum-cost $s - t$ path in G_f uses the arc with lowest cost first. Using arc a_i (the $(i + 1)$st arc) causes a "violation" with the i previously used arcs. Thus, for a feasible flow f, which corresponds to an assignment of $x_1, \ldots, x_n$, $\sum_{a \in A} w(a)f(a)$ measures exactly violation$(x_1, \ldots, x_n)$. Hence, a minimum-cost flow minimizes violation$(x_1, \ldots, x_n)$. □

Consider again the graph G in Figure 1. A bold arc a in G denotes $f(a) = 1$. This particular flow f has value$(f) = 4$ and cost$(f) = 1$. Indeed, the only violation is $x_1 = a = x_2$.

Next we describe the behaviour of Algorithm 1 to compute a minimum-cost flow in G. We need to compute a sequence of minimum-cost $s - t$ paths in G_f, maintaining extreme intermediate flows. Note that along each minimum-cost $s-t$ path in G_f we can increase the flow by a maximum of $\varepsilon = 1$. Hence all extreme flows in G are integer. By construction, there are exactly n such paths, each containing one arc in A_s (in fact, the paths may as well be computed starting from the vertices x_i instead of s, using only arcs in A_X and A_t). Further, each minimum-cost $s - t$ path contains exactly one arc in A_t. Namely, consider a minimum-cost path P using multiple arcs in A_t. Then P consists of an $s-t$ path with one arc in A_s, followed by a $t-t$ path. If the $t-t$ path has cost 0, we may omit this part, and use only the $s-t$ path with one arc in A_s. If the $t-t$ path, which is a circuit, has negative cost, it contradicts Theorem 1. Effectively, it means that the $t-t$ path could have been used to improve the preceding intermediate solution, thus contradicting the extremity of that solution. To conclude, the minimum-cost paths we need to compute use exactly one arc in A_s and one arc in A_t. It follows that these paths can be computed in $O(m)$ time, and the total time complexity for finding a maximum flow of minimum cost in G is $O(nm)$. Hence it follows, by Theorem 3, that consistency of the soft_alldifferent constraint can be checked in $O(nm)$ time.

4 The Filtering Algorithm

The following theorem identifies hyper-arc consistent domain values for the soft_alldifferent constraint. For an arc a of G, let G^a arise from G by enforcing $f(a) = 1$ for every flow f in G.

Theorem 4. *The constraint* soft_alldifferent$(x_1, \ldots, x_n, z)$ *is hyper-arc consistent if and only if*

(i) *for all all arcs $a \in A_X$ a minimum-cost flow of maximum value in G^a has cost at most $\max D_z$,*
(ii) *all values in D_z are not smaller than the cost of a minimum-cost flow of maximum value in G.*

Proof. Enforcing $f(a) = 1$ for arc $a = (x_i, d)$ corresponds to assigning $x_i = d$. The result follows from Definition 1 and Theorem 3. Namely, property (i) checks consistency for all domain values in $D_1, \ldots, D_n$. Property (ii) checks consistency of the domain values of D_z. □

Algorithm 2 Naive hyper-arc consistency.

---
set minimum = ∞
for $x_i \in X$ do
  for $d \in D_i$ do
    compute minimum-cost $s - t$ flow f in G^a where $a = (x_i, d)$
    if cost$(f) > \max D_z$ **then**
      remove d from D_i
    end if
    if cost$(f) <$ minimum **then**
      set minimum $=$ cost(f)
    end if
  end for
end for
if $\min D_z <$ minimum **then**
  set $\min D_z =$ minimum
end if

Using Theorem 4, we can construct an algorithm that enforces hyper-arc consistency for the soft_alldifferent constraint, presented as Algorithm 2. For all variables $x_i \in X$, the algorithm scans all domain values $d \in D_i$, and checks whether there exists a minimum-cost $s - t$ flow in G^a, where $a = (x_i, d)$, of maximum value with cost at most $\max D_z$. If such a flow does not exist, then, by Theorem 4, d is removed from D_i. Finally, we remove all values of D_z which are smaller than the cost of a minimum-cost flow in G. The time complexity of Algorithm 2 is $O(m^2 n)$.

We can construct a more efficient filtering algorithm, however. It is presented as Algorithm 3, and makes use of the following theorem. We follow the notation introduced in Section 3.1.

Theorem 5. *Let f be an extreme flow of maximum value in G. Let $a = (x_i, d) \in A_X$ and P a minimum-cost $d - x_i$ path in G_f. Let $f^\star$ be an extreme flow of maximum value in G^a. Then* cost$(f^\star) =$ cost$(f) +$ cost(P).

Proof. Either $f(a) = 1$ or $f(a) = 0$. In case $f(a) = 1$, $f^\star(a) = 1$, $P = d, x_i$, cost$(P) = 0$ and we are done. In case $f(a) = 0$, first note that there exists a $d - x_i$ path in G_f. Namely, there is exactly one $d' \in D_i$ for which $f((x_i, d')) = 1$, which allows the path d, t, d', x_i. Let P be a minimum-cost $d - x_i$ path in G_f. Together with arc (x_i, d) P forms a circuit C. The directed circuit C in G_f gives an undirected circuit in G^a. For all $b \in A$, define flow $f^\star$ in G^a as follows:

$$f^\star(b) = \begin{cases} 0 & \text{if } b^{-1} \in C \\ 1 & \text{if } b \in C \\ f(b) & \text{else.} \end{cases}$$

It is easy to check that $f^\star$ is again a flow of maximum value.

Because f is extreme, we may assume that P enters and leaves t only once, say via arcs b_{in} and b_{out} respectively (where $b_{\text{in}} = (d, t)$). It follows that cost$(P) =$

Algorithm 3 More efficient hyper-arc consistency.
---
compute minimum-cost flow f in G
if $\text{cost}(f) > \max D_z$ then
    return INCONSISTENT
end if
if $\min D_z < \text{cost}(f)$ then
    set $\min D_z = \text{cost}(f)$
end if
for $a = (x_i, d)$ with $f(a) = 0$ do
    compute minimum-cost $d - x_i$ path P in G_f
    if $\text{cost}(f) + \text{cost}(P) > \max D_z$ then
        remove d from D_i
    end if
end for

$w(b_{\text{in}}) - w(b_{\text{out}})$. From Theorem 1 we know that $\text{cost}(P) \geq 0$. Similarly,

$$\begin{aligned}\text{cost}(f^\star) &= \sum_{b \in A} f^\star(b) w(b) \\ &= \sum_{b \in A} f(b) w(b) + w(b_{\text{in}}) - w(b_{\text{out}}) \\ &= \text{cost}(f) + \text{cost}(P)\end{aligned}$$

It remains to show that $f^\star$ is extreme in G^a. Suppose not, i.e. there exists a flow g in G^a with maximum value and $\text{cost}(g) < \text{cost}(f^\star)$. As $\text{cost}(f^\star) = \text{cost}(f) + \text{cost}(P)$ and $\text{cost}(P) \geq 0$, there are two possibilities. The first is that $\text{cost}(g) < \text{cost}(f)$, which is not possible because f is extreme. The second is that there exists an $x_i - d$ path P' in G_f with $\text{cost}(P') < \text{cost}(P)$ which also leads to a contradiction because P is a minimum-cost path. Hence $f^\star$ is extreme. $\square$

Algorithm 3 first computes a minimum-cost flow f in G. This takes $O(nm)$ time, as we have seen in Section 3.2. If $\text{cost}(f) > \max D_z$, we know that the soft_alldifferent constraint is inconsistent. If this is not the case, we update $\min D_z$. Next, we scan all arcs $a = (x_i, d)$ for which $f(a) = 0$. For each of these arcs, we compute a minimum-cost $d - x_i$ path P in G_f. By Theorem 5 and Theorem 4, we remove d from D_i if $\text{cost}(f) + \text{cost}(P) > \max D_z$. This can be done efficiently, as shown by the following theorem.

Theorem 6. *Let* soft_alldifferent$(x_1, \ldots, x_n, z)$ *be consistent and f an integer minimum-cost flow in G. Then* soft_alldifferent$(x_1, \ldots, x_n, z)$ *can be made hyper-arc consistent in $O(m)$ time.*

Proof. The complexity of the filtering algorithm depends on the computation of the minimum-cost $d - x_i$ paths for arcs (x_i, d). We make use of the fact that only arcs $a \in A_t$ contribute to the cost of such a path.

Consider the strongly connected components[2] of the graph $\tilde{G}_f$ which is a copy of G_f where s and t and all their incident arcs are removed. Let P be a minimum-cost $d - x_i$ path P in G_f. If P is equal to d, x_i then $f(x_i, d) = 1$ and $\text{cost}(P) = 0$.

---
[2] A strongly connected component in a directed graph $G = (V, A)$ is a subset of vertices $S \subseteq V$ such that there exists a directed $u - v$ path in G for all $u, v \in S$.

Otherwise, either x_i and d are in the same strongly connected component of $\tilde{G}_f$, or not. In case they are in the same strongly connected component, P can avoid t in G_f, and $\text{cost}(P) = 0$. In case x_i and d are in different strongly connected components of $\tilde{G}_f$, say $x_i \in S_1$ and $d \in S_2$, we have

$$\text{cost}(P) = \min_{\substack{a \in \{(d',t) \mid (d',t) \in A_f, \\ d' \in S_2\}}} w(a) + \min_{\substack{a \in \{(t,d'') \mid (t,d'') \in A_f, \\ d'' \in S_1 \text{ or } (d'',x_i) \in A_f\}}} w(a). \quad (3)$$

Property (3) follows from the fact that P uses exactly one ingoing and one outgoing arc for t.

Arcs a with $f(a) = 1$ or within a strongly connected component will all use a minimum-cost path with cost equal to 0, and will therefore be all consistent if $\text{cost}(f) \leq \max D_z$. For all other arcs, we can resort to property (3). For this we only have to compute once for each strongly connected component S of $\tilde{G}_f$ the minimum-cost arc going from S to t and the minimum-cost arc going from t to S (if such arcs exist), which takes in total $O(m)$ time. The strongly connected components of $\tilde{G}_f$ can be computed in $O(n+m)$ time, following Tarjan [14]. Hence the total time complexity of achieving hyper-arc consistency is $O(m)$, as $n < m$. □

The proof of Theorem 6 applies to any constraint whose graph representation resembles G and has only costs on arcs from D_X to t. For all such constraints that are consistent, hyper-arc consistency can be achieved in $O(m)$ time. Note that this is equal to the complexity of achieving hyper-arc consistency on these constraints if no costs are involved.

5 Conclusion and Discussion

We have presented an algorithm that checks consistency of the soft_alldifferent constraint on n variables in $O(nm)$ time and achieves hyper-arc consistency in $O(m)$ time, where m is the sum of the cardinalities of the domains. A previous method for removing domain values that are inconsistent with the soft_alldifferent constraint did not ensure hyper-arc consistency [7]. Moreover, that method has a time complexity of $O(m^2n\sqrt{n})$. Hence our algorithm improves on this in terms of quality as well as time complexity.

The soft_alldifferent constraint is related to the standard alldifferent constraint [8] and the minimum weight alldifferent constraint [3]. The minimum weight alldifferent constraint is a particular instance of the global cardinality constraint with costs [9, 10]. For that constraint, hyper-arc consistency can be achieved in $O(n(m + d \log d))$ time, where d is the cardinality of the union of all domains [9, 10, 13]. It is achieved by finding n shortest paths, each taking $O(m + d \log d)$ time to compute. Although our algorithm has a similar flavour, the underlying graphs have a different cost structure. We improve the efficiency by exploiting the cost structure of our particular graph when computing the shortest paths. Our result can be applied to other constraints with a similar graph representation and cost structure.

Acknowledgements

Many thanks to Bert Gerards for valuable comments. Thanks also go to Sebastian Brand for fruitful discussion. Finally, the constructive remarks of Jean-Charles Régin were highly appreciated.

References

1. K.R. Apt. *Principles of Constraint Programming*. Cambridge University Press, 2003.
2. S. Bistarelli, U. Montanari, and F. Rossi. Semiring-based Constraint Satisfaction and Optimization. *Journal of the ACM*, 44(2):201–236, 1997.
3. Y. Caseau and F. Laburthe. Solving Various Weighted Matching Problems with Constraints. In G. Smolka, editor, *Proceedings of the Third International Conference on Principles and Practice of Constraint Programming (CP'97)*, volume 1330 of *LNCS*, pages 17–31. Springer, 1997.
4. M.C. Cooper and T. Schiex. Arc consistency for soft constraints. *Artificial Intelligence*, 2004. To appear.
5. L.R. Ford and D.R. Fulkerson. Constructing maximal dynamic flows from static flows. *Operations Research*, 6:419–433, 1958.
6. E.C. Freuder and R.J. Wallace. Partial constraint satisfaction. *Artificial Intelligence*, 58(1-3):21–70, 1992.
7. T. Petit, J.-C. Régin, and C. Bessière. Specific Filtering Algorithms for Over-Constrained Problems. In T. Walsh, editor, *Proceedings of the Seventh International Conference on Principles and Practice of Constraint Programming (CP 2001)*, volume 2239 of *LNCS*, pages 451–463. Springer, 2001.
8. J.-C. Régin. A Filtering Algorithm for Constraints of Difference in CSPs. In *Proceedings of the Twelfth National Conference on Artificial Intelligence (AAAI-94)*, volume 1, pages 362–367, 1994.
9. J.-C. Régin. Arc Consistency for Global Cardinality Constraints with Costs. In J. Jaffar, editor, *Proceedings of the Fifth International Conference on Principles and Practice of Constraint Programming (CP'99)*, volume 1713 of *LNCS*, pages 390–404. Springer, 1999.
10. J.-C. Régin. Cost-Based Arc Consistency for Global Cardinality Constraints. *Constraints*, 7:387–405, 2002.
11. J.-C. Régin, T. Petit, C. Bessière, and J.-F. Puget. An Original Constraint Based Approach for Solving over Constrained Problems. In R. Dechter, editor, *Proceedings of the Sixth International Conference on Principles and Practice of Constraint Programming (CP 2000)*, volume 1894 of *LNCS*, pages 543–548. Springer, 2000.
12. A. Schrijver. *Combinatorial Optimization - Polyhedra and Efficiency*. Springer, 2003.
13. M. Sellmann. An Arc-Consistency Algorithm for the Minimum Weight All Different Constraint. In P. Van Hentenryck, editor, *Proceedings of the Eighth International Conference on Principles and Practice of Constraint Programming (CP 2002)*, volume 2470 of *LNCS*, pages 744–749. Springer, 2002.
14. R. Tarjan. Depth-first search and linear graph algorithms. *SIAM Journal on Computing*, 1:146–160, 1972.

Efficient Strategies for (Weighted) Maximum Satisfiability*

Zhao Xing and Weixiong Zhang

Department of Computer Science and Engineering
Washington University in St. Louis
St. Louis, MO 63130, USA

Abstract. It is well known that the Davis-Putnam-Logemann-Loveland (DPLL) algorithm for satisfiability (SAT) can be extended to an algorithm for maximum SAT (max-SAT). In this paper, we propose a number of strategies to significantly improve this max-SAT method. The first strategy is a set of unit propagation rules; the second is an effective lookahead heuristic based on linear programming; and the third strategy is a dynamic variable ordering that exploits problem constrainedness during search. We integrate these strategies in an efficient complete solver for both max-SAT and weighted max-SAT. Our experimental results on random problem instances and many instances from SATLIB demonstrate the efficacy of these strategies and show that the new solver is able to significantly outperform most of the existing complete max-SAT solvers, with a few orders of magnitude of improvement in running time in many cases.

1 Introduction and Overview

Given a set of clauses of Boolean variables, the aim of maximum satisfiability (max-SAT) is to satisfy the maximum number of clauses [5], an NP-hard optimization problem. Weighted max-SAT is an extension of max-SAT in which a clause carries a weight, representing the significance of the clause or the induced penalty if it is violated. Weighted max-SAT maximizes the total weight of the satisfied clauses, and is more general than its unweighted counterpart max-SAT. For simplicity, in the following discussions, when we mention max-SAT, we refer to both weighted and unweighted max-SAT. Max-SAT has many real-world applications [8, 10] such as in scheduling, configuration problems, probabilistic reasoning, auction, and pattern recognition.

It is known that the Davis-Putnam-Logemann-Loveland (DPLL) algorithm for SAT [4] can be extended to a branch-and-bound (BnB) algorithm for max-SAT. BnB-based DPLL has been shown to be one of the best algorithms for max-SAT [23]. Much effort has been devoted to improving the performance of a BnB-based DPLL algorithm for max-SAT by combining the techniques previously developed for SAT [23, 15, 2] and many methods in operations research, such as linear programming (LP) and cutting plane methods [12, 15, 6]. However, these researches have enjoyed a limited success,

---

* This research was supported in part by NSF grants IIS-0196057 and ITR/EIA-0113618, and in part by DARPA Cooperative Agreement F30602-00-2-0531. We thank Zhongsheng Guo for an early implementation of the DPLL algorithm and Fadi Aloul, Javier Larrosa and Jordi Plane for making their programs available to us for this research.

especially on large, complex problems. In particular, the current OR-based approaches are more effective than the DPLL-based algorithms only on max-2-SAT [15]. On the other hand, even if a BnB-based DPLL algorithm is competitive for max-SAT, it can handle relatively small problems with moderate degrees of constrainedness.

Therefore, despite the previous effort, much work is still needed to develop efficient algorithms for both max-SAT and weighted max-SAT, and special care is required to extend the techniques previously developed for SAT. Note that most techniques for SAT take advantage of the fact that SAT is a decision problem, so that a search avenue can be abandoned whenever a constraint violation becomes evident. This fact has been properly captured in the unit resolution or unit propagation methods and different variable ordering rules used by the DPLL algorithm and its variants. In contrast, the study of unit propagation methods and variable ordering for max-SAT is limited, except the work of [8, 23]. It is important to note that max-SAT has its own intrinsic features that are remarkably different from its decision counterpart. Many existing techniques for SAT must be reconsidered carefully when being applied to max-SAT. Overall, it is much harder to develop effective and efficient algorithms for max-SAT than for SAT, and the research of developing efficient max-SAT solver deserves much attention, due to the generality and importance of the problem.

Aiming to solve difficult max-SAT and weighted max-SAT problems *optimally*, we develop an efficient exact max-SAT algorithm based on the DPLL algorithm for SAT. Our algorithm has three ingredients, which can be viewed as novel extensions to the main ideas behind the existing methods for SAT. The first method consists of a set of unit propagation methods for max-SAT. This is important because the unit propagation for SAT cannot be directly applied to max-SAT and the lack of efficient unit propagation methods is one of the major roadblocks to efficient max-SAT algorithms. One of our unit propagation methods is based on a novel nonlinear integer programming formulation of max-SAT. The second element of our algorithm is an effective lookahead heuristic based on linear programming (LP) [11] to estimate the minimum number of clauses unsatisfiable at a node during the search. This is a remarkable contribution, as it is perhaps the first successful application of LP to max-SAT, despite similar (but not successful) previous effort to apply integer LP (ILP) to max-SAT [12, 15, 6]. The third ingredient is a dynamic weighted variable ordering that was motivated by the two successful variable ordering methods for SAT, namely, the Mom's heuristic rule [16] and the two-side Jeroslow-Wang rule [13]. We extensively analyze the performance of the new algorithm and compare it with most, if not all, existing max-SAT solvers that are available to us. The experimental analysis was carried out on random unweighted and weighted max-SAT as well as unsatisfiable problem instances from SATLIB [14].

2 Linear and Nonlinear Programming Formulation of Max-SAT

In this section, we formulate max-SAT in linear and nonlinear programming.

2.1 Linear Programming Formulation

Max-SAT can be formulated in an integer linear program (ILP) [15] or pseudo-Boolean formula [24, 6]. We map a Boolean variable v to an integer variable x that takes value

1 when v is True or 0 when it is False, i.e., $x = 1$ or 0 when $v = T$ or F, respectively. We then map $\bar{v}$ to $1 - x$. With these mappings, we can formulate a clause as a linear inequality. For example, clause $(v_1 \vee \bar{v}_2 \vee v_3)$ can be mapped to $x_1 + (1 - x_2) + x_3 \geq 1$. Here, the inequality means that the clause must be satisfied in order for the left side of the inequality to have a value no less than one.

However, a clause in a max-SAT may not be satisfied, so that the corresponding inequality may be violated. To address this issue, we introduce an auxiliary integer variable y to the left side of a mapped inequality. Variable $y = 1$ if the corresponding clause is unsatisfied, making the inequality valid; otherwise, $y = 0$. Since the objective is to minimize the total weights of violated clauses, it is equivalent to minimize the sum of the products of the clause weights and the auxiliary variables that are forced to take value 1. For example, $(v_1 \vee \bar{v}_2 \vee v_3)$ (weight 2), $(v_2 \vee \bar{v}_4)$ (weight 3) can be written as an ILP of minimizing $W = 2y_1 + 3y_2$, subject to the constraints of $x_1 + (1 - x_2) + x_3 + y_1 \geq 1$ and $x_2 + (1 - x_4) + y_2 \geq 1$.

The linear 0-1 programming formulation of max-SAT suggests that the problem could be solved by integer linear programming (ILP). However, ILP is still NP-hard. Furthermore, as shown in [15], except for max-2-SAT, a direct application of ILP to other max-SAT problems does not seem to be effective.

2.2 Nonlinear Programming Formulation

The ILP formulation of max-SAT can be extended to a nonlinear programming formulation by applying the inclusion-exclusion principle [17], so that inequalities in an ILP can be turned into equalities in an integer nonlinear program. Here we introduce an integer expression to represent a *literal*. For example, for $(v_1 \vee \bar{v}_2 \vee v_3)$, we introduce integer expressions $x_1, 1 - x_2$ and x_3 for the literals $v_1, \bar{v}_2$ and v_3. Such an integer expression takes value 1 if its corresponding literal is set to true, or value 0 otherwise. Using the inclusion-exclusion principle, for the i-th 3-literal clause of a given formula, e.g., $(v_1 \vee \bar{v}_2 \vee v_3)$, we then write a nonlinear equation $f + y_i = 1$. For this example of $(v_1 \vee \bar{v}_2 \vee v_3)$, we have

$$f = [x_1 + 1 - x_2 + x_3] - [x_1(1 - x_2) + x_1 x_3 + (1 - x_2)x_3] + x_1(1 - x_2)x_3$$

It is important to note that f can take either value 1 or 0. Specifically, $f = 0$ if no literal in the clause is set to true, or $f = 1$ otherwise. As in the ILP formulation, we introduce auxiliary variables, y_i's, to count for unsatisfied clauses. Here, $y_i = 1$ if $f = 0$, and $y_i = 0$ if $f = 1$. For a binary clause, e.g., $(v_1 \vee v_3)$ or a unit clause, e.g., $(\bar{v}_2)$, the corresponding nonlinear equation becomes $x_1 + x_3 - x_1 x_3 + y_i = 1$ or $1 - x_2 + y_i = 1$. The objective of this nonlinear integer program is the same as ILP, i.e., minimizing $W = \sum_{i=1}^{m} w_i y_i$, where w_i is the weight of the i-th clause and y_i is the auxiliary variable introduced to the i-th clause of a formula of m clauses.

3 DPLL Algorithm for Max-SAT

The DPLL algorithm [4] for SAT is a backtracking algorithm that progressively instantiates one variable at a time in searching for a satisfying variable assignment. In each step, the algorithm selects a variable and branches to two possible values, T and F.

Whenever a contradiction occurs by setting a variable to T or F, the algorithm backtracks. The process continues until either a satisfying assignment is found or it can conclude that no such assignment exists.

DPLL for SAT can be extended to max-SAT using depth-first branch-and-bound (DFBnB). Due to the space limit, here we only point out the two main differences between DFBnB for max-SAT and DPLL for SAT. First, DFBnB uses an upper bound α on the minimum total weight of clauses that cannot be satisfied, which may not be zero for max-SAT. In other words, DPLL for SAT can be viewed as a special DFBnB with $\alpha = 0$ throughout the search, disallowing any clause violation, and making unit propagation very effective for SAT. Second, DFBnB can abandon a node during the search only if the total weight of violated clauses so far (the g value in the A* algorithm) plus a lower bound on the minimum total weight of clauses that cannot be satisfied in the remaining clauses (the h value in the A* algorithm) at the node exceeds α. This indicates that max-SAT becomes more difficult when the constrainedness increases, allowing more clauses to be unsatisfied and causing a larger upper bound α. This also implies that one method to reduce search cost is to accurately estimate the weight cost of the clauses that cannot be satisfied in the remaining clauses at a node (the h value), so as to increase the possibility of pruning the node if it indeed cannot lead to a better solution. This last observation has motivated us to develop an LP-based heuristic in this paper.

A step of DPLL involves instantiating a variable. Strategies to choose the next variable and its value are referred to as *variable ordering*, which greatly affect a DPLL algorithm. We call a variable ordering that assigns different weights to variables appearing in clauses of different sizes *weighted variable ordering*. A well-known weighted variable ordering for 3-SAT is the two-sided Jeroslow-Wang rule (J-W rule) [13]. Let $\{C_1, C_2, \cdots, C_m\}$ be the set of clauses. The J-W rule selects a variable v to maximize $J(v) + J(\bar{v})$ over all unspecified variables, where $J(v) = \sum_{v \in C_i} 2^{-n_i}$ and n_i is the number of literals in C_i. Another popular variable ordering for 3-SAT is the Mom's heuristic rule (Mom's rule), which branches next on the variable having the Maximum Occurrence in the clauses of Minimum size [16]. In [7, 16], the Mom's rule was represented as a formula for weighted variable ordering where a clause of length i has a weight that is 5 times as large as the weight of a clause of length $i + 1$, i.e., the Mom's rule has weight ratios of 25:5:1 instead of 4:2:1 as in the J-W rule. Unfortunately, variable ordering for max-SAT has not been studied extensively.

4 Unit Propagation for Max-SAT

Unit propagation is perhaps the most powerful strategy for SAT, and often the core piece of a DPLL-based SAT solver. It forces the variable in a unit clause, a clause of exactly one literal, to take the value that makes the clause satisfied immediately and ignores the other value entirely. Furthermore, all the clauses containing the literal are removed (satisfied) and all negations of the literal are eliminated from all clauses, resulting in a simplified formula. More importantly, the power of unit propagation comes largely from a cascade effect, i.e., fixing the value of a literal in a unit clause may subsequently generate more unit clauses, which may further simplify the formula at hand. Conversely, if two unit clauses with opposite literals occur, forming a contradiction, the formula is obviously unsatisfiable and the current node of the search can be abandoned.

In max-SAT, a clause may not be satisfied at all. Such an unsatisfiable clause may be simplified to a unit clause during the search. Therefore, we cannot restrict the literal in a unit clause to value T, but rather have to consider setting it to F as well, as long as doing so does not cause the total weight of violated clauses to exceed the current upper bound α. Therefore, unit propagation for SAT in its pure form does not apply to max-SAT. Nonetheless, the principles of unit propagation can be extended to max-SAT. For a max-k-SAT problem where each clause has k literals, consider a node N of a DFBnB search tree explored by the extended DPLL algorithm, and an uninstantiated variable v and its corresponding integer variable x in N. Let g be the total weights of clauses that have been violated at N, and $p_i(v)$ and $n_i(v)$ be the total weights of clauses of i literals in N which have v as a positive and negative literal, respectively. Let $UB(x)$ and $LB(x)$ be upper and lower bounds of coefficient of x (to be explained below), respectively. We then have the following unit propagation (UP) rules.

- **UP1 rule:** If $\sum_{i=1}^{k} n_i(v) = 0$, set v only to T; if $\sum_{i=1}^{k} p_i(v) = 0$, set v only to F.
- **UP2 rule:** If $p_1(v) + g \geq \alpha$, set v only to T; if $n_1(v) + g \geq \alpha$, set v only to F; if both conditions hold, prune node N.
- **UP3 rule:** If $p_1(v) \geq \sum_{i=1}^{k} n_i(v)$, set v only to T; if $n_1(v) \geq \sum_{i=1}^{k} p_i(v)$, set v only to F; if both conditions hold, i.e., $p_1(v) = n_1(v)$, take either one of them.
- **UP4 rule:** if $LB(x) \geq 0$, set v only to F; if $UB(x) \leq 0$, set v only to T; if both conditions hold, take either one of them.

Among the rules listed above, UP1 is subsumed by UP3 which is subsumed by UP4. (The proof will be provided in the final journal version of the paper.) UP1 and UP2 are self-evident. UP3 is valid since setting $v = F$ leads to p_1 cost increase, which is no better than $\sum_{i=1}^{k} n_1(v)$ cost increase if $v = T$. A formal proof of this rule is a special case of the proof to UP4. UP4 is a new rule based on a nonlinear programming formulation, which can be proved by systematically exploiting the coefficients of uninstantiated variables in the nonlinear formulation. For simplicity, we only prove this rule for max-2-SAT in the following discussion. The same idea applies to max-3-SAT, while it is technically more involved to prove and implement.

Proof First of all, we represent a max-2-SAT problem instance by a nonlinear formula f (Section 2.2) in such a way that the final formula contains only variables $x_i (1 \leq i \leq n)$, i.e.,

$$f = \sum_{i=1}^{m} w_i y_i = c + \sum_{i=1}^{n} (c_i x_i) + \sum_{1 \leq i,j \leq n, i \neq j} (c_{i,j} x_i x_j), \tag{1}$$

where c is a constant, $c_{i,j}$ the coefficient of item $x_i x_j$, and c_i the coefficient of item x_i. We now derive the coefficient for variable x_i, denoted as F_{x_i}. Let $UB(x_i)$ and $LB(x_i)$ be the upper bound and the lower bound for F_{x_i}, respectively, U the set of variables that have been instantiated, and V the set of variables that are to be instantiated. We then have

$$F_{x_i} = c_i + \sum_{x_j \in U \cup V - \{x_i\}} c_{i,j} x_j \tag{2}$$

Since some of the variables x_j in F_{x_i} have not been instantiated, most of the time during the search, F_{x_i} is not fixed. To this end, we rewrite F_{x_i} as follows:

$$F_{x_i} = c_i + \sum_{x_j \in U - \{x_i\}} c_{i,j} x_j + \sum_{x_j \in V - \{x_i\}} c_{i,j} x_j$$

$$= c_i + \sum_{x_j \in U - \{x_i\}} c_{i,j} x_j + \sum_{x_j \in V - \{x_i\}, c_{i,j} > 0} c_{i,j} x_j + \sum_{x_j \in V - \{x_i\}, c_{i,j} < 0} c_{i,j} x_j$$

Note that $\sum_{x_j \in V - \{x_i\}, c_{i,j} > 0} c_{i,j} x_j \geq 0$ and $\sum_{x_j \in V - \{x_i\}, c_{i,j} < 0} c_{i,j} x_j \leq 0$, which lead to

$$\begin{cases} LB(x_i) \leq F_{x_i} \leq UB(x_i) \\ UB(x_i) = c_i + \sum_{x_j \in U - \{x_i\}} c_{i,j} x_j + \sum_{x_j \in V - \{x_i\}, c_{i,j} > 0} c_{i,j} \\ LB(x_i) = c_i + \sum_{x_j \in U - \{x_i\}} c_{i,j} x_j + \sum_{x_j \in V - \{x_i\}, c_{i,j} < 0} c_{i,j} \end{cases} \quad (3)$$

If $UB(x_i) \leq 0$, F_{x_i} cannot be positive, thus to minimize the objective $W = \sum_{i=1}^{m} w_i y_i$, x_i should take value 1, i.e., $v_i = T$. If $LB(x_i) \geq 0$, F_{x_i} cannot be negative. To minimize W, x_i should take value 0, i.e., $v_i = F$. □

5 LP-Based Lower Bound

As mentioned in Section 3, an effective way to improve DPLL for max-SAT is to introduce an admissible heuristic function h to estimate the total weights of clauses that cannot be satisfied at a node during the search. If the heuristic estimate h plus the total weight g of clauses already violated is greater than or equal to the current upper bound α, i.e., $g + h \geq \alpha$, the node can be pruned.

To compute the h value of a node N, we adopt the ILP formulation for the remaining max-SAT at N (see Section 2). Rather than solving the ILP at N, we apply linear programming (LP) to it instead. In other words, we do not restrict the mapped variables to integers 0 or 1, but instead allow them to be real variables in $[0, 1]$. As a result, we settle for a less accurate estimate of the actual solution cost to the ILP instance since LP is less restricted. By relaxing the problem to LP, we reduce computation cost.

However, the LP-based heuristic needs to be handled with further care. Note that the solution to an LP relaxation problem at a node may have many variables having values in the middle of $[0, 1]$, i.e., taking values close to 1/2. Such "fractional" variables are problematic in binary clauses. Two variables in a binary clause can take values slightly more than 1/2, forcing the auxiliary variable (the y variable in the LP formulation, see Section 2) for the clause to take value 0, yielding no contribution to the overall heuristic estimate. Similar scenarios can occur to three-literal clauses. Fortunately, such situations will not occur in unit clauses because the only literals there must be set to 0 or 1. Therefore, *we only apply the LP heuristic to the nodes where unit clauses exist in the remaining problem*, making it more accurate and more efficient to compute. Moreover, during the search, unit clauses do not need to be eliminated, since an increase in the expected lower bound from eliminating unit clauses has already been calculated by applying the LP heuristic, i.e., if we apply the LP heuristic to compute h, any expected gain on the g value from unit clauses has already been taken into account in the h value.

6 Dynamic-Weight Variable Ordering

The existing variable ordering rules, e.g., the Mom's and J-W rules described in section 3, use static weights, in that the weights are fixed throughout search regardless of problem constrainedness. As we will see in the next section, these variable orderings are effective within different ranges of problem constrainedness.

Comparing to SAT, max-SAT can contain problem instances with various constrainedness. The existing variable orderings for SAT may not be effective for max-SAT. To address this problem, we propose a dynamic-weight variable ordering. For a max-SAT problem with the total number of clauses C and the total number of variables V, at a node of a search tree, select a variable v that has the maximum value of $J(v) + J(\overline{v})$ over all unspecified variables, where $J(u) = \sum_{u \in C_i} w_i \beta(r)^{-n_i}$, w_i is the weight of the i-th clause, and β takes values $5, 26 - 3.33r$ or 2 when the ratio (r=C/V) satisfies $r \leq 6.3, 6.3 \leq r \leq 7.2$ or $r \geq 7.2$, respectively. Therefore, this method can switch weighting ratio β in variable ordering from that close to the Mom's rule to that similar to the J-W rule as constrainedness increases, thus having good performance in all cases. This will be experimentally analyzed in the next section.

7 Experimental Evaluation and Applications

The combination of the above three strategies leads to an integrated algorithm for max-SAT, which we shorthand as *MaxSolver*. In this section, we experimentally evaluate its performance by using various problem instances, including those from the SATLIB [14], and by comparing it with many existing complete algorithms for max-SAT. We adopted the following conditions in our experiments. First, an initial upper bound was applied to all algorithms considered, which was obtained using Walksat local search [21] with 100 random restarts and 10,000 flips per try. Second, random problem instances were generated by uniformly randomly choosing literals for all non-duplicate clauses. Third, a lower bound rule LB2 based on the number of unit clauses [1] was applied. Fourth, all algorithms were run on a PC workstation with Athlon 1.9 MHZ CPU and 756 MB memory. For our MaxSolver, we used CPLEX 8.0 (www.ilog.com/products/cplex) for the LP lookahead heuristic. Due to the page limit, for the most of experiments, we only present the results in terms of CPU time here and omit the results on node generated.

We start with an investigation on the efficacy of the three improving strategies, and then compare our MaxSolver directly with some existing max-SAT algorithms that we are aware of and able to get source code from their authors.

7.1 Evaluation of New Strategies

We first compared extended DPLL with and without unit propagations and extended DPLL with LP heuristic in combinations of the two variable orderings. We ran three sets of experiments: DPLL, DPLL with different unit propagation rules (DPLL+UPs), and DPLL with LP heuristic (DPLL+LP). Each combination was tested with the Mom's and J-W rules. As an efficient implementation of UP4 for max-3-SAT is still under development, we only applied the UP4 rule to max-2-SAT.

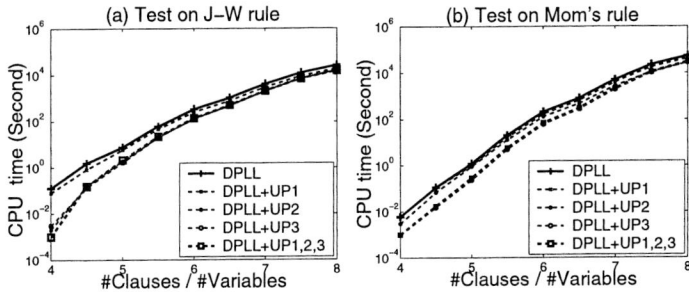

Fig. 1. Effects of unit propagations (UP) on unweighted max-3-SAT.

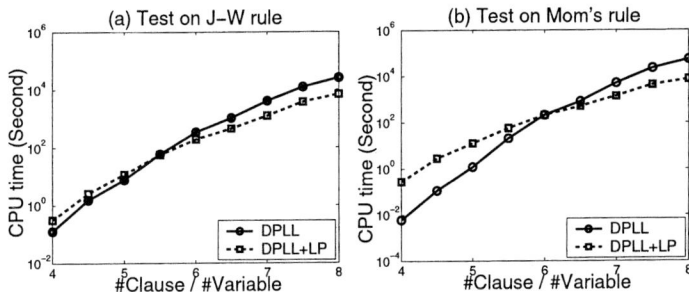

Fig. 2. Effects of LP lookahead heuristic on unweighted max-3-SAT.

Unweighted max-3-SAT. The experiments were carried out on random unweighted max-3-SAT with 80 variables and clause/variable (C/V) ratios ranging from 4 to 8 in an increment of 0.5. For C/V ratios from 4 to 6 and from 6.5 to 8, 100 and 10 problem instances were used, respectively.

The unit propagation rules are effective on certain ranges of low-constrainedness as shown in Figure 1, where the CPU times are shown in a logarithmic scale. When the C/V ratio is low, the initial upper bound α is 0 or close to 0, thanks to the effectiveness of the Walksat algorithm. As a result, solving max-3-SAT is similar to solving 3-SAT. In this case, the percentage of unit clauses is relatively high throughout the search, making the conditions of unit propagations easy to satisfy.

DPLL with LP heuristic (DPLL+LP), however, is ineffective in low-constrainedness regions, due to the overhead of LP calls. However, as shown in Figure 2, the running time overhead of LP is gradually compensated by the amount of pruning it provides as C/V ratio increases, making LP effective on over-constrained problems. To understand this phenomenon, it is important to notice that the computation time required by an LP call increases with the number of constraints of the problem at hand [11]. When constrainedness is low, such an overhead may be still too costly compared to a single DPLL node expansion. On the other hand, in a highly constrained situation where the upper bound α is large, DPLL without LP heuristic may have to search sufficiently deep along a search avenue before it can backtrack, resulting in a large amount of search cost, which is typically exponential in search depth. DPLL+LP, on the other hand, can estimate a reasonably accurate h value with a relatively small overhead for over-constrained

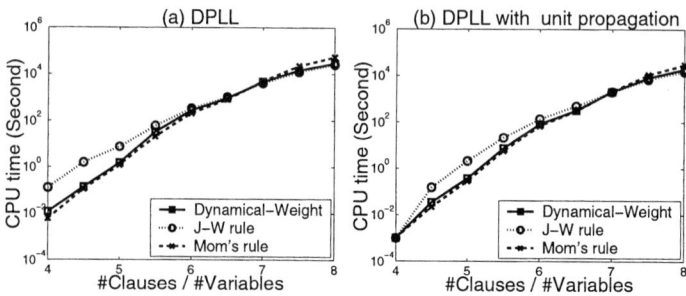

Fig. 3. Effects of variable ordering rules on unweighted max-3-SAT.

problems. The time difference between using LP or not using LP makes DPLL+LP outperform the DPLL on over-constrained problems.

The Mom's and J-W rules affect the unit propagations and the LP heuristic differently. As shown in Figures 3(a) and 3(b), the Mom's rule combined with DPLL and DPLL+UP has relatively better performance in not highly constrained regions (C/V < 7); while it is outperformed by the J-W rule as C/V ratio increases. (Note that the vertical axes of the figures are logarithmic, so the actual difference on running time is substantial.) In DPLL and DPLL+UPs, the Mom's rule tends to get rid of unit clauses quickly. If the C/V ratio is low, so is the upper bound α. It is more likely that an early increase in the number of violated constraints g will result in a lower bound value exceeding α, forcing the search to backtrack early. However, if the C/V ratio and upper bound α are high, it is not so easy for the value of $g + h$ to exceed α. Therefore, although the Mom's rule can increase g value in an early stage of the search, it actually produces fewer unit clauses to contribute to the g value as the search progresses. This is mainly because in the Mom's rule, the weights on binary and three literal clauses are smaller than that in the J-W rule, making it more difficult for non-unit clauses to be turned into unit clauses. Therefore, the Mom's rule performs better than the J-W rule in under-constrained regions, but worse in over-constrained regions.

In short, our results showed that the Mom's and J-W rules are effective under different problem constrainedness. Our new dynamic-weight variable ordering rule was developed to combine their strengths under different conditions. Moreover, instead of statically setting the weighting ratio β in variable ordering, the new rule dynamically adjusts β based on the current situation of the search. As the results in Figure 3 show, the new rule is nearly always the winner under different constraint tightness.

Unweighted max-2-SAT. Compared to unweighted max-3-SAT, unweighted max-2-SAT is simple. Because there are only two literals per clause, a simplification to a max-2-SAT formula by instantiating a variable will very likely result in some unit clauses, which, in turn, can recursively produce more unit clauses and make unit propagation happen more often. In addition, a higher percentage of unit clauses helps produce more accurate h values, making the LP heuristic more effective. In the experiments, we used random instances with 80 variables and C/V ratios from 2 to 5 in an increment of 0.5. For C/V ratios from 2 to 3 and from 3.5 to 5, 100 and 10 problem instances were used,

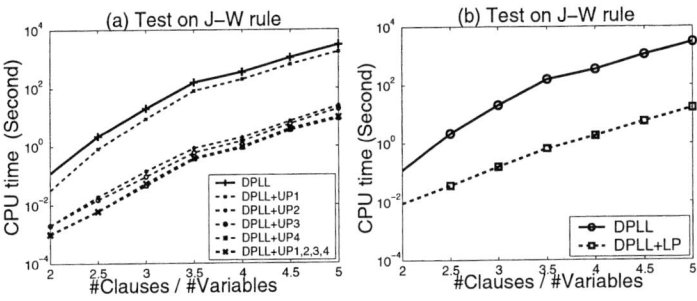

Fig. 4. Effects of (a) unit propagations, (b) LP heuristic on unweighted max-2-SAT.

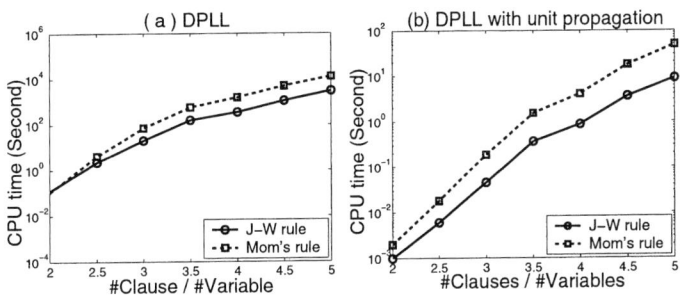

Fig. 5. Effects of variable orderings on unweighted max-2-SAT.

respectively. As shown in Figure 4(a), unit propagation rules are very effective on all constrainedness ranges of unweighted max-2-SAT, and their combination provides the best performance. When combined with the J-W rule, the unit propagation rules can reduce DPLL's running time by 10-1000 times. Furthermore, the LP heuristic is also very effective in all constrainedness ranges, as shown in Figure 4(b). In addition, the J-W rule is superior to the Mom's rule in nearly all cases, as shown in Figure 5.

Weighted max-SAT. We used the same set of random max-SAT problems that we experimented with in the unweighted case, except that each clause was randomly given an integer weight uniformly distributed between one and ten. Due to the page limit, here we only show the results of UP2 and UP3 on weighted max-3-SAT (Figure 6), and UP4 on weighted max-2-SAT (Figure 7). Experimental results show that the results on unweighted max-SAT are almost equally valid on weighted max-SAT, i.e., unit propagation rules are effective on weighted max-2-SAT or moderately constrained weighted max-3-SAT, LP lookahead heuristic is effective on weighted max-2-SAT or highly constrained weighted max-3-SAT, and the new dynamic-weight variable ordering is still effective on weighted max-3-SAT. One additional observation is that for the same problem size, weighted problems are usually easier than the corresponding unweighted problems, which can be seen by comparing Figures 1 and 4 with Figures 6 and 7.

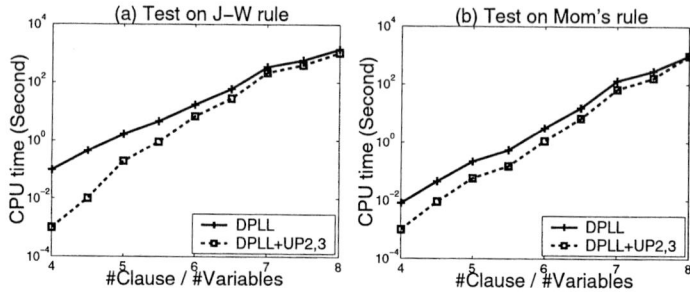

Fig. 6. Effects of unit propagations (UP) on weighted max-3-SAT.

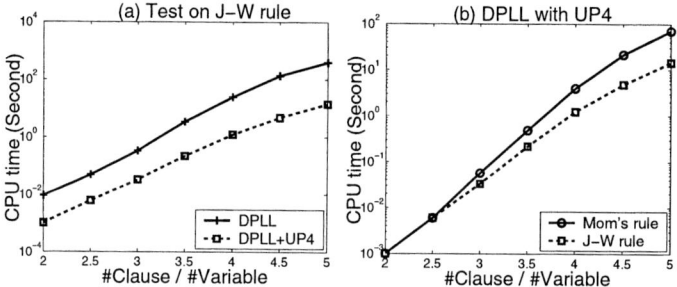

Fig. 7. Effects of (a) unit propagations, (b) variable ordering on weighted max-2-SAT.

7.2 Integrated Algorithm and Its Comparison to the Existing Methods

The remaining and important issue is the efficacy of MaxSolver which integrates the three new strategies. Based on the results in the previous section, in our experiments with MaxSolver, we applied the unit propagation rules only to max-2-SAT or moderately constrained max-3-SAT, the LP lookahead heuristic to max-2-SAT or highly constrained max-3-SAT, and our new dynamic-weight variable ordering to max-3-SAT.

To fully evaluate its performance, we compared MaxSolver with all the existing algorithms for max-SAT and maximum CSP (max-CSP) which we are aware of and whose source codes are available to us: (1) DPLL-based solver BF [2]; (2) DPLL-based solver AMF [1]; (3) pseudo Boolean optimization-based PBS2.1 [6]; (4) weighted CSP-based solver WCSP [9]. These algorithms contain most of the known techniques for SAT, max-SAT and max-CSP. BF is an extended DPLL with Mom's rule and a simple unit propagation that is similar but weaker than our UP2 rule. AMP is derived from BF and includes a lower bound function that counts unit clauses [23] and uses the J-W rule. PBS is a specialized 0-1 ILP solver and uses advanced techniques such as conflict diagnosis, random restarts, improved backtracking, and cutting plane. WCSP encodes a max-CSP (and max-SAT) into a weighted constraint network and solves the problem using state-of-the-art algorithms for weighted CSP. Among these four solvers, BF and WCSP can solve both weighted and unweighted max-SAT problems, while AMP and PBS can only handle unweighted max-SAT problems. The results presented below can be viewed as a comprehensive evaluation of these existing algorithms on max-SAT.

Table 1. Average CPU times on unweighted max-2-SAT of 80 variables.

C/V	MaxSolver	BF		AMP		PBS		WCSP	
2.0	0.00	0.04	(36)	0.07	(66)	3.01	(3013)	0.03	(27)
2.5	0.01	1.21	(207)	1.04	(179)	186.00	(320612)	0.14	(14)
3.0	0.04	51.79	(1300)	11.87	(298)	—		0.57	(14)
3.5	0.18	687.55	(3900)	80.00	(449)	—		1.59	(9)
4.0	0.85	12228.00	(14000)	485.10	(575)	—		5.80	(7)
4.5	3.89	—		2073.52	(532)	—		17.28	(4)
5.0	13.00	—		4617.56	(355)	—		45.47	(3)

We used random unweighted max-SAT instances generated by the MWFF package of Selman [20], weighted max-SAT instances from Borcher's max-SAT library [3], and unsatisfiable instances in SATLIB [14], which were generated from applications such as planning and model checking. The results are respectively in Tables 1 to 5, where "-" indicates an incomplete run after 5 hours of CPU time. For each problem class, the tables list either the C/V ratio r or the numbers of variables V and clauses C, followed by columns for the running times of the five solvers in seconds. #Unsat in Table 5 and Cost in Table 3,4 are the number of violated clauses in unweighted max-SAT and total weights of violated clauses in weighted max-SAT, respectively. The numbers in parentheses are MaxSolver's relative speedups over the existing methods.

Table 2. Average CPU times on unweighted max-3-SAT of 80 variables.

C/V	MaxSolver	BF		AMP		PBS		WCSP	
4.0	0.00	0.00	(1.0)	0.00	(1.0)	0.01	(16)	0.03	(48.0)
4.5	0.01	0.01	(1.0)	1.14	(87.3)	44.90	(3563)	1.18	(90.4)
5.0	0.15	0.19	(1.3)	7.43	(50.5)	—		6.60	(44.0)
5.5	4.26	6.95	(1.6)	64.79	(15.2)	—		27.54	(6.5)
6.0	38.00	104.00	(2.7)	386.00	(10.2)	—		107.25	(2.8)
6.5	228.00	629.00	(2.8)	1342.52	(5.9)	—		379.49	(1.7)
7.0	1723.00	9498.00	(5.5)	7937.17	(4.6)	—		877.17	(0.5)
7.5	7493.00	—		—		—		3792.67	(0.5)

For random unweighted max-2-SAT (Table 1), MaxSolver is significantly superior to the other DPLL based solvers, BF and AMP, indicating that our UP rules and LP heuristic are effective for over-constrained max-2-SAT. WCSP is the second fastest. The pseudo Boolean solver, PBS, performs much worse than DPLL-based solvers. PBS is unable to solve problems with more than 240 clauses. For random unweighted max-3-SAT (Table 2), BF performs better than it does on unweighted max-2-SAT and is sometimes competitive when the C/V ratio is low. However, it still degrades faster than MaxSolver and even AMP as C/V ratio increases, indicating that the Mom's rule on max-3-SAT becomes less effective. PBS is still not competitive at all on unweighted max-3-SAT. WCSP performs best only if C/V ratio reaches a very high value.

For random weighted max-2-SAT (Table 3) and weighted max-3-SAT (Table 4) instances from Borcher's max-SAT library [3], we compared MaxSolver with BF and WCSP, since the other two algorithms cannot apply. In Table 3, WCSP outperforms MaxSolver and BF on 10 out of 17 instances. Note that most of the instances that WCSP wins have small sizes or high constrainedness; MaxSolver is still the winner on large problems with moderate constrainedness. MaxSolver is significantly superior to BF in

Table 3. Computation results for weighted max-2-SAT test problems.

Problem instances				MaxSolver		BF				WCSP			
Name	V	C	Cost	Time	Nodes	Time		Nodes		Time		Nodes	
wp2100	50	100	16	**0.00**	98	0.00	—	138	(1.4)	0.01	—	77	(0.79)
wp2150	50	150	34	**0.00**	123	0.01	—	1.31e+3	(10.7)	0.01	—	64	(0.52)
wp2200	50	200	69	**0.02**	1.07e+3	0.30	(15.0)	4.61e+4	(43.1)	0.02	(1.00)	2.35e+2	(0.22)
wp2250	50	250	96	**0.06**	4.45e+3	3.23	(53.8)	4.30e+5	(96.6)	0.06	(1.00)	8.13e+2	(0.18)
wp2300	50	300	132	0.13	9.72e+3	12.33	(94.8)	1.44e+6	(148.1)	**0.06**	(0.46)	8.41e+2	(0.09)
wp2350	50	350	211	1.52	1.15e+5	587.01	(386.2)	6.53e+6	(567.8)	**0.51**	(0.34)	6.69e+3	(0.06)
wp2400	50	400	211	0.42	2.89e+4	292.40	(696.2)	2.82e+7	(975.8)	**0.13**	(0.31)	1.36e+3	(0.05)
wp2450	50	450	257	0.86	5.75e+4	945.05	(1098.9)	8.14e+7	(1415.7)	**0.16**	(0.19)	1.95e+3	(0.03)
wp2500	50	500	318	3.00	1.98e+5	2806.92	(935.6)	2.26e+8	(1141.4)	**0.64**	(0.21)	6.94e+3	(0.04)
wp2200	100	200	7	**0.00**	23	0.00	—	13	(0.6)	0.02	(6.67)	14	(0.61)
wp2300	100	300	67	**0.40**	1.73e+4	46.42	(116.1)	4.79e+6	(276.9)	0.88	(2.20)	3.79e+3	(0.22)
wp2400	100	400	119	**25.56**	1.09e+6	16625.91	(650.5)	1.45e+9	(13303)	27.79	(1.09)	1.42e+5	(0.13)
wp2500	100	500	241	9446.43	4.26e+8	—	—	—	—	**339.73**	(0.04)	1.80e+6	(0.00)
wp2600	100	600	266	2330.63	9.71e+7	—	—	—	—	**228.74**	(0.10)	1.00e+6	(0.01)
wp2300	150	300	24	**0.07**	2.63e+3	0.12	(1.7)	1.06e+4	(4.0)	1.90	(27.14)	3.55e+3	(1.35)
wp2450	150	450	79	**51.82**	1.83e+6	3689.28	(71.2)	2.69e+8	(147.0)	59.43	(1.15)	1.08e+5	(0.06)
wp2600	150	600	189	18809.23	6.64e+8	—	—	—	—	**8591.86**	(0.46)	2.24e+7	(0.03)

Table 4. Computation results for the weighted max-3-SAT test problems.

Problem instances				MaxSolver		BF				WCSP			
Name	V	C	Cost	Time	Nodes	Time		Nodes		Time		Nodes	
wp3250	50	250	1	**0.00**	39	0.00	-	55	(1.4)	0.01	—	2.64e+2	(6.8)
wp3300	50	300	13	**0.01**	859	0.02	(2.0)	1.56e+3	(1.8)	0.13	(13.0)	1.90e+3	(2.2)
wp3350	50	350	25	**0.18**	1.15e+4	0.36	(2.0)	2.78e+4	(2.4)	0.54	(2.8)	7.29e+3	(0.6)
wp3400	50	400	33	**0.51**	3.67e+4	0.95	(1.9)	7.22e+4	(2.0)	0.90	(1.8)	1.20e+4	(0.3)
wp3450	50	450	35	**0.32**	2.11e+4	0.85	(2.7)	5.84e+4	(2.8)	0.51	(1.6)	6.02e+3	(0.3)
wp3500	50	500	77	19.76	1.66e+6	86.48	(4.4)	6.68e+6	(4.0)	**6.94**	(0.4)	8.20e+4	(0.0)
wp3500	100	300	6	**0.07**	1.84e+3	0.22	(3.1)	7.38e+3	(4.0)	2.63	(37.6)	1.42e+4	(7.7)
wp3600	100	600	26	**36.61**	1.53e+6	127.72	(3.5)	5.98e+6	(3.9)	477.05	(13.0)	2.38e+6	(1.6)
wp3675	150	675	2	**0.13**	2.54e+3	2.18	(16.8)	5.07e+4	(20.0)	15.45	(51.5)	4.04e+4	(15.9)
wp3700	150	750	5	**2.00**	4.86e+4	9.98	(5.0)	2.21e+5	(4.5)	167.50	(83.8)	4.40e+5	(9.1)

Table 3, mainly due to the tremendous effects of our UP4 rule. Moreover, the power of UP4 rule becomes increasingly more effective as the constrainedness increases. In Table 4, when UP4 rule is not applied to weighted max-3-SAT due to its complicated implementation, MaxSolver can still substantially outperform BF and WCSP in all but one case.

MaxSolver also outperforms the other solvers on many instances from SATLIB. As shown in Table 5, *jnh* instances are best solved using MaxSolver. For *pret* instances and *dubois25*, PBS is the winner. Note that PBS is many orders of magnitude slower than MaxSolver on *jnh* instances, each of which has at least 2 unsatisfiable clauses. This matches the results in Tables 1 and 2 where PBS is the worst on highly over-constrained problems. Therefore, PBS is not suitable for hard max-SAT. MaxSolver still outperforms BP and AMP for these problems, and solves every one of them in a reasonable amount of time. Therefore, the results indicate that our MaxSolver, although developed based on random max-SAT, works fairly well on these instances with special structures embedded. Finally, WCSP is much worse than MaxSolver on all the instances.

In summary, our results show that MaxSolver and its three improving strategies are effective on max-SAT problems, outperforming the four existing algorithms on many instances from random weighted and unweighted max-SAT and from SATLIB, often with orders of magnitude reduction on running time.

Table 5. CPU times on unsatisfiable SATLIB instances.

Instance	V	C	#Unsat	MaxSolver	BF		AMP		PBS		WCSP	
jnh8	100	850	2	**0.001**	0.03	(30.0)	0.04	(40.0)	439.80	(439800.000)	2.33	(2330)
jnh9	100	850	2	**0.010**	0.04	(4.0)	0.53	(5.3)	40.69	(4069.000)	3.31	(331)
jnh14	100	850	2	**0.001**	0.03	(30.0)	0.04	(41.0)	13.21	(13210.000)	6.19	(6190)
jnh211	100	800	2	**0.001**	0.03	(30.0)	0.04	(37.0)	26.77	(26770.000)	1.78	(1780)
jnh307	100	900	3	**0.010**	0.32	(32.0)	0.41	(41.0)	1391.60	(139160.000)	7.77	(777)
aim50−2.0no1	50	100	1	0.040	0.02	(0.5)	0.07	(1.8)	**0.00**	**(0.000)**	0.25	(6)
aim50−2.0no2	50	100	1	0.010	0.01	(1.0)	0.03	(3.0)	**0.01**	**(1.000)**	0.01	(1)
aim50−2.0no3	50	100	1	0.010	0.02	(2.0)	0.05	(5.0)	**0.01**	**(1.000)**	0.10	(10)
pret60−40	60	160	1	3.850	5.65	(1.5)	14.25	(3.7)	**0.02**	**(0.005)**	134.45	(35)
pret60−60	60	160	1	3.970	5.67	(1.4)	14.26	(3.6)	**0.01**	**(0.003)**	136.64	(34)
pret60−75	60	160	1	4.830	5.63	(1.2)	14.19	(2.9)	**0.02**	**(0.004)**	137.50	(28)
dubois25	75	200	1	18.600	121.80	(6.6)	319.70	(17.2)	**0.27**	**(0.001)**	3820.75	(205)

8 Related Work

Hansen [10] surveyed several heuristics and approximation algorithms for max-SAT. Freuder and Wallace [8, 23] carried out an early and the most significant research on over-constrained satisfaction problems by directly extending the techniques for constraint satisfaction. They proposed a number of basic ideas of how to construct a DPLL-based exact max-SAT solver, most of which we have briefly discussed in section 3.

Our unit propagation UP1 rule and a rule similar to our UP2 rule were mentioned in [25, 22, 1]. UP3 rule was first proposed by Niedermeier and Rossmanith in [18], and was applied to max-2-SAT in [25]. Niedermeier and Rossmanith also presented a set of transformation and splitting rules in order to obtain a worst case complexity for max-SAT. However, conditions for using most of those rules are too restrictive to satisfy. Our new UP4 rule was developed based on an idea of formulating max-SAT as a nonlinear program. The combination of all these four rules has been shown to be very efficient and powerful in our experiments.

[15] is perhaps the first to apply ILP to max-SAT. It developed an ILP-based solver outperforming DPLL-based solvers on max-2-SAT. However, when applied to max-3-SAT, it is much slower than a DPLL-based algorithm. In this paper, we proposed to use LP instead, and successfully showed its power on max-3-SAT for the first time.

Little work has been done on variable ordering for max-SAT, except the work in [23] on the effects of applying in-most-unit-clause and in-most-shortest-clause heuristics on small random unweighted max-SAT of 25 variables. Our dynamic-weight variable ordering is novel in that it is able to adjust itself according to problem characteristics to cope with different constraint situations.

In contrast to the amount of effort devoted to SAT and unweighted max-SAT, research on weighted max-SAT is rather limited. In addition to the BF and WCSP algorithms we compared in this paper, the most relevant previous work is the branch-and-cut algorithm for weighted max-SAT [15]. We did not include this branch-and-cut algorithm in our analysis because it is compatible with the BF algorithm, as discussed in [15].

9 Conclusions and Future Work

Max-SAT is an important problem that has many real-world applications. However, the existing algorithms for max-SAT are typically restricted to simple problems with small numbers of variables and low clause/variable ratios. The main contributions of this paper are three effective methods for max-SAT and an integrated algorithm for solving hard max-SAT instances. These methods include a set of unit propagation rules, a linear-programming based lookahead heuristic and a dynamic-weight variable ordering rule, and constitute the main building blocks of a new max-SAT solver, called MaxSolver.

We experimentally showed that these new strategies and MaxSolver are effective on hard weighted and unweighted max-SAT problems. MaxSolver is significantly superior to four best existing algorithms for the max-SAT instances that we considered. MaxSolver runs significantly faster than the existing algorithms, sometimes with a few orders of magnitude CPU time reduction, on many instances from random max-SAT and instances derived from real application domains.

We will apply MaxSolver to over-constrained real-world applications. For example, the Maximum Probable Explanation (MPE) problem in Bayesian Networks has been formulated as a weighted max-SAT and subsequently solved, approximately, by an approximation algorithm [19]. We plan to optimally solve large MPE problems using our new MaxSolver.

References

1. T. Alsinet, F. Manya, and J. Planes. Improved branch and bound algorithms for Max-SAT. In *Proc. SAT2003*, 2003.
2. B. Borchers and J. Furman. A two-phase exact algorithm for Max-SAT and weighted Max-SAT problems. *J. Combinatorial Optimization*, 2(4):299–306, 1999.
3. http://www.nmt.edu/ borchers/maxsat.html.
4. M. Davis, G. Logemann, and D. Loveland. A machine program for theorem proving. *CACM*, 5:394–397, 1962.
5. R. Dechter. *Constraint Processing*. Morgan Kaufmann, 2003.
6. H. Dixon and M. L. Ginsberg. Inference methods for a pseudo-boolean satisfiability solver. In *Proc. AAAI-02*, pages 635–640.
7. J. W. Freeman. *Improvements to Propositional Satisfiability Search Algorithms*. PhD thesis, Univ. of Pennsylvania, 1995.
8. E. C. Freuder and R. J. Wallace. Partial constraint satisfaction. *Artificial Intelligence*, 58:21–70, 1992.
9. S.d. Givry, J. Larrosa, P. Meseguer, and T. Schiex. Solving Max-SAT as weighted CSP. In *Proc. CP-2003*, 2003.
10. P. Hansen and B. Jaumard. Algorithm for the maximum satisfiability problem. *Computing*, 44:279–303, 1990.
11. F. S. Hillier and G. J. Lieberman. *Introduction to Operations Research*. McGraw-Hill, 2001.
12. J. N. Hooker and G. Fedjki. Branch-and-cut solution of inference problems in prepositional logic. *Annals of Math. and Artificial Intelligence*, 1:123–139, 1990.
13. J.N. Hooker and V. Vinay. Branching rules for satisfiability. *J. Automated Reasoning*, 15:359–383, 1995.
14. H.H. Hoos and T. Stuzle. http://www.satlib.org, 1999.
15. S. Joy, J. Mitchell, and B. Borchers. A branch and cut algorithm for Max-SAT and weighted Max-SAT. In D. Du, J. Gu, and P.M. Pardalos, editors, *Satisfiability Problem: Theory and Applications*, pages 519–536. 1997.
16. C.M. Li and Anbulagan. Heuristics based on unit propagation for satisfiability problems. In *Proc. IJCAI-97*, pages 366–371.

17. C.L. Liu. *Introduction to Combinatorial Mathematics*. McGraw-Hill, 1968.
18. R. Niedermeier and P. Rossmanith. New upper bounds for maximum satisfiability. *J. Algorithm*, 36:63–88, 2000.
19. James D. Park. Using weighted max-sat engines to solve mpe. In *Proc. AAAI-02*, pages 682–687.
20. B. Selman. Mwff: Program for generating random max k-SAT instances. Available from DIMACS.
21. B. Selman, H. Kautz, and B. Cohen. Noise strategies for local search. In *Proc. AAAI-94*, pages 337–343, 1994.
22. R. J. Wallace. Enhancing maximum satisfiability algorithms with pure literal strategies. In *11th Canadian Conf. on AI*, 1996.
23. R.J. Wallace and E.C. Freuder. Comparative study of constraint satisfaction and davis-putnam algorithms for maximum satisfiability problems. In D. Johnson and M. Trick, editors, *Cliques, Coloring, and Satisfiability*, pages 587–615. 1996.
24. J.P. Walser. *Integer Optimization Local Search*. Springer, 1999.
25. H. Zhang, H. Shen, and F. Manya. Exact algorithms for Max-SAT. In *Workshop on First-Order Theorem Proving (FTP-03)*.

Preprocessing Techniques for Distributed Constraint Optimization

Syed Muhammad Ali*, Sven Koenig, and Milind Tambe

USC, CS Department, 941 W 37th Street, Los Angeles, CA 90089-0781, USA
{syedmuha,skoenig,tambe}@usc.edu

Abstract. Although algorithms for Distributed Constraint Optimization Problems (DCOPs) have emerged as a key technique for distributed reasoning, their application faces significant hurdles in many multiagent domains due to their inefficiency. Preprocessing techniques have been successfully used to speed up algorithms for centralized constraint satisfaction problems. This paper introduces a framework of very different preprocessing techniques that speed up ADOPT, an asynchronous optimal DCOP algorithm that significantly outperforms competing DCOP algorithms by more than one order of magnitude.

1 Introduction

Algorithms for Distributed Constraint Optimization Problems (DCOPs) [1, 2] have emerged as a key technique for distributed reasoning, given their ability to optimize over a set of distributed constraints. For example, DCOP algorithms have been used in distributed sensor networks [3] to optimize the allocation of sensors to targets so as to maximize the value of the tracked targets or the area covered by the sensors [3, 1]. Solving DCOPs optimally is known to be NP-hard, yet one often needs to develop DCOP algorithms that provide optimal solutions as efficiently as possible. For example, researchers have recently developed ADOPT, an asynchronous optimal DCOP algorithm that significantly outperforms competing optimal DCOP algorithms (that do not allow partial or complete centralization of value assignments) [1]. This paper introduces a framework of preprocessing techniques that make algorithms like ADOPT even more efficient. The idea of preprocessing is not new in the context of CSPs, where arc-consistency, path-consistency and general k-consistency algorithms can speed up CSP algorithms dramatically [4, 5]. However, preprocessing algorithms have not yet been investigated in the context of DCOPs. In this paper, we close this gap with preprocessing algorithms that are very different from preprocessing algorithms for CSPs. Our preprocessing algorithms demonstrate for the first time that preprocessing can indeed speed up DCOP algorithms. In fact, they can speed up ADOPT by more than one order of magnitude.

---

* This research was supported in part by a subcontract from NASA's Jet Propulsion Laboratory (JPL) and in part by an NSF award under contract IIS-0350584. The views and conclusions contained in this document are those of the authors and should not be interpreted as representing the official policies, either expressed or implied, of the sponsoring organizations or the U.S. government.

2 DCOPs and ADOPT

DCOPs consist of a set of agents N. $D(n)$ denotes the set of possible values that agent $n \in N$ can assign to itself. The other agents cannot directly read this value, but the agent can communicate the value to its neighbors. $c(d(n), d(n'))$ denotes the cost of a soft binary constraint between agents $n \in N$ and $n' \in N$ if agent n is assigned value $d(n) \in D(n)$ and agent n' is assigned value $d(n') \in D(n')$. We refer to these cost functions simply as constraints. The objective is to assign a value to every agent so that the sum of the costs of the constraints is minimal.

In this paper, we build on ADOPT, the first optimal DCOP algorithm that uses only localized asynchronous communication and polynomial space for each agent [1]. ADOPT constructs a constraint tree, which is a tree of agents with the property that any two agents that are involved in some constraint are in a predecessor-successor (but not necessarily parent-child) relationship in the tree. ADOPT searches the constraint tree in a way that resembles uninformed and memory-bounded versions of A*, but does so in a distributed fashion, where every agent sends messages only to its parent or successors in the constraint tree. ADOPT begins by all agents choosing their values concurrently. Agents can send their values to those successors they are neighbors with. When an agent receives a value message, it computes and sends a cost message to its parent in the constraint tree. This cost message is an estimate of the total cost of the constraints for the best complete assignment of values to the message-sending-agent's successors (and to the agent itself) that is: (i) guaranteed to be a lower bound on the real cost, and (ii) guaranteed to be consistent with the current assignment of values to its predecessors. The agent calculates this lower bound estimate by adding the exact costs of all constraints that involve agents with known values (namely its predecessors with whom it has constraints) and a lower bound estimate of the smallest sum of the costs of all constraints in the subtree rooted at the agent (received from its children via cost messages). Initially, all agents use zero as lower bound estimates. The agents increase these lower bound estimates as they receive cost messages from their children. The agents set them back to zero whenever they receive a value message that indicates that one of their predecessors has changed its value.

3 Preprocessing Framework

Our preprocessing framework consists of a preprocessing phase followed by the main phase which just runs ADOPT. The preprocessing phase supplies ADOPT with non-zero lower bound estimates to focus its search. They are calculated by solving a relaxed version of the DCOP, which is why we refer to them in the following as heuristic values. The heuristic values can be calculated by using either ADOPT itself to solve the relaxed DCOP or specialized preprocessing algorithms. Our specialized preprocessing algorithms DP0, DP1 and DP2 are dynamic programming algorithms that assign heuristic values to the agents, starting at the leaves of the constraint tree and then proceeding from each agent to its parent. We use the following additional notation to describe them formally: $C(n) \in N$ denotes the set of children of agent $n \in N$. $A(n)$ denotes the set of predecessors of agent $n \in N$ with which the agent has constraints. Finally, the heuristic value $h(d(n))$ is a lower bound estimate of the smallest sum of the costs of all constraints in the subtree rooted at the agent $n \in N$, provided that agent n is assigned the value $d(n) \in D(n)$. DP0, DP1 and DP2 set $h(d(n)) := 0$ for all $d(n) \in D(n)$ and $n \in N$ with $C(n) = \emptyset$, that is, the heuristic values of all leaves to zero. They calculate the remaining heuristic values $h(d(n))$ for all $d(n) \in D(n)$ and $n \in N$ with $C(n) = \emptyset$ as follows:

DP0	$h(d(n)) := \sum_{n' \in C(n)} \sum_{n'' \in A(n')} \min_{d(n') \in D(n')} \min_{d(n'') \in D(n'')} c(d(n'), d(n''))$
DP1	$h(d(n)) := \sum_{n' \in C(n)} \min_{d(n') \in D(n')} (h(d(n')) + c(d(n'), d(n)))$
DP2	$h(d(n)) := \sum_{n' \in C(n)} (\min_{d(n') \in D(n')} (h(d(n')) + c(d(n'), d(n)))$ $+ \sum_{n'' \in A(n') \setminus \{n\}} \min_{d(n'') \in D(n'')} c(d(n'), d(n''))))$

DP0, DP1 and DP2 calculate different heuristic values and differ in their computation and communication overhead. Each heuristic value of DP2 is guaranteed to be at least as large as the corresponding heuristic value of both DP0 and DP1. Thus, the heuristic values of DP2 are at least as informed as the ones of DP0 and DP1.

4 Experimental Results

In the following, we refer to ADOPT0, ADOPT1 and ADOPT2 as the combination of DP0, DP1 and DP2, respectively, in the preprocessing phase and ADOPT in the main phase. It is obvious that these versions solve DCOPs optimally since they use lower bound estimates as heuristic values. Since the processing times of DP0, DP1, and DP2 per iteration are polynomial and their number of iterations is polynomial as well, their runtimes are polynomial. Since solving DCOPs is NP-hard, the runtimes of the preprocessing algorithms do not contribute to the overall runtime in a major way. However, it is not immediately obvious whether the preprocessing algorithms are able to reduce the total runtime, that is, the sum of the runtimes of the preprocessing phase and the main phase. Hence, it is crucial to perform an experimental investigation of the different preprocessing algorithms.

Our test domains are three-coloring problems with a link density of two. The values of the agents correspond to the colors, and the costs of all pairs of values of any two neighboring agents are drawn from the integers from 1 to 100 with uniform probability. We follow other researchers and use cycles to measure the runtimes, where every agent is allowed to process all of its messages in each cycle. Figure 1 (left) shows the overall number of cycles of ADOPT and our three new versions of ADOPT as a function of the number of agents. When we report cycles, we penalize ADOPT1 and ADOPT2 for their larger messages in the preprocessing phase by increasing their cycle count in the preprocessing phase by a factor that equals the number of heuristic values they send per message, namely 3. ADOPT2 outperforms all other versions of ADOPT and its speedups increase with the number of agents. For example, ADOPT2 speeds up ADOPT by a factor of 9.8 for 12 agents.

To illustrate the advantage of our preprocessing algorithms, Figure 1 (right) compares the number of cycles taken by DP1 and the number of cycles that ADOPT would need if it were used in the preprocessing phase on the DCOP after all of its constraints that are not in a parent-child relationship in the constraint tree are deleted. These two

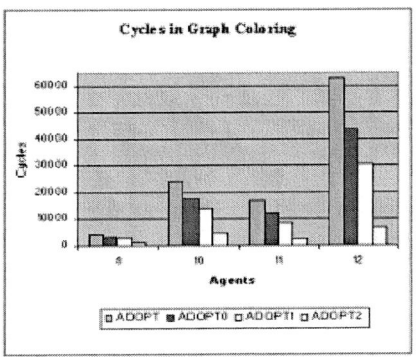
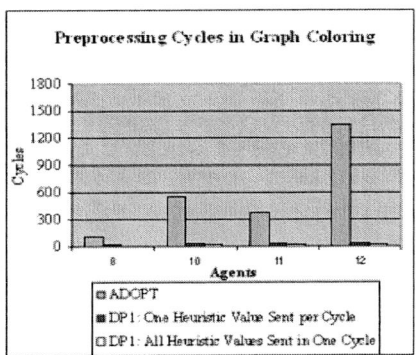

Fig. 1. Total Cycles (left) and Preprocessing Cycles (right).

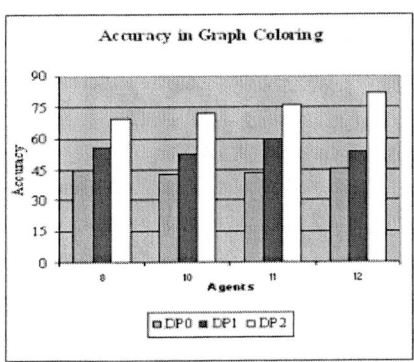
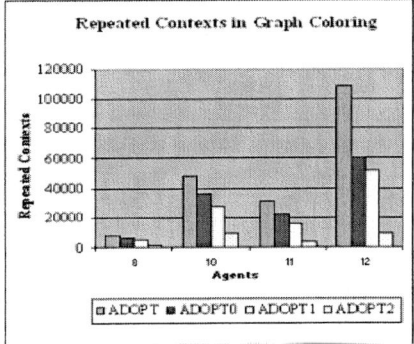

Fig. 2. Accuracy (left) and Regenerated Contexts (right).

preprocessing algorithms calculate the same heuristic values. However, the number of cycles of DP1 is smaller than the one of ADOPT by a factor of 52.5 for 12 agents. If we did not penalize DP1 for its larger messages by increasing its cycle count, its number of cycles would even be smaller than the one of ADOPT by a factor of 157.4.

To understand better why the speedups depend on the preprocessing algorithm, remember that the heuristic values computed by the preprocessing algorithms are used to seed lower bounds of ADOPT for the main phase. ADOPT can raise these lower bounds during its operation. We therefore computed the average ratio of the lower bounds provided by the preprocessing algorithms and the lower bounds after ADOPT terminated. We refer to this ratio as the accuracy. The larger the accuracy, the more informed the lower bounds are. An accuracy of 0 percent means that the lower bounds provided by the preprocessing phase were zero and thus no better than the lower bounds used by ADOPT itself. In this case, the preprocessing algorithm does not speed up ADOPT. On the other hand, an accuracy of 100 percent means that the lower bounds provided by the preprocessing algorithm were so good that ADOPT was not able to raise them. Figure 2 (left) shows the accuracies of DP0, DP1 and DP2. The accuracy of DP0 is 45.1 percent for 12 agents, the accuracy of DP1 is 53.4 percent, and the accuracy of DP2 is 81.6

percent. Figure 2 (left) shows that the accuracies are closely correlated with the number of cycles from Figure 1 (left). The overall number of cycles decreases as the accuracies and thus the informedness of the heuristic values increase.

ADOPT is a memory-bounded DCOP algorithm and thus has to regenerate partial solutions (contexts) when it backtracks to a previously explored part of the search space. We therefore measured the average number of regenerated contexts at each agent, where a context assigns a value to each predecessor of the agent in the constraint tree. Thus, a regenerated context is in effect a regenerated partial solution. Figure 2 (right) shows that the numbers of regenerated contexts are indeed closely correlated with the accuracies from Figure 2 (left) as well as the number of cycles from Figure 1 (left). It appears that more informed heuristic values reduce the amount of backtracking and thus the number of regenerated partial solutions, resulting in a smaller number of cycles. For example, ADOPT2 uses far more informed heuristic values than ADOPT and thus repeats far fewer contexts and, correspondingly, provides high speedups.

References

1. Modi, P., Shen, W., Tambe, M., Yokoo, M.: An asynchronous complete method for distributed constraint optimization. In: AAMAS. (2003) 161–168
2. Mailler, R., Lesser, V.: Solving distributed constraint optimization problems using cooperative mediation. In: AAMAS. (2004) (to appear)
3. Lesser, V., Ortiz, C., Tambe, M., eds.: Distributed sensor networks: A multiagent perspective. Kluwer (2003)
4. Dechter, R., Meiri, I.: Experimental evaluation of preprocessing techniques in constraint satisfaction problems. In: IJCAI. (1989) 271–277
5. Bistarelli, S., Gennari, R., Rossi, F.: Constraint propagation for soft constraints: generalization and termination conditions. In: CP. (2000) 83–97

Variable Ordering Heuristics Show Promise*

J. Christopher Beck[1], Patrick Prosser[2], and Richard J. Wallace[1]

[1] Cork Constraint Computation Centre, Department of Computer Science,
University College Cork, Cork, Ireland
{c.beck,e.freuder}@4c.ucc.ie
[2] Department of Computing Science, University of Glasgow, Scotland
pat@dcs.gla.ac.uk

1 Introduction

Promise is the ability to make choices that lead to a solution when one exists. The traditional intuition behind variable ordering heuristics is Haralick and Elliott's fail-first principle: choose the variable such that assigning it is most likely to lead to a domain wipe-out (in AIJ 14, 1980). In contrast, the standard belief about value ordering heuristics is based on Geelen's discussion (in ECAI'92): choose a value that is most likely to participate in a solution. It is not clear *a priori* that changes in variable ordering change the likelihood of finding a solution in a way that will affect overall performance significantly. In this paper we show that promise does have a meaning for variable ordering heuristics and that the level of promise of a variable ordering heuristic can be measured. In addition, we show that the promise of different variable ordering heuristics is different and that the level of promise of a variable ordering heuristic correlates with search cost for problems with many solutions.

2 A Measure of Promise

A reasonable approach to measuring promise is to assess the extent to which a variable ordering heuristic increases or decreases the likelihood of finding a solution. It is critical that this measurement is independent of a heuristic's ability to escape bad subtrees, i.e. we must ensure that any measure of promise is not contaminated by the fail-firstness of a heuristic. The "likelihood of finding a solution" can be treated probabilistically. For a given decision there is some probability over all possible subsequent decisions that the choice will lead to a solution. We can also consider promise with respect to an entire problem, i.e. as an expected value over all possible sequences of choices. In this sense we can speak of the promise of a problem in terms of its relation to a perfect selection. This measure of promise has a natural minimum and maximum: 0 (for insoluble problems) and 1 (if every n-tuple is a solution). This gives us a universal measure across all problems. These points can be illustrated with the following toy problem. We have three variables v_1, v_2 and v_3 with domains $d_1 = \{a,b\}$, $d_2 = \{a,b,c\}$, and $d_3 = \{a,b,c\}$, and the constraints $C_{1,2} = \{(a,b),(b,b),(b,c)\}$, $C_{1,3} = \{(a,a),(a,b),(b,b),(b,c)\}$,

---

* This work has received support from Science Foundation Ireland under Grant 00/PI.1/C075 and ILOG, SA.

and $C_{2,3} = \{(a,a),(b,c),(c,a),(c,b),(c,c)\}$. To calculate promise, we consider the probability of choosing each viable value from a domain, when any value is equally likely to be chosen. For simple backtracking we get the tree in Figure (a), and from this we can calculate the overall promise for backtracking on this problem by summing the path-products (shown in Figure (b)), giving a value of $0 + \frac{1}{18} + \frac{2}{18} = \frac{1}{6}$. The overall promise for this problem and this consistency algorithm is then $\frac{1}{6}$, and for backtracking this is the same as the solution density. Consider forward checking (fc) using the smallest-domain-first (sdf) ordering. The search tree is shown in Figure (c) and we again compute promise by summing the path products in tree (c) giving the sum: $0 + \frac{1}{4} + \frac{1}{4} = \frac{1}{2}$. If we use a different variable ordering, say 3-2-1 instead of 1-2-3, we get a different search tree, Figure (d), and a different measure of promise: $0 + \frac{1}{3} + \frac{1}{6} + \frac{1}{6} = \frac{2}{3}$.

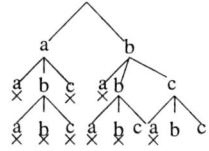

(a) Backtrack Tree

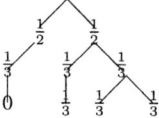

(b) Probability Tree of (a)

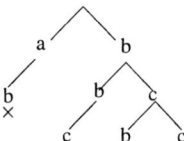

(c) Forward Checking Tree, ordered 1-2-3

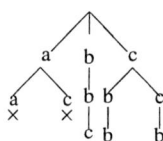

(d) Forward Checking Tree, ordered 3-2-1

From these examples we now draw some conclusions: (1) Promise can vary depending on the variable ordering and the consistency algorithm. (2) Promise is not in general equivalent to solution density; the equivalence holds only if there is no consistency maintenance. (3) There does not appear to be a particular variable ordering that is guaranteed to maximize promise. Therefore, the level of promise of a variable ordering heuristics will probably have to be decided empirically.

It is possible to assess the overall promise of a problem under a given variable ordering with the following *probing* procedure. Use a heuristic to select an uninstantiated variable, randomly select a value for this variable, and then enforce some level (possibly none) of consistency. Repeat these steps until all variables are consistently instantiated or a deadend is encountered. At a deadend the probing process re-starts from the beginning with a new random seed. This is repeated until a complete solution is found. The number of probes required gives us a measure of promise: the greater the promise the fewer the number of probes required on average to obtain a solution. (In fact, in the limit the expected number of probes is the reciprocal of the promise.)

This procedure avoids contamination by fail-firstness because we never try to recover from a deadend: the number of probes are a reflection of promise alone. If used with a random value ordering heuristic over many runs, this technique also avoids effects of value selection on promise. We can use any consistency enforcement algorithm as part of the probing procedure.

3 Empirical Investigations

We use the probing procedure to investigate two hypotheses: (1) *Different variable ordering heuristics exhibit different levels of promise*, and (2) *Promise is inversely correlated with search effort*. We expect that for easier problems promise will be strongly correlated with search cost and as problems become more difficult, the effect of promise will decrease and fail-firstness should be more important to search effort.

We use a set of well-known variable ordering heuristics together with their corresponding anti-heuristics: sdf (smallest domain first) and ldf (largest domain first); max- and min-static-degree; max- and min-forward-degree; Brélaz heuristic and anti-brelaz (i.e. choose the variable with the smallest (resp. largest) domain and break ties by choosing the variable with maximum (resp. minimum) forward degree (CACM 22, 1979)); domdeg and anti-domdeg (i.e. choose the variable that minimizes (resp. maximizes) the ratio of domain size to forward degree (Bessiere & Régin, CP'96)); and finally random (i.e. randomly select an unassigned variable).

Haralick and Elliott's Forward checking (fc) is used with each heuristic. We conduct the probing procedure 100 times for each problem and variable ordering heuristic, with different seeds for the random number generator. The mean reciprocal of the number of probes over the 100 runs is our estimate of promise for that problem and heuristic. For problems with no solutions, we define the promise to be 0. For a set of problems and a variable ordering heuristic, we calculate promise by finding the arithmetic mean of the promise estimate over each problem in the set for that heuristic.

To estimate the search effort for a problem and a variable ordering heuristic we follow a similar procedure as for estimating promise. The difference is that instead of probing for solutions we simply use a complete backtracking search with forward checking. Our measure of search effort is the number of consistency checks required to find a solution. Again, for a given problem and variable ordering heuristic, we run this algorithm 100 times with differing random seeds for value selection, and define the search cost to be the median number of constraint checks over the 100 runs. For a set of problems the mean search cost is the arithmetic mean of the search cost for each problem.

We first test our hypotheses on randomly generated CSPs. The test problems are generated using the $\langle n, m, p_1, p_2 \rangle$ model of Smith and Grant (ECAI'98), with 15 variables and 10 values per variable. Density p_1 is fixed at 0.7, and tightness p_2 varies from 0.30 to 0.39 in steps of 0.01. There are 100 problems at each value of p_2. Problems are not filtered and therefore samples may contain a mix of soluble and insoluble problems.

The left graph in Figure 1 presents the mean promise estimates for each variable ordering heuristic. A log-scale is used on the y-axis to make the rankings of the heuristics easier to see. The right graph in Figure 1 presents the search cost for each variable ordering heuristic.

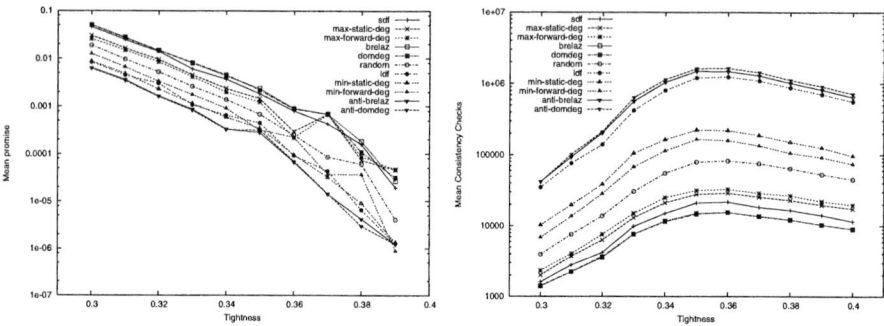

Fig. 1. Mean promise estimates (left) and mean search cost (right) for each random problem set.

The promise graph clearly shows that different variable ordering heuristics do exhibit different levels of promise. As the tightness increases there are fewer soluble problems and the level of promise correspondingly decreases. Even when we remove the insoluble problems (not shown) the promise decreases with increasing tightness as fewer solutions result in a lower promise for a given variable ordering heuristic. Comparing the two plots in Figure 1, we can see that the most successful heuristics (i.e. those with lowest search cost: domdeg, brelaz, and sdf) also exhibit the highest levels of promise. Furthermore, the rankings seem relatively consistent: with some exceptions that may be due to noise from problem sets with few soluble problems, the ith best heuristic exhibits the ith highest level of promise.

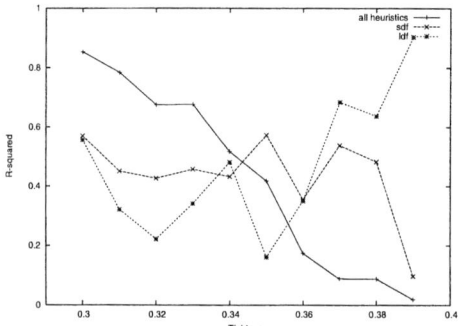

Fig. 2. R^2 values for the correlations between promise and the reciprocal of search cost for each random problem set and selected variable ordering heuristics.

Figure 2 presents a measure of the correlation between promise and search cost. The plot labeled "all" examines 1100 points for each problem set composed of the search cost and promise values for each of the 100 test problems and 11 variable ordering heuristics. For low values of tightness, the variation in promise accounts for 70-80% of the variation in search cost. As the problems become tighter the R^2 value drops to close to 0.

Figure 2 also presents the R^2 values for sdf and its anti-heuristic ldf. This plot is similar to that seen with the other heuristic/anti-heuristic pairs based on domain size (i.e., domdeg and brelaz): at low values of tightness the R^2 values are somewhat noisy and around 0.4. For the tighter problem sets, the anti-heuristic ldf starts to have a much stronger correlation with search cost while the correlation of the heuristic sdf declines. The reason for this effect is that the anti-heuristics perform uniformly poorly across the insoluble problems at a tightness value. Given that there are very few soluble problems at high tightness values (i.e. one for set 0.39) this leads to a strong correlation between promise and search cost. Another surprising result is that for the problem sets with low tightness, the R^2 values for individual heuristics are much lower than the "all" plot. This occurs because the relationship between promise and search cost is weaker within any single heuristic, but over all heuristics the trend of higher promise corresponding to lower search cost for loose problems is clear.

The heuristics and anti-heuristics based only on variable degree have a similar behavior as the domain-based heuristics for low values of tightness. As the tightness increases the R^2 values of both the heuristics and anti-heuristics drop as expected. Lending support to our above explanation of the domain-based anti-heuristics, the degree-based anti-heuristics have large variances on insoluble problems.

4 Observations, Discussion, and Conclusion

Using random CSPs, we have demonstrated a definite inverse relation between promise and search effort across different variable ordering heuristics. We have also shown that promise has a high (inverse) correlation with search effort for problems with many solutions but a low correlation when the number of solutions decreases. There is no question, then, about having to consider promise as well as fail-firstness in trying to account for differences in the performance of these heuristics.

Why should heuristics such as sdf, domdeg, and brelaz show greater degrees of promise than other variable orderings? These heuristics give preference to variables with small domain sizes. If we assume that each value in the domain of a variable has equal probability of occurring in a solution, when domain sizes are small the probability of any value in that domain being in a solution is relatively high. That is, *the values are more promising*. Therefore we should expect that heuristics that prefer variables with small domains will have higher promise, and this is just what we have seen. This explanation may also account for the differences between heuristics and anti-heuristics that are based on degree alone, although this has not yet been tested.

A full understanding of search heuristics will require further work. By focusing on promise, we have neglected the fail-first principle in this paper. The development of a method of measurement of fail-firstness and the investigation of its correlation with search cost is a key area for future work. Our intuition is that it is the combination of promise and fail-firstness that, to a large extent, determines the search efficiency of heuristics.

The Tractability of Global Constraints

Christian Bessiere[1], Emmanuel Hebrard[2], Brahim Hnich[2], and Toby Walsh[2]

[1] LIRMM-CNRS, Montpelier, France
bessiere@lirmm.fr
[2] Cork Constraint Computation Center, University College Cork, Ireland
{e.hebrard,b.hnich,tw}@4c.ucc.ie

Abstract. Constraint propagation is one of the techniques central to the success of constraint programming. Fast algorithms are used to prune the search space either before or during backtracking search. Propagating global constraints is intractable in general. In this paper, we characterize a number of important questions related to constraint propagation. For example, we consider the two questions: "Is this problem generalized arc-consistent?" and "What are the maximal generalized arc-consistent domains?". We identify dependencies between the tractability and intractability of these questions for finite domain variables. Finally, we prove intractability for a range of global constraints.

1 Introduction

It is well known that constraint propagation on binary (or bounded arity) constraints is polynomial. However, constraint toolkits support an increasing number of non-binary or global constraints. Global constraints permit users to model problems compactly and solvers to prune the search space efficiently and effectively. In many problems, the arity of such global constraints can grow with the problem size. Such global constraints may therefore exhibit complexities far beyond the quadratic propagation cost of binary constraints. Indeed, it is easy to see that reasoning with global constraints is intractable in general. In this paper, we characterize the different reasoning tasks related to constraint propagation. For example, does this value have support? As a second example, what are the maximal generalized arc-consistent domains? We identify dependencies between the tractability and intractability of these different questions. Afterwards, we study a range of existing and new global constraints We show that they are NP-hard to propagate. Thus, we expect that any decomposition will hinder propagation (unless P=NP).

2 Theoretical Background

A *constraint satisfaction problem* (CSP) involves a set of variables, each with a domain of values, and a set of constraints that specify allowed combinations of values for subsets of variables. We will denote variables with upper case letters and values with lower case. We assume a constraint C is given intensionally by a function of the form $f_C : D(X_1) \times \ldots \times D(X_n) \mapsto \{True, False\}$ where $D(X_i)$ are the domains of the variables in the scope $var(C) = (X_1, \ldots, X_n)$ of the constraint C. (We say that D is a domain on $var(C)$.) We only consider constraints C for which f_C is computable in polynomial time.

Constraint toolkits usually contain a library of predefined *constraint types* with a particular semantics that can be applied to sets of variables with various arities and domains. A constraint is only an instance of a constraint type on given variables and domains. For instance, *alldifferent* is a constraint type. *alldifferent*$(X_1, .., X_3)$ with $D(X_1) = D(X_2) = \{1,2\}, D(X_3) = \{1,2,3\}$ is an instance of constraint of the type *alldifferent*.

A solution to a CSP is an assignment of values to the variables satisfying the constraints. To find such solutions, we often use tree search algorithms that construct partial assignments and enforce a local consistency to prune the search space. One of the oldest and most commonly used local consistencies is generalized arc consistency. A constraint C is *generalized arc consistent* (GAC) iff, when a variable in the scope of C is assigned any value, there exists an assignment to the other variables in C such that C is satisfied [5]. This satisfying assignment is called *support* for the value. In general, applying GAC can remove any value anywhere in the domain of a variable. This is why GAC is usually applied to constraints that involve *finite domain* variables. In the following, we will consider finite domain integer variables in which every value in the domain is given extensionally.

3 Complexity of Generalized Arc Consistency

We characterize five different problems related to genaralized arc consistency reasoning. These problems can be adapted to any other local consistency as long as it rules out values in domains (e.g., bounds consistency, singleton arc consistency, etc.) and not non-unary tuples of values (e.g., path consistency, relational-k-consistency, etc.)

In the following, PROBLEM(C) represents the class of problems defined by PROBLEM on constraints of the type C. PROBLEM(C) will sometimes be written PROBLEM when no confusion is possible. Note also that we use the notation PROBLEM[data] to refer to the instance of PROBLEM(C) with the input 'data'. $\mathcal{U}$ denotes the set of all constraint types.

Table 1 contains the five problems. The first problem we consider is GACSUPPORT. It is at the core of all the generic arc consistency algorithms. The second problem, ISITGAC, is not directly related with operations used in basic propagation algorithms. It is largely introduced for academic purposes. The third question, NOGACWIPEOUT, can be used to decide if we do not need to backtrack at a given node in the search tree. (Note that $D' \subseteq D$ stands for: $\forall X_i \in var(C), D'(X_i) \subseteq D(X_i)$.) An algorithm like GAC-Schema [4] removes values from the initial domains of variables till we have the *maximal* generalized arc consistent subdomains. That is, the set of subdomains that are GAC and any larger set of subdomains are not GAC. MAXGAC characterizes this "maximality" problem. We finally consider GACDOMAIN, the non-decision problem of returning the domains that a GAC algorithm computes.

In the following, we describe the relationships between the tractability and intractability of the different problems defined above.

Table 1. The five problems related to genaralized arc consistency.

Problem	Instance	Question/Output
GACSUPPORT($\mathcal{C}$)	$C \in \mathcal{C}$, D on $var(C)$, $X \in var(C)$, and $v \in D(X)$	Does value v for X have a support on C in D?
ISITGAC($\mathcal{C}$)	$C \in \mathcal{C}$, D on $var(C)$	Does GACSUPPORT$[C, D, X, v]$ answer "yes" for each variable $X \in var(C)$ and each value $v \in D(X)$?
NOGACWIPEOUT($\mathcal{C}$)	$C \in \mathcal{C}$, D on $var(C)$	Is there any non empty $D' \subseteq D$ on which ISITGAC$[C, D']$ answers "yes"?
MAXGAC($\mathcal{C}$)	$C \in \mathcal{C}$, D on $var(C)$, and $D \subseteq D_0$	Is it the case that ISITGAC$[C, D]$ answers "yes" and $\not\exists D', D \subset D' \subseteq D_0$, on which ISITGAC$[C, D']$ answers "yes"?
GACDOMAIN($\mathcal{C}$)	$C \in \mathcal{C}$, D_0 on $var(C)$	The domain D such that MAXGAC$[C, D_0, D]$ answers "yes"

3.1 Tractable Cases

The five problems defined above are not independent. Knowledge about the tractability of one can give information on the tractability of others. We identify here the dependencies between the tractabilities of the different questions.

Theorem 1. *Given a constraint type $\mathcal{C}$,*

1. *GACSUPPORT $\in P$ iff NOGACWIPEOUT $\in P$ iff GACDOMAIN $\in P$*
2. *{GACSUPPORT, NOGACWIPEOUT, GACDOMAIN} $\in P \Rightarrow$ ISITGAC $\in P$*
3. *{GACSUPPORT, NOGACWIPEOUT, GACDOMAIN} $\in P \Rightarrow$ MAXGAC $\in P$*
4. *MAXGAC $\in P \Rightarrow$ ISITGAC $\in P$*

Proof. (1) If GACSUPPORT is in P, then we can answer NOGACWIPEOUT just by checking that at least one value in the domain of a variable X in $var(C)$ has support. Indeed, all the values in the support themselves have support.

If NOGACWIPEOUT is in P, we can check that (X, v) has support just by calling NOGACWIPEOUT with only v in the domain of X.

It is trivial that if GACSUPPORT is in P, using a generic GAC algorithm that calls GACSUPPORT a polynomial number of times, we will have the output of GACDOMAIN in polynomial time.

By calling GACDOMAIN with only (X, v) in the domain of X, the obtained domain will be non empty iff (X, v) has a support, then answering GACSUPPORT in polynomial time if GACDOMAIN was in P.

(2) Trivial.
(3) Trivial.
(4) If MAXGAC is in P, it is sufficient to call it with D both as the initial and current domain to answer ISITGAC on D. □

3.2 Intractable Cases

We can identify similar dependencies between these questions when they are intractable. Interestingly, we have only been able to identify the inverse relationships between MAX-

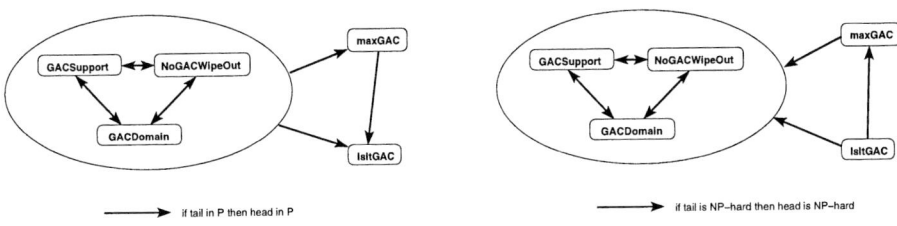

Fig. 1. Summary of the dependencies between problems.

GAC, IsItGAC and the other three problems. It is a challenging open question to prove either that one of these results which is just an implication reverses or that it does not reverse in general.

Theorem 2. *Given a constraint type $\mathcal{C}$,*

1. *GACSUPPORT is NP-complete iff NOGACWIPEOUT is NP-complete iff GAC-DOMAIN is NP-hard*
2. *ISITGAC is NP-complete $\Rightarrow$ GACSUPPORT, NOGACWIPEOUT, GACDOMAIN are NP-hard*
3. *MAXGAC is NP-hard $\Rightarrow$ GACSUPPORT, NOGACWIPEOUT, GACDOMAIN are NP-hard*
4. *ISITGAC is NP-complete $\Rightarrow$ MAXGAC is NP-hard*

Proof. (1) GACSUPPORT($\mathcal{C}$) can be transformed in NOGACWIPEOUT($\mathcal{C}$): Given $C \in \mathcal{C}$, GACSUPPORT$[C,D,X,v]$ is solved by calling NOGACWIPEOUT$[C, D|_{D(X)=\{v\}}]$.

NOGACWIPEOUT$[C, D]$ can be reduced to GACSUPPORT by calling GACSUPPORT$[C, D, X, v]$ for each value v in $D(X)$ for one of the X in $var(C)$. GAC leads to a wipe out iff none of these values has a support.

GACSUPPORT($\mathcal{C}$) can be reduced to GACDOMAIN($\mathcal{C}$) since GACSUPPORT$[C, D, X, v]$ answers "yes" iff GACDOMAIN$[C, D|_{D(X)=\{v\}}]$ doesn't return empty domain.

GACDOMAIN$[C, D]$ can be reduced to GACSUPPORT by performing a polynomial number of calls to GACSUPPORT$[C, D, X, v]$, one for each $v \in D(X)$, $X \in var(C)$. When the answer is "no" the value v is removed from $D(X)$, otherwise it is kept. The domain obtained at the end of this process represents the output of GACDOMAIN.

(2) ISITGAC$[C, D]$ can be reduced to GACSUPPORT by performing a polynomial number of calls to GACSUPPORT$[C, D, X, v]$, one for each $v \in D(X)$, $X \in var(C)$. If one of them answers "no" ISITGAC answers "no", otherwise it answers "yes".

(3) MAXGAC$[C, D_0, D]$ can be reduced to GACSUPPORT. We perform a polynomial number of calls to GACSUPPORT$[C, D_0, X, v]$, one for each $v \in D_0(X)$, $X \in var(C)$. When the answer is "yes" the value v is added to a (initially empty) set $D'(X)$. MAXGAC answers "yes" if and only if the domain D' obtained at the end of the process is equal to D.

(4) ISITGAC$[C, D]$ can be transformed in MAXGAC$[C, D, D]$. □

Table 2. A list of counting constraints that are intractable to propagate with GAC.

Name	Definition
nvalue($N, [X_1, \ldots, X_n]$)	$N = \{X_i \mid 1 \leq i \leq n\}$
egcc($[X_1, \ldots, X_n], [O_1, \ldots, O_m]$)	$\forall j, O_j = \sum_i |X_i = j|$
rgcc($[[X_1, \ldots, X_n]], [o_1, \ldots, o_m]$)	$\forall j, o_j = \sum_i |X_i = j|$
common($N, M, [X_1, \ldots, X_n], [Y_1, \ldots, Y_m]$)	$N = \{i \mid X_i = Y_j\}$ and $M = \{j \mid X_i = Y_j\}$
cardpath($N, [X_1, \ldots, X_m], C$)	$N = \sum_{i=1}^{m-k+1} |C(X_i, \ldots, X_{i+k-1})|$

4 Examples of Intractable Constraints

In the long version of this paper [3], we give a number of constraints for which the complexity of GAC was not known. We use the basic tools of computational complexity to show their tractability or intractability. Table 2 gives some of the intractability results we obtained for counting constraints on integer variables. Proofs are in [3].

The nvalue constraint was proposed in [6]. The extended global cardinality constraint, egcc, allows the O_j to be variables and not just fixed intervals as in [8]. egcc has been proved intractable in [7]. The rgcc constraint is a simple gcc in which repetitions of variables are allowed in the sequence $[[X_1, \ldots, X_n]]$. The common constraint was introduced in [1]. The cardpath constraint [2], ensures that when we slide C down the sequence $X_1, \ldots, X_m$ it holds N times. cardpath is intractable even if enforcing GAC on C is polynomial and the sequence of variables $[X_1, \ldots, X_m]$ does not contain any repetition.

Acknowledgements

The last three authors are supported by Science Foundation Ireland and an ILOG software grant. We thank Marie-Christine Lagasquie for some advice on reducibility notions.

References

1. N. Beldiceanu. Global constraints as graph properties on a structured network of elementary constraints of the same type. SICS Technical Report T2000/01.
2. N. Beldiceanu and M. Carlsson. Revisiting the cardinality operator and introducing cardinality-path constraint family. In *Proceedings ICLP'01*, pages 59–73, 2001.
3. C. Bessiere, E. Hebrard, , B. Hnich, and T. Walsh. The tractability of global constraints. Technical Report APES-83-2004, APES Research Group, May 2004.
4. C. Bessiere and J.C. Régin. Arc consistency for general constraint networks: Preliminary results. In *Proceedings IJCAI'97*, pages 398–404, 1997.
5. R. Mohr and G. Masini. Good old discrete relaxation. In *Proceedings ECAI'88*, pages 651–656, 1988.
6. F. Pachet and P. Roy. Automatic generation of music programs. In *Proceedings CP'99*, pages 331–345, 1999.
7. C. Quimper. Enforcing domain consistency on the extended global cardinality constraint is NP-hard. TR CS-2003-39, School of Computer Science, University of Waterloo, 2003.
8. J-C. Régin. Generalized arc consistency for global cardinality constraints. In *Proceedings AAAI'96*, pages 209–215, 1996.

Support Inference for Generic Filtering

Frederic Boussemart, Fred Hemery, Christophe Lecoutre, and Lakhdar Sais

CRIL (Centre de Recherche en Informatique de Lens)
CNRS FRE 2499
rue de l'université, SP 16
62307 Lens cedex, France
{boussemart,hemery,lecoutre,sais}@cril.univ-artois.fr

Abstract. In this paper, we show that a static analysis of constraints can deliver interesting structural knowledge. Such knowledge, viewed as some general constraint properties, is very useful in achieving support inference, thereby reducing the cost of consistency checking. Indeed, exploiting during search some properties established in a preprocessing step can lead to substantial improvements of backtracking algorithms that maintain a form of local consistency such as arc consistency.

1 Introduction

One challenge of the Constraint Programming (CP) community is to develop efficient general approaches to solve CSP instances. As constraint propagation is recognized as an important component in the design of efficient search procedures, many filtering techniques have been introduced by the CP community. In this paper, we are interested in exploiting new general constraint properties in order to improve generic filtering, thereby reducing the gap between generic and specific approaches.

Arc consistency is a general property of constraint networks which can be established stand-alone or maintained during search. When arc consistency is maintained during search, an initialization phase is generally achieved by a preprocessing step, and a propagation phase is repeated at each step of the search process. The idea behind this paper is to propose new improvements in order to reduce the cost of the propagation phase. In other words, the idea is to achieve substantial computations during the preprocessing step in order to avoid useless consistency checking during search.

More precisely, we present a static analysis of the structure of each constraint in order to extract interesting properties, namely, conflict sets, covering sets and substitutability. Then, we show how it is possible to exploit such knowledge in a search algorithm that maintains a domain filtering consistency such as arc consistency.

2 Formal Background

An instance of the Constraint Satisfaction Problem (CSP) is defined by a constraint network. A constraint network is a pair $(\mathscr{X}, \mathscr{C})$ where $\mathscr{X}$ is a finite set of variables such that each variable $X \in \mathcal{X}$ has an associated domain $dom(X)$ denoting the set of values allowed for X, and $\mathcal{C}$ is a finite set of constraints such that each constraint $C \in \mathcal{C}$ has an associated relation $rel(C)$ denoting the set of tuples allowed for the variables $vars(C)$ involved in the constraint C.

Let C be a k-ary constraint such that $vars(C) = \{X_{i_1}, \ldots, X_{i_k}\}$, $dom(C)$ represents the domain of C, i.e. the Cartesian product $\prod_{j=1}^{k} dom(X_{i_j})$. A k-tuple t is a support of C iff $t \in rel(C)$ and a conflict of C iff $t \in dom(C) - rel(C)$. The set of supports of C restricted to $X = a$ is denoted $supports(C)_{X=a}$ and the set of conflicts of C restricted to $X = a$ is denoted $conflicts(C)_{X=a}$.

Now, we introduce some properties (given in the binary case) that can be exploited by any backtracking algorithm that alternates variable instantiation and constraint propagation enforcing a domain filtering consistency [5] such as arc-consistency, restricted path consistency, singleton arc consistency, etc. The properties that we have identified permit inferences that reduce the cost of looking for constraint supports. As a result, the number of constraint checks performed by propagation can be significantly decreased.

A first mechanism to infer supports involves (the cardinality of) conflict sets.

Proposition 1. *Let $C \in \mathcal{C}$ s.t. $vars(C) = \{X, Y\}$ and $a \in dom(X)$. At any step of the search, if $|dom(Y)| > \lambda$ then $supports(C)_{X=a} \neq \emptyset$ where λ is the size of the initial set of conflicts of C restricted to $X = a$.*

A second mechanism to infer supports is based on covering sets.

Definition 1. *Let $C \in \mathcal{C}$ s.t. $vars(C) = \{X, Y\}$ and $S \subseteq dom(Y)$. S is a covering set from Y for C iff $\forall a \in dom(X), \exists b \in S$ s.t. (a, b) is a support of C.*

Proposition 2. *Let $C \in \mathcal{C}$ s.t. $vars(C) = \{X, Y\}$ and S a covering set from Y for C. At any step of the search, if any element of S still remains in $dom(Y)$ then $\forall a \in dom(X)$ $supports(C)_{X=a} \neq \emptyset$.*

The last mechanism is called substitutability that has been introduced by [6] and defined with respect to all constraints of a CSP. In this paper, we are interested in a restricted form of substitutability that is defined independently for each constraint of a CSP. Restricting such a property to a given constraint might lead to a great number of substitutable values.

Definition 2. *Let $C \in \mathcal{C}$, $X \in vars(C)$ and $\{a, b\} \subseteq dom(X)$. a is substitutable for b wrt X in C, denoted $a \succeq_{C,X} b$, iff $supports(C)_{X=a} \supseteq supports(C)_{X=b}$.*

Proposition 3. *Let $C \in \mathcal{C}$, $X \in vars(C)$ and $a \in dom(X)$.*

- $supports(C)_{X=a} \neq \emptyset \Rightarrow \forall b \in dom(X)$ s.t. $b \succeq_{C,X} a$, $supports(C)_{X=b} \neq \emptyset$.
- $supports(C)_{X=a} = \emptyset \Rightarrow \forall b \in dom(X)$ s.t. $a \succeq_{C,X} b$, $supports(C)_{X=b} = \emptyset$.

3 Support Inference in Arc Consistency Algorithms

It is possible to exploit the properties that have been identified in the previous section when using an algorithm establishing arc consistency. More precisely, we have chosen to illustrate our approach with respect to AC3 [9]. Indeed, AC3 is quite simple to present, and all extensions introduced here can be directly integrated in other coarse-grained arc consistency algorithms such as AC2001/3.1, AC3.2 and AC3.3 (and also, for some of them, adapted to fine-grained ones).

We have developed the three following versions:

- $AC3^{R0}$ corresponds to AC3.
- $AC3^{R1}$ is the variant of AC3 that exploits conflict sets and covering sets.
- $AC3^{R2}$ is the variant of AC3 that exploits conflict sets, covering sets and substitutability.

The two variants of AC3 that we have introduced above are not very interesting when one just establishes arc consistency. Indeed, the initialization phase is heavy, and then penalizing if no search is performed. Clearly, the variants we propose must be used with a MAC (or GAC) algorithm. Initializing the new data structures before or after preprocessing and exploiting them all along search is a good compromise between the cost of the initialization and the benefit that can be obtained.

4 Experiments

To prove the practical interest of the properties introduced in this paper, we have implemented the different algorithms described in the previous section and conducted an experimentation with respect to significant classes of random and real-world instances. Performances have been measured in terms of the number of constraint checks (#ccks) and the cpu time in seconds (cpu). Also, on some problems involving 100 instances, performance criteria are given on average.

We have used a MAC algorithm which maintains arc consistency by using AC3 [9], AC2001/3.1 [3, 11] or AC3.2 [8]. Also, we have used the variable ordering heuristic $dom/wdeg$ [4] as it has been shown to be a quite efficient generic heuristic.

First, we have experimented some realistic scheduling problems. We have selected 4 representative instances from the set of 60 job shop instances proposed by [10]. One can observe on Table 1 the significant gain obtained wrt AC3 when exploiting unidirectionality (AC3.1/AC2001) and (partial) bidirectionality (AC3.2), conflict and covering sets (R1) and substitutability (R2). As illustrated by the behavior of $AC3.2^{R2}$, on this example the more exploited constraint knowledge is, the more efficient the search algorithm is.

Finally, to study the behaviour of the different variants wrt random problems, we have considered five classes $<n, d, m, t>$ of 100 random instances located at the phase transition where n denotes the number of variables, d the uniform domain size, m the number of binary constraints and t the constraint tightness (number of unallowed tuples). These classes have been selected such that the tightness ranges from 5% to 88%. It is interesting to note in Table 2 that the smaller the tightness is, the more efficient variants $R1$ and $R2$ are.

Table 1. Job shop instances.

instances			MAC3		MAC3.1		MAC3.2	
			cpu	#ccks	cpu	#ccks	cpu	#ccks
$<RG=0.1, BK=1>$		R0	251.64	1,449,387K	192.22	611,045K	98.37	242,679K
(sat)		R1	123.26	600,751K	91.38	266,557K	80.81	215,979K
		R2	100.55	375,148K	80.59	173,698K	75.69	152,896K
$<RG=0.1, BK=2>$		R0	374.49	2,281,435K	169.28	522,253K	116.64	291,574K
(sat)		R1	262.59	1,448,883K	145.67	427,742K	113.24	278,557K
		R2	189.27	778,953K	147.63	257,601K	116.98	172,229K
$<RG=0.0, BK=1>$		R0	497.57	2,883,037K	350.90	1,158,383K	175.21	425,669K
(sat)		R1	228.72	1,042,013K	176.96	493,222K	146.39	383,073K
		R2	179.69	695,099K	147.10	335,314K	131.83	277,671K
$<RG=0.0, BK=2>$		R0	418.46	2,454,923K	222.26	727,814K	154.72	429,273K
(sat)		R1	298.89	1,563,852K	194.98	588,483K	152.37	398,453K
		R2	226.73	880,159K	188.48	341,490K	159.91	241,383K

Table 2. Random instances.

instances		MAC3		MAC3.1		MAC3.2	
		cpu	#ccks	cpu	#ccks	cpu	#ccks
$<30,10,1330,5>$	R0	39.52	58,253K	46.47	32,047K	42.98	16,611K
(32/100 sat)	R1	26.40	2,723K	28.93	2,636K	27.99	1,738K
	R2	27.42	2,409K	29.52	2,331K	28.54	1,512K
$<30,14,725,20>$	R0	93.20	150,315K	105.16	80,536K	92.25	42,699K
(49/100 sat)	R1	57.17	24,380K	71.56	20,916K	68.14	15,228K
	R2	66.10	22,357K	79.20	18,951K	77.69	13,597K
$<50,10,494,20>$	R0	208.39	348,812K	240.57	196,167K	198.85	97,260K
(70/100 sat)	R1	157.22	109,300K	197.82	85,754K	180.89	55,579K
	R2	186.94	97,946K	222.95	75,997K	209.97	48,575K
$<40,20,200,175>$	R0	14.49	25,037K	12.32	12,827K	9.10	6,848K
(51/100 sat)	R1	12.28	16,918K	11.63	9,977K	9.60	6,243K
	R2	13.73	16,359K	12.88	9,705K	11.12	6,123K
$<150,50,230,2200>$	R0	26.78	60,057K	14.70	25,687K	9.95	13,089K
(31/100 sat)	R1	24.34	51,818K	14.62	24,348K	9.79	13,569K
	R2	24.11	50,183K	14.84	23,726K	10.39	13,389K

5 Related Work

An arc consistency algorithm schema, AC-Inference, has been described [2] that allows exploiting generic and specific properties of constraints so as to save useless constraint checks. AC7 is a derivation of AC-Inference that simply utilizes bidirectionality. We have shown, in this paper, that (a local form of) substitutability is another generic constraint property that allows support inference. Hence, it should be possible to build from AC-Inference a general-purpose fine-grained arc consistency algorithm exploiting both bidirectionaly and substitutability.

Interchangeability and its extended forms has been introduced by [6]. Simply removing interchangeable values at the preprocessing stage has been experimentally shown productive under certain conditions [1]. And using interchangeability independently for each constraint in order to save constraint checks has been proposed by [7]. Our exploitation of substitutability can then be seen as a refinement of the piece of work of [7] related to constraint propagation.

6 Conclusion

In this paper, we have introduced new general properties that allow support inference for any backtracking algorithm maintaining a domain filtering consistency. Exploiting such properties can be seen as a tentative to reduce the gap between generic and specific approaches.

We have shown that coarse-grained arc-consistency algorithms can significantly benefit from these properties since the variants that we have presented:

- are easy to implement (new data structures are not dynamically updated),
- have a limited space requirement ($O(md)$ versus $O(md^2)$ for AC-Inference),
- are competitive.

Acknowledgements

This paper has been supported by the CNRS, the "programme COCOA de la Région Nord/Pas-de-Calais" and by the "IUT de Lens".

References

1. B.W. Benson and E.C. Freuder. Interchangeability preprocessing can improve forward checking search. In *Proceedings of ECAI'92*, pages 28–30, 1992.
2. C. Bessière, E.C. Freuder, and J. Régin. Using constraint metaknowledge to reduce arc consistency computation. *Artificial Intelligence*, 107:125–148, 1999.
3. C. Bessière and J. Régin. Refining the basic constraint propagation algorithm. In *Proceedings of IJCAI'01*, pages 309–315, 2001.
4. F. Boussemart, F. Hemery, C. Lecoutre, and L. Sais. Boosting systematic search by weighting constraints. In *Proceedings of ECAI'04 (to appear)*, 2004.
5. R. Debruyne and C. Bessière. Domain filtering consistencies. *Journal of Artificial Intelligence Research*, 14:205–230, 2001.
6. E.C. Freuder. Eliminating interchangeable values in constraint satisfaction problems. In *Proceedings of AAAI'91*, pages 227–233, 1991.
7. A. Haselbock. Exploiting interchangeabilities in constraint satisfaction problems. In *Proceedings of IJCAI'93*, pages 282–287, 1993.
8. C. Lecoutre, F. Boussemart, and F. Hemery. Exploiting multidirectionality in coarse-grained arc consistency algorithms. In *Proceedings of CP'03*, pages 480–494, 2003.
9. A.K. Mackworth. Consistency in networks of relations. *Artificial Intelligence*, 8:118–126, 1977.
10. N. Sadeh and M.S. Fox. Variable and value ordering heuristics for the job shop scheduling constraint satisfaction problem. *Artificial Intelligence*, 86:1–41, 1996.
11. Y. Zhang and R.H.C. Yap. Making AC3 an optimal algorithm. In *Proceedings of IJCAI'01*, pages 316–321, Seattle WA, 2001.

Strong Cost-Based Filtering for Lagrange Decomposition Applied to Network Design

Wilhelm Cronholm and Farid Ajili

IC-Parc, Imperial College London, London SW7 2AZ, UK
{w.cronholm,f.ajili}@icparc.imperial.ac.uk

Abstract. This paper describes a new hybrid algorithm for a multicast network design application. The problem consists of finding a minimum-cost topology and link dimensions subject to capacity and multicast routing constraints. The algorithm exploits Lagrange Decomposition (LD) to yield separable subproblems. Each subproblem has a Constraint Programming relaxation. We derive a sharper cost bound and stronger cost-based filtering rules. The results indicate that our solver outperforms the pure LD approach.

1 Introduction

Several hybrids [9] have suggested the benefits of cost-based filtering [3, 9, 10]. Its main idea is that Constraint Programming (CP) focuses not only on excluding inconsistent values but also non-optimal values as these will not appear at optimality. Our work is motivated by a large-scale multicast network design problem ($\mathcal{P}$) arising in the telecoms sector [2, 11].

Lagrange Relaxation (LR) is a natural approach to exploit problem structure [1]. It dualises "complicating" constraints in order to yield a manageable relaxation. [12] proposes one way of coupling LR with CP, where at each dual iteration only one substructure is used. If the problem consists of two linear sub-structures A and B, then the algorithm dualises A and propagates B. At convergence, the optimal dual information is then used to propagate A. This seriously restricts its application in our context for several reasons including 1) it requires structure A to have a *reasonably sized linear* formulation with *easily obtainable dual values*, 2) convergence is often computationally expensive.

To overcome these restrictions, we present a new hybrid algorithm based on Lagrange Decomposition [5], also named variable splitting. It creates "copies" of some variables, using one copy per sub-structure and dualising the equality of a variable to its copy. As it preserves the problem sub-structures, LD provides a bound which is at least as good as the LR bound, and is particularly useful if there are no apparent complicating constraints [5]. Additionally, our hybrid enables the propagation of *all* sub-structures at *every* dual iteration and also offers desirable ingredients to design strong cost-based filtering.

This paper is organised as follows. Section 2 defines $\mathcal{P}$. Section 3 presents a pure LD algorithm to solve $\mathcal{P}$ and Section 4 extends this with cost-based filtering. Section 5 summarises results. Section 6 concludes.

2 The Multicast Network Design Problem

The input of $\mathcal{P}$ consists of 1) an *undirected* graph $G = (V, E)$ where V and E are respectively its set of nodes (routers) and edges (links), 2) a set F_e of facilities for each edge e, each facility $f_e \in F_e$ is defined by its capacity b_e^f, and installation cost c_e^f, 3) a set $\mathcal{K}$ of (multicast) demands, where each $k \in \mathcal{K}$ is defined by its set $R^k \subseteq V$ of terminals, and requested bandwidth d^k. A solution to $\mathcal{P}$ is assigning, at minimum cost, one facility $f \in F_e$ for each e, and multicast tree S^k for each demand k in $\mathcal{K}$, such that the used capacity does not exceed the installed capacity for each edge. See [11] for more details about $\mathcal{P}$.

We now introduce the decision variables. For every $e \in E$ and $k \in \mathcal{K}$, let x_e^k be a binary variable that is 1 iff edge e is used by the tree associated to demand k. For every edge e and facility f, let z_e^f be a binary variable that is 1 iff facility f is installed on e. Let x^k designate the variables $(x_e^k), e \in E$. The integer programming model of $\mathcal{P}$ is then:

$$(\mathcal{P}): \quad Z^* = \text{Minimise } Z = \sum_{e \in E} \sum_{f \in F_e} c_e^f z_e^f \quad (1)$$

$$\text{Subject to: } \sum_{f \in F_e} z_e^f = 1, \ e \in E \quad (2)$$

$$\sum_{k \in \mathcal{K}} d^k x_e^k \leq \sum_{f \in F_e} b_e^f z_e^f, \ e \in E \quad (3)$$

$$x^k \in \mathbf{X}^G(R^k), \ k \in \mathcal{K} \quad (4)$$

$$x_e^k \in \{0,1\}, \ z_e^f \subset \{0,1\}, \ e \in E, \ k \in \mathcal{K}, \ f \in F_e \quad (5)$$

(1) minimises the total installation cost Z. (2) force exactly one selected facility per edge. (3) constrain the edge utilisation not to exceed the installed capacity. (4) require the vector x^k to define a tree in G that belongs to the set $\mathbf{X}^G(R^k)$ of multicast trees spanning nodes R^k. (5) are integrality constraints of the variables.

3 Lagrange Decomposition Based Algorithm

As in [11], the algorithm implements a branch-and-bound search by solving an LD relaxation with a subgradient (SG) dual solver.

For each $e \in E$ and each $k \in \mathcal{K}$, the routing variable x_e^k is "split" by introducing a new binary variable y_e^k. It plays the role of its *copy* in constraints (3). To preserve the solution set of $\mathcal{P}$ the split equalities $x_e^k - y_e^k = 0$, for every $e \in E$ and $k \in \mathcal{K}$, are added. Each of these is then dualised with an associated Lagrange multiplier $\lambda_e^k \in \mathbb{R}$. To get a good bound within reasonable time, we also relax the integrality of both x and y.

The resulting relaxation decomposes into *separable* subproblems, $|E|$ *dimensioning* subproblems, one per edge, and $|\mathcal{K}|$ *routing* subproblems, one per demand. The e-th (dimensioning) subproblem consists of (2), (3), as well as domain constraints. It decomposes into a *disjunction* of continuous knapsacks, one per facility f. The f-th knapsack corresponds to setting z_e^f to 1. The continuous knapsacks are solved sequentially by Dantzig's method [8] and the least-cost solution is retained. The k-th (routing) subproblem consists of (4) and is equivalent to the Steiner tree problem (see e.g. [7]). It is solved by a continuous variant of the solver in [7].

For every fixed multiplier $\lambda \in \mathbb{R}^{|E||\mathcal{K}|}$, the optimal cost $L(\lambda)$ is *additively* computed from the optima of the subproblems. The relaxed cost $L(\lambda)$ is a lower bound on Z^*. The best lower bound corresponding to the optimal multipliers λ^* is obtained by solving the Lagrange dual problem. The iterative SG of [10] is invoked to yield good multipliers, convergence is not guaranteed. An iteration *separately* solves all subproblems *to optimality* and updates the multipliers.

The search monitors both the splitting equalities and integrality of x and y for violation. If there are no violations, then a primal solution is found and the incumbent cost UB is updated accordingly. Otherwise, the pair of variables having the largest $\lambda_e^k(x_e^k - y_e^k)$ is selected. The search branches by posting $x_e^k = y_e^k = 0$, and its negation $x_e^k = y_e^k = 1$ on backtrack.

4 CP-Based Lagrange Decomposition Algorithm

To keep a reasonably sized CP component, the dualised splitting constraints are excluded from the CP store. It follows that the CP relaxations attached to the subproblems are *disjoint*, they share no variables. The CP store of the e-th subproblem contains (3) but the installed capacity is modelled as one variable. The capacity selection (2) is then included as the `element` constraint [4]. Integrality of y is also added. For the k-th subproblem it contains a slightly strengthened version of the flow inequalities of [7] and integrality of x. Each node propagates its CP stores *one by one* with the aim of removing inconsistent values from the variables' domains. This is done after the last SG and immediately *before* branching. There is no need to memorise all CP stores throughout the search since only one store is considered at a time. By using a concept of *generic* models [3], our implementation carefully avoids the overhead caused by setting up a CP store every time the subproblem is propagated.

We now focus on cost-based filtering rules. They aim at removing *non-optimal* domain values. These domain changes will be further propagated by the CP reduction step. This cost-filtering is run at *every* dual iteration and the fixing is done *between* two SG iterations.

The current dual iteration gives a lower bound $LB = L(\lambda)$ and also suggests a solution value $\bar{v}$ for every problem variable v. Also, let $rc(v)$ designate the reduced cost associated with v and denote by UB the incumbent cost.

We start by adapting standard cost-based filtering [9]. It is well known that $LB + |rc(x_e^k)|$ is a valid lower bound on Z^*, if we were to set x_e^k to v at the current node provided that $v \in \{0,1\}$. If we fix x_e^k to a value v then we can also fix y_e^k to v since $x_e^k = y_e^k$ is satisfied in any solution. This is captured by:

$$\text{If } \bar{x}_e^k = v, \ LB + |rc(x_e^k)| \geq UB \text{ then } x_e^k = y_e^k = v \qquad (6)$$

Similar rules apply to the y and z variables. However, it turned out that these rules are weak in practise. Instead we will derive stronger filtering rules below.

Suppose that the integer values $\bar{x}_e^k$ and $\bar{y}_e^k$ assigned to two given variables x_e^k and y_e^k are *equal*, i.e. $\bar{x}_e^k = \bar{y}_e^k$. If we fix x_e^k to $1 - \bar{x}_e^k$ in the k-th subproblem, we should also restrict y_e^k to that same value in the e-th subproblem. This means that we incur not only a cost in the k-th subproblem, but also one in the e-th subproblem. Since the subproblems are disjoint, the cost incurred by switching *both variables* is the sum of the individual costs incurred in the two subproblems. Thus, if such a sum exceeds UB we infer that $x_e^k = y_e^k = v$ must hold in the subtree rooted at the current node. This is reflected by the following rule:

$$\text{If } \bar{x}_e^k = \bar{y}_e^k = v, \ LB + |rc(x_e^k)| + |rc(y_e^k)| \geq UB \text{ then } x_e^k = y_e^k = v \quad (7)$$

This rule strengthens (6) with no extra overhead. The soundness of the rule *only* requires the incurred cost estimates to be valid. For the k-th subproblem, the reduced costs are obtained from its solver. However, the reduced costs of the y and z are not readily available, because of the integrality of z. Dropping these and solving the resulting relaxation lead to poor reduced costs. We adopted a rather technical, but interesting option to estimate the incurred costs. With regard to $rc(y_e^k)$, this includes 1) the least-cost effect of all knapsacks 2) the value $rc(x_e^k)$ when $\bar{x}_e^k = \bar{y}_e^k$ because of (7). For z, we adapt the penalty tests of [6]. For details we refer to [3].

So far, the reduced cost is viewed as an incurred cost. Another view interprets it as the amount the *cost coefficient* for the variable can be decreased without losing optimality of the SG solution, say s. Here, we use them to "adjust" the SG multipliers so that LB increases. Again, see [3] for more details.

We vary the multiplier λ_e^k subject to preserving the fact that s is still an optimal solution to the subproblems even with the "new" multipliers. This would yield an increased bound without re-optimising the subproblems with the new multipliers. The sharpest bound is found by considering all pairs (e, k). This is done by formulating a linear program where the multipliers are the variables. Thanks to the splitting equalities, this problem decomposes nicely into trivial independent subproblems. Its solution yields a stronger bound LB_s:

Proposition 1. *Let LB be the lower bound returned by the SG at the current iteration. If we define $\mathcal{V} = \{(e, k) \mid e \in E, k \in \mathcal{K}, \bar{x}_e^k \neq \bar{y}_e^k\}$, then $LB_s = LB + \sum_{(e,k) \in \mathcal{V}} \min\{|rc(x_e^k)|, |rc(y_e^k)|\}$ is a lower bound on Z^*.*

LB_s, which is as least as good as LB, is used for pruning. Since LB_s is constructed with variables where (7) does not apply, we also use it in (7) instead of LB to yield a more powerful filtering at *every* dual iteration. Note that $LB_s = LB$ with optimal multipliers.

5 Summary of Results

We compare several algorithm variants implemented in *ECLiPSe* [4] and summarise the findings on commercially generated test data. Comprehensive results can be found in [3]. If propagation and cost-filtering are enabled, then optimality is certified on more tests and often faster compared to a pure LD approach. Thus, our filtering rules guide the search to optimal areas. However, on some instances, the hybrid algorithm has a larger search tree indicating that the branching is unstable and the primal heuristics is not sufficiently effective. These require deeper study. Furthermore, a sharper bound is almost always obtained when including cost-filtering. This validates the use of fixing in between SG iterations as well as the importance of propagation. Also, LB_s is significantly sharper than LB for the first dual iterations and less fluctuating. Hence, the stronger bound can be used to speed up the dual solver.

6 Conclusion

We introduce a hybridisation of Lagrange decomposition and constraint programming. By contrast to Lagrange relaxation, our hybrid enables the propagation of *all* sub-structures at every dual iteration without requiring optimal dual information from one of them. Our main contribution is a strong form of cost-based propagation that combines gradient information from several sub-structures. The encouraging results for a network design application indicate the benefits of the new hybrid. Future work include extensions of the cost-based techniques to other approaches and further study of branching strategies.

References

1. R.K. Ahuja, T.L. Magnanti, and J.B. Orlin. *Network Flows: Theory, Algorithms and Applications*. Prentice-Hall, New Jersey, 1993.
2. D. Bienstock and A. Bley. Capacitated network design with multicast commodities. Tech. Rep. ZIB 00–14, Konrad-Zuse-Zentrum für Inform., Berlin, 2000.
3. W. Cronholm. CP-based lagrange decomposition applied to multicast network design. PhD transfer thesis, IC-Parc, Imperial, London UK, 2004.
4. ECLiPSe. Introduction. Tech. Rep. IC-PARC-03-01, Imperial, London UK, 2002.
5. M. Guignard and S. Kim. Lagrangean decomposition: A model yielding stronger Lagrangean bounds. *Math. Program.*, 39, 1987.
6. K. Holmberg and D. Yuan. A Lagrangian heuristic based branch-and-bound approach for the capacitated network design problem. *Oper. Res.*, 48(3), 2000.
7. T. Koch and A. Martin. Solving Steiner tree problems in graphs to optimality. *Networks*, 32(3), 1998.
8. S. Martello and P. Toth. *Knapsack Problems: Algorithms and Computer Implementations*. John Wiley and Sons Ltd, 1990.
9. M. Milano, editor. *Constraint and Integer Programming: Toward a Unified Methodology*. Kluwer Academic Publishers, 2003.
10. W. Ouaja and B. Richards. A hybrid multicommodity routing algorithm for traffic engineering. *Networks*, 43(3), 2004.
11. M. Prytz and A. Forsgren. Dimensioning multicast-enabled communications networks. *Networks*, 39(4), 2002.
12. M. Sellmann and T. Fahle. CP-based Lagrangian relaxation for the automatic recording problem. *Ann. Oper. Res.*, 118(1), 2003.

The Impact of AND/OR Search Spaces on Constraint Satisfaction and Counting

Rina Dechter and Robert Mateescu

Donald Bren School of Information and Computer Science
University of California, Irvine, CA 92697-3425
{dechter,mateescu}@ics.uci.edu

Abstract. The contribution of this paper is in demonstrating the impact of AND/OR search spaces view on solutions counting. In contrast to the traditional (OR) search space view, the AND/OR search space displays independencies present in the graphical model explicitly and may sometimes reduce the search space exponentially. Empirical evaluation focusing on counting demonstrates the spectrum of search and inference within the AND/OR search spaces.

1 Introduction

The primary contribution of this paper is in viewing search for constraint processing in the context of *AND/OR search spaces* rather than *OR spaces*. We demonstrate how the AND/OR principle can exploit independencies in the graph model to yield exponentially smaller search spaces. The notion of AND/OR search tree is closely related to the notion of pseudo-tree rearrangement introduced in [1] for constraint satisfaction. In recent work we revive this idea, extend it to various tasks for any graphical model and extend AND/OR spaces to search graphs as well, thus allowing caching. In this paper we focus on counting for constraint networks and provide initial empirical evaluation along the full spectrum of space and time.

2 AND/OR Search Trees

In the following sections we will use the common definitions and notations for constraint networks and their associated parameters. For more details see [2].

Definition 1 (AND/OR search tree based on a DFS tree). *Consider a constraint network $\mathcal{R}$ and a DFS spanning tree T of its primal graph. The AND/OR search tree of $\mathcal{R}$ based on T, denoted S_T, has alternating levels of OR nodes (labeled with variable names, e.g. X) and AND nodes (labeled with variable values, e.g. $\langle X, v \rangle$). The root of S_T is an OR node labeled with the root of T. The children of an OR node X are AND nodes, each labeled with a value of X, $\langle X, v \rangle$. The children of an AND node $\langle X, v \rangle$ are OR nodes, labeled with the variables that are children of X in T.*

Consider the tree T in Fig. 1 describing a graph coloring problem over domains $\{1, 2, 3\}$. Its traditional OR search tree along the DFS ordering $d = (X, Y, T, R, Z, L, M)$ is given in Fig. 2, its AND/OR search tree based on the DFS tree T and a highlighted solution subtree are given in Fig. 3.

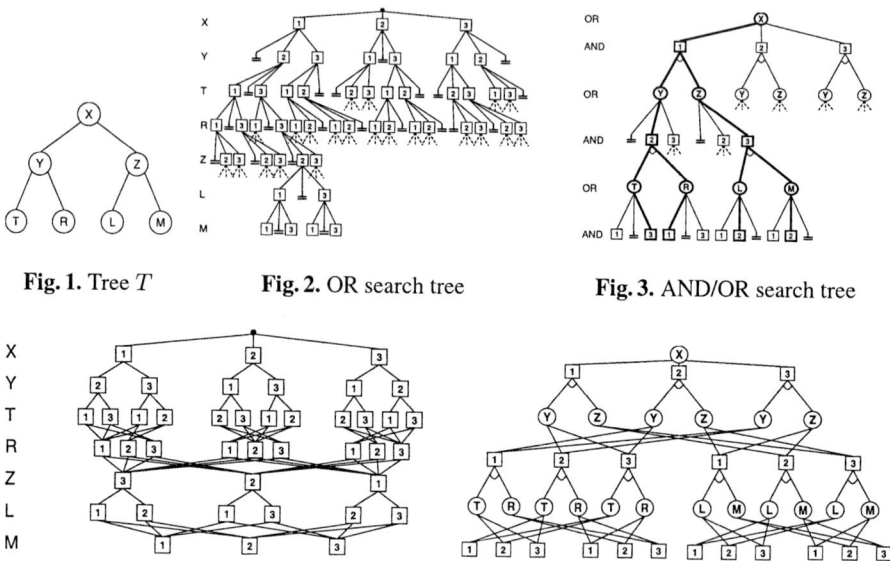

Fig. 1. Tree T **Fig. 2.** OR search tree   **Fig. 3.** AND/OR search tree

Fig. 4. Minimal OR search graph of the tree problem in Fig. 1

Fig. 5. Minimal AND/OR search graph of the tree problem in Fig. 1

Pseudo-trees. The construction of AND/OR search trees can use as its basis not just DFS spanning trees, but also the more general *pseudo-trees* [1, 3]. They have the property that every arc of the original primal graph is a back-arc in the pseudo-tree (i.e. it doesn't connect across different branches). Clearly, any DFS tree and any chain are pseudo-trees. Searching the OR space corresponds to searching a chain. It is easy to see that searching an AND/OR tree is exponential in the depth of the pseudo-tree. Also, it is known that the minimal depth over pseudo-trees, m^*, satisfies $m^* \leq w^* \log n$ [3].

Theorem 1. *Given a constraint network $\mathcal{R}$ and a pseudo-tree T, its AND/OR search tree S_T is sound and complete (contains all and only solutions) and its size is $O(n \cdot \exp(m))$ where m is the depth of the pseudo-tree. A constraint network that has a treewidth w^* has an AND/OR search tree whose size is $O(\exp(w^* \cdot \log n))$.*

3 AND/OR Search Graphs

It is often the case that certain states in the search tree can be merged because the subtrees they root are identical. Any two such nodes are called *unifiable*, and when merged, transform the search tree into a search graph. It can be shown that the closure of an AND/OR search graph under the merging of unifiable states yields a unique fixed point, called the *minimal AND/OR search graph*. Merging is applicable to the OR search space as well. However, in many cases it will not be able to reach the compression we see in the AND/OR search graph. Fig. 4 and Fig. 5 show a comparison between minimal OR and AND/OR search graphs for the problem in Fig. 1. Note that in the AND/OR graph only the AND levels are relevant, the OR levels serving only for clarity.

```
procedure AND-OR-COUNTING
Input: A constraint network; a pseudo-tree T of its constraint graph; parents pa_i and parent-separators psa_i.
Output: The number of solutions g(X_0). π denotes the current partial assignment path.
1.  Initialize: X_0 = root(T), type(X_0) = OR, OPEN ← X_0, cache ← φ;
2.  Expand: n ← first node in OPEN; generate all successors of n as follows:
      if (type(n) == OR), denote n = X
        succ(X) ← {⟨X, v⟩ | consistent(⟨X, v⟩)}
        if (succ(X) = φ) then g(X) = 0; (dead-end)
          [ cache(π_{pa_X}) = 0 , update constraints and go to step 3 ]
        for each ⟨X, v⟩ ∈ succ(X) do π' ← π ∪ (⟨X, v⟩)
          [ if (cache(π'_{psa_X}) ≠ φ) then g(⟨X, v⟩) = cache(π'_{psa_X})  else ]   add ⟨X, v⟩ to OPEN
      if (type(n) == AND), denote n = ⟨X, v⟩
        if X is a leaf in T then, g(⟨X, v⟩) = 1, go to step 3
        succ(⟨X, v⟩) ← {Y | Y ∈ children(X) in T}
        for each Y ∈ succ(⟨X, v⟩) do
          [ if (cache(π_{pa_Y}) ≠ φ) then g(Y) = cache(π_{pa_Y})  else ]   add Y to OPEN
3.  Propagate: while you can propagate g values:
      a. For a non-terminal AND node ⟨X, v⟩:
        if (Y ∈ succ(⟨X, v⟩) and g(Y) = 0), remove siblings of Y from OPEN, g(⟨X, v⟩) = 0.
        if all succ(⟨X, v⟩) are evaluated, g(⟨X, v⟩) = Π_{Y ∈ succ(⟨X,v⟩)} g(Y)
          [ if (⟨X, v⟩ is evaluated) then cache(π_{psa_X}) = g(⟨X, v⟩) ]
      b. For a non-terminal OR node X:
        if all succ(X) have g values, g(X) = Σ_{⟨X,v⟩ ∈ succ(X)} g(⟨X, v⟩)
OR        [ if (X is evaluated) then cache(π_{pa_X}) = g(X) ]
4.  if X_0 was evaluated, exit with g(X_0) else go to step 2.
```

Fig. 6. The counting algorithm

We will now describe some efficient rules for generating AND/OR search graphs. The idea is to extract from each path only the relevant *context* that completely determines the unexplored portion of the space. Subsequently, if memory allows, the subgraph is only solved once and the results are indexed by the context and cached. We will need some more definitions.

Definition 2 (induced-width relative to a pseudo-tree). *Given G^T, which is an extended graph of G that includes all the arcs in the pseudo-tree T, the induced width of G relative to the pseudo-tree T, $w_T(G)$, is the induced-width of G^T along the DFS ordering of T.*

Definition 3 (parents, parent-separators). *Given the induced-graph, G^{*T} of an extended graph G^T, the parents of X denoted pa_X, are its earlier neighbors in the induced-graph. Its parent-separators, psa_X are its parents that are also neighbors of future variables in T.*

In G^{*T}, the parent-separators of every node X_i separate in T its ancestors on the path from the root, and all its descendents in G^T. Therefore, any two nodes having the same context, that is, the same assignments to their parent-separators, can be merged.

Theorem 2. *Given G, a pseudo-tree T and its induced width $w = w_T(G)$, the size of the AND/OR search graph based on T obtained when every two nodes in S_T having the same context are merged is $O(n \cdot k^w)$, when k bounds the domain size.*

Thus, the minimal AND/OR search graph of G relative to T is $O(n \cdot k^w)$ where $w = w_T(G)$. Since, as can be shown, $\min_T\{w_T(G)\}$ equals the tree-width w^* and since $\min_{T \in chain}\{w_T(G)\}$ equals the path-width pw^* we obtain that the minimal

Table 1. A/O FC, N=60, K=3

N=40, K=3, C=50, S=3, 20 inst., w*=13, d=20							
		Time			Number of dead-ends		
tightness		20%	40%	60%	20%	40%	60%
# solutions		0	0	147898575	0	0	147898575
	BE	8.714	8.709	8.637			
i=0	A/O FC	0.030	0.454	32.931	533	9,229	1,711,947
	OR FC	0.031	0.511	9737.823	533	9,897	324,545,908
i=6	A/O FC	0.029	0.454	25.140	533	8,991	917,612
	OR FC	0.032	0.508	7293.472	533	9,897	208,159,068
i=13	A/O FC	0.030	0.457	**11.974**	533	8,533	**181,157**
	OR FC	0.032	0.494	1170.203	533	9,283	20,018,823

Table 2. A/O FC, N=100, K=2

N=100, K=2, C=130, S=3, 20 inst., w*=32, d=43				
tightness	10%	30%	50%	70%
# solutions	0	0	0	0
Time (seconds)				
i=20	0.069	0.193	3.572	677.045
Number of nodes				
i=20	70	406	4,264	1,139,860
Number of dead-ends				
i=20	72	204	4,266	1,043,692

AND/OR search graph is bounded exponentially by the primal graph's tree-width, while the minimal OR search graph is bounded exponentially by its path-width. It is well known [4] that for any graph $w^* \leq pw^* \leq w^* \cdot \log n$. It is also easy to place m^* (the minimal pseudo-tree depth) yielding $w^* \leq pw^* \leq m^* \leq w^* \cdot \log n$.

4 AND/OR Algorithms for Counting

Figure 6 presents the basic DFS traversal of the AND/OR search space. The square bracketed lines allow different levels of caching. The nodes in the search graph are labeled by g-values. These stand for the number of solutions below that variable (or variable-value). The computation of the number of solutions is done at step 3 by multiplication (for AND nodes) and summation (for OR nodes). The complexity is, [2]:

Theorem 3. AND-OR-COUNTING *with linear space has time complexity* $O(n \cdot \exp(w^* \cdot \log n))$, *where* w^* *is the tree-width of the problem. With full caching, it is time and space exponential in* w^*. *For OR space, the complexity is exponential in the path-width.*

5 Empirical Demonstration

We ran a version of the counting algorithm, which uses forward checking (FC) as the constraint propagation method, defined by the *consistent* function in step 2 of the algorithm. We compared AND/OR and OR search spaces, resulting in two algorithms: A/O FC and OR FC. We tried different levels of caching, controlled by an *i-bound* which defines the maximum context size that can be cached. We also compared against bucket elimination (BE) in some cases, where space was available. We report average measures over 20 instances. Also, $w*$ is the induced width and d is the depth of the pseudo-tree. The constraint networks were generated randomly uniformly given a number of input parameters: N - number of variables; K - number of values per variable; C - number of constraints; S - the scope size of the constraints; t - the tightness (percentage of allowed tuples per constraint). For extended results see [2].

Table 1 shows a comparison on moderate size problems which allowed bucket elimination to run. The bolded time numbers show the best values in each column. The most important thing to note is the vast superiority of AND/OR space over the traditional

OR space. A/O FC and OR FC are comparable only on inconsistent problems (up to $t = 40\%$). When the problems are consistent, the difference becomes greater with increasing number of solutions. For BE we only report time, which is not sensitive to the tightness of the problems.

Table 2 shows examples of large networks for which BE and traditional OR search were infeasible. We ran only A/O FC with the maximum cache size possible for our machine. This shows that AND/OR search is more flexible, being able to solve problems of much larger size than inference algorithms or the traditional OR search.

6 Conclusions, Discussion and Related Work

The paper shows how counting algorithms can be affected when formulated as searching AND/OR search trees and graphs rather than searching their OR counterparts. We present and analyze counting algorithms and provide initial empirical evaluation along the full spectrum of space and time. We compare counting algorithms on the AND/OR search space when pruning is accomplished by forward-checking and show how their performance is affected by different levels of caching and how it is compared to bucket-elimination, as a function of problem tightness. The empirical evaluation shows that AND/OR search space is always better than the traditional OR space, often yielding exponential improvements. Compared to inference based algorithms (bucket elimination), AND/OR search is more flexible and able to adapt to the amount of available space. All the existing constraint propagation techniques are readily available for AND/OR search. Coupling this with the possibility of caching makes AND/OR search a very powerful scheme. For full details see [2].

Related Work. It can be shown that graph-based backjumping [5,6] mimics the exploration of an AND/OR search tree. Indeed, it was shown that the depth of a DFS-tree or a pseudo-tree [7,3] plays an important role in bounding backjumping complexity. Memory-intensive algorithms can be viewed as searching the AND/OR search graph, such as recent work [8] which performs search guided by a tree-decomposition for constraint satisfaction and optimization. A similar approach was introduced recently in [9, 10] both for belief updating and counting models of a CNF formula. Relationship between minimal AND/OR graphs and tree-OBDDs can be shown.

Acknowledgments

This work was supported in part by the NSF grant IIS-0086529 and the MURI ONR award N00014-00-1-0617.

References

1. Freuder, E.C., Quinn, M.J.: Taking advantage of stable sets of variables in constraint satisfaction problems. In: International Joint Conference on Artificial Intelligene. (1985) 1076–1078
2. Dechter, R., Mateescu, R.: The impact of AND/OR search spaces on constraint satisfaction and counting. Technical report, UCI (2004)

3. Bayardo, R., Miranker, D.: A complexity analysis of space-bound learning algorithms for the constraint satisfaction problem. In: AAAI'96. (1996) 298–304
4. Bodlaender, H., Gilbert, J.R.: Approximating treewidth, pathwidth and minimum elimination tree-height. Technical Report RUU-CS-91-1, Utrecht University (1991)
5. Dechter, R.: Enhancement schemes for constraint processing: Backjumping, learning and cutset decomposition. Artificial Intelligence **41** (1990) 273–312
6. Dechter, R.: Constraint Processing. Morgan Kaufmann Publishers (2003)
7. Freuder, E.C., Quinn, M.J.: The use of lineal spanning trees to represent constraint satisfaction problems. Technical Report 87-41, University of New Hampshire, Durham (1987)
8. Terrioux, C., Jegou, P.: Hybrid backtracking bounded by tree-decomposition of constraint networks. Artificial Intelligence **146** (2003) 43–75
9. Darwiche, A.: Recursive conditioning. In: Proceedings of the 15th Conference on Uncertainty in Artificial Intelligence. (1999)
10. F. Bacchus, S.D., Piassi, T.: Value elimination: Bayesian inference via backtracking search. In: Proceedings of the 19th Conference on Uncertainty in Artificial Intelligence. (2003)

A General Extension of Constraint Propagation for Constraint Optimization

Xiaofei Huang

CallVista, Inc.
Foster City, CA 94404, USA
huangxiaofei@ieee.org

Abstract. In this paper, we propose a general extension of constraint propagation for constraint optimization based on cooperative computation. It is similar both in principle and operations to constraint propagation. In principle, it eliminates variable values by checking the feasibility that they can be in any global optimum. In operations, it is based on parallel, local iterative computations. The proposed algorithm returns both a solution and a global lower bound at each iteration. As an approximation algorithm for optimization, it significantly outperform classical optimization methods, such as simulated annealing and local search with multi-restarts in practice.

1 Introduction

Constraint programming formalization [1] has been an important and productive tool within artificial intelligence and related areas. Typically, a constraint satisfaction problem (CSP) is posed as follows. Given a set of discrete variables of finite domains and a set of constraints, each specifying a relation on a particular subset of the variables, find the relation on the set of all the variables which satisfies all the given constraints. Constraint propagation [1] has been widely used as a technique for reducing the domains of variables.

Constraint optimization [2–4] (also referred as weighted MAX-CSP) generalizes constraint satisfaction by assigning a real value to each tuple of a constraint to describe degrees of quality, cost, or probability. That is, each constraint is a real-valued function on a particular subset of the variables, termed soft constraint. A constraint optimization problem (COP) becomes an optimization task, i.e., to find the global optimum of a multivariate function, which is a summation of those real valued functions.

Constraint propagation for constraint satisfaction is a technique for reducing the search space by eliminating variable values. By reducing the search space, we can greatly improve the efficiency of other combinatorial optimization techniques, such as backtracking, in solving the original problem. If one value left for each variable, then they constitute a solution for the problem. One of the biggest advantages of constraint propagation is its inherent parallel operations. The values for each variable can be eliminated fully in parallel at each iteration.

The value elimination is based on the principle that any value for any variable can be eliminated if those values can not be in any solutions to the problem.

To the soft constraint programming, the principle for value elimination used in constraint propagation can be generalized as eliminating those values for each variable which can not be in any global optimal solution. However, there is no straightforward way to generalize the operations of constraint propagation so that we can check if a value is contained in a global optimum or not. For constraint satisfaction, it is a simple task by checking the violation of any local constraints. For constraint optimization, however, it is a challenge task. A variable value that optimize local constraints, may not necessarily be contained in a global optimum due to the NP-hardness of the problem.

In this paper, we propose an algorithm based on cooperative computation [5] to accomplish this task. It is similar both in principle and operations to constraint propagation. In principle, it eliminates variable values by checking the feasibility that they can be in any global optimum. In operations, it is based on parallel, local iterative computations. At each iteration, it eliminates variable values fully in parallel by computing the lower bound of the problem's cost function and uses it to judge if a variable value can be in any global optimal solution. The lower bound is guaranteed to be tightened as the iteration proceeds so that more and more variable values can be eliminated.

Different from many existing methods based on local propagation for COP, our algorithm introduces the cooperation among the local operations. When the cooperation level is reduced to zero, our algorithm is equivalent in principle to the method proposed by T. Schiex [6] for soft constraints. When dealing with MAX-CSP (a special case of COP), by dropping cooperation, the lower bounds computed by our algorithm are the same as those computed by the integer programming method proposed by M. Affane and H. Bennaceur [7]. However, the power of our algorithm comes from the cooperation. Both theory and experiments show that the cooperation can greatly tighten the lower bound so that much more values can be eliminated. Under certain conditions, the lower bound can approach the optimal value of the cost function. In this case, all values for each variable except the one in the optimal solution will be eliminated after a certain number of iterations and the global optimum is found.

Many algorithms have been developed for MAX-CSP using Branch and Bound method [8]. The cooperative optimization proposed in this paper for COP is fundamentally different from it both in principle and operations. Branch and Bound method is based on the idea of intelligently enumerating all the feasible solutions. The branch refers to intelligently select the order of the variables to be instantiated and the bound refers to lower bounds used for eliminating branches of instantiated variables. The number of the branches may grow exponentially with the number of instantiated variables. It was found that Branch and Bound method does not scale well when we deal with thousands to millions of variables in practice.

2 Constraint Optimization Problem

The constraint optimization problem we deal with in this paper can be formulated as the minimization (or maximization) of a multivariate objective function of the following aggregate form

$$E(x_1, x_2, \ldots, x_n) = \sum_{i=1}^{n} C_{X_i}, \quad (1)$$

where each variable x_i, for $1 \leq i \leq n$, has a finite domain D_i of size m_i ($m_i = |D_i|$), and C_j is a constraint, that is, a real valued function defined on a particular subset of variables, X_i, $X_i \subset X$, where $X = \{x_1, x_2, \ldots, x_n\}$. The objective function is also simply denoted as $E(x)$.

If each constraint involves at most two variables, the objective function (1) becomes

$$E(x_1, x_2, \ldots, x_n) = \sum_{i} C_i(x_i) + \sum_{i,j,i \neq j} C_{ij}(x_i, x_j), \quad (2)$$

where C_i is a unary constraint on variable x_i and C_{ij} is a binary constraint on variable x_i and x_j. In this paper, we do not assume the symmetry of the binary constraints, i.e., we do not assume $C_{ij} = C_{ji}$.

3 Lower Bound and the Cooperative Computation

The lower bound is obtained by decomposing a problem into n subproblems, one for each variable and its neighborhood. Following that, we find out the lower bounds for all subproblems together in a cooperative way. The global lower bound is the summation of the lower bounds of the subproblems. The cooperation is introduced to improve the quality of the global lower bound.

For example, a binary COP (2) has a straight-forward decomposition:

$$E_i = C_i(x_i) + \sum_{j,\ j \neq i} C_{ij}(x_i, x_j) \quad \text{for } i = 1, 2, \ldots, n. \quad (3)$$

The lower bound for each sub-problem can be obtained directly by

$$\min_{x_j \in X_i} E_i, \quad \text{for } i = 1, 2, \ldots, n, \quad (4)$$

where X_i is the set of variables that sub-objective function E_i contains. Obviously, the summation of those lower bounds for the subproblems is a global lower bound because $\sum_i E_i = E$.

In general, the quality of the global lower bound obtained in this way is poor. To improve the quality, we introduce cooperation among the minimization of the subproblems (see (4)) by computing the following difference equations iteratively,

$$c_i^{(k)}(x_i) = \min_{x_j \in X_i \setminus x_i} \left((1 - \lambda_k) E_i + \lambda_k \sum_j w_{ij} c_j^{(k-1)}(x_j) \right) \quad \text{for } i = 1, 2, \ldots, n, \quad (5)$$

where $c_i(x_i)$ is an unary constraint introduced by the algorithm on the variable x_i, called the assignment constraint on variable x_i. k is the iteration step, w_{ij} are non-negative weight values satisfying $\sum_i w_{ij} = 1$. It has been found [5] that such a choice of w_{ij} makes sure the iterative update functions converge. For binary COP, by substituting (3) into (5), it can be found that the complexity of the computation at each iteration is $O(m^2n^2)$.

Parameter λ_k in (5) controls the level of the cooperation at step k and is called the cooperation strength, satisfying $0 \leq \lambda_k < 1$. A higher value for λ_k in (5) will weigh the solutions of the other sub-problems $c_j(x_j)$ more than the one of the current sub-problem E_i. In other words, the solution of each sub-problem will compromise more with the solutions of other sub-problems. As a consequence, a higher level of cooperation in the optimization is reached in this case.

Theory tells us that the summation of $c_i(x_i)$ provides a lower bound function of $E(x)$. To be more specific, we have

$$\sum_i c_i(x_i) \leq E(x_1, x_2, \ldots, x_n), \quad \text{for } \forall x_i \ \forall i. \qquad (6)$$

In particular,

$$\sum_i \min_{x_i} c_i(x_i) \leq E^*,$$

where E^* is the optimal value of the function $E(x)$. Note that $\min_{x_i} c_i(x_i)$ is the lower bound for the ith subproblem E_i. That is, the summation of lower bounds of subproblems, denoted as E_-^*, is a global lower bound of $E(x)$.

Given a constant cooperation strength and the initial condition $c^{(0)}(x_i) = 0$ for any i, theory also tells us that such a lower bound is guaranteed to be improved as the iteration proceeds. That is,

$$E_-^{*(1)} \leq E_-^{*(2)} \leq \ldots \leq E_-^{*(k)} \leq E^*.$$

The global lower bound $E_-^{*(k)}$ is used for value elimination. For any variable value, say x_i, if

$$c_i^{(k)}(x_i) > (E^* - E_-^{*(k)}) + \min_{x_i} c_i^{(k)}(x_i), \qquad (7)$$

then that value can be eliminated since it can not be in any global optimum, guaranteed by theory. For CSP, which is a special case of COP with a boolean return value for each constraint, the above elimination criteria falls back to arc-consistency checking used by constraint propagation.

The proposed algorithm also returns a solution at each iteration besides the lower bounds. Let $\tilde{x}_i^{(k)} = \arg\min_{x_i} c_i^{(k)}(x_i)$, $(\tilde{x}_1^{(k)}, \tilde{x}_2^{(k)}, \ldots, \tilde{x}_n^{(k)})$ is a solution returned by the algorithm at iteration k. Hence, it is also an approximation algorithm for COP. Unlike many existing optimization techniques, it has a solid theoretical foundation, including convergence property. It guarantees both the existence and the uniqueness of solutions as well as an exponential convergence rate of λ. It knows if the solution is the global optimum or not, and the quality of solutions. It has been generalized using the lattice concept from abstract algebra to be more powerful and complete [5]. It has also been generalized to cover the classic local search as its special case by extending its cooperation schemes [9].

The cooperative optimization has been successfully applied to many problems in computer vision [5, 9], such as shape from shading, stereo matching, and image segmentation. All of them are modeled by constraint programming using soft constraints. Many of those problems are very large in scale, involving hundred thousands of variables and hundreds of values for each variable.

4 Conclusions

This paper presented a general extension of constraint propagation for constraint optimization. Both of them follow the same principle of eliminating values not feasibly in any global solutions. To achieve that goal, the algorithm proposed in this paper computes lower bounds for a set of subproblems and their summation is a global lower bound. Those lower bounds are used to derive rules to eliminate variable values. Similar to constraint propagation, the computation of the generalized algorithm is also based on parallel, local iterative operations. Since the generalized algorithm returns a solution at each iteration as well, it can be used as an approximation algorithm for solving large scale optimization problems modeled by constraint programming.

References

1. Freuder, E.C., Mackworth, A.K.: Constraint-based Reasoning. MIT/Elsevier, London, England (1994)
2. Schiex, T., Fargier, H., Verfaillie, G.: Valued constraint satisfaction problems: Hard and easy problems. In: Proc. of the 14th IJCAI, Montreal, Canada (1995) 631–637
3. Modi, P.J.: Distributed Constraint Optimization for Multiagent Systems. PhD thesis, University of Southern California, Los Angles, U.S.A. (2003)
4. Rudová, H., Matyska, L.: Uniform framework for solving over-constrained and optimization problems. In: CP'99 Post-Conference Workshop on Modelling and Solving Soft Constraints. (1999)
5. Huang, X.: A general framework for constructing cooperative global optimization algorithms. 4th International Conference on Frontiers in Global Optimization (2003)
6. Schiex, T.: Arc consistency for soft constraints. In: Proc. of CP'2000. (September, 2000)
7. Affane, M.S., Bennaceur, H.: Exploiting integer programming tools to solve max-csp. In: Proc. of the Workshop on Integration of AI and OR techniques in Constraint Programming for Combinatorial Optimisation Problem. (1999)
8. Wallace, R.J.: enhancements of branch and bound methods for the maximal constraint satisfaction problem. In: Proc. of AAAI. (1996) 188–195
9. Huang, X.: Cooperative optimization for solving large scale combinatorial problems. In Grundel, D., Murphey, R., Pardalos, P., eds.: 4th International Conference on Cooperative Control and Optimization, Destin, Florida, U.S.A. (2003)

How Much Backtracking Does It Take to Color Random Graphs? Rigorous Results on Heavy Tails

Haixia Jia and Cristopher Moore

Computer Science Department, University of New Mexico, Albuquerque NM 87131
{hjia,moore}@cs.unm.edu

Abstract. For many backtracking search algorithms, the running time has been found experimentally to have a heavy-tailed distribution, in which it is often much greater than its median. We analyze two natural variants of the Davis-Putnam-Logemann-Loveland (DPLL) algorithm for Graph 3-Coloring on sparse random graphs of average degree c. Let $P_c(b)$ be the probability that DPLL backtracks b times. First, we calculate analytically the probability $P_c(0)$ that these algorithms find a 3-coloring with no backtracking at all, and show that it goes to zero faster than any analytic function as $c \to c^* = 3.847...$ Then we show that even in the "easy" regime $1 < c < c^*$ where $P_c(0) > 0$ — including just above the degree $c = 1$ where the giant component first appears — the expected number of backtrackings is exponentially large with positive probability. To our knowledge this is the first rigorous proof that the running time of a natural backtracking algorithm has a heavy tail for graph coloring.

1 Introduction

Many common search algorithms for combinatorial problems have been found to exhibit a heavy-tailed distribution in their running times; for instance, in the number of backtracks performed by the Davis-Putnam-Logemann-Loveland (DPLL) algorithm and its variants on constraint satisfaction problems, including Satisfiability, Graph Coloring, and Quasigroup Completion [7–10, 12]. In such a distribution, with significant probability, the running time is much larger than its median, and indeed its expectation can be exponentially large even if the median is only polynomial. These distributions typically take a power-law form, in which the probability $P(b)$ that the algorithm backtracks b times behaves as $b^{-\gamma}$ for some exponent γ. One consequence of this is that if a run of the algorithm has taken longer than expected, it is likely to take much longer still, and it would be a good idea to restart it (and follow a new random branch of the tree) rather than continuing to search in the same part of the search space.

For Graph 3-Coloring, in particular, these heavy tails were found experimentally by Hogg and Williams [10] and Davenport and Tsang [5]. At first, it was thought that this heavy tail indicated that many *instances* are exceptionally hard. A clearer picture emerged when Gomes, Selman and Crato [8] showed that the running times of randomized search algorithms on a typical *fixed* instance show a heavy tail. In Figure 1 we show our own experimental data on the distribution of the number of backtracks for two versions of DPLL described below. In both cases the log-log plot follows a straight line, indicating a power law. As n increases, the slopes appear to converge to -1, and we conjecture that $P_c(b) \sim b^{-1}$ up to some exponential cutoff.

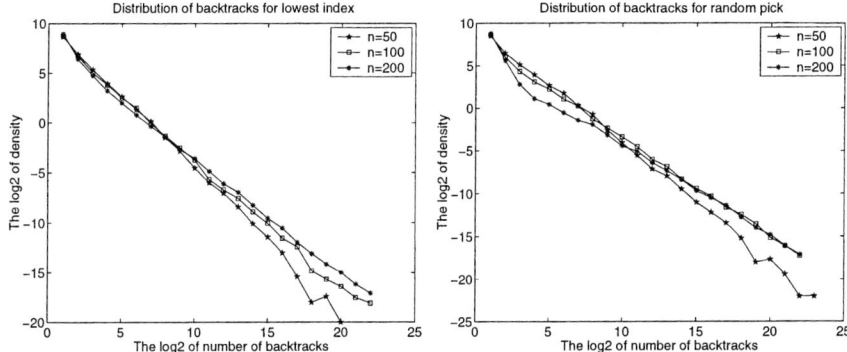

Fig. 1. Log-log plots of the distribution of the number of backtracks $P_c(b)$ for the two DPLL algorithms A and B described in the text on random graphs with $c = 3.5$. The data appears to follow a power law $P_c(b) \sim b^{-1}$ in the limit $n \to \infty$.

A fair amount of theoretical work has been done on heavy tails, including optimal restart strategies [11] and formal models [4]. However, there are relatively few rigorous results establishing that these tails exist. One exception is Achlioptas, Beame, and Molloy [1], who showed using lower bounds on resolution proof complexity that DPLL takes exponential time on random instances of 3-SAT, even at some densities below the satisfiability threshold. Our results appear to be the first on Graph Coloring, and they rely on much simpler reasoning.

Our results hold for two variants of DPLL. Both of them are greedy, in the sense that they branch on a vertex with the smallest available number of colors; in particular, they perform *unit propagation*, in which any 1-color vertex is immediately assigned that color. They are distinguished by which 2-color vertex they branch on when there are no 1-color vertices (we focus on the algorithm's performance on the giant component, during which there is always a 1- or 2-color vertex). In algorithm A, the vertices are given a fixed uniformly random ordering, and we branch on the 2-color vertex of lowest index. In algorithm B, we choose a vertex uniformly at random from among the 2-color vertices. In both variants, we try the two possible colors of the chosen 2-color vertex in random order.

Our main result is the following:

Theorem 1. *For algorithms A and B, let b be the number of times the algorithm backtracks on $G(n, c/n)$. If $1 < c < c^* = 3.847...$, there exist constants $\beta, q > 0$ such that $\Pr[b > 2^{\beta n}] \geq q$. In particular, $\mathrm{E}[b] = 2^{\Theta(n)}$.*

Note that this theorem does not show that this tail has a power-law form (although we believe our arguments could be refined to do that); it simply shows that with positive probability the amount of backtracking is exponentially large.

We rely heavily on the fact that for both these variants of DPLL, a single random branch is equivalent to a linear-time greedy heuristic, 3-GL, analyzed by Achlioptas and Molloy [2]. They showed that if $1 < c < c^* = 3.847...$ then 3-GL colors $G(n, c/n)$ with positive probability. (If $c < 1$ then the graph w.h.p. has no bicyclic component and it is easy to color.) This shows that $P_c(0) > 0$ for c in this range, i.e., with positive probability these variants of DPLL succeed with no backtracking at all. However, as our results show, the expected amount of backtracking is exponentially large even for random graphs with c in this "easy" regime, and indeed just above the appearance of the giant component at $c = 1$.

2 The Probability of Success Without Backtracking

We follow an approach of Achlioptas and Moore [3] and separate the algorithm's progress into rounds, where each round consists of coloring a 2-color vertex and the resulting cascade of 1-color vertices. We use generating functions to calculate exactly the probability that a given round will fail (and backtrack) by creating a 0-color vertex. This gives the following result:

$$P_c(0) = \exp\left(-\int_0^{t_0} dt \, \frac{c\lambda^2}{2(1-\lambda)(2+\lambda)}\right) + o(1) \ . \tag{1}$$

Here t_0 is the unique positive root of $1 - t - e^{-ct} = 0$ and $\lambda = (2/3)c(1 - t - e^{-ct})$. Figure 2 shows that (1) fits our experimental data for graphs of size 10^4 perfectly.

As c approaches the unique positive root c^* of $c - \ln c = 5/2$, the integral in (1) diverges and $P_c(0) \to 0$ faster than any analytic function. Specifically, for $c = c^* - \epsilon$ we have $P_c(0) \sim \exp(-A/\sqrt{\epsilon})$. Using methods from statistical physics,

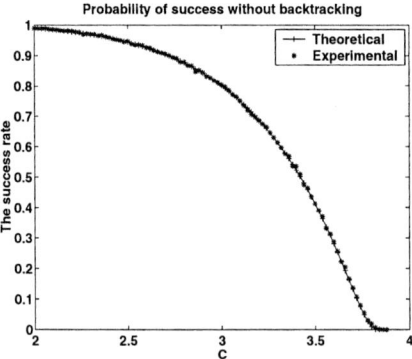

Fig. 2. A comparison of our calculation (1) of the probability of success (the solid line) with experimental results with $n = 10^4$. Each point is the average of 10^4 trials.

Deroulers and Monasson [6] found the same critical behavior for heuristics on random 3-SAT; we expect it for other graph coloring heuristics as well, such as the smoothed Brelaz heuristic analyzed by Achlioptas and Moore [3] which succeeds with positive probability for $c < c^* \approx 4.03$.

3 Exponential Backtracking with Positive Probability

In this section we sketch the proof of Theorem 1. We focus on variant A of DPLL; the reasoning for B is similar.

Let t_1 be a constant such that $0 < t_1 < t_0$ where t_0, given in the previous section, is the expected time for the algorithm to color the giant component if it does so without backtracking. Run the algorithm for $t_1 n$ steps, conditioning on not having created a 0-color vertex so far; this is equivalent to running 3-GL conditioned on its success. At the end of these $t_1 n$ steps there are w.h.p. $s_3(t_1)n + o(n)$ 3-color vertices and $s_2(t_1)/3 + o(n)$ 2-color vertices of each color pair, where $s_3(t_1)$ and $s_2(t_1)$ are given by the differential equations of [2]. In addition, the uncolored part of the graph G' is uniformly random in $G(n', p)$ where n' is the total number of uncolored vertices.

Let us call a triangle *bad* if it is composed of 2-color vertices whose allowed colors are red and green, it is disconnected from the rest of G', and the indices of its vertices are all greater than the median index of the 2-color vertices in G'. The number of bad triangles in G' is essentially Poisson distributed with expectation $\Theta(1)$, so with positive probability there is exactly one of them.

Let us call this bad triangle Δ. It is important to us in the following ways:

1. It is not 2-colorable, so every branch of the subtree below the step creating Δ will fail, and the algorithm will be forced to backtrack at least to the $(t_1 n)$th step and uncolor one of Δ's blue neighbors.
2. Since Δ is isolated from rest of G', we will find this contradiction only if we choose one of Δ's vertices from the pool of 2-color vertices. In particular, we will not be led to Δ by a chain of forced steps.
3. A will not color any of Δ's vertices until it runs out of 2-color vertices of lower index, and this will not happen for at least $s_2(t_1)n/2$ more steps.

Therefore, Δ will cause the entire subtree starting with these $t_1 n$ steps to fail, but we won't find out about it until we explore the tree $\Theta(n)$ more deeply, and this forces us visit an exponential number of nodes.

Overall, what we are saying is that the events that different branches of the search tree fail are far from independent; they have a strong positive correlation since a single bad triangle dooms an entire subtree to failure, and the probability they all fail is positive even though a random branch succeeds with positive probability $P_c(0)$. The DPLL algorithm naively tries to 2-color Δ an exponential number of times, hoping that recoloring other vertices will render Δ 2-colorable. In terms of restarts, once Δ has "spoiled" an entire section of the search space, it makes more sense to start over with a new random branch.

We would like to go beyond Theorem 1 and prove a power-law distribution, $P_c(b) \sim b^{-1}$. Intuitively, suppose that Δ appears at a uniformly random depth

d up to a maximum of n, and that the running time b scales as 2^{Ad} for some A. Then the probability that b is between 2^{Ad} and $2^{A(d+1)}$ is $1/n$, giving a probability density $P(b) = 1/(2^{Ad}(2^A-1)n) \sim 1/b$. Any distribution of d which varies slowly from $\Theta(1)$ to $\Theta(n)$ would give the same qualitative result.

A logical question is what happens to the running time if we backtrack immediately whenever we create an odd 2-color cycle, rather than waiting to bump into it deeper in the search. While this obviates our proof of Theorem 1, we find experimentally that this variant of DPLL still has a heavy-tailed distribution of running times. We propose this as a direction for further work.

Acknowledgments

We are grateful to Dimitris Achlioptas, Sinan Al-Saffar, Paul Beame, Tracy Conrad, Michael Molloy, Remi Monasson, Vishal Sanwalani and Bart Selman for helpful comments and conversations. This work was supported by NSF grant PHY-0200909 and the Los Alamos National Laboratory.

References

1. Dimitris Achlioptas, Paul Beame, and Michael Molloy, "A sharp threshold in proof complexity." *Proc. 33rd Symp. on Theory of Computing* 337–346.
2. D. Achlioptas and M. Molloy, "Analysis of a list-colouring algorithm on a random graph." *Proc. 38th Foundations of Computer Science* 204–212.
3. D. Achlioptas and C. Moore, "Almost all graphs of degree 4 are 3-colorable." *Proc. 34th Symp. on Theory of Computing* 199–208, and *J. Comp. & Sys. Sci.* 67 (2003) 441–471, special issue for STOC 2002.
4. H. Chen, C.P. Gomes and B. Selman, "Formal models of heavy-tailed behavior in combinatorial search." *Proc. 7th Intl. Conf. on the Principles and Practice of Constraint Programming* (2001) 408–422.
5. A. Davenport and E.P.K. Tsang, "An empirical investigation into the exceptionally hard problems." *Proc. Workshop on Constraint-based Reasoning* 46–53.
6. C. Deroulers and R. Monasson, "Critical behaviour of combinatorial search algorithms, and the unitary-propagation universality class." Preprint, cond-mat/0405319.
7. I. Gent, and T. Walsh, "Easy problems are sometimes hard." *Artificial Intelligence* 70 (1993) 335–345.
8. C.P. Gomes, B. Selman and N. Crato, "Heavy-Tailed Distributions in Combinatorial Search." *Proc. 3rd Intl. Conf. on Principles and Practices of Constraint Programming* (1997) 121–135.
9. C.P. Gomes, B. Selman and H.A. Kautz, "Boosting Combinatorial Search Through Randomization." *Proc. 15th Natl. Conf. on Artificial Intelligence* (1998) 431–437.
10. T. Hogg and C.P. Williams, "The Hardest Constraint Problems: A Double Phase Transition." *Artificial Intelligence* 69(1-2) (1994) 359–377.
11. M. Luby, A. Sinclair, and D. Zuckerman, "Optimal speedup of las vegas algorithms." *Information Processing Letters* (1993) 173–180.
12. B. Selman, H. Kautz, and B. Cohen, "Local search strategies for satisfiability testing." In D. Johnson and M. Trick, Eds., *DIMACS Series in Discrete Mathematics and Theoretical Computer Science* 26 (1993) 521–532.

Solving the Crane Scheduling Problem Using Intelligent Search Schemes

(Extended Abstract)

Andrew Lim[1], Brian Rodrigues[2], and Zhou Xu[1],*

[1] Department of Industrial Engineering and Engineering Management, Hong Kong University of Science and Technology, Clear Water Bay, Kowloon, Hong Kong
xuzhou@ust.hk
[2] School of Business, Singapore Management University

1 Introduction

Cranes are central to port operations where cargo throughput and port efficiency is often determined by how well loading and unloading is performed. In ports, the effectiveness of any logistics management system which includes operating cranes is often impacted by pressures of limited port size, high cargo transshipment volumes and limited physical facilities and equipment [6]. It is therefore not surprising that emphasis has been placed on efficient crane scheduling in many ports, including the Port of Singapore [1], the Port of Hong Kong [8] and Australian ports [4].

Cranes are at the interface between land and sea, and because of operating space boundaries and crane structures cranes can only move in a limited areas, usually in one dimension along tracks. A typical operating scheme for quay cranes is illustrated as follows. Containers on vessels to be unloaded are usually partitioned into non-preemptive job parcels in some order on ship decks or holds and are moved to vehicles which transport them to stack yards for storage. In the reverse operation, cargo is loaded onto the ships from trucks out of yards. In this scenario, cranes and vehicles move through fixed channels or routes and bottlenecks occur when movement along these routes becomes congested [5].

There has been little research on crane scheduling. [2] proposed a principle-based heuristic for various type crane scheduling problems while [6] described a branch and bound method to solve a mathematical programming crane scheduling model. It is interesting to note that spatial constraints on the movement of cranes had not been considered before they were studied in [5]. This, especially, since such constraints are prevalent in all crane operations where cranes are positioned next to each other. In the latter study, the authors used a constraint which did not allow cranes to cross over each other when processing parcels of cargo at the same time. This spatial constraint was basic since cranes which operate on the same rail path cannot move in opposite directions. Schedulers in crane traffic operations realize that the possibility that cranes cannot cross

---

* Corresponding Author.

each other is a real constraint to be accounted for. We call this constraint a "non-crossing" constraint. Recently, a model was used and analyzed by [9] who devised a branch and bound search scheme and a simulated annealing algorithm for randomly-generated instances which accounted for processing times for job parcels. However, their search schemes had limited success in experiments and the simulated annealing could not ensure good performance when the size of the instance became large.

This short paper reformulates the crane scheduling as a constraint programming model. By decomposing this model, we find an efficient way to obtain the best time-allocation for job processing when their crane-allocations are given. Based on this, two intelligent search schemes are devised to compute the crane-allocation. One is a highly optimized backtracking scheme whose performance is improved through domain reductions and pruning strategies. The other is a simulated annealing algorithm, which obtained near-optimum scheduling by a local search within a stochastic neighborhood. Extensive experiments shows that these schemes perform well even in large scale instances and improve on methods currently available.

2 Problem Formulation

The crane scheduling problem can be regarded as a multiple machine (multiprocessor) scheduling problem [3] with considerations of the non-crossing constraint.

For ease of notation, we take the set of jobs in our problem to be $J = \{1, 2, ..., n\}$ and the m cranes to be given by $I = \{1, 2, ..., m\}$, both ordered from the ordering induced from the real line and assumed to be in parallel on a plane. Here, for any $a, b \in J$, $a < b$ means a precedes b or a is to the left of b. Cranes are ordered likewise. Because crane movement relatively takes little time [6], the work for job $j \in J$ is measured only by the number of crane-hours, $P_j \in Z_+$ (the set of non-negative integers), needed to complete the job. Assuming jobs are non-preemptive, we seek a crane scheduling scheme which includes a starting-time-allocation map s and a job-to-crane allocation map σ, where $s : J \to Z_+$ and $\sigma : J \to I$ indicate that every job $j \in J$ is processed on crane σ_j during the time period of $[s_j, s_j + P_j)$. Because of the non-crossing constraint, a scheme is feasible if and only if for any $k, j \in J$, where $k < j$, either k and j are executed separately in time, i.e. $[s_k, s_k + P_k) \cap [s_j, s_j + P_j) = \emptyset$, or k and j are executed on cranes which do not cross, i.e. $\sigma_k < \sigma_j$. The *Crane Scheduling Problem* is to obtain a feasible schedule, consisting of s and σ, which minimizes the latest completion time, i.e. which minimizes $\max_{j \in J} s_j + P_j$. Hence, a constraint programming model can be given as follows.

minimize $\max_{j \in J} s_j + P_j$
subject to for all $k, j \in J$ and $k < j$,
$\quad (\sigma_j \leq \sigma_k) \to [(s_j + P_j \leq s_k) \vee (s_k + P_k \leq s_j)]$
where $\quad$ for all $j \in J$, $\sigma_j \in I$ and $s_j \in Z_+$

The crane scheduling problem can easily solved if only one crane is considered, but is intractable otherwise. The proof of its NP-hardness is extended from the reduction proposed by [9].

3 Model Decomposition

Because constraints on the time-allocation map depend on the crane-allocation map, we can decompose the decisions for σ and s. When a crane-allocation map σ is given, the optimum time-allocation map s can be obtained implicitly by the following theorem.

Theorem 1. *Given the crane-allocation σ_j for $j \in J$, the optimum time-allocation s_j which minimizes the latest completion time (i.e. $\max_{j \in J} s_j + P_j$) can be obtained as follows,*

$$s_j = \begin{cases} 0 & \text{when } j = 1 \\ \max_{\forall k < j, \sigma_k \geq \sigma_j} s_k + P_k & \text{when } j = 2, ..., n. \end{cases} \quad (1)$$

This allows the decision problem for the crane-allocation map to be described by the constraint programming model:

$$\text{minimize } \max_{j \in J} s_j + P_j$$
$$\text{subject to } (1)$$
$$\text{where} \quad \text{for all } j \in J, \sigma_j \in I$$

To solve this problem efficiently, we propose two intelligent search schemes which are backtracking and simulated annealing.

4 Backtracking

We use a tree search to obtain the optimum crane-allocation map. Each path in the search tree consists of n cranes, i.e. $\sigma_1, \sigma_2, ..., \sigma_n$, corresponding to a relevant crane-allocation map. The motivation behind this approach is to avoid redundant enumerations of crane allocations, to generate nodes in the search tree rapidly, and to prune branches effectively by estimation functions. From this, a global optimum crane-allocation map is produced.

- Domain Reduction
  For every job $j \in J$, the original domain of its crane-allocation σ_j is $\{1, 2, ..., m\}$. This can be reduced if σ_k are decided for all jobs k left of j, as follows.
  Given σ_k for all $1 \leq k \leq j - 1$, let $T[i] = \max\{s_k + P_k | \sigma_k \geq i, k = 1, 2, ..., j - 1\}$ for each crane $i \in I$, and $T[0] = -1$ for consistency. According to (1), s_j must be equal to $T[i]$ if we allocate crane i to job j. Moreover, it is easy to see that $T[i] \leq T[i-1]$ for $i \in I$. Let $D(\sigma_j)$ indicate the domain of σ_j to be sufficiently considered, without delaying the minimum latest completion time. Thus, we have $D(\sigma_j) = \{i | T[i] < T[i-1], i \in I\}$.

- Node generation
  We adopt a depth-first order to generate nodes in the search tree. If we suppose σ_k for $1 \leq k \leq j-1$ are decided along the path sequentially, the domain $D(\sigma_j)$ for job j can be obtained by $T[i]$ of $i \in I$. Enumerate every crane allocation $i \in D(\sigma_j)$ to job j sequentially. For each attempt, the corresponding time-allocation s_j equals to $T[\sigma_j]$ by virtue of (1). Consequently, $T[i]$ is updated and new enumeration is completed for job $j+1$, unless j equals to n. If j equals to n, the current best schedule is updated (if necessary), and then backtracking happens. After all nodes are generated, the global optimum schedule is found.
- Pruning conditions
  Suppose crane allocations are determined for jobs $1, 2, ..., j-1$. Before enumerating cranes for σ_j, it is prudent to estimate the lower bounds (EST) of the latest completion time that can be obtained in later times. If EST is not less than the current smallest objective value, any attempt for σ_j can be pruned. Let $MAX[j]$ for $j \in J$ denotes the longest processing time among jobs equal or right to j, and RDT represents the number of free time slots of the m cranes before $T[1]$ which is the current latest completion time to process jobs $1, 2, ..., j-1$. Let $LEFT[j]$ denote the total processing time of jobs $j, j+1, ..., n$. If $LEFT[j] > RDT$, in order to complete all the remaining $n-j+1$ jobs, at least one crane cannot stop until $T[1] + \lceil (LEFT[j] - RDT)/\min\{m, n-j+1\} \rceil$. Formally, the estimation function is defined by:

$$EST = \max \left\{ \begin{array}{c} T[n] + MAX[j], \\ T[1] + \min\{0, \lceil \frac{LEFT[j] - RDT}{\min\{m, n-j+1\}} \rceil\} \end{array} \right\}. \qquad (2)$$

5 Simulated Annealing

We propose a model which uses simulated annealing (SA) for the crane scheduling problem. This is similar to the standard SA [7], where feasible solutions are encoded by the crane-allocation map $\sigma = \langle \sigma_1, \sigma_2, ..., \sigma_m \rangle$. The SA starts with an initial σ by an earliest-fit policy (EF), which assigns the earliest free crane to jobs $1, 2, ..., n$ sequentially. To improve σ iteratively, a new schedule σ' is generated in the neighborhood of σ. We accept the move from σ to σ' with a probability $p = exp(-\Delta/T)$ where Δ denote the difference between the costs of σ' and σ. The parameter T is so-called the temperature. It begins with the value of T_0 and is decreased exponentially by a cooling factor r. Under a certain value of T, the solution σ might be moved for at most L_N times. As T reaches a terminating value T_e, the best obtained scheduling is output.

Different from the standard SA, we devise here a stochastic mechanism for generating σ' within the neighborhood of σ. A subset $W(\sigma) \subseteq I$ of jobs is first selected using some random factors. Then, by reallocating cranes to jobs in $W(\sigma)$, a new schedule is produced. Iterating the selection and reallocation for a constant number N_N of times, we then choose the new schedule with the minimum latest completion time as σ'. Details are omitted for the lack of space.

6 Experimental Results

We conducted extensive experiments on a Pentium IV 2.40GHZ computer and all the programs are coded by C++. In this section, let BT and SA represent the the backtracking algorithm and the simulated annealing algorithm, respectively and let BT-H denote the heuristic procedure which returns the partial optimum solution by restricting the number of search nodes in BT to be 2×10^8. In addition, as a comparison, use ZL-BB and ZL-SA to denote the branch and bound algorithm and the SA that is proposed by [9] for the crane scheduling problem. Four sets of test instances are published by [9]. Experiments shows that our new approaches significantly improved the solutions. Among four groups of 24 instances, the SA has achieved the best near-optimum solutions for 22 instances whose average gap from lower bounds is less than 1%. The BT-H also over-performs the previous ZL-SA in most cases, since solutions produced by BT-H are around 2% from lower bounds while solutions by ZL-SA are around 5%. In addition, the search ability of BT is significantly better than ZL-BB, since for small-scale instances, the B obtain optimum solutions almost instantly, while ZL-BB will consume relatively long times (say hundreds of seconds).

References

1. Erbu K. Bish, Thin-Yin Leong, Chung-Lun Li, Jonanthan W.C.Ng, and David Simchi-Levi. Analysis of a new vehicle scheduling and location problem. *Naval Research Logistics*, 48(5):1002–2024, 2001.
2. C.F. Daganzo. The crane scheduling problem. *Transportation Research B*, 23(3):159–175, 1989.
3. R.L. Graham. Bounds for certain multiprocessing anomalies. *Bell System Technical Journal*, 45:1563–1581, 1966.
4. E Kozan. Increasing the operational efficiency of container terminals in australia. *Journal of the Operational Research Society*, 48:151–161, 1997.
5. Andrew Lim, Fei Xiao, B. Rodrigues, and Yi Zhu. Crane scheduling using tabu-search. In *14th IEEE International Conference on Tools with Artificial Intelligence*, Washington DC, USA, 2002.
6. R.I. Peterkofsky and C.F. Daganzo. A branch and bound solution method for the crane scheduling problem. *Transportation Research*, 24B:159–172, 1990.
7. V.J. Rayward-Smith, I.H. Osman, C.R. Reeves, and G.D. Smith, editors. *Modern Heuristic Search Methods*. John Wiley & Sons Ltd, Baffins Lane, Chichester, West Susses PO19 1UD, England, 1996.
8. Chuqian Zhang, Yat wah Wan, Jiyin Liu, and Richard J. Linn. Dynamic crane deployment in container storage yards. *Transportation Resarch Part B*, 36:537–555, 2002.
9. Yi Zhu and Andrew Lim. Crane scheduling with spatial constraints: Mathematical model and solving approaches. In *Proceedings of the Eighth International Symposium on Artificial Intelligence and Mathematics*, 2003.

Algorithms for Quantified Constraint Satisfaction Problems

Nikos Mamoulis[1] and Kostas Stergiou[2]

[1] Department of Computer Science and Information Systems
University of Hong Kong
[2] Department of Information and Communication Systems Engineering
University of the Aegean

Abstract. Many propagation and search algorithms have been developed for constraint satisfaction problems (CSPs). In a standard CSP all variables are existentially quantified. The CSP formalism can be extended to allow universally quantified variables, in which case the complexity of the basic reasoning tasks rises from **NP**-complete to **PSPACE**-complete. Such problems have, so far, been studied mainly in the context of quantified Boolean formulae. Little work has been done on problems with discrete non-Boolean domains. We attempt to fill this gap by extending propagation and search algorithms from standard CSPs to the quantified case. We also show how the notion of value interchangeability can be exploited to break symmetries and speed up search by orders of magnitude. Finally, we test experimentally the algorithms and methods proposed.

1 Introduction

The basic decision task in a CSP is to determine whether there exist values for all variables such that all constraints in the problem are satisfied. It is well known that in standard CSPs, where all variables are existentially quantified, this task is **NP**-complete. A natural generalization of the standard CSP formalism is to consider the case where some of the variables may be universally quantified. A CSP that allows universal quantification of variables is called a Quantified Constraint Satisfaction Problem (QCSP) [3, 2]. The generalization of CSPs to QCSPs increases the expressiveness of the framework, but at the same time the complexity of the decision task rises from **NP**-complete to **PSPACE**-complete [2]. As an example consider the problem $\exists x_i \exists x_j \forall x_k$ ($x_i > x_k \wedge x_j \neq x_k$). This is a CSP where one of the variables is universally quantified, and it reads "there exist values for x_i and x_j such that for every value of x_k the constraints $x_i > x_k$ and $x_j \neq x_k$ are satisfied".

QCSPs can be used to model various **PSPACE**-complete problems from domains like game playing, planning, and belief revision. Recently, there is an increasing interest in algorithms for quantified constraint reasoning, especially in the case of QSAT. Most of the proposed algorithms are extensions of already existing algorithms from the standard case (e.g. SAT) to the quantified one. However, very little has been done as far as algorithms for QCSPs with discrete non-Boolean domains are concerned. The only work we are aware of is [3], where ways to implement arc consistency (AC) for some classes of constraints in QCSPs are proposed. We now give a formal definition of QCSPs.

Definition 1. ([3]) A *Quantified Constraint Satisfaction Problem* (QCSP) is a formula of the form $Q_1 x_1 \ldots Q_n x_n \, (c_1 \wedge \ldots \wedge c_m)$, where each Q_i denotes a quantifier ($\forall$ or $\exists$) and each c_i is a constraint relating some variables among $x_1, \ldots, x_n$.

The goal in a QCSP can be either to determine satisfiability or to find a consistent instantiation of the existential variables for all instantiations of the universal ones. The quantification formula $Q_1 x_1 \ldots Q_n x_n$ specifies a certain order on the variables. Note that this definition of quantification is essentially the same as the corresponding definition in QSAT. We can group together consecutive variables with the same quantification resulting in a formula with alternating quantifiers where a $\forall$ follows a $\exists$ and vice-versa. In this way we rewrite the previous example as $\exists x_i, x_j \forall x_k \, (x_i > x_k \wedge x_j \neq x_k)$.

In this paper we extend standard propagation and search algorithms for binary CSPs to the case of binary QCSPs. We describe an AC algorithm that can deal with arbitrary binary constraints. We extend the BT, FC, and MAC algorithms so that they can handle quantification. We then show how the notion of value interchangeability can be exploited in QCSPs to break symmetries and speed up search by orders of magnitude. Finally, we give some preliminary experimental results.

2 Arc Consistency

[3] extends the definition of AC to QCSPs and gives rules to compute AC for constraints on 0-1 variables (e.g. $\neg x = y$) and numerical constraints (e.g. $x + y = z$). We complement the work of [3] by describing simple rules that can be used to devise a generic AC algorithm for QCSPs. When applying AC on a constraint c_{ij}, the filtering achieved depends on the type of quantification for variables x_i, x_j and on the order in which the variables appear in the quantification formula. For a binary constraint there are four possible orders. We can define AC for a constraint c_{ij} using the following general rules.

$\exists x_i \, \exists x_j$: This is the case of standard CSPs. Constraint c_{ij} is AC iff each value $a \in D(x_i)$ is supported by at least one value $b \in D(x_j)$. If a value $a \in D(x_i)$ has no support in $D(x_j)$ then AC will remove a from $D(x_i)$. If $D(x_i)$ becomes empty then the problem is unsatisfiable.

$\forall x_i \, \forall x_j$: Constraint c_{ij} is AC iff each value $a \in D(x_i)$ is supported by all values in $D(x_j)$. If a value $a \in D(x_i)$ is not supported by all values in $D(x_j)$ then the problem is unsatisfiable.

$\forall x_i \, \exists x_j$: Constraint c_{ij} is AC iff each value $a \in D(x_i)$ is supported by at least one value in $D(x_j)$. If a value $a \in D(x_i)$ has no support in $D(x_j)$ then the problem is unsatisfiable.

$\exists x_i \, \forall x_j$: Constraint c_{ij} is AC iff each value $a \in D(x_i)$ is supported by all values in $D(x_j)$. If a value $a \in D(x_i)$ is not supported by all values in $D(x_j)$ then AC will remove a from $D(x_i)$. If $D(x_i)$ becomes empty then the problem is unsatisfiable.

Based on the above rules we can easily devise an AC algorithm for quantified binary CSPs. The algorithm takes a QCSP with a set of existentially or universally quantified variables in a given order, and and a set of binary constraints, and computes the AC subdomains in case the problem is AC or returns FALSE in case the problem is not AC. The algorithm uses the previously defined rules to check the consistency of a constraint according to the type and order of quantification of the variables involved in the constraint. The structure of the algorithm we have used in based on AC-2001 [1]. Details of the algorithm can be found in [6].

3 Search Algorithms

Algorithms BT and FC for binary QCSPs can be easily devised by extending the corresponding CSP algorithms. If we apply AC before search, we do not have to consider constraints of the form $\exists x_i \forall x_j, c_{ij}$ or $\forall x_i \forall x_j, c_{ij}$ in the algorithms. All values of variable x_i, in such constraints, are definitely consistent with all values of variable x_j. If some value was not consistent then it would have been removed by AC.

BT is a straightforward extension of the corresponding algorithm for standard CSPs. It proceeds by checking assignments of values to variables until the truthness of the quantified problem is proved or disproved. The extension of standard FC to QCSPs, which we call FC0, operates in a way similar to BT with the difference that each variable assignment is forward checked against values of future existential variables constrained with the current one. We have also experimented with a modified version of FC, which we call FC1, that is better suited to QCSPs. FC1 has the exactly same behavior as FC0 when the current variable is existentially quantified. If the current variable x_i is universally quantified then we forward check each value of x_i against all future variables before assigning a specific value to x_i. If one of x_i's values causes a domain wipeout then we backtrack to the last existential variable. Otherwise, we proceed in the usual way. In this way we can discover dead-ends earlier and avoid fruitless exploration of search tree branches. It is easy to see that FC1 will always visit at most the same number of search tree nodes as FC0. The two algorithms are incomparable in the number of consistency checks they perform. That is, depending on the problem, FC0 may perform less checks than FC1 and vice versa.

Based on the above, we can easily adapt the MAC algorithm to QCSPs. MAC can also be modified in the same way as FC to yield MAC1, an algorithm analogous to FC1. That is, when the current variable x_i is universally quantified we can apply AC for each instantiation $(x_i, a_j), j \in \{1, \ldots, d\}$ before committing to a particular instantiation. If one of the instantiations causes a domain wipe-out then we backtrack. Otherwise, we commit to one of the values and proceed with the next variable. Details of all these algorithms can be found in [6].

4 Symmetry Breaking via Value Interchangeability

Many CSPs contain symmetries which means that for a given solution there are equivalent solutions. This can have a profound effect on the search cost when looking for one or (mainly) all solutions to a CSP. We propose the exploitation of value interchangeability as a dynamic symmetry breaking technique in QCSPs.

A value a of a variable x_i is *neighborhood interchangeable* (NI) with a value b of x_i, if a and b are supported by exactly the same values of all variables adjacent to x_i [4] A set of NI values can be replaced by a single representative of the set without in effect losing any solutions. In the context of QCSPs we can exploit interchangeability to break symmetries by "pruning" the domains of universal variables. That is, for each set (sometimes called bundle) of NI values we can keep one representative and remove the others, either permanently before search, or temporarily during search. If the algorithm proves that the representative value is consistent (i.e. satisfies the QCSP) then so are the rest of the NI values. Therefore, checking the consistency of such values is redundant. Consider the following example. We have the formula $\forall x_i \exists x_j, x_k$ ($x_i \neq x_j, x_i \neq x_k$), where the domains of the variables are $D(x_i) = \{0, 1, 2, 3, 4\}$, $D(x_j) = \{0, 1\}$, $D(x_k) = \{0, 2\}$. Values 3 and 4 of x_i are NI since they are supported by the same values in both x_j and x_k. Therefore, they can be replaced by a single value or to put it differently one of them can be pruned out of the domain. NI values can be detected and removed as a preprocessing step. They can also be detected and removed dynamically during search to avoid repeated exploration of similar subtrees. This can be combined with FC or MAC.

5 Experimental Evaluation

To compare the performance of the algorithms presented is the previous sections, we ran experiments on randomly generated QCSPs. The random generator we used takes five parameters: $< n, n_\forall, d, p, q >$, where n is the total number of variables, $n_\forall$ is the number of universally quantified variables, d is the uniform domain size of the variables, p is the density of the constraint graph, and q is the uniform looseness of the constraints. To generate an instance, we first randomly assign universal quantification to $n_\forall$ out of the n variables, and then generate the constraint graph and the constraint matrices according to the widely used model B of standard CSPs. For each generated constraint c_{ij} the quantification of the variables is either $\exists x_i \exists x_j$ or $\forall x_i \exists x_j$. That is, we do not generate constraints that can be handled by preprocessing alone.

Figures 1 and 2 present a comparison of algorithms FC0, FC1, MAC0, MAC1, FC1+NI (FC1 + dynamic removal of NI values), MAC1+NI on problems with $n = 20$, $d = 5$, $p = 0.15$, $n_\forall = 5$, and varying q. For each value of q shown in the figures, 100 problem instances were generated. We measure the number of node visits and consistency checks performed. As we can see, there is an easy-hard-easy pattern in the search cost as in standard CSPs and QSAT.

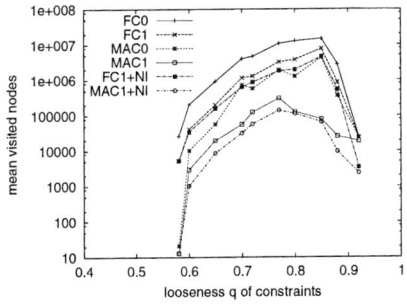

Fig. 1. Average visited nodes.

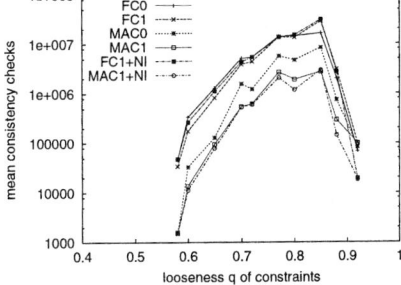

Fig. 2. Average consistency checks.

The MAC variants outperform the corresponding FC ones, as expected. FC1 and MAC1 are able to detect dead-ends early, which makes them considerably better than FC0 and MAC0 respectively. The best algorithm is MAC1+NI, followed by MAC1. Note that MAC1+NI is competitive with the QSAT solver operating on encodings of QCSPs into QSAT used in [5]. While FC1+NI was significantly outperformed by the QSAT solver, preliminary experiments showed that MAC1+NI is five times faster (median cpu times) in $< 20, 5, 5, 0.15, 0.72 >$ problems. However, mean cpu times showed a similar advantage in favor of the QSAT solver.

6 Conclusion

In this paper we studied algorithms for QCSPs with discrete non-Boolean domains. The QCSP framework can be used to model various **PSPACE**-complete problems from domains such as planning and game playing. We first described simple rules fo defining an AC algorithm that can deal with arbitrary binary constraints. We then extended the BT, FC, and MAC algorithms so that they can handle quantification. We also proposed modifications of FC and MAC that are better suited to QCSPs. We showed how value interchangeability can be exploited in QCSPs to break symmetries. Finally, we tested experimentally the algorithms and methods proposed. There is a lot of future work to be done. We intend to follow two directions; first to further improve the presented algorithms through dynamic variable ordering heuristics and techniques like backjumping and learning, and second to apply the QCSP framework in real problems, such as planning under uncertainty, and compare it with existing approaches.

Acknowledgements

We would like to thank I. Gent, P. Nightingale, and A. Rowley for their help and useful comments.

References

1. C. Bessière and J.C. Régin. Refining the basic constraint propagation algorithm. In *Proceedings of IJCAI-2001*, pages 309–315, 2001.
2. F. Boerner, A. Bulatov, P. Jeavons, and A. Krokhin. Quantified constraints: algorithms and complexity. In *Proceedings of CSL-2003*, pages 244–258, 2003.
3. L. Bordeaux and E. Monfroy. Beyond NP: Arc-consistency for quantified constraints. In *Proceedings of CP-2002*, 2002.
4. E. Freuder. Eliminating interchangeable values in constraint satisfaction problems. In *Proceedings of AAAI-91*, pages 227–233, 1991.
5. I. Gent, P. Nightingale, and A. Rowley. Encoding quantified csps as quantified boolean formulae. In *Proceedings of ECAI-2004*, 2004.
6. N. Mamoulis and K. Stergiou. Algorithms for quantified csps. Technical Report APES-78-2004, APES Research Group, February 2004. Available from http://www.dcs.st-and.ac.uk/~apes/apesreports.html.

Improving the Applicability of Adaptive Consistency: Preliminary Results*

Martí Sánchez[1], Pedro Meseguer[1], and Javier Larrosa[2]

[1] Institut d'Investigació en Intel.ligència Artificial
Consejo Superior de Investigaciones Científicas
Campus UAB, 08193 Bellaterra, Spain
{marti,pedro}@iiia.csic.es

[2] Dep. Llenguatges i Sistemes Informàtics
Universitat Politècnica de Catalunya
Jordi Girona, 08028 Barcelona, Spain
larrosa@lsi.upc.es

Abstract. We incorporate two ideas in ADC. The first one, *delaying variable elimination*, permits performing joins in different buckets, not forcing to eliminate one variable before start processing the bucket of another variable. It may cause exponential savings in space. The second idea, *join with filtering*, consists in taking into account the effect of other constraints when performing the join of two constraints. If a tuple resulting from this join is going to be removed by an existing constraint, this tuple is not produced. It can also produce exponential savings. We have tested these techniques on two classical problems, n-queens and Schur's lemma, showing very promising benefits.

1 Introduction

ADC is the reference algorithm to solve CSP by complete inference. ADC is also a specialization of bucket elimination [6], a more general algorithm used in optimization. The time and space complexity of ADC is exponential on the problem induced width. It is the high space requirement that comes as the first practical limitation. Since search algorithms are space polynomial, they are the option of choice in almost all cases. In addition, most CSP researchers think that complete inference algorithms have only theoretical interest, with little practical use. However, some recent research has shown that complete inference in general, and ADC in particular, should not be completely discarded in practice. For instance, [5,3,1] showed that a restricted use of inference can be successfully combined with search. More recently, [4] showed that plain bucket elimination could be competitive in a challenging soft constraints benchmark.

In this paper we contribute to extend the practical applicability of ADC by relaxing the order in which ADC performs computations permitting joins in different buckets, not forcing to eliminate one variable completely before starting

---

* This research is supported by the REPLI project TIC-2002-04470-C03.

to process another bucket. We call this idea *delaying variable elimination*. In addition, we take into account the effect of other constraints when performing a join of two constraints; if a tuple resulting from this join is going to be removed by an existing constraint, this tuple is not produced. We call this second idea *join with filtering*. Both ideas may produce exponential savings and are developed inside the ADC algorithm in Section 3.

2 Preliminaries

A constraint network is defined by a triple (X, D, C), where $X = \{x_1, \ldots, x_n\}$ is a set of n variables, $D = \{D_1, \ldots, D_n\}$ is a collection of finite domains, such that each variable x_i takes values in D_i, and C is a set of constraints. A constraint $c \in C$ is a relation defined on a subset of variables $var(c) \subset X$, called its *scope*. c is a set containing the permitted tuples. A tuple t is a sequence of values corresponding to variables in $var(c)$. Each value is called a component. The pair (x, a) means that the component of variable x takes value a. A tuple t can be projected over a subset A of its variables, which is noted $t[A]$. Projecting t over the empty set, $t[\emptyset]$, produces the empty tuple λ. Given two tuples t and t' without common variables, their concatenation is written $t \cdot t'$. We assume that checking if a tuple t belongs to a constraint is a constant time operation.

In this paper, letters c, r, p, q will denote constraints, x, y, z will denote variables, and a, b will denote values. We will refer to c_{ijk} as a constraint with $var(c) = \{x_i, x_j, x_k\}$. In figures, a triangle represents a hyperedge with its arity written inside. We define two operations on constraints: projection and join. Projecting out variable x, denoted $c \Downarrow_x$, is a new constraint that does not mention x. It is defined by the set of tuples of $t \in c$ removing the x component of every tuple and eliminating duplicates. The join $c \bowtie r$ of two constraints is a new constraint with scope $var(c) \cup var(r)$ defined as follows: a tuple t is permitted in the new constraint iff $t[var(c)]$ is permitted by c and $t[var(r)]$ is permitted by r. The projection of a variable out of c has complexity $O(|c|)$, $|c|$ being the number of tuples of c. The complexity of $c \bowtie r$ is dominated by $O(|c||r|)$. There is a special case when $var(r) \subseteq var(c)$ which has complexity $O(|c|)$, since the only effect of r is to discard some tuples of c, we say that r acts as a filter of the tuples in c. ADC [7] is an algorithm to solve constraint networks. The algorithm selects a variable, joins all the constraints in which it appears, and projects it from the resulting constraint, eliminating the variable from the problem. ADC processes each variable in turn, until no variable remains. The time and space complexity of ADC is $O(n.(2d)^{w^*+1})$ and $O(n.d^{w^*})$ respectively, where n is the number of variables, d bounds the domain size and w^* is the induced-width along the order of processing.

3 Delaying Variable Elimination and Filtering

To keep memory usage as low as possible, we aim at performing the most restrictive joins first. With this motivation, the idea of *delaying variable elimination*

function ADC-DVE-F(X, D, C)
1   **if** $X = \emptyset$ **then return** λ
2   **else if** $\exists x \in X \land \exists c \in C$ such that $x \in var(c) \land x \notin var(c'), \forall c' \in C, c' \neq c$
3        $t :=$ ADC-DVE-F$(X - \{x\}, D - \{D_x\}, C \cup \{c \Downarrow x\} - \{c\})$
4        $a :=$ feasible extension of t w.r.t. c
5   **return** $t \cdot (x, a)$
6   **else**
7        $x :=$ selectVar(X)
8        $B := \{c \in C| \; x \in var(c)\}$
9        $\{p, q\} :=$ selectTwo(B)
10      $F := \{c \in C| \; var(c) \subset var(p) \cup var(q)\}$
11      $r := p \bowtie^F q$
12   **if** $r = \emptyset$ **then return** NIL
13   **else return** ADC-DVE-F$(X, D, C \cup \{r\} - (\{p, q\} \cup F))$

Fig. 1. ADC-DVE-F: Adaptive consistency delaying variable elimination with filtering. λ is the empty tuple, extendible to other solutions. NIL is non extendible.

decouples joins and variable eliminations. Differently from ADC, one can start joining two constraints in one bucket, continue joining in another bucket, etc. The only condition that is imposed is that as soon as one variable is mentioned by one constraint only, this variable is eliminated. This strategy produces a correct and complete algorithm that terminates.

In addition, we can avoid storing some intermediate tuples which later are discovered as infeasible. This is the *join with filtering* idea. Given two constraints c and r and a set of constraints F where $\forall p \in F (var(p) \subset (var(c) \cup var(r)))$, the join with filtering F, $c \bowtie^F r$, is the usual join where tuples forbidden by any $p \in F$ do not appear in the resulting join. If $var(p) \subseteq var(c) \cup var(r)$ $(c \bowtie^{\{p\}} r) = ((c \bowtie r) \bowtie p)$. The complexity of adding a filter set $|F|$ in the join is $O(|c||r||F|)$ where $|F|$ is the number of constraints in the filter. This is equivalent to performing $|F|$ joins. For example if $F = \{p, q\}$, $c \bowtie^{\{p,q\}} r = (((c \bowtie r) \bowtie p) \bowtie q)$. The advantage of using filters is that intermediate tuples that will be filtered out are not stored at any moment. Joining with filters never uses more space than standard join, and it may produce exponential savings in space.

Combining both ideas we obtain the ADC-DVE-F algorithm, which appears in Figure 1. In line 10 we compute the set F of constraints that can act as filters and in line 13, filters are removed from the set C^1.

As an example, we observe the execution of the ADC-DVE-F on the 5-queens problem, showing the advantages of delayed variable evaluation and filtering. The first graph is the initial problem with the number of permitted tuples written for all the constraints involving x_1. The algorithm first selects variable x_1 and its two tightest constraints. In n-queens the tightest constraints are the ones between one variable and its two immediate neighbors in the board. For x_1 these are c_{12} and c_{13}. A filter exists for this join $F = \{c_{23}\}$. The result $c_{12} \bowtie^{\{c_{23}\}} c_{13}$ is in the

---
[1] Filters can be maintained as a set of constraints on which join will not be performed acting as filters for future joins. A somehow similar idea was presented in [2].

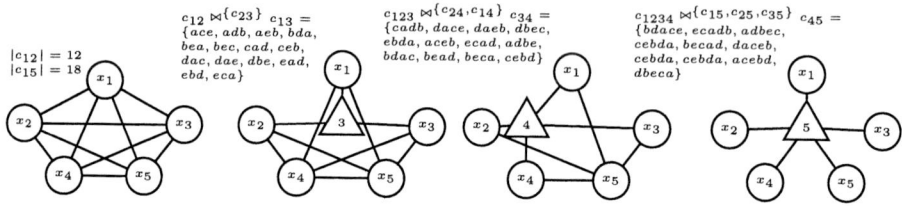

next graph on the right. The constraint that has acted as filter disappears. If we had used no filter the resulting constraint would have $|c_{12} \bowtie c_{13}| = 34$ tuples, of which 20 would have been discarded later. Let us see now the advantages of DVE. Following ADC algorithm we would now be obliged to join one of these three constraints $B_1 = \{c_{123}, c_{14}, c_{15}\}$. As we are in ADC-DVE we have the freedom to join two constraints of another variable. We will now choose x_3 which in fact has a tighter constraint than x_1, namely c_{34}, that involves consecutive variables. A filter exists for this join $F = \{c_{24}, c_{14}\}$. In the final step we perform the join with the tighter constraint c_{45} of variable x_5. A filter exists for this join $F = \{c_{15}, c_{35}, c_{25}\}$. The result are all the solutions without removing the symmetries of the problem. Notice that no elimination (projection) of a variable was necessary. In fact the algorithm can stop when there is only one constraint left in the problem.

4 Experimental Results

We tested ADC and ADC-DVE-F on two classes of problems, n-queens and Schur's lemma, but we only report results on n-queens for lack of space. The usual cause of non-solvability of an instance was always running out of memory (with a memory limit of 2,000,000 tuples) for all the algorithms and both problems.

ADC runs out of memory at $n = 8$, so the last line appearing in the first plot of Figure 2 is $n = 7$. In ADC, the number of tuples after the first variable elimination corresponds to the maximum number of tuples of the plot. The first elimination is always the most expensive in number of tuples and for increasing n it grows exponentially. In the second plot, we report results for ADC-DVE-F. Observe that last point in each line has a number of joins equal to the $n - 2$. The last point in each line for n-queens also represents the total number of solutions without removing symmetries. We observe that it grows exponentially as n grows. Instances up to $n = 13$ could be solved, so ADC-DVE-F can solve instances of dimensions increased in 6 with respect to standard ADC. In a n-clique binary graph ADC-DVE-F performs $n-2$ joins with 1 to $n-1$ filters each one. The fact that the tuples of temporal joins are not stored and that all the constraints in the filter can be deleted from the problem gives a clear advantage in time and memory space to ADC-DVE-F.

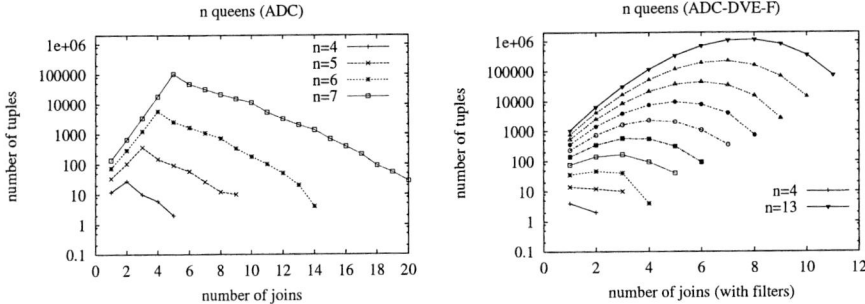

Fig. 2. Stored tuples in ADC and in ADC-DVE-F, for the n-queens problem.

5 Conclusions

The importance of ADC is often considered as purely theoretical, since most constraint satisfaction problems have a high induced width. While this is true in general, we believe that their true potential is still to be discovered. In this paper, we have proposed two modifications to the standard ADC definition with which its time and space efficiency can be improved. First, we have shown that computations can be re-arranged and the expensive ones can be delayed with the hope that the involved relations may have their size decreased. Second, we have shown that joins involving small arity constraints, which can be efficiently computed, can be anticipated in order to detect and filter out tuples from large arity constraints, where the exponential cost of the algorithm is more likely to become apparent. Any of these ideas can bring exponential saving over ADC. Our preliminary experimental results are very promising.

References

1. El Fattah Y. Dechter, R. Topological parameters for time-space tradeoff. *Artifical Intelligence*, 2000.
2. G. Gottlob, N. Leone, and F. Scarcello. A comparison of structural csp decomposition methods. *Artificial Intelligence*, 124(2):243–282, 2000.
3. Larrosa J. Boosting search with variable elimination. In *Proc. of the 6th CP*, pages 291–305, 2000.
4. Larrosa J. and Morancho E. Solving still life with soft constraints and variable elimination. In *Proc. of the 9th CP*, pages 466–479, 2003.
5. Kask K. New search heuristics for max-csp. In *Proc. of the 6th CP*, pages 262–277, 2000.
6. Dechter R. Bucket elimination: A unifying framework for reasoning. *Artifical Intelligence*, 113:41–85, 1999.
7. Dechter R. and Pearl J. Network-based heuristics for constraint satisfaction problems. *Artifical Intelligence*, 34:1–38, 1987.

On-Demand Bound Computation for Best-First Constraint Optimization

Martin Sachenbacher and Brian C. Williams

MIT Computer Science and Artificial Intelligence Laboratory
Cambridge, MA 02139, USA
{sachenba,williams}@mit.edu

Abstract. An important class of algorithms for constraint optimization searches for solutions guided by a heuristic evaluation function (bound). When only a few best solutions are required, significant effort can be wasted pre-computing bounds that are not used during the search. We introduce a method that generates – based on lazy, best-first variants of constraint projection and combination operators – only those bounds that are specifically required in order to generate a next best solution.

1 Introduction

Many problems in Artificial Intelligence can be framed as constraint optimization problems where only a few best ("leading") solutions are needed. For instance, in fault diagnosis it might be sufficient to compute the most likely diagnoses that cover most of the probability density space [6]. In planning, it might be sufficient to compute the best plan, and a few backup plans in case the best plan fails. When only a few leading solutions need to be generated, algorithms that search through the space of possible assignments guided by a pre-computed heuristic evaluation function (bound) [4] become inefficient, because only some of the bounds will typically be needed to compute the best solutions. We present a method called *best-first search with on-demand bound computation* (BFOB) that efficiently computes leading solutions for semiring-based CSPs [1]. BFOB optimally interleaves bound computation and best-first search, such that bounds are computed and assignments are expanded only as required to generate each next best solution. The algorithm can still generate all solutions and its complexity is never worse than performing bound computation as a separate pre-processing step, yet it can derive the best solutions much faster. The approach involves lazy, best-first variants of constraint combination and projection operators, and a streamed computation scheme that coordinates these operators by exploiting a tree decomposition [3, 5] of the optimization problem.

2 Semiring-Based Constraint Optimization Problems

A constraint optimization problem (COP) over a c-semiring $S = (A, +, \times, \mathbf{0}, \mathbf{1})$ [1] is a triple (X, D, F) where $X = \{x_1, \ldots, x_n\}$ is a set of variables, $D = \{D_1,$

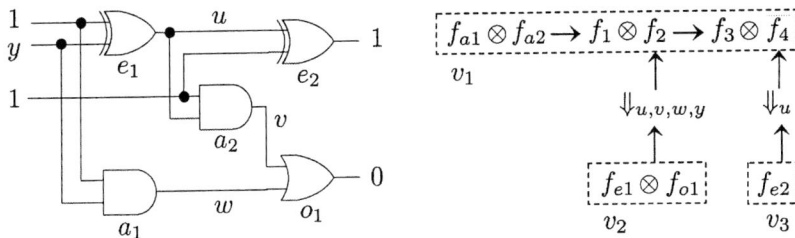

Fig. 1. Full adder example (*left*), consisting of two AND gates, one OR gate and two XOR gates, and computational scheme (*right*) for a tree decomposition of the example.

..., D_n} is a set of finite domains, and $F = \{f_1, \ldots, f_m\}$ is a set of constraints. The constraints $f_j \in F$ are functions defined over var(f_j) assigning to each tuple a value in A. The $+$ operation of the c-semiring induces an order $\leq_S$ over A as follows: $a \leq_S b$ iff $a + b = b$. In this paper, we assume that $\leq_S$ is a total order.

Example. Diagnosis of the full adder circuit in Fig. 1 can be framed as a COP over the probabilistic c-semiring $S_p = ([0,1], \max, \cdot, 0, 1)$ with variables $X = \{u, v, w, y, a_1, a_2, e_1, e_2, o_1\}$. Variables u to y have domain $\{0, 1\}$. Variables a_1 to o_1 describe the mode of a component and have domain $\{G,B\}$. If a component is good (G) then it correctly performs its boolean function; if it is broken (B) then no assumption is made about its behavior. Assume AND gates have a 1% probability of failure, and OR and XOR gates have a 5% probability of failure. Table 1 shows the resulting constraints, where each tuple is assigned the probability of its corresponding mode.

3 Optimization Using Bound-Guided Search

Solutions to a COP can be found by searching through the space of possible assignments in best first order, guided by a heuristic evaluation function [4]. In A* search, the evaluation function is $f = g \times h$, composed of the value of the partial assignment made so far, g, and a heuristic h that provides an optimistic estimate (bound) on the value that can be achieved when completing the assignment. Kask and Dechter [4] show how h can be derived from a decomposition

Table 1. Constraints for the example (tuples with value **0** are not shown).

f_{a1}: a1 w y	f_{a2}: a2 u v	f_{e1}: e1 u y	f_{e2}: e2 u	f_{o1}: o1 v w
G 0 0 .99	G 0 0 .99	G 1 0 .95	G 0 .95	G 0 0 .95
G 1 1 .99	G 1 1 .99	G 0 1 .95	B 0 .05	B 0 0 .05
B 0 0 .01	B 0 0 .01	B 0 0 .05	B 1 .05	B 0 1 .05
B 0 1 .01	B 0 1 .01	B 0 1 .05		B 1 0 .05
B 1 0 .01	B 1 0 .01	B 1 0 .05		B 1 1 .05
B 1 1 .01	B 1 1 .01	B 1 1 .05		

of the constraint network into an acyclic instance called a *bucket tree* [5]. The tree is evaluated bottom-up (that is, in post-order) using dynamic programming to compute a constraint h_{v_i} for each tree node v_i. Let function $g^{(i)}$ be defined as the combination of all functions of the nodes $v_1, \ldots, v_i$ of the bucket tree, and let function $h^{(i)}$ be defined as the combination of all functions of the nodes $c_1, \ldots, c_l$ that are children of $v_1, \ldots, v_i$:

$$g^{(i)} = \bigotimes_{j=1}^{i} (\bigotimes_{f_k \in v_j} f_k), \quad h^{(i)} = \bigotimes_{j=1}^{l} h_{c_j}.$$

Then the value $g^{(i)}(x_1^0, \ldots, x_i^0) \times (h^{(i)} \Downarrow_{x_{i+1}})(x_{i+1}^0)$ is an upper bound (with respect to $\leq_S$) on the value that can be achieved when extending the assignment $x_1 = x_1^0, \ldots, x_i = x_i^0$ by $x_{i+1} = x_{i+1}^0$. We generalize the derivation of bounds from bucket trees to tree decompositions [3, 5] by assigning variables in groups: Let $p = v_1, \ldots, v_n$ be a pre-order of the nodes V of a tree decomposition. Then p defines an ordering on groups of variables $G_1, \ldots, G_{|V|} \subseteq X$, by letting $G_1 = \text{var}(h_{v_1})$, $G_{i+1} = \text{var}(h_{v_{i+1}}) \setminus (G_1 \cup \ldots \cup G_i)$. Consider the tree decomposition in Fig. 1, consisting of three nodes v_1, v_2, and v_3. If the variables in the group $G_1 = \{u, v, w, y, a_1, a_2\}$ have been assigned (that is, node v_1 has been traversed), then $g^{(1)} \otimes h^{(1)}$ with $g^{(1)} = f_{a1} \otimes f_{a2}$ and $h^{(1)} = h_{v_2} \otimes h_{v_3}$ is a bounding function for the value that can be achieved when extending the assignment by assigning the variables in the group $G_2 = \{e_1, o_1\}$.

4 On-Demand Bound Computation

When only a few best solutions are required, computing bounds for all assignments is wasteful, since typically a large percentage of the bounds is not needed in order to compute the best solutions. The key to capturing this intuition formally is the following monotonicity property of c-semirings, which is an instance of preferential independence [2]:

Proposition 1. *If $h_0 \leq_S h_1$ for $h_0, h_1 \in A$, then for $g_0 \in A$, $g_0 \times h_0 \leq_S g_0 \times h_1$.*

It implies that in best-first search, it is sufficient to consider only the expansion with the best value (and keeping a reference to its next best sibling). This is sufficient because all other expansions cannot lead to solutions that have a better value with respect to the order $\leq_S$. The constraint-based A* scheme in [7] exploits this principle in order to significantly limit the successor nodes created at each expansion step. The idea pursued in this paper is to generalize on this: if it is unnecessary to create all possible expansions of a node, then it is also unnecessary to compute bounds on all possible expansions of a node. This allows us to interleave best-first search and the computation of a bounding function h, such that h is computed only to an extent that it is actually needed in order to generate a next best solution. We call this approach *best-first search with on-demand bound computation* (BFOB).

```
function nextBestComb(f1, f2)                function nextBestProj(f)
  while (queue ≠ ∅) do                         while (index ≠ 0) do
    ⟨i, j, v⟩ ← pop(queue)                       ⟨t, v⟩ ← at(f, index)
    ⟨t1, v1⟩ ← at(f1, i)                         if (⟨t, v⟩ ≠ nil) then
    if (⟨t1, v1⟩ ≠ nil) then                       t1 ← t ⇓_{var(f_result)}
      ⟨t2, v2⟩ ← at(f2, j)                         index ← index + 1
      if (⟨t2, v2⟩ ≠ nil) then                     for each ⟨t2, v2⟩ in f_result do
        t ← t1 ⊗ t2                                  if (t1 = t2) then goto while
        if (var(f1) ⊉ var(f2)) then                end if
          ⟨t1', v1'⟩ ← at(f1, i+1)               end for
          if (⟨t1', v1'⟩ ≠ nil) then             return ⟨t1, v⟩
            push(queue, ⟨i+1, j, v1'×v2⟩)      else
          end if                                   index ← 0
        end if                                   end if
        if (i = 1) then                        end while
          ⟨t2', v2'⟩ ← at(f2, j+1)             return nil
          if (⟨t2', v2'⟩ ≠ nil) then
            push(queue, ⟨i, j+1, v1×v2'⟩)
          end if
        end if
        if (t ≠ nil) then return ⟨t, v1 × v2⟩
      end if
    end if
  end while
  return nil
```

Fig. 2. Best-first variants of constraint combination and constraint projection.

The approach requires to compute the functions h_{v_i} incrementally and in best-first order. We achieve this – akin to streamed, on-demand computation in distributed databases – by applying constraint projection and combination operations only partially, that is, to subsets of the tuples of the constraints. Consider the scheme of functions and operations shown in Fig. 1. The best tuple of function f_{e2} is $\langle e_2{=}G, u{=}0\rangle$ with value .95 (first tuple of f_{e2} in Table 1). The projection of this tuple on u, which is $\langle u{=}0\rangle$ with value .95, is necessarily a best tuple of f_4. Similarly, a best tuple of f_{a1} can be combined with a best tuple of f_{a2}, for instance the first tuples of f_{a1} and f_{a2} in Table 1. The resulting tuple $\langle u{=}0, v{=}0, w{=}0, y{=}0, a_1{=}G, a_2{=}G\rangle$ with value .98 is necessarily a best tuple of constraint f_1. Eventually, a best tuple for h_{v_1} can be computed from the scheme without visiting large parts of the constraints f_{a1}, f_{a2}, f_{e1}, f_{e2}, and f_{o1}.

The functions nextBestProj() and nextBestComb() shown in Fig. 2 implement such best-first variants of the constraint operators $\Downarrow$ and $\otimes$, respectively. The helper function $at(f, i)$ returns the i-th best tuple of a constraint f, or generates it, if necessary, by calling the constraint operator producing f. For each projection operator, index is initially 1, and for each combination operator, queue is initially $\{\langle 1, 1, 1\rangle\}$. Initially, the tuples of the constraints are sorted and inserted at the inputs (leafs) of the scheme. BFOB then assigns variables

Table 2. Results for random Max-CSPs (10 instances each).

T	C	N	K	BFPB (% time)	BFOB (% time)
4 (25%)	20	15	4	100%	1.4%
8 (50%)	20	15	4	100%	3.2%
4 (25%)	15	10	4	100%	4.5%
8 (50%)	15	10	4	100%	14.3%
4 (25%)	20	10	4	100%	9.7%
8 (50%)	20	10	4	100%	38.8%

in groups following a pre-order traversal of the tree as described in Sec. 3, and when expanding a search node, it computes a bound on-demand for the best expansion using function at(). The best-first variants of the constraint operators have the same worst-case complexity as their counterparts $\Downarrow$ and $\otimes$. However, the average complexity of on-demand function computation can be much lower if only some best tuples of the resulting function are required.

5 Experimental Results

We compared the performance of BFOB *relative* to the alternative approach of pre-computing all functions h_{v_i}. We call this alternative algorithm BFPB (it is analogous to the algorithm BFMB described in [4]). Table 2 shows the results of experiments with three classes of Max-CSP problems for the task of generating a single best solution. The results indicate that BFOB leads to significant savings especially when computing best solutions to problems with low constraint tightness and sparse to medium network density.

References

1. Bistarelli, S., Montanari, U., Rossi, F.: Semiring-based Constraint Solving and Optimization. Journal of ACM, **44** (2) (1997) 201–236
2. Debreu, C.: Topological methods in cardinal utility theory. In: Mathematical Methods in the Social Sciences, Stanford University Press (1959)
3. Gottlob, G., Leone, N., Scarcello, F.: A comparison of structural CSP decomposition methods. Artificial Intelligence **124** (2) (2000) 243–282
4. Kask, K., Dechter, R.: A General Scheme for Automatic Generation of Search Heuristics from Specification Dependencies. Artificial Intelligence **129** (2001) 91–131
5. Kask, K., et al.: Unifying Tree-Decomposition Schemes for Automated Reasoning. Technical Report, University of California, Irvine (2001)
6. de Kleer, J.: Focusing on Probable Diagnoses. Proc. AAAI-91 (1991) 842–848
7. Williams, B., Ragno, R.: Conflict-directed A* and its Role in Model-based Embedded Systems. Journal of Discrete Applied Mathematics, to appear.

A New Algorithm for Maintaining Arc Consistency After Constraint Retraction

Pavel Surynek and Roman Barták[*]

Charles University in Prague, Faculty of Mathematics and Physics
Institute for Theoretical Computer Science
Malostranské nám. 2/25, 118 00 Praha 1, Czech Republic
`pavel.surynek@seznam.cz, roman.bartak@mff.cuni.cz`

Abstract. Dynamic Constraint Satisfaction Problems play a very important role in modeling and solving real-life problems where the set of constraints is changing. The paper addresses a problem of maintaining arc consistency after removing a constraint from the constraint model. A new dynamic arc consistency algorithm is proposed that improves the practical time efficiency of the existing AC|DC algorithm by using additional data-structures. The algorithm achieves real time efficiency close to the so far fastest DynAC-6 algorithm while keeping the memory consumption low.

1 Introduction

For solving many real-life problems, the traditional static formulation of the constraint satisfaction problem (CSP) is not sufficient because the problem formulation is changing dynamically [5]. To model such problems Dechter and Dechter [4] proposed a notion of *Dynamic Constraint Satisfaction Problem* (DCSP) that is a sequence of static CSPs, where each CSP is a result of addition or retraction of a constraint in the preceding problem. Several techniques have been proposed to solve Dynamic CSP, including searching for robust solutions that are valid after small problem changes, reusing the original solution to produce a new solution, and reusing the reasoning process. A typical representative of the last technique is *maintaining dynamic arc consistency*. The goal of maintaining dynamic arc consistency is keeping the problem arc consistent after constraint addition and constraint retraction. Adding a new constraint is a monotonic process which means that domains can only be pruned and existing arc consistency algorithms can be applied there. When a constraint is retracted from the problem then the problem remains arc consistent. However, some solutions of the new problem might be lost because the values from the original problem that were directly or indirectly inconsistent with the retracted constraint are missing in the domains. Consequently, such values should be returned to the domains after constraint retraction. Then we are speaking about *maximal arc consistency*.

---

[*] Supported by the Czech Science Foundation under the contract No. 201/04/1102.

In this paper we address the problem of maintaining maximal arc consistency after constraint retraction. Dynamic versions of popular arc consistency algorithms have been proposed to solve this problem, namely DnAC-4 [2] and DnAC-6 [3] based on extended data structures of AC-4 and AC-6, and AC|DC algorithm [1] as a reverse version of the AC-3 algorithm. DnAC-4 and DnAC-6 are very fast algorithms thanks to minimizing the number of constraint checks but they are also memory consuming and complicated for implementation. On the other hand, AC|DC is easy to implement, it has minimal memory requirements but it is less time efficient. The main reason for its time inefficiency is restoring too many values in the domains that are immediately pruned in the completion stage of the algorithm. In our work, we focused on removing this drawback by keeping additional data structures. Our hope was to improve significantly the practical time efficiency of AC|DC without increasing much the space complexity. This makes our approach different from AC-3.1|DC [6] that only substitutes AC-3.1 for AC-3 in the AC|DC scheme which increases space complexity.

2 Algorithm AC|DC-2

We extend the original AC|DC algorithm with additional data structures that record a justification and a timestamp for every value eliminated from the variable domain. By the *justification* we mean the first neighboring variable in which the eliminated value lost all supports. The *timestamp* describes the time when the value has been removed – a global counter which is incremented after every manipulation of the variable domains is used to model time. Using the timestamps is the original contribution of this paper. To prepare the above data structures (stored in the compound structure data) we propose a slightly modified AC-3 based algorithm that we call AC-3' (Figure 1).

```
function propagate-ac3'(P, data, revise)
1    queue := revise
2    while queue not empty do
3        select and remove a constraint c from queue
4        {u,v} := the variables constrained by c
5        (P,data,revise_u) := filter-arc-ac3'(P, data, c, u, v)
6        (P,data,revise_v) := filter-arc-ac3'(P, data, c, v, u)
7        queue := queue ∪ revise_u ∪ revise_v
8    return (P,data)

function filter-arc-ac3'(P, data, c, u, v)
1    modified := false
2    for each d in P.D[u] do
3        if d has no support in P.D[v] w.r.t. c then
4            P.D[v] := P.D[v] - {d}
5            data.justif[u,d].var := v
6            data.justif[u,d].time := data.time
7            data.time := data.time + 1
8            modified := true
9    if not modified then
10       return (P,data,∅)
11   return (P,data,{e in P.C|u is constrained by e and e≠c})
```

Fig. 1. A pseudo code of the modified arc-consistency algorithm AC-3'

When a constraint is retracted from the problem the algorithm uses the justifications and timestamps to determine the set of values which have been removed possibly because of the retracted constraint and that should be restored in the relaxed problem. As in the case of AC|DC algorithm the constraint retraction using AC|DC-2 is carried out in three phases. In the first phase (initialize-ac|dc2) the algorithm puts back the values into the variable domains that have been removed directly because of the retracted constraint. The second phase (propagate-ac|dc2) consists of a propagation of the initial restorations from the first phase. Finally, in the last phase (propagate-ac3') the algorithm removes the inconsistent values that have been incorrectly restored in the previous phases. Notice that in addition to the description of the current domains (P.D) we keep the original domains of the variables (P.D_0). For a detail description of the algorithms we kindly ask the reader to see [7].

```
function retract-constraint-ac|dc2(P, data, c)
1      (P,data,restored_u) :=
2          initialize-ac|dc2(P, data, c, u, v)
3      (P,data,restored_v) :=
4          initialize-ac|dc2(P, data, c, v, u)
5      P.C := P.C - {c}
6      (P,data,revise) :=
7          propagate-ac|dc2(P, data, {restored_u,restored_v})
8      (P,data) := propagate-ac3'(P, data, revise)
9      return (P,data)

function initialize-ac|dc2(P, data, c, u, v)
1      restored_u := ∅
2      time_u := ∞
3      for each d in (P.D_0[u] - P.D[u]) do
4          if data.justif[u,d].var = v then
5              P.D[u] := P.D[u] ∪ {d}
6              data.justif[u,d].var := NIL
7              restored_u := restored_u ∪ {d}
8              time_u := min(time_u, data.justif[u,d].time)
9      return (P,data,(u,time_u,restored_u))

function propagate-ac|dc2(P, data, restore)
1      revise := ∅
2      while restore not empty do
3          select and remove (u,time_u,restored_u) from restore
4          for each c in P.C|u is constrained by c do
5              {u,v} := the variables constrained by c
6              restored_v := ∅
7              time_v := ∞
8              for each d in (P.D_0[v] - P.D[v]) do
9                  if data.justif[v, d].var = u then
10                     if data.justif[v, d].time > time_u then
11                         if d has a support in restored_u w.r.t. c then
12                             P.D[v] := P.D[v] ∪ {d}
13                             data.justif[v,d].var := NIL
14                             restored_v := restored_v ∪ {d}
15                             time_v := min(time_v, data.justif[v,d].time)
16             restore := restore ∪ {(v,time_v,restored_v)}
17         revise := revise ∪ {e in P.C|u is constrained by e})
18     return (P,data,revise)
```

Fig. 2. A pseudo code of the dynamic arc-consistency algorithm AC|DC-2

The algorithm AC|DC-2 performs a correct retraction of a constraint with respect to maximal arc consistency (constraint addition can be easily done via `propagate-ac3'`). Moreover, it performs at most as many consistency checks as the existing algorithm AC|DC. Formally, the space complexity of AC|DC-2 is $O(nd+e)$ and the worst case time complexity of AC|DC-2 is $O(ed^3)$, where n is the number of variables, d is the size of the domains of variables, and e is the number of constraints. The formal proofs can be found in [7]. The theoretical complexities are thus identical to the original AC|DC algorithm, but in practice AC|DC-2 is much faster and performs much less consistency checks than AC|DC as the experiments showed.

3 Experimental Results

We compared the new algorithm AC|DC-2 to the existing algorithms AC|DC and DnAC-6 under Red Hat Linux 9.0 on 2 GHz Pentium 4 with 512 MB of memory. We performed the experiments on a set of randomly generated binary constraint satisfaction problems. For each problem, ten random instances were generated and the mean values of runtime are presented here. Constraints were added incrementally to the problem until a given density was reached or an inconsistent state was encountered. After this step, 10% of randomly selected constraints were retracted from the problem. Figure 3 shows the total runtime; AC|DC-2 is much faster than AC|DC and almost as fast as DnAC-6. A similar result was obtained for the number of constraint checks [7].

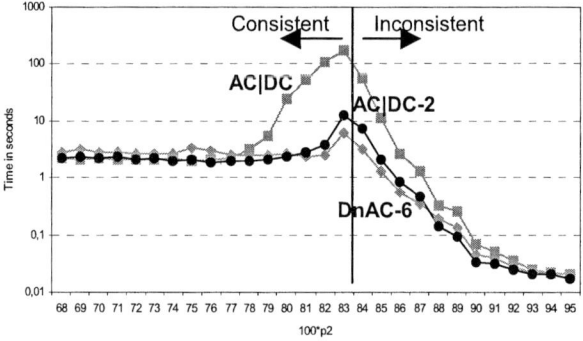

Fig. 3. Runtime (logarithmic scale in seconds) as a function of tightness for random constraint satisfaction problems $\langle 100, 50, 0.3, p_2 \rangle$

We also compared the memory consumption of the algorithms. We measured the memory consumption of the data structures specific for the algorithms so the representation of the constraints is not included. The memory consumption was measured at the time point just before the constraint causing inconsistency was added because the memory consumption is largest there. The results (Table 1) show that the memory consumption of AC|DC-2 and AC|DC is neglecting and it is much smaller than the memory consumption of DnAC-6.

Table 1. Memory consumption depending on the size of variable domains for random constraint satisfaction problems $\langle 100, d, 0.3, p_2 \rangle$

Domain size (d)	20	30	40	50	60	70	80
100*p_2	68%	77%	80%	82%	84%	85%	85%
AC|DC	<1MB	<1MB	<1MB	<1MB	<1MB	<1MB	<1MB
DnAC-6	21MB	32MB	49MB	64MB	77MB	94MB	120MB
AC|DC-2	<1MB	<1MB	<1MB	<1MB	<1MB	<1MB	<1MB

4 Conclusions

In the paper, we proposed a new algorithm AC|DC-2 for maintaining maximal arc consistency in dynamic environments where the constraints are added and retracted incrementally. As the experiments showed we improved significantly the practical time efficiency of the AC|DC algorithm and the time is now comparable to the so far fastest DnAC-6 algorithm. Moreover, the additional data structures did not increase much the space complexity of AC|DC which remains much smaller than for DnAC-6. Additionally, AC|DC is easier to implement than DnAC-6. We did not perform yet the experiments with AC-3.1|DC but we expect behavior similar to DnAC-6.

References

1. Berlandier, P. and Neveu, B.: Arc-Consistency for Dynamic Constraint Satisfaction Problems: a RMS free approach. In Proceedings of the ECAI-94 Workshop on "Constraint Satisfaction Issues Raised by Practical Applications", Amsterdam, The Netherlands, 1994.
2. Bessière Ch.: Arc-Consistency in Dynamic Constraint Satisfaction Problems. In Proc. of the 9th National Conference on Artificial Intelligence (AAAI-91), Anaheim, CA, USA. AAAI Press, 1991, 221–226.
3. Debruyne R.: Arc-Consistency in Dynamic CSPs is no more prohibitive. In Proc. of the 8th IEEE International Conference on Tools with Artificial Intelligence (ICTAI-96), Toulouse, France, 1996, 239–267.
4. Dechter, R. and Dechter, A.: Belief Maintenance in Dynamic Constraint Networks. In Proc. of the 7th National Conference on Artificial Intelligence (AAAI-88), St. Paul, MN, USA. AAAI Press, 1988, 37–42.
5. Kocjan, W.: Dynamic scheduling: State of the art report, SICS Technical Report T2002:28, ISSN 100-3154, 2002.
6. Mouhoub, M.: Arc Consistency for Dynamic CSPs. In Vasile Palade, Robert J. Howlett, Lakhmi C. Jain (Eds.): Proceedings of the 7th International Conference on Knowledge-Based Intelligent Information and Engineering Systems – Part I (KES 2003), Oxford, UK. Springer Verlag LNCS 2773, 2003, 393–400.
7. Surynek, P. and Barták, R. A New Algorithm for Maintaining Arc Consistency after Constraint Retraction. ITI Series 2004-205, Institute for Theoretical Computer Science, 2004.

Computing the Frequency of Partial Orders

Marc R.C. van Dongen[*]

Centre for Efficiency Orientated Languages, University College Cork
dongen@cs.ucc.ie

Abstract. In this paper we study four algorithms for computing the *frequency* of a given partial order. Here the *frequency* of a partial order is the number of standard labellings respecting that partial order. The first two algorithms count by enumerating all solutions to a CSP. However, large numbers of solutions to CSPs soon make algorithms based on enumeration infeasible. The third and fourth algorithm, to a degree, overcome this problem. They avoid repeatedly solving problems with certain kinds of isomorphic solutions. A prototype implementation of the fourth algorithm was significantly more efficient than an enumeration based counting implementation using OPL.

1 Introduction

We study four algorithms for computing the *frequency* of partial orders. The problem of frequency computation is posed in [4], where it is called *counting labellings* (see also [5, Page 316]).

Our first two algorithms count by enumerating the solutions of a Constraint Satisfaction Problem (CSP). This soon becomes infeasible due to large numbers of solutions. At the time of writing the best known general purpose algorithm for counting solutions to binary CSPs has a time complexity ranging from $\mathcal{O}\left((d\alpha^4/4)^n\right)$ to $\mathcal{O}\left((\alpha^5 + \alpha + \lfloor d/4 - 1 \rfloor \alpha^4)^n\right)$, where n is the number of variables, d is the size of the largest domain, and $\alpha \approx 1.2561$ [1]. Counting solutions to CSPs is known to be #P-complete in general [2]. The third and fourth algorithm overcome some of the weaknesses of search based algorithms. Both algorithms avoid labelling the same suborder with *different* label sets. The fourth algorithm also avoids repeatedly labelling the same suborder with *the same* label set.

Section 2 presents mathematical background. Section 3 encodes frequency computation as enumeration CSPs. Section 4 presents two improvements to the CSP-based algorithms. Results are presented in Section 5. Section 6 presents conclusions.

2 Mathematical Background

A *partial order* is an ordered pair $\mathcal{P} = \langle N, \sqsubseteq \rangle$, where N is a set and $\sqsubseteq$ is a reflexive and transitive relation on N such that $v \sqsubseteq w \wedge w \sqsubseteq v \implies v = w$ for all $v, w \in N$. We will write $v \sqsubset w$ for $v \sqsubseteq w \wedge v \neq w$. A bijection $l : N \mapsto \mathcal{L}$ is called a *labelling* of $\mathcal{P}$

---

[*] This work has received support from Science Foundation Ireland under Grant 02/IN.1/181.

if $v \sqsubset w \implies l(v) < l(w)$, for all $v, w \in N$. If in addition $\mathcal{L} = \{1, \ldots, |N|\}$ then l is called a *standard* labelling of $\mathcal{P}$. The *frequency* of $\mathcal{P}$, denoted $f(\mathcal{P})$, is the number of standard labellings of $\mathcal{P}$.

3 Formulating the Labelling Problem as a CSP

A *constraint satisfaction problem* (CSP) is a tuple $\langle X, D, C \rangle$, where X is a set of variables, D is a function that maps each variable to its domain, and C is a set of constraints. Here a *constraint* is a pair $\langle S, R \rangle$, where S is an ordered sequence of variables and R is a subset of the Cartesian product of the variables in S. A *solution* of CSP $\langle X, D, C \rangle$ is a function s such that $s(x_1, \ldots, x_m) \in R$ for all $\langle \langle x_1, \ldots, x_m \rangle, R \rangle \in C$.

Let $\langle X, \sqsubseteq \rangle$ be a partial order. Furthermore, let $D(x) = \{1, \ldots, |X|\}$, for $x \in X$, and let C be given by $C = \{ \langle \langle v, w \rangle, R_{vw} \rangle : \langle v, w \rangle \in X^2 \wedge v < w \}$, where

$$R_{vw} = \begin{cases} \{ \langle i, j \rangle \in D(v) \times D(w) : i \neq j \} & \text{if } \neg(v \sqsubseteq w) \wedge \neg(w \sqsubseteq v), \\ \{ \langle i, j \rangle \in D(v) \times D(w) : i < j \} & \text{if } v \sqsubset w, \\ \{ \langle i, j \rangle \in D(v) \times D(w) : j < i \} & \text{if } w \sqsubset v. \end{cases}$$

It is left as an exercise to the reader to prove that $\langle X, D, C \rangle$ is a CSP whose solutions are exactly the standard labellings of $\langle X, \sqsubseteq \rangle$.

An alternative formulation is to replace all disequality constraints $\cdot \neq \cdot$ by a global alldifferent constraint. This has the advantage that efficient algorithms are known for enforcing hyper-arc consistency for this global constraint [3].

We implemented the algorithms using OPL [7] and MAC-3_d [6]. The MAC-3_d implementation uses binary disequality constraints, whereas the OPL implementation uses Régin's filtering constraint [3]. The MAC-3_d version was about ten times faster.

4 Counting by Removing One or Several Nodes

The *restriction* of $\mathcal{P} = \langle N, R \rangle$ to $M \subseteq N$ is defined as $\langle M, R \cap M^2 \rangle$. The restriction $\langle N', \sqsubseteq \rangle$ of $\mathcal{P}$ to $N' \subseteq N$ is called a *(connected) component* of $\mathcal{P}$ if both of the following are true:

- For all $u, w \in N'$ there exist a (possibly empty) set $\{v_1, \ldots, v_m\} \subseteq N'$ and $\preceq_i \in \{\sqsubseteq, \sqsupseteq\}$, for $1 \leq i \leq m+1$, such that $u \preceq_1 v_1 \preceq_2 \cdots \preceq_m v_m \preceq_{m+1} w$.
- For all $u \in N'$ and all $w \in N \setminus N'$ there do not exist a set $\{v_1, \ldots, v_m\} \subseteq N$ and $\preceq_i \in \{\sqsubseteq, \sqsupseteq\}$, for $1 \leq i \leq m+1$, such that $u \preceq_1 v_1 \preceq_2 \cdots \preceq_m v_m \preceq_{m+1} w$.

Theorem 1 (Multinomial Property). *Let $\mathcal{P} = \langle N, R \rangle$ be a partial order and let $N_1, \ldots, N_m$ be pairwise disjoint non-empty sets such that $\langle N, R \rangle = \langle \bigcup_{i=1}^m N_i, \bigcup_{i=1}^m R \cap N_i^2 \rangle$, then $f(\mathcal{P}) = \frac{(|N_1|+\cdots+|N_m|)!}{(|N_1|!)\times\cdots\times(|N_m|!)} \times \prod_{i=1}^m f(\langle N_i, R \cap N_i^2 \rangle)$.*

The *minima* of $\mathcal{P} = \langle N, R \rangle$, denoted minima($\mathcal{P}$), are defined as minima($\mathcal{P}$) = $\{v \in N : (N \times \{v\}) \cap R = \{\langle v, v \rangle\}\}$. The *maxima* of $\mathcal{P}$, denoted maxima($\mathcal{P}$), are defined as maxima($\mathcal{P}$) = $\{v \in N : (\{v\} \times N) \cap R = \{\langle v, v \rangle\}\}$.

```
Function frequency(Partial Order of Integer ⟨ N, E ⟩): Integer;
    Integer product, sum;
Begin
    product := | N |!;
    Foreach ⟨ N', E' ⟩ In connected_components(⟨ N, E ⟩) Do
        If | N' | > 1 Then Begin
            sum := 0;
            Foreach m ∈ minima(⟨ N', E' ⟩) Do
                sum := sum + frequency(⟨ N' \ { m } , E' ∩ (N' \ { m })² ⟩);
            product := product × sum/| N' |!;
        End;
    Return product;
End;
```

Fig. 1. Algorithm for computing the frequency of a partial order.

The multinomial property lets us reduce a problem having *several* connected components to several smaller labelling problems. The following lemma allows us to reduce a problem having only *one* connected component to a smaller problem.

Lemma 2. *Let* $\mathcal{P} = \langle N, \sqsubseteq \rangle$ *and let* $m \in N$. $\mathcal{P}$ *has a standard labelling* $f(\cdot)$ *such that* $f(m) = |N| \ (f(m) = 1)$ *if and only if* $m \in \text{maxima}(\mathcal{P}) \ (m \in \text{minima}(\mathcal{P}))$.

Theorem 3. *Let* $\mathcal{P} = \langle N, R \rangle$ *be a partial order and let* $M = \text{maxima}(\mathcal{P})$, *then*

$$f(\mathcal{P}) = \sum_{m \in M} f(\langle N \setminus \{m\}, R \cap (N \setminus \{m\})^2 \rangle).$$

Proof. By Lemma 2 only the maxima can be assigned the largest label. The number of standard labellings of $\mathcal{P}$ where a given maximal node m is labelled with the largest label is equal to the number of standard labellings of the restriction of $\mathcal{P}$ to $N \setminus \{m\}$.

Theorem 3 remains true when substituting minima for maxima. Theorems 1 and 3 suggest an algorithm for computing frequencies of partial orders. Pseudo-code for this algorithm is depicted in Figure 1. It maintains global consistency and exploits the multinomial property to avoid labelling the same partial order with different label sets. Unfortunately, *frequency* frequently (implicitly) labels sub-orders with the same label set.

Let let $\emptyset \subset S \subseteq N$. S is *maximal* (*minimal*) with respect to $\mathcal{P} = \langle N, \sqsubseteq \rangle$ if there is a standard labelling $l(\cdot)$ of $\mathcal{P}$ such that $\{l(s) : s \in S\} = \{|N| - |S| + 1, \ldots, |N|\}$. (such that $\{l(s) : s \in S\} = \{1, \ldots, |S|\}$).

Theorem 4. *Let* $P = \langle N, R \rangle$ *be a partial order let* $1 \leq s \leq |N|$ *and let* M *be the set constaining all maximal sets of* $\mathcal{P}$ *that have a Cardinality of* s, *then*

$$f(P) = \sum_{S \in M} f(\langle N \setminus S, R \cap (N \setminus S)^2 \rangle) \times f(\langle S, R \cap S^2 \rangle).$$

Proof. By induction on s and application of Theorem 3.

Theorem 4 remains true if minimal is substituted for maximal. The algorithm called *frequency'* (depicted in Figure 2) uses Theorem 4 for frequency computation. The parameter *size* is the *size-parameter* of the algorithm. It corresponds to s in Theorem 4.

```
Function frequency'(Integer size, Partial Order of Integer ⟨ N, E ⟩): Integer;
    Integer product;
    Function freq(Integer size, Partial Order of Integer ⟨ N, E ⟩): Integer;
        Integer sum;
        Set of Integer D;
    Begin
        If | N | ≤ 1 Then
            Return 1;
        Else If size ≥ | N | Then
            Return freq(size/2, ⟨ N, E ⟩);
        Else Begin
            sum := 0;
            Foreach M ∈ minimal_sets(size, ⟨ N, E ⟩) Do Begin
                D := N \ M;
                sum := sum + frequency'(size, ⟨ M, E ∩ M² ⟩) × frequency'(size, ⟨ D, E ∩ D² ⟩);
            End;
            Return sum;
        End;
    End;
    Begin
        product := | N |!;
        Foreach ⟨ N', E' ⟩ In connected_components(⟨ N, E ⟩) Do
            product := product × freq(size, ⟨ N', E' ⟩)/| N' |!;
        Return product;
    End;
```

Fig. 2. Improved algorithm for computing the frequency of partial orders.

5 Experimental Results

Let $K_{m,n} = \langle \{1, \ldots, m+n\}, \sqsubseteq \rangle$, where $i \sqsubset j \iff i \leq m < j$. These orders are difficult to count for *frequency* and *frequency'*. "Tree shaped orders" are among the easiest connected orders count. Let B_n^+ (B_n^-) denote the partial order whose Hasse diagram corresponds to the complete binary tree with $2^{1+n} - 1$ nodes, that is rooted at the bottom (top). Note that $f(B_n^+) = f(B_n^-)$.

We implemented *frequency* and *frequency'* in Prolog. They improved significantly over the MAC-based algorithms. MAC-3_d our best MAC-based algorithm required more than 6 hours for computing $f(K_{8,8})$. An implementation with OPL did not terminate after many hours and required an intermediate memory size of more than 60MB. However, *frequency'* required 0.01 seconds for computing $f(K_{8,8})$ with a size-parameter of 8. and fewer than 2 seconds with a size-parameter of 2.

Table 1 lists the results of applying *frequency'*. All results were obtained with a 1000 MHz DELL Latitude. The results for B_n^- with a size-parameter of 1 demonstrate the advantage of using Theorem 1. Each time a node is removed from B_n^- this results in two B_{n-1}^-, for $n > 0$. The results for the $K_{n,n}$ and B_n^+ demonstrate the advantage of Theorem 4 because as the size-parameter increases less and less time is required.

The differences in time for computing the frequencies of B_n^+ and B_n^- demonstrates that *frequency'* is not clever at exploiting structural properties of partial orders. It should be possible to improve the algorithm by allowing it to also remove maximal sets.

6 Conclusions

We studied four algorithms for computing the frequency of a given partial order. The first two algorithms are based on the correspondence between partial orders and con-

Table 1. Timing results for *frequency'* algorithm.

Problem Size		Frequency	Time in Seconds
B_3^+	1–3	stack overflow	—
B_3^+	4	21964800	3.45
B_3^-	1	21964800	0.00
B_6^-	1	$10^{163.61}$	0.21
B_8^-	1	$10^{9568.46}$	3.96
$K_{8,8}$	1	stack overflow	—
$K_{8,8}$	2	1625702400	1.96
$K_{8,8}$	8	1625702400	0.01
$K_{10,10}$	10	13168189440000	0.06
$K_{16,16}$	16	4377631366973950525440000000	9.30

straint satisfaction problems (CSPs). They use backtrack search while maintaining arc consistency to enumerate and count all solutions. A disadvantage of these algorithms is that they soon become infeasible due to there being many solutions.

The third and fourth algorithm overcome some of the weaknesses of the search based algorithms. They eliminate a class of permutations acting upon the *entire* label set of a given partial order $\mathcal{P}$. For moderately sized problems the techniques presented in this paper significantly reduce the total solution time.

References

1. O. Angelsmark and P. Jonsson. Improved algorithms for counting solutions in constraint satisfaction problems. In F. Rossi, editor, *Proceedings of the ninth International Conference on Principles and Practice of Constraint Programming (CP'2003)*, pages 81–95, 2003.
2. A.A. Bulatov and V. Dalmau. Towards a dichotomy for the counting constraint satisfaction problem. In *Proceedings of the 41st Annual Symposium on Foundations of Computer Science (FOCS 2003)*, pages 272–282, 2003.
3. Jean-Charles Régin. A filtering algorithm for constraints of difference in CSPs. In *Proceedings of the 12th National Conference on Artificial Intelligence (AAAI'94)*, pages 362–367, 1994.
4. M.P. Schellekens. Compositional average time analysis *toward a calculus for software timing*. Technical report, Centre for Efficiency Orientated Languages, 2004. In Preparation.
5. R. Sedgewick and P. Flajolet. *An Introduction to the Analysis of Algorithms*. Addison-Wesley Publishing Company, 1996.
6. M.R.C. van Dongen. Saving support-checks does not always save time. *Artificial Intelligence Review*, 2004. Accepted for publication.
7. P. Van Hentenryck. *The OPL Programming Language*. MIT Press, 1999.

On Tightness of Constraints*

Yuanlin Zhang

Cork Constraint Computation Center
University College Cork
Cork, Republic of Ireland
y.zhang@4c.ucc.ie

Abstract. The *tightness* of a constraint refers to how restricted the constraint is. The existing work shows that there exists a relationship between tightness and global consistency of a constraint network. In this paper, we conduct a comprehensive study on this relationship. Under the concept of k-consistency (k is a number), we strengthen the existing results by establishing that only some of the tightest, *not all*, binary constraints are used to predict a number k such that strong k-consistency ensures global consistency of an arbitrary constraint network which may include non-binary constraints. More importantly, we have identified a lower bound of the number of the tightest constraints we *have to* consider in predicting the number k. To make better use of the tightness of constraints, we propose a new type of consistency: *dually adaptive consistency*. Under this concept, only the tightest *directionally relevant* constraint on each variable (and thus in total $n-1$ such constraints where n is the number of variables) will be used to predict the level of "consistency" ensuring global consistency of a network.

1 Introduction

Informally, the *tightness* of a binary constraint is the *maximum number of compatible values* allowed for each value of the constrained variables. For example, let $x, y \in 1..10$ be two variables and consider the constraint $x = y$. For any value of x, the constraint allows at most one compatible value for y. The constraint is also said 1-tight. There is a very interesting relationship between the tightness and the global consistency of a constraint network. (When we say a network is *globally consistent*, we mean it is satisfiable.) For example, if all the constraints in a binary network is 1-tight, path consistency (i.e., strongly 3-consistency) is sufficient to determine the global consistency of the network. If *not all* constraints are 1-tight, the existing method will use the least tight constraint to determine the level of consistency sufficient for global consistency. *This level is higher (and thus more expensive) if the constraints are less tight.* The motivation of this paper is to determine the level of consistency by using less number of and possibly tighter constraints. For example, by our results, if a constraint network with n variables has n 1-tight constraints on "correct" variables, a local consistency similar to path consistency is able to ensure its global consistency.

---

* This work has received support from Science Foundation Ireland under Grant 00/PI.1/C075.

2 Tightness Under k-Consistency

In this section, we show that we can use a smaller number of m-tight constraint to determine the weak m-tightness of a constraint network and thus the local level of consistency ensuring the global consistency of the network. On the other hand, we identify a lower bound on the number of m-tight constraints in a weakly m-tight network.

In this paper, n denotes the number of variables in a constraint network. A constraint is represented as c_S where S is the set of variables involved in the constraint.

m-Tightness. [4] Given a number m, a constraint c_S is m-tight on x if and only if any instantiation of $S - \{x\}$ is compatible with all or at most m values of x. If a constraint is m-tight on x, its tightness on x is m. A constraint is m-tight if it is m-tight on each of its variables.

Relevant Constraints. A *relevant constraint* on a variable x with respect to a set of variables Y is one whose scope consists of only x and variables from Y. In other words, it involves x, but does not involve any variable outside Y. $R_Y(x)$ is used to denote the set of relevant constraints on x wrt Y. When Y is clear from the context, $R(x)$, rather than $R_Y(x)$, will be used.

Weakly m-Tight Constraint Networks. A constraint network is *weakly m-tight* at level k iff for every set of variables $Y = \{x_1, \cdots, x_k\}$ and a new variable x, there exists an m-tight relevant constraint on x wrt Y.

This definition is simpler than the one given in [5] where every set Y of size k or greater than k is considered. The Proposition 1 below shows that the two definitions are equivalent.

Remark. The definition needs the assumption that given a network, there is a universal constraint among any set of variables on which there is no explicit constraint. A universal constraint on a set of variables allows any instantiation of the variables. In this section, we need to keep in mind that there is a constraint among any set of variables.

For a weakly tight network, we have this consistency result.

Theorem 1. [5] *If for some m, a constraint network with constraints of arity at most r is strongly $((m+1)(r-1)+1)$-consistent and weakly m-tight at level $((m+1)(r-1)+1)$, it is strongly n-consistent.*

There is a strong relationship among different levels of weak tightness in a network.

Proposition 1. *If a constraint network is weakly m-tight at level k for some m, it is weakly m-tight at any level $j > k$.*

The following result gives a sufficient condition for a constraint network to be weakly m-tight at level k.

Theorem 2. *A constraint network is weakly m-tight at level k if for every variable in the network, there are at least $n - k + 1$ m-tight binary constraints on it for some m and k.*

The next result shows a lower bound on the number of m-tight constraints in a network weakly tight at level 3.

Theorem 3. *For a constraint network to be weakly m-tight at level 3, it needs at least $n(n-1)/2 - 2\lfloor n/3 \rfloor$ when $n = 0, 1 \pmod 3$, or $(n-2)(3n-1)/6$ when $n = 2 \pmod 3$, m-tight binary or ternary constraints.*

3 Tightness Under Directional Consistency

From the results in the previous section, under the concept of k-consistency we can not reduce, by much, the number of m-tight constraints required to predict the k-consistency ensuring global consistency. In this section, we examine tightness under directional consistency [2].

Directionally Relevant Constraints. Given an ordering of variables, a relevant constraint on x with respect to a set of variables Y is *directionally relevant* if it involves x and only variables before x.

Definition 1. *A constraint network is* directionally weakly m-tight at level k *with respect to an order of variables iff for every set of variables $Y = \{x_1, \cdots, x_l\}$ ($l : k..n - 1$) and a new variable x, there exists an m-tight directionally relevant constraint on x.*

Directional weak m-tightness does not require a constraint to be tight on *each* of its variables. It is related to global consistency in the following way.

Theorem 4. *Given a network, let r be the maximum arity of its constraints. If it is directionally weakly m-tight at level $(m+1)(r-1)+1$ and is strongly directionally $(m+1)(r-1)+1$-consistent, then it is strongly directionally n-consistent.*

The next result presents a sufficient condition for a network to be directionally weakly m-tight.

Theorem 5. *A network of arbitrary constraints is directionally weakly m-tight at level k with respect to a variable ordering if for all $i > k$, there are at least $i - k$ directionally relevant binary constraints which are m-tight on the i_{th} variable.*

4 Dually Adaptive Consistency

One main purpose of our characterization of weakly m-tight network is to help identify a consistency condition under which a solution of a network can be found without backtracking (i.e., efficiently).

Motivated by the idea of adaptive consistency [2], we propose a concept of dually adaptive consistency which makes use of both topological structure and the semantics of a constraint network. In the following definition, the *width* of a variable with respect to a variable ordering is the number of the directionally relevant constraints on it.

Given a network, a variable ordering, and a variable x, let $DR(x)$ be the set of directionally relevant constraints on x and S be the union of the scopes of the constraints of $DR(x)$. The constraints of $DR(x)$ are *consistent* on x, if and only if for any consistent instantiation $\bar{a}$ of $S - \{x\}$, there exists $u \in D_x$ such that $(\bar{a}, u)$ satisfies all the constraints in $DR(x)$.

Definition 2. *Given a constraint network and an ordering of its variables, let c_x be one of the tightest directionally relevant constraints on x and m_x be its tightness. It is* dually adaptively consistent *if and only if*

1) for any variable x whose width is not greater than m_x, the directionally relevant constraints on it are consistent, and

2) for any variable x whose width is greater than m_x, c_x is consistent with every other m_x directionally relevant constraints on x.

Lemma 1. *Given a number m and a collection of sets $\{E_1, \cdots, E_l\}$, assume there is a set E among them such that $|E| \leq m$. $\bigcap_{i \in 1..l} E_i \neq \emptyset$ iff the intersection of E and every other m sets is not empty.*

This lemma results in the result that a dually adaptive consistent constraint network is globally consistent.

Theorem 6. *Given a constraint network and an ordering of its variables, it is strongly directionally n-consistent if it is dually adaptively consistent.*

Proof. We only need to prove that the network is adaptively consistent: For any variable x, its directionally relevant constraints $DR(x)$ are consistent on x. Let S be the variables involved in $DR(x)$. Consider any consistent instantiation $\bar{a}$ of $S - \{x\}$. We show that there exists $u \in D_x$ such that $(\bar{a}, u)$ satisfies constraints in $DR(x)$. Let l be the number of constraints in $DR(x)$, and let c_x be one of the tightest constraint in $DR(x)$ with tightness m_x. For any constraint $c_i \in DR(x)(i : 1..l)$, let $\bar{a}$'s support set on x under c_i be E_i. It is sufficient to show $\bigcap_{i \in 1..l} E_i \neq \emptyset$. We know c_x is consistent with every other m_x constraints. Hence, E_x, $\bar{a}$'s support set under c_x, intersects with every other m_x support sets of $\bar{a}$. By the set intersection lemma, $\bigcap_{i \in 1..l} E_i \neq \emptyset$. □

Improving Bucket Elimination on Constraint Networks. For a variable x, the fact that we enforce all its directionally relevant constraints consistent on x, is described as joining (a Database operation of *natural join*) all the constraints (taken as relations) and projecting away x (and thus eliminating x) in bucket elimination. We know that both time and space complexity of the join operation is exponential to the number of constraints involved. In terms of dually adaptive consistency, if one of the constraints c_x is m-tight and m is smaller than the number of constraints of concern, we only need to join c_x and every other m constraints and then project away x. An extreme case is that if a constraint c_x is 1-tight, it is sufficient to join c_x and every other constraint of concern, and then project away x.

5 Conclusion

The theme of this paper is to study the impact of the tightness of constraints on the global consistency of a network. Specifically, the tightness of the constraints determines the level of local consistency sufficient to guarantee global consistency. Under the concept of k-consistency, to determine the local consistency ensuring global consistency, we show that it is sufficient to consider only some of the binary constraints. We also show that a weakly tight constraint network *does* need a significant number of constraints to be tight. After studying directional consistency, we propose a new type of consistency – dually adaptive consistency – which considers not only the topological structure, but also the tightness of the constraints in a network. Based on this concept, only the tightest (in a local sense) constraints or the widths of variables, depending on which are smaller, determine the local consistency ensuring global consistency.

Dually adaptive consistency immediately leads to a more efficient version of *bucket elimination* algorithm for constraint networks [1], and may be helpful where the heuristics from bucket elimination have shown some promise (e.g., [3]). Having shown that theoretically there is a close relationship between the tightness of constraints and global consistency, in the future, we will explore whether the tightness of constraints can play greater role in solving practical constraint networks.

Acknowledgement

I thank Fengming Dong, Angela Glover, Georg Ringwelski, and other members at 4C for their helpful comments on an earlier draft of this paper.

References

1. R. Dechter. Bucket elimination: A unifying framework for reasoning. *Artificial Intelligence*, 113:41–85, 1999.
2. R. Dechter and J. Pearl. Network-based heuristics for constraint satisfaction problems. *Artificial Intelligence*, 34:1–38, 1987.
3. J. Larrosa and R. Dechter. Boosting search with variable elimination in constraint optimization and constraint satisfaction problems. *Constraints*, 8(3):303–326, 2003.
4. P. van Beek and R. Dechter. Constraint tightness and looseness versus local and global consistency. *Journal of The ACM*, 44(4):549–566, 1997.
5. Yuanlin Zhang and Roland H. C. Yap. Consistency and set intersection. In *Proceedings of IJCAI-03*, pages 263–268, Acapulco, Mexico, 2003. IJCAI Inc.

Concurrent Dynamic Backtracking for Distributed CSPs

Roie Zivan and Amnon Meisels

Department of Computer Science, Ben-Gurion University of the Negev
Beer-Sheva, 84-105, Israel
{zivanr,am}@cs.bgu.ac.il

Abstract. A distributed concurrent search algorithm for distributed constraint satisfaction problems (*DisCSPs*) is presented. Concurrent search algorithms are composed of multiple search processes (*SPs*) that operate concurrently and scan non-intersecting parts of the global search space. Search processes are generated *dynamically*, started by the initializing agent, and by any number of agents during search. In the proposed, $ConcDB$, algorithm, all search processes perform dynamic backtracking (DB). As a consequence of DB, a search space scanned by one search process can be found unsolvable by a different search process. This enhances the efficiency of the $ConcDB$ algorithm. Concurrent search is an asynchronous distributed algorithm and is shown to be faster than asynchronous backtracking (ABT). The network load of $ConcDB$ is also much lower than that of ABT.

1 Introduction

Distributed constraint satisfaction problems (*DisCSPs*) are composed of agents, each holding its local constraints network, that are connected by constraints among variables of different agents.

A search procedure for a consistent assignment of all agents in a $DisCSP$, is a distributed algorithm. All agents cooperate in search for a globally consistent solution. An intuitive way to make the distributed search process on DisCSPs efficient is to enable agents to compute concurrently. Concurrent computation by agents can result in a shorter overall time of computation for finding a solution.

One method for achieving concurrency in search on Distributed CSPs is to enable agents to cooperate in a single backtrack procedure. In order to avoid the waiting time of a single backtrack search, agents compute assignments to their variables asynchronously. In asynchronous backtracking algorithms, agents assign their variables without waiting to receive information about all relevant assignments of other agents [Yokoo2000,Silaghi2002]. In order to make asynchronous backtracking correct and complete, all agents share a static order of variables and the algorithm keeps data structures for *Nogoods* that are discovered during search (cf. [Bessiere et. al.2001]).

In [Zivan and Meisels2004] we presented a different way of achieving concurrency for search. In order to achieve shorter overall runtime, concurrent search runs multiple search processes on a *DisCSP*. All agents participate in all search processes, assigning their variables and checking for consistency with constraining agents. All search processes are performed asynchronously by all agents, thereby achieving concurrency of computation and shortening the overall time of run for finding a global solution [Zivan and Meisels2004]. Agents and variables are ordered randomly on each of the search processes, diversifying the sampling of the search space. Agents generate and terminate search processes dynamically during the run of the algorithm, thus creating a distributed asynchronous algorithm. The degree of concurrency during search changes dynamically and enables automatic load balancing [Zivan and Meisels2004].

The present paper proposes Concurrent Dynamic Backtracking $ConcDB$ that performs dynamic backtracking [Ginsberg1993] on each of its concurrent sub-search spaces. Since search processes are dynamically generated by $ConcDB$, the performance of backjumping in one search space can indicate that other search spaces are unsolvable. This feature, combined with the random ordering of agents in each search process, enables early termination of search processes discovered by DB to be unsolvable.

For the principles, and a detailed description of *Concurrent Search* along with examples of the algorithm run and dynamic splitting, we encourage the reader to refer to [Zivan and Meisels2004,Zivan and Meisels2004b]. The $ConcDB$ algorithm is described in section 2. For a correctness and completeness proof for $ConcDB$, the reader is referred to [Zivan and Meisels2004b]. Section 3 presents an experimental comparison of $ConcDB$ to asynchronous backtracking (ABT) [Yokoo2000,Bessiere et. al.2001]. For all measures of concurrent performance, from number of steps through number of concurrent constraints checks, to number of messages sent, $ConcDB$ outperforms *ABT* and its advantage is more pronounced for harder problem instances. For all measures of performance, run-time and network load, the difference between $ConcDB$ and *ABT grows with message delay*. In other words, $ConcDB$ is more robust to message delay than asynchronous backtracking (see also [Fernandez et. al.2002]).

2 Concurrent Dynamic Backtracking

The backjumping method that is used in the Concurrent Dynamic Backtracking algorithm is based on $Dynamic\ Backtracking$ [Ginsberg1993,Bessiere et. al.2001]. Each agent that removes a value from its current domain stores the partial assignment that caused the removal of the value. This stored partial assignment is called an *eliminating explanation* by [Ginsberg1993]. When the current domain of an agent empties, the agent constructs a backtrack message from the union of all assignments in its stored removal explanations. The union of all removal explanations is an inconsistent partial assignment, or a *Nogood* [Ginsberg1993,Bessiere et. al.2001]. The backtrack message is sent to the agent which is the owner of the most recently assigned variable in the $Nogood$.

In $ConcDB$, a short $nogood$ can belong to multiple search spaces, all of which contain no solution and are thus unsolvable. In order to terminate the corresponding search processes, an agent that receives a backtrack message performs the following procedure:

- detect the SP to which the received CPA either belongs or was split from.
- check if the SP was split.

– if it was:
      • send an *unsolvable* message to the *next_agent* of the related CPA.
      • choose a new unique ID for the CPA received and its related SP.
      • continue the search using the SP and CPA with the new ID.
  – check if there are other SPs which contain the inconsistent partial assignment received, send corresponding *unsolvable* messages and resume the search on them with newly generated $CPAs$.

The change of ID makes the process independent of whether the backtrack message included the *original CPA* or one of its split offsprings.

The **unsolvable** message used by the $ConcDB$ algorithm, is a message not used in general *Concurrent Search*, which indicates an unsolvable sub-search-space. An agent that receives an *unsolvable* message performs the following operations for the unsolvable SP and each of the SPs split from it:

  – mark the SP as unsolvable.
  – send an *unsolvable* message which carries the ID of the SP to the agent to whom the related CPA was last sent.

Agents that receive a CPA first check if the related SP was not marked *unsolvable*. If so, they terminate the CPA and its related SP.

3 Experimental Evaluation

The common approach in evaluating the performance of distributed algorithms is to compare two independent measures of performance - time, in the form of steps of computation [Lynch1997,Yokoo2000], and communication load, in the form of the total number of messages sent [Lynch1997]. Comparing the number of concurrent steps of computation of the search algorithms for DisCSPs, measures their time of run. Concurrent steps of computation, in systems with no message delay, are counted by a method similar to that of [Lamport1978,Meisels et. al.2002].

An important part of the experimental evaluation is to measure the impact of imperfect communication on the performance of concurrent search. Message delay can change the behavior of distributed search algorithms [Fernandez et. al.2002]. In the presence of concurrent computation, the time of message delays must be added to the total algorithm time *only if no computation was performed concurrently*. To achieve this goal, we use a simulator which counts message delays in terms of computation steps and adds them to the accumulated run-time when no computation is performed concurrently [Zivan and Meisels2004a].

Experiments were conducted on random constraints networks of n variables, k values in each domain, constraints density p_1 and tightness p_2 (cf. [Prosser1996, Smith1996]). All of the experiments were conducted on networks with 15 agents ($n = 15$), 10 values for each variable ($k = 10$) and a value of constraints density $p_1 = 0.7$. The tightness value p_2 is varied between 0.1 and 0.9, to cover all ranges of problem difficulty.

In [Zivan and Meisels2004] we have evaluated the effectiveness of concurrent search by comparing Concurrent Search with different levels of concurrency. The results show conclusively the strong advantage of dynamically increasing the level of concurrency when ever needed during search over a fixed level of concurrency.

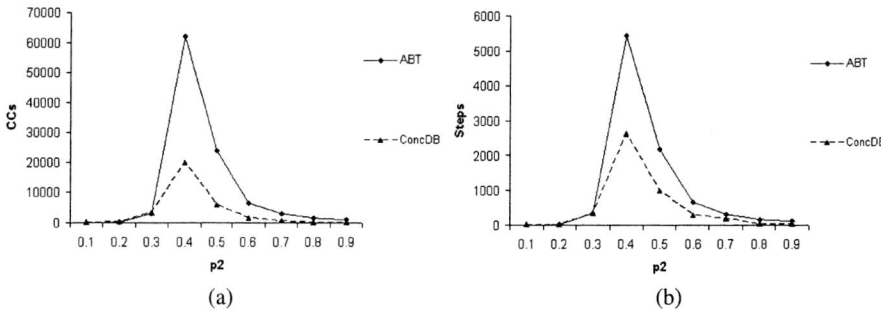

Fig. 1. (a) Number of concurrent constraints checks performed by ConcDB and ABT, (b) Number of concurrent steps for both algorithms.

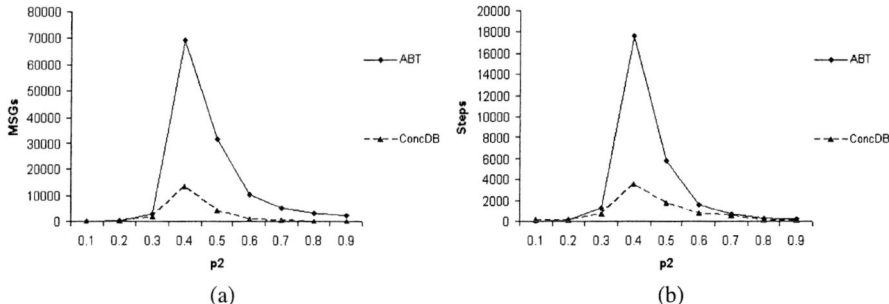

Fig. 2. (a) Total number of messages sent by ConcDB and ABT. (b) Number of logical concurrent steps performed by ConcDB and ABT.

The performance of concurrent dynamic backtracking (*ConcDB*) is compared to asynchronous backtracking (*ABT*) [Yokoo2000]. In *ABT* agents assign their variables asynchronously, and send their assignments in *ok?* messages to other agents to check against constraints. A fixed priority order among agents is used to break conflicts. Agents inform higher priority agents of their inconsistent assignment by sending them the inconsistent partial assignment in a *Nogood* message. In our implementation of *ABT*, the *Nogoods* are resolved and stored according to the method presented in [Bessiere et. al.2001]. Based on Yokoo's suggestions [Yokoo2000] the agents read, in every step, all messages received before performing computation.

Figure 1(a) presents a comparison of the number of concurrent constraints checks performed by *ConcDB* and *ABT*. For the harder problem instances, *ConcDB* outperforms *ABT* by a factor of 4. In figure 1(b), the results are presented by the number of concurrent steps of computation. The smaller factor of difference can be related to the larger amount of local computation *ABT* performs in each step since it reads all the messages which it received up to this step. The full version of the paper [Zivan and Meisels2004b] includes similar results for DisCSPs with lower density ($p_1 = 0.4$). Figure 2(a) presents the total number of messages sent by both algorithms. When it comes to network load the advantage of *ConcDB* is larger (a factor of 5).

Figure 2(b) presents the results of the set of experiments in which the algorithms were run on a system with random message delay. Each message was delayed between 5 to 10 steps of computation. Random message delay degrades the performance of asynchronous backtracking while the effect on $ConcDB$ is minor. The results show a larger factor of difference between the two algorithms.

4 Conclusion

Concurrent search algorithms maintain multiple search processes on non intersecting parts of the global search space of a DisCSP ([Zivan and Meisels2004]). All agents in concurrent search participate in every search process, since each agent holds some variables of the search space. Search processes are dynamically generated by agents in an asynchronous distributed process. Concurrent dynamic backtracking ($ConcDB$) provides an efficient method for several search processes to search concurrently a DisCSP. Dynamic backtracking enables concurrent search an early termination of search processes on sub-spaces which do not lead to a solution. An inconsistent subset can be found in one sub-space and rule out other sub-spaces as unsolvable. In such a case, the search on the obsolete sub-search-spaces is terminated by an elegant procedure which does not affect viable search processes in progress.

The experimental behavior of $ConcDB$ on random DisCSPs clearly indicates its efficiency, compared to algorithms of a single search process like asynchronous backtracking (ABT). Experiments were conducted for a wide range of constraints tightness and in systems with random message delays. In all experiments and for three different measures of performance, $ConcDB$ outperforms ABT by a large margin.

References

[Bessiere et. al.2001] C. Bessiere, A. Maestre and P. Messeguer. Distributed Dynamic Backtracking. *Proc. Workshop on Distributed Constraints, IJCAI-01*, Seattle, 2001.

[Fernandez et. al.2002] C. Fernandez, R. Bejar, B. Krishnamachari, K. Gomes Communication and Computation in Distributed CSP Algorithms. *Proc. Principles and Practice of Constraint Programming, CP-2002*, pp. 664-679, Ithaca NY USA, July, 2002.

[Ginsberg1993] M. L. Ginsberg Dynamic Backtracking. *Artificial Intelligence Research*, vol.1, pp. 25-46, 1993

[Lamport1978] L. Lamport Time, clocks and the ordering of events in a distributed system. *Comm. of ACM*, vol. 21, pp.558-565, 1978.

[Lynch1997] N. A. Lynch. Distributed Algorithms. *Morgan Kaufmann Series*, 1997.

[Meisels et. al.2002] A. Meisels et. al. Comparing performance of Distributed Constraints Processing Algorithms. *Proc. DCR Workshop, AAMAS-2002*, pp. 86-93, Bologna, July, 2002.

[Prosser1996] P. Prosser An empirical study of phase transition in binary constraint satisfaction problems *Artificial Intelligence*, vol. 81, pp. 81-109, 1996.

[Silaghi2002] M.C. Silaghi Asynchronously Solving Problems with Privacy Requirements. *PhD Thesis*,Swiss Federal Institute of Technology (EPFL), 2002.

[Smith1996] B. M. Smith. Locating the phase transition in binary constraint satisfaction problems. In *Artificial Intelligence*, vol. 81, pp. 155-181, 1996.

[Solotorevsky et. al.1996] G. Solotorevsky, E. Gudes and A. Meisels. Modeling and Solving Distributed Constraint Satisfaction Problems (DCSPs). *Constraint Processing-96*, New Hampshire, October 1996.

[Yokoo2000] M. Yokoo. Algorithms for Distributed Constraint Satisfaction: A Review. *Autons Agents Multi-Agent Sys 2000*, vol. 3(2), pp. 198-212, 2000.

[Zivan and Meisels2004] R. Zivan and A. Meisels. Concurrent Backtrack search on DisCSPs. proc. of *FLAIRS 2004*, pp.776-81, Miami-Beach, May 2004.

[Zivan and Meisels2004a] R. Zivan and A. Meisels. Message delay and DisCSP search algorithms. submit to *DCR 2004*, September 2004.

[Zivan and Meisels2004b] R. Zivan and A. Meisels. Concurrent Dynamic Backtracking for DisCSPs. (full version http://www.cs.bgu.ac.il/ zivanr)

Set Variables and Local Search
Abstract

Magnus Ågren

Information Technology, Uppsala University, Box 337, S – 751 05 Uppsala, Sweden
agren@it.uu.se

For some time now, set variables and set constraints have been around in the *Constraint Programming (CP)* area. Most of the popular CP systems of today for global search have features for modelling problems using set variables, i.e., decision variables taking values that are subsets of some universe. Consider, for instance, the work by Gervet[1] and Puget[2].

Many problems have natural models using set variables. Classical examples include the set partitioning problem and the set covering problem. However, such problems also appear frequently as sub-problems in many real-life applications. Examples include airline-crew rostering, tournament scheduling, and time-tabling. To be able to reason about these problems at the higher level that set variables mean may reduce the modelling and solving time and increase the understanding of an application considerably. Since this is already known from global search, we believe that it should be put also in a local search framework.

Local search is becoming more and more popular as an alternative or complement to global search when it comes to tackling hard combinatorial problems. The technique has proven to be very efficient and often outperforms others[3,5].

In recent years, there has been much research on the integration of CP with local search, investigating such concepts as high declarativeness, incrementality, and global constraints. Consider, for instance, the work by Michel and Van Hentenryck[4,5] and Nareyek[6].

This paper introduces set decision variables and set constraints in the local search area. It presents a way of representing set variables in the local search context, where we deal with concepts like transition functions, neighbourhoods, and penalty costs. Furthermore, some common (global) set constraints and their penalty costs are defined. These are then used to provide set-based models for three combinatorial problems, showcasing the benefit of set variables.

---

[1] Carmen Gervet. *Set Intervals in Constraint Logic Programming: Definition and Implementation of a Language*. PhD thesis, Université de Franche-Comté, 1995.

[2] Jean-François Puget. *Finite set intervals*. Workshop on Set Constraints, 1996.

[3] Philippe Galinier and Jin-Kao Hao. *Solving the progressive party problem by local search*. Advances and Trends in Local Search Paradigms for Optimization, 1998.

[4] Laurent Michel and Pascal Van Hentenryck. *Localizer: A modeling language for local search*. Principles and Practice of Constraint Programming – CP 1997, 1997.

[5] Laurent Michel and Pascal Van Hentenryck. *A constraint-based architecture for local search*. OOPSLA'02, 2002.

[6] Alexander Nareyek. *Using global constraints for local search*. DIMACS Workshop on Constraint Programming and Large Scale Discrete Optimization, 1998.

N–Kings for Dynamic Systems

Konstantin Artiouchine[1,2]

[1] CNRS LIX FRE 2653, Ecole Polytechnique, 91128 Palaiseau CEDEX, France
Konstantin.Artiouchine@polytechnique.org
[2] Thales TRT, Domaine de Corbeville, 91404 Orsay CEDEX, France

Abstract. We study the problem of scheduling a set of aircraft in the surtoundings of an airport. Aircraft are subjected to dynamic and spatial constraints and the runway is a single ressource that cannot be simultaneously shared. We elaborate and study a simplified model of the problem: The "$N-$King" problem.

Motivated by an aicraft scheduling problem, we study the situation where kings (aircrafts) on a chessboard have to reach a target square (the runway) within a minimum amount of time. The problem is to find a sequence of moves of K kings on a $N \times N$ chessboard from a given initial layout with the goal to "empty" the board. A king leaves the board when it reaches a target square.

The following constraints have to be satisfied :

- Distance between any pair of kings on the board is at least one.
- A king can be taken off the board at the time step following its arrival onto the target square (marked with a cross on the figure 1).
- Each king on the board **must** move to an adjacent square.
- All moves are compulsory and **simultaneous**.
- All kings must be took off the board in a finite number of steps.

In the optimization variant of the problem we aim to minimize the number of steps required to empty the chessboard. Despite our simplifications, this problem is not trivial even for relatively small instances it is not easy to compute the optimal solution. Note that it can also happen that no move at all is possible (see Figure 2).

 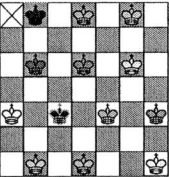

Fig. 1. An instance of the problem **Fig. 2.** Instance without solution

In order to solve this problem we use a CP model mixing both combinatorial and dynamics parts of the problem. Constraints modeling the dynamics are necessary to solve this type of problems because of tight interaction between the combinatorial part of initial problem (i.e. scheduling part) and trajectory determination (i.e. control problem which could be modeled and/or discretized by the means of viability theory[1]).

---

[1] Jean-Pierre Aubin, **Viability Theory**, Birkhäuser, 1991.

Relation Variables
in Qualitative Spatial Reasoning

Sebastian Brand

National Research Institute for Mathematics and Computer Science (CWI)
P.O. Box 94079, 1090 GB, Amsterdam, The Netherlands

Qualitative spatial representation and reasoning (QSR) [1] lends itself well to modelling by constraints. In the standard modelling approach, a spatial object, such as a region, is described by a variable, and the qualitative relation between spatial objects, such as the topological relation between two regions, contributes a constraint. We study here an alternative constraint-based formulation of QSR. In this approach, a spatial object is a constant, and the relation between spatial objects is a variable. We call this the *relation-variable* approach, in contrast to the conventional *relation-constraint* approach.

Although modelling qualitative relations with variables is not original – see [2] for an application to qualitative temporal reasoning – it has practically been ignored in the field of QSR so far. This fact surprises in view of the advantages of this approach. In particular, the following important issues are tackled. **Aspect integration:** Space has several aspects that can be characterised qualitatively, such as topology, size, shape, absolute and relative orientation. These aspects are interdependent, but no convenient canonical representation exists that provides a link. This is in contrast to temporal reasoning, in which the concepts can be defined in terms of time points. **Context embedding:** In practice, spatial reasoning problems are not likely to arise in pure form but embedded into a context. **Systems:** Knowledge in the relation-constraint approach is not stated declaratively but in algorithmic or at best in meta-constraint form. However, typical current constraint solving systems focus on domain reduction, and rarely provide facilities to easily access and modify the constraint network.

The relation-variable approach to modelling QSR responds to these points. It results in a plain, single-level constraint satisfaction problem. Aspect integration is facilitated by stating inter-aspect constraints, and embedding means simply stating additional context constraints. The resulting problem can be solved by any constraint solver that supports extensionally defined constraints.

We study diverse instances of QSR problems, such as aspect integration and evolution of spatial scenarios. The modelling task and the implementation is greatly simplified by using relation variables.

References

1. A. G. Cohn and S. M. Hazarika. Qualitative spatial representation and reasoning: An overview. *Fundamenta Informaticae*, 46(1-2):1–29, 2001.
2. E. P. K. Tsang. The consistent labeling problem in temporal reasoning. In K. S. H. Forbus, editor, *Proc. of 6th National Conference on Artificial Intelligence (AAAI'87)*, pages 251–255. AAAI Press, 1987.

Synchronous, Asynchronous and Hybrid Algorithms for DisCSP*

Ismel Brito

Institut d'Investigació en Intel.ligència Artificial
Consejo Superior de Investigationes Científicas
Campus UAB, 08193 Bellaterra, Spain
ismel@iiia.csic.es

There is some debate around the efficiency of synchronous and asynchronous backtracking algorithms for solving DisCSP. The general opinion was that asynchronous algorithms were more efficient than the synchronous ones, because of their higher concurrency. In this work we continue this line of research, and we study the performance of three different procedures, one synchronous, one asynchronous and one hybrid, for solving sparse, medium and dense binary random DisCSP. The synchronous algorithm is *SCBJ*, a distributed version of the Conflict-Based Backjumping (*CBJ*) algorithm. The asynchronous algorithm is the standard *ABT* [2] enhanced with some heuristic. The hybrid algorithm is *ABT-Hyb*, a novel *ABT*-like algorithm, where some synchronization is introduced to avoid resending redundant messages. *ABT-Hyb* behaves like *ABT* when no backtracking is performed. However, when an agent has to backtrack, it sends a *Back* message and enters in a *waiting* state until receiving: a message that allows it to have a value consistent with its agent view, an *Info* message from the receiver of the last *Back* message or a *Stop* message informing that the problem has no solution. During the *waiting* state, the agent accept any received *Info* message and rejects as obsolete any received *Back* message. No matter the synchronous backtracking, *ABT-Hyb* inherits the good theoretical properties of *ABT*: it is sound, complete and terminates.

In this work, we provide a formal protocol for processing messages by packets, in *ABT* and *ABT-Hyb*, instead messages one by one. On *SCBJ* we also propose two approximations for the minimum domain heuristic. From preliminary results, we observe that *ABT-Hyb* clearly improves over *ABT*, in both computation effort and communication costs. Comparing *SCBJ* with *ABT-Hyb*, we observe that *SCBJ* always requires less messages than *ABT-Hyb*. Considering computation effort, *SCBJ* requires more effort than *ABT-Hyb* for binary random problems. However, when enhanced with minimum domain approximation for dynamic variable ordering, *SCBJ* is the best algorithm in terms computation effort and in number of messages exchanged.

An extended version of this abstract is available at [1].

References

1. Brito I., Meseguer P. Synchronous, Asynchronous and Hybrid Algorithms for DisCSP *available at* http://www.iiia.csic.es/~ismel/
2. Yokoo M., Durfee E.H., Ishida T., Kuwabara K. The Distributed Constraint Satisfaction Problem: Formalization and Algorithms. *IEEE Trans. Knowledge and Data Engineering* **10**, 1998.

---

* This research is supported by the REPLI project TIC-2002-04470-C03-03.

Long-Term Learning for Algorithm Control*

Tom Carchrae

Cork Constraint Computation Centre
University College Cork, Ireland
t.carchrae@4c.ucc.ie

Despite both the commercial and academic success of optimization technology and specifically constraint programming, using the technology still requires significant expertise. For non-trivial applications the quality of a system still has much to do with the quality of the person that implemented it. We investigate algorithm control techniques aimed at achieving strong scheduling performance using off-the-shelf algorithms without requiring significant human expertise. Rather than building knowledge-intensive models relating algorithm performance to problem features, we base the control decisions on the evolution of solution quality over time. Such an approach is crucial to our goal of the reduction of expertise.

The aim is to find the best solution possible to a problem instance within a given time limit T. In [1] we introduced the idea of low-knowledge algorithm control and explored two approaches to algorithm control. The most promising approach is a *switching* paradigm, where control decisions allocate computational resources to each algorithm over a series of iterations such that the total run-time is T. Each algorithm is run, one after another, passing the best known solution to the next run. Reinforcement learning is used during the solving to allocate the run-time of each run of an algorithm.

The algorithm control problem can be viewed as an optimization problem where we want to maximize the improvement in solution cost over time. We wish to discover the optimal time allocation to algorithms during each iteration. So far, we have only looked at online learning so that on each problem the learning starts from scratch. The focus of our current work is to see how effectively we can utilize all of the past solving experience for more effective control. Our approach is to learn the optimal allocation, by brute force, for a set of problem instances. We will then use these 'optimal' examples to train a pattern matching algorithm, such as a neural network. We expect to discover trends which can be used to make control decisions that will maximize the improvement in solution cost.

References

1. Carchrae, T., Beck, J.: Low-knowledge algorithm control. In: Proceedings of the Nineteenth National Conference on Artificial Intelligence (AAAI-04). (2004)

---

* This work has received support from SFI under Grant 00/PI.1/C075, the Embark Initiative of IRCSET under Grant PD2002/21 and ILOG, SA.

Solution Extraction with the "Critical Path" in Graphplan-Based Optimal Temporal Planning

Tien Ba Dinh

School of Computing and Engineering
University of Huddersfield, UK
t.b.dinh@hud.ac.uk

In AI planning, given the initial state, the goal state and a set of actions, a solution of the problem is a sequence of actions which takes the initial state to the goal state, i.e. a plan. The field has been studied and significantly improved since the past few years. Many state of the art planning systems, such as Graphplan, FF, GP-CSP, TGP, TPSYS, TP4, TLPlan, STAN, LPGP, have shown their good performance on different planning domains. Scientists continue studying to deal with bigger and more complex planning domains which include the explicit modelling of time, resources.

In the search for optimal solutions to planning problems, Graphplan, introduced by Blum and Furst [1], is known as one of the best approaches. Since the introduction in 1995, it has been the framework in many optimal planning systems, such as GP-CSP, TGP, TPSYS.

I am developing the planning system, CPPlanner, which based on the Graphplan approach to find an optimal solution in terms of time (*makespan*) for temporal planning domains. Unlike TGP and TPSYS, in CPPlanner, the action representation has been extended to deal with effects which can happen at any time during their execution. As other Graphplan-based planners, it consists of two phases: the graph expansion and the solution extraction. The graph expansion advances the graph in time until all the sub goals appear and are pair wise non-mutex. Then, the solution extraction is called to look for a solution. If it fails to find a solution, the planner runs the expansion phase again to move to the next possible timepoint. Otherwise, the planner terminates with an optimal solution.

The main contribution of our planning system is the use of "critical paths" in the solution extraction phase. At first, the planner retrieves all the paths which start from a proposition in the initial state to a sub goal in the current state. These paths are used as "critical paths" candidates. The planner chooses these candidates one by one to act as the "critical path" for the search. This helps to prune irrelevant branches in the search tree early. In addition, the solution extraction uses the time as a bound and the conflict-directed backjumping to speed up the backtracking search.

References

1. A. L. Blum and M. L. Furst, "Fast planning through Planning Graph Analysis," *Artificial Intelligence*, 90:281-300, 1997.

Machine Learning for Portfolio Selection Using Structure at the Instance Level*

Cormac Gebruers[1] and Alessio Guerri[2]

[1] Cork Constraint Computation Centre, University College Cork, Cork, Ireland
c.gebruers@4c.ucc.ie

[2] DEIS, University of Bologna, Viale Risorgimento 2, 40136 Bologna, Italy
aguerri@deis.unibo.it

Many combinatorial optimization problems do not have a clear structure, may present many side constraints, and may include subproblems. In addition, different instances within the same domain can have different structure and characteristics. As a consequence it is commonplace that a single algorithm is not the best performer on every problem instance. We consider an algorithm portfolio approach to try to help us select the best algorithm for a given problem instance. Our purpose is twofold: firstly, to show that *structure at the instance level* is tightly connected to algorithm performance, and secondly to demonstrate that different machine learning and modelling methodologies, specifically Decision Trees (DT), Case Based Reasoning (CBR) and Multinomial Logistic Regression (MLR), can be used to perform effective algorithm portfolio selection. We test our claims by applying the above mentioned techniques to a large set of instances of the Bid Evaluation Problem (BEP) in Combinatorial Auctions. A BEP consists of a *Winner Determination Problem* (a well-known NP-hard problem best solved by a IP-based approach), and additional temporal information and precedence constraints (which favour a CP-based approach). We solved the BEP instances using a set of different algorithms. We observed that two algorithms; one IP-based and the other a hybrid combining both CP and IP elements, outperformed all the others on all instances. Hence we divided the instances into 2 classes based on which of these 2 algorithms solves them best. In order to perform our analysis we extract a set of structure-based features, that are cheap to determine, from each instance . We apply the Machine Learning methodologies using the extracted features as input data and the best algorithms as prediction classes. Table 1 shows the prediction rates we obtain. They are compared to Weighted Random (WR), a prediction technique based on the frequency distribution of the solution strategy where the strategy that is best most often is suggested most often and so on. The results in Table 1 suggest that, in the context of the BEP, we are able to build a practical and useful system that can often select the best algorithm. Using a small number of features that are cheap to extract means the overhead of this approach is small. Furthermore, adding new algorithm choices doesn't increase the number of features required to choose among the algorithms. Thus, the system is flexible and extendible.

Table 1. Summary of results.

	DT	CBR	MLR	WR
Prediction rate	90%	85%	79%	49%

---

* This work has received support from Science Foundation Ireland under Grant 00/PI.1/C075. This work was partially supported by the SOCS project, funded by the CEC, contract IST-2001-32530.

Local Search with Maximal Independent Sets

Joel M. Gompert

Constraint Systems Laboratory
University of Nebraska-Lincoln
jgompert@cse.unl.edu

When solving Constraint Satisfaction Problems (CSPs), it is desirable to find multiple solutions, or to find solutions that are robust, allowing us to modify the values of variables without breaking the solution. Furthermore, we would like to be able to represent these multiple solutions in a compact manner. We present a method for improving the performance of, and solutions returned by, stochastic local search using *maximal independent sets*[1] of the constraint graph. Given an independent set, this information can be used to significantly speed up the process of solving a CSP by reducing the search space. The CSP is partitioned into two sets of variables I and $\bar{I}$, where I is a maximal independent set of the constraint graph. In this way, search is concentrated only on the variables of $\bar{I}$, reducing the search space by a factor exponential in the size of I. Also this technique can provide multiple solutions in a compact form with no extra cost, since if we find a set of valid domain values for each variable in I, every element of the Cartesian product of these sets is a solution to the CSP. We focus on exploiting this information in local search. This technique is limited to low-density graphs, since dense graphs are less likely to contain a large independent set. The resulting solutions are robust with respect to the variables in the independent set. We compare the technique with WalkSAT, as defined for CSPs by [2], on low-density random CSP instances generated according to model B, with 16 variables, domain size 8, tightness 0.3 and density 0.1. The average CPU run-time for WalkSAT was 96.5 seconds, while the average for WalkSAT_IS was 0.36 seconds. Also, while WalkSAT returns one solution, the average number of solutions returned by WalkSAT_IS per instance was 47,536,305 solutions This is a dramatic improvement in performance, as well as in the number of solutions returned. This technique falls in the category of algorithms exploiting backdoor variables [3]. A related technique is the cycle-cutset technique [2]. Related work on SAT problems can be found in [4]. Future work will involve a wider range of experiments. Also we plan to perform a comparison with the cycle-cutset technique.

Acknowledgments. This research is supported by NSF CAREER Award #0133568.

References

1. Boppana, R., Halldórsson, M.M.: Approximating maximum independent sets by excluding subgraphs. In: 2nd Scandinavian Workshop on Algorithm Theory. Volume 447. (1990) 13–25
2. Dechter, R.: Constraint Processing. Morgan Kaufmann (2003)
3. Williams, R., Gomes, C.P., Selman, B.: Backdoors to typical case complexity. In: Artificial Intelligence. (2003)
4. Kautz, H., McAllester, D., Selman, B.: Exploiting variable dependency in local search. Poster session abstract, IJCAI (1997)

---

[1] We used the CliqueRemoval algorithm [1], which executes in linear-time.

A Dynamic Restart Strategy for Randomized BT Search

Venkata Praveen Guddeti

Constraint Systems Laboratory, University of Nebraska-Lincoln
vguddeti@cse.unl.edu

Local search (LS) and multi-agent-based search (ERA [1]) are stochastic and incomplete procedures for solving a Constraint Satisfaction Problem (CSP). Their performance is seriously undermined by local optima and deadlocks, respectively. Although complete, backtrack (BT) search suffers from thrashing and a high degree of unpredictability in its run-time even within the same problem domain. Further, when the problem is large, the completeness of BT cannot be guaranteed in practice. Gomes et al. [2] proposed to use randomization and rapid restarts (RRR) to overcome the heavy tail behavior of BT. RRR requires the specification of a cutoff value determined from an overall profile of the cost of search for solving the problem. When no such profile is known, the cutoff value is chosen by trial-and-error. Walsh [3] proposed the strategy Randomization and Geometric Restart (RGR), which does not rely on a cost profile but determines the cutoff value as a function of a constant parameter and the number of variables in the problem. Neither RRR nor RGR takes into account the intermediate results of search (i.e., across restarts). We propose an improved restart strategy, Randomization and *Dynamic* Geometric Restarts (RDGR), which dynamically adapts the value of the cutoff parameter to the results of the search process. This is done by geometrically increasing the cutoff value for the following restart only when the quality of the current best solution is improved upon. We empirically evaluate the performance of RDGR by comparing it against a deterministic BT with various ordering heuristics, local search, ERA, and RGR in the context of a real-world resource allocation problem [4]. Our experiments show that, for the same execution time, RDGR always outperforms RGR in terms of percentage of test runs and yields more stable results. Our results can be summarized as follows (where $\succ$ denotes algorithm dominance): On tight but solvable instances, ERA $\succ$ RDGR $\succ$ RGR $\succ$ BT $\succ$ LS; and on over-constrained instances, RDGR $\succ$ RGR $\succ$ BT $\succ$ LS $\succ$ ERA. We are currently validating our findings on randomly generated problems. We will also use the insight gained from the distinction between tight (but solvable) and over-constrained problem instances uncovered in our case-study to build new hybrid search strategies. This work is supported by NSF grants #EPS-0091900 and CAREER #0133568. The experiments were conducted utilizing the Research Computing Facility of UNL.

References

1. Liu, J., Jing, H., Tang, Y.: Multi-agent oriented constraint satisfaction. Artificial Intelligence **136** (2002) 101–144
2. Gomes, C.P., Selman, B., Kautz, H.: Boosting combinatorial search through randomization. In: AAAI 98. (1998) 431–437
3. Walsh, T.: Search in a small world. In: IJCAI 99. (1999) 1172–1177
4. Lim, R., Guddeti, P., Choueiry, B.: An Interactive System for Hiring and Managing Graduate Teaching Assistants. In: Prestigious Applications of Intelligent Systems (ECAI 04). (2004)

A BDD-Based Approach to Interactive Configuration

Tarik Hadzic

Department of Innovation, IT University of Copenhagen, Denmark
tarik@itu.dk

Configuration problems emerged as a research topic in the late 1980s as the result of a manufacturing shift from mass-production to mass-customization. *Interactive configuration* is an important application area where a user interactively tailors a product (a car, a PC, a device driver,...) to his specific needs using a supporting program called the *configurator*. Each step in user-configurator interaction includes a user selecting a setting for some specific component or property of his product, and the configurator calculating a list of valid choices for the other unspecified components of the product. The configurator's calculation of valid choices should satisfy the following requirements:

- Any value that can be extended to a valid product specification should be included in the list of valid choices (i.e., we can specify any valid product specification).
- Valid choices should contain only those values that could be extended to a valid specification (i.e., the user will never be forced to backtrack).
- The configurator's response time should be fast enough to provide a truly interactive user experience.

Most of the formalisms describing configuration problems come from the CSP framework. However, all general CSP solving techniques have exponential time complexity and they are not able to deliver on all three requirements listed above. The way around this complexity barrier is in the *compilation* of the original problem as suggested in [2].

Our approach is to compile the original configuration problem *offline* to a structure called Binary Decision Diagrams (BDDs) [1], and to perform online interaction using that structure. We are providing efficient online algorithms that are polynomial in the size of the resulting BDD. Initial experimental results indicate that small BDD representations can be obtained for large search spaces.

In the future, we hope to generate more experimental results to evaluate our approach, and to combine it with existing CSP techniques.

References

1. Bryant, R.: Graph-based algorithms for boolean function manipulation. IEEE Transactions on Computers (1986) 35:677–691
2. Dechter, R., Pearl, J.: Tree Clustering for Constraint Networks. Artificial Intelligence (1989) 38:353–366

Extending Super-solutions*

Emmanuel Hebrard

Cork Constraint Computation Center, University College Cork, Ireland
e.hebrard@4c.ucc.ie

Super solutions, introduced first for SAT problems in [1], are solutions in which, if a small number of variables lose their values, we are guaranteed to be able to repair the solution with only a few changes. In this paper, we stress the need to extend the super-solution framework along several dimensions to make it more useful practically.

For instance, consider the jobshop scheduling problem (jsp). A jsp involves a set of jobs (sequences of activities) and a set of machines. The objective is to schedule the jobs such that no machine is required by two activities that overlap, and the makespan is minimized. A jsp can be formulated as a CSP, with one variable for each activity, and a domain size equal to the makespan minus its duration. To find the minimal makespan, one starts with the makespan equal to a lower bound and increase it till a solution exists.

The first figure represents a $(1, 0)$-super-solution of a jsp with 4 jobs and 4 machines. Bars are activities, organized in jobs. Their length are proportional to their duration and colors correspond to machines.

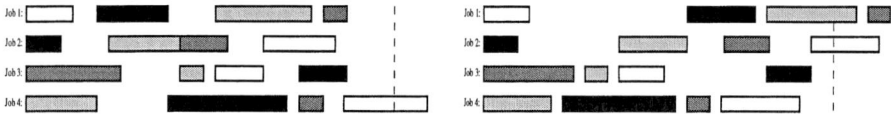

With a small increase in the makespan, we observe that a super-solution for a jsp contains more slacks between activities, making it more robust. However, this may not be completely satisfactory. Indeed, the values are time points, the breakages may not be known till we attempt to execute the job, and so any repair to the schedule must be restricted to future time points. The last figure shows a super-solution with this restriction. The dashed lines correspond to the optimal makespan, there is of course a trade-off between robustness and optimality. Since the jsp involves temporal constraints it is worth noticing that the notion of *weak controllability* [2] relates closely to our work.

There are a number of such improvements upon classical super-solution that we can gather from our knowledge of the problem. For instance, some machines may be reliable, or some may be more costly to repair, one would then restrict the break-set and repair-set accordingly. Moreover, the slacks should be linked to the duration for repairing a particular machine, or to the expected delay of an activity.

References

1. M. Ginsberg, A. Parkes, and A. Roy. Supermodels and robustness. In *Proceedings AAAI'98*, pages 334–339, Madison WI, 1998.
2. T.Vidal and H.Fargier. Contingent durations in temporal csps: from consistency to controllabilities. In *TIME'97*, Daytona Beach, USA, 1997.

---

* The author is supported by Science Foundation Ireland and an ILOG grant.

Choosing Efficient Representations of Abstract Variables

Christopher Jefferson

AI Group, Department of Computer Science
University of York, UK
caj@cs.york.ac.uk

Constraint programming is a powerful and general purpose tool which is used to solve many useful real world problems. The *constraint satisfaction problem* (CSP) is to assign values to variables such that all constraints among them are satisfied and, potentially, some objective is optimal. The process of transforming an abstract specification of a problem into an efficient CSP (known as modelling) is unfortunately more an art than a science at present and must be learnt by years of experience. This prevents constraint programming from being truly widespread. Even among experts the tradeoffs involved in the various modelling decisions are sometimes poorly understood.

Of the decisions that must be made while modelling a problem, one of the most important is how to represent high level constructs such as sets, functions and relations as CSP variables. Work in this area includes how to implement most efficiently a particular transformation to sets [1] and multisets [5]. The more general problem of choosing among a set of different transformations has been investigated by Hnich [3] for functions, and Hnich et al. [4] for permutations.

To understand further the modelling process, we are working on CONJURE, an automatic modelling system [2], which will formalise the methods used by expert modellers. Within this framework, we are studying the most influential of these decisions in the presence of arbitrarily nested variables and arbitrarily complex constraints.CONJURE is designed to generate a large number of CSPs, some of which are more effective than others, so it is necessary to rank them. This goal is being achieved by developing methods of comparing and categorising transformation choices, and comparing them to the theoretically best choices under various metrics such as memory requirement and size of search tree. Among the results obtained so far are a set of sufficient conditions for transformations to perform as well as the best possible in terms of search size.

References

1. Gervet C.: Constraint Logic Programming with Finite Set Domains. *Proceedings of the International Logical Programming Symposium, 1994*
2. Frisch A., Jefferson C., Martínez Heránndez B. and Miguel I.: *The Rules of Constraint Modelling*. APES Technical Report 85
3. Hnich, B.: *Function Variables for Constraint Programming*. Phd Thesis, Uppsala University, 2004
4. Hnich, B., Smith, B.M. and Walsh T.: Dual Modelling of Permutation and Injection Problems. *Journal of Artifical Intelligence Research, volumne 21*
5. Walsh, T.: Consistency and Propagation with Multiset Constraints: A Formal Viewpoint. *Proceedings of CP-2003*

A Hypergraph Separator Based Variable Ordering Heuristic for Solving Real World SAT

Wei Li

University of Waterloo, Waterloo, Canada
w22li@math.uwaterloo.ca

Problem structure has been used to guide the variable ordering heuristic in backtracking search since [1]. Recent experimental results show that guiding the variable ordering heuristic using tree decompositions can improve the performance of SAT and CSP solvers. Huang and Darwiche's [2] variable ordering heuristic uses a Dtree, a static binary tree decomposition, to compute the variable group ordering. Since the Dtree has to be constructed before search, the pre-established variable groupings never change during the execution of the solving. Boolean Constraint Propagation (BCP) is the look-ahead strategy for all of the cutting-edge SAT solvers. Because long implication chains exist in real world instances and a large number of variables on the implication chains can be instantiated after making a relatively small number of decisions, the internal structure of real world instances often changes dramatically in different parts of the search tree.

In this paper, we use a dynamic decomposition method based on hypergraph separators. A separator of a hypergraph H is a set of hyper-edges whose removal chops H into disjoint sub-hypergraphs whose sizes stand in some sought relation. Finding hypergraph separators naturally leads to a divide-and-conquer strategy. We report our effort of using hypergraph separator decomposition to guide the variable ordering of a SAT solver dynamically, which includes (i) highly ranked variables are added to the current separator dynamically; (ii) various subproblem ordering heuristics are tried; and (iii) hypergraph separators are generated dynamically during backtracking search rather than statically prior to search. Our primary focus is to achieve speedups on large real world satisfiability problems. We combined the state-of-the-art SAT solver zChaff [3] with hypergraph separator decomposition and tested it on SAT 2002 competition benchmarks. Our results show that the new solver often outperforms both the regular zChaff and the zChaff integrated with Dtree decomposition in solving real-world problems. Furthermore, the new solver solved more hard instances than the Dtree decomposition within a given cutoff time limit.

References

1. E. C. Freuder. A sufficient condition for backtrack-bounded search. *J. ACM*, 32:755–761, 1985.
2. J. Huang and A. Darwiche. A structure-based variable ordering heuristic for SAT. In *IJCAI-03*, pages 1167–1172, 2003.
3. zChaff. http://www.ee.princeton.edu/~chaff/zchaff.php

Exploiting Symmetries via Permutations for PC Board Manufacturing

Roland Martin

Technical University Darmstadt, 64283 Darmstadt, Germany
martin@algo.informatik.tu-darmstadt.de

Our version of the PC board manufacturing problem (originated from a cooperation with Philips/Assembléon, Netherlands) consists of two subproblems:(1) determining the setup of the mounting machine in terms of assigning component types to the individual worktables of the machine and (2) find a distribution of the mounting tasks to the individual worktables based on the setup of these worktables. This means a mounting task can be assigned to a worktable (which we call *placeable*) if its component type is present at this worktable.

Since the worktables are identical in terms of the component type assignment (a feasible assignment for one worktable is also feasible on any other) there is a symmetry in the setup problem.

Unfortunately each worktable has access to a different set of mounting tasks such that an assignment on different worktables implies a different mounting task distribution. The drawback is that the symmetry of worktables cannot be handled in the usual way without losing solutions and in the worst case lose all optimal solutions.

Therefore we introduce a modelling feature, which we call *Symmetry Object (SymObj)*. An instance of a SymObj represents a worktable and there are as many SymObjs as worktables. The setup problem now is to find a setup for each SymObj. To solve the mounting task distribution problem, each SymObj is assigned to a different slot on the machine such that the order of the worktables is permuted. Each permutation now implies a specific mounting task distribution. Using SymObjs now enables us to exclude the worktable symmetry without losing solutions. The solutions for each symmetry class of the worktable setup are now the permutations of the SymObjs. It is now possible to consider different heuristics for the permutations. The heuristic used in our approach is to maximise the number of placeable mounting tasks.

References

1. Barbara M. Smith: Modelling a Permutation Problem. School of Computing Research Report 2000.18, June 2000;
   http://scom.hud.ac.uk/staff/scombms/papers.html
2. Zeynep Kiziltan and Barbara M. Smith: Symmetry-Breaking Constraints for Matrix Models. Presented at the second International Workshop on Symmetry in Constraint Satiafaction Problems, September 2002.
3. Siamak Tazari: Solving a core scheduling problem in modern assembly-line balancing. Technical Report, TU Darmstadt, Oktober 2003.

Iterative Forward Search Algorithm: Combining Local Search with Maintaining Arc Consistency and a Conflict-Based Statistics

Tomáš Müller

Faculty of Mathematics and Physics, Charles University
Malostranské nám. 2/25, Prague, Czech Republic
muller@ktiml.mff.cuni.cz

Abstract. The paper presents an iterative forward search framework for solving constraint satisfaction and optimization problems. This framework combines ideas of local search, namely improving a solution by local steps, with principles of depth-first search, in particular extending a partial feasible assignment towards a solution. Within this framework, a conflict-based statistics and explanations-based maintenance of arc consistency is proposed as well.

We present an iterative forward search framework to solve CSPs. This framework is close to local search methods; however, it maintains a partial feasible solution as opposed to the complete conflicting assignment characteristic of local search. Similarly to local search, we process local changes in the solution. We also describe how to extend the presented algorithm by dynamic maintaining arc consistency and conflict-based statistics.

In our approach, the conflict-based statistics works as an advice in the value selection criterion. It helps to avoid repetitive, unsuitable assignments of the same value to a variable by memorizing conflicts caused by this assignment in the past. In contrast to the *weighting-conflict* heuristics proposed in [2], conflict assignments are memorized together with the causal assignment which impacted them. Also, we propose the presented statistics to be unlimited, to prevent short-term as well as long-term cycles.

Because the iterative forward search algorithm works with partial feasible solutions, it can be easily extended to dynamically maintain arc consistency during the search. This can be done by using well known dynamic arc consistency (MAC) algorithms (e.g., by AC|DC algorithm or DnAC6). Moreover, since the only constraints describing assignments can be added and removed during the search, approaches based on explanations [1] can be used as well.

References

1. Narendra Jussien, Romuald Debruyne, and Patrice Boizumault. Maintaining arc-consistency within dynamic backtracking. In *Principles and Practice of Constraint Programming*, pages 249–261, 2000.
2. Narendra Jussien and Olivier Lhomme. Local search with constraint propagation and conflict-based heuristics. *Artificial Intelligence*, 139(1):21–45, 2002.

Programming Robotic Devices with a Timed Concurrent Constraint Language

María del Pilar Muñoz and Andrés René Hurtado

Universidad Javeriana, Colombia
{mpmunoz,arhurtado}@puj.edu.co

This work shows the implementation of *ntcc-lman* [1], a framework for ntcc [2], a non deterministic timed concurrent constraint process calculus. This calculus provides a formal model in which concepts proper to robotic control can be conveniently represented. The *ntcc-lman* framework includes a ntcc based kernel language, a compiler, a constraint system, a formal abstract machine based on ntcc reduction rules and a virtual machine. We show how the framework can be used to program typical robotic tasks to control *LEGO* robots in real time using *timed ccp* technology. To our knowledge, this is the first *timed ccp* framework for programming robotic devices.

The *ntcc-lman* framework was motivated by the increasing interest and the theoretical work in process-calculi as a formal framework for concurrent constraint languages. The goal of our project was to develop a formal framework for ntcc and to analyze its expressiveness in programming robotic devices. In efficiency, the work presented is quite competitive with other programming languages for *LEGO* robots, such as LUSTRE and ESTEREL, both synchronous languages for *LEGO* robots and *jcc*, of relevance to our work as an implementation of tcc that compiles tcc into Java. The novelty of the *ntcc-lman* approach is to offer a very robust framework combining the benefits of a formal foundation in process-calculi with a real-world application in which it is possible to program robotic tasks and prove their temporal properties.

We believe the *ntcc-lman* framework is also suitable for other type of applications. We are currently including a *midi* interface in order to test some non-trivial music improvisation processes that have already been successfully modeled in ntcc . These kind of applications are interesting for our framework because they are inherently non deterministic and temporal. Finally we are exploring the use of the framework as a tool to introduce constraints and concurrency in computer science undergraduate courses.

References

1. M.P. Muñoz, A.R. Hurtado.: LMAN: *ntcc* Abstract Machine for concurrent programming of *LEGO* robots. (In Spanish). Systems Engineering Degree, Department of Computing and Systems Engineering, Universidad Javeriana (2004) http://www.brics.dk/~fvalenci/lman/
2. M. Nielsen and C. Palamidessi, F. Valencia.: Temporal Concurrent Constraint Programming: Denotation, Logic and Applications. Nordic Journal of Computing (2002)

Heuristics for the Distributed Breakout Algorithm

Adrian Petcu

Ecole Politechnique Federale de Lausanne (EPFL), CH-1015 Lausanne, Switzerland
adrian.petcu@epfl.ch
http://liawww.epfl.ch/

Extended Abstract

Distributed Constraint Satisfaction Problems (DisCSP) is a very powerful paradigm applicable for a wide range of coordination and problem solving tasks in distributed artificial intelligence.

There are a number of distributed algorithms that were developed for this kind of problems. One of these, the Distributed Breakout Algorithm (DBA), is an extension of the original centralized Breakout Algorithm. This algorithm is a local search method, with an innovative technique for escaping from local minima: the constraints have weights, which are dynamically increased to force the agents to adjust their values while in a local minimum. While having a number of interesting properties, local search algorithms also have a common drawback: choosing indiscriminately between the possible values of the local variable (only considering the cost of the immediate improvements) can lead to "chain-reactions" (one conflict originating in one part of the constraint graph needlessly propagates throughout the whole graph, only to (hopefully) be resolved in a completely different part of the graph).

We developed techniques that can determine what values from the local domain will not cause such conflict propagations, and use one of those values as the next variable assignment. In this way, we look for a "local resolution" to all conflicts, in the sense that we keep them contained as much as possible, and involve "external parties" only when there is no other way.

We see from the experimental results that such techniques can yield significant improvements in terms of the number of cycles required to solve the problem (and therefore improvements in terms of communication and time requirements), especially when the problems are very difficult. Moreover, these techniques are able to guide the search towards a solution even in many cases where the standard DBA will cycle forever.

In the following, we will concentrate on the problem of *distributed constraint optimization* (DCOP), as a paradigm that is more useful for real-world problems. DCOP is a generalization of the Distributed Constraint Satisfaction Problems (DisCSP) framework, where the constraints are valued (functions returning a range of values, not just true or false). As such, solutions have varying degrees of quality or cost, and the objective is to minimize/maximize these costs.

Explanations and Numeric CSPs

Guillaume Rochart

École des Mines de Nantes – LINA, FRE CNRS 2729
4, rue Alfred Kastler - B.P. 20722 – F-44307 Nantes Cedex 3
grochart@emn.fr

Numerous industrial problems can be modelled as MINLP (*Mixed Integer Non-Linear Programming*) problems combining both numeric and integer variables: design of water transmission networks, automobile, aircraft, etc. [1]. These problems are really hard to solve since they combine both the combinatorial nature of mixed integer programming and the intrinsic difficulty of nonlinear programs. Several methods were proposed to solve these problems: branch-and-bound, extended cutting plane methods, and generalised Bender's decomposition, etc. But industrial applications need more than solving problems. Problems can be dynamic, this implies that constraints may be added or removed dynamically. Moreover, if no solution is found, the user often needs to know why the problem is over-constrained, or why the expected solution is inconsistent.

Constraint programming offers generic models and tools to solve combinatorial problems. Furthermore, explanation-based constraint programming provides tools to dynamically solve problems and maintain explanations about the resolution. Such features are now well known for constraint programming over integer variables. However only few works proposed solutions to extend it to real variables. [2] proposed to extend `mac-dbt` to solve numeric problems thanks to a dynamic domain splitting mechanism. But these works solve separately integer problems and numeric problems. Moreover, no solution is proposed for the main drawback about explanations for numeric problems: slow convergence of propagation may need to store a huge amount of explanations.

Here, we propose both a generic framework to solve MINLP problems with explanation-based constraint programming: indeed since `mac-dbt` and `dynamic domain splitting` are very similar, these algorithms can be abstracted in order to form a generic one. Moreover some ideas are exposed to decrease the number of explanations to store, by filtering redundant or useless explanations. Some first experiments show that using explanations with MINLP problems does not imply a great overhead for computing and managing explanations; it can even improve the resolution time. Last, these results show that filtering explanations can effectively reduce the time needed to maintain these explanations.

References

1. Michael R. Bussieck and Armin Pruessner. Mixed-integer nonlinear programming. In *SIAG/OPT Newsletter: Views & News*, 2003.
2. Narendra Jussien and Olivier Lhomme. Dynamic domain splitting for numeric CSP. In *European Conference on Artificial Intelligence*, pages 224–228, 1998.

Softly Constrained CP Nets

Kristen Brent Venable

University of Padova, Italy
kvenable@math.unipd.it

Abstract. In this paper a novel approach to deal with preferences expressed as a mixture of soft constraints and CP nets is presented. We construct a set of hard constraints whose solutions, if optimal for the soft constraints, are the optimal solutions of the set of preferences. This allows us to avoid dominance testing (is one outcome better than another?) which is a very expensive operation often used when finding optimal solutions or testing optimality. This simple and elegant technique permits conventional constraint and SAT solvers to solve problems involving both preferences and soft constraints.

Preferences and constraints are ubiquitous in real-life scenarios. We often have hard constraints (as "I must be at the office before 9am") as well as some preferences (as "I would prefer to be at the office around 8:30am") Among the many existing approaches to represent preferences, we will consider CP nets [2], which is a qualitative approach where preferences are given by ordering outcomes (as in "I like meat over fish") and soft constraints [1], which is a quantitative approach where preferences are given to each statement in absolute terms (as in "My preference for fish is 0.5 and for meat is 0.9").

At present, not much is understood about reasoning with CP nets and soft constraints. One of our aims is to tackle this problem. We define a structure called a constrained CP net. This is just a CP net plus a set of soft constraints. We give a semantics for this structure (based on the original flipping semantics of CP nets) which gives priority to the soft constraints. We show how to obtain the optimal solutions of such a constrained CP net by compiling the preferences into a set of hard constraints whose solutions, which are optimal for the soft constraints, are exactly the optimal solutions of the constrained CP net. Finding an optimal solution of a constrained CP net is NP-hard (as it is in CP nets and in soft constraints), but testing if an outcome is optimal is linear after the first test.

Acknowledgements. This is a joint work with Francesca Rossi (University of Padova, Italy), Steve Prestwich (University College Cork, Ireland) and Toby Walsh (Cork Constraint Computation Centre, Ireland).

References

1. S. Bistarelli, U. Montanari, F. Rossi. Semiring-based Constraint Solving and Optimization. Journal of ACM, vol.44, n.2, pp. 201-236, March 1997.
2. C. Boutilier, R. Brafman, H. Hoos, and D. Poole. Reasoning with conditional ceteris paribus preference statements. In *Proceedings of 15th Annual Conference on Uncertainty in Artificial Intelligence (UAI-99)*, 1999.

Online Constraint Solving and Rectangle Packing

Alfio Vidotto*

Cork Constraint Computation Centre
Dept. of Computer Science, UCC, Cork, Ireland
av1@student.cs.ucc.ie

In Online Problem Solving, partial solutions must be generated and executed before the complete problem is known. Many potential applications of constraint programming turn out to be online problems – for example, dynamic scheduling. How should we decide which values to assign to variables before all the variables and constraints are known? If we have some knowledge of the possible future developments of the problem, can we use that knowledge to make our initial assignments?

As a first step towards answering such questions, I have focused on one problem domain. Assume there is a conveyor belt carrying items into a machine. We must place items within a "window" on the belt. Items have different (rectangular) shapes and cannot overlap. Each time step, the belt moves to the left, carrying the leftmost items into the machine. We are also given new items which we must place in the window, or reject. We know the set of possible items. How should we place the items to maximize the number passed into the machine?

As an initial constraint model, I represent the belt as a grid. The grid squares are the variables, the values indicate whether or not the squares are occupied and may identify which shape is used, and the constraints ensure that the shapes are placed properly on the grid (i.e. occupy the correct amount of space, and do not overlap). The objective is to place as many shapes as possible. For the online problem, new variables are added to the right of the grid each time step, and variables to the left are removed. Variables which have been assigned values in the previous steps now have their values fixed. A new set of values become available to reflect the new items. The aim is to make a decision this time step which helps maximize the total final reward. Our first version uses a heuristic, balancing the reward obtained by placing a shape with the flexibility to place future shapes. The flexibility is measured by studying the effect of a decision on the domains of the remaining variables. The balance can be tuned using a parameter.

Future work will concentrate on different heuristics, probabilistic models of arrivals, e.g. in the style of [1, 2], and on a controller for adaptive problem solving.

References

1. D. W. Fowler and K. N. Brown, "Branching constraint satisfaction problems and Markov Decision Problems compared", *Annals of Operations Research*, Volume 118, Issue 1-4, pp85-100, 2003.
2. S. Manandhar, A. Tarim, and T. Walsh. Scenario-based Stochastic Constraint Programming. In *Proceedings of IJCAI-2003*, 2003.

---

* Funded by Enterprise Ireland (SC/2003/81) and supervised by Ken Brown and Chris Beck.

Modelling Chemical Reactions Using Constraint Programming and Molecular Graphs

Christine Wei Wu[*]

Cork Constraint Computation Center
Department of Computer Science, University College Cork, Cork, Ireland
cww1@cs.ucc.ie

Generating all *constitutional isomers* (chemical compounds that have the same molecular formula but different chemical structures) is a challenging problem. The structures are normally represented by molecular graphs, where vertices are atoms and edges are chemical bonds. The degree of a vertex in the graph represents the valency of the corresponding atom. The problem can be extended to generating all sets of molecules that can result from a reaction.

I have formulated this chemistry problem as a constraint satisfaction problem (CSP). As an initial representation of the problem, I represent each bond as a pair of variables. The atoms are represented by integers and connected by the bonds. The domain of each variable is all of the atoms in the problem. Each atom must appear a fixed number of times (its valency). For example, consider a problem that consists of two oxygens, two carbons and four hydrogens, i.e. eight atoms in three types. The number of bonds is half the sum of the atoms' valencies. For the sample problem we need 8 bonds. It is easy to specify the valency constraint with help of the **Ilog Solver** constraint *IloDistribute*, which restricts the appearance of variables that take a given value in an array. We believe this is the first constraint encoding of the problem.

However, there are millions of symmetrical duplicates. Those symmetries are caused by the nature of the model and can be classified into three kinds: (i) the two atoms on each side of a bond can be swapped; (ii) as the bonds are represented by an array of undistinguished variables, permuting the assignments produces symmetrical solutions; (iii) for multiple atoms of the same element, swapping all of the assignments of one instance with assignments of the other produces symmetrical solutions. We use symmetry breaking constraints to increase solving speed and reduce the number of duplicate solutions. The first two symmetries can be broken by enforcing a lexicographical order[1,2]. The third can be partially broken by giving the same value for all of the instances of an element with valency 1 (e.g. hydrogen) and increasing its valency.

Future work will concentrate on breaking the remaining symmetry, and on extending to include more chemistry constraints.

---

[*] Funded by Enterprise Ireland SC/2003/81, supervised by Ken Brown and Chris Beck.
[1] A. Frisch, B. Hnich, Z. Kiziltan, I. Miguel & T. Walsh: Global constraints for lexicographic orderings. Proceedings CP-2002.
[2] I. Gent, P. Prosser & B. Smith.: A 0/1 encoding of the GACLex constraint for pairs of vectors. Proc. ECAI2002 workshop on Modelling and Solving Problems with Constraints.

Constraining Special-Purpose Domain Types

Peter Zoeteweij

CWI, Amsterdam, The Netherlands
P.Zoeteweij@cwi.nl

With an open-ended constraint solver it is possible to introduce new facilities for modeling a problem. To illustrate this approach, we present as a case study how OpenSolver [2] can be configured as a solver for the job-shop scheduling problem (JSSP). OpenSolver is configured using plug-ins for several aspects of constraint solving. Here we use special-purpose domain types (sets of domains that can be associated with a variable) and reduction operators.

A JSSP instance consists of several jobs that themselves consist of a number of activities. Activities are characterized by a resource that is needed to process the activity, and by how long the activity claims this resource. The constraints are: all activities of a job must be processed in a specified order, and no two activities can use the same resource simultaneously. The goal is to find starting times for all activities such that the total processing time (makespan) is minimal.

A CP model for this problem uses a variable for the starting time and completion time of each activity [1]. When doing a complete search for the minimal makespan, branching is on the order in which resources are assigned to the activities that require them. The nodes of the search tree correspond to partial schedules, for which constraint propagation verifies feasibility. Search can be implemented by posting and retracting precedence constraints.

Because posting and retracting is not directly supported in OpenSolver, we introduced a special-purpose domain type Ranking. The possible values for variables of this type are all permutations of the numbers $0 \ldots n-1$, for n activities that require the same resource. Branching on such variables is binary: the left branch fixes a particular number to be the next element of the permutation. The right branch corresponds to all permutations where this number is not the next element. In addition, a domain type Activity represents the time window for an activity of a given duration. Special reduction operators constrain the precedences among a set of Activities according to a Ranking variable domain.

Together with a reduction operator for enforcing an order among the activities of a job, this yields a basic JSSP solver. Reduction operators for the "disjunctive" constraint and edge finding [1] were added to achieve realistic performance. The benefit of our approach is that we only have to program a few plug-ins. OpenSolver provides the propagation, search, and optimization.

References

1. P. Baptiste, C. Le Pape, W. Nuijten. *Constraint-Based Scheduling: Applying Constraint Programming to Scheduling Problems*. Kluwer Academic Publishers, 2001.
2. P. Zoeteweij. OpenSolver: a Coordination-Enabled Abstract Branch-and-Prune Tree Search Engine (doctoral program abstract). In F. Rossi (ed.) *Proceedings of CP 2003*, LNCS 2833, Springer-Verlag, 2003.

PLASMA: A Constraint Based Planning Architecture

Andrew Bachmann[*], Tania Bedrax-Weiss[*], Jeremy Frank, Michael Iatauro[*],
Conor McGann[*], and Will Taylor

Computational Sciences Division[*]
NASA Ames Research Center, MS 269-3
Moffett Field, CA 94035
frank@email.arc.nasa.gov

Until recently, planning research focused on solving problems of feasibility using models consisting of causal rules. Propositional logic is sufficient for representing such rules. However, many planning problems also contain *time* and *resource* constraints. It is often impractical to represent such planning domains with propositions. Large time horizons and possible resource states lead to enormous domain representations. Propositional representations can often obscure information that is useful during search. Finally, propositional representations can make it difficult for human modelers to express the domain in a convenient and natural way. The *Constraint-based Planning* paradigm employs constraints as the building blocks of both planning domain rules and plans. The building blocks of such plans are intervals of time over which some state holds or an action occurs in a plan. Each interval is represented by variables describing its properties (e.g. start, end, duration). At each step of the planning process, a mapping is maintained between the plan under construction and an underlying constraint network. As actions are added to the plan, constraints are posted on variables representing the action, its preconditions and its effects (a generalization of causal links). The domain rules contain directives for adding new intervals and for posting constraints over the variables on those intervals as plans are modified. Employing constraints in rules makes it easy to represent disjunctive preconditions, conditional effects, and mutual exclusions directly. The semantics of this mapping ensure that logical inference (e.g. propagation) on the constraint network can be used directly by search engines operating on plans,

Plan State Management Architecture (PLASMA) is a constraint-based planning and scheduling architecture. Model rules are written using NDDL, an object-oriented language for specifying model components, relationships such as is-a and has-a, and constraint-template rules defining the set of legal plans. Planner activity is all interpreted as restriction or relaxation of a dynamic constraint network. PLASMA is built from highly customized components for plan representation, generic constraint propagators, rule enforcement, heuristic enforcement and plan completion. PLASMA uses a strong transaction model of the entire planning process, including adding and removing parts of the constraint network, variable assignment, and constraint propagation. We have developed *PlanWorks*, a comprehensive tool suite for PLASMA. PlanWorks includes visualization components specialized for different components (e.g. constraints, activities, states, resources, causal links, search trees and heuristics), inter-view navigation features, transaction query mechanisms across the entire planning process, and test-case capture system.

---

[*] Authors listed in alphabetical order. [*] QSS Group Inc.

Applying Constraint Satisfaction Techniques to 3D Camera Control

Owen Bourne and Abdul Sattar

Institute for Integrated and Intelligent Systems
Griffith University
PMB50 Gold Coast Mail Centre
QLD 9726
{o.bourne,a.sattar}@griffith.edu.au

Controlling an autonomous camera in three-dimensional (3D) virtual environments is a difficult task which manifests itself in many interactive computer graphics applications. Computer games [2] and guided exploration [1] are examples where autonomous cameras are required to provide suitable views of the scene as the user interacts with the environment. The camera system is expected to consistently provide a suitable view of the target object(s) for the user.

Fig. 1. Screenshots of the test application.

The camera control problem is often over-constrained. We successfully applied local search strategies to generate solutions to the problem in real-time. A cost is associated with each constraint (current constraints are: *distance*, *height*, *occlusion*, *frame coherence rotation*, and *frame coherence distance*), making some constraints more likely to be satisfied than others. A 3D game engine was developed to evaluate the camera's real-time performance. Preliminary comparisons with related works indicate significant performance benefits from the use of local search.

References

1. Steffi Beckhaus, Felix Ritter, and Thomas Strothotte, *CubicalPath - dynamic potential fields for guided exploration in virtual environments*, Pacific Graphics 2000 (Hong Kong) (Brian A. Barsky, Yoshihisa Shinagawa, and Wenping Wang, eds.), IEEE Press, October 3-5 2000, pp. 387–395.
2. Nicolas Halper, Ralf Helbing, and Thomas Strothotte, *A camera engine for computer games: Managing the trade-off between constraint satisfaction and frame coherence*, Computer Graphics Forum **20** (2001), no. 3.

Adaptive Enterprise Optimization Framework: AEO Server and AEO Studio

Alexander Brodsky[1] and X. Sean Wang[2]

[1] Dept. of Info. & Software Eng., George Mason Univ. and Adaptive Decisions, Inc.
[2] Dept. of Computer Science, University of Vermont

Adaptive Enterprise Optimization (AEO) is an object-oriented framework for quick development of modular and extensible optimization solutions. AEO framework raises the level of modeling abstraction, allowing easy extensibility. In the framework, AEO Server is the run-time environment and AEO Studio the development environment. AEO Server and Studio have been used in various optimization applications, including Gas Pipeline Optimizer, Bid Optimizer for strategic sourcing, and Power Generation Commitment Optimizer. In this demo, we focus on the Gas Pipeline Optimizer solution, currently deployed in a major gas pipeline transportation company in North America.

AEO Studio supports the development of optimization solution components: Business Entity Models (BEM), Resource Models (RM), and Decision Models (DM). Intuitively, a BEM describes a transformation of one set of resources into another, an RM describes a resource in terms of its constraint variables, and resource matching rules and constraints, and a DM describes an objective function and high-level global constraints. At run time, instead of receiving constraints, variables, and an objective function as seen in a usual optimization solver, AEO Server receives BEM instances, including input and output resources (i.e., RM instances), and a single DM instance. AEO server uses resource matching rules across BEM instances to identify which output resource "flows to" which input resources. AEO server then constructs the constraint that is the conjunction of (1) all constraints from BEM and RM instances, (2) all constraints from the DM instance, and (3) the constraints regarding resources, specifying the "flow" of an output resource to an input resource, as well as constraints on sets of resources that a particular resource "flows" to or from. The optimization problem, with the above constraint and the objective function in the DM instance, is handled either by an existing solver (e.g., LP, MIP, or NLP) integrated in AEO Server, or by a customized algorithm developed in AEO Studio.

A gas pipeline network transports natural gas from exploration to distribution areas by using compressor stations, each having multiple compressor units using the same gas or electric power as fuel. Gas Pipeline Optimization solution recommends which compressor units must be on at exactly what target discharge pressures to achieve minimum fuel consumption. Gas Pipeline Optimization is implemented in the AEO framework, and deploys a custom-built optimization algorithm. The main algorithmic challenge is the combination of non-linearity and combinatorial nature of constraints. A performance study demonstrated high scalability and significantly better results than both historic pipeline operation and previously used optimization approach based on dynamic programming.

CRE2: A CP Application for Reconfiguring a Power Distribution Network for Power Losses Reduction*

Juan Francisco Díaz[2], Gustavo Gutierrez[1], Carlos Alberto Olarte[1], and Camilo Rueda[1]

[1] Pontificia Universidad Javeriana, Cali, Colombia
{crueda,caolarte,ggutierrez}@atlas.puj.edu.co
[2] Universidad del Valle, Cali, Colombia
jdiaz@univalle.edu.co

CRE2 is a CP application written in *MOzArt* (www.mozart-oz.org) for reconfiguring power distribution networks for power losses reduction. This includes two distinct interacting processes: load flow computation and selecting switches to open or close. Load flow is computed for each *radial* network obtained from switching operations. We developed a real intervals constraint system (XRI) and integrated it to *MOzArt* . *CRE2* uses XRI for load flow and the *MOzArt* finite domain constraint system for switch state changes.

An electric distribution network consists of four main components: (1) Power Transformers, that supply the energy to the system; (2) Feeders, that are nodes attached to the power transformers; (3) Internal nodes, some with (active (P) and reactive (Q) customer loads; (4) Branches, connecting feeders and nodes in the network, each having a resistance (R), a reactance (X) and (optionally) a Switch.

The *load flow problem* consists of finding values for the current in each branch (I), the voltage (V) in each node, load currents in nodes (I_q) having customer loads and, with these, compute active and reactive losses (L_p, L_q). Input data includes impedance ($Z = R + Xj$) and active and reactive loads (P, Q). Values found must satisfy fundamental electrical laws:the Ohm law equations on each branch (relating node voltages, current in branches, and resistance and reactance), Kirchoff laws (relating input and output currents in nodes) and an equation relating load current $w.r.t$ P, Q and node voltage.

On the other hand, the target configuration (network topology) must satisfy the following additional constraints: (1) Node voltage cannot drop below a fixed limit; (2) Current in branches cannot exceed a given limit; (3) The number of branches supplying current into a given node must be equal to one (Radiality); (4) Current must flow to all nodes in the new configuration(Service Continuity); (5) The number of switches that can be changed is limited; (6) Power losses in the reconfigured network must be a given percentage lower than in the original network.

A user interacts with *CRE2* via a graphic interface. It contains a power distribution network editor offering widgets to represent electrical components. Properties of each component can be entered (and visualized) by clicking on it. Edited networks can be saved or processed launching load flow or reconfiguration tasks by choosing appropriate options in a menu. Large networks can be defined in an XML file and then loaded into the GUI.

---

* This work was partially supported by COLCIENCIAS and EPSA, under contract No.254-2002 and by COLCIENCIAS and Parquesoft, under contract No.298-2002.

Our model has been tested successfully in canonical reconfiguration problems of networks up to 60 nodes. While our approach is arguably less efficient than some existing approximation schemes, we think using CP provides definite advantages: (1) all electrical and operational power system constraints are always satisfied, (2) provides a simpler computational model, directly related to fundamental electric laws of the system, (3) allows more flexible parameter control, such as maximum number of switching operations and (4) leaves more room to introduction of additional operational constraints or search control strategies.

A Constraint-Based Planner Applied to Data Processing Domains

Keith Golden[1] and Wanlin Pang[2]

[1] Computational Science Division, NASA Ames Research Center, Moffett Field, CA 94035
[2] QSS Group Inc., NASA Ames Research Center, Moffett Field, CA 94035

Earth-science data processing at NASA is the problem of transforming low-level observations of the Earth system, such as data from Earth-observing satellites, into high-level observations or predictions, such as crop failure or high fire risk. Given the large number of socially and economically important variables that can be derived from the data, the complexity of the data processing needed to derive them and the many terabytes of data that must be processed each day, there are great challenges and opportunities in processing the data in a timely manner, and a need for more effective automation. Our approach to providing this automation is to cast it as a constraint-based planning problem: we represent data-processing operations as planner actions and desired data products as planner goals, and use a planner to generate data-flow programs that produce the requested data. The planning problem is translated into a constraint satisfaction problem (CSP) and solved by constraint propagation and search algorithms.

As a demonstration of our approach, we are developing a constraint-based planning agent, called IMAGEbot, and applying it to the Terrestrial Observation and Prediction System (TOPS, http://ecocast.arc.nasa.gov). The architecture of the agent is described in Figure 1. In the following, we describe a few of the components in more detail:

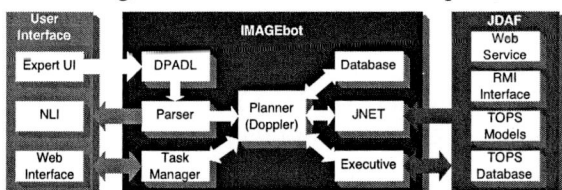

Fig. 1. The architecture of IMAGEbot

DPADL: The Data Processing Action Description Language is used to provide action descriptions of models, filters and other programs as well as of available data sources. Goals, in the forms of data product requests, can also be described in DPADL.
User Interface: We provide a simplified form-based Web interface to allow users to submit typical requests. For more advanced use, we are also developing a natural language interface which allows complex data requests to be posed in an intuitive manner.
DoPPLER: The Data Processing Planner accepts goals in the form of data descriptions and synthesizes data-flow programs using the action descriptions read in by the DPADL parser. It reduces the planning problem to a CSP whose solution provides a solution to the original planning problem.
JNET: The constraint solver can handle numeric and symbolic constraints, as well as constraints over strings and even arbitrary Java objects. Additionally, it can solve a limited class of universally quantified constraints.
JDAF: JDAF is a framework that provides a common API for all TOPS data-processing programs and scientific models for ecosystem forecasting.

CLab: A C++ Library for Fast Backtrack-Free Interactive Product Configuration

Rune M. Jensen[*]

IT University of Copenhagen, Rued Langgaards Vej 7, 2300 Copenhagen S, Denmark
rmj@itu.dk

Product configuration is a successful application area of constraint programming. CLab [1, 2] is an open source C++ library for building fast backtrack-free interactive product configurators. It contains functions that support a two-phase approach to interactive product configuration described by Hadzic et al. [3]. In the first phase, a Binary Decision Diagram (BDD) representing the set of valid configurations is compiled offline. In the second phase, this BDD is accessed by the online interactive product configurator. The library has two major functions: one that builds the BDD from a declarative product model (M_1), and one that computes the set of possible ways a current partial configuration can be extended to a valid product (M_2). The latter function is fast (polynomial) and used to make the interactive product configuration process complete and backtrack-free. It allows the user to choose freely between any possible continuation of the partial configuration. The approach is illustrated by the procedure

    INTERACTIVE-CONFIGURATION(C)
1    $S \leftarrow M_1(C)$
2   **while** $|S| > 1$
3   **do choose** $(x_i = v) \in M_2(S)$ $\triangleright M_2(S) = \{a : c \in S, a \in c\}$
4        $S \leftarrow \{c \in S : (x_i = v) \in c\}.$

Line 1 denotes the offline phase, where a BDD S of the solution space is computed from the product model C. Line 2-4 denote the online phase. In each iteration, the user chooses a value v of a product variable x_i that belongs to the set of possible assignments (Line 3). The solution space is then reduced accordingly (Line 4). Future work includes adding explanation faciletes to CLab.

References

1. Jensen, R.M.: CLab user manual. Technical Report ITU-TR-2004-46, IT University of Copenhagen (2004)
2. Jensen, R.M.: CLab 1.0. (http://www.itu.dk/people/rmj/clab/)
3. Hadzic, T., Subbarayan, S., Jensen, R.M., Andersen, H.R., Møller, J., Hulgaard, H.: Fast backtrack-free product configuration using a precompiled solution space representation. In: Proceedings of the International Conference on Economic, Technical and Organizational aspects of Product Configuration Systems, DTU-tryk (2004) 131–138

---

[*] Thanks to the members of the VeCoS Group at the IT University of Copenhagen for rewarding discussions on this work.

A Constraint-Based System for Hiring and Managing Graduate Teaching Assistants

Ryan Lim, Venkata Praveen Guddeti, and Berthe Y. Choueiry

Constraint Systems Laboratory, University of Nebraska-Lincoln
{rlim,vguddeti,choueiry}@cse.unl.edu

We have designed and implemented a system for the management of Graduate Teaching Assistants (GTAs) in our department. The system is based on Constraint Processing techniques and is operated through web-based interfaces. The task is to assign GTAs, based on their qualifications, availability, and preferences, to academic tasks over a semester such as grading, supervising labs and recitations, and teaching introductory classes. Typically, every semester, the department has about 70 different academic tasks and can hire between 25 and 40 GTAs. The problem is often tight and sometimes over-constrained. In the past, this task has been performed manually by members of the staff and faculty. Tentative schedules were iteratively refined based on feedback from faculty and the GTAs themselves, in a tedious and error-prone process lingering over 3 weeks. We have built web-based interfaces to streamline the collection of data and specification of constraints. Further, we have implemented a number of constraint-based functionalities that assist the human manager in generating solutions interactively and automatically [1]. The modeling efforts started in Spring 2001 [2]. The prototype system has been used since Fall 2001 and is continually being enhanced. The current system has decreased the amount of time and effort spent on the task and yielded assignments that gained everyone's approval. The interactive component consists of an interface for viewing and manipulating the constraint model from a task-centered and a resource-centered perspectives. The set of algorithms for automatic problem-solving includes a (deterministic) backtrack search with various ordering heuristics [2], a local search [3], a multi-agent based search [3], and a randomized backtrack search with a new restart strategy [4]. Future work includes extending this set of algorithms, designing an 'algorithm driver' for allowing them to collaborate, and implementing functionalities for allowing the user to visualize and combine (sets of) solutions. This work is supported by the Department of Computer Science and Engineering, and NSF grants #EPS-0091900 and CAREER #0133568.

References

1. Lim, R., Guddeti, P., Choueiry, B.: An Interactive System for Hiring and Managing Graduate Teaching Assistants. In: PAIS/ECAI 04. (2004)
2. Glaubius, R., Choueiry, B.Y.: Constraint Constraint Modeling and Reformulation in the Context of Academic Task Assignment. In: Workshop Modelling and Solving Problems with Constraints (ECAI 02). (2002)
3. Zou, H., Choueiry, B.Y.: Characterizing the Behavior of a Multi-Agent Search by Using it to Solve a Tight, Real-World Resource Allocation Problem. In: Workshop on Applications of Constraint Programming (ACP 03). (2003) 81–101
4. Guddeti, P., Choueiry, B.Y.: A Dynamic Restart Strategy for Randomized BT Search. In: CP 04. (2004)

A Web-Based Meeting Scheduling Solver With Privacy Guarantees, Without Trusted Servers

Marius-Călin Silaghi[1], Vaibhav Rajeshirke[1], and Richard Wallace[2]

[1] Florida Institute of Technology
[2] University College Cork

Some problems having privacy requirements can be modeled with distributed (weighted) constraint satisfaction frameworks [3]. Previous approaches to such problems used trusted servers or some kind of argumentation, inherently leaking data about the secret constraints [5]. We developed techniques[patent pending] and a system for solving these problems where an agent does not divulge absolutely any secret information to any attacker controlling less than half of the participants. Agents and servers only learn a randomly picked solution.

We identify the following privacy attacks on distributed CSP techniques:
1. S-attacks against secure multiparty computation-backtracking hybrids. [1]
2. Shadow CSPs against argumentation based solvers. [5]
3. Attacks against search with known orders on variables and domains. [2]
4. Statistical attacks against DisCSP solvers that shuffle domains. [4]

To achieve resistance to these attacks we invented two fundamental cryptographic techniques: a) S-mixnets for shuffling shared secrets; b) Two alternative functions for solving WCSPs using solely '+/*' operations (with no comparison).

We also developed three secure multiparty protocols that combine S-mixnets with the aforementioned functions, obtaining MPC-DisWCSP1 and MPC-DisWCSP2 (resistant to attacks 1-3), and MPC-DisWCSP3 (resistant to attacks 1-4). MPC-DisWCSP1 can be parametrized between polynomial space and linear logic time, but is slower. Only MPC-DisWCSP3 can exploit public constraints.

Results: An applet-based secure meeting scheduling system is deployed at www.cs.fit.edu/~msilaghi/secure. The methods also apply for incentive auctions and stable matchings problems [3]. Our solution to the 4th attack can be used to improve the privacy offered by other computation techniques based on DisCSPs (e.g with trusted servers, choosing a solution randomly among all solutions).

References

1. M. Silaghi. *Asynchronously Solving Problems with Privacy Requirements*. PhD thesis, EPFL, 2002. www.cs.fit.edu/~msilaghi/teza.
2. M. Silaghi. Solving a DisCSP with cryptographic multi-party computations, without revealing constraints and without involving trusted servers. In *IJCAI DCR Workshop*, 2003.
3. M. Silaghi. Incentive auctions and stable marriages problems solved with $\lfloor n/2 \rfloor$-privacy of human preferences. Technical Report CS-2004-11, FIT, 2004.
4. M. Silaghi and V. Rajeshirke. The effect of reordering policies on privacy. In *AAMAS (to appear)*, 2004.
5. R. Wallace. Reasoning with possibilities in multiagent graph coloring. In *IJCAI DCR Workshop*, 2003.

A Constraint-Based Graphics Library for B-Prolog

Neng-Fa Zhou

The City University of New York and
Afany Software
zhou@sci.brooklyn.cuny.edu

Introduction

CGLIB is a high-level graphics library for B-Prolog, a constraint logic programming system. The library provides primitives for creating and manipulating graphical objects and a set of constraints including non-overlap, grid, table, and tree constraints that facilitates the specification of the layouts of objects. The library adopts a construct called action rules available in B-Prolog for creating agents and programming interactions among agents or between agents and the user. The library is a fully working system implemented in B-Prolog, Java and C. It can be used in many areas such as drawing editors, interactive user interfaces, document authoring, animation, information visualization, intelligent agents, and games. The high-level abstraction of the library and the use of constraints and action rules in the specification of layouts and behaviors can significantly enhance the productivity of the development of graphics. We demonstrate through several examples the effectiveness of the library as a tool for developing graphics-rich and interactive user interfaces. The system is available from *www.bprolog.com* and the details of the library can be found in [1].

References

1. Neng-Fa Zhou, CGLIB – A Constraint-based Graphics Library, Software – Practice and Experience, Vol. 33, No.13, pp.1199-1216, 2003.

Author Index

Ågren, Magnus 788
Ajili, Farid 726
Ali, Syed Muhammad 706
Artiouchine, Konstantin 789
Atserias, Albert 77

Bacchus, Fahiem 663
Bachmann, Andrew 408, 810
Barták, Roman 62, 767
Beck, J. Christopher 92, 711
Bedrax-Weiss, Tania 810
Beldiceanu, Nicolas 107
Bessiere, Christian 32, 123, 138, 716
Bourne, Owen 811
Boussemart, Frederic 721
Brand, Sebastian 790
Brito, Ismel 791
Brodsky, Alexander 812

Cambazard, Hadrien 153
Carchrae, Tom 92, 792
Carlsson, Mats 107
Čepek, Ondrej 62
Cesta, Amedeo 496
Chen, Hubie 168, 182
Choueiry, Berthe Y. 817
Cicirello, Vincent A. 197
Cohen, David 212
Coletta, Remi 123
Cooper, Martin 212
Cronholm, Wilhelm 726
Culberson, Joseph 17

Dalmau, Víctor 182
Dechter, Rina 317, 731
Déplanche, Anne-Marie 153
Devkar, Alex 438
Díaz, Juan Francisco 813
Dinh, Tien Ba 793

Fernández, Cèsar 32
Flener, Pierre 227
Frank, Jeremy 242, 810
Freuder, Eugene C. 92, 123
Furnon, Vincent 468

Gao, Yong 17
Gebruers, Cormac 794
Gervet, Carmen 604
Giunchiglia, Enrico 260
Glover, Fred 423
Gogate, Vibhav 317
Golden, Keith 815
Golynski, Alexander 542
Gomes, Carla P. 32, 274, 377, 572
Gompert, Joel M. 795
Guddeti, Venkata Praveen 796, 817
Guerri, Alessio 794
Gutierrez, Gustavo 813

Hadzic, Tarik 797
Hebrard, Emmanuel 138, 716, 798
Hellsten, Lars 290
Hemery, Fred 721
Hladik, Pierre-Emmanuel 153
Hnich, Brahim 138, 716
Hooker, John N. 305
Hoos, Holger H. 438
Huang, Xiaofei 737
Hurtado, Andrés René 803

Iatauro, Michael 810

Jeavons, Peter 212
Jefferson, Christopher 799
Jensen, Rune M. 816
Jia, Haixia 742
Jussien, Narendra 153

Kask, Kalev 317
Khatib, Lina 408
Koenig, Sven 706
Kolaitis, Phokion G. 77
Kovács, András 332

Lagoon, Vitaly 347
Larrosa, Javier 757
Law, Yat Chiu 362
Leahu, Lucian 377
Lecoutre, Christophe 721
Lee, Jimmy H.M. 362
Leyton-Brown, Kevin 438

Li, Wei 800
Lim, Andrew 747
Lim, Ryan 817
Liu, Liyuan 47
López-Ortiz, Alejandro 542

Mamoulis, Nikos 393, 752
Martin, Roland 801
Mateescu, Robert 731
McGann, Conor 810
Meisels, Amnon 782
Meseguer, Pedro 757
Michel, Laurent 47
Moore, Cristopher 742
Morris, Paul 408
Morris, Robert 408
Müller, Tomáš 802
Muñoz, María del Pilar 803

Narizzano, Massimo 260
Neveu, Bertrand 423
Nudelman, Eugene 438

Oddi, Angelo 496
Olarte, Carlos Alberto 813
O'Sullivan, Barry 123

Pan, Guoqiang 453
Pang, Wanlin 815
Pearson, Justin 227
Perron, Laurent 468
Pesant, Gilles 290, 482
Petcu, Adrian 804
Petit, Thierry 107
Podelski, Andreas 1
Policella, Nicola 496
Prestwich, Steven 512
Prosser, Patrick 711
Puget, Jean-Francois 5, 527

Quimper, Claude-Guy 542

Rajeshirke, Vaibhav 818
Ramakrishnan, Sailesh 408
Régin, Jean-Charles 572
Refalo, Philippe 557
Reyna, Luis G. 227
Ringwelski, Georg 92
Rochart, Guillaume 805
Rodrigues, Brian 747
Rossi, Francesca 588
Rueda, Camilo 813

Sachenbacher, Martin 762
Sadler, Andrew 604
Sais, Lakhdar 721
Sánchez, Martí 757
Sattar, Abdul 811
Schulte, Christian 619
Sellmann, Meinolf 274, 634
Selman, Bart 9, 32
Shaw, Paul 468, 648
Shoham, Yoav 438
Silaghi, Marius-Călin 818
Simonis, Helmut 13
Smith, Stephen F. 197, 496
Stergiou, Kostas 393, 752
Stuckey, Peter J. 347, 619
Surynek, Pavel 767

Tacchella, Armando 260
Tambe, Milind 706
Taylor, Will 810
Thiffault, Christian 663
Trinquet, Yvon 153
Trombettoni, Gilles 423

van Beek, Peter 290, 542
Váncza, József 332
van Dongen, Marc R.C. 772
Van Hentenryck, Pascal 47
van Hoeve, Willem Jan 679
Vardi, Moshe Y. 77, 453
Venable, Kristen Brent 588, 806
Vidotto, Alfio 807
Vilím, Petr 62

Wallace, Richard J. 711, 818
Walsh, Toby 138, 663, 716
Wang, X. Sean 812
Williams, Brian C. 762
Wu, Christine Wei 808

Xing, Zhao 690
Xu, Zhou 747

Yorke-Smith, Neil 588

Zhang, Yuanlin 777
Zhang, Weixiong 690
Zhou, Neng-Fa 819
Zivan, Roie 782
Zoeteweij, Peter 809

Lecture Notes in Computer Science

For information about Vols. 1–3129

please contact your bookseller or Springer

Vol. 3263: M. Weske, P. Liggesmeyer (Eds.), Object-Oriented and Internet-Based Technologies. XII, 239 pages. 2004.

Vol. 3260: I. Niemegeers, S.H. de Groot (Eds.), Personal Wireless Communications. XIV, 478 pages. 2004.

Vol. 3258: M. Wallace (Ed.), Principles and Practice of Constraint Programming – CP 2004. XVII, 822 pages. 2004.

Vol. 3255: A. Benczúr, J. Demetrovics, G. Gottlob (Eds.), Advances in Databases and Information Systems. XI, 423 pages. 2004.

Vol. 3254: E. Macii, V. Paliouras, O. Koufopavlou (Eds.), Integrated Circuit and System Design. XVI, 910 pages. 2004.

Vol. 3253: Y. Lakhnech, S. Yovine (Eds.), Formal Techniques in Timed, Real-Time, and Fault-Tolerant Systems. X, 397 pages. 2004.

Vol. 3249: B. Buchberger, J.A. Campbell (Eds.), Artificial Intelligence and Symbolic Computation. X, 285 pages. 2004. (Subseries LNAI).

Vol. 3246: A. Apostolico, M. Melucci (Eds.), String Processing and Information Retrieval. XIV, 316 pages. 2004.

Vol. 3242: X. Yao (Ed.), Parallel Problem Solving from Nature - PPSN VIII. XX, 1185 pages. 2004.

Vol. 3241: D. Kranzlmüller, P. Kacsuk, J.J. Dongarra (Eds.), Recent Advances in Parallel Virtual Machine and Message Passing Interface. XIII, 452 pages. 2004.

Vol. 3240: I. Jonassen, J. Kim (Eds.), Algorithms in Bioinformatics. IX, 476 pages. 2004. (Subseries LNBI).

Vol. 3239: G. Nicosia, V. Cutello, P.J. Bentley, J. Timmis (Eds.), Artificial Immune Systems. XII, 444 pages. 2004.

Vol. 3238: S. Biundo, T. Frühwirth, G. Palm (Eds.), KI 2004: Advances in Artificial Intelligence. XI, 467 pages. 2004. (Subseries LNAI).

Vol. 3232: R. Heery, L. Lyon (Eds.), Research and Advanced Technology for Digital Libraries. XV, 528 pages. 2004.

Vol. 3229: J.J. Alferes, J. Leite (Eds.), Logics in Artificial Intelligence. XIV, 744 pages. 2004. (Subseries LNAI).

Vol. 3224: E. Jonsson, A. Valdes, M. Almgren (Eds.), Recent Advances in Intrusion Detection. XII, 315 pages. 2004.

Vol. 3223: K. Slind, A. Bunker, G. Gopalakrishnan (Eds.), Theorem Proving in Higher Order Logics. VIII, 337 pages. 2004.

Vol. 3221: S. Albers, T. Radzik (Eds.), Algorithms – ESA 2004. XVIII, 836 pages. 2004.

Vol. 3220: J.C. Lester, R.M. Vicari, F. Paraguaçu (Eds.), Intelligent Tutoring Systems. XXI, 920 pages. 2004.

Vol. 3217: C. Barillot, D.R. Haynor, P. Hellier (Eds.), Medical Image Computing and Computer-Assisted Intervention – MICCAI 2004. XXXVIII, 1114 pages. 2004.

Vol. 3216: C. Barillot, D.R. Haynor, P. Hellier (Eds.), Medical Image Computing and Computer-Assisted Intervention – MICCAI 2004. XXXVIII, 930 pages. 2004.

Vol. 3210: J. Marcinkowski, A. Tarlecki (Eds.), Computer Science Logic. XI, 520 pages. 2004.

Vol. 3208: H.J. Ohlbach, S. Schaffert (Eds.), Principles and Practice of Semantic Web Reasoning. VII, 165 pages. 2004.

Vol. 3207: L.T. Yang, M. Guo, G.R. Gao, N.K. Jha (Eds.), Embedded and Ubiquitous Computing. XX, 1116 pages. 2004.

Vol. 3206: P. Sojka, I. Kopecek, K. Pala (Eds.), Text, Speech and Dialogue. XIII, 667 pages. 2004. (Subseries LNAI).

Vol. 3205: N. Davies, E. Mynatt, I. Siio (Eds.), UbiComp 2004: Ubiquitous Computing. XVI, 452 pages. 2004.

Vol. 3203: J. Becker, M. Platzner, S. Vernalde (Eds.), Field Programmable Logic and Application. XXX, 1198 pages. 2004.

Vol. 3202: J.-F. Boulicaut, F. Esposito, F. Giannotti, D. Pedreschi (Eds.), Knowledge Discovery in Databases: PKDD 2004. XIX, 560 pages. 2004. (Subseries LNAI).

Vol. 3201: J.-F. Boulicaut, F. Esposito, F. Giannotti, D. Pedreschi (Eds.), Machine Learning: ECML 2004. XVIII, 580 pages. 2004. (Subseries LNAI).

Vol. 3199: H. Schepers (Ed.), Software and Compilers for Embedded Systems. X, 259 pages. 2004.

Vol. 3198: G.-J. de Vreede, L.A. Guerrero, G. Marín Raventós (Eds.), Groupware: Design, Implementation and Use. XI, 378 pages. 2004.

Vol. 3194: R. Camacho, R. King, A. Srinivasan (Eds.), Inductive Logic Programming. XI, 361 pages. 2004. (Subseries LNAI).

Vol. 3193: P. Samarati, P. Ryan, D. Gollmann, R. Molva (Eds.), Computer Security – ESORICS 2004. X, 457 pages. 2004.

Vol. 3192: C. Bussler, D. Fensel (Eds.), Artificial Intelligence: Methodology, Systems, and Applications. XIII, 522 pages. 2004. (Subseries LNAI).

Vol. 3190: Y. Luo (Ed.), Cooperative Design, Visualization, and Engineering. IX, 248 pages. 2004.

Vol. 3189: P.-C. Yew, J. Xue (Eds.), Advances in Computer Systems Architecture. XVII, 598 pages. 2004.

Vol. 3186: Z. Bellahsène, T. Milo, M. Rys, D. Suciu, R. Unland (Eds.), Database and XML Technologies. X, 235 pages. 2004.

Vol. 3185: M. Bernardo, F. Corradini (Eds.), Formal Methods for the Design of Real-Time Systems. VII, 295 pages. 2004.

Vol. 3184: S. Katsikas, J. Lopez, G. Pernul (Eds.), Trust and Privacy in Digital Business. XI, 299 pages. 2004.

Vol. 3183: R. Traunmüller (Ed.), Electronic Government. XIX, 583 pages. 2004.

Vol. 3182: K. Bauknecht, M. Bichler, B. Pröll (Eds.), E-Commerce and Web Technologies. XI, 370 pages. 2004.

Vol. 3181: Y. Kambayashi, M. Mohania, W. Wöß (Eds.), Data Warehousing and Knowledge Discovery. XIV, 412 pages. 2004.

Vol. 3180: F. Galindo, M. Takizawa, R. Traunmüller (Eds.), Database and Expert Systems Applications. XXI, 972 pages. 2004.

Vol. 3179: F.J. Perales, B.A. Draper (Eds.), Articulated Motion and Deformable Objects. XI, 270 pages. 2004.

Vol. 3178: W. Jonker, M. Petkovic (Eds.), Secure Data Management. VIII, 219 pages. 2004.

Vol. 3177: Z.R. Yang, H. Yin, R. Everson (Eds.), Intelligent Data Engineering and Automated Learning – IDEAL 2004. XVIII, 852 pages. 2004.

Vol. 3176: O. Bousquet, U. von Luxburg, G. Rätsch (Eds.), Advanced Lectures on Machine Learning. IX, 241 pages. 2004. (Subseries LNAI).

Vol. 3175: C.E. Rasmussen, H.H. Bülthoff, B. Schölkopf, M.A. Giese (Eds.), Pattern Recognition. XVIII, 581 pages. 2004.

Vol. 3174: F. Yin, J. Wang, C. Guo (Eds.), Advances in Neural Networks - ISNN 2004. XXXV, 1021 pages. 2004.

Vol. 3173: F. Yin, J. Wang, C. Guo (Eds.), Advances in Neural Networks – ISNN 2004. XXXV, 1041 pages. 2004.

Vol. 3172: M. Dorigo, M. Birattari, C. Blum, L. M. Gambardella, F. Mondada, T. Stützle (Eds.), Ant Colony, Optimization and Swarm Intelligence. XII, 434 pages. 2004.

Vol. 3170: P. Gardner, N. Yoshida (Eds.), CONCUR 2004 - Concurrency Theory. XIII, 529 pages. 2004.

Vol. 3166: M. Rauterberg (Ed.), Entertainment Computing – ICEC 2004. XXIII, 617 pages. 2004.

Vol. 3163: S. Marinai, A. Dengel (Eds.), Document Analysis Systems VI. XI, 564 pages. 2004.

Vol. 3162: R. Downey, M. Fellows, F. Dehne (Eds.), Parameterized and Exact Computation. X, 293 pages. 2004.

Vol. 3160: S. Brewster, M. Dunlop (Eds.), Mobile Human-Computer Interaction – MobileHCI 2004. XVII, 541 pages. 2004.

Vol. 3159: U. Visser, Intelligent Information Integration for the Semantic Web. XIV, 150 pages. 2004. (Subseries LNAI).

Vol. 3158: I. Nikolaidis, M. Barbeau, E. Kranakis (Eds.), Ad-Hoc, Mobile, and Wireless Networks. IX, 344 pages. 2004.

Vol. 3157: C. Zhang, H. W. Guesgen, W.K. Yeap (Eds.), PRICAI 2004: Trends in Artificial Intelligence. XX, 1023 pages. 2004. (Subseries LNAI).

Vol. 3156: M. Joye, J.-J. Quisquater (Eds.), Cryptographic Hardware and Embedded Systems - CHES 2004. XIII, 455 pages. 2004.

Vol. 3155: P. Funk, P.A. González Calero (Eds.), Advances in Case-Based Reasoning. XIII, 822 pages. 2004. (Subseries LNAI).

Vol. 3154: R.L. Nord (Ed.), Software Product Lines. XIV, 334 pages. 2004.

Vol. 3153: J. Fiala, V. Koubek, J. Kratochvíl (Eds.), Mathematical Foundations of Computer Science 2004. XIV, 902 pages. 2004.

Vol. 3152: M. Franklin (Ed.), Advances in Cryptology – CRYPTO 2004. XI, 579 pages. 2004.

Vol. 3150: G.-Z. Yang, T. Jiang (Eds.), Medical Imaging and Augmented Reality. XII, 378 pages. 2004.

Vol. 3149: M. Danelutto, M. Vanneschi, D. Laforenza (Eds.), Euro-Par 2004 Parallel Processing. XXXIV, 1081 pages. 2004.

Vol. 3148: R. Giacobazzi (Ed.), Static Analysis. XI, 393 pages. 2004.

Vol. 3147: H. Ehrig, W. Damm, J. Desel, M. Große-Rhode, W. Reif, E. Schnieder, E. Westkämper (Eds.), Integration of Software Specification Techniques for Applications in Engineering. X, 628 pages. 2004.

Vol. 3146: P. Érdi, A. Esposito, M. Marinaro, S. Scarpetta (Eds.), Computational Neuroscience: Cortical Dynamics. XI, 161 pages. 2004.

Vol. 3144: M. Papatriantafilou, P. Hunel (Eds.), Principles of Distributed Systems. XI, 246 pages. 2004.

Vol. 3143: W. Liu, Y. Shi, Q. Li (Eds.), Advances in Web-Based Learning – ICWL 2004. XIV, 459 pages. 2004.

Vol. 3142: J. Diaz, J. Karhumäki, A. Lepistö, D. Sannella (Eds.), Automata, Languages and Programming. XIX, 1253 pages. 2004.

Vol. 3140: N. Koch, P. Fraternali, M. Wirsing (Eds.), Web Engineering. XXI, 623 pages. 2004.

Vol. 3139: F. Iida, R. Pfeifer, L. Steels, Y. Kuniyoshi (Eds.), Embodied Artificial Intelligence. IX, 331 pages. 2004. (Subseries LNAI).

Vol. 3138: A. Fred, T. Caelli, R.P.W. Duin, A. Campilho, D.d. Ridder (Eds.), Structural, Syntactic, and Statistical Pattern Recognition. XXII, 1168 pages. 2004.

Vol. 3137: P. De Bra, W. Nejdl (Eds.), Adaptive Hypermedia and Adaptive Web-Based Systems. XIV, 442 pages. 2004.

Vol. 3136: F. Meziane, E. Métais (Eds.), Natural Language Processing and Information Systems. XII, 436 pages. 2004.

Vol. 3134: C. Zannier, H. Erdogmus, L. Lindstrom (Eds.), Extreme Programming and Agile Methods - XP/Agile Universe 2004. XIV, 233 pages. 2004.

Vol. 3133: A.D. Pimentel, S. Vassiliadis (Eds.), Computer Systems: Architectures, Modeling, and Simulation. XIII, 562 pages. 2004.

Vol. 3132: B. Demoen, V. Lifschitz (Eds.), Logic Programming. XII, 480 pages. 2004.

Vol. 3131: V. Torra, Y. Narukawa (Eds.), Modeling Decisions for Artificial Intelligence. XI, 327 pages. 2004. (Subseries LNAI).

Vol. 3130: A. Syropoulos, K. Berry, Y. Haralambous, B. Hughes, S. Peter, J. Plaice (Eds.), TeX, XML, and Digital Typography. VIII, 265 pages. 2004.